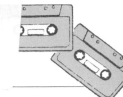

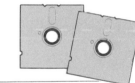

BUSINESS REPLY MAIL
FIRST CLASS   PERMIT NO. 2277   NEW YORK, NY

POSTAGE WILL BE PAID BY

JOHN WILEY & SONS, INC.
CPA EXAMINATION REVIEW
P.O. Box 886
DeKalb, IL 60115-0886

BUSINESS REPLY MAIL
FIRST CLASS   PERMIT NO. 2277   NEW YORK, NY

POSTAGE WILL BE PAID BY

JOHN WILEY & SONS, INC.
CPA EXAMINATION REVIEW
P.O. Box 886
DeKalb, IL 60115-0886

IF FOUND, please notify and arrange return to owner. This text is important for the owner's preparation for the Uniform Certified Public Accountant Examination.

Name of CPA Candidate _____

Address   _____

City, State, Zip   _____

Telephone   ( )_____

Additional texts are available at your local bookstore

or directly from John Wiley and Sons, Inc.

Order information and order forms can be found at the front of the book

——————————————†† ——————————————

CPA
EXAMINATION REVIEW
VOLUME I
OUTLINES and STUDY GUIDES

16th EDITION

Irvin N. Gleim, Ph.D., CPA
University of Florida
Gainesville, Florida

&

Patrick R. Delaney, Ph.D., CPA
Northern Illinois University
DeKalb, Illinois

JOHN WILEY & SONS

New York Chichester Brisbane Toronto Singapore

WILEY

Permissions

Material from Uniform CPA Examination Questions and Unofficial Answers, Copyright @ 1973, 1978, 1980, 1983, 1985, 1986, 1987, 1988 and 1989 by American Institute of Certified Public Accountants, Inc., is reprinted (or adapted) with permission.

The following items copyright © by the American Institute of Certified Public Accountants, Inc., are reprinted (or adapted) with permission:

1. Information for CPA Candidates and Revised Content Specification Outlines for the Uniform Certified Public Accountant Examination, Board of Examiners, 1985.

2. Definitions, examples, etc. from The Code of Professional Conduct.

3. Example audit reports from Statements on Auditing Standards and Statements on Standards for Accounting and Review Services.

4. Example financial statements from Industry Audit Guides: Audits of Colleges and Universities, Audits of Voluntary Health and Welfare Organizations, and Hospital Audit Guide.

5. Example Statement of Activity from SOP 78-10.

Chart adapted from C.E. Arrington and K. Pany, "SAS No. 30: Clarifying and Extending the Accountant's Involvement with Reporting on Internal Accounting Control," Journal of Accounting Auditing and Finance (Summer, 1981) p. 369, Warren, Gorham, and Lamont, reprinted with permission.

Reproduction and adaption of pronouncements, copyright © Financial Accounting Standards Board, Norwalk, Connecticut 06856-5116, with permission.

Reproduction of "Combined Statement of Revenues, Expenditures, and Changes in Fund Balances--All Governmental Fund Types and Expendable Trust Funds," copyright © Governmental Accounting Standards Board, Norwalk, Connecticut 06856-5116, with permission.

Several examples in Chapter 11, "Taxes," are taken from Internal Revenue Service Publication 17.

The following material in this manual was taken, with permission, from Intermediate Accounting, Sixth Edition, by Donald E. Kieso and Jerry J. Weygandt, John Wiley & Sons, Inc., 1989: Table entitled "Summary of APB Opinions and FASB Standards Pertaining to the Income Statement."

ISBN 0-471-50341-X
10 9 8 7 6 5 4 3 2 1

PREFACE

The objective of this volume is to provide, in an easily readable format, study outlines of all areas tested on the Uniform CPA Examination. The clear, concise phraseology supplemented by brief examples and illustrations is designed to help candidates quickly understand and retain the material. To make the task of preparing for the examination more manageable, we have structured both review volumes into 44 modules (manageable study units). The modular organization commences in Chapter 5 of this volume and in Chapter 2 of Volume II. Also, the multiple choice questions in Volume II have been grouped into topical categories within each module. These categories correspond to the sequencing of material as it appears within each of the corresponding modules in this volume. A significant feature of this volume concerns the tables summarizing the frequency and extent to which topical areas have been tested on each of the last nine exams. Our classification of the coverage of these exams is based on the AICPA's Revised Content Specification Outlines for the Uniform Certified Public Accountant Examination which were effective beginning with the May 1986 exam.

The Sixteenth Edition has been updated and revised to include changes in applicable law and new authoritative pronouncements through May 15, 1989. Additionally, other areas have been revised to improve the pedagogical treatment of the materials. Finally, coverage of some areas has either been reduced or expanded to reflect changes in exam coverage.

The authors are indebted to the American Institute of Certified Public Accountants and the Financial Accounting Standards Board for permission to reproduce and adapt their publications.

The authors deeply appreciate the enthusiastic and dedicated attitude of the many CPA candidates with whom the authors have had the pleasure to work. As always, the authors welcome any comments concerning materials contained in or omitted from this text. Please send these to Patrick R. Delaney, c/o CPA Examination Review, P.O. Box 886, DeKalb, Illinois 60115.

Please read Chapter 1 carefully, especially "Attributes of Examination Success" and "Purpose and Organization of These Review Textbooks."

Good Luck on the Exam,

Irvin N. Gleim
Patrick R. Delaney

May 15, 1989

ABOUT THE AUTHORS

Patrick R. Delaney is the Arthur Andersen & Co. Alumni Professor of Accountancy at Northern Illinois University. He received his PhD in Accountancy from the University of Illinois. He has public accounting experience with Arthur Andersen & Co. and is coauthor of **GAAP: Interpretation and Application**, also published by John Wiley & Sons, Inc. He is on the Illinois CPA Society's Board of Directors and was Chairman of its Accounting Principles Committee; is a past president of the Rockford Chapter, National Association of Accountants; and has served on numerous other professional committees. He is a member of the American Accounting Association, American Institute of Certified Public Accountants, and National Association of Accountants. Professor Delaney has published in The Accounting Review and is a recipient of NIU's Excellence in Teaching Award and Lewis University's Distinguished Alumnus Award. He has been involved in NIU's CPA Review Course as director and instructor.

Irvin N. Gleim is Professor Emeritus of Accounting at the University of Florida and is a CPA, CIA, and CMA. He received his PhD in Accountancy from the University of Illinois. He is a member of the American Institute of Certified Public Accountants, Florida Institute of Certified Public Accountants, American Accounting Association, American Business Law Association, Institute of Internal Auditors, Institute of Management Accounting, and National Association of Accountants. He has published professional articles in the Journal of Accountancy, The Accounting Review, and The American Business Law Journal. He has developed and taught both proprietary and university CPA review courses. He is author of CIA Examination Review and CMA Examination Review, both published by Accounting Publications, Inc.

ABOUT THE CONTRIBUTORS

Richard E. Baker, PhD, CPA, is Professor of Accountancy at Northern Illinois University and teaches in the NIU CPA Review Course. Professor Baker prepared the Business Combinations and Consolidations Module. He has received several teaching awards at NIU. He has also prepared revisions for the Business Combination and Consolidations Module.

John C. Borke, MAS, CPA, is an Assistant Professor of Accounting at the University of Wisconsin-Platteville. He has worked as a staff auditor with Peat, Marwick, Mitchell, & Co. Professor Borke prepared several other sections in Financial Accounting including the section in Chapter 8 on the Conceptual Framework; and prepared the revision of Chapter 9, Cost Accounting.

William Cummings, PhD, CPA, CDP, is an Assistant Professor of Accounting at Northern Illinois University. He has a background in accounting systems and has worked and consulted in industrial accounting. Professor Cummings has contributed to the revision of the Auditing EDP module.

John H. Engstrom, DBA, CPA, is Professor of Accountancy at Northern Illinois University. He is the coauthor of Essentials of Accounting for Governmental and Not for Profit Organizations, Richard D. Irwin, Inc. He revised Chapter 10, Governmental and Nonprofit Accounting.

Edward C. Foth, PhD, CPA, is an Associate Professor and Administrator of the Master of Science in Taxation Program at DePaul University. He has public accounting experience with Arthur Andersen & Co. and teaches in their Basic and Intermediate U.S. Tax School. Professor Foth is the author of Commerce Clearing House's Study Guide For Federal Tax Course, Study Guide for CCH Federal Taxation: Basic Principles, and coauthor of their S Corporations Guide. He prepared Chapter 11.

William T. Geary, PhD, CPA, is an Associate Professor at The College of William and Mary. He has taught in several CPA Review Programs and the NASBA Critique Program and is presently the director of the William and Mary CPA Review Program. Professor Geary prepared the revision of Leases in Module 26.

Duane R. Lambert, JD, MBA, CPA, is Professor of Business Administration at California State University, Hayward where he teaches courses in Business Law and Accounting. He also has been a Visiting Lecturer and a Visiting Associate Professor at the University of California, Berkeley. Professor Lambert has "Big Eight" experience and has taught CPA review courses for the past several CPA examinations. He rewrote and revised modules to reflect current treatment in Chapter 6, Business Law.

Kurt Pany, PhD, CPA, is a Professor of Accounting at Arizona State University. Prior to entering academe, he worked as a staff auditor for Touche Ross & Co. Professor Pany prepared the Professional Responsibilities, Internal Control, Evidence, and Reporting Modules and revised the SAS Outlines in Chapter 5.

James H. Perkins, MS, MIS, CIA, CISA, CPA, EDP Director of Internal Auditing, General Electric Data Security, Cleveland. He previously worked as Audit Manager, Federal Reserve Bank of Cleveland, a Principal Research Manager--Audit Programs for the Bank Administration Institute in Rolling Meadows, Illinois, and as a staff auditor for Deloitte Haskins & Sells. Mr. Perkins has contributed to the revision of the Auditing EDP Module.

Kurt F. Reding, DBA, CPA, is an Assistant Professor of Accountancy at Northern Illinois University. Mr. Reding has experience as a staff auditor with Arthur Young and Company. He prepared the revision of the Audit Sampling module in Chapter 5, Auditing.

W. Max Rexroad, PhD, CPA, is Professor of Accounting at Illinois State University and teaches in the ISU CPA Review Course. He has received the Distinguished Teaching Award from the College of Business at ISU as well as other teaching awards. He has taught numerous CPE courses for the Illinois CPA Society and other state societies. He prepared a revision of the Pensions section of Module 26.

John R. Simon, PhD, CPA, is Professor of Accountancy at Northern Illinois University. He has taught in NIU's CPA Review Course for the past twelve years and is presently the director of the course. He is a recipient of NIU's Excellence in Teaching Award. Professor Simon prepared the Earnings Per Share section of the Stockholders' Equity Module, the Foreign Currency Translation portion of the Changing Prices and Foreign Currency Translation Module, and expanded topical coverage in several other modules in Chapter 8.

Douglas M. Stein, MAS, CMA, CPA, is a candidate for the PhD degree at the University of Wisconsin--Madison. Mr. Stein has contributed to the revision of the Auditing EDP module.

Harold Wright, JD, is Coordinator and Assistant Professor of Business Law at Northern Illinois University. He has taught in NIU's CPA Review Course for the past fourteen years and is a recipient of NIU's Excellence in Teaching Award. Professor Wright prepared revisions in Chapter 6, Business Law.

TABLE OF CONTENTS

*As explained in Chapter 1, this volume is organized into 44 modules (manageable study units). Volume II is organized in a parallel fashion. For easy reference, both Volumes I and II have numbered index tabs indicating the first page of each module.

Acknowledgements

Writing an annualized text is always a publishing event and a rejuvenating human experience. The authors are most grateful to the many users of previous editions, both instructors and students who have so generously shared with us their satisfaction with our work and their suggestions for changes and improvements. We hope that this will continue for we have benefited from those communications.

This work continues to be a "community effort." In addition to those colleagues cited as contributors, we would like to acknowledge and thank those many friends who gave us so many devoted hours to bring this edition to you so quickly after the May 1989 Examination: Lee Gampfer, Penelope LeFew, Pam Miller, Nancy O'Connor, Norma Rodriguez, Sara Sawyer, Linda Tatro, and Lorrie Wildenradt.

We are very appreciative of the many comments we have received from users of our books.

Several of our colleagues allowed us to use their charts or summaries in the text; these credits are noted with their contributions.

OTHER CONTRIBUTORS AND REVIEWERS

The following individuals assisted in the preparation of this volume by drafting and reviewing answer explanations for the financial and managerial accounting questions from the Theory and Practice examinations.

John Coffey, BS, CPA, is a candidate for the MAS degree at Northern Illinois University.

Bill Griensenauer, MAS, CPA, is Assistant Controller, Forsythe McArthur and Associates, Inc.

Ken Groetsema, BS, CPA, is employed by Ernst and Whinney.

Rebecca A. Hoger, BS, CPA, is a candidate for a MAS degree in Accountancy at Northern Illinois University.

John C. Pintozzi, BS, CPA, is a staff accountant with Touche Ross & Co.

Lori Wetzel, BS, MAS, CPA, CMA, is a staff accountant with Peat Marwick Main.

Dee Wolter, BS, is a candidate for the MAS degree at Northern Illinois University.

CHAPTER ONE
BEGINNING YOUR CPA REVIEW PROGRAM

To maximize the efficiency of your review program, begin by studying (not merely reading) this chapter and the next three chapters of this volume. They have been carefully organized and written to provide you with important information to assist you in successfully completing the CPA exam. Beyond providing a comprehensive outline of the material tested on the exam, Chapter 1 will assist you in organizing a study program to prepare for the exam. Self-discipline is essential.

GENERAL COMMENTS ON THE EXAMINATION

Successful completion of the Uniform CPA Examination is an attainable goal. Keep this point foremost in your mind as you study the first four chapters in this volume and develop your study plan.

Purpose of the Examination*

The CPA examination is designed to measure basic technical competence, including

1. Technical knowledge and application of such knowledge
2. Exercise of good judgment
3. Understanding of professional responsibilities

The CPA examination is one of many screening devices to assure the competence of those licensed to perform the attest function and to render professional accounting services. Other screening devices are educational requirements, ethics examinations, etc.

The examination appears to test the material covered in accounting programs of the better business schools. It also appears to be based upon the body of knowledge essential for the practice of public accounting and, perhaps specifically, the audit of a medium-sized client. Since the examination is primarily a textbook or academic examination, you should plan on taking it as soon as possible after completing your undergraduate accounting education. Take the examination with the idea of passing all parts of the exam, since studying for the whole exam is synergistic. For example, while studying for the accounting theory exam, you often study material tested on the accounting practice exams, and vice versa.

Examination Content

Guidance concerning topical content of the CPA exam can be found in a document prepared by the Board of Examiners of the AICPA entitled Revised Content Specification Outlines for the Uniform Certified Public Accountant Examination.

The Board's objective in preparing this detailed listing of topics tested on the exam is to help "in assuring the continuing validity and reliability of the Uniform CPA Examination." These outlines are an excellent source of guidance concerning the areas and the emphasis to be given each area on future exams.

---

*The following general comments are largely adapted from Information for CPA Candidates published by the American Institute of Certified Public Accountants. Information for CPA Candidates is usually sent to CPA candidates by their State Board of Accountancy as they apply to sit for the CPA examination. If you will not be immediately applying to your State Board of Accountancy to sit for the exam, you may wish to request a complimentary copy from your board or the AICPA. (Write to AICPA, Examination Division, 1211 Avenue of the Americas, New York, New York 10036-8775.)

We have included the content outlines in this volume by placing each outline (Accounting Practice, Accounting Theory, Auditing, and Business Law), or portion thereof, in the chapter containing related topical areas. Additionally, we have used the outlines as the basis for our frequency analysis of the last nine exams (May 1985 - May 1989). These outlines/frequency analyses should be used as an indication of the topics' relative importance on past exams.

The AICPA does not require knowledge of new accounting and auditing pronouncements until approximately 12 months after they are issued. When a question appears on a topic on which a pronouncement has been issued in the previous 12 months, the graders give credit for the old rule as well as the new rule. CPA exam coverage of business law and tax law changes appears in Chapter 6 and Chapter 11, respectively.

Schedule of Examinations

The Uniform Certified Public Accountant Examination is given twice a year, usually the first consecutive Wednesday-Thursday-Friday in May and November.

The dates for future CPA examinations are

1989	November	1, 2, 3	1990	May	2, 3, 4
				November	7, 8, 9

1991	May	8, 9, 10
	November	6, 7, 8

Recent exams have followed the format presented in the schedule on the next page. Currently, the exam consists of 60% multiple choice (M/C) questions in all parts, but the time allocations within each part are different. For example, the 3 multiple choice question sections on the Practice I exam were given 45-55 minutes each, for an average of about 2 1/2 minutes per individual multiple choice item. The 60 multiple choice questions in Theory were assigned a time range of 90-110 minutes, or about 1 2/3 minutes per question. You should note the suggested time limits for each question as you begin working the exam. The subject and time schedules are at the top of the next page.

You receive four scores; accounting practice is considered one section. Seventy-five is considered passing. Rules for partial credit on the examination vary from state to state (see "State Boards of Accountancy" below).

CPA EXAM SCHEDULE AND EXPECTED FORMAT

	Wednesday	Thursday	Friday
A.M.		Auditing 8:30 a.m. - 12 noon 5 Questions: 1 Question of 60 M/C 4 Essays	Business Law 8:30 a.m. - 12 noon 5 Questions: 1 Question of 60 M/C 4 Essays
P.M.	Practice I 1:30 - 6:00 p.m. 5 Questions: 3 Questions of 20 M/C each 2 Problems	Practice II 1:30 - 6:00 p.m. 5 Questions: 3 Questions of 20 M/C each 2 Problems	Theory 1:30 - 5:00 p.m. 5 Questions: 1 Question of 60 M/C 4 Essays

State Boards of Accountancy

The right to practice public accounting as a CPA is governed by individual state statutes. While some rules regarding the practice of public accounting vary from state to state, all State Boards of Accountancy use the Uniform CPA Examination and AICPA advisory grading service as one of the requirements to practice public accounting. Every candidate should inquire of his/her State Board of Accountancy to determine the requirements to sit for the exam, e.g., education, filing dates, references, and fees. A frequent problem candidates encounter is failure to apply by the deadline. APPLY TO SIT FOR THE EXAMINATION EARLY. ALSO, YOU SHOULD USE EXTREME CARE IN FILLING OUT THE APPLICATION AND MAILING THE REQUIRED MATERIALS TO YOUR STATE BOARD OF ACCOUNTANCY. If possible, have a friend review your completed application before mailing with check, photo, etc. Too many candidates are turned down for sitting for a particular CPA examination simply because of minor technical details that were overlooked (photos not signed, check not enclosed, question not answered on application, etc.). BECAUSE OF THE VERY HIGH VOLUME OF APPLICATIONS RECEIVED IN THE MORE POPULOUS STATES, THE ADMINISTRATIVE STAFF DOES NOT HAVE TIME TO CALL OR WRITE TO CORRECT MINOR DETAILS AND WILL SIMPLY REJECT YOUR APPLICATION. This can be extremely disappointing particularly after spending many hours in preparing to sit for a particular exam.

The various state requirements to take the CPA exam are listed on the following page. The data are based on the CCH Accountancy Law Reporter, AICPA Legislative Reference Service, and a survey of state boards. Note that the presentation is condensed and generalized; there are numerous "alternatives," etc. Be sure to inquire to your state board for specific and current requirements.

It is possible for candidates to sit for the examination in another state as an out-of-state candidate. Candidates desiring to do so should contact the State Board of Accountancy in their home state. Addresses of all 54 Boards of Accountancy appear below.

INDIVIDUAL STATE CPA REQUIREMENTS
Compiled May 1, 1989

State Board address	Educ.[1]	Application deadline First time	Re-exam	Exam[2] fee	Cond. re-[3] quirements	Life of[4] condition	Yrs. exp.	Cont. ed. re- quirements hrs./yrs.	
AL 12 Commerce Row, 529 S. Perry St., Montgomery 36104	4	2-28,8-31	3-31,9-30	$175	2 or P	4NE	2-3	40	1
AK P.O. Box D, Juneau 99811	2-4	60 days	same	$100	2 or P	5Y	2-4	60	2
AZ 3110 N. 19th Ave., Suite 140, Phoenix 85015	4	2-28,8-31	same	$175	2 or P	3Y	2	80[5]	2[5]
AR 1515 W. Seventh St., Ste. 320, Little Rock 72201	4	60 days	30 days	$150	2 or P,50	5NE	1-2	40	1
								120	3
CA 2135 Butano Dr., Ste. 112, Sacramento 95825	0-4	3-1,9-1	same	$100	2 or P	6NE	2-4	80	2
CO 617 State Services Bldg., Denver 80203	4	3-1,9-1	same	varies	2 or P	5NE	0-1	80	2
CT 30 Trinity St., Hartford 06106	4	60 days	same	$170	2 or P,50	3Y	3	40	1
DE P.O. Box 1401, Dover 19903	2-4	3-1,9-1	same	$125	2 or P,50	5NE	2-4	Yes[5]	
DC 614 H St. NW, Rm. 923, Washington 20001	4	90 days	60 days	$100	2 or P	5NE	2	Yes	
FL 4001 NW 43rd St., Ste. 16, Gainesville 32606	4+[5]	2-1,8-1	3-1,9-1	$175	2 or P,50	5NE	0-1	20-80	2[5]
GA 166 Pryor St. SW, Atlanta 30303	4	2-1,8-1	3-1,9-1	$140	2,40[5]	5NE	2-5	60	2
GU P.O. Box P, Agana 96910	4	60 days	same	$ 35	2 or P,50	6NE	1-2		
HI P.O. Box 3469, Honolulu 96801	5	3-1,9-1	same	$100	2 or P,50	6NE	2	80[5]	2
ID 500 S. Tenth St., Ste 104, Statehouse Mail, Boise 83720	4	3-1,9-1	same	$100	2 or P,50	6NE	1-2	80	2
IL 10 Administration Bldg., 506 S. Wright, Urbana 61801	4	3-1,9-1	same	$180[6]	2 or P,50	3 of N6E	0		
IN 1021 State Office Bldg., Indianapolis 46204	4	3-1,9-1	same	$135	2,50	6NE	2-6	80	2
IA 1918 SE Hulsizer, Ankeny 50021	4	2-28,8-31	same	$ 90	2 or P,50	5NE	1-3	120	3
KS 900 W. Jackson St., Topeka 66612	4-5	3-15,9-15	same	$125	2,50	4 of N6E	2[5]	40	1
KY 332 W. Broadway, Ste. 310, Louisville 40202	4	3-1,9-1	same	$125	2 or P,50	6NE	2-4	20	1
LA 1515 WTC, 2 Canal St., New Orleans 70130	4[5]	3-1,9-1	same	$125	2,50	1 of N4E	2-4	120	3
ME State House Station 35, Augusta 04333	4	4-15,10-1	same	$ 80	2 or P	3Y	1-2	12	1
MD 501 St. Paul Place, Rm. 902, Baltimore 21202	4	60 days	same	$ 80	2 or P,50	5NE	0	80	2
MA 100 Cambridge St., Rm. 1524, Boston 02202	4	3-15,9-15	same	$200	2 or P,50	6NE	2-9	80	2
MI P.O. Box 30018, Lansing 48909	4	60 days	same	$120	2 or P,50	6NE	2	40	1
MN Metro Square Bldg., 5th Fl., St. Paul 55101	4[5]	60 days	same	$115	2,50	5NE	1 6	120	3
MS P.O. Box 55447, Jackson 39296-5447	4	3-15,9-15	same	$107	2 or P,45	8NE	1-4	120	3
MO P.O. Box 613, Jefferson City 65102	4[5]	3-1,9-1	same	$130	2 or P,50	6NE	0	120	3[5]
MT 1424 9th Ave., Helena 59620-0407	4	3-15,9-15	same	$100	2 or P,50	5NE	1-2	120	3
NE P.O. Box 94725, Lincoln 68509	4	3-31,9-30	same	$120[6]	2 or P,50	5NE	2-4	120	3
NV One East Liberty St., Suite 311, Reno 89501	4	3-1,9-1	same	$100	2 or P,35	6NE	2-4	80	2[5]
NH Two and One-Half Beacon St., Concord 03301-4447	4	3-15,9-15	same	$125	2,50	5Y	1-2	80	2[5]
NJ 1100 Raymond Blvd., Rm. 507-A, Newark 07102	4	3-1,9-1	same	$100	2 or P,50[5]	6NE	2-4	48	2
NM 4125 Carlisle NE, Alburquerque 87107	4	3-1,9-1	same	$125	2	3Y	1	120	3
NY Cultural Education Center, Albany 12230	4	90 days	60 days	$370	2 or P	6NE	1-2	120	3[5]
NC P.O. Box 12827, Raleigh 27605-2827	2	2-28,8-31	same	$140[5]	2 or P	5NE	1-5	40[5]	1
ND Box 8104, Univ. Sta., Grand Forks 58202	0	3-15,9-15	same	$125	2 or P	5NE	0-4	120	3
OH 77 S. High St., 18th Floor, Columbus 43266-0301	4[5]	3-1,9-1	4-1,10-1[5]	$140	1,40	8Y	1-4	120[5]	3[5]
OK 6600 North Harvey, Suite 130, Oklahoma City 73116	0-4[5]	60 days	same	$100	2 or P	1 of 3 N6E	0-3	24	1
OR Commerce Building, First Floor, Salem 97310	0-4	3-1,9-1	same	$ 75	2 or P,50	6NE	1-2	80	2
PA P.O. Box 2649, Harrisburg 17105-2649	4	2-15,8-15	3-1,9-1	$104	1,20	Unlimited	1-2	80	2
PR Box 3271, San Juan 00904	0-4[5]	60 days	same	$ 50	2	Unlimited	0-6		
RI 233 Richmond St., Providence 02903	4	3-15,9-15	same	$150	2 or P	Unlimited	1-2	120	3
SC Dutch Plaza, Ste 260, 800 Dutch Square Blvd., Columbia 29210	4	3-15,9-15	same	$140	2 or P,40	3NE	2	60	2
SD 301 E. 14th St., Ste. 200, Sioux Falls 57104	2-4	3-1,9-1	same	$175	2 or P,50	4Y	2	120	3
TN 500 James Robertson Pkwy., 2nd. Floor, Nashville 37219	4	3-1,9-1	same	$ 75	2 or P,50	6NE or 3Y	2-3	80	2
TX 1033 LaPosada, Ste. 340, Austin 78752-3892	2	2-28,8-31	same	$100	2	5Y	1-6	40	1
UT Heber M. Wells Bldg., 160 E. 300 S., Box 45802, Salt Lake City 84145	4	60 days	same	$165	2 or P,50	6NE	1-3	80	2
VT 109 State St., Montpelier 05602	0	4-1,10-1	same	$170	2 or P,50	6NE	2	80	2
VI Prop. & Procure. Bldg., No. 1 Sub Base, Rm. 205, St. Thomas 00801	0	3-15,9-15	same	$100	2	Unlimited	2-6		
VA 3600 West Broad St., Richmond 23230	4[5]	60 days	same	$100	2 or P,50	5NE	2,3		
WA 210 E. Union St., EP-21, Box 9131, Olympia 98504	4	3-1,9-1	same	$125	2 or P,50	6NE	1	80	2
WV 201 L&S Bldg., 812 Quarrier St., Charleston 25301	4	2-15,8-15	same	$ 40[5]	1	3Y	0		
WI P.O. Box 8935, Madison 53708	4	3-1,9-1	same	$115	2,50	2 of N4E	3[5]		
WY Barrett Bldg., 3rd Fl., Cheyenne 82002	4	3-15,9-15	same	$150	2 or P	3Y	2	120	3

[1]Years of higher education

[2]First-time fee

[3]Number of parts, specific parts, and minimum scores on parts failed

[4]Y = years; NE = next exams

[5]Check with your local State Board for specific requirements

[6]Effective in Nov. 1988

NOTE: The publisher does not assume responsibility for errors in the above information. You should request information concerning requirements in your state at least 6 months in advance of the exam dates.

ATTRIBUTES OF EXAMINATION SUCCESS

Your primary objective in preparing for the CPA exam is to pass. Other objectives such as learning new and reviewing old material should be considered secondary. The five attributes of examination success discussed below are essential. You should study the attributes and work toward achieving/developing each of them before taking the examination.

1. Knowledge of Material

Two points are relevant to "knowledge of material" as an attribute of examination success. First, there is a distinct difference between being familiar with material and knowing the material. Frequently we (you) confuse familiarity with knowledge. Can you remember when you just could not answer an examination question or did poorly on an examination, but maintained to yourself or your instructor that you knew the material? You probably were only familiar with the material. On the CPA examination, familiarity is insufficient; you must know the material. For example, you may be familiar with the concepts in accounting for leases (SFAS 13), but can you compute the present value of an annuity due under a lease agreement and record entries for the lessee and lessor? Once again, a very major concern must be to know the material rather than just being familiar with it. Knowledgable discussion of the material is required on the CPA examination. Second, the Uniform Certified Public Accountant Examination tests a literally overwhelming amount of material at a rigorous level. From an undergraduate point of view, the CPA examination includes material from the following courses.

    Accounting
        Auditing (including EDP and Audit Sampling)
        Intermediate Financial
        Advanced Financial
        Cost/Managerial
        Governmental/Nonprofit
        Tax
    Business Law

Furthermore, as noted earlier, the CPA exam tests material in all of these areas. In other words, you are not only responsible for material in the above courses, but also for all new developments in each of these areas.

This text contains outlines of accounting topics from FASB pronouncements, financial accounting courses, cost accounting courses, etc. Return to the original material (e.g., FASBs, your accounting textbooks, etc.) when the outlines less than reinforce topical areas you should know for the exam.

2. Solutions Approach

The solutions approach is a systematic approach to solving the problems found on the CPA examination. Many candidates know the material fairly well when they sit for the CPA exam, but they do not know how to take the examination. Candidates generally neither work nor answer problems efficiently in terms of time or grades.

The solutions approach permits you to avoid drawing "blanks" on CPA exam problems; using the solutions approach coupled with grader orientation (see the next section heading) allows you to pick up a sizable number of points on questions testing material with which you are not familiar.

Chapter 3 outlines the solutions approach for practice problems, essay questions, and multiple choice questions. Example problems are worked as well as explained.

3. Grader Orientation

Your score on each section of the exam is determined by the sum of points assigned to individual questions. Thus, you must attempt to maximize your points on each individual question. The name of the game is to satisfy the grader, as s/he is the one who awards you points. Your answer and the grading guide (which conforms closely to the unofficial answer) are the basis for the assignment of points.

This text helps you develop grader orientation by analyzing AICPA grading procedures and grading guides (this is explained further in Chapter 2). The authors believe that the solutions approach and grader orientation, properly developed, are worth at least 10 to 15 points on each section to most candidates.

4. Examination Strategy

Prior to sitting for the examination, it is important to develop an examination strategy, i.e., a preliminary inventory of the questions, the order of working questions, etc.

Your ability to cope successfully with 19 1/2 hours of examination can be improved by

a. Recognizing the importance and usefulness of an examination strategy
b. Using Chapter 4 "Taking the Examination" and previous examination experience to develop a "personal strategy" for the exam
c. Testing your "personal strategy" on recent CPA questions under examination conditions (using no reference material and within a time limit)

5. Examination Confidence

You need confidence to endure the physical and mental demands of 19 1/2 hours of problem solving under tremendous pressure. Examination confidence develops from proper preparation for the exam which includes mastering the first four attributes of examination success. Examination confidence is also necessary to enable you to overcome the initial frustration with problems for which you may not be specifically prepared.

This study manual (in conjunction with Volume II), properly used, should contribute to your examination confidence. The systematic outlines herein will provide you with a sense of organization such that as you sit for the examination, you will feel reasonably prepared (it is impossible to be completely prepared).

Reasons for Failure

The Uniform Certified Public Accountant Examination is a formidable hurdle in your accounting career. Candidates, generally with a college degree and an accounting major, face about a 30% pass rate nationally on each section of the exam. About 20% of all candidates (first-time and re-exam) sitting for each examination successfully complete that examination. The cumulative pass rate on the exam is about 70-75%; that is, the percentage of first-time candidates who eventually pass the exam. It is even higher for serious candidates (80%-90%) because a significant number of candidates "drop out" after failing the exam the first time.

Attempt to identify and correct your weaknesses before you sit for the examination based on your experience with undergraduate and previous CPA examinations. Also, analyze the contributing factors to incomplete or incorrect solutions to CPA problems prepared during your study program. The more common reasons for failure are

1. Failure to understand the requirements
2. Misunderstanding the text of the problem
3. Lack of knowledge of material tested
4. Inability to apply the solutions approach
5. Lack of an exam strategy, e.g., time budgeting
6. Sloppiness, computational errors, etc.
7. Failure to proofread and edit

These are not mutually exclusive categories. Some candidates get in such a hurry that they misread the requirements and the problem text, fail to use a solutions approach, make computational errors, and omit proofreading and editing.

PURPOSE AND ORGANIZATION OF THESE REVIEW TEXTBOOKS

Volume I and Volume II of CPA EXAMINATION REVIEW are designed to help you prepare adequately for the examination. There is no easy approach to prepare for the successful completion of the CPA Examination; however, through the use of Volumes I and II, your approach will be systematic and logical.

The objective of Volume I is to provide study materials supportive to CPA candidates. While no guarantees are made concerning the success of those using this text, this volume promotes efficient preparation by

1. Explaining how to "satisfy the grader" through analysis of examination grading and illustration of the solutions approach.

2. Defining areas tested previously through the use of the content specification outlines/frequency analyses described earlier. Note that predictions of future exams are not made. You should prepare yourself for all possible topics rather than gambling on the appearance of certain questions.
3. Organizing your study program by comprehensively outlining all of the subject matter tested on the examination in 44 easy-to-use study modules. Each study module is a manageable task which facilitates your exam preparation. Turn to the TABLE OF CONTENTS and peruse it to get a feel for the organization of this volume.

As you read the next few paragraphs which describe the contents of this book (Volume I), flip through the chapters to gain a general familiarity with the book's organization and contents.

Chapters 2, 3, and 4 of Volume I will help you "satisfy the grader."

Chapter 2   Examination Grading and Grader Orientation
Chapter 3   The Solutions Approach
Chapter 4   Taking the Examination

Chapters 2, 3, and 4 contain material that should be kept in mind throughout your study program. Refer back to them frequently. Reread them for a final time just before you sit for the exam.

Chapter 5 (Auditing) and Chapter 6 (Business Law) each contain

1. AICPA Content Specification Outlines combined with the authors' frequency analysis thereof
2. Outlines of material tested on that section of the examination

Chapters 7 through 11 outline the practice and theory sections of the CPA examination. Chapter 7, Accounting Theory and Accounting Practice, discusses the general coverage of the theory and practice sections of the examination. This chapter also contains the AICPA Content Specification Outlines combined with the frequency analyses for all the financial accounting topics tested in the theory and practice parts of the exam. The content specification outlines and frequency analyses of the other topics tested in the theory and practice parts of the exam are located at the beginning of Chapters 9 (Cost Accounting), 10 (Governmental and Nonprofit Accounting), and 11 (Taxes). Note that Chapter 13, Taxes, is currently tested only in the practice section. Also note that the official pronouncements (ARBs, APBs, SFASs), which are tested in the accounting theory and accounting practice parts of the exam, are presented in outline form at the end of Chapter 8, Financial Accounting.

The first objective of Volume II is to provide CPA candidates with recent examination problems organized by topic, e.g., audit reports, secured transactions, consolidations, etc. In addition to the traditional approach of printing practice problems and essay questions, Volume II includes over 2,100 multiple choice questions (largely May 1983 to May 1989). Multiple choice questions are an effective means of studying the material tested on the exam (in contrast to studying the solutions approach). It is also necessary, however, to work with practice problems and essay questions to develop the solutions approach (the ability to solve CPA essay questions and practice problems efficiently).

The second objective of Volume II is to provide (1) the AICPA Unofficial Answers for each essay question/problem, (2) an outline of the solution for each essay question, (3) an explanation and solution guide of how to solve each practice problem, and (4) a one-paragraph explanation for each multiple choice question. The essay questions, multiple choice questions, and problems are arranged in 44 modules which parallel the modules in Volume I.

A significant feature of these volumes is the grouping of multiple choice questions into topical categories. These categories correspond to the sequencing of material as it appears within the text of each corresponding module in Volume I. In the answer explanations for the multiple choice questions in Volume II, we have included headings which provide cross-references to the text material in Volume I. For example, in Module 24, Fixed Assets, a heading appears above the answers to those questions dealing with depreciation. This heading is identified by the letter "F." To find the topical coverage of depreciation in Volume I, the candidate would refer to the Table of Contents for Financial Accounting (Chapter 8) and look under the module title (Fixed Assets) for the letter "F." At the right on the line marked "F." would be the appropriate page number in Fixed Assets related to depreciation.

Other Textbooks

Since this text is a compilation of study guides and outlines, it may be necessary to supplement it with accounting textbooks and other materials. You probably already have some of these texts or earlier editions of them. In such a case, you must make the decision whether to replace them and trade familiarity (including notes therein, etc.), with the cost and inconvenience of obtaining the newer texts containing a more updated presentation.

Before spending time and money acquiring new texts, begin your study program with CPA EXAMINATION REVIEW to determine your need for supplemental texts.

Ordering Other Textual Materials

You probably already have intermediate, advanced, and cost accounting texts for theory and practice. Governmental accounting is generally covered sufficiently in one or two chapters of an advanced accounting text. A law text and an auditing text may also be needed to prepare for their respective sections. If you cannot order desired texts through a local bookstore, write the publisher directly.

The pervasive need of candidates will be AICPA materials. Candidates should locate an AICPA member to order their materials, since members are entitled to a 20% discount (educators obtain a 40% discount) and may place telephone orders. The backlog at the order department is substantial; telephone orders decrease delivery time from a month or more to about a week. The telephone number and address of the AICPA are as follows:

Telephone: (800) 334-6961   Address: Order Department
American Institute of Certified
Public Accountants
1211 Avenue of the Americas
New York, New York 10036-8775

You may request shipment by first class, which is billed separately.

Working CPA Problems

The content outlines/frequency analyses, study outlines, etc., in Volume I will be used to acquire and assimilate the knowledge tested on the examination. This, however, should be only <u>one-half</u> of your preparation program. The other half should be spent practicing how to work problems using Volume II, "Problems and Solutions."

Most candidates probably spend over 90% of their time reviewing material tested on the CPA exam. Much more time should be allocated to working old examination problems <u>under exam conditions</u>.

Working old examination problems (including essay questions) serves two functions. First, it helps you develop a solutions approach as well as solutions that will satisfy the grader. Second, it provides the best test of your knowledge of the material.

At a minimum, candidates should work one of the more complex and difficult problems (e.g., statement of cash flows, consolidated financial statement worksheet, process cost report) in each area or module.

The multiple choice questions and answers can be used in many ways. First, they may be used as a diagnostic evaluation of your knowledge. For example, before beginning to review deferred taxes you may wish to answer 10 to 15 multiple choice questions to determine your ability to answer CPA examination questions on deferred taxes. The apparent difficulty of the questions and the correctness of your answers will allow you to determine the necessary breadth and depth of your review. Additionally, exposure to examination questions prior to review and study of the material should provide motivation. You will develop a feel for your level of proficiency and an understanding of the scope and difficulty of past examination questions. Moreover, your review materials will explain concepts encountered in the diagnostic multiple choice questions.

Second, the multiple choice questions can be used as a post-study or post-review evaluation. You should attempt to understand all concepts mentioned (even in incorrect answers) as you answer the questions. Refer to the explanation of the answer for discussion of the alternatives even though you selected the correct response. Thus, you should read the explanation of the unofficial answer unless you completely understand the question and all of the alternative answers.

Third, you may wish to use the multiple choice questions as a primary study vehicle. This is probably the quickest, but least thorough approach in preparing for the exam. Make a sincere effort to understand the question and to select the correct response before referring to the unofficial answer and explanation. In many cases, the explanations will appear inadequate because of your unfamiliarity with the topic. Always refer back to an appropriate study source, such as the outlines and text in this volume, your accounting textbooks, FASB pronouncements, etc.

The multiple choice questions outnumber the essay questions/practice problems by greater than 10 to 1 in this book. This is similar to a typical CPA exam. The November 1988 exam contained

	Multiple Choice	Essay/Problem
Practice I	60	2
Auditing	60	4
Practice II	60	2
Business Law	60	4
Theory	60	4
Total	300	16

The numbers are somewhat misleading in that many essay questions/practice problems contain multiple (and often unrelated) parts.

One problem with so many multiple choice questions is that you may overemphasize them. Candidates generally prefer to work multiple choice questions because they are
1. Shorter and less time consuming
2. Solvable with less effort
3. Less frustrating than essay questions and practice problems

Another problem with the large number of multiple choice questions is that you may tend to become overly familiar with the questions. The result may be that you begin reading the facts and assumptions of previously studied questions into the questions on your examination. Guard against this potential problem by reading each multiple choice question with extra care.

Multiple choice questions from the most recent exam appear at the end of each module. Questions labeled "Identical/similar" are either identical to or have been changed only slightly from the question to which it is referred.

Essay questions require the ability to organize and compose a solution, as well as knowledge of the subject matter. Remember, working essay questions/practice problems from start to finish is just as important as, if not more important than, working multiple choice questions.

The essay questions and unofficial answers may also be used for study purposes without preparation of answers. Before turning to the unofficial answers, study the question and outline the solution (either mentally or in the margin of the book). Look at our answer outline preceding the unofficial answer for each question and compare it to your own. Next, read the unofficial answer, underlining keywords and phrases. The underlining should reinforce your study of the answer's content and also assist you in learning how to structure your solutions. Answer outlines representing the major concepts found in the unofficial answer are provided for each theory essay question. These will facilitate your study of essay questions.

REMEMBER! The AICPA does not accept solutions in outline form. THE AICPA EXPECTS THE GRADING CONCEPTS TO BE EXPLAINED IN CLEAR, CONCISE, WELL-ORGANIZED SENTENCES. However, you may prepare answers in list form as long as the listed items complete a sentence that begins with a lead-in phrase.

The problems and solutions in Volume II provide you with an opportunity to diagnose and correct any exam-taking weaknesses prior to sitting for the examination. Continually analyze your incorrect solutions to determine the cause of the error(s) during your preparation for the exam. Treat each incorrect solution as a mistake that will not be repeated (especially on the examination). Also attempt to generalize your weaknesses so that you may change, reinforce, or develop new approaches to exam preparation and exam taking.

After you have finished reviewing for each part of the exam, work the complete sample exam for that part of the exam. A complete sample exam is provided in the Appendix to Volume II.

SELF-STUDY PROGRAM

The following suggestions will assist you in developing a systematic, comprehensive, and successful self-study program to help you complete the exam.

CPA candidates generally find it difficult to organize and complete their own self-study program. A major problem is determining what and how to study. Another major problem is developing the self-discipline to stick to a study program. Relatedly, it is often difficult for CPA candidates to determine how much to study, i.e., determining when they are sufficiently prepared. The following self-study suggestions will address these and other problems that you face in preparing for the CPA exam. Remember that these are only suggestions. You should modify them to suit your personality, available study time, and other constraints. Some of the suggestions may appear trivial, but CPA candidates generally need all the assistance they can get to systemize their study program.

Study Facilities and Available Time

Locate study facilities that will be conducive to concentrated study. Factors that you should consider include

1. Noise distraction
2. Interruptions
3. Lighting
4. Availability, e.g., a local library is not available at 5:00 a.m.
5. Accessibility, e.g., your kitchen table vs. your local library
6. Desk or table space

You will probably find different study facilities optimal for different times, e.g., your kitchen table during early morning hours and local libraries during early evening hours.

Next review your personal and professional commitments from now until the exam to determine regularly available study time. Formalize a schedule to which you can reasonably commit yourself. In the appendix to this chapter, you will find a detailed approach to managing your time available for the exam preparation program.

Self-Evaluation

The CPA EXAMINATION REVIEW self-study program is partitioned into 44 topics or modules. Since each module is clearly defined and should be studied separately, you have the task of preparing for the CPA exam partitioned into 44 manageable tasks. Partitioning the overall project into 44 modules makes preparation psychologically easier, since you sense yourself completing one small step at a time rather than seemingly never completing one or a few large steps.

By completing the following "Preliminary Estimate of Your Knowledge of Subject" inventory, organized by the 44 modules in this program, you will have a tabulation of your strong and weak areas at the beginning of your study program. This will help you budget your limited study time. Note that you should begin studying the material in each module by answering up to 1/4 of the total multiple choice questions in Volume II covering that module's topics (see instruction "5.A." in the next section). This "mini-exam" should constitute a diagnostic evaluation as to the amount of review and study you need.

Preliminary Estimate of Your Present Knowledge of Subject

No.	Module	Proficient	Fairly Proficient	Generally Familiar	Not Familiar
	AUDITING				
1	Professional Responsibilities				
2	Internal Control		X		
3	Evidence		X		
4	Reporting			X	
5	Audit Sampling	X			
6	Auditing EDP		X		

No.	Module	Proficient	Fairly Proficient	Generally Familiar	Not Familiar
	BUSINESS LAW			X	
7	Contracts			X	
8	Sales			X	
9	Commercial Paper			X	
10	Secured Transactions			X	
11	Bankruptcy				
12	Suretyship				
13	Agency			X	
14	Partnerships and Joint Ventures			X	
15	Corporations			X	
16	Federal Securities Acts			X	
17	Accountant's Legal Liability		X		
18	Regulation of Employment				
19	Property				
20	Insurance				
21	Trusts and Estates				
	THEORY AND PRACTICE				
22	Basic Theory and Financial Reporting				
23	Inventory				
24	Fixed Assets				
25	Monetary Current Assets and Current Liabilities				
26	Present Value				
27	Deferred Taxes				
28	Stockholders' Equity				
29	Investments				
30	Statement of Cash Flows		X		
31	Business Combinations and Consolidations			X	
32	Changing Prices and Foreign Currency Translation			X	
33	Miscellaneous				
34	Costing Systems				
35	Planning, Control, and Analysis				
36	Standards and Variances				
37	Nonroutine Decisions				
38	Governmental Accounting				
39	Nonprofit Accounting				
40	Taxes: Individual				
41	Taxes: Transactions in Property				
42	Taxes: Partnership				
43	Taxes: Corporate				
44	Taxes: Gift and Estate				

Time Allocation

The study program below entails an average of 250 hours (Step "6." below) of study time. The breakdown of total hours is indicated in the left margin.

$\begin{bmatrix} 3 \\ hrs. \end{bmatrix}$ 1. Study Chapters 2-4 in this volume and Chapter 1 in Volume II. These chapters are essential to your efficient preparation program.

Time estimate includes candidate's review of the examples of the solutions approach in Chapters 2 and 3.

2. Determine the order of studying for the four sections of the exam.

	Volume I	Volume II
Auditing	Chap 5	Chap 2
Business Law	Chap 6	Chap 3
Practice	Chap 7-11	Chap 4-7
Theory	Chap 7-10	Chap 4-6

If you have no preference, use the chronological order in the book. Note that you should study for practice and theory concurrently (recall that federal income taxes are not tested on theory).

$\begin{bmatrix} 1 \\ hr. \end{bmatrix}$ 3. Begin Auditing and Business Law by studying the introductory material at the beginning of Chapters 5 and 6. Begin Practice/Theory by studying Chapter 7.

Time estimate: 15-30 minutes for each section.

4. For each section (Auditing, Law, and Practice/Theory) study one module at a time. The modules for each section of the exam are listed on the previous page in the self-evaluation section.

5. For each module

$\begin{bmatrix} 38 \\ hrs. \end{bmatrix}$ A. Work 1/4 of the multiple choice questions in Volume II (e.g., if there are 40 multiple choice questions in a module, you should work every 4th question). Score yourself.

This diagnostic routine will provide you with an index of your proficiency and familiarity with the type and difficulty of questions.

Time estimate: 3 minutes each, not to exceed 1 hour total.

$\begin{bmatrix} 72 \\ hrs. \end{bmatrix}$ B. Study the outlines and illustrations in Volume I. Refer to outlines of authoritative pronouncements per instructions in Volume I. Also refer to your accounting textbooks and original authoritative pronouncements (this will occur more frequently for topics in which you have a weak background).

Time estimate: 1 hour minimum per module, with more time devoted to topics less familiar to you.

$\begin{bmatrix} 60 \\ hrs. \end{bmatrix}$ C. Work the remaining multiple choice questions in Volume II. Study the explanations of the multiple choice questions you missed or had trouble answering.

Time estimate: 3 minutes to answer each question and 2 minutes to study the answer explanation of each question missed.

$\begin{bmatrix} 48 \\ hrs. \end{bmatrix}$ D. Under exam conditions, work at least 2 essay questions and/or practice problems. Work additional essay/problems as time permits.

Time estimate: 20 minutes for each essay question, 45 minutes for each practice problem, and 10 minutes to review the unofficial answer and solution guide for each problem worked.

[28 hrs.]   E. Work through the sample CPA examinations presented at the end of Volume II. Each exam should be taken in one sitting.

Take the examination under simulated exam conditions, i.e., in a strange place with other people present (e.g., your local municipal library). Apply your solutions approach to each problem and your exam strategy to the overall exam.

You should limit yourself to the allotted exam times, and spend time afterwards grading your work and reviewing your effort. It might be helpful to do this with other CPA candidates. Another person looking over your exam might be more objective and notice things such as clarity of essays, logic of problem presentations, etc.

Time estimate: To take the exams and review them later, approximately 5-6 hours for each part.

6. The total suggested time of 250 hours is only an average. Allocation of time will vary candidate by candidate. Time requirements vary due to the diverse backgrounds and abilities of CPA candidates.

Allocate your time so you gain the most proficiency in the least time. Remember that while several hundred hours will be required, you should break the overall project down into 44 more manageable tasks. Do not study more than one module during each study session.

Using Notecards

Key definitions, formulas, lists, etc. can be summarized on notecards to illustrate important concepts. Candidates can organize the notecards into three sections: Business Law, Auditing, and Practice/Theory. During your study program, you can frequently review your notecards to refresh your memory on certain topics and to evaluate your progress. The following examples illustrate on one candidate's notecards various exam topics.

Practice and Theory

RETAIL INVENTORY	INCLUDE Bi	EXCLUDE Bi
MKUP + MKdwN	AVE COST	FIFO COST
MKUPS ONLY	CONVENTIONAL AVE L-C-M	FIFO L-C-M

CONSOLIDATIONS

Primary purpose of Consolidated F/S is to present for benefit of shareholders, CR of parent, the ni and B/S of a parent and its sub-"substance over form."

LIMITATIONS OF CONSOLIDATING —
• SUB INFO NOT DISCLOSED
• DIVERSIFICATION ELEMENTS HIDDEN
• LOSE INFO AS YOU AGGREGATE

Prepared by Cindy Johnson, former student, Northern Illinois University

Auditing

Tolerable misstatement—
Max $ misstatement for
a bal.

Audit risk—risk of the
existence of a monetary
misstatement greater than
the tolerable misstatement

Nonsampling risk—
— wrong audit procedure
— audit error   con't.

Sampling risk—may
cause result diff. than
pop. as a whole.
— Substantive tests
   1) incorrect accep. β
   2) incorrect rejec. α
— Tests of Controls
   1) risk of assessing control
      risk too low (overreliance)
   2) risk of assessing control
      risk too high (underreliance)

Prepared by Rebecca A. Hoger, Master's degree candidate, Northern Illinois University

Business Law

NEGOTIABLE INSTRUMENT

- in writing
  semi permeable movable form
- signed by appropriate person
- unconditional promise to pay
  sum certain in money

- words of negotiability
- no 2nd promise (collateral—OK)
- payable on demand or at
  definite date.

ELEMENTS OF A BINDING AGREEMENT

1) Manifestation of Mutual Assent
   a) offer
   b) acceptance
2) Reality of consent
3) consideration
4) capacity of parties
5) legality of object
6) compliance w/ statute of frauds

Prepared by Cindy Johnson, former student, Northern Illinois University

Stop Using Calculators

As you know, calculators are not permitted on the CPA exam due to security problems (you can see the cathode ray answer displays at a considerable distance). Most CPA candidates are not used to working problems without calculators. Eliminate your dependence on a calculator throughout your CPA exam preparation program so you will be able to make necessary computations quickly and accurately on the exam. To eliminate this dependence, practice computing the required answers utilizing mathematical shortcuts.

Levels of Proficiency Required

What level of proficiency do you have to develop with respect to each of the topics to pass the exam? You should work toward a minimum correct rate on the Volume II multiple choice questions of 60 to 70% in accounting practice and 70 to 75% in other areas.

In accounting practice, only 60 to 70% rather than 75% is recommended, because this section of the CPA exam is "curved." We recommend 70 to 75% for the other areas (accounting theory, auditing, and business law), because they are graded on the basis of raw points. As explained in Chapter 2, recent exams in auditing, business law, and accounting theory have been graded by adding "difficulty points" to the candidates' raw scores.

Warning: Disproportional study time devoted to multiple choice questions (relative to essay questions/practice problems) can be disastrous on the exam. You should work a substantial number of essay questions and practice problems under exam conditions, even though multiple choice questions are easier to work and are used to gauge your proficiency. The authors believe that a serious effort on essay questions and problems will also improve your proficiency on the multiple choice questions.

Conditional Candidates

If you have received conditional status on the examination, you must concentrate on the remaining part(s). Unfortunately, many candidates do not study after conditioning the exam, relying on luck to get them through the remaining part(s). Conditional candidates will find that material contained in Chapters 1-4 and the information contained in the appropriate modules will benefit them in preparing for the remaining part(s) of the examination.

PLANNING FOR THE EXAMINATION

Overall Strategy

An overriding concern should be an orderly, systematic approach toward both your preparation program and your examination strategy. A major objective should be to avoid any surprises or anything else that would rattle you during the 2 1/2 days of taking the examination. In other words, you want to be in complete control as much as possible. "Control" is of paramount importance from both positive and negative viewpoints. The presence of "control" on your part will add to your confidence and your ability to prepare for and take the exam. Moreover, the presence of "control" will make your preparation program more enjoyable (or at least less distasteful). On the other hand, a lack of organization will result in inefficiency in preparing and taking the examination, with a highly predictable outcome. Likewise, distractions during the examination (e.g., inadequate lodging, long drive) are generally disastrous.

In summary, your establishment of a systematic, orderly approach to the examination is of paramount importance.

1. Develop an overall strategy at the beginning of your preparation program (see below)
2. Supplement your overall strategy with outlines of material tested on each section of the CPA examination (see Chapters 5 through 11)
3. Supplement your overall strategy with an explicitly stated set of problem-solving procedures--the solutions approach
4. Supplement your overall strategy with an explicitly stated approach to each examination session (see Chapter 4)
5. Evaluate your preparation progress on a regular basis and prepare lists of things "to do" (see Weekly Review of Preparation Program Progress on following page)
6. RELAX: You can pass the exam. About 10,000 candidates successfully complete the exam each sitting. You will be one of them if you complete an efficient preparation program and execute well (i.e., use your solutions approach and exam strategy) while writing the exam.

The following outline is designed to provide you with a general framework of the tasks before you. You should tailor the outline to your needs by adding specific items and comments.

A. Preparation Program (refer to Self-Study Program discussed previously)

1. Obtain and organize study materials
2. Locate facilities conducive for studying and block out study time
3. During your study program, if it becomes apparent that you will not be adequately prepared for all four parts of the upcoming exam, concentrate the majority of your study on your two strongest parts. For the two parts selected, devote much of your time to correcting weaknesses and the remainder for reviewing your strengths. CANDIDATES ADOPTING THIS STRATEGY MUST DO SO ONLY IN LIGHT OF THE PASS AND/OR CONDITION REQUIREMENTS APPLICABLE IN THE STATE IN WHICH THEY PLAN TO SIT.
4. Develop your solutions approach (including solving essay questions and practice problems as well as multiple choice questions)
5. Prepare an examination strategy
6. Study the material tested recently and prepare answers to actual exam questions on these topics under examination conditions
7. Periodically evaluate your progress

B. Physical Arrangements

1. Apply to and obtain acceptance from your State Board
2. Reserve lodging for examination nights

C. Taking the Examination (covered in detail in Chapter 4)

1. Become familiar with exam facilities and procedures
2. Implement examination strategies and the solutions approach

Weekly Review of Preparation Program Progress

The following pages contain a hypothetical weekly review of program progress. You should prepare a similar progress chart. This procedure, which takes only about five minutes per week, will help you proceed through a more efficient, complete preparation program.

Make notes of materials and topics
1. That you have studied
2. That you have completed
3. That need additional study

WEEKS TO GO	COMMENTS ON PROGRESS, "to do" ITEMS, ETC.
12	1. COMPLETED READINGS ON SFASs, APBs, SFACs, AND TOOK NOTECARDS. 2. COMPLETED READING OF BASIC THEORY, INVENTORY, CONTRACTS, AND FIXED ASSETS MODS. 3. NEED WORK AT MULTIPLE CHOICE AND SOLUTIONS APPROACH TO PRACTICE PROBLEMS IN MODS.
11	1. READ PROFESSIONAL RESP., INTERNAL CONTROL, AND EVIDENCE MODS. PREPARED AUDIT PROGRAMS FOR RECEIVABLES, PAYROLL CYCLES 2. READ SALES/COMMERCIAL PAPER MODULES - WORKED SOME M/C AND A FEW ESSAYS. 3. WORKED ON BUS. LAW ESSAY PROBLEMS & SOLUTIONS APPROACH TO SOLVING THEM.
10	1. WORKED THROUGH MONETARY CA AND CL, PRESENT VALUE, AND DEFERRED TAXES MODS. DID A FEW M/C & PROBLEMS FROM EACH. 2. NEED WORK ON COMMERCIAL PAPER REQUIREMENTS. 3. READ SECURED TRANSACTIONS AND BANKRUPTCY MODS. 4. WORK NEEDED ON SOLUTIONS APPROACH FOR AUDITING ESSAYS.
9	1. WORKED ON STOCKHOLDERS' EQUITY, INVESTMENTS, STATEMENT OF CASH FLOWS, AND BUSINESS COMBINATIONS MODULES. 2. WORKED AT SOME M/C AND ESSAYS FOR EACH MOD. 3. NEED WORK ON TIME BANK ON ESSAY PROBLEMS -- CUT DOWN ON TIME. 4. NEED TO READ REPORTING MODULE AND PREPARE A STANDARD UNQUALIFIED AUDIT REPORT.

WEEKS TO GO	COMMENTS ON PROGRESS, "to do" ITEMS, ETC.
8	1. READ SURETYSHIP, AGENCY, PARTNERSHIP LAW MODULES -- WORKED THRU MULTIPLE CHOICE -- TRY A FEW ESSAYS. 2. WORKED ON AUDIT SAMPLING MODULE. 3. TAKE NOTECARDS ON AUDIT SAMPLING TERMS 4. READ GOVERNMENTAL AND NONPROFIT ACCOUNTING MODULES.
7	1. FINISHED AUDIT EDP, CORPORATIONS, CHANGING PRICES/FOREIGN CURRENCY, AND MISCELLANEOUS FINANCIAL MODS. 2. WORKED THROUGH AUDIT AND BUS. LAW ESSAYS. 3. START READING THE COST ACCOUNTING AND TAX MODULES.
6	1. WORKED ON COST SYSTEMS, PLANNING, AND STANDARD MODS FOR COST. 2. FINISHED INDIVIDUAL TAX MODULE. 3. WORK ON PROBLEMS/ESSAYS FOR COST MODS. 4. REVIEW NEEDED ON CONTRACT REQUIREMENTS.
5	1. READ PROPERTY TAX, PARTNERSHIP TAX, AND FEDERAL SECURITIES LAW MODS. 2. WORKED AT MULTIPLE CHOICE FOR THE ABOVE MODS. 3. DO A FEW ESSAYS FOR TAX/BUS. LAW MODULES. 4. TAKE NOTECARDS ON TAXABLE INCOME, AGI CALCULATION.
4	1. MODS COMPLETED: NONROUTINE DECISIONS, CORPORATE TAX, GIFT AND ESTATE TAX, AND ACCOUNTANT'S LEGAL LIABILITY. 2. WORKED ON MULTIPLE CHOICE AND PROBLEMS FOR COST MODS. 3. WORK ON TAX PROBLEMS.
3	1. TOOK PRACTICE/THEORY SAMPLE EXAM. 2. STILL NEED WORK ON TIME BANK. 3. WENT OVER SASs, AND SSARSs -- TAKE NOTECARDS FOR. 4. GO OVER AUDITING MULTIPLE CHOICE -- A FEW IN EACH MODULE.

WEEKS TO GO	COMMENTS ON PROGRESS, "to do" ITEMS, ETC.
2	1. READ REGULATION OF EMPLOYMENT, PROPERTY, INSURANCE, AND TRUST MODS IN BUSINESS LAW. 2. WORK THROUGH BUSINESS LAW MULTIPLE CHOICE AND ESSAYS FROM EACH MOD. 3. TAKE THE AUDITING SAMPLE EXAM.
1	1. TOOK BUSINESS LAW PRACTICE EXAM. 2. REVIEW NOTECARDS FOR LAW, PRACTICE/THEORY AND AUDITING. 3. REVIEW SOLUTIONS APPROACH, TIME BANK, INDIVIDUAL AND CORPORATE TAX MODS.
0	1. TOOK SAMPLE EXAMS FOR ALL MODULES. 2. REVIEW EXAMINATION POLICIES AND PROCEDURES. 3. REVIEW NOTECARDS. 4. REVIEW AUDIT REPORTS. 5. PREPARED INVENTORY AUDIT PROGRAM, QUALIFIED AUDIT REPORT. 6. WORKED THROUGH A STATEMENT OF CASH FLOWS.

APPENDIX

TIME MANAGEMENT FOR CPA CANDIDATES

Twice a year, candidates begin preparing for the CPA exam. They buy CPA review manuals, notebooks, dividers, pens, pencils, erasers, and even books that say to "keep a positive mental attitude toward this new and difficult assignment." All this is important to you as you begin studying for the exam. However, let us raise a note of caution--do not charge into your studies with such enthusiasm that you neglect to consider the magnitude of the task.

We know you have heard "war stories" from previous CPA candidates about the hundreds of hours that you will have to spend during the next three to four months working problems and reading official pronouncements. We know that all too often candidates do not realize the extent to which their time will be committed to studying for the exam. Common sense should tell you that finding those hundreds of hours for study will not be a simple task.

In this section of your CPA review program, we will help you to identify the hours you have available for studying for the CPA exam. We ask that you complete a short exercise using the "Time Analysis Matrix." After completing this exercise, you will have indentified the "time blocks" that are currently available to you for study. This is an important exercise for you, whether you are a full-time student or a full-time practitioner.

Time Analysis Matrix.

The "Time Analysis Matrix" (last page of this appendix) covers one complete week (i.e., seven days, twenty-four hours per day). The days of the week move across the matrix, while the hours of the day are listed down the left-hand side of the matrix. Each box represents a one-hour time block that is available to you. You have 168 (7 days x 24 hours) one-hour time blocks to work with every week.

Analyzing Your Fixed Time.

Fixed time is the time you have allocated for SPECIFIC PURPOSES throughout your CURRENT WEEKLY SCHEDULE. For example, if you are a full-time student, your CURRENT CLASS SCHEDULE should represent fixed time. When you are in class, you cannot be in the library or the coffee shop. You are committed to using this time in a specific way. If you are working full-time, your normal working hours should be considered fixed time. Additionally, hours allotted to normal sleep time should be considered fixed time. IN SHORT, ANY HOURS YOU HAVE SPECIFICALLY COMMITTED TO USING REGULARLY DURING THE WEEK SHOULD BE CONSIDERED FIXED TIME.

Take a few moments and examine the TIME ANALYSIS MATRIX. Use a colored pencil or pen and shade in the time blocks that represent FIXED TIME in your CURRENT WEEKLY SCHEDULE. After you have finished shading in the time blocks, COUNT the shaded blocks and complete the following equations

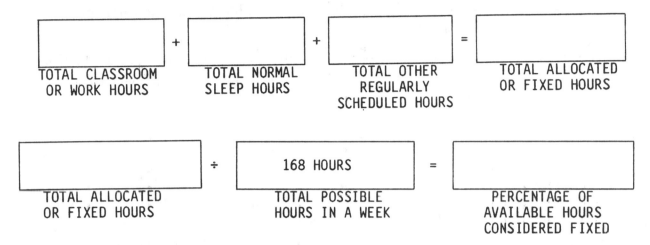

Now for the Moment of Truth.

If you are like most <u>undergraduate students</u>, your percentage of fixed hours should be around 46%. If this is true, you probably have approximately 54% or 91 hours per week that can be used in a DISCRETIONARY manner. It is with these DISCRETIONARY HOURS that PERSONAL TIME MANAGEMENT techniques can really be of help to you. If you can make the discretionary hours productive, you will find there is more than enough time to adequately prepare for the CPA exam.

If you are <u>working full-time</u> and studying for the exam through a review course or on your own, you will probably find that approximately 70% of your time will be fixed. Therefore, you have approximately 30% or 50 hours per week to use at your DISCRETION. You will have to work even harder at making the discretionary hours productive hours.

Approaching Your Discretionary Hours.

CPA CANDIDATES DO NOT LIVE BY SOLVING PROBLEMS ALONE! Believe it or not, even CPA candidates need time to relax and refresh their minds. However, you must carefully limit and properly sequence the discretionary time you spend relaxing and refreshing your mind.

Each hour on the TIME ANALYSIS MATRIX that is not shaded is considered discretionary. For each of these time blocks, you have to make an important decision. HOW DO YOU WANT TO USE EACH DISCRETIONARY HOUR? Take a few moments and shade in the discretionary time blocks.   (Use a light-colored pencil which is a different color than the one used for FIXED TIME.) This will make them stand out so you can see the impact of this free time and where it is located on the matrix.

How do you make a discretionary hour become a PRODUCTIVE HOUR? As you look at the discretionary hours on the time analysis matrix, where do you need both a PHYSICAL and a MENTAL break? Think about your personal needs, since no two people work, study, or rest in exactly the same way. Where you need BOTH the PHYSICAL and MENTAL break period, WRITE THE LETTER "B" in the time block. Now the discretionary time period has become a PRODUCTIVE-FIXED time period.

Review the time analysis matrix. At this point, you have allocated time blocks to "fixed hours" and to "break hours." The REMAINING hours are what you have to work with as you begin to set the remainder of your schedule.

Now--What Time Do You Have Left?

At this point, any time blocks that are shaded as DISCRETIONARY and do not contain the letter "B" are available for scheduling. LOOK FOR TIME PERIODS THAT ARE AVAILABLE CONSISTENTLY FROM DAY TO DAY. For example, you might find that 7-9 P.M. is open Monday through Friday. This would be a perfect time slot for allocating to STUDY TIME. It is a reasonable length of study time, and it is available every day. REASONABLENESS OF THE STUDY PERIOD AND CONSISTENCY OF AVAILABILITY ARE "CRUCIAL" TO USING THE TIME BLOCKS AS PRODUCTIVE STUDY PERIODS. Take a few moments and mark the time blocks you want to designate as STUDY PERIODS. WRITE THE LETTER "S" in these time blocks.

The Final Analysis.

Review the time analysis matrix and count the number of hours you have designated as being FIXED. Next, count the number of hours you originally designated as DISCRETIONARY, but which have now been marked as being DISCRETIONARY-USED FOR BREAKS (i.e., the letter "B"). Finally, count the number of hours you have marked as being DISCRETIONARY-USED FOR STUDY (i.e., the letter "S"). Complete the following equation and see how you have allocated your time. ARE YOU GETTING THE MOST OUT OF YOUR TIME? IF NOT, STEP BACK AND REWORK YOUR SCHEDULE.

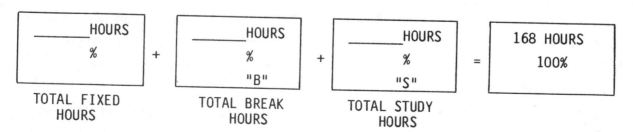

NOTE: For the FINAL ANALYSIS, consider time designated as neither FIXED nor DISCRETIONARY-USED FOR STUDY to be DISCRETIONARY-USED FOR BREAKS. Therefore, "Break Time" will be used both for relaxation and for time not otherwise assigned for a specific purpose.

Time Analysis Matrix

	MON	TUES	WED	THURS	FRI		SAT	SUN
1 am								
2 am								
3 am								
4 am								
5 am								
6 am								
7 am								
8 am								
9 am								
10 am								
11 am								
12 pm								
1 pm								
2 pm								
3 pm								
4 pm								
5 pm								
6 pm								
7 pm								
8 pm								
9 pm								
10 pm								
11 pm								
12 am								

NOW IS THE TIME
TO MAKE A COMMITMENT

CHAPTER TWO
EXAMINATION GRADING AND GRADER ORIENTATION

All State Boards of Accountancy use the AICPA advisory grading service. As your grade is to be determined by this process, it is very important that you understand the AICPA grading process and its implications for your preparation program and for the solution techniques you will use during the examination.

The AICPA has a full-time staff of CPA examination personnel whose responsibilities include

1. Preparing questions for the examination
2. Working with outside consultants who prepare questions
3. Preparation of grading guides and unofficial answers
4. Supervising and reviewing the work of examination graders

The AICPA examination staff is under the supervision of the AICPA Board of Examiners which has the responsibility for the CPA examination.

This chapter contains a description of the AICPA grading process based on the description of AICPA grading in Information for CPA Candidates, AICPA grading guides, etc.

The AICPA Grading Process

The AICPA exercises very tight control over all the examination papers during the grading process and prior to their return to individual State Boards of Accountancy. Upon receipt from the exam sites, papers are assigned to control groups, reviewed for candidate numbers, and checked against state board records of examination papers submitted.

Multiple choice questions are graded electronically. Essay questions and practice problems are graded individually on the basis of grading guides. Grading guides consist of grading concepts, which are ideas, constructs, principles, etc., that can be clearly defined. Grading concepts for practice problems include amounts such as equivalent units of production or goodwill, as well as particular debits and credits in journal entries.

While tentative grading guides (answers) are prepared prior to the examination, the final grading guides are based upon two test gradings of samples of actual examinations. Once grading guides are fully developed, "production graders" perform the first grading of the examination. The "production graders" are practicing CPAs, university professors, attorneys, etc., commissioned by the AICPA on a per diem basis to grade the examination. These graders specialize in a single essay question or practice problem, and grade answers to that question for about six weeks. About 200 graders, some full-time, some part-time, are required for each examination.

After the multiple choice questions are machine-graded and returned to their respective examinations, the first grading of essay questions and practice problems begins. The control group of papers moves from grader to grader. Attached to each examination is a grading guide similar to the "Hypothetical Grading Guide" on page 34. The purpose of the first grading is to separate examinations as to pass, fail, and marginal.

The second grading is performed by reviewers who generally inspect the work of the "production graders" but emphasize review of the marginal examinations, i.e., papers with grades of 70 to 74. Papers with grades of 70 to 74 are regraded to grades of 69 or 75. One of the major reasons for this procedure is to relieve State Boards of Accountancy of requests for regrading failing papers "very near" 75. Most 72s, 73s, and 74s are regraded to 75. All of the questions on papers selected for regrading are reevaluated. Grade changes (when made) are made to the essay questions or practice problems. An analysis is undertaken of all essay questions and practice problems to differentiate sophisticated grading concepts (those included by most candidates passing the exam) from rudimentary grading concepts (those included by candidates both passing and failing the exam). Answers which include sophisticated grading concepts are generally graded up, and papers with only rudimentary grading concepts are generally graded down. Note this procedure is only applied to papers in the 70 through 74 range. In all cases, as throughout the grading procedure, the candidate is given the benefit of the doubt.

The third grading is administered to papers that have several passing parts but have a failing score on a particular part. A fourth and final grading may be per-formed on papers that continue to have inconsistent grades after the third grading, e.g., 88, 84, 68, 89.

Note that the first grading is directed to individual questions while the second grading is directed to individual sections, e.g., Theory, Law, etc. The third grading is a review of failing parts written by candidates who have done well on other remaining parts (or for example, conditional candidates with one part to go). The fourth and final grading is directed to any remaining inconsistencies. It should be emphasized that answer format, presentation, logic, etc., are given more consider-ation on the regradings than on the first grading.

A tape totaling the grade on individual questions for each section is then prepared. The examination papers, grades, and grading tapes are returned to the individual state boards several weeks prior to the official grade release date. The grade release date is usually at the end of January for the November exam, and at the end of July for the May exam.

What Graders Are Looking For

Based on Information for CPA Candidates, the examination instructions, examination questions, unofficial answers, etc., the examiners appear to be looking for

1. Knowledge of the academic content of the typical undergraduate accounting major (including business law)
2. Ability to apply this knowledge to specific situations with good judgment
3. Precise and concise use of the English language
4. Examination, evaluation, and classification of data in complex situations
5. Organization and presentation of accounting data
6. Application of accounting and auditing standards, procedures, etc., to specific situations

Multiple Choice Grading

Conversion tables are developed for each overall question which consists of a number of individual multiple choice questions. These tables assign one point for each correct response on the auditing, business law, and theory sections of the examination. Grades on these parts have been modified by "difficulty points" whereby candidates are "spotted" points for attempting the multiple choice questions (note that this is a means of "curving" the grades on the entire section).

The November 1988 multiple choice point allocation and grading were typical of recent exams. Auditing, Business Law, and Theory presented all their multiple choice questions as Problem 1. For these sections, each correct response was worth 1 point. "Difficulty points" were awarded on the November 1988 exam as summarized in the following table.

	No. of MC	% of section grade	"Difficulty points"	No. of correct responses for 75% on MC	Correct response rate req.
Auditing	60	60%	5	40	67%
Business Law	60	60%	6	39	65%
Theory	60	60%	3	42	70%
Practice	120	60%	7	76	63%

Practice I and Practice II each had three problems consisting of 20 multiple choice items with each question worth one-half of a point. Each problem made up 10% of the total grade of the practice portion of the exam. The conversion tables for the six multiple choice problems in Practice I and II for November 1988 appear below.

Practice I

Problem 1		Problem 2		Problem 3	
No. correct	Grade	No. correct	Grade	No. correct	Grade
20-18	10	20-18	10	20-18	10
17	9.5	17	9.5	17	9.5
16	9	16	9	16	9
15	8.5	15	8.5	15	8.5
14	8	14	8	14	8
13*	7.5	13*	7.5	13*	7.5
12	7	12	7	12	7
11	6.5	11	6.5	11	6.5
10	6	10	6	10	6
9	5.5	9	5.5	9	5.5
8	5	8	5	8	5
7	4.5	7	4.5	7	4.5
6	4	6	4	6	4
5	3.5	5	3.5	5	3.5
4	3	4	3	4	3
3	2.5	3	2.5	3	2.5
2	2	2	2	2	2
1	1.5	1	1.5	1	1.5
0	0	0	0	0	0

Practice II

Problem 1		Problem 2		Problem 3	
No. correct	Grade	No. correct	Grade	No. correct	Grade
20-18	10	20-17	10	20-17	10
17	9.5	16	9.5	16	9.5
16	9	15	9	15	9
15	8.5	14	8.5	14	8.5
14	8	13	8	13	8
13*	7.5	12*	7.5	12*	7.5
12	7	11	7	11	7
11	6.5	10	6.5	10	6.5
10	6	9	6	9	6
9	5.5	8	5.5	8	5.5
8	5	7	5	7	5
7	4.5	6	4.5	6	4.5
6	4	5	4	5	4
5	3.5	4	3.5	4	3.5
4	3	3	3	3	3
3	2.5	2	2.5	2	2.5
2	2	1	2	1	2
1	1.5	0	0	0	0
0	0				

*Number of correct responses to achieve 75% on this problem.

Consistent with the other sections of the examination, "difficulty points" are awarded for the practice multiple choice problems. As can be seen, the ratio of correct responses over total questions required for "75%" on each question (marked by asterisk) - 13/20, 13/20, 13/20, 13/20, 12/20, and 12/20, respectively - was cumulatively 76/120, for an overall 63% correct response rate. Because a "non-curved" exam requires a total of 90 correct responses (75% of 120 questions), 14 questions or 7 points were "spotted" to the candidates sitting for the practice portion of the November 1988 exam (remember that each question is worth one-half of a point).

Implications: Since grading is on a relative basis, do your best regardless of the difficulty of the questions. Perfect and use a "multiple choice question solutions approach" which is discussed in Chapter 3. If you are unsure about a particular question, you should make an educated guess, i.e., pick the "best" answer. Your grade is based on your total correct answers, i.e., no penalty exists for incorrect answers. The grading procedure for multiple choice questions is explained in the instructions at the beginning of each section of the exam. The importance of carefully reading and following these, and all other instructions, cannot be overemphasized.

Essay Grading

To illustrate the grading of essay questions, we have included question Number 3 from the November 1985 Business Law Examination in this section. Following the question are the AICPA Unofficial Answer and a hypothetical grading guide.

Number 3

John Nolan, a partner in Nolan, Stein, & Wolf partnership, transferred his interest in the partnership to Simon and withdrew from the partnership. Although the partnership will continue, Stein and Wolf have refused to admit Simon as a partner.

Subsequently, the partnership appointed Ed Lemon as its agent to market its various product lines. Lemon entered into a two-year written agency contract with the partnership which provided that Lemon would receive a 10% sales commission. The agency contract was signed by Lemon and, on behalf of the partnership, by Stein and Wolf.

After six months, Lemon was terminated without cause. Lemon asserts that:

• He is an agent coupled with an interest.

• The agency relationship may not be terminated without cause prior to the expiration of its term.

• He is entitled to damages because of the termination of the agency relationship.

Required:

Answer the following, setting forth reasons for any conclusions stated.

a. Discuss Nolan's property rights in the partnership prior to his withdrawal and the property rights acquired by Simon as a result of his transaction with Nolan.

b. Discuss the merits of Lemon's assertions.

UNOFFICIAL ANSWER

a. Nolan's property rights in the partnership prior to the conveyance of his partnership interest consisted of:

• His rights in specific partnership property. This right permitted Nolan to possess any item of partnership property for partnership purposes.

• His interest in the partnership. This interest is classified as personal property and is defined as the partner's share of the profits and surplus (including capital).

• His right to participate in the management of the partnership. This right entitles Nolan to an equal voice in the management and conduct of the partnership business.

Nolan's transfer of his partnership interest to Simon merely entitles Simon to receive Nolan's share of the profits and Nolan's interest in any property distributed by the partnership. Since Stein and Wolf have refused to admit Simon as a partner, Simon will not be entitled to participate in the management of the partnership or to acquire Nolan's right to possess specific partnership property.

b. Lemon's first assertion that he is an agent coupled with an interest is incorrect. An agency coupled with an interest in the subject matter arises when the agent has an interest in the property that is the subject of the agency. The fact that Lemon entered into a two-year written agency agreement with the partnership that would pay Lemon a commission clearly will not establish an interest in the subject matter of the agency. The mere expectation of profits to be realized or proceeds to be derived from the sale of the partnership's products is not sufficient to create an agency coupled with an interest. As a result, the principal-agency relationship may be terminated at any time.

Lemon's second assertion that the principal-agency relationship may not be terminated without cause prior to the expiration of its term is incorrect. Where a principal-agency relationship is based upon a contract to engage the agent for a specified period of time, the principal may discharge the agent despite the fact such discharge is wrongful. Although the principal does not have the right to discharge the agent, he does have the power to do so. Thus, Lemon may be discharged without cause.

Lemon's third assertion that he is entitled to damages because of the termination of the agency relationship is correct. Where a principal wrongfully discharges its agent, the principal is liable for damages based on breach of contract. Under the facts, Lemon's discharge by the partnership without cause constitutes a breach of contract for which Lemon may recover damages.

Essay questions are generally graded based on the number of <u>grading concepts</u> in the candidate's solution. The grading guide is a list of the grading concepts and raw point(s) assigned to each concept. The total raw points listed are usually in

excess of the maximum points which a candidate may earn on the question. A
hypothetical grading guide for the preceding business law essay question appears
below.

November 1985 Business Law, Number 3
Hypothetical Grading Guide*

		Grading points
a.	Nolan's property rights in partnership	
	Right to possess partnership property for partnership purposes	1
	Partnership interest is personal property	1
	Right to equal voice in management	1
	Simon's property rights in partnership	
	Right to share in profits	1
	Entitled to share in property distributed by the partnership	1
	No right to specific partnership property	1
	No right to participate in management	1
b.	Validity of Lemon's assertions	
	Assertion 1 is incorrect	1
	Agency coupled with an interest requires agent to have an interest in subject of agency	1
	Commission does not qualify as agency coupled with an interest	1
	Can terminate at any time since lacking an agency coupled with an interest	1
	Assertion 2 is incorrect	1
	Principal always has power to terminate the agent	1
	Principal does not have necessarily have the right to terminate the agent	1
	Assertion 3 is correct	1
	If principal wrongfully discharges agent, principal is liable for damages under breach of contract	1
Grading Points Possible		16

The conversion scale below converts the "raw" grading points shown above to the grade
earned on the question.

CONVERSION SCALE

Grading Points Earned	16-13	12	11	10	9-8	7-6	5-4	3	2	1	0
Grade	10	9	8	7.5	7	6.5	5	4	3	2	1

TOTAL GRADE: NUMBER 3
Grade from Conversion Scale
Demerit for form, etc.   _____
                                                          _____
                                                          ======

Note: To obtain a passing grade (7.5) on this question, a candidate would need to
earn 10 of the possible 16 points (62.5%).

*The AICPA Board of Examiners does not release the grading guides used for scoring
essay questions. The grading guide above was prepared by the authors to illustrate
to candidates the manner in which points are allocated to grading concepts.*

In the above grading guide, note that each grading concept is summarized by several keywords. Graders undoubtedly scan for these keywords during the first grading.

Another consideration is "cross-grading." Often candidates answer one requirement elsewhere than required; i.e., the answer to requirement "a" may be written as part of the answer to requirement "b." Frequently, the grading guides permit "cross-grading," i.e., giving credit in one part of the answer for a correct response in another part of the answer. To assure full credit, however, candidates should be very careful to organize their answers to meet the question requirements; i.e., you should answer requirement "a" in answer "a," answer requirement "b" in answer "b," etc. Additionally, the efficient use of time is of the utmost importance. If you have included grading concepts in one part of a question that are applicable to another part of the same question, do not repeat them. Simply refer the grader to your previous answer.

Two common misconceptions about the AICPA grading of essay questions have cost candidates points in recent years. First, answers should not consist of a listing (or outline) of keywords. Answers should be set forth in short, concise sentences, organized per the requirements of the question. However, it is acceptable to prepare answers in list form, so long as the listed items complete a sentence that begins with a lead-in phrase. Second, a candidate should not answer only one or two parts of a question very thoroughly and leave the remaining parts blank. Even though the grading guide may have more grading concepts than there are points available, each part of a question may have a limited number of attainable points.

Notice that the last grading concept in the example grading guide is "Demerit for form, etc." Grading guides may provide a penalty for sloppiness, inadequate form, etc. Alternatively, they may provide a bonus for good form and appearance. A closely related matter is the examiner's consideration of the candidates' ability to express themselves in acceptable written language. Recent examinations have contained the following paragraph in the instructions for each section of the exam.

> A CPA is continually confronted with the necessity of expressing opinions and conclusions in written reports in clear, unequivocal language. Although the primary purpose of the examination is to test the candidate's knowledge and application of the subject matter, the ability to organize and present such knowledge in acceptable written language may be considered by the examiners.

The grading guide might be thought of as a brief outline of the unofficial answer. Note the similarities between the grading guide and the unofficial answer.

Problem Grading

Problem grading guides are more structured than the grading guides for essay questions, because essay questions have an open-ended nature. Although some alternative calculations may be acceptable for practice problems, relatively little latitude is available in the problem solutions. Problem grading guides consist of check figures from throughout the unofficial answer. The grading of a practice problem is illustrated in the next chapter, The Solutions Approach.

Allocation of Points to Questions

Information for CPA Candidates states that the "maximum point values for each question are approximately proportional to the minutes allotted to the question in the suggested time budget printed in the examination booklet." Candidates should be concerned with point allocations for the purpose of allocating their time on the exam.

Grading Implications for CPA Candidates

Analysis of the grading process helps you understand what graders are looking for and how you can present solutions to "satisfy the grader." Before turning to Chapter 3 for a discussion of how to prepare solutions, consider the following conclusions derived from the foregoing grading analysis.

1. Your solutions should be neat and orderly to avoid demerits and to obtain bonuses
2. Allocate your time based on AICPA minimum suggested times
3. Do your best on every question, no matter how difficult

    a. Remember the exam is graded on a relative basis
    b. If a question is difficult for you, it probably is difficult for others also
    c. Develop a "solutions approach" to assist you

4. No supporting notes or computations are required for the multiple choice questions; however, you may use scratch paper to perform computations, etc. The multiple choice answers are machine-graded, and any related work on scratch paper is ignored.

    a. Conversely, supplementary computation sheets should be prepared for practice problems for submission to the grader

5. Essay solutions should be numbered and organized according to the problem requirements, e.g., a, b1, b2, c1, c2, c3, d1, d2

    a. Label your solutions parallel to the requirements
    b. Emphasize keywords
    c. Separate grading concepts into individual sentences or short paragraphs

        1) Do not bury grading concepts in lengthy paragraphs that might be missed by the grader. Include as many sensible grading concepts as possible.
        2) Use short, uncomplicated sentence structure
        3) DO NOT PRESENT YOUR ANSWER IN OUTLINE FORMAT

    d. Do not omit any requirements

6. Problem solutions should also be numbered and organized according to the requirements of the problem

   a. Solutions should be complete because of the finite number of grading concepts

   b. Label solutions neatly to help the grader find the required grading concepts (check figures)

      1) Reasonable abbreviations are fine, e.g., A/P for accounts payable

      2) Headings should be prepared for all schedules and statements

      3) Assumptions should be briefly stated indicating knowledge of alternative treatments

   c. All supporting calculations should be prepared on answer sheets or computational sheets

      1) All such supporting calculations and schedules should be labeled

      2) In your answer, you should use references such as "See sched. A"

In summary, SATISFY THE GRADER. You need neat, readable solutions organized according to the requirements, which will also be the organization of the grading guides. Remember that a legible, well-organized solution gives a professional appearance. Additionally, recognize the plight of the grader having to decipher one mess after another, day after day. Give him/her a break with a neat, orderly solution. The "halo" effect will be rewarded by additional consideration (and hopefully points!).

NOW IS THE TIME
TO MAKE A COMMITMENT

CHAPTER THREE
THE SOLUTIONS APPROACH

The solutions approach is a systematic problem-solving methodology. The purpose is to assure efficient, complete solutions to CPA exam problems, some of which are complex and confusing relative to most undergraduate accounting problems.

Unfortunately, there appears to be a widespread lack of emphasis on problem-solving techniques in accounting courses. Most accounting books and courses merely provide solutions to specific types of problems. Memorization of these solutions for examinations and preparation of homework problems from examples is "cookbooking."

"Cookbooking" is perhaps a necessary step in the learning process, but it is certainly not sufficient training for the complexities of the business world. Professional accountants need to be adaptive to a rapidly changing complex environment. For example, CPAs have been called on to interpret and issue reports on new concepts such as price controls, energy allocations, and new taxes. These CPAs rely on their problem-solving expertise to understand these problems and to formulate solutions to them.

Practice Problem Solutions Approach Algorithm

The steps outlined below are only one of many possible series of solution steps. Admittedly, the procedures suggested are very structured; thus, you should adapt the suggestions to your needs. You may find that some steps are occasionally unnecessary, or that certain additional procedures increase your own problem-solving efficiency. Whatever the case, substantial time should be allocated to developing an efficient solutions approach before taking the examination. You should develop your solutions approach by working old CPA problems.

Note that the steps below relate to any specific problem; overall examination or section strategies are discussed in Chapter 4.

1. **Glance over the problem.** Only scan the problem. Get a feel for the type or category of problem. Do not read it. Until you understand the requirements, you cannot discriminate important data from irrelevant data.

2. **Study the requirements.** "Study" as differentiated from "read." Candidates continually lose points due to misunderstanding the requirements. Underline key phrases and words.

2a. **Visualize the solution format.** Determine the expected format of the required solution. Develop an awareness of "schedule and statement format." Put headings on the required statements and schedules. Often a single require- ment will require two or more statements, schedules, etc. A common example is a question followed by "why" or "explain." Explicitly recognize multiple requirements by numbering or lettering them on your examination booklet, expanding on the letters already assigned to problem parts.

3. **Outline the required procedures mentally.** Interrelate any data given (e.g., a trial balance or comparative balance sheets) in the problem to the expected solution format, mentally noting a "to do" list. Determine what it is you are going to do before you get started doing it. You will usually be working through the requirements in order. However, be watchful for problems with interrelated requirements (e.g., each paragraph of information given in the problem is needed to solve more than one requirement). An alternative solutions approach for these types of problems is to make all required computations for each piece of information at one time. By using this time saving approach, you will be solving a part of each requirement as each piece of information is covered, but not necessarily in the same order as given on the exam.

3a. **Review applicable principles, knowledge.** Before immersing yourself in the details of the problem, quickly (30-60 seconds) review and organize your knowledge of the principles applicable to the problem. Jot down any acronyms, formulas, or other memory aids relevant to the topic of the question. Otherwise, the details of the problem may confuse and overshadow your previous knowledge of the applicable principles.

4. **Study the text of the problem.** Read the problem carefully. With the requirements in mind, you can now begin to sort out relevant from irrelevant data. Underline and circle important data. The data necessary for answering each requirement may be scattered throughout the problem. As you study the text, use arrows, etc. to connect data pertaining to a common requirement. List the requirements (a, b, etc.) in the margin alongside the data to which they pertain. Use a bright colored pen to mark up the problem. Heavy colored underlining and comments are attention getting and give you confidence.

4a. **Prepare intermediary solutions as you study the problem.** E.g., calculate goodwill, reconstruct accounts, prepare time diagrams, timelines, journal entries, etc. You are able to perceive these required intermediary solutions because you already understand the problem requirements. These intermediary solutions, along with your underlining and your notes in the text of the problem, will drastically decrease re-reading time.

5. **Prepare the solution.** You now are in a position to write a neat, complete, organized, labeled solution. Label computations, intermediary solutions,

assumptions made, etc., on your scratch sheets and turn them in with your solution (Note: but not for multiple choice questions).

6. **Proofread and edit.** Do not underestimate the utility of this step. Just recall all of the "silly" mistakes you made on undergraduate examinations. Corrections of errors and completion of oversights during this step can easily be the difference between passing and failing.

7. **Review the requirements.** Assure yourself that you have answered them all.

Time Requirements for the Solutions Approach. Many candidates bypass the solutions approach because they feel it is too time consuming. Actually, the solutions approach is a time saver, and more importantly, it helps you prepare better solutions to all problems.

Without committing yourself to using the solutions approach, try it step-by-step on several essay questions and practice problems. After you conscientiously go through the step-by-step routine a few times, you will begin to adopt and modify aspects of the technique which will benefit you. Subsequent usage will become subconscious and painless. The important point is that you have to try the solutions approach several times to accrue any benefits.

Schedule Layout. Many candidates are concerned with how to "lay out" schedules and "set up" problems. As you visualize the solution formats, prepare the statement and schedule headings. This will help you understand the requirements and develop the necessary intermediary solutions, analyses, etc. Put the "headed" answer sheets aside until you have worked through the entire problem and are ready to "write up" your final solution.

In preparation for the examination, you should continually be concerned with schedule and statement formats. As you study topics, e.g., consolidations, leases, nonprofit accounting, etc., and work recent CPA problems, always note the schedule and statement formats. To assist you, numerous formats are illustrated throughout these texts. Recognize that there generally are several acceptable formats for most presentations. Become comfortable with the alternate presentations by comparing and contrasting unfamiliar formats to the format(s) with which you are familiar.

It is not necessary to "memorize" the format to be able to solve many financial accounting problems because the necessary components are often listed in the requirements. For example, assume a problem has the following requirement.

a. Prepare a comparative schedule of <u>pretax accounting income</u> and <u>taxable income</u>, including supporting schedules of <u>sales, cost of goods sold, present-value computations</u>, and <u>investment income</u>.

Analysis: The requirement calls for a schedule with two columns as follows.

Dom Corp.

COMPARATIVE SCHEDULE OF PRETAX ACCOUNTING
INCOME AND TAXABLE INCOME
For the Year Ended December 31, 19X7

	Pretax Accounting	Taxable

Note that the necessary supporting schedules are also listed in the requirement.

Diagrams are very important to help you understand interrelationships within a problem setting. You should practice using diagrams to analyze problems. For example, if the Sterling Company has investments in Turner, Grotex, and Scott Companies, this may be diagramed as

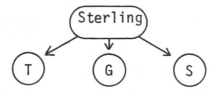

A very important diagram form is the time diagram or time line as shown below. Time diagrams are frequently helpful to sort out a series of transactions occurring over several time periods.

```
_____|_____19X7_____|_____19X8_____|_____
```

Diagrams are recommended for three reasons. First, diagrams help to organize your analysis of the information in the problem. Second, diagrams create a firmer impression in your mind so as to prevent confusion while you are working the problem. A simple diagram, such as O ⟶ S indicating that Operating Corp. invested in Service Corp., will often aid your solution. Third, time diagrams promote preparation of solutions in chronological order, which tends to make them more orderly and complete.

T-accounts (representing ledger accounts) are extremely useful to reconstruct account balances and flow of information from account to account. One example of information flows arises in cost accounting as shown below. Material, labor, and overhead costs flow into the work-in-process account; then to finished goods inventory; then to cost of goods sold.

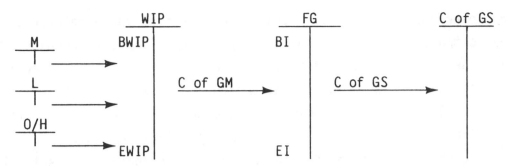

An example of T-account analysis to reconstruct ledger accounts is inherent in the solution to the multiple-choice question below.

> With certain of its products, Hite Foods, Inc. includes coupons having no expiration date which are redeemable in merchandise. In the company's experience, 40% of such coupons are redeemed. The liability for unredeemed coupons at December 31, 19X6 was $9,000. During 19X7, coupons worth $18,000 were issued and merchandise worth $8,000 was distributed in exchange for coupons redeemed. The December 31, 19X7, balance sheet should include a liability of
>
>> a. $7,600.
>> b. $8,200.   (correct per the T-account below)
>> c. $9,800.
>> d. $13,000.

	Liability	
Beginning		9,000
40% of Issued		7,200 (18,000 x .40)
Redeemed	8,000	
Ending		8,200

Journal Entries. Many candidates have trouble with journal entries. When you come upon a seemingly difficult entry, diagram the economic event that occurred. Most economic events are transactions with third parties. Therefore, ask yourself, "What did we give up?" and "What did we receive?"

Also, always start with the easy elements of a journal entry. If we sold something for cash, debit cash and then worry about the credit. This is particularly important with compound/complex entries.

Journal entries are often a "solutions approach" in themselves. When you do not understand a transaction, e.g., amount of profit on a combined sale-financing lease, prepare the journal entries. Furthermore, journal entries can constitute a solutions approach even though they are not explicitly required in the solution, as in the preparation of consolidated worksheets.

Practice Problem Solutions Approach Example

The problem on the next two pages is Problem 4 from Part I of the May 1985 Examination in Accounting Practice. This problem will be worked using the solutions approach. Following this solution guide is the AICPA Unofficial Answer.

First, glance over the problem noting that it consists of three related parts requiring various computations and schedules for property, plant, and equipment.

Second, study the requirements. Part a. is essentially two subrequirements requiring a schedule showing depreciation and amortization expense (requirement a1.) for the year ended 12/31/86 and a schedule showing accumulated depreciation and amortization (requirement a2.) at 12/31/86 for the depreciable assets.

Part b. requires the computation of gain or loss from disposal of assets that would appear in Blake's income statement for the year ended 12/31/86.

The requirement in part c. is the preparation of the property, plant, and equipment section of the 12/31/86 balance sheet.

Third, determine the steps to your solution. The standard solutions approach for most problems is to complete each requirement in order before moving on to the next requirement. This approach will, of course, work for this problem. However, you may wish to modify your solutions approach for problems of this type in which the requirements are interrelated. This alternative solutions approach is to prepare time lines for each depreciable asset, make all computations for each asset at one time, and label each computation according to the requirement to which it relates. For example, if a number or computation relates to requirement b., it can be labeled "b." Numbers can be added to designate subrequirements contained in each lettered requirement (e.g. a1., a2.). Using this approach, the candidate will be solving a part of each requirement as each asset is covered, but not necessarily in the same order as given on the exam. Once you have worked through all the information given, the formal required schedules can be prepared.

Fourth, study the text of the problem preparing intermediary solutions as you proceed.

1. Go through the problem using a felt tip pen to make marginal notes setting out key information (e.g., useful life) and underlining key points (e.g., salvage value of the depreciable assets is immaterial). Set up time lines for each depreciable asset and transfer data from the text of the problem to the time lines.

Number 4 (Estimated time – 45 to 55 minutes)

Information pertaining to Blake Corporation's property, plant and equipment for 1986 is presented below.

Account balances at January 1, 1986

	Debit	Credit
Land	$ 150,000	
Building	1,200,000	
Accumulated depreciation		$263,100
Machinery and equipment	900,000	
Accumulated depreciation		250,000
Automotive equipment	115,000	
Accumulated depreciation		84,600

Depreciation method and useful life

Building – 150% declining balance; 25 years.
Machinery and equipment – Straight-line; ten years.
Automotive equipment – Sum-of-the-years'-digits; four years.
Leasehold improvements – Straight-line.

The salvage value of the depreciable assets is immaterial. Depreciation is computed to the nearest month.

(handwritten) $\frac{1}{25} \times 1.50 \times (1,200,000 - 263100)$
$\frac{1}{10} \times cost$
$\rightarrow$ remaining / $\frac{n(n+1)}{2}$ years
$\rightarrow$ 1/shorter of useful life or life of leasehold

Transactions during 1986 and other information

• On January 2, 1986, Blake purchased a new car for $10,000 cash and trade-in of a two-year-old car with a cost of $9,000 and a book value of $2,700. The new car has a cash price of $12,000; the market value of the trade-in is not known.

(handwritten)
Auto → Trade In   2000   [12,000-10,000]
       – B.V   -2700
       Gain/Loss (700) loss (b.)
→ 12,000 × 4/10 (a.)

• On April 1, 1986 a machine purchased for $23,000 on April 1, 1981, was destroyed by fire. Blake recovered $15,500 from its insurance company.

(handwritten)
Mach. → Ins. Recovery 15500   [23,000-(5 years × 4/10 × 23,000)]
        – B.V   -11500
        Gain/Loss   4000 Gain (b.)

• On May 1, 1986, costs of $168,000 were incurred to improve leased office premises. The leasehold improvements have a useful life of eight years. The related lease, which terminates on December 31, 1992, is renewable for an additional six-year term. The decision to renew will be made in 1992 based on office space needs at that time.

(handwritten)
Leasehold → use shorter of 80 months or 96 months
168,000 ÷ 80 × 8 months = 16,800 depreciation
+ A/D
(a) Balance in A/D 12-31-86
→ ½ year

• On July 1, 1986 machinery and equipment were purchased at a total invoice cost of $280,000; additional costs of $5,000 for freight and $25,000 for installation were incurred.

(handwritten)
Mach. → 280,000 + 5000 + 25,000 = 310,000
310,000 ÷ 10 × ½ = 15500 deprec. (a.)
+ A/D
+ Depreciation on destroyed mach.
(a.) Balance A/D 12-31-86

• Blake determined that the automotive equipment comprising the $115,000 balance at January 1, 1986, would have been depreciated at a total amount of $18,000 for the year ended December 31, 1986.

(handwritten)
Auto
(a.) depreciation – deprec. on car traded in + deprec. on car purchased

Required:

a. For each asset classification prepare schedules 1) showing depreciation and amortization expense, and 2) accumulated depreciation and amortization that would appear on Blake's income statement for the year ended December 31, 1986, and balance sheet at December 31, 1986, respectively.

b. Prepare a schedule showing gain or loss from disposal of assets that would appear in Blake's income statement for the year ended December 31, 1986.

c. Prepare the property, plant and equipment section of Blake's December 31, 1986, balance sheet.

2. No 1986 transactions affected the land account; it will still be reported at $150,000 on 12/31/86.

3. The only transaction affecting the building accounts was the recording of 1986 depreciation. The building is still reported at $1,200,000.

Building

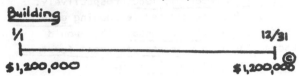

¹⁄₁   12/31

$1,200,000 $1,200,000

4. The 1/1/86 balance of accumulated depreciation (building) is $263,100. Depreciation is computed using the 150% declining balance method. Using this method, depreciation expense is computed by multiplying the beginning of the year book value ($1,200,000 − $263,100 = $936,900) by 150% of the straight-line rate (1/25 x 150% = 6%). This results in 1986 depreciation expense of $56,214 and 12/31/86 accumulated depreciation of $319,314 ($263,100 + $56,214).

Accumulated Depreciation—Building

V₁   12/31

$263,100 ⓐ₂

1984 Depreciation:
$1,200,000
  − 263,100
$936,900 x 150% x 1/25 = $56,214 ⓐ₁
                          +263,100
                          $319,314
                          ⓐ₂+ⓒ

5. Machinery and equipment was reported at $900,000 at 1/1/86. This amount must be reduced by the cost of the machine destroyed ($23,000) and increased by the purchases of machinery ($310,000), resulting in a 12/31/86 balance of $1,187,000. (See time lines after 7.)

6. The insurance proceeds from the destroyed machine total $15,500. The machine was in service for 5 years (4/1/81 − 4/1/86) of its 10-year useful life. Using the straight-line method with no salvage value, the book value of the machine at the time of the fire was $11,500 (5/10 x $23,000). Therefore, the gain on disposal is $4,000 ($15,500 − $11,500). (See time lines after 7.)

7. The 1/1/86 balance of accumulated depreciation (machinery and equipment) is $250,000. 1986 depreciation (straight-line method) must be computed in three parts: on the machine destroyed by fire ($23,000 x 1/10 x 3/12 = $575), on the remainder of the equipment owned at 1/1/86 [($900,000 − $23,000) x 1/10 = $87,700], and on the new equipment purchased [($280,000 + $5,000 + $25,000) x 1/10 x 6/12 = $15,500]. Note that the cost of the new equipment includes the total cost of preparing it for use. The 12/31/86 balance of accumulated depreciation is $342,275. This is computed by taking the beginning balance ($250,000), adding 1986 depreciation expense ($575 + $87,700 + $15,500 = $103,775), and subtracting the accumulated depreciation taken off the books for the destroyed machine ($23,500 x 5/10 = $11,500).

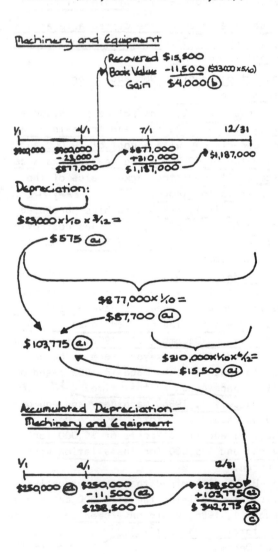

Machinery and Equipment

Recovered $15,500
Book Value −11,500 ($23000 x 5/10)
Gain $4,000 ⓑ

V₁   4/1   7/1   12/31
$900,000 $900,000 $877,000 $1,187,000
          −23,000   +310,000
          $877,000 $1,187,000

Depreciation:

$23,000 x 1/10 x 3/12 =
$575 ⓐ₁

$877,000 x 1/10 =
$87,700 ⓐ₁

$103,775 ⓐ₁

$310,000 x 1/10 x 6/12 =
$15,500 ⓐ₁

Accumulated Depreciation—Machinery and Equipment

V₁   4/1   12/31
$250,000 ⓐ₁ $250,000 $238,500
             −11,500 ⓐ₂   +103,775 ⓐ₁
             $238,500 $342,275 ⓐ₁
                                 ⓒ

8. The automotive equipment was reported at
    $115,000 at 1/1/86. This amount must be
    reduced by the cost of the car traded in
    ($9,000) and increased by the cost of
    the new car acquired ($12,000), result-
    ing in a 12/31/86 balance of $118,000.
    (See time line after 10.)

9. The market value of the car traded in is
    unknown, so the normal cash price of the
    new car ($12,000) is used to value the
    transaction. The $12,000 car is obtain-
    ed in exchange for $10,000 cash and the
    car traded in; therefore, the trade-in
    must be worth $2,000. Since its book
    value is $2,700, a loss of $700 results.
    (See time line after 10.) The journal
    entry to record the exchange is

New car	12,000	
Loss on disposal	700	
Accumulated depreciation	6,300	
Old car		9,000
Cash		10,000

10. The 1/1/86 balance of accumulated depre-
    ciation (automotive equipment) is
    $84,600. The problem states that <u>total</u>
    depreciation on the automotive equipment
    on hand at 1/1/86 would have been
    $18,000. However, one car was traded in
    on 1/2/86. Depreciation on this car
    would have been $1,800 ($9,000 x 2/10,
    using the sum-of-the-years'-digits
    method); therefore depreciation on the
    remaining 1/1/86 automotive equipment is
    $16,200 ($18,000 - $1,800). The new car
    cost $12,000; depreciation on it for
    1986 is $4,800 ($12,000 x 4/10). There-
    fore, total 1986 depreciation is $21,000
    ($16,200 + $4,800). The 12/31/86 bal-
    ance in accumulated depreciation
    ($99,300) is computed by taking the
    1/1/86 balance ($84,600), subtracting
    the accumulated depreciation taken off
    the books for the trade-in [$9,000 -
    $2,700 = $6,300], and adding 1986
    depreciation ($21,000).

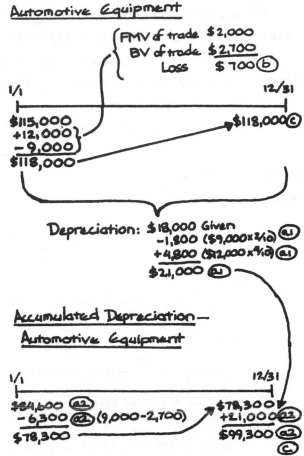

11. The leasehold improvement costs were
    incurred on 5/1/86. These costs should
    be amortized over the <u>shorter</u> of the
    remaining lease life (80 months) or the
    useful life of the improvements (8 years
    or 96 months). The lease term should
    <u>not</u> include the option period unless
    renewal is relatively certain. There-
    fore, 1986 amortization expense is 8/80
    of $168,000, or $16,800.

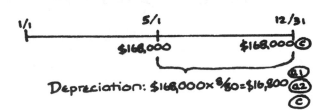

12. Leasehold improvements are reported at
    their $168,000 cost less the $16,800
    amortization.

Fifth, prepare the solution (see the following pages). Place your lettered computations in the appropriate schedule. All schedules should have a heading which includes the name of the company, schedule title, and period covered. Supporting schedules should be appropriately titled and referenced, e.g., "See Schedule 1."

Sixth, proofread and edit.

Seventh, review later, time permitting.

Unofficial Answer
Number 4

a.

Blake Corporation
Depreciation and Amortization Expense
For the Year Ended December 31, 1986

Building			
Book value 1/1/86 ($1,200,000 - $263,100)		$936,900	
150% declining balance rate [(100% ÷ 25) x 1.5]		x 6%	
Total depreciation on building			$ 56,214
Machinery and equipment			
Balance, 1/1/86	$900,000		
Deduct machine destroyed by fire	23,000	$877,000	
Depreciation		x 10%	87,700
Machine destroyed by fire, 4/1/86		$ 23,000	
Depreciation from 1/1 to 4/1/86 (10% x 3/12)		x 2.5%	575
Purchased 7/1/86		$310,000	
Depreciation from 7/1 to 12/31/86 (10% x 6/12)		x 5%	15,500
Total depreciation on machinery and equipment			103,775
Automotive equipment			
Depreciation on $115,000 balance, 1/1/86		$ 18,000	
Deduct depreciation on car traded in 1/2/86			
(SYD 3rd year 2/10 x $9,000)		1,800	16,200
Car purchased 1/2/86		12,000	
Depreciation SYD 1st year		x 4/10	4,800
Total depreciation on automotive equipment			21,000
Leasehold improvements			
Cost 5/1/86		$168,000	
Amortization period (5/1/86 to 12/31/92)		÷ 80 mos.	
Amortization per month		$ 2,100	
Amortization for 1986 (5/1 to 12/31/86)		x 8 mos.	
Total amortization on leasehold improvements			16,800
Total depreciation and amortization expense for 1986			$197,789

Blake Corporation
Accumulated Depreciation and Amortization
December 31, 1986

Accumulated depreciation--building at 12/31/86
  Balance, 1/1/86 $263,100
  Depreciation for 1986   56,214
  Balance, 12/31/86 $319,314

Accumulated depreciation--machinery and equipment at 12/31/86
  Balance, 1/1/86 $250,000
  Depreciation for 1986   103,775
                                                                         353,775
  Deduct machine destroyed by fire (5 x 10% x $23,000)   11,500
  Balance, 12/31/86 $342,275

Accumulated depreciation--automotive equipment at 12/31/86
  Balance, 1/1/86 $ 84,600
  Depreciation for 1986   21,000
                                                                         105,600
  Deduct car traded in ($9,000 - $2,700)   6,300
  Balance, 12/31/86 $ 99,300

Accumulated amortization--leasehold improvements at 12/31/86
  Amortization for 1986 $ 16,800
  Balance, 12/31/86 $ 16,800

Total accumulated depreciation and amortization 12/31/86 $777,689

b.

Blake Corporation
Gain or Loss From Disposal of Assets
For the Year Ended December 31, 1986

Gain on machine destroyed by fire
  Insurance recovery $15,500
  Book value of machine destroyed
    [$23,000 - (5 x 10% x $23,000)]   11,500 $ 4,000

Loss on car traded in on new car purchase
  Book value of car traded in $ 2,700
  Trade-in allowed ($12,000 - $10,000)   2,000   700

Net gain on asset disposals for 1986 $ 3,300

c.

Blake Corporation
Property, Plant, and Equipment Section
of Balance Sheet
December 31, 1986

	Cost	Accumulated depreciation and amortization	Book value
Land	$ 150,000	$ --	$ 150,000
Building	1,200,000	319,314	880,686
Machinery and equipment	1,187,000 [1]	342,275	844,725
Automotive equipment	118,000 [2]	99,300	18,700
Leasehold improvements	168,000	16,800	151,200
Totals	$2,823,000	$777,689	$2,045,311

Explanations of Amounts

[1] Machinery and equipment at 12/31/86

Balance, 1/1/86	$ 900,000
Purchased, 7/1/86 ($280,000 + $5,000 + $25,000)	310,000
	1,210,000
Deduct machine destroyed by fire 4/1/86	23,000
Balance, 12/31/86	$1,187,000

[2] Automotive equipment at 12/31/86

Balance, 1/1/86	$ 115,000
Car purchased, 1/2/86	12,000
	127,000
Deduct car traded in	9,000
Balance, 12/31/86	$ 118,000

The hypothetical grading guide on the next page is a schedule of key solution figures showing the "raw" grading points assigned to these key figures.

May 1985 Practice I, Number 4
Hypothetical Grading Guide*

			Grading points
Part a.			
	Depreciation/amortization for 1986		
	Building	$ 56,214	1
	Machinery and equipment	103,775	1
	Automotive equipment	21,000	1
	Leasehold improvements	16,800	1
	Accumulated depreciation/amortization at 12/31/86		
	Building	319,314	1
	Machinery and equipment	342,275	1
	Automotive equipment	99,300	1
	Leasehold improvements	16,800	1
Part b.			
	Gain on machine destroyed	4,000	1
	Loss on car traded in	700	1
Part c.			
	Cost of machinery and equipment at 12/31/86	1,187,000	1
	Cost of automotive equipment at 12/31/86	118,000	1
	Cost figures (column) at 12/31/86		1
	Accumulated depreciation and amortization figures (column) at 12/31/86		1
	Book value figures (column) at 12/31/86		1
	Grading points possible		15

The conversion scale below converts the "raw" grading points shown above to the grade earned on the problem.

CONVERSION SCALE

Grading Points Earned	15-13	12	11	10	9	8	7	6	5	4	3	2	1	0
Grade	10	9.5	9	8.5	8	7.5	7	6	5	4	3	2	1	0

TOTAL GRADE: NUMBER 4
Grade from Conversion Scale
Demerit for form, etc.   _____
                                                         _____
                                                         _____

*The AICPA Board of Examiners does not release the grading guides used for scoring essay questions and practice problems. The grading guide below was prepared by the authors to illustrate to candidates the manner in which points are allocated to grading concepts.

Essay Question Solutions Approach Algorithm

The major difference between the solutions approach for problems and the one for essay questions is the use of a <u>keyword</u> outline. The <u>keyword</u> outline in the essay solutions approach takes the place of the intermediary solution in the problem solutions approach. Substitute the following two steps for step 4a, "Prepare intermediary solutions as you study the problem," from the practice problem "solutions approach."

4a. **Write down keywords (concepts).** Jot down a list of keywords (grading concepts) in the margin of the examination. The proximity of the keywords to the text of the question will be more efficient than making notes on a separate sheet of paper which may be misplaced.

4b. **Organize the keywords into a solution outline.** After you have noted all of the grading concepts that bear on the requirements, reorganize the outline for the entire answer. Make sure that you respond to each requirement and do not preempt answers to other requirements.

Essay Questions Solutions Approach Example

To illustrate the use of the solutions approach in answering essay questions, we have included Question 3 from the November 1985 Examination in Business Law (same question that was used to illustrate grading in Chapter 2). The illustration appears on the next three pages.

Highlights of the Solutions Approach to Essay Questions

After studying the requirements and visualizing the format of the unofficial answer, study the text of the question making notes and also preparing a <u>keyword</u> outline. After the keyword outline has been prepared, a basic distinction must be made as to the type of essay question presented. The first type of essay question contains one fact situation from which two or more requirements cover the <u>same</u> or similar auditing topics, points of law, or accounting rules. The proper method of answering this type of question is to handle the requirements simultaneously. In other words, apply each step in the solutions approach to all of the requirements before moving on to the next step.

The second type of essay question contains one fact situation from which two or more requirements cover <u>different</u> topics or rules. The proper method of answering this type of question is to handle the requirements independently, following each step of the solutions approach separately for each requirement. Thus, after the first requirement is completed, repeat the solutions approach for each remaining requirement. The benefit to handling the requirements independently is to keep the different topics or rules separate in your mind. This allows you to complete one requirement before moving on to another requirement and mentally "changing gears."

Make sure that you have answered each requirement (and only that requirement) completely. Be careful not to preempt an answer to another requirement. The keyword outline for the example question should be similar to the grading guide in Chapter 2. Next, write up your solution and edit as needed.   If you have time later, review your solution again.

Revisions may be made in the margin of your answer sheet. Or, you might use only 3/4 of each page to write up your solution. The remaining 1/4 can then be used to add material and to make revisions which can be keyed to the text with asterisks. Alternatively, write on every other line. The solution will thus be easier for the grader to read. It will also be easier for you to proofread and edit. Remember, there is no limit on the number of answer sheets you may use.

Number 3 (Estimated time - 15 to 20 minutes)

John Nolan, a partner in Nolan, Stein, & Wolf partnership, transferred his interest in the partnership to Simon and withdrew from the partnership. Although the partnership will continue, Stein and Wolf have refused to admit Simon as a partner.

Subsequently, the partnership appointed Ed Lemon as its agent to market its various product lines. Lemon entered into a two-year written agency contract with the partnership which provided that Lemon would receive a 10% sales commission. The agency contract was signed by Lemon and, on behalf of the partnership, by Stein and Wolf.

After six months, Lemon was terminated without cause. Lemon asserts that

• He is an agent coupled with an interest.
• The agency relationship may not be terminated without cause prior to the expiration of its term.
• He is entitled to damages because of the termination of the agency relationship.

Required:

Answer the following, setting forth reasons for any conclusions stated.
a. Discuss Nolan's property rights in the partnership prior to his withdrawal and the property rights acquired by Simon as a result of his transaction with Nolan.
b. Discuss the merits of Lemon's assertions.

KEYWORD OUTLINE
Assignor
Assignment of Partnership Interest
Assignee

Fewer rights as an Assignee

Principal
Agent

Improper Termination

No, since agent needs interest in property that's subject of the agency
No, because principal has power, not right.
Yes, damages because of breach

Step 1:

Glance over quickly

Step 2:

Study requirements

Step 2A:

Visualize solution format

1. The solution will be in paragraph form
2. For Part a. one may expect the solution to discuss property rights before and after an assignment
3. For Part b. consider the validity for Lemon's assertions

For steps 3 - 7, each requirement should be addressed and fully answered <u>before</u> the next requirement is addressed. As an example, the requirement for Part a. should be answered in its entirety before Part b. is started.

For Part a.

Step 3:

Outline required procedures mentally.
Approach for Part a.
Read the question very carefully to first obtain an understanding of the relationship between the partnership and Nolan and Simon.

Step 3A:

Review applicable principles with regard to property rights in a partnership.

a. Partner can possess partnership property for partnership purposes
b. Partner's interest in partnership is personal property
c. Partner has the right to participate in management
d. Assignment of a partnership interest only allows the assignee to receive share of profits and distributed property

e. Assignee cannot participate in management or possess specific partnership property

Step 4:

Study the text

Step 4A:

Keyword outline (see previous page containing the question)

Step 4B:

Organize key words into solutions Outline
Because this question is organized around the discussion of specific rights, a possible approach is to discuss each right in a separate paragraph

1. Nolan's specific property rights
   a. Possession
   b. Interest as personal property
   c. Participation in management
2. Simon's specific property rights
   a. Share profits and distribution
   b. No right to participate in management
   c. No right to possess specific property

*Step 5:

Prepare solution

*Step 6:

Proofread and edit

*Step 7:

Review

For Part b.

Step 3:

Outline required procedures

Approach for Part b. will be to consider the validity of each of Lemon's assertions considering his termination

*See Unofficial Answer in Chapter 2

STep 3A:

Review applicable principles with regard to assertions about an agency termination

    a. Generally principal always has the power to terminate, but not necessarily the right to terminate

    b. However, principal does not have the power to an agency coupled with an interest

    c. Agency coupled with an interest exists when agent has interest in property of agency

    d. Principal liable under breach of contract for wrongful discharge

STep 4:

Study the text

STep 4A:

Keyword outline (see previous page containing the question)

STep 4B:

Organize keywords into solutions outline

Because this question is organized around the discussion of specific assumptions, a possible approach is to discuss each assumption in a separate paragraph

1. Agency coupled with an interest

    a. Deals with subject of agency

    b. Commission does not qualify

2. Termination without cause

    a. Principal has the power, but not necessarily the right, to terminate

    b. Can terminate without cause

3. Damages

    a. Termination was breach of contract

    b. Partnership liable for damages

*STep 5:

Prepare solution

*STep 6:

Proofread and edit

*STep 7:

Review

*See Unofficial Answer in Chapter 2

NOTE: You <u>must write out</u> the answers to essay questions. <u>Keyword</u> outlines are not sufficient. The AICPA requires you to show an understanding of the grading concepts, not merely a listing of grading concepts. However, you may prepare answers in list form, as long as the listed items complete a sentence that begins with a lead-in phrase.

Prepare brief paragraphs consisting of several concise sentences about each grading concept. The paragraphs may be numbered in an outline format similar to that of the unofficial answers.

<u>Multiple Choice Questions Solutions Approach Algorithm</u>

1. **Work individual questions in order**

   a. If a question appears lengthy or difficult, skip it until you can determine that extra time is available. Put a big question mark in the margin to remind you to return to questions you have skipped or need to review.

2. **Cover up the choices before reading each question**

   a. The answers are sometimes misleading and may cause you to misread or misinterpret the question

3. **Read each question <u>carefully</u> to determine the topical area**

   a. Study the requirements <u>first</u> so you know which data are important
   b. Underline keywords and important data
   c. Identify pertinent information with notations in the margin of the exam
   d. Be especially careful to note when the requirement is an <u>exception</u>, e.g., "Which of the following is <u>not</u> an accounting change handled by the cumulative effect method?"
   e. If a set of data is the basis for two or more questions, read the requirements of each of the questions before beginning to work the first question (sometimes it is more efficient to work the questions out of order or simultaneously)
   f. Be alert to read questions as they are, not as you would like them to be; you may encounter a familiar looking item; don't jump to the conclusion that you know what it is
   g. For accounting practice questions, prepare intermediary solutions as you read the question.

4. **Anticipate the answer before looking at the alternative answers**

   a. Recall the applicable principle (e.g., change in estimate); the applicable model (e.g., net present value); or the applicable code section (e.g., 1245)
   b. If accounting practice questions deal with a complex area like earnings per share, set them up like full-blown problems on scratch paper, if necessary, using abbreviations that enable you to follow your work (remember that these questions are machine-graded)

5. **Read the answers and select the <u>best</u> alternative**

   a. For accounting practice questions, if the answer you have computed is not among the choices, quickly check your math and the logic of your solution. If you don't arrive at one of the given answers in the allotted time, make an educated guess.

6. Mark the correct answer (or educated guess) on the examination booklet itself

7. After completing all of the individual questions in an overall question, transfer the answers to the machine gradable answer sheet with extreme care

   a. Be very careful not to fall out of sequence with the answer sheet. A mistake would cause most of your answers to be wrong. SINCE THE AICPA USES ANSWER SHEETS WITH VARYING FORMATS, IT WOULD BE VERY EASY TO GO ACROSS THE SHEET INSTEAD OF DOWN OR VICE VERSA. Read the instructions carefully!

   b. Review to check that you have transferred the answers correctly

   c. Do not leave this step until the end of the exam as you may find yourself with too little time to transfer your answers to the answer sheet. THE EXAM PROCTORS ARE NOT PERMITTED TO GIVE YOU EXTRA TIME TO TRANSFER YOUR ANSWERS.

Multiple Choice Question Solutions Approach Example

A good example of the multiple choice solutions approach is provided, using multiple choice question number 18 from the November 1985 Examination in Auditing

Step 3:
Topical area? Auditor's consideration of internal control

Step 4:
Principle? When dealing with internal control, the auditor must obtain an understanding of structure

Step 5:
a. Incorrect--not required.
b. Correct--required procedures.
c. Incorrect--analytical procedures part of substantive testing.
d. Incorrect--not required.

Obtaining understanding → *Tests of Controls*

18. When evaluating an internal control structure to determine whether the necessary procedures are prescribed and are followed satisfactorily, an auditor must

   a. Develop questionnaires and checklists.
   b. Obtain an understanding of the structure and perform tests of controls.
   c. Perform tests of controls and analytical procedures.
   d. Evaluate administrative policies.

Currently, all multiple choice questions are scored based on the number correct; i.e., there is no penalty for guessing. The rationale is that a "good guess" indicates knowledge. Thus, you should answer all multiple choice questions.

Efficiency of the Solutions Approach

The mark of an inefficient solution is one wherein the candidate immediately begins to write an essay/problem solution. Remember, the final solution is one of the last steps in the solutions approach. You should have the solution under complete control (with the keyword outline or intermediary solutions) before you begin your final solution.

While the large amount of intermediary work in the solutions approach may appear burdensome and time-consuming, the technique results in more complete solutions in less time than with haphazard approaches. Moreover, the solutions approach really allows you to work out problems that you feel unfamiliar with at first reading. The solutions approach, however, must be mastered prior to sitting for the CPA examination. In other words, the candidate must be willing to invest a reasonable amount of time toward perfecting his/her own solutions approach.

In summary, the solutions approach may appear foreign and somewhat cumbersome. At the same time, if you have worked through the material in this chapter, you should have some appreciation for it. Develop the solutions approach by writing down the seven steps in the solutions approach algorithm at the beginning of this chapter, and keep them before you as you work recent CPA exam problems. Remember that even though the suggested procedures appear <u>very structured</u> and <u>time-consuming</u>, integration of these procedures into your own style of problem solving will help improve <u>your</u> solutions approach. The next chapter discusses strategies for the overall examination.

NOW IS THE TIME
TO MAKE A COMMITMENT

CHAPTER FOUR
TAKING THE EXAMINATION

This chapter is concerned with developing an examination strategy, e.g., how to cope with the environment at the examination site, what order to work problems, etc.

EXAMINATION STRATEGIES

Your performance during the 2 1/2 day examination is final and not subject to revision. While you may sit for the examination again if you are unsuccessful, the majority of your preparation will have to be repeated, requiring substantial, additional amounts of time. Thus, examination strategies (discussed in this chapter) which maximize your exam-taking efficiency are very important.

Getting "Psyched Up"

The CPA exam is quite challenging and worthy of your best effort. Explicitly develop your own psychological strategy to get yourself "up" for the exam. Pace your study program such that you will be able to operate at peak performance when you are actually taking the exam. Many candidates "give up" because they have a bad day or encounter a rough problem. Do the best you can; the other candidates are probably no better prepared than you.

Examination Supplies

The AICPA recommends that candidates prepare their solutions in pencil. As you practice your solutions approach, experiment with pencils, lead types, erasers, etc., that are comfortable to use and also result in good copy for the grader.

In addition to an adequate supply of pencils and erasers, it is very important to take a watch to the examination. Also, take refreshments (as permitted), which are conducive to your exam efficiency. Finally, dress to assure your comfort during the exam. Layered clothing is recommended for possible variations in temperature at the examination site.

Do not take study materials into the examination room. You will not be able to use them. They will only muddle your mind and get you "uptight." Finally, DO NOT carry notes or crib sheets upon your person: this can only result in the gravest of problems. If you choose to bring study materials to the examination site, you are only permitted to review these materials before or after the examination session, not during the session.

Lodging, Meals, Exercise

Make advance reservations for comfortable lodging convenient to the examination facilities. Do not stay with friends, relatives, etc. Both uninterrupted sleep and total concentration on the exam are a must. Consider the following in making your lodging plans.

1. Proximity to exam facilities
2. Lodging and exam parking facilities
3. Availability of meals and snacks
4. Recreational facilities

Plan your meal schedule to provide maximum energy and alertness during the day and maximum rest at night.

Do not experiment with new foods, drinks, etc., during the examination time period. Within reasonable limits, observe your normal eating and drinking habits. Recognize that overconsumption of coffee during the exam could lead to a hyperactive state and disaster. Likewise, overindulgence in alcohol to overcome nervousness and induce sleep the night before might contribute to other difficulties the following morning.

Tenseness should be expected before and during the examination. Rely on a regular exercise program to unwind yourself at the end of the day. As you select your lodging for the examination, try to accommodate your exercise pleasure, e.g., running, swimming, etc. Continue to indulge in your exercise program on the days of the examination.

To relieve tension or stress while studying, try breathing or stretching exercises. Use these exercises before and during the examination to start and to keep your adrenaline flowing. Do not hesitate to attract attention by doing pushups, jumping jacks, etc., in a lobby outside of the examination room if it will improve your exam efficiency. Remain determined not to go through another examination to obtain your certificate.

A problem you will probably experience during the exam related to general fatigue and tenseness is writer's cramp. Experiment with alternate methods of holding your pencil, rubbing your hand, etc., during your preparation program.

In summary, the examination is likely to be both rigorous and fatiguing. Expect it and prepare for it by getting in shape, planning methods of relaxation during the exam and exam evenings, and finally building the courage and competence to complete the exam (successfully).

Examination Facilities and Procedures

Visit the examination facilities at least the evening before the examination to assure knowledge of the location. Remember: no surprises. Having a general familiarity with the facilities will lessen anxiety prior to the examination.

Talking to a recent veteran of the examination will give you background for the general examination procedures, such as

1. Procedure for distributing exam booklets, papers, etc.
2. Accessibility of restrooms
3. Availability of coffee and snacks at exam location
4. Admissibility of coffee and snacks in the exam room
5. Peculiar problems of exam facilities, e.g., noise, lighting, temperature, etc.
6. Permissibility of early departure from exam
7. A copy of his/her exam booklet
8. His/her experience in taking the exam
9. Any other suggestions s/he might make

As you might see, it is important to talk with someone who recently sat for the examination at the same location where you intend to sit. The objective is to reduce your anxiety just prior to the examination and to minimize any possible distractions. Finally, if you have any remaining questions regarding examination procedure, call or write your state board.

On a related point, do not be distracted by other candidates who show up at the examination completely relaxed and greet others with confidence. These are most likely candidates who have been there before. Probably the only thing they are confident of is a few days' vacation from work. Also, do not become distracted when they leave early: some candidates may leave after signing in for that session.

Arrive at the Examination Early

On the day of the exam, be sure to get to the examination site at least 30 minutes early to reduce tension and to get yourself situated. Most states have assigned seating. If this is the case, you will be seated by your candidate ID number. However, if you have a choice, it probably is wise to sit away from the door and the administration table to avoid being distracted by candidates who arrive late, leave early, ask questions, etc., and proctors who occasionally converse. AVOID ALL

POSSIBLE DISTRACTIONS.   <u>Stay away from friends.</u> Find a seat that will be comfortable: consider sunlight, interior lighting, heating/air conditioning, pedestrian traffic, etc.

Usually the proctors open the sealed boxes of exams and distribute the booklets to candidates 10 minutes before the scheduled beginning of the examination. You are not permitted to open the booklet, but you should study the instructions printed on the front cover. The instructions generally explain

1. How to turn in examination papers
2. Handling of

    a. Multiple choice answer sheets
    b. Scratch sheets
    c. Columnar work sheets

3. Examiners' consideration of the candidate's ability to express him/herself in acceptable written language

You will be given a supply of answer paper as you enter the exam room or as the test booklets are passed out. You will not be permitted to write anything except filling in the headings on an adequate supply of columnar and lined answer paper. The heading preprinted in the top right hand corner of each sheet of paper is

Candidate's No. _____

Date _____

State _____

Subject _____

Problem _____ Page _____

Do not use your name; write <u>only your candidate number</u>, which will be assigned to you at the beginning of the exam. If a problem requires a name signature, e.g., on an audit report, do not use your own name or initials.

You probably will not work the examination problems in order. There is a possibility of confusion since you cannot number your answer sheets consecutively until the end of the exam. To alleviate this problem, take 10 or 15 paper clips to the exam room to keep the answer sheets of each question separate and in order, while you answer other questions. At the end of the exam, put the packets of answer sheets in proper order and number them consecutively.

Inventory of the Examination Content

When you receive your examination booklet, carefully read the instructions. The objective is to review the standard instructions and to note any new or special instructions. After reviewing the instructions on the front of your examination booklet, make note of the number of questions/problems and the time allocated to each. Immediately after receiving permission to open the examination booklet, glance over each of the questions sufficiently and jot down the topics on the time schedule

on the front of the exam booklet. This will give you an overview of the ensuing 3
1/2 or 4 1/2 hours of work.

You may find it to your advantage to write down keywords, acronyms, etc. on the
front of the examination booklet <u>before</u> you forget them, but only <u>after</u> you have been
told to begin the examination. For example, you would write down the acronym for the
ten generally accepted auditing standards on the front page of the auditing
examination.

Allocation of Time

Budget your time. Time should be carefully allocated in your attempt to maximize
your points. Remember the maximum points available on each question are proportional
to the suggested time allotments on the front of each exam booklet. Theoretically,
time should be allocated so that you maximize points per minute.

While you have to develop your own strategy with respect to time allocation, some
suggestions may be useful. First, consider the three sections that have essay questions (Auditing, Law, Theory) and are 210 minutes long. Allocate 5 minutes to
reading the instructions and to taking an inventory, jotting the topics tested by
question on the front cover. Write the topic next to the time allotment. Assuming
60 individual multiple choice and 4 essay questions, you should spend about 10
minutes <u>keyword</u> outlining each of the 4 essay questions. Then, plan on spending
about 1 1/2 minutes working each of the individual multiple choice questions. (Do
not prepare the final solutions to the essay questions until you work all of the
multiple choice questions. Frequently, multiple choice questions will jog your
memory of additional grading concepts for the essays.) Next, complete the multiple
choice answer sheet by CAREFULLY transferring your answers from the exam booklet to
the machine gradable form. This should take about 5 minutes. The answers must be
transferred before the exam session ends. THE PROCTORS ARE NOT ALLOWED TO GIVE YOU
EXTRA TIME TO DO THIS.

After completing these tasks, you now have spent 2 1/4 hours and have substantially completed both the multiple choice questions and essay questions. Revise the
<u>keyword</u> outline and prepare the final solutions of the essay questions one at a time.
Allocate about 15 minutes to each solution. Recognize that you can write all the
grader will care to read in 15 minutes from a well-developed outline.

Finally, you have 10 minutes to proofread and edit. Remember that this hypothetical time allocation is for illustrative purposes only.

Hypothetical Time Budget
210-Minute Essay Exam
(60 individual multiple choice, 4 essay questions)

	Minutes
Inventory of exam	5
Keyword outline of 4 essay questions	40
Answer 60 multiple choice questions	90
Completion of multiple choice answer sheet	5
Final solution of 4 essay questions	60
Extra time	10
Total	210

Now consider the time allocation in the two practice parts which are 4 1/2 hours (270 minutes) in length. For a 4 1/2 hour practice section, consisting of three sets of multiple choice questions (each set containing 20 items), and 2 problems (that require schedules, entries, etc.), you should allocate 2 1/2 hours to the 60 multiple choice questions (2 1/2 minutes each) and about 1 1/2 hours (45 minutes each) to the 2 problems--which leaves about 1/2 hour of "extra time." The nature of practice problems does not lend itself to as precise a time allocation as the essay questions. It is important to keep track of the time spent on each problem during the examination. Write the time you start each problem near the top of the question to preclude your spending more than the suggested time on any one problem.

Order of Working Questions/Problems

Select the question/problem that you are going to work first from the notes you made on the front of your examination. Some candidates will select the question/problem that appears easiest to get started and build confidence. Others will begin with the question/problem they feel is most difficult to get it out of the way. Multiple choice questions generally should not be worked first on the auditing, business law, and theory exams, since each question may contain 4 or 5 grading concepts (for possible inclusion in your essay solutions) as alternate answers. You should, therefore, work through the multiple choice questions only after you have keyword outlined all of the essay questions (but before you write up your final solutions). This way, when doing the multiple choice questions, you may pick up a grading concept or keyword which you did not have in your initial keyword outline.

Once you select a question/problem, you should apply the solutions approach. Practice problems should be worked through to the final stage, and all calculations and schedules should be labeled before leaving the problem. If you start another practice problem before completing one, you will have to rework (or at a minimum, waste time becoming familiar again with) the unfinished problem.

You should, however, leave a problem if you get stuck, rather than just "spinning your wheels." Later, when you come back and retool the problem, you may be able to think of a new approach to "unlock" the solution. Likewise, proofreading and editing should be undertaken after working on one or more other problems, so you have a fresh perspective as you evaluate your own solution.

On the other hand, essay questions should be worked only through the <u>keyword</u> outline prior to moving on to the next question. Recall that essay questions are generally graded with an open-ended grading guide. Thus, you want to include as many grading concepts as possible in your solution. Waiting to write your essay solution until after all other questions have been dealt with will force you to take a fresh look at the question. As a result, additional grading concepts are often found. As you recognize grading concepts applicable to other questions, turn to the respective question and jot down the <u>keywords</u> (remember that the <u>keyword</u> outlines should be prepared in the margin of your exam booklet).

Note that the AICPA grading curves generally reflect decreasing returns to scale. That is to say, candidates get more credit for the first correct answer than for the last correct answer. This comes about through the use of base points; i.e., a relatively large amount of credit is given to the initial stages of the solution.

The existence of decreasing returns to scale in the AICPA grading curves implies that candidates should allocate more time to the questions/problems which are troublesome. The natural tendency is to write on and on for questions/problems with which you are conversant. Remember to do the opposite: spend more time where more points are available; i.e., you may already have earned the maximum allowable on the question/problem familiar to you.

Never, but never, leave a question blank, as this almost certainly precludes a passing grade on that section. Some candidates talk about "giving certain types of questions to the AICPA," i.e., no answer. The only thing being given to the AICPA is grading time since the grader will not have to read a solution. Expect a couple of "far out" or seemingly "insurmountable" questions/problems. Apply the solutions approach--imagine yourself having to make a similar decision, computation, explanation, etc., in an actual situation and come up with as much as possible to answer the question.

Page Numbering

Carefully follow the instructions on the front of each exam booklet with regard to turning in papers. Remember that a lost answer is a zero. The typical instructions include

    1. Arrange your answers in numerical order and number them consecutively, e.g., if you have 15 sheets answering Practice I, number them 1 through 15

2. The multiple choice answer sheet should be numbered page 1 and the numbering of your other pages should start with page 2
3. For practice problems, include scratch sheets (label all computations) as part of the answer
4. Write "continued" on the bottom of sheets when another answer sheet for the same problem follows

Postmortem of Your Performance

DON'T DO IT and especially don't do it until Friday evening. Do not speak to other candidates about the exam after completing sections on Wednesday evening, Thursday noon, Thursday evening, and Friday noon. Exam postmortem will only upset, confuse, and frustrate you. Besides, the other candidates probably will not be as well prepared as you, and they certainly cannot influence your grade. Often, those candidates who seem very confident have overlooked an important requirement(s) or fact(s). As you leave the exam room after each session, think only ahead to achieve the best possible performance on each of the remaining sections.

AICPA GENERAL RULES
GOVERNING EXAMINATION

1. The only aids you are allowed to take to the examination tables are pens, pencils, and erasers. Rulers, slide rules, and calculators are prohibited.

2. You will be furnished an identification card containing your candidate identification number. Make a note of the identification number for future reference. Use this identification number on all of your papers. The importance of remembering this number and recording it on your examination papers correctly cannot be overemphasized. If a question calls for an answer involving a signature, do not sign your own name or initials. The required form of identification must be available for inspection by the proctors throughout the examination.

3. Any reference during the examination to books or other matters or the exchange of information with other persons shall be considered misconduct sufficient to bar you from further participation in the examination.

4. Answers must be written on paper furnished by the Board. Heading up answer papers is allowed prior to the start of the examination. Extra time is not allowed for this at the end of the session. All unused paper must be returned to the Board at the end of each examination session.

5. You must observe the fixed time for each session which will start and end promptly. It is your responsibility to be ready at the start of the period and to stop writing when told to do so.

6. Question booklets will be distributed shortly before each session begins. You are not permitted to look at the booklet until the starting signal is given.

7. All answers (including the blackening of spaces on the multiple choice answer sheets) should be written in pencil, preferably with No. 2 lead.

8. Identify your answers by using the proper question number. Begin your answer to each question on a separate page and number pages in accordance with the instructions on the printed examination booklets. Use only one side of each sheet. Arrange your answers in the order of the questions.

9. The estimated minimum and maximum time that you may need for giving adequate answers to each question is printed in the examination booklet. These estimates should be used as a guide to allot your time. It is recommended that you not spend more than the estimated maximum time on any one question until the others have been completed except to the extent that the maximum time has not been used on prior questions. Point values for the individual questions are

printed in the examination booklet. The
following is an example of time
estimates as they might appear in a
printed examination booklet:

All questions are required:

	Point Value	Estimated Minutes Minimum	Maximum
No.1	60	90	110
No.2	10	15	25
No.3	10	15	25
No.4	10	15	25
No.5	10	15	25
Total	100	150	210

10.   All amounts given in a question are to
be considered material unless otherwise
stated.

11.   Answer sheets for the multiple choice
items may vary for each part of the
examination. It is important to pay
strict attention to the manner in which
your answer sheet is structured. As you
proceed with the examination, be absolutely certain that the space in which
you have indicated your answer corresponds directly in number with the item
in your question booklet. If you mark
your answers on the examination booklet,
be certain you transfer them to the multiple choice answer sheet before the
session ends.

12.   You should attempt to answer all multiple choice items. There is no penalty
for incorrect responses. Since objective items are computer-graded, your
comments and calculations associated
with them are not considered and should
not be submitted.

13.   Attach all computations to the papers
containing your answers for Accounting
Practice I and Accounting Practice II.
Identify them as to the questions to
which they relate. The rough calculations and notes may assist the graders
in understanding your answers.

14.   The CPA is continually confronted with
the necessity of expressing opinions and
conclusions in written reports in clear,
unequivocal language. Although the
primary purpose of the examination is to
test your knowledge and application of
the subject matter, the ability to
organize and present such knowledge in
acceptable written language may be considered by the graders. Neatness and
orderly presentation of work are also
very important. Credit cannot be given
for answers that are illegible.

15.   Formal journal entries should not be
prepared unless specifically required.
Time may be saved by entering adjustments, reclassifications, etc., directly
on working papers. Elaborate working
papers should not be prepared unless
they are of assistance in meeting the
stated requirements. If both working
papers and formal statements are required and time is not adequate to complete both, the working papers should be
completed.

16.   You should avoid explaining how to
answer a question instead of actually
attempting a solution. If time grows
short, a brief statement to the point is
permissible, but full credit cannot be
obtained by doing this. A partial
answer is better than none and will be
awarded appropriate credit.

17.   Due consideration and credit, if appropriate, will be given to alternative
answers which can arise because there
are slight variations in practical accounting procedures or techniques and
there are different schools of thought
on certain accounting matters.

18.   You may retain your examination booklet
providing you do not leave the examination room before one-half hour prior to
scheduled completion time. You are not
permitted to take the question booklet
or examination papers when you leave
your table temporarily. You are responsible for protecting your papers at all
times and should turn them face down
when temporarily leaving for any reason.

19.   Penalties will be imposed on any candidate who is caught cheating before or
during an examination. These penalties
may include expulsion from this and
future examination sessions.

In addition to the above general rules, oral instructions will be given by the examination supervisor shortly before the start of each session. They should include the location and/or rules concerning

    a. Storage of briefcases, handbags, books, personal belongings, etc.
    b. Food and beverages
    c. Smoking
    d. Rest rooms
    e. Telephone calls and messages
    f. Requirements (if any) that candidates must take all parts not previously passed each time they sit for the examination. Minimum grades (if any) needed on parts failed to get credit on parts passed.
    g. Official clock, if any
    h. Additional supplies
    i. Assembly, turn-in, inspection, and stapling of solutions

The next section is a detailed listing (mind jogger) of things to do for your last-minute preparation. It also contains a list of strategies for the exam.

CPA EXAM CHECKLIST

One week before exam

___ 1. Look over major topical areas, concentrating on schedule formats and the information flow of the formats.
      E.g.:
      Accounting Changes and Error Correction
      Income Statement Format
      Long-Term Construction Accounting
      Inventory Methods
      Cost vs. Equity Method Investments
      Lessee-Lessor Accounting
      EPS Calculations
      Purchase, Pooling, Consolidation Methods
      Cost of Goods Manufactured Schedule
      FIFO and Wtd. Avg. Process Costing Flow
      Capital Budgeting Models
      Governmental Fund Accounting
      Individual and Corporate Tax Formats

___ 2. Reread outlines (your own or those in CPA Examination Review) of most important SASs, underlining buzz words.

___ 3. Review law notes, committing important terms and lists to notecards or abbreviated outlines.

___ 4. If time permits, work through a few questions in your weakest areas so that techniques/concepts are fresh in your mind.

___ 5. Assemble notecards and key outlines of major topical areas into a manageable "last review" notebook to be taken with you to the exam.

What to bring

___ 1. Registration material for the CPA exam.

___ 2. Hotel confirmation.

___ 3. Cash--payment for anything by personal check is rarely accepted.

___ 4. Major credit card--American Express, Master Card, Visa, etc.

___ 5. Alarm clock--this is too important an event to trust to a hotel wake-up call that might be overlooked.

___ 6. Food--candidates may wish to pack a sack lunch for Thursday and Friday. Time is often limited between the conclusion of the morning session and the beginning of the afternoon session. Since it is suggested that candidates arrive no later than 30 minutes prior to each session's starting time, this will allow you plenty of time to check in. Bring snack foods that will provide energy and sustenance, such as fruit and cheese.

___ 7. Clothing that is comfortable and that can be layered to suit the temperature range over the three-day period and the examination room conditions.

___ 8. Watch--it is imperative that you be aware of the time remaining for each session.

___ 9. Earplugs--even though an examination
     is being given, there is constant
     activity in the examination room,
     e.g., people walking around, rustling
     of paper, people coughing, etc. The
     use of earplugs would block out this
     distraction and help you concentrate
     to your fullest extent.

___ 10. Other--"last review" materials, pen-
     cils, erasers, leads, sharpeners,
     pens, paperclips, etc.

While waiting for the exam to begin

1. Put ID card on table for ready reference
   to your number. Fill out attendance form
   that proctor will pick up prior to distributing exam booklet.

2. Fill out all page headings (except for
   question and page number) and divide
   papers on table into computational forms,
   essay sheets (use every other line when
   writing essay answers), and columnar
   workpaper. Make sure your ID number is
   CORRECT on each answer sheet. Fill in ID
   number on M/C answer form, filling in
   circles that correspond to your ID
   number.

3. Realize that proctors will be constantly
   circulating throughout each exam session.
   You need only raise your hand to receive
   more paper at any time or paper will be
   available at nearby tables.

4. Take a few deep breaths and compose yourself. Resolve to do your very best and
   to go after every point you can get!

Before leaving for exam each day

1. Put ID card in wallet, purse, or on person for entry to take the exam. This is
   your official entrance permit that allows
   you to participate in all sections of the
   exam.

2. Remember your hotel room key.

3. Pack snack items and lunch (optional).

4. Limit consumption of liquids.

5. Realize that on Friday morning you must
   check out and arrange for storage of your
   luggage (most hotels have such a service)
   PRIOR TO departing for the Law and Theory
   sections in order to prevent late charges
   on your hotel bill.

Evenings before exams

1. Reviewing the evenings before the exams
   could earn you the extra points needed to
   pass a section. Just keep this last-
   minute effort in perspective and do NOT
   panic yourself into staying up all night
   trying to cover every possible point.
   This could lead to disaster by sapping
   your body of the endurance needed to
   attack questions creatively during the
   next 7-8 hour day.

2. Before the practice sessions, scan the
   general schedule formats to imprint the
   flow of information on your mind (e.g.:
   income statement and EPS formats, partnership "safe payment" schedule, lease
   formats, indiv. and corp. tax formats,
   etc.).

3. Scan tax notes, imprinting required
   percentages used for figuring charitable
   contributions, tax credit for the
   elderly, etc., on your mind.

4. Read over KEY notecards or the most important outlines on topics in which you
   feel deficient.

5. Go over acronyms you have developed as
   study aids (i.e., TIP, PIE, GODC for the
   ten GAAS in auditing). Test yourself by
   writing out the letters on paper while
   verbally giving a brief explanation of
   what the letters stand for.

6. Reread key outlines of important SASs on
   Wednesday evening so that buzz words will
   be fresh in your mind on Thursday
   morning.

7. Reread key outlines or notecards for law
   on Thursday evening, reviewing important
   terms, key phrases, and lists (i.e.,
   essential elements for a contract, requirements for a holder in due course,
   etc.) so that they will be fresh in your
   mind Friday morning.

8. Scan outlines of SFACs 1, 2, 5, 6, and
   any other notes pertinent to answering
   theory questions, in order to imprint
   keywords.

9. Avoid postmortems during the examination
   period. Nothing you can do will affect
   your grade on sections of the exam you
   have already completed. Concentrate only
   on the work ahead in remaining sections.

10. GET A GOOD NIGHT'S REST! Being well rested will permit you to meet each day's challenge with a fresh burst of creative energy.

Practice

1. Open the exam booklet, noting the number of M/C questions (60 per part have been asked on recent exams) and the areas they cover (various financial, individual tax, managerial, etc.).

2. Scan the "required" sections of all non-M/C problems to get a feel for the nature of the topics covered, making a mental note of the time allotted to each section (exam point allotments parallel time allocation). Remember to divide allotted time per question proportionately over ALL parts to a question (parts are often unrelated, so don't forget that if 40-50 minutes are allowed for Problem 5, that much time must be divided among all required parts). Knowing the nature of these problems that you will tackle later allows your subconscious to sort out needed facts for solving them as you work the M/C.

3. Reconcile the problem numbers with the questions listed on the front of the exam booklet and check consecutive page numbers in your booklet to reassure yourself that your booklet is complete, that no pages are stuck together, etc.

4. Begin working the M/C questions, noting the time begun at the start of each set. Realize that you have approximately 1 1/2 to 2 1/2 minutes per question. Use computational sheets rather than the exam booklet itself for computations so that you have ample room to develop mini-schedules, time lines, etc. Do not waste time labeling computations because the grader will not use M/C computation sheets. It is wise to number your computations for your own use if you come back to a question, however.

5. Read each question carefully! Dates are extremely important! (E.g., a long-term contract problem using the percentage-of-completion method may give information for a contract begun in 19X6 but ask for income recognized for year ended Dec. 31 19X7.)

6. If you are struggling with problems beyond your time limit, divide M/C into 2 categories and use this strategy

   a. Questions for which you know you lack knowledge to answer: Drawing from any resources you have, narrow answers down to as few as possible; then make an EDUCATED GUESS.

   b. Questions for which you feel you should be getting a correct answer: Put "?" by M/C number on exam booklet and label computational sheet so you can return to it later. Your mental block may clear, or you may spot a simple math error that now can be corrected, thus giving you extra points.

7. Remember: NEVER change a first impulse M/C answer later unless you are absolutely certain you are right. It is a proven fact that your subconscious often guides you to the correct answer.

8. Go on to problems while you are "hot!" You can transfer M/C answers to the computer form later when you are tired.

9. Work problems that you consider easiest first, noting time begun and time allotted. Your goal is to pick up extra time to allocate to problems you are weaker on.

10. Read "required" section, underlining and noting EVERY requirement that you are asked for.

11. Read the information given, underlining key facts, circling percentages and interest rates that you plan to use, crossing out extraneous information, etc.

12. Draw time lines, visualize schedule headings, schedule formats, etc., that will help you respond to requirements. Do not forget to put a heading on each schedule or statement.

13. Computations should be made on computation sheets which WILL be used by the grader as an "audit trail" to support your work. Label and cross-reference to schedules and work sheets as necessary. (E.g., when asked to show comparative balance sheets for 19X6 and 19X7 with the correct valuation of Investment in Subsidiary, show supporting computations by stating "See Schedule A on page ...".)

14. Write legibly; be neat and organized. Leave space on schedules, etc., to add information that you might think of later.

15. For practice problems, format, organization, technique, disclosure, etc., are of critical importance.

16. Constantly compare your progress with the time remaining. NEVER spend more than the maximum time on any problem until ALL problems are answered and time remains. Fight the urge to complete one problem at the expense of another problem. Remember that there are more gradable points in the beginning stages of problems than toward the end (the law of diminishing returns applies!). Ten points is the maximum you can earn, so once you feel you have answered sufficiently, move on!

17. As each problem is completed, quickly reread the "required" section again to make sure you have responded to each requirement. Check off each completed problem on the form provided; this should prevent you from inadvertently leaving a problem unanswered. Paper clip together the pages used to answer each individual related part of a question and set them aside for final assembly before handing in.

18. Each test will include a problem or question for which you may feel unprepared. Accept the challenge and go after the points! Draw from all your resources. Ask yourself how GAAP would be applied to similar situations, scan the M/C for clues, look for relationships in all the available information given in the problem, try "backing into" the problem from another angle, etc. Every problem (no matter how impossible it may look at first glance) contains some points that are yours for the taking. Make your best effort. You may be on the right track and not even know it!

19. The cardinal rule is NEVER, but NEVER, leave an answer blank.

20. When you see alternate routes to take in problem solving, explain to the grader any assumptions you are making and why. Should you run out of time on a problem that you know how to complete, write a note to the grader briefly describing what you would have done had time permitted.

21. If time permits, go back to any M/C question that you "guessed" on.

22. Double check to make certain you have answered ALL parts of EVERY problem to the best of your ability.

23. Transfer M/C answers to the form provided. Be especially careful to follow the numbers exactly because number patterns differ on each answer form! Don't wait until it's too late to make this transfer.

24. Assemble paper-clipped answer sheets in the correct order. Count total number of pages, counting M/C answer form as page 1. Consecutively number pages (i.e., Page 3 of 20).

25. Take assembled answers with "Degree of Completion" form to front of exam room where a proctor will staple them together.

Auditing

1. Check exam booklet for completeness as you note the number of M/C questions (you can expect 60), and read "required" sections of essay questions, noting the time allotted to each question.

2. Reconcile the question numbers with the questions listed on the front of the exam booklet and check consecutive page numbers in your booklet.

3. Use the solutions approach to briefly outline key concepts or acronyms that apply to each requirement. These are fresh in your mind now and can be supplemented later after answering M/C questions. Your subconscious will also be working on added ideas.

4. The crucial technique to use for auditing M/C is to read each question CAREFULLY, underlining keywords such as "most," "least," "primary," "special report," "interim report," etc. Then READ EACH CHOICE before you start eliminating inappropriate answers. In auditing, often the 1st or 2nd answer may sound correct but a later answer may be MORE CORRECT! Be discriminating! NEVER choose (a) or (b) BEFORE reading (c) and (d).

5. Begin the essay questions, carefully monitoring your time. Read all parts (a, b, c, etc.) of "required" section and organize your answer around the key concepts, acronyms, and buzz words that are responsive to part a, b, c, etc.

6. The most important technique to use for ALL essay questions is to constantly remind yourself that the grader assumes you know nothing (s/he cannot read your

mind) and you, as a candidate for a professional designation, must convince him/her of your knowledge of the subject matter under question. NEVER OMIT THE OBVIOUS! Explain each answer as if you were explaining the concept to a beginning business student.

7. Recognize that some questions ask for general, rather than specific, responses allowing you to bring out many relevant points.

8. Using the key "buzz word" outline, develop well-organized, complete sentences that are responsive to each part of the question. Always answer essay questions using every other line of answer paper.

9. Points are allocated to quantity as well as quality of related ideas presented in an answer, so state in brief form as many relevant ideas as you can possibly think of in the time allowed. BE CREATIVE!

10. Auditing answers are often "list" oriented, so do not fall into the trap of developing only 2 or 3 ideas at the expense of running out of time to present more gradable concepts.

11. When an auditing question calls for audit procedures or programs to use in a certain business setting (such as a university book store buy-back revolving cash fund), you must BE SPECIFIC and tailor your procedures to the factual situation described. For example, it is not enough to tell the grader that proper segregation of duties is required; you must specify that where Jones has custody of cash, Smith should have recording responsibilities, etc.

12. Constantly compare your progress with the time remaining. NEVER spend more than the maximum time on any question until ALL questions are answered and time remains.

13. As each question is completed, quickly reread the "required" section to make sure you have responded to each requirement.

14. Double check to make certain you have answered ALL parts of EVERY question to the best of your ability.

15. Transfer M/C answers to the form provided. Be especially careful to follow the numbers exactly, because number

patterns differ on each answer form! Don't wait until it's too late. The proctors are not authorized to give you extra time for this.

16. Remember: A legible, well-organized, grammatically correct answer--using as many buzz words as appropriate--gives a professional appearance.

17. Take assembled answers with "Degree of Completion" form to the front of exam room where a proctor will staple them together.

Business Law

1. Check exam booklet for completeness as you note the number of M/C questions (you can expect 60), and read "required" sections of essay questions, noting the time allotted to each question.

2. Reconcile the question numbers with the questions listed on the front of the exam booklet and check consecutive page numbers in your booklet.

3. Use the solutions approach to briefly outline key concepts that apply to each requirement. These are fresh in your mind now and can be supplemented later after answering M/C questions. Your subconscious will also be working on added ideas.

4. You will need the maximum time available for the law essay questions because they usually consist of 8 unrelated yet involved fact situations that you must address. Thus, you must use the minimum time allotted in answering the law M/C.

5. The crucial technique to use for business law M/C is to read through each fact situation CAREFULLY, underlining keywords such as "oral," "without disclosing," "subject to mortgage," etc. Then read EACH CHOICE carefully before you start eliminating inappropriate answers. In business law, often the 1st or 2nd answer may sound correct, but a later answer may be MORE CORRECT. Be discriminating! Reread the question and choose the right response.

6. Law essay fact situations are often lengthy and involved. Read carefully and decide which areas of law apply.

7. The most important technique to use for ALL essay questions is to constantly remind yourself that the grader assumes

you know nothing (s/he cannot read your mind) and you, as a candidate for a professional designation, must convince him/her of your knowledge of the subject matter under question. NEVER OMIT THE OBVIOUS! Explain each answer as if you were explaining the concept to a beginning business student.

8. Tell the grader that you are applying the UCC or Common Law, or the Act of 1933 or 1934, etc.

9. State the issue involved or the requirements that you are testing for (i.e., all 6 elements of a contract are present).

10. State the rule of law that applies to the issue.

11. Tell the grader how this affects the parties involved.

12. Limit discussion to relevant issues. Too often, candidates spend more time than allotted on a question they are sure of, only to sacrifice points on another question where those extra minutes are crucial.

13. Remember that on the law section you have a maximum of about 10 minutes per fact situation.

14. If you draw a blank as to a conclusion, telling the grader all the points of law that you know about the fact situation may salvage the question.

15. As each question is completed, quickly reread the "required" section to make sure you have responded to each requirement.

16. Double check to make certain you have answered ALL parts of EVERY question to the best of your ability.

17. Transfer M/C answers to the form provided. Be especially careful to follow the numbers exactly because number patterns differ on each answer form! Don't leave this until it's too late.

18. Remember: A legible, well-organized, grammatically correct answer gives a professional appearance.

19. Take assembled answers with "Degree of Completion" form to the front of exam room where a proctor will staple them together.

Theory

1. Check exam booklet for completeness as you note the number of M/C questions (you can expect 60), and read "required" sections of essay questions, noting the time allotted to each question.

2. Reconcile the question numbers with the questions listed on the front of the exam booklet and check consecutive page numbers in your booklet.

3. Use the solutions approach to briefly outline key concepts that apply to each requirement. These are fresh in your mind now and can be supplemented later after answering M/C questions. Your subconscious will also be working on added ideas.

4. Recognize that you may be feeling a little "burned out" by Friday afternoon, so fight to stay sharp and go after the available points!

5. Use all the GAAP keywords applicable to the question asked, inasmuch as the grader will be looking for these as s/he seeks to award you points. (E.g., "Revenues generally are not recognized until realized or realizable and earned.")

6. The most important technique to use for ALL essay questions is to constantly remind yourself that the grader assumes you know nothing (s/he cannot read your mind) and you, as a candidate for a professional designation, must convince him/her of your knowledge of the subject matter under question. NEVER OMIT THE OBVIOUS! Explain each answer as if you were explaining the concept to a beginning business student.

7. Limit discussion to relevant issues. Too often, candidates spend more time than allotted on a question they are sure of, only to sacrifice points on another questions where those extra minutes are crucial.

8. You've come too far to end the exam early, just because it's the last part and you feel you've written enough. Stick it out until they call for the exams.

9. As each question is completed, quickly reread the "required" section to make sure you have responded to each requirement.

10. Double check to make certain you have answered ALL parts of EVERY question to the best of your ability.

11. Transfer M/C answers to the form provided. Be especially careful to follow the numbers exactly, because number patterns differ on each answer form! Don't wait until it's too late. The proctors are not authorized to give you extra time for this.

12. Remember: A legible, well-organized, grammatically correct answer--using as many buzz words as appropriate--gives a professional appearance.

13. Take assembled answers with "Degree of Completion" form to front of exam room where a proctor will staple them together.

HAVE YOU MADE YOUR

COMMITMENT?

CHAPTER FIVE
AUDITING MODULES

Introduction

Module 1/Professional Responsibilities (RESP)

Module 2/Internal Control (IC)

Module 3/Evidence (EVID)

Module 4/Reporting (REPT)

Module 5/Audit Sampling (AUDS)

Module 6/Auditing EDP (EDP)

Statements on Auditing Standards (SASs)

Mini Outlines

SUMMARY OF AUDITING TOPICS TESTED

The auditing section of the CPA exam tests the candidate's knowledge of generally accepted auditing standards (GAAS) and procedures as they relate to the CPA's functions in the examination of financial statements. It is essential that you have a recent copy of the codification of the Statements on Auditing Standards. The codified version, as opposed to the original Statements on Auditing Standards (the SASs) as issued, eliminates all superseded portions. Commerce Clearing House, Inc., (4025 W. Peterson Ave., Chicago, Illinois 60646) publishes the codification as the AICPA Professional Standards. This codification also includes Statements on Standards for Accounting and Review Services, Code of Professional Ethics, International Accounting Standards, International Auditing Guidelines, Statements on Standards for Management Advisory Services, Quality Control, and Tax Practice. Many university bookstores carry this source as it is often required in the undergraduate auditing course. You should also have an auditing textbook to assist you in your preparation.

This chapter reviews topics tested on the auditing section of the exam. Begin by studying the content of the recent auditing examinations as suggested in the "self-study program" which is in Chapter 1 of this volume. After studying each module in this volume, work all of the multiple choice and essay questions.

Recognize that most candidates have difficulty with audit sampling and auditing EDP due to limited exposure in their undergraduate programs and in practice. Thus, you should work through the outlines presented in each study module and work the related questions. Unfortunately, this entire volume would be required to provide comprehensive textbook coverage of topics tested on the exam.

AICPA Content Specification Outline/Frequency Analysis

The AICPA Content Specification Outline of the coverage of auditing, including the authors' frequency analysis (last nine exams) thereof, appears on the following pages.

Mini Outlines/Final Review

At the end of this chapter, we have provided Mini Outlines of the modules. These outlines are to be used as a final review tool and not as a primary study source.

AICPA CONTENT SPECIFICATION OUTLINE/FREQUENCY ANALYSIS[*]
AUDITING

	May 1985	Nov. 1985	May 1986	Nov. 1986	May 1987	Nov. 1987	May 1988	Nov. 1988	May 1989
I. Professional Responsibilities									
A. General Standards and Rules of Conduct									
1. Proficiency, Independence, and Due Care	1	3	1	1	-	1	1	-	-
2. Codes of Professional Conduct	1	3	5	4	-	2	2	3	2
3. Miscellaneous**	3	-	-	-	1	-	-	1	-
B. Control of the Audit									
1. Planning and Supervision	2	5	2	2	-	2	2	2	-
2. Audit Risk and Materiality				1		1	-	-	1
3. Analytical Procedures	-	-	-	1	1	-	-	-	1
4. Quality Control	1	1	1	1	-	1	2	2	1
C. Other Responsibilities									
1. Client Errors, Management Fraud, and Defalcations	1	2	2	1	1	2	-	-	-
2. Client Illegal Acts	1	1	-	2	1	1	-	1	-
3. Responsibilities in Review and Compilation	1	1	1	1	-	2	-	1	-
4. Responsibilities in Attestation Engagements	-	-	-	-	-	-	-	-	-
5. Responsibilities in Management Advisory Services	2	2	1	-	1	-	-	1	-
6. Responsibilities in Tax Practice	2	-	-	-	-	-	-	-	-
Areas No Longer Tested	-	-	-	-	-	-	-	-	-
Total MC Questions	15	18	13	14	5	12	7	11	5
Total Essays	-	-	-	-	1	-	-	-	1
Actual Percentage[***] (AICPA 15%)	15%	18%	13%	14%	15%	12%	7%	11%	15%

[*]Except where noted, the line items in the outline are the AICPA's; the frequencies, tabulations, and actual percentages are the authors'.

**These line items in the outline have been added by the authors.

[***]The "actual percentage" is a measure of the relative coverage of the specific area (i.e., I, II, etc.) on each Auditing exam. This percentage includes both multiple choice questions and essays based on the point allocation used by the AICPA [i.e., multiple choice are assigned 1 point each and essays are 10 points each; note that in Auditing, essays are categorized by one of the four areas only (i.e., I, II, etc.)].

AICPA CONTENT SPECIFICATION OUTLINE/FREQUENCY ANALYSIS (CONTINUED)
AUDITING

	May 1985	Nov. 1985	May 1986	Nov. 1986	May 1987	Nov. 1987	May 1988	Nov. 1988	May 1989
II. Internal Control									
A. Definitions and Basic Concepts	2	3	3	1	1	1	2	2	1
B. Consideration of the Internal Control Structure	2	2	3	2	3	3	1	4	2
C. Cycles									
1. Sales, Receivables, and Cash Receipts	1	1	4	1	1	3	1	3	-
2. Purchases, Payables, and Cash Disbursements	2	-	1	-	2	-	3	2	2
3. Inventories and Production	1	-	-	1	2	1	1	1	1
4. Personnel and Payroll	2	1	-	-	2	3	1	-	1
5. Financing and Investing	1	-	-	-	1	1	1	1	1
D. Other Considerations									
1. Communication of Internal Control Structure Related Matters	2	1	1	1	1	1	1	1	2
2. Reports on Internal Control	1	1	1	1	-	2	2	2	2
3. Sampling	1	3	2	2	1	2	2	-	4
4. Effects of EDP**	3	1	5	1	2	-	4	3	3
5. Flowcharting	-	1	1	-	3	1	-	-	-
6. Effects of an Internal Audit Function**	1	1	-	-	-	-	1	-	1
Total MC Questions	19	15	21	10	19	18	20	19	20
Total Essays	1	1	1	2	1	1	1	1	1
Actual Percentage (AICPA 30%)	29%	25%	31%	30%	29%	28%	30%	29%	30%

AICPA CONTENT SPECIFICATION OUTLINE/FREQUENCY ANALYSIS (CONTINUED)
AUDITING

	May 1985	Nov. 1985	May 1986	Nov. 1986	May 1987	Nov. 1987	May 1988	Nov. 1988	May 1989
III. Evidence and Procedures									
A. Audit Evidence									
1. Nature, Competence, and Sufficiency of Evidential Matter	-	-	1	1	1	-	3	2	1
2. Evidential Matter for Financial Statement Assertions	-	1	-	1	-	-	1	-	-
3. Analytical Procedures	-	-	2	2	2	1	-	1	1
4. Client Representations	1	1	1	1	2	3	2	-	1
5. Using the Work of a Specialist	1	1	-	1	1	-	-	1	-
6. Inquiry of a Client's Lawyer	1	1	1	1	-	1	1	1	1
B. Specific Audit Objectives and Procedures									
1. Tests of Details of Transactions and Balances	5	5	1	6	7	4	5	2	7
2. Documentation	-	1	-	1	1	1	2	1	-
C. Other Specific Audit Topics									
1. Use of the Computer in Performing the Audit	2	3	2	2	2	-	1	3	2
2. Use of Statistical Sampling in Performing the Audit	1	2	-	2	-	2	3	-	2
3. Related Party Transactions	-	1	-	-	1	1	1	-	1
4. Subsequent Events	-	-	1	-	1	-	1	2	
5. Compliance Auditing	-	1	-	-	1	-	-	-	2
6. Omitted Procedures Discovered After the Report Date	-	1	-	1	1	-	1	-	1
D. Review and Compilation Procedures									
1. Understanding of Accounting Principles and Practices of the Industry	-	-	-	-	1	-	1	-	-
2. Inquiry and Analytical Review	1	-	1	1	-	1	2	-	-
3. Unusual Matters	-	-	-	-	1	-	-	-	-
4. Other Procedures	-	-	-	-	-	-	-	-	1
Total MC Questions	12	18	10	20	22	14	23	13	20
Total Essays	2	1.5	2	1	1	2	1	2	1
Actual Percentage (AICPA 30%)	32%	33%	30%	30%	32%	34%	33%	33%	30%

AICPA CONTENT SPECIFICATION OUTLINE/FREQUENCY ANALYSIS (CONTINUED)
AUDITING

	May 1985	Nov. 1985	May 1986	Nov. 1986	May 1987	Nov. 1987	May 1988	Nov. 1988	May 1989
IV. Reporting									
A. Reporting Standards and Types of Reports									
1. Unqualified	-	-	-	-	-	-	2	-	-
2. Explanatory Language Added to the Standard Report	-	-	1	-	-	-	-	-	-
3. Qualified	1	1	2	2	-	-	-	2	-
4. Adverse	1	-	-	1	1	-	-	1	-
5. Disclaimer	-	-	2	-	-	1	-	-	1
6. Consistency	1	1	3	-	-	1	2	-	1
7. Going Concern	-	-	-	-	-	1	-	1	-
8. Reporting Responsibilities	-	-	-	-	1	0	-	2	-
9. Comparative	1	-	1	2	1	-	-	-	1
10. Scope of Examination	2	3	1	-	2	1	1	1	3
11. Generally Accepted Accounting Principles	1	-	-	-	-	-	1	1	-
12. Disclosure	-	-	-	2	2	-	-	-	1
13. Review and Compilation	1	1	1	2	-	3	2	4	1
14. Review of Interim Financial Information	-	-	-	1	-	-	-	-	-
15. Special Reports	1	-	1	1	1	2	1	1	1
16. Negative Assurance	1	-	1	-	-	-	-	-	-
17. Prospective Financial Statements	2	-	-	-	2	3	-	1	2
18. Compliance with Laws and Regulations	-	-	-	-	-	1	1	-	-
B. Other Reporting Considerations									
1. Subsequent Discovery of Facts Existing at the Date of the Auditor's Report	-	2	1	-	1	-	-	-	-
2. Dating of the Auditor's Report	-	-	-	2	-	-	-	-	1
3. Part of Examination Made by Other Independent Auditors	-	-	1	1	1	-	-	1	1
4. Letters for Underwriters	-	-	-	1	-	1	-	1	1
5. Filing Under Federal Securities Statutes	-	-	-	-	1	-	-	1	-
6. Other Information in Documents Containing Audited Financial Statements	-	-	-	-	-	1	-	-	1
7. Required Supplementary Information	2	1	-	1	-	1	-	-	-
8. Information Accompanying the Basic Financial Statements	-	-	-	1	-	1	-	-	-
9. Communicating with Audit Committees	-	-	-	-	-	-	-	-	-
Total MC Questions	14	9	16	16	14	16	10	17	15
Total Essays	1	1.5	1	1	1	1	2	1	1
Actual Percentage (AICPA 25%)	24%	24%	26%	26%	24%	26%	30%	27%	25%

Summary of Essay Questions

The essay summary on the following page presents in detail the types of essay questions which have appeared during recent years. The following abbreviations are used in the summary.

Internal Control   CR--Cash Receipts

                          CD--Cash Disbursements

                          Fill-in--Candidates were required to fill in the appropriate operation represented on a flowchart (see the Internal Control Module). When no such indication was included, the flowchart required candidates to determine weaknesses in internal control.

Reports   GAAP--The report in the question related to an <u>audit</u> of a firm which used <u>generally accepted accounting principles</u>.

                          Special--The report in the question was a "special" report (see AU 621)

                          Review--The report in the question related to a review engagement.

OVERVIEW OF THE ATTEST FUNCTION

In this overview section the general nature of the attest function is first discussed. Second is a discussion of the general nature of the attest function as it relates to financial statement information. Third, a diagram is provided for understanding the nature of audits of financial statements. A section on generally accepted auditing standards (GAAS) and Statements on Auditing Standards (SASs) follows.

Attest Function--General Nature

The attest function provides independent assurance or "attestation" as to whether appropriate criteria have been met. It is helpful here to contrast an "asserter" to an "attester" of information. An asserter has primary responsibility for presenting information which follows appropriate criteria. Think of management (the asserter) as being responsible for presenting publicly available financial information. The attester (generally referred to as the "CPA," "auditor," "public accountant," or "practitioner") then performs appropriate procedures to determine whether the information has been prepared in conformity with the appropriate criteria (most frequently GAAP). Also, be aware that even in cases in which the attester assists in the preparation of the information, he or she is still not the asserter.

Currently, in the United States, attestation is most frequently performed by CPAs through financial statements audits, operational audits, and compliance audits. Yet, the attestation function also allows CPAs to provide assurance on such areas as descriptions of computer software and information on investment performance statistics. Also, the Single Audit Act of 1984 provides an example of the rapidly expanding

AUDITING
Essay Summary

Date	Prof. Resp.	Internal Control	Evidence	Reporting	Sampling	EDP
5/89	Resp. Errors, Irreg. + Illegal Acts	Prepare Questionnaire (Shipments)	Program (Accts. Rec.)	Analyze (GAAP)		
11/88			Program (related parties) General Techniques and procedures (Inventory)	Analyze (Review)	General Concepts	
5/88		Flowchart (CR)	Program (loss contingencies)	Analyze GAAP Discuss (Prospective)		
11/87		Question (Purch., Prepare)	Program (Cash)	Requiring Modific. List Generic Circumst.		Benefits of Micro Comp. Soft
5/87		Opinion on IC	Program (Planning)	Analyze (Review)	Problem (PPS Sampling)	
11/86		General (Phases, etc.)	Audit Risk and Materiality	Prepare (GAAP)		General and Application Controls
5/86		Ques. (CR, Prepare)	Program (Common and Treasury Stock)	Analyze (GAAP)	General Concepts	
11/85		Narrative (CD)	⅓ Rep Letter ⅓ Program (Other Auditor) ⅓ Program (Accts. Rec.)	Prepare (Special) ⅓ Other Auditors		

attest functions in that it requires any city or local government that receives
$100,000 or more in federal financial assistance to have an audit which includes not
only an examination of the financial statements, but also an evaluation of the
internal controls used to manage such assistance and the recipient's compliance with
the related laws and regulations. (In these areas the auditor, in addition to
following generally accepted auditing standards, must follow the General Accounting
Office's Standards for Audit of Governmental Organizations, Programs, Activities, and
Functions.) In the midst of all of these expansions of the attest function, in 1986,
the Auditing Standards Board issued its Statement on Standards for Attestation
Engagements. The Statement presents 11 attestation standards (summarized later in
this module) which provide a general framework for and set reasonable boundaries
around the attest function.

Information on financial statement audits, the bulk of the auditing portion of
the CPA exam, is presented in much greater detail throughout this module. Operational audits generally relate to evaluating whether the criteria of effectiveness
and efficiency of various accounting processes have been met; operational auditing is
considered in further detail in the Evidence module. Compliance audits are directed
at determining whether a client is in compliance with a law or an agreement (e.g.,
the criteria may be to maintain certain ratio requirements as required by a debt
agreement). Reports for compliance audits are discussed in the Reporting module.
(See "Special Reports.")

The need for independent third-party attestation arises due to possible differences between management and others (stockholders, the government, etc.) as to

1. Beliefs regarding activities in which the firm should engage
2. Beliefs regarding the manner in which these activities should be performed
3. Reward structures (management's pay, at least in part, is a salary while
    investors receive interest dividends, and/or capital gains)

Attest Function--Financial Statement Information

The purpose of third-party financial statement attestation is to provide assurance that financial statements, which have been prepared by management, follow appropriate criteria (e.g., generally accepted accounting principles). The preparation of
financial information may be viewed as consisting of inputs (source documents) being
processed (through use of journals, ledgers, etc.) to arrive at an output (the
financial information itself). Or shown diagrammatically

Inputs ⟶ Processing ⟶ Outputs

Source ⟶ Journals, ⟶ Financial
Documents   Ledgers, etc.   Information

While CPAs often assist in the preparation of the financial statements, the attestation function conceptually begins with financial information.

Financial ————————> CPA ————————————> Attested-to
Information   Attestation   Financial Information

A CPA collects various types of evidence relating to the propriety of the recording of economic events and transactions. In examining transactions CPAs must satisfy themselves that

1. All significant transactions occurring during the period have been properly recorded, classified and summarized in the statements, and
2. All significant transactions included in the financial statements did occur during the period

In short, the attestation function helps assure that all transactions have been recorded at their proper amounts. A CPA serves a "control" function in the sense that s/he helps to establish the likelihood that the entity's financial information follows the appropriate criteria to an acceptable degree.

Several forms of the attestation function are currently being performed by CPAs. The primary form is the annual financial statement audit

Annual Financial ————————> CPA ————————> Audited Annual
Statements   Audit   Financial Statements

In an _audit_ the CPA renders an opinion on whether the financial statements of the entity being audited have been prepared in conformity with generally accepted accounting principles (GAAP).

CPAs also become associated with financial information in performing engagements short of audits. For example, overall analytical and inquiry procedures may be used when CPAs perform _reviews_ of interim, annual, or forecast information. In the case of interim financial information

Interim Financial ————————> CPA ————————> Reviewed Interim
Information   Review   Financial Information

Because of the limited nature of the evidence gathering procedures in a review, the CPA's report provides _limited assurance_ with respect to whether the statements follow the appropriate criteria. In the case of reviewed interim financial information, for example, the report explicitly indicates the limited nature of the review's procedures and states that no opinion regarding the statements as a whole is expressed. The report's concluding paragraph indicates whether the CPA is aware of any material modifications which need to be made to the statements for them to be in conformity with generally accepted accounting principles.

CPAs may also provide assistance to clients in the form of _compilation_ and _unaudited_ statement services. Compilation services are performed for _nonpublic_ companies which seek assistance in the preparation of financial statements. In the

case of <u>public</u> companies which are not required to have audits (primarily certain
utilities, banks, etc., which do not report to the Securities Exchange Commission)
similar assistance may be obtained through CPA preparation of <u>unaudited</u> statements.
For both compilations and unaudited statements, note that the CPA's primary role is
to prepare the financial statements, an accounting as opposed to attestation function
(in fact, in the case of compilations, independence is not required). Accordingly,
in both cases the CPA's report disclaims any opinion and gives no assurances with
respect to whether the statements comply with the appropriate criteria. (The
Evidence and Reporting modules discuss these forms of association in further detail.)

Finally, note that while attestation (i.e., reviewing and/or auditing) is often
considered an area within accounting, it is probably more accurate to consider it a
separate function which provides assurance ("attests") to the outputs generated by
the accounting process. One must be an accountant to be an auditor (or "reviewer"),
but one is not necessarily an auditor if one is an accountant. In other words, auditors must be proficient as auditors as well as proficient as accountants.

Diagram of an Audit

In the audit process an auditor gathers evidence to support a professional
opinion. Sufficient competent evidential matter must be gathered to adequately
restrict <u>audit risk</u>, the risk of unknowingly failing to appropriately modify the
audit report on materially misstated financial statements.[1] The following diagram
outlines the steps in the evidence collection and evaluation process in which an
auditor forms an opinion.

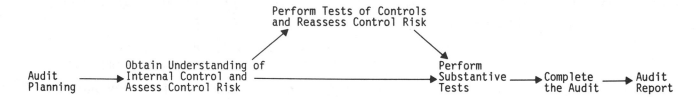

<u>Audit Planning</u>. While planning continues throughout the audit, the objective of
this first phase is to obtain an overall understanding of the entity being audited,
and to develop an overall strategy for the expected conduct and scope of the audit.
A primary goal is to assess inherent risk--the likelihood of material misstatements,
assuming no related internal controls--related to various accounts as well as the
level of risk associated with the overall engagement. Evidence gathered includes
information about the entity's characteristics and the characteristics of its

---

[1]*The concept of audit risk and its components of inherent risk, control risk and
detection risk is presented briefly in this section and is discussed in detail in
section "B.1." of the* Professional Responsibilities *module.*

industry. Also, analytical procedures are required at this stage to assist in planning the nature, timing, and extent of audit procedures.

Internal Control--General. The second generally accepted auditing standard of field work requires a consideration of internal control. The auditor's study of internal control has the two primary purposes of helping the auditor (1) to plan the audit and (2) to assess control risk, the risk that a material error will not be prevented or detected on a timely basis by the internal control structure. Based on the results obtained while obtaining an understanding of internal control primarily for planning purposes, the auditor decides whether to perform tests of controls (compliance tests) to possibly allow a reassessment of control risk.

> Note: AU 319 on internal control eliminates the term compliance tests and replaces it with tests of controls. Because conformity with AU 319 is not required until 1990, to avoid confusion, we will often include "(compliance tests)" following tests of controls.

Obtain Understanding of Internal Control and Assess Control Risk. The auditor obtains an understanding of internal controls and documents this understanding using memoranda, questionnaires, checklists, flowcharts, and/or decision tables. The emphasis at this stage is usually on obtaining an understanding of how the internal control system is purported to function to allow further planning of the audit. Indeed, it is difficult to imagine planning an audit without understanding the essentials of the internal controls.

While obtaining an understanding of the system, the auditor may or may not have chosen to perform tests of controls (compliance tests) to evaluate the effectiveness of the design and operation of internal controls. For example, for a continuing client, the auditor may believe that he already understands the controls well enough to perform some tests. If tests of controls have been performed, the auditor may be able to assess control risk at somewhat below the maximum level; if tests of controls (compliance tests) have not been performed, control risk will be assessed at the maximum level.

Regardless of whether any tests of controls (compliance tests) have been performed at this stage, the auditor must decide whether to perform (more) tests to possibly allow a lower level of control risk assessment and thereby restrict substantive testing. For internal controls that seem weak, a decision will be made to rely in large part on substantive tests--analytical procedures, and/or tests of details of transactions and balances. On the other hand, if controls seem capable of preventing, detecting and correcting material misstatements, the auditor must decide whether it is more cost effective to perform tests of controls (compliance tests) or to directly perform substantive tests.

Perform Tests of Controls and Reassess Control Risk. In situations in which the auditor believes that controls may be adequate and may be relied upon, tests of controls (compliance tests) may be performed. In these tests, auditors typically select various types of transactions which have been processed by the system and test whether the prescribed controls worked. Using test results, the auditor reassesses control risk. When an acceptable level of compliance with controls exists, less substantive testing is generally required because the control risk is lower than when there is a lower level of compliance.

Substantive Tests--General. Substantive tests are used to "substantiate" account balances. Substantive tests restrict detection risk, the risk that audit procedures will incorrectly lead to a conclusion that a material error does not exist in an account balance when in fact such an error does exist. While tests of controls, as noted above, provide evidence as to whether controls procedures and policies are being followed, substantive tests provide evidence as to whether actual account balances are proper. Two substantive tests are (1) Analytical Procedures and (2) Tests of Details of Transactions and Balances.

Substantive Tests--Analytical Procedures. In these tests auditors gather evidence about relationships among various accounting and nonaccounting data such as industry and economy information. When unexpected changes occur (or expected changes do not occur) in these relationships, an auditor investigates further and obtains an explanation. Ratio analysis is a frequently used analytical procedure. The auditor would, for example, calculate a ratio and compare it to criteria such as budgets, prior year data, and industry data.

Substantive Tests--Tests of Details of Transactions and Balances. Auditors use these tests to detect dollar errors in the financial statements. The details supporting individual financial statement agreement are tested to gain assurance that material errors do not exist in the accounts. Sending confirmations for year-end receivable accounts is an example.

Completing the Audit. Auditors perform a number of procedures near the end of the audit. For example, evidence is aggregated and evaluated for sufficiency. Analytical procedures are performed to assist the auditor in assessing conclusions reached and for evaluating overall financial statement presentation. Final decisions are made as to required financial statement disclosures and as to the appropriate audit report.

Audit Report.   There is a standard unqualified audit report (adopted in 1988) that is issued by CPAs when their examination and the results thereof are satisfactory. It is also known as a "clean opinion" and is reproduced below. This standard unqualified report is modified as the audit examination deviates from normal, or as the financial statements fail to comply with generally accepted accounting principles (GAAP).

Variations of the audit report include:

1. Standard Unqualified
2. Unqualified with additional explanatory language
3. Qualified
4. Disclaimer
5. Adverse

The purposes and examples of each are outlined and illustrated in the Reporting module of this chapter.

As a final step in this introduction, you will find it useful to read the standard unqualified report carefully, and note the key points made in it. Remember, the audit report is the primary objective and product of the audit.

Independent Auditor's Reports

TO: Board of Directors and Stockholders
     ABC Company

We have audited the accompanying balance sheets of ABC Company as of December 31, 19X7 and 19X6, and the related statements of income, retained earnings, and cash flows for the years then ended. These financial statements are the responsibility of the Company's management. Our responsibility is to express an opinion on these financial statements based on our audits.

We conducted our audits in accordance with generally accepted auditing standards. Those standards require that we plan and perform the audit to obtain reasonable assurance about whether the financial statements are free of material misstatement. An audit includes examining, on a test basis, evidence supporting the amounts and disclosures in the financial statements. An audit also includes assessing the accounting principles used and significant estimates made by management, as well as evaluating the overall financial statement presentation. We believe that our audits provide a reasonable basis for our opinion.

In our opinion, the financial statements referred to above present fairly, in all material respects, the financial position of ABC Company as of December 31, 19X7 and 19X6, and the results of its operations and its cash flows for the years then ended in conformity with generally accepted accounting principles.

                                                           Joe Smith, CPA
                                                           February 23, 19X8

Some key points in the above report include:

Required Title ("Independent Auditor's Report")
Addressee (company, board of directors and/or stockholders--not management)
Introductory paragraph

1. We have audited

2. Client's financial statements (statements listed)

3. Financial statements are the responsibility of management

4. The auditor's responsibility is to express an opinion

Scope paragraph

1. Audit conducted in accordance with GAAS

2. GAAS require that we plan and perform audit to provide reasonable assurance statements free of material misstatement

3. Audit involves
    Examining on a test basis evidence supporting amounts and disclosures
    Assessment of accounting principles
    Assessment of significant estimates
    Evaluation of overall presentation

4. Audit provides reasonable basis for opinion

Opinion paragraph

1. In our opinion
2. Statements fairly present per GAAP

Manual or printed signature (Firm name)

Date (normally last day of field work)

Generally Accepted Auditing Standards

CPAs are to perform their examinations of financial statements in compliance with generally accepted auditing standards. The figure on the following page summarizes the ten generally accepted auditing standards; for comparative purposes, the 11 attestation standards are also presented. You should memorize the ten generally accepted auditing standards (also by category) for the exam. The following mnemonics provide one way to remember the standards:

TIP (Training, Independence, Professional Care)
PIE (Planning, Internal Control, Evidence)
GODC (GAAP, Opinion, Disclosure, Consistency)

> NOTE: To form the third mnemonic (god with a soft c), one must reorder the reporting standards--1, 4, 3, 2.

The attestation standards relate to all attestation services performed by CPAs. The generally accepted auditing standards may be considered to be the appropriate interpretations as they relate to audits of financial statements. After you have memorized the generally accepted auditing standards, you will find that studying the attestation standards is easy since most are similar. Be familiar with the attestations standards since a question on them is likely.

ATTESTATION STANDARDS AND GENERALLY ACCEPTED AUDITING STANDARDS

Attestation Standards	Generally Accepted Auditing Standards

General Standards

1. The engagement shall be performed by a practitioner or practitioners having adequate technical **training** and proficiency in the attest function.	1. The examination is to be performed by a person or persons having adequate technical **training** and proficiency as an auditor.
2. The engagement shall be performed by a practitioner or practitioners having adequate **knowledge** in the subject matter of the assertion.	
3. The practitioner shall perform an engagement only if he or she has reason to believe that the following two **conditions** exist: • The assertion is capable of **evaluation against reasonable criteria** that either have been established by a recognized body or are stated in the presentation of the assertion in a sufficiently clear and comprehensive manner for a knowledgeable reader to be able to understand them. • The assertion is capable of reasonably **consistent estimation** or measurement using such criteria.	
4. In all matters relating to the engagement, an **independence** in mental attitude shall be maintained by the practitioner or practitioners.	2. In all matters relating to the assignment, an **independence** in mental attitude is to be maintained by the auditor or auditors.
5. Due **professional care** shall be exercised in the performance of the engagement.	3. Due **professional care** is to be exercised in the performance of the examination and the preparation of the report.

Standards of Field Work

1. The work shall be adequately **planned** and assistants, if any, shall be properly supervised.	1. The work is to be adequately **planned** and assistants, if any, are to be properly supervised.
	2. A sufficient understanding of the internal control structure is to be obtained to plan the audit and to determine the nature, timing, and extent of tests to be performed.
2. Sufficient **evidence** shall be obtained to provide a reasonable basis for the conclusion that is expressed in the report.	3. Sufficient competent **evidential matter** is to be obtained through inspection, observation, inquiries, and confirmations to afford a reasonable basis for an opinion regarding the financial statements under examination.

Standards of Reporting

1. The report shall **identify** the **assertion** being reported on and state the character of the engagement.	1. The report shall state whether the financial statements are presented in accordance with **generally accepted accounting principles.**
2. The report shall state the practitioner's conclusion about whether the assertion is presented in conformity with the established or stated **criteria** against which it was measured.	2. The report shall identify those circumstances in which such principles have not been consistently observed in the current period in relation to the preceding period.
	3. Informative **disclosures** in the financial statements are to be regarded as reasonably adequate unless otherwise stated in the report.
3. The report shall state all of the practitioner's significant **reservations** about the engagement and the presentation of the assertion.	4. The report shall either contain an expression of **opinion** regarding the financial statements, taken as a whole, or an assertion to the effect that an opinion cannot be expressed. When an overall opinion cannot be expressed, the reasons therefore should be stated. In all cases where an auditor's name is associated with financial statements, the report should contain a clear-cut indication of the character of the auditor's examination, if any, and the degree of responsibility he is taking.
4. The report on an engagement to evaluate an assertion that has been prepared in conformity with agreed-upon criteria or on an engagement to apply agreed-upon procedures should contain a statement **limiting** its **use** to the parties who have agreed upon such criteria or procedures.	

Statements on Auditing Standards

In 1939, the AICPA appointed the Committee on Auditing Procedure; the committee issued 54 Statements on Auditing Procedures (SAP). In 1973 the Auditing Standards Executive Committee replaced the Committee on Auditing Procedure and issued Statement on Auditing Standards (SAS) No. 1 which was a codification of SAPs which had not then been superseded. The Auditing Standards Executive Committee issued 22 other SASs and was replaced in 1978 when the AICPA created the Auditing Standards Board which now has the responsibility for issuing pronouncements on auditing matters. The Auditing Standards Board has continued the series of SASs which are considered interpretations of GAAS per Ethics Rule 2.02 which requires compliance with GAAS. SASs 2 through 61 have been issued as of May 15, 1988.

All of the SASs (except superseded sections) are outlined at the end of this chapter in their codified order. The manner in which you use these outlines depends upon your educational and practical auditing background. If you have previously read the SASs, you may be able to use the outlines directly without rereading the material. If you are unfamiliar with the SASs, you will probably need to read them, and either simultaneously study the outline, or use the outline to review the major points. In some circumstances you may find that although you haven't read the detailed SAS, your educational and/or practical experience makes studying the outline adequate. At the beginning of each module in this chapter, a study program will refer you to the appropriate SASs. The module presentation itself also provides a summary of the most important information, generally that which has received extremely heavy coverage on past exams.

Also included at the end of this chapter are outlines for the AICPA's Statement on Standards for Attestation Engagements, Financial Forecasts and Projections and Statements on Standards for Accounting and Review Services (SSARS). These too should be studied as a separate topic, as well as with the topical material presented in this chapter.

SAS 1 Section		Module in This Book	New Codified SAS Section No.
100*	Introduction	Overview	
200*	General GAAS	Overview	
310	Relationship Between Appointment and Planning	EVID	
320	Internal Control	IC	Superseded by SAS 55
331	Receivables and Inventories	EVID	
332	Long-Term Investments	EVID	
400*	First 3 Reporting GAAS	REPT	
500*	Fourth Reporting GAAS	REPT	
901	Public Warehouses	EVID	

*Contains multiple subsections

	Module in This Book	New Codified SAS Section No.
SAS 2 Audit Reports	REPT	509
SAS 3 EDP and Internal Control	EDP	Superseded by SAS 48
SAS 4 Firm Quality Controls	RESP	Superseded by SAS 25
SAS 5 Meaning of Present Fairly	REPT	411
SAS 6 Related Party Transactions	EVID	Superseded by SAS 45
SAS 7 Predecessor-Successor Communications	EVID	315
SAS 8 Other Information	REPT	550
SAS 9 Effect of an Internal Audit Function	IC	322
SAS 10 Limited Review	REPT	Superseded by SAS 24
SAS 11 Using Specialists	EVID	336
SAS 12 Inquiry of Client's Lawyer	EVID	337
SAS 13 Limited Review Reports	REPT	Superseded by SAS 24
SAS 14 Special Reports	REPT	Superseded by SAS 62
SAS 15 Comparative Financial Statements	REPT	Superseded by SAS 58
SAS 16 Detection of Errors and Irregularities	RESP	Superseded by SAS 53
SAS 17 Illegal Acts by Clients	RESP	Superseded by SAS 54
SAS 18 Replacement Costs	EVID	Deleted by Auditing Standards Board
SAS 19 Client Representations	EVID	333
SAS 20 Required Communications of Material Weaknesses in Internal Accounting Control	IC	Superseded by SAS 60
SAS 21 Segment Reporting	REPT	435
SAS 22 Planning and Supervision	EVID	311
SAS 23 Analytical Review Procedures	EVID	Superseded by SAS 56
SAS 24 Review of Interim Financial Information	EVID	Superseded by SAS 36
SAS 25 The Relationship of Generally Accepted Auditing Standards to Quality Control Standards	RESP	161
SAS 26 Association with Financial Statements	REPT	504
SAS 27 Supplementary Information Required by the Financial Accounting Standards Board	REPT	553
SAS 28 Supplementary Information on the Effects of Changing Prices	REPT	554
SAS 29 Reporting on Information Accompanying the Basic Financial Statements in Auditor-Submitted Documents	REPT	551
SAS 30 Reporting on Internal Accounting Control	REPT	642
SAS 31 Evidential Matter	EVID	326
SAS 32 Adequacy of Disclosure in Financial Statements	REPT	431
SAS 33 Supplementary Oil and Gas Reserve Information	REPT	Superseded by SAS 45
SAS 34 The Auditor's Considerations When a Question Arises about an Entity's Continued Existence	REPT	Superseded by SAS 59
SAS 35 Special Reports--Applying Agreed-Upon Procedures to Specified Elements, Accounts, or Items of a Financial Statement	REPT	622
SAS 36 Review of Interim Financial Information	EVID	722
SAS 37 Filings under Federal Securities Statutes	REPT	711
SAS 38 Letters for Underwriters	REPT	Superseded by SAS 49
SAS 39 Audit Sampling	AUDS	350
SAS 40 Supplementary Mineral Reserve Information	EVID	556
SAS 41 Working Papers	EVID	339
SAS 42 Reporting on Condensed Financial Statements and Selected Financial Data	REPT	552

		Module in This Book	New Codified SAS Section No.
SAS 43	Omnibus Statement on Auditing Standards	VARIOUS	1010**
SAS 44	Special-Purpose Reports on Internal Accounting Control at Service Organizations	IC	324
SAS 45	Omnibus Statement on Auditing Standards-- 1983	VARIOUS	1020**
SAS 46	Consideration of Omitted Procedures after the Report Date	EVID	390
SAS 47	Audit Risk and Materiality in Conducting an Audit	RESP VARIOUS	312
SAS 48	The Effects of Computer Processing on the Examination of Financial Statements	VARIOUS	1030**
SAS 49	Letters for Underwriters	REPT	634
SAS 50	Reports on the Application of Accounting Principles	REPT	625
SAS 51	Reporting on Financial Statements Prepared for Use in Other Countries	REPT	534
SAS 52	Omnibus Statement on Auditing Standards	VARIOUS	1040**
SAS 53	The Auditor's Responsibility to Detect and Report Errors and Irregularities	RESP	316
SAS 54	Illegal Acts by Clients	RESP	317
SAS 55	Consideration of the Internal Control Structure in a Financial Statement Audit	IC	319
SAS 56	Analytical Procedures	EVID	329
SAS 57	Auditing Accounting Estimates	EVID	342
SAS 58	Reports on Audited Financial Statements	REPT	508
SAS 59	The Auditor's Consideration of an Entity's Ability to Continue as a Going Concern	EVID REPT	341
SAS 60	The Communication of Internal Control Structure Related Matters Noted in an Audit	IC	325
SAS 61	Communication with Audit Committees	IC	380
SAS 62	Special Reports	REPT	623
SAS 63	Compliance Auditing Applicable to Governmental Entities and other Specified Recipients of Governmental Financial Assistance	EVID	*

*Not codified as we go to press

**Outlines of the paragraphs of this statement have been inserted in the outlines of the sections which it superseded

*Authors' Note: Changes in terminology have been made in the Auditing Modules and in the SAS Outlines to reflect changes in the AICPA's forthcoming revision of the **Codification of Auditing Standards**. These are indicated as the items are presented.*

PROFESSIONAL RESPONSIBILITIES

Professional ethics (responsibilities) have traditionally been focused at the individual practitioner level. The authoritative literature at that level includes: the Generally Accepted Auditing Standards; the AICPA Code of Professional Conduct (hereafter the Code); Statements on Responsibilities in Tax Practice; Statements on Standards for MAS; and Statements on Quality Control Standards.

Generally, multiple choice questions are used to test the candidate's knowledge of the AICPA Code of Professional Conduct and, to a lesser extent, the Statements on Responsibilities in Tax Practice, Statements on Standards for Management Advisory Services, and the Statement on Quality Control Standards. Occasionally essay questions have provided a description of a situation with ethical connotations and have required that the candidate list and describe any unethical behavior which has occurred.

Study Program for the Professional Responsibilities Module

This module is organized and should be studied in the following manner.

A. General Standards and Code of Professional Conduct

   1. General Standards
   2. Code of Professional Conduct

B. Control of the Audit

   1. Planning and Supervision
   2. Quality Control

C. Other Responsibilities

   1. Client Errors, Management Fraud, and Defalcations
   2. Client Illegal Acts
   3. Responsibilities in Compilation and Review
   4. Responsibilities in Management Advisory Services
   5. Responsibilities in Tax Practice

The above outline is based on the AICPA CPA Exam Content Specification Outline for Professional Responsibilities.

The following SAS sections pertain to Professional Responsibilities.

Section AU

110	Responsibilities and Functions of the Independent Auditor
150	Generally Accepted Auditing Standards
161	Relationship of Generally Accepted Auditing Standards to Quality Control Standards
201	Nature of the General Standards
210	Training and Proficiency of the Independent Auditor
220	Independence
230	Due Care in the Performance of Work
310	Relationship Between the Auditor's Appointment and Planning

Additionally, outlines of the Code of Professional Conduct, Statements on Quality Control, Management Advisory Services, and Tax Practice are presented in this module.

A. **General Standards and Rules of Conduct**

1. <u>General Standards (AU 210, 220, 230).</u> The three general <u>audit</u> standards (recall TIP--Training, Independence, Professional Care) are personal in nature in the sense that they are concerned with the auditor's qualifications and the quality of his/her work. The general <u>attestation</u> standards also include standards which require adequate knowledge of the subject matter of the assertion (#2) and that the attester only become involved with assertions which may be evaluated against reasonable criteria in a reasonably consistent manner (#3).

   Be aware of several overall points here. First, training includes both formal education and professional experience. Second, independence requires both actual independence and the appearance of independence to third parties. An important point to remember is that while independence is required for audits, it is not required for tax, MAS, or compilations. Third, although infallibility is not assumed by the attester, due professional care must be exerted at all levels.

2. <u>Code of Professional Conduct</u>

   a. <u>Overview.</u> The Code of Professional Conduct, passed by the AICPA membership in 1988, consists of two sections

      (1) Principles--which provide the framework
      (2) Rules--which govern the performance of professional services

      In addition, many interpretations and rulings, orginally passed with the prior Code, are in effect.
      The Code is applicable to all AICPA members, not merely those in public practice. Compliance with the Code depends primarily on members' understanding and voluntary actions, and only secondarily on (1) reinforcement by peers, (2) public opinion, and (3) disciplinary proceedings. The possible disciplinary proceedings include <u>admonishment</u>, <u>suspension</u>, or <u>expulsion</u> from the AICPA. In addition, court decisions have consistently held that even if an individual is not a member of the AICPA, that individual is still expected to follow the profession's Code of Professional Conduct. Finally, the individual state CPA board and societies monitor ethical matters.
      The Code provides <u>minimum</u> levels of acceptable conduct relating to all services performed by CPAs, unless the wording of a standard

specifically excludes some members. For example, some standards do not apply to CPAs not in public practice.

The overall structure of the Code goes from the very generally worded standards to the more specific and operational rules. The interpretations and rulings remaining from the prior Code are even more specific.

The Principles sections consists of 6 Articles:

I	Responsibilities
II	The Public Interest
III	Integrity
IV	Objectivity and Independence
V	Due Care
VI	Scope and Nature of Services

The Rules, Interpretations, and Rulings are structured as

Code of Professional Conduct Rules
and Related Interpretations and Rulings

Rules	Interpretation	Number of Rulings Issued
101 - Independence	1 - Transactions, interests, relationships	69
	1 - Director Nonprofit Organization	
	2 - Retired Partner	
	3 - Recordkeeping Assistance	
	5 - Meaning of Certain Terminology	
	6 - Litigation	
	8 - Financial Interests	
	9 - Family Relationships	
	10 - Governmental Entities	
102 - Integrity and Objectivity	1 - Financial Statement Misrepresentations	
201 - General Standards	1 - Competence	9
202 - Attestation and Other Standards	1 - Unaudited Statements	
203 - Accounting Principles	1 - Departures	
	2 - FASB Interpretations	
	3 - Other Information	
301 - Confidential Information	1 - Exceptions	15
302 - Contingent Fees	1 - Findings of governmental agencies	
501 - Acts Discreditable	1 - Client Records	182
	2 - Discrimination	
	3 - Governmental Audits	
	4 - Negligence is Discreditable	
502 - Advertising and Solicitation	1 - Good Taste and Dignified	
	2 - False, Misleading, Deceptive	
	5 - Services to Clients of Third Parties	
503 - Commissions	1 - When Commission Allowed	
505 - Form of Practice and Name	1 - Investment in Accounting Corp.	
	2 - Members Not in Public Practice	

NOTE: Gaps in sequence are due to deleted sections.

A one-sentence summary is presented later in this module for each of the ethics rulings issued by the AICPA. They are now published in Vol. 2 of the Professional Standards. While CPA candidates should read the rulings to better understand the ethics rules and interpretations, it is <u>not</u> necessary to memorize them--consider them to be illustrations.

The Code of Professional Conduct has been reproduced in most auditing texts. If you refer to the Code in your auditing text, make sure it is current. Following is an outline of the six principles (referred to in the Code as articles) included in section 1 of the Code. Next is a combined outline of Section 2 of the Code (rules) integrated with the interpretations and rulings.

b. <u>Code of Professional Conduct--Principles</u>

<u>Article I - Responsibilities.</u> In carrying out their responsibilities as professionals, members should exercise sensitive professional and moral judgments in all their activities.

<u>Article II - The Public Interest.</u> Members should accept the obligation to act in a way that will serve the public interest, honor the public trust, and demonstrate commitment to professionalism

(1) A distinguishing mark of a professional is acceptance of responsibility to public

   (a) The accounting profession's public consists of clients, credit grantors, governments, employers, investors, business and financial community, and others.

   (b) In resolving conflicting pressures among groups an accountant should consider the public interest (the collective well-being of the community)

<u>Article III - Integrity.</u> To maintain and broaden public confidence, members should perform all professional responsibilities with the highest sense of integrity

(1) Integrity can accommodate the inadvertent error and honest difference of opinion, but it cannot accommodate deceit or subordination of principle

(2) Integrity

   (a) Is measured in terms of what is right and just

   (b) Requires a member to observe <u>principles of objectivity, independence, and due care</u>

<u>Article IV - Objectivity and Independence.</u> A member should maintain objectivity and be free of conflicts of interest in discharging professional responsibilities. A member in public practice should be independent in fact and appearance when providing auditing and other attestation services

(1) Overall

   (a) Objectivity a state of mind

      1] Objectivity imposes obligation to be impartial, intellectually honest, and free of conflicts of interest

      2] Independence precludes relationships that may appear to impair objectivity in rendering attestation services

   (b) Regardless of the service performed, members should protect integrity of their work, maintain objectivity, and avoid any subordination of their judgment

(2) Members in public practice require maintenance of objectivity and independence (includes avoiding conflict of interest)

    (a) Attest services--require independence in fact and in appearance

(3) Members not in public practice

    (a) Are unable to maintain appearance of independence, but must maintain objectivity

    (b) When employed by others to prepare financial statements, or to perform auditing, tax, or consulting services, must remain objective and candid in dealings with members in public practice

Article V - Due Care. A member should observe the profession's technical and ethical standards, strive continually to improve competence and the quality of services, and discharge professional responsibility to the best of the member's ability

(1) Competence is derived from both education and experience
(2) Each member is responsible for assessing his or her own competence and for evaluating whether education, experience, and judgment are adequate for the responsibility taken

Article VI - Scope and Nature of Services. A member in public practice should observe the Principles of the Code of Professional Conduct in determining the scope and nature of services to be provided

(1) Members should

    (a) Have in place appropriate internal quality control procedures for services rendered

    (b) Determine whether scope and nature of other services provided to an audit client would create a conflict of interest in performance of audit

    (c) Assess whether activities are consistent with role as professionals

c. Code of Professional Conduct--Rules, Interpretations, and Rulings

Rule 101 Independence. A member in public practice shall be independent in the performance of professional services as required by standards promulgated by designated bodies

Interpretations 101-1. Independence is impaired if

(1) During period of professional engagement, or at time of expressing an opinion, member or a member's firm:

    (a) Had or was committed to acquire any direct or a material indirect financial interest in client

    (b) Was a trustee of any trust or executor of any estate having direct or material indirect interest in client

    (c) Had any joint investment with any client, officer, stockholder, etc., that was material

    (d) Had any loan to or from client, officer, stockholder, etc. Exceptions (independence is not impaired) include the following loans:

        1] Borrowed by CPA not material to borrower's net worth
        2] Home mortgages
        3] Other secured loans except loans guaranteed by CPA firm

   (2) During period covered by the financial statements, during period of professional engagement, or when expressing opinion

      (a) Promoter, underwriter, voting trustee, director, officer, employee, etc.

      (b) Trustee of any pension or profit sharing trust of client

<u>Interpretation 101-1</u>. (until this is recodified it is the second Interpretation 101-1) CPA who is a director of a nonprofit organization where board is large and representative of community leadership is <u>not</u> lacking independence if

(1) Position purely honorary
(2) Position identified as honorary on external materials
(3) CPA participation restricted to use of name
(4) CPA does not vote or participate in management affairs

<u>Interpretation 101-2</u>. Retired CPA's association with clients does not impair firm independence if

(1) Retired CPA no longer active in firm
(2) Client fees do not have a material effect on CPA's retirement benefits
(3) Retired CPA not associated with firm

<u>Interpretation 101-3</u>. When a CPA performs writeup services, it <u>may or may not</u> impair independence

(1) Must meet following requirements to retain appearance that CPA is not employee of client

      (a) CPA cannot have any relationship with client that impairs integrity and objectivity
      (b) Client must understand statements and accept as his own
      (c) CPA must not assume role of employee or management

         1] Cannot consummate transactions or have custody of assets, etc.
         2] Cannot prepare source documents, etc.
         3] Cannot make changes in client's data without client concurrence

      (d) When doing audit must gather sufficient competent evidence (conform to GAAS)

(2) For <u>non-SEC</u> clients can rent block computer time to clients
(3) For <u>SEC</u> clients CPA cannot maintain accounting records or rent block time

<u>Interpretation 101-4</u>. (Deleted)

<u>Interpretation 101-5</u>. Meaning of certain terminology

(1) Rule 101 prohibits client-CPA loans except for certain type which are per normal lending procedures
(2) Loan--financial transaction that generally provides for repayment terms and a rate of interest
(3) Financial Institution--one which makes loan to general public as part of normal transactions
(4) Normal lending procedures--terms for "other borrowers" including

      (a) Amount of loan and collateral
      (b) Repayment terms
      (c) Interest rate, points, closing costs, etc.

    (d) Requirement to pay closing costs as lender's usual practice

    (e) General availability of such loans to public

<u>Interpretation 101-6.</u> Effect of threatened litigation

(1) Client-CPA actual or threatened litigation

    (a) Commenced by present management alleging audit deficiencies, impairs

    (b) Commenced by auditor against present management for fraud, deceit impairs

    (c) Expressed intention by present management alleging deficiencies in audit work impairs if auditor believes <u>strong possibility</u> of claim

    (d) <u>Immaterial</u> not related to audit <u>usually</u> does <u>not</u> impair (i.e., billing disputes)

(2) Litigation by client security holders or other third parties generally does not impair unless material client-CPA cross-claims develop

(3) If independence is impaired, CPA should disassociate and/or disclaim an opinion for lack of independence

(4) CPA may re-sign report of prior year (when s/he was independent) if no material audit work is required

<u>Interpretation 101-7.</u> (Deleted)

<u>Interpretation 101-8.</u> A CPA's financial interest in nonclients may have an effect on independence when those nonclients have financial interest (investee or investor) in CPA's clients

(1) Definitions

    <u>Investor</u>--(1) a parent or (2) another investor that holds an interest in another company (investee) which gives it the ability to exercise significant influence over the investee

    <u>Material investee</u>--investor's carrying amount of investment is 5% or more of investor's total assets or investor's equity in investee's income is 5% or more of the investor's income

    <u>Material financial interest</u>--5% or more of member's net worth

(2) Provisions

    (a) Where a nonclient investee is material to a client investor, any direct or material indirect financial interest by CPA in a nonclient investee impairs independence

    (b) Where a client investee is material to a nonclient investor, any direct or material indirect financial interest of a CPA in a nonclient impairs independence

    (c) Careful consideration should be given to situations involving brother-sister common control or client-nonclient joint ventures

    (d) Where a nonclient investee is not material to a client investor, an immaterial financial interest of a CPA in the nonclient investee would not be considered to impair independence; a material one would

    (e) Where a client investee is not material to a nonclient investor, an immaterial or material financial interest of a CPA in a nonclient investor will not generally impair independence with respect to the investee; the exception case is when the member owns so much of the nonclient so as to be able to significantly influence the nonclient's actions--then not independent

Interpretation 101-9. Meaning of independence terminology and the effect of family relationships on independence

(1) "He and his firm" in Rule 101 includes

    (a) Individual practitioner performing attestation services
    (b) The proprietor of, or all partners or shareholders in a firm
    (c) All full and part time employees of a firm participating on engagement
    (d) All full and part time managerial employees of a firm in an office performing a significant portion of engagement

       Managerial employees--partner and others with authority to sign and give final approval for report issuance

    (e) Any entity whose operating, financial, or accounting policies can be significantly influenced by one or more persons in (1) to (4) above

       Examples of individuals with significant influence
       - Promoters, directors, underwriters
       - Top officers
       - APB, para 17 guidelines
       - 20% or more interest of limited partnerships

(2) Effect of family relationships on independence

    (a) Spouse and dependent persons--same as member, except spouse may be employed by client if s/he does not exert significant influence over client's operating, financial, or accounting policies. If spouse is in audit sensitive position (subject to significant internal controls--cashier, internal auditor, etc.) member should not participate in engagement
    (b) Nondependent close relatives--normally not considered, but member independence is impaired if

       1] Professional participating on job has close relative with significant influence, audit sensitive position, or material financial interest in client and professional knows
       2] A partner or managerial employee--in office has a close relative who can exert significant influence

    (c) Other family considerations--consider whether reasonable person aware of all facts and considering normal strength of character and normal behavior would question

Interpretation 101-10. A CPA's responsibility with respect to client and nonclient entities which are a part of a governmental entity's combined statements

(1) If CPA audits oversight entity (the overall governmental entity)

    (a) If nonclient component is material, CPA must be independent of it
    (b) If CPA can demonstrate that nonclient component is immaterial, CPA need not be independent of it

(2) If CPA audits a material component, must be independent of oversight entity and other components

Rule 102 Integrity and Objectivity. In performance of _any_ professional service, a member shall (a) maintain objectivity and integrity, (b) avoid conflicts of interest, and (c) not knowingly misrepresent facts or subordinate judgment

(1) In tax matters, resolving doubt in favor of client does not, by itself, impair integrity or objectivity

Interpretation 102-1. Knowingly making or permitting false and misleading entries in an entity's financial statements or records is a violation

Rule 101, 102 Ethics Rulings

Independence and Integrity Ethics Rulings

1. If a CPA accepts more than a token gift from a client, independence may be impaired.
2. A CPA may join a trade association, which is a client, without impairing independence, but not serve in a capacity of management.
3. If a CPA is cosignor of a client's checks, independence is impaired.
4. Independence is impaired if a CPA prepares a client's payroll and conditions of Interpretation 101-3 are not met.
5. If a client processes all original entry documents and transmits this data to a CPA for further processing, independence is not impaired if the conditions of Interpretation 101-3 are met.
6. If a CPA's spouse, as an employee, performs only bookkeeping services for a client, independence is not impaired.
7. Independence is impaired if a CPA supervises client office personnel on a monthly basis.
8. Extensive accounting and MAS services, including interpretation of statements, forecasts, etc., do not impair independence.
9. Independence is impaired if the CPA cosigns checks or purchase orders or exercises general supervision over budgetary controls.
10. The independence of an elected legislator (a CPA) in a local government is impaired with respect to that governmental unit.
11. Mere designation as executor or trustee, without actual services in either capacity, does not impair independence, but actual service does.
12. If a CPA is a trustee of a foundation, independence is impaired.
13. If a CPA's stock investment in a bank is not material, it does not impair independence with a client borrowing from that bank.
14. A CPA serving as director and treasurer of a local United Fund does not impair independence with respect to charities receiving money from the fund.

15. If a retired partner is still closely associated with the CPA firm, his serving on a client's board of directors impairs independence.
16. Independence is impaired if a member serves on the board of a nonprofit social club if the board has ultimate responsibility for the affairs of the club.
17. Membership in a country club does not impair independence.
18. Being chairman of a city council does not impair independence with respect to other governmental agencies not under the council's control.
19. Independence is impaired if a CPA serves on a committee administering a client's deferred compensation program.
20. Membership on governmental advisory committees does not impair independence with respect to that governmental unit.
21. A CPA serving as director of an enterprise would not be independent with respect to the enterprise's profit sharing and retirement trust.
22. Independence is impaired if the CPA's brother is a stockholder and vice-president of a closely held company.
23. Independence would not be impaired for a company owned by the uncle of a CPA's wife (infrequent personal contacts).
24. Independence would be impaired if a CPA's father serves on a school board.
25. Independence is impaired if a CPA's son is a director of a savings and loan association.
26. A CPA purchasing a public client's stock for his son's educational trust would impair independence.
27. A CPA's independence would be impaired if the CPA's spouse is trustee of a trust owning stock in the CPA's client.
29. A CPA's independence is impaired when owning bonds in a municipal authority.
31. A partner's ownership of an apartment in a co-op apartment building does not impair the firm's independence.
32. A CPA, who is president and a substantial stockholder in a company which is indebted on a mortgage loan to a S&L, does not impair the firm's independence with respect to the S&L.

33. A CPA impairs independence upon joining a client's employee benefit plan.
34. A partner's ownership of stock in a bank impairs firm independence with respect to the bank's trust fund.
35. A CPA's ownership of shares in a mutual investment fund which owns stock in the CPA's clients normally would not impair independence.
36. A CPA who is a member of an investment club, holding stock in a client, lacks independence.
38. A CPA serving with a client bank in a co-fiduciary capacity, with respect to a trust, does not impair independence with respect to the bank or trust department (if the estate's or trust's assets were not material).
39. A CPA who acts as a transfer agent and/or registrar is not independent with respect to the company.
41. A CPA may audit a mutual insurance company that provides a retirement plan for the CPA's employees if the plan is not material to the insurance company.
42. A CPA firm's independence would not be impaired if the client, a stock life insurance company, underwrites a group term life insurance policy for the firm's partners if the amount at risk is not material to the insurance company's underwriting activities.
43. A CPA's independence would be impaired upon serving as treasurer of a charitable organization.
45. A CPA can be independent of a client in bankruptcy if the CPA's claim is fixed at the date of the bankruptcy filing.
47. A CPA who is a shareholder of a company serving as a mutual fund's investment advisor or manager is not independent to the mutual fund.
48. A university faculty member cannot be independent to a student senate fund because the student senate is a part of the university which is the CPA's employer.
51. A CPA who provides legal services to a client is not independent with respect to the client.
52. Unless the amounts involved are insignificant to both the client and the auditor, fees for all prior years' professional services should be collected before issuance of the current year audit report.
53. A CPA's independence, with respect to an employee benefit plan, is not impaired by being the auditor of the sponsoring company.

54. A CPA's independence is not impaired by rendering actuarial services to a client, if the client makes or approves all significant matters of judgment.
55. A CPA's independence is not impaired if the CPA is involved in hiring and instructing new personnel during a systems implementation. The client must make all significant management decisions and the CPA must restrict supervisory activities to initial instruction and training.
56. Independence is impaired by recruiting and hiring a controller and/or cost accountant for a client company. The CPA may, however, recommend position descriptions and candidate specifications as well as initially screen and recommend qualified candidates.
57. There is a possible violation of independence if a CPA firm recommends an outside service bureau in which partners have a financial interest.
58. Independence is impaired when a CPA owns a building and leases space to a client.
59. Generally CPA's auditing employee benefit plans must be independent of the employer.
60. Participation by a CPA's spouse in an employee stock ownership plan of a client does not impair independence until a right of possession of the stock exists.
61. A CPA may own a limited partnership interest (less than 20%) in a partnership in which a client owns less than 20% if neither is active in management in the partnership. If more than one client is involved, the aggregate investment (CPA plus clients) must be less than 50% of the interest of all limited partners.
62. To be independent for compilations or reviews of prospective financial statements associated with an offering or placement of securities, a CPA must be independent with respect to all promoters, others receiving 10% or more of proceeds, and the issuer itself. A broker or sales agent who does not otherwise organize the entity is not a promoter.
63. Independence with respect to a fund-raising foundation is impaired if a CPA serves on the board of directors of the entity for whose benefit the foundation exists (unless position is purely honorary).
64. A CPA not in public practice may use the CPA designation in connection with financial statements and correspondence of his employer if his employment status is made clear and no reference to either having made a review or audit is made.
65. Independence is impaired by a member's retirement or savings plan which includes

a direct or material indirect financial interest in an attest client.

66. A client financial institution may service a member's loan that is otherwise prescribed by Rule 101 as long as there is no risk of material loss to the client with respect to the loan being serviced.

67. A member may not hold a direct financial interest in an attestation client, even when held in a blind trust.

68. A member's material investment in a limited partnership impairs independence for other limited partnerships that have the same promoter and/or general partner.

Rule 201 General Standards. Member must comply with the following standards for all professional engagements

(1) Only undertake professional services that one can reasonably expect to complete with professional competence
(2) Exercise due professional care
(3) Adequately plan and supervise engagements
(4) Obtain sufficient relevant data to afford a reasonable basis for conclusions and recommendations

Interpretation 201-1. Competence to complete an engagement includes

(1) Technical qualifications of CPA and staff
(2) Ability to supervise and evaluate work
(3) Knowledge of technical subject matter
(4) Capability to exercise judgment in its application
(5) Ability to research subject matter and consult with others

Interpretations 201-2, 3, 4. (Deleted)

Rule 202 Compliance With Standards. A member who performs auditing, review, compilation, MAS, tax or other services shall comply with standards promulgated by bodies designated by Council

NOTE: The designated bodies are:

(1) Financial Accounting Standard Board
(2) Governmental Accounting Standards Board
(3) AICPA designated bodies

(a) Accounting and Review Services Committee
(b) Auditing Standards Board
(c) Management Advisory Services Executive Committee

Interpretation 202-1. Rule 202 does not preclude a CPA from being associated with unaudited financial statement, as long as the degree of responsibility taken is clearly stated

Rule 203 Accounting Principles. Member cannot provide positive or negative assurance that financial statements are in conformity with GAAP if statements contain departures from GAAP having a material effect on statements taken as a whole except when unusual circumstances would make financial statements following GAAP misleading

(1) When unusual circumstances require a departure from GAAP, CPA must disclose in report the departure, its effects (if practicable), and reasons why compliance would result in a misleading statement

Interpretation 203-1. CPAs are to allow departure from SFAS only when results of SFAS will be misleading

(1) Requires use of professional judgment
(2) Examples of possible circumstances requiring disclosure are

(a) New legislation
(b) Conflicting industry practices

<u>Interpretation 203-2.</u> FASB Interpretations are covered by Rule 203

(1) Also unsuperseded ARBs and APBs

<u>Interpretation 203-3.</u> SFASs which stipulate that certain information should be disclosed outside the basic financial statements are not covered by Rule 203

<u>Rule 201, 202, 203 Ethics Rulings</u>

1. A practicing CPA who prepares an un-audited financial statement for a company in which he is a stockholder, is deemed to be associated with unaudited financial statements, i.e., requires a disclaimer due to lack of independence.
2. A CPA employed by a corporation may perform examinations of corporate interests for internal purposes only. Reports to outsiders cannot indicate he is a CPA and must be on the corporate letterhead.
3. A CPA cannot accept the audit opinion issued by the controller of the client who is also a CPA.
4. A CPA may express an opinion on a prior fiscal year in which he prepared un-audited financial statements provided he can satisfy himself as to their fairness and comply with GAAS.

5. Unaudited interim reports issued by clients are considered associated with a CPA if the CPA's name is listed anywhere on or in the report.
6. A practicing CPA who prepares statements for a private club of which he is a treasurer may issue the statements on CPA letterhead with proper disclaimer per Section 504.
7. A CPA who is in partnership with non-CPAs may sign the report with the firm name, his own name and indicate "certified public accountant."
8. A CPA selecting subcontractors for MAS engagements is obligated to select subcontractors on the basis of professional qualifications, technical skills, etc.
9. A CPA should be in a position to supervise and evaluate work of a specialist in his employ.

Rule 301 Confidential Client Information. Member in public practice shall not disclose confidential client information without client consent except for

(1) Compliance with Rule 202 and 203 obligations
(2) Compliance with enforceable subpeona or summons
(3) AICPA review of professional practice
(4) Initiating complaint or responding to inquiry made by a recognized investigative or disciplinary body

<u>Interpretation 301-1.</u> Confidential relationship rule cannot prohibit CPA from carrying out responsibility per GAAS

Rule 302 Contingent Fees*. Fees may not be contingent upon finding or results of services, although fees may

(1) Vary with complexity of services rendered
(2) Be fixed by courts or other public authorities
(3) In tax matters be based on results of judicial proceedings or findings of governmental agencies

*As we go to press, the AICPA has entered into a consent degree with the Federal Trade Commission that would allow contingent fees from clients that are not receiving certain compilation and attestation services from a CPA.

<u>Interpretation 302-1.</u> The findings of governmental agencies ("(3)" above) does not refer to the preparation of original tax returns, amended returns, claims for refund, and requests for private letter rulings

Rule 301, 302 Ethics Rulings

1. A member may utilize outside computer services to process tax returns as long as there is no release of confidential information.
2. With client permission, a CPA may provide P&L percentages to a trade association.
3. A CPA withdrawing from a tax engagement due to irregularities on the client's return should urge successor CPA to have client grant permission to reveal reasons for withdrawal.
4. A CPA who had audited an international union could not be retained by local unions bringing suit against the international union.
5. A CPA may use a records retention agency to store client records as long as confidentiality is maintained.
6. A CPA may be engaged by a municipality to verify taxpayer's books and records for the purpose of assessing property tax. The CPA must maintain confidentiality.
7. CPAs and their employees should not reveal the names of the CPA's non-public clients without client permission.
8. CPAs should not base their fee for work on a bond issue as a percentage of the total amount of the issue.
9. A CPA's fees for work on acquisitions of other companies should be based upon the services rendered and not a percentage of the acquisition price.
10. Expert witness fees may not be based upon the amount awarded.
11. Fees based upon the amount of mortgage commitments are contingent fees and a violation of Rule 302.
12. A fee based on taxes saved in preparing a return is a violation of Rule 302. There is a proper tax liability and no basis for tax savings.
13. Contingent fees for accounting services associated with a fire adjuster are not permitted.
14. A CPA has a responsibility to honor confidential relationships with non-clients. Accordingly, CPAs may have to withdraw from MAS engagements where the client will not permit the CPA to make recommendations without disclosing confidential information about other clients or non-clients.
15. If the CPA has conducted a similar MAS study with a negative outcome, the CPA should advise potential clients of the previous problems providing that earlier confidential relationships are not disclosed. If the earlier confidential relationship may be disclosed (through client knowledge of other clients), the CPA should seek approval from the first client.

Rule 501 Acts Discreditable. A member shall not commit an act discreditable to the profession

Interpretation 501-1. Retention of client records after client has demanded them is discreditable

Interpretation 501-2. Discrimination on basis of race, color, religion, sex, age, or national origin is discreditable

Interpretation 501-3. In audits of governmental grants, units, or other recipients of governmental monies, failure to follow appropriate governmental standards, procedures, etc. is discreditable

Interpretation 501-4. Negligently making (or permitting or directing another to make) false or misleading journal entries is discreditable

Rule 502 Advertising and Other Forms of Solicitation. In public practice, shall not seek to obtain clients by false, misleading, deceptive advertising or other forms of solicitation

Interpretation 502-1. Advertising should be in good taste and dignified

    a.   No restrictions on type style, media, frequency, art work etc.
    b.   May include names, address, telephone number, number of partners, office hours, year established, services offered, educational attainment, statements of position, etc.

Interpretation 502-2. False, misleading, and deceptive advertising is prohibited

    a.   Statements made in advertising should be verifiable

Interpretations 502-3,4. (Deleted)

Interpretation 503-5. CPA may render services to clients of third parties as long as all promotion efforts within Code

Rule 503 Commissions*. Member in public practice shall not accept payment for the referral of products or services of others and shall not pay to obtain a client

(1)   Exceptions in which member may pay to obtain a client--purchase of an accounting practice or retirement payments

*As we go to press, the AICPA has entered into a consent degree with the Federal Trade Commission that would allow a CPA to accept a commission from referring goods or services to clients that do not receive certain compilation and attestation services from the CPA. The CPA would be required to disclose to the client that a commission was involved in the referral.

Interpretation 501-1. While payment of commissions to obtain a client is prohibited, payments for professional services performed by referring CPA are allowed

Rule 504.   (Deleted)

Rule 505 Form of Practice and Name. Member may practice public accounting only in form of proprietorship, partnership, or professional corporation and may not practice under a misleading name.

(1)   May include past partners
(2)   An individual may practice in name of a former partnership for up to 2 years (applies when all other partners have died or withdrawn)
(3)   A firm name may include a fictitious name or indicate specialization if name is not misleading
(4)   Firm may not designate itself as members of AICPA unless all partners or shareholders are members

Interpretation 505-1. CPA may have an investment interest in a commercial corporation performing services similar to public accounting if it is not material to the corporation

Interpretation 505-2. CPA holding out to public as being CPA or public accountant and who participates in operation of separate business that offers services rendered by public accountants must observe Code in operation of business.

Rule 501-502, 503, 505 Ethics Rulings
Other Responsibilities Ethic Rulings

Due to rescinding the advertising and solicitation prohibition, the majority of the ethics rulings have been suspended.

2.   A CPA may permit a bank to collect notes issued by a client in payment of fees.
3.   A CPA employed by a firm with non-CPA practitioners must comply with the rules of conduct. If a partner of such a firm is a CPA, the CPA is responsible for all persons associated with the firm to comply with the rules of conduct.

33.   A CPA who is a course instructor has the responsibility to determine that the advertising materials promoting the course are within the bounds of Rule 502.
38.   A CPA who is controller of a bank may place his CPA title on bank stationery and in paid advertisements listing the officers and directors of the bank.
78.   CPAs who are also attorneys may so indicate on their letterhead.
82.   A CPA may write a financial management newsletter (being advertised for sale) with his name featured prominently.

86. A CPA may be engaged to verify financial or statistical facts used in a client's advertising and the CPA's name may be used in such advertising.

108. CPAs interviewed by the press should observe the code of professional conduct and not provide the press with any information for publication that the CPA could not publish himself.

109. A CPA who arranges for clients to purchase supplies at a discount may not accept a commission from a supplier but may only accept payment for a common effort on behalf of the clients purchasing the supplies.

110. A CPA may represent a computer tax service providing services only to tax practitioners (not clients) and receive a fee for each tax return processed within his franchise area.

111. A CPA may buy a bookkeeping practice based on a percentage of fees received over a three-year period.

112. A CPA cannot pay a management specialist to refer potential clients to him.

113. A CPA may not refer potential life insurance customers to a spouse who is a life insurance agent.

114. A CPA may pay bonuses or otherwise share profits to employees from professional accounting work where practice development is a factor in determining bonus or profit sharing.

115. A CPA firm may conduct actuarial and administrative services for a client as a separate partnership.

117. A CPA may be a director of a consumer credit company if he is not the auditor.

127. A CPA may not both work for the state controller and practice public accounting as most businesses are subject to some form of state control.

132. A non-CPA partner to a CPA who specializes in taxes should not accept a position as a public member of board of tax appeals for a recently established municipal income tax ordinance.

134. CPAs who share offices, employees, etc., may not indicate a partnership exists unless a partnership agreement is in effect.

135. CPA firms which are members of an association cannot use letterhead that indicates a partnership rather than an association.

136. Where a firm consisting of a CPA and a non-CPA is dissolved, and an audit is continued to be serviced by both, the audit opinion should be signed by both individuals, such that a partnership is not indicated.

137. The designation "non-proprietary partner" should not be used to describe personnel as it may be misleading.

138. A CPA may be a partner of a firm of public accountants when all other personnel are not certified, and at the same time practice separately as a CPA.

139. A CPA in practice with a non-CPA would have to conform to the Code of Conduct, and would not be permitted to represent itself as a partnership of CPAs.

140. A partnership practicing under the name of the managing partner who is seeking election to high office may continue to use the managing partner's name plus "and Company" if the managing partner is elected and withdraws from the partnership.

141. A CPA in partnership with a non-CPA is ethically responsible for all acts of the partnership and those of the non-CPA partner.

144. A CPA firm may use an established firm name in a different state even though there is a difference in the roster of partners.

145. Newly merged CPA firms may practice under a title which includes the name of a previously retired partner from one of the firms.

146. CPA firms may not designate themselves as Members of the American Institute of Certified Public Accountants unless all their partners or shareholders are members of the AICPA.

147. A sole proprietor may not use in his firm title the designation "and Company" or "and Associates."

148. Two CPAs may use in their firm title the designations "and Company" or "and Associates."

155. A CPA firm in partnership with a computer corporation providing services only for the clients of the CPA firm (not directly to the public) would not be a violation of the Code.

156. A CPA may assist a corporation in developing a tabulating service to be offered to the public if he has no financial interest in the corporation and the CPA is not publicly connected with the tabulating service.

158. A CPA's association with a firm providing data processing services should be limited to that of a consultant. The CPA should not be an officer or shareholder.

159. A CPA firm may buy computer time at a discount from another CPA firm and bill it to his clients at the regular rates.

167. A CPA should not recommend investments in tax-sheltered investments and receive a commission on the sale of such investments.

175. CPAs serving as bank directors should carefully consider the effect of their role as bank director with problems concerning:
     1. Confidential client information
     2. Conflict of interest (between bank and client)
     3. Independence (after bank grants material loan to client)
     4. Solicitation (using directorship to obtain clients)
176. A CPA firm's name, logo, etc., may be imprinted on newsletters and similar publications if the outside author or publisher is clearly indicated.
177. Performing centralized billing services for a doctor is a public accounting service and must be conducted in accordance with the code.
178. A CPA engaged in public accounting may operate a separate business from the same location unless a conflict of interest exists.
179. CPA firms which are members of an association (for purposes of joint advertising, training, etc.) should practice in their own names, although they may indicate membership in the association.
180. Because estate planning is a type of service performed by CPAs, a CPA engaged in public accounting who renders estate planning in a separate office must conduct that business in accordance with the Rules of Conduct.
181. A CPA may purchase a portion, or all, of another CPA's practice and that may be based on a percentage of future annual fees.
182. A member need only return records originally provided to the member by the client for a terminated engagement (in this case preparation of a tax return).

Professional Corporation Characteristics (per AICPA council)

   a. Ownership shall be by persons engaged in public accounting
   b. Provision must be made for transfer of shares from a shareholder who is no longer engaged in public accounting
   c. To extent possible, all directors and officers shall be CPAs
   d. Conduct of shareholders and employees shall comply with AICPA standards

B. Control of the Audit

1. Planning and Supervision (AU 310, 311, 312, and 315)

   a. Overall planning considerations. The first standard of fieldwork requires that work be adequately planned and supervised. The nature, timing, and extent of audit planning varies with the (1) size and complexity of the client, (2) the auditor's experience with the entity, and (3) the auditor's knowledge of the entity's business. AU 310 points out that the early appointment of the auditor allows the auditor to plan his/her work so that it may be done more efficiently than in situations in which an auditor is appointed shortly before or after a client's year end.

   Also, when a client has computer operations, the following need to be considered.

   (1) Extent of usage
   (2) Complexity of usage
   (3) Organizational structure of computer operations
   (4) Availability of data
   (5) Potential for using computer-assisted audit techniques

   The auditor must be aware that specialized computer skills (either by staff or by outside consultants) may be needed to audit a firm with a computer system.

   During the planning of an audit an auditor must determine both a preliminary measure of materiality and an acceptable level of audit risk. The materiality measure is to be based on the definition in SFAC 2 which suggests that a material misstatement is one which makes it probable that the judgment of a reasonable person relying on the information would have been changed or influenced. Although this preliminary measure of materiality may be either quantitative or nonquantitative, it is easier to think about a quantitative measure. Section 312 suggests that materiality levels include an overall level for each statement. For example, the auditor may believe that misstatements aggregating approximately $100,000 would have a material effect on income, but that such misstatements would have to aggregate approximately $200,000 to materially affect financial position. In such cases the lower measure would be used for any transactions affecting income.

After determining a materiality level for the various financial statements, the auditor would then apportion the amount among the various accounts. This apportionment may be based on factors such as the relative size of various accounts and by using professional judgment. The apportioned amount for each account is the "tolerable misstatement" discussed in the Audit Sampling Module (Section C). Tolerable misstatement, combined for the entire audit plan, should not exceed the auditor's preliminary estimate of materiality.

The auditor must also determine an appropriate level of <u>audit</u> risk, "the risk that the auditor may unknowingly fail to appropriately modify his opinion on financial statements that are materially misstated." At the overall financial statement level, audit risk is the chance that a material misstatement exists and has been missed by the auditor. At the individual account-balance level, audit risk is composed of three components--inherent risk, control risk, and detection risk.

<u>Inherent</u> risk refers to the likelihood of a material misstatement occurring in an account, assuming no related internal controls. This risk could be low, for example, for petty cash when it is known that only a very limited amount was spent during the year; it could be high for a general cash account with millions of dollars of expenditures. To assess this risk the auditor will perform overall review techniques and will use his/her overall auditing knowledge.

<u>Control</u> risk is the risk that a material misstatement will not be prevented or detected on a timely basis by the internal control structure. The auditor may assess this risk through overall review techniques, internal control review techniques (e.g., questionnaires, flowcharts, etc.), and tests of controls.

<u>Detection</u> risk is the risk that an auditor's procedures will lead him/her to conclude that a material misstatement does not exist in an account balance when in fact such a misstatement does exist. The auditor's substantive tests are primarily relied upon to control detection risk.

Note that detection risk is related to the effectiveness of the auditor's procedures, while inherent and control risk are elements of the client and its internal control structure. When an auditor believes that an account has a high level of inherent and/or control risk, detection risk should be set at a relatively low level. On the other hand, a low level of inherent and control risk (as evidenced by the auditor's evaluation and subsequent test of controls) will justify allowing a higher detection risk.

Several other considerations relating to materiality and audit risk are important. First, the two concepts have an inverse relationship--as the materiality level increases, the potential audit risk decreases. Second, both concepts may be evaluated either quantitatively or nonquantitatively. Third, know that the planning level of materiality may be modified during the performance of the audit as additional information about the client is identified.

AU 311 presents additional planning assistance. We may divide the section's overall planning considerations as follows.

Client considerations:

1. Type of business and industry
2. Accounting policies and procedures
3. Conditions requiring extension of audit procedures (e.g., related party transactions)
4. Items likely to need adjustment

Audit considerations:

1. Anticipated internal control reliance
2. Preliminary judgment about materiality levels
3. Reports to be issued
4. Methods used to process significant information (i.e., outside service center)

Auditors also perform various audit procedures at the planning stage. We may categorize them as

Information collection techniques

1. Correspondence, prior workpapers, financial statements, etc.
2. Current interim statements
3. Authoritative (especially new) pronouncements
4. Effect of nonaudit services which have been performed

Detailed planning techniques

1. Need for consultants, specialists, internal auditors, etc.
2. Establish timing of audit work
3. Coordinate staff requirements

Client involvement

1. Inquire about current developments
2. Discuss type, scope, timing, etc.
3. Coordinate client assistance in data collection

Analytical procedures

1. Perform procedures to gain understanding of business and identify areas of high risk

Note: Analytical procedures are discussed in detail in the Evidence module (Section B.1.a.)

Note also that a written audit program is to be developed and used for the audit.

b. <u>Supervision Considerations (AU 311)</u>. Supervision includes instructing assistants, being informed on significant problems, reviewing audit work, and dealing with differences of opinion among audit personnel. The complexity of the audit and qualifications of audit assistants affect the degree of supervision needed. Procedures should be established for documenting any disagreements of opinions among staff personnel; the basis for resolution of such disagreements should be documented.

c. <u>Communications Between Predecessor and Successor Auditors (AU 315)</u>. When a potential new client has been served by another auditor in the past, the successor auditor should, before accepting the engagement, obtain permission from the potential client to communicate with the predecessor auditor. The initiative in communication rests with the successor auditor; the communication may be oral or written. The successor should question the predecessor on matters concerning the integrity of management, any disagreements as to accounting principles, and the reasons for the change in auditors. The predecessor is normally to respond promptly and fully (unusual circumstances such as impending litigation may, however, cause a limited reply). If the engagement is accepted by the successor, other inquiries such as a review of the predecessor's work papers <u>may</u> be performed by the successor. Again, conditions such as litigation may preclude the predecessor from cooperating and may thus cause the successor to perform additional audit procedures.

    d. <u>Timing of Audit Procedures (AU 313)</u>. Tests of controls and substantive audit tests can be conducted at various times. The timing of tests of controls is very flexible as they are often performed at an interim period and subsequently updated through year end.

Auditors also have a certain amount of flexibility in planning the timing of substantive tests. Section 313 discusses three timing aspects:

    (1) Factors to be considered before applying tests at an interim date before year end
    (2) Auditing procedures to be followed for the remaining period between the interim date and year end, and
    (3) Coordination of the timing of audit procedures

Before applying procedures prior to year end, an auditor should consider the incremental audit risk involved as well as whether performance of such interim procedures is cost effective. While reliance on internal control is not required for the period between the interim date and year end, it may be difficult to satisfy the completeness assertion (see the Evidence module) without some degree of internal control reliance.

The auditor who performs procedures at an interim date must be satisfied that additional procedures are available which make it possible to update balances from the interim date to year end. Such tests ordinarily should compare information between the interim and year-end periods to identify unusual changes and should include other analytical review procedures and/or substantive tests of details to provide a reasonable basis for extending audit conclusions to year end. When errors have been discovered at the interim date, the auditor should carefully consider whether they have again occurred as of year end.

Concerning the coordination of timing, a properly conducted audit will reflect the fact that the performance of certain procedures needs to be synchronized. This especially applies to (1) related party transactions, (2) interrelated accounts and cutoffs, and (3) negotiable assets. For interrelated accounts and negotiable assets, the auditor is concerned that one might be substituted for another to allow the double counting of a given resource (e.g., sale of securities after they have been counted at year end and inclusion of proceeds in year end cash).

2. <u>Quality Control (QC 10-90)</u>

    a. <u>Overview</u>. The nine quality control standards (outlined at the end of this section) apply to the audit practice of all firms. As indicated earlier, while the generally accepted auditing standards and the Code are primarily directed at the individual practitioner level, the quality control standards apply to the CPA <u>firm</u> itself.

A major function of these quality control standards is to serve as the appropriate criteria for evaluation for independent <u>peer reviews</u>.

In a peer review, one's peers (other CPAs) evaluate the quality of the firm's audit work. A peer review may be performed by

(1)   Another CPA firm
(2)   An AICPA approved peer review committee
(3)   A state society of CPA's approved peer review committee

For quality control purposes the AICPA has also formed a "Division for CPA Firms" which has two sections--the SEC Practice Section and the Private Companies Practice Section. While membership in either of these sections is voluntary, member firms of either section are required to submit to peer reviews (once every three years) and may be penalized by the AICPA for work deemed to be substandard.

The peer review process is new and is still being refined as more experience is gained. In 1988 the process was expanded to require varying levels of review for CPA firms which perform any attestation or compilation services. The overall objective of the process is to help assure the performance of the attestation function in a socially desirable manner. Possible benefits of peer review include

(1)   Prevention of poor audit procedures due to the awareness of the firm's personnel regarding subsequent peer review
(2)   Detection of poor audit procedures
(3)   The reviewing firm may learn from the process
(4)   Self-regulation by the profession may be more cost effective than the alternative of governmental regulation

Possible limitations of peer review are

(1)   It is costly to the reviewed firm and to the public to whom some portion of the cost is undoubtedly passed
(2)   In cases where the roles of reviewer and reviewee switch, a lack of perceived and/or actual independence may result
(3)   While it may be possible to determine whether a firm has followed its quality control standards, evaluating the actual adequacy of an audit (presumably the "bottom line" in peer reviewing) is difficult
(4)   The effectiveness of the sanctioning (penalization) process remains largely untested

To this point there have been few questions on quality control (the frequency analysis presented earlier in this chapter indicates only 1 or 2 multiple choice questions per exam). For multiple choice questions be familiar not only with the names of the nine standards but also with what they imply (e.g., supervision policies provide assurance that work performed meets the firm's standards of quality). Essay questions on the nine quality control standards and/or on peer review may appear in the future.

b.   Outline of Quality Control Standards

(1)   A system of quality control standards is required to assure the firm is providing professional services that comply with professional standards

(a)   Includes organization structure, policies, and procedures
(b)   Should be appropriate in relation to the firm's

1]   Size
2]   Degree of operating autonomy within firm
3]   Nature of practice
4]   Organization structure

        5] Other appropriate cost-benefit considerations

    (c) The system has inherent limitations

        1] E.g., variance in individual performances, understanding of professional requirements, etc.

(2) Quality control standards apply to auditing and accounting and review services

    (a) May be applied to other areas, e.g., MAS, tax, etc.

    (b) Should apply to work done by foreign offices and domestic affiliates

(3) A firm shall consider each of the following interrelated elements of quality control in establishing quality control policies and procedures (quoted from SQCS #1)

    (a) <u>Independence.</u> "Policies and procedures should be established to provide the firm with reasonable assurance that persons at all organizational levels maintain independence to the extent required by the rules of conduct of the AICPA."

    (b) <u>Assigning Personnel to Engagements.</u> "Policies and procedures for assigning personnel to engagements should be established to provide the firm with reasonable assurance that work will be performed by persons having the degree of technical training and proficiency required in the circumstances."

    (c) <u>Consultation.</u> "Policies and procedures for consultation should be established to provide the firm with reasonable assurance that personnel will seek assistance, to the extent required, from persons having appropriate levels of knowledge, competence, judgment, and authority."

    (d) <u>Supervision.</u> "Policies and procedures for the conduct and supervision of work at all organizational levels should be established to provide the firm with reasonable assurance that the work performed meets the firm's standards of quality."

    (e) <u>Hiring.</u> "Policies and procedures for hiring should be established to provide the firm with reasonable assurance that those employed possess the appropriate characteristics to enable them to perform competently."

    (f) <u>Professional Development.</u> "Policies and procedures for professional development should be established to provide the firm with reasonable assurance that personnel will have the knowledge required to enable them to fulfill responsibilities assigned."

    (g) <u>Advancement.</u> "Policies and procedures for advancing personnel should be established to provide the firm with reasonable assurance that those selected for advancement will have the qualifications necessary for fulfillment of the responsibilities they will be called on to assume."

    (h) <u>Acceptance and Continuance of Clients.</u> "Policies and procedures should be established for deciding whether to accept or continue a client in order to minimize the likelihood of association with a client whose management lacks integrity."

    (i) <u>Inspection.</u> "Policies and procedures for inspection should be established to provide the firm with reasonable assurance that the procedures relating to the other elements of quality control are being effectively applied."

(4) Responsibility for a quality control system shall be assigned to individuals to assure effective implementation based on

    (a) Competence of individuals
    (b) Authority delegated
    (c) Extent of supervision over them

(5) Quality control policies and procedures shall be communicated to the firm's personnel

    (a) Normally in writing, but not required
    (b) Documentation expected to be more extensive in larger and multi-office firms

(6) The quality control system shall be monitored on a timely basis

    (a) Monitoring includes the quality control element of inspection
    (b) To assure effectiveness of the system
    (c) Size, structure, and nature of practice determine monitoring function
    (d) Includes timely modification of policies and procedures for

        1] New authoritative pronouncements
        2] Expansion of practice
        3] Opening of new offices, mergers, etc.

C. Other Responsibilities

1. <u>Errors and Irregularities (AU 316)</u>. Review the outline of this section carefully as errors and irregularities have been heavily examined. Distinguish between an error (an unintentional mistake such as a math error) and an irregularity (an intentional distortion such as fraud). Know that an audit should be designed to provide <u>reasonable assurance</u> of detecting material errors and irregularities. Also, a properly designed and executed audit may miss a material irregularity, particularly one involving forgery or collusion.

Section B of the outline presents a summary of factors believed to indicate a risk of financial statement misstatement (management characteristics, operating, and industry characteristics, and engagement characteristics). One might expect an essay question based on these factors. In addition, section C of the outline presents risk factors at the account balance level.

Irregularities (as well as errors) which are not properly reported will lead to a qualified or adverse opinion. When the auditor is unable to determine whether the statements are correct, a disclaimer or qualified report is necessary. Know that unless irregularities are clearly inconsequential, the audit committee is to be informed, as well as a level of management at least one level above those involved.

2. <u>Illegal Acts (AU 317)</u>. Illegal acts are also heavily examined.

   In discussing an auditor's responsibility for detecting illegal acts, know
   that the further removed an illegal act is from the events and transactions
   ordinarily reflected in financial statements, the less likely the auditor is
   to become aware of the act or to recognize its possible illegality. AU 317
   differentiates between illegal acts having a <u>direct and material effect</u> on
   the financial statements (e.g., relating to tax laws) vs. an indirect and
   material effect (e.g., securities purchased or sold based on inside
   information, OSHA violations). The auditor's responsibility for detection
   of illegal acts may be summarized as follows:

   <u>Direct</u>--Responsibility is the same as for irregularities (that is, to
   plan the audit to provide reasonable assurance of detection of
   material misstatements).

   <u>Indirect</u>--Normally, an audit in accordance with GAAS does not include
   audit procedures specifically designed to detect illegal acts with
   indirect effects. However, procedures applied for forming an
   opinion on the financial statements may bring possible illegal acts
   to the auditor's attention. If specific information comes to the
   auditor's attention concerning such an act, the auditor should
   apply audit procedures to ascertain whether an illegal act has
   occurred.

   When an auditor discovers acts which might be illegal, s/he must
   consider whether (1) it is necessary to contact legal counsel, (2) the act
   is properly reported in the financial statements (including the SFAS 5 loss
   contingency aspect) and (3) the act's implications on other portions of the
   audit. The audit committee must be provided with, unless the act is clearly
   inconsequential (1) a description of the act, (2) circumstances concerning
   the occurrence, and (3) the effects on the financial statements. When
   senior management is involved, the auditors should communicate directly with
   the audit committee. When a client refuses to give appropriate
   consideration to handling an illegal act (even an immaterial one), the
   auditor should consider withdrawing from the engagement.

3. <u>Responsibilities in Compilation and Review</u>. While the accountant's overall
   responsibilities with respect to compilations and reviews of financial
   statements are discussed in the Evidence and Reporting modules, recall that
   the accountant <u>need not</u> be independent to perform a compilation (an
   accounting service) and must be independent to perform a review (an
   attestation service).

4. Responsibilities in Management Advisory Services

   a. In 1982 a new series of pronouncements on management advisory services, Statements on Standards for Management Advisory Services (SSMAS), became effective. Know that SSMAS 1 distinguishes between a MAS consultation (usually oral and based on the CPA's existing personal knowledge--see 3.c. of the following outline) and a MAS engagement (a more thorough study--see 3.b. of outline). Also, for an audit client, a CPA shall not assume a role of management or any positions that might impair objectivity.

   b. Outline of SSMAS 1 (MS 11) Definitions and Standards for MAS Practice

      (1) Management advisory services, in general

         (a) Consist of advice and assistance on organization, personnel, planning, operations, controls, etc.
         (b) Are often closely related to auditing, tax, and review services of CPAs

      (2) Purpose of this series of statements is to

         (a) Provide compliance guidance for Rule 201 of the AICPA Code of Professional Conduct

            1] Previous statements on MAS were not enforceable under Rule 201
            2] Previous statements may be consulted until new standards are issued

         (b) Provide other appropriate standards under Rule 202 of the AICPA Rules of Conduct

      (3) Definitions

         (a) Management advisory services (MAS)--advice and technical assistance to help the client improve use of capabilities and resources
         (b) MAS engagement--MAS form where an analytical approach is applied to a study or project
         (c) MAS consultation--MAS form based on existing personal knowledge about the client, the circumstances, the technical matters involved, and the mutual intent of the parties

            1] Usually oral advice given in a short time frame
            2] Advice may be definitive (existing knowledge is adequate) or qualified (cost, time, scope, or other limitations are present)

         (d) MAS practitioner--any member of AICPA in public practice while performing a MAS service for a client

            1] Also any individual carrying out MAS for a client on behalf of an AICPA member

      (4) Standards for MAS Practice

         (a) General standards for MAS engagements and consultations

            1] Professional competence--undertake engagements which can reasonably be expected to be completed competently
            2] Due professional care
            3] Planning and supervision

            4] <u>Sufficient relevant data</u>--to afford reasonable basis for conclusions and recommendations

            5] <u>Forecasts</u>--do not vouch for achievability of results

    (b) Technical standards for MAS engagements and consultations

        NOTE: MS 11 and MS 31, combined here as technical standards for engagements and consultations, are identical

        1] <u>Role of MAS practitioner</u>--practitioner should not assume role of management or take any positions that might impair objectivity

        2] <u>Understanding with client</u>--may be oral or written concerning the nature, scope, and limitations of MAS engagement

        3] <u>Client benefit</u>--should not be explicitly or implicitly guaranteed and estimates (and their support) should be identified

        4] <u>Communication of results</u>--significant information, limitations, qualifications, or reservations should be communicated orally or in writing

c. <u>Outline of SSMAS 2 (MS 21) MAS Engagements</u>

  (1) Nature of MAS engagements

    (a) Involve gathering and analyzing appropriate information to develop conclusions and recommendations

        NOTE: A MAS engagement is more detailed in scope than is a MAS consultation. Also, recommendations and comments made as a direct result of an audit, review, or compilation are not a MAS engagement or consultation as here defined.

    (b) When a client inquires concerning a MAS matter unrelated to the engagement, the practitioner's response may fall within the definition of a consultation (see below)

  (2) <u>Details on general standards</u> for MAS engagements

    (a) <u>Professional competence</u>--in MAS engagements includes ability to

        1] Identify and define client needs

        2] Select and supervise staff

        3] Select and apply analytical process

        4] Apply relevant technical knowledge

        5] Effectively communicate and assist with implementation of recommendations

    (b) <u>Planning and supervision</u>--to provide reasonable assurance that work is in accordance with understanding of client and with professional standards

        1] A plan for the engagement should be developed and modified as necessary during the engagement

        2] The necessary level of documentation and supervision is based on skills of individuals involved and duration and complexity of engagement

    (c) <u>Sufficient relevant data</u>--to complete in manner consistent with understanding with client

           1] Data should be obtained by interview, observation, computation, research, analysis, and review of client documents
           2] Practitioner should exercise professional judgment in determining nature and quantity of information to complete engagement

    (3) Additional points on MAS engagements

        (a) Practitioners should not assume role of management
        (b) The client should understand the nature of the engagement
        (c) Practitioners should obtain understanding with client of expected benefits of engagement

           1] Results should not be guaranteed either implicitly or explicitly
           2] Reservations concerning achievability of anticipated benefits should be expressed

        (d) Communication of results may be oral or written

           1] Should include underlying assumptions and limitations
           2] If oral, practitioner should document in file

d. <u>Outline of SSMAS 3 (MS 31) MAS Consultations</u>

    (1) Nature of MAS consultations

        (a) Situations in which MAS consultations occur

           1] Concurrent with other professional services or independently
           2] May be one decision or a continuing consultation on a wide variety of matters
           3] May be via telephone, nonbusiness setting, periodic meetings, or formal writings

        (b) MAS consultations are generally based on practitioner's <u>existing</u> personal <u>knowledge</u>

        NOTE: Scope here is less than for an engagement.

        (c) Examples--recommendations, limited analysis of options, and fact finding based on limited technical research

    (2) Details on general standards for MAS consultations

        (a) <u>Due professional care</u>--should provide for clear communication and careful delineation of appropriate degree of client reliance
        (b) <u>Planning and supervision</u>--will vary with complexity of entity and inquiry
        (c) <u>Sufficient relevant data</u>--when information is provided by client to practitioner, the client should be informed that advice given is dependent on accuracy and completeness of such information

    (3) Additional points on MAS consultations

        (a) Role of MAS practitioner in a consultation is as a general business advisor
        (b) Practitioner should recognize possibility of misunderstanding of results and take steps to prevent it
        (c) Form of communication with client may be oral or written

5. <u>Responsibilities in Tax Practice</u>

   a. <u>Overview.</u> On most exams one or two multiple choice questions deal with
      issues raised in the Statements on Responsibilities in Tax Practice.
      Each of the Statements raises one major issue (e.g., how estimates are
      to be handled). Be aware that the standards related to the signature of
      a preparer and of a reviewer (TX 111 and TX 121) have been deleted.
      Read the following remaining outlines. You will be able to grasp the
      nature of the statements in a short period of time, and any questions on
      the exam will probably be quite easy to answer.

   b. <u>Outline of Tax Statements</u>

      <u>TX Section 101 - Introduction</u>

      (1) Series of statements setting good standards of tax practice out-
          lining CPA's responsibility to

          (a) His/her client
          (b) The public
          (c) The government
          (d) His/her profession

      (2) Each statement will cover a particular tax aspect
      (3) Objectives of statements

          (a) Identify and develop appropriate standards of responsibilities
              and promote uniform application
          (b) Encourage increased understanding of CPA's responsibilities by
              the Treasury Department and IRS
          (c) Foster increased public compliance with and confidence in our
              tax system

      (4) CPA has no separate written statement of standards of conduct
          relating solely to tax practice, a number of guides to assist
          him/her are available

          (a) CPA is guided by

              1] Statutes
              2] Regulations
              3] Rules governing practice before the IRS and
              4] Institute's Code of Professsional Conduct

          (b) It is in the public interest and in the self-interest of the
              CPA to develop separate statements on responsibility in tax
              practice

      (5) The primary effect of the program will be educational

          (a) Statements will not have the force of authority as the rules
              contained in Treasury Circular 230
          (b) Statements are not intended to be retroactive

      <u>TX Section 131 - Answers to Questions on Returns</u>

      (1) CPA should sign the preparer's declaration on a federal tax return
          only if s/he is satisfied that a reasonable effort has been made to
          provide appropriate answers

          (a) Where such a question is left unanswered the reason for such
              omission should be stated

      (b) Possibility that an answer to a question might prove disadvantageous to the client does not justify omission or a statement of the reason for such omission

(2) CPA should satisfy him/herself that a reasonable effort was made to provide appropriate answers to the questions because

      (a) The question may be important in determining taxable income or loss, or tax liability

      (b) It is not consistent with the CPA's professional stature to sign an incomplete return

(3) Reasonable ground may exist for omitting an answer

      (a) Information not readily available and answer is not significant in terms of taxable income or loss, or tax liability

      (b) Answer may be significant but

          1] Uncertainty exists regarding the meaning of the question
          2] Information is not sufficiently reliable to report

      (c) Answer to the question is voluminous but data will be supplied to the revenue agent in the course of his/her examination

(4) Where reasonable grounds exist for omission of an answer, a brief explanation should be provided on return

(5) Statement should not be construed to have any bearing on whether a return which contains unanswered questions is complete to start the running of the statute of limitations

(6) A member may resolve doubt in favor of client if there is reasonable support for position

TX Section 141 - Recognition of Administrative Proceedings of a Prior Year

(1) Selection of the treatment of an item on a tax return should be based upon facts and rules as of the time the return is prepared

      (a) Unless the taxpayer is bound as to the treatment in the later year, the disposition of an item for a prior year does not govern the treatment of a similar item in a later year's return

      (b) A CPA may sign the return containing a departure from the treatment of an item arrived at as a part of an administrative proceeding regarding a prior year's return

(2) No requirement that a disclosure of the dissimilarity be made in a later year's return, when valid reasons exist

TX Section 151 - Use of Estimates

(1) A CPA may prepare tax returns using estimates if they are not unreasonable and

      (a) Use is generally acceptable or
      (b) It is impracticable to obtain exact data

(2) Explanations

      (a) Accounting requires the exercise of judgment, e.g., useful life and salvage value
      (b) It is permissible to make a reasonable estimate of accruals

       (c) Accuracy in recording transactions involving small expenditure is difficult to achieve

       (d) Unavailable data requires use of estimates

(3) Estimated amounts should not be presented in such a way as to imply greater accuracy than exists

       (a) Estimates should be presented in any manner which will avoid deception

       (b) Use of a round amount or an amount suggested in a Treasury Department guideline may be sufficient

       (c) If a tax return entry is an aggregation of items which includes a significant estimated amount, such estimated amount should be disclosed

(4) CPA should encourage the use of appropriate records to support, where practical, all entries on a client's tax return

TX Section 161 - Knowledge of Error: Return Preparation

(1) A CPA should advise his/her client promptly upon learning of an error (which includes omission) in a previously filed return or upon learning of a client's failure to file

       (a) His/her advice should include recommendations of measures to be taken

           1] May be oral advice

       (b) CPA is neither obligated to inform the IRS nor may s/he do so without his/her client's permission

(2) A CPA should consider whether to proceed with the preparation of the current year's return if the client has not taken appropriate action to rectify a prior year's error that has resulted or may result in a material understatement of tax

       (a) If s/he does prepare such return, the CPA should assure him/herself the error is not repeated

       (b) Items associated with the uncorrected prior error should not be allowed except as specifically permitted by

           1] Internal Revenue Code

           2] IRS pronouncements and court decisions

(3) Item 2 is concerned only with errors that have resulted or may result in a material understatement of tax liability

(4) It is the client's responsibility to decide whether to correct the error

(5) When the error is discovered during an engagement which does not involve taxes, the CPA should

       (a) Advise the client of the existence of the error

       (b) Recommend that the matter be taken up with the client's tax advisor

(6) Whether an error is material should be left to the judgment of the individual CPA

(7) It is not recommended that a client compensate in a current tax return for a prior year's understatement

TX Section 171 - Knowledge of Error: Administrative Proceedings

(1) Statement is concerned with errors that have resulted or may result in a material understatement of tax liability
(2) The CPA should request the client's agreement to disclose the error to the IRS

    (a) If client refuses, the CPA may be under a duty to withdraw from the engagement

(3) It is appropriate for the CPA to serve as an advocate for her/his client with respect to any position for which s/he has reasonable support
(4) CPA may not make disclosures to IRS without client agreement due to confidential relationship

    (a) CPA withdrawal, itself, during proceedings may also be construed as a violation of confidential relationship. Indicates existence of client problems to IRS.

TX Section 181 - Advice to Clients

(1) CPA must use judgment to assure that his/her advice reflects professional competence and appropriately serves the client's needs
(2) CPA may communicate with his/her client when subsequent developments affect advice previously provided with respect to significant matters

    (a) CPA cannot be expected to assume responsibility for initiating such communication

        1] Except while s/he is assisting a client with the advice provided

    (b) CPA may undertake this obligation by specific agreement

(3) Written communications are recommended in important unusual transactions

    (a) Oral advice is acceptable in usual transactions

(4) CPA should consider such factors as

    (a) Importance of transaction and amounts
    (b) Specific or general nature of inquiry
    (c) Time available to develop and submit advice
    (d) Technical complications
    (e) Existence of authority and precedents
    (f) Tax sophistication of client

(5) CPA may wish to advise client that

    (a) Advice reflects professional judgment
    (b) Subsequent developments may affect previous advice

TX Section 191 - Certain Procedural Aspects of Preparing Returns

(1) CPA may rely on information furnished by his/her client

    (a) CPA is not required to examine or review documents or other evidence in order to sign
    (b) CPA should encourage clients to provide him/her with supporting data where appropriate

    (c) CPA should make use of client's return of prior years whenever feasible

    (d) CPA is required to make reasonable inquiries where information appears incorrect or incomplete

    (e) CPA should sign return without modifying the preparer's declaration

        1] Unusual circumstances may be disclosed in the return by a rider not constituting a modification of the declaration

TX Section 201 - Positions Contrary to Treasury Department or Internal Revenue Service Interpretations of the Code

(1) A CPA may take a position contrary to Treasury Department or IRS interpretations of the Code

    (a) There must be reasonable support

    (b) Disclosure is not required

(2) A CPA may take a position contrary to a specific section of the Internal Revenue Code

    (a) There must be reasonable support, e.g.,

        1] Legal opinions as to constitutionality of specific provisions

        2] Published writings of tax specialists asserting the possibility of a lack of constitutionality

        3] Possible conflicts between two sections of the Code

    (b) There must be disclosure

(3) In no event may a CPA take a position that lacks reasonable support even when this position is disclosed

(4) CPA may wish to make disclosure even if not required due to

    (a) Fraud and negligence penalties per section 6653

    (b) Six-year statutory assessment period per section 6501(e)

    (c) Various preparer penalties

    (d) Treasury Department regulations are promulgated per IRS Code direction, i.e., quasi-legislative (see sections 1502 and 472)

(5) Tax returns are client representations

    (a) Client has final responsibility for positions taken

    (b) Positions taken must be with full client acquiescence

INTERNAL CONTROL

The second field work standard, as restated by AU 319, states:

> A sufficient understanding of the internal control structure is to be obtained to <u>plan the audit</u> and to <u>determine the nature, timing, and extent of tests</u> to be performed.

AU 319 provides auditors with information on the relationship between a client's internal control structure[*] and financial statement audits. For purposes of audits, the study of internal control has two primary objectives (1) aid in planning the remainder of the audit and (2) assess control risk (this assessment leads to the auditor's determination of the nature, timing and extent of tests to be performed).

On page 86 of the auditing overview section, the following "Diagram of an Audit" was presented and explained.

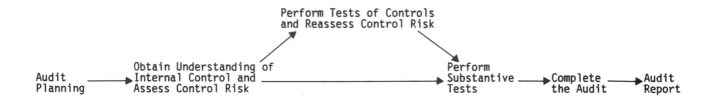

This module covers internal control and develops the relationships among internal control, tests of controls (compliance tests), and substantive tests.

Every CPA examination includes questions on internal control. Often an overall question presents a system or organization and requires the candidate to list weaknesses and make recommendations for improvements in internal control. Occasionally a question requires the preparation of an internal control questionnaire with prescribed internal controls. Multiple choice questions frequently require specification of a control which would, if present and operating properly, detect a stated weakness or error. Objective questions also have appeared regarding organization responsibility, e.g., who should distribute payroll checks?

---

[*]*AU 319, "Consideration of the Internal Control Structure in a Financial Statement Audit," uses the term "internal control structure." Other references (including prior auditing references) use "internal control system." We will use the terms, as well as the abbreviation "ICS," interchangeably in this module.*

Study Program for the Internal Control Module

This module is organized and should be studied in the following manner:

A. The Nature of Internal Control

  1. The Internal Control Structure
  2. Major elements of the Internal Control Structure

     a. Control environment
     b. Accounting system
     c. Control procedures

  3. Related topics

B. The Auditor's Consideration of Internal Control

C. Accounting Cycles

  1. Sales, Receivables, and Cash Receipts
  2. Purchases, Payable, and Cash Disbursements
  3. Inventories and Production
  4. Personnel and Payroll
  5. Property, Plant, and Equipment
  6. Overall Internal Control Checklists

D. Other Considerations

  1. Communicating with the Audit Committee
  2. Other reports on Internal Control
  3. Effects of an Internal Audit Function

In section A we begin with the key concepts related to an entity's internal control structure as presented in AU 319. It is especially important that you read and understand AU 319--the outline following the modules should be helpful. Section B of this module reviews the approach suggested by AU 319 by which auditors are to consider internal control when performing audits. The Section C discussion is meant to provide you with information that will help you to respond to "applied type" questions which involve actual accounting cycles. Section D involves communications with audit committees, reports on internal control, and the effects of an internal audit function on an audit.

The following SAS sections pertain to internal control and are discussed in this module.

Section AU

319	Consideration of the Internal Control Structure in a Financial Statement Audit
322	The effect of an Internal Audit Function on the Scope of the Independent Auditor's Examination
324	Special-Purpose Reports on Internal Accounting Control of Service Organizations
325	Communication of Internal Control Structure Related Matters Noted in an Audit
380	Communication with Audit Committees
642	Reporting on Internal Accounting Control

A. The Nature of Internal Control

AU 319 presents information on both the nature of an entity's internal control structure and also on the auditor's overall approach for considering internal control. In this section we begin by discussing material related to the first area--the internal control structure. Finally, we present several important, related topics.

1. The Internal Control Structure

AU 319 defines an entity's internal control structure as the policies and procedures established to provide reasonable assurance that specific entity objectives will be achieved. The concept of reasonable assurance recognizes that the cost of internal controls should not exceed their expected benefits. The definition of the ICS thus recognizes that the system is not meant to provide a guarantee or to provide absolute assurance that objectives will be met.

The portion of the ICS that is most relevant to audits is the set of policies and procedures that pertain to the entity's ability to record, process, summarize, and report financial data consistent with assertions in financial statements. The portion not generally relevant to financial statement audits includes policies and procedures concerning the effectiveness, economy, and efficiency of the management decision-making process. Typically, policies and procedures over financial data are relevant to the audit. Policies and procedures over nonfinancial data are relevant only if the auditor uses the nonfinancial data to apply auditing procedures. For example, policies relating to number of salespersons hired would not usually be relevant to the audit, yet, be aware, if the auditor uses analytical procedures to help determine the reasonableness of sales (by calculating sales per salesperson) then the policies and procedures over number of salespersons are relevant because number of salespersons is used to help determine financial information (sales).

2. Major elements of the Internal Control Structure

You need to know that AU 319 divides the ICS into three elements, and the nature of each--the control environment, the accounting system, and the 5 control procedures. Although you should study these in section A of the outline of AU 319, we provide a brief summary of each of them at this point.

> a. The control environment. The control environment factors reflect the overall attitude, awareness, and actions of the firm's leaders concerning the importance of control. The 7 factors, which you may remember using the mnemonic O CPA CPE, are:
>
> O - Organizational structure
>
> C - Communication methods

P - Philosophy and operating style
A - Audit committee

C - Control methods for performance monitoring and follow-up
P - Personnel policies and procedures
E - External influences

b. The accounting system. The accounting system consists of the methods
    and records established to identify, assemble, analyze, classify,
    record, and report an entity's transactions and to maintain
    accountability for the related assets and liabilities. As such, for
    audit purposes, the accounting system is a major part of the ICS. To be
    effective, the accounting system must accomplish the following goals for
    transactions:

    (1) Identify and record all valid transactions
    (2) Describe on a timely basis
    (3) Measure the value properly
    (4) Record in the proper time period
    (5) Properly present and disclose

c. Control procedures. The third element of the ICS is the control
    procedures, in addition to the control environment and the accounting
    system, that have been established to provide reasonable assurance that
    specific entity objectives will be achieved. These procedures are
    especially important to you since we will later use them as a primary
    means of finding weaknesses in internal control structure. Those
    procedures, for which we use the mnemonic IS SAD, are:

    I - Independent checks on performance and proper valuation of recorded
        amounts
    S - Segregation of duties (separate authorization, recordkeeping and
        custody)

    S - Safeguards over access to assets and records
    A - Authorization of transactions and activities
    D - Documents that are adequate and records to ensure proper recording

3. Related Topics

    a. Financial statement assertions. As is discussed in further detail in
        the Evidence module, assertions are management representations that are
        embodied in the account balance, transaction class, and disclosure
        components of financial statements. They include (1) presentation and
        disclosure, (2) existence or occurrence, (3) rights and obligations, (4)
        completeness, and (5) valuation. The AU 319 approach is one of
        suggesting that for each account or transaction class the auditor
        determines assertions of primary importance and then considers the
        related controls. A control often relates to less than all important
        assertions. Thus, a control over processing sales orders might, for
        example, be effective at determining that the existence of receivables
        (e.g., there was a sale), but not provide adequate evidence pertaining
        to their valuation (e.g., because collection may be questionable), or on
        completeness (whether all receivables have been recorded).

    b. Limitations of internal control. As we have suggested earlier, the
        internal control structure provides reasonable, but not absolute
        assurance. Even the best ICS may break down due to:

        (1) Misunderstandings
        (2) Mistakes of judgment
        (3) Personal carelessness, distraction, fatigue

      (4) Collusion

      (5) Management override--management is often not subject to many of the controls and may "override" them

      Be familiar with these limitations!

c. Accounting vs. administrative control. Section AU 320, which preceded AU 319, distinguished between administrative and accounting controls and suggested that auditors should generally emphasize the latter. As noted on the outline of AU 319, the distinction is no longer used in audits. The distinction does, however, still apply to other portions of the professional literature, as well as laws such as the Foreign Corrupt Practices Act.

      Administrative controls include the plan of organization, procedure, records, etc., over the process which leads to management's authorization of transactions. Accounting control is the plan of organization and the procedures and records to (a) safeguard assets and (b) safeguard the reliability of the financial records and is designed to provide reasonable assurance that

      (1) Transactions are executed in accordance with management's authorization

      (2) Transactions are recorded to permit financial statements per GAAP and to maintain accountability over assets

      (3) Access to assets is controlled

      (4) Assets are periodically compared to recorded accountability

d. Foreign Corrupt Practices Act. A law passed by Congress in 1977 with provisions

      (1) Requiring every corporation registered under the Securities Exchange Act of 1934 to maintain a system of strong internal accounting control (as defined above),

      (2) Requiring corporations [defined in (1)] to maintain accurate books and records, and

      (3) Making payments (by individuals as well as by business entities) to foreign officials to secure business (i.e., bribes) illegal

      Violations of the act can result in fines (up to $1 million for SEC registrants and $10,000 for individuals) and imprisonment (up to five years) of the responsible individuals. Thus, a strong ICS is required under federal law.

e. Essential characteristics of internal control. Section 320 presented six essential characteristics (SPACER--segregation of function, personnel, access to assets, comparison of accountability with assets, execution of transactions, recording of transactions). In prior editions of this manual we have suggested that you use them to identify weaknesses in internal control for applied type problems. AU 319 replaces these characteristics with the 5 categories of control procedures--IS SAD (independent checks, segregation, safeguards over access to assets, authorization, and documents adequate).

B. **The Auditor's Consideration of the Internal Control Structure**

    AU 319 presents the auditor's consideration of internal control (this begins at "B" in the SAS outline). Recall that AU 319 identifies two major objectives of the auditor's consideration of internal control--(1) Aid in planning the remainder of the audit and (2) assess control risk.

While AU 319, Appendix C presents a very involved flowchart of the overall process, we will summarize the auditor's approach used to study internal control using 4 steps:

1. Obtain and document understanding of ICS to plan the audit
2. Assess control risk
3. Perform (additional) tests of controls
4. Reassess control risk

The relationships among these four steps are presented in the flowchart on the next page. We now discuss them in detail.

1. <u>Obtain and document understanding of ICS to plan the audit</u>. In determining the level of understanding necessary to plan the audit, an auditor uses sources such as past experience with the client, and an understanding of the industry in which the client operates to determine the risk of material misstatements. An auditor will also consider his/her assessments of inherent risk, materiality, and the complexity of the client's ICS. AU 319 provides information on the level of necessary understanding for the (a) control environment, (b) accounting system, and (c) control procedures.

    a. <u>Control environment</u>. The auditor must obtain sufficient knowledge to understand management's and the board of director's attitude, awareness, and actions concerning the control environment. The substance of the policies, procedures, and actions are more important than the form. Thus, for example, a budget reporting system that provides adequate reports which are not used is of little value.

    b. <u>Accounting system</u>. The auditor needs to obtain a level of knowledge of the accounting system adequate to understand (1) the major transaction classes, (2) how those transactions are initiated, (3) the available accounting records and support, (4) the manner of processing of transactions, and (5) the financial reporting process used to prepare financial statements.

    c. <u>Control procedures</u>. Ordinarily, an understanding of the control procedures related to <u>each</u> account balance, transaction class, and disclosure component in the footnotes is <u>not</u> required. The level of understanding required depends largely upon the degree of complexity of the accounting system. Also, while obtaining an understanding of the control environment and the accounting systems, the auditor will often have obtained information on a number of control procedures.

    <u>Procedures for obtaining an understanding</u>. The auditor relies primarily upon a combination of (1) previous experience with the entity, (2) inquiries, (3) inspection of documents and records, and (4) observation of entity activities to obtain the needed understanding of the ICS. At this point in the audit, these procedures are performed primarily to help the auditor to understand the design and whether the controls have been <u>placed in operation</u>. AU 319 distinguishes between determining that controls are placed in operation vs. evaluating their operating effectiveness. In

SUMMARY FLOWCHART OF SAS 55 CONSIDERATION
OF INTERNAL CONTROL DURING A FINANCIAL STATEMENT AUDIT

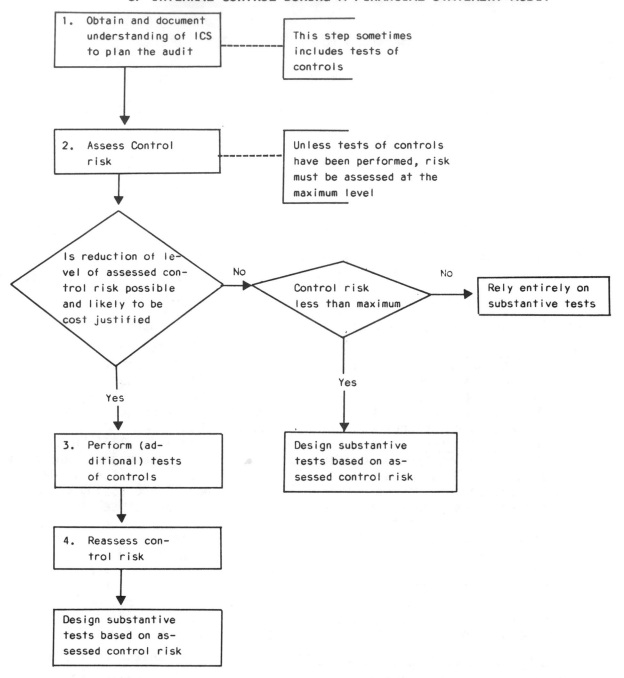

determining whether controls have been placed in operation, the auditor determines that the entity is using them. This is all that is necessary for planning the audit.

In evaluating operating effectiveness, the auditor goes further and considers (1) how the policy, procedure, or record was applied; (2) the consistency with which it was applied; and (3) by whom. Tests of controls (described in detail in section 3 below) address the effectiveness of the design and operation of a control. Tests of controls are necessary to assess control risk below the maximum level.

AU 319 points out that while obtaining an understanding of the design of a control, including whether it has been placed in operation, an auditor may either by plan or by chance obtain some information on operating effectiveness. For example, while making inquiries about the design of the client's budgeting system and whether it has been placed in operation, an auditor may have obtained evidence on the effectiveness of the system in preventing or detecting expense misclassifications. Thus, its operating effectiveness has been tested. In this manner, in essence, some <u>tests of controls</u> may have been concurrently performed with obtaining an understanding of the ICS.

<u>Documentation of Understanding of ICS</u>. The auditor's documentation of his/her understanding of the ICS for purposes of planning the audit is influenced by the size and complexity of the entity, as well as the nature of the entity's ICS. For a small client a memorandum may be sufficient. For a larger client, flowcharts, questionnaires, and decision tables may be needed. The more complex the ICS and the more extensive the procedures performed by the auditor, the more extensive should be the documentation.

The advantages and disadvantages of using questionnaires, memoranda, and/or flowchart methods are

Method	Advantages	Disadvantages
Questionnaire	1. Easy to complete 2. Comprehensive list of questions make it unlikely that important portions of internal control will be overlooked 3. Weaknesses become obvious (generally those questions answered with a "no")	1. May be answered without adequate thought being given to questions 2. Questions may not "fit" client adequately
Memoranda	1. Tailor-made for engagement 2. Requires a detailed analysis and thus forces auditor to understand functioning of structure	1. May become very long and time consuming 2. Weaknesses in structure not always obvious 3. Auditor may overlook important portions of internal control structure

| Flowchart | 1. Graphic representation of structure
2. Usually makes it unlikely that important portions of internal control will be overlooked
3. Good for EDP systems
4. No long wording (as in case of memoranda) | 1. Preparation is time consuming
2. Weaknesses in structure not always obvious (especially to inexperienced auditor) |

(Note: Flowcharts, including symbols, are discussed in the Auditing EDP module.)

In addition to questionnaires, memoranda, and flowcharts, auditors may prepare "decision tables" to document their understanding of internal control. Decision tables are graphic methods of describing the logic of decisions. Various combinations of <u>conditions</u> are matched to one of several <u>actions</u>. In an internal control setting, the various important controls are reviewed and, based on the combination of answers received, an action is taken, perhaps a decision on whether to perform tests of controls. The following extremely simplified table will provide you with the information you need for the CPA exam (note, for example, in the case of segregation of functions, a series of detailed segregation conditions--not one summary--would be used).

<u>Conditions</u>

		Rules
		1 2 3 4 5 6 7
1)	Segregation of function adequate	y y y y n n n
2)	Adequate documents	y y n n y y n
3)	Independent checks on performance	y n y n y n -

<u>Actions</u>

1)	Perform all relevant tests of controls	x
2)	Perform limited tests of controls	x x x
3)	Perform no tests of controls	x x x

Note that for decision rule 7, after the first two conditions have received "no's" it doesn't matter what the third condition is--tests of controls will not be used. Also, while a decision table is an efficient means of describing the logic of an internal control process, it does not provide an analysis of document flow as does a flowchart.

2. <u>Assess control risk</u>. After obtaining and documenting the understanding of the ICS system to plan the audit, the first assessment of control risk is made. This assessment should be based in terms of the financial statement assertions (see A3a in this module and A of the Evidence Module). If the effectiveness of controls has <u>not</u> been tested, control risk must be assessed at the maximum level. If the auditor has tested the effectiveness of some controls (i.e., some tests of control have been performed), a lower assessment may be possible. Yet, because in most circumstances the testing of effectiveness of controls will be quite limited at this point, without additional tests of controls (compliance tests) the assessment of control risk will generally still be quite high.

After the assessment of control risk, the auditor must decide whether the performance of additional tests of controls (compliance tests) are likely to result in a cost-justified reduction in the assessment of control risk.

3. Perform (additional) tests of controls. Tests of controls are used to test either the effectiveness of the design or operation of an ICS policy or procedure. Approaches include

    a. Inquiries of appropriate personnel
    b. Inspection of documents and reports
    c. Observation of the application of policies and procedures
    d. Reperformance of the policy or procedure by the auditor (when evaluating operation)

    To illustrate the nature of tests of controls, assume that the client has implemented the control procedure of requiring a second person to review the quantities, prices, extensions, and footing of each sales invoice. The purpose of this control procedure is to prevent material errors in the billing of customers and the recording of sales transactions. By using the first approach, inquiry, the auditor would discuss with appropriate client personnel the manner in which the control functions. Generally, because of the indirect nature of the information obtained, inquiry alone is not considered to provide credible enough evidence to support a reduced level of assessed control risk.

    The remaining approaches, inspection, observation, and reperformance, may be illustrated by assuming that a sample of 60 sales invoices has been selected from throughout the year. The auditor might inspect the invoices and determine whether evidence exists that the procedures have been performed (e.g., invoices bearing initials of the individual who reviewed them). Another option is to observe applications of the procedures being applied to the invoices. Finally, the auditors may reperform the procedure by comparing quantities shown on each invoice to the quantities listed on the related shipping documents, comparing unit prices to the client's price lists, and by verifying the extensions and footings.

    Timeliness of evidential matter. For reasons of efficiency and practicality, auditors often perform tests of controls at a date prior to year end. Also, pertaining to observation, note that for many situations only a limited number of observations of individuals performing control procedures are practical. The auditor must realize that generalizing tests of controls results beyond the periods sampled is risky. It is for this reason that auditors must consider whether additional tests should be performed over untested periods to provide assurance that controls functioned over the entire period. Relatedly, while auditors may consider evidential matter obtained from prior audits, they should obtain evidential matter in the current period to determine whether changes have occurred in the ICS.

4. <u>Reassess control risk</u>. Based on the results of the tests of controls (compliance tests), the auditor will reassess control risk related to the various assertions. If the controls are functioning to prevent or detect misstatements in an area, the controls may be relied upon to a greater extent than in the case in which controls are found to be ineffective. Controls which are found to be ineffective will result in a higher control risk assessment, and therefore a greater dependence upon substantive testing (i.e., there is an inverse relationship). For financial statement assertions in which the assessed level of control risk is at the maximum level, the auditor need not document the basis for that conclusion. For those assertions where it is below the maximum, the auditor should document the basis for the conclusion that the design and operation of the ICS support that assessed level.

The entire four-step approach for the consideration of internal control (understand, assess control risk, perform tests of controls, reassess control risk) may be illustrated through use of an example. Assume that you have been told by the controller that two secretaries are present and open all mail together each morning. These secretaries are supposed to prepare a list of all cash receipts, which is then to be forwarded to the accounts receivable clerk. The cash, according to the controller, is then given to the cashier who deposits it each day. Because you work in the area where the secretaries work, you have observed them following these procedures and conclude that the process seems to have been placed in operation. To keep the example simple, assume that based on this and other internal control information you gathered while obtaining an understanding of the structure, internal control over receivables seems to be strong. Assume that to this point you have performed no tests of controls. Thus, you must document your understanding of the structure and make a decision as to whether controls should be tested. Because no tests of controls have been performed, your initial assessment is that control risk is at the maximum level.

Subsequently, you decide to perform tests of controls (compliance tests) with the objective of determining whether the structure is actually in operation and may be relied upon to limit control risk. Also, assume you have decided that, if the results of your tests of controls (compliance tests) indicate that the controls are operating as described, one substantive test will be to confirm 30 of the firm's 250 accounts receivable to verify their existence. That is, despite strong internal controls, substantive tests must generally still be performed.

However, when you performed your tests of controls (compliance tests) of observing the opening of the mail, you discovered that the secretaries, in circumstances in which one is "busy," had decided to minimize their work by having the other individually perform the task periodically. Also, you discovered that the secretaries, when only a "limited" amount of cash is received, decided to omit the step of preparing a list of cash receipts and simply forward the receipts to the accounts receivable clerk who then forwards them to the cashier who deposits them periodically.

You have discovered that the controls over cash receipts are not as strong as was indicated when you were gaining an understanding of the structure. In this situation, you might decide that a higher than acceptable likelihood exists that an embezzlement of cash receipts could occur--that is control risk is high. You might then decide to increase the scope of your substantive tests; you could, for example, confirm more accounts than originally had been planned. You might also decide to expand your investigation of bad debt write-offs to determine that accounts have not been collected and subsequently been fraudulently written off. Note that if you had originally obtained a more accurate description of the actual functioning of the internal control over cash receipts, you might have decided to omit the tests of controls (compliance tests) and might have initially assessed control risk at the maximum level, thus resulting in complete reliance upon substantive tests.

5. Summary. The approach presented above may be summarized as follows:

   1. Obtain and document understanding of ICS to plan the audit

      a. Study the control environment, accounting system, and control procedures
      b. Decide whether to perform any tests of controls at this first stage
      c. Document understanding of system--use flowcharts, memoranda, questionnaires, decision tables, etc.

   2. Assess control risk

    a.   If no tests of controls have been performed, control risk must be assessed at the maximum level

    b.   If tests of controls have been performed, a somewhat lower level of assessment of control risk may be possible

    c.   Determine whether to perform additional tests of controls

3.   Tests of controls (tests of compliance)

    a.   Tests whether internal controls are functioning adequately (through inquiry, inspection, observation, and reperformance)

    b.   Document results of tests by transaction type and assertion

4.   Reassess control risk

    a.   Based on results of tests of controls, assess control risk

    b.   If the assessment is less than the maximum level of risk, document the basis for that conclusion

    d.   Plan substantive tests

C. Accounting Cycles

We now consider CPA exam questions which require the candidate to determine an audit test which will meet some specified objective or to identify internal control weaknesses or to prepare an internal control questionnaire. For many candidates, these questions are especially difficult. The difficulty is frequently the result of the fact that the candidate (1) does not have an understanding of the various source documents and accounting records and how they relate to one another in an accounting system, and (2) does not know what types of detailed internal controls over the source documents and accounting records should exist. To help you prepare for these questions, we are presenting information on both directional testing (which is also helpful for evidence questions) and a summary of transaction cycles.

Directional Testing. As a starting point, you should understand the notion of directional testing. The basic idea is that testing from source documents forward to recorded entries accomplishes a different objective than testing from recorded entries back to source documents. Diagrammatically directional testing suggests:

                Test of completeness (detect understatements)   ⟶

Source Document   ⟵   ⟶   Recorded Entry

  ⟵   Test of existence (detect overstatements)

In sentence form, the rules are:

1.   Tracing forward (source document to recorded entry) primarily tests completeness of recording, and has a primary objective of detecting understatements

2. Tracing (vouching) backwards--recorded entry to source document--
    primarily tests existence and has a primary objective of detecting
    overstatements.

To understand the basic concept here think about sales invoices (a source
document) and the sales journal (the recorded entry):

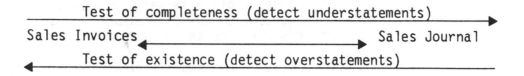

An auditor may select a group of sales invoices and compare them to the
sales journal. On the other hand, the auditor may also vouch sales journal
entries back to the sales invoices (and other support such as shipping
documents, customer purchase orders). If an auditor is testing for <u>understated</u>
sales, it would be best to start with possible sales, not those that were
already recorded in the sales journal. Thus, for finding understatements of
sales, a CPA would sample from the sales invoices (which are prepared when a
sale occurs) in an effort to determine whether individual sales are being
recorded. On the other hand, when testing for overstated sales, the CPA would
test back from the sales recorded in the sales journal back to sales invoices
(as well as other source documents such as shipping documents, customer purchase
orders). This is because for each recorded sale there should be support. We
will apply the concept of directional testing in our discussion of the detailed
transaction cycles.

   <u>Financial Accounting Reporting Cycle</u>. In the overview section we suggested
that an accounting system may be viewed as follows:

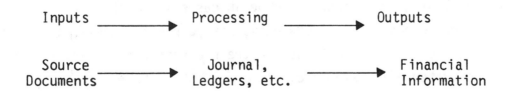

At this point review "The Financial Accounting Reporting Cycle" (page 141)
and simply look it over and note the various <u>source documents</u> (inputs), and
<u>accounting records</u> such as journals and ledgers which are used to process the
inputs (processing), and financial statements (outputs). Recall that our
objectives are to (1) learn an approach for addressing questions pertaining to
internal control weaknesses and for preparing internal control questionnaires,

and (2) learn how to answer other questions pertaining to the effectiveness of audit tests.

One approach for questions pertaining to internal control weaknesses is to:

(1) Read the problem to identify the type of transaction cycle
(2) Obtain an understanding of how the accounting system works by carefully reading the problem in detail (and possibly informally flowcharting it if the description is very detailed)
(3) Use the control procedures (IS SAD--Independent checks, segregation, safeguards over access to assets, authorization, and documents adequate)
(4) Recall typical weaknesses (presented subsequently) for the transaction cycle involved to find additional internal control weaknesses

Steps 1 and 2 are clearly necessary since you need to understand the problem and its requirements. When performing the second step, realize that on an overall basis internal controls are aimed at both safeguarding assets and financial records. Also, be aware of each department's operational objective (e.g., the shipping department ships goods). Also, know that one way of considering controls is to classify them by whether they are (1) preventive, (2) detective, and/or (3) corrective.

Preventive controls are typically most effective since they are designed to prevent an error or irregularity from occurring (e.g., two persons opening the mail which includes cash receipts may prevent embezzlements). Detective and corrective controls most frequently occur together. They detect and correct an error or irregularity which has already occurred (e.g., bank account reconciliation by an individual not otherwise involved with cash receipts or cash disbursements). While these controls are typically less expensive to implement than preventive controls, they may detect errors too late. They may detect that an employee embezzled $1,000,000, but may only be corrective in the sense that an embezzlement loss journal entry is made in cases where the employee has disappeared. For purposes of the CPA exam, ask yourself how effective each of the detective and corrective controls is--their effectiveness depends on the details of the system being examined.

When using the control procedures to find internal control weaknesses (step 3), segregation of duties is especially important since many of the weaknesses relate to inadequate segregation. Recall that inadequate segregation exists whenever one individual is performing two or more of the following: authorization, recordkeeping, and custodianship. For example, when a cashier (custodian) authorizes the write-off of bad debts (authorization), a weakness exists.

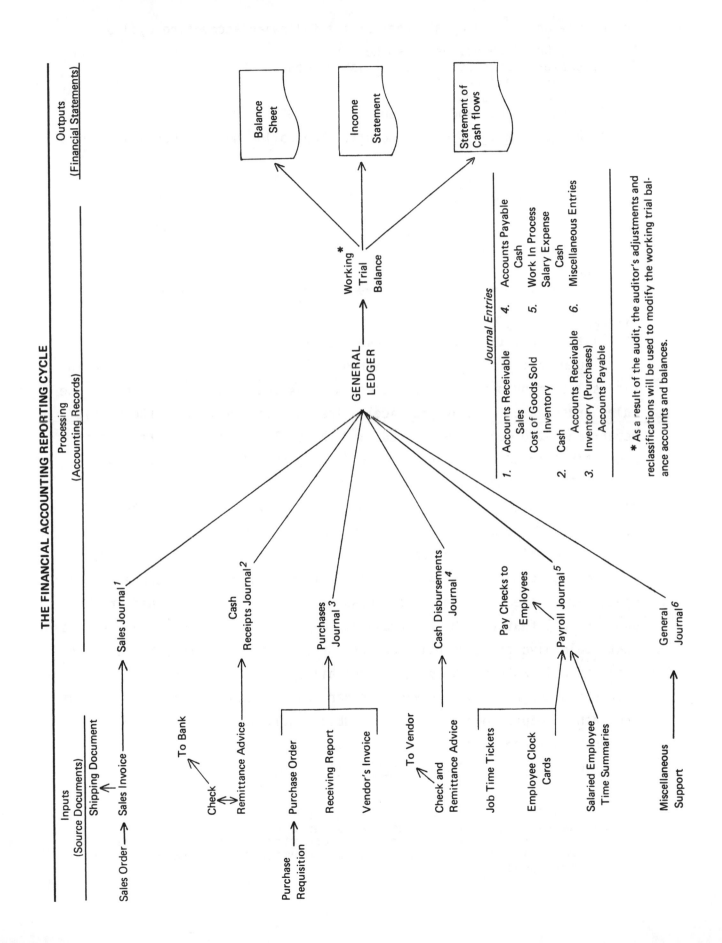

THE FINANCIAL ACCOUNTING REPORTING CYCLE

We may now analyze in detail each of the following accounting cycles

1. Sales, Receivables, and Cash Receipts
2. Purchases, Payables, and Cash Disbursements
3. Inventories and Production
4. Personnel and Payroll
5. Property, Plant, and Equipment

1. <u>Sales, Receivables, and Cash Receipts</u>. The following is a possible flow of documents

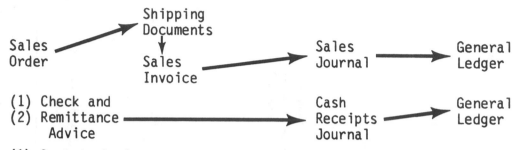

(1) Sent to banks
(2) List or remittance advice is used to make entries

Assume that the firm's sales personnel prepare sales orders for potential sales (many other possibilities, such as the customer filling out the sales order, are found in practice). The sale is approved by the credit department, the goods are shipped, and the billing department (a part of accounting) prepares a sales invoice (a copy of which becomes the customer's "bill"). After the sales invoice is prepared, the sales journal, the general ledger, and the accounts receivable subsidiary ledger are posted. The customer pays the account with a check, and a remittance advice is enclosed to describe which invoice the check is paying. As a preventive control, two individuals open the mail which includes these customer remittances. The checks are listed and sent to the cashier who daily deposits them in the bank (recall that the checks should not go to the accounting department, as that would give the accounting department custody of assets [checks in this case] as well as recordkeeping responsibility). Another copy of the list of checks and the remittance advices is sent to accounting to be used to post the cash receipts journal, which is subsequently posted to the general and accounts receivable subsidiary ledgers.

<u>Major Controls Frequently Missing in CPA Exam Questions</u>

Sales

1) Credit granted by a credit department
2) Sales orders and invoices prenumbered and controlled
3) Sales returns are presented to receiving clerk who prepares a receiving report which supports prenumbered sales return credit memoranda

Accounts Receivable

1) Subsidiary ledger reconciled to control ledger regularly
2) Individual independent of receivable posting reviews statements before sending to customers
3) Monthly statements sent to all customers
4) Write-offs approved by management official independent of recordkeeping responsibility

Cash Receipts

1) Cash receipts received in mail listed by individuals with no recordkeeping responsibility

   a) Cash goes to cashier
   b) Remittance advices go to accounting

2) Over-the-counter cash receipts controlled (cash register tapes)
3) Cash deposited daily
4) Employees handling cash are bonded
5) Bank reconciliation prepared by individuals independent of cash receipts recordkeeping

Sales, Receivables, and Cash Receipts Questions

Multiple Choice

Question

Answer

1. (579,A1,15) An auditor is testing sales transactions. One step is to trace a sample of debit entries from the accounts receivable subsidiary ledger back to the supporting sales invoices. What would the auditor intend to establish by this step?
   a. Sales invoices represent bona fide sales.
   b. All sales have been recorded.
   c. All sales invoices have been properly posted to customer accounts.
   d. Debit entries in the accounts receivable subsidiary ledger are properly supported by sales invoices.

(d) The question is about directional testing. By undertaking this step, the auditor would determine that the entries in the accounts receivable subsidiary ledger are properly supported by sales invoices. Therefore, answer (d) is the correct answer. Answer (a) would address the question: "What would the auditor accomplish by tracing sales invoices back to customers' purchase orders, sales orders, shipping documents and sales agreements?" Answer (b) would address: "What would the auditor accomplish when tracing approved customer purchase orders to credit entries in sales?" Answer (c) would address: "What would the auditor accomplish by tracing sales invoices to the accounts receivable subsidiary ledger?"

2. (578,A1,3) A client's physical count of inventories was lower than the inventory quantities shown in its perpetual records. This situation could be the result of the failure to record
   a. Sales.
   b. Sales returns.
   c. Purchases.
   d. Purchase discounts.

(a) The question is asking what situation could cause the actual inventory to be lower than the amount recorded in the perpetual records. If sales had not been recorded, the perpetual inventory records would not reflect the shipment of inventory resulting in inventory overstatement. Therefore, answer (a) is the correct answer. Answers (b) and (c) would address cases for which the physical count is higher than the perpetual records since physical goods would be in inventory with no recordkeeping having been performed. Purchase discounts, answer (d), relates to the cost of items involved as opposed to the quantity.

3. How would you test credit sales for understatements?

ANSWER: Compare a sample of approved sales orders to the subsequent posting in the sales journal (and through to the general ledger). You are interested in finding out whether the approved sales order made it all the way to the general ledger. Note that you may find over-statements by this audit procedure (e.g., a $10 sale recorded for a higher amount) but that the primary emphasis is in finding understatements.

4. How would you test credit sales for overstatements?

ANSWER: Opposite of 3 above.

5. Are you mainly testing for over or understatements of cash when you agree remittance advices to the cash receipts journal?

ANSWER: Understatements. That is, did the cash which the firm received get recorded?

6. What could cause a remittance advice with no subsequent cash receipt entry?

ANSWER: An embezzlement.

7. Should there be a sales invoice for each sales order?

ANSWER: No. Sales in process and sales not approved will not be invoiced.

Problems

The following page presents a sales, receivables, and cash receipts transaction cycle problem from the May 1985 exam. We have detailed some of the internal control weaknesses on the flowchart. Exam questions which provide such a detailed flowchart often cause candidates significant problems. While reading the problem to identify the type of transaction cycle is not difficult, obtaining an understanding of how the structure works requires careful thought, especially for those with very limited audit experience. When presented with a detailed flowchart such as this one, it is helpful to determine the point at which the transactions originate and to follow one through the structure.

In this flowchart, as is typically the case, the transactions originate in the top left corner. Here a customer order is received by phone. Then a 4-copy sales order is prepared by a sales clerk. It is helpful to think about the actual function being performed. Recall that a sales order is typically prepared to assist with subsequent preparation of a sales invoice and to begin the shipping process, if credit is approved. You should also think about the various documents and departments involved and work through the entire system.

The next step is to study the flowchart again, this time using your knowledge of internal control to find weaknesses. As indicated earlier, the control procedures (IS SAD) and the above list of typical control weaknesses will help. Using IS SAD, the solution's weaknesses (which follow the flowchart) may be derived as

Number 3 (Estimated time — 15 to 25 minutes)

The following flowchart depicts the activities relating to the shipping, billing, and collecting processes used by Smallco Lumber, Inc.

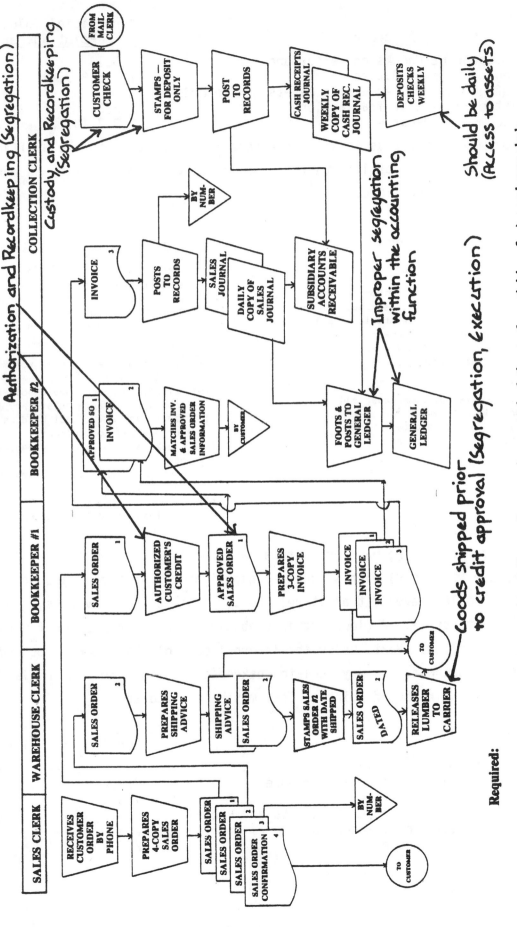

Required:

Identify weaknesses in the system of internal accounting control relating to the activities of a.) warehouse clerk, b.) bookkeeper #1, c.) bookkeeper #2, and d.) collection clerk.

Control Procedure	"Unofficial Solution" Point Number
Independent Checks on Performance	3,5,13
Segregation of Duties	1,4,6,8,9,11
Safeguards over Access to Assets and Records	12
Authorization of Transactions	1,2,3
Documents Adequate	2,3,7,10,13

You may disagree as to which characteristic pertains to the unofficial solution. This is not important as the objective is to identify as many key concepts as possible.

Answer 3 (10 points)

The weaknesses in Smallco Lumber's internal controls are:

Warehouse Clerk
(1) Releases lumber prior to authorization, e.g., approval of customer's credit.
(2) Copies of shipping advice should be prepared and forwarded to Bookkeeper #1.
(3) Lacks documentation that lumber was given to the carrier.

Bookkeeper #1
(4) Credit authorized by bookkeeper and not a responsible officer.
(5) Prepares and mails invoice without knowledge of what was shipped.

Bookkeeper #2
(6) Bookkeeper who maintains general ledger should not be responsible for footing and crossfooting of journals, i.e., sales and cash receipts journals.
(7) Subsidiary accounts receivable ledger should be reconciled to general ledger.

Collection Clerk
(8) Collection clerk should not maintain sales journal.
(9) Collection clerk should not maintain accounts receivable subsidiary ledger.
(10) Remittance advice not used as the basis for posting collections.
(11) Checks are not promptly endorsed by the mail clerk.
(12) Cash receipts are not promptly deposited.
(13) Deposit slips are not reconciled to cash receipts journal or debits to general ledger.

The following page presents a cash receipts problem (Internal Control module Problem 9) with weaknesses highlighted. Note that a quick reading of the problem reveals that it relates to the sales, receivables, and cash receipts cycle. A flowchart is probably not necessary since few documents are involved. Next, using the internal control characteristics and the major controls, you may isolate weaknesses. Also, the "unofficial solution" contains 7 numbered points. They may be derived as:

Control Procedure	"Unofficial Solution" Point Number
Independent Checks on Performance	2,3,6
Segregation of Duties	1,3
Safeguards over Access to Assets and Records	2,5,7
Authorization of Transactions	2,3
Documents Adequate	2,3,4

Cash Receipts IC Weaknesses (1180,A4)

(15 to 25 minutes)

MAJOR PROBLEM
2 CLERKS CONTROL
AUTHORIZATION, ←
CUSTODY, AND
RECORDKEEPING (NO
ENTRY MADE IF CASH
DISAPPEARS).

INADEQUATE SEGRE-
GATION -- ONE
SHOULD COLLECT CASH,
OTHER SHOULD AUTHORIZE
ADMISSION.

CASH NOT DEPOSITED
DAILY (ACCESS TO
ASSETS)

CASH REGISTER WITH
TAPE NEEDED HERE

NO INDEPENDENT
COUNT OF PAYING
PATRONS

ONLY ONE ENTRY
PER WEEK
(RECORDING)

OTHER
IS BONDING
POSSIBLE OR
REASONABLE?

WHO RECONCILES
THE BANK
ACCOUNT?

The Art Appreciation Society operates a museum for the benefit and enjoyment of the community. During hours when the museum is open to the public, two clerks who are positioned at the entrance collect a five dollar admission fee from each nonmember patron. Members of the Art Appreciation Society are permitted to enter free of charge upon presentation of their membership cards.

At the end of each day one of the clerks delivers the proceeds to the treasurer. The treasurer counts the cash in the presence of the clerk and places it in a safe. Each Friday afternoon the treasurer and one of the clerks deliver all cash held in the safe to the bank, and receive an authenticated deposit slip which provides the basis for the weekly entry in the cash receipts journal.

The board of directors of the Art Appreciation Society has identified a need to improve their system of internal control over cash admission fees. The board has determined that the cost of installing turnstiles, sales booths or otherwise altering the physical layout of the museum will greatly exceed any benefits which may be derived. However, the board has agreed that the sale of admission tickets must be an integral part of its improvement efforts.

Smith has been asked by the board of directors of the Art Appreciation Society to review the internal control over cash admission fees and provide suggestions for improvement.

Required:

Indicate weakness in the existing system of internal control over cash admission fees, which Smith should identify, and recommend one improvement for each of the weaknesses identified.

Organize the answer as indicated in the following illustrative example:

Weakness	Recommendation
1. There is no basis for establishing the documentation of the number of paying patrons.	1. Prenumbered admission tickets should be issued upon payment of the admission fee.

Note: Refer to the Unofficial Answer to Problem 9 for a complete solution to this problem.

In most cases more than one of the control procedures could help you to arrive at the points in the "unofficial solution." Also, you will probably (hopefully) find that, even though you haven't memorized the major controls, they come to your attention when the problem provides information such as the fact that deposits are only made on Fridays.

2. <u>Purchases, Payables, and Cash Disbursements</u>. The following is a possible flow of documents

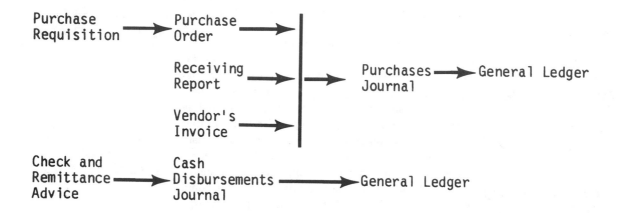

Assume that the purchase requisition is an internal document sent by the department in need of the supplies to the purchasing department. The purchasing department determines the proper quantity and vendor for the purchase and prepares a purchase order. One copy of the purchase order is sent to the vendor. Another copy is sent to the receiving department to allow receiving personnel to know that items received have been ordered; however, the copy of the purchase order sent to receiving will not have a quantity of items on it so as to encourage personnel to count the goods when they are received. When the goods are received, a receiving report is prepared by the receiving department and forwarded to the accounting department. A vendor's invoice or "bill" is received by the accounting department from the vendor. When the accounting department has the purchase order, receiving report, and vendor's invoice, the payment is approved and then recorded in the purchases journal since evidence exists that the item was ordered, received, and billed. A check and remittance advice is subsequently sent to the vendor in accordance with the terms of the sale. The purchase order, receiving report, and vendor's invoice are stamped paid to prevent duplicate payments.

Major Controls Frequently Missing in CPA Exam Questions

Purchases

1) Prenumbered purchase orders used
2) Separate purchasing department makes purchases
3) Purchasing personnel independent of receiving and recordkeeping
4) Suppliers' monthly statements compared with recorded payables

Accounts Payable

1) Accounts payable personnel independent of purchasing, receiving, and disbursements
2) Clerical accuracy of vendors' invoices tested
3) Purchase order, receiving report, and vendor's invoice matched

Cash Disbursements

1) Prenumbered checks with a mechanical check protector used
2) Two signatures on large check amounts
3) Checks signed only with appropriate support (purchase order, receiving report, vendor's invoice). Treasurer is check signer
4) Support for checks canceled after payment
5) Voided checks mutilated, retained, and accounted for
6) Bank reconciliations prepared by individual independent of cash disbursements recordkeeping
7) Physical control of unused checks

Purchases, Payables, and Cash Disbursement CPA Exam Questions

Short Answers

1. Which documents need to be present before payment is approved?

   ANSWER: Purchase order, receiving report, vendor's invoice. (This shows that the firm ordered the goods, received the goods, and has been billed for the goods.)

2. How can a firm control disbursements so that if a duplicate invoice is sent by the supplier the payment will not be made a second time?

   ANSWER: Cancel the required supporting documents in "1." after the invoice is paid the first time.

3. What audit test could be used to determine whether recorded purchases represent valid business expenses?

   ANSWER: Compare a sample of recorded disbursements with properly approved purchase orders, purchase requisitions, vendors' invoices, and receiving reports.

4. What audit procedure would test whether actual purchases are recorded?

   ANSWER: Select a sample of purchase requisitions and agree them to the purchase orders and to the purchases journal (as well as to subsequent general ledger posting).

5. Should there be a purchase order for each purchase requisition?

   ANSWER: No. Several requisitions may be summarized on one purchase order and some requisitions may not be approved.

The above are meant to assist you in obtaining an overall understanding of auditing procedures and internal controls. Note that entire courses (and majors) in systems analysis address these issues. The purpose of the above is to give the individual who has a very limited systems background a starting point for analysis.

Problem

On the following page is a purchase/disbursements problem (Internal Control module, Problem 4). This question is typical of a number of questions which have presented a flowchart with certain information on operations omitted--the candidate is to determine what description belongs in the blocks, circles, etc. which simply contain a number or letter. This type of question does not require a knowledge of internal control weaknesses. What is necessary is an understanding of how accounting systems generally work.

First, you must know the common flowchart symbols (presented in the Auditing EDP module under "Flowcharting"). This information will be helpful to you because when you see, for example, a trapezoid, you will know that a manual operation has been performed. Additionally, for such problems, you should consider the department the missing information is in and that department's purpose (e.g., the purchasing department purchases appropriate goods from vendors at acceptable prices). Finally, consider both the step preceding and succeeding the missing information to provide you with a clue as to what is being represented.

Starting with A in the purchasing department, we note that an approved requisition has been received from stores. Step A represents some form of manual operation (due to the existence of a trapezoid) out of which a 5-copied purchase order as well as the requisition come. The only possible manual operation here is the preparation of a 5-part purchase order. At this point, the various copies are either filed or sent elsewhere (the circles represent connectors to other portions of the flowchart or possibly represent a document leaving the system). In this case, we see the various copies being filed and sent to receiving and vouchers payable. Step B represents a copy being sent elsewhere. When we consider the fact that the purpose of the purchasing department is to purchase the items, it becomes obvious that this copy must be sent to the vendor--otherwise no order would occur.

Because a receiving report appears for the first time under step C, it obviously represents the preparation of a receiving report. Next are connectors D and E. We know that the use of the circle indicates that something--probably a document or form of some sort--has been received. For D, a clue is given in that requisition 1 has also been received. We know that this is from purchasing by recalling that requisition 1 and purchase order 5 were sent to vouchers payable--this is shown on the flowchart under

Problem 4: Purchases and Disbursements Flowchart (583,A5).

(15 to 25 minutes)

The following illustrates a Manual System for Executing Purchases and Cash Disbursements Transactions.

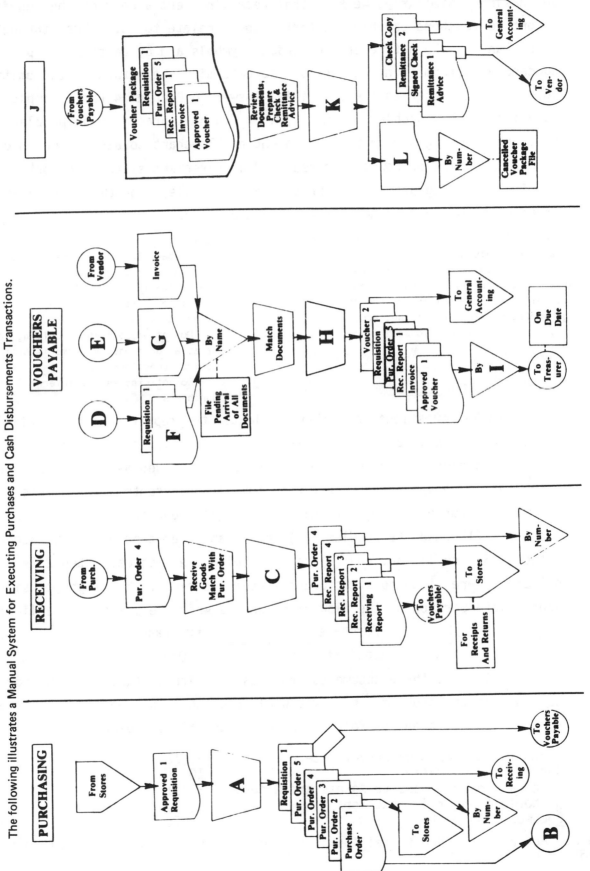

Required: Indicate what each of the letters (A) through (L) represent. Do not discuss adequacies or inadequacies in the system of internal control.

purchasing. Similarly, we know that receiving sent a copy of the receiving report to vouchers payable and that E and G relate to it. Thus, through understanding the nature of the various symbols and by considering preceding and succeeding information, we are able to determine the nature of the omitted information. Refer to the Unofficial Answer to Problem 4 for a complete solution to this problem. Finally, when you have practiced on problems such as this one, you might wish to use the entire flowchart to assist you in obtaining an understanding of how a purchases and disbursement system can work.

The following problem (Internal Control Module, Problem 1) requires preparation of an internal control questionnaire:

Green, CPA, has been engaged to audit the financial statements of Star Manufacturing, Inc. Star is a medium-sized entity that produces a wide variety of household goods. All acquisitions of materials are processed through the purchasing, receiving, accounts payable, and treasury functions.

Required:
Prepare the "Purchases" segment of the internal control questionnaire to be used in the evaluation of Star's internal control structure. Each question should elicit either a yes or no response.

Do not prepare the receiving, accounts payable, or treasury segments of the internal control questionnaire.

Do not discuss the internal controls over purchases

Recently, questions requiring candidates to prepare internal control questionnaires have become more frequent. A question such as the above is difficult because it doesn't provide any obvious clues as to the appropriate responses. The approach we have used for internal control weaknesses is also appropriate for preparing internal control questionnaires. Recall that the steps are (1) read the problem, (2) obtain an understanding of the accounting system, (3) use IS SAD, and (4) recall typical weaknesses. Step 2 is a bit different here since no structure has been described. You might consider the appropriate portion of the flow of documents which we presented earlier:

Purchase ⟶ Purchase
Requisition   Order

Roughing out these documents provides you with a starting point for considering the problem. Next you would use the IS SAD mnemonic to determine appropriate questions as follows (keyed to unofficial solution)

Independent Checks on Performance	9, 12
Segregation of Duties	10
Safeguard over Access to Assets and Records	8, 11
Authorization of Transactions	1, 2, 3, 4
Documents Adequate	5, 6, 7

Note: Refer to the Unofficial Answer to Problem 1 for a complete solution to this problem.

There will always be points on segregation of duties. Concerning safeguarding of assets and records, simply consider the documents and assets involved. Also, on these questions you will typically be able to gain a number of points by simply including a question for each document to determine whether it exists (documents adequate) and is properly authorized. Finally, if you are able to recall the "typical weaknesses" for the area you might be able to derive questions you missed when you used IS SAD.

3. <u>Inventories and Production</u>. Inventories and production fit under the first two cycles. However, due to the unique nature of inventories, separate coverage is warranted. Two cases will be considered here: a non-manufacturing firm and a manufacturing firm.

   Assume you are auditing a retailer who purchases products from a wholesaler and then sells the goods to the public. As in the acquisitions and payments cycle, purchase requisitions and purchase orders are used and controlled to purchase the inventory items which are of a "finished goods" nature. Likewise, when ordered goods are received, a receiving report is filled out by personnel in the receiving department. Perpetual inventory records are maintained for large dollar items. The firm has calculated economic reorder points and quantities. When quantities on hand reach the reorder point, a purchase requisition is prepared and sent to the purchasing department which places the order.

   At the end of the year, a physical inventory is taken during which items on hand are counted. In the case of items for which perpetual records exist, the perpetuals are corrected for any errors--large errors must be explained. For items without perpetual records, the total on hand is used to adjust the cost of goods sold at year end (beginning inventory + purchases - ending inventory = cost of goods sold).

   The case of the manufacturing firm is somewhat more involved. Recall that basically three types of inventory accounts are involved. First, supplies and raw materials are purchased from suppliers in much the same manner as described above for the nonmanufacturing firm. Second, work in process is the combination of raw materials, direct labor, and factory overhead. Third, when the items in process have been completed, they are transferred at their cost (typically standard cost) to finished goods. Finally, when the goods are sold, the entry is to credit finished goods and to debit cost of goods sold.

Work in process is controlled through use of a standard cost system as described in elementary cost accounting courses. Recall that raw materials are those which typically can be directly identified with the product (e.g., transistors in a radio). Direct labor is also identified with the product (e.g., assembly line labor). Overhead includes materials not specifically identified with the product (amount of glue used) and supervisory, non-administrative labor. Variances may be calculated for all three components--raw materials, direct labor, and overhead. Variances will be allocated between cost of goods sold and ending inventory (finished goods and work in process) based on the proportion of items sold and those remaining in inventory, although any "abnormal" waste will be directly expensed. This allocation is necessary because generally accepted accounting principles require that the firm report inventory based on the lower of actual cost or market--not standard cost.

Major Controls Frequently Missing in CPA Exam Questions

1) Perpetual inventory records for large dollar items
2) Prenumbered receiving reports prepared when inventory received; receiving reports accounted for
3) Adequate standard cost system to cost inventory items
4) Physical controls against theft
5) Written inventory requisitions used
6) Proper authorization of purchases and use of prenumbered purchase orders

Inventories and Production CPA Exam Questions

Multiple Choice

(578,A1,12) When verifying debits to the perpetual inventory records of a non-manufacturing company, an auditor would be most interested in examining a sample of purchase
  a. Approvals.
  b. Requisitions.
  c. Invoices.
  d. Orders.

(c) The question is asking what an auditor would be most interested in for the verification of debits to the perpetual inventory records. The invoice from the vendor (purchase invoice) will show the number and cost of items sent to the client company. Therefore, answer (c) is the correct answer. Answer (a) would address a question relating to internal controls over purchases. Answer (b) would address: "When verifying that recorded purchases of inventory were asked for by stores an auditor would be most interested in examining a sample of purchase?" Answer (d) would address: "When verifying that recorded purchases in inventory have been properly ordered an auditor would be most interested in examining a sample of purchase?"

(578,A1,50) To best ascertain that a company has properly included merchandise that it owns in its ending inventory, the auditor should review and test the
  a. Terms of the open purchase orders.
  b. Purchase cut-off procedures.
  c. Contractual commitments made by the purchasing department.
  d. Purchase invoices received on or around year end.

(b) The question is asking how to best ascertain that a company has properly included merchandise that it owns in its ending inventory. Purchase cut-off procedures include the other choices and is thus more complete. Therefore, answer (b) is the correct answer. Answers (a) and (c) would be especially good answers for a question such as "To ascertain the amount of future purchase commitments a firm has an auditor should review and test the?" Answer (d) would address: "An effective procedure for determining that a proper year-end cut-off of purchases has occurred is to review and test the?"

On the next page is an example of an inventory problem with weaknesses highlighted. Also, using internal control characteristics, weaknesses may be derived as

Control Procedure	"Unofficial Solution" Point Number
Independent Checks on Performance	6
Segregation of Duties	2,4,6,7
Safeguards over Access to Assets and Records	6
Authorization of Transactions	1,3,5
Documents Adequate	1,2,4,6,7

4. Personnel and Payroll. The following is a possible flow of documents

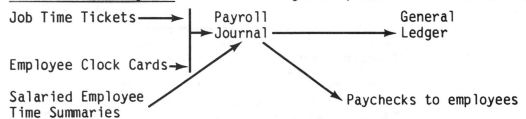

Assume that a separate personnel department maintains complete, up-to-date records for each employee. Included in such records is information on level of education, basic payroll information, experience, and authorization for any changes in pay rates. Assume that the firm's factory, direct labor personnel use a time clock to punch in each morning and out each evening. Their employee clock card thus shows the total hours worked each day. These direct labor personnel also fill out job time tickets for each job they work on each day. At the end of each week their supervisor compares job time tickets with employee clock cards which have already been signed by the employees. Assume also that salaried and other employees fill out weekly time summaries indicating hours worked. All of the above information is sent to the payroll accounting department whose responsibility is to prepare the payroll journal and to prepare the unsigned payroll checks. The checks are then signed by the treasurer and distributed by an independent paymaster who has no other payroll functions. The summary payroll entry is then posted to the general ledger in the accounting department.

Internal Control Weaknesses
(1173,A6)

(25 to 30 minutes)

INTRODUCTORY MATERIAL

> You have been engaged by the management of Alden, Inc., to review its internal control over the purchase, receipt, storage, and issue of raw materials. You have prepared the following comments which describe Alden's procedures.

Raw materials, which consist mainly of high-cost electronic components, are kept in a locked storeroom. Storeroom personnel include a supervisor and four clerks. All are well trained, competent, and adequately bonded. Raw materials are removed from the storeroom only upon written or oral authorization of one of the production foremen.

GOOD PERSONNEL POLICIES! (PERSONNEL)

ORAL AUTHORIZATION MAKES REMOVAL WITHOUT WRITTEN ENTRY POSSIBLE (RECORDING OF TRANSACTIONS, ACCESS TO ASSETS)

INADEQUATE RECORDING, PERPETUAL RECORDS NEEDED FOR VALUABLE INVENTORY ITEMS (HIGH COST ELECTRONIC COMPONENTS) (RECORDING OF TRANSACTIONS, COMPARISON OF ACCOUNTABILITY WITH ASSETS)

There are no perpetual-inventory records; hence, the storeroom clerks do not keep records of goods received or issued. To compensate for the lack of perpetual records, a physical-inventory count is taken monthly by the storeroom clerks who are well supervised. Appropriate procedures are followed in making the inventory count.

MAY NOT BE AN ECONOMICAL QUANTITY (AN ADMINISTRATIVE CONTROL)

After the physical count, the storeroom supervisor matches quantities counted against predetermined reorder level. If the count for a given part is below the reorder level, the supervisor enters the part number on a materials-requisition list and sends this list to the accounts-payable clerk. The accounts-payable clerk prepares a purchase order for a predetermined reorder quantity for each part and mails the purchase order to the vendor from whom the part was last purchased.

INADEQUATE SEGREGATION, ACCOUNTS PAYABLE PERFORMS PURCHASING FUNCTION AND PAYABLE FUNCTION (SEGREGATION OF FUNCTIONS)

MAY NOT BE BEST VENDOR (EXECUTION OF TRANSACTIONS)

INADEQUATE SEGREGATION, STOREROOM SHOULD NOT BE FIRST TO RECEIVE GOODS. (SEGREGATION OF FUNCTIONS)

HIGH COST ITEMS NEED QUALITY INSPECTION

When ordered materials arrive at Alden, they are received by the storeroom clerks. The clerks count the merchandise and agree the counts to the shipper's bill of lading. All vendors' bills of lading are initialed, dated, and filed in the storeroom to serve as receiving reports.

NO PRENUMBERED RECEIVING REPORTS (RECORDING OF TRANSACTIONS)

The internal auditing department periodically compares the payroll department's file on each employee with that in the personnel department's file to determine that no unauthorized changes in payroll records have been made. Employees with cash handling and recordkeeping responsibilities should be covered by fidelity bonds, a form of insurance which protects an employer against losses caused by dishonest employees (fidelity bonds also serve as a control when new employees are hired since the insurer will typically perform a background check on prospective employees).

Major Personnel and Payroll Controls Frequently Missing in CPA Exam Questions

1) Segregate: Timekeeping
                Payroll Preparation
                Personnel
                Paycheck Distribution
2) Time clocks used where possible
3) Job time tickets reconciled to time clock cards
4) Time clock cards approved by supervisors (overtime and regular hours)
5) Treasurer signs paychecks
6) Unclaimed paychecks controlled by someone otherwise independent of the payroll function (locked up and eventually destroyed if not claimed). In cases in which employees are paid cash (as opposed to checks) unclaimed pay should be deposited into a special bank account.

Personnel and Payroll CPA Exam Questions

Multiple Choice

17. (1179,A1,5) For internal control purposes, which of the following individuals should preferably be responsible for the distribution of payroll checks?
   a. Bookkeeper.
   b. Payroll clerk.
   c. Cashier.
   d. Receptionist.

17. (d)   From an internal control viewpoint, the person to distribute payroll checks should follow the dictum of separation of functional responsibilities: record keeping, custodianship, authorization, and operations. The receptionist would be independent of those keeping payroll records [answer (a)], preparing the payroll [answer (b)], and those with custodianship over cash [answer (c)].

35. (579,A1,37) Effective internal control over the payroll function would include which of the following?

    a. Total time recorded on time clock punch cards should be reconciled to job reports by employees responsible for those specific jobs.

    b. Payroll department employees should be supervised by the management of the personnel department.

    c. Payroll department employees should be responsible for maintaining employee personnel records.

    d. Total time spent on jobs should be compared with total time indicated on time clock punch cards.

35. (d) The requirement is an effective internal control technique over the payroll function. Note that you are looking for the best answer of the four alternatives. Total time spent on individual jobs should be compared with total time per the time clock. This will insure that all time is properly allocated to individual jobs, and excess time was not incurred that was not chargeable to specific jobs. Answer (a) is incorrect because employees should not be permitted to reconcile or check their own job reports, i.e., there should be a separate review. Answers (b) and (c) are incorrect because the payroll department and the personnel department should be separate, as they have separate functional responsibilities. The personnel department authorizes the hiring and pay levels of employees whereas the payroll department expends funds.

A payroll problem (Internal Control module, Problem 8) in a flowchart format with weaknesses highlighted is presented below. The approach for this problem is the same as for the flowchart question discussed in the sales, receivables, and cash receipts transaction cycle (Number 3 from the May 1985 exam). As we suggested earlier, first follow a transaction through the system.

Payroll IC Weaknesses
(580,A5)

(15 to 20 minutes)

A CPA's audit working papers contain a narrative description of a _segment_ of the Croyden Factory, Inc. payroll system and an accompanying flowchart as follows:

The internal control structure with respect to the personnel department is well-functioning and is _not_ included in the accompanying flowchart.

At the beginning of each work week payroll clerk No. 1 reviews the payroll department files to determine the employment status of factory employees and then prepares time cards and distributes them as each individual arrives at work. This payroll clerk, who is also responsible for custody of the signature stamp machine, verifies the identity of each payee before delivering signed checks to the foreman.

At the end of each work week, the foreman distributes payroll checks for the preceding work week. Concurrent with this activity, the foreman reviews the current week's employee time cards, notes the regular and overtime hours worked on a summary form, and initials the aforementioned time cards. The foreman then delivers all time cards and unclaimed payroll checks to payroll clerk No. 2.

Required:

    a. Based upon the narrative and accompanying flowchart, what are the weaknesses in the internal control structure?

    b. Based upon the narrative and accompanying flowchart, what inquiries should be made with respect to clarifying the existence of _possible additional weaknesses_ in the internal control structure?

Note: Do not discuss the internal control structure of the personnel department.

The narrative background for Problem 8 makes clear that this flowchart starts with payroll clerk Number 1 determining the employment status of factory employees and then preparing clock cards. Give thought to the actual operation being performed. Here, for example, the clerk has

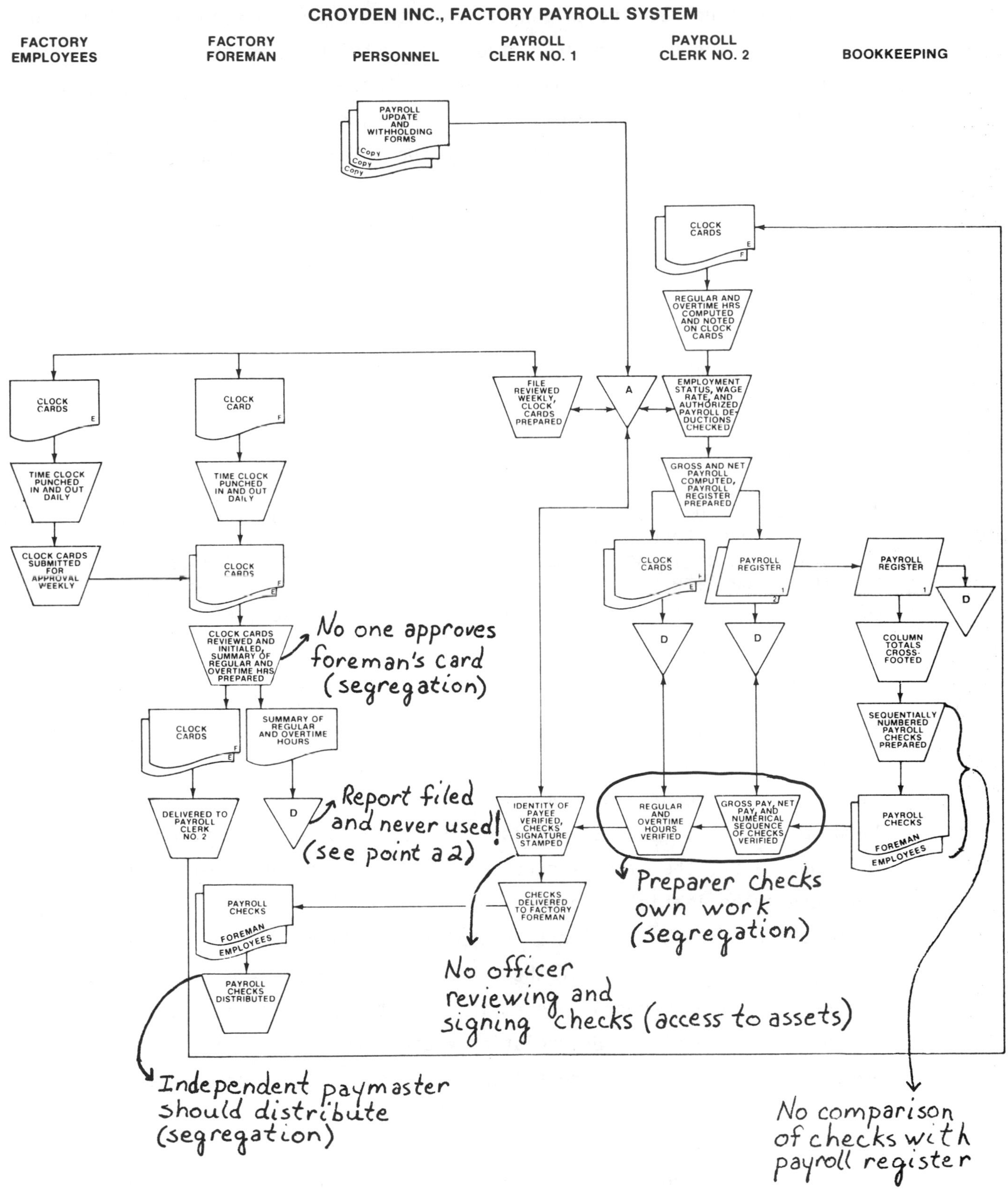

CROYDEN INC., FACTORY PAYROLL SYSTEM

| FACTORY EMPLOYEES | FACTORY FOREMAN | PERSONNEL | PAYROLL CLERK NO. 1 | PAYROLL CLERK NO. 2 | BOOKKEEPING |

Handwritten annotations on the flowchart:

No one approves foreman's card (segregation)

Report filed and never used! (see point a2)

Preparer checks own work (segregation)

No officer reviewing and signing checks (access to assets)

Independent paymaster should distribute (segregation)

No comparison of checks with payroll register

information (such as withholding data) obtained from personnel. After the
clock cards have been prepared, they are distributed to the factory.
Consider for yourself what happens in the factory--think about the daily
punching in and out and submission of time cards to the factory foreman. It
might help you to imagine that you are the foreman, for example, and that
you are reviewing the clock cards and preparing the summary (which is filed
and never used again--a sure sign that the report is either unnecessary, or,
as in this case, not properly utilized). In like manner, work through the
entire system.

The next step is to study the flowchart in detail, using your knowledge
of internal control to find weaknesses. Using IS SAD, the solution's
weaknesses may be derived as follows:

Control Procedure	"Unofficial Solution" Point Number
Independent Checks on Performance	a4,b3,b4,b5
Segregation of Duties	a1,a2,a3,a6,a7,a8,a9,a10,b1
Safeguards over Access to Assets	a5
Authorization of Transactions	a1,a2,a3,a4,b2
Documents Adequate	a1

Again, recall that it is not important which characteristic jogs your memory
as to a weakness.

Note: Refer to Problem 8 for a complete solution to this problem.

5. Property, Plant, and Equipment. This cycle is a subset of the acquisition
and payment cycle. Assume that a firm must obtain board of directors'
approval for purchases over a certain amount. Otherwise, the purchase is
handled similarly to a merchandise purchase. As in the case of merchandise purchases, the item is recorded as an addition when some form of
purchase authorization is present with a vendor's invoice and a receiving
report. The firm then selects an appropriate life and depreciation method
(e.g., straight-line, sum-of-the-years'-digits, double-declining balance)
for depreciation purposes. Depreciation entries are made in the general
journal with a debit to depreciation expense (manufacturing overhead for
manufacturing equipment) and a credit to accumulated depreciation. The firm
must also have controls to determine that repair and maintenance expenses
have not been capitalized.

Asset retirements are recorded by removing the asset and accumulated
depreciation from the general ledger--a gain (loss) may occur on the
transaction. In the case of an exchange of assets, the firm has policies to
determine that GAAP is properly followed in recording the transaction.

Major Property, Plant, and Equipment Controls Frequently Missing in CPA Exam
Questions

1) Major asset acquisitions are properly approved by the firm's board of directors and properly controlled through capital budgeting techniques
2) Detailed records are available for property assets and accumulated depreciation
3) Written policies exist for capitalization vs. expensing decisions
4) Depreciation properly calculated
5) Retirements approved by an appropriate level of management
6) Physical control over assets to prevent theft

6. Overall Internal Control Questionnaires (checklists). The following internal control questionnaires (in checklist form) outline the controls which are typically necessary in various transaction cycles and accounts. While the lists are clearly too lengthy to memorize, review them and obtain a general familiarity. Candidates with little actual business experience will probably find them especially helpful for questions which require the preparation of an internal control questionnaire. Study in detail the questionnaire checklists on cash receipts (#3), cash disbursements (#4) and on payroll (#14)--as indicated above, a large percentage of the internal control weakness type questions relate to these three areas.

The checklists are organized into subtopics--generally by category of balance sheet account, e.g., cash, receivables, fixed assets, liabilities, shareholders' equity, etc. The related nominal accounts should be considered with the real accounts, e.g., depreciation and fixed assets, sales and accounts receivable.

1. General

Chart of accounts
Accounting procedures manual
Organizational chart to define responsibilities
Absence of entries direct to ledgers
Posting references in ledgers
Review of journal entries
Use of standard journal entries
Use of prenumbered forms
Support for all journal entries
Access to records limited to authorized persons
Rotation of accounting personnel
Required vacations
Review of system at every level
Appropriate revision of chart of accounts
Appropriate revision of procedures
Separation of recordkeeping from operations
Separation of recordkeeping from custodianship
Record retention policy
Bonding of employees
A conflict of interest policy

2. Cash funds

Imprest system
Reasonable amount
Completeness of vouchers
Custodian responsible for fund
Reimbursement checks to order of custodian
Surprise audits
No employee check cashing
Physically secure
Custodian has no access to cash receipts
Custodian has no access to accounting records

3. Cash receipts

Detail listing of mail receipts
Restrictive endorsement of checks
Special handling of postdated checks

Daily deposit
Cash custodians bonded
Cash custodians apart from negotiable
  instruments
Bank accounts properly authorized
Handling of returned NSF items
Comparison of duplicate deposit slips
  with cash book
Comparison of duplicate deposit slips
  with detail A/R
Banks instructed not to cash checks
  to company
Control over cash from other sources
Separation of cashier personnel from
  accounting duties
Separation of cashier personnel from
  credit duties
Use of cash registers
Cash register tapes
Numbered cash receipt tickets
Outside salesmen cash control
Daily reconciliation of cash collec-
  tions

4. Cash disbursements

Numbered checks
Sufficient support for check
Limited authorization to sign checks
No signing of blank checks
All checks accounted for
Detail listing of checks
Mutilation of voided checks
Specific approval for unusually large
  checks
Proper authorization of persons sign-
  ing checks
Control over signature machines
Check listing compared with cash book
Control over interbank transfers
Prompt accounting for interbank
  transfers
Checks not payable to cash
Physical control of unused checks
Cancelation of supporting documents
Control over long outstanding checks
Reconciliation of bank account
Independence of person reconciling
  bank statement
Bank statement direct to person
  reconciling
No access to cash records or receipts
  by check signers

5. Investments

Proper authorization of transactions
Under control of a custodian
Custodian bonded
Custodian separate from cash receipts
Custodian separate from investment
  records

Safety deposit box
Record of all safety deposit visits
Access limited
Presence of two required for access
Periodic reconciliation of detail
  with control
Record of all aspects of all secur-
  ities
Availability of brokerage advices,
  etc.
Periodic internal audit
Securities in name of company
Proper segregation of collateral
Physical control of collateral
Periodic appraisal of collateral
Periodic appraisal of investments
Adequate records of investments for
  application of equity method

6. Accounts receivable and sales

Sales orders prenumbered
Credit approval
Credit and sales departments in-
  dependent
Control of back orders
Sales order and sales invoice com-
  parison
Shipping invoices prenumbered
Names and addresses on shipping in-
  voice
Review of sales invoices
Control over returned merchandise
Credit memoranda prenumbered
Matching of credit memoranda and re-
  ceiving reports
Control over credit memoranda
Control over scrap sales
Control over sales to employees
Control over C.O.D. sales
Sales reconciled with cash receipts
  and A/R
Sales reconciled with inventory
  change
A/R statement to all customers
Periodic preparation of aging
  schedule
Control over collections of written-
  off receivables
Control over A/R write offs, e.g.,
  proper authorization
Control over A/R written off, i.e.,
  review for possible collection
Independence of sales, A/R, receipts,
  billing, and shipping personnel

7. Notes receivable

Proper authorization of notes
Detailed records of notes
Periodic detail to control comparison
Periodic confirmation with makers
Control over notes discounted

Control over delinquent notes
Physical safety of notes
Periodic count of notes
Control over collateral
Control over revenue from notes
Custodian of notes independent from
cash and recordkeeping

8. Inventory and cost of sales

Periodic inventory counts
Written inventory instructions
Counts by noncustodians
Control over count tags
Control over inventory adjustments
Use of perpetual records
Periodic comparison of G/L and per-
petual records
Investigation of discrepancies
Control over consignment inventory
Control over inventory stored at
warehouses
Control over returnable containers
left with customers
Preparation of receiving reports
Prenumbered receiving reports
Receiving reports in numerical order
Independence of custodian from
recordkeeping
Adequacy of insurance
Physical safeguards against theft
Physical safeguards against fire
Adequacy of cost system
Cost system tied into general ledger
Periodic review of overhead rates
Use of standard costs
Use of inventory requisitions
Periodic summaries of inventory usage
Control over intracompany inventory
transfers
Purchase orders prenumbered
Proper authorization for purchases
Review of open purchase orders

9. Prepaid expenses and deferred charges

Proper authorization to incur
Authorization and support of amorti-
zation
Detailed records
Periodic review of amortization poli-
cies
Control over insurance policies
Periodic review of insurance needs
Control over premium refunds
Beneficiaries of company policies
Physical control of policies

10. Intangibles

Authorization to incur
Detailed records
Authorization to amortize
Periodic review of amortization

11. Fixed assets

Detailed property records
Periodic comparison with control
accounts
Proper authorization for acquisition
Written policies for acquisition
Control over expenditures for self-
construction
Use of work orders
Individual asset identification
plates
Written authorization for sale
Written authorization for retirement
Physical safeguard from theft
Control over fully depreciated assets
Written capitalization--expense poli-
cies
Responsibilities charged for asset
and depreciation records
Written, detailed depreciation
records
Depreciation adjustments for sales
and retirements
Control over intracompany transfers
Adequacy of insurance
Control over returnable containers

12. Accounts payable

Designation of responsibility
Independence of A/P personnel from
purchasing, cashier, receiving
functions
Periodic comparison of detail and
control
Control over purchase returns
Clerical accuracy of vendors' in-
voices
Matching of purchase order, receiving
report, and vendor invoice
Reconciliation of vendor statements
with A/P detail
Control over debit memos
Control over advance payments
Review of unmatched receiving reports
Mutilation of supporting documents at
payment
Review of debit balances
Investigation of discounts not taken

13. Accrued liabilities and other expenses

Proper authorization for expenditure
and incurrence
Control over partial deliveries
Postage meter
Purchasing department
Bids from vendors
Verification of invoices
Imprest cash account
Detailed records
Responsibility charged

Independence from G/L and cashier
functions
Periodic comparison with budget

14. Payroll

Authorization to employ
Personnel data records
Tax records
Time clock
Supervisor review of time cards
Review of payroll calculations
Comparison of time cards to job
sheets
Imprest payroll account
Responsibility for payroll records
Compliance with labor statutes
Distribution of payroll checks
Control over unclaimed wages
Profit sharing authorization
Responsibility for profit sharing
computations

15. Long-term liabilities

Authorization to incur
Executed in company name
Detailed records of long-term debt
Reports of independent transfer agent
Reports of independent registrar
Otherwise adequate records of credi-
tors
Control over unissued instruments

Signers independent of each other
Adequacy of records of collateral
Periodic review of debt agreement
compliance
Recordkeeping of detachable warrants
Recordkeeping of conversion features

16. Shareholders' equity

Use of registrar
Use of transfer agent
Adequacy of detailed records
Comparison of transfer agent's report
with records
Physical control over blank certifi-
cates
Physical control over treasury certi-
ficates
Authorization for transactions
Tax stamp compliance for canceled
certificates
Independent dividend agent
Imprest dividend account
Periodic reconciliation of dividend
account
Adequacy of stockholders' ledger
Review of stock restrictions and pro-
visions
Valuation procedures for stock
issuances
Other paid-in capital entries
Other retained earnings entries

D. Other Considerations

1. Communicating with the Audit Committee. Recall that the existence of an
audit committee is a factor in the control environment (see section A,
outline of AU 319, section 1.c). An audit committee is a group of outside
(nonmanagement) directors whose functions typically include

(a) Nominating, terminating, and negotiating CPA firm audit fees
(b) Discussing broad, general matters concerning the type, scope, and
timing of the audit with the public accounting firm
(c) Discussing internal control weaknesses with the public accounting firm
(d) Reviewing the financial statements and the public accounting firm's
audit report
(e) Working with the company's internal auditors

CPAs communicate with audit committees on a variety of matters. We have
discussed in the Professional Responsibilities module that irregularities and
illegal acts must be communicated to the audit committee. In addition, AU 325
requires auditors to communicate reportable conditions to the audit committee.
A reportable condition is a significant deficiency in the design or function of
the internal control structure that could adversely affect the organization's
ability to record, process, summarize, and report financial data. These

reportable conditions may be communicated orally (with the discussion documented in the working papers), or as is more frequently the case, in a written letter to the audit committee.

A reportable condition may be so significant as to be considered a <u>material weakness in internal control</u>. A material weakness is a condition that does not reduce to a relatively low level the risk that material misstatements might occur and not be detected within a timely period by employees in the normal course of performing their assigned functions. Auditors, unless a different arrangement is made with the client, are not required to classify reportable conditions as being material weaknesses.

The report issued on reportable conditions should indicate that it is intended solely for the audit committee, management, and others in the organization (unless requirements established by governmental authorities require such reports in which case the report may be provided). Because of the potential for misinterpretation, when no reportable weaknesses are noted, the auditor should **not** issue a report indicating that no such conditions were noted. Know that communicating information on weaknesses in internal control has long been considered a "secondary" purpose or a "by-product" of audits.

The following is an example of the form of a report which might be issued when reportable conditions have been found:

> In planning and performing our audit of the financial statements of the ABC Corporation for the year ended December 31, 19XX, we considered its internal control structure in order to determine our auditing procedures for the purpose of expressing our opinion on the financial statements and not to provide assurance on the internal control structure. However, we noted certain matters involving the internal control structure and its operation that we consider to be reportable conditions under standards established by the American Institute of Certified Public Accountants. Reportable conditions involve matters coming to our attention relating to significant deficiencies in the design or operation of the internal control structure that, in our judgment, could adversely affect the organization's ability to record, process, summarize, and report financial data consistent with the assertions of management in the financial statements.

> [Include paragraphs to describe the reportable conditions noted.]

> This report is intended solely for the information and use of the audit committee (board of directors, board of trustees, or owners in owner-managed enterprises), management, and others within the organization (or specified regulatory agency or other specified third party).

Finally, AU 380 requires the communication of certain information on SEC engagements, as well as engagements of other companies with active audit committees or boards of directors. The nature of the items, also presented in the outline of AU 380, may be summarized, using our categories, as follows:

Audit related matters

1. Auditor responsibility under GAAS audits
2. Significant audit adjustments
3. Auditor responsibility for other information in documents containing audited financial statements (see Reports module)

Accounting matters

4. Significant accounting policies
5. Important management judgments and accounting estimates

Auditor relationships with management

6. Disagreements with management
7. Management consultation with other accountants
8. Major issues discussed with management prior to retention
9. Difficulties encountered in performing the audit

2. Reports on Internal Control. AU 642 outlines four general types of reports on internal accounting control. Review carefully the entire outline.

  a. Separate opinion on internal accounting control. AU 642 allows accountants to issue an opinion on internal accounting control. The publicly available report addresses the issue of whether the firm's internal accounting control system can prevent or detect material errors or irregularities.   The report issued, to be addressed to the company, its board of directors or stockholders, should

   (1) Describe the scope of the engagement
   (2) Include the date to which the opinion relates
   (3) Indicate that establishment and maintenance of the system is management's responsibility
   (4) Briefly explain the broad objectives and inherent limitations of internal accounting control.
   (5) Provide opinion on whether the system meets the objectives of internal accounting control.
   (6) Be dated the date of completion of field work.

  The following is an example of such a report:

  We have made a study and evaluation of the system of internal account control of XYZ Company and subsidiaries in effect at December 31, 19X1. Our study and evaluation was conducted in accordance with standards established by the American Institute of Certified Public Accountants.

  The management of XYZ Company is responsible for establishing and maintaining a system of internal accounting control. In fulfilling this responsibility, estimates and judgments by management are required to assess the expected benefits and related costs of control procedures. The objectives of a system are to provide management with reasonable, but not absolute, assurance that assets are safeguarded against loss from unauthorized use or disposition, and that transactions are executed in accordance with management's authorization and recorded properly to permit the preparation of financial statements in accordance with generally accepted accounting principles.

  Because of inherent limitations in any system of internal accounting control, errors or irregularities may occur and not be detected. Also, projection of any evaluation of the system to future periods is subject to the risk that procedures may become inadequate because of changes in condition, or that the degree of compliance with the procedures may deteriorate.

In our opinion, the system of internal accounting control of XYZ Company and subsidiaries in effect at December 31, 19X1, taken as a whole, was sufficient to meet the objectives stated above insofar as those objectives pertain to the prevention or detection or errors or irregularities in amounts that would be material in relation to the consolidated financial statements.

b. Report made as part of a financial statement audit. As indicated in the prior section on communications with audit committees, auditors must communicate reportable conditions. A sample report is presented in D.1.

c. Report based on criteria established by regulatory agencies. AU 642 allows reporting on internal accounting control when the criteria have been prescribed by a regulatory agency. While CPAs do not assume responsibility for the criteria, they should report any weakness discovered which is not covered by the prescribed criteria.

d. Other special purpose reports. These reports, described briefly in the outline of AU 642, Section G, are for management, another independent accountant, or other specified third parties. While no specific report form is suggested, the accountant must disclaim an opinion on whether the system meets the overall objectives of internal control. AU 324 provides more specific guidance on the preparation and use of those reports for service centers (e.g., EDP Service Centers and bank trust departments holding assets for employee benefit plans).

3. Effects of an Internal Audit Function. AU 322 discusses the effect of an internal audit function on the CPA's audit. While a CPA may use the work of internal auditors, the CPA remains responsible for such work. The CPA should evaluate the competence, objectivity, and work performance of internal auditors when such work is being used. Competence is evaluated through inquiries about internal audit staff educational backgrounds, training, and supervision. Objectivity relates primarily to the organizational level to which the internal audit function reports (e.g., all other factors held constant, an internal audit function which periodically reports to the audit committee is considered more objective than one which reports only the controller). Work performance may be evaluated by review and tests of internal auditor work.

EVIDENCE

The entire financial statement audit may be described as a process of evidence accumulation and evaluation. This process enables the auditor to formulate an informed opinion as to whether the financial statements are presented fairly in accordance with generally accepted accounting principles. The following "Diagram of an Audit" was first presented and explained in the auditing overview section.

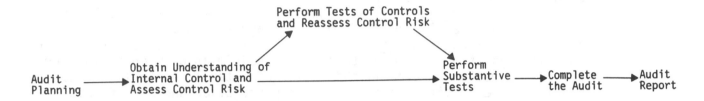

This module covers "evidential matter" as a concept and discusses types of evidential matter generated through performance of substantive tests--both analytical procedures and tests of details of transactions and balances--and discusses completing the audit.

Numerous questions on evidence appear on each CPA Exam. Multiple choice questions frequently ask the candidate to select the audit procedure most likely to detect errors which have occurred in given accounting records. Essay as well as multiple choice questions are used to test whether the candidate can distinguish among various concepts such as

1) Competent vs. sufficient evidence
2) Analytical procedures vs. tests of details of transactions and balances
3) Audit objectives vs. audit procedures

Additionally, candidates may be required to prepare an audit program.

Study Program for Evidence Module

This module is organized and should be studied in the following manner

A. Evidence--General

1. Competent and Sufficient Evidential Matter
2. Types of Evidence

B. Evidence--Specific (Substantive Tests)

1. Types of Substantive Tests
2. Preparing Substantive Test Audit Programs
3. Documentation

C. Other Specific Evidence Topics

1. Cash
2. Receivables
3. Inventory
4. Marketable Securities
5. Property, Plant, and Equipment
6. Prepaids
7. Payables (Current)
8. Long-Term Debt

9. Owners' Equity
10. Engagement Letters
11. Client Representation Letters
12. Using the Work of a Specialist
13. Inquiry of a Client's Lawyer
14. Related Party Transactions
15. Going Concern Considerations
16. Subsequent Events
17. Omitted Procedures

D. Completing the Audit

E. Compilation and Review Procedures

1. Compilation Procedures
2. Review Procedures
3. Overall Comments

F. Other Related Topics

1. Compliance Audits
2. Operational Auditing

This module covers information included in the Evidence and Procedures section of the AICPA Content Specification Outline with the following exceptions: (1) Use of the Computer in Performing the Audit is covered in the Auditing EDP module; and (2) Use of Statistical Sampling in Performing the Audit is covered in the Audit Sampling module:

The following SAS sections pertain to audit evidence

Section AU

326	Evidential Matter
329	Analytical Procedures
331	Receivables and Inventories
332	Long-Term Investments
333	Client Representations
334	Related Party Transactions
336	Using the Work of a Specialist
337	Inquiry of a Client's Lawyer Concerning Litigation, Claims, and Assessments
339	Working Papers
341	The Auditor's Consideration of an Entity's Ability to Continue as a Going Concern

Read the various sections and study the outlines for each of the above SASs separately. After studying each outline, attempt to summarize in your own words the "sum and substance" of the pronouncement. If you cannot explain the pronouncement in your own words, you do not understand it. Go back and study it again.

A. **Evidence--General**

The second attestation standard, as well as the third audit field work standard, both require the collection of sufficient evidence to provide a reasonable basis for the conclusion to be issued in the report. As background pertaining to financial statements, bear in mind that when management prepares financial statements which purport to be in conformity with generally accepted accounting principles, certain assertions (implicit or explicit) are made. Section 326.03 identifies and classifies these assertions as:

1) <u>Presentation</u> and disclosure--components of financial statements are properly classified, described, and disclosed (e.g., inventories are properly classified on the balance sheet)
2) <u>Existence</u> or occurrence--assets and liabilities exist at a given date and transactions have occurred during a given period (e.g., inventories physically exist)
3) <u>Rights</u> and obligations--assets are rights of the entity and liabilities are obligations at a given date (e.g., firm has legal title to inventory)
4) <u>Completeness</u>--all transactions and accounts are included (e.g., all inventory items included on balance sheet)
5) <u>Valuation</u> or allocation--components of financial statements included at appropriate amounts (e.g., inventories are properly stated at lower of cost or market)

(PERCV--as in, "I perceive the need to pass the CPA exam.")

Note the relationship between existence and completeness. The existence assertion relates to whether the recorded amount is bona fide (e.g., recorded receivables are legitimate). Completeness, on the other hand, addresses the issue of whether all transactions have been recorded (e.g., are all receivables recorded?). An auditor must test for both existence and completeness. This concept of "directional testing" is discussed in Section C of the Internal Control module.

The Statement on Attestation Standards suggests two basic types of evidence collection procedures: (1) search and verification and (2) internal inquiries and comparisons. Search and verification procedures include procedures such as inspecting assets, confirming receivables, and observing the counting of inventory. Internal inquiry and comparison procedures include discussions with firm representatives and analytical review procedures such as ratio analysis.

As described in greater detail in the Reporting module, accountants perform (1) examinations, (2) reviews, (3) agreed-upon procedures attest engagements as well as (4) compilation accounting engagements. Of these forms of association, an examination offers the highest level of assurance. (An "audit" is considered to be an examination of financial statements.) In examinations, accountants select from among all available audit procedures to determine whether the appropriate assertions (generally PERCV in the case of financial statements) have been met.

A review offers limited assurance (also referred to as negative assurance) with respect to information. It is composed primarily of internal inquiries and comparisons. However, when evidence with respect to an assertion seems incomplete or inaccurate, search and verification procedures may be performed.

Agreed-upon procedures result in a report in which a summary of findings and/or negative assurance is provided. The extent of the procedures are specified by the user, but must exceed the attester's mere reading of the assertions.

Compilations, which are considered accounting and not attestation services, result in a report which provides no explicit assurance on the information. While the accountant who performs a compilation should understand the nature of the client's business and its accounting records, s/he is not required to make any inquiries or perform any other verification procedures beyond reading the information. As is the case with all other forms of association, material known errors or omissions must be disclosed in the accountant's report which is expanded to disclose the situation.

Three presumptions (asked directly and indirectly on several previous exams) relate to evidence:

1) Evidence from independent sources provides more assurance than evidence secured solely from within the entity.
2) Information from direct personal knowledge is more persuasive than information obtained indirectly.
3) Assertions developed under effective internal controls are more reliable than those developed in the absence of internal controls.

1. Competent and Sufficient Evidential Matter. The amount of evidence necessary depends upon the form of accountant association--examination, review, agreed-upon procedures, compilation. Competent evidential matter

may be thought of as being reliable. Section 326 states that to be competent, evidential matter must be both valid and relevant (know these criteria). The concept of sufficient evidence refers to the quantity of evidence that an accountant must gather. Sufficient evidence has been gathered when attestation risk (audit risk in the case of financial statement examinations--see Planning and Supervision in the Professional Responsibilities module) is considered to be at an acceptable level.

Section 326.20 suggests that in the great majority of cases the auditor finds it necessary to rely on evidence that is persuasive rather than convincing. An acceptable level of audit risk does not indicate that all uncertainty be eliminated for sufficient evidence to have been gathered. The auditor must be able to form an opinion within a reasonable length of time, at a reasonable cost. However, the difficulty or expense involved in testing a particular item is not in itself a valid reason for omitting a test. Auditors use professional judgment to determine the extent of tests necessary to obtain sufficient evidence. In exercising this professional judgment, auditors consider both the materiality of the item in question (e.g., dollar size) as well as the inherent risk of the item (e.g., cash, due to its liquidity, may have a higher inherent risk than do certain property, plant, and equipment items).

The following example distinguishes between competent vs. sufficient evidence. Assume that an auditor has highly credible evidence on one account receivable for $400 out of a total receivable balance of $1,000,000. While this evidence is competent, most auditors would suggest that it is not sufficient evidence for the $1,000,000 balance; to be sufficient, more evidence verifying the account's total value must be collected.

Obtaining sufficient competent evidence is particularly difficult when auditing client accounting estimates (e.g., allowance for doubtful accounts, loss reserves, pension expenses). In 1988, the Auditing Standards Board through AU 342 provided guidance on auditing estimates. The SAS suggests that the auditor's objectives are to determine that all estimates (1) have been developed, (2) are reasonable and (3) follow GAAP. Typically these estimates are needed because the valuation of some accounts is based on future events or because certain evidence can not be accumulated on a timely, cost-effective basis. Know that the three basic approaches for evaluating the reasonableness of these estimates are (1) to review and test management's process of deriving the estimate (consider the reasonableness and accuracy of management's approach), (2) develop one's own expectation of the accounting estimate and compare it to management's and (3) review subsequent events or transactions occurring prior to the completion of field work which bear on the estimate.

2. Types of Evidence. Recall from the Professional Responsibilities module (Section B.1.a) that at the account level audit risk has three components-- inherent risk, control risk, and detection risk. Inherent risk refers to the fact that certain accounts are riskier than others (e.g., cash has more inherent risk than an inventory of coal). Most frequently inherent risk is assessed by auditors performing overall review techniques and using overall auditing knowledge. As is discussed in detail in the Internal Control module, control risk is assessed through the auditor's consideration of internal control.

    Detection risk is controlled primarily by the auditor's substantive tests. AU 326.14-.16 distinguishes between underlying accounting data and all corroborating (supporting) information available to the auditor. Underlying accounting data includes books of original entry (journals), general and subsidiary ledgers, related accounting manuals, and informal and memorandum records such as worksheets supporting cost allocations, computations, and reconciliations.

    Corroborating evidence is the supporting documentation that is the basis for a transaction being recorded in the journals and ledgers. While every text seems to have its own list of types of corroborating evidence, the following list seems adequate (memorize them by remembering the first letter of each category--AICPA S).

> Authoritative documents
> Interrelationships
> Calculations
> Physical existence
> Authoritative statements--by client and by third parties
> Subsequent events
>
> (Note: some sources include internal control in such lists--this makes the mnemonic AICPA IS)

    Authoritative documents such as truck titles, vendors' invoices, etc., support ownership and transaction occurrence.

    Interrelationships within the data such as interest expense and accrued interest payable, unusual items, etc., provide assurance as to the reasonableness of items and the absence of material irregularities or errors.

Calculations by auditor such as calculation of depreciation expense, tax liabilities, etc., support the application of GAAP.

Physical existence is determined by observation and count.

Authoritative statements by a client provide support for the treatment of certain items in the recording and aggregation of transaction data. Authoritative statements by third parties such as confirmations provide evidence concerning the existence of transactions with third parties.

Subsequent events confirm the status of estimates and assertions at the financial statement date. For example, subsequent collection of receivables gives evidence as to their valuation and collectibility. Court award of a lawsuit pending at year end is evidence of the year-end payable or receivable.

Since the competency of evidence depends upon the financial statement assertion under consideration (recall PERCV), the auditor must use professional judgment when deciding which type of evidence is most appropriate in a specific situation. Conceptually, the auditor should attempt to gather a sufficient quantity of competent evidence at a minimum cost.

Audit procedures (acts to be performed) are undertaken by the auditor to obtain the corroborating evidence discussed above. Some of the terms (i.e., "buzz words") that you will find in written audit procedures are listed below. Review the terms and relate them to one or more of the categories of corroborative evidence. (Note: each "buzz word" indicates a specific action that the auditor would take while performing an audit procedure.)

> Agree (schedule balances to general ledger, financial
>   statement balances to schedules)
> Analyze (account transactions)
> Compare (beginning balances with last year's audit figures)
> Confirm (payables and receivables)
> Count (cash, inventory, etc.)
> Examine (authoritative documents)
> Foot (totals)
> Inquire (for explanations of accounting treatments)
> Inspect (legal documents)
> Interrelate (interest expense with liabilities)
> Observe (inventories)
> Prove (totals)
> Read (minutes of directors' meetings)
> Recalculate (client's figures)
> Reconcile (beginning and ending balance)
> Review (disclosures for compliance with GAAP)
> Review (legal documents)
> Scan (for unusual items)
> Trace or retrace (bookkeeping procedures)
> Vouch (transactions)

B. **Evidence--Specific (Substantive Tests)**

As noted earlier, the objective of an audit is to express an opinion on whether the firm's financial statements are fairly presented in conformity with generally accepted accounting principles. Substantive tests are designed to assist the auditor in reaching this goal by ascertaining whether the specific balances of financial statement accounts are in conformity with generally accepted accounting principles. While tests of controls (compliance tests) are used to test the "means" of processing (the internal control system), substantive tests are used to directly test the "ends" of processing--the financial statements.

When evaluating evidence, the objective is to obtain an estimate of the total error in the financial statements and to determine whether it exceeds a material amount. The auditor estimates the likely error in the financial statements and attempts to determine whether an unacceptably high audit risk exists. Note here that in the evaluation of audit evidence, because of information obtained during the audit, the auditor <u>may</u> revise his/her preliminary estimate of materiality (see discussion in Planning and Supervision section in the Professional Responsibilities module).

1. <u>Types of Substantive Tests</u>. Substantive tests are of two types: (1) Analytical procedures (2) Tests of details of transactions and balances.

a. <u>Analytical procedures</u>. Analytical procedures consist of evaluations of financial information made by a study of plausible relationships among financial and nonfinancial data. Analytical procedures are used for the following purposes:

<u>Planning</u>--determine the nature, timing, and extent of tests (Required)

<u>Substantive</u>--substantiate accounts for which overall comparisons are helpful

Note, GAAS requires the use of analytical procedures during the planning stage and the final review stage. Analytical procedures are <u>not</u> a required substantive test.

<u>Overall Review</u>--assess conclusions reached and evaluate overall financial statement presentation (Required)

Perhaps the most familiar example of analytical procedures used in auditing is the calculation of ratios. However, analytical procedures range from simple comparisons of information through the use of complex models such as regression and time series analysis. The typical approach is

1) Develop an expectation for the account balance
2) Determine the amount of difference from the expectation that can be accepted without investigation
3) Compare the company's account balance (or ratio) with the expected account balance
4) Investigate significant differences from the expected account balance

When developing an expectation, the auditor must attempt to identify plausible relationships. These expectations may be derived from:

1) The information itself in prior periods
2) Anticipated results such as budgets and forecasts
3) Relationships among elements of financial information within the period
4) Industry information
5) Relevant nonfinancial information

Relationships differ in their predictability. Be familiar with the following principles:

1) Relationships in a dynamic or unstable environment are less predictable than those in a stable environment
2) Relationships involving balance sheet accounts are less predictable than income statement accounts (because balance sheet accounts represent balances at one arbitrary point in time)
3) Relationships involving management discretion are sometimes less predictable (e.g., decision to incur maintenance expense rather than replace plant).

Recall from earlier in this module (section A) that the reliability of evidence varies based on whether it is obtained (from) (1) independent sources, (2) personal knowledge, or (3) developed under strong internal control. In addition, in the case of analytical procedures be aware that use of data that has been subjected to audit testing and data available from a variety of sources increases the reliability of the data used in the analysis.

Principal limitations concerning analytical procedures include

1) The guidelines for evaluation may be inadequate (e.g., Why is an industry average good? Why should the ratio be the same as last year?)
2) It is difficult to determine whether a change is due to a misstatement or is the result of random change in the account
3) Cost-based accounting records hinder comparisons between firms of different ages and/or asset compositions
4) Accounting differences hinder comparisons between firms (e.g., if one firm uses LIFO and another uses FIFO the information is not comparable)
5) Analytical procedures present only "circumstantial" evidence in that a "significant" difference will lead to additional audit procedures as opposed to direct detection of a misstatement.

b. Tests of details of transactions and balances. These tests are used to examine the actual details making up the various account balances. For example, if receivables total $1,000,000 at year end, tests of details may be made of the individual components of the total account. Assume the $1,000,000 is the accumulation of 250 individual accounts. As a test of details, an auditor might decide to confirm a sample of these 250 accounts. Based on the results of the auditor's consideration of internal control and tests of controls, the auditor might determine that 60 accounts should be confirmed. Thus, when responses are received and when the balances have been reconciled, the auditor has actually tested the detail supporting the account; the existence of the accounts has been confirmed. As an additional test (and also as an alternative procedure when confirmation replies have not been received from debtors), the auditor may examine cash receipts received subsequent to year end on individual accounts. This substantive test provides evidence pertaining to both the existence and the valuation of the account.

2. Preparing Substantive Test Audit Programs. The CPA exam frequently requires the candidate to prepare an audit program. This skill, obviously necessary in practice, is generally tested through essay questions. Recently two approaches have been used in these problems.

   a. The exam describes a financial statement account(s) of a company and requires the candidate to prepare a substantive test program
   b. The exam asks questions on an area in which a SAS prescribes specific audit procedures and requires the candidate to prepare an audit program

   Approach for a Substantive Test Program. As noted earlier under "Evidence--Specific (Substantive Tests)," statements which purport to be in conformity with generally accepted accounting principles contain certain assertions: presentation and disclosure, existence or occurrence, rights and obligations, completeness, and valuation or allocation (PERCV). Auditors gather evidence to form an opinion with respect to these assertions. The experienced auditor should be able to prepare an audit program for an audit area (e.g., inventory) to test whether these assertions are supportable. The process is one in which specific audit objectives are developed (also either explicitly or implicitly) based on the assertions being made in the financial statements. Finally, audit procedures to meet these audit objectives are formulated and listed in an audit program. These relationships may be illustrated as

Financial Statements

Assertions

Audit Objectives

Audit Procedures

Audit Program

For purposes of the CPA exam, consider two possible approaches for auditing an account: (1) direct tests of ending balance ("tests of balances"), and (2) tests of inputs and outputs during the year ("tests of details of transactions"). First, the auditor may directly test ending balances for high turnover accounts such as cash, accounts receivable, accounts payable, etc. (e.g., confirm year-end balances). The second approach, tests of transactions (inputs and outputs during the year), is used most extensively for lower turnover accounts (e.g., fixed assets, long-term debt, etc.). For example, for fixed assets, a low turnover account, the emphasis will be on vouching additions or retirements--not on auditing the entire account for a continuing audit engagement. While the distinction between approaches will probably help you on audit program problems, bear in mind that during an audit it is not an either/or proposition--a combination of approaches with an emphasis of one approach over the other will generally be used.

To prepare a substantive test audit program use the following three step approach.

(1)   Determine whether the program should have an ending balance or transactions (input/output) emphasis
(2)   Write as the first step of your audit program: "Use understanding of the internal control structure, and assessment of control risk to plan the nature, timing, and extent of tests to be performed for (name account).
(3)   Use the PERCV assertions (including the overall framework presented below) to develop your audit program

The following tables present summarized substantive audit programs for the major balance sheet accounts. Although the programs are constructed to present the pertinent procedures under only one assertion, be aware that many audit procedures provide support for multiple assertions. For example, while receivable confirmations are listed under the "existence or occurrence" assertion, it may be argued that confirmations provide evidence with respect to all five assertions. The purpose is to use the PERCV assertions as an aid to organizing your thoughts; do not worry about which assertion an audit procedure "bests fits under." Also, you should understand the listed procedures well enough to be able to explain them in detail on the CPA exam. Section C of this module should help you with this information.

In reviewing the summary audit procedures, you will find a number of similarities between areas. We have provided the following "overall framework" to help you identify the similarities.

Overall: Use understanding of the internal control structure and assessment of control risk to plan the nature, timing, and extent of tests to be performed for (name account).

Presentation and Disclosure:
  Review disclosure. Always include a general disclosure requirement
        related to overall compliance with GAAP.
  Inquire about disclosures. Consider specific disclosure
        requirements for the account, as well as for related
        accounts. Example: for receivables, you would recall from
        your accounting courses such possibilities as factoring,
        pledging, or discounting.

Existence or Occurrence:
  Confirmation. Often an account will lend itself to confirmation
        (e.g., bank for cash, debtor for receivables, stock
        registrar and transfer agent for stock authorized and
        outstanding).
  Observation. Always consider whether you can observe the item
        itself and/or a legal document representing the item.
        Examples: cash on hand, inventory, loan agreements.
  Vouch transactions. This step relates directly to "directional
        testing" as presented in Section C of the Internal Control
        Module. Example: for receivables the auditor may examine
        shipping documents, invoices, credit, and credit memos.

Rights and Obligations:
  Cutoffs. Auditors must consider whether transactions have been
        reported in the proper period. Think about the transactions
        affecting the account to determine the proper cutoff. For
        example, cash cutoffs will relate to receipts and
        disbursements of cash, while receivables will relate to
        credit sales and cash receipts.
  Authorization. Consider whether there are transactions which
        require specific authorization. Authorization of
        transactions relates to whether proper rights and
        obligations have been established. This step is not always
        included, but programs for accounts such as receivables,
        debt, and owners' equity accounts are affected.

Completeness:
  Analytical procedures. Always include a step on analytical
        procedures. Also, mention specific procedures for the
        account being audited. Section C of this module provides
        examples for the various accounts.
  Omissions. Consider how transactions (adjustment) could improperly
        have been omitted from the account. Examples here include
        inventory count sheets not included, accruals not made, debt
        not recorded.

Valuation:
  Foot schedules. Consider the actual schedules involved with the
        account and include a step to foot and cross-foot them.

  Agree schedules balances to general ledger balances.

  Agree financial statement balances to schedules. Because financial
        statements are derived from accounting information, the
        general and subsidiary ledgers as well as other accounting
        records must be summarized. Examples: accounts receivable,
        inventory count sheets.
  Consider valuation method of account. You should consider the
        accounting method used, and whether it has been properly

applied. Most accounts have a number of steps here.
Examples: Receivables must be valued net of an appropriate
allowance, inventory costing methods (e.g., LIFO, FIFO), and
application of the lower of cost or market rule. Always
integrate your accounting knowledge with auditing procedures
here.

Consider related accounts. When you are preparing an audit program
for a balance sheet account, include procedures used to
audit the related income statement accounts. Examples:
analytical procedures for bad debt expense may provide
evidence as to the valuation of receivables; recalculating
interest expense may provide evidence as to the existence of
long-term debt; and recalculation depreciation and
analytical procedures applied to repairs and maintenance
expense may provide evidence as to the completeness and/or
valuation of property, plant, and equipment.

You may wish to use the above steps as a starting point to tailor your
audit program. However, be careful here since you are unlikely to receive
credit for them unless you tailor them to the account involved. Detailed
information on the actual audit procedures is presented in Section C of this
module.

Although using the PERCV assertions is never detrimental, in several
circumstances you may find them unnecessary. First, if you have a
significant amount of audit experience, you may not need to explicitly
consider assertions. Second, if a problem asks for procedures relating to
specific parts of an account (e.g., for cash, the bank balance, or the
checks outstanding) you may not need to use the assertions since you may be
able to directly derive procedures. The assertions (including the above
framework) are especially helpful in those cases for which you need a
logical starting point and/or need to organize your approach.

Approach for Developing Account Audit Objectives. The CPA exam may ask
for the auditor's "objectives" in the audit of an account. The approach for
developing a substantive test audit program may be easily adapted to answer
this type of question. In the case of long-term debt, for example, the
following could serve as objectives:

1. Determine whether internal control over long-term debt is adequate
2. Determine whether long-term debt disclosures comply with GAAP
    (presentation and disclosure)
3. Determine whether recorded long-term debt exists at year end (existence
    or occurrence)
4. Determine whether long-term debt represents an obligation to the firm at
    year end (rights and obligations)
5. Determine whether all long-term debt has been completely recorded at
    year end (completeness)
6. Determine whether all long-term debt has been properly valued at year
    end (valuation)

SUMMARY AUDIT PROCEDURES*:
CASH, RECEIVABLES, INVENTORY

	Cash	Receivables	Inventory
Presentation and Disclosure	1. Review disclosures for compliance with GAAP 2. Inquire about compensating balance requirements and restrictions	1. Review disclosures for compliance with GAAP 2. Inquire about pledging, discounting 3. Review loan agreements for pledging, factoring	1. Review disclosures for compliance with GAAP 2. Inquire about pledging 3. Review purchase commitments
Existence or Occurrence	3. Confirmation 4. Count cash on hand 5. Prepare bank transfer schedule	4. Confirmation 5. Inspect notes 6. Vouch (examine shipping documents, invoices, credit memos)	4. Confirmation of consigned inventory and inventory in warehouses 5. Observe inventory count
Rights and Obligations Completeness	6. Review cutoffs (receipts and disbursements) 7. Review passbooks, bank statements 8. Perform analytical procedures 9. Review bank reconciliation 10. Obtain bank cutoff statement to verify reconciling items on bank reconciliation	7. Review cutoffs (sales, sales returns) 8. Inquire about factoring of receivables 9. Perform analytical procedures	6. Review cutoffs (sales, sales returns, purchases, purchase returns) 7. Perform test counts and compare with client's counts/summary 8. Inquire about consigned inventory 9. Perform analytical procedures 10. Account for all inventory tags and count sheets
Valuation	11. Foot summary schedules 12. Reconcile summary schedules to general ledger 13. Test translation of any foreign currencies	10. Foot subsidiary ledger 11. Reconcile subsidiary ledger to general ledger 12. Examine subsequent cash receipts 13. Age receivables to test adequacy of allowance for doubtful accounts 14. Discuss adequacy of allowance for doubtful accounts with management and compare to historical experience	11. Foot and extend summary schedules 12. Reconcile summary schedules to general ledger 13. Test inventory costing method 14. Determine that inventory is valued at lower of cost or market 15. Examine inventory quality (salable condition) 16. Test inventory obsolescence

*Audit procedures are described in detail in Section C.

SUMMARY AUDIT PROCEDURES:
MARKETABLE SECURITIES, PROPERTY, PLANT AND EQUIPMENT, PREPAIDS

	Marketable Securities	Property, Plant, Equipment	Prepaids
Presentation and Disclosure	1. Review disclosures for compliance with GAAP 2. Inquire about pledging 3. Review loan agreements for pledging	1. Review disclosures for compliance with GAAP 2. Inquire about liens and restrictions 3. Review loan agreements for liens and restrictions	1. Review disclosures for compliance with GAAP 2. Review adequacy of insurance coverage
Existence or Occurrence	4. Confirmation of securities held by third parties 5. Inspect and count 6. Vouch (to available documentation)	4. Inspect additions 5. Vouch additions 6. Review any leases for proper accounting 7. Perform search for unrecorded retirements	3. Confirmation of deposits and insurance 4. Vouch (examine) insurance polices (miscellaneous support for deposit)
Rights and Obligations	7. Review cutoffs (examine transactions near year end)	8. Review minutes for proper approval of additions	(See existence or occurrence)
Completeness	8. Perform analytical procedures 9. Reconcile dividends received to published records	9. Perform analytical procedures 10. Vouch major entries to repairs and maintenance expense	5. Perform analytical procedures
Valuation	10. Foot summary schedules 11. Reconcile summary schedules to general ledger 12. Test amortization of premiums and discounts 13. Recompute long- vs. short-term portions 14. Perform lower of cost or market tests 15. Review audited financial statements of major investees	11. Foot summary schedules 12. Reconcile summary schedules to general ledger 13. Recalculate depreciation	6. Foot summary schedules 7. Reconcile summary schedules to general ledger 8. Recalculate prepaid portions

SUMMARY AUDIT PROCEDURES:
PAYABLES (CURRENT), LONG-TERM DEBT, OWNERS' EQUITY

	Payables (Current)	Long-Term Debt	Owners' Equity
Presentation and Disclosure	1. Review disclosures for compliance with GAAP 2. Review purchase commitments	1. Review disclosures for compliance with GAAP 2. Inquire about pledging of assets 3. Review debt agreements for pledging and events causing default	1. Review disclosures for compliance with GAAP 2. Review information on stock options, dividend restrictions
Existence or Occurrence	3. Confirmation 4. Inspect copies of notes and note agreements 5. Vouch payables (examine purchase order, receiving reports, invoices)	4. Confirmation 5. Inspect copies of notes and note agreements 6. Trace receipt of funds (and payment) to bank account and cash receipts journal	3. Confirmation with registrar and transfer agent (if applicable) 4. Inspect stock certificate book (when no registrar or transfer agent) 5. Vouch capital stock entries
Rights and Obligations	6. Review cutoffs (purchases, purchase returns, disbursements)	7. Review cutoffs (examine transactions near year end) 8. Review minutes for proper authorization (and completeness)	6. Review minutes for proper authorization 7. Inquire of legal counsel on legal issues 8. Review articles of incorporation and bylaws for propriety of equity securities
Completeness	7. Perform analytical procedures 8. Perform search for unrecorded payables (examine unrecorded invoices, receiving reports, purchase orders) 9. Inquire of management as to completeness	9. Perform analytical procedures 10. Inquire of management as to completeness 11. Review bank confirmations for unrecorded debt	9. Perform analytical procedures 10. Inspect treasury stock certificates
Valuation	10. Foot subsidiary ledger 11. Reconcile subsidiary ledger to general ledger 12. Recalculate interest expense (if any) 13. For payroll, review year-end accrual 14. Recalculate other accrued liabilities	12. Foot summary schedules 13. Reconcile summary schedules to general ledger 14. Vouch entries to account 15. Recalculate interest expense and accrued interest payable	11. Agree amounts to general ledger 12. Vouch dividend payments 13. Vouch all entries to retained earnings 14. Recalculate treasury stock transactions

Approach for a Program for Areas in which SASs Prescribe Procedures. The following are areas for which the SASs list specific procedures which the auditor is to apply.

Specific Types of Transactions

Illegal Acts	317.08, 317.10- .11
Related Parties	334.07- .10
Litigation (Loss Contingencies)	337.04- .07

Information with which "limited" procedures are required

Other Information in Documents Containing Audited Statements	550.04
Interim Reviews	722.06
Compilations	AR100.12- .13
Reviews	AR100.27

Supplemental Information Required
  by the FASB

General Procedures	553.07

Areas in which "audit" procedures are required

Receivables and Inventories	331.03- .14
Long-Term Investments	332.04- .08
Segment Information	435.04- .07
Subsequent Events	560.10- .12

Other

Other Auditors Involved	543.10- .13
Public Warehouses	901.03, 331.14

While we discuss these areas throughout the various modules, the Summary of Prescribed Audit Procedures: Other Areas (see the following pages) presents lists of the primary procedures for several of the areas for which you may expect an exam question. Do not try to memorize the procedures for each of the areas. Instead, review them well before the exam and then, again, shortly before the exam. Note the similarities within areas of the required procedures. For example, procedures for illegal acts and related parties certainly overlap. Be careful not to cover these topics too "lightly." This is the type of problem for which, without adequate preparation, a candidate may "blank out" and receive little or no credit for his/her solution.

3. Documentation (AU ¶339). Candidates should be familiar with the information in the outline of Section 339 as to the function and types of workpapers, factors affecting the structure and content of workpapers, and the guidelines as to what workpapers should include. You should know the primary objectives of workpapers: (1) to aid in the conduct of the examination; (2) to provide support for the auditor's opinion. Relatedly, the workpapers must document

that the financial statements support the client's records and that the field work standards (PIE--planning, internal control, evidence) have been adhered to.

Additionally, candidates should be aware of the following terms.

Working Trial Balance--A listing of ledger accounts with current year-end balances (as well as last year's ending balances), with columns for adjusting and reclassifying entries as well as for final balances for the current year. Typically both balance sheet and income statement accounts are included.

Lead Schedules--Schedules which summarize like accounts, the total of which is typically transferred to the working trial balance. For example, a client's various cash accounts may be summarized on a lead schedule with only the total cash being transferred to the working trial balance.

Index--The combination of numbers and/or letters given to a workpaper page for identification and organization purposes. For example, cash workpaper may be indexed A-1.

Cross-Reference--When the same information is included on two workpapers, auditors indicate on each workpaper the index of the other workpaper containing the identical information. For example, if Schedule A-1 includes a bank reconciliation with total outstanding checks listed, while Schedule A-2 has a detailed list of these outstanding checks plus the total figure, the totals on the two workpapers will be cross-referenced to one another.

Current Workpaper Files--Files which contain corroborating information pertaining to the current year's audit program (e.g., cash confirmation)

Permanent Workpaper Files--Files which contain information that is expected to be used by the auditor on many future audits of a client (e.g., schedules of ratios by year)

C. **Other Specific Evidence Topics**

1. Cash

    a. Special audit considerations for cash

        (1) Kiting. Kiting is an irregularity that overstates cash by causing it to be simultaneously included in two or more bank accounts. Kiting is possible because a check takes several days to clear the bank on which it is drawn (the "float period"). Following is an example of how kiting can be used to conceal a prior embezzlement in a company that has two bank accounts (one in Valley State Bank and one in First City Bank).

Date	Situation
12/15	Bookkeeper writes himself a $10,000 check on the Valley account, and cashes it--no journal entry is made
12/16	Bookkeeper loses the money gambling in Bullhead City
12/31	Bookkeeper, fearing the auditors will detect the irregularity, conceals the shortage by

SUMMARY OF PRESCRIBED AUDIT

	Illegal Acts	Related Parties-- Identifying Transactions	Related Parties-- Determining Existence
Professional Standard Section	AU 317.08	AU 334.08	AU 334.07
1. Discuss with Management	a. Policies for prevention b. Policies for identifying, evaluating, and accounting c. Inquire as to existence NOTE--Audits do not include procedures designed specifically to detect illegal acts. However, normal audit procedures may bring illegal acts to the auditor's attention.	a. Inquire as to existence	a. Policies for identifying and accounting b. Obtain list of related parties c. Inquire as to existence
2. Examine	a. Consider laws and regulations b. Normal tests of controls (compliance tests) and substantive test examination procedures	a. SEC filings b. Minutes of Board of Directors and others c. Conflict of interest statements	a. SEC filings b. Pensions, other trusts, and identify officers thereof c. Stockholder listings (for closely-held firms) d. Prior year audit workpapers
3. Other Procedures	a. Coordinate with loss contingency procedures b. Consideration of internal control c. Read minutes d. Overall substantive tests e. Include in representation letter	a. Review business with major customers, suppliers, etc. b. Consider services being provided (received) at unreasonable prices c. Review accounting records for large, unusual transactions d. Review confirmations e. Review invoices from lawyers f. Consideration of internal control g. Provide audit personnel with names of known related parties	a. Contact predecessor and other auditors b. Review material investment transactions c. Know that such transactions are more likely for firms in financial difficulty

PROCEDURES: OTHER AREAS

Litigation, Claims, and Assessments	Segment Information	Required Supplemental Information	Subsequent Events
AU 337.05-.07	AU 435.05-.07	AU 553.07	AU 560.10-12
a. Policies for identifying, evaluating, and accounting for b. Obtain description	a. Methods for determining segments b. Basis of accounting for sales/transfers between segments c. Methods for allocations d. Consistency with prior periods	a. Measurement methods, significant assumptions, consistency with prior periods	a. Contingent liabilities b. Significant changes in capital stock, debt, working capital c. Current status of estimated items d. Unusual items after balance sheet date
a. Correspondence & invoices from lawyers b. Minutes--stockholders, directors, others c. Read contracts, agreements, etc. d. Other documents	a. FASB 14 requirements	a. Compare with financial statements and other information	a. Latest interim statements b. Minutes of stockholders, directors, etc.

a. Letters of audit inquiry to client's lawyers	a. Evaluate FASB % rule compliance
	b. Analytical procedures:
	  1. compare to last year
	  2. compare to budget
	  3. study overall relationships
		a. Add to representation letter
		b. Perform further inquiries if information seems incorrect
		c. Apply any other required procedures for specific area being considered
			a. Include in representation letter
			b. Coordinate with loss contingency procedures
			c. Cutoff procedures (sales, purchases)

1. Writing a $10,000 unrecorded check on First City account and depositing it in the Valley account. This will cover up the shortage because Valley will credit the account for the $10,000, and the check will not clear the First City account until January--no journal entry is made until after year end
2. When the First City bank reconciliation is prepared at 12/31, the check is not listed as outstanding.

Kiting may be detected by preparing a bank transfer schedule, by preparing a four column bank reconciliation for the First City account, or by obtaining a cutoff statement for the First City account.

(2) Bank Transfer Schedule. A bank transfer schedule shows the dates of all transfers of cash among the client's various bank accounts. Know that its primary purpose is to help auditors to detect kiting. The schedule is prepared by using bank statements for the periods before and after year end and by using the firm's cash receipts and disbursements journals. The following is an example of a bank transfer schedule which will help an auditor to detect the kiting described in (1) above:

		Date			Date	
Amount	Bank Drawn on	Books	Bank	Bank Deposited in	Books	Bank
$10,000	First City	1/2	1/2	Valley	1/2	12/31

Note that analysis of the schedule reveals that at December 31, the cash is double counted: it is included in both the Valley account (the bank gave credit for the deposit on 12/31) and in the First City account.

(3) Bank Reconciliations. Auditors generally prepare either a two or a four column bank reconciliation for the difference between the cash per bank and per books. The four column approach (also called a proof of cash) will allow the auditor to reconcile:

(a) all cash receipts and disbursements recorded on the books to those on the bank statement and
(b) all deposits and disbursements recorded on the bank statement to the books.

A four column reconciliation will not allow the auditor to verify whether:

(a) checks written have been for the wrong amounts and so recorded on both the books and the bank statement and
(b) unrecorded check or deposits exist that have not cleared the bank.

In the earlier kiting example, note that the Valley four column reconciliation will detect the kiting because the 12/15 credit for the check used in the embezzlement will have been included in the Valley bank statement disbursements, but not on the books as of 12/31. This is because the embezzlement will result in a $10,000 unreconciled difference between the book and bank totals in the disbursements column of the reconciliation. The First City reconciliation, by itself, will not assist in detection of the kiting because both book and bank entries occur after year end.

(4) <u>Bank cutoff statements</u>. A cutoff statement is a bank statement for the first 8-10 business days after year end. Know that is primary purpose is to help auditors to <u>verify reconciling items</u> on the year-end bank reconciliation. Tests performed using a cutoff statement include verifying that outstanding checks have been completely and accurately recorded as of year end, and that deposits in transit have cleared within a reasonable period. The statement is sent directly by the bank to the auditor. In the above kiting example, the cutoff statement for the First City account will allow the auditor to detect the irregularity since it will include the December 31 unrecorded check.

b. <u>Typical substantive audit procedures for cash</u>

(1) <u>Review disclosures for compliance with generally accepted accounting principles.</u>

(2) <u>Inquire of management concerning compensating balance requirements and restrictions on cash</u>. A compensating balance is an account with a bank in which a company has agreed to maintain a specified minimum amount; compensating balances are typically required under the terms of bank loan agreements. Such restrictions on cash, when material, should be disclosed in the financial statements.

(3) <u>Send confirmation letters to banks</u> to verify the amounts on deposit. A standard confirmation form is currently sent to all banks with which the client deals. Also, be aware that the form asks for replies from the bank as to <u>loans outstanding, contingent liabilities</u>, and <u>various security agreements</u> under the Uniform Commercial Code. The confirmation letter is mailed to the bank by the auditor.

(4) <u>Count cash on hand at year end</u> to verify its existence.

(5) <u>Prepare a bank transfer schedule for the last week of the audit year and the first week of the following year</u> to disclose misstatements of cash balances resulting from <u>kiting</u>. See section "a" above.

(6) <u>Review the cutoff of cash receipts and cash disbursements around year end</u> to verify that transactions affecting cash are recorded in the proper period.

(7) <u>Review passbooks and bank statements</u> to verify that book balances represent amounts to which the client has rights.

(8) <u>Perform analytical procedures</u> to test the reasonableness of cash balances. Tests here may include comparisons to prior year cash balances.

(9) <u>Review year-end bank reconciliations</u> to verify that cash has been properly stated as of year end. See section "a" above.

(10) <u>Obtain a bank cutoff statement</u> to verify whether the reconciling items on the year-end bank reconciliation have been properly reflected. See section "a" above.

(11) <u>Foot summary schedules of cash and agree their total to the amount which will appear on the financial statements.</u>

(12) <u>Reconcile summary schedules of cash to the general ledger.</u>

(13) <u>Test translation of any foreign currencies.</u>

2. Receivables (AU 331.03 - .08)

    a. Special audit considerations for receivables

        (1) Lapping. Lapping is an embezzlement scheme in which cash
             collections from customers are stolen and the shortage is concealed
             by delaying the recording of subsequent cash receipts. A
             simplified lapping scheme is shown below.

Date	Situation	Bookkeeping Entry		
1/7	Jones pays $500 on account	No entry, bookkeeper cashes check and keeps proceeds		
1/8	Smith pays $200 on account	Cash	500	
		Accounts Receivable--Jones		500
	Adam pays $300 on account			
1/9	Brock pays $500 on account	Cash	500	
		Accounts Receivable--Smith		200
		Accounts Receivable--Adams		300
1/10	Bookkeeper determines Brock is unlikely to purchase from company in the future	Allowance for Doubtful Accts.	500	
		Accounts Receivable--Brock		500

Lapping most frequently occurs when one individual has
responsibility for both recordkeeping and custody of cash.
Although the best way to control lapping is to segregate duties and
thereby make its occurrence difficult, it may be detected by using
the following procedures:

(a) Analytical procedures--calculate age of receivables and
     turnover of receivables (lapping increases the age and
     decreases turnover)

(b) Confirm receivables--investigate all exceptions noted,
     emphasize accounts that have been written off and old
     accounts. For all accounts watch for postings of cash
     receipts which have taken an unusually long time. For
     example, when a reply to a confirmation suggests that the
     account was paid on December 29, investigate when the posting
     occurred.

(c) Deposit slips

     1] Obtain authenticated deposit slips from bank and compare
         names, dates, and amounts on remittance advices to
         information on deposit slips (where possible)

     2] Perform surprise inspection of deposits, and compare
         deposit slip with remittances

(d) Bookkeeping system

     1] Compare remittance advices with information recorded
     2] Verify propriety of noncash credits to accounts receivable
     3] Foot cash receipts journal, customers' ledger accounts,
         and accounts receivable control account
     4] Reconcile individual customer accounts to accounts
         receivable control account

> 5] Compare copies of monthly statements with customer accounts

(2) <u>Confirmations</u>. Review the outline of AU 331.03–.08. Confirmations are a generally accepted auditing procedure and a CPA must be able to justify a decision not to use them. Confirmations are used to test the <u>existence</u> assertion, and only to a limited extent the <u>valuation</u> assertion. Know the difference between <u>positive</u> and <u>negative</u> confirmations as well as when each is to be used.

Positive confirmations request a reply from debtors, regardless of whether a debtor agrees with the amount on the confirmation. Negative confirmations only require a response when the debtor disagrees with the amount on the confirmation. In both cases the auditor mails the confirmation to the debtors who are asked to reply directly to the auditors.

AU 331 suggests use of the <u>positive</u> form
  (a) for large accounts and
  (b) when a large number of accounts with errors are expected

AU 331 states that the <u>negative</u> form is useful
  (a) when there is good internal control
  (b) for accounts with small dollar balances, and
  (c) when those receiving the confirmations are expected to give them adequate consideration.

Note that when no reply is received to a negative confirmation the assumption is made that the debtor agrees that s/he owes the amount on the confirmation. When no reply is received to a positive confirmation a second request is normally mailed to the debtor; if no reply to the second request is still received, the auditor performs alternate procedures (e.g., examination of shipping documents, subsequent cash receipts, sales agreements).

b. <u>Typical substantive audit procedures for receivables</u>

(1) <u>Review disclosures for compliance with generally accepted accounting principles.</u>

(2) <u>Inquire of management about pledging, or discounting of receivables</u> to verify that appropriate disclosure is provided.

(3) <u>Review loan agreements for pledging and factoring of receivables</u> to verify that appropriate disclosure is provided.

(4) <u>Confirm accounts and notes receivable by direct communication with debtors</u> to verify the existence of the accounts. See "a" above.

(5) <u>Inspect notes on hand and confirm those not on hand by direct communication with holders.</u> For notes receivable, the auditor will generally be able to inspect the actual note. This procedure is particularly important in situations in which the note is negotiable (i.e., salable) to third parties.

(6) <u>Vouch receivables to supporting customer orders, sales orders, invoices, shipping documents and credit memos</u> to verify the existence of accounts.

(7) <u>Review the cutoff of sales and cash receipts around year end</u> to verify that transactions affecting accounts receivable are recorded

in the proper period. A sale is properly recorded when title passes on the items being sold. Title passes for items sold FOB shipping point when the item is shipped from inventory; title passes for items sold FOB destination when the item is received by the purchaser. You should realize that a proper credit sales cutoff generally affects at least four components of the financial statements: accounts receivable, sales, cost of goods sold, and inventory. Cash receipts should be recorded when the check (or cash) is received from a customer.

(8) <u>Inquire about factoring of receivables</u> to verify that the client maintains rights to the accounts.

(9) <u>Perform analytical procedures for accounts receivable, sales, notes receivable, and interest revenue.</u> Typical ratios include: (a) the gross profit rate, (b) accounts receivable turnover, (c) the ratio of accounts receivable to credit sales, (d) the ratio of accounts written off to the ending accounts receivable, and (e) the ratio of interest revenue to notes receivable.

(10) <u>Foot the accounts and notes receivable subsidiary ledgers</u> to verify clerical accuracy.

(11) <u>Reconcile subsidiary ledgers to the general ledger control accounts</u> to verify clerical accuracy.

(12) <u>Examine cash receipts subsequent to year end</u> to test the adequacy of the allowance for doubtful accounts.

(13) <u>Age accounts receivable</u> to test the adequacy of the allowance for doubtful accounts. An <u>aging schedule</u> is used to address the receivable <u>valuation</u> assertion. Such a schedule summarizes receivables by their age (e.g., 0-30 days since sale, 31-60 days since sale...). Estimates of the likely amount of bad debts in each age group are then made (typically based on historical experience) to estimate whether the amount in the allowance for doubtful accounts is adequate at year end.

(14) <u>Discuss the adequacy of the allowance for doubtful accounts with management and the credit department and compare it to historical experience</u> to verify valuation.

3. <u>Inventory (AU 331.09-.13)</u>

   a. <u>Special audit consideration for inventory</u>

     (1) <u>Observation.</u> Observation by the auditor of the client's counting of inventory (which primarily addresses the <u>existence</u> assertion) is a generally accepted auditing procedure and departure from it must be justified. You should be familiar with various situations that may affect the auditor's observation:

      (a) When a client uses statistical methods in determining inventory quantities, the auditor must be satisfied that the sampling plan has statistical validity.

      (b) The existence of good internal control may allow an effective count to be made prior to year end. In such circumstances, the auditor will rely upon the internal control structure and tests of updating of inventory through year end to determine that year-end inventory is properly stated.

      (c)   For a first-year client the auditor will probably not have been present for the count of the beginning inventory, a necessary input to determining cost of goods sold. If adequate evidence is available (e.g., acceptable predecessor workpapers), no report modification may be necessary. When adequate evidence is not available, the auditor may be required to qualify his/her audit report due to the scope limitation. Any resulting misstatement affects both current and prior year income and is therefore likely to result in qualification of the opinion on the income statement. The balance sheet at year end will be unaffected due to the self-correcting nature of such an error.

      (d)   Related to (c), a first-year client may have engaged the auditor subsequent to year end and the auditor may also have missed the year-end inventory count. In addition, other events may make it impossible for the auditor to be present for the client's count of inventory. In such circumstances, alternate procedures may sometimes be used to establish the accuracy of the count (e.g., good internal control); however, these alternate procedures <u>must include some physical counts of inventory items</u> and must include appropriate tests of intervening transactions.

b. <u>Typical substantive audit procedures for inventory</u>

    (1) <u>Review disclosures for compliance with generally accepted accounting principles</u>.

    (2) <u>Inquire of management about pledging of inventory</u> and verify the adequacy of disclosure.

    (3) <u>Review purchase and sales commitments</u> to verify whether there may be a need to either accrue a loss and/or provide disclosure. Generally, commitments are not disclosed in the financial statements unless uneconomic commitments result in a need to accrue significant losses (due to current price changes).

    (4) <u>Confirm consigned inventory and inventory in warehouses</u>. Some companies store inventory items in public warehouses. In such a situation, the auditor should <u>confirm</u> in writing with the custodian that the goods are being held. Additionally, if such holdings are significant, the auditor should apply one or more of the following procedures:

      (a)   Review the client's control procedures relating to the warehouseman

      (b)   Obtain a CPA's report on the warehouseman's internal control structure

      (c)   Observe physical counts of the goods

      (d)   If warehouse receipts have been pledged as collateral, confirm with lenders details of the pledged receipts

    (5) <u>Observe the taking of the physical inventory and make text counts</u> to verify the existence (and to a limited extent the ownership) of inventory. See "a" above.

    (6) <u>Review cutoffs of sales, sales returns, purchases, and purchase returns around year end</u> to verify that transactions affecting inventory are recorded in the proper period. Know here that the

objective is to include in inventory those items for which the client has legal title.

(7) Perform test counts during the observation of the taking of the inventory and compare them to the client's counts and subsequently to the accumulated inventory to verify the accuracy of the count and its accumulation. See "a" above.

(8) Inquire of management as to the existence of consigned inventory to verify the adequacy of its disclosure. Know that inventory consigned out remains the property of the client until it is sold. Inventory consigned to the client must not be included in the physical count since it belongs to the consignor.

(9) Perform analytical procedures to test the reasonableness of inventory. Analytical procedures include calculation of gross profit margins by product, and inventory turnover rates.

(10) Account for all inventory tags and count sheets to verify that inventory has been completely recorded.

(11) Foot and extend summary inventory schedules to verify clerical accuracy.

(12) Reconcile inventory summary schedules to the general ledger to verify clerical accuracy.

(13) Test the inventory cost method to verify that it is in conformity with generally accepted accounting principles. Here the auditor will determine the method of pricing used and whether it is acceptable and consistent with the prior years--e.g., LIFO, FIFO.

(14) Test the pricing of inventory to verify that it is valued at the lower of cost or market. As a general rule, inventories should not be carried in excess of their net realizable value. In certain circumstances a specialist may be needed to assist in valuation of inventory (see section 12, Using the Work of a Specialist, below).

(15) Examine inventory quality and condition to assess whether there may be evidence suggesting that it is in unsatisfactory condition.

(16) Perform any necessary additional tests of inventory obsolescence to verify the valuation of inventory.

4. Marketable Securities (AU 332)
   (Review outline of AU 332 at this point)

   a. Special audit considerations for marketable securities

      (1) GAAP Requirements. Recall the criteria for deciding whether the cost, equity, or consolidated basis should be used for the investments (see outline of APB 18 and SFAS 94). Also recall the distinction in accounting treatment for applying the lower of cost or market valuation rule for long-term vs. short-term investments in marketable equity securities.

      (2) Audit Approach. Evidence related to the existence assertion is obtained by inspecting any securities that are held by a client (often in a safe deposit box) and by confirming securities held by third parties (e.g., a bank). A client employee should be present during the inspection to avoid confusion over any missing securities. In examining the security certificates, the auditor

determines whether securities held are identical to the recorded securities (certificate numbers, number of shares, fact value, etc.).

Evidence pertaining to <u>valuation</u> (carrying amount) for long-term investments for an investee may be obtained by examining investee (a) audited financial statements, (b) unaudited financial statements [insufficient evidence in and of itself] (c) market quotations, and (d) other evidential matter.

(3) <u>Simultaneous verification</u>. Because of the liquid nature of securities, the auditor's inspection is generally performed at year end simultaneously with the audit of cash, bank loans (e.g., a revolving credit agreement), and other related items.

b. <u>Typical substantive audit procedures for marketable securities</u>

(1) <u>Review disclosures for compliance with generally accepted accounting principles</u>.

(2) <u>Inquire of management about pledging of marketable securities</u> and verify that appropriate disclosure is provided.

(3) <u>Review loan agreements for pledging of marketable securities</u> and verify that appropriate disclosure is provided.

(4) <u>Obtain confirmation of securities in the custody of others</u> to verify their existence.

(5) <u>Inspect and count securities on hand and compare serial numbers with those shown on the records and, if appropriate, with prior year audit working papers</u>. This procedure addresses the existence of the securities and provides evidence that no irregularity involving "substitution" (e.g., unauthorized sale and subsequent repurchase) of securities has occurred during the year. When an auditor is unable to inspect and count securities held in a safe deposit box at a bank until after the balance sheet date, a bank representative should be asked to confirm that there has been no access between the balance sheet date and the security count date.

(6) <u>Vouch purchases and sales of securities during the year</u>. This audit procedure will provide evidence relating to all financial statement assertions. Included here will be recomputation of gains and losses on security sales.

(7) <u>Review the cutoff of cash receipts and disbursements around year end</u> to verify that transactions affecting marketable securities transactions are recorded in the proper period.

(8) <u>Perform analytical procedures</u> to test the reasonableness of marketable securities. A typical analytical procedure is to verify the relationship between interest and dividend income to the securities.

(9) <u>Reconcile amounts of dividends received to published dividend records</u>.

(10) <u>Foot and extend summary marketable security schedules</u> to verify clerical accuracy.

(11) <u>Reconcile summary inventory schedules to the general ledger</u> to verify clerical accuracy.

(12) <u>Test amortization of premiums and discounts</u> to verify that investments are properly valued.

(13) <u>Recompute the long- vs. short-term portion of marketable securities</u> to verify their propriety.

(14) <u>Determine the market value of securities at the date of the balance sheet</u> and perform lower of cost or market tests.

(15) <u>Review audited financial statements of major investments</u> to test whether they are properly valued at year end.

5. <u>Property, Plant, and Equipment (PP&E)</u>

   a. <u>Special audit considerations for PP&E</u>

     (1) <u>Accounting considerations.</u> Many PP&E acquisitions involve trades of used assets. Recall APB 29 which requires that no gain be recognized when a plant asset is exchanged for a similar plant asset; gains are properly recognized for dissimilar trades.

        Assets constructed by a company for its own use should be recorded at the cost of direct material, direct labor, and applicable overhead. Recall that interest may be capitalized.

     (2) <u>Overall approach.</u> The reasonableness of the entire account balance must be audited in detail for a client that has not previously been audited. When a predecessor auditor exists, the successor will normally review that auditor's work papers.

        For a continuing audit client, the audit of PP&E consists largely of an analysis of the year's acquisitions and disposals (an input and output approach). Subsequent to the first year, the account's slow rate of turnover generally permits effective auditing of the account in less time than accounts of comparable size.

     (3) <u>Relationship with Repairs and Maintenance.</u> A number of CPA questions address this area. A PP&E acquisition may improperly be recorded in the repair and maintenance expense account. Therefore, an analysis of repairs and maintenance may detect <u>understatements</u> of PP&E. Alternatively, an analysis of PP&E may disclose repairs and maintenance that have improperly been capitalized, thereby resulting in <u>overstatements</u> of PP&E.

     (4) <u>Unrecorded retirements.</u> Disposals may occur due to retirements or thefts of PP&E items. Simple retirements of equipment are often difficult to detect since no journal entry may have been recorded to reflect the event. Unrecorded or improperly recorded retirements (and thefts) may be discovered through examination of changes in insurance policies, consideration of the purpose of recorded acquisition, examination of property tax files, discussions, observation, or through an examination of debits to accumulated depreciation and of credits to miscellaneous revenue accounts. Inquiry of the plant manager may disclose unrecorded retirements and/or obsolete equipment.

   b. <u>Typical substantive audit procedures for PP&E</u>

     (1) <u>Review disclosures for compliance with generally accepted accounting principles.</u>

(2) Inquire of management concerning any liens and restrictions on PP&E. PP&E may be pledged as security on a loan agreement. Such restrictions are disclosed in the notes to the financial statements.

(3) Review loan agreements for liens and restrictions on PP&E and verify that appropriate disclosure is provided.

(4) Inspect major acquisitions of PP&E to verify their existence.

(5) Vouch additions and retirements to PP&E to verify their existence and the client's rights to them. Typically large PP&E transactions support will include original documents such as contracts, deeds, construction work orders, invoices, and authorization by the directors.

(6) Review any leases for proper accounting to determine whether the related PP&E assets should be capitalized.

(7) Perform search for unrecorded retirements and for obsolete equipment. See "a" above.

(8) Review minutes of the board of directors (and shareholders) to verify that additions have been properly approved.

(9) Perform analytical procedures to test the reasonableness of PP&E. Typical analytical procedures involved a (a) comparision of total cost of PP&E divided by cost of goods sold, (b) comparison of repairs and maintenance on a monthly and annual basis (c) comparison of acquisitions and retirements for the current year with prior years.

(10) Obtain or prepare an analysis of repairs and maintenance expense and vouch transactions to discover items that should have been capitalized. See "a" above.

(11) Foot PP&E summary schedules to verify clerical accuracy.

(12) Reconcile summary PP&E schedules to the general ledger to verify clerical accuracy.

(13) Recalculate depreciation to verify its clerical accuracy. In addition, the existence of recurring losses on retired assets may indicate that depreciation charges are generally insufficient.

6. Prepaid Assets

  a. Special audit considerations for prepaid assets

   (1) Overall. Prepaid assets typically consist of items such as insurance and deposits. Insurance policies may be examined and the prepaid portion of any expenditure may be recalculated. Additionally, policies may be confirmed with the company's insurance agent and/or payments may be vouched. Deposits and other prepaid amounts are typically immaterial. When they are considered material, an auditor may confirm their existence, recalculate prepaid portions, and examine any available support.

   (2) Self-insurance. The lack of insurance on a asset (or inadequate insurance) will not typically result in report modification, although this may be disclosed in the notes to the financial statements. Also, an auditor may serve an advisory role by pointing out assets which, unknown to management, may have inadequate insurance.

b. Typical substantive audit procedures for prepaid assets

(1) Review disclosures for compliance with generally accepted accounting principles.

(2) Review the adequacy of insurance coverage.

(3) Confirm deposits and insurance with third party to verify their existence.

(4) Vouch additions to accounts (examine insurance policies and miscellaneous other support for deposit) to verify existence.

(5) Perform analytical procedures to test the reasonableness of prepaid assets. A primary procedure here is comparison with prior year balances and obtaining explanations for any significant changes.

(6) Foot prepaid summary schedules to verify clerical accuracy.

(7) Reconcile summary schedules to the general ledger to verify proper valuation.

(8) Recalculate prepaid portions of prepaid assets to verify proper valuation.

7. Payables (Current)

a. Special audit considerations for payables

(1) Confirmation. Confirmations may be sent to vendors. However, such confirmation procedures are sometimes omitted due to the availability of externally generated evidence (e.g., both purchase agreements and vendors' invoices) and due to the inability of confirmations to adequately address the completeness assertion. (Auditors are primarily concerned about the possibility of understated payables; a major payable will not in general be confirmed if the client completely omits it from the trial balance of payables).

Accounts payable confirmations are most frequently used in circumstances involving (1) bad internal control, (2) bad financial position, and (3) situations when vendors do not send month-end statements. However, when an auditor has chosen to confirm payables despite the existence of vendor statements, the confirmation will generally request the vendor to send the month-end statement to the auditor. For this reason, the balance per the client's books is not included on such a confirmation.

Confirmations are sent to (1) major suppliers, (2) disputed accounts, and (3) a sample of other suppliers. Major suppliers are selected because they represent a possible source of large understatement: the client will normally have established large credit lines. The size of the recorded payable at year end is of less importance than for receivables. While as a practical matter large year-end recorded balances will normally be confirmed, the emphasis on detecting understated payables may lead the auditor to also confirm accounts with relatively low recorded year-end balances.

(2) The search for unrecorded liabilities. The search for unrecorded liabilities is an effort to discover any liabilities which may have been omitted from recorded year-end payables. Typical procedures include the following.

(a) Examination of vendors' invoices and statements both immediately prior to and following year end.

      (b) Examination, <u>after year end</u>, of the following to test whether proper cutoffs have occurred:

         1.] Cash disbursements
         2.] Purchases
         3.] Unrecorded vouchers (receiving reports, vendor's invoices, purchase orders)

      (c) Analytical procedures
      (d) The internal control structure is analyzed to evaluate its likely effectiveness in preventing and detecting the occurrence of such errors.

  b. <u>Typical substantive audit procedures for payables</u>

    (1) <u>Review disclosures for compliance with generally accepted accounting principles.</u>
    (2) <u>Review purchase commitments</u> to determine whether there may be a need to either accrue a loss and/or provide disclosure (see also step 3 of inventory program).
    (3) <u>Confirm accounts payable by direct correspondence with vendors.</u> Confirmation of payables provides evidence relating to the occurrence, obligation, completeness, and valuation assertions. See "a" above.
    (4) <u>Inspect copies of notes and note agreements.</u>
    (5) <u>Vouch balances payable to selected creditors by inspecting purchase orders, receiving reports, and invoices.</u>
    (6) <u>Review the cutoff of purchases, purchase returns, and disbursements around year end</u> to verify that transactions are recorded in the proper period.
    (7) <u>Perform analytical procedures</u> to test the reasonableness of payables. Examples here are ratios such as accounts payable divided by purchases, and accounts payable divided by total current liabilities.
    (8) <u>Perform search for unrecorded payables</u> to determine whether liabilities have been completely recorded. See "a" above.
    (9) <u>Inquire of management as to the completeness of payables.</u>
  (10) <u>Foot the subsidiary accounts payable ledger</u> to test clerical accuracy.
  (11) <u>Reconcile the subsidiary ledger to the general ledger control account</u> to verify clerical accuracy.
  (12) <u>Recalculate interest expense on interest bearing debt.</u>
  (13) <u>Recalculate year-end accrual for payroll.</u> A typical procedure here is to allocate the total days in the payroll subsequent to year end between the old and new years and to determine whether the accrual is reasonable.
  (14) <u>Recalculate other accrued liabilities.</u> The approach for accruals is largely one of (1) testing computations made by the client in setting up the accrual and (2) determining that the accruals have been treated consistently with the past. Note that the audit approach here is somewhat different than for accounts payable which, because one or more transactions usually directly indicate the year-end liability, do not require such a computation. Examples of accounts requiring accrual include property taxes, pension plans, vacation pay, service guarantees, commissions, and income taxes payable.

8. Long-Term Debt

   a. Special audit considerations for long-term debt

      (1) Overall approach. Despite the fact that this account's turnover rate is low, considerable analysis is performed on its ending balance. Confirmations are frequently used; recall that when the debt is owed to banks, confirmation is obtained with the standard bank confirmation. In addition, minutes of director and/or stockholder meetings will be reviewed to determine whether new borrowings have properly authorized.

      The proceeds of any new borrowings are traced to the cash receipts journal, deposit slips, and bank statements. Repayments are traced to the cash disbursements journal, canceled checks, and canceled notes. If a debt trustee is used, it will be possible to obtain information through use of a confirmation whether the repayments have been made.

   b. Typical substantive audit procedures for long-term debt

      (1) Review disclosures for compliance with generally accepted accounting principles.
      (2) Inquire of management concerning pledging of assets related to debt.
      (3) Review debt agreements for details on pledged assets and for events which may result in default on the loan.
      (4) Confirm long-term debt with payees or appropriate third parties.
      (5) Obtain and inspect copies of debt agreements to verify whether provisions have been met and disclosed.
      (6) Trace receipt of funds (and payments) to the bank account and to the cash receipts journal to verify that the funds were properly received (or disbursed) by the company.
      (7) Review the cutoff of cash receipts and disbursements around year end to verify that transactions affecting debt are recorded in the proper period.
      (8) Review minutes of board of directors and/or shareholders to verify that transactions have been properly authorized.
      (9) Perform analytical procedures to verify the overall reasonableness of long-term debt and interest expense.
      (10) Inquire of management as to the completeness of debt.
      (11) Review bank confirmation for any indication of unrecorded debt.
      (12) Foot summary schedules of long-term debt to test clerical accuracy.
      (13) Reconcile summary schedules of long-term debt to the general ledger to verify clerical accuracy.
      (14) Vouch entries in long-term debt accounts.
      (15) Recalculate interest expense and accrued interest payable.

9. Owners' Equity

   a. Special audit considerations for owner's equity

      (1) Control of capital stock transactions. Clients use one of two approaches for capital stock transactions. First, a stock certificate book may be used which summarizes shares issued through use of "stubs" which remain after a certificate has been removed. The certificates for outstanding shares are held by the stockholders; canceled certificates (for repurchased stock or received when a change in stock ownership occurs) are held by the

client. When a stock certificate book is used auditors reconcile outstanding shares, par value, etc., with the "stubs" in the book. Confirmations are sometimes sent to stockholders.

The second approach, typically used by large clients, is to engage a transfer agent and registrar to manage the company's stock transactions. In such cases the number of shares authorized, issued, and outstanding will usually be confirmed to the auditor directly by the transfer agent and registrar.

(2) Retained earnings. Little effort will be exerted in auditing the retained earnings of a continued client. The audit procedures for dividends will allow the auditor to verify the propriety of that debit to retained earnings. The entry to record the year's net income (loss) is readily available. Finally, the nature of any prior period adjustments is examined to determine whether they meet the criteria for an adjustment to retained earnings. Recall that the type of adjustment typically encountered is a correction of prior years' income.

b. Typical substantive audit procedures for stockholders' equity

(1) Review disclosures for compliance with generally accepted accounting principles.

(2) Review articles of incorporation, bylaws, and minutes for provisions relating to stock options, and dividends restriction.

(3) Confirm stocks authorized, issued, and outstanding with the independent registrar and stock transfer agent (if applicable).

(4) For a corporation which acts as its own stock registrar and transfer agent, reconcile the stock certificate book to transactions recorded in the general ledger.

(5) Vouch transactions and trace receipt of funds (and payment) to the bank account and to the cash receipts journal to verify that the funds were properly received (or disbursed) by the company.

(6) Review minutes of the board of directors and/or shareholders to verify that stock transactions have been properly authorized.

(7) Inquire of the client's legal counsel to obtain information concerning any unresolved legal issues.

(8) Review the articles of incorporation, and bylaws for the propriety of equity transactions.

(9) Perform analytical procedures to test the reasonableness of dividends.

(10) Inspect treasury stock certificates to verify that transactions have been completely recorded and that client has control of certificates.

(11) Agree amounts which will appear on the financial statements to the general leger.

(12) Vouch dividend payments to verify that amounts have been paid.

(13) Vouch all entries affecting retained earnings.

(14) Recalculate treasury stock transactions.

10. Engagement letters. Engagement letters are essentially contracts that document and confirm the auditor's acceptance of the appointment, outline the objectives and scope of the audit, outline the extent of auditor responsibility to the client, and indicate the form of report to be issued by the auditor. Engagement letters are recommended on both audits and

reviews and should be issued each year to new and existing clients. While the Auditing Standards Board has not issued a sample engagement letter, the following list includes some important factors to be included in an engagement letter.

a. Confirmation that an audit or review is to be performed (as well as any other services)
b. Period under examination
c. Financial statements to be examined or reviewed
d. Set of standards the work is to be performed in accordance with (e.g., GAAS)
e. Form of the report to be issued
f. Appropriate tests and procedures to be performed
g. Details of responsibility to detect errors and irregularities
h. Management's responsibility for preparing the financial statements
i. Fee and billing arrangements
j. Copy of the letter is included for the client to sign and return to the auditor if the terms are agreeable
k. Signature of the auditor
l. Date of the letter

11. <u>Client Representation Letters (AU ¶333)</u>. Review the outline and note that representation letters are required for audits. Representation letters, while <u>not a substitute for other audit procedures</u>, ordinarily confirm oral representations which have been made by management to the auditor and thereby reduce the likelihood of misunderstandings. They are to be signed by the chief executive officer and the chief financial officer at the close of the audit (dated last day of significant field work). Management refusal to provide such written representation is a limitation on the scope of the audit sufficient to preclude an unqualified opinion. Although the exact content of the letter varies by engagement, the following is a sample representation letter.

(Date of Auditor's Report)

(To Independent Auditor)

    In connection with your examination of the (identification of financial statements) of (name of client) as of (date) and for the (period of examination) for the purpose of expressing an opinion as to whether the (consolidated) financial statements present fairly the financial position, results of operations, and cash flows of (name of client) in conformity with generally accepted accounting principles (other comprehensive basis of accounting), we confirm, to the best of our knowledge and belief, the following representations made to you during your examination.

1. We are responsible for the fair presentation in the (consolidated) financial statements of financial position, results of operations, and cash flows in conformity with generally accepted accounting principles (other comprehensive basis of accounting).

2. We have made available to you all
   a. Financial records and related data.
   b. Minutes of the meetings of stockholders, directors, and committees of directors, or summaries of actions of recent meetings for which minutes have not yet been prepared.

3. There have been no
   a. Irregularities involving management or employees who have significant roles in the internal control structure.
   b. Irregularities involving other employees that could have a material effect on the financial statements.
   c. Communications from regulatory agencies concerning noncompliance with, or deficiencies in, financial reporting practices that could have a material effect on the financial statements.

4. We have no plans or intentions that may materially affect the carrying value or classification of assets and liabilities.

5. The following have been properly recorded or disclosed in the financial statements:
   a. Related party transactions and related amounts receivable or payable, including sales, purchases, loans, transfers, leasing arrangements, and guarantees.
   b. Capital stock repurchase options or agreements or capital stock reserved for options, warrants, conversions, or other requirements.
   c. Arrangements with financial institutions involving compensating balances or other arrangements involving restrictions on cash balances and line-of-credit or similar arrangements.
   d. Agreements to repurchase assets previously sold.

6. There are no
   a. Violations or possible violations of laws or regulations whose effects should be considered for disclosure in the financial statements or as a basis for recording a loss contingency.
   b. Other material liabilities or gain or loss contingencies that are required to be accrued or disclosed by Statement of Financial Accounting Standards No. 5.

7. There are no unasserted claims or assessments that our lawyer has advised us are probable of assertion and must be disclosed in accordance with Statement of Financial Accounting Standards No. 5.

8. There are no material transactions that have not been properly recorded in the accounting records underlying the financial statements.

9. Provision, when material, has been made to reduce excess or obsolete inventories to their estimated net realizable value.

10. The company has satisfactory title to all owned assets, and there are no liens or encumbrances on such assets nor has any asset been pledged.

11. Provision has been made for any material loss to be sustained in the fulfillment of, or from inability to fulfill, any sales commitments.

12. Provision has been made for any material loss to be sustained as a result of purchase commitments for inventory quantities in excess of normal requirements or at prices in excess of the prevailing market prices.

13. We have complied with all aspects of contractual agreements that would have a material effect on the financial statements in the event of noncompliance.

14. No events have occurred subsequent to the balance sheet date that would require adjustment to, or disclosure in, the financial statements.

(Name of Chief Executive   (Name of Chief Financial
Officer and Title)   Officer and Title)

(Section 333, Appendix)

12. Using the Work of a Specialist (AU ¶336). Read the outline and note especially that the auditor may use the work of a specialist in cases such as the valuation of inventory. The specialist is not referred to in the

audit report unless his/her report is the basis for an opinion other than unqualified.

13.   <u>Inquiry of a Client's Lawyer (AU ¶337)</u>.   Read the key points in the outline as well as the summary table in Section "B.2." of this module.   The client's lawyer is the primary source for corroboration of information obtained from the client concerning loss contingencies.   Therefore, the client prepares a list and describes claims, litigation, assessments, and unasserted claims pending against the firm.   This information is sent by the auditor to the attorney who is to review it and provide additional input, if possible.

Refusal of the lawyer to reply is a scope limitation which may affect the audit report.   If the lawyer is unable to estimate the effect of litigation, claims, and assessments on the financial statements, it may result in an uncertainty that would also have an effect on the audit report. In the case of unasserted claims which the client has not disclosed, the lawyer is <u>not</u> required to note them in his/her reply to the auditor. However, the lawyer is generally required to inform the client of the omission and to consider withdrawing if the client fails to inform the auditor.   The following is a sample lawyer's letter.

In connection with an examination of our financial statements at (balance sheet date) and for the (period) then ended, management of the Company has prepared, and furnished to our auditors (name and address of auditors), a description and evaluation of certain contingencies, including those set forth below involving matters with respect to which you have been engaged and to which you have devoted substantive attention on behalf of the Company in the form of legal consultation or representation.   These contingencies are regarded by management of the Company as material for this purpose (management may indicate a materiality limit if an understanding has been reached with the auditor).   Your response should include matters that existed at (balance sheet date) and during the period from that date to the date of your response.

Pending or Threatened Litigation (excluding unasserted claims)

[Ordinarily the information would include the following: (1) the nature of the litigation, (2) the progress of the case to date, (3) how management is responding or intends to respond to the litigation (for example, to contest the case vigorously or to seek an out-of-court settlement), and (4) an evaluation of the likelihood of an unfavorable outcome and an estimate, if one can be made, of the amount or range of potential loss.]   Please furnish to our auditors such explanation, if any, that you consider necessary to supplement the foregoing information, including an explanation of those matters as to which your views may differ from those stated and an identification of the omission of any pending or threatened litigation, claims, and assessments or a statement that the list of such matters is complete.

Unasserted Claims and Assessments (considered by management to be probable of assertion, and that, if asserted, would have at least a reasonable possibility of an unfavorable outcome)

[Ordinarily management's information would include the following: (1) the nature of the matter, (2) how management intends to respond if the claim is asserted, and (3) an evaluation of the likelihood of an unfavorable outcome and an estimate, if one can be made, of the amount or range of potential loss.]   Please furnish to our auditors such explanation, if any, that you consider necessary to supplement the foregoing information, including an explanation of those matters as to which your views may differ from those stated.

  We understand that whenever, in the course of performing legal services for us with respect to a matter recognized to involve an unasserted possible claim or assessment that may call for financial statement disclosure, if you have formed a professional conclusion that we should disclose or consider disclosure concerning such possible claim or assessment, as a matter of professional responsibility to us, you will so advise us and will consult with us concerning the question of such disclosure and the applicable requirements of Statement of Financial Accounting Standards No. 5. Please specifically confirm to our auditors that our understanding is correct.

  Please specifically identify the nature of and reasons for any limitation on your response.

  [The auditor may request the client to inquire about additional matters, for example, unpaid or unbilled charges or specified information on certain contractually assumed obligations of the company, such as guarantees of indebtedness of others.]

(Section 337, Appendix)

14. <u>Related Party Transactions (AU ¶334)</u>. Review the outline and the summary table in Section "B.2." of this module. The main issue with related party transactions concerns the price at which a transaction occurs. This price may not be the one which would have resulted from an "arm's length bargaining." Note the procedures suggested in Section 334 for discovering related party transactions. Further note that it is generally not possible for the auditor to determine whether such a transaction would have occurred, if no related party had existed, and, if so, the price thereof.

15. <u>Going Concern Considerations (AU 341)</u>. The use of accruals by generally accepted accounting principles relies on an assumption that an entity will continue indefinitely as a going concern. For example, capitalizing assets and depreciating them over future periods is justified on the basis that the costs will be "matched" against future revenues. While audits do not contain specific procedures to test the appropriateness of this going concern assumption, procedures performed for other objectives (i.e., the PERCV objectives) may identify conditions and events indicating substantial doubt as to whether an entity will remain a going concern. AU 341 suggests that such procedures include (1) analytical procedures, (2) the review of subsequent events, (3) (non)compliance with debt agreements, (4) reading of minutes, (5) inquiry of legal counsel, and (6) confirmation of arrangements with various organizations to maintain financial support. When such procedures indicate that substantial doubt may exist as to whether an entity will remain a going concern, the auditor must obtain management's plans (including significant prospective financial information) for dealing with the situation and assess the likelihood that these plans can be implemented.

As we will discuss in further detail in the Reporting module, when substantial doubt remains, the auditor must determine that it is properly disclosed in the notes to the financial statements and must either add an explanatory paragraph to his/her unqualified audit report or must disclaim an opinion. At this point you should review the outline of AU 341.

16. <u>Subsequent Events and Subsequent Discovery of Facts Existing at the Date of the Audit Report (AU 560, 561)</u>. These two sections deal with accounting issues (e.g., how to measure and disclose certain events) as well as audit responsibility with respect to subsequent events. Section 560 classifies subsequent events into two types.

   a. Those events that provide additional evidence with respect to conditions that existed at the date of the balance sheet (for which the financial statements are to be adjusted for any changes in estimates)
   b. Those events that provide evidence with respect to conditions that did <u>not</u> exist at the date of the balance sheet but arose subsequent to that date (for which there is to be footnote disclosure).

Section 560 also deals with the auditing issues involved when these types of events are noted prior to release of the audit report. Be familiar with the audit procedures that may reveal the existence of subsequent events--see outline section C. In the Reports module we discuss dating of the audit report when a subsequent event has occurred.

Section 561 deals with the auditing of events existing at the report date that are not discovered until after the release of the financial statements. Read carefully the outline of the auditor's responsibilities with respect to these events--a number of questions have been asked concerning to subsequent events.

17. <u>Omitted Procedures Discovered After the Report Date (AU ¶390)</u>. Subsequent to issuance of an audit report, an auditor may realize that one or more necessary procedures were omitted from the audit. When this occurs, the auditor should first assess its importance. If omission is considered important (i.e., it affects present ability to support the previously expressed opinion) and if the auditor believes individuals are relying or are likely to rely on the financial statements, the procedures or alternate procedures should be promptly applied. If the procedure is then applied and errors are detected, the auditor should review his/her responsibilities under AU 561 on subsequent discovery of facts existing at the date of the auditor's report. If the client does not allow the auditor to apply the necessary procedure(s), the auditor should consult his/her attorney as to appropriate action.

D. **Completing the Audit**

A number of audit procedures are involved in completing the audit. These procedures are completed on, or near, the last date of field work. First, some of the topics discussed in sections "B" and "C" are generally completed near the end of the audit--analytical procedures performed as an overall review, obtaining a representation letter, inquiry of the client's lawyer, procedures to identify subsequent events, the search for unrecorded liabilities, and the review of working papers. In addition, a review of the adequacy of overall financial statement disclosures is performed often using a disclosure checklist that lists all specific disclosures required by GAAP and the SEC, if appropriate.

To issue an unqualified opinion the auditor must determine that audit risk is at an appropriately low level. The materiality of known and likely errors is considered. Finally, as discussed in the Internal Control module, certain communications are made with the audit committee. Reportable conditions not previously disclosed are communicated to the audit committee and management. Also, for SEC engagements, various other matters concerning the nature of the audit need to be communicated.

E. **Compilation and Review Procedures (AR 100 - 600)**

In 1978 the AICPA developed procedures which are to be applied for (1) compilations and (2) reviews of financial statements of a nonpublic entity. In this module we discuss those procedures relating to evidence. In the Reporting module (Section "C.1.b.") we discuss the related reporting procedures.

1. Compilation Procedures. To perform a compilation the accountant must

    a. Possess an understanding of the accounting principles and practices in the client's industry to enable performance of the compilation

    b. Possess a general understanding of the client's

        (1) Business transactions,
        (2) Accounting records,
        (3) Accounting personnel qualifications,
        (4) Financial statement accounting basis, and
        (5) Financial statement form and content.

    c. Read the compiled statements and consider whether they appear to be appropriate and free from obvious material errors

The accountant is not required to make inquiries or perform other procedures to verify, corroborate, or review the information supplied by the client. However, whenever an accountant becomes aware of information which is incorrect, incomplete, or otherwise unsatisfactory, the accountant should obtain additional or revised information. If the entity refuses to provide (or correct) such information, the accountant should withdraw from the compilation. Finally, recall from the Overview section that independence is not required when performing a compilation.

2. <u>Review Procedures</u>. To perform a review, an accountant must
   a. Inquire about
      (1) The client's accounting principles and practices
      (2) The client's procedures for recording, classifying, and summarizing transactions, and accumulating information for disclosure in financial statements
      (3) Actions taken at meetings of stockholders, board of directors, etc.
      (4) Whether financial statements follow GAAP, changes in business activities or accounting principles, subsequent events, other matters (ask those responsible for financial and accounting)
   b. Perform analytical procedures to identify unusual items and relationships comparing with prior periods, budgets, and predictable relationships
   c. Read the financial statements to determine whether they seem to follow GAAP
   d. Obtain reports from other accountants who have audited or reviewed components

3. <u>Overall Comments</u>. Compilations and reviews are primarily for nonpublic entities which are not required to have annual audits. Note, however, that public companies may choose to have a review of their quarterly financial information. The procedures are virtually identical to those presented above.

   The CPA exam multiple choice questions concerning compilations and review procedures have most frequently provided a list of procedures and asked which one is not a compilation or review procedure. The answer is usually a procedure relative to reviewing internal control or a detailed test of balances such as sending a receivable confirmation. On the November 1979 exam, candidates were asked to recite the various review procedures.

F. **Other Related Topics**
   1. <u>Compliance Audits (Government Audits)</u>.
      Increasingly costly government programs have led to demands for accountability of those with program administrative responsibility. This demand has resulted in increased CPA audit responsibility. The approach taken for the development of this increased responsibility has been to use GAAS as a starting point, but then to supplement GAAS responsibility with additional auditor performance and reporting requirements. Because many of the supplemental requirements relate to assessing compliance with various laws, regulations etc., the area is commonly referred to as compliance auditing.

In 1988 the Comptroller General of the United States (the top executive within the General Accounting Office) published <u>Governmental Auditing Standards</u>, also referred to as the "yellow book." This book presents the generally accepted government auditing standards (GAGAS); the importance of this information is emphasized by the fact that the book is listed in <u>Information For CPA Candidates</u> as a publication which should be studied. In addition, in 1989, the Auditing Standards Board released SAS No. 63 to provide more detailed guidance for CPAs involved with compliance auditing. The related outlines are presented in this manual (immediately following SAS, Section 901). You should review the outlines carefully as an increasing number of questions on compliance auditing (i.e., government financial auditing) is expected. In this section we will present a brief overview of the important information so as to allow you to more efficiently review the outlines.

<u>Government Auditing Standards</u> divide audits into two broad types-- financial and performance. These two types of audits are further subdivided as follows:

In reviewing <u>Government Auditing Standards</u> make certain that you are familiar with the general nature of each of these types of audits. The reporting requirements for financial audits deserve special attention. You need to know that in addition to an audit report stating whether <u>both GAAP and GAGAS</u> has been followed, a report on <u>compliance</u> with applicable laws and regulations, and one on <u>internal control</u> are required. The <u>report on compliance</u> should contain a statement of positive assurance on items tested for compliance with laws and regulations, and negative assurance on those items not tested; it should also include all material instances of noncompliance and of illegal acts. The <u>report on internal control</u> includes, as a minimum, (1) the scope of the auditor's work in obtaining an understanding of the internal control structure and in assessing control risk, (2) a description of the entity's significant internal controls and (3) reportable conditions, including material weaknesses identified as a result of the audit.

SAS 63 operationalizes the financial audit standards presented in <u>Government Auditing Standards</u> as well as interprets other important requirements established by the Office of Management and Budget relating to the Single Audit Act of 1984. While the GAGAS apply to a variety of governmental organizations (including cities, states, hospitals, universities) and certain nongovernmental recipients of governmental financial assistance (e.g., grants, loan guarantees) the Single Audit Act begins with GAAS and GAGAS and adds more requirements for audits of state and local governments that annually receive $100,000 and over in federal financial assistance. In addition to the GAGAS reporting requirements (i.e., reports on [1] financial statements, [2] compliance and [3] internal control) auditors must perform additional procedures and report on federal financial assistance programs. In reviewing the outline of SAS 63 make certain that you are able to distinguish between the requirements relating to "major" and "nonmajor" federal financial assistance programs. For example, you need to know that major programs require auditors to perform specific procedures using a materiality consideration determined specifically for each program; nonmajor programs only require reporting on transactions identified by tests performed for other purposes. Also, distinguish between specific and general requirements under these programs. Specific requirements relate to details of the program being considered (e.g., the purposes for which funds are to be expended), while general requirements relate to overall requirements for all government programs (e.g., no civil rights violations).

2. Operational Auditing.

Operational audits, generally performed by internal auditors, typically evaluate the effectiveness and efficiency of various operational processes. As such they are similar to "performance audits" as presented in the outline of Government Auditing Standards. In fact, the topic "operational auditing" was dropped from the AICPA Content Specification Outline when compliance auditing was added.

As an example of an operational audit, consider an auditor's examination of the sales, receivables, and cash receipts cycle to consider whether policies and procedures concerning the effectiveness and efficiency of related management decision-making processes. A financial statement audit on the other hand would deal more directly with controls relating to the entity's ability to record, process, summarize, and report financial data consistent with the assertions in the financial statements.

REPORTING

The report represents the end product of the auditor's association with the client's financial statements. The following "Diagram of an Audit," originally presented in the auditing overview section, shows the relationship of the audit report to the entire financial statement audit.

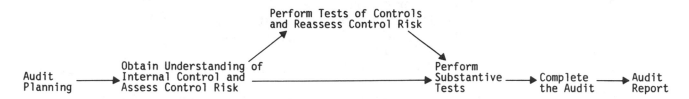

This module primarily addresses audit reports, but also includes information on other reports (e.g., compilation reports, review reports, special reports). Candidate knowledge of reports is tested on every examination. While most of the report questions refer to audit reports, a significant number of questions refer to the other types of reports which auditors issue. Essay questions in this area often describe a situation and ask the candidate to prepare an appropriate audit report. Multiple choice questions present a circumstance which calls for a departure from the standard short-form report and ask specifically what type of report is to be issued.

Study Program for the Reporting Module

This module is organized and should be studied in the following manner.

A. Financial Statement Audit Reports--General

B. Financial Statement Audit Reports--Detailed

    1. Circumstances Resulting in Departure from the Auditor's Standard Report

    2. Report Preparation

C. Accountant Association Other Than Audit

    1. Other Forms of Auditor Association with Historical Financial Statements

    2. Other Reports

All of the following sections of Statements on Auditing Standards apply to reports.

Section (AU)

341	The Auditor's Consideration of an Entity's Ability to Continue as a Going Concern
410	Adherence to GAAP
411	The Meaning of "Present Fairly"
420	Consistency of Application of GAAP
431	Adequacy of Informative Disclosure
435	Segment Information
504	Association with Financial Statements
508	Reports on Audited Financial Statements
530	Dating of Report
534	Reporting on Financial Statements Prepared for Use in Other Countries
543	Part of Examination Made by Other Independent Auditors
550	Other Information in Documents Containing Audited Financial Statements
551	Information in Auditor Submitted Documents
552	Reporting on Condensed Financial Statements and Selected Financial Data
553	Supplementary Information Required by the FASB
560	Subsequent Events
561	Subsequent Discovery of Facts Existing at the Report Date
622	Special Reports--Applying Agreed-Upon Procedures to Specified Elements, Accounts or Items of a Financial Statement
623	Special Reports
625	Reports on the Application of Accounting Principles
634	Letters for Underwriters
722	Review of Interim Financial Information

You should also read the outlines of AT 200 on prospective financial information and AT 300 on pro forma information. These outlines precede the outlines of the Statements on Auditing Standards. Finally, you should read the outlines of the Statements on Standards for Accounting and Review Services, following the outlines of the Statements on Auditing Standards:

Statements on Standards for Accounting and Review Services (SSARS)

SSARS 1 Compilation and Review of Financial Statements
SSARS 2 Reporting on Comparative Financial Statements
SSARS 3 Compilation Reports on Financial Statements Included in Certain Prescribed Forms
SSARS 4 Communications Between Predecessor and Successor Accountants
SSARS 5 Reporting on Compiled Financial Statements (consists solely of changes to SSARS 1 which have been integrated into the outline of that statement)
SSARS 6 Reporting on Personal Financial Statements Included in Written Personal Financial Plans

The above SAS sections are very detailed. In this module we present an overview of the information contained in these sections. In order to simplify the discussion, the topics are covered in a sequence which is different than the order in which they are presented in the codified professional standards. The best way to cover this material is to read the background material first on each SAS presented in this module. Then, read the actual SAS section together with the SAS outline presented subsequently in this volume. The purpose of this module is to give you an overview of the information which will make it easier for you to understand the actual SASs.

This module covers the topics listed in the Reporting area of the AICPA Content Specification Outline plus subsequent events which the AICPA includes in the Audit Evidence and Procedures area of the Outline.

A. **Reports--General**

1. Overall issues

The attestation reporting standards require that reports:

a. Identify the assertion being reported on (usually GAAP in the case of financial statements) and state the character of the engagement
b. State the accountant's conclusion
c. State the accountant's significant reservations
d. Limit the distribution of agreed-upon criteria and agreed-upon procedures engagement reports to parties who agreed to them

When thinking about reports, it is useful to think about the distinction between the asserter and the attester. Recall from the Overview in Chapter 5 (Attest Function--General Nature) that the asserter makes the assertion (e.g., financial statements follow GAAP) while the attester gathers evidence to support the assertion and to assess the measurements and communications of the asserter. Management is normally the asserter while the CPA is the attester.

As indicated in the Evidence module, it is useful to think about four forms of accountant association with information. Examinations (referred to as audits in the case of financial statements) provide a positive opinion on whether assertions follow the appropriate criteria. While the unqualified report for financial statement audits includes three paragraphs-- introductory, scope and opinion--unqualified examination reports for other types of information sometimes include only a scope paragraph and an opinion paragraph.

Reviews provide a report which includes limited assurance. Limited assurance is also referred to as "negative assurance" because a phrase such as "nothing came to our attention" is included in the report. The first paragraph of the report states that a review in accordance with AICPA standards was performed. The second paragraph indicates the limited scope of the review and the third paragraph provides the limited assurance. The procedures of a review are largely limited to internal inquiries and comparisons and are thus significantly more limited than an examination (see Evidence module).

Agreed-upon procedures result in a report which summarizes findings, provides negative assurance, or both. The first paragraph states that agreed upon procedures have been applied, that the report is to assist a specified user, and that the report should not be used by others. The second paragraph enumerates the agreed-upon procedures. The third paragraph indicates the limited scope of the engagement. The fourth paragraph summarizes findings and/or provides negative assurance. Because agreed-upon procedures will ordinarily be less in scope than examinations, the report disclaims a positive opinion on the financial statements.

Finally, because compilations are considered an accounting service (not attestation), no assurance is provided in the report. The first paragraph states that a compilation in conformity with AICPA standards has been performed; the second paragraph states that no opinion or assurance is provided.

2. Financial Statement Audit Reports. Most CPA exam questions pertain to audits (examinations) of financial statements. The following standard short-form report was originally presented in the overview section:

Independent Auditor's Report

To: Board of Directors and Stockholders
ABC Company

We have audited the accompanying balance sheets of ABC Company as of December 31, 19X7 and 19X6 and the related statements of income, retained earnings, and cash flows for the years then ended. These financial statements are the responsibility of the Company's management. Our responsibility is to express an opinion on these financial statements based on our audits.

We conducted our audits in accordance with generally accepted auditing standards. Those standards require that we plan and perform the audit to obtain reasonable assurance about whether the financial statements are free of material misstatement. An audit includes examining, on a test basis, evidence supporting the amounts and disclosures in the financial statements. An audit also includes assessing the accounting principles used and significant estimates made by management, as well as evaluating the overall financial statement presentation. We believe that our audits provide a reasonable basis for our opinion.

In our opinion, the financial statements referred to above present fairly, in all material respects, the financial position of ABC Company as of December 31, 19X7 and 19X6, and the results of its operations and its cash flows for the years then ended in conformity with generally accepted accounting principles.

Joe Smith, CPA
February 23, 19X8

Some key details relating to the above report (adopted in 1988 by the ASB) include:

Title ("Independent Auditor's Report")

Addressee (company, board of directors and/or stockholders--not management)

Introductory paragraph

    1. We have audited
    2. Client's financial statements (statements listed)
    3. Financial statements are the responsibility of management
    4. The auditor's responsibility is to express an opinion

Scope paragraph

    1. Audit conducted in accordance with GAAS
    2. GAAS require that we plan and perform audit to provide reasonable assurance statements free of material misstatement
    3. Audit involves
        Examining on a test basis evidence supporting amounts and disclosures
        Assessment of accounting principles
        Assessment of significant estimates
        Evaluation of overall presentation
    4. Audit provides reasonable basis for opinion

Opinion paragraph

    1. In our opinion
    2. Statements fairly present per GAAP

Manual or printed signature (Firm name)

Date (normally last day of field work)

Remember that the generally accepted auditing standards (GAAS) include four reporting standards (GAAP, Opinion, Disclosure, Consistency--the GODC mnemonic presented in the Overview Section). Read Sections 410, 411, and 431 (we will cover numerous other sections on audit reports following). Note especially in Section 411 that the "present fairly" term in the opinion paragraph is generally to be interpreted within the framework of GAAP. That is, if financial statements are in conformity with GAAP, they generally are presented fairly. Also, note from Section 411, when alternate acceptable principles exist (e.g., LIFO and FIFO), the auditor may conclude that more than one accounting principle is appropriate--that is, the auditor does not have to decide whether the client is using the "best" one. There may be, however, unusual circumstances in which accounting principles may cause the financial statements to be misleading (e.g., new legislation); in such cases, the principle is not to be followed.

Section 411 addresses the issue of the authority of various sources of GAAP. The sources, originally introduced in 1982, were modified in 1987 to clarify for state and local governmental agencies that Governmental Accounting Standards Board (GASB) pronouncements are authoritative. The modification also states when no GASB standard exists for a transaction or event of such a governmental entity, the pronouncements of the FASB are presumed to apply. Following are the current sources.

Category	Included items
a. Authoritative body pronouncements	FASB and GASB Statements FASB and GASB Interpretations APB Opinions AICPA Accounting Research Bulletins
b. Other expert pronouncements	AICPA Industry Audit Guides and Accounting Guides
c. Widely recognized pronouncements and practices	AICPA Statements of Position FASB and GASB Technical Bulletins AICPA Accounting Interpretations Widely accepted industry practices
d. Other accounting literature	APB Statements AICPA Issues Papers AcSEC Practice Bulletins Minutes of the FASB Emerging Issues Task Force FASB Concepts Statements International Accounting Standards Other Professional Association and Regulatory Pronouncements Accounting textbooks and articles

In cases of conflict between the accounting treatment suggested by the categories, category "a" prevails over all categories. Categories "b" and "c" are considered to be of equivalent authority, while category "d" is of lesser authority. For conflicts within a category (or between "b" and "c"), the treatment most closely approximating the transaction's economic substance prevails (i.e., substance over form).

When the auditor issues a qualified or an adverse opinion, the report should provide, if practicable, the information causing the departure from an unqualified report. Thus, if the client omits information in the footnotes concerning a loan agreement's restriction of future dividends, the auditor would provide the additional information. However, if the client has omitted a statement of cash flows, the auditor would not be required to prepare it, since it is not practicable to easily/directly obtain this information from the client's records.

As indicated earlier in this module, the date of the report is normally the last day of field work. AU 530 discusses an often-tested exception to this rule pertaining to subsequent events (discussed in section C.16. of the Evidence module). When a subsequent event requiring disclosure has occurred after the close of field work, the auditor may either dual date the report (for example, assuming that March 2 was the last day of significant field work, "March 2, 19X8, except for footnote X as to which the date is March 6, 19X8"), or may change the report date to the date of the subsequent event (March 6 in our example). Note when using the second option, the auditor increases his/her responsibility for all material events through the latter date, and audit procedures must, therefore, be extended through that date.

B. **Financial Statement Audit Reports--Detailed**

1. Circumstances resulting in Departure from the Auditor's Standard Report.

The AICPA does not present a list of necessary conditions for an auditor to render a standard, unqualified report. The approach is one of presenting circumstances that may require departure from the standard report. These situations may be divided into circumstances requiring additional explanatory language be added to an unqualified report, and those which result in other than an unqualified report as follows:

Circumstances requiring unqualified report with additional

explanatory language

a. Opinion based, in part, on report of another auditor
b. Unusual circumstances requiring a departure from promulgated GAAP
c. Uncertainties (may also lead to a disclaimer)
d. Substantial doubt about ability to remain a going concern (may also lead to a disclaimer)
e. Inconsistency in application of GAAP
f. Certain circumstances affecting comparative statements
g. Required quarterly data for SEC reporting companies
h. Supplementary information required by FASB or GASB
i. Other information in document containing audited financial statements
j. Emphasis of a matter

Circumstances requiring other than an unqualified report
k. Departure from GAAP
l. Scope limitation
m. Lack of independence

You should be familiar with the effect that each of the above circumstances has on an audit report. The following pages contain a summary of some of the most important "must know" material. While the outlines of the various audit report sections present the information in more detail, we provide you with a more structured, organized approach to these topics than is possible with the outlines alone. Section B.2. of this module presents examples of the actual modifications made to audit reports to reflect the circumstances.

a. <u>Opinion based, in part, on report of another auditor (AU 543, 508.12-.13)</u>. Opinions based, in part, on the report of another auditor may differ from the standard report. This situation arises when two or more auditors are involved in the audit of a single entity. An example of this is the case in which one audits the entire firm except for a subsidiary in a distant location. The auditor who audited the single subsidiary will generally render a report on the subsidiary. The auditor who audited the remainder of the firm could give a report on that portion of the entity examined. However, there will generally be a preference (and indeed often a legal requirement) for an audit report on the overall entity.

The overall audit report must be signed by the principal auditor. The principal auditor is designated based on the materiality of the portion of financial statements examined, knowledge of the overall financial statements, and the importance of the components audited. The principal auditor is required to

(1) Make inquiries regarding the other auditor's reputation (e.g., contact AICPA, state society of CPAs, other practitioners, bankers, etc.)
(2) Obtain representation from other auditor concerning independence
(3) Ascertain that other auditor knows U.S. auditing standards, SEC standards (if appropriate), and knows that financial statements are a representation of the overall firm

If the results of any of the above inquiries are unsatisfactory, the principal auditor must either modify the overall audit report (qualify or disclaim), or audit the component. If the results of the inquiries are satisfactory, the following summarizes the principal auditor's required decisions and responsibilities.

PRINCIPAL - OTHER AUDITOR RELATIONSHIP

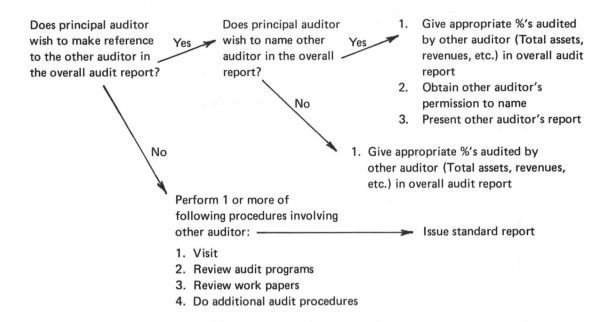

The decision to make reference to the other auditor indicates <u>divided responsibility</u> between the auditors and is <u>not</u> considered an audit report qualification. The decision <u>not</u> to make reference to the other report indicates that the principal auditor assumes responsibility for the work of the other auditor. Reasons for assuming responsibility include

(1)   The other auditor is an affiliate of the principal auditor
(2)   The principal auditor hired the other auditor
(3)   The portion audited by the other auditor is not material
(4)   Other miscellaneous reasons as the principal auditor (or client) desires

Finally, note that in situations in which the other auditor's report is other than unqualified, the materiality of the matter (causing a departure from the standard report of the other auditor) to the overall financial statements determines whether the principal auditor's report must be modified.

b.   <u>Unusual circumstances requiring a departure from promulgated GAAP (AU 508.14-.15)</u>. This case, which relates to Ethics Rule 203 (see Professional Responsibilities module), requires the auditor to <u>agree</u> with the client that a departure from GAAP is justified due to unusual circumstances (e.g., new legislation or a new type of transaction). An unqualified report is issued which includes a separate explanatory paragraph describing the departure.

c.   <u>Uncertainties (AU 508.16-.33)</u>. When the outcome of a significant matter is not susceptible to reasonable estimation, an explanatory paragraph or a disclaimer may be appropriate. For example, uncertainties may exist regarding the outcome of lawsuits pending against the company.

The need for an explanatory paragraph is directly related to the SFAS 5 treatment for loss contingencies as follows:

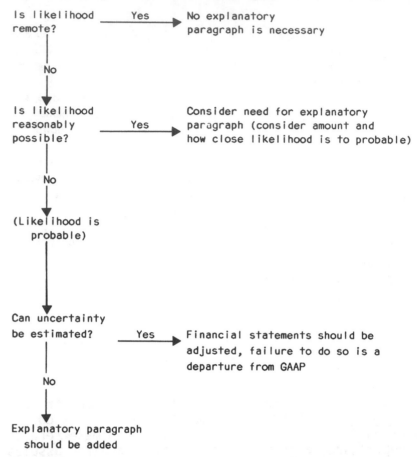

d. <u>Substantial doubt about ability to remain a going concern (AU 341)</u>. A special type of uncertainty concerns the situation in which substantial doubt about the ability of a client to continue as a going concern exists. When audit procedures raise such a question, the auditors consider whether management's plans for dealing with the conditions and events causing the uncertainty are likely to negate the problem. If, after evaluating management's plans, substantial doubt still exists, the auditors should either add explanatory language to their unqualified report or disclaim an opinion. Recall that we discussed this section in C-15 of the Evidence Module.

NOTE: Prior to 1988 uncertainties and going concern questions resulted in a "subject to " qualified report (or a disclaimer). The 1988 changes made by the Auditing Standards Board eliminated "subject to's" and replaced them with unqualified reports with explanatory paragraphs.

e. <u>Inconsistency in application of GAAP (AU 420, AU 508.34-.36)</u>. The 1988 change in reporting removed any mention of consistency from the standard unqualified report. A lack of consistency in following accounting principles usually results in an unqualified report with explanatory language. Review APB 20 on accounting changes when studying this section. The actual explanatory language for consistency is presented in a separate paragraph following the opinion paragraph.

The general rule is that changes in accounting principles result in the addition of explanatory language, while changes in accounting estimates, corrections of clerical errors, and minor reclassifications of accounts from one year to the next do not. Changes in business entities, and changes among carrying bases (cost, equity, consolidated) for continuing subsidiaries result in explanatory language; creation, cessation, purchase, or disposition of subsidiaries do not result in explanatory language.

Bear in mind that consistency pertains to the accounting treatment for items between periods. Also, in comparative reports for changes which are not accounted for by retroactive restatement, the explanatory paragraph is retained as long as the year of change is presented. Retroactive changes require the explanatory paragraph only in the year of the change.

Here are several other important points relating to consistency.

(1)   Differing accounting principles may be used for different portions of an account. For example, a client may choose to use FIFO for valuation of a portion of its inventory and LIFO for the remainder. Similarly, for fixed assets, differing depreciation methods may be used for differing classes (types) of assets.

(2)   A change which is immaterial this year, but is expected to become material in the future, does not result in explanatory language if the client has properly disclosed it in the notes to the financial statements.

(3)   If the auditor does not concur with a change in principle, or if the change has not been properly accounted for, a qualified report is required because this represents a departure from GAAP.

(4)   The audit report does not mention consistency when there has been no change in principle.

The most frequent changes in principle relating to consistency are summarized on the following page.

Type of change	Consistency explanatory paragraph	Restate prior year
I. Change in Accounting Principle		
1. GAAP to GAAP	Yes	No[1]
2. Non-GAAP to GAAP	Yes	Yes
3. GAAP to non-GAAP	Yes[2]	No
4. For newly acquired assets in an existing class of assets (whether 1, 2, or 3 above)	Yes	No[1]
5. For a new class of asset (whether 1, 2, or 3 above)	No	No[1]
II. Change in Accounting Estimate		
1. Judgmental adjustments	No	No
2. Inseparable estimate and principle change	Yes	No
III. Change in Entity		
1. Changes between carrying basis (cost, equity, consol.)	Yes	Yes
2. Pooling	No	Yes
3. Changes in subsidiaries (creation, cessation, purchase or disposition)	No	No
IV. Correction of Error		
1. Error in principle (1.2., above)	Yes	Yes
2. Error not involving application of a principle	No	Yes
V. Change in Statement Format		
1. Classifications and reclassifications	No	Yes

[1]The following "exceptions" call for restatement
    a. LIFO to another method
    b. Method of accounting for long-term construction-type contracts
    c. To or from "full cost" method in extractive industries

[2]Note that "1.3." will also result in a departure from GAAP exception

f. **Certain circumstances affecting comparative financial statements (AU 508.76-.83).** When comparative statements are issued (that is, financial statements for two or more periods are presented), the auditor must report on the statements for all years presented. One overall report, dated as of the last day of field work for the most recent audit, addressing the years presented, is issued. Two major situations may result in an unqualified report with explanatory language:

(1) An opinion on the prior-period financial statements may differ from the opinion previously issued. For example, an auditor may previously have qualified the opinion on the prior period statements because of a departure from GAAP, and the prior-period statements may be restated in the current period to follow GAAP. In such a circumstance the auditor's updated report on the prior period statements should indicate that the statements have been restated and should express an unqualified opinion with respect to the restated statements. Whenever an updated report has an opinion different from that previously expressed, the auditor should disclose all substantive reasons from the different opinion in a separate explanatory paragraph. The explanatory paragraph should disclose

          (a)   The date of the previous report
          (b)   The type of opinion previously expressed
          (c)   The circumstances causing the auditor to express a different opinion
          (d)   That the updated opinion is different from the previous opinion

(2)   When a predecessor auditor has examined the prior period statements, a decision needs to be made as to whether the predecessor's report is to be reissued. If the report is <u>not</u> to be reissued, the successor auditor's report should indicate in the introductory paragraph

          (a)   That the financial statements of the prior period were examined by other auditors
          (b)   The date of the predecessors' report
          (c)   Type of report issued by the predecessor
          (d)   The substantive reasons therefore, if it was other than a standard unqualified report

If the predecessor's report is to be reissued, the predecessor should read the current statements, compare the prior-period statements to the current statements, and obtain from the successor a letter of representation as to whether any material matters concerning the prior period statements have arisen.

Regardless of whether the predecessor's report is being reissued, the opinion paragraph of the successor auditor's report refers only to the second year.

g. <u>Required quarterly data for SEC reporting companies (AU 722)</u>. Certain SEC reporting companies are required to include unaudited quarterly information in their annual reports or other documents filed with the SEC that contain audited financial statements. Auditors are engaged to perform review procedures either at the conclusion of each quarter, or at the end of the year when the information is included with the annual information. When dealing with the annual financial statements, omission, misstatement, or auditor inability to review the quarterly information all lead to inclusion of an explanatory paragraph in the annual audit report. Be aware that the information is to be reviewed, not audited. Therefore, its misstatement will <u>not</u> lead to a qualified or an adverse opinion.

h. <u>Supplementary information required by the FASB or GASB (AU 553)</u>. This information is treated identically to the required quarterly data for SEC reporting companies (see the prior section). Omission, misstatement, or auditor inability to review the information will lead to the inclusion of an explanatory paragraph in the audit report.

i. <u>Other information in a document containing audited financial statements (AU 550-552)</u>. Several types of information are included here. Section 550 deals with other information in documents containing audited statements. This refers to the case where the audited financial statements are included in a published annual report which includes other information (e.g., president's letter, graphs, pictures). The auditor is to read the annual report and note any inconsistencies between the financial statements and the other information provided. If the audited financial statements are inconsistent with the other information, one or both of the following must be true:

(1) Financial statements are incorrect--this will lead to a qualified opinion or an adverse opinion since it is a departure from GAAP (see "k." below)
(2) Other information is incorrect--this will lead to an unqualified report with an explanatory paragraph, and/or withholding use of the audit report and/or withdrawal from the engagement

Finally, the auditor may note no inconsistency, but may believe that the other information seems incorrect. In such cases the auditor is to discuss the matter with the client, consult with other parties such as legal counsel, and use judgment as to the resolution of the matter.

Section 551 deals with reporting on information in auditor-submitted documents. When an auditor submits a document containing audited financial statements, s/he has the responsibility to report on all the information included in the document. The auditor is to either explicitly disclaim an opinion on this additional information or, if s/he has audited it in detail, expand the audit report to include reference to it. If the information is to be audited, the measure of materiality is in relation to the financial statements taken as a whole.

Section 552 (para .09-.11) addresses the situation for which selected financial data, derived from audited financial statements, are presented in a client prepared document (e.g., annual report) which also includes the audited financial statements. The auditor may report only on the financial data which is derived from the audited financial statements. In this situation, an explanatory paragraph is added in which the auditor states whether the selected financial data are fairly stated in all material respects in relation to the financial statements.

j. Emphasis of a matter (AU 508.37). The auditor may wish to emphasize a matter regarding the financial statements, but, nevertheless, may intend to render an unqualified opinion. Examples include cases in which the entity is a component of a larger entity, or in which significant related party transactions exist, or the auditor wishes to draw attention to an important subsequent event. Such information is included in an explanatory paragraph.

NOTE: The following sections require other than an unqualified report.

k. Departures from generally accepted accounting principles (AU 508.49-.66). Departures from GAAP result in either a qualified opinion or an adverse opinion. Examples of departures from GAAP include the use of an unacceptable inventory valuation method (e.g., current sales value) or incorrectly treating a capital lease as an operating lease.
    The type of report depends on the materiality of the departure. Know that materiality depends on

(1) Dollar magnitude of effects
(2) Significance of item to enterprise
(3) Pervasiveness of misstatement
(4) Impact of misstatement on financial statements taken as a whole

Conceptually, as departures become more material, the likelihood of an adverse opinion increases. If the departure from GAAP consists of inadequate disclosure of required information, the correct information, if available, is to be included in an explanatory paragraph which <u>precedes</u> the qualified or adverse opinion paragraph. When the information is not available, the explanatory paragraph of the report should so state.

Be familiar with two specific types of departures from GAAP-- incorrect segmental information and omission of the statement of cash flows. AU 435 discusses reporting for segment information (generally required for SEC reporting companies). Inaccurate (or omitted) segment information constitutes a departure from GAAP and leads to a qualified opinion or an adverse opinion. The measure of materiality for segment information is in relation to the financial statements taken as a whole; thus, the auditor is not required to apply auditing procedures that would be necessary to express a separate opinion on the segment information.

The unjustified omission of a statement of cash flows is also a departure from GAAP. Know, however, that for this type of departure, the Professional Standards require issuance of a qualified opinion, <u>not</u> an adverse opinion; additionally, the auditor need not present the missing statement in an explanatory paragraph of his/her report.

1. <u>Scope limitations (AU 508.40-.48)</u>. Scope limitations result in either a qualified opinion or a disclaimer. In both cases, the opinion paragraph indicates that the opinion modification is based on the possible effects on the financial statements, and not due to the scope limitation itself. The type of report issued depends on the importance of the omitted procedures. This assessment is affected by the nature and magnitude of the potential effects of the matters in question and by their significance to the financial statements (e.g., number of accounts involved).

Two types of scope limitations must be considered--client imposed and circumstance imposed. Client imposed limitations result when a client will not allow the auditor to perform an audit procedure (e.g., confirm receivables). Circumstance imposed limitations occur in situations <u>other</u> than the client saying, "No, I will not allow you to perform that procedure." For example, a weak internal control structure may make it impossible for the auditor to perform the audit. This is considered a circumstance imposed limitation. The following diagram summarizes the effect of scope limitations on the report.

SCOPE LIMITATION DECISIONS

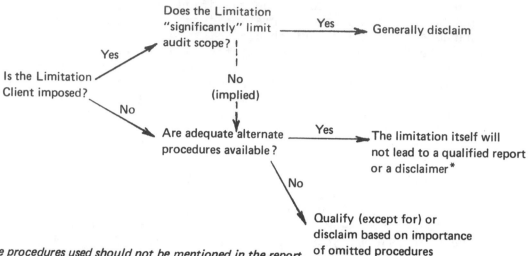

*The alternative procedures used should not be mentioned in the report.

Know that scope limitations may result in different opinions on individual financial statements. For example, if the auditor of a first-year client has been unable to verify the accuracy of the beginning inventory, the scope limitation will affect the current year's income statement (through cost of goods sold) but not the year-end balance sheet. In such a situation, the auditor might issue an unqualified opinion on the balance sheet and a disclaimer on the income statement.

Note the distinction between scope limitations and limited reporting objectives. Consider two circumstances. First, the auditor may, when requested, report on only one statement (e.g., the balance sheet). If access to information underlying the financial statements is not limited, such a situation does not involve a scope limitation. The auditor may report on the financial statement.

Second, the auditor has performed an audit of the overall financial statements and is issuing either a disclaimer or an adverse opinion may <u>not</u> express an opinion stating that certain identified items (accounts) in the financial statements are fairly presented. Such "piecemeal opinions" are considered inappropriate because of the belief that the positive piecemeal opinion might overshadow or contradict the overall disclaimer or adverse report.

m. <u>Lack of independence</u> (AU 504.08-.10). When an auditor is not independent, a disclaimer must be issued stating that the auditor is not independent. No mention of the reason for the lack of independence nor any audit procedures followed is to be given in the report. These circumstances might occur when the CPA firm has neglected to sell an equity (e.g., common stock) interest in the client being audited.

<u>Summary</u>. Know that circumstances "a" through "j" may result in unqualified reports with additional explanatory language. Circumstances "c" and "d," uncertainties and doubt about ability to remain a going concern, may also result in disclaimers. The circumstances requiring other than an unqualified opinion may be summarized as:

Circumstances	Type of opinion
k. Departure from GAAP	Qualified or adverse
l. Scope limitation	
1. Client imposed	"generally disclaim," otherwise qualified
2. Circumstance imposed	Qualified or disclaimer
m. Lack of independence	Disclaimer

The actual wording of the required modifications to the reports are discussed in the next section.

2. <u>Report Preparation.</u> Questions frequently require the candidate to prepare an audit report which reflects certain departures from the standard form, or to list deficiencies in a given report.

The best approach to preparing a report is to start with the standard short-form report and modify it as appropriate for the circumstances presented. You should have the standard short-form report memorized. While the various SASs present numerous types of reports which are other than the standard short-form, it is <u>not</u> necessary to memorize them. Use the following approach to prepare (or evaluate) reports:

Step 1. Determine the overall type of report to be issued
Step 2   Determine whether the introductory paragraph needs to be modified
Step 3. Determine whether the scope paragraph needs to be modified
Step 4. Determine whether an explanatory paragraph needs to be added
Step 5. Determine whether the opinion paragraph needs to be modified

<u>Step 1.</u> <u>Determine the overall type of report to be issued.</u> To accomplish this, use the information presented earlier in this module to determine whether a standard unqualified, an unqualified with explanatory language, a qualified, adverse, or disclaimer report is necessary

<u>Step 2.</u> <u>Determine whether the introductory paragraph needs to be modified.</u>

Standard unqualified introductory paragraph

We have audited the accompanying balance sheets of ABC Company as of December 31, 19X7 and 19X6 and the related statements of income, retained earnings, and cash flows for the years then ended. These financial statements are the responsibility of the Company's management. Our responsibility is to express an opinion on these financial statements based on our audits.

The introductory paragraph is modified (1) when an uncertainty disclaimer is being issued, (2) when the auditor is asked to report on one basic financial statement and not the others, and (3) when the report of another auditor is being referred to. For uncertainty disclaimers, the "We have audited" beginning of the paragraph is changed to "We were engaged to audit"; also, the last sentence of the paragraph is deleted. When one statement (e.g., the balance sheet) is being reported on, the other statements are simply not referred to. In the case of reference to other auditors, the standard introductory paragraph is supplemented with information such as the following:

> We did not audit the financial statements of M Company, a wholly-owned subsidiary, which statements reflect total assets of $____ and $____ as of December 31, 19X7 and 19X6, and total revenue of $____ and $____ for the years then ended. Those statements were audited by other auditors whose report has been furnished to us, and our opinion, insofar as it relates to the amounts included for M Company, is based solely on the report of the other auditors.

Step 3.   Determine whether the scope paragraph needs to be modified.

Standard unqualified scope paragraph

> We conducted our audits in accordance with generally accepted auditing standards. Those standards require that we plan and perform the audit to obtain reasonable assurance about whether the financial statements are free of material misstatement. An audit includes examining, on a test basis, evidence supporting the amounts and disclosures in the financial statements. An audit also includes assessing the accounting principles used and significant estimates made by management, as well as evaluating the overall financial statement presentation. We believe that our audits provide a reasonable basis for our opinion.

When considering the need to modify the scope paragraph, ask yourself: Did the matter(s) of concern significantly restrict the scope of the audit procedures which were performed? If the answer is yes, unless the auditor is satisfied with the adequacy of alternative procedures, the scope paragraph is modified.

Scope limitations and references to other auditors result in modification of the scope paragraph. Disclaimers due to a scope limitation omit the scope paragraph. When the scope limitation leads to a qualified report, the only required modification is

> "Except as discussed in the following paragraph" we conducted our audits in accordance with generally accepted auditing standards. Those standards require ... (no further modification).

When other auditors are referred to, the final sentence becomes:

> We believe that our audits and the report of other auditors provide a reasonable basis for our opinion.

Step 4.   Determine whether an explanatory paragraph needs to be added.

The general rule states that any departure from the standard report will require an explanatory paragraph. The exceptions to this rule are 1) other auditor involvement, and 2) the lack of independence (when a brief one paragraph disclaimer is issued). The explanatory paragraph simply explains the matter of concern. The 1988 revisions to the reporting standards require the explanatory paragraph to be placed before or after the opinion paragraph depending upon the circumstances. The rules are as follow:

a. Explanatory paragraphs for qualified reports, disclaimers, and adverse opinions precede the opinion paragraph.

b. Explanatory paragraphs for consistency and uncertainties in unqualified reports follow the opinion paragraph.

c. All other explanatory paragraphs may either precede or follow the opinion paragraph.

Following are several sample explanatory paragraphs:

Scope limitation

We were unable to obtain audited financial statements supporting the Company's investment in a foreign affiliate stated at $____ and $____ at December 31, 19X2 and 19X1, respectively, or its equity in earnings of that affiliate of $____ and $____, which is included in net income for the years then ended as described in Note X to the financial statements; nor were we able to satisfy ourselves as to the carrying value of the investment in the foreign affiliate or the equity in its earnings by other auditing procedures.

Consistency

As discussed in Note X to the financial statements, the Company changed its method of computing depreciation in 19X2.

Departure from GAAP

The Company has excluded from property and debt in the accompanying balance sheets, certain lease obligations that, in our opinion, should be capitalized in order to conform with generally accepted accounting principles. If these lease obligations were capitalized, property would be increased by $____ and $____, long-term debt by $____ and $____, and retained earnings by $____ and $____ as of December 31, 19X2 and 19X1, respectively. Additionally, net income would be decreased by $____ and $____ and earnings per share would be decreased by $____ and $____, respectively for the years then ended.

Step 5.   Determine whether the opinion paragraph needs to be
modified.

Standard unqualified opinion paragraph

In our opinion, the financial statements referred to above present
fairly, in all material respects, the financial position of ABC Company
as of December 31, 19X7 and 19X6, and the results of its operations and
its cash flows for the years then ended in conformity with generally
accepted accounting principles.

The general rule states for reports other than
unqualified, the opinion paragraph will require
modification. In addition, if the principal auditor makes
reference to other auditors, a modification is required.
For all other unqualified reports with additional
explanatory language, the standard opinion paragraph is
issued. Here are some examples of modifications for
various circumstances:

Other auditors

In our opinion, based on our audits and the report of other auditors,
the financial statements ...

GAAP departure qualified

In our opinion, except for the effects of not capitalizing certain lease
obligations as discussed in the preceding paragraph, the financial
statements

Scope limitation qualified

In our opinion, except for the effects of such adjustments, if any, as
might have been determined to be necessary had we been able to examine
evidence regarding the foreign affiliate investment and earnings, the
financial statements ...

> NOTE: Notice that the report modification con-
> cerns the effect on the financial state-
> ments, not the nature of the scope
> limitation itself.

Scope limitation disclaimer

Since the Company did not take physical inventories and we were not able
to apply other auditing procedures to satisfy ourselves as to the
inventory quantities and the cost of property and equipment, the scope
of our work was not sufficient to enable us to express, and we do not
express an opinion on these statements.

Adverse Opinion

In our opinion, because of the effects of the matters discussed in the
preceding paragraphs, the financial statements referred to above do not
present fairly, in conformity with generally accepted accounting
principles, ...

SUMMARY OF DEPARTURES FROM STANDARD REPORT

Circumstance	Introductory paragraph modified?	Scope paragraph modified	Opinion paragraph modified	Explanatory paragraph added
UNQUALIFIED WITH EXPLANATORY LANGUAGE				
a. Other Auditor--Make reference	Yes	Yes	Yes	No
b. Justified GAAP Departure				
c. Uncertainties				
d. Going concern				
e. Inconsistency				
f. Report reissued (f2)	No	No	No	Yes
g. Required SEC quarterly data				
h. Supplementary information				
i. Other information				
j. Emphasis of a matter				
f. Predecessor report not reissued (f1)	Yes	No	No	No
QUALIFIED OPINIONS				
k. Departure from GAAP	No	No	Yes	Yes
l. Scope limitation	No	Yes	Yes	Yes
DISCLAIMER				
c. Uncertainties*	Yes	Yes	Yes	Yes
d. Going concern*	Yes	Yes	Yes	Yes
l. Scope limitation	Yes	Omit	Yes	Yes
m. Lack of independence	(A one paragraph disclaimer is issued)			
ADVERSE				
b. Departure from GAAP	No	No	Yes	Yes

*No sample report presented in Professional Standards

C. Accountant Association Other than Audit

As indicated in the overview section, accountants become involved with financial information on engagements less than "full" audits. These forms may be categorized as: (1) other forms of auditor association with historical financial statements, and (2) other reports.

1. Other Forms of Auditor Association with Historical Financial Statements. Here we discuss four primary "other" forms of auditor association. The candidate should be very familiar with each of these forms of association.

   a. Unaudited statements (AU 504). For those relatively few public firms which are not required to have an annual audit, the option of unaudited statements exists. In this case, a simple disclaimer of opinion is generally issued; also each page of the financial statements should be marked "unaudited." However, if the auditor is aware of any significant departures from GAAP, s/he should suggest that the statements be revised and, failing that, should include such information in the disclaimer.

   b. Compiled or reviewed statements (AR 100 - 500). When a CPA has compiled financial statements for a nonpublic entity, a disclaimer of opinion is issued--it is dated as of the date of completion of the compilation. Each page of the financial statements is to be marked "See Accountant's Compilation Report." If management elects to exclude disclosures such as footnotes from the financial statements, a special form of the disclaimer is available (AR 100.21). Other departures from GAAP are to be described in an explanatory paragraph to the report.

Compilation report examples

Accountant's Compilation Report

I (we) have compiled the accompanying balance sheet of XYZ Company as of December 31, 19XX, and the related statements of income, retained earnings, and cash flows for the year then ended, in accordance with standards established by the American Institute of Certified Public Accountants.

A compilation is limited to presenting in the form of financial statements information that is the representation of management (owners). I (we) have not audited or reviewed the accompanying financial statements and, accordingly, do not express an opinion or any other form of assurance on them.

Third Paragraph if Disclosures Are Omitted

Management has elected to omit substantially all of the disclosures (and the statement of cash flows) required by generally accepted accounting principles. If the omitted disclosures were included in the financial statements, they might influence the user's conclusions about the company's financial position, results of operations, and cash flows. Accordingly, these financial statements are not designed for those who are not informed about such matters.

The following paragraph is added to the compilation report if the financial statements have been prepared on a comprehensive basis other than GAAP.

These financial statements (including related disclosures) are presented in accordance with the requirements of (name of body), which differ from generally accepted accounting principles. Accordingly, these financial statements are not designed for those who are not informed about such differences.

Recall that the <u>review</u> form of association, which calls for audit procedures far short of an audit (see Evidence module, Section D), may be performed for a public or for a nonpublic firm. The review report provides limited assurance to users, as expressed in the statement that the auditor is not aware of any material modifications which need to be made to the financial statements. Departures from GAAP are to be treated the same as in compilation reporting.

Review report examples

Accountant's Review Report

I (we) have reviewed the accompanying balance sheet of XYZ Company as of December 31, 19XX, and the related statements of income, retained earnings, and cash flows for the year then ended, in accordance with standards established by the American Institute of Certified Public Accountants. All information included in these financial statements is the representation of the management (owners) of XYZ Company.

A review consists principally of inquiries of company personnel and analytical procedures applied to financial data. It is substantially less in scope than an examination in accordance with generally accepted auditing standards, the objective of which is the expression of an opinion regarding the financial statements taken as a whole. Accordingly, I (we) do not express such an opinion.

Based on my (our) review, I am (we are) not aware of any material modifications that should be made to the accompanying financial statements in order for them to be in conformity with generally accepted accounting principles.

Accountant's Review Report with Exception

I (we) have reviewed the accompanying balance sheet of XYZ Company as of December 31, 19XX, and the related statements of income, retained earnings, and cash flows for the year then ended, in accordance with standards established by the American Institute of Certified Public Accountants. All information included in these financial statements is the representation of the management (owners) of XYZ Company.

A review consists principally of inquiries of company personnel and analytical procedures applied to financial data. It is substantially less in scope than an examination in accordance with generally accepted auditing standards, the objective of which is the expression of an opinion regarding the financial statements taken as a whole. Accordingly, I (we) do not express such an opinion.

Based on my (our) review, with the exception of the matter(s) described in the following paragraph(s), I am (we are) not aware of any material modifications that should be made to the accompanying financial statements in order for them to be in conformity with generally accepted accounting principles.

As disclosed in note X to the financial statements, generally accepted accounting principles require that inventory cost consist of material, labor, and overhead. Management has informed me (us) that the inventory of finished goods and work in process is stated in the accompanying financial statements at material and labor cost only, and that the effects of this departure from generally accepted accounting principles on financial position, results of operations, and cash flows have not been determined.
                        (or)
As disclosed in note X to the financial statements, the company has adopted [description of newly adopted method], whereas it previously used [description of previous method]. Although the [description of newly adopted method] is in conformity with generally accepted accounting principles, the company does not appear to have reasonable justification for making a change as required by Opinion No. 20 of the Accounting Principles Board.

c. Reviewed quarterly statements (AU 722). The review form of association discussed above is also appropriate for firms wishing to have quarterly financial statement reviews. The reports issued are essentially the same as those presented above, except that they are modified to relate to one quarter.

d. Condensed financial statements (AU 552.01-.08). A client which must file a set of audited financial statements at least annually with a regulatory agency may choose to prepare condensed financial statements for other purposes. In such cases the auditor's report on such condensed statements should disclose

   (1) That the auditor has expressed an opinion on the complete audited financial statements
   (2) The date of the audit report on the complete statements
   (3) The type of opinion expressed on the complete statements
   (4) Whether the condensed statements are fairly stated in relation to the complete financial statements

On the other hand, for a client which is not a public entity and, therefore, is not required to file complete annual audited financial statements, an adverse opinion is recommended for condensed statements (see footnote 6 of AU 552).

e. <u>Financial statements prepared for use in other countries (AU 534)</u>. An auditor may be asked to report on the financial statements of a United States client which follow the accounting principles of a foreign country. The general rule is that in such circumstances the auditor must follow U.S. general and field work standards to the extent that they are appropriate. Certain procedures, however, may <u>not</u> be appropriate (e.g., procedures related to the tax deferral account in a country which does not allow tax deferral). Also, the auditor may be requested to apply the other country's auditing standards. This may be done if U.S. standards have been followed and if the auditor is familiar with the standards of the other country.

The report issued depends on whether it is for use primarily outside the U.S. (the most frequent case) or within the U.S. If it is intended primarily for outside the U.S., a modified U.S. report may be issued which: 1) describes the basis followed, 2) states that U.S. standards (and other national standards if appropriate) were followed, and 3) states whether the statements present fairly and consistently the basis followed. If, however, the auditor has made certain that s/he understands the responsibilities relating to the standard report of the other country, then such report may be issued. Financial statements for use primarily outside of the U.S. may be distributed to limited U.S. individuals and organizations (such as banks) if differences between the U.S. and the foreign country standards are understood.

If distribution within the U.S. is <u>more than limited</u>, the auditor should use the U.S. standard report and modify it as necessary for any departures from GAAP. Additionally, for distribution outside the U.S., a report may be prepared as indicated in the prior paragraph.

2. <u>Other Reports.</u> Auditors also become involved with a variety of other types of information which result in the following reports.

a. Special reports
b. Letters for underwriters
c. Financial forecasts and projections
d. Application of accounting principles
e. Pro forma financial information

In addition, recall that auditors may issue reports on internal control. This topic is summarized in the internal control module.

a. <u>Special reports (AU 622, 623 [SAS No. 63])</u>. The information on special reports was revised in 1989 to update and align it with the SASs passed in 1988 (SAS Nos. 52-61). AU 623 presents guidance on five basic types of reports. You should have a general familiarity with each. Your approach here should be to study the information in this section in combination with the outline of AU 623. Here we present only summary information and sample reports; details are presented in the outline of AU 623.

The first type of special report deals with reporting on financial statements which follow a comprehensive basis other than GAAP (e.g., cash basis, tax basis or a basis prescribed by a regulatory agency). In general, the report issued parallels the standard audit report, with a fourth paragraph added indicating the basis being followed, and that it is a comprehensive basis of accounting other than GAAP. When the basis is prescribed by a regulatory agency, an additional paragraph limiting distribution to the company and to the regulatory agency is added at the end of the report. Terms such as "balance sheet," and "income statement" are not used for comprehensive statements--use, for example, "statement of assets and liabilities arising from cash transactions."

The following is the suggested standard form for cash basis statements:

Financial Statements Prepared on the Cash Basis

Independent Auditor's Report

We have audited the accompanying statements of assets and liabilities arising from cash transactions of XYZ Company as of December 31, 19X2 and 19X1, and the related statements of revenue collected and expenses paid for the years then ended. These financial statements are the responsibility of the Company's management. Our responsibility is to express an opinion on these financial statements based on our audits.

We conducted our audits in accordance with generally accepted auditing standards. Those standards require that we plan and perform the audit to obtain reasonable assurance about whether the financial statements are free of material misstatement. An audit includes examining, on a test basis, evidence supporting the amounts and disclosures in the financial statements. An audit also includes assessing the accounting principles used and significant estimates made by management, as well as evaluating the overall financial statement presentation. We believe that our audits provide a reasonable basis for our opinion.

As described in Note X, these financial statements were prepared on the basis of cash receipts and disbursements, which is a comprehensive basis of accounting other than generally accepted accounting principles.

In our opinion, the financial statements referred to above present fairly, in all material respects, the assets and liabilities arising from cash transactions of XYZ Company as of December 31, 19X2 and 19X1, and its revenue collected and expenses paid during the years then ended, on the basis of accounting described in Note X.

A comprehensive basis report prepared solely for filing with a regulatory agency, following a basis prescribed by that agency, would be similar to the above report, but would also add the following as a final paragraph:

> This report is intended solely for the information and use of the board of directors and management of XYZ Insurance Company and for filing with the [name of regulatory agency] and should not be used for any other purpose.

The second type of special report is that on special elements, accounts, or items. An auditor may, if allowed to perform the procedures s/he believe necessary, issue an opinion on one or more accounts (e.g., receivables or rentals). On the other hand, if the auditor is hired to perform only agreed-upon procedures, negative assurance is provided.

Special Elements Report Examples

Report Relating to Accounts Receivable

Independent Auditor's Report

We have audited the accompanying schedule of accounts receivable of ABC Company as of December 31, 19X2. This schedule is the responsibility of the Company's management. Our responsibility is to express an opinion on this schedule based on our audit.

We conducted our audit in accordance with generally accepted auditing standards. Those standards require that we plan and perform the audit to obtain reasonable assurance about whether the schedule of accounts receivable is free of material misstatement. An audit includes examining, on a test basis, evidence supporting the amounts and disclosures in the schedule of accounts receivable. An audit also includes assessing the accounting principles used and significant estimates made by management, as well as evaluating the overall schedule presentation. We believe that our audit provides a reasonable basis for our opinion.

In our opinion, the schedule of accounts receivable referred to above presents fairly, in all material respects, the accounts receivable of ABC Company as of December 31, 19X2, in conformity with generally accepted accounting principles.

NOTE: As is the case with all special reports, an additional paragraph is added limiting distribution when a basis which is not GAAP or another comprehensive basis is used.

Agreed-Upon Procedures

Trustee
XYZ Company

At your request, we have performed the procedures enumerated below with respect to the claims of creditors of XYZ Company as of May 31, 19XX, set forth in the accompanying schedules. Our review was made solely to assist you in evaluating the reasonableness of those claims, and our report is not to be used for any other purpose. The procedures we performed are summarized as follows:

a. We compared the total of the trial balance of accounts payable at May 31, 19XX, prepared by the company, to the balance in the company's related general ledger account.

b. We compared the claims received from creditors to the trial balance of accounts payable.

c. We examined documentation submitted by the creditors in support of their claims and compared it to documentation in the company's files, including invoices, receiving records, and other evidence of receipt of goods or services.

Our findings are presented in the accompanying schedules. Schedule A lists claims that are in agreement with the company's records. Schedule B lists claims that are not in agreement with the company's records and sets forth the differences in amounts.

Because the above procedures do not constitute an audit made in accordance with generally accepted auditing standards, we do not express an opinion on the accounts payable balance as of May 31, 19XX. In connection with the procedures referred to above, except as set forth in Schedule B, no matters came to our attention that caused us to believe that the accounts payable balance might require adjustment. Had we performed additional procedures or had we made an audit of the financial statements in accordance with generally accepted auditing standards, other matters might have come to our attention that would have been reported to you. This report relates only to the accounts and items specified above and does not extend to any financial statements of XYZ Company, taken as a whole.

The third type of special report is one which results from an engagement in which the auditor is hired to test whether a client is in compliance with some form of agreement. For example, an auditor may give negative assurance to a bank on whether a client is in conformity with restrictions contained in a debt agreement.

Compliance Report Examples
Contractual Compliance
Independent Auditors' Report

Compliance Report as a
Separate Report

Compliance Report Included
in Unqualified Report

We have audited, in accordance with generally accepted auditing standards, the balance sheet of XYZ Company as of December 31, 19X2 and the related statement of income, retained earnings, and cash flows for the year then ended, and have issued our report thereon dated February 16, 19X3.

Standard Unqualified Report

In connection with our audit, nothing came to our attention that caused us to believe that the Company failed to comply with the terms, covenants, provisions, or conditions of sections XX to XX, inclusive, of the Indenture dated July 21, 19X0 with ABC Bank insofar as they relate to accounting matters. However, our audit was not directed primarily toward obtaining knowledge of such noncompliance.

This report is intended solely for the information and use of the boards of directors and managements of XYZ Company and ABC Bank and should not be used for any other purpose.

Then add these two paragraphs

The fourth type of special report is for client special purpose financial presentations that have been prepared by the client to comply with an agreement (e.g., a loan agreement). The information presented is more substantial than specified elements, but is different in some ways, and generally less complete than required by a comprehensive basis of accounting. Unless the report is to be filed with a regulatory agency such as the SEC and to be included in a publicly available document (e.g., a prospectus), a paragraph limiting distribution is added to the report.

Special Purpose Financial Presentation Examples

Loan agreement
(GAAP not followed)

[Introductory paragraph
refers to specific report]

[Standard scope paragraph]

The accompanying special-purpose financial statements were prepared for the purpose of complying with Section 4 of a loan agreement between DEF Bank and the Company as discussed in Note X, and are not intended to be a presentation in conformity with generally accepted accounting principles.

Schedule of Apartment Revenues and Expenses Included in a document to be distributed to the general public

[Introductory paragraph refers
to specific report]

[Standard scope paragraph]

The accompanying Historical Summaries were prepared for the purpose of complying with the rules and regulations of the Securities and Exchange Commission (for inclusion in the registration statement on Form S-11 of DEF Corporation) as described in Note X and are not intended to be a complete presentation of the Apartments' revenues and expenses.

In our opinion, the special-purpose financial statements referred to above present fairly, in all material respects, the assets and liabilities of ABC Company at December 31, 19X2 and 19X1, and the revenues, expenses and cash flows for the years then ended, on the basis of accounting described in Note X.

This report is intended solely for the information and use of the boards of directors and managements of ABC Company and DEF Bank and should not be used for any other purpose.

In our opinion, the Historical Summaries referred to above present fairly, in all material respects, the gross income and direct operating expenses described in Note X of ABC Apartments for each of the three years in the period ended December 31, 19XX, in conformity with generally accepted accounting principles.

The fifth special report is that for which a client is required to present information on prescribed forms or schedules. For example, a state corporate commission may require all corporations within its jurisdiction to report assets, liabilities, and equities per a standard form. If that form calls for the auditor to make an assertion which s/he believes to be unjustified, s/he is to either reword the form or attach a separate report to the form.

b. Letters for underwriters (AU 634). When a public firm wishes to issue new securities to the public, the underwriters of the securities will generally ask the firm's auditor to give "comfort" on the financial and accounting data in the prospectus which is not covered by the audit opinion. In these cases, the auditor may give negative assurance (a statement that nothing came to the CPA's attention that caused him/her to believe that the information does not meet a specified standard) on accounting related matters. The letter to the underwriter will refer to one or more of the following: CPA independence, compliance of the CPA's audit with various requirements, unaudited interim financial information, changes subsequent to the balance sheet date, and various tables of date examined.

c. Financial forecasts and projections (AT 300). In October 1985 the Auditing Standards Board released its Statement on Standards for Accountants' Services on Prospective Financial Information. While it retains the AICPA's long-held policy that a CPA should not vouch for the achievability of a forecast (see Responsibilities module), the Statement presents three forms of accountant association with forecasts or projections--compilation, examination, and application of agreed-upon procedures.

The following are the standard report forms suggested for compilation and examination of forecasts or projections.

Compilation Report

We have compiled the accompanying forecasted balance sheet, statements of income, retained earnings, and cash flows of XYZ Company as of December 31, 19XX, and for the year then ending, in accordance with standards established by the American Institute of Certified Public Accountants.

A compilation is limited to presenting in the form of a forecast information that is the representation of management and does not include evaluation of the support for the assumptions underlying the forecast. We have not examined the forecast and, accordingly, do not express an opinion or any other form of assurance on the accompanying statements or assumptions. Furthermore, there will usually be differences between the forecasted and actual results, because events and circumstances frequently do not occur as expected, and those differences may be material. We have no responsibility to update this report for events and circumstances occurring after the date of this report.

Examination Report

We have examined the accompanying forecasted balance sheet, statements of income, retained earnings, and cash flows of XYZ Company as of December 31, 19XX, and for the year then ending. Our examination was made in accordance with standards for an examination of a forecast established by the American Institute of Certified Public Accountants and, accordingly, included such procedures as we considered necessary to evaluate both the assumptions used by management and the preparation and presentation of the forecast.

In our opinion, the accompanying forecast is presented in conformity with guidelines for presentation of a forecast established by the American Institute of Certified Public Accountants, and the underlying assumptions provide a reasonable basis for management's forecast. However, there will usually be differences between the forecasted and actual results, because events and circumstances frequently do not occur as expected, and those differences may be material. We have no responsibility to update this report for events and circumstances occurring after the date of this report.

Departures from the standard report for forecasts/projections are very similar to those for historical financial statement audit reports (presented in section "B.4." of this module). While it is not necessary that you read the entire Statement (on forecasts/projections), you should at this point turn to the outline of the Statement which begins on page 302. Several extremely important points relative to that outline are:

(1) An accountant should not be associated with projections which do not disclose assumptions

(2) Forecasts may be for general or limited use, while projections are for limited use only (see Point "A.1." of outline for discussion)

(3) Independence is not required for compilations (recall this is also the case for financial statement compilations)

(4) Concerning assurance provided: Know that a compilation report provides no assurance (again, this is also the case with financial statement compilations); an examination report provides assurance with respect to the reasonableness of assumptions; and an agreed-upon procedures report provides negative assurance

Finally note that past exams have asked very few questions on prospective information, but the issuance of this Statement may lead to an increase.

d. Application of Accounting Principles (AU 625). Accountants are occasionally asked by prospective clients or intermediaries (e.g., lawyers, commercial banks): 1) to report on certain completed or proposed transactions, 2) the type of opinion which would be rendered based on certain facts provided, or 3) the appropriate application of accounting principles to hypothetical transactions. In such circumstances the auditor should 1) obtain the prospective client's permission, 2) contact the prospective client's current accountant and 3) follow the procedures outlined for Predecessor/Successor Auditors (see "B.1.c." in the Professional Responsibilities module) to determine that s/he is aware of all pertinent information. Once accomplished, a report may be issued which describes the accountant's beliefs pertaining to the transactions or financial statements.

e. Reporting on Pro Forma Financial Information (AT 300). High levels of business combinations, and various types of changes in capitalization created a significant demand for auditor association with "pro forma financial information" which adjusts earlier historical financial information prospectively for the effects of an actual or proposed transaction (or event). The standard relating to this situation was released by the Auditing Standards Board in September of 1988 as a Statement on Standards for Attestation Engagements. Accountants may either review or examine the information. The following is an example of an examination report:

Pro Forma Financial Information

Independent Auditor's Report

We have examined the pro forma adjustments reflecting the transaction described in Note 1 and the application of those adjustments to the historical amounts in the accompanying pro forma condensed balance sheet of X Company as of December 31, 19X1, and the pro forma condensed statement of income for the year then ended. The historical condensed financial statements are derived from the historical financial statements of X Company, which were audited by us, and of Y Company, which were audited by other accountants, appearing elsewhere herein. Such pro forma adjustments are based upon management's assumptions described in Note 2. Our examination was made in accordance with standards established by the American Institute of Certified Public Accountants and, accordingly, included such procedures as we considered necessary in the circumstances.

The objective of this pro forma financial information is to show what the significant effects on the historical financial information might have been had the transaction [or event] occurred at an earlier date. However, the pro forma condensed financial statements are not necessarily indicative of the results of operations or related effects on financial position that would have been attained had the above-mentioned transaction [or event] actually occurred earlier.

[Additional paragraphs(s) may be added to emphasize certain matters relating to the attest engagement.]

In our opinion, management's assumptions provide a reasonable basis for presenting the significant effects directly attributable to the above-mentioned transaction described in Note 1, the related pro forma adjustments give appropriate effect to those assumptions, and the pro forma column reflects the proper application of those adjustments to the historical financial statement amounts in the pro forma condensed balance sheet as of December 31, 19X1, and the pro forma condensed statement of income for the year then ended.

Review reports, as is the case with reviews of historical financial information, indicate that they are less in scope than examinations, and provide negative assurance (e.g., "nothing came to our attention..."

Scope restrictions, uncertainties, departures from AICPA standards, etc., are treated in a manner similar to that for reviews and audits of historical financial statements. At this point review the outline of the section which precedes the SAS outline.

Summary

The CPA exam has recently asked questions which have required candidates to either prepare or be aware of information provided in reports other than the standard unqualified report. For example, in May 1985, candidates were required to identify the deficiencies contained in an auditor's report; in November 1985, candidates were required to prepare a report on comparative financial statements. Memorizing all of the miscellaneous reports is difficult and time consuming. The following table summarizes most of the key elements of the types of reports on which questions have been asked in the recent past. The candidate should not attempt to memorize the details of each report.

OTHER REPORTS SUMMARY*

	Comprehensive basis	Specified elements — a. Opinion	Specified elements — b. Agreed upon procedures	Compliance reports — a. Within standard report	Compliance reports — b. Separate report	Special Purpose Presentation	Nonpublic Entity — Compilation	Nonpublic Entity — Review
Introductory Paragraph	1. Standard report except for, in first sentence (a) names of statements (b) name reporting basis used	1. Standard report except for, in first sentence (a) names of accounts (b) name reporting basis used	1. We have applied agreed upon procedures 2. Report solely for your information 3. Describe procedures applied	1. Standard report	1. Standard report except for, add "and have issued our report thereon dated ___" (to end of first sentence)	1. Standard report except for, in first sentence (a) names of statements	1. We have compiled (list statements) in accordance with standards established by AICPA	1. We have reviewed (list statements) in accordance with AICPA standards. All information is representation of management
Scope Paragraph	1. Standard report	1. Standard report except for naming of accounts		1. Standard report		1. Standard report except for names of accounts		1. Review principally inquiry and analytical procedures 2. Less in scope than audit 3. Do not express an opinion
Explanatory Paragraph	1. Mention basis and refer to footnote which describes	Description of reporting basis if not given in scope paragraph	No explanatory paragraph	No explanatory paragraph	No explanatory paragraph	Mention basis and refer to footnote which describes	No explanatory paragraph	No explanatory paragraph
Opinion (Assurance) Paragraph	Opinion 1. Standard report except for (a) names of statements (b) refer to reporting basis used	Opinion 1. Standard report except for (a) names of accounts (b) name reporting basis used	Negative Assurance 1. We do not express an opinion 2. No matters came to our attention which need adjustment 3. If additional procedures had been performed other matters might have come to our attention 4. Report relates only to above accounts and items	Opinion and negative assurance 2 paragraphs: A. Standard opinion para B. Negative assurance on compliance para 1. Nothing came to our attention to lead us to believe not in compliance 2. Exam was not directed primarily toward obtaining knowledge of such noncompliance	Negative assurance 1. Nothing came to our attention to lead us to believe not in compliance 2. Exam was not directed primarily toward obtaining knowledge of such noncompliance	Opinion 1. Standard report except for (a) names of statements (b) refer to reporting basis used	Disclaimer 1. Compilation only presents financial statements which are management's representations 2. Have not audited or reviewed, express no opinion	Negative Assurance 1. Not aware of material modifications to be in conformity with GAAP
How to Report Departures from Reporting Criteria**	1. Same as standard report	1. Add comment to opinion para and add explanatory para describing 2. If significant client interpretations of criteria have been made add explanatory para describing	1. Prepare schedules summarizing accounts 2. Add comment to negative assurance para and add explanatory para describing	1. Add comment to negative assurance para and add explanatory para describing	1. Add comment to negative assurance para and add explanatory para describing	1. Same as standard report	1. Add sentence to disclaimer para disclosing departure and add explanatory para (after disclaimer) describing 2. If footnotes omitted, add explanatory para (after disclaimer) so stating and state that they might influence a user's conclusions	1. Add comment to negative assurance para and add explanatory para (after negative assurance) describing

*Note that no report form has been proposed for the Special Report based on Prescribed Forms or Schedules. Prospective financial statements are summarized in the outline section (following the SAS (AU) outlines).

**All special reports include an additional paragraph when distribution is limited (see outline of AU 623).

AUDIT SAMPLING

Sampling is essential throughout audits as auditors attempt to gather sufficient competent evidence in a cost efficient manner. The following "Diagram of an Audit" was originally presented in the auditing overview section.

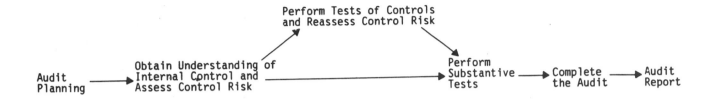

Audit sampling is used for both tests of controls, that is, compliance tests ("attribute sampling") and for tests of details of transactions and balances (usually, "variables sampling"). In both attribute sampling and variables sampling, the plans may be either nonstatistical or statistical. The following chart summarizes methods of audit sampling.

Audit sampling has been tested on most recent auditing examinations, usually in the form of multiple choice questions. Occasionally an essay question has appeared. The adoption of SAS 39 (Section 350) and the related <u>Audit Sampling</u> guide increases the likelihood of statistical sampling questions.

One might anticipate additional questions dealing with concepts such as sampling risk, nonsampling risk, tolerable misstatement (previously "tolerable error"), and the projection of sample results to an overall population. Also, as in the past, one might expect exam questions dealing with the relationships between statistical concepts and basic audit concepts such as reliance on internal controls, materiality, and audit decision making.

Authors' Note: Changes in terminology have been made in this module and in the SAS Outline of AU 350 to reflect changes in the AICPA's forthcoming revision of the **Codification of Auditing Standards**. *These are indicated as the terms are presented.*

Composer diagram should go here-"Detailed Audit Sampling Techniques".

Detailed Audit Sampling Techniques

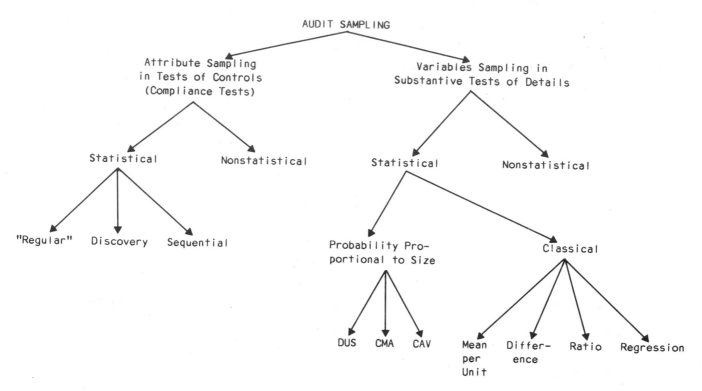

*Probability proportional to size sampling may also be used for attribute sampling.

Study Program for Audit Sampling Module

This module is organized and should be studied in the following manner.

A.   Basic Audit Sampling Concepts

1.   Definition of Sampling
2.   General Approaches to Audit Sampling--Nonstatistical and Statistical
3.   Uncertainty and Audit Sampling
4.   Categories of Audit Tests for Which Sampling May Be Used
5.   Categories of Statistical Sampling Plans

B.   Sampling in Tests of Controls (Compliance Tests)

1.   Risk of Assessing Control Risk Too High or Too Low (Risk of Underreliance and Overreliance)
2.   Statistical Sampling in Tests of Controls (Compliance Tests)
3.   Nonstatistical Sampling in Tests of Controls (Compliance Tests)

C.   Sampling in Substantive Tests of Details

1.   Overall Issues
2.   Probability-Proportional-to-Size (PPS) Sampling
3.   Classical Variables Sampling
4.   Comparison of PPS Sampling to Classical Variables Sampling

The outline is based on the content specification outline that includes sampling

under internal control as topic "II.D.3." and under evidence as topic "III.C.2."

AU 350 and the AICPA Audit and Accounting Guide entitled Audit Sampling (published in 1983) pertain most directly to audit sampling. Additionally, AU 312 on audit risk and materiality relates to this area. When reviewing this section make certain that you have clear the relationship between audit risk and its components (inherent risk, control risk, and detection risk) and sampling risk. Sampling risk, in the case of substantive tests of account balances, includes the risks of incorrect rejection and acceptance, which relate to detection risk. The terminology for sampling risk for tests of internal control has been changed as a result of the SASs which were passed in 1988 to the risk of assessing control risk too high and the risk of assessing control risk too low; these risks obviously relate to control risk. Those risks previously were referred to as the risk of underreliance (overreliance) on internal accounting control. Throughout this module we will use the new terminology, generally supplemented by the old term in parentheses.

The material in this module is primarily organized around both AU 350 and the Audit Sampling guide. It is presented in outline form to allow an efficient review of the material.

A. **Basic Audit Sampling Concepts**

1. Definition of Sampling

    a. Audit sampling is the application of an audit procedure to less than 100% of the items within an account balance or class of transactions for the purpose of evaluating some characteristic of the balance or class (AU 350.01)

    b. The AICPA Audit and Accounting Guide, Audit Sampling, groups procedures that do not involve sampling as follows

        (1) Inquiry and observation

            (a) Procedures that depend on segregation of duties or that otherwise provide no documentary evidence
            (b) Tracing one or a few transactions to obtain an understanding of an accounting system and its internal controls

        (2) Analytical procedures
        (3) One-hundred-percent examination

            (a) For example, some audit plans include the audit of all "large" accounts and a portion of the small accounts. In such situations only the "small" accounts would be subject to sampling.

        (4) Untested balances

        Note: Procedures performed to obtain an understanding of the internal control structure sufficient to plan an audit generally do not involve sampling. However, many "tests of controls" used to assess control risk do involve sampling.

2. General Approaches to Audit Sampling--Nonstatistical and Statistical

    a. Both involve judgment in planning, executing the sampling plan, and in evaluating the results of the sample

    b. Both can provide sufficient competent evidential matter

    c. The choice of a sampling approach is independent of the auditor's decisions concerning

        (1) The audit procedures to be applied

        (2) The competence of the evidential matter obtained

        (3) The actions to be taken when errors are found

    d. Statistical sampling helps the auditor to

        (1) Design an efficient sample

        (2) Measure the sufficiency of the evidential matter obtained

        (3) Evaluate the sample results

            (a) The auditor can quantify sampling risk to limit it to a level considered acceptable

    e. Cost of statistical sampling

        (1) Training auditors

        (2) Designing samples

        (3) Selecting items to be tested

3. Uncertainty and Audit Sampling--Uncertainty is implicit in the concept of a "reasonable basis for an opinion" referred to in the third field work standard. Eliminating all uncertainty, even if possible, would delay release of audited information and greatly increase audit cost.

    a. Audit risk is the risk of the existence of a monetary misstatement greater than the tolerable misstatement. It consists of (a) the risk (inherent risk and control risk) that the balance or class and related assertions contain misstatements that could be material when aggregated with other misstatements and (b) the risk (detection risk) that the auditor will not detect such misstatement. Recall our discussion of audit risk in the Professional Responsibilities module (section "B.1.a").

        (1) Audit risk may be expressed using the following model

$$AR = IR \times CR \times AP \times TD$$

            where: AR = Audit risk
                       IR = Inherent risk
                       AP = Analytical procedures risk
                       TD = Test of details allowable risk of incorrect acceptance

        Note: The above model is presented in the Appendix to AU 350. This model separates detection risk into the two components of AP and TD.

        (2) Nonsampling risk includes all aspects of audit risk that are not due to sampling. It is controlled by adequate planning and supervision of audit work and proper adherence to quality control standards. The following are examples of nonsampling risk.

(a) The failure to select appropriate audit procedures
(b) The failure to recognize errors in documents examined
(c) Misinterpreting the results of audit tests

(3) Sampling risk is the risk that the auditor's conclusion, based on a sample, might be different from the conclusion which would be reached if the test were applied in the same way to the entire population (AU 350.10)

    (a) Tests of controls (compliance tests) sampling risks (AU 350.12, as revised)

        1] The risk of assessing control risk too high (under-reliance) is the risk that the assessed level of control risk based on the sample is greater than the true operating effectiveness of the control structure policy or procedure

        2] The risk of assessing control risk too low (overreliance) is the risk that the assessed level of control risk based on the sample is less than the true operating effectiveness of the control structure policy or procedure

    (b) Substantive test sampling risks (AU 350.12)

        1] The risk of incorrect rejection is the risk that the sample supports the conclusion that the recorded account balance is materially misstated when it is not materially misstated

        2] The risk of incorrect acceptance is the risk that the sample supports the conclusion that the recorded account balance is not materially misstated when it is materially misstated

4. Categories of Audit Tests in Which Sampling May Be Used

    a. Tests of controls (compliance tests) are directed toward the design or operation of an internal control structure policy or procedure to assess its effectiveness in preventing or detecting material misstatements in a financial statement assertion

    b. Substantive tests are used to obtain evidence about the validity and propriety of the accounting treatment of transactions and balances

    c. Dual-purpose tests are used to test operation of internal control policies or procedures and test whether a recorded balance or class of transactions is correct

5. Categories of Statistical Sampling Plans

    a. Attribute sampling (used in tests of controls) reaches a conclusion in terms of a rate of occurrence

        (1) It tests the rate of deviation from a prescribed internal control procedure to determine whether the assessed level of control risk is appropriate

        (2) Attribute sampling is discussed further in section "B."

    b. Variables sampling (used in substantive testing) reaches a conclusion in dollar amounts (or possibly in units)

        (1) Probability-proportional-to-size (PPS) sampling [dollar-unit sampling, cumulative monetary amount (CMA) sampling] is a variables sampling procedure that uses attribute theory to express a con-

clusion in dollar amounts. PPS is discussed further in section "C.2."

(2) <u>Classical variables sampling techniques</u> use normal distribution theory to evaluate selected characteristics of a population on the basis of a sample of the items constituting the population. Classical techniques are discussed in section "C.3."

c. On the following page is an outline organized around the audit guide's steps involved in attribute and variables sampling. At this point you may also wish to review the outline of AU 312 on Audit Risk and Materiality.

B. Sampling in Tests of Controls (Compliance Tests)

1. <u>Risk of assessing control risk too high (underreliance, alpha risk, type I error)</u>. This risk relates to <u>audit efficiency</u>. If the auditor assesses control risk too high, substantive tests will consequently be expanded beyond the necessary level, leading to audit inefficiency.

2. <u>Risk of assessing control risk too low (overreliance, beta risk, type II error)</u>. This risk relates to <u>audit effectiveness</u>. If the auditor assesses control risk too low, substantive tests will not be expanded to the necessary level to ensure an effective audit. Because materially misstated financial statements may result from this situation, controlling this risk is generally considered of greater audit concern than controlling the risk of assessing control risk too high.

AUDIT AND ACCOUNTING GUIDE SAMPLING STEPS

<u>Tests of Controls (Compliance Tests)</u>	<u>Substantive Tests</u>
1. <u>Determine</u> the objectives of the test	<u>Determine</u> the objectives of the test
2. <u>Define</u> the deviation conditions	<u>Define</u> the population a. Define the sampling unit b. Consider the completeness of the population c. Identify individually significant items

3. <u>Define</u> the population
   a. Define the period covered by the test
   b. Define the sampling unit
   c. Consider the completeness of the population
	<u>Select</u> an audit sampling technique

4. <u>Determine</u> the method of selecting the sample
    a. Random-number sampling
    b. Systematic sampling
    c. Other sampling

<u>Determine</u> the sample size
a. Consider the variation within the population
b. Consider the acceptable level of risk
c. Consider the tolerable misstatement
d. Consider the expected amount of misstatement
e. Consider the population size

5. <u>Determine</u> the sample size
    a. Consider the acceptable risk of assessing control risk too low (overreliance)
    b. Consider the tolerable rate
    c. Consider the expected population deviation rate
    d. Consider the effect of population size
    e. Consider a sequential or a fixed sample-size approach

<u>Determine</u> the method of selecting the sample

6. <u>Perform</u> the sampling plan

7. <u>Evaluate</u> the sample results
    a. Calculate the deviation rate
    b. Consider sampling risk
    c. Consider the qualitative aspects of the deviations
    d. Reach an overall conclusion

<u>Perform</u> the sampling plan

<u>Evaluate</u> the sample results
a. Project the misstatement to the population and consider sampling risk
b. Consider the qualitative aspects of the misstatements and reach an overall conclusion

8. <u>Document</u> the sampling procedure

<u>Document</u> the sampling procedure

3. <u>Statistical (Attribute) Sampling in Tests of Controls (Compliance Tests)</u>

    a. <u>Steps involved in attribute sampling</u>

        (1) <u>Determine the objectives of the test</u>--Remember that tests of controls are designed to provide reasonable assurance that internal controls are operating effectively

            (a) Attribute sampling is generally used when there is a trail of documentary evidence

        (2) <u>Define the deviation conditions</u>--An auditor should identify characteristics (attributes) that would indicate operation of the internal control procedures on which s/he plans to rely. The auditor next defines the possible deviation conditions. A deviation is a departure from the prescribed internal control policy or procedure.

            EXAMPLE: If the prescribed procedure to be tested requires the cancelation of each paid voucher, a paid but uncanceled voucher would constitute a deviation.

(3) Define the population--For tests of controls, the population is the class of transactions being tested. Conclusions based on sample results can be projected only to the population from which the sample was selected. Three steps are involved in defining the population.

   (a) Define the period covered by the test--Ideally, tests of controls should be applied to transactions executed during the entire period under audit. In some cases it is more efficient to test transactions at an interim date and use supplemental procedures to obtain reasonable assurance regarding the remaining period.

   (b) Define the sampling unit--The sampling unit is one of the individual elements, as defined by the auditor, that constitute the population. In our earlier example, the sampling unit is the voucher.

   (c) Consider the completeness of the population--The auditor actually selects sampling units from a physical representation of the population (in our example, paid vouchers). Because subsequent statistical conclusions relate to the physical representation, the auditor should consider whether it includes the entire population.

(4) Determine the method of selecting the sample--The sample should be representative of the population. All items in the population should have an opportunity to be selected. Methods include

   (a) Random number sampling--Every sampling unit has the same probability of being selected, and every combination of sampling units of equal size has the same probability of being selected. Random numbers can be generated using a random number table or a computer program.

   (b) Systematic sampling--Every nth (population size/sample size) item is selected after a random start. When a random starting point is used, this method provides every sampling unit in the population an equal chance of being selected. If the population is arranged randomly, systematic selection is essentially the same as random number selection.

      1] One problem with systematic sampling is that the population may be systematically ordered (for example, the identification number of all large items ends with a 9). A biased sample may result since 9s may be selected either too frequently or never. This limitation may be overcome by using multiple random starts or by using an interval that does not coincide with the pattern in the population.

      2] An advantage of systematic sampling, as compared to random number sampling, is that the population items do not have to be prenumbered for the auditor to use this method.

   (c) Block sampling--A sample consisting of contiguous units.

      EXAMPLE: An auditor selects 3 blocks of 10 vouchers for examination.

      The advantage of block sampling is the ease of sample unit selection. The disadvantage is that the sample selected may not be representative of the overall population. Because of this disadvantage, use of this method is <u>generally not desirable</u> in statistical sampling.

(d) <u>Haphazard sampling</u>--A sample consisting of units selected without any conscious bias, that is, without any special reason for including or omitting items from the sample. It does not consist of sampling units selected in a "careless" manner, but in a manner that the auditor hopes to be representative of the population. Like block sampling, it is generally not used for statistical sampling because it does not allow the auditor to measure the probability of selecting a given combination of sampling units.

(5) <u>Determine the sample size</u>--A series of decisions must be made.

   (a) <u>Allowable risk of assessing control risk too low (overreliance)</u>. Since the auditor usually uses the results of tests of controls (compliance tests) as the primary source of evidence for assessing control risk, a low level of risk is normally selected

      1] Risk levels between 1% and 10% are normally used
      2] There is an inverse relationship (e.g., as one increases the other decreases) between the risk of assessing control risk too low and sample size

   (b) <u>Tolerable rate (tolerable deviation rate)</u>--The maximum rate of deviation from a prescribed control structure policy or procedure that an auditor is willing to accept without modifying the planned assessed level of control risk

      1] The auditor's determination of the tolerable deviation rate is a function of

         a] The planned assessed level of control risk and
         b] The degree of assurance desired by the sample

      2] When the auditor's planned assessed level of control risk is low, and the degree of assurance desired from the sample is high, the tolerable rate should be low

         a] This will be the case, for example, when the auditor does not perform other tests of controls for an assertion

   (c) <u>Expected population deviation rate (Expected rate of occurrence)</u>--An estimate of the deviation rate in the entire population

      1] If the expected population deviation rate exceeds the tolerable rate, tests (tests of controls/attribute sampling) will not be performed
      2] Although the risk of assessing control risk too low is often not explicitly controlled when determining attribute sample size, it can be controlled to some extent by specifying a conservative (larger) expected deviation rate
      3] There is a direct relationship (e.g., as one increases, the other increases) between the expected deviation rate and sample size
      4] The expected population deviation rate is typically determined by

a] Last year's deviation rate adjusted judgmentally for current year changes in the control procedure, or

b] Determining the deviation rate in a small preliminary sample

c] This factor is used only to determine sample size and not to evaluate sample results, so the estimate need not be exact

(d) Population effect--Increases in the size of the population normally increase the sample size. However, it is generally appropriate to treat any population of more than 5,000 sample units as if it were infinite.

(e) Fixed vs. a sequential sample size approach--Audit samples may be designed using either a fixed or a sequential sample size approach. Supplementing traditional attribute (fixed size) sampling approaches are

1] Sequential (stop-or-go) sampling--a sampling plan for which the sample is selected in several steps, with the need to perform each step conditional on the results of the previous steps. That is, the results may either be so poor as to indicate that the control may not be relied upon, or so good as to justify reliance at each step.

2] Discovery sampling--a procedure for determining the sample size required to have a stipulated probability of observing at least one occurrence when the expected population occurrence rate is at a designated level. It is most appropriate when the expected occurrence rate is zero or near zero. If a deviation is detected, the auditor must either (1) use an alternate approach or, (2) if the deviation is of sufficient importance, audit all transactions.

(f) Once the factors listed above have been quantified, the sample size can be easily determined through the use of sample size tables. For the CPA exam remember the following relationships.

ATTRIBUTE SAMPLING
SUMMARY OF FACTOR RELATIONSHIPS TO SAMPLE SIZE

Factor	Relationship
Population	Direct
Risk of assessing control risk too low	Inverse
Tolerable rate	Inverse
Expected population deviation rate	Direct

(6) Perform the sampling plan--The auditor should apply the appropriate audit procedures to all items in the sample to determine if there are any deviations from the prescribed control procedures being tested. Each deviation should be analyzed to determine whether it is an isolated or recurring type of occurrence.

(a) The auditor should select extra sample items (more than the needed sample size) so that voided, unused, or inapplicable documents can be excluded from the sample and be replaced

       (b)   If the auditor is unable to examine a selected item (e.g., a document has been misplaced) it should be considered a deviation for evaluation purposes. The auditor should consider the reasons for this limitation and its implications for the audit.

       (c)   In some cases the auditor may find enough deviations early in the sampling process to indicate that a control cannot be relied upon. The auditor need not continue the tests in such circumstances.

       (d)   If a dual purpose test is being used, a larger sample size should be used

(7)   <u>Evaluate the sample results</u>--Once audit procedures have been performed on all sample items, the sample results must be evaluated and projected to the entire population from which the sample was selected

       (a)   Calculate the sample deviation rate

           1] $\text{Deviation rate} = \dfrac{\text{Number of observed deviations}}{\text{Sample size}}$

           2]   The deviation rate is the auditor's best estimate of the true (but unknown) deviation rate in the population

       (b)   Consider the sampling risk

           Determine (by reference to tables) the upper deviation limit (upper occurrence limit, achieved upper precision limit) actually achieved for the specified risk level and actual number of deviations observed. This upper limit represents the sample deviation rate plus an allowance for sampling risk (precision) based on the risk of overreliance specified.

           1]   <u>The allowance for sampling risk (precision)</u> is a measure of the difference between the sample estimate and the corresponding population characteristic at a specified sampling risk

       (c)   Compare the upper deviation limit to the tolerable rate specified in designing the sample

           1]   If the upper deviation limit is less than or equal to the tolerable rate, the sample results support reliance on the control procedure tested

           EXAMPLE: Assume that the auditor established the following criteria for an attribute sampling plan.

           - Population size: over 5,000 units
           - Allowable risk of assessing control risk too low: 5%
           - Tolerable deviation rate: 6%
           - Estimated population deviation rate: 2.5%

           By referencing the appropriate sample size table (not included here) the auditor determined that the required sample size was 150 units.

           The auditor applied appropriate audit procedures to the 150 sample units and found 8 deviations.

           a]   The sample deviation rate $= \dfrac{8}{150} = 5.3\%$

        b] The upper deviation limit found from the table for a
5% risk of assessing control risk too low and 8
deviations = 9.5%

        c] The allowance for sampling risk = 9.5 - 5.3 = 4.2%

        d] The conclusions that can be drawn include

            i] There is a 95% chance of the true population de-
viation rate being less than or equal to 9.5% (5%
chance of it being greater than 9.5%)

          ii] Since the upper deviation limit (9.5%) exceeds the
tolerable deviation rate (6%), the sample results
indicate that control risk for the control
procedure being tested is higher than planned,
and, therefore, the resulting substantive tests
must be expanded

    (d) In addition to the frequency of deviations found, the auditor
should consider the qualitative aspects of each deviation

        1] The nature and cause of each deviation should be
analyzed. For example, are the deviations due to a
misunderstanding of instructions or to carelessness?

        2] The possible relationship of the deviations to other
phases of the audit should be considered. For example,
the discovery of an irregularity ordinarily requires
broader consideration than does the discovery of an error.

    (e) Reach an overall conclusion by applying audit judgment

        1] If all evidence obtained, including sample results,
supports the auditor's planned assessed level of control
risk, the auditor generally does not need to modify
planned substantive tests

        2] If the planned level is not supported the auditor will

            a] Test other related controls, or

            b] Modify the related substantive tests to reflect
increased control risk assessment

  (8) Document the sampling procedure. Each of the prior 7 steps, as
well as the basis for overall conclusions, should be documented in
the workpapers

4. Nonstatistical Sampling for Tests of Controls (Compliance Tests)--The steps
involved in the design and implementation of a nonstatistical sampling plan
are similar to statistical plans. Differences in determining sample size,
sample selection, and evaluating sample results are discussed below.

  a. Determine sample size--As in statistical sampling, the major factors are
the risk of assessing control risk too low, the tolerable rate, and the
expected population deviation rate

    (1) In nonstatistical sampling it is not necessary to quantify these
factors

    (2) The auditor should still consider the effects on sample size as
described in section "B.2.a.(5)"

  b. Sample selection--As indicated earlier, random number sampling and
systematic sampling are most frequently used with statistical

sampling. Block sampling and haphazard sampling are frequently used with nonstatistical sampling.

  c. <u>Evaluate sample results</u>--In nonstatistical sampling it is impossible to determine an upper deviation limit or to quantify sampling risk

    (1) The auditor should relate the deviation rate in the sample to the tolerable rate established in the design stage to determine whether an adequate allowance for sampling risk has been provided to draw the conclusion that the sample provides an acceptably low level of risk

      (a) <u>Rule of thumb</u>--If the deviation rate in the sample does not exceed the expected population deviation rate used in determining sample size, the auditor can generally conclude that the risk that the true deviation rate exceeds the tolerable deviation rate, is consistent with the risk considered acceptable when the sample was planned

    (2) As in statistical sampling the qualitative aspects of deviations should be considered in addition to the frequency of deviations

    (3) Again the auditor must use his/her professional judgment to reach an overall conclusion as to the assessed level of control risk for the assertion(s) related to the internal control procedure tested

C. Sampling in Substantive Tests of Details

  1. <u>Overall Issues</u>

    a. Review the following risks described in "A.3.a.(3)" as they relate to substantive testing

      (1) <u>Risk of incorrect rejection (alpha risk, type I error)</u>. Like the risk of assessing control risk too high, this risk relates to <u>audit efficiency</u>. If the sample results incorrectly indicate that an account balance is materially misstated, the performance of additional audit procedures will generally lead to the correct conclusion.

      (2) <u>Risk of incorrect acceptance (beta risk, type II error)</u>. Like the risk of assessing control risk too low, this risk relates to <u>audit effectiveness</u>. If the sample results indicate that an account balance is not misstated, when it is misstated, the auditor will not perform additional procedures and the financial statements may include such misstatements.

      (3) Although the two risks are mutually exclusive (the auditor cannot incorrectly decide to reject an account balance at the same time s/he incorrectly decides to accept an account balance), both risks may be considered in the sample design stage

      (4) The following portions of this outline summarize the steps involved in substantive testing (topic "C.1.b."), probability-proportional-to-size sampling (topic "C.2."), and classical variables sampling (topic "C.3."). Finally, PPS and classical variables sampling are compared (topic "C.4.").

    b. <u>Steps involved in variables sampling</u>

      (1) <u>Determine the objectives of the test</u>--Remember that variables sampling is used primarily for substantive testing and that its conclusion is generally stated in dollar terms (although conclusions in terms of units [e.g., inventory] are possible).

Variables sampling might test, for example, the recorded amount of accounts receivable.

(2) Define the population--The population consists of the items constituting the account balance or class of transactions of interest. Three areas need be considered.

   (a) Sampling unit--The sampling unit is any of the individual elements that constitute the population

   EXAMPLE: If the population to be tested is defined as total accounts receivable, the sampling unit used to confirm the balance of accounts receivable could be each subsidiary account receivable.

   (b) Consider the completeness of the population--Since sampling units are selected from a physical representation (e.g., a trial balance of receivables) the auditor should consider whether the physical representation includes the entire population

   (c) Identify individually significant items--Items which are individually significant for which sampling risk is not justified should be tested separately and not be subjected to sampling. These are items in which potential errors could individually equal or exceed tolerable misstatement.

(3) Select an audit sampling technique--Either nonstatistical or statistical sampling may be used. If statistical sampling is used, either PPS or classical variables techniques are appropriate.

(4) Determine the sample size--Five items need to be considered.

   (a) Variation within the population--Increases in variation (standard deviation in classical sampling) result in increases in sample size

   (b) Acceptable level of risk--The risk of incorrect acceptance is related to audit risk (see AU 312 outline and Professional Responsibilities module section "B.1.a."). The auditor may also control the risk of incorrect rejection so as to allow an efficiently performed audit. Increases in these risks result in decreases in sample size.

   (c) Tolerable misstatement (error)--An estimate of the maximum monetary misstatement that may exist in an account balance or class of transactions, when combined with misstatements in other accounts, without causing the financial statements to be materially misstated. As tolerable misstatement increases, sample size decreases.

   (d) Expected amount of misstatement (error)--Expected misstatement is estimated using an understanding of the business, prior year information, a pilot sample, and/or the results of the review and evaluation of internal control. As expected misstatement increases a larger sample size is required.

   (e) Population size--Sample size increases as population size increases. The effect is more significant in classical variables sampling than PPS sampling.

   (f) For the CPA exam remember the following relationships:

SUMMARY OF VARIABLES SAMPLING RELATIONSHIPS TO SAMPLE SIZE

Factor	Relationship
Variation	Direct
Risk - Incorrect Acceptance	Inverse
- Incorrect Rejection	Inverse
Tolerable Misstatement (Error)	Inverse
Expected Misstatement (Error)	Direct
Population	Direct

(5) <u>Determine the method of selecting the sample</u>--Generally random number or systematic sampling [see "B.2.a.(4)"]

(6) <u>Perform the sampling plan</u>--Perform appropriate audit procedures to determine an audit value for each sample item

(7) <u>Evaluate the sample results</u>--The auditor should project the results of the sample to the population. The total projected misstatement, after any adjustments made by the entity, should be compared with the tolerable misstatement and the auditor should consider whether the risk of misstatement in excess of the tolerable amount is at an acceptably low level. Also, qualitative factors (such as the nature of the misstatements and their relationship to other phases of the audit) should be considered. For example, when irregularities have been discussed, a simple projection of them will not in general be sufficient as the auditor will need to obtain a thorough understanding of them and of their likely effects.

(8) <u>Document the sampling procedure</u>--Each of the prior 7 steps, as well as the basis for overall conclusions, should be documented

c. <u>Comments on nonstatistical sampling</u>--Both statistical and nonstatistical sampling require judgment. The major differences between statistical and nonstatistical sampling in substantive testing are in the steps for determining sample size and evaluating sample results.

    (1) <u>Determination of sample size</u>--There is no requirement to explicitly quantify the factors that are considered in determining sample size. However, be aware of the relationships summarized in "C.4.f." Also, know that the statistical tables <u>may</u> be used to assist in the determination of sample size.

    (2) <u>Evaluation of sample results</u>--The auditor should project misstatements found in the sample to the population and consider sampling risk

        (a) Projecting misstatements can be accomplished by

            1] Dividing the total dollar amount of misstatement in the sample by the fraction of total dollars from the population included in the sample, or

            2] Multiplying the average difference between audit and book values for sample items times the number of units in the population

        (b) If tolerable misstatement exceeds projected misstatement by a large amount, the auditor may be reasonably sure that an acceptably low level of sampling risk exists. Sampling risk increases as projected misstatement approaches tolerable error.

        (c) When sampling results do not support the book value, the auditor can

            1] Examine additional sampling units
            2] Apply alternative auditing procedures, or
            3] Ask the client to investigate and, if appropriate, make necessary adjustments

        (d) Qualitative aspects of misstatements need to be considered as well as frequency and amounts of misstatements (see C.1.b.(7) above)

2. <u>Probability-Proportional-to-Size (PPS) Sampling [dollar-unit, cumulative monetary amount (CMA) sampling]</u>

    a. Uses attribute sampling theory to express a conclusion in dollar amounts. PPS sampling is gaining popularity in practice because it is easier to apply than classical variables sampling

    b. Steps in PPS sampling

        (1) <u>Determine the objectives of the test</u>--PPS tests the reasonableness of a recorded account balance or class of transactions. PPS is primarily applicable in testing account balances and transactions for <u>overstatement.</u>

        (2) <u>Define the population</u>--The population is the account balance or class of transactions being tested

            (a) <u>Define the sampling unit</u>--The sampling units in PPS are the individual dollars in the population. Actually, the auditor examines the individual account or transaction (called a <u>logical unit</u>) which includes the dollars sampled

            (b) <u>Consider the completeness of the population</u>--As with other sampling plans, the auditor must assure him/herself that the physical representation of the population being tested includes the entire population

            (c) <u>Identify individually significant items</u>--PPS automatically includes in the sample any unit that is individually significant

        (3) <u>Select an audit sampling technique</u>--Here we have selected PPS
        (4) <u>Determine the sample size</u>--A PPS sample divides the population into sampling intervals and selects a logical unit from each sampling interval

            (a)

$$\text{Sample size} = \frac{\text{Recorded amount of population}}{\text{Sampling interval}}$$

where:

$$\text{Sampling interval} = \frac{\left[\text{Tolerable Misstatement} - (\text{Expected misstatement} \times \text{Expansion factor})\right]}{\text{Reliability factor}}$$

Expansion Factors (from the <u>Audit Sampling</u> guide) for expected misstatements

	Risk of Incorrect Acceptance								
	1%	5%	10%	15%	20%	25%	30%	37%	50%
Factor	1.9	1.6	1.5	1.4	1.3	1.25	1.2	1.15	1.0

Reliability Factors (from the <u>Audit Sampling</u> guide) for misstatements of overstatement. (Use 0 errors for determining Reliability Factor.)

Number of Overstatements	Risk of Incorrect Acceptance								
	1%	5%	10%	15%	20%	25%	30%	37%	50%
0	4.61	3.00	2.31	1.90	1.61	1.39	1.21	1.00	.70
1	6.64	4.75	3.89	3.38	3.00	2.70	2.44	2.14	1.68
2	8.41	6.30	5.33	4.72	4.28	3.93	3.62	3.25	2.68
3	10.05	7.76	6.69	6.02	5.52	5.11	4.77	4.34	3.68

(b) Observations

  1] The size of the <u>sampling interval</u> is related to the risk of incorrect acceptance and tolerable misstatement. The auditor controls the risk of incorrect rejection by making an allowance for expected misstatements. The auditor specifies a planned allowance for sampling risk so that the estimate of projected misstatement plus the allowance for sampling risk will be less than or equal to tolerable misstatement

  2] If no misstatements are expected, the sampling interval is determined by dividing tolerable misstatement by a factor that corresponds to the risk of incorrect acceptance, i.e., the reliability factor

(5) <u>Determine the method of selecting the sample</u>--PPS samples are generally selected using <u>systematic sampling</u> with a random start. All logical units with dollar amounts greater than or equal to the sampling interval are certain to be selected.

(6) <u>Perform the sampling plan</u>--The auditor must apply appropriate audit procedures to determine an audit value for each logical unit included in the sample

(7) <u>Evaluate the sample results</u>--Misstatements found should be projected to the population and an allowance for sampling risk should be calculated. When the logical unit contains 100 percent misstatements, the <u>upper limit on misstatements</u> is the total of projected misstatement and the allowance for sampling risk. The allowance for sampling risk consists of <u>basic precision</u> and an incremental <u>allowance for projected misstatements</u>.

$$\begin{matrix} \text{Upper limit} \\ \text{on misstatements} \end{matrix} = \begin{matrix} \text{Projected} \\ \text{misstatement} \end{matrix} + \begin{matrix} \text{Allowance for} \\ \text{sampling risk} \end{matrix}$$

When the logical unit contains less than 100 percent misstatements, the upper limit on misstatements is calculated as follows:

$$\begin{matrix} \text{Upper limit} \\ \text{on misstatements} \end{matrix} = \begin{matrix} \text{Projected} \\ \text{misstatement} \end{matrix} + \begin{matrix} \text{Basic} \\ \text{precision} \end{matrix} + \begin{matrix} \text{Incremental} \\ \text{allowance} \\ \text{for projected} \\ \text{misstatements} \end{matrix}$$

Projected misstatement is calculated for each logical unit containing misstatements and totalled. For logical units less than the size of the sampling interval, the projected misstatement is calculated by multiplying the percentage of misstatement ("the tainting") times the sampling interval. For logical units greater in size than the sampling interval, the actual amount of misstatement is found.

Basic precision is found by multiplying the reliability factor [see "2.b.(4)" above] times the sampling interval.

Incremental allowance for projected misstatements is determined by ranking the misstatements for logical units which are less than the sampling interval from highest to lowest and considering the incremental changes in reliability factors for the actual number of misstatements found. The table of Reliability Factors presented earlier ["2.b.(4)"] presents values for 0 through 3 misstatements. Table 1 of Appendix D of the Audit Sampling guide presents additional values for situations in which more misstatements are detected. One must subtract 1.00 from each incremental change to isolate the incremental allowance for projected misstatements.

(a) Decision rule: Compare the upper limit on misstatements to tolerable misstatement

    1] If the upper limit on misstatements is less than or equal to tolerable misstatement, the sample results support the conclusion that the population is not misstated by more than tolerable misstatement at the specified risk of incorrect acceptance

    2] If the upper limit on misstatements is greater than the tolerable misstatement, the sample results do not support the conclusion that the population is not misstated by more than the tolerable misstatement. This may be due to the fact that (a) the population is misstated, (b) the auditor's expectation of misstatement was low and resulted in too small of a sample, or (c) the sample is not representative of the population.

    3] The auditor should consider qualitative aspects of errors found as well as quantitative factors

(b) Observation: If no misstatements are found, projected misstatement and the incremental allowance for projected misstatements will equal zero, leaving the basic precision as the only nonzero component of the upper limit on misstatements. No further calculations are needed since the tolerable misstatement will be greater than this amount.

(8) Document the sampling procedure--Each of the prior 7 steps, as well as the basis for overall conclusions, should be documented

The following example illustrates the probability proportional to size method.

Probability Proportional to Size Sampling Example

Step 1. Objective of test--determine reasonableness of accounts receivable
Step 2. Define population--individual dollars in account
Step 3. Select sampling technique--probability proportional to size
Step 4. Determine sample size--

"Given"

Tolerable misstatement (TM)	$50,000
Risk of incorrect acceptance	.05
Expected misstatement (EM)	$10,000

$$\text{Calculation sample size} = \frac{\text{Recorded amount of population}}{\text{Sampling interval}}$$

$$\text{Sampling interval} = \frac{\text{TM} - (\text{EM} \times \text{Expansion factor})}{\text{Reliability factor}}$$

$$= \frac{\$50,000 - (\$10,000 \times 1.6)}{3.0} = \$11,333.33$$

$$\text{Sample size} = \frac{\text{Recorded amount of population}}{\text{Sampling interval}} = \frac{\$1,000,000}{\$11,333.33} = 88$$

Step 5. Determine method of selecting sample--systematic
Step 6. Perform sampling plan
Step 7. Evaluate and project results

Projected misstatement--Assume 3 misstatements.

Book value	Audited value	Taint %	Sampling interval	Projected misstatement
$ 100	$ 95	5%	$11,333	$ 567
11,700	212	--*	NA	11,488
65	58.50	10%	11,333	1,133
		Projected misstatement		$13,188

* Not applicable; book value larger than sampling interval

Basic precision = Reliability factor x Sampling interval = 3.0 x

$11,333.33 = $34,000

Incremental allowance for projected misstatements

Reliability factor	(Increm - 1)	Misstatements	Incremental allowance
3.00	--	--	--
4.75	.75	$1,133	$ 850
6.30	.55	567	312
Incremental allowance for projected misstatements			$1,162

Upper limit on misstatements	=	Projected misstatement	+	Basic precision	+	Incremental allowance for projected misstatements
	=	$13,188	+	$34,000	+	$1,162
	=	$48,350	(Accept, this is less than tolerable than tolerable misstatement)			

3. Classical Variables Sampling
    a. Classical variables sampling models use normal distribution theory to evaluate selected characteristics of a population on the basis of a sample of the items constituting the population

(1) For any normal distribution, the following fixed relationships exist concerning the area under the curve and the distance from the mean in standard deviations. This table assumes a two-tailed approach which is appropriate since classical variables sampling models generally test for both overstatement and understatement.

Distance in Stan. Dev. (Reliability coefficient)	Area Under the Curve (Reliability level)	
±1.0	68%	
1.64	90%	*
1.96	95%	
2.0	95.5%	
2.7	99%	

* Most frequently employed on CPA exam

Example where the mean = 250 and the standard deviation = 10:
Small graph goes here, lift from 12th edition.

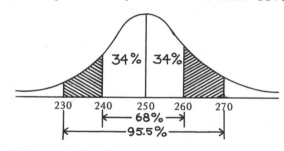

(2) For large samples (greater than or equal to 30) the distribution of sample means tends to be normally distributed about its own mean which is equal to the true population mean, even if the population is not normally distributed (Central Limit Theorem). Since many populations sampled in auditing are not normally distributed, this is important.

(3) The standard deviation in the above model measures the dispersion among the respective amounts of a particular characteristic, for all items in the population for which a sample estimate is developed

b. Variations of classical variables sampling

(1) Mean-per-unit estimation is a classical variables sampling technique that projects the sample average to the total population by multiplying the sample average by the number of items in the population

(a) Determine audit values for each sample item
(b) Calculate the average audit amount
(c) Multiply this average audit amount times the number of units in the population to obtain the estimated population value

(2) Difference estimation is a classical variables sampling technique that uses the average difference between audited amounts and individual recorded amounts to estimate the total audited amount of a population and an allowance for sampling risk

(a) Determine audit values for each sample item
(b) Calculate the difference between the audit value and book value for each sample item
(c) Calculate the average difference

        (d) Determine the estimated population value by multiplying the average difference by the total population units and adding or subtracting this value from the recorded book value

    (3) Ratio estimation is a classical variables sampling technique that uses the ratio of audited amounts to recorded amounts in the sample to estimate the total dollar amount of the population and an allowance for sampling risk

        (a) Determine audit values for each sample item
        (b) Calculate the ratio between the sum of sample audit values and sample book values
        (c) Determine the estimated population value by multiplying the total population book value times this ratio

    (4) The regression approach is similar to the difference and ratio approaches. This approach has the effect of using both the average ratio and the average difference in calculating an estimate of the total amount for the population.

    (5) Difference and ratio estimation are used as alternatives to mean-per-unit estimation. The auditor should use these approaches when applicable because they require a smaller sample size (i.e., they are more efficient than mean-per-unit estimation).

        (a) One factor in the calculation of sample size for classical variables sampling models is the estimated standard deviation. If the standard deviation of differences or ratios is smaller than the standard deviation of audit values, these two methods will produce a smaller sample size.

           1] Difference estimation will be used if the differences between sample audit values and book values are a relatively constant dollar amount, regardless of account size
           2] Ratio estimation will be used if the differences are a constant percentage of book values

        (b) The following constraints must be met if either difference or ratio estimation is to be used

           1] The individual book values must be known and must sum to the total book value
           2] There must be more than a few (20-50) differences between audit and book values

        (c) These two methods will usually be more efficient than mean-per-unit estimation when stratification of the population is not possible

c. Variables sampling steps applied to classical variables sampling

    (1) Determine the objectives of the test--Recall that variables sampling models are designed to draw conclusions in dollar amounts
    (2) Define the population--The population consists of the items constituting the account balance or class of transactions

        (a) Sampling unit--As with PPS sampling, the sampling unit is any of the individual elements that constitute the population. For example, the sampling unit in receivables is often an individual customer's account
        (b) Consider the completeness of the population--As discussed in PPS, the auditor must consider whether the physical representation includes the entire population

(c) Identify individually significant items--Items which are individually significant for which sampling risk is not justified, should be tested separately and not be subject to sampling. These are items for which potential error could individually equal or exceed tolerable misstatement. Note that in PPS these items were automatically selected

(3) Select an audit sampling technique--Here we would select among mean-per-unit, difference, ratio, and regression estimation

(4) Determine the sample size--The following factors are included in the sample size calculation

(a) The population size is directly related to sample size

(b) Estimated standard deviation--An estimate must be made of the dispersion of audit values for the units constituting the population. This value can be estimated by

1] Calculating the standard deviation of recorded amounts
2] Auditing a small pilot sample, or
3] Using the standard deviation found in the previous audit
4] A population's standard deviation may be reduced through stratification. Stratification divides the population into relatively homogeneous groups. This minimizes the effect of variation within the population. The mean-per-unit approach requires sample sizes for an unstratified population that may be too large to be cost effective for ordinary audit applications

(c) Tolerable misstatement--An estimate of the maximum monetary misstatement that may exist in an account balance or class of transactions, when combined with error in other accounts, without causing the financial statements to be materially misstated

(d) Risk of incorrect rejection (alpha risk)--Since the risk of incorrect rejection is inversely related to sample size, the auditor must weigh the costs of a larger sample size against the potential incurrence of additional costs associated with expanded audit procedures following the initial rejection resulting from a sample size that was too small

(e) Risk of incorrect acceptance (beta risk)--In specifying an acceptable level of risk of incorrect acceptance, the auditor considers the level of audit risk that s/he is willing to accept. Recall this discussion in section "B.1.a." of the Professional Responsibilities module

(f) Planned allowance for sampling risk (desired precision)--The allowance is a function of the auditor's estimates of tolerable misstatement, risk of incorrect rejection, and risk of incorrect acceptance. The risk of incorrect acceptance is not explicitly included in the sample size equation, but the allowance for sampling risk controls the level of risk the auditor is assuming

1] The following equation can be used to calculate the allowance for sampling risk:

A = TM x R

A = planned allowance for sampling risk
TM = tolerable misstatement
R = ratio of desired allowance for sampling risk to tolerable error at a specified risk of incorrect acceptance and a specified risk of incorrect rejection. The following table is from the Audit Sampling Guide - Appendix C

Ratio of Desired Allowance for Sampling Risk to Tolerable Misstatement

Risk of Incorrect Acceptance	Risk of Incorrect Rejection			
	.20	.10	.05	.01
.01	.355	.413	.457	.525
.025	.395	.456	.500	.568
.05	.437	.500	.543	.609
.075	.471	.532	.576	.641
.10	.500	.561	.605	.668
.15	.511	.612	.653	.712
.20	.603	.661	.700	.753
.25	.653	.708	.742	.791
.30	.707	.756	.787	.829
.35	.766	.808	.834	.868
.40	.831	.863	.883	.908
.45	.907	.926	.937	.952
.50	1.000	1.000	1.000	1.000

2] *EXAMPLE: If tolerable misstatement is determined to be $50,000, and the risks of incorrect acceptance and incorrect rejection are set at 5% and 10%, respectively, then*

   A = $50,000 x .500 = $25,000

3] Notice that if the planned allowance is set equal to tolerable misstatement, the risk of incorrect acceptance assumed will always be 50%. If the planned allowance is equal to half of tolerable misstatement, then the risk of incorrect acceptance will be equal to 50% of the specified risk of incorrect rejection

(g) Sample size equation

$$n = \left(\frac{N \times SD \times U_R}{A} \right)^2$$

n = sample size
N = population size
SD = estimated population standard deviation
U_R = the standard normal deviate for the acceptable risk of incorrect rejection
A = planned allowance for sampling risk

(h) The above formula assumes sampling with replacement and may be adjusted by a finite correction factor (thereby reducing sample size) when sampling without replacement

$$n' = \frac{n}{1 + n/N}$$ n' = sample size adjusted for finite correction factor

(5) <u>Determine the method of selecting the sample</u>--Classical samples are generally selected using random sampling or stratified random sampling

(6) <u>Perform the sampling plan</u>--Perform appropriate audit procedures to determine an audit value for each item

   (a) If the auditor is unable to examine selected items (i.e., accounts receivable confirmations are not returned) the auditor should perform alternative procedures that provide sufficient evidence to form a conclusion

(7) <u>Evaluate and project the sample results</u>--As was the case with sample selection, the actual evaluation and projection of sample results is affected by the method used. Here we will assume mean per unit. Additionally, the various auditing textbooks do not agree on the approach for evaluating sample results. The decision rules presented here are simplified.

   (a) Calculate the estimated audited population value (EAPV)

      $$EAPV = N \times \overline{X}$$

      N = population size

      $\overline{X}$ = average of audit sample values

   (b) Calculate the achieved allowance for sampling risk (this holds the risk of incorrect rejection at its planned level)

      $$A' = N \times U_R \times \frac{SD \times \sqrt{1 - (n'/N)}}{\sqrt{n'}}$$

      N = population size
      U_R = standard normal deviate for planned risk of incorrect rejection (reliability)
      SD = standard deviation of audit sample values

   (c) Calculate the adjusted allowance for sampling risk (this holds the risk of incorrect acceptance at its planned level)

      $$A'' = A' + TM (1 - A'/A)$$

      TM = tolerable misstatement

   (d) Use the following decision rule. If the book value falls in the interval created by the estimated population value, plus or minus the adjusted allowance for sampling risk, accept the population as not having a material misstatement. If it does not, reject the population

      NOTE: This decision rule assumes that the risk of incorrect acceptance is the most important risk to control and that the auditor has properly calculated the required

sample size. Also, the auditor should consider qualitative aspects of the misstatements as well as quantitative factors

The following example illustrates the unstratified mean per unit classical
method.

Classical Variables (Mean Per Unit) Sampling Example

Step 1. Objective of test--determine existence of accounts receivable
Step 2. Define population--individual accounts
Step 3. Select sampling technique--mean per unit
Step 4. Determine sample size--

"Given" -- a through f

a. Population size   10,000 accounts
b. Estimated standard deviation $30
c. Tolerable misstatement $50,000
d. Risk of incorrect rejection   .05
e. Risk of incorrect acceptance   .05
f. Planned allowance for sampling risk $27,150

$$A = TM \times R = \$50,000 \times .543^* = \$27,150$$

* From Ratio of Desired Allowance for Sampling Risk to Tolerable
   Misstatement Table

g. Calculate sample size

$$n = \left(\frac{N \times SD \times U_R}{A}\right)^2 = \left(\frac{10,000 \times 30 \times 1.96}{\$27,150}\right)^2 = 469$$

$$n' = \frac{n}{1 +(n/N)} = \frac{469}{1 + (469/10,000)} = 448$$

Step 5. Determine method of selecting sample - random
Step 6. Perform sampling plan
Step 7. Evaluate and project sample results

Assume $\overline{X}$ (average audited value) = $98
       SD (standard deviation)   = $29

EAPV = 10,000 x $98 = $980,000

$$A' = N \times U_R \times \frac{SD \times \sqrt{1-(n'/N)}}{\sqrt{n'}} = 10,000 \times 1.96 \times \frac{29 \times \sqrt{1 -(448/10,000)}}{\sqrt{448}} = \$26,246$$

$$A'' = A' + TM (1-A'/A) = 26,246 + 50,000 (1 - 26,246/27,150) = \$27,911$$

$980,000 ± $27,911

[$952,089, $1,007,911] [Accept, since book value ($1,000,000) is in this
interval]

4. Comparison of PPS Sampling to Classical Variables Sampling

a. PPS sampling is generally easier to use than classical variables
    sampling. Classical variables sampling requires more familiarity with
    statistical theory and generally requires the assistance of computer
    programs to design an efficient sample and evaluate sample results

b. If the auditor expects no misstatements, PPS sampling will generally result in a smaller sample size. As the expected amount of misstatement increases, the appropriate PPS sample size increases. If there are many differences between recorded and audited amounts, classical variables sampling may be more efficient

c. PPS sampling automatically results in a stratified sample and identifies individually significant items because items are selected for testing in proportion to their dollar amounts

d. A PPS sample can be designed more easily and sample selection can begin before the complete population is available, but classical variables samples may be easier to expand if that becomes necessary

e. PPS sampling includes an assumption that the audited amount of a sample unit should not be negative nor greater than the recorded amount. Selection of zero balances also requires special sample design considerations. Classical variables sampling can be used to test for understatement as well as overstatement without modification. Selection of zero or negative balances does not necessitate special design considerations

f. PPS sampling is not based on any measure of the estimated variation of audited amounts. Classical variables sampling requires an estimate of the population standard deviation.

g. When misstatements are found, PPS evaluation might overstate the allowance for sampling risk, leading to rejection of an acceptable recorded amount

h. In classical variables sampling, when there are very large items in the population or very large differences between recorded and audited amounts and the sample size is not large, the normal distribution theory might not be appropriate leading to the acceptance of an unacceptable recorded amount

AUDITING EDP

Computers have become the primary means used to process financial accounting information in most businesses. Thus, to conduct a proper audit, the auditor must be
able to evaluate and test a client's electronic data processing (EDP) system. Consistent with this situation, knowledge of EDP terminology, systems, and audit procedures is tested on the auditing portion of the CPA exam. The following "diagram" of
an Audit was first presented and explained in the auditing overview section.

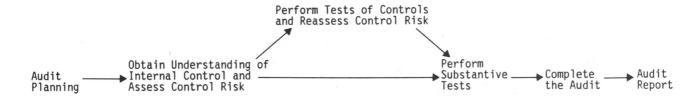

EDP does not necessitate modification of the diagram. However, note that the
internal controls to be reviewed and evaluated may be computer rather than manual
controls. Similarly, EDP procedures may be used to test compliance with various
internal controls. Also, at the substantive test stage, audit procedures will very
obviously be affected when a client's records (e.g., general ledger) are maintained
on a computer.

The EDP questions on past CPA exams have been very basic in nature. In fact, the
candidate could answer a large percentage of questions with information from four
sources: (1) SAS No. 55 (to a limited extent); (2) the AICPA Audit Guide, <u>Computer
Assisted Audit Techniques</u>; (3) the AICPA Audit Guide, <u>The Auditor's Study and
Evaluation of Internal Control in EDP Systems</u>; and (4) the information presented in
any basic auditing text's chapter on EDP. For example, essay questions have typically required candidates to describe the effects of EDP on internal control, enumerate the types of auditing procedures that auditors use when EDP is involved, and
relate EDP considerations to an internal control question.

Multiple choice questions have also addressed the effect of EDP on internal control and audit procedures. Additionally, multiple choice questions have tested candidate's knowledge of basic EDP concepts and terms.

If you are not familiar with basic EDP terminology, refer to the glossary at the end of this module (Section "D."). If you have very limited time to study, you should concentrate on understanding flowcharting (part "A." of this module) and how EDP affects the review of internal control and basic audit procedures (part "B."). This will allow you to answer questions that test internal control evaluation using EDP concepts. To become more fully prepared, the information in the remainder of this module should also be studied.

If you have not previously studied EDP, realize that to be fully prepared, a complete review of this module and reference to supplementary materials (i.e., beginning EDP texts) will likely be necessary. We do not believe, however, that reviewing such text material is efficient for most candidates. The information in this module should prepare you to perform reasonably well on the exam. Keep in mind that the review of these materials cannot make you an expert. However, this material should help you to understand the complexities of EDP in sufficient detail to answer most essay and multiple choice questions.

Study Program for Auditing EDP Module

This module is organized and should be studied in the following order. Refer to Section "D." first if you are not familiar with basic EDP terminology.

A. Flowcharting

    1. Flowcharting Symbols
    2. Types and Definitions

B. Principles of Auditing EDP Systems

    1. The Auditor's Review and Evaluation of Internal Control When EDP is Involved
    2. General Controls
    3. Application Controls
    4. Audit Techniques Using EDP

C. Unique Characteristics of Specific EDP Systems

    1. Batch Processing
    2. Direct or Random Access Processing
    3. Data Base Processing
    4. Small Computer Environment
    5. Service Bureau/Center
    6. Distributed Systems

D. EDP Definitions

    1. Hardware
    2. Software
    3. Data Organization for EDP Operations
    4. Documentation

5. Modes of EDP Operation
6. Systems Analysis and Design

A. **Flowcharting**

Flowcharting is a procedure to graphically show the sequential flows of data and/or operations. The data and operations portrayed include document preparation, authorization, storage, and decision making. The more common flowcharting symbols are illustrated below.

1. Common Flowcharting Symbols

Symbol	Name	Description
	Document	This can be a manual form or a computer printout
	Computer Operation	Computer process which transforms input data into useful information
	Manual Operation	Manual (human) process to prepare documents, make entries, check output, etc.
	Decision	Determines which alternative path is followed (IF/THEN/ELSE Conditions)
	Input/Output	General input or output to a process. Often used to represent accounting journals and ledgers on document flowcharts
	Online Storage	Refers to direct access computer storage connected directly to the CPU. Data is available on a random access basis.
	Offline Storage	Refers to a file or indicates the mailing of a document, i.e., invoices or statements to customers. A letter in the symbol below the line indicates the order in which the file is stored. (N-Numerical, C-Chronological, A-Alphabetical)

Symbol	Name	Description
	Display	Visual display of data and/or output on a terminal screen
	Batch Total Tape	Manually computed total before processing (such as the number of records to be processed). This total is recomputed by the computer and compared after processing is completed.
	Magnetic Tape	Used for reading, writing, or storage on sequential storage media
	Manual Data Entry	Refers to data entered through a terminal keyboard or key-to-tape or key-to-disk device
	Annotation	Provides additional description or information connected to symbol to which it annotates by a dotted line (not a flowline)
	Flowline	Shows direction of data flow, operations, and documents
	Communication Link	Telecommunication line linking computer system to remote locations
	Start/Termination	Used to begin or end a flowchart. (Not always used or shown in flowcharts on the CPA exam.) May be used to show connections to other procedures or receipt/sending of documents to/from outsiders

◯   On Page Connector   Connects parts of flow chart on the same page

⬠   Off Page Connector   Connects parts of flow chart on separate pages

2. Types and Definitions

Flowcharts may be one of several types.

a. System flowchart--A graphic representation of a data processing appli-
    cation which depicts the interaction of all the computer programs for a
    given system, rather than the logic for an individual computer program
b. Program flowchart--A graphic representation of the logic (procedural
    steps) of a computer program
c. Internal control (audit) flowcharts or document flowchart--A graphic
    representation of the flow of documents from one department to another,
    showing the source flow and final disposition of the various copies of
    all documents. (See the flowchart from Problem 3 of the May 1985 exam
    in Section "C.1." of Internal Control. Note that the flowchart tests
    the candidate's knowledge of internal control, not his/her knowledge of
    EDP. A candidate should also be able to develop a flowchart from a
    description given.)

3. Other Documentation Charting Techniques

a. Decision table--Decision tables are logic diagrams that present decision
    choices, in matrix form, that are too complex to be clearly shown in a
    flowchart. Decision tables often supplement complex flowcharts. See
    Module 2, page 140, on internal control for an example of a decision
    table.
b. Data Flow Diagram (DFD)--Documents logical flows of data and functions
    in a system
c. HIPO Chart (Hierarchy, Input, Process, Output)--Shows the hierarchy of
    system subtasks or modules. Input, Processing, and Output requirements
    are then described for each module.

B. **Principles of Auditing EDP Systems**

1. The Auditor's Consideration of Internal Control When EDP is Involved

    The auditor's responsibilities with respect to internal control over EDP

systems remains the same as with manual systems, that is, to obtain an

understanding adequate (1) to aid in planning the remainder of the audit and

(2) to assess control risk. Yet, factors such as the following may affect

the study of internal control in that computer systems may

    (1) result in transaction trails that exist for a short period of time
         or only in computer readable form

  (2) include program errors that cause uniform mishandling of
       transactions--clerical errors become less frequent
  (3) include computer controls that need to be relied upon instead of
       segregation of functions
  (4) involve increased difficulty in detecting unauthorized access
  (5) allow increased management supervisory potential resulting from
       more timely reports
  (6) include less documentation of initiation and execution of
       transactions
  (7) include computer controls that affect the effectiveness of related
       manual control procedures that use computer output

The overall process used to consider internal control is the same in EDP
vs. manual systems in that auditors must obtain an overall understanding of
the control structure. The AICPA Audit Guide, The Auditor's Study and
Evaluation of Internal Control in EDP Systems, points out that computer
controls may be divided between general and application controls. These
controls are an integral part of the internal control structure and the
auditor must obtain an understanding of them to perform the audit. The
Audit Guide, issued prior to SAS No. 55 on internal control, includes the
flowchart which appears on page 276. A review of the flowchart will reveal
that it is essentially consistent with SAS No. 55, although the assessment
of control risk is implicit.

Following the consideration of internal control, the auditor performs
various substantive tests necessary to evaluate the reasonableness of
records produced by the EDP system. The nature, timing, and extent of these
tests, like all other tests, depends upon the auditor's assessment of
control risk.

2. General Controls

In an EDP environment, general controls are controls that affect multiple application systems, e.g., payroll, accounts payable, and accounts
receivable. Five categories of general controls are presented in the AICPA
audit guide. The five categories are (a) organization and operation controls, (b) systems development and documentation controls, (c) hardware and
systems software controls, (d) access controls, and (e) data and procedural
controls. Each category described here includes a discussion of the control, as well as detailed examples.

a. Organization and operation controls

  (1) Controls

      (a) Segregate functions between the EDP department and user
           departments

       (b) Do not allow the EDP department to initiate or authorize transactions

       (c) Segregate functions within the EDP department

(2)   <u>Discussion</u>--Segregation of duties provides the control mechanism for maintaining an independent processing environment, thus meeting the control objectives. In addition to organizationally segregating the EDP department from the user departments, the key functions within EDP should be segregated to ensure maximum separation of duties. The key functions are

       (a) <u>Systems analyst</u>--The systems analyst is responsible for analyzing the present user environment and requirements and (1) recommending the specific changes which can be made, (2) recommending the purchase of a new system, or (3) designing a new EDP system. The analyst is in constant contact with the user department and the programming staff to ensure the user's actual and ongoing needs are being met. A system flowchart is one tool used by the analyst to define the system requirement.

       (b) <u>Applications programmer</u>--The applications programmer is responsible for writing, testing, and debugging the application programs from the specifications (whether general or specific) provided by the systems analyst. A program flowchart is one tool used by the applications programmer to define the program logic.

       (c) <u>Systems programmer</u>--The systems programmer is responsible for implementing, modifying, and debugging the software necessary for making the hardware work (such as the operating system, telecommunications monitor, and the data base management system)

       (d) <u>Operator</u>--The operator is responsible for the daily computer operations of both the hardware and the software. S/he mounts magnetic tapes on the tape drives, supervises operations on the operator's console (a special CRT), accepts any required input, and distributes any generated output.

       (e) <u>Data Librarian</u>--The librarian is responsible for the custody of the removable media, i.e., magnetic tapes or disks, and for the maintenance of program and system documentation

       (f) <u>Quality assurance</u>--The quality assurance function is a relatively new function established primarily to ensure that new systems under development and old systems being changed are adequately controlled and that they meet the user's specifications and follow department documentation standards

       (g) <u>Control group</u>--The control group acts as liaison between users and the processing center. This group records input data in a control log, follows the progress of processing, distributes output, and ensures compliance with control totals.

       (h) <u>Data security</u>--The data security function is responsible for maintaining the integrity of the online access control security software. Passwords and IDs are issued to users and follow up is done on all security violations. Review of the work of the data security function can minimize testing.

       (i) <u>Data base administrator</u>--In a data base environment, a data base administrator (DBA) may exist as another key function. The DBA is responsible for maintaining the data base and restricting access to the data base to authorized personnel.

Auditor's Evaluation of Internal Control, EDP

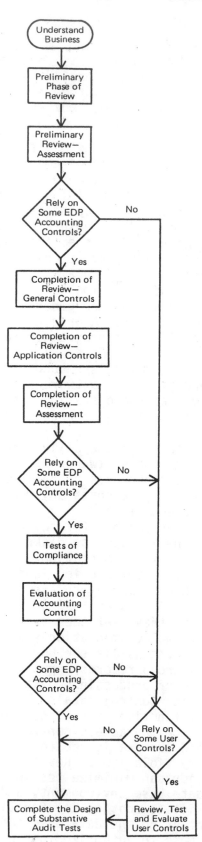

OBJECTIVES:

1. Flow of transactions and significance of output.
2. Extent to which EDP is used in significant accounting applications.
3. Basic structure of accounting control, including both EDP and user controls.

1. Assess significance of EDP and non-EDP accounting controls.
2. Determine extent of additional review within EDP.
3. Develop preliminary design of substantive tests.

1. Determine the effect of strengths and weaknesses on application controls.
2. Identify general controls on which reliance is planned and determine how they operate.
3. Design tests of compliance.

1. Identify applications and related controls on which reliance is planned, and determine how the controls operate.
2. Design tests of compliance.

1. Assess effectiveness of EDP and non-EDP accounting controls.
2. Review preliminary design of substantive procedures.

1. Provide reasonable assurance that controls are functioning properly.
2. Determine and document when, how, and by whom.

1. Consider the types of errors and irregularities that could occur.
2. Determine the accounting control procedures that prevent or detect such errors and irregularities.
3. Determine whether the necessary control procedures are pre-scribed and followed satisfactorily.
4. Evaluate weaknesses and assess their effect on the nature, timing, and extent of substantive procedures.

NOTE: User controls are those outside the EDP system, i.e., traditional controls such as total payroll, dollars of inventory, etc., kept by user departments.

(j)   Network technician--The network technician is fast becoming the most powerful position in a MIS organization. Using line monitoring equipment, they can see each key stroke made by any user. This group must have strict accountability controls.

From an ideal standpoint, all of the key functions should be segregated; however, in a small EDP environment, many of the key functions are concentrated in a small number of employees. In this situation, two key functions that should be segregated are the applications programmer and the operator. When these functions are not segregated, irregularities in EDP can be perpetrated and concealed and the auditor should not rely on the controls within EDP.

The auditor's tests of controls (compliance tests) of the organization and operation controls should include inquiry, observation, discussion, and review of an appropriate organization chart, responsibility for initiating and authorizing transactions, and custody of electronic records or documentation. Any discrepancies should be reported and the appropriate controls recommended.

b.   Systems development and documentation controls

(1)   Controls

(a)   User departments must participate in systems design
(b)   Each system must have written specifications which are reviewed and approved by management and by user departments
(c)   Both users and EDP personnel must test new systems
(d)   Management, users, and EDP personnel must approve new systems before they are placed into operation
(e)   All master and transaction file conversion should be controlled to prevent unauthorized changes and to verify the results on a 100% basis.
(f)   After a new system is operating, there should be proper approval of all program changes
(g)   Proper documentation standards should exist to assure continuity of the system

(2)   Discussion--Within EDP, new systems are developed that either replace old systems or enhance present systems. This environment requires unique controls to ensure that the integrity of the overall system is maintained. Two common controls over system change include the following.

(a)   Design methodology--All new systems being developed should flow through a documented process that has specific control points where the overall direction of the system can be evaluated and changes, if needed, can be made
(b)   Change control process--To effect a change on a system that is presently operating, a formal change process should exist that requires formal approval before any change is implemented. Once approved, the change is developed and tested before it is incorporated into the present system. Programmers should not have access to live data files or production programs. All program changes and maintenance should be done with copies of the programs using test data only. This control process applies to any system or program changes, as well as any changes to a file structure or file content.

that individual, calls back the individual, and reestab-
lishes communications. This system is the primary preven-
tative technique for stopping unauthorized dial-up access
to EDP by an individual trying to masquerade as an
authorized user from an unauthorized telephone number. It
can not be utilized if the dial-in users call in from
multiple locations, e.g., salespeople.

3] Encryption boards--Encryption boards are new devices that
are installed in the back of a microcomputer or stand
alone devices for larger systems. The board is programmed
with a unique "key" that makes data unreadable to anyone
who might intercept a data transmission.

Access controls are tested by attempting to violate the
system, either physically or electronically, or reviewing any
unauthorized access that has been recorded. The auditor must
use tests of controls (compliance tests) to ensure that all
security violations are followed up on to ensure they are
errors.

e. Data and procedural controls

(1) Controls

(a) A control group should

1] Receive all data to be processed
2] Ensure that all data are recorded
3] Follow up on errors during processing, and determine that
transactions are corrected and resubmitted by the proper
user personnel
4] Verify the proper distribution of output

(b) A written manual of systems and procedures should be prepared
for all computer operations and should provide for management's general or specific authorization to process transactions

(c) Internal auditors (or another independent group in the
organization; e.g., quality assurance) should review and
evaluate proposed systems at critical stages of development
and review and test computer processing activities

(2) Discussion--The EDP environment should be clearly defined in detail
and appropriately documented so each individual responsible for
processing knows what to do in each situation that may arise. To
prevent unnecessary stoppages or errors in processing, the
following specific controls should be implemented.

(a) Operations run manual--The operations manual specifies, in
detail, the "how to's" for each application to enable the
computer operator to respond to any errors that may occur

(b) Backup and recovery--To ensure the preservation of historical
records and the ability to recover from an unexpected error,
files created within EDP are backed up in a systematic
manner. The most common method used in a batch processing
environment is called the Grandfather-Father-Son method. In
this environment, detail files are updated with each run. The
detail file being updated is the father. The new file is the
son. The file from which the father was developed is the

grandfather. The father, grandfather, and great-grandfather are backup files that should be stored both on- and off-premises. If the son were destroyed, for example, it could be reconstructed by rerunning the father file and the related transaction file. For data base systems, a daily "snap shot" of the data files is taken, which is retained until the weekly files are created, which are retained until the monthly files are created, which are retained until the yearly files are created. All critical data files, programs, and documentation should be backed up and stored offsite to facilitate a timely restart of processing should a disaster occur.

(c) <u>Contingency processing</u>--Detailed contingency processing plans should be developed to prepare for natural disasters (such as a lightning strike), man-made disasters (such as arson), or general hardware failures that disable the data center. The plans should detail the responsibilities of individuals, as well as the alternate processing sites that should be utilized. There is a new service being sold that allows EDP centers to pay a service fee to be allowed access to an unused facility for backup if they incur an emergency. Backup centers already equipped with hardware are called "hot sites." A center not equipped with hardware but ready for hardware to be brought in is called a "cold site" or "shell site."

(d) <u>Processing control</u>--Processing controls should be monitored by the control group to ensure that processing is completed in a timely manner (controlled through a production schedule of the EDP department), all hardware errors have been corrected (controlled through an operators log), and output has been properly distributed (controlled through distribution logs).

(e) <u>File protection ring</u>--A file protection ring is a processing control to ensure that an operator does not use a magnetic tape as a tape to write on when it actually has critical information on it. If the ring is on the tape, data can be written on the tape.

(f) <u>Internal and external labels</u>--External labels are gummed-paper labels attached to a reel of tape or other storage medium which identify the file. Internal labels perform the same function through the use of machine readable identification in the first record of a file. The use of labels allows the computer operator to determine whether the correct file has been selected for processing. Trailer labels are often used on the end of a magnetic tape file to maintain information on the number of records processed.

These controls are tested mainly through identification, observation, and inquiry. While some of these controls, such as protection rings and labels, are easily implemented, other controls, such as contingency processing, are more difficult and costly to implement. The auditor should determine that these controls are either present or that management has accepted the related risks and that all exceptions are scrutinized.

3. Application Controls

Another set of specialized controls in an EDP system is application controls. Application controls are controls that relate to a specific application instead of multiple applications.

Each accounting application that is processed in an EDP system is controlled during three steps within EDP: input, processing, and output. The input step converts human readable information into computer readable information. Ensuring the integrity of the information in the computer is critical during the processing step. Presentation of the results of processing to the user and retention of data for future use occurs in the output step. Common controls relating to input, processing, and output are presented and discussed with specific examples. The candidate should be prepared to identify these controls in a multiple choice question or use several of them in an essay question.

a. Input controls

(1) Controls

(a) Input data should be properly authorized and approved
(b) The system should verify all significant data fields used to record information (editing the data)
(c) Conversion of data into machine readable form should be controlled and verified for accuracy
(d) Movement of data between processing steps and departments should be controlled
(e) The correction of errors and resubmission of corrected transactions should be reviewed and controlled

(2) Discussion--To ensure the integrity of the human readable data into a computer readable format, there are many common controls that can be used

(a) Preprinted form--Information is preassigned a place and a format on the input form used. The form reduces the possibility that computer input operators will miss or ignore input data recorded by users. This control is used when a large quantity of repetitive data is inputted.
(b) Check digit--An extra digit is added to an identification number to detect certain types of data transmission or transposition errors. It is used to verify that the number was entered into the computer system correctly (within the application program there is a software code that recomputes the check digit), e.g., an extra number on an account number that is calculated as a mathematical combination of the other digits. For example, a bank may add a check digit to individuals' 7 digit account numbers. The computer will calculate the correct check digit based on performing predetermined mathematical operations on the 7 digit account number and will then compare it to the check digit which has been inputted.

      (c) <u>Control, batch, or proof total</u>--A total of one numerical field for all the records of a batch that normally would be added, e.g., total sales dollars

      (d) <u>Hash total</u>--A total of one field for all the records of a batch where the total is a meaningless total for financial purposes, e.g., a mathematical sum of account numbers added together

      (e) <u>Record count</u>--A control total used for accountability to ensure all the records received are processed

      (f) <u>Reasonableness and limit tests</u>--These tests determine if amounts are too high, too low, or unreasonable (e.g., for a field that indicates auditing exam scores, a limit check would test for scores over 100). A reasonableness check is similar to a validity check (see below).

      (g) <u>Menu driven input</u>--If input is being entered into a CRT, then the operator should be greeted by a menu and prompted as to the proper response to make [e.g., What score did you get on the Auditing part of the CPA Exam (75-100)?]

      (h) <u>Field checks</u>--Checks that make certain only numbers, alphabetical characters, special characters, and proper positive and negative signs are accepted into a specific data field where they are required (e.g., a pay rate should include only numerical data; a numeric check would assure that only numbers will be accepted into these columns. If alphabetical information is erroneously input, an error message would result.)

      (i) <u>Validity check</u>--A check which allows only "valid" transactions or data to be entered into the system (e.g., a field indicating sex of an individual where 1=male and 2=female if coded with a "3" would not be accepted)

      (j) <u>Missing data check</u>--If blanks exist in input data where they should not (e.g., an employee's division number) an error message would result

      (k) <u>Field size check</u>--If an exact number of characters is to be inputted (e.g., employee numbers all have six digits) an error message would result if < 6 or > 6 characters are inputted

      (l) <u>Logic check</u>--Ensures that illogical combinations of inputs are not accepted into the computer (e.g., the field total for raw material is validated by footing price times quantity).

  b. <u>Processing controls</u>

    (1) <u>Controls</u>

      (a) Control totals should be produced and reconciled with input control totals--proof of batch totals

      (b) Controls should prevent processing the wrong file and detect errors in file manipulation--label checks

      (c) Limit and reasonableness checks should be incorporated into programs to prevent illogical results such as reducing inventory to a negative value

      (d) Run-to-run totals should be verified at appropriate points in the processing cycle. This ensures that records are not added or lost during the processing runs.

(2) Discussion--Once the input has been accepted by the computer, it usually is processed through multiple steps. Processing controls are essential to ensure the integrity of the data through all of the processing steps. Examples of processing controls that are established during the input step and are revised or checked during processing include record counts, hash totals, and control totals. Two additional controls that should be established are

    (a) Checkpoint/restart capacity--If a particular program requires a significant amount of time to process, it is desirable to have software within the application that allows the operator the ability to restart the application at the last checkpoint passed as opposed to restarting the entire application

    (b) Error resolution procedure--Individual transactions may be rejected during processing as a result of the error detection controls in place. There should be complementary controls that ensure those records are corrected and reentered into the system. Logging of errors in a suspense file of "suspended" transactions is often used to control error resolution.

c. Output controls

  (1) Controls--Visual review of the output should be done by the user or an independent control group

    (a) Output control totals should be reconciled with input and processing control totals

    (b) Output should be scanned and tested by comparison to original source documents

    (c) Systems output should be distributed only to authorized users

  (2) Discussion--Prior to the release of output to the user, there should be appropriate controls in place to ensure that processing was accomplished according to specifications. The following controls are frequently used to maintain the integrity of processing.

    (a) Control total--The user of the application will frequently give the operator the expected result of processing ahead of time to allow the operator to verify that processing was completed properly and to notify the user if the totals did not agree

    (b) Limiting the quantity of output and total processing time-- Time restraints and output page generation constraints are often automated within the job being run to ensure that, if processing is being done in error, the job will not utilize resources needlessly

    (c) Error message resolution--Following each job the system provides technical codes indicating the perceived success of the job run. The operator should be trained to recognize these codes and take the appropriate action detailed in the operations run manual.

4. Audit Techniques Using EDP

The first decision an auditor must make is whether to audit around (examine inputs into and outputs from the computer while ignoring processing) or through the computer (in some manner directly utilize the computer's processing ability). Auditing through the computer gains importance as client EDP systems become more sophisticated. There are many techniques which auditors can use to audit through the computer to test EDP applications. Some of the more common techniques are described below.

a. Audit software--The auditor may use various types of software on either microcomputers or main frame computers. For example, auditors often use microcomputer electronic spread sheets to prepare working trial balances, lead, and other schedules. Such spreadsheets may significantly simplify the computational aspects of tasks such as incorporating adjustments and reclassifications on a worksheet.
Three other types of software may be used on either a microcomputer or a main frame computer: generalized audit software, system utility software, and customized (written specially for one client) audit programs. Generalized audit software is used most frequently because it allows the auditor to access various clients' computer files. Some of the audit procedures that may be performed by generalized audit software include:

(1) Testing client calculations
(2) Making additional calculations
(3) Extracting data from the client files
(4) Examining records which meet criteria specified by the auditor (e.g., property acquisitions in excess of $10,000)
(5) Selecting audit samples
(6) Comparing data that exist on separate files
(7) Summarizing data
(8) Printing reports and various analyses
(9) Comparing data obtained through other audit procedures with client records
(10) Identify weaknesses in internal control
(11) Prepare flowcharts of client transaction cycles and of client programs
(12) Prepare graphic displays of data for easier analysis
(13) Correspondence (engagement letters, representation letters, attorney's letters)

b. Test data--A set of dummy transactions is developed by the auditor and processed by the client's computer programs to determine whether the controls which the auditor intends to rely upon are functioning as expected. Some of these transactions may include errors to test the effectiveness of programmed controls and to determine how transactions are handled. Every possible transaction value need not be tested. In fact, prior exam questions have suggested that each control need only be tested once. Several possible problems associated with test data are that the auditor must

(1) Make certain the test data is not included in the client's accounting records
(2) Determine that the program tested is actually used by the client to process data
(3) Devote the necessary time to develop adequate data to test key controls

c. Integrated test facility (ITF)--This method introduces dummy transactions into a system in the midst of live transactions and is usually built into the system during the original design. One way to accomplish this is to incorporate a simulated division or subsidiary into the accounting system with the sole purpose of running test data through it. The test data approach is similar, therefore its limitations are also similar, yet the test data approach does not run simultaneously through the live system. The running of dummy transactions in the midst of live transactions makes the task of keeping the two transaction types separate more difficult.

d. Parallel simulation (Also known as controlled processing/reprocessing)-- This method processes actual client data through an auditor's software program (and frequently, although not necessarily, the auditor's computer). After processing the data, the auditor compares the output obtained with output obtained from the client. This method verifies processing of actual transactions (as opposed to test data and ITF that use dummy transactions) and allows the auditor to verify actual client results. The limitations of this method include

    (1)   The time it takes the auditor to build an exact duplicate of the client's system

    (2)   Incompatability between auditor and client software

    (3)   The time involved in reprocessing large quantities of data

However, the auditor can simply test portions of the system to reduce the overall time and concentrate on key controls.

e. Audit workstation--More internal audit departments and a few external auditing firms are ending their dependence on audit software programs run on a mainframe by using an audit workstation. Using a microcomputer and the necessary software, the auditor extracts the necessary data from the client's files and performs the desired tests directly on the micro-computer. There are seven steps in the use of an audit workstation.

    (1)   Determine data needed--At this step the auditor analyzes the information stored on the mainframe and determines what information would be useful

    (2)   Write extract routine--On a one-time basis, the auditor writes specifications that extract the information required and place it in a format that can be transferred to the audit microcomputer

    (3)   Run extract program--As often as required the extract program is run to create the file that will be transferred to the microcomputer

    (4)   Download extracted file--Moving the files from the mainframe to the microcomputer makes this the most technical step in the process. However, there are new software packages available for the mainframe and the microcomputer that make this process relatively simple.

    (5)   Perform analysis--The auditor is now free of the mainframe and is able to perform the desired analysis. Using a spreadsheet package, the auditor can prepare financial statements, generate ratios, and prepare totals. Using a data-base package the auditor can run statistical analyses.

    (6)   Prepare report--The auditor now has the necessary analyses to develop a more substantial analytical report

    (7)   Workpapers--To document the process, the auditor can write a report using a word processing package and can save the results electronically

The audit workstation may eventually replace manual workpapers. Every auditor would then have his/her own lap computer.

C. Unique Characteristics of Specific EDP Systems

Section "B." described the definitional approach to general and application controls. The purpose of this section is to describe EDP systems that are commonly found in the business environment so the candidate will be able to apply the appropriate controls to the system in question.

1. Batch Processing

Batch processing is a common EDP system. If the question does not specify the EDP system, then the candidate may assume that batch processing is used. Three key points in a batch processing system are

a. Transactions flow through the system in batches (groups of like transactions). In any particular batch, transactions may add, change, or delete information in the master file.
b. If CRTs are used in batch processing, it may appear to the user that changes are occurring immediately to the master file. Often a temporary batch file is set up and the transactions are processed later in the day (online system but not real-time).
c. Batch processing normally leaves a relatively easy to follow audit trail

2. Direct or Random Access Processing

Most newer systems employ direct access processing techniques. Instead of processing transactions in batches, the data is processed as the transactions occur and are entered into the system. Transactions can be input in any order because master file records are available in a random access fashion.

a. Transaction data is entered through online terminals and stored on direct access, disk storage
b. Edit routines immediately check the data for errors. Messages on the display prompt the user to correct and reenter the data.
c. Master files and programs are stored online so that updating can take place as the edited data flows to the application
d. Output comes in the form of CRT displays and hardcopy reports produced periodically
e. Direct access processing is often referred to as online real-time (OLRT) because the response by the system to data input can arrive back to the user in time to affect the user's decision process and files are updated immediately (i.e., an airline reservation system)
f. System security must be in place to restrict access to programs and data to authorized persons only

3. Data Base Processing

Data base processing is the most difficult EDP system to understand. A data base is a set of interconnected files that users can access to obtain specific information. A data base eliminates the need for separate, and often repetitive, application-specific files. For example, instead of payroll and personnel maintaining separate files that contain basically the same information, a data base may be used that contains both the payroll and personnel information and combines like files (e.g., one employee name and number). Such storage of information may alter the audit trail.

Data base processing is dependent on an online real-time (OLRT) EDP system. CRTs can be used to directly access the data base.

The emphasis on controls shifts from batch-type controls to OLRT-type controls, which include the following.

a. User department--Controls in this EDP system must start at the user department, with strict controls over who is authorized to read and/or change the data base

b. Access controls--In addition to the usual controls over terminals and access to the system, data base processing also maintains controls within the data base itself. These controls limit the user to reading and/or changing (updating) only authorized sections of the data base.

c. Backup and recovery--Because the data base is being updated on a continuous basis during the day, a magnetic tape backup of the data base should be made at the end of each day. This tape(s) can be used for backup and recovery. Many times each night only the changes are saved; then, once a week the total data base is saved.

d. Data base administrator--See "B.2.a." above

e. Audit software--Audit software usually tests a backup copy of a data base that has been stored on magnetic tape

4. Small Computer Environments

With the proliferation of micro and minicomputers, controls over these environments (often termed "end-user computing") tend to be "forgotten" or considered unnecessary. No matter how small the computer may become, the control objectives remain the same. Segregation of duties becomes especially difficult in small computer environments because one individual may perform all recordkeeping (processing) as well as maintain other non-recordkeeping responsibilities. Thus, segregation both within the recordkeeping function and with transaction authorization, and asset custody may become a problem.

The emphasis in this environment should center around the following points:

a. Security--In a small computer environment, security over the hardware is not as critical as security over the software and data. Most companies can easily replace the hardware, but may suffer a severe setback if the software and/or data is lost. Access to the software diskettes should be controlled while in storage for the night and in use during the day. Backup copies should also be made, with periodic updating and storage at a different location. If a fixed disk (hard disk) is used, access controls must be present since anyone turning on the power switch can read the data stored on those files. Also, a control problem may exist because the computer operator often understands the system and also has access to the diskettes. The manager of the company may need to become more directly involved in supervising the data processing function where a lack of separation of duties exists in EDP.

b. Verification of processing--Periodically, an independent verification of the applications being processed on the small computer system should be made to prevent the system from being used for personal projects. Also, verification helps prevent errors in internally developed software from going undetected, resulting in inaccurate records or erroneous management decisions.

c. Personnel--Centralized authorization to purchase hardware and software should be required to ensure that "fly-by-night" equipment and "garage-developed" software are not purchased and that corporate-wide discounts can be obtained

5. Service Bureau/Center

Service bureaus are independent computer centers from which companies rent computer time. These bureaus allow companies (users) to do away with most of their data processing departments and/or computer hardware.

Certain controls should be maintained at both the user and the service bureau locations.

a. Contract--In the service bureau contract, ownership of data files and records by the user should be explicitly stated

b. Processing verification--Either batch controls or online controls (depending upon the particular system being rented) should be maintained at the user's location. This includes data transmitted, information received, and data base information.

c. Backup and recovery--Backup files should be under the control of the user, not the service bureau. Likewise, documented recovery procedures should be maintained at the user's location in the event the service bureau abruptly closes or is unable to process data.

d. Timesharing systems--If the service bureau has online access, many users may access and use the computer simultaneously. Controls applicable to in-house batch processing are also applicable to service bureaus. Standard online controls also apply to timesharing systems. The major concern is protection of user data (both stored and in-process) from destruction and unauthorized access. Data protection controls include the following features:

(1) Boundary protection--Reserves a set of addresses for use by a particular job
(2) Passwords on header labels--Access is not allowed without the correct password
(3) Physical security of library storage safeguards the files
(4) Access control--Unique identification and confidential passwords

6. Distributed Systems

Distributed systems represent a network of remote computer sites each having a small computer connected to the main computer system. For example, payroll could have a small computer which communicates with the main system. Distributed systems reduce the load on the main computer system by transferring edit or simple processing functions to the remote sites. Faster turnaround of information is also a feature of distributed systems.

Controls in this system include

a. Audit unit--Each remote location should be well controlled and audited as a separate unit to verify the integrity of the data processed
b. Segregation--Compensating controls over each location should exist as users may have both authorization and recording functions
c. Uniform standards--A set of uniform standards should be established. The auditor should review the document and perform compliance tests on it

D. EDP Definitions

This section reviews the basic terminology that is used in EDP environments.

1. Hardware

a. Computer hardware--Consists of the configuration of physical EDP equipment. (Software consists of the computer programs that tell hardware what to do.)

(1) CPU (Central Processing Unit)--The central processing unit is the principal hardware component of a computer. It contains an arithmetic/logic unit, primary storage, and a control unit. The major function of the CPU is to fetch stored instructions and data, decode the instructions, and carry out the instructions in the arithmetic/logic unit. The CPU is often called a microprocessor in a microcomputer.

(a) The arithmetic/logic unit adds, subtracts, multiplies, compares, etc.
(b) The primary storage contains the data and program steps that are being processed by the CPU divided into ROM (read only memory) and RAM (random access memory). Application programs and data are stored in the RAM at execution time.
(c) The control unit keeps track of addresses in the computer, status of programs, what to do next, etc.

(2) Console--A special CRT used for communication between the operator and the computer.
(3) Peripheral equipment--All non-CPU hardware that may be placed under the control of the central processor. Classified as online or offline (see below), this equipment consists of input, storage, output, and communication devices.
(4) Controllers--Hardware units designed to operate (control) specific input/output units, i.e., card reader controllers, magnetic tape controllers, etc. These devices eliminate the need for the central processing unit to operate the input/output devices.
(5) Channels--Hardware units designed to handle the transfer of data into or out of primary storage (memory). Thus, the central processing unit need not handle the transfer of data.
(6) Buffer memory (or Buffer)--Temporary storage unit used to hold data during input/output operations. This unit compensates for the vast differences in speed between the CPU and the input/output units.

       (7)   Offline--Peripheral equipment not in direct communication with the CPU, e.g., dial-up terminal. The operator generally must intervene to connect offline equipment or data to the CPU.

       (8)   Online--Peripheral equipment in direct communication with, and under the control of, the CPU, e.g., disk drives controlled by the CPU

b. Input devices--Provide a means of transferring data into CPU storage

       (1)   Magnetic tape reader--A device capable of sensing information recorded as magnetized spots on magnetic tape. May also be an output device and storage medium.

       (2)   Magnetic ink character reader (MICR)--Device that reads characters by scanning characters which have been temporarily magnetized using magnetic ink, e.g., bank check readers

       (3)   Optical character recognition (OCR)--Reads characters directly from documents based on their shapes and position on the source document and converts the characters to binary form

       (4)   CRT (Cathrode ray tube)--Typewriter-like device that decodes key strokes into electronic impulses. May be used with an accoustic coupler if telephone communications are used instead of a direct hard wire to the CPU.

       (5)   Key-to-tape and Key-to-disk--Systems in which input data can be entered (keyed) directly onto magnetic tape (to tape), magnetic disk (to disk), or floppy disk through a CRT (key)

c. Storage devices--Devices which store data that can be subsequently used by the CPU. Classified as random or sequential access.

       (1)   Random access--Data can be accessed directly regardless of how it is physically stored. Disks are random access devices which can also process data sequentially.

       (2)   Sequential access--Data must be processed in the order in which it is physically stored. Magnetic tape is a sequential storage device.

       (3)   Primary memory--Primary random storage directly accessed and utilized by the CPU using ROM (read only memory) and RAM (random access memory). User software is temporarily stored in RAM.

       (4)   Magnetic tape or cartridge tape--Can either be an input or an output device. Retrieval of information on magnetic tape is limited to sequential access. Cheapest type of storage available. It is the primary media for backing up direct access disk files.

       (5)   Magnetic disk (Disk)--Disks are secondary random access devices which allow data to be retrieved directly without searching through other stored data. In addition, magnetic disks also allow the transfer of data to the CPU at a faster rate. Microcomputers make extensive use of floppy and hard disk units.

d. Output devices--Devices to produce readable data (or machine readable data, when further processing is required)

       (1)   Cathode ray tube (CRT)--Combination keyboard/display screen device for sending and receiving data

       (2)   Printer--Prints data on computer paper, or directly onto invoices, checks, etc., one character, line, or page at a time

(3) COM (Computer output to microfilm or microfiche)--A device which records output directly on microfilm or microfiche. This frequently takes the place of a printer.

e. Remote systems--In some companies, in addition to hardware located at a centralized site or in the central EDP room, access and sometimes processing capabilities are provided in other rooms or even in other buildings or cities

   (1) Terminals--CRT devices or microcomputers used for input/output (communication) with the CPU
   (2) Point-of-sale devices--A terminal connected to a computer which takes the place of a cash register or similar device. It allows instant recording of transactions (e.g., checks) and has the ability to keep a perpetual inventory.
   (3) Modem (Accoustic coupler)--A hardware device used to convert digital signals from terminals and the CPU into analog signals for transmission across data lines and then to convert the signal back to digital for use by the receiving terminal or CPU
   (4) Distributed systems--Processing is performed at the location closest to the user

2. Software

Software consists of the instructions (programs) which tell the computer hardware how to perform the desired processing.

a. Types of programs

   (1) Operating system--The instructions which control the overall functioning of the CPU and its peripheral equipment. Several different operating systems permit a single configuration of hardware to function in the following modes.

      (a) Multiprogramming--Key Word Program. The operating system processes a program until an input/output operation is required. Since input or output can be handled by peripheral hardware (channels and controllers), the CPU can begin executing another program's instructions. Several programs appear to be concurrently processing.
      (b) Multiprocessing--Key Word Process. Multiple CPUs process data while sharing peripheral units, allowing two or more programs to be executed simultaneously
      (c) Virtual storage--The operating system separates user programs into segment pages automatically. To the user it appears as though there is unlimited memory available for programs, even though the program is still confined to a physical segment of memory. The system brings to primary storage from secondary storage the "page" of the program that the user is working on.

   (2) Utility program--A standard program for performing a commonly required process, such as sorting, merging, and other file maintenance
   (3) Application program--Used to perform the desired data processing tasks, e.g., preparation of payroll, updating of accounts receivable, etc.
   (4) Source program--Program written by a programmer in a source language (FORTRAN, COBOL, etc.) that will be converted into an object program

(5) <u>Object program</u>--The converted source program that was changed using a compiler to create a set of machine readable instructions that the CPU understands

(6) <u>Compiler program</u>--Produces a machine language object program from a source program language in one basic step (e.g., COBOL compiler)

(7) <u>Interpretive program</u>--Each source code instruction is converted to object code each time it is executed. Therefore, a program loop would be very inefficient.

(8) <u>Data base management system</u> (DBMS)--A comprehensive software package for the purpose of creating, accessing, and maintaining a data base

(9) <u>Telecommunications monitor program</u>--Provides edit capabilities and file maintenance to users, monitors online terminals, and handles input to application programs.

b. <u>Programming terminology</u>

(1) <u>Edit</u>--To correct input data prior to processing

(2) <u>Loop</u>--A set of program instructions performed repetitively. Repetition continues a predetermined number of times, or until all data have been processed.

(3) <u>Desk checking</u>--Review of a program by the programmer for errors before the program is run and debugged on the computer

(4) <u>Memory dump</u>--A listing of the contents of storage in hexadecimal (base 16) code

(5) <u>Run</u>--A complete cycle of a program, including input, processing, and output

(6) <u>Debug</u>--To find and eliminate errors in a computer program. Many compilers assist debugging by listing errors in the program such as invalid commands.

(7) <u>Patch</u>--A section of coding inserted into a routine to correct a mistake or alter a routine

(8) <u>Address</u>--A location in main CPU storage

3. <u>Data Organization for EDP Operations</u>

a. <u>Bit</u>--A binary digit (0 or 1 represented by a positive or negative charge, on or off, etc.) the smallest unit of data possible

b. <u>Byte (Character)</u>--A group of bits (usually 8) which represents a single character, whether alphabetic, numeric, or alphanumeric

c. <u>Wordsize</u>--The amount of data handled by the CPU at one time. 32 bits for mainframe computers, usually 16 bits for microcomputers.

d. <u>Alphabetic</u>--Characters from the alphabet

e. <u>Numeric</u>--Digits 0-9

f. <u>Alphanumeric</u>--Alphabetic, numeric, and special characters. Special characters are pluses, minuses, dollar signs, etc.

g. <u>Field, Item</u>--A group of related characters (e.g, a social security number)

h. <u>Record</u>--A group of related fields handled as a unit, e.g., an employee's pay record for one week

i. <u>File</u>--A group of related records (e.g, all the weekly pay records year-to-date), which is usually arranged in sequence

j. <u>Master file</u>--A file containing relatively permanent information used as a source of reference and periodically updated with a detail (transaction) file (e.g., permanent payroll records)

    k. <u>Detail or transaction file</u>--A file containing current transaction information used to update the master file (e.g, hours worked by each employee during the current period used to update the payroll master file)

    l. <u>Data base</u>--A series of interrelated files combined to eliminate redundancy of data items and to establish logical connections between data items, e.g., payroll and personnel files are combined eliminating redundant SSN, name, etc.

4. <u>Documentation</u>

Documentation is the written description of a system, application, or program designed to substantiate or to explain some aspect of the system, application, or program.

    a. <u>Program documentation</u>--Describes a single program. Program documentation usually consists of the following sections.

        (1) <u>Problem statement or program specifications</u>--Clear statement of the problem to be solved and the objectives of the program

        (2) <u>Operating instructions</u>--To be used by the operator when running the program

        (3) <u>Record layouts</u>--Sample input documents and report formats

        (4) <u>Program flowcharts</u>--Including the logic

        (5) <u>Program listing</u>--In the source language

        (6) <u>Test data</u>--To test the controls and accuracy of the program

        (7) <u>Approval and change sheet</u>--Includes initial authorization to use, record of periodic review, and proper authorization of any changes

    b. <u>System</u>--Overall description of a related set of programs (an application, e.g, payroll, inventory, etc.)

    c. <u>Operations</u>--The operating instructions taken from the program documentation. Note that the operator is not given access to the other parts of the run manual, e.g., programs. This control precludes tampering with the program, the test data, etc.

    d. <u>User instructions</u>--To personnel preparing input or receiving output: how to prepare input and what to expect as output

    e. <u>Library or file control instructions</u>--Relate to the structure, storage, and safeguarding of files

5. <u>Modes of EDP Operation</u>

EDP operations can be classified several ways.

    a. Systems can be differentiated based on the timing of transaction processing. Two types of systems using this basis for differentiation are

        (1) <u>Batch processing</u>--Records are collected into groups (batches) before processing

        (2) <u>Online real-time systems</u> (OLRT)--Processing time is instantaneous in these systems. This requires related records and programs to be online (disk files), not in an offline library.

           (a) Definition of terms

               1] <u>Online</u>--A terminal or input device in direct communication with the central processing unit

               2] <u>Real-time</u>--The data files are updated immediately after data input. Response is received by user in time to affect the decision process.

3] Integrated systems--Multiple files or a data base. Each transaction that affects multiple files updates all files in one processing run rather than separate runs for each file, i.e., duplicate operations are minimized.

4] Virtual storage--A technique which simulates increased RAM storage by dividing large programs into frames or pages. The pages being executed are held in RAM memory until they are no longer needed. The unneeded pages are then "swapped" for needed pages being stored on direct access storage (disk packs).

(b) Operation of OLRT systems

1] Communications controller--An input device that electronically scans incoming messages from terminals for correctness, assigns priorities, and puts them into an input queue for later processing by the CPU. May also be called: concentrator, multiplexor, cluster, controller.

2] Supervisory program--The operating system in an online real-time system. It takes the messages produced by the communications controller, determines which files and which programs are needed for processing those transactions, and controls the actual processing of the transactions.

3] Input terminals--Any device used as a source for the transactions, usually a CRT

4] Location of files and programs--In an online real-time system, active files and programs are stored on magnetic disk as opposed to the usual library storage procedures of a batch processing system. The files and programs are obtained by the supervisory program after analysis of required files and programs.

b. Systems may also be differentiated based on the physical location of the equipment. Using this criterion, the following are the two major categories:

(1) In-house systems--Computer hardware and personnel are maintained by the company which utilizes them

(2) Non-in-house systems--Main processing hardware belongs to another organization. The most common off-premise systems are

(a) Block time--Rental of time by one firm of another organization's computer

(b) Timesharing--Access to another organization's computer is provided through terminal devices. User has the impression of being the sole user of the system, when in reality the computer is sharing its time with a number of users.

(c) Service bureaus--Use of an outside organization to provide a wide range of data-processing services (from systems analysis and design to the actual running of programs with data) for a fee. Also called Facilities Management if the company uses an outside management team to run its internal EDP operation under contract.

6. Systems Analysis and Design

A general knowledge of systems analysis and design is tested on the auditing section of the exam. Note that these areas can apply to noncomputer areas as well. The following list comprises the components of a typical analysis and design process. This process is often referred to as the Application Development Life Cycle. The specific terms may be different on the exam but the objectives will not change. This same methodology can be used if buying packaged software. Testing should be even more exacting than for an inhouse developed system.

a. Feasibility study--A preliminary investigation of the problem area raised by a user of the system. The current system is investigated by interviewing key user personnel and examining documentation. Alternative actions are examined and the feasibility of each in economic, technical, and scheduling terms is enumerated.

b. Detailed investigation and requirements definition--A thorough examination of user needs and requirements. Further interviews, reviews of documentation, and observation of procedures are undertaken. Detailed alternatives with associated costs and benefits are developed for user and management review. Upon management approval of one alternative, the process moves into systems design of the new system.

c. System design--At this point the detailed specifications of the new system are developed. Documents, inputs, output designs, file formats, major work flows, and processing requirements are specified. User personnel must be kept in close touch as this phase progresses. Controls for the new system should be developed at this time. Management approves and signs off on the specifications prior to further development of the system.

d. Systems development--The detailed specifications are now developed into a working system. Needed hardware and software are obtained (software may be written in-house or purchased), documentation is written and the system is thoroughly tested. Training of user personnel begins during this phase.

e. Implementation of the system--Schedules are arranged to begin the start-up of the new system. File conversion and user training are completed before cut-over to the new system. Four methods of implementation are in common use

(1) Parallel operation--The old and new systems are run side-by-side for a period of time to ensure that the new system is producing the proper output. This method is expensive and may be impossible because of time and cost constraints.

(2) Pilot operation--The entire system is implemented for only one segment of the business such as one location or division. When all the problems have been resolved, implementation is expanded to other segments of the company.

(3) Piecemeal implementation--The new system is divided into logical modules and implemented in the entire company one module at a time. New modules are added as the preceding one begins to run smoothly.

(4) Cold turkey implementation-(sometimes called the "plunge" method)--The old system is shut off and the new one turned on during a

weekend or other down period. The company must proceed on faith
that the new system has no undetected defects. Obviously this
method has the greatest risk and should be avoided if at all
possible. Some notable systems failures have occurred using this
approach! Fallback plans are developed to determine which problems
might cause the implementation team to fall back to the old system.

f. Post implementation review and maintenance--The implemented system is
evaluated by users and systems personnel. The main purpose is to see if
the system is fulfilling user needs and specifications. Maintenance
activity is ongoing over the life of the system to correct errors and
adapt the system to changing environmental conditions.

OUTLINES OF PROFESSIONAL STANDARDS

This section begins with an outline of the first three Statements on Standards for Attestation Engagements. The next 130 pages outline the nonsuperseded sections of SAS 1 through SAS 63 as of May 1989. Note that the outlines are presented in codified sequence rather than chronological sequence (see listing of SAS Sections on pages 92-94). Study these SAS outlines in conjunction with the related topical material, e.g., ethics, reports, etc., in this chapter. Finally, outlines are presented of SSARS 1-6.

STATEMENTS ON STANDARDS FOR ATTESTATION ENGAGEMENTS

AT 100 Attestation Standards

Overall Objectives and Approach--This section provides a general framework (composed of 11 attestation standards) and sets boundaries around the attest function. These standards are meant to serve as a general framework for all attest engagements. As such, they are meant to (1) guide CPAs engaged in new and evolving attest services, and (2) guide AICPA standards-setting bodies.

Since financial statement audits are attest services, the attest standards apply. Thus, the ten generally accepted auditing standards provide more specific guidance, while the attest standards are meant to apply at a more general level.

The following outline has four sections. Section A defines attest engagements, and provides examples. Sections B, C, and D present the general, field work, and reporting standards, respectively. Note that the first numbered subheadings under sectionS B, C, and D are the standards.

A. Attest engagements

    1. Definition: An attest engagement is one in which a practitioner is engaged to issue or does issue a written communication that expresses a conclusion about the reliability of a written assertion that is the responsibility of another party.

    2. Examples of attest engagements

        a. Reports on internal control
        b. Descriptions of computer software
        c. Compliance with statutory, regulatory, and contractual requirements
        d. Investment performance statistics
        e. Information supplementary to financial statements

    3. Examples of professional services not considered to be attest engagements

        a. Management consulting engagements which provide advice or recommendations.
        b. Tax engagements (advocacy, return preparation, and advice)
        c. Financial statement compilations
        d. Assisting client in preparing nonfinancial statement information (e.g., acting as the company accountant)

      e. Serving as an expert witness

      f. Providing expert opinion on points of principle, given specific facts (e.g., application of tax laws, or accounting standards)

   4. Attestation standards are divided into (1) general, (2) field work, (3) reporting standards.

B. General standards

   1. The engagement shall be performed by practitioner with adequate technical training and proficiency in the attest function

      a. Preparing and presenting assertions vs. performing attestation

         (1) Preparing and presenting assertions (the <u>asserter</u>)--collecting, classifying, summarizing, and communicating information

         (2) Attesting (the <u>attester</u>)--gathering evidence to support assertion and assessing the measurements and communications of asserter

   2. Engagements shall be performed by practitioner with adequate knowledge of subject matter

      a. The requirement may be met, in part, through use of specialists if practitioner can communicate work objectives and evaluate work of specialist

   3. The engagements shall be performed only if assertion(s) is(are) (1) capable of evaluation against reasonable criteria, and (2) capable of reasonably consistent estimation or measurement using those criteria

      a. Examples of reasonable criteria setting bodies--those authorized under AICPA Code of Professional Conduct or by the regulatory agencies

      b. Criteria established by industry associations or similar groups do not follow due process and the practitioner should evaluate whether they are reasonable

      c. Evaluation of the usefulness of criteria should consider the relevance and reliability of the information

      d. An assertion estimated using criteria of a body designated by AICPA Code of Professional Conduct is, by definition, capable of reasonably consistent estimation

> *NOTE: The following bodies have been authorized to promulgate technical standards:*
> *(1) The Auditing Standards Board*
> *(2) The Accounting and Review Services Committee*
> *(3) The Management Advisory Services Executive Committee*
> *(4) The Financial Accounting Standards Board*
> *(5) The Governmental Accounting Standards Board*

      e. Assurance should not be provided on extremely subjective assertions (e.g., this is the "best" software product)

   4. The practitioner is to maintain an independent mental attitude

      a. Also, avoid situations that may impair appearance of independence

   5. Due professional care shall be exercised

C. Standards of field work

   1. Work shall be adequately planned and assistants properly supervised

      a. Factors to be considered in planning an attest engagement

        (1) Presentation criteria
        (2) Anticipated attestation risk (risk of unknowingly failing to appropriately modify attest report on a materially misstated assertion)
        (3) Preliminary judgments about materiality levels
        (4) Likelihood items will need revision or adjustment
        (5) Conditions that may require extension or modification of attest procedures
        (6) Nature of report to be issued

2. Sufficient evidence shall be obtained to provide reasonable basis for conclusion in report

    a. Presumptions (subject to important exceptions)

        (1) Evidence from independent sources provides more assurance than evidence secured solely from within entity
        (2) Information from direct personal knowledge is more persuasive than information obtained indirectly
        (3) Assertions developed under effective internal control are more reliable than those developed in absence of internal control

        NOTE: Recall that the above presumptions are also presented in AU 326.19

    b. Procedures that involve <u>search and verification</u> (they generally are more costly ones such as inspection, confirmation, observation) are more effective in reducing attestation risk than those involving <u>internal inquiries and comparisons</u> (e.g., analytical procedures, discussions with involved individuals)

    c. Levels of acceptable attestation risk

        (1) <u>Examination</u> (highest level of assurance)--low level of attestation risk, achieved by selecting from all available procedures
        (2) <u>Review</u> (moderate level of assurance)--moderate level of attestation risk, achieved by inquiries and analytical procedures (and additional procedures when evidence with respect to assertions seems incomplete or inaccurate)
        (3) <u>Agreed-Upon Procedures</u> (most frequently negative assurance)--specified by specific user, but must exceed mere reading of assertions

D. Standards of reporting

  1. The report shall identify assertion being reported on and state character of the examination

    a. It is the responsibility of the asserter (generally management) to identify the assertions being made. The assertions should generally be bound with and accompany the practitioner's (attester's) report
    b. A practitioner's general distribution report should include (1) description of scope of work performed, and (2) reference to appropriate profes-sional standards

        (1) When a form is prescribed by authoritative standards (e.g., GAAS) it should be used
        (2) When no form exists, terms "examination" or "review" should be used with a reference to "standards established by AICPA" included

    c. For agreed-upon procedures the practitioner should refer to arrangements made with the specified user(s)

2. The report shall state practitioner's conclusion about whether assertion is presented in conformity with criteria

   a. General-distribution attest reports should be limited to 2 levels: (1) examinations (low level of attestation risk) and (2) reviews (moderate level of risk)

   b. Examinations provide a positive opinion on whether assertions are presented in conformity with criteria. Form of the report

      (1) First paragraph identifies information and states that examination was conducted in accordance with AICPA standards
      (2) Additional paragraphs may be added to emphasize matters relating to engagement or presentation of assertions
      (3) Final paragraph identifies information and whether (in our opinion) statements are in conformity with criteria

   c. Reviews provide negative assurance on whether any information came to practitioner's attention that assertions are not presented in conformity with criteria. Form of the report

      (1) First paragraph identifies information and states that review was conducted in accordance with AICPA standards
      (2) Second paragraph states that scope of review is less than an examination and that no opinion is expressed
      (3) Additional paragraphs may be added to emphasize certain matters relating to review or presentation of assertions
      (4) Final paragraph identifies information and provides negative assurance (nothing came to our attention) on statements being in conformity with criteria

   NOTE: When criteria have been specified by user and agreed upon by asserter and user, the examination and review reports are modified to include (1) statement of limitations on use of report to specified parties and (2) indication, when applicable, that presentation of assertions differs from criteria used for general-distribution reports

   d. Agreed-upon procedures provide a summary of findings, negative assurance, or both. Form of the report

      (1) First paragraph states that (1) agreed-upon procedures have been applied, (2) purpose solely to assist specified user, and (3) report should not be used by others
      (2) Second paragraph enumerates agreed-upon procedures
      (3) Third paragraph states that scope of agreed-upon procedures less in scope than an examination and that no opinion is expressed
      (4) Final paragraph identifies information and provides negative assurance, a summary of findings or both on statements being in conformity with criteria

   NOTE: Be aware of the three forms of attestation reports--examinations, reviews, and agreed-upon procedures

3. Report shall state all of practitioner's significant reservations about the engagement and the presentation of the assertion

   a. Scope limitations may require practitioner to qualify, disclaim any assurance, or to withdraw from engagement

      (1) Reasons should be described in practitioner's report

(2) If many assertions are affected, or if performing a review, a disclaimer or withdrawal is more likely to be appropriate
(3) Client imposed restrictions generally result in a disclaimer or withdrawal

b. Reservations about the presentation (e.g., measurement, form, arrangement, content, underlying judgments, assumptions) can result in either a qualified or an adverse report

4. Report on conformity with agreed-upon criteria or agreed-upon procedures should include statement limiting its use to parties who have agreed upon such criteria or procedures

AT 200 Financial Forecasts and Projections

Overall Objective and Approach--This section presents guidance on accountant's association with financial forecasts and projections. The standard outlines procedures and reporting requirements for various forms of accountant association with prospective financial information. As a starting point, it is important that you understand the basic information presented in section A of the outline. That information is used throughout the remainder of the outline. Sections B, C, and D of the outline provide information on the three basic forms of accountant association with prospective financial information--compilations, examinations, and agreed-upon procedures. (CPAs do not perform reviews on quarterly information.) Section E presents miscellaneous related information.

A. Definition and basic concepts

1. Prospective financial statements--financial forecasts and financial projections

a. Types

(1) Financial forecasts--prospective financial statements that present the responsible party's [person(s) responsible for assumptions, usually management] beliefs about the entity's expected financial position, results of operations, and cash flows
(2) Financial projection--prospective financial statements that present expected results, to the best of the responsible party's knowledge and belief, given one or more hypothetical assumptions. A projection is a "what would happen if..?" statement

b. Minimum disclosures

(1) Financial statement information: sales, gross profit (or cost of goods sold), unusual or infrequently occurring items, provision for income taxes, discontinued operations, extraordinary items, income from continuing operations, net income, earnings per share, and significant cash flows
(2) Background information: purpose of prospective statements, assumptions, and significant accounting policies
(3) Assumptions

NOTE: Omission of group 1 items creates a "partial presentation" not considered in the Statement. Omission of group 2 items in the presence of group 1 items results in a presentation subject to the provisions of this Statement. The accountant should not compile or examine statements lacking disclosure of assumptions (group 3).

    c. <u>Pro forma statements</u> (those which show how a hypothetical transaction might have affected historical statements) and accountant financial analysis of a particular project are not included under provisions of this statement

    d. Financial forecasts and projections may both be in the form of single point estimates or ranges (in which case a paragraph discussing the estimates or ranges is added to report)

    e. Uses of prospective financial statements

        (1) <u>General</u>--may be used by persons with whom the responsible party is not negotiating directly (e.g., in an offering statement for debt or equity interests). Only a forecast is appropriate for general use

        (2) <u>Limited</u>--may only be used by responsible party or by responsible party and third parties with whom responsible party is negotiating directly. A forecast or a projection is appropriate for limited use

  2. Accountant independence--an accountant need <u>not</u> be independent to perform a compilation, but must be independent to perform a review or agreed-upon procedures

  3. The accountant's report should not indicate that engagement included "preparation" of prospective financial statements

B. Compilations of prospective financial statements

  1. Compilation procedures

    a. Assemble, to extent necessary, based on responsible party's assumptions

    b. <u>Perform required compilation procedures</u>

        (1) Establish understanding with client (preferably in writing) about services to be performed

        (2) Inquire about accounting principles used

        (3) Ask how responsible party identifies key factors and assumptions

        (4) List (or obtain a list of) significant assumptions and consider its completeness

        (5) Consider whether there are obvious inconsistencies in assumptions

        (6) Test mathematical accuracy

        (7) Read statements for conformity with AICPA guidelines and determine that asssumptions are not obviously inappropriate

        (8) If a significant portion of prospective period has expired, inquire about actual results

        (9) Obtain written client representation letter (signed by responsible party at highest level of authority)

      (10) Attempt to obtain additional or revised information when above procedures make errors seem likely

  2. Compilation reports (see the standard report in the Reporting module)

    a. Key elements of standard compilation report

        (1) Scope paragraph--identify statements, compilation in accordance with AICPA standards

        (2) Opinion paragraph--a compilation is limited in scope, <u>no opinion or assurance</u> is provided, an indication is provided that prospective results <u>may not</u> be achieved and that the accountant takes <u>no responsibility for updating</u> statements or assumptions

(3) For projections, a paragraph should be added describing limited use of nature of form of association
(4) Date of report--date of completion of compilation procedures

  b. Circumstances resulting in departure from standard compilation report

(1) Presentation deficiencies or disclosure omissions, other than a significant assumption (clearly indicate deficiency in report)
(2) Comprehensive basis statements which do not disclose the basis used (disclose the basis in the report)
(3) Summary of significant accounting policies omitted (a paragraph is needed which discloses that the policies have been omitted)

C. Examinations of prospective financial statements

  1. Examination procedures

    a. Evaluate preparation
    b. Perform examination procedures

(1) Reach an <u>understanding with client</u> (ordinarily confirmed in an engagement letter)
(2) <u>Evaluate the support for underlying assumptions</u> (consider available support, consistency, reliability of underlying historical information, logical arguments or theory)
(3) <u>Obtain written representation letter</u> (signed by responsible party at highest level of authority)

    c. Evaluate presentation for conformity with AICPA presentation guidelines (especially, that presentations reflect assumptions)

  2. Examination reports (see the standard report in the Reporting module)

    a. Key elements of standard examination report

(1) <u>Scope paragraph</u>--identify statements, examination in accordance with AICPA standards
(2) <u>Opinion paragraph</u>--the opinion indicates that the statements are in <u>conformity with AICPA presentation standards</u>, that assumptions provide a reasonable basis, that prospective results may not be achieved, and that the accountant has no responsibility to update statements

    (a) When a projection has been examined, the opinion should state whether the assumptions provide a reasonable basis for the projection given the hypothetical assumptions

(3) For projections, a paragraph should be added that describes the limitations on the usefulness of the presentation
(4) <u>Date of report</u>--date of completion of examination procedures

    b. Circumstances resulting in departure from standard review report

(1) Departure from AICPA presentation guidelines (result in a qualified or adverse opinion)
(2) Unreasonable assumptions (adverse opinion)
(3) Scope limitation (disclaimer)
(4) Emphasis of a matter (unqualified)
(5) Evaluation based in part on report of another auditor (unqualified--divided responsibility)

D. Application of agreed-upon procedures to prospective financial statements

1. Procedures performed when applying agreed-upon procedures

a. Procedures are those the <u>specified users</u> desire, as long as the specified users take responsibility for their adequacy (but, the procedures must include more than mere reading of the statements)

b. The accountant should normally meet with specified users to establish nature and scope of procedures

(1) If this is impossible, the accountant should

(a) Discuss nature/scope of procedures with specified user's legal counsel or other representative

(b) Review correspondence with users

(c) Compare procedures with any supervisory agency written requirements, or

(d) Distribute copy of engagement letter to specified users

2. Reports for agreed-upon procedures

a. Key elements of unqualified report (no standard report exists)

(1) <u>Scope paragraph</u>--identify statements, indicate that the report is limited in use and intended solely for specified users, and enumerate procedures that have been performed

(2) <u>Middle paragraph</u>--indicate that the work performed is less in scope than an examination and disclaim an opinion on whether the statements conform with AICPA presentation guidelines

(3) <u>Opinion paragraph</u>--indicate findings (<u>negative assurance--no matters came to our attention</u>), that prospective results may not be achieved, and that no responsibility to update statements is taken

E. Other information

1. <u>Accountant-submitted documents</u> containing prospective (with <u>no</u> accountant association) and historical financial statements (with accountant association)

NOTE: Accountant submitted documents are those which the CPA actually prepares for a client. For more on this, see the outline on AU 551, especially the introduction.

a. When an accountant's compilation, review, or audit report on historical financial statements is included in an accountant-submitted document containing prospective financial statements, the accountant should examine, compile, or apply agree-upon procedures to prospective statements unless

(1) They are labeled as a "budget,"

(2) The budget does not extend beyond the end of the current fiscal year, and

(3) The budget is presented with interim historical financial statements for the current year

NOTE: In such cases, a disclaimer paragraph on the budget information is added to the accountant's report on the financial information. Also, if management elects to omit summaries of significant assumptions, this is disclosed in an additional paragraph.

2. Client-prepared documents

    a. Prospective statements (<u>no</u> accountant association) and historical financial statements (<u>with</u> accountant association)

      (1) Accountant should not consent to the use of his/her name in the document unless

        (a) S/he (or another accountant) has examined, compiled, or applied agreed-upon procedures to prospective statements and the report accompanies them, or

        (b) The prospective statements are accompanied by an indication that the accountant assumes no responsibility for them

    b. Prospective statements (with accountant association) and historical financial statements (<u>no</u> accountant association)

      (1) The accountant should not consent to use of his/her name in document unless

        (a) S/he (or another accountant) has compiled, reviewed, or examined the historical financial statements and the report accompanies them, or

        (b) The historical financial statements are accompanied by an indication that the accountant assumes no responsibility for them

    c. Prospective statements (with accountant association) and other nonfinancial statement information (<u>no</u> accountant association)

      (1) The accountant need only read the other information to consider its consistency with prospective financial statement information

      (2) If inconsistencies exist, the accountant should consider whether prospective report needs modification

        (a) If client refuses to provide additional or revised information, the accountant should withhold use of report or withdraw

      (3) If no inconsistencies exist, but the information seems materially misstated, the matter should be discussed with the responsible party and, possibly, with the entity's legal counsel. If the problem remains, notify responsible party in writing and notify own legal counsel

AT 300 Reporting on Pro Forma Financial Information

Overall Objective and Approach--This section presents guidance on appropriate procedures and for reporting on certain pro forma financial information. As a starting point, this section <u>does not</u> apply to circumstances in which (1) pro forma information is presented within the same document, but not with financial statements (see the outline of AU 550) or (2) financial statements footnote information includes pro forma information (e.g., to show a revision of debt maturities, or a revision of earnings per share for a stock split).

    This section <u>does</u> apply to pro forma financial information, presented with the basic financial statements, used to show the effects of an underlying transaction or event (hereafter, simply transaction). Such transactions include possible (1) business combinations, (2) changes in capitalization, (3) disposition of a significant portion of a business and (4) proposed sale of securities and the application of proceeds. For example, a company which is considering issuing debt might prepare pro forma financial information to indicate what the effect of granting a loan in the prior period would have been. The pro forma financial information must be included with the historical financial statements. Thus, financial statements would generally have a column for historical information, and one for pro forma information.

This section divides much of the procedural and reporting advice into three areas--(1) determining that the assumptions are reasonable, (2) determining that the assumptions lead to the adjustments, and (3) determining that the adjustments have been properly reflected in the "pro forma column." The outline is divided into (a) procedural requirements and (b) reporting requirements.

A. Procedural requirements

 1. The overall approach is to apply pro forma adjustments to historical financial information

    a. Such adjustments should be based on management's assumptions and give effect to all significant effects attributable to the transaction
    b. Pro forma financial information should be labeled as such to distinguish it from historical financial information

 2. The following information should be included with any pro forma disclosures with which an accountant is associated

    a. Description of the transaction being reflected
    b. Source of the historical financial information on which it is based
    c. Significant assumptions used to develop pro forma adjustments
    d. Significant uncertainties about the assumptions
    e. Indication that the information should be read in conjunction with the related historical financial information
    f. Indication that the pro forma is not necessarily indicative of the result that would have been attained had the transaction actually taken place earlier

 3. An accountant may agree to report on an <u>examination</u> or a <u>review</u> of pro forma financial information if the following conditions are met

    a. The document with the pro forma financial information includes (or incorporates by reference) complete financial statements for the most recent period
    b. The historical financial statements on which the pro forma financial information is based have been audited or reviewed

       (1) The level of assurance for the pro forma financial information should be limited to the level of assurance provided on the historical financial statements

       EXAMPLE: When the historical financial statements have been audited, the pro forma financial information may be examined or reviewed. When the historical financial statements have been reviewed, the pro forma financial information may only be reviewed.

    c. The accountant must have an appropriate level of knowledge of the accounting and financial reporting practices of each significant part of the combined entity

       (1) If another accountant has performed an audit or a review of a part of the combined entity, the accountant reporting on the pro forma financial information must still obtain the above knowledge

       EXAMPLE: In a business combination between Company A and Company B, the accountant reporting on the pro forma financial information must obtain the knowledge relating to both companies, even if s/he has only audited one of them.

4. The objective of an accountant's examination or review procedures relates to whether

   a. Management's assumptions are reasonable
   b. The pro forma adjustments appropriately follow from the assumptions
   c. The pro forma financial information column of numbers reflects proper application of the adjustments

   NOTE: When performing an examination, or review, reasonable assurance and negative assurance, respectively, are provided

5. The following procedures should be applied to assumptions and pro forma adjustments for either an examination or a review

   a. Obtain knowledge of each part of the combined entity in a business combination
   b. Obtain an understanding of the underlying transaction (e.g., read contracts, minutes of meetings, make inquiries)
   c. Procedures applied to the assumptions

      (1) Discuss with management
      (2) Evaluate whether they are presented in a clear and comprehensive manner and are consistent with one another

   d. Procedures applied to the adjustments and their accumulation

      (1) Obtain sufficient evidence in support of adjustments
      (2) Evaluate whether pro forma adjustments are included for all significant effects of the transaction
      (3) Evaluate whether adjustments are consistent with one another and with the data used to develop them
      (4) Determine that computation of pro forma adjustments are mathematically correct and properly accumulated

   e. Obtain written representations from management concerning their

      (1) Responsibility for the assumptions
      (2) Belief the assumptions are reasonable, that adjustments give effect to the assumptions, and that pro forma column reflects application of those adjustments
      (3) Belief that significant effects attributable to the transactions are properly disclosed

   f. Read the pro forma financial information and determine that the following disclosures are presented

      (1) Underlying transaction, pro forma adjustments, significant assumptions, and significant uncertainties
      (2) The source of the historical financial information on which the pro forma financial information is based has been appropriately identified

B. Reporting on Pro Forma Financial Information

   1. Overall issues

      a. The report on the pro forma financial information may be added to the accountant's report on the historical financial information, or it may appear separately
      b. The report on pro forma financial information should be dated as of the completion of the appropriate procedures

(1) When the report on the historical and the pro forma financial information are combined, and when the completion of the pro forma procedures is after the completion of field work for the audit or review of the historical financial information, the report should be dual dated

(a) For example, "March 1, 19X2, except for the paragraphs referring to the pro forma financial information as to which the date is March 20, 19X2"

2. An accountant's report on pro forma financial information should include

a. An identification of the pro forma financial information
b. Reference to the historical financial information

(1) Any modification in the report on the historical statements should be referred to

c. A statement that AICPA standards have been followed

(1) A review report should indicate that it is less in scope than an examination

d. A separate paragraph explaining the objective of pro forma financial information and its limitations
e. Opinion

(1) Examination--opinion as to whether (a) management's assumptions provide a reasonable basis for presenting the significant effects directly attributable to the transaction (b) whether the pro forma adjustments give appropriate effect to those assumptions, and (c) the pro forma column reflects those adjustments properly
(2) Review--negative assurance on those items in (1) above

3. The accountant may qualify the opinion, render an adverse opinion, disclaim or withdraw due to circumstances such as scope limitations, uncertainties about the assumptions, conformity of presentation with assumptions, or other reservations

STATEMENTS ON AUDITING STANDARDS

110 Responsibilities and Functions of the Independent Auditor

Paras 110.05-.08 superseded

<u>Overall Objective and Approach</u>--This section presents the objective of audits, compares the responsibilities of the auditor with those of management, and discusses the professional requirements necessary for an auditor.

A. Objective of a financial statement audit--the expression of an opinion on the fairness with which the financial statements present financial position, results of operations, and cash flows in conformity with GAAP

B. Responsibilities:

1. Management--adopting sound accounting policies and internal controls which will safeguard assets and assure the production of proper financial statements

2. Auditor--expression of an opinion on the financial statements

> *NOTE: A number of exam questions have addressed the idea that management's role includes the preparation of the statements while that of the auditor is expressing an opinion.*

C. An independent auditor must have adequate levels of education and experience

150 Generally Accepted Auditing Standards

Para. 150.06 amended by SAS 43

<u>Overall Objective and Approach</u>--This section (a) distinguishes between auditing standards and auditing procedures, (b) presents the 10 generally accepted auditing standards (GAAS), and (c) briefly discusses the concepts of relative risk and materiality.

A. Distinguishing between auditing procedures and auditing standards

1. Auditing procedures--acts to be performed (e.g., confirming receivables)

2. Auditing standards--measures of the quality of the performance of auditing procedures and the objectives to be attained by the use of the procedures undertaken

> *NOTE: The CPA exam has asked a number of multiple choice questions that are based on the above definitions*

3. As indicated in the next 3 sections, the auditing standards are divided into three categories--general, field work, and reporting

B. General standards

1. <u>T</u>raining--the examination is to be performed by a person or persons having adequate technical <u>training</u> and proficiency as an auditor

2. <u>I</u>ndependence--in all matters relating to the assignment, an <u>independence</u> in mental attitude is to be maintained by the auditor or auditors

3. <u>P</u>rofesional Care--due <u>professional care</u> is to be exercised in the performance of the examination and the preparation of the report

C. Standards of field work

1. <u>P</u>lanning--the work is to be adequately <u>planned</u> and assistants, if any, are to be properly supervised

2. <u>I</u>nternal Control--a sufficient understanding of the <u>internal control</u> structure is to be obtained to plan the audit and to determine the nature, timing, and extent of tests to be performed

3. <u>E</u>vidential matters--Sufficient competent <u>evidential matter</u> is to be obtained through inspection, observation, inquiries, and confirmations to afford a reasonable basis for an opinion regarding the financial statements under examination

D. Standards of reporting

1. <u>G</u>enerally accepted accounting principles--the report shall state whether the financial statements are presented in accordance with <u>generally accepted accounting principles</u>

2. Consistency--the report shall identify those circumstances in which such principles have not been <u>consistently</u> observed in the current period in relation to the preceding period

3. Disclosures--informative <u>disclosures</u> in the financial statements are to be regarded as reasonably adequate unless otherwise stated in the report

4. Opinion--the report shall either contain an expression of <u>opinion</u> regarding the financial statements, taken as a whole, or an assertion to the effect that an opinion cannot be expressed. When an overall opinion cannot be expressed, the reasons therefore should be stated. In all cases where an auditor's name is associated with financial statements, the report should contain a clear-cut indication of the character of the auditor's examination, if any, and the degree of responsibility s/he is taking

NOTE: You need not memorize the exact wording, but know the 10 standards. Recall TIP, PIE, and GODC (reordered standards of reporting--1, 4, 3, 2)

E. The section presents a brief, very general discussion of "relative risk" and materiality.

1. These concepts underlie the application of all GAAS, but particularly the standards of field work and reporting

2. Materiality suggests that the degree of risk related to an account may vary due to both the nature of the company (e.g., manufacturing inventories are often more important than inventories of a public utility) and by type of account (e.g., accounts receivable are generally more risky than prepaid insurance)

3. Relative risk suggests that some types of accounts and transactions are more risky than others (cash transactions are more susceptible to irregularities than certain inventories)

Note: The information in this section is extremely general. Subsequent to this section, AU 312 provided much more information on materiality. In addition, the AU 312 concept of relative risk is largely consistent with AU 312's "inherent risk."

161 The Relationship of Generally Accepted Auditing Standards to Quality Control Standards (SAS 25)

Overall Objective and Approach--This section requires that both individual CPAs and CPA firms comply with GAAS. CPA firms must also establish quality control policies and procedures to provide reasonable assurance that GAAS will be followed during audit engagements. Although this section provides no detailed guidance on quality control standards, it does point out that the existence of such standards is required by firms which perform audits. For details on the actual quality control standards that have been promulgated, see the Professional Responsibilities module.

A. Rule 202 of the Code of Professional Conduct requires that individual CPAs comply with GAAS

B. CPA firms should comply with GAAS and establish quality control policies and procedures

    1. The nature and extent of quality control policies and procedures depends on the firm's

        a. Size
        b. Autonomy of personnel and practice offices
        c. Nature of the firm's practice
        d. Firm's organizational structure
        e. Appropriate cost-benefit considerations

C. GAAS and quality control standards are related

    1. GAAS related to the conduct of <u>individual audits</u>

    2. Quality control standards relate to <u>overall audit practice</u>

    3. GAAS and quality control standards may affect both the conduct of individual audits and the conduct of a firm's entire audit practice

201 through 230 The General Standards

<u>**Overall Objective and Approach**</u>--These brief sections present information on the general group (training, independence, professional care) of GAAS. We combine discussion of these sections.

A. The general standards are personal in nature and are concerned with the qualifications of the auditor and the quality of the auditor's work

B. Training--The examination is to be performed by a person or persons having adequate technical training and proficiency as an auditor

    1. Both proper <u>education</u> and <u>professional experience</u> are necessary

    2. A CPA must exercise <u>objectivity</u> and <u>professional judgment</u> when performing an audit

C. Independence--in all matters relating to the assignment, an <u>independence</u> in mental attitude is to be maintained by the auditor or auditors

    1. The CPA should not only be <u>independent in fact</u>, but should also <u>appear independent</u> (i.e., avoid situations that may lead outsiders to doubt their independence)

    2. To stress the CPA's independence, many companies follow the practice of having the independent auditor appointed by the board of directors or the stockholders

D. Professional Care--due <u>professional care</u> is to be exercised in the performance of the examination and the preparation of the report; due professional care

    1. <u>Requires</u> that a professional perform a service with <u>reasonable care</u> and <u>diligence</u>

    2. <u>Does not require</u> infallibility, nor liability for losses due to pure errors of judgment

310 and 311 Planning

<u>Overall Objective and Approach</u>--These sections present information on planning. Section 310 discusses advantages of early appointment of the auditor, while Section 311 presents actual planning considerations

A. Planning--the work is to be adequately <u>planned</u> and assistants, if any, are to be properly supervised

    1. Early appointment of the auditor enables the auditor to plan work so that it may be done expeditiously and to determine the extent to which it can be done before year end

    2. When appointed close to year end or after year end, the auditor should make certain whether an adequate examination and the expression of an unqualified opinion is possible

B. Approach for planning the audit

    1. Overall considerations

        a. Entity's type of business and industry
        b. Entity's accounting policies and procedures
        c. Methods used to process accounting information, including the use of service centers
        d. Anticipated reliance on internal control
        e. Preliminary materiality judgments
        f. Financial statement items likely to require adjustment
        g. Conditions likely to require extension of audit tests
        h. Nature of reports to be issued for the audit

    2. Audit procedures applicable to planning the examination

        a. Review correspondence, prior year's workpapers, statements, etc.
        b. Determine the effect of nonaudit services to the client on the examination
        c. Inquire about current business developments
        d. Read current interim statements
        e. Discuss type, scope, timing, etc., of examination with client
        f. Consider effects of applicable authoritative pronouncements
        g. Coordinate client's preparation of data needed by auditor
        h. Determine need for consultants, specialists, and internal auditors
        i. Establish timing of audit work
        j. Coordinate staff requirements

        NOTE: Be familiar with the above

    3. A <u>written audit program should be prepared</u>

        a. Instructs assistants on the work to be done
        b. Details audit procedures which are necessary
        c. Reflects the results of planning considerations and procedures
        d. May require modifications due to changing conditions

    4. Knowledge of the entity's business helps the auditor in

        a. Identifying problem areas
        b. Assessing conditions in which accounting data are developed
        c. Evaluating reasonableness of estimates

       d. Evaluating reasonableness of management representations
       e. Evaluating appropriateness of GAAP

  5. The auditor should consider the manner in which the computer is used in processing data

  6. The auditor must adequately understand and audit computer operations

C. Supervision

  1. Assistants should be adequately supervised

  2. When a difference about an auditing or accounting issue arises among firm personnel, such difference should be documented in the workpapers and, if necessary, the subordinate whose views are <u>not</u> being followed should be allowed to disassociate himself/herself from the resolution of the matter

> *EXAMPLE: Assume that an assistant does not believe that an adequate number of receivable confirmations have been sent. The assistant and the others involved should document their views in the working papers. Also, from the perspective of the CPA firm, know that it is important that the working papers document the manner in which (including reasons) the issue was resolved.*

312 Audit Risk and Materiality in Conducting an Audit (SAS 47)

Overall Objective and Approach--This section presents information on how the CPA should consider both audit risk and materiality when conducting an audit. Because the SASs issued subsequent to this one (after June of 1984) have used the components of audit risk presented in this section, it is extremely important. The section discusses the auditor's consideration of audit risk and materiality while (1) planning the audit, and (2) evaluating audit findings. For both planning the audit and evaluating findings, considerations at the financial statement and individual account balance levels are discussed.

A. Definitions and key concepts

  1. <u>Audit risk</u>--the risk that the auditor may <u>unknowingly fail to modify his/her opinion</u> on the financial statements that are materially misstated

> *NOTE: Not included in this definition are risks relating to losses from litigation, adverse publicity, or other such events. Also not included is the risk of incorrect rejection of a materially correct population--see outline of AU 350 for information on this risk.*

  2. <u>Materiality</u> (per SFAC 2)--magnitude of omission or misstatement of accounting information that, in light of surrounding circumstances, makes it <u>probable that the judgment of a reasonable person relying on the information would have been changed or influenced</u>

       a. Financial statements are materially misstated when errors or irregularities individually or in aggregate cause departures from GAAP due to

           (1) Misapplications of GAAP
           (2) Departures from fact
           (3) Omissions

        b. Materiality judgments are made based on an interaction of both quantitative and qualitative considerations

           (1) Example: An illegal payment for an otherwise immaterial amount could be material if there is a reasonable possibility that it could lead to a material contingent liability or a material loss of revenue

   3. Both audit risk and materiality should be considered in (1) <u>planning</u> the audit, and in (2) <u>evaluating</u> audit findings as to whether financial statements follow GAAP

B. <u>Planning the Audit</u>: Consider audit risk and materiality at the <u>Financial Statement Level</u>

   1. When planning the audit the auditor should determine appropriate levels of materiality and audit risk

        a. These judgments may be in either quantitative or nonquantitative terms

   2. <u>Audit risk consideration at the financial statement level</u>

        a. The auditor should use his/her judgment as to an appropriately low level of audit risk for the financial statements

   3. <u>Materiality considerations at the financial statement level</u>

        a. While an auditor may determine an appropriate materiality level to include for each financial statement, for planning purposes the lowest amount so obtained would ordinarily be considered material to any one of the financial statements

EXAMPLE: If $100,000 would have a material effect on income, but $200,000 to materially affect financial position, the lower amount would normally be used in planning. This lower amount is normally used because in planning, the auditor will not in general be able to distinguish the types of misstatements which will be detected, and because the statements are interrelated. A $100,000 misstatement may thus materially affect the income statement and immaterially affect the balance sheet.

        b. During planning, materiality is largely a <u>quantitative</u> concept, although throughout the performance of the audit the auditor must be alert for misstatements that could be <u>qualitatively</u> material

NOTE: The need for relying largely on quantitative considerations is because of difficulties in anticipating likely qualitative characteristics of misstatements which will subsequently be discovered.

        c. Theoretically, if the auditor's judgment about materiality at the planning stage was based on the same information available to him/her while evaluating audit findings, materiality for planning and evaluation purposes would be the same

           (1) The planning vs. evaluation materiality levels will, however, ordinarily differ because circumstances encountered on the audit will influence the judgment

           (2) If significantly lower materiality levels become appropriate in evaluating audit findings, the auditor should reevaluate the sufficiency of the auditing procedures she has performed

C. <u>Planning the Audit</u>: Consider audit risk and materiality at the <u>individual</u> <u>account-balance or class-of-transactions level</u> (hereafter, "account-level")

1. Holding other planning considerations equal, either a decrease in the level of audit risk acceptable to the auditor or a decrease in the amount considered material will cause

    a. Selection of a more effective auditing procedure
    b. Performance of auditing procedures closer to balance sheet date
    c. Increasing extent of a particular auditing procedure

2. Audit risk at the account level must be controlled to allow an overall financial statement low level of risk

3. Audit risk

    a. Components

        (1) <u>Inherent risk</u>--risk that an account could be materially misstated, when aggregated with other misstatements, assuming there were no related internal controls. This risk varies by account (e.g., cash is more susceptible to theft than an inventory of coal)
        (2) <u>Control risk</u>--risk that internal control will not prevent or detect misstatements which could be material when aggregated with other misstatements
        (3) <u>Detection risk</u>--risk that auditing procedures will not detect a misstatement which could be material when aggregated with other errors

    NOTE: Know that, at the account level, audit risk is composed of these 3 risks. AU 312 does not discuss these three risks at the overall financial statement level.

    b. Relationships among components

        (1) Inherent and control risks exist independently of the audit while detection risk relates to auditor's procedures

            NOTE: Auditors <u>assess</u> inherent and control risk, and <u>restrict</u> detection risk

        (2) <u>Acceptable detection risk should vary inversely with the inherent</u> <u>and control risks</u>

    c. Professional judgment is used to assess inherent risk and control risk

        (1) Separate or combined assessments are acceptable
        (2) If either is assumed to be at less than maximum level of risk, the basis for the assessment should be disclosed (e.g., questionnaires, checklists)

4. It is <u>not appropriate to use assessments of inherent risk and control risk</u> <u>to eliminate substantive tests</u>

    a. <u>Substantive tests for material accounts are necessary</u>

D. Evaluating audit findings

1. The auditor should aggregate misstatements in a manner so as to determine whether financial statements are materially misstated at either the account or financial statement level

2. The aggregation of misstatments should include the auditor's best estimate
    of the total misstatement in the accounts that s/he has examined

    a. This is known as "likely misstatement"

        (1) Likely misstatement should be distinguished from "known misstate-
             ment," which is the total amount of the misstatements identified by
             the auditor which have not been corrected

        *EXAMPLE: Assume an auditor has used a number of substantive tests to
        audit in detail 50% of an account and has discovered $1,000 of misstate-
        ments. If not corrected, the known misstatement is $1,000; likely
        misstatement is $2,000 since, all things considered equal, one would
        expect the unexamined portion of the account to also include approxi-
        mately $1,000 of misstatement.*

3. When an auditor uses audit sampling to test an account balance, s/he pro-
    jects the amount of known misstatements identified in the sample to the
    entire portion under consideration

    a. In audit sampling, this is known as "projected misstatement"
    b. Projected misstatement, along with the results of other substantive
        tests, contributes to the auditor's assessment of likely misstatement in
        the account

4. Inherent subjectivity generally makes the likelihood of material
    misstatement greater in accounts which include accounting estimates as
    compared to those based essentially on factual data (e.g., transactions)

    a. Examples

        (1) Estimates: Inventory obsolescence, uncollectible receivables,
             warranty obligations
        (2) Essentially factual data: cash balance, notes payable, outstanding
             common stock

    b. If the auditor believes that the estimate is unreasonable, s/he should
        treat the difference between that estimate and the closest reasonable
        estimate as a likely misstatement and aggregate it with other likely
        misstatements

        *NOTE: Subsequent to issuance of this section, AU 342 was issued to
        provide further guidance on auditing estimates*

5. When total likely misstatement is material, the auditor should request
    management to eliminate the material misstatement

    a. Failure by management to eliminate the misstatement will result in
        either a qualified or adverse opinion on the financial statements

6. When likely misstatement is immaterial the auditor should recognize that the
    financial statements may be materially misstated due to further misstatement
    remaining undetected

    a. If audit risk is considered unacceptably high, the auditor should
        perform additional auditing procedures

313 Substantive Tests Prior to the Balance Sheet Date (SAS 45)

<u>Overall Objective and Approach</u>--This section presents guidance related to performing substantive tests at a date prior to the balance sheet date ("interim testing"). For example, in certain circumstances an auditor might wish to audit an account as of November 30, and then apply certain procedures for the period through December 31, the balance sheet date. In addition to discussing the effect of interim procedures on audit risk, the section provides guidance on (1) factors to be considered prior to applying such procedures at an interim date, (2) extending interim date audit conclusions to the balance sheet date, and (3) coordinating the timing of auditing procedures.

A. Overall relationship of interim substantive testing on audit risk

    1. Potentially increases audit risk (the risk that the auditor may <u>unknowingly fail to modify his/her opinion</u> on financial statements that are materially misstated--see outline of AU 312)

    2. Potential for increased audit risk increases as interim period is lengthened

    3. To control for the potentially increased audit risk, effective substantive tests to cover the remaining period should be designed

B. Performing substantive tests at an interim date

    1. Factors to be considered before performing tests at an interim date

       a. Difficulty in controlling the incremental audit risk due to performing test early

       b. Cost of subsequent tests necessary in remaining period (period after principal substantive tests through year end)

       c. Effectiveness of remaining period substantive tests if internal controls are not being relied upon

       d. Existence of rapidly changing business conditions which might cause management to misstate financial statements

       e. Predictability of year-end balances

    2. <u>Extending interim date audit conclusions</u> to balance sheet date

       a. <u>Compare interim balances with year-end balances for unusual changes</u> and perform other analytical procedures and/or substantive tests of detail

       b. Consider implications of interim period errors in determining scope of remaining period tests

    3. Coordinate timing of audit procedures such as

       a. Related party transactions

       b. Interrelated accounts and accounting cutoffs (e.g., cash with marketable securities)

       c. Negotiable assets (e.g., cash) and liabilities (e.g.,loans)

315 Communications Between Predecessor and Successor Auditors (SAS 7)

<u>Overall Objective and Approach</u>--This section presents guidance on communications between predecessor and successor auditors when a change of auditors has taken place or is in process. The section presents information on (a) several definitions and key concepts, (b) a <u>required</u> communication by the potential successor <u>before</u> accepting the engagement, and (c) other communications after the successor auditor has accepted the engagement.

A. Definitions and key concepts

1. <u>Predecessor auditor</u>--auditor who has resigned or has been notified that his/her services have been terminated

2. <u>Successor auditor</u>--auditor who has accepted an engagement or has been invited to make a proposal for an engagement

3. The responsibility for beginning the communication process is with the successor

4. The communication may be written or oral

B. <u>Required</u> communications <u>before</u> successor accepts engagement

1. The successor should obtain prospective client's permission to contact the predecessor

   a. If the prospective client refuses permission, the successor should inquire as to the reasons and consider the implications of such refusal in deciding whether to accept the engagement

2. Successor's inquiries of the predecessor should include

   a. Facts bearing on <u>integrity</u> of management
   b. <u>Disagreements</u> with management as to accounting principles, auditing procedures, or other significant matters
   c. The predecessor's understanding of the <u>reasons for change</u> in auditors

   NOTE: *You should know (1) that these inquiries are required, and (2) their nature.*

3. The predecessor should normally respond promptly and fully, on the basis of facts known

   a. Unusual circumstances such as impending litigation may result in a limited reply from the predecessor; in such circumstance the predecessor should indicate that his/her response is limited

C. Other communications after acceptance of the engagement

1. The purpose of most other communications is to obtain information on

   a. Consistency of application of accounting principles
   b. Audit areas that have required an inordinate amount of time
   c. Audit problems that arose from the condition of the accounting system and records
   d. Reviewing predecessor working papers for matters of continuing accounting significance

      (1) Examples: working paper analysis of balance sheet accounts, and those related to contingencies

2. Valid business reasons may lead the predecessor auditor to decide not to allow a review of his/her working papers

3. When more than one successor auditor is considering acceptance of an engagement, the predecessor auditor should not be expected to make himself/herself or his working papers available until the successor has accepted the engagement

4. If the successor becomes aware of information relevant to the predecessor auditor, that information should be disclosed at a meeting of the client, the predecessor auditor, and the successor auditor

316 The Auditor's Responsibility to Detect and Report Errors and Irregularities

<u>Overall Objective and Approach</u>--This section presents guidance on the auditor's responsibility to detect and report errors and irregularities and provides guidance for their detection. The guidance is in the form of overall client, as well as account characteristics that are believed to affect the risk of such misstatements.

A. Section provides guidance on auditor's responsibility to detect errors and irregularities during audits

  1. Definitions

     a. <u>Error--unintentional</u> misstatements or omissions in financial statements. Examples:

        (1) Mistakes in gathering or processing accounting data
        (2) Incorrect accounting estimates
        (3) Misapplication of GAAP

     b. <u>Irregularities--intentional</u> misstatements or omissions in financial statements. Examples:

        (1) Manipulation, falsification, alteration of accounting records
        (2) Misrepresentation or intentional omissions
        (3) Intentional misapplication of accounting principles

     NOTE: Intent is the fundamental difference between errors and irregularities. Because intent is difficult to determine, distinguishing between errors and irregularities is sometimes difficult.

  2. Auditor's responsibility for errors and irregularities

     a. Audit should be designed to provide <u>reasonable assurance</u> of detecting material errors and irregularities

     NOTE: Know the above responsibility

     b. A properly designed and executed audit may miss a material irregularity, particularly one involving forgery or collusion
     c. Auditor should exercise

        (1) <u>Due care</u> in planning, performing, and evaluating result of procedures
        (2) <u>Proper degree of professional skepticism</u> to achieve reasonable assurance material errors and irregularities will be detected

     d. Audit does not constitute a guarantee that misstatements will be detected

B. During planning, an assessment of the risks of material misstatements should be made at both the overall financial statement level and at the account balance or class-of transactions level (hereafter, simply "account level"). (Know enough of the following factors to be able to reply to an essay question.)

  1. Financial statement level risk factors

     a. <u>Management characteristics</u>

      (1) <u>Domination</u> of operating and financing decisions by one person
      (2) <u>Aggressive</u> management <u>attitude</u> toward <u>financial reporting</u>
      (3) High management <u>turnover</u>
      (4) Management's <u>undue emphasis</u> on meeting <u>earnings projections</u>
      (5) <u>Poor</u> management <u>reputation</u>

   b. <u>Operating and industry characteristics</u>

      (1) <u>Profitability inadequate</u> or inconsistent
      (2) High <u>sensitivity to economic factors</u> (inflation, interest rates, etc.)
      (3) <u>Rapid change in industry</u>
      (4) <u>Declining industry</u>
      (5) Organization <u>decentralized without adequate monitoring</u>
      (6) Internal or external matters raise substantial <u>doubt</u> as to ability to continue as a <u>going concern</u>

   c. Engagement characteristics

      (1) <u>Difficult accounting issues</u>
      (2) <u>Difficult to audit transactions</u> or balances
      (3) <u>Significant errors</u> found in <u>prior audits</u>
      (4) <u>New client</u> with no prior audit or insufficient information available from predecessor

NOTE: Be familiar with the above financial statement level risk factors

2. The size, complexity, and ownership characteristics of the entity have a significant influence on the risk factors

   a. For a large entity the auditor would consider factors that constrain improper conduct by senior management--e.g., effectiveness of the board of directors, audit committee, internal audit function
   b. For a small entity some of the above matters may be inapplicable or unimportant

3. The auditor should access the risk of management misrepresentation by reviewing information about the risk factors. Matters such as the following may be considered

   a. Known circumstances relating to financial statement distortion
   b. Lack of management policies for providing accounting estimates
   c. Lack of control, leading to crisis conditions, disorganized work areas, etc.
   d. Lack of control over computer processing
   e. Lack of security of data or assets (e.g., inadequate investigation of new employees, no fidelity bonds)

4. Response to risk at financial statement level

   a. Use more experienced personnel or more supervision
   b. Apply procedures closer to balance sheet date
   c. Heightened degree of professional skepticism

C. Audit risk at the balance or class of transactions level

  1. Factors

    a. Financial statement risk factors
    b. Complexity of accounting issues

   c. Difficult transactions
   d. Misstatements detected in prior audits
   e. Susceptibility of assets to misappropriation
   f. Competence of personnel
   g. Judgment involved in determining account balance
   h. Size and volume of individual items in account
   i. Complexity of calculations

D. Professional skepticism

  1. An audit should be planned and performed with an attitude of <u>professional skepticism</u>

   a. The auditor neither assumes that management is dishonest nor assumes unquestioned honesty
   b. The auditor recognizes that conditions observed and evidential matter obtained, including information from prior audits, need to be objectively evaluated to determine whether the financial statements are free of material misstatement

  2. Professional skepticism <u>during audit planning</u>, when the auditor believes the risk of misstatement is high

   a. The auditor will consider the assessment in determining the nature, timing, or extent of procedures, assigning staff, and requiring appropriate levels of supervision
   b. Should devote increased attention to determining whether the accounting principles are appropriate in the circumstances (e.g., revenue recognition, asset realization, capitalization vs. expensing)
   c. More evidence is required for material transactions

  3. Professional skepticism <u>during the performance of the audit</u>

   a. Conditions such as the following may cause the auditor to consider whether material misstatements exist

    (1) Analytical procedures disclose significant differences from expectation
    (2) Significant unreconciled differences between control account and subsidiary records or between physical count and a related account are not appropriately investigated and corrected on a timely basis
    (3) Confirmation requests disclose significant differences or fewer responses than expected
    (4) Transactions selected for testing are not supported by proper documentation or are not appropriately authorized
    (5) Supporting records or files that should be readily available are not promptly produced when requested
    (6) Audit tests detect errors apparently known to client personnel, but not voluntarily disclosed to the auditor

   b. As the number of the above conditions increases, the auditor should consider whether it is necessary to reassess the planning assessment of risk of material misstatement in the financial statements

E. Evaluation of audit test results

  1. Because irregularities are intentional, they may have implications beyond their monetary effect

2. When <u>immaterial irregularities</u> are suspected

   a. <u>Consider implications</u> for audit
   b. <u>Take to appropriate level of management</u> at least one above those involved

3. When possible <u>material irregularities</u> are suspected

   a. <u>Consider implications</u> for audit
   b. <u>Take to appropriate level of management</u> at least one above those involved
   c. <u>Attempt to obtain evidential matter</u> on whether in fact material
   d. If appropriate, <u>suggest client consult legal counsel</u>

F. Effect of irregularities on audit report

  1. When auditor knows <u>statements are incorrect</u>

   a. Insist on <u>financial statement revision</u>
   b. <u>If not revised, issue qualified or adverse opinion</u>, disclosing substantive reasons

  2. <u>When unable to conclude</u> whether statements incorrect

   a. <u>Disclaim or qualify</u>
   b. <u>Communicate findings to audit committee</u> or board of directors
   c. <u>If client refuses to accept report, withdraw</u> and indicate reasons to audit committee or board of directors

G. Communications concerning errors or irregularities

  1. Unless irregularities are clearly inconsequential, the auditor must inform the audit committee

  2. Irregularities involving senior management should be reported directly to the audit committee

  3. Irregularities that are individually immaterial may be reported to the audit committee on an aggregate basis

  4. Situations in which a duty exists to report beyond management and audit committee

   a. Form 8-K disclosures (change of auditors)
   b. Disclosure to successor auditor
   c. Disclosure in response to subpoena
   d. Disclosure to funding agency for entities receiving governmental financial assistance

H. Responsibilities in other circumstances

  1. More responsibility may exist for audits of governmental organizations under the Single Audit Act of 1984

  2. Less responsibility may exist for examinations not including complete set of financial statements (e.g., specified elements) or for reviews and agreed-upon procedure engagements

I. Characteristics of errors and irregularities (Appendix)

  1. Materiality--plan audit to detect misstatements that could be large enough to be quantitatively material

2. Level of involvement

    a. Employees

        (1) Defalcations often immaterial and do not misstate net assets or net income
        (2) These irregularities are generally controlled through internal control structure and fidelity bonding

    b. Senior management, including owner-manager of small business

        (1) Infrequent
        (2) Often not susceptible to internal control structure
        (3) Culture, custom, and corporate governance may control, but are not infallible

3. <u>Concealment</u>

    a. Irregularities often involve manipulation of accounting records
    b. <u>Unrecorded transactions normally more difficult to detect than concealment</u>
    c. Concealment may make detection difficult or impossible to detect

4. Internal control structure

    a. If a lack of controls exists, audit should be planned to detect potential error or irregularity
    b. Nonrecurring breakdown of specific control procedures difficult to detect
    c. Management may circumvent

5. Effects on financial statements

    a. Overstatements of accounts are easier to detect
    b. Misstatements charged to balance sheet easier to detect than those to income statement

317 Illegal Acts by Clients

(Supersedes AU 328)

Overall Objective and Approach--This section presents guidance on the nature and extent of consideration given to client illegal acts during audits. The guidance relates both to considering the possibility of illegal acts, and to the responsibility when such illegal acts are detected.

A. Overall definition of illegal acts and summary of auditor responsibility

    1. Illegal acts--violations of laws or governmental regulations

        a. Illegal acts by clients are acts attributable to entity under audit acts of management or employees acting on behalf of entity
        b. Illegal acts by clients do not include personal misconduct by entity's personnel that is unrelated to business

    2. Determination of legality of act is normally beyond auditor's professional competence and depends on legal judgment

    3. The further removed illegal act is from the events and transactions ordinarily reflected in financial statements the less likely it is that the auditor will become aware

        a. Examples of illegal acts more likely to be detected (have direct and material effect on determination of financial statement amounts)

       (1)   Tax laws affecting accruals
       (2)   Revenue accrued on governmental contracts

  b. Examples of illegal acts less likely to be detected (have indirect effects on financial statements--often a contingent liability)

       (1)   Laws related to securities trading
       (2)   Occupational safety and health
       (3)   Price fixing

NOTE: "a." items typically relate to financial and accounting aspects; "b." items typically relate more to an entity's operating aspects.

The auditor's responsibility for illegal acts having a direct and material effect on determination of financial statement amounts ("a.") is the same as for errors and irregularities--to design the audit to provide reasonable assurance of their detection when they are material, see AU 316. An auditor does not ordinarily have a sufficient basis for recognizing possible violations of those illegal acts having only indirect effects ("b.").

  c. The remainder of this section is only on illegal acts having material, but indirect effect on the financial statements ("b.", above).

B. Auditor's consideration of possibility of illegal acts <u>on all audits</u>

  1. Summary of the auditor's responsibility

     a. Be aware of possibility of such illegal acts
     b. If specific information comes to the auditor's attention concerning the existence of illegal acts, apply audit procedures specifically directed to ascertaining whether such an illegal act has occurred
     c. An audit provides no assurance that illegal acts will be detected or that any contingent liabilities that may result will be disclosed

  2. <u>Audit procedures when there is no evidence</u> concerning the existence of possible illegal acts

     a. Audits normally do not include procedures designed to detect illegal acts, but other procedures may identify such acts (e.g., reading minutes, inquiries to management and legal counsel, substantive tests)
     b. The auditor should make inquiries of management concerning the client's compliance with laws and regulations. Where applicable, the auditor should inquire of management concerning

       (1)   Client's policies related to prevention of illegal acts
       (2)   Directives issued by client and representations obtained by client from management on compliance with laws

     c. The auditor should ordinarily also obtain written representations from management concerning the absence of violations of laws whose effects should be considered for disclosure in the financial statements or as a basis for recording a loss contingency

NOTE: The section states that audits <u>do not</u> include procedures designed to detect illegal acts ("a." above) and then suggests several inquiry type procedures ("b." and "c." above)

  3. <u>Information</u> that <u>may suggest</u> that possibility of <u>illegal acts</u>

     a. Unauthorized, improperly recorded, or unrecorded transactions
     b. Investigation by a governmental agency
     c. Reports of regulatory agencies citing law violations

        d. Large payments for unspecified services to consultants, affiliates, or employees

        e. Excessive sales commissions

        f. Unusually large payment to cash, bearer, transfers to numbered bank accounts

        g. Unexplained payments to government officials or employees

        h. Failure to file tax returns or pay other fees

   4. Audit procedures required <u>when the auditor becomes aware</u> of information concerning a <u>possible illegal act</u>

        a. Obtain an understanding of the act and its implications

            (1) Inquire of management at a level above those involved

        b. If management <u>does not</u> provide satisfactory information that there has been no illegal act

            (1) Consult client's legal counsel or other specialists (client arranges this consultation)

            (2) Apply additional necessary procedures such as

                (a) Examine supporting documents

                (b) Confirm significant information

                (c) Determine whether transaction authorized

                (d) Consider whether other similar transactions have occurred and apply procedures to identify

C. Auditor's response to detected illegal acts

NOTE: This section only relates to audits in which the procedures followed in "B." above have revealed that an illegal act is likely to have occurred

   1. If necessary contact legal counsel

   2. Consider financial statement effect

        a. Quantitative and qualitative aspects

        b. Determine that act adequately disclosed in financial statements

            (1) Consider possible loss contingency--e.g., threat of expropriation of assets, enforced discontinuance of operations in another country, and litigation

   3. Consider implications of illegal act on other aspects of audit (e.g., reliability of management representations)

D. Communication with audit committee

   1. <u>Determine that audit committee is informed</u>, unless clearly inconsequential

   2. Communication should include

        a. <u>Description of act</u>

        b. <u>Circumstances of occurrence</u>

        c. <u>Effects on financial statements</u>

   3. If senior management is involved, auditor should communicate directly with audit committee

   4. <u>Communication may be written or oral (if oral, document)</u>

E. Effect on auditor's report

1. Improper accounting, a qualified or adverse opinion due to the departure from GAAP

2. If auditor precluded from obtaining sufficient information (i.e., a scope limitation exists), generally disclaim

3. If client refuses to accept report, withdraw and indicate reasons in writing to audit committee or board of directors

4. When circumstances (not the client) make it impossible to determine legality, the auditor should consider the effect on the report

    NOTE: In this circumstance either a "circumstance imposed" scope limitation or an "uncertainty" may be involved. See the outline of AU 508.

F. Other considerations

1. Withdrawal may be necessary, even when client does not take remedial actions for illegal acts having an immaterial effect on the financial statements (auditor may wish to contact legal counsel)

2. Situations in which there may be a duty to notify parties outside the client

    a. Form 8-K disclosures (change of auditors)
    b. Disclosure to successor auditor (AU 315)
    c. Disclosure in response to subpoena
    d. Disclosure to funding agency for entities receiving governmental financial assistance

3. Additional responsibilities may exist for audits of governmental units under the Single Audit Act of 1984

319 Consideration of the Internal Control Structure in a Financial Statement Audit (Supersedes AU 320)

Overall Objective and Approach--This section provides guidance on the auditor's responsibility with respect to a client's internal control structure. It suggests that a client's internal control structure is composed of three elements--the control environment, the accounting system, and control procedures--and describes them.

Auditors consider the internal control structure for two primary purposes-- (1) to plan the audit by performing procedures to obtain an understanding of the design of policies and procedures relevant to audit planning and to determine whether they have been placed in operation, and (2) to assess control risk. Recall that control risk, combined with inherent risk and detection risk are the components of audit risk--see outline of AU 312 and section B.1.a. of the Professional Responsibilities module for more on this.

This perhaps is the most complex of the various AU sections. Know that its major concepts are summarized in sections A and B of the Internal Control module. In the event that you have difficulties following this outline we suggest that you first read the module presentation.

A. Internal control structure

1. Definition of an Internal Control Structure (ICS)-- the policies and procedures established to provide reasonable assurance that specific entity objectives will be achieved

a. The portion of the ICS most relevant to audits are those policies and procedures that pertain to entity's ability to <u>record, process, summarize, and report financial data consistent with assertions in financial statements</u> (see Evidence module and outline of AU 326 for PERVC assertions)

b. Other policies and procedures may also be considered on audits (e.g., nonfinancial data such as production statistics are used in analytical procedures)

c. Certain ICS policies and procedures are generally not relevant to audits

   (1) Those concerning effectiveness, economy, efficiency, (e.g., determining appropriate price to charge for products)

NOTE: SAS No. 55 eliminates the distinction between accounting vs. administrative controls (for purposes of audits) and replaces them with the above description of audit relevant controls

2. For purposes of audits, an entity's ICS may be divided into three elements

   a. Control environment
   b. Accounting system
   c. Control procedures

3. <u>Control environment</u> factors (including appendix discussion, order altered)

   a. <u>Organizational structure</u>--provides overall framework for planning, directing, and controlling operations
   b. <u>Communication</u> methods for the assignment of authority and reponsibility
   c. <u>Philosophy and operating style</u> of management

      (1) Approach to taking and monitoring business risks
      (2) Attitude and actions toward financial reporting
      (3) Emphasis on meeting budget, profit, and other financial and operating goals

   d. <u>Audit committee</u>

      (1) Should assist board of directors
      (2) Should maintain communication between the board and the entity's internal and external auditors

   e. <u>Control methods</u> of management, including consideration of

      (1) Planning and reporting systems such as budgets, forecasts, responsibility accounting
      (2) Method for identifying actual vs. planned performance
      (3) Using (1) and (2) to investigate variances
      (4) Policies for developing and modifying accounting systems and control procedures

   f. <u>Personnel</u> policies and procedures--to employ sufficient competent personnel to accomplish the entity's goals and objectives
   g. <u>External</u> influences, including

      (1) Monitoring and compliance requirements imposed by legislative and regulatory bodies (e.g., examinations by bank regulatory agencies)
      (2) Review and follow-up by parties outside the entity concerning entity actions (e.g., follow-up by creditors on amounts due to them)

NOTE: Use the mnemonic "O CPA CPE" to remember these control environment factors

4. Accounting system

   a. Methods and records established to identify, assemble, analyze, classify, record, and report entity's transactions and maintaining accountability for assets and liabilities

   b. An effective accounting system will establish methods and records that will

      (1) Identify and record all valid transactions
      (2) Describe transactions on a timely basis and in sufficient detail to permit proper classification for financial reporting
      (3) Measure value of transactions per GAAP
      (4) Record in proper time period
      (5) Properly present transactions and related disclosures in the financial statements

5. Control procedures

   a. Those policies and procedures in addition to control environment and accounting system that management has established to provide reasonable assurance that specific entity objectives will be achieved

   b. Categories of control procedures (order altered)

      (1) Independent checks on performance and proper valuation of recorded amounts (e.g., clerical checks, reconciliations)
      (2) Segregation of duties (authorization, recording, custody of assets)
      (3) Safeguards over access to assets and records
      (4) Authorization of transactions and activities proper
      (5) Documents adequate and records ensure proper recording of transactions and events (e.g., prenumbered shipping documents)

   NOTE: Remember these procedures using the mnemonic "IS SAD." We will use these procedures and the control environment factors (O CPA CPE) to identify weaknesses in internal control.

6. General considerations related to ICS

   a. The following factors affect the required ICS--entity size, organization, and ownership characteristics, nature of business, diversity, and regulatory requirements

   b. Reasonable assurance recognizes that cost of ICS should not exceed the benefits expected to be derived

   c. Limitations of ICS

      (1) Misunderstanding of instructions
      (2) Mistakes of judgment
      (3) Personal carelessness, distraction, fatigue
      (4) COLLUSION
      (5) Management override--management is often not subject to many of the controls and may "override" them

   NOTE: Know these limitations!

B. Effects of ICS on audit planning

   1. Overall--auditor should obtain sufficient understanding of each of three elements of ICS (control environment, accounting system, control procedures) to plan the audit

2. The understanding should include knowledge about the <u>design</u> of policies, procedures and records and whether they have been placed in <u>operation</u> by the entity

    NOTE: Distinguishing between determining that controls have been "placed in operation" (which is required for both audit planning and assessing control risk) and evaluating their "operating effectiveness" (which is detailed below in section C.2.) is only required for assessing control risk. An auditor may simply observe that the client is using a control to determine that the control has been placed in operation. Operating effectiveness is concerned with (1) how the control was applied, (2) the consistency with which it was applied, and (3) by whom.

3. In determining how much understanding is needed to plan the audit, the auditor considers types of misstatements that could occur, and their risk of occurring. Sources of this information include the auditor's

    a. Previous audits
    b. Understanding of the industry in which the entity operates
    c. Assessment of inherent risk
    d. Judgments about materiality
    e. Complexity of client's operations and systems

        (1) As they become more complex, it may be necessary to devote more attention to the ICS elements to gain understanding necessary to design effective substantive tests

4. Knowledge required by auditor for each of ICS elements

    a. Control environment--auditor should obtain knowledge to understand management's and board of director's attitude, awareness, and actions

        (1) The substance of the various policies, procedures, and related actions is more important than the form

            EXAMPLE: A budgeting system may provide adequate report, but if the reports are not analyzed and acted on, no real control exists.

    b. Accounting system--obtain knowledge on

        (1) Significant classes of transactions
        (2) How transactions are initiated
        (3) Accounting records and supporting documents
        (4) Accounting processing involved from initiation of transaction to inclusion in financial statements
        (5) Financial reporting process, including estimates and disclosures

    c. Control procedures--auditor obtains some information when gaining understanding of control environment and accounting system

        EXAMPLE: While obtaining an understanding of the <u>accounting system's</u> processing of cash transactions, the auditor may become aware of whether the control procedure of preparing bank reconciliations has been placed in operation.

        (1) Ordinarily audit planning does not require understanding of all control procedures related to each account or assertion

5. Procedures to obtain understanding of ICS

    a. Previous experience

        b. Inquiries of management, supervisory, staff
        c. Inspection of documents and records
        d. Observation of entity activities and operations

6. Documentation of understanding of ICS

    a. Depends on entity, for a large client may include flowcharts, questionnaires, or decision tables; for a small client a memorandum may be sufficient

      NOTE: At this point you should be able to summarize

      (1) The required knowledge of each of the 3 ICS elements,
      (2) The procedures used to obtain this knowledge, and
      (3) The required level of documentation for purposes of planning the audit

C. Effect of ICS on assessing control risk

  1. Overall--control risk is the risk of material misstatement not being prevented or detected by ICS

  NOTE: Recall that auditors consider control risk for two purposes--(1) to aid in planning the audit, and (2) to assess control risk (which is what this section of the outline is about).

  2. Assessing control risk at below the maximum involves

    a. Identifying policies and procedures relevant to assertions that are likely to prevent or detect misstatements
    b. Performing tests of controls to evaluate effectiveness of ICS policies and procedures

      NOTE: Prior to issuance of this section tests of controls were referred to as "compliance tests".

  3. Control risk should be assessed in terms of the financial statement assertions--PERVC

      Presentation and disclosure
      Existence or occurrence
      Rights and obligations
      Completeness
      Valuation

  NOTE: For more on PERVC assertions see the Evidence module and the outline of AU 326.

    a. The control environment and accounting system often have a pervasive effect on a number of accounts, and therefore can often affect many assertions

      EXAMPLE: An auditor's conclusion that a highly effective control environment exists may influence decisions about the number of the entity's locations at which auditing procedures are to be performed, and whether to perform certain procedures for some accounts at an interim date.

    b. Some control procedures have a specific effect on an individual assertion in a particular account

EXAMPLE: A control procedure to ensure that employee personnel are properly counting the annual physical inventory may relate to the existence assertion for inventory.

4. Tests of controls--procedures directed toward either the effectiveness of both the design or operation ("operating effectiveness") of an ICS policy or procedure

    a. Approaches

        (1) Inquiries of appropriate personnel

        (2) Inspection of documents and reports indicating performance of policy or procedure

        (3) Observation of the application of the policy or procedure

        (4) Reperformance of the application of the policy or procedure by the auditor (used for testing operation of system, not for testing design)

NOTE: Generally, inquiries alone will not provide sufficient evidential matter to support a conclusion about the effectiveness of the design or operation of a specific control procedure. Also be able to recall the above 4 approaches.

    b. The conclusion reached is referred to as the "assessed level of control risk"

        (1) It is based on effectiveness of design and of operation

        (2) Lower assessments of risk require more evidential matter support

        (3) The assessed levels of control risk and inherent risk determine the acceptable level of detection risk

        (4) As acceptable level of detection risk decreases, more substantive tests are necessary

        EXAMPLES:

        (a) A change from less effective to more effective tests (e.g., use tests directed toward independent parties outside the entity rather than tests directed toward parties or documents within the entity)

        (b) Less reliance on interim testing

        (c) More substantive tests (larger samples)

5. Documentation--as reliance increases, required documentation of effectiveness of design and operation increases

D. Other points

1. Relationship of understanding the control structure to assessing control risk

    a. Auditors often plan to perform some tests of control concurrently with obtaining the understanding of the ICS

    b. Audit tests aimed at obtaining an understanding of the ICS may also address effectiveness of design and operation (tests thus become tests of controls)

    c. Additional tests of controls may be performed to justify a lower assessed level of control risk

2. Evidential matter to support assessment of control risk
   a. No one specific test of controls is always appropriate, and the auditor selects among inquiry, inspection, observation, and reperformance
   b. When no documentation is available to substantiate performance (e.g., inspection is not possible), observation, inquiry, or computer-assisted audit techniques may be used
      (1) The auditor must be aware that procedures observed may not be performed in same manner when auditor is not present
      (2) When evidential matter has been gathered at an interim period, the importance of the related assertion, length of remaining period, and other evidence should be used to help auditor determine if remainder of period should be tested
      (3) Inquiry alone generally will not provide sufficient evidential matter to support a conclusion about the effectiveness of the design or operation of a specific control procedure

3. Control risk and detection risk (substantive tests)
   a. The ultimate purpose of assessing control risk is to contribute to the auditor's evaluation of the risk that material misstatements exist in the financial statements
   b. As the assessed level of control risk decreases, the acceptable level of detection risk increases (an "inverse" relationship)
   c. Ordinarily, the assessed level of control risk cannot be so low as to eliminate need for substantive tests for all assertions relevant to significant accounts
   d. Recall that substantive tests are (1) tests of detail of transactions and balances and (2) analytical procedures
   e. In some circumstances the results of tests of details of transactions may also serve as tests of controls
      (1) Although the objective of tests of details of transactions for substantive tests is to detect material misstatements in financial statements, such tests may also provide evidential matter on whether a control has operated effectively

      NOTE: Such tests are often referred to as "dual purpose" tests

322 The Effect of an Internal Audit Function on the Scope of the Independent Auditor's Examination (SAS 9)

Supersedes Section 320.74 of SAS 1

Overall Objective and Approach-- This section presents information on the manner in which CPAs may use the work of internal auditors. In addition to providing general information, it requires that to use internal auditor's work, CPAs must review internal auditor's (1) competence, (2) objectivity, and (3) work performance.

A. Overall
   1. The work of internal auditors cannot be substituted for the work of the CPA in determining the nature, timing, and extent of his/her own auditing procedures
   2. This section applies whether the work performed by internal auditors (a) is a part of their normal duties, (b) is performed at the request of the CPA, or (c) when internal auditors work directly with the CPA

B. If the CPA believes that the work performed by internal auditors may have a bearing on his/her own procedures, the CPA should evaluate the competence, objectivity, and work performance of the internal auditors

   1. Evaluating competence--inquire about client's practices for hiring, training, and supervising staff

   2. Evaluating objectivity

      a. Consider organizational level to which internal auditors report the results of their work and the organizational level to which they report administratively

      b. Review recommendations made in their reports

   3. Evaluating work performance

      a. Examine documentary evidence on a test basis to determine whether

         (1) Scope is appropriate?
         (2) Auditor programs are adequate?
         (3) Working papers are documented?
         (4) Conclusions are appropriate?
         (5) Reports are consistent with work?

      b. The auditor should also perform some tests of the work of the internal auditor, e.g., examine transactions or balances the internal auditor examined

      NOTE: As indicated above, CPAs evaluate internal audit competence, objectivity, and work performance. Be able to identify how CPAs evaluate competence vs. objectivity.

C. When the work of the internal auditors on internal control is significant, the auditor should arrange to have access to internal auditor's workpapers and reports

   1. The internal auditor's work frequently is more useful when discussed with the auditor prior to performance

D. Internal auditors may also be used in performing substantive tests and tests of controls

   1. The competence and objectivity of internal auditors should be considered

   2. The work of internal auditors should be supervised and tested

E. The auditor must make all of the judgments concerning matters affecting the audit report

324 Special Purpose Reports on Internal Accounting Control at Service Organizations (SAS 44)

Overall Objective and Approach--This section provides guidance related to service organizations. As an example, consider a service organization which provides bookkeeping and/or data processing services. Also, consider a trust department of a bank that invests and holds assets for employee benefit plans of various entities.

   The first portion of the section discusses audit responsibilities of a CPA whose client engages a service organization to provide services; such services may include (1) executing transactions and maintaining related accountability, and (2)

recording transactions and processing related data. Such an engagement often creates a situation in which a portion of the client's internal control structure has in actuality been transferred to the service organization. The basic decision to be made is whether the CPA should (1) audit inputs to and outputs from the service organization, (2) perform audit procedures at the actual service organization or (3) receive a special-purpose report on the service organization's internal accounting control.

The final portion of the section presents guidance for a CPA whose client is a service organization whose management desires a report on the service organization's internal control.

A. Definitions and background

1. Definitions

a. Client organization--entity whose financial statements are being examined

b. User auditor--the auditor who reports on the financial statements of the client organization

c. Service organizatic -the entity (or a segment of that entity) that provides services to the client organization

d. Service auditor--the auditor who reports on certain aspects of the system of internal accounting control of the service organization

2. The section divides the user auditor's considerations into two situations depending upon whether the service organization's controls

a. Interact with the client organization's controls (e.g., service organization processing of payroll, orders, billings, etc.)

b. Do not interact with the client organization's controls (e.g., trustees of employee benefit plans that hold and invest assets)

B. Appropriate auditing approaches

1. Situation in which client controls interact with service organization controls

a. Test client organization's controls--this approach may be used when client maintains strong control over transactions

b. Test client organization's controls and apply appropriate procedures at the service organization

c. Test client organization's controls and obtain service organization's auditor's report on the service organization's system of internal control covering both the design of the service organization's system and tests of controls directed to the specific objectives of internal accounting control

2. Situation in which client controls do not interact with service organization controls

a. Apply appropriate auditing procedures at the service organization and/or

b. Obtain a service auditor's opinion on the system of internal control

C. Consideration in using the service auditor's report

1. Process of obtaining and evaluating the service auditor's report

a. Contact the service organization through the client

b. If there is no report, or if the report is not appropriate, the auditor may either

    (1) Apply procedures at the service organization, or
    (2) Request that the service auditor apply the required procedures

  c. Make inquiries concerning the service auditor's professional reputation, as per AU 508 procedures for when other auditors are involved

  d. If unable to achieve audit objectives, qualify or disclaim an opinion due to scope limitations

2. If the data of the service auditor's report does not coincide with the period covered by the financial statements, the auditor needs to consider whether it will be necessary to update tests of the service organization

3. Reference to the service auditor's report

  a. For financial statement audits, make no reference

  b. For opinions on client's internal control, refer to the service auditor's report (AU 642.45)

D. Service auditor responsibilities for special-purpose reports

NOTE: The remainder of this outline relates to responsibilities taken by a CPA who is ISSUING a Special-Purpose report on a service organization

1. The service should be performed in accordance with GAAS, as appropriate

2. The service auditor need not be independent of each <u>client organization</u> (organizations for whom the service organization is performing services)

3. A service auditor may issue reports on (a) the design of the system, (b) the design of the system and tests of controls directed to specific objectives of internal control, and (c) reports on the system of a segment of the service organization

  a. Reports on design of system

    (1) Useful for

      (a) Providing user auditor with understanding of system
      (b) Designing tests of controls and substantive tests
      (c) Do not provide basis for reliance on controls

    (2) Required information is obtained through discussion with service organization personnel, reference to documentation, and walk-through

      (a) Tests of compliance are not required

    (3) Opinion as of specified date should include description of

      (a) Significant changes in system that auditor becomes aware of
      (b) Circumstances in which control objectives are not achieved

    (4) Elements of special-purpose reports in addition to those described in SAS 30, para 61 (AU 642.61)

    (5) Sample report on design of system (AU 324.35)

      (a) Description of system
      (b) Description of specific control objectives
      (c) Purpose of procedures performed
      (d) Inherent limitations of internal control

(e) Service auditor's opinion concerning control procedures described

Example:

To the Blank Service Center:

We have reviewed the accompanying description of the operations and control procedures of the Blank Service Center related to its payroll processing system as of (date) and identified specific control objectives and the procedures that achieve those objectives. Our review included procedures we considered necessary in the circumstances to evaluate the design of the control procedures specified in section 2. We did not test compliance with the control procedures and, accordingly, we do not express an opinion on whether those controls were being applied as prescribed for any period of time or on whether the system, taken as a whole, meets the objectives of internal accounting control. A further description of our review and its objections is attached.

Because of inherent limitations in any system of internal control, errors or irregularities may occur and not be detected. Also, projection of any evaluation of the system to future periods is subject to the risk that procedures may become inadequate because of changes in conditions.

In our opinion, the control procedures included in the accompanying description of the payroll processing system of the Blank Service Center as of (date) are suitably designed to provide reasonable, but not absolute, assurance that the control objectives specified in section 2 would be achieved if the control procedures were complied with satisfactorily.

This report is intended solely for use by management of Blank Service Center, its customers, and the independent auditors of its customers.

b. Reports on both design of system and certain tests of controls

   (1) Useful for

       (a) Providing user auditor with understanding of system including relationship of service organization's controls to those of client
       (b) Providing basis for reliance on service organization's internal controls
       (c) Designing compliance and substantive tests at client organization

   (2) Required information is obtained through discussion with service personnel, reference to documentation, tests of controls, and other procedures

       (a) Circumstances found where control objectives are not achieved should be described
       (b) Report will not necessarily include list of each compliance deviation

   (3) Elements of special-purpose reports in addition to those described in SAS 30, para 61 (AU 642.61)

       (a) Description of system
       (b) Description of specific control objectives
       (c) Inherent limitations of internal control
       (d) Service auditor's opinion concerning control procedures described and degree of compliance therewith

(4) Report on design and tests of controls is similar to D.3.a.(5)
     (AU 324.43)

c. Reports on system of segment of service organization

   (1) May be useful when it is unlikely that client organizations will
     maintain controls that interact with those of service organization

     (a) Do not ordinarily include description of design of system
     (b) Includes service auditor's opinion on internal controls
        applied by segment of service organization [SAS 30, paras 3-46
        (AU 642.03-.46)]
     (c) In report on system, basis for assessing materiality of poten-
        tial errors or irregularities is financial statements of ser-
        vice organization rather than segment
     (d) Report will not necessarily include list of each compliance
        deviation error found
     (e) Service auditor must also consider materiality of errors or
        irregularities found in relation to assets held for affected
        client organization

        1] If material, service auditor should request service
           organization to report this, and
        2] If service organization does not report errors or irregu-
           larities, service auditor should describe them in report

   (2) For sample report on system of a segment see 324.46

325 The Communication of Internal Control Structure Related Matters Noted in an Audit

(Supersedes AU 323, and AU 642.47-.53)

Overall Objective and Approach--This section provides guidance for CPAs as to how to
(1) identify and (2) report conditions that relate to an entity's internal control
structure that are observed during an audit.

A. Definitions and overall requirements

   1. Definitions

     a. <u>Reportable conditions</u>--<u>significant deficiencies</u> in the design or
       operation of the internal control structure which could adversely affect
       the organization's ability to <u>record, process, summarize, and report</u>
       <u>financial data</u> consistent with the <u>assertions of management</u> in the
       financial statements.

       *NOTE: See outline of AU 326 and Evidence module for information on the
       PERVC "assertions of management."*

       <u>Material weakness in the internal control structure</u>--a reportable
       condition in which the design or operation of the specific internal
       control structure elements do not reduce to a relatively low level the
       risk that material errors or irregularities could occur and not be
       detected within a timely period by employees in the normal course of
       performing their assigned functions.

       *NOTE: These two definitions actually outline three types of weaknesses
       in internal control*

       (1) A weakness too minor to be considered reportable
       (2) A reportable condition (i.e., it adversely affects ability to
           record, process, summarize, and report...)

       (3) A material weakness (a reportable condition that does not reduce to a relatively low level the risk of material errors...)

      Thus, a material weakness is always also a reportable condition; but, some reportable conditions are not important enough to qualify as material weaknesses. Most of AU 325 relates to reportable conditions.

B. Auditor responsibility

  1. The auditor is not obligated to identify reportable conditions beyond those coming to his/her attention during an audit

  2. The communication is to the audit committee (or to individuals with equivalent authority and responsibility when entity does not have an audit committee)

     a. When the audit committee is already aware of reportable conditions, and has acknowledged so, the auditor may decide not to report them

  3. The auditor may form an agreement with the client to disclose additional conditions which differ from those contemplated in this section

     a. For example, the client may want the auditor to disclose the existence of matters of less significance
     b. These are referred to as agreed-upon criteria

C. Form and content of the report on reportable conditions

  1. The report should preferably be written, but if communicated orally, the discussion should be documented in the working papers

  2. The report issued should state that it is intended for the audit committee management, and others in the organization

     a. When requirements state that governmental authorities are to receive the report, this may be done
     b. Report should also

       (1) Indicate that the purpose of the audit was to report on financial statements
       (2) Include the definition of reportable conditions

  3. <u>No report should be issued when no reportable conditions were noted</u> during audit (don't say "No reportable conditions were noted.")

  4. When extremely significant matters were noted, the communication should be made as soon as reasonably possible

  5. The report does <u>not</u> require the identification of whether a reportable condition is of such a magnitude as to be considered a material weakness in the control structure

     a. The auditor may choose, or the client may request, that the auditor separately identify and communicate material weaknesses

    NOTE: See the Internal Control module for a sample report

326 Evidential Matter (SAS 31)

<u>Overall Objective and Approach</u>--This section presents information related to the third standard of field work which requires that sufficient competent evidential matter be obtained. The statement suggests that management makes various assertions, either implicitly or explicitly, that are embodied in the financial statements. The role of the auditor is to obtain sufficient competent evidence to determine that the various assertions have been met. These assertions are <u>extremely</u> important since they have been integrated into a number of subsequent sections (e.g., AU 319, which requires that control risk be assessed by assertion).

   After discussing the financial statement assertions, the section presents infor-mation related to the competency and sufficiency of audit evidence.

A. Assertions (explicit or implicit) are representations made by management and include several types

   1. <u>Existence or occurrence</u> assertions state whether

      a. Assets or liabilities existed at a specific date, e.g., inventories on the balance sheet are available for sale
      b. Recorded transactions occurred during the period, e.g., sales on the income statement are the results of exchanges of goods or services for a valid asset

   2. <u>Completeness</u> assertions state whether all appropriate transactions and appropriate accounts are included in the financial statements, e.g., all purchases have been recorded and are included in financial statements

   3. <u>Rights and obligations</u> assertions state whether assets are rights of the entity and liabilities are obligations of the entity as of the balance sheet date, e.g., captial leases

   4. <u>Valuation or allocation</u> assertions state whether asset, liability, revenue, and expense elements are shown in the financial statements at the proper amounts, e.g., accounts receivable at net realization value and fixed assets at cost less accumulated depreciation

   5. <u>Presentation and disclosure</u> assertions state whether elements of financial statements are properly classified, described, and disclosed, e.g., extraordinary items meet the criteria of APB 30

   Note: Know these "PERCV" assertions (reordered as <u>P</u>resentation, <u>E</u>xistence, <u>R</u>ights, <u>C</u>ompleteness, and <u>V</u>aluation). In the text we use them to help us prepare audit progress.

B. Assertions are used to develop audit objectives and to design substantive tests

   1. The relationship between audit objectives and audit procedures is not always one-to-one

      a. An audit objective may require application of more than one procedure
      b. An audit procedure may relate to more than one objective

   2. While methods of applying audit procedures may be influenced by existence of computer, auditor's objectives do <u>not</u> change

        a. The existence of a computer may make inspection, inquiry, or confirmation impossible without computer assistance

   3. Professional judgment of the auditor considering specific circumstances determines the nature, timing, and extent of the procedures to be used on a given audit

        a. Procedures used should be adequate to fulfill specific audit objectives
        b. Evidential matter secured should be sufficient for auditor to assess validity of specific assertions contained in the elements of the financial statements

C. Evidential matter supporting the financial statements consists of

   1. <u>Underlying accounting data</u> including books of original entry, general and subsidiary ledgers, accounting manuals, informal and memorandum records

        a. Presence of the above alone is not sufficient support for the financial statements; however, in the absence of evidence regarding propriety and accuracy of this underlying data, an opinion is not justified
        b. Auditor tests underlying accounting data using analysis and review by

           (1) Retracing procedural steps of accounting process including worksheets, allocations, etc.
           (2) Recalculating allocations, etc.
           (3) Reconciling related types and applications of common information

        c. If system is properly designed and maintained, above tests will provide persuasive evidence regarding presentation of financial statements in conformity with GAAP

   2. <u>Corroborating evidence</u> which provides additional support and includes

        a. Documentary items (e.g., checks, invoices, contracts, minutes of meetings)
        b. Confirmations and other written representations
        c. Information gathered by the auditor through inquiry, observation, inspections, and physical examination
        d. Other information available or developed by auditor which allows him/her to form conclusions using valid reasoning

D. Competent evidential matter is valid and relevant

   1. Since the validity of evidence is influenced so heavily by circumstances, the generalizations below are subject to exceptions

        a. External evidential matter gathered from unbiased outsiders gives greater assurance than internally obtained evidence
        b. Financial statements processed from accounting data under conditions of adequate internal control are more reliable than those processed in entities with weak internal control
        c. Corroborating evidential matter obtained directly is more persuasive than that obtained indirectly

           (1) E.g., physical examination, observation, computation, and inspection

        NOTE: Know that competent evidence is valid and relevant. Also, the above 3 generalizations concerning validity of evidence have been asked in essay questions.

E. Sufficient competent evidential matter must be obtained to give the auditor a basis for forming an opinion

    1. Auditors use professional judgment to assess whether the quantities and types of evidential matter are sufficient

        a. Usually it is necessary to rely on persuasive rather than convincing evidence for both

            (1) Individual financial statement assertions, and
            (2) The assertion that the financial statements taken as a whole present financial position, results of operations, and its cash flows in accordance with GAAP

329 Analytical Procedures

Supersedes AU 318

Overall Objective and Approach--This section presents information on analytical procedures. It suggests that they are normally used at three stages of the audit: (1) planning, (2) substantive testing, and (3) overall review at the conclusion of an audit. Procedures (1) and (3), planning and overall review are required stages. In addition, the section presents information on the manner in which analytical procedures are applied.

A. Analytical procedures consist of <u>evaluations of financial information made by a study of plausible relationships among financial and nonfinancial data</u>

    1. <u>Basic premise--plausible relationships</u> among data may be expected to exist in the absence of known conditions to the contrary

    2. Analytical procedures used for <u>3 purposes</u>:

        a. <u>Planning</u> nature, timing, and extent of other auditing procedures
        b. <u>Substantive tests</u> about particular assertions
        c. <u>Overall review</u> in the final stage on audit

        NOTE: The section requires the use of analytical procedures in "a." and "c." above

    3. The auditor <u>compares recorded amounts to expectations</u> developed from sources such as

        a. <u>Prior period</u> financial information
        b. <u>Anticipated results</u> such as projections or forecasts
        c. <u>Relationships among elements</u> of financial information within the period
        d. <u>Industry</u> information
        e. <u>Relevant nonfinancial information</u> (e.g., number of employees, volume of goods produced)

B. Analytical procedures for <u>planning</u>

    1. The purpose is to assist in planning the nature, timing, and extent of other substantive tests and therefore should

        a. Enhance auditor's understanding of client's business and events since last audit
        b. Identify high risk areas (e.g., <u>unusual transactions</u>)

    2. Generally use data aggregated at a high level

C. Analytical procedures for <u>substantive tests</u>

1. Especially effective for assertions for which detailed evidence does not make misstatement apparent (e.g., comparing aggregate wages paid to number of employees)

2. Auditors must understand the reasons that relationships are plausible

   a. For higher assurance more predictable relationships are required to develop an expectation
   b. Principles involving <u>usual</u> predictability of relationships:

   (1) Relationships in a <u>dynamic</u> or unstable environment are <u>less predictable</u> than those in a stable environment
   (2) Relationships involving <u>balance sheet accounts are less predictable</u> than income statement accounts (because balance sheet accounts represent balances at one arbitrary point in time)
   (3) Relationships involving management discretion are sometimes less predictable (e.g., decision to incur maintenance expense rather than replace plant)

   NOTE: Know the above 3 principles

3. The following factors generally <u>increase the reliability</u> of data used to develop an expectation

   a. Data generated from <u>independent sources outside entity</u>
   b. <u>Internal data</u> developed by <u>sources independent</u> of amount being audited
   c. <u>Internal data</u> developed under an <u>effective internal control</u> structure
   d. <u>Data subjected to audit testing</u> in current or prior year
   e. <u>Expectations developed</u> using data from a <u>variety of sources</u>

4. Expectations developed at a detailed level generally have a greater chance of detecting misstatement

   a. Monthly amounts will generally be more effective than annual amounts
   b. Comparisons by line of business usually more effective than company-wide comparisons

5. The auditor should use the materiality amount and level of assurance desired from the procedure to determine the amount of difference from expectation that can be accepted without further investigation

D. Analytical procedures in <u>overall review</u>

1. Purposes are to assist auditor in

   a. <u>Assessing the conclusions</u> reached
   b. <u>Evaluating the overall financial statement presentation</u>

2. Should include reading the financial statements and notes to consider:

   a. Adequacy of data gathered in response to unusual or unexpected balances identified during preliminary analysis
   b. Unusual or unexpected balances or relationships not identified during the audit

331 Receivables and Inventories

Overall Objective and Approach-- This section establishes confirmation of receivables and observation of inventories as generally accepted auditing procedures. An auditor who omits these procedures must be able to justify the decision (in the working papers--not in the report). The section presents information on positive and negative confirmation techniques, and when each is appropriate. The section on inventories discusses a number of complications that may arise when observing the client's inventory count, and establishes procedures which may be necessary when inventories are held in public warehouses.

A. Confirmation of receivable

   1. Positive confirmation method

      a. The debtor is asked to reply whether s/he agrees or disagrees with information on confirmation

      b. Approach for nonreplies

        (1) A second and possibly a third request is normally sent
        (2) When there is still no reply, alternate procedures are applied for significant non-responding accounts; examples are examination of

          (a) Subsequent cash receipts
          (b) Cash receipts
          (c) Sales and shipping documents
          (d) Other records

        NOTE: As a practical matter, alternative procedures are generally applied to all nonresponding accounts

      c. When to use

        (1) Relatively large individual account balances
        (2) When there is reason to believe there may be a substantial number of accounts in dispute with inaccuracies or irregularities

   2. Negative confirmation method

      a. The debtor is asked to reply only when s/her disagrees with information on confirmation

      b. Approach for nonreplies--typically there is no auditor follow up since a non reply is assumed to indicate debtor agreement

      c. When to use

        (1) Internal control is satisfactory
        (2) A large number of small receivables exist
        (3) When the auditor has no reason to believe that the persons receiving the requests are unlikely to give them consideration

   3. Overall comments on receivable confirmations

      a. A combination of positive and negative confirmations is often used
      b. When negatives are used by themselves, the number of requests sent, or the extent of other auditing procedures applied to the receivable balance should normally be greater than when positives are used
      c. Receivable confirmations primarily address the existence assertion from AU 326; valuation is addressed to a much lesser extent since the amounts due may never be received

B. Inventories--held by clients

1. It is normally necessary for the CPA to be present when inventory quantities are determined by means of a physical count

2. When perpetual records are well maintained and checked by the client periodically by comparisons with physical counts, the auditor may perform observation procedures either during or after the end of the period under audit

3. When a client uses statistical sampling to determine inventory quantities, the auditor must determine that
   a. It is reasonable and has statistical validity
   b. It has been properly applied
   c. The results are reasonable in the circumstances

4. When a CPA has not observed the counting of inventory
   a. It will **always** be necessary to make some physical counts of the inventory and apply appropriate tests of intervening transactions subsequent to the client's count

      EXAMPLE: Assume the client counted inventory on December 31, and the auditor was not present. At some point, say January 15, the auditor must make some physical counts and reconcile the January 15 quantities back to those of December 31.

5. When a CPA is satisfied as to the current inventory, s/he may satisfy him/herself as to a <u>prior period's inventory</u> (e.g., the beginning inventory for the year under audit) by
   a. Tests of prior transactions
   b. Review of prior count records
   c. Gross profit tests

C. Inventories--held in public warehouses

   1. Direct confirmation in writing from custodian is ordinarily obtained

   2. If such inventories represent a significant portion of current or total assets, auditor should
      a. Review and test owner's control procedures for investigating and evaluating performance of the warehouseman
      b. Obtain report from independent accountant as to the reliability of the internal control structure relevant to custody of goods and, if applicable, pledging of receipts
         (1) Alternatively, test the structure to gain assurance that information received is reliable
      c. Observe physical counts where reasonable and practical
      d. Confirm pertinent details of pledged receipts with lenders, if any

332 Long-Term Investments

Overall Objective and Approach--This section presents guidance on appropriate audit objectives and procedures for long-term investments. The guidance relates to carrying values of investments as well as related earnings and disclosures.

A. The auditor's objectives in auditing long-term investments may be derived from the AU 326 "PERVC" assertions. For more on this see the outline of AU 326 and the Evidence module.

B. Evidential matter for the <u>existence, ownership, and cost</u> of long-term investments

1. Accounting records and documents of the investor relating to the acquisition

2. Investments in the form of securities (e.g., stocks, bonds, notes) <u>should be corroborated by inspection of the securities</u>

3. It may also be possible to obtain written <u>confirmation</u> from an independent custodian

C. Evidential matter for the <u>carrying amount</u> of investments, <u>earnings</u> therefrom, and <u>other transactions</u>

1. Audited statements are generally sufficient

2. Unaudited statements are not, by themselves, sufficient

   a. The extent and nature of audit procedures which need to be performed on the investee's financial statements are determined by materiality of investment
   b. The investee's CPA may be used to perform any necessary procedures

3. Market quotations when based on reasonably broad and active market constitute sufficient competent evidential matter for purposes of determining a market value

4. Personal evaluations (by client personnel or others) of an investment with a carrying value greater than book value are acceptable

   a. This may occur because the book value may differ significantly from the market value
   b. Evaluations of market value made by independent persons provide greater assurance of reliability than those made by persons within the companies

5. When collateral is important with regard to collectibility, ascertain

   a. Existence
   b. Market value
   c. Transferability

D. Equity method

1. CPA must satisfy him/herself as to client's methods of accounting for investments in common stock

   a. Investor's ability to exercise significant influence
   b. Circumstances that are basis for conclusion

c. When 20% to 50% presumption is not followed, obtain evidence to satisfy that presumption has been overcome, and disclose appropriately

2. Investor includes proportionate share of investee's earnings from investee's most recent reliable statements

a. May use unaudited interim statements which may in turn require audit procedures
b. Any time lag should be consistent from year to year

(1) If change in time lag has material effect express consistency exception in opinion

3. Events subsequent to investee's most recent reliable statements should be treated (in accounts or disclosed) in the same manner as subsequent events of investor

a. Such events may be so significant as to cause a loss in the value of the investment which should be recognized

4. Any material intercompany profits and losses should be eliminated

333 Client Representation

Overall Objective and Approach--This section presents guidance on obtaining written representations from management ("representation letters"). The first subsection requires the obtaining of such representations and states that they complement other procedures, but are not a substitute for the application of any necessary audit procedures. The remainder of the section provides guidance as to written representations normally obtained, and provides miscellaneous related information.

A. Auditors must obtain a representation letter from management on all audits

1. The representation letter is not to be viewed as a substitute for other auditing procedures

NOTE: This has been asked on a number of exams

2. Advantages of having obtained such a representation letter

a. It reduces the possibility of auditor-client misunderstandings
b. It confirms and documents oral representations that have been made

3. In some cases representations made by management are the only evidence available (e.g., a dicision to discontinue a line of business)

B. Written representations normally obtained from management include

1. Acknowledgement of responsibility for financial statement presentation per GAAP
2. Availability to the auditor of all financial and related data
3. Completeness and availability to the auditor of all minutes of meetings
4. Absence of errors and unrecorded transactions
5. Information on related party transactions
6. Company noncompliance with contractual agreements
7. Information concerning subsequent events

8. Management or employee irregularities

9. Noncompliance with regulatory requirements

10. Management's intentions affecting statement items, e.g., current assets

11. Disclosure of compensating balances

12. Obsolete inventories

13. Sales commitment losses

14. Satisfactory title, liens, etc., on assets

15. Repurchase agreements

16. Purchase commitment losses

17. Violations of laws, regulations, etc.

18. Other disclosures required per SFAS 5, "Accounting for Contingencies"

19. Unasserted claims probable of assertion

20. Capital stock options, repurchase agreements, etc.

> NOTE: Past exams have required a list of items included in a representation letter. Don't try to memorize them all, but be familiar with them. Also, section C of the Evidence module presents a sample representation letter.

C. Miscellaneous matters

1. Representations may be limited to matters that are considered either individually or collectively material to the financial statements, provided that the auditor and management have reached an understanding on the limits of materiality

   a. Exceptions to this rule are items, 1., 2., 3., and 8. above, which are always considered material for purposes of the letter

2. The nature of the engagement may lead the auditor to conclude that representations on other matters are also necessary

3. Details of the representation letter

   a. It should be addressed to the auditor
   b. It should be <u>dated as of the date of the auditor's report</u>
   c. It should be <u>signed by the chief executive officer and the chief financial officer</u>

      (1) In some cases representations may also be obtained from others (e.g., the completeness of minutes from the person responsible for keeping such minutes)

4. Management's refusal to furnish written representations <u>constitutes a limitation on the scope of the auditor's examination sufficient to preclude an unqualified opinion</u>

   a. This limitation will normally result in a qualified opinion or a disclaimer of opinion

   > NOTE: This relates to AU 508, on scope limitations. This is a management imposed restriction which will lead the auditor to a situation in which s/he will "generally disclaim."

334 Related Parties (SAS 45)

Overall Objective and Approach--This section presents guidance on <u>accounting</u> and <u>auditing</u> considerations for related party transactions. The subsection on audit procedures, after providing some general advice, provides guidance on (1) identifying <u>conditions</u> in which related party transactions are likely, (2) identifying <u>parties</u> that are related to the entity, (3) identifying <u>transactions</u> with related parties, and (4) <u>examining related party transactions</u> that have been <u>identified</u>. The section closes with information on required disclosures.

A. Accounting (including disclosures) considerations for related party transactions

    1. SFAS 57 provides accounting requirements for related party disclosures

        a. Nature of relationship(s)
        b. Description of transaction(s)
        c. Dollar amount of transactions
        d. Amounts due to/from related parties, including terms

      NOTE: See outline of SFAS 57 for more details

    2. Transactions should reflect their substance (rather than their form)

    3. Except for routine transactions, it will generally <u>not be possible</u> to determine whether a particular transaction would have taken place, or what its terms would have been

        a. If management makes such a representation, <u>and if it is unsubstantiated</u>, it may result in either a qualified or an adverse opinion due to a departure from GAAP--see outline of AU 508 and Reporting module for information on departures from GAAP

      NOTE: Points 3. and 3a. have been asked several times in multiple choice questions.

    4. Example transactions that may be indicative of related party transactions

        a. Borrowing or lending at interest rates above or below the market rate
        b. Selling real estate at a price significantly different from its appraised value
        c. Exchanging property for similar property in a nonmonetary transaction
        d. Making loans with no scheduled repayment terms

      NOTE: Several multiple choice questions have asked for a situation in which the existence of related parties is likely, and have used one of the above as the correct reply.

B. <u>Auditing considerations</u> for related party transactions

    1. An audit cannot be expected to provide assurance that all related party transactions will be discovered

        a. Nevertheless, an auditor should be aware of the possible existence of material related party transactions

    2. <u>Conditions in which related party transactions are likely</u>

        a. Lack of sufficient working capital or credit to continue the business
        b. An urgent desire for favorable EPS trends
        c. Overly optimistic EPS forecast
        d. Dependence on a few products, customers, or transactions
        e. Declining industry profitability

    f. Excess capacity
    g. Significant litigation
    h. Significant obsolescence

3. Procedures to identify <u>parties</u> that are related to the entity

    a. Evaluate the client's procedures for related party transactions
    b. Ask client for names of all related parties and whether there have been any transactions with these parties
    c. Review SEC filings
    d. Determine names of officers of all employee trusts
    e. Review stockholder listings of closely held companies
    f. Review prior workpapers for the names of related parties
    g. Inquire of predecessor and/or principal auditors
    h. Review material investment transactions

4. Procedures to identify <u>transactions</u> with related parties

    a. Provide audit personnel with related party names
    b. Review Board of Directors' minutes (and other committees)
    c. Review SEC filings
    d. Review client "conflict of interest" statements obtained by company from management
    e. Review nature of transactions with major customers, suppliers, etc.
    f. Consider whether unrecorded transactions exist
    g. Review accounting records for large, nonrecurring transactions
    h. Review confirmations of compensating balances for indications that balances are maintained for or by related parties
    i. Review legal invoices
    j. Review confirmations of loans receivable and payable for guarantees

5. Procedures (beyond management inquiry) for <u>examining</u> related party transactions that have been <u>identified</u>

    a. Obtain understanding of the purpose of the transaction
    b. Examine supporting documents
    c. Verify existence of required approval
    d. Evaluate reasonableness of amounts to be disclosed
    e. Consider simultaneous or joint audit of intercompany balances
    f. Inspect/confirm transferability and value of collateral
    g. Extend auditing procedures further as necessary to understand transactions

        (1) Confirm transaction details with other party
        (2) Inspect evidence held by other party
        (3) Confirm information with intermediaries, e.g., banks
        (4) Refer to trade journals, credit agencies, etc.
        (5) Seek assurance on material uncollected balances

336 Using the Work of a Specialist (SAS 11)

<u>Overall Objective and Approach</u>--This section presents guidance on using the work of a specialist during an audit. For example, an auditor may engage an appraiser to help verify a client's valuation of an inventory of diamond rings. The first subsection gives examples of specialists, reviews circumstances in which an auditor may decide to use the work of a specialist. The next subsection provides guidance on selecting a specialist. Next, the manner in which specialist's findings may be used, and the possible effects on the audit report are presented.

A. Examples of specialists, and circumstances which may lead the auditor to use the work of a specialist

1. A specialist is a person (firm) possessing special skills or knowledge other than auditing or accounting

a. Examples: actuaries, appraisers, attorneys, engineers

NOTE: The <u>CPA's staff</u>, the client's <u>internal auditors</u>, or persons such as a client's credit or plant manager are <u>not</u> considered specialists. Knowledge of this exclusion has been required for several multiple choice questions.

2. Specialists are often used for

a. <u>Valuation</u> (works of art, special drugs, restricted securities)
b. Determination of <u>quantities</u> (minerals in ground, or material stored in piles)
c. Amounts derived using <u>specialized techniques</u> (actuarial determinations)
d. <u>Interpretation of technical requirements</u> (contracts, legal documents)

B. Selecting a specialist

1. Through inquiry, consider

a. Professional certification, license, etc.
b. Reputation and standing
c. Relationship to client

2. A specialist related to the client may be acceptable, but an unrelated specialist is better

3. A documented understanding of the work should exist among auditor, client, and specialist

a. Objectives and scope
b. Specialist's relationship to client
c. Methods or assumptions used
d. Comparison of methods or assumptions with those used last year
e. Specialist's understanding of auditor's use of specialist's findings
f. Form and content of specialist's report

C. Using the work of a specialist

1. The auditor should obtain an understanding of the methods or assumptions used by the specialist to determine whether the findings are suitable for corroborating the financial statement representations

2. The auditor will ordinarily use the work of the specialist unless the above procedures (1., above) lead him/her to believe the specialist's findings are unreasonable

3. If the specialist is related to the client, the auditor should consider performing additional procedures with respect to the specialist's

    a. Assumptions
    b. Methods, and/or
    c. Findings

D. Possible effects on the audit report

    1. Situation in which the specialist's findings <u>agree</u> with the financial statement representations--<u>no reference to the specialist is to be made</u>

        NOTE: *The above point has been asked on the exam a number of times.*

    2. Situation in which the specialist's findings <u>do not agree</u> with the financial statement representations--if the auditor is unable to determine which is correct, s/he should, if possible, apply additional procedures

        a. If the matter is still not resolved, a <u>scope limitation</u> is involved and the auditor may have to either qualify or disclaim an opinion
        b. If the auditor believes the financial statement representation is incorrect, a <u>departure from GAAP</u> is involved and s/he may have to either qualify opinion or issue an adverse opinion

        NOTE: *See AU 508, and section B of the Reporting module for details on scope limitations and departures from GAAP.*

337 Inquiry of a Client's Lawyer Concerning Litigation, Claims, and Assessments (LCA)

<u>Overall Objective and Approach</u>--This section presents guidance on the manner in which a CPA is to obtain information from a client's lawyer concerning litigation, claims, and assessments (LCA) that affect a client. LCA may result in contingent, as well as direct liabilities. At this point, if you are unable to recall the SFAS 5 accounting standard related to consistency, we suggest that you review that outline.

After a brief reference to SFAS 5, the section presents information on the types of evidential matter that should be gathered, and the appropriate audit procedures to be followed. Next, details of the inquiry which is to be sent to the client's lawyer are provided. The section concludes by discussing how CPAs should handle various limitations in the lawyer's response to the inquiry.

A. Evidential matter and appropriate audit procedures

    1. The auditor should obtain evidential matter relating to LCA relevant to the following factors:

        a. Conditions indicating a possible loss from LCA
        b. The period in which the underlying cause occurred
        c. The degree of probability of an unfavorable outcome
        d. The amount or range of potential loss

    2. Because <u>management</u> is the primary source of information about such contingencies, the CPA's procedures for LCA should include

        a. Inquiring as to the policies and procedures adopted for identifying, evaluating, and accounting for contingencies

      b. Obtaining a description and evaluation of all pending contingencies at the balance sheet date and any contingencies arising after the balance sheet date

      c. Examining relevant documents including correspondence and invoices from lawyers

      d. Obtaining management's written assurance that all unasserted claims require to be disclosed by SFAS 5 (per client's lawyer) are disclosed

         (1) Obtain client's permission to inform lawyer that client has given this assurance

   3. Other audit procedures which may reveal pending or possible contingencies

      a. Reading Board of Directors' and other appropriate meeting minutes

      b. Reading contracts, leases, correspondence, and other similar documents

      c. Guarantees of indebtedness on bank confirmations

      d. Inspecting other documents for possible client-made guarantees

B. Inquiry <u>sent to</u> the client's lawyer

NOTE: Although not explicitly stated in the section, the auditor mails this inquiry (typed on the client's letterhead) to the lawyer

   1. This inquiry may be sent to the client's <u>inside general counsel</u> or legal department (i.e., lawyers that are employees of the client) <u>and outside counsel</u>

      a. Information obtained from inside counsel is <u>not</u> a substitute for information outside counsel refuses to furnish

   2. Information included in the inquiry to the lawyer

      a. Identification of the client and the date of the audit

      b. A list prepared by management (or a request by management that the lawyer prepare a list) describing pending or threatened LCA for which the lawyer has been engaged and devoted substantive attention with a request that the <u>lawyer indicate</u>

         (1) A description of the <u>nature</u> of the matter, <u>progress</u> of the case to date, and the <u>action</u> the company intends to take (e.g., contest vigorously)

         (2) If possible, an evaluation of the likelihood and amount of potential loss

         (3) Identification of any omissions from list, or a statement that the list is complete with respect to LCA

      c. A list prepared by management that describes and evaluates <u>unasserted claims and assessments</u> which management considers <u>probable of assertion</u>, and that, <u>if asserted</u>, would have a <u>reasonable possibility</u> of an unfavorable outcome and a request that the lawyer indicate any disagreements with the description or evaluation

         (1) For unasserted claims, the lawyer <u>will not</u> inform the CPA of omissions from management's list

            (a) The lawyer is to advise the client of the omission

            (b) If the client does not then inform the CPA about the omission, the lawyer is generally required to resign

         NOTE: Several exam multiple choice questions have addressed the idea that resignation of a lawyer is to be investigated by the auditor; such resignation may indicate the existence of undisclosed

unasserted claims.   The auditor should inquire about reasons for
changes in or resignations of lawyers.

    (c)   A request that the lawyer specifically identify the nature of
and reasons for any limitations in his/her response

3.   The client and CPA should agree on materiality limits, and inquiry then need
not be made of immaterial items

4.   In some circumstances the auditor may obtain a response to the inquiry in a
conference with the lawyer

    a.   The CPA should appropriately document the conference

C.   Limitations on the lawyer's response to the inquiry

1.   A lawyer may limit his/her response to material matters to which s/he has
devoted substantive attention--such limitations are not considered audit
scope limitations

2.   <u>Refusal to furnish either in writing or orally information</u> requested in the
inquiry letter is a <u>scope limitation sufficient to preclude an unqualified
opinion</u>

    a.   Scope limitations lead to either qualified opinions or disclaimers of
opinion

3.   Inherent uncertainties involving the situation may make it impossible for
the lawyer to respond as to the likelihood of loss, or the amount

    a.   This is an uncertainty situation which, if material, may lead to an
unqualified opinion with an explanatory paragraph, or a disclaimer of
opinion

NOTE: For more on scope limitations and uncertainties, see outline of
AU 508 and section B of Reporting module.

339 Working Papers (SAS 41)

<u>Overall Objective and Approach</u>--This section presents general information about the
following aspects of working papers: (a) functions and nature, (b) content, and (c)
ownership and custody

A.   Functions and nature of working papers

1.   Main functions of working papers are to

    a.   Support auditor's opinion
    b.   Aid auditor in the conduct and supervision of the engagement

2.   Working papers are records kept of

    a.   Procedures applied
    b.   Tests performed
    c.   Information obtained
    d.   Pertinent conclusions reached

3.   Examples of working papers

    a.   Audit programs
    b.   Memoranda
    c.   Letters of confirmation and representation

     d. Schedules or commentaries prepared or obtained
     e. Data stored on tapes, films, or other media

  4. Factors affecting auditor's judgment or quantity, type, and content of working papers

     a. Nature of the engagement
     b. Nature of the auditor's report
     c. Nature of the financial statements, schedules, or other information being reported on
     d. Nature and condition of client's records
     e. Planned level of control risk assessment
     f. Needs in particular circumstance for supervision and review of work

B. Consent of working papers

  1. Working papers should be sufficient to document that (a) accounting records agree or can be reconciled to financial statements, and (b) GAAS field work standards have been observed

     a. Adequate <u>planning</u> and supervision
     b. Consideration of <u>internal control</u>
     c. Sufficient competent <u>evidential matter</u>

C. Ownership and custody of working papers

  1. The working papers are the property of the auditor

  2. Working papers should be safeguarded and retained for a reasonable period of time

341 The Auditor's Consideration of an Entity's Ability to Continue as a Going Concern

<u>Overall Objective and Approach</u>--This section presents guidance on CPA responsibility for evaluating whether there is <u>substantial doubt</u> about a client's ability to continue as a going concern. The section suggests that continuation as a going concern is assumed in the absence of information to the contrary. The section first discusses an auditor's responsibility related to a client. Second, audit procedures which may identify conditions and events which raise a question about going concern status are presented. The third subsection, which is only appropriate after such conditions and/or events have been identified, discusses the manner in which an auditor evaluates management's plans for dealing with such adverse circumstances. The fourth and fifth subsections discuss proper financial statement and audit report reflections of such conditions and events.

A. The auditor's responsibility

  1. The auditor must evaluate whether there is <u>substantial doubt about the entity's ability to continue as a going concern for a period not to exceed one year from the date of the financial statements being audited</u>

     a. Ordinarily, information that significantly <u>contradicts the going concern assumption</u> relates to inability to meet obligations as they become due without:

       (1) Substantial disposition of assets
       (2) Restructuring debt
       (3) Externally forced revisions of operations

(4) Similar actions

2. The evaluation is based on audit procedures planned and performed to achieve the audit objectives related to the management assertions--for more on the assertions see AU 326 outline and section A of the Evidence module

3. The process for evaluating whether there is substantial doubt

    a. Consider whether audit procedures identify conditions and events suggesting substantial doubt

    b. If substantial doubt from a.,

        (1) Obtain management's plans,
        (2) Assess likelihood plans can be implemented

    c. If substantial doubt remains, consider

        (1) Adequacy of disclosures on inability to continue and
        (2) Include explanatory paragraph following opinion paragraph in audit report

    NOTE: Be familiar with this process.

4. <u>Auditors are not responsible for predicting future</u> conditions and events

    a. The fact that an entity ceases to exist after an audit report which does not refer to substantial doubt does not in itself indicate inadequate auditor performance

    b. Absence of reference to substantial doubt in an audit report should not be viewed as providing assurance entity will continue as a going concern

B. Audit procedures and consideration of conditions and events

  1. <u>It is not necessary to design audit procedures for identifying substantial doubt</u>

  2. <u>Procedures for other objectives are sufficient</u> to identify conditions and events indicating substantial doubt. Examples of procedures

    a. Analytical procedures
    b. Review of subsequent events
    c. Compliance with terms of debt and loan agreements
    d. Reading minutes of shareholders' and board of directors' meetings
    e. Inquiry of legal counsel on litigation, claims, and assessments
    f. Confirmation of arrangements to maintain financial support

  3. <u>Conditions</u> and events that may <u>indicate substantial doubt</u>

    a. Negative trends--e.g., losses, working capital deficiencies
    b. Other indications of financial difficulties--e.g., defaults
    c. Internal matters--e.g., work stoppages, dependence on one project
    d. External matters--e.g., legal proceedings, loss of key franchise

C. Consideration of management's plans

  1. Auditor's consideration of management's plans may include the following

    a. <u>Plans to dispose</u> of assets--consider restrictions, marketability, effects of disposal

    b. <u>Plans to borrow</u> money or restructure debt--consider availability of financing, existing arrangements, possible effects of borrowing

    c. <u>Plans to reduce</u> or delay <u>expenditures</u>--consider feasibility, possible effects

       d. <u>Plans to increase ownership equity</u>--consider feasibility and existing arrangements to reduce dividend requirements, etc.

  2. When prospective financial information is significant to management's plans

       a. Request such information
       b. Consider adequacy of support for assumptions
       c. If important factors are not considered, request revision

D. Financial statement effects

  1. <u>When substantial doubt exists consider</u> need for following <u>disclosures</u>

       a. <u>Conditions</u> and events giving rise to substantial doubt
       b. <u>Possible effects</u> of such conditions and events
       c. <u>Management's evaluation</u> of conditions and events
       d. <u>Possible discontinuance</u> of operations
       e. <u>Information on recoverability and classification</u> of assets and liabilities

  2. When, primarily because of auditor's consideration of management's plans, no substantial doubt remains, still consider need for appropriate disclosures

E. Effects on auditor's report

  1. When substantial doubt exists, modify report to include an explanatory paragraph following opinion paragraph

  2. If disclosures are inadequate, a departure from GAAP exists which may result in qualified or adverse opinion

  3. When issuing comparative statements, resolution of prior substantial doubt eliminates need for modification

  4. The auditor may also choose to disclaim an opinion when substantial doubt remains

342 Auditing Accounting Estimates (SAS 57)

<u>Overall Objective and Approach</u>--This section provides guidance on auditing accounting estimates (e.g., allowance for doubtful accounts, revenues recognized on construction contracts accounted for by the percentage of completion method). The section discusses (a) the need for and characteristics of accounting estimates (b) management's role in developing accounting estimates, and (c) the auditor's evaluation of accounting estimates

A. The need for and characteristics of accounting estimates

  1. Accounting estimates are needed because

       a. Measurement or valuation of some accounts is based on future events
       b. Evidence on some accounts cannot be accumulated on a timely, cost-effective basis

  2. Examples of accounting estimates: net realizable values of inventory and accounts receivable, loss reserves, percentage-of-completion revenues, pension and warranty expenses

  3. Estimates are based on subjective as well as objective factors

       a. Difficult for management to establish controls over them

4. <u>Responsibility of the auditor</u> with respect to estimates

    a. Evaluate the reasonableness of accounting estimates in the context of the financial statements taken as a whole

    b. Plan and perform procedures with attitude of <u>professional skepticism</u>

B. Management's role in developing accounting estimates

  1. Steps involved in making estimates

    a. Identify situations for which estimates are needed

    b. Identify relevant factors affecting estimate

    c. Accumulate data on which to base estimate

    d. Develop assumptions based on most likely circumstance and events

    e. Determine estimated amount

    f. Determine estimate follows GAAP and that disclosure is adequate

  2. The risk of misstatement of accounting estimates is affected by

    a. Complexity and subjectivity involved in process

    b. Availability and reliability of relevant data

    c. The number and significance of assumptions made

    d. Degree of uncertainty associated with assumptions

  3. An entity's internal control structure (ICS) may reduce the likelihood of material misstatements of estimate. Relevant aspects of the ICS include

    a. Communication to management need for estimate

    b. Accumulation of accurate data on which to base estimate

    c. Preparation of estimate by qualified personnel

    d. Adequate review and approval of estimates

    e. Comparison of prior estimates with subsequent results

    f. Consideration by management of whether estimates consistent with operational plans of entity

C. Auditor's evaluation of accounting estimates

  1. Auditor's objectives are to provide reasonable assurance that

    a. All estimates have been developed

    b. Estimates are reasonable

    c. Estimates follow GAAP and are properly disclosed

  NOTE: Know the above objectives.

  2. Procedures for determining all estimates have been developed (C.1.a. above)

    a. <u>Consider assertions</u> in financial statements to determine need for estimates

    b. <u>Evaluate information from other procedures</u> such as

      (1) Changes in entity's business or operating strategy

      (2) Change in methods of accumulating information

      (3) Information concerning litigation, claims and assessments

      (4) Minutes of stockholder, directors, and appropriate committees

      (5) Information in regulatory reports

    c. <u>Inquiry of management</u>

  3. Evaluating reasonableness (C.1.b. above)

    a. Three basic approaches (of which a combination may be used)

      (1) <u>Review and test management's process</u>

(a) Identify related controls
(b) Identify sources of data and factors used and consider whether appropriate
(c) Consider whether there are additional key factors or alternate assumptions about the factors
(d) Evaluate consistency of assumptions with one another, supporting data, historical data, and industry data
(e) Analyze historical data used
(f) Consider changes in business or industry
(g) Review documentation of assumptions and inquire about other plans etc.
(h) Consider using a specialist (see outline of AU 336)
(i) Test management calculations

(2) Develop own expectation of estimate

(a) Auditor independently develops an expectation

(3) Review subsequent events or transactions prior to completion of field work

NOTE: Know the above 3 approaches.

350 Audit Sampling (SAS 39)

Overall Objective and Approach--This section presents guidance on the use of sampling while planning, performing, and evaluating results of an audit of financial statements. The objective is to provide the conceptual background for audit sampling. Subsequent to issuance of this section, the AICPA issued the Audit Sampling Guide which provides more detailed guidance. Both this section and the Guide are summarized in the Audit Sampling module which includes detailed examples.

The various subsections of our outline are divided as follows: A. General background information, B., C., D. Sampling in substantive tests of details, E., F., G. Sampling in tests of controls, and H. Dual purpose testing, and I. selecting a sampling approach.

A. General background information

1. Audit sampling is the application of an audit procedure to less than 100 percent of the items within an account balance or class of transactions (hereafter, "account")

   a. The purpose of audit sampling is to evaluate some characteristics of an account (e.g., its balance)
   b. The use of a few items to obtain an understanding of a system or operation is not covered by the guidance in this section

2. Both nonstatistical and statistical approaches to sampling are addressed in this statement, and both

   a. Are considered acceptable
   b. May be used to provide sufficient competent evidential matter
   c. Require the use of judgment

3. The relationship of uncertainty to audit sampling

   a. The third standard of field work ("...sufficient competent evidential matter...") implies some degree of uncertainty

b.   Some items do not justify the acceptance of any uncertainty, and must be examined 100 percent (e.g., individually material items)

c.   This section refers to uncertainty as audit risk, the risk that material misstatements will occur in the accounting process and the risk that any material misstatements will not be detected by the auditor

   (1)   The auditor relies on internal control to reduce the first risk

   (2)   The auditor relies on substantive tests to reduce the second risk. Substantive tests include

      (a)   Detail tests (tests of transactions)

      (b)   Analytical procedures

      (c)   Tests of ending balances

   (3)   <u>Audit risk</u> may be expressed using the following model

$$AR = IR \times CR \times AP \times TD$$

Where: AR = Audit risk
          CR = Control risk
          AP = Analytical procedure risk
          IR = Inherent risk
          TD = Substantive tests of details risk

      (a)   Model is mathematical expression of formula which includes all factors affecting the determination of audit risk

      (b)   Model is useful when assessing the general relationships among risk factors but should not be relied on exclusively

      (c)   Model is useful when planning risk levels for audit procedures to achieve desired audit risk

NOTE: This formulation of the components of audit risk varies from that in AU 312. AU 312 combines AP and TD as detection risk.

4.   Audit risk includes uncertainties due to sampling, called sampling risk, and uncertainties due to factors other than sampling, called nonsampling risk

a.   Sampling risk arises from the possibility that the conclusions derived from the sample will differ from the conclusions that would be derived from the population (the sample is nonrepresentative of the population). Sampling risk varies inversely with sample size.

b.   Nonsampling risk arises from uncertainties due to factors other than sampling. For example

   (1)   Inappropriate audit procedures for a given objective, and

   (2)   The failure to recognize errors

c.   Nonsampling risk can be reduced through adequate planning and supervision (SAS 22) and adherence to quality control standards (SAS 25).

5.   In performing substantive tests, the auditor is concerned with two aspects of sampling

a.   The risk of incorrect acceptance

b.   The risk of incorrect rejection

6.   In performing tests of controls, the auditor is concerned with two aspects of sampling

a.   The risk of assessing control risk too low (previously referred to as risk of overreliance)

b.   The risk of assessing control risk too high (previously referred to as risk of underreliance)

NOTE: Risks 5.a. and 6.a. relate to the effectiveness and are most important of the audit. Risks 5.b. and 6.b. relate to the efficiency of the audit.

B. Sampling in substantive tests of details--planning

1. In planning a sample the auditor should consider

a. The relationship of the sample to the relevant audit objective
b. Preliminary estimates of materiality levels (the maximum error is called tolerable misstatement for the sample)
c. The auditor's allowable risk of incorrect acceptance
d. Characteristics of items comprising the account balance or class of transactions to be sampled

2. The auditor must select a population from which to sample and which is consistent with the specified audit objective of concern

a. The population consists of items in the account balance or transaction class of interest
b. E.g., understatement due to omission could not be detected by sampling recorded items. Sampling from subsequent activities records would be preferred.

3. The extent of substantive tests required will vary inversely with the auditor's assessment of inherent risk and control risk

4. The greater the reliance on analytical procedures and other substantive tests of a nonsampling nature, the greater the allowable risk of incorrect acceptance and, thus, the smaller the required sample size for substantive tests

5. The auditor uses his/her judgment in determining which items should be individually tested and which items should be subject to sampling

a. The efficiency of a sample may be improved by separating items subject to sampling into relatively homogeneous groups

C. Sampling in substantive tests of details--in selecting sample items, the auditor should ensure that

1. The sample is representative of the population
2. All the items have an equal chance of being chosen
3. Acceptable random-based selection techniques include

a. Random sampling
b. Stratified random smapling
c. Probability-proportional-to-size
d. Systematic sampling

D. Sampling in substantive tests of details--in performing audit procedures on selected items and when evaluating sampling results, the auditor should

1. Apply auditing procedures to each sample item

a. Unexamined items should be evaluated to determine their effect on the sample results
b. In addition, the auditor should consider the reasons for his/her inability to examine the item (e.g., a lack of supporting documentation)

2. Project the misstatement results from the sample to the population from which the sample was selected

3. Compare projected population misstatement results (including misstatements from the 100 percent examined items) to the tolerable misstatement

   a. This evaluation requires the use of judgment in both statistical and nonstatistical sampling

   b. The auditor should also consider the qualitative aspects of the misstatements

      (1) The nature and cause of the misstatement
      (2) The possible relationship of the misstatement to other phases of the audit

   c. An irregularity usually requires more consideration than a misstatement

4. The auditor should consider projected misstatement results in the aggregate from statistical and nonstatistical sources when evaluating whether the financial statements as a whole may be misstated

E. Sampling in tests of controls--planning

   1. In planning a sample the auditor should consider

      a. The relationship of the sample to the objective of the test
      b. The maximum rate of deviation from (tolerable rate) prescribed control procedures that would support his/her allowable risk of assessing control risk too low.
      c. The auditor's allowable risk of overreliance

         (1) Low levels usually required because tests of controls are the primary source of evidence about whether a control procedure is being applied as prescribed
         (2) Quantitatively the auditor might consider 5% to 10% risk of assessing control risk too low as acceptable

      d. The characteristics of the population of interest

         (1) The auditor should consider the likely rate of deviation
         (2) The auditor should consider whether to test controls singly or in combination

   2. The auditor should realize that deviations from important control procedures at a given rate ordinarily result in misstatements or irregularities at a lower rate

F. Sampling in tests of controls--sample selection should ensure that

   1. The sample is representative of the population

   2. The probability of inclusion of every item in the population is <u>known</u>

G. Sampling in tests of controls--performance and evaluation

   1. The auditor should apply auditing procedures to each sample item

      a. If the auditor cannot apply procedures to all sample items, s/he should consider reasons for the limitations
      b. Items to which procedures cannot be applied should be considered deviations for sample evaluation

2. Whether statistical or nonstatistical sampling is used, if the auditor decides that s/he is not going to rely on internal controls, the planned substantive tests should be adjusted

H. Dual purpose samples have two purposes

    1. To aid in assessing control risk (test of control)

    2. To test whether the recorded dollar amount of a transaction is correct (substantive tests)

        a. The auditor usually assumes that there is an acceptably small planned assessed level of control risk which is greater than the tolerable level

        b. The size of the sample should be the larger of the samples otherwise designed for two separate purposes

I. Selecting a sampling approach

    1. Statistical or nonstatistical approaches can provide sufficient evidential matter

    2. Choice between statistical and nonstatistical approach depends on relative

        a. Cost
        b. Effectiveness

    3. Statistical sampling helps

        a. Design efficient sampling plans
        b. Measure sufficiently of evidential matter
        c. To quantatively evaluate sample results

380 Communication with Audit Committees (SAS 61)

Overall Objective and Approach--This section establishes a requirement that CPAs communicate certain matters (more precisely, nine matters) related to an audit to the audit committee. The first section of our outline presents background information, while the second provides the nine matters to be communicated.

A. Background information

    1. Applicability--the section only applies to

        a. SEC engagements
        b. Other entities that have audit committees or equivalent oversight group

    2. Form--may be oral or written

        a. If oral, document in working papers
        b. If written, the report should indicate that it is solely for the audit committee, board of directors, and (if appropriate) management

    3. The communication is considered incidental to the audit, but should be communicated on a timely basis, not necessarily prior to issuance of the audit report

    4. Situations in which the matters need not be communicated by the CPA

        a. When the CPA is satisfied that management has communicated them
        b. When they have been communicated in prior years, although the CPA may choose to repeat them due to changes in the audit committee or due to the passage of time

5. The CPA may also choose to communicate additional matters

B. Matters to be communicated

1. <u>Auditor responsibility</u> taken under GAAS audits

2. <u>Significant accounting policies</u>

    a. Management's initial selection and changes
    b. Methods used for unusual transactions
    c. Effects of accounting policies in controversial areas or areas in which there is a lack of authoritative guidance

3. <u>Process used in obtaining management judgments</u> and accounting estimates

4. Significant <u>audit adjustments</u>

5. <u>Auditor responsibility for other information</u> in documents containing audited financial statements (see AU 550)

6. Auditor <u>disagreements</u> with management

    a. Examples

        (1) Application of accounting principles
        (2) Basis for management's accounting estimates
        (3) Scope of audit
        (4) Disclosures in financial statements
        (5) Wording of audit report

    b. Resolution of disagreements
    c. Disagreements do not include differences of opinion based upon incomplete facts or preliminary information later resolved

7. <u>Auditor views</u> on auditing and accounting <u>matters for which other auditors were contacted</u> (see AU 625)

8. <u>Major issues</u> discussed with management <u>prior to retention</u>

9. <u>Difficulties</u> encountered in performing audit

Examples:

    a. Delays by management in allowing audit commencement
    b. Unavailability of client personnel
    c. Delays in preparation of client-prepared schedules

390 Consideration of Omitted Procedures After Report Date (SAS 46)

<u>Overall Objective and Approach</u>--This brief section presents guidance on how to approach a situation in which subsequent to issuance of an audit report, an auditor determines that one or more necessary procedures may have been omitted. Also, the guidance only relates to a situation in which there is no indication that the financial statements depart from GAAP--when known departures exist see the outline of AU 561 and section C. of the Evidence module. While the auditor has no responsibility to retroactively review his/her work, the section does address the situation in which a postissuance review (e.g., an internal inspection of a peer review) may have disclosed such an omitted procedure(s).

A. When it is determined that a procedure has been omitted, the auditor should assess its importance, considering other procedures which may have compensated for its omission

1. This section only covers cases in which there is <u>no</u> indication that financial statements depart from GAAP. (See AU 561 when errors exist)

2. Although auditor has no responsibility to retroactively review his/her work, such postissuance review may occur as part of internal inspection, or peer review

3. In all such circumstances, the auditor may be well advised to consult attorney

B. When it is determined that a procedure has been omitted, auditor must

1. <u>Assess its importance</u>. (Consider other procedures which may have compensated for its omission)

    a. If omission is considered important and if auditor believes individuals are relying on financial statements, procedures (or alternate procedures) should be promptly applied

    b. If financial statement errors are detected, consult AU 561

    c. If the auditor is unable to apply procedures, consult attorney

410 Adherence to Generally Accepted Accounting Principles

Overall Objective and Approach--This very brief section states that (1) GAAP, as used in the reporting standards includes not only accounting principles, but also the methods of applying them, and (2) that the auditor's report does not represent a statement of fact by the auditor, but an opinion.

411 The Meaning of Present Fairly in Conformity with GAAP in the Independent Auditor's Report

Overall Objective and Approach--This section presents information which may be summarized as relating to (a) the meaning of conformity with GAAP, (b) the relative authority of various sources of GAAP, and (c) overall points.

A. The meaning of conformity with GAAP

1. GAAP is a technical term that encompasses the conventions, rules, and procedures necessary to define accepted accounting practice at a particular time; it includes not only broad guidelines, but also detailed practices and procedures

2. The auditor's opinion that the financial statements "present fairly an entity's financial position, results of operations, and cash flows in conformity with GAAP" should be based on a judgment of whether

    a. The accounting principles have general acceptance

    b. The accounting principles are appropriate in the circumstances

    c. The financial statements (including the notes) are informative of matters that may affect their use, understanding, and interpretation

    d. Disclosure is neither too detailed nor too condensed

    e. The financial statements reflect the underlying events and transactions in a reasonable manner

B. The relative authority of various sources of GAAP

1. The following is a summary of the relative authority of GAAP from section A. of the Reporting module

Category	Included items
a. Authoritative body pronouncements	FASB and GASB Statements FASB and GASB Interpretations APB Opinions AICPA Accounting Research Bulletins
b. Other expert pronouncements	AICPA Industry Audit Guides and Accounting Guides
c. Widely recognized pronouncements and practices	AICPA Statements of Position FASB and GASB Technical Bulletins AICPA Accounting Interpretations Widely accepted industry practices
d. Other accounting literature	APB Statements AICPA Issues Papers AcSEC Practice Bulletins Minutes of the FASB Emerging Issues Task Force FASB Concepts Statements International Accounting Standards Other Professional Association and Regulatory Pronouncements Accounting textbooks and articles

In cases of conflict between the accounting treatment suggested by the categories, category "a" prevails over all categories. Categories "b." and "c." are considered to be of equivalent authority, while category "d." is of less authority. For conflicts within a category (or between "b." and "c."), the treatment most closely approximating the transaction's economic substance prevails.

C. Overall points

1. Principle selection should be based on the substance of the transaction, and not merely its form

2. Specifying the circumstances in which one accounting principle should be selected from among alternatives is the function of bodies having authority to establish accounting principles (e.g., the FASB)

   a. When criteria for selection among alternative principles have not been established, the auditor may conclude that more than one principle is appropriate in the circumstances

   EXAMPLE: Established principles do not include criteria for choosing between inventory methods (e.g., LIFO or FIFO). Therefore the auditor would not in general question a client's continuing use of a method, say LIFO. Note, however, that this is not the case when a change in principles is involved--see outline of AU 420.

   b. There may be unusual circumstances in which the selection and application of specific accounting principles among alternative principles may make the financial statements as a whole misleading

   NOTE: Although the section doesn't suggest the manner in which this should be handled, it would seem appropriate that the auditor suggest to the client that a change in method be made. If the client refuses, in

many circumstances it would seem appropriate for the auditor to seek legal counsel and/or disassociation from the financial statements (i.e., resign).

420 Consistency of Application of GAAP

Overall Objective and Approach--This section presents guidance on applying the consistency reporting standard, which was revised in 1988 (it now reads, "The report shall identify those circumstances in which such principles have not been consistently observed in the current period in relation to the preceding period"). This section relates very directly to APB 20 which prescribes accounting for three types of accounting changes--change in principles, change in estimate, and change in reporting entity--and for corrections of errors in prior statements.

The general rule is that changes in accounting principles, changes in the reporting entity, and correction of error in principles require explanatory language as to consistency (i.e., an explanatory paragraph added to an unqualified report); changes in estimates do not. Yet, there are several exceptions to the rules (described below) with which you need to be familiar.

A. Changes that require the addition of an explanatory paragraph referring to the inconsistency

    1. <u>Change in accounting principle</u>

        a. As a typical example, consider changing from straight-line to the sum of the years' digits method

        b. Special cases of changes in accounting principles (which still require an explanatory paragraph)

            (1) <u>Correction of an error in principle</u>--for example, assume that in the preceding year a client used an unacceptable method for valuing inventory; changing to a proper method (e.g., LIFO) still requires an explanatory paragraph. There is a tendency to <u>incorrectly</u> think that since the client is eliminating an error, no mention of the inconsistency is necessary.

            (2) <u>Change in principle inseparable from a change in estimate</u>--for example, changing from deferring a cost to expensing it in the year incurred represents a change in principle from capitalization to expensing; but it also represents a change in estimate in that the life is now assessed at 1 year or less.

    2. <u>Change in the reporting entity</u>

        a. The following require an explanatory paragraph

            (1) Presenting consolidated or combined statements in place of individual company statements

            (2) Changing the specific subsidiaries in the group for which consolidated statements are presented

            (3) Changing the companies included in combined statements

            (4) Changing among the cost, equity, and consolidation methods of accounting for subsidiaries

B. Changes that <u>do not</u> require the addition of a explanatory paragraph referring to the inconsistency

    1. Change in estimate

        a. For example changing either the life or salvage value of fixed assets

2. Correction of an error <u>not involving a principle</u>

    a. For example, correction of a mathematical error in previously issued financial statements

3. Change in classification

    a. For example, adding an additional line item expense to this year's income statement which in the preceding year was included in "miscellaneous expense"

4. Creation, cessation, purchase, or disposition of a subsidiary or business unit

    NOTE: Be careful here to distinguish the above circumstances from those described in A. 2. above. These situations are normal business events. Those described in A. 2. above may be viewed as using different accounting methods.

5. Properly accounted for pooling of interest combinations

    a. Proper application of the pooling of interests methods requires restatement of prior year financial statements (APB 16)

    b. When such restatement <u>has not</u> been properly applied, a departure from GAAP exists

        (1) An explanatory paragraph would then be added to the audit report (prior to the opinion paragraph) describing the departure, and that the financial statements are inconsistent; the opinion paragraph would also be qualified to indicate the departure from GAAP

6. Changes in principles that <u>do not materially</u> affect this year's financial statements, even when reasonably certain the change will materially affect them in later years

    NOTE: The above exception ("6.") is rather unexpected, given the "conservative" nature of many of the standards. Remember it!

7. Accounting principles are adopted when events or transactions first become material in their effect

    a. Modification or adoption of a principle at this point does not require a paragraph referring to consistency

C. Miscellaneous

1. Accounting changes may also lead to a departure from GAAP situation

    a. When a material change in principles occurs, with which the auditor does not concur, a departure from GAAP exists and a qualified opinion or an adverse opinion is appropriate--see outline of AU 508

    b. Whenever an accounting change has not been appropriately described in the financial statements, a departure from GAAP exists (in this case, inadequate disclosure) and a qualified opinion or an adverse opinion is appropriate--see outline of AU 508

431 Adequacy of Disclosure in Financial Statements (SAS 32)

<u>Overall Objective and Approach</u>--This brief section interprets the third standard of reporting which states that informative disclosures are to be regarded as reasonably adequate unless otherwise stated in the report. Omission of required information is a departure from GAAP which requires the auditor to issue either a qualified or an adverse opinion--see outline of AU 508 for details. If practicable, the auditor should provide the omitted information in his/her report; practicable means that the information is reasonably obtainable from the accounts and records and does not require the auditor to assume the position of a preparer of financial information. Thus, the auditor would <u>not</u> be expected to prepare a basic financial statement (e.g., a statement of cash flows) or segment information and include it in his/her report.

435 Segment Information (SAS 21)

<u>Overall Objective and Approach</u>--This section presents guidance on examining and reporting on segment disclosures required by SFAS 14--operations in different <u>industries, foreign operations</u> and export sales, and <u>major customers</u>. Two general types of guidance are provided: (a) auditing procedures, and (b) reporting requirements.

A. Auditing procedures

   1. The objective of auditing procedures applied to segment information is to provide the auditor with a reasonable basis for concluding on whether the information is presented in conformity with SFAS 14 in relation to the financial statements taken as a whole

      a. The overall scope of procedures is in relation to providing an opinion on the <u>financial statements taken as a whole</u>, and <u>not</u> in relation to procedures that would be <u>necessary to express a separate opinion on the segment information</u>

        (1) Accordingly, materiality of segment information is evaluated by relating the dollar magnitude of the information to the financial statements taken as a whole

   2. While the scope of procedures necessary may be affected by factors such as a client's internal control, number of segments, etc., the following procedures should be applied

      a. Inquire of management concerning its methods for determining segment information, and evaluate the reasonableness of the methods
      b. Inquire of and test the method of accounting for intersegment sales and transfers
      c. Perform appropriate analytical procedures on segment information
      d. Inquire as to the methods of allocating common costs, evaluate their reasonableness, and test their application
      e. Determine whether segment information has been presented consistently from period to period

B. Reporting requirements

   1. When the segment information follows GAAP, it is not referred to in the audit report

2. If a misstatement or omission (hereafter, "misstatement") is <u>material to the</u> <u>segment information</u>, but <u>immaterial to the financial statements</u>, no report modification is necessary

    NOTE: In the above situation it would seem that the best approach would be to suggest to the client that such information be corrected

3. A material misstatement is treated like any other departure from GAAP--it will result in either a qualified or adverse opinion, see outline of AU 508

    a. The auditor need not present omitted segment information in the audit report

        (1) The audit report would state that the client has declined to present the segment information

4. Inconsistencies in the preparation of segment information

    a. Such inconsistencies may occur due to

        (1) A change in the accounting for intersegment sales or allocation of joint expenses
        (2) A change in the method of determining segment profitability
        (3) A change in accounting principle
        (4) A change requiring retroactive restatement such as the method of grouping products or foreign operations

    b. When matters such as those in "a." above are <u>properly treated</u>, explanatory language with respect to consistency only needs to be added to the audit report when the change materially affects the financial statements taken as a whole

    c. When such information is <u>not properly treated</u>, including when it is omitted, a departure from GAAP exists--this will lead to either a qualified or an adverse opinion--see outline of AU 508

5. The auditor may issue a "special report" which only relates to the segment information--see outline of AU 621

504 Association with Financial Statements (SAS 26)

<u>Overall Objective and Approach</u>--This section defines what is meant by a CPA being "associated with financial statements," and discusses "unaudited statements." The issue of being "associated with financial statements" is important because the fourth standard of reporting (which requires an opinion, or a statement that an opinion cannot be expressed) requires that a CPA must make clear the character of his/her examination, and the responsibility taken, when s/he is <u>associated</u> with financial statements.

The section related to "unaudited statements" is of limited use at this point. There are no "unaudited statements" for nonpublic companies--statements for such companies are compiled, reviewed, or audited. Thus, "unaudited statements" are only relevant for the occasional public company which for some reason does not require audited financial statements. In this outline we present information on (a) general association with financial information and (b) reporting on unaudited statements and (c) reporting on comparative statements when one period is unaudited and when one period is audited.

A. General association with financial information

1. The objective of the fourth standard of reporting is <u>to prevent misinterpretation of the degree of responsibility</u> assumed by the accountant when his/her name is <u>associated</u> with financial statements

    NOTE: Knowledge of this objective has been required on several multiple choice questions

2. An accountant is <u>associated</u> with financial statements when s/he

    a. Has consented to the use of his/her name in a report, document, or written communication containing the statements or

    b. Submits to a client financial statements that s/he has prepared or assisted in preparing, even though the accountant does not append his/her name to the statements

3. Procedure which must be followed before issuing a report--<u>the accountant has a responsibility to read the statements for obvious material misstatements</u>; no other procedural requirements exist

    a. When other procedures have been performed, mention of them should <u>not</u> be made in the report issued

B. Reporting on unaudited statements

    1. The following disclaimer may accompany or be on the statements:

       The accompanying balance sheet of X Company as of December 31, 19X1, and the related statement of income, retained earnings, and cash flows for the year then ended were not audited by us and accordingly, we do not express an opinion on them.

    2. Each page of the statements <u>should be marked as "unaudited"</u>

    3. When the client has prepared a document which includes unaudited statements, the auditor should request that

       a. His/her name not be included in the communication <u>or</u>

       b. That the financial statement be marked as unaudited and that there be a notation that s/he does not express an opinion on them

    4. If the accountant is <u>not</u> independent, the disclaimer issued should indicate such nonindependence, but should <u>not</u> indicate any procedures performed or the reason for nonindependence

    5. When the accountant believes that the unaudited statements do not follow GAAP

       a. S/he should request appropriate revision

       b. If unsuccessful, modify the disclaimer to refer to the departure

       NOTE: Some CPA exam questions have suggested that a qualified or adverse opinion is appropriate when such statements do not follow GAAP. This is incorrect since an audit has not been performed. A disclaimer with the appropriate information is appropriate. If the client refuses to accept such a report, the accountant should disassociate himself/herself from the statements.

6. In no case should a report on unaudited statements include negative assurance (e.g., "nothing came to our attention"--see the outline of AU 621 for more information on negative assurance)

7. When reporting on comparative statements in which unaudited financial statements are presented with audited statements (of a different year), the unaudited statements should be marked as unaudited and the comparative report should clearly disclaim an opinion on the unaudited statements

508 Reports on Audited Financial Statements

Overall Objective and Approach--This section presents guidance on the nature of audit reports. The information presented in this section constitutes the primary reporting guidance for normal GAAP GAAS audits. It is also summarized in the Reporting module, which includes sample reports.

You should know that the objective of the fourth reporting standard (i.e., the report is to contain an opinion on the financial statements taken as a whole or an assertion that an opinion cannot be expressed) is to prevent misinterpretation of the degree of responsibility taken by the auditor. Also, the phrase "taken as a whole," applies equally to the complete set of financial statements and to the individual financial statements.

Section A. of this outline summarizes information relating to the auditor's standard report. Section B. also deals with circumstances in which an auditor issues an unqualified report with explanatory language added. Qualified, adverse, and disclaimers of opinion are considered in sections C. through E. Sections F. and G. relate to comparative statements.

A. The auditor's standard report

1. Basic elements

    a. Title that includes word "independent"
    b. Statements were audited
    c. Financial statements are management's responsibility; expressing an opinion is the auditor's responsibility
    d. Audit conducted in accordance with GAAS
    e. GAAS require planning and performing audit to obtain reasonable assurance financial statements free of material misstatement
    f. Statement that an audit includes

        (1) Examining, on a test basis, evidence
        (2) Assessing accounting principles and estimates
        (3) Evaluating financial statement presentation

    g. Statement that auditor believes audit provides reasonable basis for opinion
    h. Opinion
    i. Manual or printed signature of firm
    j. Date of report

2. The report is addressed to company, board of directors, or shareholders

    a. When an auditor is engaged by a client to report on statements of a nonclient, the report is addressed to client (e.g., a client may hire the auditor to audit statements of an acquisition candidate)

B. Explanatory language added to the auditor's standard report

NOTE: The report issued may still be unqualified in the following circumstances. The unqualified report includes an explanatory paragraph (or other explanatory language).

1. Opinion based in part on report of another auditor

    a. Reference is made to other auditor in all three paragraphs

2. Departure from a promulgated accounting principle

    a. Pertains to situations in which unusual circumstances result in a situation in which following GAAP would lead to misleading results
    b. An explanatory paragraph added (either preceding or following opinion paragraph)

3. Uncertainties

    a. Uncertainties vs. scope limitations

        (1) Uncertainties--the matter is expected to be resolved in future, at which time evidential matter will become available
        (2) Scope limitations--sufficient evidential matter does or did exist, but is not now available (e.g., management's record retention policies or restrictions)

    b. Uncertainties vs. departures from GAAP

        (1) Departures from GAAP--inadequate disclosure, inappropriate principles, unreasonable estimates
        (2) Such departures lead to qualified or adverse opinions

    c. Deciding whether to add an explanatory paragraph (following opinion paragraph) for uncertainty

        (1) Remote likelihood--do not add an explanatory paragraph
        (2) Reasonably possible--consider adding an explanatory paragraph

            (a) Consider the magnitude of the loss and its likelihood
            (b) Auditors are more likely to add an explanatory paragraph as magnitude and likelihood increases

        (3) Probable but cannot estimate--add an explanatory paragraph

    d. Considering materiality of uncertainties

        (1) When unusual or infrequent, consider them in relation to stockholder's equity and other balance sheet items
        (2) When more related to normal, recurring operations, compare them to the income statement

4. Consistency

    a. The auditor must concur with the change

        (1) If the auditor does not concur, a departure from GAAP exists which leads to either a qualified or adverse opinion

    b. Explanatory paragraph added (following opinion paragraph)

        (1) Non-restatement cases--as long as year of change presented
        (2) Restatements--only in year of change

    c. See AU 420 outline

    5. Emphasis of a matter

        a. Pertains to situations in which <u>auditor wishes to draw attention</u> to a matter concerning financial statements (e.g., when client is component of larger entity, related party transactions, subsequent events, matter affecting comparability)

        b. <u>Explanatory paragraph</u> added (either preceding or following opinion paragraph)

C. Qualified opinions

    1. Scope limitation

        a. Types--<u>client and circumstance imposed</u>

        b. Type of report (unqualified, qualified, or disclaimer)

            (1) Depends upon importance of omitted procedure (consider nature, magnitude, potential effect, and number of accounts involved)

            (2) <u>Generally disclaim for client imposed scope restrictions</u>

        c. <u>Limitation described in scope, explanatory, and opinion paragraphs</u>

            (1) Explanatory paragraph preceding opinion paragraph

        d. Opinion qualification pertains to possible effects on financial statements, not to scope limitation itself

        e. A <u>report on only one statement</u> (e.g., balance sheet) <u>is not a scope restriction</u> if auditor has access to necessary information

    2. Departure from generally accepted accounting principle

        a. Type of report (unqualified, qualified, or adverse)

            (1) Depends on dollar magnitude, significance to operations, pervasiveness, and impact on statements as a whole

            (2) Inadequate disclosure is a departure from GAAP

        b. <u>Explanatory paragraph added</u> (preceding opinion paragraph), and <u>opinion paragraph altered</u>

        c. <u>Omission of statement of cash flows</u>

            (1) Auditor not required to prepare one

            (2) Ordinarily qualify report

        d. Accounting principle changes

            (1) Auditor evaluates whether

                (a) New principle is GAAP

                (b) Method of accounting for change is GAAP

                (c) Management justification is reasonable

            (2) If any of (1) are "no," a departure from GAAP exists

            (3) Qualification (or adverse) remains as long as statements provided

D. Adverse opinion

    1. Statements taken as a whole are not fairly presented

    2. Explanatory paragraph (preceding opinion paragraph), opinion paragraph altered

E. Disclaimer

    1. No opinion

2. When due to a scope limitation replace scope paragraph with explanatory paragraph indicating why audit did not comply with GAAS

F. Comparative financial statements

1. Continuing auditors should update report to cover comparative statements

2. Ordinarily date report as of completion of most recent audit

3. Updating prior-period reports

   a. Example--departure from GAAP in prior year statements eliminated
   b. If opinion different from previous period, explanatory paragraph should disclose

      (1) Date of previous report
      (2) Type of opinion previously expressed
      (3) Circumstances calling for changed report
      (4) State that updated opinion differs from previous opinion

G. Comparative statements--report of predecessor auditor

1. Before reissuing report predecessor should

   a. Read the current statements
   b. Compare prior statements with current
   c. Obtain letter of representations from successor indicating any matters that might have effect on prior statements
   d. If predecessor is aware of events affecting previous opinion, s/he should perform necessary audit procedures
   e. Dating report

      (1) Not revised--used original report date
      (2) Revised--dual date

2. Predecessor's report not presented

   a. Successor's report should indicate

      (1) Prior statements audited by other auditors
      (2) Date of their report
      (3) Type of report issued by predecessor
      (4) Substantive reasons if other than unqualified

         (a) Also, if other than standard, give reasons for explanatory paragraph

530 Dating the Independent Auditor's Report

Overall Objective and Approach--This section presents guidance on dating of the auditor's report. The general rule is that the report is dated as of the date of the completion of field work. The section discusses two exceptions--(a) events have occurred after field work, but before issuance of the report, and (b) certain circumstances in which an audit report is being reissued.

A. Dating the audit report when subsequent events have occurred after field work, but before issuance of the report

NOTE: An understanding of this section requires knowledge of AU 560 on subsequent events. That section distinguishes between the "event" (i.e., the subsequent event) which occurred after the balance-sheet date, but prior to the issuance of the financial statements, and the "condition" which caused the event. The basic accounting rule developed in AU 560 is that when a subsequent event occurs the auditor must determine whether the condition which caused the event existed at the date of the balance sheet. When the condition existed at the balance sheet date, adjustment of the financial statements is appropriate. When the condition came into effect after year end, note disclosure is appropriate. For more information on this, see the outline of AU 560.

1. Dating of the audit report when the <u>condition came into effect before year end</u>

    a. When an adjustment is all that is needed, and no note disclosure is needed, the audit report need not be changed
    b. When an adjustment <u>and</u> note disclosure is needed, the auditor must change the report date as indicated in "3." below

2. Dating of the audit report when the condition came into existence after year end

    a. Note disclosure is needed, and the auditor must change the report date as indicated in "3." below

3. When the report date must be changed (from the date of completion of field work), two methods are available

    a. <u>A dual date</u> in which the overall report is dated as of the last day of field work, but a note such as "except for Note X, which is dated as of _____ is added following the date."

       EXAMPLE: A report might be dated as follows: February 17, 19X1, except for Note 1, as to which the date is February 27, 19X1

    b. The report date might be changed to the <u>date of the subsequent event</u>

       EXAMPLE: Using the above example: February 27, 19X1

       (1) When the report date is changed in this manner, the CPA's responsibility for subsequent events extends to the date of his/her report--see outline of AU 560 for these procedures

B. Dating the audit report when it is being reissued

   BACKGROUND: The situation here is one in which an auditor has already issued a report, and is being asked to reissue it. This may occur for example, when the financial statements are included in a report being filed with the SEC, or, more simply, when a client asks the CPA to furnish additional copies of a previously issued report. The overall rule is that the CPA has no responsibility to make any further investigation as to events which may have occurred during the period between the original report date and the date of the release of the additional reports. The original report date is retained for the reissued report. A complicating factor arises when the CPA becomes aware of an event subsequent to the date of the original report that requires adjustment and/or disclosure.

1. When the auditor is asked to reissue his/her report, and s/he

    a. Is <u>not</u> aware of the existence of any subsequent event, the original report date should be used
    b. Is aware of the existence of a subsequent event which requires adjustment or disclosure, the report should be dated in accordance with the "A.3." above
    c. Is aware of an event which requires disclosure only (i.e., no adjustment) which has occurred <u>between the date of the original report and the date of reissuance</u>, the event may be disclosed in a separate

unaudited note to the financial statements; the audit report date is <u>not</u> changed from that used for the original report

534 Reporting on Financial Statements Prepared for Use in Other Countries (SAS No. 51)

<u>Overall Objective and Approach</u>--This section presents guidance for a CPA practicing <u>in the U.S.</u> who is engaged to report on the <u>financial statements of a U.S. entity</u> that have been prepared in conformity with the <u>accounting principles of another country</u>. For example, consider a U.S. subsidiary of a multinational corporation with a non-U.S. parent. Often such a subsidiary issues GAAP based financial statements intended for use in the U.S., and other financial statements that are prepared in conformity with accounting principles generally accepted in another country. This section addresses the approach the CPA should use for the financial statements prepared following the principles of the other country. The guidance provided in section A. of this outline deals with the applicability of the following standards--(1) U.S. GAAS, (2) other country accounting standards, and (3) other country auditing standards. Section B. of this outline provides information on reporting requirements.

A. Applicable standards and procedures other than reporting

   Overall requirements--before reporting on the statements, the auditor should have a clear understanding of, and obtain written representations from, management regarding the purpose and uses of the financial statements

   1. Applicability of <u>U.S. GAAS</u>

      a. The general rule is that the CPA must perform U.S. <u>general</u> and <u>field work</u> standards

         (1) Exceptions to the rule occur when differences in the other country's accounting principles require modification of the procedures that are followed:

         Examples

         (a) When the principles of the other country do not require deferred taxes, procedures for testing deferred tax balances would not be applicable
         (b) When principles of the other country do not require or permit disclosure of related party transactions, audit procedures related to meeting U.S. disclosure standards would not be appropriate

   2. Other country <u>accounting</u> standards

      a. The auditor should understand the accounting principles of the other country; this knowledge may be obtained by considering

         (1) The professional literature of that country
         (2) Information obtained by consulting with individuals with the necessary expertise
         (3) International Accounting Standards (when the other country's principles are not well established)

   3. Other country auditing standards

      a. When the auditor is requested to apply the other country's auditing standards s/he may do so if

         (1) U.S. standards are also applied
         (2) S/he has read pertinent literature, and to the extent necessary, has consulted with persons having the necessary expertise

B. Reporting requirements

1. Report issued for financial statements which are <u>only to be used outside the U.S.</u>--either a modified U.S. report or the standard report of the other country <u>may</u> be appropriate

a. Modified U.S. report should

(1) Identify the financial statements that have been audited
(2) Refer to the note in the financial statements that describes the basis of presentation (including the nationality) of the principles
(3) State that the audit followed U.S. auditing standards (and other country standards if appropriate)
(4) Include a paragraph on whether the statements present fairly in conformity with the basis being followed

b. The standard report of the other country may be used if

(1) Such a report would be used by auditors in the other country in similar circumstances
(2) The auditor understands the attestations contained in the report

c. Limited distribution of the reports described above in (a.) and (b.) is acceptable (e.g., to banks, institutional investors) if the statements are to be allowed in a manner that permits such parties to discuss differences in U.S. and other country reporting practices

(1) If the distribution in the U.S. is more than limited, the auditor should report using the U.S. standard form of report, modified as appropriate for departures from GAAP

(a) The CPA may choose to include a separate report expressing an opinion on whether the financial statements are in conformity with the other country's standards <u>or</u>
(b) May issue a U.S. report for distribution in the U.S., and a report as described in "B.1.a." and "B.1.b." above in the other country

NOTE: The above section is actually requiring that when the statements following the other country basis are being used on more than a limited basis in the U.S. the auditor must indicate departures from GAAP in a U.S. style report. This will <u>not</u> normally be necessary because the statements will not in general be used in the U.S. Recall from our introduction of this section that more typically, when there is a U.S. demand for such statements dual statements will be issued--one set following U.S. GAAP and the other set following other country accounting principles. The auditor would then issue a standard U.S. report on the first set of statements, and one of the reports described in "B.1." for the other country statements.

543 Part of the Examination Made by Other Independent Auditors

<u>Overall Objective and Approach</u>--This section presents guidance on reporting requirements when more than one CPA firm is involved with the audit of a particular company. As an example, consider a situation in which a parent company owns four subsidiaries. CPA firm A has audited the parent (a holding company with no operations of its own) and three of the subsidiaries; CPA firm B has audited the fourth subsidiary. This situation may occur, for example, when the parent has

recently purchased the subsidiary and as a part of the purchase agreement the acquired subsidiary is allowed to keep its CPA firm for some period of time.

In such a situation a number of audit reports may be issued. First, reports might be issued for each of the four subsidiaries. The reporting for those is quite straightforward--CPA firm A would issue three reports while CPA firm B would issue one.

The situation with respect to the parent is more complicated. After consolidation, the parent will be composed of the three subsidiaries audited by CPA firm A, and one audited by CPA firm B. It is the reporting for this situation that AU 543 addresses. The section requires that a "principal" auditor be determined to report on the consolidated parent's overall financial statements and prescribes certain requirements of the CPA firm--section A. of the outline presents that material. Two basic approaches to presenting the audit report are presented--section B. discusses a decision by the principal auditor <u>not</u> to make reference to the other auditor; section C. discusses a decision <u>to make reference</u> to the other auditor. Section D. of the outline provides miscellaneous related points.

A. Determining the principal auditor and his/her responsibilities

    1. The following factors should be considered in determining which firm is to serve as the principal auditor

        a. Materiality of the portion of the financial statements audited by each CPA

        b. Each CPA's relative knowledge of the overall financial statements

        c. The importance of the components audited by each CPA

NOTE: This will normally be an easy decision since in practice one CPA will normally have much more than 1/2 of the overall work

    2. The principal auditor is required to make the following types of inquiries about the other auditor

        a. His/her <u>reputation</u>*--contact

            (1) AICPA, state society, local chapter
            (2) Other CPAs
            (3) Bankers and other credit grantors
            (4) Others

        b. Obtain representation from the other CPA that s/he is independent per AICPA requirements, and if appropriate, per the requirements of the SEC

        c. Ascertain through communication with the other auditor that s/he

            (1) Knows the statements and his/her report will be used by the principal CPA
            (2) *Is familiar with GAAP and GAAS
            (3) *Is familiar with SEC rules (if applicable)
            (4) Knows a review of matters affecting elimination of intercompany transactions will be made by the principal CPA

*These items are ordinarily unnecessary if the principal auditor already knows the professional reputation and standing of the other auditor and if the other auditor's primary place of business is in the U.S.

NOTE: If the CPA determines that s/he can neither assume responsibility nor rely on the work of the other CPA, s/he should qualify or disclaim an opinion, stating the reasons and the magnitude of the financial statements affected. As a practical matter, in such a situation one would expect that the principal CPA would perform the procedures necessary to eliminate the problem.

3. The principal CPA must determine whether s/he wishes to refer to the other CPA in the audit report

    a. When no reference is made, the principal auditor is assuming responsibility for the work of the other auditor

B. Deciding not to make reference to the other CPA

1. No mention of the other CPA or of the procedures indicated in "A.2." above are made in the report--e.g., if a standard unqualified report is appropriate, the report would be identical to that issued if no other CPA were involved

2. Situations in which a principal auditor might choose this course of action (not making reference)

    a. The other CPA is associated with the principal auditor in some manner
    b. The other CPA was retained by the principal auditor (e.g., the principal auditor did not have a branch, and did not wish to travel to the city in which the subsidiary was headquartered)
    c. The principal auditor is satisfied with the other auditor's work
    d. The portion of the statement examined by the other CPA is not material to the overall financial statements

3. When the principal auditor is following this course of action (not making reference), s/he should also consider whether to perform one or more of the following

    a. Visit the other CPA and discuss the audit
    b. Review the other CPA's audit programs
    c. Review the other CPA's working papers
    d. Perform additional auditing procedures

C. Deciding to make reference to the other CPA

1. The audit report will indicate the other auditor involvement in the introductory, scope, and opinion paragraphs

    a. The report should indicate the dollar amount of assets, income, and other appropriate criteria included in the other CPA's audit
    b. The other auditor may be named, but only

        (1) With his/her permission
        (2) When his/her report is presented with the principal CPA's report

    c. Absent other circumstances (e.g., a scope limitation or a departure from GAAP), the report issued is unqualified with explanatory language

        NOTE: When studying how to actually write audit reports, it is most efficient to study the various modifications of the standard report together. Section B.2. of the Reporting module presents the necessary information.

D. Miscellaneous

1. Principal auditor treatment of a situation in which the other auditor's report is not standard unqualified in form

a. If the matter is material to the overall financial statements it will require modification of the principal auditor's report

b. If the matter is not material to the overall financial statements, and if the other auditor's report is not presented, the principal auditor need not make reference to the matter

    (1) If the other auditor's report is presented, the principal auditor may wish to make reference to it as to its disposition

2. The advice in this section may also relate to the situation in which an investment is accounted for by use of the equity method; reference to the other auditor who is associated with the investee may be appropriate

3. Following a pooling, a CPA may express an opinion on the restated statements of prior periods; several complications may arise

    a. If the CPA cannot satisfy him/herself with respect to the restated statements

        (1) The CPA should issue the appropriate report on the current year statements (e.g., a standard unqualified one year report), with an additional paragraph following the opinion paragraph in which the CPA expresses an opinion solely on the proper combination of the pooled companies

        (2) In these circumstances the CPA does not take responsibility for the work of the other CPAs nor for expressing an opinion on the restated statements taken as a whole; procedures should be taken to enable him/her to express an opinion as to the proper combination of the statements

550 Other Information in Documents Containing Audited Financial Statements (SAS 8)

Overall Objective and Approach--This section presents guidance on the CPA's responsibility when audited financial statements (which include the CPA's audit report) are included in a document which includes other information. For example, consider a public company's annual report which includes audited financial statements and additional information such as a president's letter, as well as various other unaudited financial and nonfinancial information. It is important to realize that this section is dealing with the situation in which the document in which the audited statements are included is being prepared by the client, and not by the auditor. Also, while the section does apply to annual reports filed with the SEC under the 1934 Securities Exchange Act as well as to other documents to which the auditor devotes attention, it does not apply to SEC registration statements under the 1933 Securities Act (dealing with initial offerings).

    Section A. of the outline does not require the CPA to perform any audit procedures beyond reading the other information for obvious errors and inconsistencies. Section B. discusses the proper action to be taken when the auditor believes that inconsistencies exist between the audited statements and the other information; Section C. addresses the situation in which the auditor believes that some of the other information may be misstated, although no inconsistency with the financial statements exists.

A. Overall auditor responsibility with respect to information in a document containing audited financial statements may be summarized as

    1. Audited financial statements--the auditor assumes normal responsibility taken on an audit

2. _Other information_--the auditor has no obligation to perform any procedures, beyond reading, to corroborate the information

NOTE: _In all of the circumstances described in sections B. and C. below, the CPA will first attempt to determine that the information in question is actually incorrect. When the information is determined to be incorrect, the auditor will attempt to convince the client to correct any misstated information. The following only applies when the misstatements are not eliminated by the client._

B. Material inconsistency between the financial statements and the other information

1. If the financial statements are incorrect a departure from GAAP exists which will lead to either a qualified or adverse opinion--see outline of AU 508 and section B. of Reporting module

2. If the other information is incorrect the auditor should consider (depending upon the circumstances)

    a. Insertion of an explanatory paragraph in the audit report
    b. Withholding use of the audit report
    c. Withdrawing from the engagement

C. No inconsistency, but the other information seems incorrect

1. The appropriate action will depend upon the circumstances, but might include notification of the client in writing and consulting with legal counsel

NOTE: _Know that the circumstances described in "B.2." and "C.1." do not result in a report which is qualified or adverse. This is because the financial statements follow GAAP--it is the other information which is incorrect._

551 Reporting on Information Accompanying the Basic Financial Statements in Auditor-Submitted Documents (SAS 29)

Overall Objective and Approach--This section presents guidance on the CPA's responsibility when audited financial statements are included in an auditor-submitted document which also includes other information. An auditor-submitted document is one that the auditor submits to his/her client or to others. The other information covered by this statement is presented outside the basic financial statements and is not necessary for the presentation of the statements--for example, consolidating information, historical summaries, and statistical data.

The distinction between this section, and the preceding section (AU 550) is that here _the auditor_, and _not the client_, is preparing the document which includes an audit report, financial statements and other information. For example, a small client may ask the CPA to prepare the report and provide it to the company. AU 550 provides guidance for when the client is preparing a report in which the auditor's report is to be included.

The basic requirement for an auditor-submitted document is that the CPA must make clear his/her association with any information which is being submitted to the client (or third party). The information, depending upon the client's needs, may either be audited or unaudited. The report on the accompanying information may be added to the CPA's standard report on the basic financial statements, or may appear separately in auditor-submitted document.

In this outline we summarize the material as follows: (a) overall responsibility, and (b) details of reporting responsibility, and (c) miscellaneous points.

A. Overall responsibility

1. When the auditor submits a document containing audited financial statements, s/he must report on all information included in the document

2. The auditor's report on accompanying information should

    a. State that the examination was made for the purpose of forming an opinion on the basic financial statements taken as a whole

    b. Identify the accompanying information

    c. State that accompanying information is presented for purposes of additional analysis and is not a part of the basic financial statements

    d. Include an opinion on the accompanying information or a disclaimer (if audit procedures are not applied)

        (1) If an opinion is given, the report should indicate that the accompanying information is fairly stated in all material respects as it relates to the basic financial statements taken as a whole

        (2) An opinion may be expressed on portions of the accompanying information and a disclaimer on the remainder

        (3) Any accompanying information on which the auditor disclaims an opinion should be marked as "unaudited"

       NOTE: Recall from our introduction that the above information may either be added to the standard report or may be included in a separate report.

3. Because the materiality level for the accompanying information is the same as that used for forming an opinion on the financial statements taken as a whole, the auditor need not apply procedures as extensive as would be necessary for a separate opinion on the information taken alone

4. When a client asks for inclusion of nonaccounting information, the auditor should generally disclaim an opinion on this accompanying information unless the records supporting it were tested

B. Details of reporting responsibility

1. If the auditor concludes that accompanying information is materially misstated, s/he should propose revisions to the client

    a. If the revision is not accepted, the audit report should be modified or the misstated information should be omitted

    b. Since it is the accompanying information that is misstated, the audit report opinion would still be unqualified

2. The auditor must consider the effect of any modification in his/her standard report when reporting on the accompanying information

    a. If a qualified opinion is issued on the basic financial statements, the impact on the accompanying information should be indicated

    b. If an opinion on the financial statements is adverse or disclaimed, no opinion should be expressed on any accompanying information

C. Miscellaneous points

1. When supplementary information required by the FASB or GASB is presented outside the basic financial statements,

     a. An opinion should be disclaimed unless the auditor is engaged to express an opinion on it

     b. The auditor's report should be expanded if

        (1) The information is omitted
        (2) The required information departs from guidelines
        (3) The auditor is unable to complete required procedures, or
        (4) The auditor is unable to remove substantial doubt about whether the information conforms to guidelines

NOTE: See the outline of AU 558 for more information on FASB and GASB required information

2. When consolidated financial statements and/or consolidating information is presented, the CPA should report appropriately in a manner consistent with the responsibility being taken

     a. This responsibility may range from ascertaining that the consolidating information is suitably identified to auditing individual components presented in the consolidating financial statements

3. Any comments made by the CPA describing procedures applied to specific items in the financial statements should be placed apart from the accompanying information

     a. This is done to maintain a clear distinction between management's representations and the CPA's representations

552 Reporting on Condensed Financial Statements and Selected Financial Date (SAS 42)

Overall Objective and Approach--This section presents guidance on reporting on a client prepared document which contains <u>condensed financial statements</u> or <u>selected financial data</u> derived from the complete audited financial statements. This section only applies when the CPA has reported on the overall financial statements from which the information is being abstracted. The section provides for separate reports on condensed financial statements and on selected financial data. Sections A. and B. of the outline discuss the nature of the CPA's report on condensed financial statements and selected financial data respectively. Section C. discusses miscellaneous related points.

A. Reporting on <u>condensed financial statements</u>

   1. The report should indicate

     a. That the complete financial statements have been audited and that the auditor has expressed an opinion on them
     b. The date of the auditor's report on the complete financial statements
     c. The type of opinion expressed on the complete financial statements
     d. Whether the information in the condensed financial statements is fairly presented in all material respects in relation to the complete financial statements from which it is derived

   2. Example report

     We have audited, in accordance with generally accepted auditing standards, the consolidated balance sheet of X Company and subsidiaries as of December 3, 19X0, and the related consolidated statements of income, retained earnings, and cash flows for the year then ended (not presented herein); and in our report dated February 15, 19X1 we expressed an unqualified opinion on those consolidated financial statements. In our opinion, the information set forth in the accompanying condensed consolidated financial statements is fairly stated in all material respects in relation to the consolidated financial statements from which it has been derived.

B. Reporting on selected financial data

    1. The report should be limited to data derived from the audited complete financial statements

    2. The CPA's report should indicate items "a.", "c." and "d." above

        a. The reference in "d." is changed from condensed financial statements to the selected financial data

    3. When comparative selected financial data are presented and some of the data were derived from financial statements audited by another CPA the report should so state, and the auditor should not express an opinion on that data

C. Miscellaneous

    1. When a client prepares a document with condensed financial statements or selected financial data which names the CPA but does not present the complete financial statements the CPA should request that the client

        a. Not include the CPA's name in the document or
        b. Engage the CPA to report on the information or
        c. Include the complete financial statements in the document

558 Required Supplementary Information (SAS 52)

Overall Objective and Approach--This section presents guidance for audits where supplementary information required by the FASB or GASB is presented. The FASB or GASB periodically require certain disclosures considered to be supplementary to the financial statements. Such information is not considered audited, although CPAs are required to perform certain limited procedures on it. The information should normally be distinct from both the audited financial statements and from other information not required by the FASB or GASB. However, when it is placed inside the audited financial statements it should be marked "unaudited" or the CPA's report should include a disclaimer on the information.

    The section also applies when a company not subject to the requirements voluntarily issues such information, unless the information indicates that the CPA did not apply any procedures or the CPA expands his/her report to include a disclaimer on the information. The section does not apply when a company voluntarily discloses information no longer required of any firms--e.g., the FASB rescinded the required disclosures of the effects of changing prices; such information is considered using the AU 550 requirements.

    This section provides guidance on both (a) procedures to be applied by CPAs, and (b) reporting considerations.

A. Procedures to be applied by CPAs

    1. Inquire of management about the methods of preparing the information, including

        a. Whether it is measured and presented within the guidelines
        b. Whether methods of measurement or presentation have changed from those used in the prior period and the reasons for any such changes

    c. Any significant assumptions or interpretations underlying the measurement or presentation

  2. Compare the information for consistency with

    a. Management's responses to the inquiries in "1." above
    b. Audited financial statements
    c. Other knowledge obtained during the audit of the financial statements

  3. Consider the need to include representations on the supplementary information in the presentation letter (see outline AU 333)

  4. Apply additional procedures that other guides (e.g., other SASs, interpretation, guides) prescribe for the specific type of supplementary information

  5. Make additional inquiries if foregoing procedures indicate possible deviations from the appropriate guidelines

B. Reporting on supplementary information

  1. The auditor only reports on information when the

    a. Information is omitted
    b. Information departs from guidelines
    c. Auditor is unable to perform prescribed procedures
    d. Auditor is unable to remove substantial doubts about whether information conforms to guidelines

  2. The actual report modification is in the form of an explanatory paragraph, with no opinion paragraph modification

560 Subsequent Events

Overall Objective and Approach--This section presents guidance on accounting for and auditing "subsequent events." Carefully distinguish between the information presented in this section and that of section 561. This section relates to proper accounting and auditing procedures related to events occurring subsequent to the balance sheet date, but prior to issuance of the audit report. Section 561 relates to events occurring after the date of the auditor's report, most frequently when the financial statements have been issued.

    This outline first defines the relevant terms from throughout the section. Section B. summarizes proper accounting for subsequent events. Section C. lists normal audit procedures which should be performed to detect subsequent events.

A. Definitions

  1. <u>Subsequent events</u>--events or transactions having a material effect on the financial statements that occur subsequent to the balance-sheet date, but prior to issuance of the financial statements and auditor's report

    a. <u>Type 1 subsequent events</u>--those events that provide additional evidence about <u>conditions that existed</u> at the date of the balance sheet and effect the estimates used in preparing financial statements
    b. <u>Type 2 subsequent events</u>--those events that provide evidence with respect to <u>conditions that did not exist</u> at the date of the balance sheet being reported on, but arose after that date

2. <u>Subsequent period</u>--the period after the balance sheet date, extending to the date of the auditor's report

B. Proper accounting for subsequent events

1. <u>Type 1</u>--make an adjusting entry to adjust the financial statements

a. Examples

(1) Settlement of litigation for an amount different from the liability recorded in the accounts, assuming the event causing the litigation occurred before year end

(2) Loss on an uncollectible account receivable as a result of a customer's deteriorating financial condition that led to bankruptcy subsequent to the balance sheet data

NOTE: Think about the above example. Although the customer filed for bankruptcy after year end, an adjustment is appropriate because filing for bankruptcy was simply the conclusion of the condition--deteriorating financial position--which began prior to year end.

2. <u>Type 2</u>--<u>disclose in notes</u> to the financial statements

a. Examples

(1) Sale of bond or stock issue
(2) Purchase of a business
(3) Litigation settlement, but only when the litigation is based on a post-balance sheet event

(a) Because of the time involved with litigation, this would presumably be rare

(4) Fire or flood loss
(5) Receivable loss, but only when the loss occurred due to a post balance sheet event such as a customer's major casualty arising after the balance sheet date

NOTE: Distinguish between this example and example 1.(a.)(2.) above

3. Several related points for Type 2 subsequent events

a. The disclosures related to subsequent event may include pro forma statements included in the notes

b. An auditor may wish to add an explanatory paragraph to an unqualified report to emphasize the subsequent event matter--see Emphasis of a Matter in the outline of AU 508 and Section B. of the Reporting module

c. When statements are reissued (for example, in an SEC filing) the statements should not be adjusted for events occurring after the original issuance date

C. Subsequent period auditing procedures

1. Certain procedures are applied to transactions after year end

a. To assure proper year-end cutoff
b. To help evaluate asset and liability valuation

2. In addition, the CPA should perform other procedures near completion of field work to identify subsequent events

a. Read latest interim statements

(1) Make comparison with other data

b. Discuss with management

(1) Existence of contingent liabilities
(2) Significant changes in shareholders' equity items
(3) Statement items accounted for on tentative data
(4) Unusual adjustments in the subsequent period

c. Read minutes of Board of Directors and other committees

(1) Make inquiries when minutes are not available

d. Obtain lawyer's letter on

(1) Litigation
(2) Impending litigation, claims
(3) Contingent liabilities

e. Include in management representation letter representations on subsequent events

561 Subsequent Discovery of Facts Existing at the Date of the Auditor's Report

Overall Objective and Approach--This section presents guidance on procedures to be followed by the CPA who, after the date of his/her audit report, becomes aware of facts that may have existed when the audit report was issued and that might have affected that report. You might wish to study and compare this section with Section 560, which deals with events occurring subsequent to the balance sheet date, but prior to issuance of the audit report.

This outline summarizes the section's procedural guidance in a series of four steps. The outline deviates from a strict format to make obvious the sequence of audit procedures.

A. Appropriate procedures for events discovered subsequent to the date of the audit report

NOTE: The auditor has no obligation to perform additional procedures after the audit report date, <u>unless</u> s/he becomes aware of facts that may have existed at the report date. As overall advice, when any of these circumstances arise, the CPA should consult with his/her attorney.

Step 1. The CPA should determine if the subsequently discovered information is reliable and existed at the date of the audit report

a. To accomplish this, the auditor should discuss the matter with the appropriate level(s) of management, the board of directors (if deemed necessary), and should request cooperation in whatever investigation is necessary

Step 2. When the CPA determines that the information is reliable and did exist at the date of the audit report, the following procedures are required

a. Determine whether the audit report would have been affected if the information had been known at the time of report issuance
b. Assess whether persons are likely to still be relying upon the report

(1) The auditor will consider, among other things, the time that has elapsed since the financial statements were issued

Step 3. When the CPA believes that the report would be affected, and that persons are relying upon the information, the CPA should insist that the client undertake appropriate disclosure, which may vary with the circumstances

    a. If the effect on the financial statements and/or the auditor's report can be promptly determined, the statements should be revised and reissued

        (1) The reason for the revision should be described in a note to the financial statements and referred to in the auditor's report

        (2) Generally, only the most recently issued audited statements would need to be revised, even though the revision resulted from events that had happened in prior years

    b. If issuance of statements of a subsequent period is imminent, appropriate revision can be made in those statements; disclosures should be similar to those in a. above

    c. If the effect can not be promptly determined and it appears that the statements will be revised after the investigation, persons known to be relying or who are likely to rely on the financial statements should be notified

        (1) If appropriate, the client should disclose the information to the proper regulatory bodies (e.g., SEC)

Step 4. This step is appropriate only if the client refuses to cooperate with the CPA

    a. Notify each member of the board of directors of the client's refusal to make disclosures and that the CPA will take the steps outlined in b., below

    b. Unless the CPA's attorney recommends a different course of action, the CPA should undertake the following steps (to the extent applicable)

        (1) Notify the client that the audit report cannot be associated with the financial statements

        (2) Notify regulatory agencies that the audit report should not be relied upon

        (3) Notify each person known to be relying on the statements that the report should not be relied upon

        NOTE: Know that the notification is limited to the client, regulatory agencies (e.g., the SEC), and persons known to be relying on the statements. It will not in general be practicable to notify all stockholders or investors at large.

    c. Appropriate disclosures

        (1) If the CPA makes a satisfactory investigation and believes the information is reliable

            (a) Disclose the nature of the information and effect on the report and statements

            (b) Disclosures should be precise and factual, and should not comment on the motives of any person who is involved

(2) If the client has not cooperated, and the auditor has been unable to conduct a satisfactory investigation the auditor should disclose that the

   (a) Information has come to his/her attention and that
   (b) The client has not cooperated in attempting to substantiate it, and if true, the auditor believes his report should no longer be relied upon

622 Special Reports--Applying Agreed-Upon Procedures to Specific Elements, Accounts or Items of a Financial Statement

Overall Objective and Approach--This section presents guidance on applying agreed-upon procedures to a financial statement element, account or item (hereafter, element). AU 623 presents guidance on expressing an opinion on financial statement elements and suggests that negative assurance may be provided based on performing agreed-upon procedures. This section presents guidance on that latter form of association, which is also considered a special report.

Agreed-upon procedures are normally conceived as being lesser in scope than would be applied in forming an opinion. For example, a company considering purchasing another company's receivables might request an auditor to confirm and age certain receivables it is considering purchasing.

The outline divides the material as follows: (a) procedural requirements and (b) reporting requirements.

A. Procedural requirements

  1. Agreed-upon procedures engagements may be accepted when

    a. The involved parties have a clear understanding of the procedures to be applied and
    b. Distribution of the CPA's report is restricted to the named parties

  2. Normally these requirements are satisfied by meeting with the named parties to discuss the procedures to be applied

    a. When the CPA is unable to meet with a named party, s/he may apply one or more of the following procedures

      (1) Discuss the procedures with legal counsel or with an appropriate representative of the parties
      (2) Review relevant correspondence from the parties
      (3) Compare procedures to be applied with any written requirements of a supervisory agency that receives the report
      (4) Distribute a draft of the report or a copy of the client's engagement letter to the parties involved, and a request for their comments before the report is issued

  3. The general GAAS standards and the first standard of field work (planning) apply

B. Accountant's report on results of agreed-upon procedures should

  1. Indicate specified elements, accounts, or items to which procedures were applied

  2. Indicate the intended distribution of the report

  3. List procedures performed

  4. State accountant's finding

5. Disclaim an opinion with respect to elements, accounts, or items

6. State that the report relates only to the item specified and not to the
    entity's financial statements taken as a whole

7. Provide negative assurance when the accountant has no adjustments to propose
    related to the element

    a. When exceptions have been noted, the report should indicate the
        exception, and then provide negative assurance with respect to the
        result of the other tests (e.g., "except as set forth in Schedule B, no
        matters came to our attention...")

    *NOTE: Periodically knowledge of these reports is examined through either a
    multiple choice or an essay question. See section C. of the Reporting
    module for a sample report.*

AU 623 Special Reports (SAS 63)

Overall Objective and Approach--This section was passed in 1989 to update the area
of "special reports" to reflect the 1988 statements (SAS No. 52-61). It describes
five specific types of special reports issued by auditors which are based on--(a)
financial statements prepared using a comprehensive basis of accounting other than
GAAP (hereafter, simply a comprehensive basis), (b) Specified elements, accounts or
items of statements (e.g., cash, accounts receivable), (c) Compliance with aspects
of contractual or regulatory requirements related to audited financial statements,
(d) Financial presentations to comply with contractual or regulatory requirements,
and (e) Financial information presented in prescribed forms or schedules that
require a prescribed form of auditor's report. Be aware that the above 5 types of
reports are the only types of special reports. Thus, for example, reviews of
interim statements (AU 722) and forecast examinations (AU 2100) are not "special
reports." (A number of multiple choice questions have presented 3 special reports,
plus another type of report and have asked "which is not a special report?")

   A confusing portion of this section relates to whether the distribution of the
various reports is limited (generally to the preparer, appropriate regulatory agency
and/or party to a contract), or is available to the general public. The following
are the primary types of reports not publicly available:

1. Presentations prepared following a basis other than GAAP or a comprehensive
    basis

2. Comprehensive basis statements prepared using a basis of accounting used to
    comply with requirements of a governmental regulatory agency (A.2.a. below)

3. Incomplete GAAP or comprehensive basis presentations unless the presentation
    is to be filed with a regulatory agency (e.g., the SEC) and to be included
    in a document that is distributed to the general public (D.1.a.(1) below)

4. Report on compliance with contractual agreements or regulatory requirements
    related to audited financial statements (C. below)

   The sections of the following outline summarize proper reporting and procedural
requirements for each of the five types of special reports as well as a discussion
of circumstances that require explanatory language in an auditor's special report.

A. Reports prepared following a comprehensive basis of accounting

    1. GAAS apply when an auditor conducts an audit of and reports on any financial
        statement; financial statements include

a. The basic financial statements (balance sheet, statements of income, retained earnings, cash flows, owners' equity)
b. Statement of assets and liabilities excluding owners' equity
c. Statement of revenue and expenses
d. Summary of operations
e. Statement of operations by product lines
f. Statement of cash receipts and disbursements

2. A comprehensive basis is one of the following

a. A basis of accounting used to comply with governmental regulatory agency (e.g., rules of state insurance commission)
b. The basis of accounting used for tax purposes
c. The cash receipts and disbursements basis of accounting, including a method with widely accepted modifications of the method (e.g., recording depreciation, accruing income taxes)
d. A definite set of criteria with <u>substantial authoritative support</u> applied to all material items (e.g., price level basis of accounting)

NOTE: The effect of the above section is to limit comprehensive basis statements to regulatory basis, tax basis, cash basis, or another one with <u>substantial authoritative support</u>. Thus, a basis developed by a client or another party (e.g., a bank for use in assessing a company's compliance with debt covenants) will not in general qualify.

3. Reports on statements per a comprehensive basis

a. A title that includes the word independent
b. A paragraph stating that the financial statements
   (1) Were audited
   (2) Are the responsibility of management and that the auditor is responsible for expressing an opinion on them

c. A paragraph stating that

   (1) The audit was conducted per GAAS
   (2) GAAS require that the auditor plan and perform the audit to obtain reasonable assurance about whether the financial statements are free of material misstatement
   (3) An audit includes

      (a) Examining on a test basis evidence supporting the amounts and disclosures in the financial statements
      (b) Assessing the accounting principles used and significant estimates and
      (c) Evaluating overall financial statement presentation

   (4) The auditor believes that the audit provides a reasonable basis for the opinion

d. A paragraph indicating

   (1) The basis of presentation and refers to the note in the financial statement describing the basis
   (2) That the basis is a comprehensive basis of accounting other than GAAP

e. A paragraph with an opinion on whether the financial statements are presented fairly, in all material respects, in conformity with the basis of accounting described

f. When statements are prepared in conformity with a regulatory agency's principles, a paragraph that restricts distribution of report solely to those within the entity and for filing with the regulatory agency--see A.2.a. above

g. The manual or printed firm signature

h. The date (generally the last day of field work--see AU 530 outline)

NOTE: Periodically an essay question requires preparation of a comprehensive basis report. Notice how closely it parallels the standard audit report on whether financial statements follow GAAP. Also, an example of the report is provided in the reporting module, section C.2.a.

4. Terms such as statement of financial position, statement of income (or operations), and statement of cash flows should not be used for comprehensive basis statements

a. Examples of appropriate (cash basis) titles: statements of assets and liabilities arising from cash flows, statement of revenue collected and expenses paid

NOTE: Different titles are used so as to prevent misleading anyone into believing that the statements follow GAAP.

5. While comprehensive basis statement notes should include a summary of significant accounting policies and describe how the basis differs from GAAP, the differences need not be quantified

6. When evaluating the adequacy of disclosures, the auditor should consider disclosure of matters such as related party transactions, restrictions on assets and owners' equity, subsequent events, and uncertainties

B. Reports on specified elements, accounts or items of a financial statement

1. Examples--rentals, royalties, a profit participation, provision for income tax, accounts receivable

2. There are two basic approaches

a. Express an opinion on one or more elements

b. Provide "negative assurance" relating to the results of applying agreed-upon procedures to one or more elements

NOTE: This section only deals with expressing an opinion (2.a.). Section AU 622 presents guidance for expressing negative assurance as a result of applying agreed-upon procedures.

3. GAAS apply, except that the reporting requirement that the audit report state whether financial statements follow GAAP is only applicable when elements of a financial statements are intended to follow GAAP

4. The interrelated nature of various financial statement accounts may require a scope of procedures well beyond the specific account involved

5. The measure of materiality must be related to the individual element, not the financial statements taken as a whole

6. A special report may <u>only</u> be issued on specific elements in statements upon which an adverse opinion or a disclaimer was issued when

   a. The elements(s) are not a major part of the financial statements

   b. The special report does not accompany the financial statements of the entity

7. Reports on specific elements

   a. The report issued is similar to that for comprehensive basis statements (see A.3. above); major exceptions

      (1) The terms relating to the financial statements are replaced with a term relating to the elements, accounts or items presented

      (2) The "opinion paragraph" (A.3.d. above) should include

         (a) A description of the basis on which the elements are presented, and when applicable, any agreements specifying such basis

         (b) If considered necessary, a description and the source of significant interpretations made by management relating to the agreement

   NOTE: *Review both A.3. and this section since periodically an exam will require preparation of such a report. Section C.2.a. of the Reporting module provides a sample report.*

8. If a specified element, account or item is based on income or stockholders' equity, the auditor should have audited the complete financial statements to express an opinion on it

C. Reports on <u>compliance with contractual agreements</u> or with regulatory requirements related to <u>audited</u> financial statements

1. The situation being considered here is one in which an audit has been performed on the financial statements, and some organization (e.g., a bank) wants assurance with respect to compliance with the conditions of an agreement

   a. Examples--loan agreements often require restriction of dividend payments and maintenance of the current ratio at a specific level

2. The auditor provides negative assurance as to compliance with the agreement, either

   a. As a separate report, or

   b. As one or more paragraphs added to the auditor's report accompanying the financial statements

      (1) In either case indication that the negative assurance is given in connection with the audit

      (2) When a separate report is issued, it should indicate that an audit has been performed, the date of the report, and whether GAAS were followed

3. Negative assurance should <u>not</u> be provided

       a. For covenants that relate to matters that have not been subjected to the audit procedures applied in the audit of the financial statements

       b. When the auditor has expressed an adverse opinion or disclaimed an opinion on the financial statements to which the covenants relate

4. A separate report on compliance with contractual agreements should include

    a. A title that includes the word independent

    b. A paragraph stating that the financial statements were audited per GAAP, the date of that report, and describing any departures from standard report

    c. A paragraph that includes reference to the specific covenants, provides negative assurance relative to compliance, and specifies that the negative assurance is being given in connection with the audit

    d. A paragraph that includes a description and the source of any significant interpretations (if needed)

    e. A paragraph that restricts distribution of report solely to those within the entity and for filing with the regulatory agency

    f. The manual or printed firm signature

    g. The date

5. When the report on compliance is included in the audit report, the auditor should include paragraphs similar to 3.c., d. and e. above (following the opinion paragraph)

    NOTE: See section C. of the Reporting module for a sample report

D. <u>Special-purpose financial presentations</u> to comply with contractual agreements or regulatory provisions

1. The situation here is one in which financial statements have been prepared to comply with some agreement (e.g., a loan agreement) or regulatory provision and are intended solely for the use of the parties to the agreement, regulatory bodies, or other specified parties; two types of special purpose presentations are discussed

    a. Special purpose financial presentations that do not constitute complete presentation of assets and liabilities, revenues and expenses, but otherwise are presented per GAAP or other comprehensive basis

       (1) The procedural and reporting requirements are similar to those for comprehensive basis statements (A. above), although a paragraph restricting distribution of the report is necessary unless the information is filed with a regulatory agency (e.g., the SEC) and is to be included in a publicly available report

    b. Special purpose financial presentations which may or may not be a complete set of financial statements that do <u>not</u> follow GAAP or an other comprehensive basis of accounting

       (1) As an example, consider an acquisition agreement that requires the borrower to prepare financial statements per GAAP, except for certain assets such as receivables, inventories, and properties for which a net realizable valuation basis is specified in the agreement

(2) The report, while similar to that for comprehensive basis statements (A. above) includes an opinion paragraph that explains what the presentation is intended to present and refers to the note describing that basis, and states that the presentation is not per GAAP

(3) A paragraph limiting distribution is included

E. Reports on information in prescribed forms or schedules

1. Printed forms or schedules (hereafter, forms) that are designed by the bodies with which they are filed often suggest a required wording for an auditor's report

   EXAMPLE: Assume that a state has a balance sheet form which companies incorporated in that state are to fill out with appropriate financial information. Also, assume that the state requires a standard unqualified report be filed with the report. The difficulty here is that the form may not provide adequate, or proper disclosures. This section deals with the manner in which an auditor should report on such forms.

2. When a schedule requires that an auditor make a statement that is incorrect, the auditor should respond in a manner such as the following

   a. Revise the form so that it complies with the required statement to be made by the auditor
   b. Attach a separate report

3. In no case should an auditor make an assertion that is not justified

   EXAMPLE: Continuing the above example, if the information can be made to follow GAAP an unqualified report could be issued. Otherwise, the auditor would not be able to meet the legal requirement as his/her report would include departures from the standard form

F. Circumstances requiring explanatory language in an auditor's special report

   NOTE: Throughout the special reports, in general the circumstances which lead auditors to qualified, adverse and disclaimers of opinions in GAAP audits generally apply. Several special considerations apply to the following circumstances which normally result in the auditor adding additional explanatory language to an unqualified report

1. Lack of consistency

   a. An explanatory paragraph is added
   b. When financial statements (or specified elements, accounts or items) have been prepared in conformity with GAAP in prior years, and the basis is changed to another comprehensive basis, the auditor is not required to add an explanatory paragraph of consistency (although s/he may choose to do so)

2. Uncertainties (including going-concern uncertainties)

   a. An explanatory paragraph is only added when the uncertainties are relevant to the presentation

      (1) For example, an explanatory paragraph may be necessary for cash basis statements, but may not be necessary for a report based on compliance with loan covenants

3. Other auditors

   a. When reference is made to other auditors whose report is being relied upon, the AU 508 requirements for other auditors apply (mention them in introductory, scope and opinion paragraphs)

4. Comparative financial statements when a different opinion than originally issued is being issued

   a. The auditor should disclose that the opinion is different, with all reasons therefore in a separate explanatory paragraph preceding the opinion paragraph

625 Reports on the Application of Accounting Principles (SAS 50)

Overall Objective and Approach--This section presents guidance on a CPA's responsibilities when s/he is asked to reply as to proper accounting for various transactions and/or as to the type of audit report that would be presented in certain circumstances. The section was developed to control "opinion shopping," the practice of going from one CPA to another until one finds an accountant who agrees with an accounting procedure which might be considered questionable.

   The guidance in the section relates to: (A) applicability, (B) performance standards, and (C) reporting standards.

A. Applicability

1. This section provides guidance on the procedures a CPA in public practice should apply in connection with a proposal to obtain a new client, or for other purposes as follows

   a. When preparing a written report on the application of GAAP to specified completed or proposed transactions
   b. When requested to provide a written report on the type of opinion that may be rendered on an entity's financial statements
   c. When preparing a written report to intermediaries (e.g., a lawyer) on the application of GAAP not involving facts or circumstances of a particular principal entity

2. Applies to oral advice on "a." and "b." above when accountant concludes the advice is an important factor used by a principal to the transaction

3. Does not apply to regular reporting engagements, litigation assistance, expert testimony, and position papers (e.g., newsletters, articles, speeches)

B. Performance standards

1. Procedures

   a. <u>Obtain an understanding</u> of form and substance of transaction(s)
   b. <u>Review applicable GAAP</u>
   c. <u>If appropriate, consult other professionals</u> and experts or perform necessary research

2. If another accountant is involved, contact and follow AU 315 (Predecessor/Successor Auditor) procedures

C. Reporting standards

   1. Report should include a

      a. Description of nature of engagement and statement that AICPA standards were followed

      b. Description of transaction(s), relevant facts, circumstances, assumptions, source(s) of information, and principles relevant to transactions

      c. Description of appropriate accounting principles to be followed

      d. Statement that responsibility for accounting treatment rests with preparers who should consult their continuing accountants

      e. Statement that any difference in facts, circumstances, or assumptions might change report

634 Letters for Underwriters (SAS 49)

Overall Objective and Approach--This section presents guidance on letters to underwriters (also referred to as "comfort letters") which CPAs may prepare to assist underwriters who are involved with the selling of securities under the Securities Act of 1933. Consider, for example, a company selling stock to the public. The underwriter will assist the company in meeting the various legal requirements, and may even purchase and then resell the stock to the public. Under the Securities Act of 1933 the underwriter is required to perform a "reasonable investigation" of the financial and accounting data that is not audited. A comfort letter is issued by the CPA to the underwriter related to certain of this information.

    This section is very detailed. However, in the past the CPA exam has only asked a few questions from it, therefore less detail is provided than has been included in prior outlines. The outline is organized as follows: (A) overall issues, (B) general requirements, and (C) detailed requirements.

A. Overall issues

   1. The statement deals with the relationship of the CPA with the client and underwriters under the Securities Act of 1933

   2. Underwriters wish to perform a "reasonable investigation" of the information in registration statements (this is a defense under the 1933 Act)

      a. The criteria for a "reasonable investigation" are not clearly established

      b. Underwriters rely on a letter (comfort letter) from CPAs to assist

   3. <u>When a CPA has audited the historical financial statements</u>, s/he may give comfort in a letter with respect to the following

      a. The CPA's independence (explicitly stated)

      b. Compliance of statements with SEC requirements (explicitly stated)

      c. Unaudited statements in registration statement (negative assurance provided)

      d. Changes in statement items subsequent to latest statements (negative assurance provided)

      e. Tables, statistics, and other financial data (negative assurance provided)

   4. <u>A CPA can give comfort only on matters in which his/her professional competence is substantially relevant</u>

      a. The CPA, client, and underwriter should meet to agree on comfort letter content

  5. SEC <u>usually accepts only unqualified reports, including those with explanatory language on uncertainties</u> (type of report issued on annual financial statements is disclosed in comfort letter)

> *NOTE: Prior to the 1988 standards, "subject to " qualified reports were issued for uncertainties. Now the report issued in such circumstances is considered unqualified with explanatory language.*

  6. When a shelf filing (one which allows for continuous or delayed offerings) is registered and no underwriter has been selected, a comfort letter may be provided to the client or legal counsel

      a. It should <u>not</u> be addressed to the client, legal counsel, or to any non-specific addressee (e.g., "underwriters to be selected")

      b. It is a draft and the text of a final letter may depend on additional procedures performed for the underwriter eventually selected

B. General comfort letter requirements

  1. Dates

      a. Closing date--securities delivered to underwriter (letter normally so dated)

      b. Cutoff date--last date of CPA's procedures related to comfort letter

      c. Effective date--securities registration becomes effective

      d. Filing date--securities registration first filed (recorded) with SEC

  2. Addressee is client, underwriter, or both

  3. Letter identifies statements, data examined, and registration statement; CPA's independence; and compliance with the SEC requirements in <u>separate</u> paragraphs

  4. Letter should <u>not</u> repeat report on audited statements and should <u>not</u> provide negative assurance about opinion

C. Detailed comfort letter requirements

  1. <u>Unaudited statements in registration statement</u> (condensed financial statements and capsule information)

      a. Agreed-upon <u>procedures should be outlined</u>

      b. Do not use terms such as general review, limited review, test, or check

      c. Negative assurance provided only if CPA has audited past annual statements or will audit them

  2. Changes in statement items subsequent to latest statements

      a. Do <u>not make opinionated statements such as "adverse changes"</u> or "nothing of interest arose"; make objective statements only

  3. Tables, statistics, and other financial data

      a. Comment only on matters for which CPA competence has relevance (accounting related--typically under the internal control structure)

(1)   One would not, for example, provide negative assurance with respect to square footage of facilities

4.   Comfort letters should indicate CPA makes no representations concerning legal matters and should indicate that report is for underwriter

642 Reporting on Internal Control (SAS 30)

Overall Objective and Approach--This section (as amended to reflect the 1988 SASs) presents guidance on three types of reports on internal control (presented in part A. of the outline). A fourth report, the one based on an audit, has been eliminated from this section and is now included in AU 325.

The general approach is one of describing appropriate procedures, and then the related report to be issued by the CPA. Section A. of the outline presents overview information. Section B. addresses opinions on internal control, the area to which most of the section relates. Sections C. and D. address internal control reports based on criteria established by regulatory agencies and other reports respectively.

A.   Overview information

1.   Accountant may be engaged to report on entity's internal control structure in several ways; accountant may be engaged to

   a.   Express an <u>opinion on entity's system of internal control</u> on a specified date or for a specified period of time
   b.   Report on all or part of entity's system, for restricted use of management or <u>specified regulatory agencies</u>, based on regulatory agencies, guidelines
   c.   Issue <u>other special-purpose reports</u> on part or all of an entity's system for restricted use of management, regulatory agencies, or other specified parties

2.   Accountant may also be involved with entity's internal control structure (ICS) in ways that do not involve reporting in accordance with this statement, e.g., consulting

   a.   In these circumstances, accountant may communicate results of engagement by letters, memoranda, and other less formal means solely for internal information of management

B.   Expression of opinion on entity's internal control structure

1.   General considerations

   a.   Objectives of internal control are to provide management with reasonable assurance that assets are safeguarded from unauthorized use and that financial records are reliable to permit preparation of financial statements; objectives are achieved when

      (1)   Transactions are executed in accordance with management's authorization
      (2)   Transactions are recorded as necessary to

         (a)   Permit preparation of financial statements in conformity with GAAP and
         (b)   Maintain accountability for assets

      (3)   Access to assets permitted only in accordance with management's authorization

(4) Recorded accountability for assets is compared to existing assets and all discrepancies resolved

b. Safeguarding of assets refers to protection against loss arising from errors and irregularities in processing transactions and handling related assets

(1) Does not refer to losses stemming from management's operating decisions

c. Objective of reliability of financial records relates to financial statements issued to external users

d. Internal control as it relates to estimates and judgments involves procedures to provide assurance that estimators review relevant information when making the required estimates and judgments

e. Inherent limitations exist which should be recognized in assessing the effectiveness of internal control structures, e.g.

(1) Projection of current evaluation of system to future periods is subject to risk that

(a) Procedures may become inadequate because of changes in conditions, or

(b) The effectiveness of the design or operation of prescribed procedures may deteriorate

f. Engagements to express opinion on internal control and the consideration of internal control for an audit in accordance with GAAS differ in purpose and scope

(1) Auditor's study of internal control establishes basis for determining extent to which auditing procedures are to be restricted and assists in planning and performing examination

(2) In GAAS audit, auditor may decide not to rely on prescribed control procedures because

(a) Procedures are not satisfactory for his/her purposes, or

(b) Audit effort required to test the policies and procedures would exceed the reduction in effort achieved

(3) Accordingly, obtaining an understanding of the ICS and assessing control risk in an audit is generally more limited (therefore weaknesses may go unnoticed) than that made in an engagement to express an opinion on the internal control structure

(4) However, accountant's opinion of structure of internal control does not increase reliability of entity's audited financial statements

g. Although scope of engagement to express opinion on the ICS differs from scope of audit, procedures are similar in nature

(1) The study and evaluation made in connection with engagement to express opinion on structure may also serve as basis for obtaining an understanding of the ICS and assessing control risk in determining the nature, timing and extent of audit tests

(2) The accountant need not apply procedures in audit that duplicate procedures applied for purpose of expressing opinion on entity's internal control structure

h. The auditor's opinion does not indicate compliance or noncompliance with Foreign Corrupt Practices Act; this is a legal determination

2. Study and evaluation for purpose of expressing an opinion on internal control includes

    a. Planning scope of engagement in which auditor must consider

        (1) Nature of entity's operations, e.g., volume of transactions and risk of asset misuse or misappropriation
        (2) Overall control environment, e.g., organizational structure, communication methods, management's financial reports, management's supervision of system, and competence of personnel
        (3) Extent of recent changes in operations or control procedures
        (4) Relative significance of various classes of transactions
        (5) Knowledge obtained in past engagements
        (6) Which locations to study in multiple location firms
        (7) Work performed by internal auditors (follow guidance in AU 322)
        (8) Documentation of specific control objectives and related procedures

    b. Reviewing the design of the ICS to secure information to judge whether control procedures are suitably designed to achieve objectives of internal control, the accountant should consider

        (1) Flow of transactions through accounting system

            (a) Identify classes of transactions, e.g., by cycle of activity
            (b) Understand flow from authorization through execution

        (2) Specific objectives that relate to points in processing of transactions and handling of assets where errors or irregularities could occur
        (3) Specific control procedures established to achieve specific control objectives

            (a) Primary ICS policies and procedures are applied at points where errors or irregularities could occur in the processing of transactions and the handling of assets (e.g., monthly bank account reconciliation)
            (b) Secondary ICS policies and procedures are those administrative controls which also help to achieve a specific internal control objective (they are not a part of the processing of transactions or the handling of assets--e.g., comparison of actual to budgeted costs)

    c. Testing effectiveness of ICS policies and procedures with prescribed procedures to provide basis for conclusions on application of prescribed procedures

        (1) Nature and extent of tests of controls essentially same considerations as tests of controls in audit
        (2) In engagement to express opinion on an ICS as of a specified date, the period of time necessary for testing the effectiveness of design and operation varies with nature of control tested
        (3) If management has changed its ICS to correct weaknesses, accountant need not consider superseded controls

    d. Evaluating results of review of the design of ICS and tests of controls

        (1) Accountant should identify weaknesses in ICS and evaluate whether they are material, either individually or in combination
        (2) Weakness is material if condition results in more than a relatively low risk of errors or irregularities in amounts that would be material in relation to financial statements

        (3)   In evaluating an individual weakness, accountant should recognize that

            (a)   The amounts of errors or irregularities that may occur and remain undetected range from zero to the gross amount of assets or transactions exposed to weakness

            (b)   The risk of errors or irregularities is likely to be different for the different possible amounts within that range (i.e., risk of errors or irregularities in amounts equal to gross exposure may be low, but risk of smaller amounts may be greater)

        (4)   In evaluating combined effect of individually immaterial weaknesses, accountant should consider

            (a)   Range of amount of errors or irregularities that may result during same accounting period from two or more individual weaknesses

            (b)   Probability that such combination of errors or irregularities would be material

        (5)   Evaluation of identified weaknesses is a subjective process that depends on such factors as nature of accounting process and assets exposed to weaknesses, overall control environment, experience and judgment of those making estimates, and extent that historical data are available

            (a)   Historical data provide more reasonable basis for estimating risk of errors than they do for estimating risk of irregularities

                1] Errors are unintentional, underlying causes tend to result in predictable level of occurrence

                2] Irregularities are intentional, underlying causes less predictible

3. Accountant should ordinarily obtain management's written representations that

    a. Acknowledge management's responsibility for establishing and monitoring the ICS

    b. State that management has disclosed all material weaknesses of which they are aware

    c. Describe any irregularities by individuals having key roles in the ICS

    d. State whether there were any changes since report date that would have a significant impact on the ICS and any changes by management to correct material weaknesses

4. Extent to which accountant documents engagement to express opinion on ICS is a matter of professional judgment

    a. Documents prepared by entity to describe its ICS may be used by accountant in his/her working papers

5. Form of accountant's report

    a. Independent accountant may express opinion on an ICS of any entity for which financial statements in conformity with GAAP, or any other criteria applicable to such statements can be prepared

    b. Accountant's report expressing opinion on entity's ICS should contain

        (1) Description of scope of engagement
        (2) Date to which opinion relates
        (3) Statement that establishment and maintenance of ICS is responsibility of management
        (4) Explanation of broad objectives and inherent limitations of internal control
        (5) Opinion on whether ICS taken as a whole was sufficient to meet broad objectives of internal control

c. Report should be dated as of date of completion of field work and be addressed to entity, board of directors, or stockholders

d. If study and evaluation discloses conditions that, individually or in combination, result in one or more material weaknesses, accountant should modify opinion paragraph of his/her report by

        (1) Describing material weaknesses
        (2) Stating whether they result from absence of control procedures or degree of the effectiveness of the design or operation of control procedures
        (3) Describing general nature of potential errors or irregularities that may occur as result of weaknesses
        (4) Accountant may also report to management other weaknesses even though they are not considered to be material

e. If a document that contains an accountant's opinion identifying a material weakness also includes statement by management asserting that cost of correction of weakness would exceed benefits of reducing risk of errors or irregularities, the accountant

        (1) Should not express any opinion on management's assertion
        (2) May disclaim an opinion on such assertion

f. Accountant should not mention corrective action implemented by management unless s/he is satisfied such procedures are suitably designed and being applied as prescribed

g. If study and evaluation of internal control indicates a material weakness <u>and</u> if opinion on ICS is issued in conjunction with examination of entity's financial statements

        (1) Accountant should indicate that opinion on internal control does not affect report on financial statements

h. Significant scope limitations caused by circumstances and/or client restrictions may require qualified opinion or disclaimer

        (1) If client-imposed, accountant should generally issue a disclaimer

i. Opinions which are formed, in part, by relying on another accountant's report should be referred to in describing scope and in expressing opinion (see AU 543)

j. If subsequent information becomes known to the accountant which might have affected the opinion, follow AU 561

C. Reports based on criteria established by regulatory agencies

  1. Agency may set forth specific criteria for evaluation of adequacy of internal control structure policies and procedures for their purposes and may require report based on those criteria

2. Criteria established by agency may be set forth in audit guides, question-naires, or other publications

   a. Criteria may encompass specified aspects of internal control, specified aspects of administrative control, or compliance with grants, regulations, or statutes

3. For accountant to be able to issue report, criteria should be in reasonable detail and in terms susceptible to objective application

4. Accountant's report should

   a. Clearly identify matters covered by study
   b. Indicate whether study included tests of controls with policies and procedures studied in engagement
   c. Describe objectives and limitations of internal control and accountant's evaluation of it
   d. State accountant's conclusions, based on agency's criteria, concerning adequacy of procedures studied, with exception concerning any material weaknesses
   e. State its specific purpose, e.g., for a grant, and that it should not be used for any other purpose

      (1) If agency requires accountant to report on all conditions not in conformity with agency's criteria, accountant must do so regardless of materiality
      (2) Accountant may report on immaterial items and make recommendations for corrective action even if not required by agency

5. For purposes of these reports, a material weakness includes a

   a. Condition that results in more than a relatively low risk that errors or irregularities which are material in relation to applicable grant or program may occur and not be detected by employees in performance of their duties
   b. Condition in which lack of conformity with agency criteria is material in accordance with agency's guidelines for determining materiality

6. Accountant is not responsible for comprehensiveness of agency's criteria

   a. However, s/he should report any relevant condition even if not covered by agency's criteria

D. Other special purpose reports

1. Accountant may be engaged to issue special report for restricted use of man-agement, another independent accountant, or other specified third parties

2. Report may be on all or part of entity's ICS or proposed ICS

3. Form of report in these circumstances is flexible; however, it should

   a. Describe scope and nature of accountant's procedures
   b. Disclaim opinion on whether ICS, taken as a whole, meets objectives of internal control
   c. State accountant's findings
   d. Indicate that report is solely intended for management or specified third party

711 Filings Under Federal Securities Statutes (SAS 37)

Overall Objective and Approach--This section presents overall information on a CPA's responsibilities when s/he is associated with information included in a client's filing with the SEC.   Section A. of the outline presents overall responsibilities. Section B. provides information on subsequent events in 1933 Act filings--this supplements the guidance in AU 560.   Section C. relates to the appropriate response when subsequent events have been discovered--this supplements the guidance in both AU 560 and AU 561.

A. Overall responsibilities under Federal Securities Statutes

   1. An accountant has a defense against lawsuits filed under section 11 of the 1933 Securities Act if s/he can prove that s/he had, after a _reasonable_ investigation, _reasonable_ grounds to believe and did believe that the statements were true and not misleading at the effective date of the financial statements

      a. The standard of _reasonableness_ is that of a prudent person in the management of his/her own property

   2. CPA should read the _experts section_ of the prospectus under a 1933 Securities Act filing to make certain that his/her name is not used in a misleading manner

   3. When a CPA's review report is included with interim financial information in a registration statement a statement should be included that this is not a _report_ under the meaning of section 7 or 11 of the Securities Act of 1933

      NOTE: The effect of the above statement is to limit CPA responsibility with respect to interim information contained in a registration statement

   4. When an independent audit report is incorporated in a registration statement by reference, the CPA is described as an "expert in auditing and accounting"

B. Procedures for finding subsequent events under a 1933 Securities Act Filing

   1. A CPA should extend his/her investigation from that of his/her report to the effective date of the filing, or as close as possible; this investigation should include

      a. Subsequent event procedures in AU 560--see outline of AU 560
      b. Additional procedures

         (1) Reading of the prospectus and relevant portions of the registration statement
         (2) Obtaining written confirmation from managerial and accounting officers as to any subsequent events not mentioned in the registration statement

   2. A predecessor accountant who has not examined the most current statements should

      a. Read applicable portions of the prospectus and registration statement
      b. Obtain a letter of representation from the successor CPA regarding the existence of any subsequent events

C. Appropriate response when subsequent events have been discovered

    1. Use any AU 560 or 561 guidance--see outlines of AU 560 and AU 561

    2. Overall

        a. Insist upon revision
        b. Comment on the matter in the audit report
        c. Inquire of attorney, and consider withholding opinion if client will not correct financial statements

    3. If the unaudited financial statements are not in conformity with GAAP, insist on revision, and failing that

        a. If CPA has issued a review report, refer to AU 561 and AU 722 for guidance
        b. If no review has been performed, modify report on audited financial statements to describe the departure

722 Review of Interim Financial Information (SAS 36)

Overall Objective and Approach--This section presents guidance on procedures to be applied when conducting a review of interim financial information and on the appropriate CPA's review report. The section's objective is to provide the CPA with a basis for providing negative assurance about whether material modificiations need be made to the interim information. Section A. of the outline presents overall information and describes appropriate procedures. Section B. describes review report considerations. Section C. describes reporting for interim information included with <u>annual</u> financial statements as an "unaudited footnote."

A. Overall information and procedures

    1. The guidance in this section applies both to interim information presented alone, and to interim information presented along with the audited financial statements

    2. The scope of procedures is affected because of the need for timely reporting of interim information and the greater need for reliance upon estimates on a quarterly basis as compared to at year end

    3. Procedures--primarily inquiries concerning significant accounting matters and analytical procedures; examples

        a. Inquire about the accounting system
        b. Inquire about significant changes in ICS
        c. Identify and provide a basis for inquiry about related and independent items that appear unusual
        d. Compare results with preceding interim period, anticipated, results, and its relationship to predictive patterns
        e. Read minutes of meetings
        f. Read interim information to determine if it conforms with GAAP
        g. Read reports prepared by other accountants
        h. Inquire of officers and executives if they changed accounting procedures or if they applied GAAP in a consistent manner
        i. Events subsequent to interim date with material effect
        j. Obtain written representation from management concerning its responsibility for financial information

        NOTE: Be familiar with the nature of the above procedures

    4. Extent to procedures depends on

        a. Accountant's knowledge of accounting and reporting practices
        b. Accountant's knowledge of weaknesses in internal control

            (1) Changes in ICS
            (2) Changes in procedures from prior annual year end
            (3) If weakness could prevent interim information from conforming with
                 GAAP, determine if it represents a restriction on scope of engage-
                 ment

        c. Accountant's knowledge of changes in nature and volume of activities or
            accounting changes
        d. Application of new or old accounting pronouncements
        e. Accounting records maintained at multiple locations

            (1) Similar to making an examination of client's financial statements
                 in accordance with GAAP

        f. Questions raised in performing other procedures

B. Accountant's report

    1. Report should include

        a. Statement that <u>review in accordance with AICPA standards</u>
        b. <u>Identification</u> of information reviewed
        c. <u>Description of interim review procedures</u>
        d. <u>Statement</u> that an interim review is substantially less in scope than
            examination per GAAS, and that no opinion is expressed
        e. <u>Statement on awareness of any material modifications</u> needed for confor-
            mity with GAAP

    2. <u>Dated as of completion of review</u>

    3. <u>Each page of information marked "unaudited"</u>

    4. May refer to review of other accountants

    5. Circumstances requiring modification

        a. Departures from GAAP

            (1) Describe nature and effects

        b. Inadequate disclosure
        c. <u>Uncertainties and a lack of consistency do not require disclosure if
            properly disclosed in financial statements</u>

    6. No report should be issued when significant scope restrictions have occurred

C. Interim information accompanying the audited financial statements

    1. The interim information may be provided as supplementary information outside
        the annual financial statements or as a note to the statements which is
        marked "unaudited"

    2. No separate report is provided on the interim information

    3. The audit is not modified unless the interim data is omitted, not reviewed,
        not appropriately marked "unaudited," or departs from GAAP

        a. In each of these circumstances an explanatory paragraph is added to the
            audit report to describe the situation
        b. Note that since this information is "unaudited," it will not lead to an
            opinion that is other than unqualified

901 Public Warehouses--Controls and Procedures for Goods Held

<u>Overall Objective and Approach</u>--This section presents guidance on internal control for a public warehouse, auditing a public warehouse and on auditing procedures to be performed by the independent auditor of the owner of goods in a warehouse. Historically, few CPA exam questions have come from this section. This outline is included for completeness sake, and on the chance that it may be examined more heavily in the future.

A. Public warehouse operations

    1. Types

        a. Terminal warehouse--principal function is furnishing storage, but may provide packaging, etc. Usually stores a wide variety of goods

        b. Field warehouse--principal function is financing arrangement. It is usually established on premises of owner of goods and warehouseman's personnel are those of owner. Purpose is to allow warehouseman to take possession of goods and issue warehouse receipts to owner to be used as collateral for loans.

        c. Warehouses may also be classified as to physical configuration, e.g.,

            (1) Refrigerated
            (2) Bulk

    2. Warehouse receipts

        a. Negotiable

            (1) Article 7 of UCC
            (2) Certain terms to provide for negotiation and transfer
            (3) Goods may be surrendered by warehouseman only on basis of receipt

        b. Nonnegotiable

            (1) Not required for withdrawal of goods
            (2) Allows partial withdrawal

    3. Government regulation

        a. U.S. Warehouse Act
        b. U.S. Commodity Exchange
        c. Tariff Act of 1930

B. Warehouseman

    1. Internal controls

        a. Goods of others are not assets or liabilities, but contingent liability exists for

            (1) Loss or improper release of goods
            (2) Improper issuance of warehouse receipts
            (3) Failure to maintain effective custody of goods

        b. Study and evaluate accounting control and administrative control

            (1) Administrative control relating to custodial responsibility

        c. Receiving, storing, delivering controls

            (1) Receipts issued for goods stored
            (2) Receiving reports for all goods stored
            (3) Goods stored should be weighed, counted, etc.
            (4) Goods stored separately unless fungible (interchangeable)
            (5) Instruction that goods are released only on proper authorization; surrender of receipt if negotiable

      (6) Limit access to storage area and control keys
      (7) Periodic statements to owners asking for notification of discrepancies
      (8) Stored goods counted periodically
      (9) Regular inspection of perishable goods
    (10) Protective devices; sprinklers, burglar alarms, etc.
    (11) Goods released only on basis of authorized written instruction
    (12) Counts per stock clerks checked by shipping clerks

  d. Warehouse receipts

      (1) Prenumbered receipts and account for numbers
      (2) Safeguard unused forms
      (3) Receipts forms issued only to authorized persons
      (4) Signer of receipts ascertains support of receiving reports
      (5) Receipts prepared to deter alteration
      (6) Limited number of signers

  e. Insurance

      (1) Review amount and type of coverage

2. Additional controls for field warehouses

  a. Controls at both central office and field warehouse
  b. Only nonnegotiable receipts issued from field warehouse
  c. Investigate and approve field arrangements

      (1) Consider reputation and financial standing of depositor
      (2) Prepare contract to meet requirements of depositors and lender
      (3) Evaluate physical effectiveness of facilities
      (4) Satisfy legal matters of field facilities lease
      (5) Bonding of field employees
      (6) Written instructions of field employees
      (7) Maintenance of detail records at central office
      (8) Examination of field facilities by central employees

3. Procedures of CPA

  a. Study and evaluate accounting and administrative controls
  b. Test warehouseman's records of all goods held
  c. Test accountability under recorded outstanding warehouse receipts
  d. Observe physical counts and reconcile to records

      (1) May not be possible if negotiable: then confirm with original holder

  e. Review insurance coverage

C. Controls and procedures for clients' goods stored at public warehouses

  1. Internal controls (by client)

    a. Consider reputation and financial standing of warehouseman
    b. Inspect physical facilities
    c. Inquire of warehouseman's control procedures
    d. Inquire of warehouseman's insurance
    e. Inquire of government licensing, inspection, etc.
    f. Review of warehouseman's statements and CPA report
    g. Physical count of stored goods
    h. Reconciliation of warehouseman's statements and owner's records

  2. Procedures of CPA (see outline of AU 331)

SAS No. 63 Compliance Auditing Applicable to Governmental Entities and Other Specified Recipients of Governmental Financial Assistance

Overall Objective and Approach--This section provides guidance on the auditor's responsibilities with respect to audits performed in accordance with government auditing standards, also referred to as generally accepted government auditing standards (GAGAS). To keep perspective on this know that:

1. GAGAS are established by the Comptroller General of the United States--the top executive within the General Accounting Office--in Government Auditing Standards (the "yellow book"). GAGAS apply to government agencies and to certain nongovernment organizations that have received governmental financial assistance

2. Certain state and local governments, in addition to being under the above requirements, are under the Single Audit Act and the related Circular A-128 issued by the Office of Management and Budget

Everything in this section relates to what Government Auditing Standards refers to as "financial audits," as opposed to "performance audits." It is important to realize that, when performing a government financial audit, the auditor must not only report on the financial statements, but also on compliance with various laws and regulations, and on the entity's internal control structure. Either separate reports on internal control and compliance may be issued, or they may be appended to the audit report.

Section A. of the outline details auditor responsibilities under AU 316 and AU 317 for illegal acts as applied to government audits; included is guidance for audit consideration related to possible violations of laws and regulations on government financial assistance programs. Section B. relates to reporting on compliance with laws and regulations, while Section C. is on reporting on the internal control structure. Sections D., E., and F. all deal with state and local government compliance with the Single Audit Act.

A. The following is guidance on applying AU 316 and AU 317 for illegal acts with a direct and material effect on the determination of financial statement amounts in audits of governmental agencies and nongovernmental agencies receiving governmental financial assistance

   1. Governmental entities

      a. The auditor should assess audit risk associated with possible violations of laws and regulations that have a direct and material effect on financial statement amounts

      b. The auditor should also assess whether management has identified relevant laws and regulations by

         (1) Considering knowledge obtained in prior years' audits
         (2) Discussing such laws and regulations with chief financial officer, legal counsel, or grant administrators and obtaining a representation letter

        (3) Reviewing agreements such as grants and loans
        (4) Reviewing minutes of meetings of the legislative body of the entity being audited
        (5) Inquiring of appropriate governmental auditors (or other audit oversight organization) about applicable laws
        (6) Inquiring of program administrators of other governmental entities that provided grants about restrictions, etc.
        (7) Reviewing information about compliance requirements from state CPA societies or associations of governments

2. Nongovernmental entities that receive governmental financial assistance

    a. <u>Examples of assistance</u>--grants of cash and other assets, loans, loan guarantees, interest rate subsidies

    b. Accepting governmental assistance may subject both the nongovernmental entity and the governmental entity to laws and regulations having a direct and material effect on financial statements; such laws and regulations may deal with

        (1) Types of services allowed or not allowed
        (2) Eligibility for financial assistance
        (3) Required matching to be made by the nongovernmental entity

3. In audits when this section applies, auditors should consider obtaining additional client representations (beyond those described in the outline of AU 333) that

    a. Management has responsibility for entity compliance with laws and regulations

    b. Management has identified and disclosed all laws and regulations having a direct and material effect on the financial statements to the auditor

B. Reporting on compliance with laws and regulations

1. Auditors must prepare a written report on their <u>tests of compliance</u> with applicable laws and regulations

    a. Positive assurance is provided for items tested through compliance tests
    b. Negative assurance is provided for items not tested
    c. The report indicates that it is intended for audit committee, management, and specific legislative or regulatory bodies, but that this restriction is not intended to limit distribution of the report

    NOTE: Know that the report on compliance with laws and regulations must be somewhat limited since the auditor's main objective was to obtain reasonable assurance about whether the financial statements are free of material misstatement. That is, the objective is <u>not</u> to provide an opinion on overall compliance with laws and regulations, but to form an opinion on the financial statements.

    Also, know that while the report is primarily for the company and regulatory bodies, distribution of the report is generally not limited. Finally, the term "compliance test" is used with respect to whether the entity is in compliance with laws and regulations--this is one reason that the term "compliance tests" pertaining to internal control in financial statement audits was replaced by the term "tests of controls."

2. Material noncompliance with laws and regulations must be reported; GAGAS require the auditor to report illegal acts that could result in criminal prosecution

    a. Because the auditor will not ordinarily possess the expertise to form a conclusion on the likelihood of criminal prosecution, the auditor may choose to report all illegal acts or possible illegal acts noted

C. Reporting on the internal control structure

1. GAGAS requires a <u>written</u> report on the internal control structure (ICS) <u>on all audits</u>; the following must be disclosed <u>in addition to</u> AU 325 requirements

    a. The elements of the ICS must be identified (e.g., transaction cycles or financial statement accounts)
    b. The scope of the auditor's work must be described
    c. Deficiencies in the ICS not considered significant enough to be reportable conditions must be reported
    d. Material weaknesses must be defined, and described (recall that for "normal" audits AU 325 makes the identification of material weaknesses optional)
    e. Report must indicate that it is intended for audit committee, management, and specific legislative or regulatory bodies, but that this restriction is not intended to limit distribution of the report

D. Overall Responsibilities under the Single Audit Act (SAA)

NOTE: This section of the outline applies only to state and local governments, whereas sections A. through C. deal with various governmental and nongovernmental entities (including state and local governments).

1. The Single Audit Act and Circular A-128, "Audits of State and Local Governments" (by the Office of Management and Budget) require state and local governments that receive $100,000 and over in federal financial assistance in a year to have an audit performed in accordance with the Single Audit Act

    a. A state or local government receiving between $25,000-$100,000 has an option of a SAA audit or one as required by the federal laws and regulations governing the federal financial assistance programs (hereafter, programs) in which the government participates
    b. The SAA does not require state or local governments receiving less than $25,000 to have a SAA audit

2. The SAA and Circular A-128 require the auditor to report on compliance with laws and regulations having a material effect on the financial statements and <u>major</u> programs, and on certain laws affecting <u>nonmajor</u> programs

NOTE: A major financial program is defined in terms of a government's expenditure of federal financial assistance under that program relative to its total expenditures of federal financial assistance. Note that the major vs. minor program distinction is determined by the organization receiving the funds, and <u>not</u> by the federal government. Thus, for example, because of difference in the level of funds received, what may be a major program to one city may be nonmajor to another.

3. The SAA and Circular A-128 also require the auditor to report on

    a. The financial statements

    b. The supplementary schedule of federal financial assistance

       (1) This schedule is used by management to identify major and nonmajor programs

    c. Internal controls over federal assistance programs

E. Single Audit Act--<u>Compliance Auditing for Major Programs</u> (D.2.b. above)

  1. To determine whether the organization has complied with laws or regulations the auditor should

    a. Perform audit procedures <u>designed to provide reasonable assurance</u> of detecting material noncompliance with <u>specific requirements</u> of programs

    b. Test and report on compliance with <u>general requirements</u>

  2. <u>Major</u> programs

    a. In auditing, the auditor considers materiality in relation to <u>each such program</u>

       (1) An amount material to one major federal program may not be material to another one

       (2) This responsibility is more demanding than for a GAAS audit which requires that materiality be considered in relation to the financial statements

    b. The auditor should test whether the entity has met the following specific requirements

       (1) Types of services allowed or not allowed

       (2) Eligibility of those to whom entity gave assistance

       (3) Matching necessary by entity

       (4) Reporting requirements entities must meet

       (5) Special tests and provisions relating to the program (many of these requirements are outlined in the <u>Compliance Supplement</u> of Circular A-128)

    c. The auditor should also determine whether

       (1) Federal financial reports and claims for advances and reimbursements are supported by accounting system

       (2) Amounts claimed or used for matching were calculated per requirements

    d. The overall risk here is that the auditor may unknowingly fail to modify the opinion on compliance

       (1) Inherent risk, control risk, and detection risk (see outline of AU 312) here relate to <u>compliance with requirements of the major federal financial assistance programs</u>

    e. When an entity passes $25,000 or more through to a subrecipient, the entity is responsible for determining that the subrecipient expends the assistance in accordance with applicable laws and regulations

       NOTE: As an example here, consider a state which receives federal assistance which is "passed down" to city governments

(1) While the entity's auditor is required to evaluate controls for monitoring subrecipient use of funds, the auditor need not perform an audit of the subrecipient

f. The auditor should obtain written representations from management on compliance with major federal financial assistance program requirements

   (1) Refusal to furnish written representations will require a qualified opinion or disclaimer on compliance

g. In performing these compliance audits questioned costs often pertain to

   (1) Unallowable costs
   (2) Undocumented costs
   (3) Unapproved costs
   (4) Unreasonable costs

h. Included in the report issued will be known questioned costs (not likely questioned costs) and an opinion on whether the entity complied in all material respects with requirements having a material effect on major federal programs

   (1) Likely questioned costs are the auditor's best estimate of total costs questioned
   (2) Known question costs are those specifically identified

i. Example of unqualified opinion paragraph for major program specific requirements:

   In our opinion, the City of Tombstone, Arizona, complied, in all material respects, with the requirements governing types of services allowed or unallowed; eligibility; matching, level of effort, or earmarking; reporting; claims for advances and reimbursements; and amount claimed or used for matching that are applicable to each of its major federal financial assistance programs for the year ended June 30, 19X1.

j. The auditor must also test compliance with general requirements (e.g., funds were not used for partisan political activity, no violations of civil rights)

   (1) A separate report is issued

      (a) A statement is included saying that procedures were substantially less in scope than an audit
      (b) Positive assurance is provided on items tested, and negative assurance is provided with respect to items not tested
      (c) Instances of noncompliance are noted

k. Example unqualified opinion paragraph for major program general requirements

   With respect to the items tested, the results of those procedures disclosed no material instances of noncompliance with the requirements listed in the first paragraph of this report. With respect to items not tested, nothing came to our attention that casued us to believe that Tombstone, Arizona, had not complied, in all material respects, with those requirements. However, the result of our procedures disclosed immaterial instances of noncompliance with those requirements, which are described in the accompanying schedule of findings and questioned costs.

F. Single Audit Act--Compliance Auditing for Nonmajor Programs (point D.2.c. above)

    1. Transactions are only tested for nonmajor programs when they are selected as a part of other required procedures (e.g., for purposes of the financial statement audit)

        a. When such transactions have been selected, tests should relate to allowability of the expenditure and eligibility of recipients

        NOTE: This requirement for specific requirements of nonmajor programs is less than what is required for major programs (which require that procedures be designed to provide reasonable assurance of detecting material noncompliance with specific requirements). Specific requirements of nonmajor programs are only tested when transactions have been selected for other purposes. For example, while auditing payroll for financial statement purposes, the auditor may have selected a payroll transaction that was charged to a nonmajor program. In such a circumstance compliance tests should be performed on that transaction.

    2. The report issued provides positive assurance for transactions tested, and negative assurance for items not tested

    3. The auditor need not address the general requirements for nonmajor programs

G. Responsibilities in Other Compliance Auditing Engagements

    1. Due professional care should be exercised and the auditor should determine appropriate requirements

Government Auditing Standards (Issued by the Comptroller General of the United States, General Accounting Office)

Background--In 1988, the Comptroller General of the United States issued a revision of Government Accounting Standards, also referred to as the "yellow book." These "generally accepted government auditing standards" (GAGAS) are meant to guide auditors and allow others to rely on auditors' work in assessing government accountability. When studying this information also review the outline of SAS No. 63 on auditing requirements in this area. In this outline we present a brief outline of the information as follows: A. financial audits, and B. performance audits.

A. Financial audits

    1. Types

        a. Financial statement audits--purposes are to determine whether the

            (1) Financial statements follow GAAP and
            (2) Entity has complied with laws and regulations for those transactions and events having a material effect on the financial statements

        b. Financial related audits--purposes are to determine whether the

            (1) Financial information is fairly presented
            (2) Financial information is presented in accordance with established or stated criteria
            (3) Entity has adhered to specific financial compliance requirements

        Examples of financial related audits: Segments of financial statements, schedules of financial matters, contracts, grants

2. General standards

   a. Qualifications--staff should possess adequate professional proficiency

      (1) All auditors with government auditing responsibility must complete at least 80 hours of CPE every two years

         (a) At least 20 of those hours must be in one of the years
         (b) At least 24 of those hours must be directly related to government and government auditing

   b. Independence
   c. Due professional care
   d. Quality control--audit organizations conducting government audits should have <u>both</u> an appropriate <u>internal</u> quality control system and participate in an <u>external</u> quality control review program (e.g., peer review)

3. Field work standards--AICPA field work standards apply, plus the following

   a. Planning

      (1) Audits, planning should include consideration of audit requirements of all levels of government
      (2) Tests should be made of compliance with applicable laws and regulations; the auditor should

         (a) Include procedures to provide reasonable assurance of detecting errors, irregularities, and illegal acts that could have a direct and material effect on financial amounts
         (b) Be aware of the possibility of illegal acts which could have an indirect and material effect on financial statements

   b. Evidence--additional standards are added to require additional documentation (e.g., appropriate cross referencing, evidence of review)

4. Reporting Standards--AICPA reporting standards (GODC) are applied plus the following

   a. <u>Report on financial statements</u>--A statement should be included in audit report stating that audit followed GAAS and GAGAS
   b. <u>Report on compliance</u>--prepare a written report on the tests of compliance with applicable laws and regulations
   c. <u>Report on internal controls</u>--prepare a written report on understanding of internal control structure and assessment of control risk made as part of a financial audit

     NOTE: The effect of b. and c. is to add information on compliance with laws and on the internal control structure to the information normally provided in financial statement audits. This information may be presented in three types of reports either separate or added to the audit report. Frequently, three separate reports may be expected. Details of the reports are presented in the outline of SAS No. 63.

   d. If general disclosure of certain information is prohibited by law, the report should state the nature of the omitted information and the requirement that makes omission necessary
   e. The report should be distributed to appropriate officials in the organization and to those with oversight authority; unless restricted by law or regulation, copies should be made available for public inspection

B. Performance Audits

    1. Types

        a. <u>Economy and efficiency audits</u> (of an entity)

            (1) Whether entity acquiring, protecting, and using resources
economically and efficiently
            (2) Causes of inefficiencies or uneconomic practices
            (3) Compliance with laws and regulations concerning economy and
efficiency

        b. <u>Program audits</u> to determine whether desired benefits are being achieved,
and compliance with laws

            (1) Whether desired benefits being achieved
            (2) Effectiveness
            (3) Entity receiving program compliance with laws and regulations
related to program

    2. General standards--these are the same as for financial audits (see A.2.

       above)

    3. Field work standards--the work is to be

        a. Adequately planned,
        b. Properly supervised,
        c. Internal control is to be assessed when necessary,
        d. An assessment of compliance with laws and regulations is required, and
        e. Sufficient competent and relevant evidence is to be obtained

    4. Reporting standards--in general, similar to financial audits plus the

       following

        a. Audit objectives and scope
        b. Audit findings and conclusions
        c. Cause of problem areas noted in audit and recommendations
        d. Include

            (1) Views of responsible officials,
            (2) Noteworthy accomplishments by management,
            (3) Issues needing further study

STATEMENTS ON STANDARDS FOR ACCOUNTING AND REVIEW SERVICES

AR 100 Compilation and Review of Financial Statements (SSARS 1)

<u>Overall Objective and Approach</u>--This section presents guidance on appropriate
procedures and reporting for <u>compilation</u> and <u>review</u> engagements of <u>nonpublic</u> entity
financial statements. In general terms, a nonpublic entity is one whose securities
are not traded in a public market; related, an entity which is in the process of
registering securities for sale to the public, or is a subsidiary, joint venture,
etc. of a public entity, does <u>not</u> qualify as a nonpublic entity.

The section states that an accountant should not submit unaudited financial
statements of a nonpublic entity to his client or others unless, as a minimum, s/he
compiles the statements. This, for example, prohibits CPAs from merely typing or
reproducing client financial statements. Also, because compilations, review, and
audits are distinctly different, the accountant should establish an understanding
with the entity, preferably in writing, regarding the services to be performed.
This understanding should also make clear that a compilation (or review) cannot be

relied upon to disclose misstatements, but that the accountant will inform the entity of any such matters that come to his/her attention.

The introduction to the auditing modules (immediately preceding the Professional Responsibilities module) presents a discussion of the nature of the attest function and explains that compilations are an accounting service, while reviews are an attest service. For that reason, compilation reports provide no explicit assurance with respect to the financial information, while reviews provide limited (negative) assurance.

The outline is organized as follows: (a) Compilations, (b) Reviews, (c) Information relevant to both compilations and reviews.

A. Compilation of financial statements

    1. Definition-- A <u>compilation</u> involves presenting in the form of financial statements information that is the representation of management (owners) without undertaking to express any assurance on the statements

    2. Compilation performance requirements

        a. The accountant should understand the accounting principles and practices of the industry in which the entity operates

        NOTE: This knowledge is normally obtained through past experience, AICPA guides, industry publications, financial statements of other entities in the industry, textbooks, periodicals, or individuals knowledgeable about the industry

        b. The accountant should understand the following relating to the entity's business

            (1) The nature of its business transactions
            (2) The form of its accounting records
            (3) The stated qualifications of its accounting personnel
            (4) The accounting basis on which the financial statements are to be presented
            (5) The form and content of the financial statements

            NOTE: This knowledge is normally obtained through experience with the entity or inquiry of the entity's personnel

        c. The accountant <u>is not required</u> to make any inquiries or perform any other verification procedures
        d. Before issuing a report, the accountant <u>is required</u> to read the compiled statements and consider whether such financial statements appear to be appropriate in form and free from obvious misstatements

    3. A compilation report should explicitly state that

        a. A compilation has been performed in accordance with <u>standards established by the AICPA</u>
        b. A compilation is limited to presenting in the form of financial statements information that is the representation of management (owners)
        c. The financial statements <u>have not been audited or reviewed</u> and accordingly, the accountant does not express an opinion or any other form of assurance on them

        NOTE: See section C of the Reporting module for a sample compilation report. Also, you should know the above 3 requirements

    4. Other reporting requirements for compilations

a. Any procedures performed by the accountant should <u>not</u> be described in the report

b. The accountant's report should be dated as of the date of completion of the compilation

c. Each page of the statements should be marked "See Accountant's Compilation Report"

d. The accountant may issue a report on only one of the financial statements, if so requested

e. If the financial statements do not have the disclosures required per GAAP or other basis of accounting being followed, the auditor should so indicate in a separate paragraph of the report

EXAMPLE PARAGRAPH:

Management has elected to omit substantially all of the disclosures (and the statement of cash flows) required by generally accepted accounting principles. If the omitted disclosures were included in the financial statements, they might influence the user's conclusions about the company's financial position, results of operations, and cash flows. Accordingly, these financial statements are not designed for those who are not informed about such matters.

f. If only limited note disclosures are provided, the accountant should make certain that they are labeled "Selection Information--Substantially All Disclosures Required by GAAP Are Not Included"

NOTE: "e" and "f" above relate to the situation in which a client wishes to present financial statements, often without any additional note disclosures. Consider, for example, a client who is a dentist who simply wants compiled financial statements but has no need for note disclosures.

g. If the accountant is not independent, the following should be included as the last paragraph to the report--I am not independent with respect to XYZ Company

(1) The accountant is not to describe the reason for a lack of independence

NOTE: Because compilations are accounting, and not attestation services, the accountant who is not independent is allowed to report on them

B. Review on financial statements

1. Definition--a <u>review</u> involves performing <u>inquiry</u> and <u>analytical procedures</u> that provide the accountant with a reasonable basis for expressing limited assurance that there are no material modifications that should be made to the statements for them to be in conformity with GAAP, or if applicable, with another comprehensive basis of accounting

2. Requirements relating to performing a review

a. The accountant <u>needs sufficient knowledge of the client industry and client company</u> to perform inquiry and analytical procedures to provide a reasonable basis for expressing limited assurance on the statements

NOTE: Industry knowledge may be obtained from AICPA guides, industry publications, financial statements of other entities in the industry, textbooks, periodicals, or individuals knowledgeable about the industry. The knowledge of the entity's business should include a general under- standing of the entity's organization, its operating characteristics, and the nature of its assets, liabilities, revenues, and expenses; this knowledge is ordinarily obtained through experience with the entity or its industry and inquiry of the entity's personnel.

3. Accountant's inquiry and analytical procedures consist of

    a. Inquiries concerning client's accounting principles and practices
    b. Inquiries concerning client's procedures for recording, classifying, and summarizing accounting transactions
    c. Analytical procedures to identify unusual items and relationships

        (1) Comparison of statements with prior periods
        (2) Comparison of statements with anticipated results, e.g., budgets
        (3) Study of predictable patterns of elements in the statements

    d. Inquiries concerning stockholders', board of directors', and other com- mittee meetings
    e. Reading the statements to determine whether they conform to GAAP
    f. Obtaining reports from other accountants, if any, who have audited or reviewed statements or significant components of the client
    g. Inquiries of persons responsible for statements

        (1) Whether statements are per GAAP or another comprehesive method of accounting
        (2) Changes in the client's business activities or accounting methods
        (3) Any exceptions concerning other analytical procedures
        (4) Subsequent events having a material effect on statements

        NOTE: Several essay questions and many multiple choice questions have required knowledge of the above procedures

4. A review does not contemplate

    a. A consideration of internal control
    b. Tests of accounting records, and
    c. Any other audit procedures
    d. However, additional procedures to achieve limited assurance are required if auditor finds mistakes, incomplete presentations, etc.

5. The working papers should contain

    a. Accountant's inquiry and analytical procedures
    b. Unusual matters arising in the review, including their disposition
    c. Possibly a representation letter from chief executive officer and chief financial officers

6. A review report should explicitly state that

    a. A review was performed in accordance with standards established by the AICPA
    b. All information included in the financial statements is the representation of the management (owners) of the entity
    c. A review consists principally of inquiries of company personnel and analytical procedures applied to financial data
    d. A review is substantially less in scope than an audit, the objective of which is the expression of an opinion regarding the financial statements taken as a whole and, accordingly, no such opinion is expressed

e. The accountant is not aware of any material modifications that should be made to the financial statements in order for them to be in conformity with GAAP, other than those modifications, if any, indicated in his/her report

NOTE: Know the above 5 elements of a review report. Also know that the first 2 elements are in the report's first paragraph, the second two in the second paragraph; the last one is in the third paragraph.

7. Other overall reporting requirements for reviews

   a. Any other procedures performed by the accountant should <u>not</u> be described
   b. The date of the report should be the date of completion of the procedures
   c. Each page of the statements should be marked "See Accountant's Review Report"
   d. A separate paragraph is used for modifying the standard report

C. Information relevant to both compilations and reviews

1. Departures from GAAP should be treated as follows

   a. The client should be asked to revise the statements to comply with GAAP

   b. <u>If the information is not revised</u>, the report should be modified

      (1) Modify the final standard paragraph of the report to indicate that a misstatement has been discovered and add an additional paragraph which follows describing the departure (including its effect <u>if</u> management has calculated it)

   c. If the accountant believes that modification of the standard report is not adequate to indicate the financial statement deficiencies taken as a whole, the accountant should withdraw from the engagement and provide no further services with respect to those financial statements

      (1) The accountant may wish to consult with legal counsel in those circumstances

      NOTE: Recall that for compilations, when note disclosures are omitted, the accountant can modify the compilation report to so cite their omission (see points A.4.e. and f. above). For reviews (as well as audits), such omissions are treated as departures from GAAP which will lead to reports which are other than unqualified.

2. Subsequent discovery of facts existing at the date of the report

   a. Consult with AU 561 (see outline)
   b. Consult with an attorney

3. Supplementary information

   a. The accountant should clearly indicate any responsibility being taken for the supplementary data

      NOTE: If you do not recall the nature of supplementary information (e.g., quarterly information included in the annual report) see the outline of AU 553

   b. When the accountant has compiled the financial statements and other data, the compilation report should also include the other data
   c. When the accountant has reviewed the financial statements, the report (or a separate report) should state that

    (1)   The review has been made primarily to express limited assurance that there are no material modifications that should be made to the financial statements

    (2)   The other information is presented only for supplementary analysis purposes and either

        (a)   Has been subject to inquiry and analytical procedures, and the accountant did not become aware of any material misstatements, or

        (b)   Has <u>not</u> been subjected to the inquiry and analytical procedures and the accountant does not express an opinion or any other form of assurance on such data

AR 200 Reporting on Comparative Financial Statements (SSARS 2)

<u>Overall Objective and Approach</u>--This section presents guidance for reporting on comparative statements of a nonpublic entity, at least a portion of which are not audited (i.e., one or more years is compiled or reviewed). The existence of compiled, reviewed, and audited financial statements, as well as financial statements with which the auditor has had no association presents a situation in which there are numerous implementation issues related to compiled statements. For example, perhaps the first year's statements have been reviewed, and the second year's compiled.

This section presents and resolves an overwhelming number of situations which may occur in practice. In the outline we attempt to provide information on the most frequent cases which one would expect to see on the CPA exam. You should be aware that several questions on the exam have required candidates either to prepare or to critique comparative reports of this nature.

The outline provides (a) overall guidance as well as (b) enumerating important situations.

A. Overall guidance

    1. The accountant's report should cover each period presented as a comparative statement

        a. An entity may include financial information with which the accountant is not associated (e.g., last year's statements) in a report that also includes information with which the accountant is associated (e.g., this year's compiled or reviewed statements)

            (1)   When the information is presented on separate pages, the information should clearly indicate that the accountant is not associated

            (2)   The accountant should not allow his/her name to be associated with such financial statements (i.e., the year which s/he is not associated) that are presented in columnar form with financial statements on which s/he has reported

                (a)   If the entity still intends to use the accountant's name, the accountant should consult with his/her attorney

    2. When compiled statements of one year omit most of the disclosures required per GAAP (e.g., do not include footnotes) they should not be presented with another year's which do have such disclosures, and the accountant should <u>not</u> issue a report on such comparative statements

3. Each page of comparative financial statements compiled or reviewed by an accountant should include a reference such as "See Accountant's Report"

4. The following is general guidance on the overall form of comparative reports

    a. When both years have been compiled or reviewed, the report uses the standard form, modified to include both years

    b. A continuing accountant who performs the same or a <u>higher level of service</u> with respect to financial statements of the current period (e.g., review this year, compilation last year) should update his report on the financial statements of a prior period presented with those of the current period

       EXAMPLE: Issue a standard review report supplemented with the following paragraph

          "The accompanying 19X1 financial statements of XYZ were compiled by me. A compilation is limited to representing in the form of financial statements information that is the representation of management. I have not audited or reviewed the 19X1 financial statements and accordingly, do not express an opinion or any other form of assurance on them.

    c. A continuing accountant who performs a <u>lower level of service</u> with respect to the financial statements of the current period (e.g., compilation this year, review last year) should either

       (1) Include a separate paragraph in his/her report with a description of the responsibility assumed for the prior period statements or

       (2) Reissue his/her report on the financial statements of the prior period

    d. EXAMPLES: Approaches (1) and (2)

       (1) Issue a compilation report on 19X2 which includes a paragraph summarizing the responsibility assumed for the 19X1 financial statements. The description should include the original date of the review report and should state that no procedures have been performed on the review after that date.

       (2) Combine the compilation report on 19X2 with the reissued report on the financial statements of the prior period <u>or</u> print them separately. The combined report should state that the accountant has not performed any procedures in connection with that review engagement after the date of the review report.

B. Other situations

  1. <u>Existence of a predecessor auditor</u>--as is the case with audited financial statements, a decision must be made as to whether the predecessor will reissue his/her compilation or review report

    NOTE: The situation here is one in which a choice is made as to whether two reports will be associated with the comparative information (19X1 the predecessor's, 19X2 the successor's) <u>or</u> one report in which the successor summarizes the predecessor's findings

    a. <u>Reissuance of the predecessor's report</u>

    (1)   The predecessor must determine whether his/her report is appropriate based on

        (a)   Current vs. prior period statement format

        (b)   Newly discovered subsequent events

        (c)   Changes in the financial statements affecting the report

    (2)   The predecessor should also perform the following procedures

        (a)   Read the current statements and the successor's report

        (b)   Compare prior and current statements

        (c)   Obtain representation letter from successor suggesting that s/he knows of no problems with the prior statements

    (3)   If anything comes to the predecessor's attention that affects the report, the predecessor should

        (a)   Make any necessary inquiries and perform any necessary procedures

        (b)   If necessary insist that the client revise the statements and revise the report as appropriate (normally add an explanatory paragraph)

            1] The report will be "dual dated"--see outline of AU 530 on dual dating

b. No reissuance of predecessor's report (i.e., it is not presented)

    (1)   The successor auditor should add a paragraph stating that the

        (a)   Prior (comparative) statements were compiled (or reviewed) by another accountant

        (b)   Date of the predecessor's report

        (c)   Assurance, if any, provided in the predecessor's report

        (d)   Reasons for any modification of the predecessor's report

2. <u>19X2 reviewed (or compiled) and 19X2 audited</u>--The situation here is similar to above with a predecessor auditor in that the prior years report may be reissued, or a summary of it included in the 19X2 report

3. When an accountant is reporting on financial statements that now omit substantially all disclosures (i.e., notes), which when originally issued did not omit such disclosures, a paragraph is added to the report indicating that the disclosures have been omitted; also, the final paragraph indicates the accountant's former form of association with the information

EXAMPLE: 19X1 has been reviewed, and now, in 19X2, 19X1 statements have been compiled from the previously reviewed statements. A compilation report is issued on 19X2, with a paragraph on the omitted disclosures (see A.4.e. above) and with a paragraph on the 19X1 statements such as the following:

> *The accompanying 19X1 financial statements were compiled by me from financial statements that did not omit substantially all of the disclosures required by generally accepted accounting principles and that I previously reviewed as indicated in my report dated March 1, 19X2.*

4.   When a company changes its status (i.e., nonpublic to public, or vice versa) the proper reporting responsibility is determined by the status at the time of reporting

AR 300 Compilation Reports on Financial Statements Included in Certain Prescribed Forms

Overall Objective and Approach--This section presents guidance on issuing compilation reports related to information presented on prescribed forms, designed by the bodies with which they filed (e.g., governmental bodies, trade associations, banks). For example, assume that a state governmental body has a balance sheet form which all companies incorporated in that state are required to fill out with appropriate financial information. Also, assume that the state requires that a compilation report be filed with the report. This section deals with the manner in which the auditor should report on such forms. This section also relates directly to the material presented in AU 621, special reports, on prescribed forms (in that section some form of association other than compilation for a nonpublic entity is assumed). The following outline provides general guidance on the report issued.

A.   General guidance on compilation reports for prescribed forms

1.   An overall presumption is made that the form is sufficient to meet the needs of the body which has designed or adopted it

2.   Departures from GAAP

a.   <u>Required to appropriately complete the form</u>--There is <u>no need</u> to advise such bodies of this type of departure

EXAMPLE: If, because of the requirements of the form, inventory is included on the form at cost, rather than the lower of cost and market, no indication would be provided that this departure from GAAP existed.

3.   Departures from the requirements of the prescribed form--treat in the same manner as 2.b above (add a final paragraph)

4.   When a prescribed form does not conform to the guidance provided in either AR 100 or AR 300, the accountant should not sign it, but should append an appropriate report to the prescribed form

AR 400 Communications between Predecessor and Successor Accountants

Overall Objective and Approach--This section presents guidance for situations in which a successor accountant <u>decides to communicate</u> with a predecessor accountant concerning acceptance of a compilation or a review engagement of a nonpublic entity; such communication is <u>not</u> required.

The guidance provided is similar to that in AU 315, which requires such communication prior to accepting an <u>audit</u>. As is the case with that section, inquiries of a predecessor may occur: (a) in conjunction with acceptance of the engagement, and (b) other inquiries, subsequent to acceptance of the engagement. The section also provides guidance for situations in which the successor becomes aware of information indicating the need for revision of the statements with which the predecessor is associated.

A.   Inquiries in conjunction with accepting an engagement

1.   Circumstances in which a successor might choose to communicate

      a. Information concerning client, principals, and management is limited or appears to be in need of special attention

      b. Change in accountants occurs substantially after end of period for which financial statements are to be compiled or reviewed

      c. There have been frequent changes in accountants

2. An accountant may not disclose confidential information without consent of client

      a. Except as permitted by AICPA Code of Conduct

      b. Successor accountant should request client to

         (1) Permit him/her to make inquiries

         (2) Authorize predecessor to respond completely

      c. If client refuses to comply with request for inquiry, accountant should consider reasons for, and implications of, such denial as they relate to accepting the engagement

3. May be oral or written and typically would include requests for information on

      a. Matters which might affect the integrity of management (owners)

      b. Disagreement about accounting principles or necessity of certain procedures

      c. If necessary, cooperation of management (owners) in providing additional or revised information

      d. Predecessor's understanding of reason for change in accountants

4. The predecessor should respond promptly and completely to requests made in connection with engagements

      a. If, due to unusual circumstances, response must be limited, accountant should so indicate

         (1) E.g., unusual circumstances include pending litigation but do not include unpaid fees

B. Other inquiries

1. May be made before/after acceptance of engagement to facilitate a compilation or review

2. Might include questions about prior periods' circumstances such as

      a. Deficiencies in underlying financial data

      b. Necessity of performing other accounting services

      c. Areas requiring inordinate amounts of time

3. May include request for access to predecessor's working papers

      a. Successor should request client authorization

      b. Customary for predecessor to be available for consultation and provide certain of his/her workpapers

      c. Predecessor and successor should agree on which workpapers

         (1) Will be available

         (2) May be copied

      d. Generally predecessor should provide access to workpapers relating to

         (1) Matters of continuing accounting significance

(2) Contingencies

e. Predecessor may refuse for valid business reasons, including but not limited to, unpaid fees

f. If client is considering several successors

(1) Predecessor and working papers need not be made available until client names an accountant as successor

g. Successor should not reference report on work of predecessor in his/her report except when comparative statements are being issued--see outline of AR 200.

C. Predecessor accountant's financial statements

1. If successor becomes aware of information indicating the need for revision of financial statements reported on by predecessor, the successor should

a. Request that the client inform the predecessor accountant

2. If the client refuses to inform the predecessor or the successor is not satisfied with the predecessor's actions, the successor should consult his/her attorney

AR 500 Reporting on Compiled Financial Statements (SSARS 5)

(This section amends AR 100. The amended paragraphs of SSARS 1 have been revised to reflect changes in SSARS 5)

AR 600 Reporting on Personal Financial Statements Included in Written Personal Financial Plans

Overall Objective and Approach--This section provides an exception to the AR 100 requirement that accountants either compile, review, or audit financial statements with which they are associated. The section allows accountant association with unaudited statements included in written personal financial plans prepared by the accountant. The outline presents related details.

A. Requirements relating to "unaudited" association with personal financial plans

1. Financial statements in personal financial plans need not be compiled, reviewed, or audited if

a. The accountant establishes an understanding (preferably in writing) with the client that statements will be used solely to assist the client and the client's advisors to develop and achieve personal financial goals and objectives

b. Nothing came to accountant's attention to cause him/her to believe that the financial statements will be used for other purposes

2. The accountant's report should state that the financial statements

a. Are for the financial plan,

b. May be incomplete or contain GAAP departures and should not be used for other purposes, and

c. Have not been audited, reviewed, or compiled

MINI OUTLINES

We have developed a set of Mini Outlines to assist candidates in testing their memory of essential auditing principles. These can be used after studying each module in depth and as a final review immediately prior to the CPA exam. In no way are these outlines intended to be a complete coverage of the subject matter. Candidates should use them to jog their memories and should then recall as much information as possible about the subject matter. Finally, because these outlines include only the very most essential auditing information, the lettering and numbering of the levels in the Mini Outlines at some points do not correspond to that found in module outlines. For those points in the Mini Outlines which you have forgotten, use the index to find the page(s) where that principle is discussed. However, if you are confused about a number of points, go back to the module and work through it again.

PROFESSIONAL RESPONSIBILITIES (1)*

A. General Standards and Rules of conduct
  1. General Standards--TIP
    a. Training
    b. Independence
    c. Professional Care
  2. Code of Professional Conduct
    a. Principles and rules (with interpretations and rulings)
    b. Principles and overall
      (1) Minimum levels of conduct
      (2) All members observe principles of objectivity, independence and due care
        (a) But members not in practice are not independent
        (b) Members in practice must be independent for attest services
      (3) Confidential relationship with client, not privileged communication
      (4) No false, misleading or deceptive advertising
      (5) No forwarding fees for referring client
    c. Code--Rules (with Interpretations and Rulings)
      (1) No direct or material indirect financial interest in a client
      (2) Spouse and dependents same as CPA's investment
      (3) Do not vouch for achievability of a forecast
      (4) Retention of client records is discreditable
      (5) Name should not mislead as to whether sole proprietorship, partnership, or corporation

B. Control of the Audit
  1. Planning and supervision
    a. Early appointment of auditor aids efficiency
    b. Determine preliminary materiality and audit risk
    c. Audit risk components
      (1) Inherent risk
      (2) Control risk
      (3) Detection risk
    d. Predecessor/successor auditors
      (1) Potential successor (with client permission) inquires about
        (a) Management integrity
        (b) Disagreements
        (c) Reasons for change
      (2) Successor later may wish to review predecessor workpapers
  2. Quality control
    a. Peer review advantages
      (1) Prevent poor auditing
      (2) Detect poor auditing
      (3) Self-regulation
    b. Quality control standards
      (1) Independence
      (2) Assigning personnel to engagements
      (3) Consultation
      (4) Supervision
      (5) Hiring
      (6) Professional development
      (7) Advancement
      (8) Acceptance and continuance of clients
      (9) Inspection
C. Other responsibilities
  1. Errors, management fraud, and defalcations

*Numbers in parentheses refer to Modules.

a. Design to provide reasonable
   assurance detect material errors
   and irregularities
b. If fraud suspected, report to
   appropriate management level
c. If fraud known report to audit
   committee
2. Illegal acts
   a. Recorded transactions easiest to
      detect
   b. Report to audit committee
   c. Consider withdrawing if client
      does not take appropriate action
   d. For materiality consider SFAS 5
      loss contingency criteria
3. MAS
   a. Primary services
      (1) Consultation
          (a) Use existing knowlege,
              oral, or written report

     (2) Engagement
        (a) Analytical approach
           applied to project
        (b) Greater in scope than
           consultation
  b. Do not make management decisions
4. Tax
   a. Sign if reasonable effort made to
      obtain answers
   b. Estimates OK, but indicate
   c. Errors in previous returns
      (1) Inform management
      (2) If client doesn't correct
          (a) Consider withdrawing
          (b) Do not inform regula-
              tory agencies
   d. May rely on data provided by
      client unless seems incorrect
   e. Do not modify preparer's declara-
      tion

INTERNAL CONTROL (2)

A. Outline of SAS 55
1. Internal control structure (ICS)
   a. Audit concern with controls to
      record, process, summarize and
      report financial data
   b. Elements
      (1) Control environment
      (2) Accounting system
      (3) Control procedures
   c. Control environment (O CPA CPE)
      (1) Organizational structure
      (2) Communication methods
      (3) Philosophy and operating
          style
      (4) Audit Committee
      (5) Control methods
      (6) Personnel policies and
          procedures
      (7) External influences
   d. Accounting system--identify,
      assemble, analyze, classify,
      record and report
   e. Control Procedures (IS SAD)
      (1) Independent checks
      (2) Segregation of duties
      (3) Safeguards over access
      (4) Authorization
      (5) Documents adequate
   f. General considerations
      (1) Reasonable assurance
      (2) Limitations
2. Effect of ICS on audit planning
   a. Understand design and if placed
      in operation
   b. Document
      (1) Memorandum for small client
      (2) Flowcharts, questionnaires,
          decision tables large client

3. Effect of ICS on assessing control
   risk
   a. Second purpose of consideration
      of ICS
   b. Tests of controls to evaluate
      design and operating
      effectiveness
   c. Documentation increases as
      reliance increase
B. Overall points
1. Terminology
   a. Financial Statement assertions
   b. Placed in operation vs. operating
      effectiveness
2. Other concepts
   a. Accounting vs. administrative
      controls
   b. Foreign Corrupt Practices Act
3. ICS in an audit
   a. Obtain and document understanding
      to plan
   b. Assess control risk
   c. Perform tests of controls
   d. Reassess control risk
C. Accounting cycles
1. Directional testing
2. Controls
   a. Preventive
   b. Detective
   c. Corrective
3. Transaction cycles
   a. Sales, receivable, and cash
      receipts
   b. Purchases, payables, and cash
      disbursements
   c. Inventories and production
   d. Personnel and payroll
   e. Property, plans, and equipment

D. Other Considerations
   1. Communicating with Audit Committee
      a. Reportable conditions
      b. Material weaknesses
   2. Reports on internal control

      a. Separate opinion
      b. Part of audit
      c. Regulatory agency criteria
      d. Special purpose reports
   3. Internal audit function

EVIDENCE (3)

A. General Evidence
   1. Assertions (PERCV)
      a. Presentation
      b. Existence or occurrence
      c. Rights and obligations
      d. Completeness
      e. Valuation or allocation
   2. Competent and sufficient evidential matter
      a. Valid
         (1) Direct vs. indirect
         (2) Independent sources vs. inside sources
         (3) Strong internal control vs. weak internal control
      b. Relevant
      c. Persuasive vs. convincing
      d. Accounting estimates
         (1) Determine all have been developed, are reasonable and follow GAAP
         (2) Recalculate, calculate own expectation, or review subsequent events
   3. Types of evidence
      a. Underlying accounting data
         (1) Journals
         (2) Ledgers
         (3) Manuals
         (4) Memoranda
      b. Corroborative evidence
         (1) Authoritative documents
         (2) Interrelationships
         (3) Calculations
         (4) Physical existence
         (5) Authoritative statements
         (6) Subsequent events
   4. Procedures used to gather types of evidence
         (1) Confirm
         (2) Inquire
         (3) Inspect
         (4) Observe
         (5) Reconcile
         (6) Review
         (7) Trace
         (8) Vouch
B. Specific evidence
   1. Types of substantive tests
      a. Analytical Procedures
         (1) Data relationships
         (2) Ratios

      b. Tests of details of transactions and balances
   2. Preparing substantive test audit programs
      a. Ending balance vs. input/output approach
      b. Test adequacy of I/C
      c. PERCV assertions
      d. Required procedures
   3. Documentation
      a. Purpose
         (1) Aid in audit
         (2) Support opinion
      b. Types
C. Other specific evidence topics
   1. Audit areas
      a. Cash
         (1) Kiting
         (2) Cutoff
      b. Receivables
         (1) Confirmations
         (2) Lapping
      c. Inventory
         (1) Observation is generally accepted auditing procedure
      d. Marketable securities
         (1) Coordinate with cash
      e. Property, plant, and equipment
      f. Prepaids
      g. Payables (current)
      h. Long-term debt
      i. Owner's equity
   2. Other
      a. Engagement letters
      b. Required client representation letters
      c. Using the work of a specialist
      d. Inquiry of client's lawyer
         (1) Loss contingencies
      e. Related party transactions
      f. Compliance audits
      g. Operational audits
      h. Omitted procedures discovered after the report date
D. Compilation and review procedures
   1. Primarily nonpublic entities
   2. General understanding of client's business and environment
   3. Compilation
      a. Read statements
      b. Independence not required
   4. Review
      a. Analytical procedures
      b. Read statements
      c. Reports of other auditors

REPORTS (4)

A. Financial Statement Audit Reports--
General
1. Overall issues
   a. Attestation reporting standards
      state that reports should
      (1) Identify assertion being
          reported on and nature of
          engagement
      (2) State accountant's
          conclusion
   b. Types of reports
      (1) Examinations
      (2) Reviews
      (3) Agreed-upon procedures
      (4) Compilations
2. Financial statement audit reports
   a. Standard unqualified report
   b. Disclosure and consistency not
      explicitly mentioned in report
   c. If practicable, qualified or
      adverse reports should provide
      information causing departure
B. Financial statement audit reports--
Detailed
1. Circumstances resulting in departure
   from standard report
   a. Opinion based in part on report
      of another auditor
      (1) Principal auditor reviews
          other auditor's
          independence, reputation and
          knowledge
      (2) Decision on whether to
          reference other auditor
   b. Unusual circumstances require
      GAAP departure
   c. Uncertainties
   d. Going concern question
   e. Consistency
      (1) Principle change result in
          modification
      (2) No mention of consistency if
          no changes
   f. Comparative statements
      (1) Restate past reports
      (2) Predecessor auditor involved
   g. Quarterly information incorrect,
      omitted, or not reviewed

h. Supplementary information
   required by FASB or GASB
i. Other Information included with
   financial statements
j. Emphasis of a matter

NOTE: a - j usually are unqualified
with additional explanatory language

k. Departures from GAAP--qualified
   or adverse
l. Scope limitations
   (1) Client imposed generally
       disclaim
   (2) Circumstance imposed qualify
       or disclaim
   (3) Reporting on one statement
       is not a scope limitation
m. Lack of independence--disclaimer
2. Report preparation
C. Accountant association other than audits
1. Other forms with historical financial
   statements
   a. Unaudited
   b. Compiled or reviewed
   c. Reviewed quarterly statements
   d. Condensed financial statements
2. Other reports
   a. Special reports
      (1) Comprehensive basis
          (a) Report similar to GAAP
              audit report
          (b) Statements not to be
              titled "balance sheet,"
              income statement, etc.
      (2) Special elements
      (3) Compliance reports
          (a) Negative assurance
      (4) Special purpose financial
          presentations
      (5) Prescribed forms
   b. Letters for underwriters (comfort
      letters)
      (1) Negative assurance on
          accounting related informa-
          tion
   c. Financial forecasts and projec-
      tions
      (1) Compilation
      (2) Examination

AUDIT SAMPLING (5)

A. Basic audit sampling concepts
1. Application of an audit procedure to
   less than 100%
2. Nonstatistical and statistical
   a. Advantages of statistical
      (1) Objectively quantify results
      (2) Measure sufficiency of
          evidence
      (3) Evaluate sample results
      (4) Efficient sample
   b. Disadvantages of statistical

   (1) Training auditors
   (2) Designing samples
   (3) Selecting items to be tested
3. Uncertainty and audit sampling
   a. Audit risk components
      (1) Inherent risk, control risk,
          detection risk, or
      (2) Detection risk composed of
          analytical procedure risk
          and test of details risk
   b. Nonsampling risk

(1) Risk not due to sampling process
(2) Inappropriate audit procedures
(3) Failure to recognize errors in documents examined
(4) Misinterpreting test results
c. Sampling risk
   (1) Test of controls sampling risks
       (a) Risk of assessing control risk too high
       (b) Risk of assessing control risk too low (more serious)

(2) Substantive test risks
   (a) Risk of incorrect rejection
   (b) Risk of incorrect acceptance (more serious)
d. Attribute sampling primarily for tests of controls and variables sampling for substantive tests
   (1) Attribute example--discovery sampling
   (2) Variables examples--classical (mean per unit, difference ratio) and probability-proportional-to-size

AUDITING EDP (6)

A. Flowcharting
B. Principles of auditing EDP systems
   1. Internal control consideration
      a. Must make evaluation of general and application controls
   2. General controls
      a. Organization and operation
      b. Systems development and documentation
      c. Hardware and systems software
      d. Access
      e. Data and procedural
   3. Application controls
      a. Input
      b. Processing
      c. Output
   4. Audit techniques using EDP
      a. Audit software (generalized audit software)
         (1) Approach--use auditor's software, generally with client's computer
         (2) Applications
             (a) Examine records
             (b) Test calculations
             (c) Select and print samples
             (d) Compare data in separate files
      b. Test data
         (1) Approach--auditor processes dummy transactions through client's hardware and software
         (2) Limitations
             (a) May be difficult to keep test data out of client's records
             (b) Use proper client program
             (c) Time to develop

      c. Integrated test facility--similar to test data but for data base environment

d. Parallel simulation (controlled re-processing)
   (1) Approach--recalculate actual client data using auditor's software
   (2) Limitations
       (a) Time-consuming to integrate with client's system
       (b) Compatibility problems
       (c) Processing time
C. Unique characteristics of specific EDP systems
   1. Batch processing
   2. Data base processing
   3. Small computer environments
   4. Service bureau/center

CHAPTER SIX
BUSINESS LAW MODULES

Introduction

Module 7/Contracts (CONT)

Module 8/Sales (SALE)

Module 9/Commercial Paper (CPAP)

Module 10/Secured Transactions (SECU)

Module 11/Bankruptcy (BANK)

Module 12/Suretyship (SURE)

Module 13/Agency (AGEN)

Mini Outlines

INTRODUCTION

The business law section of the CPA examination tests the candidate's

1. Ability to recognize legal problems
2. Knowledge of legal principles with respect to the topics listed above
3. Ability to apply the legal principles to the problem situation in order to derive the textbook solution

Refer to "Self-Study Program" in Chapter 1 for detailed suggestions on how to study the business law outlines and business law questions. The basic procedure for each of the 15 business law modules is

1. Work 10 to 15 multiple choice questions to indicate your proficiency and familiarity with the type and difficulty of questions.
2. Study the outlines in this volume.
3. Work the remaining multiple choice questions. Study the answer explanations of those you missed or had trouble with.
4. Work the essay questions.

Answering Business Law Questions

Law essay questions frequently require a conclusion, e.g.,

> *Is the instrument in question negotiable commercial paper?*

> *Assuming the instrument is negotiable, does Meglo qualify as a holder in due course entitled to collect the full $3,000?*

In many cases, you will be asked to begin your answer with an unequivocal yes or no followed by a period. Recognize that you are not used to this type of situation. Follow the solutions approach for essay questions as outlined in Chapter 3.

Virtually all of these questions requiring conclusions also require the reasons for the conclusions. Clearly, an unsupported yes or no will be worth little more than a blank answer. Always explain the legal principle(s) involved, and justify your application of the principle(s). Do not wander into other areas or deal with legal principles not specifically required by the question. Once again, "what will appear on the unofficial solution?"

The AICPA Content Specification Outline of the coverage of business law, including the authors' frequency analysis thereof (last nine exams), appears on the following pages.

Immediately following the frequency analysis is a summary of business law essay questions referenced to our study modules.

Sources of the Law

Law comes from two sources: statutes and common law. Common law is that which has evolved through court decisions. Decisions of higher courts are binding on lower courts in the same jurisdiction. Common law is applied where there is no statute covering the issue and also to help interpret statutes.

AICPA CONTENT SPECIFICATION OUTLINE/FREQUENCY ANALYSIS[*]
BUSINESS LAW

	May 1985	Nov. 1985	May 1986	Nov. 1986	May 1987	Nov. 1987	May 1988	Nov. 1988	May 1989
I. The CPA and the Law									
A. Common Law Liability to Clients and Third Persons	– [.50]	– [1]	– [1]	5	– [.75]	5	2 [.50]	– [.50]	5
B. Federal Statutory Liability									
1. Securities Acts	– [.50]	–	–	2	–	2	1	– [.50]	2
2. Internal Revenue Code	–	–	–	1	–	2	1	–	2
C. Workpapers, Privileged Communication, and Confidentiality	–	–	–	2	– [.25]	1	1	–	1
Total MC	–	–	–	10	–	10	5	0	10
Total Essays	1	1	1	–	1	–	.5	1	–
Actual Percentage[**] (AICPA 10%)	10%	10%	10%	10%	10%	10%	10%	10%	10%
II. Business Organizations									
A. Agency									
1. Formation and Termination	3	– [.50]	–	–	1	1	1	3	1
2. Liabilities of Principal	–	–	1	–	1	–	–	–	–
3. Disclosed and Undisclosed Principals	–	–	1	–	–	2	–	–	–
4. Agency Authority and Liability	2	–	–	–	1	–	2	–	2
B. Partnerships and Joint Ventures									
1. Formation and Existence	1	–	–	–	–	–	–	–	1
2. Liabilities and Authority of Partners and Joint Owners	–	–	–	–	–	1	1	– [.75]	1
3. Allocation of Profit or Loss	–	–	–	–	1	1	1	–	–
4. Transfer of Interest	2	– [.50]	2	–	–	1	–	–	1
5. Termination, Winding Up, and Dissolution	1	–	1	–	–	–	1	– [.25]	–
6. Joint Ventures***	–	–	1	–	–	–	–	–	–
7. Limited Partnership***	2	–	–	–	3 [1]	1	– [.50]	1	–

[*] Except where noted, the line items in the outline are the AICPA's; the frequencies, tabulations, and actual percentages are the authors'.

[**] The "actual percentage" is a measure of the relative coverage of the specific area (i.e., I, II, etc.) on each Business Law exam. This percentage includes both multiple choice questions and essays/problems based on the point allocation used by the AICPA (i.e., multiple choice are assigned 1 point each and essays are 10 points each; note that the number of essays, or portions thereof, for each topic is shown in brackets right below questions for that topic.

*** These line items in the outline have been added by the authors.

AICPA CONTENT SPECIFICATION OUTLINE/FREQUENCY ANALYSIS (CONTINUED)
BUSINESS LAW

	May 1985	Nov. 1985	May 1986	Nov. 1986	May 1987	Nov. 1987	May 1988	Nov. 1988	May 1989
C. Corporations									
1. Formation, Purposes, and Powers	1	1	- [.25]	-	1	-	-	1	- [.33]
2. Stockholders, Directors, and Officers	2	2	- [.50]	- [1]	1	- [.50]	-	1 [.10]	- [.67]
3. Financial Structure, Capital, and Dividends	1	1	- [.25]	-	1	- [1]	1	-	-
4. Merger, Consolidation, and Dissolution	-	-	-	-	-	-	-	-	-
D. Estates and Trusts									
1. Formation and Purposes	1	1	1	-	- [.50]	-	1	1	-
2. Allocation Between Principal and Income	-	-	1	-	- [.50]	1	1	1	1
3. Fiduciary Responsibilities	-	-	1	-	-	1	1	1	1
4. Distributions and Termination	-	-	1	-	-	1	-	-	2
Areas No Longer Tested	-	-	1	-	-	-	-	-	-
Total MC	16	6	10	-	10	10	10	9	10
Total Essays	-	1	1	2	1	1	1	1.1	1
Actual Percentage (AICPA 20%)	16%	16%	20%	20%	20%	20%	20%	20%	20%
III. Contracts									
A. Offer and Acceptance	4	3	2	3	4	- [1]	2	3	4
B. Consideration	-	1	1	2	2	1	2	[.50]	1
C. Capacity, Legality, and Public Policy	-	1	2	2	1	1 [.25]	1	1	1
D. Statute of Frauds	1 [.50]	1	1	1	2	1 [.25]	1	1	2
E. Statute of Limitations	1	-	1	1	-	-	1	-	-
F. Fraud, Duress, and Undue Influence	2	3	2	2	2	2	1	1	1
G. Mistake and Misrepresentation	-	1	1	1	1	-	-	1	1
H. Parol Evidence Rule	1	1	1	-	-	-	-	1	1
I. Third-Party Rights	1	1	1	-	1	-	-	1	1
J. Assignments	1	1	1	1	-	-	1	-	1
K. Discharge, Breach, and Remedies	-	1	2	2	2	-	1	1	2
Areas No Longer Tested	1	1	-	-	-	-	-	-	-
Total MC	12	15	15	15	15	5	10	10	15
Total Essays	.50	-	-	-	-	1	.5	.5	-
Actual Percentage (AICPA 15%)	17%	15%	15%	15%	15%	15%	15%	15%	15%

AICPA CONTENT SPECIFICATION OUTLINE/FREQUENCY ANALYSIS (CONTINUED)
BUSINESS LAW

	May 1985	Nov. 1985	May 1986	Nov. 1986	May 1987	Nov. 1987	May 1988	Nov. 1988	May 1989
IV. Debtor-Creditor Relationships									
A. Suretyship									
1. Liabilities and Defenses	-	-	-	-	1	-	-	1	-
2. Release of Parties	-	1	-	1	1	-	-	-	-
3. Remedies of Parties	-	-	-	1	-	-	-	-	-
4. Co-surety***	-	1	-	1	2	-	2	1	-
B. Bankruptcy									
1. Voluntary and Involuntary Bankruptcy	-	2	- [.80]	-	1 [.67]	-	2	1	- [.5]
2. Effects of Bankruptcy on Debtor and Creditors	-	2	- [1]	1	4	- [.33]	5	6	- [.5]
3. Reorganizations	-	1	-	-	1	-	1	1	-
Areas No Longer Tested	-	3	-	-	-	-	-	-	-
Total MC	-	10	-	4	10	-	10	10	-
Total Essays	1	-	1	.80	-	1	-	-	1
Actual Percentage (AICPA 10%)	10%	10%	10%	12%	10%	10%	10%	10%	10%
V. Government Regulation of Business									
A. Regulation of Employment									
1. Federal Insurance Contributions Act	1	1	1	1	1	2	1	1	1
2. Federal Unemployment Tax Act	1	-	1	1	1	-	1	-	1
3. Workers' Compensation Acts	1	1	1	1	1	1	1	- [.5]	1
B. Federal Securities Acts									
1. Securities Registration	-	-	1	2	1	2	2	2	3
2. Reporting Requirements	-	-	1	2	2	1	1	1	1
3. Exempt Securities and Transactions	2	- [.75]	3	3	4	2	3	1	3
4. Civil Remedies***	-	-	1	-	-	1	-	-	-
5. Proxy Solicitations and Tender Offers***	-	-	-	-	-	1	1	-	-
6. Anti-fraud Provisions***	-	-	1	-	-	-	-	-	-
Areas No Longer Tested	- [1]	3 [.25]	1	-	-	-	-	-	-
Total MC	5	5	10	10	10	10	10	5	10
Total Essays	1	1	-	-	-	-	-	.5	-
Actual Percentage (AICPA 10%)	15%	15%	10%	10%	10%	10%	10%	10%	10%

AICPA CONTENT SPECIFICATION OUTLINE/FREQUENCY ANALYSIS (CONTINUED)
BUSINESS LAW

	May 1985	Nov. 1985	May 1986	Nov. 1986	May 1987	Nov. 1987	May 1988	Nov. 1988	May 1989
VI. Uniform Commercial Code									
A. Commercial Paper									
1. Types of Negotiable Instruments	2	1	1	-	-	2	1	2	2
2. Requisites for Negotiability	2	2	2	2	1	1	1	2	2
3. Transfer and Negotiation	1	2	1	1	-	1	-	1	1
4. Holders and Holders in Due Course	1	2	1	1	-	1	1	1	-
5. Liabilities, Defenses, and Rights	1	1	1	1	- [1]	1	-	1	2
6. Discharge	-	1	-	-	-	-	-	-	-
B. Documents of Title and Investment Securities									
1. Warehouse Receipts	1	-	1	1	-	1	1	1	1
2. Bills of Lading	-	-	-	-	-	-	-	-	-
3. Issuance, Transfer, and Registration of Securities	-	-	-	-	-	-	-	-	-
C. Sales									
1. Contracts Covering Goods	1 [.50]	1	2	1	1	1 [.67]	-	2	-
2. Warranties	1	-	1	1	3	1	1	2	1
3. Product Liability	-	- [1]	1	1	-	1	- [.40]	-	-
4. Risk of Loss	-	2	- [1]	-	1	1 [1]	-	2	1 [.25]
5. Performance and Obligations	-	1	-	-	1 [1]	-	-	2	2 [.25]
6. Remedies and Defenses	1	-	-	-	3	- [.33]	-	1	1
D. Secured Transactions									
1. Attachment of Security Agreements	1	-	1	1	1	1	-	1	- [.25]
2. Perfection of Security Interests	1	-	-	1	1	1	-	1	-
3. Priorities	3	1	3	1	2	1	- [1]	1	1 [.25]
4. Rights of Debtors, Creditors, and Third Parties	2	1	-	1 [.20]	1	1	-	1	1
Total MC	18	15	15	13	15	15	5	21	15
Total Essays	.50	1	1	1.20	1	1	2	.4	1
Actual Percentage (AICPA 25%)	23%	25%	25%	25%	25%	25%	25%	25%	25%

AICPA CONTENT SPECIFICATION OUTLINE/FREQUENCY ANALYSIS (CONTINUED)
BUSINESS LAW

VII. Property	May 1985	Nov. 1985	May 1986	Nov. 1986	May 1987	Nov. 1987	May 1988	Nov. 1988	May 1989
A. Real and Personal Property									
1. Distinctions Between Realty and Personalty	1	1	-	-	- [.67]	1	-	-	-
2. Types of Ownership	-	1	2	2	-	2	2	1	- [.33]
3. Lessor-Lessee	-	1	2	-	-	1	1	1	- [.33]
4. Deeds, Recording, Title Defects, and Title Insurance	2	1	2	2	-	1	1	1	-
B. Mortgages									
1. Characteristics	-	1	-	1	-	-	2	-	-
2. Recording Requirements	1	1	1	-	-	1	1	1	-
3. Priorities	1	1	3	1	-	1	1	1	-
4. Foreclosure	1	-	-	-	-	-	-	-	- [.33]
C. Fire and Casualty Insurance									
1. Coinsurance	1	1	-	1	-	1	1	- [.17]	-
2. Multiple Insurance Coverage	-	-	-	-	- [.33]	1	-	- [.17]	-
3. Insurable Interest	1	1	-	-	-	1	1	- [.16]	-
Areas No Longer Tested	1	-	-	1	-	-	-	-	-
Total MC	9	9	10	8	-	10	10	5	-
Total Essays	-	-	-	-	1	-	-	.5	1
Actual Percentage (AICPA 10%)	9%	9%	10%	8%	10%	10%	10%	10%	10%

BUSINESS LAW
Essay Summary

Date	Contracts	Uniform Commercial Code	Debtor/Creditor Relationship	Business Organizations	CPA and The Law	Gov't Regulation of Business	Property
5/89		Sales-Risk of loss (1/4); transfer of property rights (1/4) M8; Sec. Trans.-attachment (1/4); priorities (1/4) M10	Bankruptcy - Involuntary petition (1/2); claims (1/4); discharge of debt (1/4) M11	Corp.-reacquisition of stock and directors' liability (2/3); contract with officer (1/3) M15			Property-liability on mortgage (1/3); subletting (1/3); property interests (1/3) M19
11/88	Consideration (1/2) M7	Sales-Product liab. (2/5) M8		Corp.-stkhlders directors & officers (1/10) M15; Part.-liab., authority of partners (3/4); termination, winding up & dissolution (1/4) M14	Common law liab. to clients & 3rd parties (1/2) M17; Federal Statutory liab. under Securities Acts (1/2) M17	Workers' Compensation (1/2) M18	Fire & Casualty Insurance-Coinsurance (1/6); multiple insurance coverage (1/6); insurable interest (1/6) M20
5/88	Statute of Frauds (1/4); Capacity, legality, & public policy (1/4) M7	Sales - Risk of loss M8; Secured Transactions - priorities M10		Part.-limited part. (1/2) M14; Corp.-stkhlders, directors & officers (1/2) M15	Common law liab. to clients & 3rd parties (1/2) M17		
11/87	Offer & Acceptance M7	Sales - Contracts for Goods (2/3); remedies & defenses (1/3) M8	Bankruptcy - voluntary and involuntary (2/3); effects on debtor and creditors (1/3) M11	Corp.-financial structure, capital & dividends M15			
5/87		Commercial Paper - liab., defenses, & rights M9		Estates & Trusts- formation & purposes (1/2); allocation between principal and income (1/2) M21	Common law liab. to clients & 3rd parties (3/4); Workpapers, privileged communication (1/4) M17		Realty & Personalty (2/3) M19; Fire & Casualty insurance multiple insurance coverage (1/3) M20
11/86		Sales - performance & obligations M8; Secured transactions - rights of debtor, creditors, 3rd parties (1/5) M10	Bankruptcy - voluntary and involuntary (4/5) M11	Corp.-stkhlders, directors & officers M15; Part.-limited part. M14			
5/86		Sales - Risk of loss M8	Bankruptcy - effects on debtor and creditors M11	Corp.-formation, purposes, powers (1/4); stkhlders, directors & officers (1/2); financial structure, capital & dividends (1/4) M15	Common law liab. to clients & 3rd parties M17		
11/85		Sales - Product liab. M8		Agency-formation & termination (1/2) M13; Part.-transfer of interest (1/2) M14	Common law liab. to clients & 3rd parties M17 Fed. Sec. Acts-exempt securities (3/4) M16; areas no no longer tested (1/4)		
5/85	Statute of Frauds (1/2) M7	Sales - Contracts covering goods (1/2) M8	Bankruptcy - effects on debtor and creditors M11		Common law liab. to clients & 3rd parties (1/2) Fed. statutory liab. under Securities Acts (1/2) M17	Areas no longer tested	

M - Module reference

Most business law is regulated by the individual states and therefore may differ from state to state. The Uniform Commercial Code (UCC) has been adopted (sometimes with small changes) by all states except Louisiana, and also is law in the District of Columbia. The CPA exam tests the content of the 1972 Uniform Commercial Code (as amended). The UCC has caused both modernization of business law and uniformity among the states. Wherever applicable, the UCC is to be used on the CPA Examination. The UCC covers the following areas on the CPA Examination

1. Contracts--for sales of goods only
2. Negotiable Instruments
3. Secured Transactions
4. Documents of Title
5. Investment Securities

Most other areas are governed by individual state statutes and common law. Nevertheless, general rules of law can be stated for these areas and the rules provided herein are to be used on the CPA Examination. For some subjects, there are uniform acts, e.g., Uniform Partnership Act. These are not to be confused with federal law. They are uniform in that most states have enacted them as statutes either in their entirety or with small changes and therefore can be used as the general law in that area.

The areas covered by federal law are

1. Accountant's Legal Liability (as provided in the Securities Acts)
2. Federal Securities Law
3. Bankruptcy
4. Employer-Employee Relationships (except for Workers' Compensation)

Mini Outlines/Final Review

At the end of this chapter we have provided Mini Outlines of the modules in this chapter. These outlines are to be used as a final review tool and not as a primary study source.

CONTRACTS

<u>Overview</u>

The area of contracts is very heavily tested on the CPA Examination. A large portion of the contract rules serves as a basis for many other law topics; consequently, a good understanding of the material in this module will aid you in comprehending the material in other modules.

It is important that you realize that there are two sets of contract rules to learn. The first is the group of common law contract rules which, in general, apply to contracts that are not a sale of goods. Examples of contracts that come under common law are those that involve real estate, insurance, employment, and professional services. The second set is the contract rules contained in Article Two of the Uniform Commercial Code (UCC). The UCC governs transactions involving the sale of goods, i.e., tangible personal property. Hence, if the contract is for the sale or purchase of tangible personal property, the provisions of the UCC will apply, and not the common law. For every contract question, it is important that you determine which set of rules to apply. Fortunately many of the rules under the two sets are the same. The best way for you to master this area is to first study the common law rules for a topic. Then review the rules that are different under the UCC. Since the common law and the UCC rules have much in common, you will be learning contract law in the most understandable and efficient manner.

Contract law is tested by both essay and multiple choice questions. You need to know the essential elements of a contract because the CPA Examination tests heavily on offer and acceptance. Also, understand that an option is an offer supported by consideration. Distinguish between an option and a firm offer and understand how these are affected by revocations and rejections. You need to comprehend what consideration is and that it must be bargained for to be valid. The exam also requires that you understand that "past consideration" and moral obligations are not really consideration at all. You should have a solid understanding of the Statute of Frauds.

A. **Essential Elements of a Contract**

1. Offer

2. Acceptance

    a. When offer and acceptance have occurred, an agreement is said to have been made

3. Consideration

4. Legal capacity

5. Legality (legal purpose)

6. Reality of consent

    a. Technically not a true element, but important to consider because may be necessary for enforceability of contract

7. Statute of Frauds

    a. Not a true element, but each factual situation should be examined to determine whether it applies because certain contracts must be in writing as explained later

B. **Discussion of Essential Elements of a Contract**

1. Offer

    a. May be either written or oral (or sometimes by actions)

        EXAMPLE: Offeror takes can of soup to check out stand and pays for it without saying anything.

    b. Based on intent of offeror

(1)   Courts use objective test to determine intent

   (a)   I.e., would reasonable person think that offer had been intended

(2)   Subjective intent (what offeror actually intended or meant) is not considered

(3)   Promises made in apparent jest are not offers

   (a)   Promises that objectively appear real are offers

EXAMPLE: S says, "I offer to sell to you, B, my car for $5,000."
This is an offer, even though S may be actually joking, as long as
given the way it was said, a reasonable person would think that S
did intend to make the offer to sell his/her car.

(4)   Statements of opinion or of intent are not offers

EXAMPLE: A doctor tells a patient that he will fully recover in a
couple of days, but it actually takes two weeks. This is a
statement of opinion, not an offer.

EXAMPLE: "I am going to sell my car for $400." This is a state-
ment of intent, not an offer.

(5)   Invitations to negotiate (preliminary negotiations) are not offers, e.g., price tags or lists, auctions, inquiries, general advertisements

EXAMPLE: A says: "What would you think your car is worth?" B
says: "About $5,000." A says: "I accept your offer so I'll buy
it for $5,000." B never gave an offer. However, when A said that
he would accept, this is actually an offer which B may then accept
if she wishes.

c.   Offer must be definite and certain as to what will be agreed upon in contract under common law

(1)   Essential terms are parties, price, time for performance, subject matter (quantity and type)

(2)   If unclear or open terms are clarified in subsequent negotiations, contract will become valid

(3)   Courts allow some reasonable terms to be left open if customary to do so

EXAMPLE: C calls P, a plumber, to come and fix a clogged drain.
No price is mentioned. However, upon P's completion of the work,
he has right to collect customary fee from C.

d.   Must be communicated to offeree by offeror or his/her agent

(1)   Offeree may learn of a public offer, e.g., reward in any way; s/he merely needs knowledge of it

e.   Unilateral offer is one which expects acceptance by action rather than with promise

EXAMPLE: M says he will pay J $5 if she will mow his lawn. M has made
a unilateral offer which is accepted when J mows the lawn. If J never
mows the lawn, there is no contract and therefore no breach of contract.

(1)   Unilateral contract contains one promise (offer by offeror) and acceptance by action

f. Bilateral offer is one which expects acceptance by a promise from offeree

(1) Bilateral contract is formed when offeree accepts with a promise

EXAMPLE: R says to E, "Will you agree to work for me for 3 months at $5,000 per month?" This is a bilateral offer.

(2) Bilateral contract contains two promises

g. Mistakes in transmission of offer are deemed to be offeror's fault (risk) because s/he chose method of communication

h. Termination of offer

(1) Rejection by offeree

(a) Must be communicated to offeror to be effective

(b) Rejection is effective when received by offeror

(2) Revocation by offeror

(a) Generally, offeror may revoke offer at any time prior to acceptance by offeree

1] Revocation is effective when received by offeree

EXAMPLE: X offers to sell his car to Y stating that the offer will remain open for 10 days. However, on the 5th day Y receives a revocation of the offer from X. The offer would be terminated on the 5th day even though X stated that it would remain open for 10 days.

(b) If offeree learns by reliable means that offeror has already sold subject of offer, it is revoked

(c) Public offers must be revoked by same amount of publicity used in making offer

EXAMPLE: Offer of reward for apprehension of arsonist in a newspaper makes headlines. It cannot be revoked by a small notice in the back of the newspaper.

(d) An option is an offer that is supported by consideration and cannot be revoked before stated time

1] Option is actually a separate contract to keep offer open

a] Also called an option contract

EXAMPLE: O offers to sell her car to P and states that she will keep the offer open for 10 days if P will pay her $50. P pays the $50 and six days later O attempts to revoke the offer. P then accepts the offer by the seventh day. An agreement has been formed because the offer was an option and could not be revoked before the 10 days. Note that there were actually two contracts between O and P. The first one was the option to keep the offer open. The second was the actual sale of the car.

EXAMPLE: Same example as above except that O asked P to promise to pay $50 within 10 days to keep the offer open. The result is the same because a promise to pay money is also consideration (see "B.3.a.").

2] Also, rejection does not terminate option

          3] Note differences between option and firm offer by merchants concerning sale of goods under UCC as discussed later

    (e) Once offeree has substantially begun performance based on a unilateral offer, offeror may not revoke offer

(3) Counteroffer is a rejection coupled with offeree making new offer

> EXAMPLE: *An offer is made to sell a car for $3,000 and a counteroffer is, "I'll give you $2,500."*

    (a) Mere inquiry or request for additional or different terms is not a counteroffer and does not terminate offer

> EXAMPLE: *An offer is made to sell a car for $3,000 and an inquiry is, "Will you sell for $2,500?"*

(4) Lapse of time may terminate offer

    (a) Offeror may specify period of time, e.g., one week
    (b) If no time is specified, after reasonable time
    (c) Offeror may specify happening of an event

(5) Death or insanity of offeror terminates offer

    (a) Does not affect option contract since it is already binding

        1] Unless offeror has offered to perform personal services

    (b) Death or insanity of offeree also terminates private (personal) offers since only offeree can accept

(6) Illegality

    (a) Offer terminates if after making offer and before it is accepted, it becomes illegal

> EXAMPLE: *X offers to rent to Y an upstairs floor for a cabaret. Before Y accepts, the city adopts a fire code making use of the premises illegal without substantial rebuilding.*

(7) Bankruptcy or insolvency of either offeror or offeree terminates offer
(8) Impossibility

    (a) Offer terminates if after making offer and before it is accepted, performance becomes impossible

> EXAMPLE: *X offers his car to Y for $500, but before Y agrees to the purchase, X's car is destroyed by fire.*

2. Acceptance

  a. May be written or oral
  b. Offer may be accepted only by person to whom it was directed

    (1) Use objective test--to whom would a reasonable person believe it to be directed?
    (2) Rewards can usually be accepted by anyone who knows of them

  c. Offeree must have knowledge of offer in order to accept

> EXAMPLE: *D advertises a reward of $100 for the return of his pet dog. G, unaware of the offer, returns D's dog. G cannot require that D pay the $100 (if he later hears of the offer) because he was unaware of the*

*offer when he returned the dog. He could not "accept" an offer he did
not know existed.*

d. Intent to accept is required

   (1) Use objective test

e. Acceptance must generally be in form specified by offer

   (1) By a promise in a bilateral contract
   (2) By performance of requested act in a unilateral contract

      (a) Starting performance removes offeror's right to revoke offer, but offeree must fully perform to accept

f. Acceptance must be unequivocal and unconditional (mirror image rule)

   (1) An acceptance which attempts to change terms of offer is not acceptance, but is both a rejection and a counteroffer

      EXAMPLE: O offers to sell some real estate for $100,000 cash. E says "I accept. I'll give you $50,000 now and $50,000 plus 13% interest one year from now."

      (a) Mere inquiry is not a counteroffer

         EXAMPLE: O gives the same offer as above but this time E asks if O would accept $50,000 now and $50,000 plus 13% interest one year from now. The offer is neither accepted nor terminated.

   (2) A condition which does not change or add to terms of contract is not a counteroffer, i.e., a condition that is already part of contract because of law, even though not expressed in previous negotiations

g. Silence is not acceptance unless

   (1) Offer indicated silence would constitute acceptance, e.g., offer states "your silence is acceptance," and offeree intended his/her silence as acceptance

      (a) If offeree does not intend to accept, such language has no effect

         1] Offeree is under no duty to reply

   (2) Offeree has taken benefit of services or goods and exercised control over them when s/he had opportunity to reject them

      (a) However, statutes usually override common law rule by providing that unsolicited merchandise may be treated as a gift

   (3) Through prior dealings, by agreement between parties, or when dictated by custom, silence can be acceptance

h. Time of acceptance under common law

   (1) If acceptance is made by method specified in offer or by same method used by offeror to communicate the offer, acceptance is effective when sent, e.g., when placed in mail or when telegram is dispatched

      EXAMPLE: Offeror mails a written offer without stating the mode of acceptance. Offeree mails acceptance. Offeror, before receipt, calls offeree to revoke the offer. The contract exists because acceptance was effective when mailed and revocation of offer came too late.

    (a)   Exception: If offeree sends rejection and then acceptance, first received is effective even though offeree sent acceptance by same method used by offeror

(2)   Other methods of acceptance are considered effective when actually received by offeror

(3)   Late acceptance is not valid--it is a counteroffer and a valid contract is formed only if original offeror then accepts

(4)   If acceptance is valid when sent, a lost or delayed acceptance does not destroy validity

EXAMPLE: R wires an offer to E asking her to accept by mail. The acceptance is correctly mailed but never arrives. There is a valid agreement.

(5)   Offeror can change above rules by stating other rule(s) in offer

EXAMPLE: Offeror mails a written offer to offeree stating that acceptance is valid only if <u>received</u> by the offeror within 10 days. Offeree mails back the acceptance within 10 days but it arrives late. Acceptance has not occurred even though the offeree used the same method.

i.   Once there is an offer and acceptance, a contract is formed

    (1)   Minor details, e.g., closing details, can be worked out later
    (2)   Formalization often occurs later
    (3)   Attempted revocations or rejections after contract is formed are of no effect

j.   Offers, revocations, rejections, and counteroffers are valid when received (under both common law and UCC)

    (1)   Compare with rules for acceptances which are sometimes valid when sent and other times are valid when received

k.   <u>Uniform Commercial Code Rules</u> (Important differences from common law rules above for offers and acceptances)

    (1)   The UCC applies to sale of goods, i.e., tangible personal property, (not real property, services, or insurance contracts)

    (2)   A <u>written</u> and <u>signed</u> offer for sale of goods, <u>by a merchant</u> (i.e., one who regularly deals goods under contract), giving assurance that it will be held open for specified time is irrevocable for that period

        (a)   Called firm offer
        (b)   Unlike an option, no consideration needed
        (c)   If no time is specified, reasonable time is inferred

            1] In no case is period to exceed three months

EXAMPLE: Herb, an automobile dealer, offers to sell a car to Ike stating, "I promise to keep this offer open for 45 days." Since the offer is not written and signed by Herb, the firm offer rule does not apply and Herb may revoke the offer at any time prior to Ike's acceptance.

> *EXAMPLE: Same facts as above except that the offer is written and signed by Herb. In this case, the firm offer rule applies and Herb cannot revoke the offer for the stated period.*

    (d) If assurance is given on form supplied by offeree, it must be separately signed by offeror

    (e) Compare

        1] Firm offer rule does not work under common law
        2] Options are valid under UCC as well as common law and do not require a merchant seller
        3] Options are not limited to three months

> *EXAMPLE: C (not a merchant) agrees to sell an automobile to B, with the offer to remain open for four months. This is not a firm offer so C may revoke this offer at any time by communicating the revocation to B.*

> *EXAMPLE: Same facts as above except that B pays C to keep the offer open for four months. C cannot revoke this offer for four months because although it is not a firm offer, it is an option.*

> *EXAMPLE: Same facts as the first example except that C is a merchant and engages in a signed written offer. This is a firm offer that C could not revoke during the first 3 months, but could revoke the offer during the last month.*

(3) Unless otherwise indicated, an offer for sale of goods shall be construed as inviting acceptance in any manner and by any medium reasonable under circumstances

(4) Time of acceptance under UCC

    (a) Acceptance valid when sent if reasonable method used
    (b) Above rule does not apply if another rule is stated in offer

> *EXAMPLE: A telegraphs an offer to B without specifying when acceptance is valid but does state the offer will remain open for 5 days. Within the five days, B mails back the acceptance which arrives after that 5 days. If the subject matter is a sale of goods, there is a contract because the acceptance was good when sent. Under common law, however, the acceptance takes effect under these facts when received, so no contract would result.*

(5) Offer to buy goods for prompt shipment is construed to invite acceptance, either by seller's promise to promptly ship or prompt shipment unless offer specifies which is required for acceptance

    (a) Blurs distinction between unilateral and bilateral contracts
    (b) With respect to a unilateral offer, beginning of performance by offeree (i.e., part performance) will bind offeror if followed within a reasonable time by notice of acceptance

(6) Unequivocal acceptance of offer for sale of goods is not necessary under UCC (Battle of Forms Problem)

    (a) An acceptance containing additional terms is valid acceptance (unless acceptance is expressly conditional upon offeror's agreement to additional terms)

        1] Recall, under common law, this would be a rejection and counteroffer

    (b) Between nonmerchants, the additional terms are considered proposals to offeror for additions to contract, and unless offeror agrees to the additions, contract is formed on offeror's terms

    (c) Between merchants, these additional terms become part of contract and contract is formed on offeree's terms unless

        1] Original offer precludes such additions
        2] New terms materially alter original offer
        3] The original offeror gives notice of his/her objection within a reasonable time

(7) Even if terms are left open, a contract for sale of goods will not fail for indefiniteness if there was intent to contract and a reasonable basis for establishing a remedy is available

    (a) Open price term--construed as reasonable price at time of delivery

        1] Or parties can agree to allow third party to set price

    (b) Open place of delivery term--seller's place of business, if any

        1] Otherwise, seller's residence or if identified goods are elsewhere and their location is known to both parties at time of contracting, then at that location

    (c) Open time of shipment or delivery--becomes a reasonable time
    (d) Open time for payment--due at time and place of delivery of goods or at time and place of delivery of documents of title, if any

        1] If on credit, credit period begins running at time of shipment

(8) Even if writings do not establish a contract, conduct by parties recognizing a contract will establish one

    (a) The terms will be those on which writings agree and those provided for in UCC where not agreed on, e.g., reasonable price, place of delivery
    (b) Often occurs when merchants send preprinted forms to each other with conflicting terms and forms are not read for more than quantity and price

1. Auctions
    (1) Bid is offer
    (2) Bidder may retract bid until auctioneer announces sale completed
    (3) If auction is "with reserve," auctioneer may withdraw goods before s/he announces completion of sale
    (4) If auction "without reserve," goods may not be withdrawn unless no bid made within reasonable time
    (5) Auctions are "with reserve" unless specified otherwise

3. Consideration--an act, promise, or forbearance which is offered by one party and accepted by another as inducement to enter into agreement

a. A party binds him/herself to do (or actually does) something s/he is not legally obligated to do, or when s/he surrenders legal right

> EXAMPLE: A hits and injures P with his car. P agrees not to sue A when A agrees to settle out of court for $10,000. A's promise to pay the money is consideration. P's promise to refrain from bringing a lawsuit is consideration on his/her side.

> EXAMPLE: Using the fact pattern above, further assume that it is not clear whether A is at fault. The settlement (contract) is still enforceable if made in good faith because of possible liability.

b. Legal detriment does not have to be economic, e.g., giving up drinking, smoking, and swearing
c. Consideration must be bargained for
d. Preexisting legal duty is not sufficient as consideration because no new legal detriment is suffered by performing prior obligation

    (1) Agreement to pay lesser sum than already owed is unenforceable, but if debtor incurs a detriment in addition to paying, creditor's promise to accept lesser sum will be binding

    > EXAMPLE: X owes Y $1,000. Y agrees to accept $500 and X will also install Y's new furnace at no additional cost.

    (2) Agreement to pay more to finish a job, such as building a house, is unenforceable unless unforeseen difficulties are encountered, e.g., underground stream or marshy land under a house
    (3) Agreement to pay police officer to recover stolen goods is unenforceable

    > EXAMPLE: X promises to pay Y, a jockey, $50 to ride as hard as he can in the race. Y already owes his employer, Z, that duty so there is no consideration to enforce the agreement.

    (4) Promise to pay someone for refraining from doing something s/he has no right to do is unenforceable.

e. Past consideration (consideration for a prior act, forbearance, or agreement) is not sufficient for new contract because it is not bargained for
f. Moral obligation is generally not consideration except

    (1) Promise to pay or ratification of voidable antecedent debt or promise to perform voidable antecedent duty (e.g., ratification by infant upon reaching maturity)
    (2) Promise to pay debt barred by Statute of Limitations.
    (3) Promise to pay debt barred by bankruptcy. Promise must adhere to strict rules stated in Bankruptcy Reform Act of 1978 concerning reaffirmations of dischargeable debts.

g. Adequacy of consideration--courts generally do not look into amount of exchange as long as it is legal consideration and bargained for

    (1) Exceptions

        (a) An exchange of only unequal amounts of money is not enforceable
        (b) Negligible consideration may not be adequate, e.g., nominal consideration such as $1

h. Consideration must be legally sufficient

(1)   This does not refer to amount of consideration but refers to validity of consideration

> *EXAMPLE: C does not have a CPA license.   For $1,000 he promises not to hire himself out as a CPA.   This promise is not supported by legally sufficient consideration because C has no right to hire himself out as a CPA.*

i.   Mutuality of obligation--means both parties must be bound or neither is bound

(1)   Both parties must give consideration by paying or promising to pay for the act, promise, or forbearance of the other with something of legal value

j.   Promissory estoppel acts as substitute for consideration and renders promise enforceable--promisor is estopped from asserting lack of consideration

(1)   Elements

(a)   Detrimental reliance on promise
(b)   Reliance is reasonable and foreseeable
(c)   Damage results (injustice) if promise is not enforced

(2)   Usually applied to gratuitous promises but trend is to apply to commercial transactions.   At least recovery of expenses is allowed.

> *EXAMPLE: A wealthy man in the community promises to pay for a new church if it is built.   The church committee reasonably (and in good faith) relies on the promise and incurs the expenses.*

> *EXAMPLE: Uncle promises his nephew, who feels that college is too expensive, that he will pay for his education if the nephew obtains a degree.   Nephew reasonably (and in good faith) relies on the promise and incurs the expenses.*

k.   Modifying existing contracts

(1)   Modification of contract needs new consideration on both sides to be legally binding

> *EXAMPLE: S agrees in a written contract to sell a piece of land to P for $40,000.   S later changes his mind and demands $50,000 for the same piece of land.   The original contract is enforceable (at $40,000) even if P agrees to the increased price because although P has agreed to give more consideration, S has not given any new consideration.*

(2)   Under UCC, a contract (for sale of goods) may be modified orally or in writing without consideration if in good faith

> *EXAMPLE: S agrees to sell P 300 pairs of socks for $1.00 each. Due to rapid price increases in S's costs, he asks P if he will modify the price to $1.20 each.   P agrees.   The contract as modified is enforceable because it is covered under the UCC and does not need new consideration on both sides.*

l.   Requirements contracts

(1)   If one party agrees to supply what other party requires, agreement is supported by consideration

          (a) Reason: supplying party gives up right to sell to another; purchasing party gives up right to buy from another

          (b) Cannot be required to sell amounts unreasonably disproportionate to normal requirements

    m. Output contract

       (1) If one party agrees to sell all his/her output to another agreement is supported by consideration because s/he gives up right to sell that output to another

          (a) However, illusory contracts are not supported by consideration

    n. Promise to donate to charity is enforceable based on public policy reasons

4. Legal Capacity

    a. An agreement between parties in which one or both lack the capacity to contract is void or, in some cases, voidable

    b. Minors (persons under age 18 or 21)

       (1) A minor may contract, but agreement is voidable by minor only

          (a) Adult is held to contract unless minor disaffirms

       (2) Minor who disaffirms, in the case of non-necessaries, normally must return what is left of consideration received and may recover all of consideration given

       (3) Minor is liable for reasonable value of necessaries furnished to him/her

          (a) Minor may disaffirm contract if it is executory, i.e., not completed

          (b) Necessaries include food, clothing, shelter, education, etc., considering his/her age and position in life

       (4) Minor may disaffirm contract at any time until a reasonable time after reaching majority age

          (a) Failure to disaffirm within reasonable time after reaching majority acts as ratification; e.g., one year is too long in the absence of very special circumstances such as being out of the country

       (5) A minor may ratify within a reasonable time after reaching age of majority. Ratification prior to majority is not effective.

       (6) Unless s/he dies or becomes insane, disaffirmance must be by minor

       (7) If minor misrepresents his/her age, many jurisdictions will not allow minor to disaffirm contract; some allow other party to sue for fraud

       (8) A minor usually is liable for own torts (civil wrongs), but this may depend on his/her age (above 14 commonly liable). Parents are not liable for torts of minors unless they direct or condone certain conduct or were negligent themselves

    c. Incompetent persons

       (1) Agreement by person adjudicated insane is void

          (a) Insane person need not return consideration

(2) If contract is made before adjudication of insanity, it may be voidable by incompetent person

   (a) It will be enforceable provided there was no knowledge of insanity, the agreement is reasonable, and no advantage is taken of disabled party's condition

   (b) Where courts hold such agreements voidable, restitution is condition precedent to disaffirmance

d. Legal capacity of one intoxicated is determined by his/her ability to understand and by degree of intoxication

   (1) Contracts are enforceable, in general, unless extent of intoxication at time contract made was so great that intoxicated party did not understand terms or nature of contract--then contract voidable at option of one intoxicated if s/he returns items under contract

e. Corporations contract through agents and are limited by their charters

5. Legality

   a. Agreement is unenforceable if it is illegal or violates public policy
   b. When both parties are guilty (in pari delicto), neither will be aided; i.e., if one party had already given some consideration, s/he will not get it back

      (1) But if one party repudiates (repents) prior to performance, s/he may recover his/her consideration

         EXAMPLE: X contracts to buy stolen goods from Y. If X pays Y but then repents and refuses to accept the stolen goods, X may recover the money he paid Y.

   c. When one party is innocent, s/he will usually be given relief

      (1) A member of a class of people designed to be protected by statute is considered innocent; e.g., purchaser of stock issued in violation of blue-sky laws

   d. Types of illegal contracts

      (1) Agreement to commit crime or tort

         (a) If agreement calls for intentional wrongful interference with a valid contractual relationship, it is an illegal agreement

            1] However, a sale of a business containing a covenant prohibiting seller from owning or operating similar business as well as the termination of an employee who has agreed not to compete are legal and enforceable provided the agreement

               a] Protects legitimate interests of seller or employer without creating too large a burden on buyer or employee (based on ability to find other work)
               b] Is reasonable as to length of time under the circumstances to protect those interests
               c] Is reasonable as to area to protect interests of same area
               d] Same whether employer or employee initiated termination

> EXAMPLE: *Seller of a small bakery agrees not to compete in Washington, DC, for six months.*

    (2) Usury (contract for greater than legal interest rate)

    (3) Services rendered without a license when statute requires a license

        (a) Two types of licensing statutes

            1] Regulatory licensing statute--one that seeks to protect public from incapable, unskilled, or dishonest persons

                a] Contract is unenforceable by either party
                b] Even if work done, other need not pay because not a contract

> EXAMPLE: *X, falsely claiming to have a CPA license, performs an audit for ABC Company. Upon learning the true facts, ABC may legally refuse to pay X any fees or expenses.*

            2] Revenue-seeking statute--purpose is to raise revenue for government

                a] Contract is enforceable

> EXAMPLE: *Y, based on a contract, performed extensive yard work for M. M then finds out that Y failed to obtain a license required by the local government to raise revenue. M is obligated to pay Y the agreed-upon amount.*

    (4) Exculpatory clauses (party tries to relieve self of liability for own negligence) are against public policy

        (a) However, usually enforced if parties have relatively equal bargaining power

6. Reality of Consent--Mutual assent is essential to every agreement. If one of the following concepts is present, a contract may be void (i.e., no contract) or voidable (i.e., enforceable until party having right decides to pull out).

    a. Fraud--includes following elements

        (1) Misrepresentation of a material fact

            (a) Can be total falsehood, series of truths not true together, or concealment of physical defect
            (b) Silence is not misrepresentation unless there is duty to speak, e.g.,

                1] Fiduciary relationship between parties
                2] Seller of property knows there is a dangerous latent (hidden) defect

            (c) Must be statement of past or present fact

                1] Opinion, e.g., of value, is not fact unless from expert
                2] Prophecy is not fact; e.g., "Next year you will make twice as much"
                3] Dealers' talk, i.e., puffing, is not fact

                4] Presently existing intention in mind of the speaker is
                    fact

    (2) Intent to mislead--"scienter"

        (a) Need knowledge of falsity with intent to mislead, <u>or</u>
        (b) Reckless disregard for truth can be substituted

            1] If all elements "(1)" through "(4)" are present but
                reckless disregard is proven instead of actual knowledge
                of falsity, then it is called constructive fraud

    (3) Reasonable reliance by injured party

        (a) One who knows the truth or might have learned it by a
            reasonable inquiry may not recover

    (4) Resulting in injury to others

        (a) Giving rise to an action for damages by injured party

    (5) Remedies for fraud

        (a) Defrauded party may affirm agreement and sue for damages under
            tort of deceit, or if party is sued on contract, then s/he may
            set up fraud in reduction of damages, or
        (b) Defrauded party may rescind contract

    (6) Fraud may occur

        (a) In the inducement

            1] The misrepresentation occurs during contract negotiations
            2] Creates voidable contract at option of defrauded party

            *EXAMPLE: A represents to B that A's car has been driven
            50,000 miles when in fact it has been driven for 150,000
            miles. If B purchases A's car in reliance on this
            misrepresentation, fraud in the inducement in present,
            creating a voidable contract at B's option.*

        (b) In the execution

            1] Misrepresentation occurs in actual form of agreement
            2] Creates void contract

            *EXAMPLE: Larry Lawyer represents to Danny that Danny is
            signing his will, when in fact he is signing a promissory
            note payable to Larry. This promissory note is void
            because fraud in the execution is present.*

b. Innocent misrepresentation

    (1) An innocent misstatement made in good faith, i.e., no scienter
    (2) All other elements same as fraud
    (3) Creates right of rescission (cancellation) in other party--to
        return both parties to their precontract positions

        (a) All benefits must be returned by both parties
        (b) Does not allow aggrieved party to sue for damages

c. Mistake--an act done under an erroneous conviction

        (1) Mutual mistake (i.e., by both parties) about existence, identity, or important characteristics of subject matter in contract makes contract voidable by either party

            (a) Also called bilateral mistake
            (b) Mistake about value of subject matter is not grounds for voiding contract

        (2) Unilateral mistake generally does not allow party to void contract

            (a) Major exception for mistakes in computations for bids

                1] Contract based on mistake is voidable by party making mistake if calculation is far enough off so that other party should have known that a mistake was made

   d. Duress--a contract entered into because of duress can be voided because of invalid consent

        (1) Any acts or threats of violence or extreme pressure against party or member of party's family, which in fact deprives party of free will and causes him/her to agree, is duress

            EXAMPLE: X threatens to criminally prosecute Y unless he signs contract. This contract is made under duress.

        (2) Economic duress--contract is only voidable if one party puts other in desperate economic condition
        (3) Extreme duress creates void agreement
        (4) Ordinary duress creates voidable agreement

   e. Undue influence--the mental coercion of one person over another which prevents understanding or voluntary action

        (1) Usually occurs when very dominant person has extreme influence over weaker person
        (2) Also occurs through abuse of fiduciary relationship, e.g., CPA, attorney, guardian, trustee, etc.

   f. Unconscionable contract--an oppressive contract in which one party has taken severe, unfair advantage of the other, usually because of latter's absence of choice or poor education

        (1) Under these circumstances court may void contract or reform terms so as to be fair to both parties

   g. Hardship, bad economic conditions, or a "bad deal" are not conditions creating voidable contracts
   h. Infancy, incompetency, and noncompliance with Statute of Frauds may also create voidable contract
   i. Adhesion contract--offeror is in position to say "take it or leave it" because of superior bargaining power

        (1) Usually occurs when large business entity requires its customers to use their standard form contract without allowing modification

7. Conformity with the Statute of Frauds

   a. Contracts required to be in writing and signed by party to be charged-- these are said to be within the Statute

        (1) An agreement to sell land or any interest in land

(a)   Includes buildings, easements, leases longer than 1 year, mortgages, and contracts to sell real estate

(b)   Part performance typically satisfies Statute even though real estate contract was oral, but this requires

1]   Possession of the land
2]   Either part payment or making of improvements
3]   Many courts require all three

(2)   An agreement that cannot be performed within one year from the making of agreement

(a)   Contract that can be performed in exactly one year or less may be oral

EXAMPLE: W agrees to hire X for ten months starting in four months.   This contract must be in writing because it will not be performed until 14 months after the agreement is made.

(b)   Any contract which can conceivably be completed in one year, irrespective of how long the task actually takes, may be oral

EXAMPLE: A agrees to paint B's portrait for $400.   It actually is not completed until over a year later.   This contract did not have to be in writing because it was possible to complete it within one year.

(c)   If performance is contingent on something which could take place in less than one year, agreement may be oral

EXAMPLE: "I will employ you as long as you live."   Party could possibly die in less than one year.

(d)   But if its terms call for more than one year, it must be written even if there is possibility of taking place in less than one year

EXAMPLE: "I will employ you for 5 years."   The employee's death could occur before the end of five years, but the terms control for the writing requirement under the Statute of Frauds.

(e)   Generally, if one side of performance is complete but other side cannot be performed within year, it is not within Statute, i.e., may be oral. This is especially true if performance has been accepted and all that remains is the payment of money (e.g., sale with payments spread over two years).

(3)   An agreement to answer for debt or default of another (contract of guaranty)

(a)   A secondary promise is within this section of the Statute of Frauds (i.e., must be in writing)

EXAMPLE: "If Jack doesn't pay, I will."

(b)   A primary promise is not within this section of the Statute of Frauds because it is really the promisor's own contract

EXAMPLE: "Let Jack have it, and I will pay."

(c)   Promise for benefit of promisor may be oral

EXAMPLE: Promisor agrees to answer for default of X, because X is promisor's supplier and he needs X to stay in business to keep himself in business.

   (d) Promise of indemnity (will pay based on another's fault, e.g., insurance) is not within Statute

   (e) Assignor's promise to assignee, guaranteeing obligor's performance is not within Statute

(4) Agreement for sale of goods for $500 or more is required to be in writing under UCC

EXAMPLE: Oral contract for the sale of 50 calculators for $10 each is not enforceable.

EXAMPLE: Oral contract to perform management consulting services over the next six months for $100,000 is enforceable because the $500 rule does not apply to contracts that come under common law.

EXAMPLE: Same as previous example except that the agreed time was for 14 months. This one was required to be in writing to be enforceable because of the one year rule.

   (a) Exceptions to writing requirement (these are important)

      1] Oral contract involving specially manufactured goods (i.e., not saleable in ordinary course of business) if seller has made substantial start in their manufacture (or even made a contract for necessary raw materials) is enforceable

      2] Oral contract is enforceable against party who admits it in court but not beyond quantity of goods admitted

      3] Goods that have been paid for (if seller accepts payment) or goods which buyer has accepted are part of enforceable contract even if oral

EXAMPLE: B orally agrees to purchase 10,000 parts from S for $1 each. B later gives S $6,000 for a portion of the parts. S accepts the money. In absence of a written agreement, B may enforce a contract for 6,000 parts but not for the full 10,000 parts.

   (b) Modifications of written contracts involve two issues under UCC

      1] New consideration on both sides is not required under UCC although it is under common law

         a] Under UCC, modification must be done in good faith

      2] Modified contract must be in writing if contract, as modified, is within Statute of Frauds (i.e., sale of goods for $500 or more)

EXAMPLE: S agrees orally to sell B 100 widgets for $4.80 each. B later agrees, orally, to pay $5.00 for the 100 widgets due to changed business conditions. The modified contract is not enforceable because it must have been in writing. Therefore, the original contract is enforceable.

EXAMPLE: Same as above except that the modification is in writing. Now the modified contract is enforceable despite the fact that S is giving no new consideration.

EXAMPLE: X and Y have a written contract for the sale of goods for $530. They subsequently both agree orally to a price reduction of $40. The modified contract for $490 is enforceable.

    (c) Parties may exclude future oral agreements in a signed writing

  (5) Agreement for sale of intangibles over $5,000 must be in writing; e.g., patents, copyrights, or contract rights

  (6) Sale of securities must be in writing

    (a) Must include price and quantity

b. When a writing is required, it must be signed by party sought to be charged

  (1) Any form will do, e.g., letter, telegram, receipt

  (2) Need not be single document, e.g., two telegrams

  (3) Need not be made at same time as contract

    (a) Must be made before suit is brought

    (b) Need not exist at time of suit, i.e., may have been destroyed

  (4) Should include such matters as

    (a) Identity of parties

    (b) Description of subject matter

    (c) Quantity

    (d) Price

    (e) Signature

      1] Signature need not be at end nor be in a special form so long as intent to authenticate existed, e.g., initials, stamp, printed letterhead, etc. of party to be charged

  (5) Under UCC a writing is adequate if it indicates contract for sale of goods has been made between parties and is signed by party to be charged

    (a) May omit material terms (e.g., price, delivery, time for performance) as long as quantity is stated. Reasonable terms will be inferred.

    (b) Exception to signature requirement exists under UCC when both parties are merchants--one party may send signed written confirmation stating terms (especially quantity) of oral agreement to other party within reasonable time, then non-signing party must object within 10 days or the contract is enforceable against him/her

c. Noncompliance with Statute of Frauds, i.e., failure to make a writing, will make contract unenforceable

d. Other issues for signed writing

  (1) Parol evidence rule

    (a) Provides that any written agreement intended by parties to be final and complete contract (called an intregration) may not be contradicted by previous or contemporaneous oral evidence

      1] Applies to such written contracts whether Statute of Frauds required writing or not

2] Evidence of integration is often shown by a clause such as "This agreement is the complete agreement between the parties; no other representations have been made."

EXAMPLE: A and B enter into a home purchase agreement which is intended as a complete contract. B wishes to introduce oral evidence into court that the price of $150,000 that was in the home purchase agreement was put in to get a larger loan from a bank. B claims that they orally agreed the price would be $130,000. The oral evidence is not allowed to contradict the written contract under the parol evidence rule.

(b) Exceptions (party may present oral proof)

1] To show invalidity of contract between parties, e.g., fraud, forgery, duress, mistake, failure of consideration
2] To show terms not inconsistent with writing that parties would not be expected to have included

EXAMPLE: Builder promises orally to use reasonable care not to damage nearby trees when building a house.

3] To explain intended meaning of an ambiguity (proof cannot contradict terms in contract but can explain them)
4] To show condition precedent--oral proof can be presented to show a fact or event must occur before agreement is valid
5] Under UCC, written terms may be supplemented or explained by course of dealing, usage of trade, or course of performance

(c) Does not apply to subsequent transactions, e.g., oral promises made after original agreement, or separate and distinct oral agreement made at same time as written contract

EXAMPLE: M and N have a complete written employment contract. Later, M and N orally modify the contract with M agreeing to pay more and N agreeing to take on more duties. The oral evidence is allowed because it arose subsequent to the written contract.

C. Assignment and Delegation

1. Assignment is the transfer of a right under a contract by one person to another
2. Delegation is the transfer of duties under a contract
3. Generally, a party's rights in a contract are assignable and duties are delegable
   a. No consideration is needed for valid assignment
      (1) Gratuitous assignments are revocable

EXAMPLE: A owes B a debt for services B performed for A, but B has been unable to collect because A has been in financial difficulty. B may gratuitously assign this debt to X if X can collect it. If A's financial position improves, B may revoke the assignment to X and collect the debt himself or assign it to another for consideration.

b. Rights may be assigned without delegating duties, or duties may be delegated without assigning rights
c. Partial assignments may be made, e.g., only assign part of one's rights such as right to receive money
d. A delegation of duties is not an anticipatory breach

> EXAMPLE: *X Company contracted to deliver certain goods to Y. If X Company is low on these goods, it may delegate this duty to S Company, its subsidiary. It is not an anticipatory breach because X has not indicated that performance will not occur.*

e. An assignment of a contract is taken to mean both assignment of rights and delegation of duties
f. Exceptions

     (1) Contract involving personal services, credit, trust, or confidence, e.g., an artist cannot delegate his/her duty to paint a portrait

         (a) But a contractor building a house according to a blueprint can delegate his/her duty to someone qualified
         (b) With permission, personal duties can be delegated

     (2) Provision of contract or statute prohibits assignment or delegation

         (a) Trend is to look with disfavor on prohibitions against assignments where only a right to money is concerned
         (b) The UCC makes prohibition against assignment of monetary rights ineffective

     (3) If assignment would materially change risk or obligations of other party

         (a) E.g., insurance contracts, requirement and output contracts, and contracts where personal credit is involved

4. An assignment generally extinguishes any rights of assignor but a delegation does not relieve delegant of his/her duties

a. The assignee acquires assignor's rights against obligor and has exclusive right to performance
b. If obligor has notice of assignment, s/he must pay assignee, not assignor

     (1) If obligor has no notice, s/he may pay assignor and assignee can only recover from assignor

c. Unless there is a novation, delegating party is still liable if delegatee does not perform

     (1) Novation occurs when one of original parties to contract is released and new party is substituted in his/her place

         (a) Requires consent of all three parties

> EXAMPLE: *A sells a car to B and accepts payments over time. B sells the car to C who agrees to take over the payments. No novation has occurred unless A agrees to accept C and release B.*

5. Party taking an assignment generally steps into shoes of assignor--s/he gets no better rights than assignor had

a. Assignee is subject to any defenses obligor could assert against assignor

6. If assignor makes more than one assignment of same right, there are two rules to be applied depending upon the state

    a. Either first assignee to give notice to obligor prevails, or
    b. First to obtain assignment prevails

D. **Third-Party Beneficiary Contracts**

1. Contracting parties enter into agreement intended to benefit third party(ies)

    a. Creditor beneficiary--a debtor contracts with a second party to pay the debt owed to creditor (third-party beneficiary)

        EXAMPLE: X owes C $100. X contracts with Y to paint Y's house if Y will pay C $100. C is a creditor beneficiary.

        EXAMPLE: Buyer assumes the seller's mortgage. Mortgagee is a creditor beneficiary because buyer has agreed to pay mortgage.

        EXAMPLE: Buyer purchases some property subject to a mortgage that the seller owes a Bank. The bank is not a third party beneficiary because buyer did not agree to pay the mortgage. The seller is still the only debtor on the mortgage.

    b. Donee beneficiary--almost the same as creditor beneficiary except promisee's intent is to confer a gift upon third party through promisor's performance

        EXAMPLE: X contracts to buy Y's car if Y will deliver it to D, X's son. D is a donee beneficiary.

    c. Incidental beneficiary--third party who receives an unintended benefit from a contract. S/he obtains <u>no</u> rights under the contract

        EXAMPLE: X and Y contract to build an apartment building. A, a nearby store owner, would benefit from increased business and is an incidental beneficiary.

2. Only intended beneficiary (creditor or donee) can maintain an action against contracting parties for nonperformance

    a. Intent of the promisee controls
    b. Creditor beneficiary can proceed against either contracting party

        EXAMPLE: X owes C $100. X contracts with M to paint M's house if M will pay C $100. If X does not paint M's house, C may sue X because X still owes C $100. C may also sue M, because M now owes C $100 under the contract. C is a creditor beneficiary and can sue either party.

    c. Donee beneficiary can proceed against the promisor only

        EXAMPLE: X contracts to buy Y's car if Y will deliver it to D. If Y does not deliver the car, D may sue Y. However, D may not sue X because it was a gift from X, not an obligation.

3. If the third-party beneficiary contract is executory, the parties may rescind and defeat the third party's rights

EXAMPLE: X owes C $100.   X contracts with Y to paint Y's house if Y will pay C $100.   X and Y may rescind the contract before Y pays C $100.   Then there is no contract for C to enforce; however, C may still sue X for the $100 owed.   Or in other words, C has no third party rights on an executory contract.

4. The promisor can assert any defenses against third-party beneficiary that s/he has against promisee

E. **Performance of Contract**

1. Duty to perform may depend upon a condition

   a. Condition precedent is one which must occur before there is duty to perform; e.g., "I will lend you $1,000 if your credit checks out."
   b. Condition subsequent is one which removes preexisting duty to perform; e.g., "I will pay you for these goods unless I decide to return them."
   c. Conditions concurrent are mutually dependent upon performance at nearly the same time, e.g., delivery and payment for goods
   d. Satisfaction as a condition--normally when a contract guarantees satisfaction, this means agreement is performed when a reasonable person would be satisfied. However, if agreement is expressly conditioned upon personal satisfaction of one of contracting parties, then performance does not occur until that party is actually satisfied.

2. Tender of performance is an offer to perform; e.g., offer to pay debt

   EXAMPLE: X has contracted to buy goods from Y with delivery and payment to take place concurrently.   X must offer the money to Y before Y has breached the contract for failure to deliver.

3. Under the <u>doctrine of substantial performance</u> (very important), performance is satisfied if

   a. There has been substantial performance (i.e., <u>deviations are minor</u>, and
   b. There has been <u>good faith</u> effort to comply with contract
   c. Then damages for deviations are deducted from price if above are met
   d. This is often used in relation to construction contracts

4. Payment of less than agreed-upon sum does not fulfill obligation unless both parties compromise based on a bona fide dispute as to amount owed

5. Part payment when debtor owes more than one debt to same creditor

   a. Debtor may specify which debt payment applies to

6. Executory contract--has not yet been performed; only promises have been given

   a. Wholly executory when there has been no performance, e.g., each party has merely promised--aggrieved party can still sue other party if and when the other party fails to perform on a timely basis
   b. Partially executory when only part of contract is still unperformed, e.g., one party has performed and the other has not

7. Executed contract--all parties have completely performed and no obligation remains

F. **Discharge of Contracts**

1. By agreement--new consideration is necessary, but often it is supplied by a promise for a promise, e.g., both parties agreeing to release other party of contractual obligation

    a. A novation is an agreement by three parties whereby a previous agreement is discharged by creation of a new agreement

        (1) May involve substitution of creditors, debtors, or of obligations

            EXAMPLE: X has agreed to do some accounting work for Y for $2,000. Since X is very busy, X, Y, and Z all agree to let X out of the contract and insert Z in his place. This is a novation. X and Y no longer have any obligations to each other.

            EXAMPLE: A party purchases land and assumes a mortgage. The original mortgagor is still liable unless a novation has occurred.

    b. Under UCC, no consideration is needed to modify a contract (for sale of goods) if in good faith
    c. Both parties may mutually agree to rescind contract
    d. Accord and satisfaction

        (1) Accord is an agreed substitute for performance
        (2) Satisfaction is the actual performance of that substitute
        (3) Until satisfaction is started, promisee may recover under the original contract

            EXAMPLE: X sells a boat to Y who promises to pay in 30 days. Y fails. X and Y agree that Y will fix X's roof as satisfaction. Y is liable until he starts the roof repair.

2. By release or covenant not to sue

3. By performance becoming objectively impossible

    a. Performance becomes illegal
    b. Death of party where personal service is necessary
    c. Destruction of subject matter without fault of promisor
    d. Bankruptcy of party

4. By breach of contract

    a. Partial breach (minor breach)--injured party is not discharged but may sue for damages
    b. Material breach--failure to perform a term so essential that purpose of parties is defeated

        (1) Injured party discharged and may sue for damages or rescind

    c. Anticipatory breach (renunciation before performance is due)

        (1) May sue at once, or
        (2) Wait until time performance is due or for a reasonable time and then sue
        (3) If other party has not changed position in reliance upon the repudiation, repudiating party can retract repudiation and perform at appointed time, thereby discharging his/her contractual obligation

            EXAMPLE: X agrees to convey and Y agrees to pay for land on April 1. On February 1, Y learns that X has sold the land to Z. Y may sue before April 1, or he may wait and sue on April 1.

EXAMPLE: M agrees to deliver 1,000 widgets to Q by December 1. Three months before that date, M says, he will be unable to deliver on December 1.

G. Remedies

1. Rescission--cancellation of contract whereby parties are placed in position they were in before contract was formed

   a. Common remedy for voidable contract

2. Restitution--return of consideration to injured party

3. Specific performance--compels performance promised

   a. Used only when money damages will not suffice; e.g., when subject matter is unique, or rare, as in contract for sale of land
   b. Not available to compel personal services

4. Injunction--compels an act by the party (positive injunction), or restrains an act (negative injunction)

5. Damages--payment of money

   a. Purpose is to place injured party in as good a position as s/he would have occupied if contract had been performed
   b. Actual or compensatory damages are equal to amount caused by breach

      (1) This is the most common remedy under contract law
      (2) Damages must be foreseeable before being recoverable

          (a) Damages must have been within contemplation of both parties at time of contracting as natural result of breach, i.e., damages arising from special circumstances beyond normal course of events are not recoverable

   c. Punitive damages are generally not allowed in contract law
   d. Liquidated damage clause is a provision agreed to in a contract to set the amount of damages in advance if a breach occurs

      (1) These are used instead of awarding actual compensatory damages
      (2) Not enforceable if punitive; therefore, amount set in advance must be reasonably based on what actual damages are expected to be

   e. Party injured by breach must use reasonable care to minimize loss because s/he cannot recover costs that could have been avoided--called mitigation of damages

   EXAMPLE: One who receives perishables which are not the goods bargained for must take reasonable steps to prevent loss from spoilage.

   EXAMPLE: X contracts to fix Y's car. After X begins work, Y breaches and says "Stop." X cannot continue to work and incur more costs, i.e., put in more parts and labor.

6. Quasi-contract--a type of implied contract--provides a remedy where one person has been unjustly enriched to detriment of another.

   EXAMPLE: D falsely claims to be a pauper and obtains care at a home for the aged. A large estate is discovered at his death. The home may sue for the reasonable value of services rendered.

7. Arbitration--resolution of dispute, outside of judicial system, agreed to by disputing parties

H. **Statute of Limitations**

    1. Bars suit if not brought within statutory period

        a. Periods vary for different types of cases
        b. Periods vary from state to state

    2. Statute begins to run from time cause of action accrues, e.g., breach

    3. Running of statute may be stopped when defendant is absent from jurisdiction

SALES

Overview

The law of sales governs contracts for the sale of goods. Since a sale of goods is involved, Article 2 of the Uniform Commercial Code (UCC) applies. A sale of goods under the UCC is the sale of tangible, moveable property.

One of the areas tested in sales is product liability. When studying this area, you should pay particular attention to the different legal theories under which an injured party may recover. Realize that an injured party may recover under the legal theories of breach of warranty, negligence, and strict liability. It is important that you know the circumstances under which these theories may be used. Other areas which are often tested are warranties; disclaimers; risk of loss; and remedies, rights, and duties of the buyer and seller.

You should understand that a binding contract may be present under the UCC if the parties had intended to be bound, even though certain elements of a contract may be missing. These open terms will be filled by specific provisions of the UCC. The parties to a sale need not be merchants for the UCC to apply; however, some rules vary if merchants are involved in the sales contract.

As you study this area, note that it builds on much of the material under contracts in the previous module. Therefore, as you study this area you should review the contract law rules, especially those in the previous module that apply to the UCC.

A. **Contracts for Sale of Goods**

1. Article 2 of the Uniform Commercial Code, in general, controls contracts for the sale of goods

    a. "Goods" include tangible property (whether specially manufactured or not)

        (1) Do not include sales of investment securities, accounts receivable, contract rights, copyrights, or patents

             EXAMPLE: S sells B a stereo. The UCC applies.

             EXAMPLE: S sells a home to B. The common law rules rather than the UCC rules apply to this contract since it involves the sale of real property.

             EXAMPLE: F sells to M several bushels of wheat. The UCC applies to fungible goods also, i.e., goods in which one unit is considered the equivalent of the other units.

    b. UCC applies whether sale is between merchants or consumers but some rules change if merchant involved

        EXAMPLE: S sells his used refrigerator to B, a neighbor. The UCC applies to this transaction.

    c. Thrust of UCC is to find a contract in cases where it is the intent of the parties to do so, even though some technical element of contract may be missing

    d. Open terms (missing terms) will not cause a contract for sale of goods to fail for indefiniteness if there was intent to contract and a reasonable basis for establishing a remedy is available

        (1) Elements of sales contracts are generally same as common law contracts

2. General concepts

    a. Merchant--one who deals in the kind of goods being sold, or one who holds self out as having superior knowledge and skills as to the goods involved, or one who employs another who qualifies as a merchant

    b. Firm offer--a written signed offer concerning the sale of goods, by a merchant, giving assurance that it will be held open for a specified time is irrevocable for that period, not to exceed three months

        (1) Note that only offeror need be a merchant under this rule
        (2) If firm offer does not state specific time, it will remain open for reasonable time, not to exceed 3 months
        (3) Written form may be supplied by either party as long as it is signed by merchant-offeror

        EXAMPLE: M, a merchant, agrees in a letter signed by M to sell B 1,000 widgets, with the offer to remain open for five weeks. Even if M tries to revoke this offer before the five-week period, B may still accept.

        EXAMPLE: M, a merchant, agrees in signed writing to sell B 1,000 widgets, stating that the offer will remain open for 120 days. B accepts the offer on the 95th day. If nothing has occurred to terminate offer prior to acceptance, offer and acceptance are present. The irrevocable nature of this offer would end after 90 days, but the offer would not automatically terminate. The offer would remain in existence for the stated period (120 days) unless terminated by other means.

        EXAMPLE: Same facts as above except that B gives M $100 to keep the offer open for six months. This is an option supported by consideration, so the firm offer restrictions do not apply. That is, the offer remains open for the full six months. (This would be true even if M is not a merchant.)

    c. Battle of forms--between merchants, additional terms included in the acceptance become part of the contract unless

        (1) Original offer precludes such, or
        (2) New terms materially alter the original offer, or
        (3) The original offeror gives notice of his/her objection within a reasonable time

        EXAMPLE: P offers in writing to sell to Q 1,000 type xxx widgets for $10,000. Q replies, "I accept, but I will personally pick these up with my truck." Both P and Q are merchants. They have a contract with the stated delivery terms.

    d. Under the UCC, a contract may be modified without new consideration if done in good faith

        (1) Common law requires new consideration for any modification

    e. Recall that under UCC version of Statute of Frauds, contracts for sale of goods for $500 or more must be in writing with some exceptions

        (1) Writing must contain quantity and signature of party to be charged

            (a) Need not contain all details required under common law version

        (2) If contract is modified, must be in writing if after modification it is for $500 or more

8

> *EXAMPLE: B agrees in a contract to buy widgets from S for $500. Later, S agrees to a reduction in price to $490. The first contract must be in writing (absent any exceptions), but the modified contract may be oral.*

    f. Consignment--arrangement in which agent (consignee) is appointed by consignor to sell goods if all the following conditions are met

      (1) Consignor keeps title to goods,
      (2) Consignee is not obligated to buy or pay for goods,
      (3) Consignee receives a commission upon sale, and
      (4) Consignor receives proceeds of sale

    g. Document of title--any document which in the regular course of business is accepted as adequate evidence that the person in possession of the document is entitled to receive, hold, and dispose of the document and the goods it covers

    h. Bill of lading--a document of title which is issued by a private or common carrier in exchange for goods delivered to it for shipment. It may be negotiable or nonnegotiable.

    i. Warehouse receipt--a document of title issued by a person engaged in the business of storing goods, i.e., a warehouseman. It acknowledges receipt of the goods, describes the goods stored, and contains the terms of the storage contract. It may be negotiable or nonnegotiable.

B. **Product Liability**--a manufacturer or seller may be responsible when a product is defective and causes injury or damage to a person or property. There are three theories under which manufacturers and sellers may be held liable. (In each fact pattern, consider all three, although proof of any one creates liability.)

  1. Warranty Liability--purchaser of a product may sue based on the warranties made

    a. Warranty of title

      (1) Seller warrants good title, rightful transfer and freedom from any security interest or lien of which the buyer has no knowledge

> *EXAMPLE: A seller of stolen goods would be liable to a buyer for damages.*

      (2) Merchant warrants goods to be free of rightful claim of infringement, e.g., patent or trademark, unless buyer furnished specifications to seller for manufacture of the goods

      (3) Can only be disclaimed by specific language or circumstances which give buyer reason to know s/he is receiving less than full title

         (a) Cannot be disclaimed by language such as "as is"

    b. Express warranties (may be written or oral)

      (1) Any affirmation of fact or promise made by the seller to the buyer which relates to the goods and becomes part of the basis of the bargain creates an express warranty that the goods shall conform to the affirmation or promise

         (a) Sales talk, puffing, or a statement purporting to be merely the seller's opinion does not create a warranty
         (b) No reliance is necessary on part of buyer

      (c) Must form part of the basis of bargain

         1] Would include advertisements read by buyer
         2] Normally would not include warranties given after the sale or contract was made

      (d) No intent to create warranty is needed on the part of the seller
      (e) Seller or buyer may be merchant or consumer

  (2) Any description of the goods which is made part of the basis of the bargain creates an express warranty that the goods shall conform to the description

  (3) Any sample or model which is made part of the basis of the bargain creates an express warranty that the goods shall conform to the sample or model

  (4) It is not necessary to the creation of an express warranty that the seller use formal words such as "warranty" or "guarantee"

c. Implied warranties

  (1) Warranty of merchantability--goods are fit for ordinary purpose

      (a) This warranty also guarantees that goods are properly packaged and labeled
      (b) This warranty is implied if

         1] Seller is a merchant with respect to goods of the kind being sold and
         2] Warranty is not modified or excluded
         3] Then if goods not fit for ordinary use, breach of this warranty occurs

  (2) Warranty of fitness for a particular purpose

      (a) Created when the seller knows of the particular use for which the goods are required and further knows that the buyer is relying on skill and judgment of seller to select and furnish suitable goods for this particular use

         EXAMPLE: A buyer relies upon a paint salesperson to select a particular exterior house paint that will effectively cover existing siding.

      (b) Buyer must actually rely on seller's skill and judgment
      (c) Product is then warranted for the particular expressed purpose and seller may be liable if the product fails to so perform
      (d) Applicable both to merchants and nonmerchants

d. UCC, being consumer oriented, allows these warranties to extend to parties other than the purchaser even without privity of contract

  (1) Extends to a buyer's family and also to guests in the home who may reasonably be expected to use and/or be affected by the goods and who are injured

      EXAMPLE: A dinner guest breaks a tooth on a small piece of metal in the food. Note that in food, the substance causing injury normally must be foreign, not something customarily found in it (bone in fish).

e. Disclaimers--warranty liability may be escaped or modified by disclaimers (also available at common law without rules defining limits of disclaimers)

(1) A disclaimer of merchantability can be written or oral but must use the word "merchantability" unless all implied warranties are disclaimed as in "(3)" below

(2) To disclaim the implied warranty of fitness for a particular purpose, the disclaimer must be in writing and conspicuous

(3) All implied warranties (including merchantability) can be disclaimed by oral or written language such as "as is" or "with all faults" which makes plain that there is no implied warranty

(4) Written disclaimers must be clear and conspicuous

(5) If the buyer has had ample opportunity to inspect the goods or sample, there is no implied warranty as to any defects which ought reasonably to have been discovered

(6) Implied warranties may be excluded or modified by course of dealings, course of performance, or usage of trade

(7) A disclaimer inconsistent with an express warranty is not effective, i.e., a description of a warranty in a contract cannot be disclaimed

(8) Limitations on consequential damages for personal injuries are presumed to be unconscionable if on consumer goods

2. Negligence

a. Must prove the following elements

(1) Duty of manufacturer to exercise reasonable (due) care

(a) Consider likelihood of harm, seriousness of harm, and difficulty of correction

(b) May be based on violation of statute but this is not necessary

(c) If accident is type which would not normally happen without negligence, then presumption of negligence exists

(2) Breach of duty of reasonable care

(a) Insufficient instructions may cause breach of duty

(3) Damages or injury

(4) Cause in fact

(a) In general, if injury would not have happened without defendant's conduct, there is cause in fact

(5) Proximate cause

(a) General standard here is whether the type of injury was foreseeable

b. Privity of contract (contractual connection between parties) is not needed because suit not based on contract

EXAMPLE: A car manufacturer is negligent in the manufacture and design of brakes and as a result, a driver is severely injured. The driver may sue the manufacturer even if he bought the car from a retailer.

EXAMPLE: In the example above, even a pedestrian injured because of the brake problem may recover from the manufacturer.

  c. Often difficult to prove this type of negligence because facts are frequently controlled by defendant

  d. Defenses to negligence

   (1) Contributory negligence

    (a) I.e., plaintiff helped cause accident

    (b) Complete bar to recovery

    (c) Some states instead use comparative negligence in which damages are allocated between plaintiff and defendant based on relative fault

   (2) Assumption of risk

 3. Strict liability

  a. Manufacturers, sellers, and lessors who normally deal in this type of product are liable to users of products without proof of fault or lack of reasonable care

  b. Elements

   (1) Product was defective when sold

    (a) Based on poor design, inadequate warnings, improper assembly, or unsafe materials

   (2) Defect is unreasonably dangerous to user

    (a) Based on normal expectations

   (3) Product reaches user without significant changes

   (4) Defect caused the injury

  c. Defense of contributory negligence, comparative negligence, disclaimer or lack of privity is unavailable

   (1) Assumption of risk and misuse are defenses

    EXAMPLE: Herb is injured while using his power lawnmower to trim his hedges. Manufacturer would not be liable since product was not being used for intended purpose.

C. Transfer of Property Rights

 1. If party having voidable title transfers goods to a good faith purchaser for value, the latter obtains good title

  a. Examples in which there is voidable title

   (1) Goods paid for with a check subsequently dishonored

   (2) Goods obtained by fraud, mistake, duress, or undue influence

   (3) Goods obtained from minor

   (4) Thief does **not** have voidable title but void title

    EXAMPLE: B buys a stereo from S but the check bounces. P, a good faith purchaser, pays B for the stereo. S cannot get the stereo from P but must recover money from B.

    EXAMPLE: Same as above except that B stole the stereo. P does not obtain title of the stereo.

 2. If a person entrusts possession of goods to a merchant who deals in those goods, a good faith purchaser for value obtains title to these goods, unless s/he knew that this merchant did not own the goods

EXAMPLE: C leaves his watch at a shop for repairs. The shop mistakenly sells the watch to B who is unaware of C's interest. C cannot force B to turn over the watch because B now has title. Of course, C can recover monetary damages from the shop.

3. Passage of title

    a. Once goods are identified to the contract, the parties may agree as to when title passes

        (1) Sale cannot take place until goods exist and have been identified to the contract

            (a) Identification--occurs when the goods that are going to be used to perform the contract are shipped, marked or otherwise designated as such

            (b) Identification gives buyer

                1] An insurable interest in the goods once they are identified to contract

                2] Right to demand goods upon offering full contract price once other conditions are satisfied

    b. Otherwise, title generally passes when the seller completes his/her performance with respect to physical delivery

        (1) If a destination contract, title passes on tender at destination, i.e., buyer's place of business

        (2) If a shipping (point) contract, title passes when seller puts goods in the possession of the carrier

    c. If seller has no duty to move the goods

        (1) Title passes upon delivery of documents of title

            EXAMPLE: Delivery of negotiable or nonnegotiable warehouse receipt passes title to buyer.

        (2) If no document of title exists, title passes at the time and place of contracting if the goods are identifiable

        (3) If goods not identified, there is only a contract to sell; no title passes

    d. Rejection (justified or not) of goods or a justified revocation of acceptance by buyer reverts title to seller

    e. Taking a security interest is irrelevant to passage of title

D. **Risk of Loss and Title**

1. Risk of loss is independent of title under UCC, but rules regarding the transfer of both are similar

2. General rules

    a. Parties may agree as to which party bears risk of loss or has title; otherwise UCC rules below apply

    b. Shipment terms

        (1) FOB destination point--seller retains risk of loss and title and bears costs of transportation until s/he tenders delivery of goods at point of destination

            (a) FOB means free on board

(2) FOB shipping point--buyer obtains risk of loss and title and bears shipping costs once goods are in possession of appropriate carrier

> *EXAMPLE: Seller is in San Francisco and buyer is in Chicago: FOB San Francisco.*

> *EXAMPLE: Under F.O.B. shipping point contract, seller delivers perishable goods to a nonrefrigerated carrier. Seller still has risk of loss since carrier was not appropriate type.*

(3) F.A.S. vessel--free along side

    (a) Seller must deliver goods along side the named vessel at his/her own risk and expense

(4) C.I.F.--is a shipping contract (shipping point contract) in which cost, insurance, and freight included in price

    (a) Seller puts goods in hands of a carrier and obtains insurance in buyer's name, who then has risk of loss and title

(5) C. & F.--shipping contract in which cost and freight are included in price

    (a) Seller need not buy insurance for buyer
    (b) Risk of loss and title pass to buyer upon delivery of goods to carrier

(6) No arrival, no sale--seller ships but if goods do not arrive, contract fails and neither party is liable

c. Sale on approval--goods may be returned even if they conform to the contract

(1) Not considered sold until buyer approves or accepts as sale
(2) Goods bought for trial use

    (a) Notification of buyer to seller of desire not to buy goods results in no sale

(3) Seller retains title and risk of loss until buyer accepts goods
(4) Creditors of buyer cannot reach goods until buyer accepts

d. Sale or return--goods may be returned even if they conform to the contract

(1) Goods bought for use or resale
(2) Sale is final if goods not returned during period specified
(3) Buyer obtains risk of loss and title according to shipping terms in contract

    (a) Both risk of loss and title return to seller if and when goods are returned to seller
    (b) Return of goods is at buyer's expense

(4) Creditors of buyer can reach the goods while in buyer's possession, unless notice of seller's interest is posted or filed as required
(5) Also termed sale and return

e. Often difficult to distinguish sale on approval vs. sale or return

(1) Unless buyer and seller agree otherwise

    (a) Transaction is deemed to be sale on approval if goods for buyer's use

    (b) Transaction is presumed to be sale or return if goods are for buyer's resale

f. Effect of breach on risk of loss

    (1) If seller breaches

        (a) Risk of loss remains with seller until cure by seller or acceptance by buyer to extent of any deficiency in insurance coverage

    (2) If buyer breaches

        (a) Risk of loss passes to buyer to extent of deficiency in insurance for a commercially reasonable time

g. If goods are held in warehouse and seller has no right to move them, risk of loss passes to buyer

    (1) Upon proper negotiation of a negotiable document of title

    (2) Within a reasonable time after delivery of a nonnegotiable document of title

    (3) Once warehouseman acknowledges buyer's right to goods if no document of title

h. Voidable title

    (1) One who purchases in good faith from another who has voidable title takes good title

        (a) Good faith -- purchaser unaware of facts that made previous title voidable

        (b) One may obtain voidable title by purchasing with a check that is later dishonored

> EXAMPLE: A purchases 1,000 widgets from B. B had purchased these from C but B's check had been dishonored by the bank before A purchased the widgets. A was unaware of these facts. B's title was voidable but A takes good title as a good faith purchaser

i. In situations not covered above, risk of loss passes to buyer on physical receipt of goods if seller is a merchant. Otherwise, risk passes on tender of delivery.

j. Risk of loss can be covered by insurance. In general, party has an insurable interest whenever s/he can suffer damage.

    (1) Buyer usually allowed an insurable interest when goods are identified to the contract

    (2) Seller usually has an insurable interest so long as s/he has title or a security interest

E. **Performance and Remedies Under Sales Law**

1. In general, either party may, upon breach by other, cancel the contract and terminate executory obligations

    a. Unlike common law rescission, however, cancellation does not discharge a claim for damages

2. Seller's duty to perform under a contract for sale is excused if performance as agreed has been made impracticable by the occurrence of a contingency, the nonoccurrence of which was a basic assumption on which the contract was made

3. Either party may demand adequate assurance of performance when reasonable grounds for insecurity arise with respect to performance of the other party

    a. E.g., buyer falls behind in payments or seller delivers defective goods to other buyers

    b. Party may suspend performance while waiting for assurance

    c. Failure to provide assurance within a reasonable time, not to exceed 30 days, is repudiation of the contract

    d. Provision in contract, that seller may accelerate payment when s/he has a good faith belief that makes him/her insecure, is valid

4. Seller's remedies

    a. Seller has right to "cure" nonconformity, i.e., tender conforming goods

        (1) Within original time of contract or

        (2) Within reasonable time if seller thought nonconforming tender would be acceptable

        (3) Seller must notify buyer of his intention to cure

    b. Seller may resell goods if buyer breaches before acceptance

        (1) May be public or private sale

            (a) If private, must give notice to buyer who breached; otherwise, losses cannot be recovered

            (b) If seller resells in a commercially reasonable manner, s/he may recover any loss on the sale from the buyer who breached, but s/he is not responsible to buyer who breached for profits made on resale

            (c) In any event, good faith purchasers take free of original buyer's claims

    c. If seller learns that buyer is insolvent and buyer does not have the document of title, seller may stop delivery of goods in carrier's possession unless buyer pays cash

    d. Seller may recover goods received by an insolvent buyer if demand is made within 10 days of receipt

        (1) However, if the buyer has made a written misrepresentation of solvency within 3 months before delivery, this 10-day limitation does not apply

        (2) If buyer is insolvent, seller may demand cash to make delivery

    e. Seller may recover damages

        (1) If buyer repudiates agreement or refuses goods, seller may recover the difference between market price at time of tender and contract price, plus incidental damages, minus expenses saved due to buyer's breach

        (2) If the measure of damages stated above in "(1)" is inadequate to place the seller in as good a position as performance would have, then the seller can sue for the lost profits, plus incidental damages, less expenses saved due to the buyer's breach

        (3)   The seller can recover the full contract price when

            (a)   The buyer has already accepted the goods
            (b)   Conforming goods have been destroyed after the risk of loss had transferred to buyer
            (c)   The seller is unable to resell the identified goods

    f. Remedies for anticipatory breach under contract law in general apply here, i.e., sue at once or wait until time for performance

        (1)   If breach by buyer comes during manufacture of goods, seller may

            (a)   Complete goods and identify to contract,
            (b)   Cease and sell for scrap, or
            (c)   Proceed in other reasonable manner

        (2)   Any of the above must be done while exercising reasonable commercial judgment
        (3)   Buyer who breaches is then liable for damages measured by whatever course of action seller takes

5. Buyer's remedies

    a. Buyer may reject nonconforming goods, either in entirety or any commercial unit, e.g., bale, carload, etc.

        (1)   Must do so in reasonable time and give notice to seller (failure may operate as acceptance)

            (a)   Buyer must have reasonable time to inspect even after physical acceptance

        (2)   Buyer must care for goods until returned
        (3)   If buyer is a merchant, s/he must follow reasonable instructions of seller, e.g., ship, sell

            (a)   Right to indemnity for costs

        (4)   If goods are perishable or threatened with decline in value, buyer must make reasonable effort to sell
        (5)   Buyer has a security interest in any goods in his/her possession to the extent of any payments made to seller and any expenses incurred

            (a)   S/he may sell the goods as a seller may in "4.b." above

    b. Buyer may accept nonconforming goods

        (1)   Buyer must pay at contract price but may still recover damages, i.e., deduct damages from price if s/he gives seller notice
        (2)   Buyer may revoke acceptance in a reasonable time if

            (a)   Accepted expecting nonconformity to be cured
            (b)   Accepted because of difficulty of discovering defect
            (c)   Accepted because seller assured conformity

    c. Buyer may recover damages measured by the difference between the contract price and the market value of the goods at the time buyer learns of the breach, plus any incidental damages and consequential damages

        (1)   Consequential damages are damages resulting from buyer's needs which the seller was aware of at the time of contracting
        (2)   Consequential damages cannot be recovered if buyer could reasonably have prevented these (mitigation of damages)

     d. Buyer has the right of cover

        (1) Buyer can buy substitute goods from another seller--buyer will still have the right to damages after engaging in "cover"

           (a) Damages are difference between cost of cover and contract price, plus incidental and consequential damages

           (b) Failure to cover does not bar other remedies

6. Statute of Limitations for sale of goods is 4 years

    a. An action for breach must be commenced within this period

    b. Parties may agree to reduce to not less than one year but may not extend it

    c. Statute of Limitations begins running when the contract is breached

COMMERCIAL PAPER

Overview

Commercial paper is heavily tested on the CPA exam. Coverage includes the types of negotiable instruments, the requirements of negotiability, negotiation, the holder in due course concept, defenses, and the rights of parties to a negotiable instrument. The functions of commercial paper are to provide a medium of exchange which is readily transferable like money and to provide an extension of credit. It is easier to transfer than contract rights and not subject to as many defenses as contracts are. To be negotiable, an instrument must

a. Be written
b. Be signed by the maker or drawer
c. Contain an unconditional promise or order to pay
d. State a sum certain in money
e. Be payable on demand or at definite time
f. Be payable to order or bearer

These requirements must be present on the face of the instrument. Instruments which do not comply with these provisions are nonnegotiable and are transferable only by assignment. The assignee of a nonnegotiable instrument takes it subject to all defenses.

A central theme of exam questions on negotiable instruments is the liability of the primary parties and of the secondarily liable parties under various fact situations. Similar questions in different form emphasize the rights that a holder of a negotiable instrument has against primary and secondary parties. Your review of this area should emphasize the legal liability arising upon execution of negotiable commercial paper, the legal liability arising upon various types of endorsements, and the warranty liabilities of various parties upon transfer or presentment for payment. A solid understanding of the distinction between real and personal defenses is required. Also tested is the relationship between a bank and its customers.

A. General Concepts of Commercial Paper

1. Commercial paper has two important functions

   a. Used as a substitute for money

   EXAMPLE: One often pays a bill with a check instead of using cash.

   b. Used as extension of credit

   EXAMPLE: X gives a promissory note to Y for $100 that is due one year later.

2. To encourage commercial paper to be transferred more easily by making it easier to be collected, negotiable commercial paper was established

   a. If an instrument is negotiable, favorable laws of Article 3 of UCC apply as discussed in this module

   b. If an instrument is nonnegotiable, laws of ordinary contract law apply, i.e., assignment of contract rights

      (1) Assignees of contract rights can get only the rights given by the assignor and therefore are burdened by any defenses between prior parties

      EXAMPLE: C receives a nonnegotiable instrument from B. C now wishes to collect from A, the one who had issued the nonnegotiable note to B when he purchased some goods from B. Assume that A would have owed B only two-thirds of the amount stated on the instrument due to defects in the goods. Since C obtained only the rights that B had under an assignment under contract law, C can only collect two-thirds from A on this nonnegotiable instrument.

3. It is helpful to get "the big picture" of negotiable instruments (negotiable commercial paper) before covering details

a. Whether an instrument is negotiable or not is determined by looking at its form and content on the face of the instrument

    (1) This is so that individuals seeing an instrument can determine whether it is negotiable or not

    (2) If a person has a negotiable instrument and also is a holder in due course (discussed later), s/he may collect on instrument despite most defenses that may be raised such as contract defenses

B. Types of Commercial Paper

1. Article 3 of UCC lists four types of commercial paper

    a. A draft

       (1) Has three parties in which one person or entity (drawer) orders another (drawee) to pay a third party (payee) a sum of money

       EXAMPLE:

> *June 5, 1989*
>
> *On June 5, 1990, pay to the order of Bob Smith $1,000 plus 10% annual interest from June 5, 1989.*
>
> *To: ABC Corporation*
>
> *(Signed) Sue Van Deventer*

       The above is a draft in which Sue Van Deventer is the drawer, ABC Corporation is the drawee, and Bob Smith is the payee

    b. A check

       (1) Is a special type of draft that is payable on demand and drawee must be a bank

       (2) One writing check is drawer (and customer of drawee bank)

    c. A note (also called a promissory note)

       (1) Unlike a draft or check, is a two-party instrument

          (a) One party is called the maker--this party promises to pay a specified sum of money to another party called the payee

       EXAMPLE:

> *July 10, 1989*
>
> *I promise to pay to the order of Becky Hoger $5,000 plus 10% annual interest on July 10, 1990.*
>
> *(Signed) Bill Jones*

       The above is a note in which Bill Jones is the maker and Becky Hoger is the payee.

       (2) May be payable on demand or at a definite time

    d. Certificate of deposit (CD)

        (1) Is an acknowledgment by a financial institution of receipt of money and promise to repay it

            (a) Most CDs are commercial paper so that they can be easily transferred

        (2) Is actually a special type of note in which financial institution is the maker

C. Requirements of Negotiability

  1. All of the following requirements must be on face of instrument for it to be a negotiable instrument (be sure to know these)

  2. To be negotiable, the instrument must

    a. Be written
    b. Be signed by maker or drawer
    c. Contain an unconditional promise or order to pay
    d. State a sum certain in money
    e. Be payable on demand or at a definite time
    f. Be payable to order or to bearer

  3. Details of requirements of negotiability

    a. <u>Must be in writing</u>

      (1) Satisfied by printing, typing, handwriting or any other reduction to physical form that is relatively permanent and portable

    b. <u>Must be signed by maker (of a note or CD) or drawer (of a draft or check)</u>

      (1) Signature includes any symbol used with intent to authenticate instrument

         (a) Rubber stamp, initials, letterhead satisfy signing requirement
         (b) Assumed name or trade name operates as that party's signature
         (c) Signature may be anywhere on face of instrument

    c. <u>Must contain an unconditional promise or order to pay</u>

      (1) If payment depends upon (is subject to) another agreement or event, then it is conditional and therefore destroys negotiability

        EXAMPLE: An instrument that is otherwise negotiable states that it is subject to a particular contract. This condition destroys the negotiability of this instrument.

        EXAMPLE: An instrument states: "I, Janice Jones, promise to pay to the order of Richard Riley, $1,000 if the stereo delivered to me is not defective." This instrument is not negotiable whether the stereo is defective or not because it contains a conditional promise.

         (a) However, the following are permitted and do not destroy negotiability

            1] Instrument may state its purpose

               EXAMPLE: On a check, the drawer writes "for purchase of textbooks."

           2] Instrument may refer to or state that it arises from another agreement

           3] Instrument is permitted to show that it is secured by a mortgage or by collateral

           4] Instrument is permitted to contain promise to provide extra collateral

(2) If payment is to come only out of a specified fund, this destroys negotiability

> *EXAMPLE: On his check, the drawer adds "payment will come only from my checking account." This destroys negotiability because normally if the checking account has insufficient funds, payment is required anyway.*

> *EXAMPLE: W writes "I promise to pay to the order of Y, $1,000 out of the proceeds from the sale of my home. (signed) W." This instrument is not negotiable even after the sale of the home.*

    (a) However, payment may be limited to a particular fund or source when issued by a government agency or may be limited to the entire assets of a partnership, unincorporated association, trust, or estate

(3) An IOU is not a promise or order to pay but an acknowledgement of debt, thus, is not negotiable

d. <u>Must state a sum certain in money</u>

(1) Amount must be determinable from instrument without need to refer to other sources

    (a) Stated interest rates are allowed because amount can be calculated

> *EXAMPLE: A negotiable note states that $1,000 is due one year from October 1, 1989 at 14% interest.*

> *EXAMPLE: A note states that $1,000 is payable on demand and bears interest at 14%. This also is negotiable because once payment is demanded, the amount of interest can be calculated.*

    (b) Stated different rates of interest before and after default or specified dates are allowed

        1] Interest rates tied to prime rate, consumer index, market rates, etc., destroy negotiability because of need to refer to outside source

           a] If interest rate based on legal rate or judgment rate (fixed by statute), then negotiability not destroyed

    (c) Stated discounts or additions if instrument paid before or after payment dates do not destroy negotiability

    (d) Clauses allowing collection costs and attorney's fees upon default are allowed because they reduce the risk of holding instruments and promote transferability

    (e) Must be payable only in money

        1] Option to be payable in money or something else destroys negotiability because of possibility that payment will not be in money

2] Foreign currency is acceptable even though reference to exchange rates may be needed due to international trade realities

e. <u>Must be payable on demand or at a definite time</u>

(1) On demand includes

(a) Payable on sight
(b) Payable on presentation
(c) No time for payment stated

(2) It is a definite time if payable

(a) On a certain date, or
(b) A fixed period after sight, or
(c) Within a certain time, or
(d) On a certain date subject to acceleration

1] E.g., where a payment is missed, total balance may become due at once

(e) On a certain date subject to an extension of time if

1] Is at option of holder or
2] At option of maker or drawer only if extension is limited to a definite amount of time

(3) It is not definite if payable on an act or event that is not certain as to time of occurrence

EXAMPLE: An instrument contains a clause stating that it is payable ten days after drawer obtains a bank loan. This destroys negotiability.

f. <u>Must be payable to order or to bearer</u> (these are magic words of negotiability and are often a central issue on the CPA exam)

(1) Instrument is payable to order if made payable to the order of

(a) Any person, including the maker, drawer, drawee, or payee
(b) Two persons together or alternatively
(c) Any entity

(2) Instrument is also payable to order if it is payable "to A or order"

(3) Instrument is not payable to order if it is only payable to a person, e.g., "Pay John Doe"

(a) I.e., not negotiable
(b) "Pay to the order of John Doe" would be negotiable

(4) Instrument is payable to bearer if it is payable to

(a) "Bearer"
(b) "Cash"
(c) "A person or bearer"
(d) "Order of bearer" or "order of cash"

(5) Instrument cannot be made payable to persons consecutively, i.e., maker cannot specify subsequent holders

D. **Interpretation of Ambiguities in Negotiable Instruments**

1. Contradictory terms

      a. Words control over figures

      b. Handwritten terms control over typewritten and printed (typeset) terms

      c. Typewritten terms control over printed (typeset) terms

2. Omissions

      a. Omission of date does not destroy negotiability unless date necessary to determine when payable

          EXAMPLE: A check is not dated.   It is still negotiable because a check is payable on demand.

          EXAMPLE: A draft states that it is payable 30 days after its date.   If the date is left off, it is not payable at a definite time and, therefore, it is not negotiable.

      b. Omission of interest rate is allowed because the judgment rate of interest (rate used on a court judgment) is automatically used

      c. Statement of consideration or where instrument is drawn or payable not required

3. Other issues

      a. Instrument may be postdated or antedated and remain negotiable

      b. Instrument may have a provision that by endorsing or cashing it, the payee acknowledges full satisfaction of debt and remain negotiable

      c. If an instrument is payable to order of more than one person

          (1) Either payee may negotiate or enforce it if payable to him/her in the alternative

              EXAMPLE: "Pay $100 to the order of X or Y."   Either X or Y may endorse it.

          (2) All payees must negotiate or enforce it if <u>not</u> payable to them in the alternative

      d. If not clear whether instrument is draft or note, holder may treat it as either

E. **Negotiation**

1. There are two methods of transferring commercial paper

      a. By assignment

          (1) Assignment occurs when transfer does not meet all requirements of negotiation

          (2) Assignee can obtain only same rights that assignor had

      b. By negotiation

          (1) One receiving negotiable instrument by negotiation is called a holder

          (2) If holder further qualifies as a holder in due course (as discussed later) s/he can obtain <u>more rights</u> than what transferor had

          (3) There are two methods of negotiation

              (a) Negotiating order paper requires both endorsement by transferor and delivery of instrument

                 1] Order paper includes negotiable instruments made payable to the order of X

             (b) Negotiating bearer paper is accomplished by delivery alone (endorsement not necessary)

EXAMPLE: A check is made payable to the order of cash.

    1] Subsequent parties may require endorsements (even though UCC does not) for identification

    2] Holder may, in any event, endorse it if s/he chooses to do so

2. Types of Endorsements

  a. Blank endorsement

    (1) Does not specify any endorsee

EXAMPLE: A check made to the order of M on the front can be endorsed in blank by M writing only his signature on the back.

    (2) Converts order paper into bearer paper

    (3) Note that bearer paper may be negotiated by mere delivery

EXAMPLE: B endorses a check in blank that had been made payable to his order. He lost it and C found it who delivered it to D. D is a valid holder since C's endorsement was not required.

  b. Special endorsement

    (1) Indicates specific person to whom endorsee wishes to negotiate instrument

EXAMPLE: On the back of a check payable to the order of M. Jordan he signs as follows: Pay to L. Smith, (signed) M. Jordan.

      (a) Note that words "pay to the order of" are not required on back as endorsements--instrument need be payable to order or to bearer on front only

      (b) Also, note that if instrument is not payable to order or to bearer on its face, it can <u>not</u> be turned into a negotiable instrument by using these words in an endorsement on the back

EXAMPLE: A particular instrument would have been negotiable except that on the front it was payable to A. On the back, A signed it. "Pay to the order of B, (signed) A." This does not convert it into a negotiable instrument.

    (2) Bearer paper may be converted into order paper by use of special endorsement

EXAMPLE: A check made out to cash is delivered to Carp. Carp writes on the back; Pay to Durn, (signed) Carp. It was bearer paper until this special endorsement.

EXAMPLE: Continuing the previous example, Durn simply endorses it in blank. The check is bearer paper again.

    (3) If last (or only) endorsement on instrument is a blank endorsement, any holder may convert that bearer paper into order paper by writing "Pay to X," etc., above that blank endorsement

  c. Restrictive endorsement

    (1) Requires endorsees to comply with certain conditions

EXAMPLE: Endorsement reads "For deposit only, (signed) A. Bell."

EXAMPLE: Another endorsement reads "Pay to X only if X completes work to my satisfaction on my car within three days of the date on

> *this check, (signed) A." Neither X nor any subsequent holder can enforce payment until this condition has been met.*

      (2) Note that conditions in restrictive endorsements do not destroy negotiability even though conditions placed on front of instruments do destroy negotiability because they create conditional promises or orders to pay

      (3) Endorsements cannot prohibit subsequent negotiation

  d. Qualified endorsement

      (1) Normally, endorser upon signing, promises automatically to pay holder or any subsequent endorser amount of instrument if it is later dishonored

      (2) Qualified endorsement disclaims this liability

> *EXAMPLE: Ann Knolls endorses "Without recourse, (signed) Ann Knolls."*

      (3) Qualified endorsements, otherwise, have same effects as other endorsements

      (4) Combinations of endorsements occur

         (a) Special qualified endorsement

> *EXAMPLE: Pay to Pete Bell without recourse, (signed) Tom Lack." Tom Lack has limited his liability and also Pete Bell's endorsement is needed to negotiate this instrument further.*

         (b) Blank qualified endorsement

> *EXAMPLE: "Without recourse, (signed) D. Hamilton.*

         (c) Endorsement that is restrictive, qualified, and blank

> *EXAMPLE: "For deposit only, without recourse, (signed) Bill Coffey."*

         (d) Endorsement that is restrictive, qualified, and special

> *EXAMPLE: "Pay to X if she completes work today, without recourse, (signed) D. Magee."*

3. If payee's name misspelled, s/he may endorse in proper spelling or misspelling or both

  a. But endorsee may require both

4. If an order instrument is transferred for value without endorsement, transferee may require endorsement from transferor

  a. Upon obtaining endorsement, will become a holder

5. Recent federal law standardizes endorsements on checks--now endorser should turn check over (just like before) and sign in the 1½ inch portion of check next to short edge (technically called trailing edge or payee edge)

  a. Purpose is to avoid interference with bank's endorsements

  b. Incorrect endorsements may delay check clearing process

F. **Holder in Due Course**

   1. Concept of <u>holder in due course</u> (also called <u>HDC</u>) is very important for CPA Exam purposes. An HDC is entitled to payment on negotiable instrument <u>despite most defenses</u> that maker or drawer of instrument may have

       a. Recall that an assignee of contract rights receives only rights that assignor had, i.e., assignee takes subject to all defenses that could have been asserted against assignor

       b. Likewise, an ordinary holder of a negotiable instrument has same rights as assignee

   2. To be holder in due course, a taker of instrument must

       a. Be a <u>holder</u> of a properly negotiated negotiable instrument

       b. Give <u>value</u> for instrument

          (1) Holder gives value if s/he

             (a) Pays or performs agreed consideration

                 1] An executory promise (promise to give value in the future) is not value until performed

             (b) Takes as a satisfaction of a previous existing debt

             (c) Gives another negotiable instrument

             (d) Acquires a security interest in the instrument, e.g., the holder takes possession of the instrument as collateral for another debt

          (2) A bank takes for value to the extent that credit has been given for a deposit and withdrawn

             (a) FIFO method is used to determine whether it has been withdrawn (money is considered to be withdrawn from an account in the order in which it was deposited)

          (3) Value does not have to be for full amount of instrument;

             (a) Purchase at a discount is value for full face amount of instrument provided HDC took in good faith, i.e., as long as not too large a discount

                 EXAMPLE: Purchase of a $1,000 instrument in good faith for $950 is considered full value, but purchase of the same instrument for $500 is not considered full value when market conditions show that the discount is excessive.

                 EXAMPLE: Handy purchases a negotiable note that has a face value of $1,000. She gives $600 in cash now and agrees to pay $350 in one week. Handy has given value only to the extent of $600 and thus can qualify as an HDC for $600. Once she pays the remaining $350, she qualifies as an HDC for the full $1,000. Note that even though she paid only $950, she has HDC status for the entire $1,000 because it was a reasonable discount.

       c. Take in <u>good faith</u>

          (1) I.e., holder honestly believed instrument was not defective

          (2) Subjective test--based on what holder actually thought rather than an objective test based on what might be commercially reasonable under the circumstances

     d. Take <u>without notice</u> that it is overdue, has been dishonored, or that any person has a defense or claim to it

       (1) Holder has notice when s/he knows or has reason to know (measured by objective "reasonable person" standard)

       (2) Overdue

         (a) Domestic checks presumed overdue in 30 days
         (b) Acceleration of an instrument is notice

       (3) Defense or claim

         (a) So incomplete, irregular, or obvious signs of forgery or alteration
         (b) If purchaser has notice of any party's claim or that all parties have been discharged

       (4) There is no notice of a defense or claim if

         (a) It is antedated or postdated
         (b) S/he knows that there has been a default in payment of interest

       (5) But if one acquires notice <u>after</u> becoming a holder and giving value, s/he may still be an <u>HDC</u>

         (a) I.e., once one is an HDC, acquiring notice does not end HDC status

  3. Payee of a negotiable instrument may qualify as an HDC if meets all requirements

G. **Rights of a Holder in Due Course (HDC)**

  1. The general rule is that a transfer of a negotiable instrument to an HDC cuts off all <u>personal defenses</u> against an HDC

     a. Personal defenses are assertable against ordinary holders and assignees of contract rights to avoid payment

     EXAMPLE: Art Dobbs negotiates a note to Mary Price in payment of a stereo. Mary negotiates this note to D. Finch who qualifies as an HDC. When Finch seeks payment, Dobbs points out that Price breached the contract by never delivering the stereo. Finch, as an HDC, still has the right to collect. Dobbs then has to seek recourse directly against Price.

     b. EXCEPTION--HDC takes subject to all personal defenses of person with whom HDC directly dealt

  2. Some defenses are assertable against any party including an HDC--these defenses are called <u>real (or universal) defenses</u>

  3. Types of <u>personal defenses</u>

     a. Breach of contract

       (1) Includes breach of warranty

     b. Lack or failure of consideration
     c. Prior payment

     EXAMPLE: Maker of a negotiable note pays on the note but does not keep or cancel the note. A subsequent party who qualifies as a HDC seeks to collect on this same note. Maker, having only a personal defense, must pay the HDC even though it was paid previously.

d. Unauthorized completion

> EXAMPLE: X signs a check leaving the amount blank. He tells Y to fill
> in the amount necessary to buy a typewriter. Y fills in $22,000 and
> negotiates the check to an HDC. The HDC may enforce the full amount of
> the check against X.

e. Fraud in the inducement

   (1) Occurs when person signs a negotiable instrument and knows what
        s/he is signing; however, s/he was induced into doing so by
        intentional misrepresentation

f. Nondelivery

   (1) Occurs when bearer instrument is lost or stolen

        > EXAMPLE: M issues a note that is bearer paper. It is stolen by T
        > who sells it to an HDC. The HDC wins against M.

g. Ordinary duress or undue influence

   (1) Most types of duress are considered a personal defense unless they
        become very extreme and thus are considered real defenses

        > EXAMPLE: Signing a check based on fear of losing a real estate
        > deal constitutes a personal defense.

h. Mental incapacity

   (1) Personal defense if state law makes transaction voidable
   (2) Real defense if state law makes transaction void

i. Illegality

   (1) Personal defense if state law makes transaction voidable
   (2) If state law makes it void, then real defense

4. Real Defenses

a. Forgery

   (1) Forgery of maker's or drawer's signature does not act as his/her
        signature

      (a) Does allow forger to be held liable

           > EXAMPLE: X forges M's name on a note and sells it to P. P
           > cannot collect from M whether she is an HDC or not. Her
           > recourse is against X.

b. Bankruptcy
c. Fraud in the execution

   (1) Occurs when a party is tricked into signing a negotiable instrument
        believing it to be something else

      (a) This defense will not apply if signer, based on his/her age,
           experience, etc., should have known what was happening

   (2) Recall that fraud in the inducement is a personal defense

d. Minority (or infancy)

   (1) When minor may disaffirm contract under state law, then is a real
        defense for a negotiable instrument

e. Mental incapacity, illegality, or extreme duress

(1)   Real defenses if transaction is void under state law

f.   Material alteration of instrument

(1)   Is actually only partially a real defense

(a)   If dollar amount was altered, then HDC can collect according to original terms--a non-HDC collects nothing

(b)   If an instrument was incomplete originally and then completed without authorization, HDC can enforce it as completed--a non-HDC collects nothing

(2)   Material alteration exists when terms between any two parties are changed in any way including

(a)   Changes in amount, rate of interest, or days

1]   Considered "material" even if small change such as a penny

(b)   Additions to writing or removal of part of instrument
(c)   Completion of instrument without authorization

EXAMPLE: Janice Parks negotiates a $200 negotiable note to Jim Bivins. Bivins deftly changes the amount to $500 and transfers it to E. Melvin for $500 who qualifies as an HDC. The HDC can collect only the original $200 from Janice Parks.

EXAMPLE: Same facts as before except that the material alteration is poorly done by Jim Bivins so that E. Melvin could not qualify as a holder in due course because the change was obvious. E. Melvin cannot collect even the original $200.

(d)   But not material alteration if done to correct error on address or math computations, or to place marks on instrument for audit purposes

1]   Alterations that are not material are neither real nor personal defenses so all non-HDCs as well as HDCs can enforce the instrument

(e)   Not a real defense if maker's or drawer's negligence substantially contributed to the alteration--is a personal defense

5.   Holder through a holder in due course

a.   A party who does not qualify as an HDC but obtains a negotiable instrument from an HDC is called a holder through a holder in due course
b.   Obtains all rights of an HDC

(1)   Based on fact that is an assignee who gets rights of previous party
(2)   Also called shelter rule

c.   An HDC "washes" an instrument so that any holder thereafter can be a holder through a holder in due course

EXAMPLE: An HDC transfers a note to H.V. Shelter who knew that the maker of the note has a personal defense. Shelter does not qualify as an HDC but has the same rights because he is a holder through a holder in due course.

EXAMPLE: Extending the example, H.V. Shelter gives the note to B. Evans. B. Evans does not qualify as an HDC (no value given) but is a holder through a holder in due course.

    d. Exceptions

        (1) If a party reacquires an instrument, his/her status remains what it originally was

EXAMPLE: P acquires a check from the payee. Neither qualifies in this case as a holder in due course. P delivers the check to Q who qualifies as an HDC. If the check is negotiated back to P, his rights remain those of a non-HDC.

        (2) One who was involved in fraud or illegality affecting the instrument may not become a holder through a holder in due course

6. FTC holder in due course rule

    a. Applies when seller of consumer goods or services receives a note from a consumer or arranges a loan with a bank, etc., for that consumer
    b. Requires seller or lender to put a notice on these negotiable instruments that all holders take subject to any defenses which debtor could assert against seller
    c. Note that rule does not apply to any non-consumer transactions and does not apply to any consumer non-credit transactions

EXAMPLE: Connie Consumer purchases goods for consumer use and writes out a check. Subsequent holders are governed by ordinary HDC law.

H. **Liability of Parties**--there are two general types of warranties on negotiable instruments: contractual liability and warranty liability

1. Contractual liability

    a. Refers to liability of any party who signs negotiable instrument as a maker, drawer, drawee, or endorser
    b. Maker of a note has <u>primary liability</u> which means s/he has absolute liability to pay according to note's terms until it is paid or until statute of limitations (period to sue) has run
    c. No party of a draft (or check) initially has primary liability because drawee has only been ordered to pay by drawer

        (1) Drawee's obligation is to drawer to follow order but has not promised to holder of the draft to pay
        (2) Drawee obtains primary liability if s/he accepts (certifies) draft which means s/he promises to holder to pay it when due

            (a) Often, holder may simply present draft for payment without asking for acceptance
            (b) Some drafts require acceptance before they are paid
            (c) Even if draft does not require it, holder may request acceptance (especially on a time draft before due date)

    d. Drawer has secondary liability on draft--s/he is liable only if drawee fails to pay
    e. Endorsers of note or draft have secondary liability--holder can hold endorser liable if primary parties obligated to make payment fail to pay and if following conditions met

        (1) Holder must demand payment or acceptance in a timely manner

> (a) This demand is called presentment
> (b) Presentment for payment must be on or before due date or within reasonable time for demand instruments
>
>> 1] Reasonable time for most checks is considered 30 days to hold drawer liable and 7 days after endorsement to hold endorsers liable
>
> (2) Holder must give endorsers timely notice of dishonor (i.e., that note or draft was refused payment or acceptance)

f. Drawers and endorsers may avoid secondary liability by signing without recourse

g. Upon certification of check, drawer and all previous endorsers are discharged from liability

2. Warranty liability--two types under which holder can seek payment from secondary parties are transfer warranties and presentment warranties

   a. Transfer warranties--transferor gives following transfer warranties whenever negotiable instrument is transferred for consideration

      (1) Transferor has good title
      (2) All signatures are genuine or authorized
      (3) Instrument has not been materially altered
      (4) No defense of any party is good against transferor
      (5) Transferor has no notice of insolvency of maker, drawer, or acceptor

   b. These warranties generally give loss to parties that dealt face to face with wrongdoer and thus were in best position to prevent or avoid forged, altered, or stolen instruments

      (1) Party bearing loss must then seek payment if possible, from one who forged, altered, or stole instrument

   c. Qualified endorser has same five warranties except the fourth one is changed to read that s/he has no knowledge of any defense against him/her

   d. Note that transferor, if s/he did not endorse, makes all five warranties only to immediate transferee but if transferor did endorse, makes them to all subsequent holders taking in good faith

   e. Presentment warranties--holder presenting negotiable instrument for payment or acceptance makes only warranties of title, of no knowledge that drawer's signature is unauthorized, or of no material alteration

      (1) HDC does not give these three warranties to bank

   f. To recover under warranty liabilities (either transfer or presentment warranties), party does not have to meet conditions of proper presentment, dishonor, or timely notice of dishonor that are required under contractual liability against endorsers

3. Signatures by authorized agents

   a. Agent may sign on behalf of another person (principal) and that principal is liable, not agent, if signature indicates the principal is liable

      EXAMPLE: A negotiable instrument has the following signature, signed entirely by A. Underwood, the authorized agent: Mary Johnson, by A. Underwood, agent.

EXAMPLE: If A. Underwood had simply signed Mary Johnson as she had authorized, this would also bind Mary Johnson.

EXAMPLE: If A. Underwood had signed his name only, he is liable. The principal is not liable even if agent intended her to be because her name is not on the instrument.

4. Accommodation party is liable on the instrument in the capacity in which s/he has signed even if taker knows of his/her accommodation status

   EXAMPLE: Accommodating maker is liable as a maker would be.

   EXAMPLE: Accommodating endorser is liable as an endorser would be.

   a. Accommodation party is one who signs to lend his/her name to other party

      EXAMPLE: Father-in-law endorses a note for son-in-law so creditor will accept it.

      (1) Notice of default need not be given to accommodation party
      (2) The accommodation party has right of recourse against accommodated party if accommodation party is held liable

5. Holding parties liable

   a. If there are multiple endorsers, each is liable in full to subsequent endorsers or holders

      (1) I.e., liability moves from bottom up

          EXAMPLE: A negotiable note has the following endorsements on the back from top to bottom: A, B, C, D, and E. Suppose E has sought payment from the maker but was unsuccessful. E, therefore, can seek payment from any previous endorser. Assume he collects from C. C then seeks payment from B. (He may seek from B or A but not D.)

          EXAMPLE: Note that in the previous example, if A eventually pays, he may try to collect from the maker. If unsuccessful, A may not try to collect from any endorser up the line from him.

   b. Once primary party pays, all endorsers are discharged from liability

6. Liability on instruments with forged signatures

   a. Person whose signature was forged on instrument is not liable on that instrument

      (1) Unless later ratifies it

   b. Forged signature operates as signature of forger
   c. Therefore, if signature of maker or drawer is forged, instrument can still be negotiated between parties and thus a holder can acquire good title

      (1) Recall that forgery is a real defense so that innocent maker or drawer cannot be required to pay even an HDC--forger can be required to pay if found

   d. However, a forged endorsement does not transfer title; thus, persons receiving it after forgery cannot collect on it

      (1) Three important exceptions to rule that forged endorsements cannot transfer title are imposter rule, fictitious payee rule, and

negligence of maker or drawer--these cause maker or drawer to be liable

(a) <u>Imposter rule</u> applies when maker or drawer issues a note or draft to an imposter thinking s/he actually is the real payee --when that imposter forges the real payee's name, this effectively negotiates this note or draft so that a subsequent holder (if not part of scheme) can collect from maker or drawer

1] Note that this rule normally places loss on person who was in best position to avoid this scheme, i.e., maker or drawer

a] Of course, upon payment, maker or drawer may try to collect from imposter

EXAMPLE: *J. Loux owes Larsen (whom she has not met) $2,000. Sawyer, claiming to be Larsen, gets Loux to issue him a check for $2,000. Sawyer forges Larsen's endorsement and transfers the check to P. Jenkins. Jenkins can collect from Loux because of the imposter rule exception.*

EXAMPLE: *If in the example above, J. Loux had given the check to the real Larsen and he lost it, the imposter rule would not apply even if someone found the check and forged Larsen's endorsement. No one after the forgery can collect on the check.*

(b) <u>Fictitious payee rule</u> applies when maker, drawer, or his/her agent (employee) issues a note or a check to a fictitious payee--then maker, drawer, or employee forges the endorsement --subsequent parties can enforce the note or check against the maker or drawer

1] Actually payee may be a real person as long as maker, drawer, or other person supplying name never intended for that payee to ever get payment

EXAMPLE: *R. Stewart submits a time card for a nonexistent employee and the employer issues the payroll check. Stewart forges the endorsement and transfers it to L. Reed. Reed wins against the employer even though the employer was unaware of the scheme at the time.*

(c) If person's negligence substantially contributes to the forgery that person is prevented from raising the defense of forgery and thus holder wins

EXAMPLE: *D. Wolter has a signature stamp and leaves it lying around. Unauthorized use of the stamp is not a defense against a holder as Wolter's negligence substantially contributed to the forgery. If the forger could be caught, Wolter could sue the forger for losses.*

I. Additional issues

1. Certain types of draft names come up--although they follow general rules of drafts, definitions are helpful

a. Trade acceptance is a draft in which a seller of goods extends credit to buyer by drawing a draft on that buyer directing him/her to pay seller a sum of money on a specified date

    (1) Trade acceptance also requires signature of buyer on face of instrument--called acceptance--buyer is also called acceptor at this point

    (2) Then seller may negotiate trade acceptance at a discount to another party to receive immediate cash

    (3) Seller is normally both drawer and payee of a trade acceptance

b. Banker's acceptance is a draft in which drawee and drawer are a bank

c. Sight draft is one payable upon presentment to drawer

d. Time draft is one payable at a specified date or payable a certain period of time after a specified date

e. Money order is a draft purchased by one party to pay payee in which the third party is typically post office, a bank, or a company

f. Traveler's check is purchased from a bank (or company)--drawer (traveler) must sign twice for purposes of identification (once at the time s/he purchases the check and again at the time s/he uses the check)--drawee is bank or company--payee is one who gets paid

    (1) Technically, drawee must be a bank to be a true "check"--if drawee is not a bank then traveler's check is actually a draft

g. Cashier's check is a check in which drawer and drawee are the same bank with a separate party being the payee

    (1) This is still considered a "three-party" instrument even though drawer and drawee are same bank

h. Certified check is a check that payor bank has agreed in advance to pay so that bank becomes primarily liable

J. Banks

1. Relationship between bank and depositor is debtor-creditor

    a. Even though the depositor has funds in the bank, a payee cannot force a drawee to make payment

    b. Only drawer has an action against drawee-bank for wrongfully dishonoring a check--based on contract between customer (drawer) and bank

2. Checks

    a. Banks are not obligated to pay on a check presented more than 6 months after date

      (1) But they may pay in good faith and charge customer's account

    b. Even if check creates an overdraft, a bank may charge customer's account

    c. Bank is liable to drawer for damages caused by wrongful dishonor of a check

      (1) Wrongful dishonor may occur if the bank in error believes funds are insufficient when they are sufficient

    d. Payment of bad checks, e.g., forgery of drawer or altered checks

      (1) Bank is liable to drawer for payment on bad checks unless drawer's negligence contributed because bank presumed to know signatures of its drawers

      (2) Bank cannot recover from an HDC to whom bank paid on a bad check

(3)   If drawer fails to notify bank of forgery or alterations within 14 days of bank statement, the drawer is held liable on subsequent forgeries or alterations done in same way by same person

    (a)   In any event, drawer must give notice of forgeries or alterations within one year to keep bank liable or else drawer is liable

        1]   This applies to even nonrepeat cases as well as when bank was paying in bad faith

EXAMPLE: G. Wilson forges the name of M. Gibson on a check in an artful way. A subsequent HDC cashes this check at the drawee bank. The bank is liable on this check and cannot recover from either the HDC or G. Gibson as long as Gibson notifies the bank of the forgery within one year. The loss falls on the bank based on the idea that the bank should know its drawer's signature.

    (b)   Forgeries of endorsements are treated differently--depositor has three years to notify bank and also bank may charge check back to party that presented check to bank whether or not the party was an HDC

        1]   Recall that one cashing check gave warranty that all signatures are genuine

EXAMPLE: D issues a check to P. P loses the check which is found by X. X forges the endorsement and transfers it to H. Finally, H cashes the check at the drawee bank. D soon notifies the bank of the forgery. The bank may charge it back to H (whether or not an HDC) but not to D.

e.   Oral <u>stop payment order</u> is good for 14 days; written stop payment order is good for six months and is renewable

    (1)   Stop-payment order must be given so as to give bank reasonable opportunity to act on it

    (2)   Bank is liable to drawer if it pays after effective stop-payment order only when drawer can prove that the bank's failure to obey the order caused drawer's loss. If drawer has no valid defense to justify dishonoring instrument, then bank has no liability for failure to obey stop-payment order.

EXAMPLE: W. Paisley buys a T.V. set from the Burke Appliance Store and pays for the set with a check. Later in the day Paisley finds a better model for the same price at another store. Paisley telephones his bank and orders the bank to stop payment on the check. If the bank mistakenly pays Paisley's check two days after receiving the stop order, the bank will not be liable if Paisley could not rightfully rescind his agreement with debt the Burke Appliance Store. With these facts, Paisley suffered no damages from the bank's mistake.

    (3)   If drawer stops payment on the check, s/he is still liable to holder of check unless s/he has a valid defense (e.g., if holder qualifies as a holder in due course then drawer must be able to assert a real defense to free him/herself of liability)

f. Bank is entitled to a depositor's endorsement on checks deposited with the bank

(1) If missing, bank may supply endorsement to negotiate check

g. Banks may choose which checks are charged to account first when several checks received in same day

K. **Transfer of Negotiable Documents of Title**

1. Transfer of documents of title is governed by Article 7 of UCC--transfer of such documents is very similar to transfer of negotiable instruments under Article 3 of UCC

2. Types of documents of title

a. Bill of lading is a document issued by a carrier (a person engaged in the business of transporting or forwarding goods) and given to seller evidencing receipt of the goods for shipment

b. A warehouse receipt is a document issued by a warehouseman (a person engaged in the business of storing goods for hire) and given to seller evidencing receipt of goods for storage

3. Form

a. Negotiable--document of title is negotiable if face of the document contains words of negotiability (order or bearer)

(1) Order document--a document of title containing a promise to deliver goods to the order of a named person

(a) The person may be named on the face of the document or, if there are endorsements, on back of document and last endorsement is a special endorsement

(b) Proper negotiation requires delivery of the document and endorsement by named individual(s)

(2) Bearer document--a document of title containing a promise to deliver the goods to bearer

(a) "Bearer" may be stated on face of document or, if there are endorsements, on back of document and last endorsement is a blank endorsement

(b) Proper negotiation merely requires delivery of document

b. Nonnegotiable (straight) documents of title are assigned, not negotiated

(1) Assignee will never receive any better rights than assignor had

4. Due negotiation--document of title is "duly negotiated" when it is negotiated to a holder who takes it in good faith in the ordinary course of business without notice of a defense and pays value

a. Value does not include payment of a preexisting (antecedent) debt--this is an important difference from value concept required to create a holder in due course under Article 3

5. Rights acquired by due negotiation--a holder by due negotiation acquires rights very similar to those acquired by a holder in due course

a. These rights include

        (1) Title to the document
        (2) Title to the goods
        (3) All rights accruing under the law of agency or estoppel, including rights to goods delivered after the document was issued, and
        (4) The direct obligation of the issuer to hold or deliver the goods according to the terms of the document

    b. A holder by due negotiation defeats similar defenses to those defeated by a holder in due course under Article 3 of the UCC (personal but not real defenses)

    c. A document of title procured by a thief upon placing stolen goods in a warehouse confers no rights in the underlying goods. This defense is valid against a subsequent holder to whom the document of title has been duly negotiated. Therefore, the original owner of the goods can assert better title to the goods than a holder who has received the document through due negotiation.

6. Rights acquired in the absence of due negotiation

    a. A transferee of a document, whether negotiable or nonnegotiable, to whom the document has been delivered, but not duly negotiated, acquires the title and rights which his/her transferor had or had actual authority to convey

7. Warranties transferred upon negotiation--transferor for value warrants that

    a. Document is genuine
    b. S/he has no knowledge of any fact that would impair its validity or worth, and
    c. His/her negotiation or transfer is rightful and fully effective with respect to the document of title and the goods it represents

L. Transfer of Investment Securities

1. Transfer of investment securities (stocks, bonds, or other mediums of investment) is governed by Article 8 of the UCC. This Article states that investment securities are written negotiable instruments. Consequently, the rules applicable to the transfer of investment securities are very similar to the rules contained in Article 3 of the UCC which governs the transfer of promissory notes, drafts, etc.

2. Proper negotiation of investment securities

    a. If no endorsements on the back of the certificate look to the face of the security

        (1) If a registered security (names person entitled to the security) specified person must deliver and endorse
        (2) If a bearer security only delivery of the security is needed

    b. If there are endorsements on the back of the certificate proper negotiation would be

        (1) Delivery if the last endorsement is a blank endorsement
        (2) Delivery and endorsement by specified person if the last endorsement is a special endorsement

3. A bona fide purchaser (BFP) of an investment security is someone who

     a. Receives the security through proper negotiation (delivery of a bearer security or delivery and endorsement of a registered security), and

     b. Gives value (includes taking for antecedent debt) and

     c. Takes in good faith and without notice of any adverse claim

4. A bona fide purchaser acquires the security free of most adverse claims such as fraud, duress, failure of consideration, theft of a bearer security, etc.,

     a. This status is comparable to a holder in due course under Article 3 of the UCC

5. A bona fide purchaser is still subject to the defense of a forged endorsement on a stolen registered security

     a. However, if the issuer (normally a corporation) transfers the registration of the security to the BFP based upon the unauthorized endorsement, the BFP has title to the security

     b. Original owner of the security (the party the thief stole the instrument from) is also entitled to receive a new certificate from the issuer evidencing the security that was stolen

> *EXAMPLE: Herb stole from Ike an unendorsed registered certificate of stock (an order certificate). Ike gave the issuing corporation notice of loss within a reasonable period of time. Herb, the thief, forges Ike's name to the certificate and then delivers it to Danny, a bona fide purchaser who pays value and takes the certificate without knowledge of the theft or forgery. Ike is still the owner of the shares, and Herb is liable to Ike for their value. If Danny surrenders the certificate to the issuing corporation which cancels it and issues a new one in Danny's name, Danny is now owner of the shares represented by the certificate registered in his name. However, Ike is entitled to receive from the corporation a new certificate for the same number of shares.*

6. A purchaser who does not qualify as a bona fide purchaser receives rights of his/her transferor unless purchaser took part in creating the defense present or is trying to better his/her position by passing the security through the BFP (similar to the shelter provision under Article 3 of the UCC)

7. Transferor of a security for value

     a. Extends following warranties

         (1) Transfer is effective and rightful, and

         (2) The security is genuine and has not been materially altered, and

         (3) S/he knows of no fact that might impair the validity of the security

     b. Is entitled to a reissued certificate of stock without giving further compensation to the issuer, if bona fide purchaser originally received a stock certificate containing an unauthorized signature of an employee of the issuer, who had been entrusted with the responsible handling of stock certificates

SECURED TRANSACTIONS

Overview

The concept of secured transactions is important to modern business. A creditor often requires some security from the debtor beyond a mere promise to pay. In general, the creditor may require the debtor to provide some collateral to secure payment on the debt. If the debt is not paid, the creditor then can resort to the collateral. Under Article 9 of the UCC, the collateral is generally personal property or fixtures. You need to understand the concept of attachment. For attachment to occur (1) there must be a security agreement, (2) the secured party must give value, and (3) the debtor must have rights in the collateral used to secure payment.

You also need to understand the important concept of perfection discussed in this module which allows a secured party to obtain greater rights over many third parties. Be sure to understand the three methods by which perfection can be accomplished. The examination also covers rules of priorities when competing interests exist in the same collateral.

A. Scope of Secured Transactions

1. Comes from Article 9 of UCC

   a. CPA exam now tests the 1972 official text of UCC which is covered in this module

2. Applies to transactions in which creditor intends to obtain greater security in debt by taking a security interest in personal property or fixtures (which are used as collateral)

   a. Types of personal property

      (1) Tangible personal property (goods)--there are four types

         (a) Consumer goods are those for personal, family, or household use
         (b) Inventory consists of goods for lease or sale in the ordinary course of business
         (c) Equipment consists of goods used primarily in the business
         (d) Farm products are livestock, crops, and supplies used in farming
         (e) Use of collateral by debtor, not nature of collateral, determines type of tangible personal property

         EXAMPLE: B purchases a refrigerator from S, an appliance dealer, giving S a security interest. If B bought it for home use, it involves consumer goods. If B bought it for use in his restaurant, it is equipment.

         EXAMPLE: In the above example, assume that S borrows from a bank to buy the refrigerators to sell from the appliance store. S gives the bank a security interest in the refrigerators. In the hands of S, the refrigerators are inventory.

      (2) Quasi-tangible personal property (documentary collateral)

         (a) Represented by piece(s) of paper instead of property

> *EXAMPLE: Negotiable instruments, nonnegotiable instruments, documents of title, bonds, and shares of stock are in this category.*
>
> *EXAMPLE: One or more writings that together show a monetary obligation as well as a security interest can be used as collateral. These writings are referred to as chattel paper.*

      (3) Intangible personal property

         (a) Accounts (accounts receivable) not evidenced by a writing

> *EXAMPLE: The sale of accounts receivable is covered under secured transactions.*

         (b) General intangibles, e.g., copyrights, patents, goodwill

  b. Fixtures

      (1) Former personal property that has been attached to real property in a relatively permanent manner

> *EXAMPLE: An air conditioning system installed in a home. It is now a fixture.*

      (2) Detachable trade fixtures are considered personal property rather than part of the real property

3. Article 9 of the UCC does <u>not</u> apply

  a. If collateral is real property (see Mortgages in Property module)
  b. To assignment of wage claims
  c. To claims from court proceedings
  d. To statutory liens

B. Attachment of Security Interests

1. Upon attachment, security interest is enforceable against debtor by the secured party

  a. Has priority over third parties actually aware of security interest
  b. Does not have priority over third parties unaware of security interest

2. Security interest is said to attach when all of the following occur in any order (these are important)

  a. There is a security agreement
  b. Secured party gives value
  c. Debtor has rights in collateral

3. Security agreement

  a. Is a contract or agreement that creates a security interest

      (1) Secured party is one in whose favor the security interest exists

> *EXAMPLE: A bank makes a loan to D using D's personal jewelry as collateral. The bank is the secured party.*
>
> *EXAMPLE: B buys a stereo on credit from S allowing the stereo to be used as collateral for the credit purchase. S, the seller, is the secured party.*

  b. May be oral if collateral is in possession of secured party or some other third party by arrangement

       (1) Pledge is used to mean debtor gives possession of collateral to other party to secure obligation

> EXAMPLE: *D pledges his shares of stock as collateral for a bank loan. The bank holds the stock until the loan is paid. This security agreement need not be in writing.*

  c. If collateral in possession of debtor, security agreement must

       (1) Be in writing
       (2) Be signed by debtor
       (3) Contain a reasonable description of collateral

4. Value given by secured party

  a. Includes any consideration that supports a contract (see Contracts module)
  b. Preexisting claim (although not consideration) is value

> EXAMPLE: *D already owes S $5,000 on a previous debt. Subsequently, D signs a security agreement giving S an interest in some furniture owned by D. Value has been given by S based on the previous debt.*

> EXAMPLE: *A bank grants a loan to allow B to purchase a washer and dryer. This extension of credit is a typical type of value.*

5. Debtor must have rights in collateral

  a. Ownership interest or
  b. Some right to possession
  c. Need not have title

> EXAMPLE: *M obtains a loan from a bank to purchase a sofa. She signs a security agreement granting the credit union a security interest in any sofa that she will buy with this loan. Attachment cannot occur until she buys a sofa.*

C. Perfecting a Security Interest

1. Entails steps <u>in addition to</u> attachment (with one exception discussed later) to give secured party priority over many other parties that may claim collateral

  a. Attachment focuses primarily on rights between creditor and debtor
  b. However, perfection focuses on rights between various <u>other parties</u> that may claim an interest in same collateral

       (1) Generally, perfecting a security interest gives (constructive) <u>notice to other parties</u> that perfecting party claims an interest (security interest) in certain collateral

2. Three methods of perfection (know these)

  a. <u>Filing</u> a financing statement

       (1) Written notice filed in public records

  b. Secured party (creditor) taking <u>possession</u> of collateral
  c. <u>Perfection on attachment</u>

       (1) Under some conditions, once attachment takes place, perfection is automatic with no further steps

3. <u>Filing</u> a financing statement

a. For all collateral except money and instruments (they must be possessed)

    (1) Instruments include nonnegotiable and negotiable instruments in addition to investment securities

    (2) Only method for contract rights, accounts, and other intangibles (because there is nothing to possess)

b. Financing statement must

    (1) Give names of debtor and creditor

    (2) Contain addresses of both

    (3) Identify type of or describe collateral

        (a) Unlike description in security agreement, it need not identify the specific collateral. It must merely identify the type of collateral.

    (4) Be signed by the debtor (secured party need not sign)

    (5) The security agreement may suffice as financing if it complies with the above

        (a) But a copy of it must be filed as below

c. Filing

    (1) By statute, usually in county recorder's office, Secretary of State, or both

        (a) Financing statement covering fixtures or minerals must also be filed in real estate records

    (2) Has functional purpose of giving notice to the public of creditor's security interest in the collateral

    (3) Lasts for five years and may be continued for additional five-year periods (by continuation statement)

    (4) Upon full payment to the creditor, debtor may request a release from the creditor, which the debtor can then file (termination statement)

d. Filing may be done anytime, <u>even before</u> the security agreement is made. But perfection does not occur until all requirements (of attachment plus filing) are met.

EXAMPLE: Bank is going to finance the inventory of a car dealer who is beginning business. They immediately file a financing statement. When the inventory arrives, they sign a security agreement. Perfection occurs when the security agreement is signed in this case because then all requirements of attachment plus filing have taken place.

EXAMPLE: Same example as above except that the bank obtains the security agreement first, then the inventory arrives, and afterwards the bank files a financing statement. Attachment is effective when the inventory arrives. (Note that the dealer has rights in the inventory at that time.) Perfection in this case is accomplished at the time of filing.

e. Perfection is ineffective if financing statement is improper or if it is filed in wrong place

4. Perfection by <u>possession</u>

    a. Secured party takes possession of collateral

    b. For negotiable instruments, securities, and money, possession is only method allowed for perfection

        (1) For other collateral capable of possession, possession may also be used for perfection but of course debtor may not desire losing use during creditor's possession

> *EXAMPLE: P wishes to borrow money from a bank using several shares of stock that she owns. In addition to completing the three steps needed for attachment, the bank must possess the shares in order to perfect. Filing is not effective in this case.*

    c. Cross reference: When creditor has possession of collateral, an oral security agreement suffices. Furthermore, possession also accomplishes perfection

    d. Perfection is effective as long as creditor retains possession

    e. While in possession, the secured party

        (1) Must use reasonable care to preserve the property

        (2) May keep stock dividends, newborn calf, etc. as additional collateral

            (a) Dividends, interest, etc., belong to debtor

        (3) May use or lease but not sell collateral

    f. The debtor (owner)

        (1) Must bear any accidental loss to the collateral provided the secured party has used reasonable care

            (a) Each party has an insurable interest in the collateral

        (2) Is liable for reasonable expenses, e.g., taxes, insurance of the collateral

5. Perfection by attachment (automatic perfection)

    a. Under certain conditions only, perfection is accomplished by completing attachment with no further steps

        (1) Purchase money security interest in consumer goods

            (a) Purchase money security interest occurs in two important cases

                1] Seller retains security interest in same item sold on credit to secure payment

                2] Another party such as bank provides loan for and retains security interest in same item purchased by debtor

            (b) "In consumer goods" means that goods are bought primarily for personal, family, or household purposes

> *EXAMPLE: B buys a refrigerator for his home from Friendly Appliance Dealer on credit. Friendly has B sign a written security agreement. Because all three elements needed for attachment took place, this is automatic perfection. This is true because the refrigerator is a purchase money security interest in consumer goods.*

> *EXAMPLE: Same as previous example except that Second Intercity Bank provides the loan having B sign a security agreement. This is also a purchase money security interest in consumer goods. Perfection takes place when all three elements of attachment occur.*

EXAMPLE: In the two examples above, if B had purchased the refrigerator for use in a restaurant, the collateral would be equipment. Therefore, automatic perfection would not occur. However, the secured party could file a financing statement to perfect the security interest in both cases.

(c) Perfection by attachment does not occur for motor vehicles--perfected by a lien on certificate of title filed with state

(d) Automatic perfection is <u>not</u> effective against bona fide purchaser for value who buys goods from consumer for consumer use

　　1] <u>Is effective</u>, however, if secured party had <u>filed</u>

EXAMPLE: B purchases a washer and dryer from Dear Appliances for use in his home giving Dear a security interest then sells the washer and dryer to C for a fair price for C's household use. C is unaware of the security interest that Dear has in the washer and dryer. Dear's perfection on attachment is not effective against C.

EXAMPLE: Same example as above except that Dear had filed a financing statement. Dear wins because filing is effective even against a subsequent bona fide purchaser such as C even if he buys for consumer use.

EXAMPLE: In the two examples above, if C had purchased the items from B for other than consumer use, C is <u>not</u> free of Dear's security interest. This is so because the rule only applies to bona fide purchasers for consumer use. The extra step of filing would have no effect in this case.

　　2] <u>Is effective</u> if subsequent purchaser knows of security interest before buying

EXAMPLE: An appliance dealer sells a freezer to Jack for family use. Assume attachment has occurred. Jack then sells it to Cindy who is aware of the security interest that the dealer still has in the freezer. Even if Cindy is buying this for household use, she takes subject to the security interest.

D. **Other Issues Under Secured Transactions**

　1. After-acquired property and future goods may also become part of collateral if agreement so states

EXAMPLE: An agreement states that the collateral consists of all of debtor's furniture now located in his office as well as all office furniture subsequently acquired. The security interest in the new furniture cannot attach until the debtor acquires rights in the other office furniture.

　　a. Typically used for inventory and accounts receivable when debtor also has rights to sell inventory and collect accounts, e.g., a floating lien

EXAMPLE: A, an automobile dealer, to obtain a loan, grants a bank a security interest covering "all automobiles now possessed and hereafter acquired." As the dealer obtains rights in the new inventory of automobiles, the security interest attaches as to those newly acquired automobiles.

    b. Certain restrictions exist if debtor buys consumer goods to protect consumer

       (1) An after acquired property clause applying to consumer goods is only effective against the consumer for ten days from date of purchase

2. Security interest continues in identifiable proceeds from sale of secured goods unless security agreement states otherwise

    EXAMPLE: Undeposited checks, cash that has not been deposited or commingled, accounts receivable, or new property received in exchange for the collateral are automatically covered by a security agreement.

3. Field warehousing

    a. A device used to perfect a security interest in inventory by (in essence) possession

       (1) The inventory is kept on debtor's premises but under the control of a bonded warehouseman or employee of secured party

       (2) It is less expensive than renting an outside warehouse and makes the goods more accessible to debtor when it is in effect a floating lien on the inventory

    b. Warehouseman (on behalf of secured party) must have dominion and control over the security

       (1) A separate room or warehouse is used or an area is fenced off on the debtor's premises

       (2) Locks are changed

       (3) It is posted showing the secured party's possession

       (4) Temporary relinquishment of control is permissible to allow for exchange of collateral (a revolving type of collateral arrangement)

    c. Secured party can file a financing statement as to the goods rather than rely on field warehousing device

4. Consignments

    a. Amendments to the UCC set forth procedures a consignor must follow in order to prevail against his/her consignee's creditors

    b. A consignment is a type of agreement

       (1) If it is a "true consignment," consignee is simply a sales agent who does not own the goods but sells them for consignor

          (a) "True consignment" exists when

             1] Consignor retains title to goods

             2] Consignee has no obligation to buy goods

             3] Consignor has right to all proceeds (pays consignee commission)

             EXAMPLE: Manufacturer (consignor) gives possession of goods to a marketing representative (consignee) to sell those goods on commission.

          (b) To perfect his/her interest, a consignor must

             1] Comply with applicable local law by posting a sign on the consignee's premises disclosing the consignor's interest in the goods, or

        2] Establish that the consignee is generally known as selling goods owned by other individuals, or

        3] File a financing statement under secured transactions law and give notice to the consignee's creditors who have perfected security interests in the same type of goods

            a] Notice must contain description of the goods to be delivered and be given before the consignee receives possession of goods

                EXAMPLE: P delivers goods to A on consignment. The consignment is a "true consignment" in that P has title to the goods and pays A a commission for selling the goods. Any goods that are unsold, are returned by A to P. A does not pay for any unsold goods. Creditors of A can assert claims against the goods that A possesses unless P has given notice to the creditors. The general way to accomplish this is by filing under the secured transactions law.

    (2) If it is not a true consignment because it is actually a <u>sale</u> from creditor to debtor in which debtor then owns the goods, look for a security agreement

        (a) Attachment and perfection occur as in typical secured transaction

5. Temporary perfection for

    a. Proceeds of collateral for 10 days where interest in original collateral was perfected and proceeds are of type that cannot be perfected by filing or by filing in same place as original collateral

        (1) If proceeds are of same type as original collateral, they are automatically perfected if original collateral was perfected

            EXAMPLE: Debtor sells equipment for a promissory note. Secured creditor has temporary perfection for ten days in the note.

            EXAMPLE: Debtor trades equipment in on new equipment. New equipment is perfected if old equipment was. No temporary perfection is needed.

    b. Instruments and negotiable documents for 21 days to the extent new value is given under an existing written security agreement

E. Priorities

1. If more than one party claims a security interest in same collateral, rules of priority should be examined

2. Although the rules on priorities are complex with many exceptions the following will give the general, important rules to prepare you for the exam

3. General rules of priorities

    a. If both parties perfect by filing then first to file has priority

        (1) This is true even if filing takes place before attachment

EXAMPLE: K obtains a written security agreement on day 1 on collateral that D owns and possesses. On day 2, K files a financing statement but does not loan the money (value) until day 10. L obtains a written security agreement on the same collateral on day 3 and gives value on day 4 and files on day 6. Since both perfected by filing, K has priority because he filed first even though attachment and perfection did not occur until later (day 10). To test your understanding, note that for L, attachment took place on day 4 and perfection on day 6.

    b. If both do not perfect by filing, then priority is by order of perfection

        (1) This is true regardless of order of attachment

    c. Perfected security interests win over unperfected ones
    d. If neither is perfected, then the first to attach prevails
    e. General creditors (unsecured creditors) lose to secured creditors (perfected or unperfected)

4. Other principles on priorities

    a. Buyers in the ordinary course of business take free of any security interest whether perfected or not (be sure to know this one)

        (1) In general, buying in the ordinary course of business means buying from inventory of a person or company that normally deals in those goods
        (2) Buyer has priority even if knows that security agreement exists
        (3) Purpose is to allow purchasers to buy from merchants without fear of security agreements between merchants and other parties

EXAMPLE: S, a dealer in stereos, obtained financing from L by securing the loan with her inventory in stereos. B purchases one of the stereos from that inventory. B takes free of the security interest that L has in the inventory of S whether it is perfected or not.

    b. Distinguish between buyers in the ordinary course of business and the subsequent bona fide purchasers from consumers

        (1) The latter defeats only a purchase money security interest in consumer goods (perfection on attachment) unless filing takes place--applies to sale by consumer to consumer
        (2) The former applies whether buyer is consumer or not but seller is dealer in those goods

EXAMPLE: See previous example. The result is the same whether or not B was a consumer when he bought in the ordinary course of business from S.

EXAMPLE: Refer again to the same example using S, L, and B. Now let's add on one more security interest in that B is buying the stereo on credit from S and for his own personal use. Attachment has occurred. There is perfection by attachment because between B and S, it is a purchase money security interest in consumer goods. If B sells the stereo to N, his neighbor, for consumer use, then N takes free of the perfected security interest (unless S had filed or N had notice of the security interest).

c. In the case of a purchase money security interest, if the secured party files within 10 days after the debtor receives the collateral, then this defeats other security interests by use of a 10-day grace period

(1) Note that this purchase money security interest (PMSI) does not require consumer goods

EXAMPLE: On August 1, B purchased some equipment from S on credit. All elements of attachment are satisfied on this date. On August 3, B borrows money from a bank using equipment purchased from S as collateral. Attachment is accomplished and a financing statement is correctly filed by the bank on August 3. On August 7, S then files a financing statement. Because of the 10-day grace period, S has priority over the bank.

EXAMPLE: Same as above except that S files after the 10-day grace period or not at all. The bank has priority.

(2) If inventory, no 10-day grace period is allowed for perfection to have priority

(a) Party with purchase money security interest must give notice to other secured party

(b) Party with purchase money security interest must perfect prior to debtor's taking possession

(3) Knowledge of preexisting security interest has no effect

d. Holder in due course of negotiable instruments wins over perfected or unperfected security interest

e. Security interest, perfected or unperfected, wins over subsequent perfected security interest if latter party knew of previous security interest

f. Possessor of negotiable document of title has priority over others

g. Lien creditor, e.g., repairman or contractor

(1) Has priority over an unperfected security interest

(a) Knowledge of security interest is immaterial

(2) Has priority over a security interest perfected after attachment of the lien unless it is a purchase money security interest perfected within the 10-day grace period

(3) A security interest perfected before the lien usually has priority

(4) Lien by statute (not by judgment or court order) has priority over a prior perfected security interest unless state statute expressly provides otherwise

EXAMPLE: A person such as a repairman, in the ordinary course of business, furnishes services or materials with respect to goods subject to a security interest. The repairman (artisan lien) has priority.

h. Trustee in bankruptcy as a lien creditor

(1) Trustee has the rights of a lien creditor from the date of filing of petition in bankruptcy

(a) So has priority over a security interest perfected after date of filing petition unless it is a purchase money security interest perfected within the 10-day grace period

(2) Trustee also takes the position of any existing lien creditor

F. **Rights of Parties Upon Default**

   1. If collateral consists of claims, e.g., receivables, the secured party has the right of collection from third parties

      a. Secured party may notify third party to pay secured party directly
      b. Secured party must account for any surplus and debtor is liable for any deficiency
      c. Secured party may deduct his/her reasonable expenses

   2. Secured party may retain collateral already in his/her possession or may take possession from debtor

      a. May do so him/herself if can without breach of the peace
      b. Otherwise, s/he must use judicial process
      c. Secured party has duty to take reasonable care of collateral in his/her possession

        (1) Expenses to protect collateral are responsibility of debtor

   3. If secured party proposes to satisfy obligation by retaining the collateral, s/he must

      a. Send written notice to debtor
      b. Must notify other secured parties (who have sent written notice of their interest), unless consumer goods
      c. Can only retain consumer goods if debtor has paid less than 60 percent of the purchase price or obligation

        (1) If 60 percent or more has been paid, secured party must sell collateral within 90 days after taking possession or be liable to the debtor unless debtor waives this right to sale <u>after</u> the default

   4. Secured party may sell collateral

      a. May be a public or a private sale
      b. Must use commercially reasonable practices
      c. Must sell within a reasonable time
      d. Must notify debtor of time and place of public sale or time after which private sale will occur unless collateral is perishable, threatens to decline in value, or is type sold on a recognized market

        (1) Must also notify other secured parties (who have sent written notice of their interest) unless collateral consists of consumer goods

      e. Secured party may buy at any public sale and also at a private sale if rights of debtor protected
      f. Subordinate claims are entitled to any surplus

        (1) Debtor is entitled to surplus (if any) after all claims and expenses are paid or is liable for deficiency (if any)

   5. Debtor has right to redeem collateral before secured party disposes of it by paying

      a. Entire debt, and
      b. Secured party's reasonable expenses

6. Most remedies can be varied by agreement if reasonable

    a. Provision that secured party must account for any surplus to debtor cannot be varied by agreement

7. Good faith purchaser (i.e., for value and with no knowledge of defects in sale) of collateral takes free of debtor's rights and any secured interest or lien subordinate to it

    a. Receives debtor's title
    b. If sale was improper, remedy of debtor is money damages against secured party who sold collateral, not against good faith purchaser

8. Termination of security interest is normally done by having secured party file a termination statement

BANKRUPTCY

Overview
Overview

The overall objective of bankruptcy law is to allow honest insolvent debtors to surrender most of their assets and obtain release from their debts. A secondary purpose is to give creditors fair opportunity to share in the debtor's limited assets in proportion to their claims.

Bankruptcy is typically tested by either a few multiple choice questions or an essay question. These questions normally emphasize when involuntary and voluntary proceedings can be conducted, the federal exemptions, the role of the trustee in bankruptcy, preferential transfers, priorities, and conditions under which debts may be discharged in bankruptcy. Although bankruptcy under Chapter 7 is emphasized on the CPA Examination, you should also be familiar with the other portions of this module. Recently, for example, Chapter 11 on Business Reorganizations has received some increased treatment.

A. **Alternatives to Bankruptcy Proceedings**

1. Creditors may choose to do nothing

    a. Expense of collection may exceed what creditors could recover
    b. Creditors may expect debtor to pull through

2. Grab law

    a. Creditors may rush to satisfy their claims individually through legal proceedings
    b. Methods

        (1) Obtain legal judgments against debtor
        (2) Seize and sell property
        (3) Attach liens to property
        (4) Garnish debts owed to debtor
        (5) Recover property fraudulently conveyed to a third person, e.g., given to relative to put beyond creditors' reach

    c. May result in bankruptcy proceedings (especially if some creditors are dissatisfied)

3. Composition agreement with creditors

    a. Creditors agree with debtor to accept less than is due, i.e., a percentage of their claims, in full satisfaction of the debt (i.e., discharges debts)
    b. Must have consideration

        (1) Creditors' mutual promises to accept less than full amount

            (a) Must have more than one creditor because one creditor is not bound by promise to accept less, but if more than one creditor, their mutual promises bind them
            (b) All creditors need not agree unless agreement so states

        (2) Debtor pays creditors at agreed rates
        (3) All agreeing creditors need not be treated equally but treatment of all must be disclosed to and agreed by all

    c. Debts are not discharged until debtor performs agreement
    d. Creditors who do not agree are not bound and may be able to force debtor into bankruptcy

4. Receiverships

      a. This provides for the general administration of debtor's assets by a court appointee (a receiver) for the benefit of all parties

      b. Not to be confused with composition agreement in which no receiver is appointed

5. Assignment for the benefit of creditors

      a. Debtor voluntarily transfers all of his/her assets to an assignee (or trustee) to be sold for the benefit of creditors

      b. Assignee takes legal title

         (1) Debtor must cease all control of assets

         (2) Assignment is irrevocable

      c. No agreement between creditors is necessary

         (1) Dissatisfied creditors may file a petition in bankruptcy and assignments may be set aside

6. Creditors' committee

      a. Submission of business and financial affairs by the debtor to the control of a committee of creditors

      b. Creditors' committee is given management of assets or business but not necessarily title

      c. Not as severe as assignment because assets not liquidated

      d. Nevertheless, it is similar to assignment for benefit of creditors

B. Bankruptcy in General

1. Bankruptcy is based on federal law

2. Bankruptcy provides a method of protecting creditors' rights and granting the debtor relief from his/her indebtedness

      a. Debtor is permitted to have a fresh start

      b. Creditors are treated more fairly according to the priorities stated in bankruptcy laws to effect an equitable distribution of debtor's property

C. Chapter 7 Voluntary Bankruptcy Petitions

1. A voluntary bankruptcy petition is a formal request by debtor for an order of relief

      a. The petition is filed with the court along with a list of debtor's assets and liabilities

      b. Debtor need not be insolvent--merely needs to state that s/he has debts

      c. Debtor is automatically given an order of relief upon filing of petition

         (1) Under amendments to bankruptcy act, court may dismiss voluntary petition if petitioning debtor obligations are primarily consumer debts and granting of relief would be substantial abuse of Chapter 7--(debtor may then proceed under Chapter 13)

      d. Obtaining a receivership does not affect debtor's ability to file voluntary petition for bankruptcy

2. Any person, partnership, or corporation may file voluntary bankruptcy petition with some exceptions

D. **Chapter 7 Involuntary Bankruptcy Petitions**

1. An involuntary bankruptcy petition may be filed with bankruptcy court by creditors requesting an order for relief

2. Requirements to file petition

    a. If there are fewer than twelve creditors, a single creditor may file the petition as long as his/her claim aggregates $5,000 in excess of any security s/he may hold

        (1) Claims must not be contingent
        (2) If necessary, more than one creditor may join together to have combined debts of more than $5,000 of unsecured claims

        EXAMPLE: *Poor-R-Us Company is not paying its debts as they become due. Its debtors are A (owed $7,000), B (owed $4,000), and C (owed $2,000). A alone may file the involuntary petition to force the company into bankruptcy; however, if A does not wish to do so, neither B nor C separately may force the company into bankruptcy because of failure to meet the $5,000 test. B and C may join together to file the petition.*

        EXAMPLE: *XYZ Corporation is unable to pay current obligations. XYZ has three creditors: L (owed $6,000 which is secured by personal property), M (owed $20,000 of which one half is secured), and N (owed $8,000 of which none is secured). L may not file an involuntary bankruptcy petition but can use the personal property to pay off the debt. Either M or N can file the petition.*

    b. If there are twelve or more creditors, then at least three must sign the petition and they must have claims which aggregate $5,000 in excess of any security held by them

        (1) Claims must not be contingent
        (2) Claims subject to bona fide dispute are not counted in above $5,000 tests

        EXAMPLE: *Poor Inc. is unable to meet its current obligations as they are becoming due because of severe business difficulties. It owes over $20,000 to a dozen different creditors. One of the unsecured creditors, Green, is owed $6,000. Green may not force Poor Inc. into Chapter 7 bankruptcy because even though Green is owed more than $5,000 (one of the tests in "D.2.b." above), Green must be joined by two other creditors. Even though their claims may be very small, the rest of the test is met because the aggregate claims of three (or more) creditors must be greater than $5,000.*

        EXAMPLE: *Same facts as above except that Poor Inc. has only eleven creditors. Now Green alone may force Poor Inc. into bankruptcy under Chapter 7.*

    c. Creditors who file petition in bankruptcy may need to post a bond that indemnifies debtor for losses caused by contesting petition to avoid frivolous petitions

        (1) Bankruptcy court may award damages including attorneys' fees to debtor who successfully challenges involuntary bankruptcy petition against creditors filing petition

(a) If petition was made in bad faith, punitive damages may also be awarded

3. Exempt from involuntary bankruptcy are

   a. Persons (individuals, partnerships, or corporations) owing less than $5,000
   b. Farmers
   c. Charitable organizations

4. Bankruptcy not available (voluntarily or involuntarily) for deceased person's estate

   a. But once bankruptcy has begun, it is not stopped if bankrupt (debtor) dies

5. An order of relief will be granted if the requirements for filing are met, and

   a. The petition is uncontested; or
   b. The petition is contested; and

      (1) The debtor is generally not paying his/her debts as they become due; or
      (2) During the 120 days preceding the filing of the petition, a custodian was appointed or took possession of substantially all of the property of the debtor

      EXAMPLE: Debtor assigns his property for the benefit of his creditor.

   c. Note that the above rules involve a modified insolvency in the "equity sense" (i.e., debtor not paying debts as they become due). The rest of the Bankruptcy Act uses insolvency in the "bankruptcy sense" (i.e., liabilities exceed fair market value of all nonexempt assets). The use of insolvency in the equity sense for involuntary proceedings is important

E. **Chapter 7 Bankruptcy Proceedings** (also called a liquidation or straight bankruptcy)

   1. Take place under federal law

      a. An order of relief is sought
      b. Court appoints interim trustee
      c. Filing petition automatically stays other legal proceeding against debtor's estate until bankruptcy case is over or until court orders otherwise
      d. Debtor may regain property in possession of interim trustee by filing court approved bond

      EXAMPLE: Mortgage foreclosure by savings and loan will be suspended against debtor.

   2. First creditors' meeting

      a. Debtor furnishes a schedule of assets, their locations, and a list of creditors

         (1) Claims of omitted creditors who do not obtain actual notice of the bankruptcy proceedings within the 6-month period in which creditors must file claims are not discharged

b. Claims of debtors are deemed allowed unless objected to, in which case the court will determine their validity

(1) Claims must be filed within six months of first creditors meeting
(2) Contingent and unliquidated claims are estimated
(3) Any attorneys' fees above those ruled reasonable by court are disallowed when objected to by creditors

c. Trustee may be elected by creditors in Chapter 7 proceeding

(1) If no election requested by creditors, interim trustee appointed by court continues in office

3. Trustee--the representative of the estate

a. Trustee has right to receive compensation for services rendered based on value of those services (rather than only on size of estate)
b. Duties--to collect, liquidate, and distribute the estate, keeping accurate records of all transactions
c. Trustee represents estate of bankrupt (debtor)
d. Estate of debtor consists of

(1) Property presently owned by debtor (as of the filing date)
(2) Property owed to debtor by third parties that can be recovered by trustee
(3) Income from property owned by estate after petition is filed
(4) Property received by debtor within 180 days after filing of petition by following methods: inheritance, life insurance, divorce decree, property settlement with spouse, bequest, or devise

(a) Part of estate of debtor even if debtor has right to receive above within 180 days after the filing of petition

(5) Leases disguised as secured or unsecured installment sales contracts

(a) Typically happens when lessee automatically owns "leased" property for no additional consideration or when lessee has option to buy "leased" property for nominal consideration, especially when leased property has a significant market value

1] However, if agreement is a true lease, it is not part of the lessee's estate

EXAMPLE: Y has been leasing property to Z under which Z may purchase the property for $10 at the expiration of the lease. It is estimated that the property will be worth $6,000, however, at that time. If Z takes out or is forced into Chapter 7 bankruptcy, this property will be included as part of Z's estate.

EXAMPLE: Same facts as above except that Y perfects its security interest. Now Y can sell the property to satisfy Y's debt.

(6) Property acquired by debtor, other than by methods listed above, after filing is considered "new estate" and not subject to creditors' claims in bankruptcy proceeding

4. Exemptions to which debtor is entitled

a. Keeps any interests in joint tenancy property if those interests are exempt under other nonbankruptcy law, and

b. Debtor usually has option of choosing either

    (1) <u>Both</u> exemptions under state law and federal law other than under federal Bankruptcy Code

        (a) Typical state exemptions (limited in monetary value) include

            1] Small amount of money
            2] Residence
            3] Clothing
            4] Tools of trade
            5] Insurance

        (b) Examples of exemptions under federal nonbankruptcy law

            1] Veteran's benefits
            2] Social security benefits
            3] Unemployment compensation or benefits
            4] Disability benefits
            5] Alimony

    (2) Or, exemptions provided by federal Bankruptcy Code

        (a) Allowable federal exemptions include

            1] $7,500 equity in principal residence
            2] $1,200 equity in one motor vehicle
            3] $750 in books and tools of one's trade
            4] $200 per item qualifying for personal, family, or home use (has an aggregate ceiling of $4,000)
            5] $500 in jewelry
            6] Social security and alimony
            7] Prescribed health aids
            8] Interest in any property not to exceed $400 plus $3,750 of any unused portion of the homestead exemption (item 1]); can be used to protect any type of property including cash

c. When both spouses together file petition, each spouse may separately use exemptions

5. Duties of trustee under Chapter 7 bankruptcy (i.e., a liquidation)

  a. In general, to liquidate and sell assets owned to pay creditors based on priorities discussed later and to examine propriety of claims brought by creditors

    (1) Considers how best to sell, use, or lease property of estate to act in best interest of estate

    (2) Acquires all legal assets owed to estate for equitable distribution to creditors

    (3) Trustee makes interim reports and presents final accounting of the administration of the estate to the court

6. Powers of trustee

  a. Trustee may take any legal action necessary to carry out duties

    (1) Trustee may utilize any defense available to the debtor against third parties

    (2) Trustee may continue or cease any legal action started by the debtor for the benefit of the estate

b. Trustee, with court approval, may employ professionals, e.g., accountants and lawyers, to assist trustee in carrying out duties which require professional expertise

    (1) Employed professional must not hold any interest adverse to that of debtor (i.e., to avoid conflicts of interest)

    (2) Employed professional has right to receive compensation for reasonable value of services performed

        (a) Reasonable fee is based on amount and complexity of services rendered, not on size of estate

    (3) Trustee, with court approval, may act in professional capacity if capable and be compensated separately for professional services rendered

c. Trustee must within 60 days of the order for relief assume or reject any executory contract, including leases, made by the debtor

    (1) Any not assumed are deemed rejected

    (2) Trustee must perform all obligations on lease of nonresidential property until lease is either assumed or rejected

    (3) Rejection of a contract is a breach of contract and injured party may become an unsecured creditor

    (4) Trustee may assign or retain leases if good for bankrupt's estate and if allowed under lease and state law

    (5) Rejection or assumption of lease is subject to court approval

d. Trustee may set aside liens (those which arise automatically under law) if lien

    (1) Becomes effective when bankruptcy petition is filed or when debtor becomes insolvent

    (2) Is not enforceable against a bona fide purchaser when the petition is filed

    (3) In the case of a security interest, is not perfected before filing of bankruptcy petition

e. Trustee <u>may set aside transfers made within one year prior</u> to the filing of the bankruptcy petition if

    (1) The transfer was made with intent to hinder, delay, or defraud any creditor. The debtor need not be insolvent at time of transfer.

    (2) Debtor received less than a reasonably equivalent value in exchange for such transfer or obligation and the debtor

        (a) Was insolvent at the time, or became insolvent as a result of the transfer

        (b) Was engaged in business, or was about to engage in a transaction, for which debtor's property was unreasonably small capital

        (c) Intended or believed it would incur debts beyond its ability to pay them as they matured

        (d) If the fact that the transfer was a fraudulent conveyance was the only grounds for avoiding the transfer; once avoided by trustee, transferee that gave value in good faith has a lien on property transferred to the extent of value given

    f. Trustee may also set aside preferential transfers of property to a creditor made within the <u>previous 90 days</u> while insolvent in the "bankruptcy sense"

        (1) Preferential transfers are those made for <u>antecedent debts</u> which enable the creditor to receive more than s/he would have otherwise under a Chapter 7 liquidation proceeding

            (a) Includes a security interest given by debtor to secure antecedent debt

        (2) Preferential transfers <u>made to insiders</u> within the <u>previous 12 months</u> may set aside

            (a) Insiders are close blood relatives, officers, directors, controlling stockholders of corporations, or general partners of partnerships

                EXAMPLE: S is a secured creditor of XYZ Co. which is in Chapter 7 bankruptcy. S is not an insider.

                EXAMPLE: One year ago Herb purchased a car on credit from Ike. Thirty days before filing for bankruptcy, Herb, while insolvent, makes a payment to Ike concerning the auto. This is a preferential transfer. If Ike were Herb's brother, this preference could have been set aside if it had occurred, for example, 120 days before the filing of the petition while Herb was insolvent (insider preference).

        (3) Exceptions to trustee's power to avoid preferential transfers

            (a) A contemporaneous exchange between creditor and debtor whereby debtor receives new value

                EXAMPLE: Herb, while insolvent, purchases a car for cash from Ike within 90 days of filing a petition in bankruptcy. The trustee could not avoid this transaction because Herb, the debtor, received present (i.e., contemporaneous) value (the car) for the cash transferred to Ike, the creditor. This is not a voidable preference.

            (b) A payment made by debtor in the ordinary course of business is not a preference

            (c) A security interest given by debtor to acquire property that is perfected within 10 days after such security interest attaches

            (d) A consumer debtor's payment of $600 or less to any creditor

            (e) Seller who delivers to debtor while insolvent may reclaim goods within 10 days of receipt of goods and even if bankruptcy petition has been filed in meantime if demand in writing

  7. Trustee may be sued or sue on behalf of estate

F. Claims

  1. Property rights--where claimant has a property right, property is turned over to claimant, because not considered part of debtor's estate

    a. Reclamation is a claim against specific property by a person claiming it to be his/hers

EXAMPLE: A person rented a truck for a week and in the meantime he becomes bankrupt. The lessor will make a reclamation.

b. Trust claim is made by beneficiary for trust property when the trustee is bankrupt

EXAMPLE: Trustee maintains a trust account for beneficiary under a trust set up in a will. Trustee becomes bankrupt. The trust account is not part of trustee's estate. The beneficiary may claim the trust account as his property.

c. Secured claim when creditor has a security interest, e.g., mortgage, in property or security interest under Article 9 of UCC

    (1) As long as trustee does not successfully attack the security-- basically, security interest must be without defects to prevail against trustee (i.e., perfected security interests)

    (2) Secured status may be achieved by subrogation, e.g., surety is subrogated to creditor's collateral

d. Set-offs are allowed to the extent the bankrupt and creditor have mutual debts whether unsecured or not

2. Filing of claims

a. All claims must be filed within six months after the first creditors' meeting

3. Proof of claims

a. Timely claims are deemed allowed unless creditor objects

    (1) Contingent and unliquidated claims may be estimated

b. Claims below are not allowed if an objection is made

    (1) Unenforceable claims (by law or agreement)
    (2) Unmatured interest as of date of filing bankruptcy petition
    (3) Claims which may be offset
    (4) Property tax claim in excess of the property value
    (5) Insider or attorney claims in excess of reasonable value of services as determined by court
    (6) Alimony, maintenance, and support claims for amounts due after bankruptcy petition is filed (they are not dischargeable)
    (7) Landlord's damages for lease termination in excess of specified amounts
    (8) Damages for termination of an employment contract in excess of one year's wages
    (9) Certain employment tax claims

4. Priority of claims (be sure to know)

a. Property rights, e.g., secured debts

    (1) Technically, they are not a part of the priorities because they never become part of the bankrupt estate. But practically, the validity of the property right must be determined and they are the first claims to be satisfied.

b. Unsecured claims are paid at each level of priority before any lower level is paid

(1) If there are insufficient assets to pay any given level then assets are prorated at that level (the next levels get $0)

c. Levels of priority

(1) Administration costs

(a) Includes fees to accountants, attorneys, trustees, and appraisers as well as expenses incurred only in recovering, preserving, selling, or discovering property that should be included in debtor's estate

EXAMPLE: Bee, Ware, and Watch, a partnership of CPAs, performed professional services for Dee-Funct Company before it was forced into bankruptcy by its creditors. These fees are not put in the first priority but the last because they do not qualify as administration costs.

(b) Also, includes reasonable fees, salary, or wages needed for services such as operating the business after the bankruptcy action begins

(2) Claims arising in ordinary course of debtor's business after involuntary bankruptcy petition is filed but before order for relief is entered

(3) Wages of bankrupt's employees ($2,000 maximum each) accrued within 3 months before the petition in bankruptcy was filed (any excess is treated as a general claim)

(a) This priority does not include officers' salaries

(4) Contributions to employee benefit plans within the prior 180 days, limited to $2,000 per employee, reduced by amount received as wage preference

(5) Consumer deposits for undelivered goods or services limited to $900 per individual

(6) Taxes (federal, state, and local)

(7) General (unsecured) creditors that filed timely proofs of claims

(a) Includes amounts owed to secured creditors in excess of amount for which security sells

EXAMPLE: X has been forced into Chapter 7 bankruptcy proceedings. X had assets that have been sold for $10,000 cash. Fees to accountants, attorneys, and the trustee total $3,000. Expenses to sell property total $1,000. Wages owed to two employees for the previous month's work are $2,500 and $2,000 respectively. Past taxes amount to $1,000 and two general creditors have claims amounting to $1,000 and $500 respectively. Under the priorities just given, the $3,000 and the $1,000 are administrative costs and are paid first. The wages owed to the two employees are paid next but only up to $2,000 each. The $1,000 in taxes is paid next, leaving $1,000. This must now be paid out proportionately; therefore, the general creditors received $500 and $250 respectively; the employee who was not fully paid receives an additional $250 because s/he gets a proportionate share as a general creditor on her/his remaining $500.

(b) Unsecured claims filed late (unless excused) are paid after timely claims

G. Discharge of a Bankrupt

1. A discharge is the release of a debtor from all his/her debts not paid in bankruptcy except those not dischargeable

   a. Granting an order of relief to an individual is an automatic application for discharge
   b. Corporations and partnerships cannot receive a discharge

2. Debtor must be adjudged an "honest debtor" to be discharged

3. Acts that bar discharge of all debts

   a. Improper actions during bankruptcy proceeding

      (1) Making false claims against the estate
      (2) Making any false entry in or on any document of account relating to bankrupt's affairs
      (3) Concealing property
      (4) Transfer of property after filing with intent to defeat the law
      (5) Receiving money for acting or not acting in bankruptcy proceedings
      (6) These acts are also punishable by fines and imprisonment

   b. Failed to satisfactorily explain any loss of assets
   c. Refused to obey court orders
   d. Removed or destroyed property within twelve months prior to the filing of the petition
   e. Destroyed, falsified, concealed, or failed to keep books of account or records unless such act was justified under the circumstances
   f. Been discharged in bankruptcy proceedings within the past six years
   g. "Substantial abuse" of bankruptcy (under Chapter 7) by individual debtor with primarily consumer debts
   h. A preferential transfer does not bar discharge (but can be set aside)

4. Employers (both governmental and private) cannot fire employee for having declared bankruptcy

H. Debts Not Discharged by Bankruptcy (even though general discharge allowed)

1. Taxes within three years of filing bankruptcy petition

2. Liability for obtaining money or property by false pretenses

   EXAMPLE: Obtaining credit using false information such as fraudulent financial statements

3. Willful and/or malicious injuries to a person or property of another (intentional torts)

   a. Unintentional torts and breaches of contract are discharged

4. Liability incurred by driving while legally intoxicated

5. Alimony, separate maintenance, or child support

6. Unscheduled debts unless creditor had actual notice of proceedings, i.e., where bankrupt failed to list creditor and debt

7. Those created by fraud (e.g., embezzlement)

8. Governmental fines or penalties imposed within prior 3 years

9. Educational loans of a governmental unit or nonprofit institution which became due within prior 5 years unless liability would impose "undue hardship" on debtor or debtor's dependents

10. Those from a prior bankruptcy proceeding in which the debtor waived discharge or was denied discharge

11. To avoid the practice of "loading up on luxury goods" before bankruptcy, there is a presumption of nondischargeability for

    a. Consumer debts to a single debtor of $500 or more for luxury goods or services

    b. Certain cash advances based on consumer credit exceeding $1,000

I. Revocation of Discharge

1. Discharge may be revoked if

    a. Bankrupt committed fraud during bankruptcy proceedings unknown to creditors seeking revocation

        (1) Must be applied for by an interested party within one year of discharge

            (a) Interested party is someone affected., e.g., creditor who never received payment or trustee in bankruptcy

        EXAMPLE: A bankrupt conceals assets in order to defraud creditors.

    b. Bankrupt acquired rights or title to property of estate and fraudulently failed to report this

    c. Bankrupt refused to obey lawful court order or refused to testify when not in violation of his/her constitutional right against self incrimination

J. Reaffirmation

1. Debtor promises to pay a debt that will be or has been discharged. The code makes it difficult to reaffirm a dischargeable debt.

    a. Reaffirmation of a dischargeable debt to be enforceable must satisfy the following conditions

        (1) New agreement must be enforceable under appropriate state contract law

        (2) If debtor is an individual

            (a) Debtor must have received appropriate warnings from the court or attorney on effects of reaffirmation

            (b) And if also involves consumer debt not secured by real property, court must approve new agreement as being in best interests of debtor and not imposing undue hardship on debtor

K. Business Reorganization - Chapter 11

1. Goal is to keep financially troubled firm in business

    a. It is an alternative to liquidation under Chapter 7 (straight bankruptcy)

    b. In general, allows debtor to keep assets of business

2. Can be initiated by debtor (voluntary) or creditors (involuntary)

   a. Available to individuals, partnerships, or corporations including rail-roads. Other entities ineligible to be debtors under Chapter 7 are ineligible under Chapter 11.

   b. If involuntary, same requirements must be met as needed to initiate a Chapter 7 involuntary proceeding.

3. Creditors' committee is selected from unsecured creditors after court accepts petition and grants order for relief

   a. Duties include

      (1) Determine if business should continue to operate

      (2) Determine if court should be asked to appoint a trustee or examiner

      (3) Conduct an investigation of the debtor's financial affairs

      (4) Generally consult with the debtor or trustee in the administration of the case

4. A trustee may be appointed "for cause" or "in the interest of creditors"

   a. Cause shall include fraud, dishonesty, incompetence, or gross mis-management

   b. Trustee may be appointed only upon request of a party of interest and after notice and hearing

   c. Trustee often not appointed

5. Important provision is court-supervised rehabilitation plan

   a. Allows for continued operation of business unless court orders otherwise

   b. Provides for payment of part or all of debts over extended period

      (1) Payment to creditors comes primarily from future income

   c. Must divide claims into classes of similar claims and treat each class equally

      (1) All classes must receive no less than entitled to under liquidation (Chapter 7--Bankruptcy)

6. SEC has limited power to participate in bankruptcy reorganizations

7. When debtor keeps and operates business, debtor has right to retain employees and professionals it used before reorganization

   EXAMPLE: Debtor, after a Chapter 11 reorganization, wishes to keep its CPA firm. This is permitted.

8. Debtor keeping possession of business has many rights of trustee but these do not include right to compensation as such

L. Debts Adjustment Plans - Chapter 13

1. Most individuals are eligible if

   a. Have regular income, and

   b. Owe unsecured debts of less than $100,000, and

   c. Owe secured debts of less than $350,000

2. Initiated when debtor files voluntary petition in bankruptcy court

   a. Creditors may not file involuntary petition under Chapter 13

   b. Petition normally includes composition or extension plan

      (1) Composition--creditors agree to accept less than full amounts due

SURETYSHIP

Overview

Suretyship is a broad legal term describing relationships where one person agrees to be answerable for the debt or default of another person. Suretyship is a form of security so that if the principal debtor is unable or unwilling to perform, the creditor has an immediate and direct remedy against a third party, called the surety, to satisfy the obligation of the debtor. Thus, suretyship allows creditors to protect themselves against the principal debtor's defenses of lack of capacity, death, bankruptcy, or inability to pay. However, the undertaking of a surety is not absolute. The surety may defend against payment of the debt or obligation by asserting any of its available defenses.

Suretyship is typically tested by a few multiple choice questions and sometimes by a portion of an essay question. The questions emphasize the rights, remedies, and liabilities of the three parties in a suretyship relationship. You should understand which defenses can be used in this relationship. Also, be sure to understand the rights of subrogation and contribution among co-sureties.

A. Nature of Suretyship

1. A suretyship contract is a relationship whereby one person agrees to answer for debt, default, or tort of another

   a. Surety agrees with creditor to satisfy obligation if principal debtor does not

   b. Purpose of a suretyship agreement is to protect creditor by providing creditor with added security for obligation and reduce creditor's risk of loss

   EXAMPLE: In order for D to obtain a loan from C, S (who has a good credit standing) promises to C that he, S, will pay debt if D defaults.

2. Suretyship agreements involve three parties

   a. Creditor (C in above example)

      (1) Obligee of principal debtor

   b. Principal debtor (D in above example)

      (1) Has liability for debt owed to creditor

   c. Surety (S in above example)

      (1) Promises to perform or pay debt on default of principal debtor

         (a) Surety is primarily liable because promise typically is not conditional

            1] Creditor need not attempt collection from debtor first
            2] Creditor need not give notice of debtor's default
            3] Surety is liable if debtor does not perform

3. Examples of typical suretyship arrangements

   a. Seller of goods on credit requires buyer to obtain a surety to guarantee payment for goods purchased

   b. Bank requires owners or directors of closely held corporation to act as sureties for loan to corporation

   c. Indorser of negotiable instrument agrees to pay if instrument not paid (unless indorse "without recourse"). (See Commercial Paper module.)

   d. In order to transfer a check or note, transferor may be required to obtain a surety (accommodation indorser) to guarantee payment. (See Liability of Parties in Commercial Paper module.)

e. Purchaser of real property expressly assumes seller's mortgage on property (i.e., promises to pay mortgage debt). Seller becomes surety and purchaser is principal debtor.

4. Suretyship (guaranty) contracts should satisfy elements of contracts in general (See Essential Elements of a Contract in Contracts module.)

a. If surety's agreement arises at same time as the contract between creditor and debtor, no separate consideration is needed (consideration between creditor and debtor is sufficient)

(1) If creditor gave loan or credit before surety's promise, separate consideration is necessary to support surety's new promise

EXAMPLE: C loaned $200,000 to D. Terms provided that the loan is callable by C with one month notice to D. C gave the agreed notice and exercised her right to call the loan. D requested a 60-day extension. C agreed to the extension when S agreed to be a surety on this loan. There is consideration for the new surety agreement since C gave up the right to call the loan sooner.

(a) Consideration need not be received by surety--often it is principal debtor that benefits

b. Surety's agreement to answer for debt or default of another must be in writing. (See Statute of Frauds in Contracts module.)

(1) However, if surety's promise is primarily for his/her own benefit, it need not be in writing

EXAMPLE: S agrees to pay D's debt to D's creditor if he defaults. The main purpose of S is to keep D in business to assure a steady supply of an essential component. S's agreement need not be in writing.

EXAMPLE: A del credere agent is one who sells goods on credit to purchasers for the principal and agrees to pay the principal if the customers do not. Since his promise is primarily for his own benefit, it need not be in writing.

EXAMPLE: Owners and officers of a closely held corporation agreed orally to act as sureties for a corporate loan. Because the loan is primarily to benefit the corporation, the suretyship agreement must be in writing. The indirect benefit the owners and officers receive does not take this agreement out of the Statute of Frauds.

5. Third-party beneficiary contract is not a suretyship contract

a. Third-party beneficiary contract is one in which third party receives benefits from agreement made between promisor and promisee, although third person is not party to contract

EXAMPLE: Father says: "Ship goods to my son and I will pay for them." This describes a third-party beneficiary contract, not a suretyship arrangement. Father is not promising to pay the debt of another, but rather engaging in an original promise to pay (i.e., a debtor) for goods creditor delivers to son.

6. Indemnity contract is not a suretyship contract

a. An indemnity contract is between two parties (rather than three) whereby indemnitor makes a promise to a potential debtor, indemnitee, (not to creditor as in suretyship arrangement), to indemnify and reimburse debtor for payment of debt or for loss that may arise in future. Indemnitor pays because it has assumed risk of loss, not because of any default by principal debtor as in suretyship arrangement.

EXAMPLE: Under terms of standard automobile collision insurance policy, insurance company agrees to indemnify automobile owner against damage to his/her car caused by collision.

7. Warranty (sometimes called guaranty) is not same as guaranty under suretyship law

    a. Warranties arise under, for example, real property law or sales law

        (1) Involve making representations as to facts, title, quality, etc. of property

8. Surety and guarantor are generally considered to be synonymous

    a. Unconditional guaranty is the standard suretyship relationship in which there are no further conditions required for guarantor to be asked to pay if debtor does not

    EXAMPLE: G agreed in writing to act as surety when D took out a loan with C, the lender. If D does not pay, C may proceed directly against G. C need not try to collect from D first.

    b. Distinguish between unconditional guaranty and conditional guaranty

        (1) In case of conditional guaranty, specified condition(s) must be met before creditor can resort to guarantor
           (a) Typical conditions require creditor to give guarantor notice and first exhaust remedies available against principal debtor before attempting to collect from guarantor

9. Capacity to act as surety

    a. In general, individuals that have capacity to contract
    b. Partnerships may act as sureties unless partnership agreement expressly prohibits it from entering into suretyship contracts
    c. Individual partner has no authority to bind partnership as surety

        (1) Unless it is in furtherance of partnership business
        (2) Is expressly authorized in partnership agreement
        (3) Copartners expressly authorize such action

    d. Modern trend is that corporations may act as sureties

B. Creditor's Rights and Remedies

1. Against principal debtor

    a. Creditor has right to receive payment or performance specified in contract
    b. Creditor may proceed immediately against debtor upon default, unless conditions state otherwise in contract
    c. When a debtor has more than one debt outstanding with same creditor and makes a part payment, debtor may give instructions as to which debt the payment is to apply

        (1) If debtor gives no instructions, creditor is free to apply part payment to whichever debt s/he chooses; fact that one debt is guaranteed by surety and other is not makes no difference in absence of instructions by debtor

(2) Is not valid defense of surety because considered not to affect risk of surety (See "D.3.e.")

> *EXAMPLE: If debtor owes two debts to creditor and surety only guaranteed one, creditor may apply a payment from debtor to one not guaranteed (absent instructions by debtor) and surety is not released.*

2. Against surety

   a. Creditor may proceed immediately against surety upon principal debtor's default

      (1) Unless contract requires, it is not necessary to give surety notice on debtor's default
      (2) Since surety is immediately liable, s/he can be sued without creditor first attempting to collect from debtor

3. Against guarantor of collection

   a. A guarantor of collection's liability is conditioned on creditor notifying guarantor of debtor's default and creditor first attempting to collect from debtor
   b. Creditor must exhaust remedies by going against debtor before guarantor of collection's liability arises

4. On security (collateral) held by surety or creditor

   a. Upon principal debtor's default, creditor may resort to collateral to satisfy debt

      (1) If creditor does resort to collateral, any excess collateral or amount realized by its disposal over debt amount must be returned to principal debtor
      (2) If collateral is insufficient to pay debt, creditor may proceed against surety or debtor for balance due (deficiency)

   b. Creditor is not required to use collateral; creditor may instead proceed immediately against surety or principal debtor

      (1) If surety pays, surety is subrogated (see "C.1.d." below) to creditor's rights in collateral and is therefore entitled to it
      (2) If principal debtor pays obligation, collateral must be returned to debtor along with any income earned thereon

C. Surety's Rights and Remedies

1. When the debt or obligation for which surety has given promise is due

   a. Exoneration

      (1) Surety may require (by lawsuit if necessary) debtor to pay obligation if debtor is able before surety has paid

   b. Surety may request creditor to resort first to collateral if surety can show collateral is seriously depreciating in value, or if surety can show undue hardship will otherwise result

      (1) Surety may sue to compel debtor to pay obligation owed to creditor when debtor has sufficient assets and is wrongfully withholding payment
      (2) Exoneration is not available if creditor demands prompt performance from surety upon debtor's default or surety has paid creditor

2. When surety pays debt or obligation

    a. S/he is entitled to right of reimbursement from debtor when surety fulfills principal debtor's obligation pursuant to default

        (1) May recover only actual payments to creditor

        (2) Surety is entitled to resort to collateral as satisfaction of right of reimbursement

        (3) Surety's payment after having received notice of principal debtor's valid defense against creditor causes surety to lose right of reimbursement

    b. S/he has right of subrogation

        (1) Upon payment, surety obtains same rights against principal debtor that creditor had

            (a) I.e., surety steps into creditor's shoes

            (b) Permits surety to obtain rights that s/he did not have before surety's satisfaction of debtor's obligation

            (c) If debtor is bankrupt, surety is subrogated to rights of creditor's priority in bankruptcy proceeding

                EXAMPLE: C, the creditor, required D, the debtor, to put up personal property as collateral on a loan and to also use S as a surety on the same loan. Upon D's default, C chooses to resort to S for payment. Upon payment, S may now sell the collateral under the right of subrogation because the creditor could have used the same right of sale of the collateral.

    c. Right of contribution exists among co-sureties. (See "E.3." below.)

D. **Surety's Defenses**

    1. Surety may generally exercise defenses on contract which would be available <u>to debtor</u>

        a. Breach or failure of performance by <u>creditor</u>

        b. Impossibility or illegality of performance

        c. Failure of consideration

        d. Creditor obtains debtor's promise by fraud, duress, or misrepresentation

        e. Statute of Limitations

        f. Except that surety may not use debtor's personal defenses. (See "D.4." below.)

    2. Surety may take advantage of <u>own</u> contractual defenses

        a. Fraud or duress

        (1) If creditor obtains surety's promise by fraud or duress, contract is voidable at surety's option

                EXAMPLE: Creditor forces X to sign suretyship agreement at threat of great bodily harm.

        (2) If creditor gets principal debtor's promise using fraud or duress, then surety not liable

            (a) Exception: surety liable if was aware of fraud or duress before s/he became surety

        (3) Fraud by principal debtor on surety to induce a suretyship agreement will not release surety if creditor has extended credit in good faith

(a)   But if creditor had knowledge of debtor's fraudulent representations, then surety may avoid liability

> EXAMPLE: Y asked Ace to act as surety on a loan from Bank. In order to induce Ace to act as surety, Y made fraudulent representations concerning its financial position to Ace. This fraud by Y will not release surety, Ace, if the creditor, Bank, had no knowledge of the fraud and extended credit in good faith. But if Bank had knowledge of Y's fraudulent representations, then Ace has a good defense and can avoid liability. If bank finds out about Y's fraudulent representations _after_ Bank has extended credit, Ace has no defense.

b.   Suretyship contract itself is void due to illegality
c.   Incapacity of surety (e.g., surety is a minor)
d.   Failure of consideration for suretyship contract

   (1)   However, when surety's and principal debtor's obligations are incurred at same time, there is no need for any separate consideration beyond that supporting principal debtor's contract; if surety's undertaking is entered into subsequent to debtor's contract, it must be supported by separate consideration. (See "A.4.a." above.)

e.   Suretyship agreement is not written as required per Statute of Frauds
f.   Creditor fails to notify surety of any material facts within creditor's knowledge concerning debtor's ability to perform

   (1)   Material facts are those facts pertaining to risk assumed by surety such that surety may not have assumed obligation had s/he been aware of these facts because they cause an increase in surety's risk

   > EXAMPLE: Creditor's failure to report to surety that debtor has defaulted on several previous occasions.

   > EXAMPLE: Creditor's failure to report to surety that debtor submitted fraudulent financial statements to surety to induce suretyship agreement.

g.   Surety, in general, may use any obligations owed by creditor to surety as a set-off against any payments owed to creditor

   (1)   True even if set-off arises from separate transaction

3.   Acts of creditor or debtor materially affecting surety's obligations

a.   Tender of performance by debtor or surety and refusal by creditor will discharge surety

   (1)   However, tender of performance for obligation to pay money does not normally release principal debtor but stops accrual of interest on debt

b.   Release of principal debtor from liability by creditor without consent of surety will also discharge surety's liability

   (1)   But surety is not released if creditor specifically reserves his/her rights against surety

      (a)   However, surety upon paying may then seek recovery from debtor

c.   Release of surety by creditor

        (1) Requires consideration to be valid
        (2) When valid, does <u>not</u> release principal debtor because liable whether or not surety is liable

  d. Proper performance by debtor or satisfaction of creditor through collateral will discharge surety

  e. Variance in terms and conditions of contract subsequent to surety's undertaking

        (1) Accomodation (noncompensated) surety is completely discharged for any change in contract made by creditor on terms required of principal debtor

        (2) Commercial (compensated) surety is completely released if modification in principal debtor's contract materially increases risk to surety

            (a) If risk not increased materially, then surety not released but his/her obligation is reduced by amount of loss due to modification

        (3) Surety may consent to modifications so that they are not defenses
        (4) Surety is not released if creditor modifies principal debtor's duties to be beneficial to surety (i.e., decreases surety's risk)

        EXAMPLE: Creditor reduces interest rate on loan to principal debtor from 12% to 10%.

        (5) Modifications that affect rights of sureties based on above principles

            (a) Extension of time on principal debtor's obligation
            (b) Change in amount, place, or manner of principal debtor's obligations
            (c) Modification of duties of principal debtor
            (d) Substitution of debtor's or delegation of debtor's obligation to another

                1] Note how this may result in change in risk to the surety

            (e) Release, surrender, destruction, or impairment of collateral by creditor before or after debtor's default releases surety by amount decreased

            EXAMPLE: S is a compensated surety for a loan between Debtor and Creditor. The loan had also been secured by collateral. Upon default, Creditor took possession of the collateral but let it get damaged by rain. The collateral was impaired by $500. Creditor also sought payment from S, the compensated surety. S may reduce his payment to Creditor by $500.

        (6) In order to release surety, there must be an actual alteration or variance in terms of contract and not an option or election that principal debtor can exercise under express terms of original agreement which surety has guaranteed

        EXAMPLE: Tenant and landlord entered into a two year leasing agreement which expressly contained an option for an additional year which could be exercised by tenant, with X acting as surety on lease contract. If tenant exercises this option, X still remains bound as surety.

4. Following are <u>not defenses of surety</u>.

    a. Personal defenses of principal debtor

        (1) Death of debtor or debtor's lack of capacity, e.g., debtor is a minor or was legally insane when contract was made

        (2) Insolvency (or discharge in bankruptcy) of debtor

            (a) Possibility of debtor's insolvency is a primary reason for engaging in a surety arrangement

        (3) Personal debtor's set-offs

            (a) Unless debtor assigns them to surety

    b. Creditor did not give notice to surety of debtor's default or creditor did not first proceed against principal debtor

        (1) Unless a conditional guarantor and creditor violated condition

    c. Creditor does not resort to collateral

    d. Creditor delays in proceeding against debtor unless delay exceeds statute of limitations

E. Co-sureties

1. Co-sureties exist when there is more than one surety for same obligation of principal debtor to same creditor

    a. It does not matter that co-sureties do not know of each other or that they become sureties at different times; they need only share same burden

    b. Co-sureties need not be bound for same amount; they can guarantee equal or unequal amounts of debt

        (1) Collateral, if any, need not be held equally

    c. Co-sureties need not sign same document

2. Co-sureties are jointly and severally liable to creditor

    a. That is, creditor can proceed against any of the sureties jointly or against each one individually to extent surety has assumed liability

    b. If creditor sues multiple sureties, s/he may recover in any proportion from each, but may only recover total amount of debtor's obligation

    c. Proceeding against one or more sureties does not release remaining surety or sureties

3. Right of contribution exists among co-sureties

    a. Right of contribution arises when co-surety, in performance of debtor's obligation, pays more than his/her proportionate share of total liability, and thereby entitles co-surety to compel other co-sureties to compensate him/her for excess amount paid (i.e., contribution from other co-sureties for their pro rata share of liability)

4. Co-sureties are only liable in contribution for their proportionate share

    a. Co-surety's pro rata share is proportion that each surety's risk (i.e., amount each has personally guaranteed) bears to total amount of risk assumed by all sureties by using the following formula

$$\frac{\text{Dollar amount individual co-surety personally guaranteed}}{\text{Total dollar amount of risk assumed by all co-sureties}}$$

EXAMPLE: X and Y are co-sureties for $5,000 and $10,000, respectively, of a $10,000 debt. Each is liable in proportion to amount each has personally guaranteed. Since X guaranteed $5,000 of debt and Y guaranteed $10,000 of debt, then X is individually liable for 1/3 ($5,000/$15,000) of debt and Y is individually liable for 2/3 ($10,000/$15,000) of debt. If debtor defaults on only $3,000 of debt, X is liable for $1,000 (1/3 x $3,000) and Y is liable for $2,000 (2/3 x $3,000). Although creditor may recover $3,000 from either, each co-surety has right of contribution from other co-surety.

EXAMPLE: Refer to the preceding example. If the creditor recovers all of the $3,000 debt from Y, then Y, under the right of contribution, can recover $1,000 from X so that each will end up paying his/her proportionate amount.

5. Each co-surety is entitled to share in any collateral pledged (either held by creditor or other co-surety) in proportion to co-surety's liability for debtor's default

   EXAMPLE: If in above illustration, co-surety Y held collateral pledged by debtor worth $900, both co-sureties X and Y would be entitled to share in collateral in proportion to their respective liabilities. X would be entitled to 1/3 ($5,000/$15,000) of $900 collateral, or $300; and Y would be entitled to 2/3 ($10,000/$15,000) of $900 collateral, or $600.

6. Discharge or release of one co-surety by creditor results in a reduction of liability of remaining co-surety

   a. Remaining co-surety is released only to extent of released co-surety's pro rata share of debt liability (unless there is a reservation of rights by creditor against remaining co-surety)

      EXAMPLE: A and B are co-sureties for $4,000 and $12,000, respectively, on a $12,000 debt. If creditor releases co-surety A, co-surety B is released to extent of co-surety A's liability. Each is liable in proportion to amount each has personally guaranteed. Since A guaranteed $4,000 of debt and B guaranteed $12,000 of debt, then A is individually liable for 1/4 ($4,000/$16,000) of debt and B is individually liable for 3/4 ($12,000/$16,000) of debt, i.e., $9,000. Therefore, co-surety B is released of A's pro rata liability of $3,000 (1/4 x $12,000), and only remains a surety for $9,000 ($12,000 - $3,000) of debt.

7. A co-surety is not released from obligation to perform merely because another co-surety refuses to perform

   a. However, upon payment of full obligation, co-surety can demand a pro rata contribution from his/her nonperforming co-surety
   b. Co-surety is not released if other co-sureties are unable to pay--i.e., dead, bankrupt

      (1) In which case, modify the formula found at "E.4.a." by taking those co-sureties that cannot pay completely out of formula and use it with all remaining co-sureties

8. Co-sureties have rights of exoneration, reimbursement, and subrogation like any surety (See "C.")

F. **Surety Bonds**
1. An acknowledgement of an obligation to make good the performance by another of some act, duty, or responsibility
    a. Usually issued by companies which for a stated fee assume risk of performance by bonded party
    b. Performance of act, duty, or responsibility by bonded party discharges surety's obligation
2. Performance bonds are used to have surety guarantee completion of terms of contracts
    a. Construction bond guarantees builder's obligation to complete construction
        (1) If builder breaches contract, surety can be held liable for damages but not for specific performance (i.e., cannot be required to complete construction)
            (a) Surety may complete construction if chooses to
3. Fidelity bonds are form of insurance that protects an employer against losses sustained by dishonest employees (i.e., guarantees faithful performance of duties by employee)
    a. Any significant change in the employee's duties may serve to release surety bonding company from its obligation
4. Surety bonding company retains right of subrogation against bonded party

AGENCY

Overview

Agency is a relationship in which one party (agent) voluntarily acts as a business representative of another (principal) for the purpose of entering into contracts with third parties. The law of agency is concerned with the rights, duties, and liabilities of these three parties that arise as a result of the agency relationship. Important to this relationship is the fact that the agent has a fiduciary duty to act in the best interest of the principal. A good understanding of this module is important because partnership law is a special application of agency law.

The CPA exam emphasizes the creation and termination of the agency relationship, the undisclosed as well as the disclosed principal relationship, unauthorized acts or torts committed by the agent within the course and scope of the agency relationship and principal's liability for agent's unauthorized contracts.

A. Characteristics

1. Agency is a relationship by consent (agreement) between two parties, whereby one party (agent) agrees to act on behalf of the other party (principal). A contract is not required but is frequently present.

    a. Agent is subject to continuous control of the principal
    b. Agent is a fiduciary and must act for the benefit of principal
    c. Agent can be used for other purposes, but we are primarily concerned with agents that agree to act for the principal in business transactions with third parties
    d. Agent's specific authority is determined by the principal but generally agent has authority

        (1) To perform legal acts for the principal
        (2) More specifically, to bind the principal contractually with third parties

2. Employee (servant) distinguished from an agent

    a. Employee is a type of agent in which employee's physical conduct is subject to control by employer (master)

        (1) Employer is a type of principal and is called such when the agent is an employee
        (2) Agent is subject to a lesser and a more general control, i.e., what to do and when to do it, but not control of physical conduct
        (3) Employer is generally liable for employee's torts if committed within course and scope of employment relationship

            (a) Known as doctrine of respondeat superior

                EXAMPLE: S is an employee of M. One day while delivering inventory for M, she negligently hits a third party with the delivery truck. Although S is liable because she committed the tort, M is also liable

            (b) Course and scope of employment is defined broadly

                EXAMPLE: M, the employer, gives S $30 and asks him to go buy donuts for the employees who are working overtime. He takes his own car and injures a third party through his own negligence. The employer is also liable for this tort.

        (c)   Employee need not be following instructions of employer, i.e. rule applies even if employee violated employer's instructions in committing tort

> *EXAMPLE: P works for Q delivering widgets. One rule that Q has is that all employees must look behind the truck before backing out after all deliveries. P violated this rule and injures R. Q is still liable even though it had taken steps to prevent this type of accident.*

        (d)   Contributory negligence, i.e., third party's negligence, is generally a defense for both the agent and his/her principal

           1]   Some jurisdictions have adopted comparative negligence which means that the amount of damages is determined by comparing each party's negligence

3. Independent contractor distinguished from an agent

    a. Not subject to control of employer as to methods of work
    b. Not subject to regular supervision as an employee
    c. Employer seeks the results only (contractor controls the methods)

> *EXAMPLE: A builder of homes has only to produce the results.*

    d. Generally, employer is not liable for torts committed by independent contractor

        (1)   Unless independent contractor is employed to do something imminently or inherently dangerous, e.g., blasting
        (2)   Unless employer was negligent in hiring independent contractor

    e. Independent contractor may also be an agent in certain cases

> *EXAMPLE: A public accounting firm represents a client in tax court.*

4. Types of agents

    a. General--one who has broad power to act for the principal in various types of transactions

        (1)   Principal may be liable for unauthorized acts which similar general agents are authorized for

    b. Special--appointed for a limited purpose or a specific task

        (1)   If s/he performs unauthorized acts, principal is less likely to be liable than if s/he were a general agent

    c. Gratuitous--agrees to act without expectation of compensation

        (1)   Is not bound to perform, but once started must perform duties in nonnegligent manner
        (2)   Not subject to as high a degree of care as a compensated agent

    d. Subagent--one appointed by an authorized agent to perform for the agent

> *EXAMPLE: P hires A to manage a branch office and tells A to hire anyone he needs. If A hires X as an assistant, X is a subagent of P.*

        (1)   If first agent is authorized only to employ for principal, then second agent is an agent of the principal, not a subagent

> *EXAMPLE: P asks A to hire 5 people to work in P's branch office. Those hired by A are agents of P, not agents of A or subagents of P.*

1
3

(2) If first agent has no authority to employ, second agent will be an agent to first agent and not a subagent of principal

EXAMPLE: P hires A to manage a branch office but tells A not to hire anyone, that P will supply anyone needed. If A hires X as an assistant, X is an agent of A's, not a subagent of P.

5. Examples of agents--usually special agents

   a. Agency coupled with an interest--agent has an interest in subject matter of the agency: either a property interest or a security interest

      (1) E.g., mortgagee with right to sell property on default of mortgagor

         (a) Agreement stipulating agent is to receive profits or proceeds does not by itself create an agency coupled with an interest

      (2) Principal does not have the power to terminate agency coupled with an interest

   b. Attorney--typically practices law for a number of persons
   c. Broker--special agent acting for either buyer or seller in business transactions, e.g., real estate broker
   d. Del credere--a sales agent who, prior to the creation and as a condition of the agency, guarantees the accounts of the customers to his/her principal (if the customers fail to pay)

      (1) Guarantee is not within the Statute of Frauds, i.e., it is not required to be in writing

   e. Power of attorney

      (1) Principal, in writing, grants authority to agent
      (2) Agent need not be an attorney but anyone with capacity to be agent

   f. Exclusive--only agent the principal may deal with for a certain purpose during life of the contract, e.g., real estate broker who has sole right to sell property except for personal sale by principal
   g. Factor--commercial agent employed to sell goods

      (1) Factor has possession of goods and may sell in the factor's own name

6. Types of principals

   a. Disclosed--when the third party knows or should know agent is acting for a principal and who the principal is

      (1) Principal becomes a party to authorized contracts made by the agent in the principal's name
      (2) Agent is not liable under contract

   EXAMPLE: Signed, "John Doe as agent for Tom Thumb, principal." Therefore, only Tom Thumb is liable on the contract.

   b. Partially disclosed--when the third party knows or should know the agent is acting for a principal but does not know who the principal is

      (1) Both agent and principal are liable under the contract

> *EXAMPLE: Signed, "John Doe as agent."*

c. Undisclosed--when the third party has no notice that the agent is acting for a principal

(1) Both agent and principal are liable under authorized contracts if agent so intended to act for principal

> *EXAMPLE: Signed, "John Doe."*

B. Methods of Creation

1. Appointment

a. Express-by agreement between the principal and agent

(1) Need not be in writing unless

(a) Agency contract cannot be completed within one year

> *EXAMPLE: P agrees to pay A as his agent and to keep him as his agent for two years.*

(b) Agent is to buy or sell a specific piece of real estate named in the agency contract

(c) The agency contract need not be in writing in other situations where the agent enters into agreements which fall under the Statute of Frauds

> *EXAMPLE: A, in his capacity as agent of P, signs a contract for the sale of goods costing $600. Even though the sales contract must normally be in writing under the UCC version of the Statute of Frauds, the agency agreement between A and P need not be expressed in writing.*

b. Implied--created by conduct of principal showing intention that agency exists

2. Representation--principal represents to third party that someone is his/her agent

a. Creates apparent (ostensible) authority
b. Does not require reliance by third party
c. Directed toward third party causing third party to believe (as opposed to implied appointment when agent is led to believe)

> *EXAMPLE: Principal writes to a third party that A is his agent and has authority. Even if A has no actual authority, he is an apparent agent.*

3. By estoppel--principal is not allowed to deny agency relationship when s/he causes third party to believe it exists

a. Imposed by law rather than by agreement
b. The third party must rely to his/her detriment on this appearance of agency before the principal is estopped from denying it

> *EXAMPLE: A, who is not an agent of P, bargained, while in P's presence with X, to buy goods for P. If P remains silent, he will not be able to deny the agency.*

4. Necessity--when a situation arises that makes it a matter of public policy to presume an agency relationship, e.g., in an emergency to contract for medical aid

5. Ratification--approval after the fact of an unauthorized act done by an agent or one not yet an agent

    a. By affirming the act or by accepting the benefits of the act
    b. Other party to the contract can withdraw before principal ratifies
    c. Ratification is effective retroactively back to time of agent's act
    d. Ratification is not retractable
    e. Undisclosed or partially disclosed principal cannot ratify unauthorized acts of agent
    f. Requirements to be valid

        (1) Act must be one that would have been valid if agent had been authorized, i.e., lawful and delegable

            (a) Torts can be ratified, but not crimes

        (2) Principal must have been in existence and competent when the act was done
        (3) Principal must have capacity when s/he ratifies
        (4) Agent must act for a fully disclosed principal
        (5) Principal must be aware of all material facts
        (6) Act must be ratified in its entirety, i.e., cannot ratify the beneficial part and refuse the rest

EXAMPLE: Receptionist has no authority to contract for X Company but signs a service contract on behalf of X Company. Officers of X Company make use of service contract. The receptionist's act is ratified.

C. Authority

1. Actual authority

    a. Express--consists of all authority expressly given by the principal to his/her agent
    b. Implied--authority that can be reasonably implied from express authority and from the conduct of the principal. See Methods of Creation.

        (1) E.g., agent drives principal's car. Principal acquiesces by not objecting, so agent has implied authority to do it again.
        (2) E.g., principal ratifies unauthorized act. Depending on circumstances, agent may have implied authority to do similar act.
        (3) Includes authority reasonably necessary or usual to carry out express authority; e.g., authority to drive car home when s/he has authority to buy it

2. Apparent (ostensible) authority--third party(ies) must have reasonable belief based on principal's representations. Principal has clothed agent with apparent authority to do acts customary to one in the relationship of an agent to the principal.

    a. E.g., an agent insofar as third persons are concerned can do what the predecessor did or what agents in similar positions in the general business world are deemed authorized to do for their principals
    b. Secret limitations have no effect

EXAMPLE: Principal makes agent manager of his store but tells him not to purchase goods on his own. Agent has apparent authority to purchase as similar managers would.

    c. Apparent authority exists only for those who know of principal's representations whether directly or indirectly

    d. Agent has apparent authority after termination of agency until those with whom the agent has dealt are given actual notice; others who know of agency relationship require constructive notice

        (1) Notice may come from any source

3. Estoppel--not true authority, but an equitable doctrine to protect a third party who has detrimentally relied, by estopping the principal from denying the existence of authority

    a. Often indistinguishable from effects of apparent authority or ratification

        (1) Estoppel may be applied where other doctrines technically won't work

    b. Only creates rights in the third party(ies)

> *EXAMPLE: A sells P's race horse to T on P's behalf. P did not give authority, but since the race horse continues to lose races, P does not object. When the horse begins to win races, P claims A never had authority to sell. If A does not have apparent authority and if P did not technically ratify, P can be estopped from denying the authority on equitable grounds.*

D. Capacity To Be Agent or Principal

1. Principal must be able to give legal consent

    a. Infants (person under age of majority, i.e., 18 or 21) can, in most jurisdictions, appoint an agent

        (1) If not to secure necessities, the appointment can be voided at the infant-principal's option

    b. Partnerships have all the partners as agents who, in turn, may appoint other agents

    c. Corporations, being artificial persons, must act entirely through agents

    d. Unincorporated associations are not legal entities and therefore cannot appoint agents

        (1) Individual members will be responsible as principals if they appoint an agent

    e. If act requires some legal capacity, e.g., legal age to sell land, then principal must meet this requirement or agent cannot legally perform even if s/he has capacity. Capacity cannot be increased by appointment of an agent.

    f. Marriage is not a bar for either spouse to be a principal or agent for the other

    g. Insane principal's agreements are voidable if made before s/he is judicially found insane and void if made after the judicial determination

2. An agent must merely have sufficient mental and physical ability to carry out instructions of his/her principal

    a. Can bind principal even if agent is a minor or legally unable to act for himself
    b. Corporations, unincorporated associations, and partnerships may act as agents
    c. A mental incompetent or an infant of tender years may not be an agent

E. Obligations and Rights

1. Principal's obligations to agent

    a. Compensate agent as per agreement, or, in the absence of an agreement, pay a reasonable amount for the agent's service
    b. Reimburse agent for reasonable expenses and indemnify agent against loss or liability for duties performed at the principal's direction which are not illegal
    c. Not to interfere with his/her work
    d. Inform agent of risks, e.g., physical harm, pecuniary loss
    e. Only duty to subagent is indemnification. Agent has duties of principal to subagent.
    f. May have remedies of discharging agent, restitution, damages, and accounting, or an injunction

2. Agent's obligations to principal

    a. Agent is a fiduciary and must act in the best interest of the principal and with complete loyalty
    b. Carry out instructions of principal exercising reasonable care and skill
    c. To account to the principal for profits and everything which rightfully belongs to the principal and not commingle funds
    d. To indemnify principal for any damage wrongfully caused principal, e.g., tort while in course of employment
    e. Give any information to principal which s/he would want or need to know
    f. Duty not to compete or act adversely to principal

        (1) Includes not acting for oneself unless principal knows and agrees

    g. Cannot appoint subagent or delegate nonmechanical duties unless authorized, necessary, or customary
    h. After termination, must cease acting as agent

        (1) May still have duty not to reveal secrets of principal

3. Principal's liability to third parties

    a. Disclosed principal is liable on contracts

        (1) Where agent has actual authority, implied authority, apparent authority, or contract is later ratified
        (2) Also held liable for any representations made by agent with authority to make them
        (3) Principal not liable where third party has any notice that agent is exceeding his actual authority

    b. Undisclosed or partially disclosed principal is similarly liable unless

        (1) Third party holds agent responsible (third party has choice)
        (2) Agent has already fully performed contract
        (3) Undisclosed principal is expressly excluded by contract

       (4) Contract is a negotiable instrument

          (a) Only fully disclosed (in instrument) principal is liable on a negotiable instrument

  c. If a writing is required under Statute of Frauds, principal will only be liable if agent signs

  d. Principal has his/her own personal defenses, e.g., lack of capacity, and defenses on the contract, e.g., nonperformance by the third party

       (1) Principal does not have agent's personal defenses, e.g., right of setoff where third party owes agent debt

  e. Notice to agent is considered notice to the principal except where notice was given to agent before the formation of the agency relationship

       (1) If agent is acting against interest of principal, i.e., in collusion with third party, then this third party's notice to agent is not notice to principal

  f. Principal is not liable for agent's crimes (violations of statutes) unless s/he was a party to the crime or acquiesced in commission

4. Agent's liability to third parties

  a. Agent is liable on contract when

       (1) Principal is undisclosed or partially disclosed

          (a) Agent is not relieved from liability until principal performs or third party elects to hold principal liable

       (2) S/he contracts in his/her own name

       (3) S/he guarantees principal's performance and principal fails

       (4) S/he signs a negotiable instrument and does not sign in a representative capacity or does not include the principal's name (undisclosed principal)

       (5) S/he knows principal does not exist or is incompetent

          (a) Liable even if third party also knows

       (6) S/he acts without authority

          (a) But agent with apparent or implied authority is not liable to third parties

  b. Agent is not liable when

       (1) Principal is disclosed and agent signs all documents in representative capacity

       (2) Principal ratifies unauthorized act

       (3) Third party elects to hold partially disclosed or undisclosed principal liable

  c. Agent has his/her personal defenses, e.g., right of offset if third party owes him/her debt, and defenses on the contract, e.g., nonperformance by the third party

       (1) Agent does not have principal's personal defenses, e.g., lack of capacity

    d. Agent is liable if s/he does not deliver property received from third party for principal

    e. Agent is liable for his/her own crimes and torts

5. Third parties' liability to principal and agent

    a. Third party has no contractual liability to agent unless

        (1) Agent is a party to the contract, i.e., undisclosed or partially disclosed principal, or

        (2) Agent has an interest in the contract, e.g., agent invests in the contract

    b. Third party is liable to disclosed, partially disclosed, and undisclosed principals

        (1) Third party has personal defenses against principal, e.g., lack of capacity, and defenses on the contract, e.g., nonperformance by principal

        (2) Against undisclosed principal, third party also has personal defenses against agent

F. Termination of Principal-Agent Relationship

1. Acts of the parties

    a. By agreement

        (1) Time specified in original agreement, e.g., agency for one year

        (2) Mutual consent

        (3) Accomplishment of objective, e.g., agency to buy a piece of land

    b. Principal or agent may terminate agency

        (1) Party that terminates is liable for breach of contract if termination is before specified period of time

            (a) One still has power to terminate relationship even though s/he has no right to terminate (i.e., results in breach of contract)

                EXAMPLE: A and P agree to be agent and principal for six months. P terminates A after two months. P is liable to A for breach of contract for the damages that this wrongful termination causes A. However, P does have the power to remove A's authority to act on behalf of P.

        (2) If either party breaches duties owed, other party may terminate agency without liability

        (3) If no time is specified in agency, i.e., terminable at will, then either party may terminate without liability

        (4) If agency was gratuitous, agent may terminate without liability

        (5) Principal does not have power to terminate agency coupled with an interest; this is a very important concept (see "A.5.a.")

2. Third parties who have dealt with agent or have known of agency must be given notice if agency terminated by acts of the parties

    a. Otherwise, agent still binds principal by apparent authority

    b. Constructive notice, e.g., publishing in a newspaper or a trade journal, is sufficient to third parties who have not previously dealt with agent

c. Actual notice, e.g., orally informing or sending a letter, etc., must be given to third parties who have previously dealt with agent unless third party learns of termination from another source

EXAMPLE: T has previously dealt with A, while acting as agent of P. P fires A but A makes a contract with T purporting to act as P's agent. T can still hold P liable unless he received actual notice of termination.

EXAMPLE: Same as above except that the principal gave constructive notice. T may hold P liable.

EXAMPLE: Same as above except that although P only gave constructive notice through a trade journal, T happened to read it. This qualifies as actual notice. Therefore, unlike above, T may not hold P liable.

3. By operation of law
   a. If subject of agreement becomes illegal or impossible
   b. Death or insanity of either party

      (1) Principal's estate is not liable to agent or for contracts made by agent after principal's death except as provided by statute
      (2) Exception is an agency coupled with an interest

          EXAMPLE: If mortgagee has power to sell the property to recover his loan, this authority to sell as mortgagor's agent is not terminated by mortgagor's death.

   c. Bankruptcy of principal terminates the relationship

      (1) Bankruptcy of agent does not affect unless agent's solvency is needed for performance

   d. If terminated by operation of law, no notice need be given

PARTNERSHIPS AND JOINT VENTURES

Overview

The Uniform Partnership Act is the uniform statute adopted by most states and is the basis for partnership questions on the exam. A partnership is an association of two or more persons to carry on a business as co-owners for profit. For most purposes, the partnership is not considered a separate legal entity, but a specialized form of agency. The major areas tested on partnerships are the characteristics of a partnership, comparisons with corporations, the rights and liabilities of the partnership itself, the rights, duties, and liabilities of the partners among them- selves and to third parties, the allocation of profits and losses, and the rights of various parties, including creditors, upon dissolution.

The law of joint ventures is similar to that of partnerships with some exceptions. Note that the joint venture is more limited in scope than the partnership form of business. The former is typically organized to carry out one single business undertaking or a series of related undertakings; whereas, the latter is formed to conduct ongoing business.

A. Nature of Partnerships

1. A partnership is an association of two or more persons to carry on a business as co-owners for profit

   a. To carry on a business includes almost every trade, occupation, or profession

      (1) It does not include passive co-ownership of property, e.g., joint tenants of a piece of land

   b. Co-ownership of the "business" (and not merely of assets used in a business) is an important element in determining whether a partnership exists. Each partner has a proprietary interest in the business.

      (1) Co-ownership of property (including capital) is one element
      (2) The most important and necessary element of co-ownership (and thereby partnership) is profit sharing

         (a) Need not be equal and need not include loss sharing, although it usually does and is so presumed
         (b) Receipt of a share of profits is prima facie evidence (raises a presumption) of a partnership

            1] Presumption rebutted by establishing that profit sharing was only for payment of debt, interest on loan, services performed, rent, etc.

      (3) Another important element of co-ownership is joint control

         (a) Each partner has an equal right to participate in management. May be contracted away to a managing partner.

2. Partnership relationship creates a fiduciary relationship between partners

   a. Fiduciary relationship arises because each partner is an agent for partnership and for each other in partnership business

3. Partnership relationship is based on contract but arrangements may be quite informal

   a. Agreement can be inferred from conduct, e.g., allowing someone to share in management and profits may result in partnership even though actual intent to become partner is missing

4. In general, partnerships are governed by the Uniform Partnership Act (UPA) and by agency law

    a. Draws heavily on agency law because each partner is an agent as well as a principal of partnership

        (1) Most rules can be changed in individual cases by agreement between parties affected, e.g., rights and duties between partners

> *EXAMPLE: A, B, and C form a partnership in which all three partners agree that A is liable for all of the product liability cases against the partnership. This agreement is enforceable between A, B, and C but not against other parties that never agreed to this. Therefore, as long as A is solvent, B and C can collect from A even though a third party recovers from all of them on a product liability problem.*

5. Generally, any person (entity) who has the capacity to contract may become a partner

    a. Corporations
    b. Minors--but contract of partnership is voidable
    c. Partnerships can become partners

6. Common characteristics of partnerships

    a. Limited duration; when partner leaves, partnership terminates
    b. Transfer of ownership requires agreement
    c. Not a distinct separate entity for many purposes, e.g., liability and taxation

        (1) However, is a separate legal entity for purposes of ownership of property

    d. Unlimited liability of partners for partnership debts
    e. Ease of formation, can be very informal

B. Types of Partnerships and Partners

1. Limited partnership is a special statutory relationship consisting of one or more general partners and one or more limited partners

    a. Limited partners only contribute capital and are usually only liable to that extent (analogous to shareholder)

2. General partners are ones who share in management of business and have unlimited liability

3. Limited partners are ones who do not take part in management process and whose liability is limited to their capital contributions

C. Formation of Partnership

1. By agreement, express or implied

2. Creation of a partnership may be very informal, either oral or written

    a. Written partnership agreement not required unless within Statute of Frauds, e.g., partnership that cannot be completed within one year

> *EXAMPLE: A, B, and C form a partnership that, although they expect it to last for several years, has no specific time period specified. This partnership agreement may be oral.*

> *EXAMPLE: X, Y, and Z organize XYZ partnership which by agreement will last at least five years. This partnership agreement must be in writing.*

    (1) Usually wise to have in writing

  b. Filing not required

3. Anyone who receives a share of profits is presumed to be a partner. This is, however, a rebuttable presumption.

4. Articles of copartnership (partnership agreement)--not legally necessary, but a good idea to have

5. Fictitious name statutes require partners to register fictitious or assumed names

  a. Failure to comply does not invalidate partnership but may result in fine
  b. The purpose is to allow third parties to know who is in partnership

D. Partner's Rights

1. Partnership agreement, whether oral or written, would be controlling

  a. Following rules are used unless partnership agreement states otherwise

2. Partnership interest

  a. Refers to partner's right to share in profits and return of contribution on dissolution
  b. Is considered personal property

    (1) Even if partnership property is real estate

  c. Does not include specific partnership property, merely right to use it for partnership purposes
  d. Freely assignable without other partner's consent

    (1) Assignee is not substituted as a partner without consent of all other partners
    (2) Assignee does <u>not</u> receive right to manage partnership, to have an accounting, to inspect books, to possess or own any individual partnership property--merely receives rights in the assigning partner's share of profits and return of partner's capital contribution (unless partners agree otherwise)

      (a) Typically, assignments are made to secure a loan

> *EXAMPLE: C, a CPA, wishes to obtain a large loan. He is a member of a CPA firm and assigns rights in his partnership to the bank to secure the loan.*

    (3) Assignor remains liable as a partner
    (4) Does not cause dissolution unless assignor also withdraws

3. Partnership property

  a. Includes

    (1) Property acquired with partnership funds unless different intent is shown

(2) Property or capital contributed by partners, e.g., cash, land, building, fixtures, securities
(3) Partnership profits before the profits are distributed
(4) Goodwill, partnership name, etc.
(5) Factors to use in deciding if property is partnership's rather than individual's

    (a) Whether partnership funds were used to acquire it
    (b) How property is used
    (c) Who is the owner of record
    (d) Other facts that indicate ownership such as who pays taxes

> EXAMPLE: A, B, and C have a partnership. A certain piece of real estate is used for partnership business and was paid for out of partnership funds. Taxes are paid by the partnership even though B is the owner of record. By weighing the factors, this is considered partnership property rather than B's individual property.

b. All partners have equal rights to the partnership property

    (1) Each can possess or use partnership property for partnership purposes
    (2) Property owned as tenants in partnership with other partners

c. Not assignable or subject to attachment individually, only by a claim on partnership

    (1) All partners can agree and assign property
    (2) Any partner can assign or sell if for the apparent purpose of carrying on the business of the partnership in the usual way

d. Each partner has an insurable interest in partnership property
e. Upon partner's death, his/her estate is only entitled to the deceased partner's interest in partnership, not specific property

    (1) Partnership may have to be liquidated to settle his/her estate
    (2) Heirs not automatically partners
    (3) Remaining partners own property as tenants in partnership
    (4) Remaining partners have duty to account to the heirs of the deceased for value of interest

4. Participate in management

a. Right to participate equally in management

    (1) Ordinary business decisions by a majority vote
    (2) Unanimous consent needed to make fundamental changes

b. Power to act as an agent for partnership in partnership business
c. Also has right to inspect books and have full knowledge of partnership affairs

5. Share in profits and losses

a. Profits and losses are shared equally unless agreement specifies otherwise

    (1) Even if contributed capital is not equal
    (2) E.g., agreement may specify one partner to receive greater share of profits for doing more work, etc., while losses still shared equally

       b.   If partners agree on unequal profit sharing but are silent on loss sharing, losses are shared per the profit sharing proportions

           (1)   May choose to share losses in a different proportion from profits

   6.   Other monetary rights

       a.   Indemnification for expenses incurred on behalf of the partnership
       b.   Interest on loans to partnership

           (1)   No interest on capital contributions unless in partnership agreement

       c.   No right to salary for work performed because this is a duty

           (1)   Common for partners to agree to pay salaries, especially if only one or two do most of the work

   7.   Nonmonetary rights between partners

       a.   Based on fiduciary duty (this is important)

           (1)   Partners cannot gain personally from partnership transactions without agreement by other partners
           (2)   Any wrongly derived profits must be held by partner for others
           (3)   Must not compete with partnership
           (4)   May participate in other business as long as it is not competition and does not interfere with partner's duty to partnership
           (5)   Must abide by partnership agreement

       b.   Exercise of reasonable skill
       c.   Formal accounting of partnership affairs

   8.   Incoming partners new to partnership have same rights as previous partners

       a.   Requires consent of all partners to admit new partner
       b.   Profit sharing, loss sharing, and capital contributions are by agreement between all partners

E.   **Relationship to Third Parties**

   1.   Partners are agents of the partnership

       a.   Can bind partnership to contracts with third parties

           (1)   Even where no actual authority, can bind partnership where there is apparent (ostensible) authority, authority by estoppel, or implied authority

              (a)   Apparent (ostensible) partnership created when parties misrepresent to others that they are partners

                 1]   Similar in concept to apparent (ostensible) agency
                 2]   Individuals called apparent (ostensible) partners and are liable to third parties as if they were actual partners

                    a]   Usually liable even if allows others to misrepresent him/her as partner

              (b)   Partnership by estoppel created when parties misrepresent to others that they are partners and others are hurt as they rely on this

                 1]   Many courts treat partnership by estoppel and apparent partnership as essentially the same

2] Not actual partners but liable as if were actual partners
3] Individuals called partners by estoppel

EXAMPLE: A, B, and C form a partnership to sell widgets. Contrary to the wishes of B and C, A decides to buy in the partnership name some "super-widgets" from T. Even though A did not have actual authority to buy these, T can enforce the contract based on apparent authority. A, of course, breached his fiduciary duty to B and C.

b. Partners usually have authority to buy and sell goods, receive money, and pay debts
c. Partnership is not liable for acts of partners outside of express, implied, or apparent authority

EXAMPLE: A partner of a hardware store attempts to buy some real estate in the name of the partnership. Here apparent authority does not exist.

d. Partnership is liable for partner's torts committed in course and scope of business and for partner's breach of trust, i.e., misapplication of third party's funds

EXAMPLE: A partner takes a third party's money on behalf of the partnership to invest in government bonds. Instead he uses it himself to build an addition onto his home.

EXAMPLE: A partner, while driving on partnership business, injures a third party. If the partner is negligent, the partnership is also liable.

2. Unanimous consent of partners is needed (so no implied authority for)

a. Admission of a new partner
b. Assignment of partnership property
c. Disposition of partnership goodwill
d. Making partnership a surety or guarantor
e. Admitting to a claim against partnership in court
f. Submitting partnership claim to arbitrator

3. Partner's liability is personal, i.e., extends to all his/her personal assets, (not just investment in partnership,) to cover all debts and liabilities of partnership

a. Partners are jointly liable on contracts, debt, and other obligations

(1) Joint liability means all partners must be sued together. Cannot sue only one.
(2) Partnership assets must be exhausted before partner's individual assets can be reached
(3) Since majority vote rules, all partners are liable even if they did not vote or objected to the action

b. Partners are jointly and severally liable for torts and breaches of trust

(1) Several liability means a party may sue just one partner (any one) for the full amount
(2) Party has choice whether to sue one or all parties
(3) Partnership assets need not be exhausted first. Partnership need not even be sued.

     c. Partners may split losses or liability between themselves according to any proportion agreed upon; however, third parties can still hold each partner personally liable despite agreement

        (1) If any partner pays more than his/her agreed share, s/he can get reimbursed from other partners

           EXAMPLE: X, Y, and Z as partners agreed to split losses 10%, 20%, and 70% respectively. A third party recovers $100,000 from X only based on a partnership tort. X can get $20,000 from Y and $70,000 from Z so that she ends up paying only her 10%.

           EXAMPLE: Same as before except that Y is insolvent. X can recover the proportionate share from Z or $87,500 ($100,000 x 70%/80%).

           EXAMPLE: A, B, and C are partners who agree to split losses 10%, 10%, and 80%, respectively. Y sues the partners for a tort based on the partnership business. C takes out bankruptcy. Y can recover from A and B and is not bound by the agreement between A, B, and C.

     d. New partners coming into a partnership are liable for existing debts only to the extent of their capital contributions

        (1) Unless new partners assume personal liability for old debts

     e. Partners withdrawing are liable for existing liabilities

     f. Partners withdrawing are liable for subsequent liabilities unless notice of withdrawal or death is given to third parties

        (1) Actual notice to creditors who previously dealt with partnership
        (2) Constructive, e.g., published, notice is sufficient for others who merely knew of partnership's existence

     g. Estates of deceased partners are liable for partners' debts
     h. Liability of withdrawing partner may be limited by agreement between partners but agreement is not binding on third parties (unless they join in on agreement)
     i. Partners are not criminally liable unless they personally participate in some way or statute prescribes liability to all members of management, e.g., environment regulation or sale of alcohol to a minor

F. Termination of a Partnership

  1. Termination occurs when the winding up (often called liquidation) of partnership affairs is complete

     a. First, dissolution must occur--when the partners stop carrying on a business together
     b. Second, winding up takes place--the process of settling of partnership affairs

  2. Dissolution can occur by

     a. Prior agreement, e.g., partnership agreement
     b. Present agreement of partners
     c. Withdrawal of a partner

        (1) If agreement specifies a term of existence or a particular undertaking, withdrawing partner will be in breach of contract if his/her withdrawal is prior to agreed time but can still withdraw

(a) If agreement is within Statute of Frauds, must be in writing
to be enforceable

> EXAMPLE: A, B, and C form a partnership, agreeing orally that
> it will exist for at least two years. This agreement must be
> in writing as a contract that cannot be performed within one
> year of the making of the agreement. Therefore, any of the
> partners may withdraw without liability to the other partners.

(2) If no agreed length of partnership, any partner can terminate at
any time without liability

> EXAMPLE: A, B, and C form a partnership without mentioning any
> duration. Whether the partnership agreement is in writing or not,
> any partner may withdraw without liability to those remaining.

d. Death of a partner
e. Bankruptcy of a partner or partnership
f. Subject matter of partnership business becomes illegal
g. By decree of court in such cases as

(1) Partner continually or seriously breaches partnership agreement
(2) Partner guilty of conduct that harms business

h. Assignment, selling, or pledging of partnership interest does not cause
dissolution even if no consent of other partners

3. Rights of partners in dissolution

a. If partner's withdrawal is not in violation of partnership agreement,
then other partners cannot recover from withdrawing partner for losses
due to that dissolution

(1) If partner withdraws in violation of partnership agreement, then
liable to others for breach of contract

> EXAMPLE: X, Y, and Z agreed to a ten-year partnership. Y
> withdraws early. Y is liable to X and Z for breach of the partner-
> ship agreement. Y may still, however, collect any partnership
> profits and capital contribution owed him. These are all netted
> out so that he may receive money or have to pay more in.

(2) Whether partner withdrew in violation of agreement or not,
remaining partners may elect to wind up and terminate partnership
or not wind up and continue business by paying withdrawing
partner(s) value of share(s) of partnership

4. At dissolution and during winding up

a. Partners have no actual authority to act for partnership except as is
necessary to wind up and pay debts and finish old business
b. Partners are still liable to creditors

5. Distribution priority (different from limited partnerships)

a. Creditors
b. To partners for liabilities other than capital and profits
c. To partners for capital contributions after allocating any losses
d. To partners as to profits

6. Partners are personally liable to partnership for any deficits in their

capital accounts and to creditors for insufficiency of partnership assets

a. Partners must contribute toward this deficiency according to loss sharing ratio; always same as profit sharing ratio unless agreed otherwise

EXAMPLE: The partnership of Herb, Ike, and Bucky was dissolved. The partnership had liquid assets of $260,000 and liabilities of $240,000, of which $210,000 is owed to outside creditors and $30,000 is owed to Herb for a loan Herb made to the partnership. The capital contributions were: Herb, $20,000 and Ike, $15,000. Profits and losses are to be shared according to the following ratio: Herb, 50%; Ike, 30%; and Bucky, 20%. The order of distribution of firm assets of a general partnership would be as follows: First, the outside creditors are satisfied, $210,000. Second, Herb receives $30,000 representing his loan to the firm. Third, capital contributions are returned to Herb ($20,000) and Ike ($15,000). This results in a $15,000 deficit [$260,000 - ($210,000 + $30,000 + $20,000 + $15,000)]. The partners must contribute toward this deficiency according to the loss sharing ratio. Therefore, Herb must contribute $7,500 (50% x $15,000), Ike must contribute $4,500 (30% x $15,000), and Bucky must contribute $3,000 (20% x $15,000). Thus, in the final result, Herb receives a net distribution of $42,500 [($30,000 + $20,000) - $7,500], Ike receives a net distribution of $10,500 ($15,000 - $4,500), and Bucky must contribute $3,000.

If Bucky is personally insolvent, the other partners (Herb and Ike) are liable in the <u>relative</u> proportion in which they share in the profits: Herb, $1,875 ($3,000 x 50%/80%) and Ike, $1,125 ($3,000 x 30%/80%). Therefore, Herb and Ike must reduce their net distributions by these respective amounts.

b. Priority between partnership creditors and partner's personal creditors (called marshalling of assets rule)

   (1) Partnership creditors have first priority to partnership assets; any excess goes to personal creditors
   (2) Usually, personal creditors have first priority to personal assets; any excess goes to partnership creditors

      (a) But, trustee in bankruptcy of a partnership is entitled to share pro rata with unsecured creditors of a partner

7. Partnership agreement may provide for partnership to continue without winding up (e.g., after death of a partner)

8. If business is continued after dissolution, a new partnership is formed and old creditors become creditors of new partnership

   a. Frequently, same name is used

9. Partners can bind other partners and the partnership on contracts until third parties who have known of the partnership are given notice of dissolution

   a. Actual notice must be given to third parties who have dealt with the partnership prior to dissolution
   b. Constructive notice, e.g., notice in newspaper, is adequate for third parties who have only known of the partnership

10. If partner withdraws, and sells his/her interest back to partnership

   a. Loses all partner's rights and interests in partnership
   b. If sold on installment, is merely a creditor of partnership

      c. May subsequently be partner by estoppel if s/he fails to give notice to third parties

G. **Limited Partnerships**

  1. Creation of limited partnership

     a. Must file a certificate of limited partnership with Secretary of State
     b. Should file in each state where doing business to avoid treatment as a general partnership
     c. Name of business must say "limited partnership"
     d. Requires at least one general partner who retains unlimited personal liability and at least one limited partner

       (1) Liability of limited partner(s) is limited to amount of capital contributions (with some exceptions below)

         (a) Capital contributions are set by agreement and may consist of cash, property, obligations, contribution of services, and promises to contribute cash, property, and services

           1] If promised services not performed, must pay partnership value of those services unless agreed otherwise
           2] If part or all of agreed capital contribution not paid to partnership, limited partner may be required to pay it

  2. Profit or loss sharing

     a. Profits or losses are shared as agreed upon in certificate agreement

       (1) Losses and any liability are limited to capital contributions
       (2) If no agreement on profit and losses, then shared based on percentages of capital contributions

         (a) Note how this differs from a general partnership in which losses and profits are shared equally unless agreed otherwise

  3. Managing the limited partnership

     a. <u>General</u> partners have equal right to manage unless agreed otherwise
     b. <u>Limited</u> partners have no right to manage

       (1) If a limited partner does get involved in management or daily operations of partnership, then s/he has unlimited personal liability (like a general partner) but only to third parties who knew of his/her involvement in management of partnership
       (2) Following are <u>not</u> construed as managing or taking part in control of limited partnership

         (a) Acting as an agent or employee of limited partnership or of a general partner
         (b) Consulting with and advising general partner about business
         (c) Approving or disapproving amendments to limited partnership agreement
         (d) Voting on dissolution or winding up of limited partnership
         (e) Voting on loans of limited partnership
         (f) Voting on change in nature of business
         (g) Voting on removal of a general partner

       (3) If a limited partner <u>knowingly</u> allows his/her name to be part of limited partnership name, then is liable to creditors who extend credit to business (unless creditors knew that limited partner was not a general partner)

(a) Exception if limited partner has same name as a general partner

(4) Limited partner is not an implied agent or apparent agent

4. Limited partnership interests may be assigned in part or in whole

   a. If all interest assigned, then ceases to be partner unless otherwise agreed
   b. Assignee becomes actual limited partner if all other partners consent or if assignor gives assignee that status pursuant to authority (if given in certificate of partnership)

      (1) In such case, former limited partner is generally not released from liability to limited partnership

5. Admission of new limited partner requires amendment of certificate

6. Limited partner may not withdraw capital contribution if it impairs creditors

7. Limited partners may own competing interests

8. Limited partners have right to inspect partnership books and tax return information

9. Withdrawal of a limited partner requires six months prior written notice unless agreed otherwise

10. Dissolution of limited partnership

   a. May take place by agreement in certificate
   b. Takes place if a general partner dies, withdraws, becomes insane, is removed, or files for bankruptcy, unless remaining general partner(s), if any, have and exercise right to continue business

      (1) If partnership agreement provides that partnership will continue after death of a partner, then dissolution will not occur

   c. Death of a limited partner does not terminate partnership

      (1) Executor of estate of deceased limited partner obtains rights and liabilities of that limited partner to settle estate

         (a) Executor does not become an actual limited partner

   d. Creditor obtaining a judgment against limited partner does not dissolve partnership

      (1) Creditor has right to limited partners' income only

11. Can be a limited and general partner at same time

   a. Has rights, powers, and liability of a general partner
   b. Has rights against other partners with respect to contribution as a limited partner and also as a general partner

12. After dissolution, winding up typically is done by remaining general partners or in some cases by court action

   a. Upon winding up, the assets of a limited partnership are distributed based on the following priorities (this is very different from prior law)

      (1) To creditors including partners who are creditors (note also how this is different from winding up a general partnership)
      (2) Amounts before withdrawal to which partners are entitled

(3) Capital contributions of both limited and general partners (note that general and limited partners rank on the same level)
(4) Distribution of profits of both limited and general partners

H. Joint Ventures

1. Definition of joint venture--association of two or more persons (or entities) organized to carry out a single business undertaking (or series of related undertakings) for profit

    a. Distinguished from partnership because purpose is not to conduct ongoing business involving various transactions

        (1) Joint venture is more limited
        (2) Partnership is formed for indefinite period of time

    b. Also called joint enterprise or joint adventure
    c. Generally, corporations may engage in joint ventures
        EXAMPLE: X corporation, O corporation, and N corporation decide to form a joint venture to bring oil from the north to the south of Alaska.

        (1) In some states, corporations may not be partners in a partnership

2. Law of joint ventures is similar to that of partnerships with some exceptions

    a. Each joint venturer is not necessarily an agent of other joint venturers--limited power to bind others

        (1) Can be express agent by agreement

    b. Death of joint venturer does not automatically dissolve joint venture
    c. Joint venture is interpreted as special form of partnership

        (1) Fiduciary duties of partners in partnership law apply

            (a) Duty to provide full disclosure to each other
            (b) Possible conflict of interest in disclosing trade secrets between members

        (2) No formalities necessary for creation

            (a) Usually written contract anyway

        (3) Each member has right to participate in management

            (a) Management of joint venture is often placed on one member by agreement

        (4) Liability is unlimited and each joint venturer is personally liable for debts
        (5) Each is liable for own negligence as well as negligence of other joint venturers
        (6) Each member is entitled to an accounting
        (7) In general, treated as partnership for tax purposes

            (a) Profits taxable when earned whether or not distributed

CORPORATIONS

Overview

A corporation is an artificial being which is created by or under law and which operates under a common name through its elected management. It is a legal entity, separate and distinct from its shareholders. The corporation has the authority vested in it by statute and its corporate charter. The candidate should understand the characteristics and advantages of the corporate form over other forms of business organization.

Basic to preparation for questions on corporation law is an understanding of the following: the liabilities of a promoter who organizes a new corporation; the liability of shareholders; the liability of the corporation with respect to the preincorporation contracts made by the promoter; the fiduciary relationship of the promoter to the stockholders and to the corporation; the various circumstances under which a stockholder may be liable for the debts of the corporation; the rights of shareholders particularly concerning payment of dividends; the rights and duties of officers, directors, and other agents or employees of the corporation to the corporation, to stockholders, and to third persons; subscriptions; and the procedures necessary to merge, consolidate, or otherwise change the corporate structure.

A. Characteristics and Advantages of Corporate Form

1. Majority of states have adopted Model Business Corporation Act which is used in this module

2. Limited liability

    a. Generally a shareholder in a corporation risks only his/her investment

        (1) Liability for corporate affairs does not extend to his/her personal assets

3. Transferability of interest

    a. Shares in corporations are represented by stocks and can be freely bought, sold, or assigned with little effect on the operations of the company unless shareholders have agreed to restrictions

4. Continuous life

    a. Unlike a partnership, a corporation is not terminated by death of a shareholder, or his/her incapacity

        (1) Regarded as perpetual, and continues to exist until dissolved, merged, or otherwise terminated

5. Separate entity

    a. A corporation is a legal entity in itself and is treated separately from its stockholders

        (1) Can take, hold, and convey property
        (2) Can contract in own name with shareholders or third parties
        (3) Can sue and be sued

6. Financing

    a. Often easier to raise large amounts of capital than in other business organizations by issuance of stock or other securities, e.g., bonds

    b. More flexible because can issue different classes of stock and/or bonds to suit its needs and market demands

7. Corporate management

    a. Corporations can employ management personnel who are experts in their fields of business

    b. Persons who manage corporations are not necessarily shareholders

    c. Management of a corporation is usually vested in board of directors elected by shareholders

B. Disadvantages of Form

1. Taxation (can be an advantage depending on circumstances)

    a. Tax burdens may be heavier than on individuals operating sole proprietorship because of federal "double taxation"

        (1) Corporate taxation

        (2) Distributed earnings taxed to shareholders

        (3) Subchapter S status can alleviate

        (4) Various tax breaks may partially or completely avoid double taxation

    b. Many states have a state corporate income tax

2. Costs of incorporating, because must meet formal creation requirements

3. Formal operating requirements must be met

    a. Procedural and administrative details to be complied with

    b. Continuing governmental supervision

    c. Some states allow less formal operating requirements for small, closely-held corporations

C. Types of Corporations

1. Domestic corporation is one which operates and does business within the state in which it was incorporated

2. Foreign corporation is one doing business in any state except one in which it was incorporated

    a. Foreign corporations if "doing business" in a given state are not exempt from many requirements and details that domestic corporations must meet

        (1) Corporation is doing business in that state if transactions are continuous rather than an isolated transaction

    b. Model Business Corporation Act requires foreign corporation file documentation similar to that for incorporation

    c. If foreign corporation does not qualify to do business in a state

        (1) May be denied access to courts to sue

        (2) Is liable to the state for any fees, taxes, interest, and penalties as if it had qualified to do business

3. Professional corporations are ones under state laws which allow professionals to incorporate, e.g., doctors, accountants, attorneys

    a. Typically, shares may be owned only by licensed professionals

    b. Retain personal liability for their professional acts

    c. Obtain other corporation benefits, e.g., limited liability for corporate debts, some tax benefits

15

4. Closely-held corporation (also called close corporation) is one whose stock is owned by a limited number of persons usually with restrictions on the transfer of stock to keep it out of the hands of outsiders

   a. Informal administration of the corporation permitted, e.g., missing regular board of directors' meeting

5. Holding company is one that controls multiple corporations

6. <u>De facto</u> corporation has been formed in fact but has not properly been formed under the law

   a. Usually defective because of some small error

      (1) There must have been a good faith attempt to form
      (2) There must have been at least an attempt to substantially comply with the incorporation statute

      EXAMPLE: An organization filed all the necessary papers but did not pay the filing fee.

   b. It is necessary that there has been exercise of corporate power by this group

   EXAMPLE: The organization in the example above is completely idle, holds no organizational meeting, and transacts no business in the corporate name. It is not even a <u>de facto</u> corporation.

   c. Shareholders in a <u>de facto</u> corporation still have limited liability to third parties

      (1) If <u>de facto</u> incorporation is not achieved, the stockholders are treated as partners for purposes of liability

   d. A <u>de facto</u> corporation may only be challenged by the state directly (quo warranto proceeding) and may not be challenged by third parties

   e. Under Model Business Corporation Act essentially same end is achieved by providing that

      (1) Once state issues certificate of incorporation, this is conclusive evidence that all conditions have been met to be a corporation

         (a) However, state may revoke or cancel certificate of incorporation or dissolve corporation

7. <u>De jure</u> corporation has been formed correctly in compliance with the incorporation statute

8. Corporation by estoppel is a term used in equity to prevent injustice when an organization has not qualified as either a <u>de jure</u> or a <u>de facto</u> corporation but has held itself out as one or has been recognized as being a corporation

   EXAMPLE: Purchaser who makes a promissory note payable to a "corporation" cannot refuse to pay on the grounds that the "corporation" does not exist even though it was actually a partnership.

EXAMPLE: "Corporation" owes a debt to a supplier. The "corporation" cannot avoid the obligation by claiming that it is not a valid corporation.

D. Formation of Corporation

1. Promoter is person(s) who forms the corporation and arranges the capitalization to begin corporation

   a. Promoter handles the issuing of the prospectus, promoting stock subscriptions, and drawing up the charter
   b. Promoter has a fiduciary relationship with corporation, and is not permitted to act against interests of corporation

      (1) Does not prevent personal profit if fully disclosed

   c. Promoter is not an agent of the corporation, because the corporation is still not in existence

      (1) Any agreements (preincorporation contracts) made by promoter are not binding on the future corporation until adopted after corporation comes into existence

         (a) Normally promoter is personally liable on contract. Adoption by corporation does not relieve promoter; novation is required to relieve promoter

            1] Promoter has liability even if promoter's name does not appear on contract
            2] However, promoter is not liable if third party clearly states that s/he would look only to corporation for performance

         (b) The corporation may adopt the promoter's actions formally or by actions

            EXAMPLE: Promoter, P, makes a contract for a corporation which is to be formed, called C. After C is formed, it begins performance of the contract made by P. C is now liable on the contract.

            EXAMPLE: Same as above except that C formally adopts the preincorporation agreement and states so in the corporate minutes. C is liable on this contract even before the corporation begins performance of the contract.

         (c) In the absence of a statute or charter provision, the corporation is not liable to the promoter for his/her services unless later approved by the corporation

2. Formed only under state incorporation statutes

3. Incorporation

   a. Incorporator may or may not be promoter
   b. Articles of incorporation (charter) are filed with the state. They contain

      (1) Proposed name which cannot be the same or closely resemble the name of another corporation so as to be misleading
      (2) Purpose of corporation
      (3) Powers of corporation

(4) The amount of capital stock authorized and the types of stock to be issued
(5) Designation of agent for service of process

c. First shareholders' meeting

(1) Stock certificates issued to shareholders
(2) Resignation of temporary directors and election of new
(3) Adoption of bylaws--the rules governing the operation of the corporation

d. At same meeting or subsequent meeting, directors

(1) Elect officers
(2) Adopt or reject preincorporation contracts
(3) Begin business of corporation

E. Corporate Financial Structure

1. Definitions

a. Authorized stock--amount permitted to be issued in articles of incorporation; e.g., amount and types
b. Unissued stock--authorized but not yet issued
c. Issued stock--authorized and delivered to shareholders
d. Outstanding stock--issued and not repurchased by the corporation, i.e., it is still owned by shareholders
e. Treasury stock--issued but not outstanding, i.e., corporation repurchased it

(1) Are not votable and do not receive dividends
(2) Corporation does not recognize gain or loss on transactions with its own stock
(3) Must be purchased out of unreserved or unrestricted earned surplus as defined below and as permitted by state law

(a) If articles of incorporation so permit or if majority of voting shareholders permit, unrestricted capital surplus (see below) may also be used

(4) May be distributed as part of stock dividend
(5) May be resold without regard to par value
(6) Can be resold without regard to preemptive rights
(7) No purchase of treasury stock may be made if it renders corporation insolvent

f. Cancelled stock--stock purchased or received by corporation that is cancelled

(1) No longer issued or outstanding
(2) Makes room for more stock to be issued

g. Par-value stock

(1) Par value is arbitrary amount set in the articles of incorporation
(2) Stock should be issued for this amount or more
(3) May subsequently be traded for any amount
(4) Creditors may hold purchaser liable if stock originally purchased at below par

(a) Contingently liable for difference between amount paid and par value

(b) Subsequent purchaser also liable unless purchased in good faith without notice that sale was below par

h. No-par stock--stock issued without a set par value

(1) May have a stated value

i. Stated capital (legal capital)--number of shares issued times par value (or stated value)

(1) If no par or stated value, then includes total consideration received by corporation

(a) Under limited circumstances, portion may be allocated by board of directors to capital surplus as permitted by law

(2) Dividends normally may not be declared or paid out of it
(3) Following also increase stated capital by number of shares increased times par value (or stated value)

(a) Exercise of stock option
(b) Small common stock dividend

(4) Following do not change stated capital

(a) Acquisition or reissuance of treasury stock under cost method
(b) Stock splits

1] Increase number of shares issued and decrease par or stated value, e.g., 2-for-1 stock split doubles the number of shares issued and cuts in half the par or stated value

(c) Payment of organization costs

j. Earned surplus (retained earnings)--cumulative amount of income (net of dividends) retained by the corporation during its existence or since a deficit was properly eliminated

(1) Note that under modern terminology, this is correctly referred to as retained earnings as indicated above; since laws written using old terms, CPA candidates should be familiar with old as well as new terms as learned in accounting

k. Net assets--excess of total assets over total debts
l. Surplus--excess of net assets over stated capital
m. Capital surplus--entire surplus of corporation less earned surplus

(1) Note that paid-in capital is considered capital surplus

n. Contributed capital--total consideration received by corporation upon issuance of stock

2. Classes of stock

a. Common stock usually gives each shareholder one vote per share and is entitled to dividends if declared by the directors

(1) Has no priority over other stock for dividends
(2) Shareholders entitled to share in final distribution of assets
(3) Votes may be apportioned to shares in other ways, e.g., 1 vote per 10 shares
(4) Nonvoting common stock also may be issued if provided for in the articles of incorporation

b. Preferred stock is given preferred status as to liquidations and dividends, but dividends are still discretionary

   (1) Usually nonvoting stock

   (2) Dividend rate is generally a fixed rate

   (3) Cumulative preferred means that if a periodic dividend is not paid at the scheduled time, the obligation continues and accumulates; and must be satisfied before common stock may receive a dividend

      (a) Noncumulative preferred means that if the dividend is passed, it will never be paid (i.e., the obligation to pay ceases)

      (b) Held to be implicitly cumulative unless different intent shown

   (4) Participating preferred participates further in corporate earnings left after a fixed amount is paid to preferred shares. The participation with common shares is generally on a fixed percentage basis.

c. Callable (or redeemable) stock may be redeemed at a fixed price by the corporation. This call price is fixed in the articles of incorporation or may be subject to an agreement among the shareholders themselves.

d. Convertible preferred gives the owner the option to convert the preferred stock to common stock at a fixed exchange rate

3. Marketing of stock

  a. Stock subscriptions are contracts to purchase a given number of shares in an existing corporation or one to be organized

   (1) Subscription to stock is a written offer to buy and is not binding until accepted by the corporation

   (2) Under the Model Business Corporation Act, stock subscriptions are irrevocable for six months

   (3) Once accepted, the subscriber becomes liable

      (a) For the purchase, and

      (b) As a corporate shareholder

   (4) An agreement to subscribe in the future is not a subscription

  b. Watered stock

   (1) Stock is said to be watered when the cash or property exchanged is less than par value or stated value

      (a) No-par stock cannot be watered as long as issue amount is reasonable

   (2) Stock must be issued for consideration equal to or greater than the par or stated value under most state laws

      (a) No-par stock may be issued for consideration that the directors determine to be reasonable

   (3) Creditors of the corporation may recover from the stockholders the amount of water in their shares; i.e., the amount the stockholders would have paid to the corporation had they paid the full amount required (i.e., par value less amount paid)

      (a) If the corporation becomes insolvent

      (b) Subsequent purchaser of watered stock is not liable unless s/he had knowledge thereof

    c. Valid consideration or value for shares

      (1) Consists of cash, property, services performed

        (a) Directors have duty to set value on property received

          1] Directors' value set is conclusive unless fraud shown

      (2) Executory promises are <u>not</u> sufficient, e.g.

        (a) Promise to perform services cannot be counted
        (b) Promise to pay is not sufficient
        (c) Promissory note (whether negotiable or not) likewise is not sufficient

  4. Bonds

    a. Evidence of debt of the corporation. The owner of a bond is not an owner of the corporation but a creditor.
    b. Interest is paid on the debt at fixed intervals, and at a designated time, the principal is repaid

F. Powers of Corporation

  1. Types of corporate power

    a. Inherent power is that power which is necessary for corporate existence, e.g., power to contract
    b. Express powers are set out in the charter and bylaws at the time corporation is organized
    c. Implied powers are those which are necessary to carry out the express powers and the purpose of the incorporation

      EXAMPLE: Open a checking account.

    d. Acts within the corporation's implied or express power are <u>intra</u> <u>vires</u> and outside are <u>ultra</u> <u>vires</u>

  2. Corporations generally have the particular power to

    a. Acquire their own shares (treasury stock) or retire their own shares

      (1) Typically limited to amount of surplus

    b. Acquire shares of other corporations
    c. Make charitable contributions

      (1) Contributions to change laws are a valid business purpose, e.g., referendum measure

    d. To have exclusive use of its corporate name in the jurisdiction
    e. Generally, a corporation may also be a partner of a partnership under the Model Business Corporation Act
    f. To buy, own, hold, and sell real and personal property
    g. To contract through its agents in the name of the corporation
    h. To sue and be sued in its own name
    i. Loans to directors require shareholder approval
    j. Loans to employees (even employees who are also directors) do not need shareholder approval and are appropriate if they benefit corporation
    k. Guarantee obligations of others only if in reasonable furtherance of corporation's business

      (1) Does not allow indorsement for accommodation purposes only

G. **Liabilities of Corporations**

1. Crimes

   a. Corporations are liable for crimes they are capable of committing
   b. Punishment generally consists of fines or forfeiture, although recently directors have been faced with prison sentences for crimes of the corporation

2. Contracts

   a. Rules under Agency Law apply in full force here

3. Torts

   a. Corporations are liable for the damages resulting from torts committed by their officers, directors, agents, or employees within the course and scope of their corporate duties

   EXAMPLE: Fraudulent deceit against a customer.

   EXAMPLE: Employee assaults a complaining customer.

   b. Defense that the tort occurred in connection with ultra vires acts is not valid

4. Ultra vires acts

   a. Illegal and ultra vires acts are not the same

      (1) Illegal acts are acts in violation of statute or public policy

      EXAMPLE: False advertising.

      (2) Whereas ultra vires acts are merely beyond the scope of the corporate powers, i.e., a legal act may be ultra vires

      EXAMPLE: Although legal to become a surety, the articles of incorporation may not allow it.

   b. The state and stockholders have right to object to ultra vires acts

      (1) Competitor does not

   c. Ultra vires contract will be upheld to the extent of performance by both sides

      (1) Directors or officers may be sued by shareholders on behalf of the corporation or by the corporation itself if there are damages to the corporation

   d. An ultra vires contract that is wholly executory, i.e., no performance on either side, is void and neither party can enforce it
   e. If partially or fully performed on one side, then other side is estopped from raising ultra vires as a defense without being liable for damages

5. Acts of officers

   a. Corporation is liable for authorized acts
   b. Even if not authorized, if the act is of the type customarily delegated to such an officer, the corporation is liable under agency law
   c. Corporations are generally liable on contracts made by their agents within the course and scope of corporate authority

      (1) Corporations are not obligated to perform illegal contracts

(2) Preincorporation contracts must be adopted before there is liability

H. Officers and Directors of Corporations

1. Directors are elected by shareholders

2. Directors' duties and powers

   a. Generally to guide policies of company

      (1) They are generally in charge of a company's operations
      (2) Power to discharge their duties

   b. Must comply with statutes, articles of incorporation, and bylaws
   c. Select officers
   d. Declare dividends
   e. A director as an individual has no power to bind the corporation--must act as a board member at a duly constituted meeting of the board

      (1) Must hold directors' meetings at times designated in the charter
      (2) Majority vote of those present is needed for most business decisions if quorum is present

         (a) Quorum is majority of all directors
         (b) Some statutes require a majority vote of total directors to make business decisions

      (3) Action may be taken by board with no meeting

         (a) Unless prohibited by articles of incorporation or by corporate bylaws, and
         (b) There must be unanimous written consent by board members to the action to be taken

   f. May delegate some authority, e.g., day to day or routine matters, to an executive committee
   g. Directors are not entitled to compensation unless so provided in articles, bylaws, or by a resolution of the board passed before the services are rendered

      (1) May be reimbursed for expenses incurred on behalf of corporation
      (2) Entitled to compensation if acting in role as employee

3. Director's liability

   a. General rule is that directors must exercise ordinary care and due diligence in performing the duties entrusted to them by virtue of their positions as directors--trend is toward increased liability

      (1) Directors are liable for own torts committed even if acting for corporation

         (a) Under doctrine of respondeat superior (see Agency), corporation is also liable

      (2) Business judgment rule--as long as director is acting in good faith s/he will not be liable for errors of judgment unless s/he is negligent

      (3) Directors are chargeable with knowledge of the affairs of the corporation

(a) If director does not prevent (intentionally or negligently) wrongs of other directors, may be held liable

(b) Normally may rely on reports of accountants, officers, etc. if reasonable judgment used

(4) If corporation does not actually exist (not even a de facto corporation) then director as well as others in corporation have personal liability

b. Directors only liable for negligence if their action was the cause of the corporation's loss

(1) Corporation may indemnify directors (also officers, employees, agents) against suits based on their duties for the corporation

(a) Corporation may also indemnify them for legal fees if person successfully defends suit or if court determines that person should be indemnified

c. Directors owe a fiduciary duty to the corporation

(1) Owe fiduciary duties of loyalty and due care to the corporation
(2) Conflicts of interest

(a) Transactions of a corporation with director(s) or other corporation in which director(s) has interest are valid as long as at least one of the following can be established

1] Conflict of interest is disclosed or known to board and majority of disinterested members approve of transaction
2] Conflict of interest is disclosed or known to shareholders and those entitled to vote approve it by a majority
3] Transaction is fair and reasonable to corporation

EXAMPLE: A plot of land already owned by a director is sold at the fair market value to the corporation. This contract is valid even without approval if the land is needed by the corporation.

d. Directors are personally liable for <u>ultra vires</u> acts of the corporation unless they specifically dissented on the record

EXAMPLE: Loans made to stockholders by a corporation.

EXAMPLE: Dividends that impair capital.

4. Officers

a. An officer of the corporation is an agent and can bind corporation by his/her individual acts if within the scope of his/her authority

(1) The corporation is not bound by the acts of an agent beyond the scope of authority
(2) President usually has authority for transactions that are part of usual and regular course of business

(a) No authority for extraordinary transactions
(b) Rules of estoppel are applicable; e.g., corporations may not claim president had no authority if s/he acted as if s/he did

(3) Acts of officers may be ratified by board

b. Officers and directors may be the same persons
c. Officers are selected by the directors for a fixed term under the bylaws

(1) If a term is not definite, it is governed by the directors

    d. Officers have a fiduciary relationship with the corporation and are limited in business transactions

    e. Courts are recognizing a fiduciary duty owed by majority shareholders to minority shareholders based on differences in ability to control corporation

5. Officers, like directors, are liable for own torts, even if committed while acting for corporation

    a. Corporation is also liable if officer was acting within the scope of his/her authority

I. Stockholders' Rights

1. Stock can be acquired by original issue, by purchase from another stockholder or by purchase for the benefit of another

2. Right to transfer stock by indorsement and delivery or by separate assignment

    a. Stock certificates are negotiable instruments

        (1) No holders in due course, but if properly indorsed, a thief may give good title

        (2) If indorsement is forged, corporation will bear the loss against a purchaser in good faith if it has issued a new certificate

        EXAMPLE: X steals stock certificate from Y, forges Y's indorsement, submits it to the corporation for a new certificate, and transfers the new certificate to P, a purchaser in good faith. P will get to keep the certificate as a valid stockholder and the corporation will be liable to Y for the value of the shares.

    b. Corporation registers the transfer and issues new shares to transferee

    c. Limitations on transfer may be imposed, but they must be reasonable

        (1) UCC requires that any restrictions must be plainly printed on the certificate to be effective against third party

        (2) These limitations are most often imposed in closely held corporations

        EXAMPLE: Existing shareholders of the corporation may have first option to buy.

3. Stockholder has no right to manage corporation unless is also officer or director

    a. Retains limited liability unlike limited partner who participates in management

4. Right to vote for election of directors, decision to dissolve the corporation, and any other fundamental corporate changes

    a. Governed by the charter and the class of stock owned

    b. Stockholders do not vote on how to manage the corporation

        (1) Management is entrusted to the board of directors

    c. Cumulative voting may be required, i.e., a person gets as many votes as s/he has shares times the number of directors being elected

       EXAMPLE: 100 shares x 5 directors is 500 votes.

       (1) Gives minority shareholders an opportunity to get some representation by voting all shares for one or two directors

    d. Can vote by proxy--an assignment of voting rights
    e. Directors have the power to amend or repeal the bylaws unless reserved to the shareholders by the articles of incorporation
    f. Amendment of the articles of incorporation and approval of fundamental corporate changes such as a merger, consolidation, or sale of all assets generally require majority approval by shareholders

5. Right to dividends

    a. Shareholder generally has no right to dividends unless they are declared by the board of directors

       (1) Power to declare is discretionary based on the board's assessment of business needs
       (2) When there is a surplus together with available cash, the shareholders may be able to compel declaration of dividends if board's refusal to declare a dividend is in bad faith or its refusal is unreasonable, but this is difficult to establish

    b. Dividends are normally payable to stockholders of record on a given date
    c. Dividends become a liability of corporation only when declared

       (1) True for all types of stock such as common stock or even cumulative preferred stock

       EXAMPLE: Knave Corporation declares dividends of $10,000 to the 10,000 $1 cumulative preferred stockholders (there is no average on these shares) and $20,000 to the 500 common stockholders. The following year is so bad that Knave Corporation is liquidated. Furthermore, no dividends are declared and general creditors are owed more than the corporation has. None of the shareholders get any dividends in this following year.

    d. Cash dividends may be paid out of unrestricted and unreserved earned surplus (retained earnings) unless corporation already is or will be insolvent because of dividend

       (1) Some states have other regulations, sometimes allowing reductions in other accounts, too
       (2) Under Model Business Corporation Act, dividends are prohibited that cause total liabilities to exceed total assets after effect of the distribution is considered

6. Right of stockholders to inspect books and records exists

    a. Generally, any person who is holder of record of shares at least six months or owns at least 5% of all shares to examine corporate books and records
    b. These books and records include minute books, stock certificate books, stock ledgers, general account books
    c. Must have a purpose reasonably related to his/her interest as shareholder, e.g., to communicate with other shareholders

       (1) Not to compete with corporation

       (2) May get list of shareholders to help wage a proxy fight to attempt to control corporation

       (3) If shareholder, within last 2 years, has misused any information secured through prior examination, the corporation may properly refuse to allow shareholder to examine books

    d. Corporation may be subject to fines for refusal

7. Preemptive right

    a. This is the right to subscribe to new issues of stock (at FMV) so that a stockholder's ownership will not be diluted without the opportunity to maintain it

       EXAMPLE: A corporation has one class of common stock. Stockholder A owns 15%. A new issue of the same class of stock is to be made. Stockholder A has the right to buy 15% of it.

    b. This is the right of first refusal and applies to issuances of new stock of the same class or series that the shareholder owns

    c. Usually only applies to common stock, not preferred

    d. Not for treasury stock

    e. There is no preemptive right to purchase stock unless articles of incorporation so provide

8. Stockholders' right to sue

    a. Stockholder can sue in his/her own behalf where his/her interests have been directly injured, e.g.

       (1) Denial of right to inspect records

       (2) Denial of preemptive right if provided for

    b. Stockholders can sue on behalf of the corporation, i.e., a derivative suit

       (1) In cases where a duty to the corporation is violated and corporation does not enforce, e.g.

          (a) Director violates his/her fiduciary duty to corporation

          (b) Illegal declaration of dividends, e.g., rendering corporation insolvent

          (c) Fraud by officer on corporation

       (2) Unless demand would be futile, must first demand that directors sue in name of corporation and then may proceed if they refuse

          (a) Suit may be barred if directors make good faith business judgment that the suit is not in the corporation's best interests

       (3) Damages go to corporation

9. Right to a pro rata share of distribution of assets on dissolution after creditors have been paid

J. **Stockholder's Liability**

1. Generally stockholder's liability is limited to his/her price paid for stock

    a. Also true of controlling stockholders

2. May be liable to creditors for

a. Original issue stock sold at a discount (below par value). See watered stock discussion.
b. Unpaid balance on no-par stock
c. Dividends paid which impair capital if the corporation is insolvent

3. Piercing the corporate veil--courts disregard corporate entity and hold stockholders personally liable

a. Rarely happens but may occur if

(1) Corporation used to perpetrate fraud, e.g., forming an under-capitalized corporation
(2) Owners/officers do not treat corporation as separate entity
(3) Shareholders commingle assets, bank accounts, financial records with those of corporation
(4) Corporate formalities not adhered to

K. **Substantial Change in Corporate Structure**

1. The most important changes are discussed below--candidates should note that terms discussed below often involve complex negotiations and that in practice these terms are sometimes flexible

2. Merger

a. This is the union of two corporations where one is absorbed into the other

(1) One is dissolved and the other remains in existence
(2) Surviving corporation issues its own shares to the shareholders of the other corporation

b. Remaining corporation (possessor) gets all assets but is subject to all liabilities of merged corporation
c. Requires approval of board of directors of both companies
d. Requires approval of majority of shareholders of each company
e. Dissenting shareholders are paid FMV for their shares

(1) It is called the right of appraisal
(2) Right exists even if not provided for in Articles of Incorporation if state law so provides

3. Consolidation

a. This is the joining of two (or more) corporations into a single new corporation--called a "true consolidation"

(1) Consolidating corporations are terminated
(2) Only the new corporation remains

b. All assets and liabilities are acquired by the new company
c. Requires approval of board of directors of both companies
d. Requires majority vote of shareholders of each corporation
e. Dissatisfied shareholders in consolidation may dissent and assert appraisal rights, thereby receiving the FMV of their stock
f. New corporation is liable for debts of old corporations

4. Sale of substantially all assets

a. One corporation may buy all the assets of another corporation
b. Shareholders and board of directors of selling corporation must approve

    c. Fraudulent conveyances are illegal for protection of creditors

5. Reorganization

    a. Rearrangement and revamping of corporation's capital and asset structure with as little effect as possible upon creditors

        (1) It is an alternative to bankruptcy and forced liquidation

    b. Reorganization can be

        (1) Voluntary
        (2) Forced by Federal Bankruptcy Act

L. Dissolution

1. Dissolution is the termination of the corporation's status as a legal entity

    a. Liquidation is the winding up of affairs and distribution of assets
    b. Dissolution does not finally occur until liquidation is complete

2. Voluntary dissolution

    a. By expiration of time stipulated in charter

        (1) Rare, usually perpetual existence

    b. Merger or consolidation
    c. Filing a certificate with the state to surrender charter

        (1) By incorporators prior to issuance of shares
        (2) Written consent of all stockholders
        (3) Resolution at stockholders' meeting

            (a) Usually by majority vote of shareholders and directors

    d. Judicial proceedings in bankruptcy by filing voluntary petition

3. Involuntary

    a. By the state because

        (1) Fraud in original application for legal existence
        (2) Failure to pay taxes for long period
        (3) No business activity
        (4) Other substantial injury to public
        (5) State may only suspend corporation's right to do business

4. Creditors must be given notice of the dissolution or the corporation will remain liable on its debts

5. Shareholder may petition for judicial dissolution based on evidence that

    a. Directors are deadlocked, or
    b. Directors acted illegally or in oppressive manner, or
    c. Shareholders are deadlocked

        (1) Unable to elect directors for two consecutive annual meetings

6. Dissolution does not result from

    a. Sale of all assets
    b. Appointment of receiver
    c. Assignment for benefit of creditors

FEDERAL SECURITIES ACTS

Overview

The bulk of the material tested on the exam from this area comes from the Securities Act of 1933, as amended, and the Securities Exchange Act of 1934, as amended. Topics included under the scope of the 1933 Act are registration requirements, exempt securities, and exempt transactions. The purposes of the 1933 Act are to provide investors with full and fair disclosure of a security offering and to prevent fraud. The basic prohibition of the 1933 Act is that no sale of a security shall occur in interstate commerce without registration and without furnishing a prospectus to prospective purchasers unless the security or the transaction is exempt from registration.

The purpose of the 1934 Act is the establishment of the Securities Exchange Commission to assure fairness in the trading of securities subsequent to their original issuance. The basic scope of the 1934 Act is to require periodic reports of financial and other information concerning registered securities, and to prohibit manipulative and deceptive devices in both the sale and purchase of securities.

The exam often includes an essay question on the Federal Securities Acts; however, this is sometimes combined with accountant's liability or is included within a question concerning corporation or limited partnership law.

A. **Securities Act of 1933** (Generally applies to initial issuances [primary offerings] of securities)

1. Purposes of Act are to provide potential investors with full and fair disclosure of all material information relating to issuance of securities (such that a prudent decision to invest or refrain from investing can be made) and to prevent fraud or misrepresentation

   a. Accomplished by

      (1) Requiring a registration statement to be filed with Securities Exchange Commission (SEC) before either a public sale or an offer to sell securities in interstate commerce

         (a) This is the fundamental thrust of 1933 Act
         (b) SEC is government agency comprised of commissioners and its staff which was created to administer and enforce the Federal Securities Laws. The Commission interprets the acts, conducts investigations, adjudicates violations, and performs a rule-making function to implement the acts.

            1] Can subpoena witnesses
            2] Can obtain injunction preventing sale of securities
            3] Cannot assess monetary penalties without court proceedings
            4] Cannot prosecute criminal acts

      (2) Requiring prospectuses to be provided to investors with or before the sale or delivery of the securities to provide public with information given to SEC in registration statement

         (a) For definition of prospectus, see "A.2.i." below

      (3) Providing civil and criminal liabilities for failure to comply with these requirements and for misrepresentation or fraud in the sale of securities even if not required to be registered

   b. SEC does not evaluate the merits or value of securities

      (1) SEC can only compel full and fair disclosure

(2) In theory, public can evaluate merit of security when provided with full and fair disclosure

(3) SEC's function is not to detect fraud or to stop offerings where fraud or unethical conduct is suspected

c. The major items you need to know are

(1) That registration statement and prospectus are usually required
(2) Which transactions are exempt from registration
(3) Which securities are exempt from registration
(4) What the liability is for false or misleading registration statements

2. Definitions

a. Security--any note, stock, bond certificate of interest, debenture, investment contract, etc., or any interest or instrument commonly known as a security

(1) General idea is that investor intends to make a profit on the investment through the efforts of others rather than through his/her own efforts

EXAMPLE: W is a general partner of WDC partnership in Washington, D.C. Usually, W's interest would not be considered a security because a general partner's interest typically involves participation in the business rather than mere investment.

(a) Includes limited partnership interests
(b) Includes rights and warrants to subscribe for the above
(c) Includes treasury stock
(d) Investment contract is a security when money is invested in a common enterprise with profits to be derived from the effort of others

EXAMPLE: Blue Corporation in Florida owns several acres of orange trees. Blue is planning on selling a large portion of the land with the orange trees to several individuals in various states on a row-by-row basis. Each purchaser gets a deed and is required to purchase a management contract whereby Blue Corporation maintains all the land and oranges and then remits the net profits to the various purchasers. Even though it may appear that each individual purchased separately the land with the oranges and a management contract, the law looks at the "big picture" here. Since in reality the individuals are investing their money, and the profits are derived from the efforts of others, the law treats the above fact pattern as involving securities. Therefore, the Securities Acts apply.

b. Person--individual, corporation, partnership, unincorporated association, business trust, government

c. Controlling person--has power, direct/indirect, to influence the management and/or policies of an issuer, whether by stock ownership, contract, position, or otherwise

EXAMPLE: A 51% stockholder is a controlling person by virtue of a majority ownership.

EXAMPLE: A director of a corporation also owns 10% of that same corporation. By virtue of the stock ownership and position on the board of directors, he has a strong voice in the management of the corporation. Therefore, he is a controlling person.

d. Insiders--(applies to the Securities Exchange Act of 1934) include officers, directors, and owners of more than 10 percent of any class of issuer's equity securities

   (1) Note that debentures not included because not equity securities
   (2) For purposes of this law to avoid a "loophole," insiders include "beneficial owners" of more than 10 percent of the equity stock of issuer

       (a) To determine amount of "beneficial ownership," add to the individual's equity ownership, that of equity stock owned by

           1] Owner's spouse
           2] Owner's minor children
           3] Owner's relative in same house
           4] Owner's equity stock held in trust in which owner is beneficiary

           EXAMPLE: X owns 6 percent of the common stock of ABC Company in Philadelphia. Her spouse owns 3 percent of ABC Company's common stock. Stock was also placed in the name of their two minor children, each owning 1 percent of ABC Company's common stock. X has beneficial ownership of 11 percent of the equity securities of ABC Company so she is an insider for the 1934 Act. Note that her husband also qualifies as an insider.

           EXAMPLE: Use the same facts as in the previous example except that all four individuals owned debentures of ABC Company. Since these are not equity securities, none qualifies as an insider.

           EXAMPLE: L is an officer who owns 4 percent of the common stock of XYZ Company in Washington, DC. Since L is an officer, s/he is an insider even though the ownership level is below 10 percent.

e. Issuer--every person who issues or proposes to issue any security

   (1) Includes a controlling person

f. Underwriter--any person who has purchased from issuer with a view to the public distribution of any security or participates in such undertaking

   (1) Includes any person who offers or sells for issuer in connection with the distribution of any security
   (2) Does not include person who sells or distributes on commission for underwriter (i.e., dealers)
   (3) Remember, an issuer includes a controlling person

g. Dealer--agent, broker, or principal who spends either full or part time in the business of dealing or trading securities issued by another person

h. Sale--every contract for sale or disposition of security for value (consideration)

      (1) Offer to sell--every attempt to dispose of security for value

      (2) Under Rule 145, the issuance of securities as part of business re-organization (e.g., merger or consolidation) constitutes a sale and must be registered with SEC unless the issue otherwise qualifies as an exemption from the registration requirements of 1933 Act

      (3) Issuance of stock warrants is considered a sale so that requirements of 1933 Act must be met

      (4) Employee stock purchase plan is a sale and therefore must comply with the provisions of the 1933 Act

          (a) Company must also supply a prospectus to each employee to whom stock is offered

      (5) Stock dividends or splits are not sales

      (6) Includes neither preliminary negotiations nor agreements between an issuer and an underwriter

 i. Registration statement--the statement required to be filed with SEC before initial sale of securities in interstate commerce

      (1) Includes financial statements and all other relevant information about the registrant's property, business, directors, principal officers, together with prospectus

      (2) Also, includes any amendment, report, or document filed as part of the statement or incorporated therein by reference

 j. Prospectus--any notice, circular, advertisement, letter, or communication offering any security for sale (or merger)

      (1) May be a written, radio, or television communication

      (2) After the effective date of registration statement, communication (written or oral) will not be considered a prospectus if

          (a) Prior to or at same time, a written prospectus was also sent, or

          (b) If it only states from whom written prospectus is available, identifies security, states price, and who will execute orders for it (i.e., tombstone ad)

      (3) Preliminary prospectus may be sent during the waiting period (i.e., time interval between time of first filing with SEC and effective date), if so identified and states that it is subject to completion and amendment

          (a) A legend in red ink is printed on this preliminary prospectus indicating that the prospectus is "preliminary" and that a registration statement has been filed but has not become effective ("red herring" prospectus)

          (b) Note that in addition to the written offers described above, oral offers to sell may also be made between the filing date and the effective date

              1] Sales are not permitted between these dates

3. Registration requirements

   a. Registration is required under the Act if

      (1) The securities are to be offered, sold, or delivered in interstate commerce or through the mails

    (a) Interstate commerce means trade, commerce, transportation, or communication (e.g., telephone call) among more than one state or territory of U.S.

        1] Interpreted very broadly to include trade, commerce, etc. that is within one state but affects interstate commerce

EXAMPLE: A corporation issues securities to individuals living only in Philadelphia. It is further shown that this issuance affects trade in Delaware. Interstate commerce is affected because although Philadelphia is of course in one state, the effects on at least one other state allow the Federal Securities Acts to take affect under our Constitution. Therefore, registration of these securities is required under the Federal Law unless exemptions are found as discussed later.

  (2) Unless it is an exempted security or exempted transaction (see "A.4." and "A.5.")

b. Issuer has primary duty of registration

  (1) Any person who sells unregistered securities that should have been registered may be liable to a purchaser (unless transaction or security is exempt)

  (2) Liability cannot be disclaimed in writing or orally by issuer

c. Registration statements are public information

d. Information required, in general

  (1) Financial statements audited by independent CPA

  (2) Names of issuer, directors, officers, general partners, underwriters, large stockholders, counsel, etc.

  (3) Risks associated with the securities

  (4) Description of property, business, and capitalization of issuer

  (5) Information about management of issuer

  (6) Description of security to be sold and use to be made by issuer of proceeds

e. Prospectus is also filed as part of registration statement

  (1) Generally must contain same information as registration statement, but it may be condensed or summarized

f. Registration statement and prospectus are examined by SEC

  (1) Amendments are almost always required by SEC

  (2) SEC may issue stop-order suspending effectiveness of registration if statement appears incomplete or misleading

  (3) Otherwise registration becomes effective on 20th day after filing (or on 20th day after filing amendment)

    (a) 20 day period is called the waiting period

  (4) It is unlawful for company to offer or sell the securities prior to approval (effective registration date)

    (a) Except for preliminary prospectuses

g. Applies to both corporate and noncorporate issuers

h. Registration covers a single distribution, so second distribution must also be registered

    i. Shelf registration allows for registration of securities that are contemplated to be sold over a two-year period

       (1) Most changes brought up to date without need for new prospectus by use of stickers

          (a) E.g., changes in prices, interest rates

       (2) If material change in manner of distribution, then amendment to registration required

    j. State "Blue Sky" laws must also be complied with (see "C." below)

4. Exempt securities (need never be registered but still subject to antifraud provisions under the Act)

    a. Commercial paper, e.g., note, draft, check, etc., with a maturity of nine months or less

       (1) Must be for commercial purpose and not investment

> *EXAMPLE: OK Corporation in Washington, DC wishes to finance a short-term need for more cash for current operations. OK will do this by issuing some short-term notes which all have a maturity of nine months or less. These are exempt from the registration requirements.*

    b. Intrastate issues--securities offered and sold only within one state

       (1) Issuer must be resident of state and doing 80% of business in the state and must use at least 80% of sale proceeds in connection with business operations in the state

       (2) All offerees and purchasers must be residents of state

       (3) For 9 months after last sale by issuer, resales can only be made to residents of state

       (4) All of particular issue must qualify under this rule or this exemption cannot be used for any sale of the issue

> *EXAMPLE: A regional corporation in need of additional capital makes an offer to the residents of the state in which it is incorporated to purchase a new issue of its stock. The offer expressly restricts sales to only residents of the state and all purchasers are residents of the state.*

    c. Small issues (Regulation A)--issuances up to $1,500,000 may be exempt if

       (1) There is a notice filing with SEC

       (2) An offering circular (containing financial information about the corporation and descriptive information about offered securities) must be provided to offeree. Financial statements in offering circular need not be audited.

       (3) Note that an offering circular is required under Regulation A instead of the more costly and time-consuming prospectus

    d. Securities of governments, banks, quasi-governmental authorities (e.g., local hospital authorities), savings and loan associations, farmers, co-ops, and common carriers regulated by ICC

       (1) Public utilities are not exempt

    e. Security exchanged by issuer exclusively with its existing shareholders so long as

(1) No commission is paid
(2) Both sets of securities must have been issued by the same person

> *EXAMPLE: A stock split is an exempt transaction under the 1933 Act and thus, the securities need not be registered at time of split.*

 f. Securities of nonprofit religious, educational, or charitable organizations

 g. Certificates issued by receiver or trustee in bankruptcy

 h. Insurance and annuity contracts

5. Exempt transactions or offerings (still subject, however, to antifraud provisions of the Act; may also be subject to reporting requirements of the 1934 Act--See "B.")

 a. Sale or offer to sell by any person <u>other than</u> an issuer, underwriter, or dealer

  (1) Generally covers sales by individual investors on their own account

  (2) May be transaction by broker on customer's order

   (a) Does not include solicitation of these orders

  (3) Exemption does not apply to sales by controlling persons (see "2.c." above) because considered an underwriter or issuer

 b. <u>Regulation D</u> establishes three important exemptions in Rules 504, 505, and 506 under the 1933 Act

  (1) Rule 504 exempts an issuance of securities up to $500,000 sold in 12-month period to any number of investors, or up to $1,000,000 if at least $500,000 is registered at state level

   (a) No general offering or solicitation is permitted

   (b) The issuer must restrict the purchasers' right to resell the securities or else the exemption is lost

   (c) No specific disclosure is required

  (2) Rule 505 exempts issuance of up to $5,000,000 in 12-month period

   (a) No general offering or solicitation is permitted within 12-month period

   (b) Permits sales to 35 unaccredited (nonaccredited term sometimes used) investors and to unlimited number of accredited investors within 12 months

    1] Accredited investors are, for example, banks, savings and loan associations, credit unions, insurance companies, broker dealers, certain trusts, partnerships and corporations, also natural persons having joint or individual net worth exceeding $1,000,000 or having joint or individual net income of $200,000 for two most recent years

   (c) The issuer must restrict the purchasers' right to resell the securities; in general must be held for two years or else exemption is lost

   (d) These securities typically state that they have not been registered and that they have resale restrictions

   (e) Unlike under Rule 504, if nonaccredited investor purchases these securities, audited balance sheet must be supplied (i.e., disclosure is required) as well as other financial statements or information, if readily available

            1] If purchased only by accredited investors, no disclosure required

   (3) Rule 506 allows private placement of unlimited amount of securities

      (a) In general, same rules apply here as outlined under Rule 505
      (b) However, an additional requirement is that the unaccredited investors (up to 35 within 12 months) must be sophisticated investors (individuals with knowledge and experience in financial matters) or be represented by individual with such knowledge and experience

> EXAMPLE: A growing corporation is in need of additional capital and decides to make a new issuance of its stock. The stock is only offered to 10 of the president's friends who regularly make financial investments of this sort. They are interested in purchasing the stock for an investment and each of them is provided with the type of information that is regularly included in a registration statement.

   (4) Disclosures for offerings under $2,000,000 have been simplified to be similar to disclosures under Regulation A
   (5) A controlling person (See "A.2.c.") who sells restricted securities may be held to be an underwriter (and thus subject to the registration provisions) unless requirements of Rule 144 are met when controlling person is selling through a broker

      (a) Broker performs no services beyond those of typical broker who executes orders and receives customary fee
      (b) Ownership (including beneficial ownership) for at least two years
      (c) Only limited amounts of stock may be sold--the lesser of

         1] 1% of outstanding stock during 3 months, or
         2] If traded on an exchange, the average weekly volume of previous four weeks

      (d) Public must have available adequate disclosure of issuer corporation
      (e) Notice of sale must be filed with SEC
      (f) If "(a)" through "(e)" are met, the security can be sold without registration

  c. Post-registration transactions by dealer, i.e., dealer is not required to deliver prospectus

   (1) If transaction is made at least 40 days after first date security was offered to public, or
   (2) After 90 days if it is issuer's first public issue
   (3) Does not apply to sales of securities that are leftover part of an allotment from the public issue

6. Antifraud provisions

  a. Apply even if securities are exempt (see "A.4.") or the transactions are exempt (see "A.5.") as long as interstate commerce is used (use of mail or telephone qualifies) to sell or offer to sell securities
  b. Included are schemes to defraud purchaser or making sale by use of untrue statement of material fact or by omission of material fact

   (1) Proof of negligence is sometimes sufficient rather than proof of scienter
   (2) Protects purchaser, not seller

7. Civil liability (i.e., private actions brought by purchasers of securities)

   a. Purchaser may recover if can establish that

      (1) Was a purchase of a security issued under a registration statement containing a misleading statement or omission of a material fact, and

         (a) May also recover if issuer or any person sold unregistered securities for which there is no exemption

      (2) Suffered economic loss

      (3) Privity of contract is not necessary

      EXAMPLE: Third parties who have never dealt with issuer but bought securities from another party have a right to recover when the above is established despite lack of privity.

   b. Purchaser of securities may recover from

      (1) The issuer

      (2) Any directors, partners, or underwriters of issuer

      (3) Anyone who signed registration statement

      (4) Experts of authorized statements, e.g., attorneys, accountants, engineers, appraisers

   c. Burden of proof is shifted to defendant in most cases; however, except for the issuer, defendant may use "due diligence" defense

      (1) Due diligence defense can be used successfully by defendant by proving that

         (a) As an expert, s/he had reasonable grounds after reasonable investigation to believe that his/her own statements were true and/or did not contain any omissions of material facts by the time the registration statement became effective

         EXAMPLE: Whitewood, a CPA, performs a reasonable audit and discovers no irregularities.

         (b) S/he relied on an expert for the part of the registration statement in question and did believe (and had reasonable grounds for such belief) that there were no misstatements or material omissions of fact

         EXAMPLE: Greenwood, a CPA, relies on an attorney's work as a foundation for his own work on contingent liabilities.

         (c) S/he did reasonably believe that after a reasonable investigation, statements not in the province of an expert were true or that material omissions did not exist

         EXAMPLE: Lucky, an underwriter, made a reasonable investigation on the registration statement and did reasonably believe no impropriety existed even though misstatements and omissions of material facts existed. Note that the issuer is liable even if s/he exercised the same care and held the same reasonable belief because the issuer is liable without fault and cannot use the due diligence defense.

   d. Seller of security is liable to purchaser

        (1) If interstate commerce or mail is used and
        (2) If registration is not in effect and should be or
        (3) If registration statement contains misstatements or omissions of material facts
        (4) For amount paid plus interest less any income received by purchaser
        (5) Even if seller no longer owns any of the securities
        (6) Buyer may ask for rescission instead of damages

    e. Statute of limitations is

        (1) One year after discovery is made or after discovery should have reasonably been made of misstatement or omission
        (2) In any event no longer than three years after offering of securities

8. Criminal liability

    a. If person intentionally (willfully) makes an untrue statement or intentionally omits a material fact, or willfully violates SEC Act or regulation

        (1) Reckless disregard of the truth may also qualify

    b. If person uses interstate commerce or mail to fraudulently sell any security
    c. Person is subject to fine and/or imprisonment

        (1) Injunctions are also available

    d. Criminal liability available even if securities are exempt or transactions are exempt

        (1) I.e., criminal sanctions available if fraudulent means used to sell securities even though exemption available

B. **Securities Exchange Act of 1934** (Generally applies to subsequent trading of securities--must comply separately with 1933 Act if applicable, i.e., initial issuances rather than subsequent trading)

1. Purposes of the Act

    a. Federally regulate securities exchanges and securities traded thereon
    b. Require adequate information be provided in various transactions
    c. Regulate the use of credit in securities transactions
    d. Prevent unfair use of information by insiders
    e. Prevent fraud and deceptive practices

2. All of following are required to register with SEC if interstate commerce or mail is used

    a. National securities exchanges
    b. Over-the-counter and other equity securities traded in interstate commerce and where the corporation has assets of more than $3 million and 500 or more holders of record (stockholders) as of the last day of the issuer's fiscal year

        (1) Equity securities--stock, rights to subscribe to, or securities convertible into stock (not ordinary bonds)

    c. Dealers in municipal securities
    d. Securities that are traded on any national securities exchange must be registered

        (1) Securities exempted under 1933 Act may still be regulated under 1934 Act

    e. Brokers and dealers (must register whether or not members of an exchange)

    f. Any purchaser of more than 5 percent of a class of equity securities must file to disclose purpose of purchase, amount and source of money, name, and other relevant information within 10 days

> *EXAMPLE: Z purchases 7 percent of the preferred stock of U.B. Ware Corporation. Z must satisfy the above disclosure requirements since not only shares of common stock but shares of preferred stock are clearly equity securities.*

        (1) Tender offers for securities need not be approved by SEC unless the tender offer is seeking more than 5% of the outstanding equity securities of a given corporation

3. Sanctions available to SEC under the 1934 Act

    a. Revocation or suspension of registration
    b. Denial of registration
    c. Permanent or temporary suspension of trading of securities (injunction)

4. Exempt securities

    a. Obligations of U.S. government, guaranteed by, or in which U.S. government has interest
    b. Obligations of state or political subdivision, or guaranteed thereby
    c. Securities of federally chartered bank or savings and loan institution
    d. Securities of common carrier regulated by ICC

        (1) Municipal securities traded by broker or dealer are not exempt

    e. Industrial development bonds

5. Issuers of securities registered under the 1934 Act must file the following reports with SEC

    a. Annual reports (Form 10-K) must be certified by independent public accountant
    b. Quarterly reports (Form 10-Q) must be filed for each of first three fiscal quarters of each fiscal year of issuer

        (1) Not required to be certified by CPA

    c. Current reports (Form 8-K) of certain material events such as change in corporate control, revaluation of assets, or change in amount of issued securities

        (1) Filed within 10 days of the close of month in which events took place

    d. These reports are not to be confused with reports to shareholders-- company not required under 1934 Act to give reports to shareholders

6. Whether registered under 1934 Act or not, securities registered during previous year under 1933 Act must have periodic reports filed with SEC by issuers

7. Proxy solicitations

   a. Proxy--grant of authority by shareholder to someone else to vote his/her shares at meeting

   b. Proxy solicitation provisions apply to solicitation (by any means of interstate commerce or the mails) of holders of securities required to be registered under the 1934 Act--must be reported to SEC

   c. Proxy statement must be sent with proxy solicitation

     (1) Must contain disclosure of all material facts concerning matters to be voted upon

       (a) Either misstatements or omissions of material facts are violations of proxy rules

       (b) Material means that it would likely affect vote of average shareholder on proposed action

     (2) Purpose is for fairness in corporate action and election of directors

   d. Requirements of proxy itself

     (1) Shall indicate on whose behalf solicitation is made

     (2) Identify clearly and impartially each matter to be acted on

   e. Some of inclusions in proxy material

     (1) Proposals by shareholders which are a proper subject for shareholders to vote on

     (2) Financial statements for last two years, certified by independent accountant, if

       (a) Solicitation is on behalf of management, and

       (b) It is for annual meeting at which directors are to be elected

   f. Any person who owns at least 5 percent or has held stock for 6 months or more has right of access to lists of shareholders for lawful purpose

   g. The proxy statement, proxy itself, and any other soliciting material must be filed with SEC

   h. Brokers are required to forward proxies for customers' shares held by broker

   i. Incumbent management is required to mail proxy materials of insurgents to shareholders if requested and expenses are paid by the insurgents

   j. Remedies for violation of proxy solicitation rules

     (1) Civil action by aggrieved shareholder for damages caused by material misinformation or omissions of material facts

     (2) Or injunctions possible

     (3) Or court may set aside vote taken and require a new proxy solicitation with full and fair disclosure

8. Anti-fraud provisions--very broad scope

   a. Unlawful to manipulate process and create appearance of active trading (not good faith transactions by brokers)

   b. Unlawful to use any manipulative or deceptive devices in purchase or sale of securities

     (1) Applies to all securities, whether registered or not (as long as either mail, interstate commerce, or a national stock exchange is used)--this is important

     (2) Includes any act, practice, or scheme which is deceptive or manipulative (against SEC rules and/or regulations)--most

importantly, it is unlawful to make any false statement of a material fact or any omission of a material fact that is necessary to make statement(s) not misleading (in connection with purchase or sale of security, whether registered or not)

(a) This is Rule 10b-5 promulgated by the SEC under Section 10b of the Act

    1] There are no exemptions under Rule 10b-5 such as listed at "B.4."

(b) The basic test of materiality is whether a reasonable person would attach importance to the fact in determining his/her choice of action in the transaction

EXAMPLE: A broker offers to sell a stock and omits to tell the purchaser that the corporation is about to make an unfavorable merger.

(c) Scienter is a requirement

    1] Knowledge of falsity, or
    2] Reckless disregard for the truth
    3] Negligence is not sufficient
    4] Cross reference this with the anti-fraud provisions under the 1933 Act in which scienter need not necessarily be proven

(d) Applies to any seller, buyer, or person who lends his/her name to statements used in the buying and selling of securities. Cross reference this to the 1933 Act which only applies to sellers or offerors of securities

(e) Applies to insider who buys or sells on inside information until it is disseminated to public

c. SEC urges affirmative disclosure of material information affecting issuer and securities

(1) No statutory duty to do so
(2) Must forego trading if one has such knowledge until public has information

    (a) Includes insiders and anyone with knowledge, e.g., accountant, attorney, engineer
    (b) May not tip information to others, nor may tipees trade the securities

9. Civil liability

a. Any person who intentionally (willfully) manipulates a security may be liable to the buyer or seller of that security if the buyer or seller is damaged

(1) Note that both buyers and sellers may recover under the 1934 Act

b. Any person who makes a misleading (or of course false) statement about any material fact in any application, report, or document is liable to an injured purchaser or seller if s/he

(1) Relied on the statement, and
(2) Did not know it was false or misleading
(3) However, the party sued can avoid liability if s/he can prove s/he

    (a) Acted in good faith, and

           (b) Had no knowledge that the statement(s) was (were) misleading or false

    c. See "B.8.b.(2)(b)" above for materiality requirement

10. Criminal liability

    a. Available for intentional violation of the Act, regulations, or rules

    b. Also available for intentional false or misleading statements on material facts in applications, reports, or documents under the Act

11. Reporting requirements of insiders under 1934 Act

    a. Must file statement with SEC

        (1) Discloses amount of equity securities

            (a) Includes beneficial ownership (see "A.2.d.(1)(a)")

        (2) Time of statement disclosure

            (a) When securities registered, or

            (b) When registration statement becomes effective, or

            (c) Within 10 days of person attaining insider status

        (3) Insider must report any changes in ownership within 10 days

C. **State "Blue Sky" Laws**

    1. These are state statutes regulating the issuance and sale of securities

      a. They contain antifraud and registration provisions

    2. Must be complied with in addition to federal laws

    3. Exemptions from federal laws are not exemptions from state laws

ACCOUNTANT'S LEGAL LIABILITY

Overview

Accountant's legal liability is often tested on the CPA exam by use of essay questions that require the candidate to apply the legal principles contained in this module to hypothetical fact patterns. Multiple choice questions are used on some exams which also require application as well as knowledge of this material.

Accountant's civil liability arises primarily from contract law, the law of negligence, fraud, the Securities Act of 1933, and the Securities Exchange Act of 1934. The first three are common law and largely judgemade law; whereas, the latter two are federal statutory law.

The agreement between an accountant and his/her client is generally set out in a carefully drafted engagement letter. Additionally, the accountant has a duty to conduct his/her work with the same reasonable care as an average accountant. This duty defines the standard used in a negligence case. It is important to understand:

1. When an accountant can be liable to his/her client.
2. When an accountant can be liable to third parties; the courts are not in agreement on this issue when ordinary negligence is involved as discussed herein.

3. That an accountant is liable to the client and to all third parties that relied on the financial statements when the accountant committed fraud, constructive fraud, or was grossly negligent; furthermore in these cases, the accountant can be assessed punitive damages.
4. The extent of liability under the Securities Act of 1933 and the Securities Exchange Act of 1934 as well as how they differ from each other and from common law.

The CPA examination also tests the dual nature of the ownership of the accountant's working papers. Although the accountant owns the working papers and retains them as evidence of his/her work, confidentiality must be maintained. Therefore, the CPA cannot allow this information to reach another without the client's consent. In general, privileged communications between a CPA and the client are not sanctioned under federal statutory law or common law, but the privilege is in existence in states that have passed statutes granting such a right.

A. Common Law Liability to Clients

1. Liability to clients for breach of contract

    a. Occurs if accountant fails to perform substantially as agreed under contract

        (1) Duties under contract may be

            (a) Implied--accountant owes duty in contract to perform in nonnegligent manner
            (b) Express--accountant owes duty to perform under terms of the contract

                1] This duty can extend liability beyond that which is standard under a normal audit
                2] Typically terms are expressed in engagement letter which should specify clearly and in writing the following

                    a] Type and scope of engagement to avoid misunderstandings between CPA and client
                    b] Procedures and tests to be used
                    c] That engagement will not necessarily uncover fraud, mistakes, defalcations, or illegal actions unless CPA agrees to greater responsibility

d] Engagement letter should be signed by at least client (accountant will typically sign also) but oral contract for audit still enforceable without engagement letter

(2) Accountant (CPA) is said to be in privity of contract with client when contract exists between them

    (a) Reverse also true, i.e., client is in privity of contract with CPA

(3) Accountant is not an insurer of financial statements and thus does not guarantee against losses from irregularities

    (a) "Normal" audit is not intended to uncover fraud, shortages, defalcations, or irregularities in general but is meant to provide audit evidence needed to express opinion on fairness of financial statements

(4) Accountant is not normally liable for failure to detect fraud, irregularities, etc. <u>unless</u>

    (a) "Normal" audit or review would have detected it, or
    (b) Accountant by agreement has undertaken greater responsibility such as defalcation audit, or
    (c) Wording of audit report indicates greater responsibility

EXAMPLE: A CPA has been hired by a client to perform an audit. A standard engagement letter is used. During the course of the audit, the CPA fails to uncover a clever embezzlement scheme by one of the client's employees. The CPA is not liable for the losses unless a typical, reasonable audit should have resulted in discovery of the scheme.

(5) In an audit or review of financial statements, accountant is under duty to investigate when s/he discovers or becomes aware of suspicious items

    (a) Investigation should extend beyond management's explanations

b. Client should not interfere or prevent accountant from performing

EXAMPLE: A CPA firm issues its opinion a few days late because of its client's failure to supply needed information. The CPA firm is entitled to the full fee agreed upon under the contract (engagement).

c. When breach of contract occurs

(1) Accountant is not entitled to compensation if breach is major

EXAMPLE: M failed to complete the audit by the agreed date. If time is of the essence so that the client receives no benefit from the audit, M is not entitled to compensation.

(2) Accountant is entitled to compensation if there are only minor errors but client may deduct from fees paid any damages caused by breach

(3) Client may recover any damages caused by breach even if accountant not entitled to fee

(4) In general, punitive damages are not awarded for breach of contract

2. Liability to clients based on negligence

    a. Elements needed to prove negligence against accountant

        (1) Accountant had duty to perform with same degree of skill and judgment possessed by average accountant

            (a) This is standard used in cases involving ordinary negligence (or simply called negligence)

                1] Different phrases are used for this standard, i.e.,

                    a] Duty to exercise due care
                    b] Duty of skill of average, reasonable accountant (or CPA)
                    c] Duty to act as average (or reasonable) accountant (or CPA) would under similar circumstances
                    d] Duty of judgment of ordinary, prudent accountant (CPA)

            (b) Standard is similar to that imposed on other professions
            (c) Standard for accountants is guided by

                1] State and federal statutes
                2] Court decisions
                3] Contract with client
                4] GAAP and GAAS (persuasive but not conclusive)

                    a] Failure to follow GAAP or GAAS virtually establishes lack of due care but reverse not true, i.e., following GAAP and GAAS does not automatically preclude negligence but is strong evidence for presence of due care

                5] Customs of the profession (persuasive but not conclusive)

                    EXAMPLE: W, a CPA, issued an unqualified opinion on the financial statements of X Company. Included in the assets was inventory stated at cost when the market was materially below cost. This violation of GAAP can be used to establish that W was negligent. Also, the client can sue under contract law because W has an implied duty in the contract to not be negligent.

        (2) Accountant breached duty owed of average reasonable accountant
        (3) Causal relationship must exist between breached duty of accountant and damages of plaintiff

            (a) Also, cause should be proximate, i.e., foreseeable

                EXAMPLE: A CPA negligently fails to discover during an audit that several expensive watches are missing from the client's inventory. Subsequently, an employee is caught stealing some watches. He confesses to stealing several before the audit and more after the audit when he found out he did not get caught. Only five of the watches can be recovered from the employee who is unable to pay for those stolen. The CPA may be liable for those losses sustained after the audit if discovery could have prevented them. However, the CPA normally would not be liable for the watches taken before the audit when the loss is not the proximate result of the negligent audit. But if there were watches that could have

*been recovered at time of audit but can't be now, the CPA
could be liable for those watches even though they were taken
before audit.*

    (4) Damages (i.e., loss) results

        (a) Limited to losses that use of reasonable care would have
avoided

        (b) Punitive damages not normally allowed for ordinary negligence

        (c) Contributory negligence may be a complete defense by CPA in
many states if client's own negligence substantially
contributed to accountant's failure to perform audit
adequately

3. Accountant's liability is not based on honest errors of judgment--liability
requires at least negligence under common law

4. Liability to client for fraud, gross negligence or constructive fraud

    a. Fraud of accountant is established by following elements

        (1) Misrepresentation of material fact or accountant's expert opinion

        (2) Scienter, shown by either

           (a) Intent to mislead with accountant's knowledge of falsity, or

           (b) Reckless disregard of the truth

        (3) Reasonable reliance by injured party

        (4) Actual damages

    b. Called constructive fraud or gross negligence if when proving above four
elements, reckless disregard of the truth is established instead of
knowledge of falsity

        *EXAMPLE: During the course of an audit, a CPA fails to verify the
existence of the company's investments which amount to a substantial
portion of the assets. Many of these, it is subsequently found, were
nonexistent. Even in the absence of intent to defraud, the CPA is
liable for constructive fraud based on reckless disregard of the truth.*

        *EXAMPLE: Care and Less Co., CPAs, uncover suspicious items during the
course of their audit of Blue Co. Because their audit steps did not
require the additional steps needed to check into these suspicious
items, the CPAs failed to uncover material errors. Even if a typical
audit would not have required these additional audit steps, the CPAs are
liable for the damages that result because they have a duty to look into
such circumstances when they come to their attention.*

    c. Contributory negligence of client is not a defense available for
accountant in cases of fraud, constructive fraud or gross negligence

    d. Privity of contract is not required for plaintiff to prove fraud,
constructive fraud or gross negligence

B. Common Law Liability to Third Parties (Nonclients)

1. Client is in privity of contract with accountant based on contractual
relationship

    a. In a normal accountant-client relationship, there usually is no privity
of contract between the accountant and third parties

    b. Traditionally, accountants could use defense of no privity against suing third parties in contract and even negligence cases

2. More recently, many courts have expanded liability to some third parties

The following distinctions should be understood

    a. Third-party beneficiary--client and accountant intended this party to be primary beneficiary under contract

      (1) Third-party beneficiary considered in privity of contract
      (2) Accountant liable for negligence, gross negligence, or fraud

    b. Foreseen party--third party who accountant knew would rely on financial statements, or member of limited class that accountant knew would rely on financial statements for specified transaction

      (1) Accountant liable for gross negligence or fraud
      (2) Courts split on whether accountant is liable to foreseen party based on negligence, but usually held liable

EXAMPLE: A CPA agrees to perform an audit for ABC Client knowing that the financial statements will be used to obtain a loan from XYZ Bank. Relying on the financial statements, XYZ Bank loans ABC $100,000. ABC goes bankrupt. If XYZ can establish that the financial statements were not fairly stated thus causing the bank to give the loan and if negligence can be established, many courts will allow XYZ Bank to recover from the CPA.

EXAMPLE: Facts are the same as in the example above except that XYZ Bank was not specified. Since the CPA knew that some bank would rely on these financial statements, the actual bank is a foreseen party since it is a member of a limited class.

      (3) Recovery <u>not</u> allowed by an indeterminate class for an indefinite period of time under this concept

    c. Foreseeable party--nonprivity third party not identified to the accountant by specific person or member of limited class, who may foreseeably be expected to receive the accountant's audit report, and in some way to act or forebear to act in reliance upon it. Foreseeable third persons have some form of business relationship to or interest in the client which makes such reliance plausible

      (1) Accountant liable for gross negligence or fraud
      (2) Courts split on whether accountant is liable to foreseeable third party based on negligence--generally accountant not liable

    d. Other third parties

      (1) Accountant liable for fraud, constructive fraud or gross negligence

EXAMPLE: A CPA is informed that financial statements after being audited will be used to obtain a bank loan. The audited financial statements are also shown to trade creditors and potential investors. These third parties are not actually foreseen parties and generally cannot recover from the CPA for ordinary negligence. However, they may qualify as foreseeable third parties since a creditor or investor is the type of person whom an accountant should reasonably foresee as a user of the audited financial statements.

3. To recover, plaintiff must also prove

    a. Material misstatement or omission on financial statements

    b. Accountant's fault caused damages to third party

      (1) Actual damages if based on negligence

      (2) Actual damages plus punitive damages may be added if based on fraud, constructive fraud or gross negligence

C. **Statutory Liability to Third Parties**--Securities Act of 1933

  1. General information on Securities Act of 1933

    a. Covers regulation of sales of securities registered under 1933 Act

      (1) Requires registration of initial issuances of securities with SEC

      (2) Makes it unlawful for registration statement to contain untrue <u>material</u> fact or to omit <u>material</u> fact

        (a) Material fact--one about which average prudent investor should be informed

        (b) Most potential accountant liability occurs because registration statement (and prospectus) includes audited financial statements

        (c) Accountant's legal liability arises for untrue material fact or omission of material fact in registration statement (or prospectus)

        (d) 1933 Act does not include periodic reports to SEC or annual reports to stockholders (these are in the 1934 Act below)

  2. Parties that may sue

    a. Any purchaser of registered securities

      (1) Plaintiff need not be initial purchaser of security

      (2) Purchaser generally must prove that specific security was offered for sale through registration statement

        (a) Exchange and issuance of stock based on a merger counts as a sale

    b. Third parties can sue without having privity of contract with accountant under Federal Securities Acts

  3. Proof requirements

    a. Plaintiff (purchaser) must prove damages were incurred

    b. Plaintiff must prove there was material misstatement or omission in financial statements included in registration statement

    c. Plaintiff <u>need not</u> prove reliance on financial statements unless security was purchased at least 12 months after effective date of registration statement

    d. Plaintiff <u>need not</u> prove negligence or fraud

    e. If "a." and "b." above are proven, it is a <u>prima facie</u> case (sufficient to win against the CPA unless rebutted) and shifts burden of proof to accountant who may escape liability by proving

      (1) "Due diligence," that is, after reasonable investigation, accountant had reasonable grounds to believe that statements were true and there was no material misstatement

        NOTE: Although the basis of liability is not negligence, an accountant who was at least negligent will probably not be able to establish "due diligence"

(2) Plaintiff knew financial statements were incorrect when investment was made, or

(3) Lack of causation--loss was due to factors other than the misstatement or omission

f. Plaintiff may also win under anti-fraud provisions of 1933 Act

4. Damages

a. Difference between amount paid and market value at time of suit
b. If sold, difference between amount paid and sale price
c. Damages cannot exceed price at which security was offered to public
d. Plaintiff cannot recover decrease in value after suit is brought

(1) Accountant is given benefit of any increase in market value during suit

5. Statute of limitations

a. Action must be brought against accountant within one year from discovery (or when discovery should have been made) of false statement or omission
b. Or if earlier, action must be brought within three years after security offered to public

D. **Statutory Liability to Third Parties**--Securities Exchange Act of 1934

1. General information on Securities Exchange Act of 1934

a. Regulates securities sold on national stock exchanges

(1) Includes securities traded over-the-counter and other equity securities where the corporation has more than $3 million in total assets and the security is held by 500 or more persons at the end of a fiscal year

b. Requires each company to furnish to SEC an annual report (Form 10-K)

(1) Includes financial statements (not necessarily the same as an annual report to shareholders) attested to by an accountant
(2) Accountant civil liability comes from 2 sections--10 and 18

(a) Section 10 (including Rule 10b-5)--makes it unlawful to

1] Employ any device, scheme, or artifice to defraud
2] Make untrue statement of material fact or omit material fact
3] Engage in act, practice, or course of business to commit fraud or deceit in connection with purchase or sale of security

(b) Section 18--makes it unlawful to make false or misleading statement with respect to a material statement unless done in "good faith"

2. Parties who may sue

a. Purchasers _and_ sellers of registered securities

(1) Note that under the 1933 Act, only purchasers may sue
(2) Exchanges and issuances of stock based on merger included in 1934 Act

3. Proof requirements--Section 10, in general including Rule 10b-5

a. Plaintiff (purchaser or seller) must prove damages resulted

b. Plaintiff must prove there was a material misstatement or omission in information released by firm

    (1) Information may, for example, be in form of audited financial statements in report to stockholders or in Form 10-K

c. Plaintiff must prove reliance on financial information

d. Plaintiff must prove existence of <u>scienter</u> (the intent to deceive, manipulate, or defraud)

    (1) Includes reckless disregard of truth as well as knowledge of falsity

    (2) E.g., accountant involved "only" in ordinary negligence would not be liable

e. Note that these proof requirements differ in very significant ways from proof requirements under the 1933 Act

f. Plaintiff cannot recover if s/he is reckless or fraudulent

4. Proof requirements--Section 18

a. Plaintiff (purchaser or seller) must prove

    (1) Damages were incurred

    (2) There was a material misstatement or omission on a report (usually Form 10-K) filed with SEC

    (3) Reliance on Form 10-K

b. Then burden of proof is shifted to accountant who may escape liability by proving s/he acted in "good faith"

    (1) Although basis of liability here is not in negligence, an accountant who has been grossly negligent typically will not be able to establish "good faith"

    (2) An accountant who has been only negligent will probably be able to establish "good faith"

5. Damages

a. Generally, difference between amount paid and market value at time of suit

b. If sold, difference between amount paid and sale price

c. Damages may not exceed investor's actual damages

6. Statute of limitations

a. Section 10 (Rule 10b-5)--varies by state

b. Section 18--action must be brought within 1 year after discovery of facts and within 3 years after cause of action

E. Summary of Accountant's Civil Liability[1]

THE INDEPENDENT AUDITOR'S CIVIL LIABILITY--AN OVERVIEW

	Law						
	Common				1933 Act	1934 Act	
		Third Parties			Section 11	Section 10	Section 18
Elements of Proof	Client	Primary Beneficiary	Foreseen	Ordinary	Stock Purchasers	Stock Purchasers and Sellers	Stock Purchasers and Sellers
Resultant Damages	P	P	P	P	P	P	P
Material Misstatement or Omission	P	P	P	P	P	P	P
Justifiable Reliance	P	P	P	P	D[a]	P	P
Minimum Degree of Auditor Deficiency or Behavior	P(N)	P(N)	P(N or GN)	P(GN)	D(DD)	P(GN)	D(GF)

P = Burden of proof rests with plaintiff
D = Burden of proof rests with defendant
N = Ordinary negligence
GN = Gross negligence
DD = Due diligence. This term includes the auditor's ability to show good faith in the conduct of the audit and no knowledge of the material misstatement
GF = Good faith. Auditor must prove s/he had not acted with scienter
 a = Defendant may escape liability by proving plaintiff knew of error (omission) before purchase. Plaintiff must prove reliance if an earnings statement covering at least 12 months subsequent to registration was available when security was purchased

F. Legal Considerations Affecting the Accountant's Responsibility

1. Accountant's working papers

    a. Consist of notes, computations, etc. that accountant accumulates when doing professional work for client
    b. Owned by accountant unless there is agreement to the contrary
    c. Ownership is essentially custodial in nature (to serve dual purpose)

        (1) To preserve confidentiality

            (a) Absent client consent, cannot allow transmission of information in working papers to another

                1] However, accountant must produce, upon being given an enforceable subpoena, workpapers requested by court of law or government agency

                    a] Subpoenas should be limited in scope and specific in purpose
                    b] Accountant may challenge a subpoena as being too broad and unreasonably burdensome

        (2) Retention by accountant as evidence of nature and extent of work performed for legal or other reasons

2. Privileged communications between accountant and client

    a. Do not exist at common law so must be created by statute

        (1) Only a few states have privileged communications

[1]Schultz, J.J., Jr., and K. Pany, "The Independent Auditor's Civil Liability--an Overview," *The Accounting Review* (April, 1980), p. 320 (adapted).

      (2) Federal law does not recognize privileged communications
      (3) If accountant acting as agent for (hired by) one who has privileged communication such as an attorney, then accountant's communications privileged

  b. To be considered privileged, accountant-client communication must

      (1) Be located in a jurisdiction where recognized
      (2) Have been intended to be confidential at time of communication
      (3) Not be waived by client

  c. If considered privileged, valid grounds exist for accountant to refuse to testify in court concerning these matters

      (1) This privilege is, in general, for benefit of client
      (2) Can be waived by client
      (3) If part of privileged communication is allowed, all of privilege is lost

  d. Code of Professional Ethics prohibits disclosure of confidential client data unless

      (1) Client consents
      (2) To comply with GAAS and GAAP
      (3) To comply with enforceable subpoena (e.g., courts where privilege not recognized)
      (4) Quality review under AICPA authorization
      (5) Responding to AICPA or state trial board

  e. U.S. Supreme Court has held that tax accrual files are not protected by accountant-client privilege

3. CPA certificates are issued under state (not federal) jurisdiction

4. Acts of employees

  a. Accountant is liable for acts of employees in the course of employment (see Agency module)

      EXAMPLE: XYZ, a partnership of CPAs, hires Y to help perform an audit. Y is negligent in the audit causing the client damage. The partners cannot escape liability by showing they did not perform the negligent act.

  b. Insurance typically used to cover such losses

5. Duty to perform audit is not delegable because it is contract for personal services

6. Generally, basis of relationship of accountant to his/her client is that of independent contractor

7. Insurance

  a. Accountants' malpractice insurance covers their negligence
  b. Fidelity bond protects client from accountant's fraud
  c. Client's insurance company is subrogated to client's rights (i.e., has same rights of recovery of loss against accountant that client had)

8. Reliance by auditor on other auditor's work

  a. Principal auditor still liable for all work unless audit report clearly indicates divided responsibility
  b. Cannot rely on unaudited data; must disclaim or qualify opinion

9. Subsequent events and subsequent discovery

   a. Generally not liable on audit report for effect of events subsequent to last day of field work

      (1) Unless report is dated as of the subsequent event
      (2) Liability extends to effective date of registration for reports filed with SEC

   b. Liable if subsequently discovered facts that existed at report date indicate statements were misleading <u>unless</u>

      (1) Immediate investigation is conducted, and
      (2) Prompt revision of statements is possible, or
      (3) SEC and persons known to be relying on statements are notified by client or CPA

10. Liability from preparation of unaudited financial statements

   a. Financial statements are unaudited if

      (1) No auditing procedures have been applied
      (2) Insufficient audit procedures have been applied to express an opinion

   b. Failure to mark each page, "unaudited"
   c. Failure to issue a disclaimer of opinion
   d. Failure to inform client of any discovery of something amiss

      (1) E.g., circumstances indicating presence of fraud

G. Criminal Liability

1. Sources of Liability

   a. Securities Act of 1933 and Securities Exchange Act of 1934

      (1) Can be found guilty for <u>willful</u> illegal conduct

         (a) Misleading omission of material facts
         (b) Putting false information in registration statement

      (2) Subject to fine of up to $10,000 and/or up to 5 years prison
      (3) Examples of possible criminal actions

         (a) CPA aids management in a fraudulent scheme
         (b) CPA covers up prior year financial statement misstatements

   b. Criminal violations of Internal Revenue Code

      (1) For willfully preparing false return (perjury)
      (2) For willfully assisting others to evade taxes (tax evasion)

   c. Criminal liability under RICO (Racketeer Influenced and Corrupt Organizations)

      (1) Covers individuals affiliated with businesses or associations involved in a pattern of racketeering

         (a) Racketeering includes organized crime but also includes fraud under the federal securities laws as well as mail fraud

            1] Accountants subject to criminal penalty through affiliation with accounting firm or business involved in racketeering

        (b)   Pattern of racketeering means at least two illegal acts of racketeering in previous ten years

    (2)   RICO has been expanded to also allow civil suit by private parties

        (a)   Treble damages allowed (to encourage private enforcement)
        (b)   Has been held to apply against accountants even without a criminal indictment or conviction

H. Liability of Income Tax Return Preparers

1. Definitions

    a. Preparer--an individual who prepares for compensation, or who employs one or more persons to prepare for compensation, a return, or a substantial portion of a return, under Subtitle A of the Internal Revenue Code, or a claim for refund. Subtitle A of the Internal Revenue Code covers <u>income</u> tax returns; as such, the preparer of an excise tax return, a gift tax return, or an estate tax return is not considered a preparer subject to the requirements and penalties described below

        (1)   A person who prepares only a portion of a return is not considered a preparer if that portion involves gross income, deductions, or the basis of determining tax credits of (a) under $2,000, or (b) under $100,000 and also less than 20% of gross income (or 20% of AGI) of the return as a whole

        (2)   A preparer need <u>not</u> be enrolled to practice before the Internal Revenue Service. Preparation of tax returns is not included under the concept of "practice before the IRS"

    b. Compensation--must be received and can be implied or explicit [e.g., a person who does his neighbor's return and receives a gift has not been compensated. An accountant who prepares the individual return of the president of a company, for which he performs the audit, for no additional fee as part of a prior agreement <u>has</u> been compensated (implied)]

2. Requirements

    a. Preparer must sign returns done for compensation

        (1)   Must be a manual signature
        (2)   Include preparer's identification number and address

    b. Returns and claims for refund must contain the identification number of the preparer and the identification number of that preparer's employer or partnership, if any

    c. Preparer must provide a finished copy of the return or refund claim to the taxpayer before or at the time when the preparer presents a copy to the taxpayer for signing

    d. Employers of income tax preparers must retain information on all preparers employed by them as follows

        (1)   Name
        (2)   Taxpayer identification number
        (3)   Principal place of work

e. Preparer must either keep a list of those for whom returns were filed with the following information, or copies of the actual returns, for a minimum of three years

   (1) Name
   (2) Taxpayer identification number
   (3) Taxable year
   (4) Type of return or claim for refund filed

3. Preparer penalties

  a. The general period for assessing preparer penalties is three years; however, there is no statutory limitation for preparer fraud

  b. "Negligent or intentional disregard" for rules and regulations which results in an understatement of the taxpayer's liability is subject to a $100 penalty

    (1) Rules and regulations include Internal Revenue Code, Treasury Regulations, and Revenue Rulings
    (2) However, if the tax return preparer exercises due care in using information provided by taxpayer, the preparer is not liable for underpayment of taxes

      (a) Due care is satisfied here if preparer is told by taxpayer of existence (and adequacy) of documentation that supports tax return when preparer has no reason to doubt it

        1] Not sufficient to rely only on taxpayer saying what amounts are
        2] Preparer, in general, not required to examine or retain documents that support amounts for tax return

    (3) A reasonable position that is disclosed in the return and is taken contrary to existing rules and regulations in good faith is not considered to be negligence or intentional disregard

  c. "Willful disregard" for rules and regulations resulting in an understatement of the taxpayer's liability is subject to a $500 penalty

    (1) There is no statutory limitation for assessing this penalty
    (2) The IRS bears the burden of proof

  d. Additional penalties related to the requirements imposed upon a tax return preparer

    (1) Failure to furnish the taxpayer with a copy of the return or claim for refund. A $25 penalty per failure
    (2) Failure to retain copies of the returns for at least three years, or a list of clients. A $50 penalty per failure subject to a maximum of $25,000
    (3) Failure to sign a return. A $25 penalty per failure
    (4) Failure to include social security number or employer identification number. A $25 penalty per failure
    (5) Failure by an employer to prepare and make available a list of preparers. Subject to a penalty of $100 or $5 per item missing from the list
    (6) The preparer endorsing or negotiating a refund check issued to the taxpayer is subject to a $500 penalty per occurrence

  e. A 20% penalty may be imposed on any person for the substantial understatement of tax liability

        (1) Substantial understatement is a reported tax liability that understates the correct tax by at least 10% of such tax, or $5,000

        (2) Penalty may be fully or partially waived for honest mistakes

f. An overvaluation penalty may be imposed on any person if there is an underpayment of tax of at least $1,000 that is attributable to a valuation overstatement

        (1) Overstatement occurs if the claimed value of property is at least 150% more than the value (or basis) that is determined to be correct

        (2) Penalty percentage varies from 10% to 30% depending upon the extent of the overstatement

g. Penalties for aiding and abetting understatement of tax liability

        (1) Any person who assists in the preparation of a document under internal revenue laws knowing that such information will be used in connection with a material matter and that the information will result in an understatement of the tax liability

        (2) Such person will be subject to a $10,000 penalty unless the understatement applies to the liability of a corporation where the penalty is $50,000 and/or 1 year of imprisonment

h. Fraud and false statements

        (1) Any person who

            (a) Willfully subscribes to a return, statement, or other document which is verified by a written declaration that is made under the penalties of perjury, and which s/he does not believe to be true and correct as to every material matter; or

            (b) Willfully aids, counsels, advises, etc. in fraudulent preparations of such documents

        (2) Such person is guilty of a felony and upon conviction shall be fined not more than $100,000 ($500,000 in the case of a corporation) or imprisoned not more than 3 years, or both, together with the costs of prosecution

i. Disclosure or use of information by preparers of returns

        (1) Any preparer who discloses any information furnished to the preparer for the preparation of a return or uses the information for any purpose other than to prepare such return is guilty of a misdemeanor

        (2) Such preparer shall be fined no more than $1,000, or imprisoned not more than one year, or both, plus payment of the costs of prosecution

4. Injunction can be sought by IRS to prohibit an income tax preparer from engaging in the following practices

a. Actions subject to disclosure requirement penalties and understatement of liability penalties

b. Actions subject to criminal penalties under the Code

c. Misrepresentation of the preparer's eligibility to practice, experience, or education as an income tax preparer

d. Guaranteeing the payment of a tax refund or allowance of a tax credit

e. Other actions of a fraudulent or deceptive nature that substantially interfere with proper administration of the Internal Revenue Law

I. **Assessments by IRS**

1. IRS sends individual taxpayer a 90-day letter to give him/her official notice of assessment

    a. Note that 30-day letter is not official notice of assessment

2. Then taxpayer has 90 days to file Petition of Redetermination of Deficiency in Tax Court if s/he wishes to dispute assessment

3. Taxpayer may settle before going to tax court or may commence suit in tax court

REGULATION OF EMPLOYMENT

Overview
    Issues on this topic are based on the Workers' Compensation Laws and Federal Social Security Rules including the Federal Insurance Contributions Act (FICA) and the Federal Unemployment Tax Act (FUTA). These laws supplement the law of agency. In this area, emphasis is placed on the impact that state and federal laws have on the regulation of employment.

    To adequately understand these materials, you should emphasize the theory and purpose underlying the Workers' Compensation Laws. You should also focus on the effect that these laws have on employers and employees. Notice the changes these laws have made on common law.

    Upon looking at the Federal Social Security Laws, emphasize the coverage and benefits of the respective programs.

A. Federal Social Security Act

    1. Main purpose of Act is as name implies, i.e., attainment of the social security of people in our society

        a. Basic programs include

            (1) Old age insurance
            (2) Survivor's and disability insurance
            (3) Hospital insurance (Medicare)
            (4) Unemployment insurance

        b. Sources of financing for these programs

            (1) Old-age, survivor's, disability, and hospital insurance programs are financed out of taxes paid by employers, employees, and self-employed under provisions of Federal Insurance Contributions Act and Self-Employment Contributions Act
            (2) Unemployment insurance programs are financed out of taxes paid by employers under the Federal Unemployment Tax Act and various state unemployment insurance laws

    2. Federal Insurance Contributions Act (FICA)

        a. Imposes social security tax on employees, self-employed, and employers
        b. Social security tax applies to compensation received which is considered to be wages
        c. In general, tax rates are same for both employer and employee

            (1) Rates changed frequently

        d. Taxes are paid only up to base amount which is also changed frequently

            (1) If employee pays FICA tax on more than base amount, s/he has right to refund for excess

                (a) May happen when employee works for two or more employers

                    1] These two or more employers do not get refunds

        e. It is employer's duty to withhold employee's share of FICA from employee's wages and remit both employee's amount and employer's equal share to government

            (1) Employer is required to match FICA contributions of employees on dollar-for-dollar basis

        (2) If employer neglects to withhold, employer may be liable for both employee's and employer's share of taxes, i.e., to pay double tax

        (3) Employer is required to furnish employee with written statement of wages paid and FICA contributions withheld during calendar year

  f. Taxes paid by employer are deducted on tax return of employer

        (1) But employee may not deduct taxes paid on his/her tax return

  g. Neither pension plans nor any other programs may be substituted for FICA coverage

        (1) Individuals receiving payments from private pension plans may also receive social security payments

3. Self-Employment Contributions Act

  a. Self-employed persons are required to report their own taxable earnings and pay required social security tax

  b. Self-employment income is net earnings from self-employment

  c. Tax rates paid on self-employment income up to base rate

        (1) Since self-employed does not have employer to match the rate, tax rate is set to be less than amount paid by employer and employee together but more than amount paid by employee alone

        (2) Rate is amended frequently

        (3) Base rate is reduced by any wages earned during year because wages are subject to FICA

4. Unemployment Insurance (Federal Unemployment Tax Act--FUTA)

  a. Tax is used to provide unemployment compensation benefits to workers who lose jobs and cannot find replacement work

  b. Federal unemployment tax must be paid by employer if employer employs one or more persons covered by act

        (1) Deductible as business expense on employer's federal income tax return

        (2) Not deductible by employee because not paid by employee

  c. Employer must also pay a state unemployment tax

        (1) An employer is entitled to credit against his/her federal unemployment tax for state unemployment taxes paid

        (2) State unemployment tax may be raised or lowered according to number of claims against employer

        (3) If employer pays a low state unemployment tax because of good employment record, then employer is entitled to additional credit against federal unemployment tax

5. Coverage under Social Security Act is mandatory for qualifying employees

  a. Person may not elect to avoid coverage

  b. Part-time and full-time employees are covered

  c. Compensation received must be "wages"

6. Definitions

  a. Wages--all compensation for employment

        (1) Include

            (a) Money wages

            (b) Compensation in general even though not in cash

        (c) Servicemen's base pay
        (d) Bonuses and commissions
        (e) Vacation and dismissal allowances
        (f) Tips if greater than $20

    (2) Exclude

        (a) Wages greater than base amount
        (b) Travel expenses
        (c) Employee medical and hospital expenses paid by employer
        (d) Employee insurance premiums paid by employer
        (e) Payment to employee retirement plan by employer

b. Employee--person whose performance is subject to physical control by employer not only as to results but also as to methods of accomplishing those results

    (1) Partners, self-employed persons, and independent contractors are not covered by unemployment compensation provisions since they are not "employees"

        (a) Are covered as self-employed persons for old-age, survivor's, and disability insurance program purposes

    (2) Independent contractor distinguished from an employee

        (a) Independent contractor not subject to control of employer or regular supervision as employee
        (b) I.e., employer seeks results only and contractor controls method

          EXAMPLE: *A builder of homes has only to produce the results.*

    (3) Officers and directors of corporations are "employees" if they perform services and receive remuneration for these services from corporation

c. Employment--all service performed by employee for person employing him/her

    (1) Must be continuing or recurring work
    (2) Services from following are exempt from coverage

        (a) Student nurses
        (b) Certain public employees
        (c) Non-resident aliens
        (d) Ministers

    (3) Services covered if performed by employee for employer without regard to residence or citizenship

        (a) Unless employer not connected with U.S.

    (4) Domestic workers, agricultural workers, government employees, and casual workers are governed by special rules

d. Self-employment--carrying on trade or business either as individual or in partnership

    (1) Wages greater than base amount are excluded
    (2) Can be both employed (in one job) and self-employed (another business), but must meet requirements of trade or business, i.e., not a hobby, occasional investment, etc.

e. Employer

    (1) For Federal Unemployment Tax Act (FUTA) need only employ one person or more for specified short period of time

    (2) In general, may be individual, corporation, partnership, trust, or other entity

7. Old-age, survivor's, and disability insurance benefits

  a. Availability of benefits depends upon attainment by individual of "insured status"

    (1) Certain lengths of working time are required to obtain insured status

  b. An individual who is "fully insured" is eligible for following benefits

    (1) Survivor benefits for widow or widower and dependents

    (2) Benefits for disabled worker and his/her dependents

    (3) Old-age retirement benefits payable to retired worker and dependents

        (a) Reduced benefits for retirement at age 62

    (4) Lump-sum death benefits

  c. Individual who is "currently insured" is eligible for following benefits

    (1) Limited survivor benefits

        (a) In general, limited to dependent minors or those caring for dependent minors

    (2) Benefits for disabled worker and his/her dependents

    (3) Lump-sum death benefits

    (4) Survivors or dependents need not have paid in program to receive benefits

  d. Amount of benefits defined by statute which changes from time to time and depends upon

    (1) Average monthly earnings, and

    (2) Relationship of beneficiary to retired, deceased, or disabled worker

        (a) E.g., husband, wife, child, grandchild--may be entitled to different benefits

    (3) Benefits increased based on cost of living

    (4) Benefits increased for delayed retirement

8. Reduction of social security benefits

  a. Early retirement results in reduced benefits

    (1) Retirement age is increasing in steps

  b. Returning to work after retirement can affect social security benefits

    (1) Earned income, after retirement, which exceeds an annual limitation results in reduced benefits of $1 in benefits for each $2 of earnings above a specified amount of annual earned income

        (a) A person age 70 or older does not suffer a reduction in retirement benefits

          (b) Earned income in general means income from work (wages or self-employment)

      (2) Income from private pension plans, savings, investments, or insurance does not affect benefits because not earned income

      (3) Income from limited partnership is considered investment income rather than self-employment income

9. Unemployment benefits

    a. Eligibility for and amount of unemployment benefits governed by state laws

    b. Does not include self-employed

    c. Generally available only to persons unemployed through no fault of their own; however, not available to seasonal workers if paid on yearly basis, e.g., professional sports player in off-season

    d. One must have worked for specified period of time and/or earned specified amount of wages

B. **Workers' Compensation Act**

1. Workers' compensation is a form of strict liability whereby employer is liable to employee for injuries or diseases sustained by employee which arise out of and in course of employment

    a. Employee is worker subject to control and supervision of employer

    b. Distinguish independent contractor

      (1) Details of work not supervised

      (2) Final result can of course be monitored (based on contract law)

2. Purpose

    a. To give employees and their dependents benefits for job-related injuries or diseases with little difficulty

      (1) Previously, employee had to sue employer for negligence to receive any benefits in form of damages

      (2) Employee usually cannot waive his/her right to benefits

    b. Puts burden where it can be afforded, i.e., cost is passed on as an expense of production to be borne by employers (industry)

    c. <u>No fault need be shown</u>; payment is automatic upon satisfaction of requirements

      (1) Removes employer's common law defenses of

          (a) Assumption of risk--employee assumed risk of injury upon consenting to do work

          (b) Negligence of a fellow employee--employer formerly could avoid liability by proving it was another employee's fault

          (c) Contributory negligence--injured employee was also negligent

3. Regulated by states

    a. Except that federal government employees are covered by federal statute

    b. Each state has its own statute

4. Generally, there are two types of statutes

    a. Elective statutes

        (1) If employer rejects, s/he loses the three common law defenses against employee's common law suit for damages

    b. Compulsory statutes

        (1) Require that all employers within coverage of statute provide benefits

        (2) Majority of states have compulsory coverage

5. Insurance used to provide benefits

    a. In lieu of insurance policy, employer may assume liability for workers' compensation claims but must show proof of financial responsibility to carry own risk

6. Legislative scope

    a. Workers' compensation coverage extends to all employees who are injured on job or in course of employment

        (1) During authorized time;

        (2) While acting in furtherance of employer's business purpose

    b. Coverage does not extend to employee while traveling to or from work

    c. Out of state work may be covered if it meets above mentioned criteria

    d. All states have workers' compensation law; most employees covered

    e. Must be employee; coverage does not extend to independent contractors

    f. Public employees are often covered

7. Legal action for damages

    a. Employers covered by workers' compensation insurance are generally exempt from lawsuits by employees

    b. Acceptance of benefits under workers' compensation laws by employee is in lieu of action for damages against employer and such a suit is barred

        (1) Employer assumes definite liability (strict liability) in exchange for employee giving up his/her common law rights to sue employer for damages caused by the job, e.g., suit based on negligence

        (2) When employee is covered by workers' compensation law, his/her sole remedy against employer is that which is provided for under appropriate workers' compensation act

        (3) However, if employer <u>intentionally</u> injures employee, employee may proceed against employer based on intentional tort

    c. Employee is entitled to workers' compensation benefits <u>without regard to fault</u>

        (1) Negligence or even gross negligence of injured employee is not a bar to recovery

        (2) Failure of employee to follow employer's rules is not a bar to recovery

        (3) Employee's negligence plays no role in determination of amount of benefits awarded

        (4) However, injuries caused by intentional self-infliction, participation in mutual altercation, or intoxication of employee do constitute a bar to recovery

    d. When employer fails to provide workers' compensation insurance or when employer's coverage is inadequate, injured employee may sue in common law for damages, and employer cannot resort to usual common law defenses

(1) When employer uninsured, many states have a fund to pay employee for job-related injuries

    (a) State then proceeds against uninsured company

    (b) Penalties imposed

8. Actions against third parties

  a. Employee's acceptance of workers' compensation benefits does not bar suit against third party whose negligence caused injury

    (1) If employee sues and recovers from third party, employer (or its insurance carrier) is entitled to compensation for workers' compensation benefits paid to employee

      (a) Any recovery in excess of workers' compensation benefits received belongs to injured employee

      (b) To the extent that recovery duplicates benefits already obtained from employer (or carrier), that employer (or carrier) is entitled to reimbursement from employee

> EXAMPLE: *Kraig, an employee of Badger Corporation, was injured in an auto accident while on the job. The accident was due to the negligence of Todd. Kraig can recover under workers' compensation and also fully recover from Todd in a civil court case. However, Kraig must reimburse the workers' compensation carrier to the extent the recovery duplicates benefits already obtained under workers' compensation laws.*

  b. If employee accepts workers' compensation benefits, employer (or its insurance carrier) is subrogated to right of employee against third party whose negligence caused injury

    (1) Therefore, if employee elects not to sue third party, employer (or its insurance carrier) obtains employee's right of action against third person

9. Claims

  a. Employees are required to file claim forms on timely basis

    (1) In some states, failure to file claim on time may bar employee's recovery

10. Benefits

  a. Medical

    (1) Provides for medical care to injured or diseased employee

      (a) Normally unlimited with regard to time and dollar amount limitations

  b. Disability

    (1) This is partial wage continuation plan

  c. Death

    (1) Various plans and schedules provide payments to widow and minor children

  d. Special provisions

        (1)   Normally, statutes call for specific scheduled payments for loss of limb or eye

        (2)   Also, if employee's injury is of a nature which prevents his/her returning to his/her occupation, plan may pay cost of retraining

    e. Normally not subject to waiver by employee

C. Torts of Employee

    1. Employer is generally liable to third parties for torts of employee if committed within the course and scope of his/her employment

        a. Note that third party may hold both liable up to full damages

PROPERTY

Overview

Property entails items capable of being owned, i.e., the rights related to the ownership of things that society will recognize and enforce. Property is classified as real or personal, and as tangible or intangible. Protection of property and settlement of disputes concerning property is a major function of the legal system.

The candidate should be able to distinguish between personal and real property and between tenancies in common, joint tenancies, and tenancies by the entirety. The candidate also should understand that an instrument given primarily as security for real property is a mortgage and be able to distinguish between the legal results arising from "assump-

tion" of a mortgage and taking "subject to" a mortgage. Other questions concerning mortgages require basic knowledge of the concepts of novation, suretyship, subrogation, redemption, and purchase money mortgages.

Questions on deeds usually distinguish between the legal implication of warranty deeds, quitclaim deeds, and special warranty deeds. Both mortgages and deeds should be publicly recorded, and the questions frequently require the candidate to identify a priority and explain constructive notice. The most important topics under lessor-lessee law are the Statute of Frauds, the effect of a sale of leased property, assignment, and subleasing.

A. Distinctions Between Real and Personal Property

1. Real property (realty)--includes land and things attached to land in a relatively permanent manner

    EXAMPLE: *A building is erected on a parcel of land. Both the land and the building are real property.*

2. Personal property (personalty)--property not classified as real property or a fixture (see Fixture "A.3.")

    a. May be either

        (1) Tangible--subject to physical possession

             EXAMPLE: *Automobiles and books and tangible personal property.*

        (2) Intangible--not subject to physical possession but subject to legal ownership

             EXAMPLE: *Contractual rights to receive payment for automobiles sold are intangible personal property.*

3. Fixture--item that was originally personal property but which is affixed to real property in relatively permanent fashion such that it is considered to be part of real property

    a. Several factors are applied in determining whether personal property that has been attached to real property is a fixture

        (1) Affixer's objective intent as to whether property is to be regarded as personalty or realty

            (a) In general, item is a fixture if it was intention of parties that it become part of real property
            (b) If intent is clear, then this becomes controlling factor in determination of whether an item is fixture or not

    (2) Method and permanence of physical attachment (annexed to the real property)

        (a) If item cannot be removed without material injury to real property, it is generally held that item has become part of realty (i.e., a fixture)

    (3) Adaptability of use of personal property for purpose for which real property is used

        (a) If personal property is necessary or beneficial to use of real property, more likely that item is fixture

        (b) But if use or purpose of item is unusual for type of realty involved, it might be reasonable to conclude that it is personalty, and affixer intends to remove item when s/he leaves

  b. Trade fixture is a fixture installed (affixed) by tenant in connection with business on leased premises

EXAMPLE: A tenant who is leasing premises for use as grocery store installs refrigeration unit on property. Refrigeration unit is integral to conducting of business for which tenant occupies premises and therefore qualifies as trade fixture.

    (1) Trade fixtures remain personal property, giving tenant right to remove these items upon expiration of lease

        (a) If item is so affixed to real property that removing it would cause substantial damage, then it is considered part of realty

B. Interests in Real Property

  1. Present interests

    a. Fee simple absolute

      (1) Highest estate in law (has the most ownership rights)

      (2) May be transferred inter vivos (while living), by intestate succession (without will), or by will (testate at death)

      (3) May be subject to mortgages, state laws, etc.

EXAMPLE: Most private residences are fee simple absolute estates although they are commonly subject to mortgage.

    b. Fee simple defeasible

      (1) Fee simple determinable--upon the happening of the stated event the estate automatically reverts to the grantor

EXAMPLE: Conveyance to the holder of an interest was, "to A as long as A uses it for church purposes." The interest will revert back to the grantor or his heirs if the property is not used for church purposes.

      (2) Fee simple subject to condition subsequent--upon the happening of the stated event the grantor must take affirmative action to divest the grantee of the estate

EXAMPLE: Conveyance to the holder of the interest was "to A, but if liquor is ever served on the premises, the grantor has right to enter the premises." The grantor has power of termination so as to repossess the premises.

   c. Life interest--an interest whose duration is usually measured by the life of the holder but may be measured by lives of others

      EXAMPLE: Conveyance of land, "to A so long as she shall live."

     (1) Upon termination (death), property reverts to grantor or grantor's heirs, or to a named remainderman (see "B.2.b.")

     (2) Usual life interest can be transferred by deed only, i.e., not by a will because it ends on death

     (3) Holder of a life interest (life tenant) is entitled to ordinary use and profits of land but may not commit waste (injure interests of remainderman)

       (a) Must maintain property (in reasonable state of repair)

       (b) May not misuse property

   d. Leaseholds--see Lessor-Lessee at end of Property module

2. Future interest (holder of this interest has right to or possibility of possession in the future)

   a. Reversion--future interest reverts back to transferor (or his/her heirs) at end of transferee's estate

     (1) Usually kept when conveying a life interest or an interest for a definite period of time

      EXAMPLE: X conveys, "to Y for life" or "to Y for 10 years." X has a reversion.

   b. Remainder--future interest is in a third party at the end of transferee's estate

      EXAMPLE: X conveys, "to Y for life, remainder to Z and her heirs."

3. Concurrent interest--two or more persons (co-tenants) have undivided interests and concurrent possessory rights in real or personal property--each has a nonexclusive right to possess whole property

   a. Tenancy in common

     (1) A concurrent interest with no right of survivorship (interest passes to heirs, donee, or purchaser)

     (2) Unless stated otherwise, multiple grantees are presumed to be tenants in common

     (3) Tenant in common may convey individual interest in the whole but cannot convey a specific portion of property

       (a) Unless there is a judicial partition to split up ownership

        1] Creditors may sue to compel a partition to satisfy individual's debts

   b. Joint tenancy

     (1) A concurrent interest with all rights of ownership going to the surviving joint tenants (i.e., rights of survivorship)

       (a) Cannot be transferred by will because upon death, other co-tenants own it

(2) If rights in property conveyed without consent of others, new owner becomes a tenant in common rather than joint tenant; remaining co-tenants are still joint tenants

> *EXAMPLE: A, B, and C are joint tenants of Greenacre. A sells his interest to D without the consent of B and C. D is a tenant in common with a one-third interest in the whole. B and C are still joint tenants (with the right of survivorship) each having a one-third undivided interest.*

c. Tenancy by the entirety

(1) Joint interest held by husband and wife
(2) It is presumed when both spouses' names appear on title document
(3) To transfer, both must convey
(4) Each spouse has a right of survivorship
(5) Divorce creates a tenancy in common

C. Contracts for Sale of Land

1. Generally precede transfers of land. Often includes escrows. (See "E.1.c.")

> *EXAMPLE: An earnest money agreement. The purchaser puts the money down to show his seriousness while he investigates the title and arranges for a mortgage.*

a. Generally, agreement must

(1) Be in writing and signed by party to be bound

  (a) To satisfy Statute of Frauds under contract law

(2) Identify land and parties
(3) Identify purpose
(4) Contain terms or promises
(5) Contain purchase price

b. Assignable unless prohibited in contract

2. If not expressed, there is an implied promise that seller will provide a marketable title (implied warranty of marketability)

a. A marketable title is one reasonably free from doubt. Does not contain such defects as breaks in chain of title, outstanding liens, or defective instruments in past (chain of title).

(1) Zoning restrictions do not make a title unmarketable

b. Agreement may provide for marketable or "insurable" title

(1) Insurable title is one which a title insurance company will insure against defects, liens, and invalidity

c. If title is not marketable, purchaser may

(1) Rescind and recover any down payment
(2) Sue for damages
(3) Sue for specific performance with a reduction in price

3. Risk of loss before deed is conveyed, e.g., if house burns who bears the burden?

   a. General rule is purchaser bears the risk of loss, subject to terms of
       the contract
   b. Courts may look to who has the most ownership rights and benefits
       (normally buyer)
   c. Either party can insure against risk of loss

D. **Types of Deeds**

   1. Warranty deeds contain the following covenants (unconditional promises) by
       grantor

      a. Grantor has title and right to convey it
      b. Free from encumbrances except as disclosed in the deed

         *EXAMPLE: O conveys by warranty deed Blackacre to P. There is a
         mortgage still unpaid on Blackacre. Unless O discloses this mortgage to
         P, O has violated the covenant that the deed be free from encumbrances.*

      c. Quiet enjoyment--neither grantor nor third party with rightful claim
          will disturb grantee's possession

   2. Bargain and sale deed (grant deeds)

      a. Generally, only covenants that grantor has done nothing to impair title,
          e.g., s/he has not created any encumbrances
      b. Does not warrant against prior (before grantor's ownership) impairments

   3. Quitclaim deed conveys only whatever interest in land the grantor has. No
       warranty of title is made by grantor.

      a. It is insurable, recordable, and mortgagable as with any other deed

E. **Executing a Deed**

   1. There must be delivery for deed to be effective; there must be an intent on
       part of grantor to pass title (convey) to grantee

      a. Possession of the deed by grantee raises a presumption (rebuttable) of
          delivery
      b. A recorded deed raises a presumption (rebuttable) of delivery
      c. A deed given to a third party to give to grantee upon performance of a
          condition is a delivery in escrow

         (1) Escrow agent--intermediary between the two parties who holds deed
              until grantee pays, then gives deed to grantee and money to grantor

      d. Destructing of deed does not destroy <u>title</u>

F. **Recording a Deed**

   1. Gives constructive notice to the world of grantee's ownership (this is
       important)

      a. Protects grantee (new owner) against subsequent purchasers

         *EXAMPLE: X sells land to Y. Y records his deed. Later X sells land to
         Z. Z loses as against Y because Y recorded the deed giving constructive
         notice of the prior sale.*

(1) However, deed is valid between immediate parties without recording

b. Most recording statutes provide that subsequent purchaser (bona fide) who takes without notice of the first sale has priority

(1) I.e., if grantee does not record immediately, s/he may lose his/her priority

(2) Under a notice-type statute, a subsequent bona fide (good faith) purchaser, whether s/he records or not, wins over previous purchaser who did not record before that subsequent purchase

EXAMPLE: A sells the same piece of property in a state having a notice-type statute to B and C in that order. B did not record the purchase. C is unaware of the sale to B and is thus a bona fide purchaser. C defeats B. Note that C should record the purchase or run the risk of another bona fide purchaser defeating C's claim.

(3) Under a race-notice type (notice-race) statute, the subsequent bona fide purchaser wins over a previous purchaser only if s/he records first (i.e., a "race" to file first)

EXAMPLE: X sells some property to Y and then to Z, a good faith purchaser. After the sale to Z, Y records the purchase and then Z records the purchase. Although Y wins in a state having a race-notice statute, Z wins in a state having a notice-type statute.

EXAMPLE: Same as above except that Z does not record, both results above are not affected.

c. Notice refers to actual knowledge of prior sale or constructive knowledge, i.e., one is deemed to be aware of what is filed in records

d. To be a purchaser, one must give value which does not include antecedent debts (as it does in Secured Transactions module and Commercial Paper module)

G. Title Insurance

1. Generally used to insure that title is good and to cover the warranties by seller

a. Not required if contract does not require it

2. Without title insurance purchaser's only recourse is against grantor and s/he may not be able to satisfy the damages

a. Standard insurance policies generally insure against all defects of record and defects grantee may be aware of, but not defects disclosed by survey and physical inspection of premises

b. Title insurance company is liable for any damages or expenses if there is a title defect or encumbrance that is insured against

(1) Certain defects are not insured by the title policy

(a) These exceptions must be shown on face of policy

c. Title insurance does not pass to subsequent purchasers

H. Adverse Possession

1. Possessor of land who was not owner may acquire title if s/he holds it for the statutory period

    a.   The statutory period is the running of the Statute of Limitations. Varies by state from 5 to 20 years.

    b.   The statute begins to run upon the taking of possession

    c.   True owner must commence legal action before statute runs or adverse possessor obtains title

    d.   Successive possessors may tack (cumulate required time together)

       (1) Each possessor must transfer to the other. One cannot abandon or statute begins over again for the next possessor.

    e.   True owner of a future interest, e.g., a remainder, is not affected by adverse possession

> *EXAMPLE: X dies and leaves his property to A for life, remainder to B. A pays little attention to the property and a third party acquires it by adverse possession. When A dies, B is entitled to the property regardless of the adverse possession but the statute starts running against B.*

  2. Necessary elements

    a.   Open and notorious possession

       (1) Means type of possession that would give reasonable notice to owner

    b.   Hostile possession

       (1) Must indicate intentions of ownership

          (a) Does not occur when possession started permissively or as co-tenants

          (b) Not satisfied if possessor acknowledges other's ownership

       (2) Color of title satisfies this requirement. When possession is taken under good faith belief in a defective instrument or deed purporting to convey the land.

    c.   Actual possession

       (1) Possession of land consistent with its normal use, e.g., farm land is being farmed

    d.   Continuous possession

       (1) Need not be constant, but possession as normally used

    e.   Exclusive possession

       (1) Possession to exclusion of all others

I. Mortgages

  1. Definition--nonpossessory lien on real property to secure the performance of an obligation (usually a debt)

    a.   Under law of majority of states, debtor has title

    b.   Obligation or debt is usually evidenced by a promissory note which is incorporated into mortgage

    c.   Purchase-money mortgage is created when seller takes a mortgage from buyer at the time of sale

       (1) Or lender furnishes the money with which property is purchased

    d.   A mortgage may be given to secure future advances

    e.   A mortgage is an interest in real property and must be in writing, signed, etc. (must satisfy Statute of Frauds)

(1)   Recall that contract must be signed by party to be charged--in this case only by mortgagor (the one taking out mortgage)

2.   Mortgage may be recorded and receives the same benefits as recording a deed or recording an assignment of contract

    a.   Gives constructive notice of the mortgage

        (1)   But mortgage <u>is effective</u> between mortgagor and mortgagee and third parties, who have actual notice, even without recording

    b.   Protects against subsequent mortgagees (priority of mortgage), purchasers, or other takers

    c.   Recording statutes are generally similar to (or the same ones) those used in recording deeds (see "F.1.b.")

        (1)   First mortgagee to obtain a mortgage and to record it will have priority over all subsequent mortgagees subject to special rights of purchase money security interests and certain statutory liens (i.e., mechanic's or construction lien)

        (2)   The first mortgage to have priority is satisfied in full (upon default) before the next mortgage to have priority is satisfied

            (a)   Second mortgagee can require first mortgagee to resort to other property for payment if first mortgagee has other property available as security

    d.   If the first mortgagee does not record, a subsequent mortgagee who records will have priority if s/he did <u>not</u> have notice of the first mortgage

        (1)   If subsequent mortgagee had notice, s/he cannot get priority in most jurisdictions

EXAMPLE: M loans money to X on some property and becomes the first mortgagee in time. M does not record the mortgage. N loans money on the same property. N is unaware of the prior mortgage and records the second mortgage. N has priority over M.

EXAMPLE: Same as above except N is aware of the first mortgage. M wins because N had actual notice despite the lack of recordation.

    e.   Mortgage that is recorded prior to acquisition of another property interest takes priority

EXAMPLE: Mortgagee records a mortgage long after giving a loan but before the mortgagor leases the property. The mortgagee has priority over the leasehold upon default by the mortgagor.

3.   When mortgaged property is sold the buyer may

    a.   Assume the mortgage

        (1)   If "assumed," the buyer becomes personally liable (mortgage holder is third-party beneficiary)

        (2)   Seller remains liable (unless released by mortgage holder by a novation)

            (a)   But between the seller and buyer, buyer has primary responsibility and seller has the rights and responsibilities of a surety

        (3)   Normally the mortgage holder's consent is needed due to "due on sale clauses"

          (a) Terms of mortgage may permit acceleration of principal or renegotiation of interest rate upon transfer of the property

  b. Take subject to the mortgage

     (1) If buyer takes "subject to" then buyer accepts <u>no</u> liability for the mortgage and seller is still primarily liable

        (a) Buyer may pay mortgage and mortgage holder must accept

     (2) Mortgage holder may still foreclose on the property even in the hands of the buyer

        (a) Buyer has no right against seller concerning the mortgage subject to terms of contract or conveyance

     (3) Mortgage holder's consent not needed unless stipulated in mortgage and in no event can consent be unreasonably withheld, unless a "due on sale clause" is present

  c. Novation--occurs when purchaser assumes mortgage and mortgagee (lender) releases in writing the seller from the mortgage

> *EXAMPLE: O has mortgaged Redacre. He sells Redacre to T. T agrees to assume mortgage and mortgagee bank agrees in writing to substitute T as the only liable party in place of O. Because of this novation, O is no longer liable on the mortgage.*

4. Rights of parties

  a. Mortgagor (owner, debtor) retains possession and right to use land

     (1) May transfer land encumbered by mortgage

  b. Mortgagee (creditor) has a lien on the land and may assign mortgage to third parties or foreclose on land to satisfy debt upon default

     (1) Even if mortgagor transfers land, it is still subject to the mortgage if it has been properly recorded

  c. If mortgagor defaults on payment of the note, mortgagee may resort to land for payment by foreclosure

     (1) Requires judicial action that directs a foreclosure sale

        (a) Court will refuse to confirm sale if price is so low as to raise a presumption of unfairness

        (b) However, court will not refuse to confirm sale merely because higher price might have been received at a later time

     (2) Mortgagor usually can save real estate (redeem the property) by use of equity of redemption

        (a) Pays interest, debt, and expenses
        (b) Exists until foreclosure sale
        (c) Cannot be curtailed by prior agreement

     (3) After foreclosure sale debtor has right of redemption

        (a) Affords mortgagor one last chance to redeem property
        (b) Pays off loan within statutory period

     (4) If mortgagee forecloses and sells property and mortgagor does not use equity of redemption or right of redemption

        (a) Mortgagee must return any excess proceeds from sale to mortgagor

      (b) If proceeds from sale are insufficient to pay note, mortgagor is still indebted to the mortgagee for deficiency

          1] Grantee of the mortgagor who <u>assumed</u> mortgage would also be liable for deficiency but one who took <u>subject to</u> the mortgage would not be personally liable

5. Deed of trust--also a nonpossessory lien on real property to secure a debt

   a. Like a mortgage, debtor retains possession of land and creditor has a lien on it

   b. Legal title is given to a trustee to hold

      (1) Upon default, trustee may sell the land for the benefit of creditor

6. Sale on contract

   a. Unlike a mortgage or a deed of trust, the seller retains title to property

   b. Purchaser takes possession and makes payments on the contract

   c. Purchaser gets title when debt fully paid

J. Lessor-Lessee

1. Relationship which arises from contracting for possession of real property for some period of time

   a. A lease is a contract and a conveyance

      (1) Contract is the primary source of rights and duties

      (2) May be oral if less than one year

      (3) Lease is actually personal property

   b. Landlord is lessor and has ownership interest called reversion

   c. Tenant is lessee and has a possessory interest

2. Types of leaseholds

   a. Period-to-period

      (1) Lease is for a fixed time such as a month or year but it continues from period-to-period until proper notice of termination

      (2) Notice of termination must be given in the same amount of time as rent or tenancy period (i.e., if tenancy is from month-to-month then the landlord or tenant must give at least one month's notice)

   b. Definite period of time (called lease for years)

      (1) Lease is for a fixed amount of time, e.g., lease of two years or six months

      (2) Ends automatically at date of termination

   c. Holdover by tenant after definite term with express or implied approval of landlord creates a period-to-period lease

3. Lessor covenants (promises) and tenant's rights

   a. Generally, lessor's covenants are independent of lessee's rights; therefore, lessor's breach does not give lessee right to breach

   b. Right to possession--lessor makes premises available to lessee

   c. Quiet enjoyment--neither lessor nor a third party with a valid claim will evict lessee unless there has been a breach of the lease

   d. Fitness for use--premises are fit for human occupation, i.e., warranty of habitability

   e. Lessee may assign or sublease unless prohibited or restricted in lease

(1) Assignment is transfer by lessee of his/her entire interest reserving no rights

    (a) Assignee is in privity of contract with lessor and lessor may proceed against him/her for rent and breaches under lease agreement

    (b) Assignor (lessee) is still liable to lessor unless there is a novation or release

    (c) Lease may have clause that requires consent of lessor for subleases

        1] In which case, consent to each individual sublease is required

        2] Lack of consent makes sublease voidable

    (d) Clause prohibiting sublease does not prohibit assignment

(2) A sublease is the transfer by lessee of less than his/her entire interest; e.g., for three months during summer, then lessee returns to it in the fall

    (a) Lessee (sublessor) is still liable on lease

    (b) Lessor has no privity with sublessee and can take no action against him/her for rent, but certain restrictions of original lease run with the land and are enforceable against sublessee

    (c) Sublessee can assume obligations in sublease and be liable to pay landlord

    (d) Clause prohibiting assignment does not prohibit sublease

    f. Subject to lease terms, trade fixtures attached by lessee may be removed if can be removed without substantial damage to premises

    g. Tenant can use premises for any legal purpose unless lease restricts

4. Lessee's duties and lessor's rights

    a. Rent--due at end of term or period of tenancy unless otherwise agreed in lease

    (1) No right to withhold rent even if lessor is in breach (unless so provided by lease or by statute)

    (2) Nonpayment gives lessor right to sue for it or to bring an eviction suit or both

    b. Lessee has obligation to make ordinary repairs. Lease or statute may make lessor liable.

    (1) Structural repairs are lessor's duty

    c. If tenant wrongfully retains possession after termination, lessor may

    (1) Evict lessee, or

    (2) Treat as holdover tenant and charge with fair rental value, or

    (3) Tenancy becomes one of period-to-period, and lessee is liable for rent the same as in expired lease

5. Termination

    a. Expiration of lease

    b. Proper notice in a tenancy from period-to-period

    c. Surrender by lessee and acceptance by lessor

    d. Death of lessee terminates lease except for a lease for a period of years

    (1) Death of lessor generally does not terminate lease

    e. Eviction

        (1) Actual eviction--ousting directly
        (2) Constructive eviction--allowing conditions which make property
             unusable if lessor is liable for condition of premises

    f. Transfer of property does not affect tenancy

        (1) New owner cannot rightfully terminate lease unless old owner could
             have, e.g., breach by tenant

INSURANCE

Overview

Insurance is a contract whereby the insurer (insurance company) indemnifies the insured (policy-holder) against loss on designated property due to specified risks such as fire, storm, etc. The obligation of the insured under the insurance contract is the payment of the stipulated premium. Before an insured can recover under a property insurance policy, the policyholder must have an insurable interest in the property at the time it was damaged or destroyed. Basically, insurance is limited to providing protection against the risk of loss arising from a happening of events caused by the negligence of insured and negligence and intentional acts of third parties. Insurance does not protect against loss due to intentional acts of insured. Insurance contracts like others, require agreement, consideration, capacity, and legality.

Primary emphasis on the exam is placed upon knowledge of fire and casualty insurance. The exam has emphasized insurable interest, co-insurance and pro rata clauses, risks protected against, subrogation, and assignment of insurance contracts.

A. General Considerations

1. Insurance is the distribution of the cost of risk over a large number of individuals subject to the same risk, in order to reimburse the few who actually suffer from the risk

2. Insurance is designed to protect against large unexpected losses, not small everyday losses

    a. This is one reason for $50 or $100 deductible clause in auto-collision insurance

3. Intentional acts of insured usually are not insurable, e.g., fire by arson, liability for assault and battery

    a. Negligence or carelessness is insurable and is generally not a defense of the insurer
    b. Negligence of an insured's employees is also covered

4. Self-insurance is the periodic setting aside of money into a fund to provide for losses

    a. Not true insurance, because it is not a distribution of risk; it is preparation to meet possible losses

B. Insurance Contract

1. Similar to a common law contract. Must contain all essential elements, i.e., agreement, legality, capacity, and consideration

2. Generally a unilateral contract where the insured prepays the premiums and the insurer promises to indemnify insured against loss

3. Insurance is generally binding at time of unconditional acceptance of the application and communication of this to insured

    a. The application is the offer, and issuance of the policy is acceptance
    b. A company agent (as opposed to an independent agent) usually has power to issue a temporarily binding slip which obligates the insurer during

interim before issuance of policy
  c. Physical delivery of written policy is not necessary
  d. Insurer may require conditions to be met before policy becomes
      effective, e.g., pay a premium

      (1) A general agent may accept a policy for insured

  4. Policy may be voidable at option of insurer if there is

      a. Concealment--the insured failed to inform insurer at time of application
          of a fact material to insurer's risk

          *EXAMPLE: An applicant for auto insurance is unable to drive and does
          not so inform the insurer.*

          (1) Any matter specifically asked by insurer is by law material and
               failure to disclose or a misleading answer is concealment
          (2) Need not disclose facts learned after making the contract

      b. Material misrepresentation by insured, e.g., nonexistent subject matter

          (1) Representation acceptable if substantially true, e.g., value of
               subject matter does not have to be exact

      c. Breach of warranty incorporated in the policy.

          *EXAMPLE: An applicant for fire insurance warrants that a night watchman
          will be on duty at night at all times to check for fire. If he is not
          and a loss occurs, this may release the insurer.*

  5. Statute of Frauds does not require insurance contract to be in writing
      because it may fall within the one-year rule (but usually is required by
      state statutes)

  6. Insurable interest

      a. There must be a relationship between the insured and the insured event
          so that if the event occurs insured will suffer substantial loss
      b. In property, there must be both a legal interest and a possibility of
          pecuniary loss

          (1) Legal interest may be ownership or a security interest, e.g.,
               general creditors do not have an insurable interest but judgment
               lien creditors and mortgagees do
          (2) Insurable interest need not be present at inception of the policy
               so long as it is present at time of the loss
          (3) One can insure only to extent one has an insurable interest, e.g.,
               mortgagee can insure only amount still due
          (4) Contract to purchase or possession of property can give an
               insurable interest

C. Subrogation

  1. This is the right of insurer to step into the shoes of insured as to any
      cause of action relating to a third party whose conduct caused the loss

      *EXAMPLE: While driving his car, X is hit by Y. If X's insurance company
      pays X, the insurance company is subrogated to X's claim against Y.*

      a. Applies to accident, automobile collision, and fire policies

2. A general release of a third party, who caused the loss, by insured will release insurer from his/her obligation

    EXAMPLE: While driving his car, X is hit by Y. Y talks X into signing a statement that X releases Y from all liability. X will not be able to recover on his insurance. X's insurance company is released when Y is released.

    a. Because insurer's right of subrogation has been cut off
    b. A partial release will release insurer to that extent

D. **Liability Insurance**

1. Insurer agrees to protect insured against liability for accidental damage to persons or property

    a. Usually includes duty to defend in a lawsuit brought by third parties
    b. Intentional wrongs not covered, e.g., fraud
    c. Insurer has no rights against insured for causing the loss because this is what the insurance is to protect against

2. Malpractice--a form of personal liability

    a. Used by accountants, doctors, lawyers
    b. Protects against liability for harm caused by errors or negligence in work
    c. Does not protect against intentional wrongs, e.g., fraud

E. **Fire Insurance**

1. Generally covers direct fire damage and also damage as a result of fire such as smoke, water, or chemicals

2. Blanket policy applies to a class of property which may be changing (inventory) rather than a specific piece of property (specific policy)

3. Valued policy predetermines value of property which becomes the face value of the policy

4. Recovery limited to face value of policy

5. <u>Coinsurance clause</u>

    a. The insured agrees to maintain insurance equal to a specified percentage of the value of his/her property. Then when a loss occurs, insurer only pays a proportionate share if insured has not carried the specified percentage.

    b. Formula

$$\text{Total recovery} = \text{Actual loss} \times \frac{\text{Amount of insurance}}{\text{Coinsurance \%} \times \text{FMV of property at time of loss}}$$

EXAMPLE: Insured owns a building valued at $100,000. He obtains 2 insurance policies for $20,000 each and they both contain 80% coinsurance clauses. There is a fire and his loss is $40,000. He will only collect $20,000 ($10,000 each) on his insurance, calculated as follows:

$$\$40,000 \times \frac{\$20,000 + \$20,000}{80\% \text{ of } \$100,000}$$

    c. Does not apply when insured property is totally destroyed

      EXAMPLE: On October 10, Harry's warehouse was totally destroyed by fire. At the time of the fire, the warehouse had a value of $500,000 and was insured against fire for $300,000. The policy contained an 80% coinsurance clause. Harry will recover $300,000, the face value of the policy, because total destruction occurred and the coinsurance clause would not apply. If the warehouse had been only partially destroyed, with damages amounting to $300,000, Harry would only recover $225,000 (based on the formula above), because the coinsurance clause would apply.

6. Pro rata clause

    a. Someone who is insured with multiple policies can only collect, from each insurer, the proportionate amount of the loss

      (1) Proportion is the amount insured by each insurer to total amount of insurance

        EXAMPLE: Insured incurs a loss due to fire on property and is entitled to a $10,000 recovery. The property is covered by two insurance policies, one for $8,000 from Company A and one for $12,000 from Company B. Consequently, total insurance coverage on the property was $20,000. Company A will be liable for 40% ($8,000/$20,000) of fire loss, i.e., $4,000 (40% x $10,000). Company B will be liable for 60% ($12,000/$20,000) of fire loss, i.e., $6,000 (60% x $10,000).

7. Proof of loss

    a. Insured must give insurer a statement of amount of loss, cause of loss, etc., within a specified time

      (1) Failure to comply will excuse insurer's liability unless performance is made impracticable, e.g., death of insured

8. Mortgagor and mortgagee have insurable interests, and mortgagees usually require insurance for their protection

9. Fire policies are usually not assignable because risk may have changed

    a. I.e., danger that new owner would not be reliable, e.g., record of arson
    b. Even if property is sold, there can be no assignment of insurance without insurer's consent
    c. A claim against an insurer may be assigned, e.g., house burns and insurance company has not yet paid

TRUSTS AND ESTATES

Overview

This topic includes the administration of a decedent's estate and the administration of a trust.

An estate is the legal entity which comes into existence on a person's death for the purpose of succeeding to the property of the decedent, to establish liability for payment of debts of the decedent, and to distribute any remaining property. The estate is administered in accordance with the decedent's will or the intestate statutes. An executor or administrator is approved by the court and empowered to act for the estate and carry out its responsibilities. An executor or administrator may engage the necessary legal, accounting, and other services. Adequate records must be kept to show proper disposition of the assets of the estate. At the conclusion of an estate, an accounting is generally rendered and the judicial settlement is secured in probate court, thereby closing the estate.

A trust arises where one person holds legal title to certain property for the use and benefit of another. In other words, in a trust, the legal and equitable title are split so that one called a trustee holds legal title for the benefit of another person, called a beneficiary. A trust is administered by a trustee who must perform the duties imposed by law and by the trust instrument and is personally liable if s/he does not follow these requirements.

One of the most frequently tested topics in estates and trusts is allocation of trust principal and income. Candidates should be thoroughly familiar with this distinction, e.g., between cash dividends and stock dividends. Also tested are the rights of beneficiaries to a trust with particular emphasis on the distinction between the rights of income beneficiary and the residual beneficiary, the duties of an administrator or executor of an estate as well as the duties of a trustee. You should also understand for the CPA exam how and when a trust is created and terminated.

A. Estates

1. The execution and validity of a will is generally the province of lawyers. However, some general information regarding wills which pertains to administration of estates is useful to aid you in background knowledge for tested topics.

    a. Emphasis on CPA exam is now on administration of estates and trusts
    b. Preparation of tax returns and schedules used to render an accounting are frequently done by CPA firms

2. General information and definitions

    a. Will—legal declaration of person's intent concerning disposition of his/her property at death

        (1) Will takes effect upon death—may be changed or revoked until death

    b. Estate—legal entity holding title to person's property after his/her death

        (1) Pays decedent's debts
        (2) Administered by executor or administrator

    c. Testate—a person is said to die testate if there is a valid will in existence

        (1) Estate (decedent property) will pass to beneficiaries by terms of will

    d. Intestate--a person is said to die intestate if there is no will or if will is held invalid

        (1) Estate will pass by intestate succession, i.e., state statute prescribes rules of distribution of an estate

            (a) Rules are calculated to approximate probable wishes of most individuals

        (2) Any assets not disposed of by will are distributed by intestate succession laws

    e. Testator (male) or testatrix (female)--one who makes will

    f. Legacy (bequest)--gift of personal property under will

        (1) Specific legacy is gift of specified item

            EXAMPLE: Decedent willed his car specifically to his daughter.

            (a) If specific item does not exist when testator dies, then beneficiary gets nothing

        (2) General legacy is gift payable out of general assets of estate

            EXAMPLE: Decedent willed $100 to his son.

            (a) As long as estate is not insolvent, beneficiary will receive general legacy

    g. Devise--gift of real property under will

        (1) Same rules apply to general and specific devises as to legacies, above

    h. Residue--remainder of estate after all other gifts have been made and all debts paid

        EXAMPLE: "I hereby give ... to ... and the rest of my estate to A."

        (1) Its value is undetermined until an appraisal and inventory of estate is made and all other gifts have been made or accounted for and all debts discharged

    i. Probate--process of proving validity and authenticity of a will by demonstrating that an instrument purporting to be last will and testament of person was duly executed in accordance with legal requirements

  3. Validity of will

    a. Testator/testatrix must be competent when s/he executes (makes) will

        (1) Must be of legal age (normally 18) at time of execution of will

        (2) Must have mental capacity to make will

            (a) Ability to understand nature and extent of property s/he owns and nature of will

    b. Must be executed in compliance with formal requirements of state statute

        (1) Signature of testator/testatrix required

        (2) Signed by individuals who witnessed testator/testatrix signing will

            (a) Except where handwritten wills allowed

    c. Only effective on testator's/testatrix's death ("will speaks at death")

    d. Revocable and amendable during testator's/testatrix's life

B. **Administration of Estates**

1. Purpose of administration

   a. To carry out decedent's wishes as expressed in will
   b. To discover, collect, and conserve assets of decedent
   c. To protect creditors by paying from assets all claims and taxes against estate
   d. To identify beneficiaries and to properly distribute assets of estate according to testator's intentions or law of intestate succession

2. One who is authorized by probate court to administer the estate of decedent is called a personal representative

   a. Executor/executrix--personal representative named in will by testator to carry out provisions of will and empowered by probate court to act for estate

      (1) Probate court will follow testator's wishes and appoint the person named in will to be the executor, unless person named is disqualified, unavailable, or unwilling to serve
      (2) Person named as executor

         (a) Can decline to serve
         (b) Can be beneficiary of will

   b. Administrator--person appointed by court to administer estate when decedent dies intestate or if executor named in will cannot or will not serve
   c. Unless personal representative accepts appointment to serve gratuitously, s/he is entitled to reasonable compensation for services rendered
   d. Personal representative is required to file with the court an inventory of estate's assets for appraisal

      (1) Taxes also assessed

3. Probate of will is prerequisite to administration of estate

   a. Until admitted to probate, will is ineffective and inoperative insofar as transferring title to property held by estate
   b. Will becomes effective upon probate but relates back to time of decedent's death
   c. There is basic limitation period (normally three years from date of death) within which it must be determined whether decedent left a will

      (1) If no will is probated within this statutory period of time, there rises presumption that decedent died intestate

4. Petition for probate must be filed in proper court supervising distribution, usually called probate court

   a. This is necessary prior to distribution of estate
   b. Petition consists of statement of approximate value of estate and names, ages, residence, and relationship of heirs of decedent
   c. Filing generally includes a sworn statement, by original witnesses to the will, that the will being submitted is valid
   d. All executed copies of will must be presented to court before they can be admitted to probate

5. Creditors are given notice and must file their claims within statutory time period

6. Administrator or executor/executrix is fiduciary and must act as such by acting in the best interests, and by carrying out wishes of testator/testatrix or statutory scheme

   a. Responsible for collecting all debts, paying all expenses, and generally carrying out distribution to those entitled

      (1) May sell assets to pay debts; personal property must be sold before real property (unless otherwise directed by will)
      (2) May contract and engage services, e.g., attorneys, accountants, appraisers
      (3) Must post bond to ensure performance unless will provides otherwise

   b. Personally liable if s/he fails to execute his/her duties

      (1) Reasonable person standard used

   c. Must not commingle estate with his/her own property
   d. Must keep an accounting of all assets and their disposition

      (1) The final accounting rendered should include

         (a) An inventory of all assets of estate
         (b) A statement of all debts of estate
         (c) A statement of disposition of all assets and income from estate
         (d) A statement of expenses, costs, and commissions of administration

      (2) Preparation of tax returns and financial schedules used to render an accounting in estate administration are often done by CPA firms
      (3) The probate court issues a "decree of final settlement," distribution of estate assets is made pursuant to court decree, and the personal representative is discharged

7. Distribution of estate

   a. By terms of will

      (1) Surviving spouse, under the concept of statutory share, has right to denounce the provision made in will for him/her and elect instead a stated share (normally 1/3) of decedent's estate

         (a) Protects surviving spouse from being disinherited by will

   b. By intestate succession when there is no will or if will does not provide for entire estate

      (1) Laws vary from state to state
      (2) Intestate succession applies to real property as well as to personal property

   c. Property held in joint tenancy passes to surviving joint tenants and, therefore, does not pass through a will or intestate succession

      (1) Property owned as tenants in common does pass through a will or through intestate succession

    d. Abatement--process of determining distribution of estate when it is insufficient to satisfy all debts and gifts

        (1) Debts and administration expenses are paid first, taking from (in order)

            (a) Intestate property (property not provided for in will)
            (b) Residue
            (c) General devises or legacies
            (d) Specific devises or legacies

        (2) Any remaining assets are distributed as follows until they run out

            (a) Specific devises or legacies
            (b) General devises or legacies
             (c) Residue
            (d) Intestate property

        (3) Abatement attempts to fulfill wishes of testator to best extent by protecting those bequests most important to testator, such as specific bequests

8. Ademption--when specific bequest or devise becomes impossible to perform because of circumstances or events occurring after execution of will

    a. Particular property bequeathed or devised is not part of testator's estate at time of his/her death

        (1) Gift thereby fails since there is no such property in estate
        (2) Only applies to specific bequests or devises

9. Lapse--a gift in a will is said to lapse if beneficiary is living when will is executed, but beneficiary subsequently predeceases the testator (i.e., when beneficiary dies between the execution of will and death of testator)

    a. Since intended beneficiary is not living at time of estate distribution, the gift to him/her lapses and passes to residue of estate

10. Post-mortem passing of property by means other than wills

    a. Joint tenancy--concurrent ownership of same piece of property with right of survivorship

        (1) Right of survivorship means that other joint tenant(s) get property upon death of one joint tenant

            (a) Heirs do not share in property by will or by intestate succession
            (b) No estate administration involved

              EXAMPLE: M, N, and O own a piece of property as joint tenants. If O dies, then M and N become the two joint tenants even if O tried to pass this interest in a will.

    b. Tenancy in common--concurrent ownership with no right of survivorship

        (1) This interest passes to heirs in a will, or if no will exists, by intestate succession

    c. Tenancy by entirety--concurrent interest in which the owners are husband and wife with right of survivorship
    d. Life insurance--by selection of beneficiaries who directly receive insurance proceeds by contract, not by will

e. Employee benefits and pensions

(1) Provisions for direct death benefits without estate administration

C. **Trusts**

1. Definition--a trust is fiduciary relationship wherein trustee holds legal title to property for benefit of beneficiaries

a. Legal and equitable (beneficial) title are separated

(1) Trustee holds legal title
(2) Beneficiaries hold equitable title

b. Trustor or settlor is the person who creates the trust

(1) Settlor can make him/herself either trustee or beneficiary (not both), but, of course, s/he does not need to be either
(2) Settlor can reserve right to revoke trust; otherwise, trust is irrevocable

c. Trustee manages the property and distributes the income to the beneficiary(ies) if so provided in trust agreement

EXAMPLE: S desires to transfer Blackacre to her son, B, who is a minor, but does not want B to control legal title until he is older and capable of managing the property. Therefore, S creates a trust by transferring title of Blackacre to a trustee, J, who will hold and manage the property until B reaches age 18 and then will convey Blackacre to B.

2. Creation of trust

a. Elements

(1) Settlor (trustor) with legal capacity

(a) For inter vivos trusts (transfers between living persons), person must have legal capacity to transfer title of property
(b) For testamentary trusts (trusts created in wills), person must have legal capacity to make a will

(2) Settlor intends to create trust

(a) May be written or oral

1] If trust is in a will (i.e., testamentary trust) then will must comply with formalities

(b) No notice to or acceptance by beneficiaries required
(c) No notice to or acceptance by trustees required
(d) No consideration required

1] Distinguish--a contract to make a future trust does need consideration

(e) Legality

1] Purpose of trust must be legal or trust is considered void

(3) Trustee--one who holds legal title

(a) May be minor, corporation, or other person

(b) May be either settlor or beneficiary (but not both because then all three would be same person and trust would terminate)

(c) Death of trustee does not destroy trust--new trustee appointed

(4) Beneficiary (Cestui que trust)

(a) Must be identifiable at time trust is created
(b) May be minor, corporation or other person
(c) Class of persons may be beneficiaries
(d) Settlor may be beneficiary

(5) Trust property (also called res or corpus)

(a) Must exist at time of creation of trust
(b) Must be specifically identified
(c) Trust must be limited in duration so as to not violate the rule against perpetuities

1] This rule requires that trust cannot (by its terms) last longer than a life in being plus 21 years or it will fail

EXAMPLE: A forms a trust. The terms of this trust state that the income is to go to his son, B, for life unless B has a child, in which case the property will be distributed to this child at the age of 21.

2] Purpose is to prevent title to property from being tied up for an unreasonable period of time

3. Types of Trusts

a. Inter vivos trust is created by settlor while living

(1) Transfer in trust is the transferring of property by settlor to trustee for benefit of another
(2) Declaration of trust is when settlor declares him/herself trustee for beneficiary

(a) In a declaration of trust, no transfer of property is necessary

b. A testamentary trust is set up in testator's/testatrix's will to have property transferred in trust after death of settlor

(1) Requires elements of valid will

c. Charitable trust--a trust that has as its object some recognized social benefit, e.g., furthering education, religion, relief to poor

(1) Valid even if indefinite as to time and beneficiaries
(2) Cy pres (i.e., as near as possible) doctrine is used by courts to carry out general intent when specific instructions are impossible

d. Clifford Trust

(1) Rules for Clifford Trust started on or before March 1, 1986

(a) Trust in which its creator retains right to possession of trust property after a stated period of time or upon happening of stated event
(b) Based on Supreme Court's case

        (c)   Creator of trust is taxed on trust property unless Internal Revenue Code requirements are met because s/he is still treated as owner

            1]   Not treated as owner for tax purposes (i.e., not taxed on) if creator of trust will not obtain possession within 10 years from creation of trust

EXAMPLE: The Huskies decided they would like to shift some of their income to their children, Herb and Harriet. They decided to create a short-term irrevocable trust for the benefit of the children with Illini Trust Company as trustee. The duration of the trust was ten years plus one day. The trust agreement was dated August 1, 1985. The Huskies then conveyed an apartment building in trust to the trustee on October 10, 1985. The Huskies' trust was not created until October 10, 1985, when title to the building was conveyed to the trustee in writing. Consequently the duration of the trust was less than 10 years and it would not qualify as a Clifford trust. Thus the rental income would be taxed as part of the parents' income and not as part of the children's, which was the Huskies' intent when creating the trust.

    (2)   In general, transfers through a trust made after March 1, 1986 have been changed under the Tax Reform Act of 1986

        (a)   Trusts started after the above date do not allow income shifting from the grantor to the beneficiary if the grantor or grantor's spouse retains a reversionary interest in the trust property

        (b)   As of this writing, an exception is allowed from the new changes in that Clifford Trusts made under a binding property settlement on or before March 1, 1986 are able to continue to shift income to the beneficiary

            1]   However, if the beneficiary is a son or daughter and is under the age of 14, the shifted income is taxed at the parent's tax rate

            2]   Note that if the beneficiary is either over 13 years old or is not the son or daughter of the grantor, under the conditions above, the income is taxed at the beneficiary's rate

  e. Spendthrift trusts

    (1)   Trusts that prohibit beneficiary from assigning or transferring to another party any unreceived payments

    (2)   Protects beneficiary from creditors or from his/her squandering of assets

  f. Implied trusts

    (1)   Resulting trust arises when

        (a)   Beneficial interest(s) fail(s)

EXAMPLE: An income beneficiary is named but a remainderman is not named. At the end of the trust the beneficial interest will fail.

            1]   Trustee then holds for settlor or settlor's heirs, or

      (b) Title to property is taken (with consent) in name of one who did not furnish consideration

> *EXAMPLE: A prominent politician purchases some land but does not want his name associated with it. A business associate holds the land in his name for the politician.*

  g. Active trust is one wherein trustee has some specific duties to perform

     (1) Passive trust is one requiring no duties of trustee, and trustee is merely holder of legal title of trust property until ownership passes to beneficiaries

  h. Totten trusts

     (1) Totten trust pertains to a bank savings account which depositor opens as "John Smith in trust for Sam Smith"
     (2) Revocable by depositor simply by withdrawing money
     (3) Funds may be used during depositor's life in any manner
     (4) Totten trusts become irrevocable at depositor's death

  i. Constructive trust arises when person who takes legal interest in property cannot enjoy beneficial interest without violating some established (legal) principle

     (1) Therefore, the court converts legal owner into trustee for the party who is entitled to beneficial enjoyment
     (2) Arises by operation of law as remedial device
     (3) Imposed whenever court determines that one who acquired title to property is under duty to transfer it to another person because acquisition was by fraud, duress, mistake, etc. or because the holder of title would be unjustly enriched if s/he were permitted to retain it

> *EXAMPLE: S conveys property to A, but B fraudulently changes conveyance to his own name. Therefore, the court will impose a constructive trust whereby B is deemed to hold the property in trust for A.*

D. Administration of Trusts

  1. Trustee's duties

    a. Fulfill terms in express trust

     (1) Unless illegal or impossible
     (2) Or unless circumstances unanticipated by settlor occur so that fulfillment of trust terms would defeat trust's original purpose
     (3) Or unless court decree directs otherwise

    b. Trustee is fiduciary (this concept is very important)

     (1) Owes duty to act in best interests of beneficiary(ies) rather than his/her own
     (2) Duty of loyalty to beneficiary(ies)

       (a) Must upon request furnish all records and information on trust
       (b) Must keep trust property separate from own

    c. Must administer trust in reasonable manner

     (1) Use same care as reasonable person would use in care of his/her own property

        (2) Must defend actions brought against trust

        (3) Should use judgment in getting fair returns on property without unreasonable risk

        (4) Must collect claims owed to trust

        (5) Must keep reasonable records

        (6) Should make trust property productive

            (a) Unproductive property should be sold

        (7) May not delegate duties trustee can do him/herself

  2. Trustee's powers

     a. May be express

        (1) Duty to invest trust property in reasonable manner not contrary to terms of trust

     b. May be implied

        (1) Only those powers that are not prohibited under trust and are reasonably necessary to fulfill purpose of trust

        (2) Trustee has right to reimbursement for reasonable expenses incurred on behalf of trust

        (3) May prudently sell and purchase property

            (a) Diversification may be used to decrease risk of loss

        (4) May lease property if reasonable

        (5) If more than one trustee, unanimous consent needed

            (a) Charitable trusts only need consent of majority

        (6) No implied power to mortgage, pledge, or borrow on trust property

  3. Liability of trustee

     a. To beneficiaries based on breach of trust or breach of fiduciary duties

     EXAMPLE: The trustee of some income property failed to make proper roof repairs resulting in extensive water damage to the trust property. Evidence shows that there was sufficient warning of needed repairs. The trustee is liable for the loss in value of the property.

     EXAMPLE: The trustee sold some shares of stock to himself from the trust property at a price below fair market value. This is a clear breach of trust.

        (1) Discharged from liability if beneficiaries consent to breach before, during, or after breach

     b. To third parties

        (1) Liable under contract or tort law

            (a) Trustee has right of exoneration (trust property pays for liability) when in performance of trust duties

E. **Termination of Trust**

  1. At end of period stated in trust

  2. Revocation by settlor

     a. Can do so only if power of revocation is reserved in trust

(1) Exception: if settlor is sole beneficiary, may terminate trust when desires to

3. Achievement of trust purpose

EXAMPLE: X creates a trust in which his daughter, C, is to receive the income (as beneficiary) to help her become a CPA. She gets her CPA license. Since the purpose of the trust has been achieved, the trust terminates.

4. Failure of trust purpose

EXAMPLE: Same as example above, but unfortunately C dies before her goal is obtained. The trust terminates.

5. Agreement of all beneficiaries

   a. As long as trust purpose not defeated

      (1) Trust purpose may be defeated if settlor joins in to terminate trust

6. By merger

   a. If trustee and beneficiary are ever the same person, legal title and equitable title are merged, thus terminating the trust

   EXAMPLE: S creates a trust which designates A and B as co-trustees and names B as beneficiary. The trust also states that after six years B has the right to remove A as trustee. If B exercises this right, the trust would terminate because the sole trustee and sole beneficiary would be the same person and legal and equitable title would merge.

   EXAMPLE: S creates a trust in which A becomes trustee for A and B as beneficiaries. This trust would not be terminated by merger because B does not hold both legal and equitable title even though A does.

   b. If sole beneficiary is co-trustee this does not terminate trust because legal and equitable title do not merge

7. Settlor may revoke (or modify) trust only if terms of trust so state or settlor has reserved that right

   a. Reason: beneficiary has rights to beneficial interest in trust

F. **Allocation Between Principal and Income**

   1. Typically, interests are divided between an income beneficiary and a remainderman beneficiary

      a. Income beneficiary receives income from trust property (usually for specified time such as for his/her life)
      b. Remainderman gets trust property when trust terminates

      EXAMPLE: S puts income property into a trust stating that B will receive the income for life with the remainder going to R when B dies.

   2. It is duty of trustee to distribute income and principal in accordance with terms of trust

      a. In absence of specific trust provisions, allocation is governed by Uniform Principal and Income Act

          (1)   Provisions of this uniform act are applicable to both estates and trusts

   3. Principal includes

      a. Original trust property, including any income earned up to formation of the trust
      b. Proceeds and gains from sale of property, including insurance received on destruction of property
      c. New property purchased with principal or proceeds from principal
      d. Stock dividends and stock splits (cash dividends are income)
      e. Liquidating distributions
      f. Amortization of premium on property bought by trustee

   4. Payable from principal are expenses affecting principal, e.g.,

      a. Principal payment of loans
      b. Litigation over trust property
      c. Permanent (capital) improvements
      d. Costs incurred in purchase or sale of trust property
      e. Losses on sale or exchange of trust property

   5. Income includes profits from trust principal after trust begins, e.g.,

      a. Rent (including prepaid rent) less costs of collection
      b. Interest
      c. Cash dividends
      d. Royalties

   6. Payable from income are ordinary and operating expenses, e.g.,

      a. Ordinary administrative expenses
      b. Interest
      c. Insurance premiums
      d. Taxes
      e. Repairs and maintenance
      f. Depreciation

   7. Annuities are allocated between principal and income

   8. Trustee is liable to income beneficiary and remainderman for confusion or commingling of assets

      a. CPA is likely to be consulted to determine the amount of money to go to income beneficiary and amount to go to remainderman

G. Federal Estate Tax

   1. Federal estate tax is a tax imposed on the right to transfer property by death

   2. Further explanation of federal estate tax--see Module 44, Gift and Estate Taxes (GETX)

H. **Real Estate Investment Trusts (REITs)**

1. Real Estate Investment Trust Act

    a. Authorized by Congress in 1960
    b. Permits organization of unincorporated association to invest in real estate
    c. Association need not pay corporate income taxes

2. Provisions to be met

    a. 100 or more certificate holders during each year
    b. 5 or fewer holders must not own more than 50% of certificates
    c. Trustees must have centralized control
    d. Owners must have limited liability and free transferability of shares
    e. Major portion of income must be rents from real property or gains on sale of real property
    f. Must pay at least 90% of taxable income to certificate holders each year

3. Failure to meet provisions

    a. Trust taxed as if corporation

4. Tax treatment

    a. Ordinary income and capital gains pass through to investors
    b. Depreciation and other losses do not pass through

5. Trust must comply with applicable SEC securities registration laws

MINI OUTLINES

To assist candidates in testing their memory of essential legal principles, we have developed a set of **Mini Outlines.** These can be used after studying each module in depth and as a final review immediately prior to the CPA exam. **In no way are these outlines intended to be a complete coverage of the subject matter.** Candidates should use them to jog their minds by recalling as much information as possible and constructing legal examples to test their comprehension of the subject matter. Using the outlines in this fashion will serve as a barometer (or self-diagnostic tool) of your knowledge. Finally, because the outlines contain only the essential legal principles, **the lettering and numbering of the several levels in the Mini Outlines do not correspond to that found in module outlines.** For those points in the Mini Outlines which you have forgotten, use the index to find the page(s) where that principle is discussed. However, if you are confused about a number of the principles, go back to the module and work through it again.

CONTRACTS (7)*

A. Essential elements of contract**
  1. Offer and acceptance
     a. Offer
        (1) Newspaper advertisement
        (2) Termination of offer
           (a) Death
           (b) Insanity
           (c) Illegality
           (d) Destruction of subject matter
           (e) Rejection
           (f) Revocation
     b. Acceptance
        (1) Mirror image
        (2) Silence
        (3) Time of acceptance
           (a) Reasonable means rule
        (4) Offeree must intend to accept
        (5) Only offeree may accept
  2. Reality of consent
     a. Duress
     b. Fraud
     c. Undue influence
     d. Mistake
  3. Consideration
     a. Legal detriment
        (1) Preexisting legal duty
        (2) Illusory promise
     b. Bargained for element
     c. Past consideration
     d. Moral obligation
     e. Exceptions
        (1) Promissory estoppel
        (2) Promise to pay debt barred by Statute of Limitations

        (3) UCC - modification of contract for sale of goods
  4. Capacity
     a. Minors
        (1) Necessaries
        (2) Contracts for personal property
        (3) Contracts for real property
        (4) Ratification may only occur after reaching majority age
     b. Incompetent persons
     c. Intoxicated persons
  5. Legality
     a. Illegal if contract violates public policy
     b. Illegal if contract violates a statute
  6. Compliance with Statute of Frauds
     a. Promise to pay debt of another
        (1) Leading object exception
     b. An agreement made upon consideration of marriage
        (1) Exception - mutual promises of marriage
     c. Sale of any interest in land
        (1) Exception - part performance
     d. An agreement not capable of being performed within one year
     e. Sale of goods $500 or more
        (1) Exceptions
           (a) Written confirmation between merchants
           (b) Substantial start on specially manufactured goods
           (c) Admission in court
           (d) Part or full performance

*Numbers in parentheses refer to Modules.
**The mnemonic "COLLARS" may be useful in remembering the essential elements of a contract (Consideration, Offer, Legality, Legal capacity, Acceptance, Reality of consent, and Statute of Frauds).

f. The writing must be signed by the party to be charged
   (1) Can combine two documents together to create sufficient writing

B. Parol evidence rule
C. Assignment and delegation
  1. Assignee receives no better rights than the assignor had
D. Third-party beneficiary contracts
  1. Creditor beneficiary
  2. Donee beneficiary
  3. Incidental beneficiary
E. Discharge of contractual obligation
  1. By performance
    a. Doctrine of substantial performance
  2. Objective impossibility
    a. Subjective impossibility
  3. Frustration of purpose
  4. Novation
  5. Accord and satisfaction

6. Breach of contract by other party
  a. Anticipatory breach (repudiation)
7. Occurrence or nonoccurrence of contractual condition
  a. Condition precedent
  b. Condition subsequent
  c. Condition concurrent
8. Tender of performance
  a. Tender of payment of money merely stops interest running

F. Remedies
  1. Damages
    a. Compensatory
     (1) Must be foreseeable
     (2) Mitigation of damages
    b. Punitive
    c. Liquidated
  2. Specific performance
    a. Only available when item is unique
  3. Rescission and restitution

SALES (8)

A. Sale vs. bailment
B. Formation of sales contract
  1. Firm offer rule
  2. Battle of forms
  3. Modification of preexisting contract for the sale of goods
  4. Sale of goods $500 or more must be in writing
C. Identification of goods
  1. Buyer's special property interest
D. Passage of title
E. Risk of loss rules
  1. Party with title does not necessarily have risk of loss
  2. Parties can allocate through provision in contract
  3. Breaching party has risk of loss
  4. Carriage contracts
    a. FOB point of shipment
    b. FOB point of destination
  5. Merchant seller transfers risk when goods are delivered to buyer
  6. Nonmerchant seller transfers risk when seller tenders goods
  7. Concerning goods evidenced by negotiable document of title, risk transfers upon proper negotiation of document
  8. In sale on approval (goods purchased for use) risk transfers when buyer approves goods
  9. In sale or return (goods purchased for resale) risk transfers when buyer takes possession
F. Sale of goods by nonowner
  1. Thief
  2. Entrusting situation (deceptive bailment)

  3. Seller has voidable title
  4. Seller has void title
G. Product liability
  1. Negligence
  2. Warranty liability
    a. Warranty of title
     (1) Merchant seller warns against infringement of patent or trademark
    b. Express warranties
    c. Implied warranties
     (1) Merchantability--granted by merchant seller
      (a) Fit for ordinary purposes
      (b) Properly packaged
     (2) Fit for particular purpose
     (3) Disclaimers
      (a) Merchantability--can be oral or written but must contain some form of the word "merchantability"
      (b) Fit for particular purpose--must be in writing but no need for specific language
      (c) Goods sold "as is" or "with all faults" excludes both implied warranties but not the warranty of title
      (d) Offer of inspection by seller disclaims implied warranties concerning all patent defects

3. Strict liability
    a. Defense--product was not used for
        intended purpose
H. Seller's rights and remedies for breach
    of contract
    1. Seller's right to cure
    2. Seller's monetary damages
        a. Difference between market value
            at the time of tender and
            contract price plus incidental
            expenses
        b. Lost profits plus incidental
            expenses
        c. Full contract price
    3. Seller may refuse to deliver goods
        unless insolvent buyer is willing to
        pay cash
    4. Seller may stop goods in transit if
        buyer is insolvent
    5. Seller may demand return of goods
        received by insolvent buyer if done
        within 10 days of delivery

    6. Both buyer and seller have right to
        demand written assurances of per-
        formance
I. Buyer's rights and remedies for breach of
    contract
    1. Right to cover
    2. Right to reject nonconforming goods
        a. Merchant must follow seller's
            reasonable instructions concern-
            ing rejected goods
    3. Buyer may accept nonconforming goods
        a. Buyer may revoke acceptance when
            (1) Defect was hidden
            (2) Guaranteed defect was to be
                 cured and is not
    4. Recover damages
        a. Difference between market value
            at time buyer should have learned
            of breach and contract price plus
            incidental expenses plus conse-
            quential damages
J. Statute of Limitations is 4 years
    1. Parties may reduce to 1 year by
        agreement

COMMERCIAL PAPER (9)

A. Types
    1. Notes
    2. Drafts
        a. Checks--drawn on a bank and
            payable on demand
    3. Certificates of deposit
    4. Trade acceptances
B. Requirements of negotiability
    1. Written and signed
    2. Unconditional promise or order to pay
        sum certain
        a. "Subject to" vs. "in accordance
            with" another agreement
        b. Limiting payment to particular
            fund
        c. Cost of collection does not
            destroy sum certain
        d. Foreign currency okay
    3. Payment at a definite time or on de-
        mand
        a. Payable on death of someone not
            payable at definite time
    4. Words of negotiability
    5. Contain no other promise except a
        promise granting security for the
        instrument
C. Negotiation
    1. Bearer paper--delivery only
    2. Order paper--delivery and endorsement
    3. Endorsement
        a. Blank vs. special
        b. Qualified

            (1) Destroys secondary (contrac-
                 tual) liability and alters
                 warranty liability
        c. Restrictive
D. Holder in due course
    1. Must be a holder
    2. Gives executed value
        a. Discharge of prior debt
        b. Taking as security for existing
            debt
    3. Takes in good faith
    4. Takes through proper negotiation
        prior to knowledge that instrument is
        overdue or that a defense exists con-
        cerning it
E. Shelter provision
F. Defenses
    1. Real
        a. Forgery
            (1) Fictitious payee
            (2) Imposter
        b. Material alteration
        c. Fraud in the execution
        d. Minority
        e. Illegality
        f. Discharge in bankruptcy
        g. Extreme duress
    2. Personal
        a. Misdelivery
        b. Unauthorized completion of an
            incomplete instrument
        c. Fraud in the inducement
        d. Ordinary duress
        e. Undue influence

f. Breach of contract
g. Failure or nonpayment of
    consideration
G. Liability of parties
    1. Primary
        a. Acceptance by drawee
        b. Certification by bank
    2. Secondary
        a. Presentment
        b. Dishonor
        c. Notice of dishonor
    3. Warranties on transfer
    4. Warranties on presentment for payment
        or acceptance

H. Banks
    1. Relationship between banks and payee-
        holder
    2. Stop payment orders
I. Negotiable document of title
    1. Holder by due negotiation
        a. Value does not include discharge
            of preexisting debt
J. Investment securities
    1. Article 8 of UCC
    2. Bona fide purchase

SECURED TRANSACTIONS (10)

A. Types of collateral
    1. Tangible personal property
        a. Consumer goods
        b. Equipment
        c. Inventory
        d. Farm products
    2. Intangible personal property
        a. Accounts
    3. Documentary collateral
        a. Instruments
        b. Documents of title
    4. The use debtor makes of the property
        determines the type of collateral
B. Attachment of security interest
    1. Three requirements necessary
        a. There is a security agreement
            (1) When collateral possessed by
                 debtor, security agreement
                 must be in writing, signed
                 by debtor, and contain rea-
                 sonable description of col-
                 lateral
            (2) When possessed by secured
                 party, security agreement
                 may be oral
        b. Secured party gives value
        c. Debtor has rights in collateral
C. Perfection of security interest
    (3 methods)
    1. Filing a financing statement
        a. Valid for all collateral except
            money and negotiable instruments
            and securities
        b. Must be signed by debtor
    2. Possession
        a. The only method available
            concerning perfection in money
            and negotiable instruments
    3. By attachment only (automatic per-
        fection)
        a. Only available for purchase money
            security interest in consumer
            goods

        b. Not available against good faith
            purchaser for value who purchases
            from consumer for consumer use
D. Other issues
    1. After acquired property
    2. Field warehousing
        a. Perfection by possession
    3. Consignments
        a. True consignments
            (1) File a financing statement
        b. Other consignments
            (1) Look for secured transac-
                 tions
E. Priorities
    1. If both parties perfect by filing,
        then first to file has priority
    2. If both do not perfect by filing,
        then first to perfect has priority
    3. Perfected over unperfected
    4. If both unperfected, first to attach
    5. Purchase money security interest has
        priority over all other security
        interests if perfected within ten
        days of delivery except when
        collateral is inventory
    6. Purchaser in ordinary course of
        business defeats prior perfected
        security interest
F. Remedies upon default
    1. Secured party has right to take pos-
        session of collateral
        a. By self-help
        b. By judicial process
    2. Secured party may sell collateral
        a. Sale may be public or private
        b. Must be handled in commercially
            reasonable manner
        c. Debtor can require sale under
            some conditions
    3. If secured party retains collateral,
        entire obligation is discharged

F. Termination of relationship
 1. The power vs. the right to terminate
   a. Agency coupled with an interest
 2. By operation of law
   a. Death or insanity of either party
   b. Bankruptcy of principal
   c. Subject of agreement becomes illegal
 3. By acts of the parties
   a. Unilateral action by either agent or principal
   b. By mutual consent
   c. Expiration of agreement
   d. Principal must give notice of the termination
     (1) Notice by publication to all who knew of the relationship but had not dealt with agent
     (2) Actual notice to all who had previously dealt with agent

PARTNERSHIPS AND JOINT VENTURES (14)

A. General partnership
 1. Characteristics
   a. Normally not a separate entity from general partners
   b. Common law allows formation; no need for statutory authorization
   c. Easy to create
   d. Partners have unlimited liability
 2. Creation
   a. By agreement
   b. By estoppel
   c. Is presumed if parties are sharing net profits
 3. Partnership property
   a. Owned by partners as tenants in partnership
     (1) Surviving partners have right to specific partner-ship property
     (2) Heirs of deceased partner have no claim to specific partnership property
 4. Partner's partnership interest
   a. Is considered personal property
   b. Can be assigned without consent of other partners
     (1) Does not cause dissolution
     (2) Assignee is not a substitute partner
     (3) Assignee receives assigning partner's share of profits
 5. Partner's rights
   a. To share in profits
   b. To equal voice in management
     (1) Ordinary decisions by majority vote
     (2) Unanimous consent needed for certain acts
   c. To inspect books
   d. To return of capital contribution
   e. No right to salary
   f. No right to interest on capital contribution
 6. Liability to third parties
   a. Partners are agents of copartners
     (1) Partners are jointly and severally liable for torts committed by copartners within scope of partnership business
     (2) Partners are jointly liable for contracts entered into within copartners' authority
 7. Termination
   a. Dissolution occurs every time makeup of partnership changes
     (1) Admission of new partners
       (a) New partner only liable to extent of capital contribution concerning existing partnership debts
     (2) Withdrawal of partner
       (a) Withdrawing partner must give notice of withdrawal to terminate further liability
       (b) Priorities upon winding up
         (1) Creditors
         (2) To partners for loans
         (3) To partners for capital contribution
         (4) To partners for share of profits
   b. Marshalling of assets
B. Limited partnerships
 1. Need state statutory authority to create
 2. Must have at least one general partner
 3. Limited partner's liability is limited to capital contribution
 4. Limited partner cannot take part in management
 5. Limited partner's name may not be used in name of firm

6. Limited partner has right to an accounting
7. Limited partner has right to inspect books
8. Priorities on dissolution
C. Joint ventures
   1. Characteristics
      a. Association of two or more persons for single business undertaking
      b. Unlike partnership which is formed to conduct ongoing business

      c. Corporations can be joint venturers
   2. Each joint venturer has limited power to bind others
   3. Rights, duties, and liabilities
      a. Fiduciary duty
      b. Right to participate in management
      c. Unlimited liability
      d. Liability for negligence
      e. Tax treatment similar to partnership

CORPORATIONS (15)

A. Types
   1. De jure
   2. De facto
   3. Domestic
   4. Foreign
      a. Doing business outside state of incorporation requires permission from foreign state
B. Characteristics
   1. Separate entity
      a. Shareholders have limited liability
      b. Piercing corporate veil
   2. Must have state statutory authorization to create
   3. Duration may be perpetual
   4. Expensive to create
C. Creation
   1. Promoters
      a. Corporations must adopt promoter's contracts before being liable
      b. Promoter remains liable even after adoption of contracts by corporation
   2. Preincorporation stock subscriptions
      a. Subscribers unable to revoke for six months
   3. Articles of incorporation
D. Types of shares
   1. Treasury stock--may be sold at less than par value
   2. Watered stock
E. Directors
   1. Must act as a board
   2. Unable to vote by proxy
   3. No right to salary for services
   4. Individual director is not agent of corporation
   5. Declaration of dividends within directors' discretion
      a. Declaration of dividends is illegal if impairs capital
         (1) Payable out of surplus only

   6. Liable for negligence but not for bad business judgment
   7. Directors may contract with corporation
F. Officers
   1. Agents of corporation
   2. Indemnification of officers for expenses incurred in legal actions arising from officers' representation of corporation
G. Shareholders
   1. Right to transfer shares
   2. Preemptive rights
   3. Right to vote
      a. By proxy
      b. On amendments of articles of incorporation but not necessarily amendments of the bylaws
      c. For election of directors
      d. On fundamental changes (mergers, consolidations)
      e. Voting trusts
   4. Engage in derivative lawsuit
   5. Right to inspect corporate books
   6. Right to fair market value of shares from corporation if fundamental change is proposed
H. Corporate powers
   1. Corporation may become partner
   2. Corporation may lend money to employees but not to directors without shareholder approval
   3. Corporation may not act as accommodating endorser
   4. Corporation may only act as a surety if engaged in such business
   5. Ultra vires contracts
I. Fundamental changes
   1. Mergers
   2. Consolidations
   3. Must have majority shareholder approval
J. Dissolution

FEDERAL SECURITIES ACTS (16)

A. Blue Sky Laws - State Security Laws

B. 1933 Act
1. Registration statement and prospectus must be approved by SEC before offer to sell or sale of a security in interstate commerce
   a. Security includes:
      (1) Stocks
      (2) Bonds
      (3) Limited partnership interest
      (4) Investment contracts where profits are to come from the efforts of others
         (a) Shares in a citrus growing farm
         (b) Shares in a cattle raising ranch
   b. Applies primarily to original issues of securities
   c. Purpose of Act
      (1) To allow investor to make informed investment decision
      (2) Not to tell investor that security is a good buy
   d. Exempt securities
      (1) Banks
      (2) Railroads
      (3) Commercial paper - with a maturity of nine months or less
      (4) Charitable organizations
      (5) Insurance contracts
      (6) Intrastate issues
      (7) Small issuances up to 1,500,000
         (a) Notification of filing is required
   e. Exempt transactions
      (1) Stock split
      (2) Stock dividend
      (3) Sales by person other than issuer, underwriter, or dealer
         (a) Controlling person must register sale, e.g., director owning 10% of stock
      (4) Regulation D - private placement of stock
         (a) Purchasers must buy for investment purposes
   f. Registration statement
      (1) Signers, directors of issuer, underwriters, and experts are liable for omission or misrepresentation
         (a) Investor does not have to prove reliance on misrepresentation
         (b) CPA has burden of proving due diligence defense
   g. Statute of limitations - one year from the time the misrepresentation should have been discovered but never longer than three years from the sale of the security

C. 1934 Act
   1. Reporting requirements
   2. Proxy solicitations

ACCOUNTANT'S LEGAL LIABILITY (17)

A. Common law liability to clients
   1. Liability for breach of contract
      a. Based on accountant's failure to carry out contract terms
         (1) Accountant's duty to perform cannot be delegated
         (2) Client must not interfere with accountant's performance
         (3) If major breach, accountant not entitled to compensation
      b. Accountant not under duty to discover fraud or irregularities
         (1) Unless accountant's negligence prevents discovery
         (2) Unless engaged in special purpose defalcation audit and lack of reasonable professional care prevents discovery
   2. Liability for negligence
      a. Based on accountant's failure to exercise due professional care
         (1) Following GAAS and GAAP does not conclusively prove absence of negligence
      b. Client is contributorily negligent if client restricted accountant's investigation
         (1) May limit accountant's liability
   3. Liability for fraud
      a. Actual fraud
         (1) Intentional act or omission designed to deceive
      b. Constructive fraud
         (1) Gross negligence with reckless disregard for truth

B. Common law liability to third parties
   1. Accountant is liable to

a. Third-party primary beneficiary for ordinary negligence
b. Foreseen third party-courts are split
c. All third parties for fraud or gross negligence
2. Third party must prove
   a. Material misstatement or omission on financial statements
   b. Reliance on financial statements
   c. Damages resulted from such re-liance
C. Statutory liability to third parties--Securities Act of 1933
   1. Act requires filing of certified fi-nancial statements with SEC
   2. Any purchaser of security may sue accountant
   3. Purchaser establishes prima facie case if s/he proves
      a. Material misstatement or omission on financial statements
      b. Damages were incurred
         (1) Measured by difference between purchase price and market value at time of suit
      c. Need not prove reliance on finan-cial statements
   4. Accountant may avoid liability by proving
      a. Due diligence
         (1) After reasonable investiga-tion accountant had reason-able grounds to believe statements were true
      b. Purchaser knew financial state-ments were incorrect when s/he bought stock
      c. Loss caused by factor other than misstatement or omission on fi-nancial statements
D. Statutory liability to third parties--Securities Exchange Act of 1934

1. Accountant's liability arises from annual report containing certified financial statements
2. Any purchaser or seller of registered security may sue accountant
3. Third party must prove
   a. Material misstatement or omission on financial statements
   b. Accountant's intent to deceive (scienter)
   c. Reliance on financial statements
   d. Damages resulted from such re-liance
4. Accountant may avoid liability if s/he acted in good faith
E. Criminal liability
   1. Guilty of "willful and knowing" violation
      a. Federal statutes
         (1) Securities Act of 1933
         (2) Securities Exchange Act of 1934
         (3) Internal Revenue Code
      b. State statutes
F. Other potential liability of accountant from
   1. Discovery of subsequent events
G. Privileged communications
   1. Preserves confidentiality of communications between accountant and client
   2. Does not exist at common law
      a. Must be created by statute
   3. Privilege protects accountant from being required to testify in court
H. Working papers
   1. Owned by accountant
   2. Must be kept confidential
   3. Must relinquish on an enforceable subpoena
I. Preparation of income tax returns
   1. Federal law applies to all compensated preparers

REGULATION OF EMPLOYMENT (18)

A. Federal Social Security Act
   1. Provides financing for several social insurance programs
      a. Old-age, survivor's, and dis-ability coverage
      b. Hospital insurance coverage (Medicare)
      c. Unemployment insurance coverage
   2. Coverage under the Act is mandatory
      a. Must be an employee
      b. Compensation received must be wages
   3. Federal Insurance Contributions Act
      a. Imposes social security tax on wages

      b. Imposes an equal tax rate on both employee and employer
   4. Self-Employment Contributions Act
      a. Imposes social security tax on self-employment income
      b. A higher tax rate is imposed than under FICA
   5. Unemployment insurance
      a. Employer must pay both federal and state unemployment tax
      b. Employer entitled to credit against federal tax for state tax paid

6. Benefits under the Act
   a. Availability depends upon attainment of insured status
      (1) Determined by "quarters of coverage" obtained
   b. Amount depends upon
      (1) Average monthly earnings
      (2) Relationship of beneficiary to employee
7. Income tax considerations
   a. Benefits received are tax-free
      (1) Excludable from gross income
   b. Employee's portion of social security tax is nondeductible from gross income
   c. Employer's portion of social security tax is deductible from gross income

B. Workers' Compensation Acts
   1. Employer liable for injuries sustained by employee which arise in the course of employment
   2. Employer assumes liability in exchange for employee's forfeiture of right to sue employer for damages
   3. Removes employer's common law defenses
      a. Assumption of risk
      b. Fellow servant doctrine
      c. Contributory negligence
   4. Employee is entitled to benefits without regard to fault
      a. Employee's negligence or gross negligence does not bar recovery

PROPERTY (19)

A. Fixtures
   1. Trade fixtures
B. Present interest in real property
   1. Fee simple
   2. Life estate
C. Future interest
   1. Remainder
   2. Reversion
D. Concurrent ownership interest
   1. Joint tenancy--right of survivorship
   2. Tenancy in common--deceased tenant's share passes by his/her estate
   3. Tenancy by the entirety
E. Sale of land
   1. Contract
      a. Must be in writing
      b. Buyer is entitled to marketable title
      c. Buyer has risk of loss before deed is transferred
      d. Does not transfer title to buyer
      e. Specific performance is possible remedy for breach
   2. Deeds
      a. Warranty--make various guarantees, e.g., title, quiet enjoyment, etc.
      b. Bargain and sale
      c. Quitclaim
      d. Must be delivered before title passes to buyer
      e. Recording protects buyer against subsequent good faith purchasers
         (1) Notice type recording statute
         (2) Race-notice type recording statute
   3. Mortgages
      a. Must be in writing

      b. Recording protects mortgagee against subsequent purchasers
      c. Mortgagee's foreclosure rights upon default
      d. Equity of redemption
      e. Buyer who "assumes" mortgage has personal liability
      f. Buyer who purchases "subject to" mortgage has no personal liability
   4. Deeds of trust
      a. Like mortgages, but a judicial proceeding can be avoided upon default
      b. No redemption by mortgagor
   5. Land installment contract sales
      a. Allows seller to keep money paid and property upon default unless inequitable
F. Title Insurance
   1. Insures against loss due to defect of good title
   2. Title insurance company liable for damages due to title defects
G. Adverse possession
   1. Requirements
      a. Open
      b. Notorious
      c. Hostile
      d. Actual
      e. Continuous
H. Lessor--lessee
   1. Lease may be oral if less than one year
   2. Various types of leaseholds, e.g., period to period, lease for years
   3. Lessor's rights and duties
   4. Lessee's right to assign sublease

INSURANCE (20)

A. Insurance contract
1. Offer and acceptance
2. Representations
   a. Statements of fact not included as part of policy
   b. Only affect policy when material misrepresentation occurs
3. Warranties
   a. Statements of fact included in the policy
   b. Even immaterial breaches of warranty release insurer from liability
4. Statute of Frauds does not require writing
B. Property insurance
1. Insurable interest
   a. Must be present at time of loss
   b. Following have insurable interest in property:
      (1) Owners
      (2) Partners
      (3) Secured creditors
      (4) Lessees
      (5) Mortgagees
      (6) Bailees
      (7) Identification of goods gives buyer insurable interest
2. Valued or unvalued policy
3. Can insure against
   a. Own negligence
   b. Other party's negligence
   c. Other party's intentional acts
   d. But not against own intentional acts
   e. Hostile fires
   f. But not friendly fires
4. Coinsurance clause
   a. Know--usually tested
   b. Does not apply when there is total destruction of property
5. Pro rata clause
6. Loss payable clause
7. Insurer's right of subrogation

TRUSTS AND ESTATES (21)

A. Administration of an estate
1. Testate--will is present
2. Intestate--property passes by intestate succession statutes
3. Executor and administrator
   a. Right to compensation
   b. Duties and liabilities
4. Spouse's rights under dower and statutory share
5. Creditors' rights concerning decedent's estate
6. Tax considerations--particularly marital deduction
B. Trust
1. Creation
   a. By implication
      (1) Resulting trust
      (2) Constructive trust
   b. By express intent
2. Parties
   a. Trustee
      (1) Occupies fiduciary relationship
      (2) Has legal title to property
      (3) Duties and liabilities
         (a) Reasonable prudent investor standard applied to performance of the trustee
   b. Beneficiary--has beneficial title
      (1) Income
      (2) Principal
3. Types of trust
   a. Inter vivos
   b. Testamentary
   c. Charitable
   d. Constructive trust
4. Allocation of expenses and receipts to income and principal beneficiaries--very important--know
5. Tax considerations
C. Real Estate Investment Trusts
1. Must comply with SEC securities registration laws
2. Tax considerations

CHAPTER SEVEN
PREPARING FOR ACCOUNTING THEORY AND PRACTICE

This chapter is very brief because Chapters 8 through 11 discuss topics common to and tested on both practice and theory.

Chapter 8   Financial Accounting
Chapter 9   Cost Accounting
Chapter 10 Governmental and Nonprofit Accounting
Chapter 11 Taxes (tested only on practice)

Accounting Practice vs. Accounting Theory

Accounting practice tests application of accounting knowledge in a computational sense, i.e., problem solving. Also required is a knowledge of GAAP including all of the authoritative pronouncements, and industry practices where authoritative pronouncements do not exist. Most of the practice problems require problem solutions; some of the multiple choice questions only require specification of an accounting principle.

Accounting theory includes explanation and conceptual justification of accounting practices including GAAP; however, some theory multiple choice and essay questions require only regurgitation of authoritative pronouncements.

Condition Candidates

If you are preparing for either Accounting Practice or Accounting Theory only, you can still use this book effectively. The topical nature of the material tested in accounting practice does not significantly differ from that tested in accounting theory (with the exception of income taxes). It is the nature of the questions that differs, i.e., problematic vs. conceptual. We believe that in order to assure yourself of success on the remaining section of the exam you must understand both the "why" (conceptual justification) and the "how" (problem solving) of the problems. The table on the next page illustrates the difference in emphasis to be followed in your preparation program.

Examination in Accounting Practice	Examination in Accounting Theory
• Work multiple choice questions from both theory and practice	• Work multiple choice questions from both theory and practice; ignore income taxes and questions requiring extensive computations
• Work problems from prior accounting practice exams	• Work essay questions from prior theory exams
• Briefly review the pronouncements at the end of Chapter 8	• Study the outlines of the pronouncements at the end of Chapter 8; indepth knowledge is required

Preparing for Accounting Practice

First, become acquainted with the nature of the practice exam including the type and breadth of questions. Review the relative frequency of areas tested as compiled on the Content Specification outlines which follow.

Relatedly, you should evaluate your competency by working 10 to 20 multiple choice questions from each of the Modules 22-44 in this volume. This diagnostic routine will acquaint you with the specific nature of the questions tested on each topic as well as indicate the amount of study required per topic. You should work toward a 65% correct response rate as a minimum on each topic (65% is suggested as an across-the-board minimum because the multiple choice questions are graded on a curve and presumably you will do better than 65% on many topics). See discussion of self study programs and examination grading in Chapter 1 and Chapter 2.

Second, study the content of Chapters 8 through 11 emphasizing the mechanics of each topic such as inventory pricing, consolidations, equivalent units of productions, etc. Use simple examples, journal entries, and diagrams to put a handle on the basic concepts underlying each topic. You may have to refer to your textbooks, FASB pronouncements, etc. for topics with which you have had no previous exposure.

Third, work actual CPA practice problems from recent exams in this volume under examination conditions. Refer back to Chapter 3 and restudy the solutions approach for practice problems.

CPA practice problems are more involved and longer than typical problems found on undergraduate accounting examinations. CPA problems require special skills that are usually not developed in undergraduate accounting programs. You must develop these skills before the examination by applying the methodology in Chapter 3 on "live" CPA problems.

Fourth, work all of the objective questions in this volume including a review of the questions answered in your diagnostic self-evaluation.

Preparing for Accounting Theory

First, utilize the multiple choice questions in this Volume per the discussion of the first and fourth points just above, under "Preparing for Accounting Practice." Practice and theory multiple choice questions are very similar in scope and difficulty per topic. Candidates should be aware that the information in Modules 40-44, dealing with taxes, is not tested in accounting theory.

Second, emphasize the basic principles and objectives underlying accounting, e.g., revenue and expense recognition rules, etc. Study the introductory material in Chapters 8 through 11 which explains the basic concepts of each topic.

Third, read carefully the "Basic Accounting Theory" section located at the beginning of Module 22. This section integrates APB Statement 4 and SFACs 1-3 and 5-6. Note below how some chapters of Statement 4 have been replaced by an SFAC.

	APB Statement 4 Chapter	SFAC
1.	Purpose and Nature of Statement	SFAC 1
2.	Environment of Financial Acctg.	SFAC 1
3.	Objectives of Financial Acctg.	SFAC 1, SFAC 2
4.	Basic Elements of Financial Acctg.	SFAC 6
	Basic Features of Financial Acctg.	SFAC 6*
5.	GAAP - Pervasive Principles	SFAC 5
6.	GAAP - Broad Operating Principles	
7.	GAAP - Detailed Accounting Principles	
8.	Financial Accounting in the Future	

*Only partially supplants Statement 4

Fourth, compare and contrast the basic concepts of financial, accounting, cost accounting, etc., to the detailed rules for all of the specific topics. You want to understand the specific topics within the framework of the general models or rules, e.g., relating inventory valuation rules to the general theory of income recognition.

Fifth, practice the solutions approach for essay questions on recent CPA theory questions. Most CPA candidates have little experience with accounting essay questions; undergraduate accounting examinations generally consist of short problems. Be careful not to underemphasize writing out complete solutions to essay questions. Do not wait until the examination to develop answering techniques.

Sixth, recognize the value of the keyword outline (prepared in the exam margin). Practice it while answering old examination questions, and perhaps more importantly, orient your study habits to the keyword outline approach. As you review material, think of it in "outline" or "list" form. While you should use the keyword outline to organize your answer, your answer has to be written out for the grader. LISTS OF KEYWORDS, EVEN IN OUTLINE FORM, ARE NOT ACCEPTABLE TO THE AICPA.

Seventh, get yourself in good physical and mental condition. Theory, tested on Friday afternoon from 1:30 to 5:00, will follow 16 hours of practice, auditing, and law examination. Commit yourself to stay and to work until 5:00 p.m. It is very easy to get up and leave an hour early.

Summary of Accounting Practice and Accounting Theory Exam Coverage

The AICPA Content Specification Outline of the coverage of financial accounting in the Examinations in Accounting Practice and Accounting Theory including the authors' frequency analysis thereof (last nine exams), appears on the following pages. The outlines for other areas covered on the accounting practice and accounting theory exams have been placed in the chapters to which they apply.

AICPA percentage allocation of areas covered on Accounting Practice and Accounting Theory exams

		Practice	Theory
Ch. 8	Financial Accounting	60%	80%
Ch. 9	Cost-Managerial	10%	10%
Ch. 10	Governmental and Nonprofit	10%	10%
Ch. 11	Income Taxes	20%	n/a
	TOTAL	100%	100%

Immediately following the frequency analysis is a summary of accounting theory essay questions and accounting practice problems referenced to our study modules. The following symbols are used:

P = Practice I Exam Problem
Q = Practice II Exam Problem
T = Theory Exam Essay
* = Part of Essay/Problem

AICPA CONTENT SPECIFICATION OUTLINE/FREQUENCY ANALYSIS*
Financial Accounting

I. Presentation of Financial Statements or Worksheets

Practice

	M 85	N 85	M 86	N 86	M 87	N 87	M 88	N 88	M 89
A. Balance Sheet	–	[.5]	[.5]	–	[.5]	–	–	–	4
B. Income Statement	[.75]	[.5]	[1]	–	–	–	–	3	[.8]
C. Statement of Cash Flows	–	–	–	–	[1]	[.6]	7	–	7
D. Statement of Owners' Equity	–	[.5]	–	–	–	–	–	–	–
E. Consolidated Financial Statements or Worksheets	2	2	2	2 [1]	6	– [1]	8 [1]	5 [1]	4
Total Multiple Choice Questions	2	2	2	2	6	–	15	8	15
Total Problems	.75	1.5	1.5	1	1.5	1.6	1	1	.8
Actual Percentage**	8.5	16	16	11	18	16	17.5	14	15.5

(AICPA 15%)

Theory

No Comparable Theory Section

II. General Concepts, Principles, Terminology, Environment, and Other Professional Standards

Practice

No Comparable Practice Section

Theory

	M 85	N 85	M 86	N 86	M 87	N 87	M 88	N 88	M 89
A. Authority of Pronouncements (substantial authoritative support--GAAP)	–	–	–	–	–	–	–	–	–
B. Conceptual Framework	1	2	1	2	1	–	2	1	1
C. Basic Concepts and Accounting Principles	1 [.2]	–	–	–	–	1	–	–	–
D. Nature and Purpose of Basic Financial Statements	–								
E. Consolidated Financial Statements	–	– [.5]	–	1	–	–	1	–	
F. Historical Cost, Constant Dollar, Current Cost, and Other Accounting Concepts	1	1	1	1	1	–	1	–	–
Total Multiple Choice Questions	3	3	2	4	2	1	4	1	1
Total Essays	.58	.2	.5	–	–	–	–	–	–
Actual Percentage**	8.8	5	7	4	2	1	4	1	1

(AICPA 15%)

---

*Except where noted, the line items in the outline are the AICPA's; the frequencies, tabulations, and actual percentages are the authors'.

**The "actual percentage" is a measure of the relative coverage of the specific areas (i.e., I., II., etc.) on each Accounting Practice or Theory exam. This percentage includes both multiple choice questions and essays/problems based on the point allocation used by the AICPA (i.e., multiple choice are assigned ½ point each in Practice and 1 point each in Theory; essays/problems are 10 points each; note that the number of essays/problems for each topic is shown in brackets right below the multiple choice questions for that topic).

AICPA CONTENT SPECIFICATION OUTLINE/FREQUENCY ANALYSIS*
Financial Accounting

III. Measurement, Valuation, Realization, and Presentation of **Assets** in Conformity with GAAP

	P M85	P N85	P M86	P N86	P M87	P N87	P M88	P N88	P M89	T M85	T N85	T M86	T N86	T M87	T N87	T M88	T N88	T M89
A. Cash, Marketable Securities, and Investments																		
1. Cash	1	1	1	1	-	1	1	1	-	-	-	-	-	-	-	-	-	-
2. Marketable Equity Securities	1	1	1	-	1	1	2	-	-	1	1 [.25]	1	-	1	- [.33]	1	1	-
3. Other Securities	-	-	-	-	-	-	-	-	-	-	-	-	-	-	-	-	-	-
4. Investment in Bonds	1	1	1	-	-	1	-	2	-	-	-	2	-	2	-	-	2	-
5. Investment in Stocks	-	-	3	- [.5]	1	-	-	- [.1]	- [.5]	1	- [.25]	1	1	1	-	-	-	- [.8]
6. Sinking and Other Funds	-	-	-	-	-	1	-	1	-	-	-	-	-	-	-	-	1	-
B. Receivables and Accruals																		
1. Accounts and Notes Receivables	2	1	1	1	-	1 [.1]	-	1	-	- [.75]	1	-	- [.5]	-	- [.5]	-	- [.35]	1
2. Affiliated Company Receivables	-	-	-	-	-	-	-	-	-	-	-	-	-	-	-	-	-	-
3. Discounting of Notes	1	1	1	1	-	-	-	1	1	-	-	1	-	- [.5]	-	1	-	1
4. Installment Accounts	-	-	-	-	-	-	-	-	1	-	-	-	-	-	-	-	-	-
5. Interest and Other Accrued Income	-	-	-	-	-	- [.1]	-	-	-	-	-	-	-	1	-	-	-	-
6. Allowance for Doubtful Accounts	-	2	1	1	-	1	1	-	-	-	1	1	-	1	-	-	-	1
7. Lease Receivable --Lessor***	3	-	-	1	1	-	-	-	-	-	-	-	1	-	1	-	-	-
C. Inventories																		
1. Acquisition Costs	1	1	1	1	-	1	-	1	1	1	- [.2]	1	1	- [.33]	1	- [.25]	1	- [.25]
2. Costing Methods	2	-	2	-	2	-	1	1	-	1	-	1	1	- [.33]	1	- [.25]	2	-
3. Valuation Methods	-	2	-	2	-	2	1	-	1	1	- [.2]	1	1	- [.34]	1	- [.50]	1	- [.6]
D. Property, Plant, and Equipment Owned or Leased																		
1. Acquisition Costs	- [.33]	1	1	3	1	- [.5]	1	- [.6]	-	1	- [.25]	1	- [.375]	1	-	1	- [.25]	-
2. Capital Versus Revenue Expenditures	-	-	2	1	-	-	1	-	1	-	-	-	1	- [.25]	1	-	1	-
3. Depreciation, Amortization and Depletion	-	1	1	1	-	-	-	-	1	2	- [.375]	2	1	- [.125]	1	1	- [.50]	1
4. Leasehold Improvements	-	-	-	-	1	-	-	-	-	-	-	-	1	-	1 [.25]	-	1	-	1
5. Obsolescence and Write-Downs	-	-	1	-	-	-	1	-	1	-	-	-	-	-	-	-	-	-
6. Disposition	-	-	-	-	-	-	-	-	-	-	-	-	-	-	-	-	- [.25]	-
7. Capitalized Interest***	-	1	-	-	-	-	-	-	-	-	-	-	1	-	-	-	-	-
E. Capitalized Leased Assets--Lessee*																		
1. Acquisitions Costs	1	-	1	-	-	-	-	-	1	-	-	1	-	-	-	- [.5]	-	-
2. Amortization	-	-	-	-	-	-	-	-	-	-	-	1	-	-	-	-	-	-
F. Intangibles and Other Assets																		
1. Goodwill	-	-	-	-	- [.5]	-	-	1	1	-	-	-	1	-	-	1	-	1
2. Patents	1	-	-	-	1	-	1	1	1	-	-	1	-	-	1	-	-	-
3. Other Intangibles	-	-	1	-	1	-	[.1]	1	-	-	1	-	-	-	-	-	1	-
4. Prepaid Expenses	1	-	1	1	-	-	[.1]	-	-	-	1	-	-	1	-	-	-	-
5. Deferrred Income Taxes	-	-	1	-	-	-	-	-	-	-	-	-	-	-	-	-	-	-
6. Prepaid Pension Costs	-	1	-	-	-	1	-	1	-	-	-	-	-	-	-	-	-	-
Coinsurance (now covered only in Business Law Exam)	1	-	1	-	-	-	-	-	-	-	-	-	-	-	-	-	-	-
Total Multiple Choice Questions	15	15	21	14	9	10	11	12	10	8	5	17	8	8	8	6	8	6
Total Problems/Essays	.33	-	-	.5	.5	.5	.5	.6	.5	.75	1.53	-	.5	2	1.33	1.5	1.35	1.65
Actual Percentage**	10.8	7.5	10.5	12	9.5	10	10.5	12	10	15.5	20	17	13	28	21	21	21.5	22.5
	(AICPA 10%)									(AICPA 15%)								

***These line items in the outline have been added by the authors.

AICPA CONTENT SPECIFICATION OUTLINE/FREQUENCY ANALYSIS*
Financial Accounting

IV. Valuation, Recognition, and Presentation of **Liabilities** in Conformity with GAAP

	Practice M85	N85	M86	N86	M87	N87	M88	N88	M89	Theory M85	N85	M86	N86	M87	N87	M88	N88	M89
A. Payables and Accruals																		
1. Accounts Payable	-	-	1	-	-	1	1	1	1	-	-	-	1	-	-	-	-	-
2. Notes Payable	1	2	-	1	1	1	[.25]	[.15]	1	-	-	-	-	-	-	-	-	-
3. Accrued Employees' Costs	-	1	1	1	1	2	-	-	1	1	-	-	-	-	-	-	-	1
4. Interest and Other Accrued Expenses	1	1	2	1	-	1	-	2	1	1	-	-	-	1	-	1	-	-
5. Unfunded Accrued Pension Expense	-	-	-	-	1	-	1	-	1	-	-	-	-	-	-	-	-	-
6. Taxes Payable	-	-	1	1	-	1	-	-	1	-	-	-	-	1	-	-	1	-
7. Deposits and Escrows	1	-	1	1	-	-	-	-	1	-	-	1	-	-	-	-	-	-
B. Deferred Revenues																		
1. Unperformed Service Contracts	1	1	-	1	1	1	-	-	-	-	-	-	-	-	-	-	-	-
2. Subscriptions or Tickets Outstanding	1	1	-	2	2	1	2	1	1	-	1	-	-	1	-	1	-	-
3. Installment Sales	-	-	1	1	-	1	-	-	1	-	-	-	-	-	-	-	-	-
4. Sale and Leaseback	1	1	-	1	-	1	1	1	-	-	-	-	-	-	1	-	-	-
C. Deferred Income Tax Liabilities																		
1. Equity Method of Accounting for Investments	1	-	1	1	-	-	1	-	1	-	-	-	-	-	-	-	-	-
2. Depreciation of Plant Assets	-	-	-	-	1	1	-	[.15]	1 [.2]	[.17]	1	1	1	-	-	1	1	-
3. Long-Term Construction Contracts	-	-	1	-	1	-	1	-	1	-	-	-	-	-	-	-	-	-
4. Other Temporary Differences	1	-	1	1	-	-	-	-	-	-	-	1	1	1	-	1	-	1
D. Capitalized Lease Liability --Lessee ***																		
1. Measurement at Present Value	-	1	2	2	2	1	1	2	1	[.5]	2	-	-	1 [1]	1	-	1 [.5]	[.8]
2. Amortization	-	1	-	-	-	1	1	[.15]	-	-	-	1	1	-	1	-	-	[.2]
E. Bonds Payable																		
1. Issue of Bonds	-	1	2	1	1	1	1 [.15]	-	1	[.5] [.25]	1	[.5]	1	1	-	-	[.17]	[.5]
2. Issue Costs	1	-	-	-	-	1	-	-	-	[.25]	-	-	-	[.17]	-	-	1	-
3. Amortization of Discount or Premium	-	-	1	2	1	-	[.25]	-	1	[.25]	[.25]	-	1	1	-	1	-	-
4. Types of Bonds	1	-	1	-	1	-	1	1	1	-	-	-	-	-	-	-	-	-
5. Conversion of Bonds	-	-	1	-	1	1	1	1	1	-	1	-	1	-	[.33]	1	-	-
6. Detachable Stock Warrants	-	-	-	-	1	-	1	1	-	-	1 [.25]	-	-	1	-	1	-	[.25]
7. Retirement of Bonds	(See VI.D.3)									(See VI.D.3)								
F. Contingent Liabilities and Commitments	(See VII.F.)									(See VIII.G.)								
Total Multiple Choice Questions	10	10	17	17	15	16	12	9	16	2	8	4	6	9	2	7	4	2
Total Problems/Essays	-	-	-	-	-	-	.5	.6	.2	1.84	-	1	1	-	.67	.5	-	1.75
Actual Percentage**	5	5	8.5	8.5	7.5	8	11	10.5	15	20.4	8	14	16	9	9	12	4	19.5

(AICPA 10%; was 5% prior to 5/86)   (AICPA 10%)

AICPA CONTENT SPECIFICATION OUTLINE/FREQUENCY ANALYSIS*
Financial Accounting

V. Ownership Structure, Presentation, and Valuation of <u>Equity Accounts</u> in Conformity with GAAP

	Practice									Theory								
	M 85	N 85	M 86	N 86	M 87	N 87	M 88	N 88	M 89	M 85	N 85	M 86	N 86	M 87	N 87	M 88	N 88	M 89
A. Preferred and Common Stock																		
1. Issued	–	–	–	1	–	–	–	–	–	–	–	–	1	–	–	–	2	–
2. Outstanding	–	–	–	–	–	–	–	–	–	–	–	–	–	–	–	–	–	1
3. Retirement of Stock	–	–	–	1	–	–	1	–	–	–	–	–	–	–	–	–	–	–
4. Book Value Per Share	2	–	–	1	–	–	–	–	–	–	–	–	–	–	–	–	–	–
5. Classification	–	–	–	–	–	–	–	–	2	–	–	–	–	–	–	–	–	–
B. Additional Paid-In Capital	1	2	–	1	–	–	–	2	–	–	–	1	–	–	–	1	–	–
C. Retained Earnings and Dividends [.5]																		
1. Prior Period Adjustments	1	–	–	–	1	–	–	–	–	–	–	–	1	–	–	–	–	–
2. Net Income	–	–	–	–	–	–	–	–	–	–	–	–	–	–	–	–	–	–
3. Cash Dividends	–	1	–	–	–	–	–	–	–	–	–	–	–	–	1	–	–	1
4. Property Dividends [.33]	1	–	–	1	–	–	–	1	–	–	–	1	–	1	–	1	–	–
5. Liquidating Dividends	–	–	–	–	–	–	1	–	–	–	–	–	–	–	–	1	–	–
6. Stock Dividends and Splits [.16]	1	–	–	1	–	1	–	–	2	1	–	1	1	1	–	–	1	–
7. Appropriations of Retained Earnings [.33]	–	1	–	–	–	–	–	–	–	–	–	–	–	–	–	–	–	–
D. Treasury Stock and Other Contra Accounts																		
1. Cost Method [.17] / [.34]	1	–	–	1	–	–	–	1	2	2	–	1	1	–	1	–	1	–
2. Par Value Method	–	–	–	–	–	–	–	–	–	–	–	–	–	–	1	–	1	1
3. Restrictions on Acquisitions of Treasury Stock	–	–	–	–	–	–	–	–	–	–	–	–	–	–	–	–	–	–
4. Other Contra Accounts [.17]	–	–	–	–	–	–	–	–	–	–	–	–	–	–	–	–	–	–
E. Stock Options, Warrants, and Rights	–	–	–	–	–	–	–	1	2	1	–	–	1	1	2	1	1	1
F. Reorganization and Change in Entity																		
1. Incorporation of an Unincorporated Enterprise	1	–	–	–	–	–	–	–	–	–	–	–	–	–	–	–	–	–
2. Business Combinations	(See I.E.)									(See VIII.E.)								
3. Bankruptcy	–	1	–	–	–	–	1	–	1	–	–	–	–	–	–	–	–	–
G. Partnerships																		
1. Formation	1	–	–	–	–	–	–	–	1	–	–	1	–	–	–	1	–	–
2. Admission, Retirements, and Dissolution [.40]	1	2	–	1	1	–	–	2	1	1	–	–	–	1	–	–	1	–
3. Profit or Loss Distribution and Other Special Allocations	–	–	–	–	1	–	–	–	1	–	–	–	–	–	1	–	–	1
Areas No Longer Tested	–	–	–	–	–	–	–	–	–	–	–	–	–	–	–	–	–	–
Total Multiple Choice Questions	10	7	–	8	3	1	3	7	12	5	–	5	5	6	5	5	6	5
Total Problems/Essays	–	–	.5	–	–	.4	.5	–	–	–	1	–	–	–	–	–	–	–
Actual Percentage**	5	3.5	5	4	1.5	4.5	6.5	3.5	6	5	10	5	5	6	5	5	6	5
	(AICPA 5%)									(AICPA 5%)								

AICPA CONTENT SPECIFICATION OUTLINE/FREQUENCY ANALYSIS*
Financial Accounting

VI. Measurement and Presentation of Income and Expense Items, Their Relationship to Matching and Periodicity, and Their Relationship to GAAP

	Practice									Theory									
	M 85	N 85	M 86	N 86	M 87	N 87	M 88	N 88	M 89	M 85	N 85	M 86	N 86	M 87	N 87	M 88	N 88	M 89
A. Revenues and Gains																		
1. Cash Versus Accrual Basis	(See I.B.)	-	1	1	2	-	1	1	1	-	-	-	-	-	-	-	-	-
2. At Time of Sale	-	1	1	-	1	1	-	2	1	-	-	-	-	-	-	-	[.40]	
3. At Completion of Production	-	-	-	-	2	-	-	-	-	-	-	-	-	-	-	1	-	1
4. During Production (percentage-of-completion)	1	1	1	1	1	1	-	-	-	2	1	-	1	1	1	-	1	-
												[1]						
5. Installment Method or Cost Recovery	1	1	1	1	-	1	-	1	-	-	-	-	-	-	-	-	1	1
6. Equity in Earnings of Investee	-	-	1	-	-	-	-	1	-	-	-	-	-	-	-	-	1	1
				[.25]			[.1]		[.2]		[.25]				[.33]			
7. Interest	1	1	1	1	2	1	-	1	1	-	-	-	-	-	-	1	-	-
							[.2]	[.4]					[.125]				[.25]	
8. Dividends	1	1	-	-	1	1	-	1	-	-	-	-	1	-	-	-	1	-
				[.25]					[.1]						[.17]			
9. Royalties	1	1	-	1	1	1	-	1	1	-	-	-	-	-	-	-	1	1
10. Rent	-	1	1	1	1	1	-	-	1	-	-	-	-	-	-	-	1	-
11. Disposal of Assets and Liquidation of Liabilities	1	1	-	1	4	-	-	-	-	-	-	-	-	-	-	-	-	-
	[.33]																	
12. Foreign Exchange	-	-	-	-	-	-	-	-	-	-	-	-	-	-	-	-	-	-
13. Unusual Gains	-	-	-	-	-	1	-	1	-	-	-	-	-	1	1	-	-	1
									[.1]						[.17]			
B. Expenses and Losses																		
1. Cost of Sales	1	1	1	1	-	1	1	1	-	-	-	-	-	-	-	-	-	-
											[.4]							
2. General and Administrative	1	-	1	1	-	-	-	-	-	-	-	-	-	-	-	-	-	-
3. Selling	1	-	-	-	-	-	1	-	-	-	-	-	-	-	-	-	-	-
4. Financial (interest)	1	2	1	1	1	1	-	-	1	-	-	-	-	1	-	-	-	-
		[.125]								[.25]								[.25]
5. Depreciation, Amortization, and Depletion	-	1	3	2	2	1	-	-	-	1	-	-	1	-	-	1	-	1
	[.33]	[.25]			[.25]	[.2]	[.4]				[.375]							
6. Research and Development	1	-	1	1	1	1	-	-	1	-	1	-	-	-	1	-	1	-
7. Foreign Exchange		(See VII.M.)											(See VIII.N.)					
8. Uncollectible Accounts	1	1	1	1	1	1	1	-	-	-	-	-	-	-	-	-	-	-
													[.375]					
9. Royalties	1	-	1	1	-	-	-	-	-	-	-	-	-	-	-	-	-	-
10. Rent	1	-	1	1	-	-	1	-	1	-	-	-	-	-	-	-	-	-
11. Compensation	1	2	1	3	2	-	-	-	1	1	-	-	-	-	1	-	-	-
													[1]					
12. Disposal of Assets and Liquidation of Liabilities	-	-	-	-	1	-	-	-	-	-	-	-	-	-	-	-	-	-
13. Unusual Losses	-	2	1	-	3	1	-	-	-	-	-	-	-	-	-	-	-	-
						[.25]			[.1]	[.25]	[.25]							[.35]
14. Pension Costs***	1	-	-	-	-	-	1	1	1	-	2	-	-	2	1	-	1	2
																[1]		
C. Provision for Income Tax																		
1. Current	-	2	2	1	1	1	1	-	-	-	-	-	-	-	-	-	-	-
2. Deferred	-	-	1	1	1	2	-	-	1	-	1	1	1	1	1	-	1	-
	[.25]	[.125]								[.33]								
D. Recurring Versus Nonrecurring Transactions and Events																		
1. Discontinued Operations	2	-	1	-	1	1	-	1	-	1	-	-	1	-	-	-	1	-
														[.33]				
2. Extraordinary Items	-	1	-	2	-	1	-	1		-	1	-	-	-	-	1	-	1
														[.67]				
3. Debt Extinguishment or Restructure***	-	1	1	2	3	1	-	-	1	-	1	-	-	-	-	-	1	-
															[.33]			
E. Accounting Changes	2	2	2	1	2	1	-	-	1	-	-	-	-	-	-	-	1	1
												[.5]						
F. Earnings Per Share	1	2	2	2	2	2	2	2	-	1	1	1	1	1	1	1	1	1
Total Multiple Choice Questions	21	25	28	28	36	23	7	15	13	6	8	2	6	7	7	5	13	11
Total Problems/Essays	.5	.5	-	.5	-	.5	.5	.8	.5	.83	1.28	1.5	1.5	1	1	1	.65	.6
Actual Percentage**	19.7	17.5	14	19	18	16.5	8.5	15.5	11.5	14.3	21	17	21	17	17	15	19.5	17
	(AICPA 15%)									(AICPA 20%)								

AICPA CONTENT SPECIFICATION OUTLINE/FREQUENCY ANALYSIS*
Financial Accounting

VII. Other Financial Topics

	Practice									Theory								
	M 85	N 85	M 86	N 86	M 87	N 87	M 88	N 88	M 89	M 85	N 85	M 86	N 86	M 87	N 87	M 88	N 88	M 89
A. Disclosures in Notes to the Financial Statements	-	2	-	-	-	-	-	1	-									
B. Accounting Policies	-	-	-	-	-	-	-	-	-									
C. Nonmonetary Transactions	1	1	1	2	-	-	1	-	1									
D. Interim Financial Statements	2	1	1	1	1	-	1	1	1									
E. Historical Cost, Constant Dollar Accounting, and Current Cost	1	1	2	1	1	2	1	1	1									
F. Gain/Loss Contingencies	2	-	1	-	2	2	2	1	2			No Comparable						
G. Segments and Lines of Business	1	1	1	1	1	1	-	-	2			Theory Section						
H. Employee Benefits	-	-	-	-	-	2	-	-	-									
I. Analysis of Financial Statements	2	2	3	3	3	2	2	2	4									
J. Development Stage Enterprises	-	-	-	-	-	-	2	1	-									
K. Personal Financial Statements	1	2	1	1	1	-	1	1	1									
L. Combined Financial Statements	-	-	1	-	1	-	1	1	-									
M. Translation of Foreign Statements***	2	1	1	2	1	1	1	-	2									
Total Multiple Choice Questions	12	11	12	11	11	10	12	9	14									
Total Problems	-	-	-	-	-	-	-	-	-									
Actual Percentage **	6	5.5	6	5.5	5.5	5	6	4.5	7									

(AICPA 5%)

VIII. Other Financial Topics

	Practice									Theory								
	M 85	N 85	M 86	N 86	M 87	N 87	M 88	N 88	M 89	M 85	N 85	M 86	N 86	M 87	N 87	M 88	N 88	M 89
A. Statement of Cash Flows										2	2	2	2	2	2	2	2	2
B. Accounting Policies										-	1	1	-	2	1	1	-	1
C. Accounting Changes										1	2	-	1	1	2	-	-	1
											[.5]				[1]			
D. Nonmonetary Transactions										-	-	1	1	-	1	1	1	-
E. Business Combinations										1	1	-	1	-	2	2	-	2
												[.5]		[1]			[1]	
F. Interim Financial Statements										1	-	1	1	1	1	1	1	1
G. Gain/Loss Contingencies			No Comparable							1	1	1	-	1	1	1	-	2
			Practice Section									[1]		[1]		[1]		
H. Segments and Lines of Business										1	1	1	1	-	2	1	-	1
I. Employee Benefits										1	-	-	1	-	-	-	1	-
J. Analysis of Financial Statements										1	1	1	1	1	1	1	1	1
K. Development Stage Enterprises										-	1	1	-	1	-	1	-	1
L. Personal Financial Statements										1	-	-	1	-	1	1	1	1
M. Combined Financial Statements										-	-	-	-	-	1	-	-	1
N. Translation of Foreign Statements***										1	1	1	1	1	1	1	1	1
Total Multiple Choice Questions										11	11	10	11	8	17	13	8	15
Total Essays										-	-	1	1	1	1	1	2	-
Actual Percentage **										11	11	20	21	18	27	23	28	15

(AICPA 15%; was 10% prior to 5/86)

(P) - Practice I Exam
(Q) - Practice II Exam
(T) - Theory Exam
* - Part of one problem

FINANCIAL ACCOUNTING
Problem and Essay Summary

Date	Mod 22 Cash/Accrual	Mod 22 Error Correction	Mod 22 Accounting Changes/ Changes in estimates	Mod 22 Balance Sheet	Mod 22 Income Statement	Mod 22 Extraordinary Items/ Discontinued Operations
5/89					Preparation of income statement and book to tax reconciliation (P)	
11/88						
5/88			Accounting for changes in principle, estimate, rationale (T)		Preparation of income statement (Q)	
11/87						
5/87	(See Mod 22 on this line)			Recognition of implicit goodwill, adjust accounts to accrual basis, prepare balance sheet (P)		Reporting discontinued operations and extraordinary items (T)
11/86					Preparation of income statement (P)	
5/86		Worksheet to correct Balance Sheet, Income Statement (P)	Identify/report all types of changes (T)			
11/85						
5/85					Preparation of income statement and book to tax reconciliation (P)	

FINANCIAL ACCOUNTING
Problem and Essay Summary

(P) - Practice I Exam
(Q) - Practice II Exam
(T) - Theory Exam
* - Part of one problem

Date	Mod 23 Inventory	Mod 23 Long-term Contracts	Mod 24 Fixed Assets	Mod 24 Noncurrent Assets	Mod 25 Current/Noncurrent Receivables
5/89	Criteria for acquisition costs, LCM				
11/88			Cost capitalization, depreciation, disposal for fixed assets (T) Schedule of changes in plant assets, depreciation (P)		Net method of recording receivables, trade discounts, factoring of receivables (T)
5/88	Warehousing costs, LCM, retail method (T)			Schedule of changes in noncurrent assets, and related revenues and expenses (P)	
11/87			Reporting of fixed assets on income statement and balance sheet (P)		Assignment, discounting of notes receivable (T)
5/87	Insurance costs, acquisition costs, LCM, LIFO effects (T)		Costs to capitalize, depreciation policy maintenance, additions, leasehold improvements (T)		
11/86		Theory of percentage of completion method, income recognition, progress billings (T)			Direct write off vs. allowance method, reporting interest bearing notes
5/86					
11/85	Inventory costs, dollar value LIFO, consigned goods, LCM (T)		Costs to capitalize, theory of depreciation (T)	Intangible assets, long-term bonds, deferred tax (P)	
5/85			Reporting of fixed assets on income statement, balance sheet (P)		Noninterest bearing notes, assignment, factoring (T)

FINANCIAL ACCOUNTING
Problem and Essay Summary

(P) - Practice I Exam
(Q) - Practice II Exam
(T) - Theory Exam
* - Part of one problem

Date	Mod 25 & 26 Current/Noncurrent Liabilities	Mod 25 Loss Contingencies	Mod 26 Bonds	Mod 26 Pensions	Mod 26 Leases	Mod 27 Deferred Tax
5/89			Issue of bonds, nonconvertible bonds with detachable warrants		Theory of capital leases, classification of leases, acctg. for capital leases	
11/88	Long-term liabilities section of balance sheet, schedule of interest expense (Q)	Product defects promotional obligations (T)				
5/88	Long-term liabilities* section of balance sheet, compute interest expense (P)			Problems of defined benefit pensions, determine service and interest cost, actual return on plan assets (T)	Theory of capital leases, sale and leaseback, questions when lessee has a capital lease (T)	
11/87		Safety hazard warranties, product defects (T)	Issue of bonds, early extinguishment, conversion of bonds (T)			
5/87						
11/86		Warranties, expropriation, lawsuit (T)			Classify leases, reporting for capital and operating leases (T)	
5/86			Issue price, reporting on balance sheet & income statement, detachable warrants (T)			
11/85						
5/85			Selling price, reporting on balance sheet, income statement, serial bonds (T)		Theory for capital leases, reporting for capital leases (T)	Theory, depreciation, rent, timing differences, reporting (T)

FINANCIAL ACCOUNTING
Problem and Essay Summary

(P) - Practice I Exam
(Q) - Practice II Exam
(T) - Theory Exam
*   - Part of one problem

Date	Mod 28 Stockholders' Equity	Mod 29 Investments and Marketable Securities	Mod 30 Statement of Cash Flows	Mod 31 Business Combinations
5/89		Current/noncurrent portfolios, equity method (P)		
11/88		Current/noncurrent portfolios (T)		Pooling method balance sheet consolidation, statement of retained earnings (P); Rationales for purchase and pooling business combinations (T)
5/88	Preparation of stockholders' equity section (P)*			
11/87		Current portfolio, equity method (T)	Cash basis statement of changes; schedule of changes in partners' capital accounts (P)	Purchase method, balance sheet consolidation (Q)
5/87			Cash basis statement of changes in financial position (P)	Recording and reporting for a purchase and a pooling (T)
11/86	Compensatory stock options (T)	Marketable equity securities (P)		
5/86	Stockholders' equity section restated (P)			Purchase/pooling minority interest, criteria for consolidation (T)
11/85	Treasury stock, stock dividends, cash dividends (T)	Long-term portfolio, equity method (T)		Pooling method, Post-combination balance sheet and income statement (P)
5/85				

CHAPTER EIGHT
FINANCIAL ACCOUNTING

Module 33/Miscellaneous (MISC)

ARB, APB, and FASB Pronouncements

INTRODUCTION

This chapter is written to help you review intermediate and advanced accounting (financial accounting) for both the practice and theory sections of the exam. The AICPA Content Specification Outline of the coverage of financial accounting in the examinations in Accounting Practice and Accounting Theory, including the authors' frequency analysis thereof (last nine exams), appears in Chapter 7.

The chapter is organized along the lines of the traditional intermediate and advanced accounting texts. The topics are arranged per the twelve financial modules (on the previous pages). You will be referred frequently to the outlines of authoritative pronouncements on the particular topic being discussed at the end of the financial accounting modules in this chapter. These outlines can be located easily by referring to the headings identifying the pronouncements which appear at the top of each page at the end of this chapter. At first consideration, presentation might appear more comprehensive if the outlines of APBs, SFASs, etc., were integrated in this chapter rather than presented separately. Separate presentation, however, allows separate study of the pronouncements and also precludes confusion with the editorial views of the authors.

The objective is to provide you with the basic concepts, journal entries, and formulas for each topic and subtopic. Hopefully you will be able to expand, adapt, and apply the basics to specific problem situations as presented in multiple choice questions, theory essay questions, and practice problems appearing on the exam. Keep in mind the importance of working all three types of questions under exam conditions as you study the basics set forth in this chapter. Refer to the multiple choice questions, essay questions, and practice problems on each of the financial accounting topics.

As you work through this chapter, remember that there are many possible series of journal entries and account titles that can be used in accounting for a specific type of economic transaction, e.g., long-term construction contracts. Reconcile the approach illustrated in the chapter with the approach you studied as an undergraduate (or which appeared in your intermediate or advanced text).

BASIC THEORY AND FINANCIAL REPORTING

A. Basic Concepts

This module includes the basic financial statements except the Statement of Cash Flows. It also includes revenue and expense recognition rules, accounting changes, and error correction. <u>The relevant accounting pronouncements are indicated in the discussion complete with cross references to outlines of the pronouncements at the end of this chapter.</u> (Note these outlines appear in the following sequence: ARBs, APBs, APB Statements, SFASs, and SFACs. The page headers in the outlines identify the sources of the pronouncements outlined on those pages.) Turn to each outline as directed and study the outline while reviewing the related journal entries, computations, etc.

1. Basic Accounting Theory

The foundation of financial accounting is generally accepted accounting principles (GAAP). As defined in APB Statement No. 4, GAAP encompasses "the conventions, rules, and procedures necessary to define accepted accounting practice at a particular time. The standard of 'generally accepted accounting principles' includes not only broad guidelines of general application, but also detailed practices and procedures." In practice, GAAP has come to include SFASs, FASB Interpretations, APB Opinions, ARBs and SEC releases. These are the pronouncements to which practitioners look when determining if financial statements fairly present financial position, results of operations, and changes in cash flows.

Although GAAP is the current basis for financial reporting, it does not constitute a cohesive body of accounting theory. Generally, SFASs and the other authoritative pronouncements have been the result of a problem-by-problem approach. The pronouncements have dealt with specific problems as they occur and are not predicated on an underlying body of theory.

Theory can be defined as a coherent set of hypothetical, conceptual, and pragmatic principles forming a general frame of reference for a field of inquiry; thus, accounting theory should be the basic principles of accounting rather than its practice (which GAAP describes or dictates). Accounting has a definite need for conceptual theoretical structure. Such a structure is necessary if an authoritative body such as FASB is to promulgate consistent standards. A body of accounting theory should be the foundation of the standard-setting process and should provide guidance where no authoritative GAAP exists.

There have been efforts to develop such a frame of reference. Notable early attempts include ARS No. 1 (The Basic Postulates of Accounting) and ARS No. 3 (A Tentative Set of Broad Accounting Principles for Business Enterprises) issued in 1961 and 1962. In 1966, the American Accounting Association issued A Statement of Basic Accounting Theory (ASOBAT). These three endeavors were largely ignored by the authoritative standard-setting bodies. In 1970, APB Statement 4 was released, based in part on ARS Nos. 1 and 3. Being a product of the APB, it is generally considered to be a more influential document than its predecessors. It can be thought of as the "official" accounting theory in areas where more recent guidelines have not yet been issued.

The most recent attempt to develop accounting theory began with the conceptual framework project. In 1976, FASB issued Tentative Conclusions on Objectives of Financial Statements of Business Enterprises, and later the same year, Conceptual Framework for Financial Accounting and Reporting: Elements of Financial Statements and Their Measurement. These two pronouncements led to the establishment of the Statements of Financial Accounting Concepts, of which six have been issued. The purpose of this series is "to set forth fundamentals on which financial accounting and reporting standards will be based." In other words, the SFACs attempt to organize a framework that can serve as a reference point in formulating SFASs.

Definition of Accounting. Before discussing "accounting theory" further, it is important to understand what accounting is. APB Statement 4 defines accounting as "...a service activity. Its function is to provide quantitative information, primarily financial in nature, about economic entities that is intended to be useful in making economic decisions--in making reasoned choices among alternative courses of action." Financial accounting and reporting is the subset of accounting which most of the theoretical work discussed above is concerned with. "Financial reporting includes not only financial statements but also other means of communicating information that relates, directly or indirectly, to the information provided by a business enterprise's accounting system--that is, information about an enterprise's resources, obligations, earnings, etc." (SFAC 1). It is important to note that not all informational needs are met by accounting or financial reporting. The following diagram from SFAC 5 describes the information spectrum.

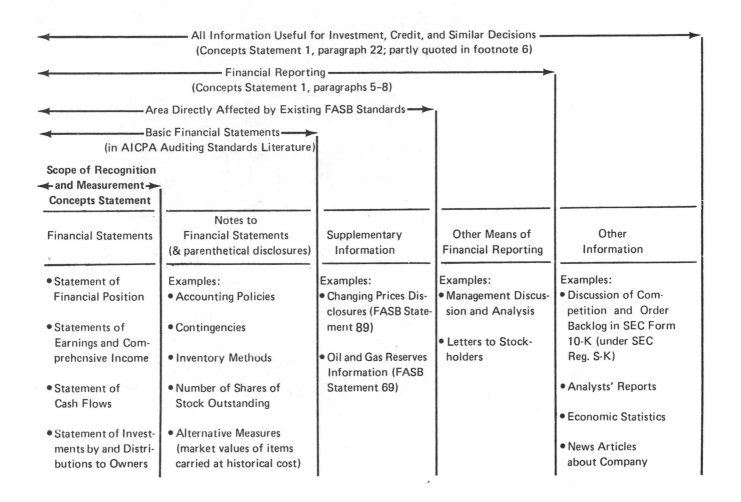

Financial Statements	Notes to Financial Statements (& parenthetical disclosures)	Supplementary Information	Other Means of Financial Reporting	Other Information
• Statement of Financial Position	Examples: • Accounting Policies	Examples: • Changing Prices Disclosures (FASB Statement 89)	Examples: • Management Discussion and Analysis	Examples: • Discussion of Competition and Order Backlog in SEC Form 10-K (under SEC Reg. S-K)
• Statements of Earnings and Comprehensive Income	• Contingencies		• Letters to Stockholders	
• Statement of Cash Flows	• Inventory Methods	• Oil and Gas Reserves Information (FASB Statement 69)		• Analysts' Reports
• Statement of Investments by and Distributions to Owners	• Number of Shares of Stock Outstanding			• Economic Statistics
	• Alternative Measures (market values of items carried at historical cost)			• News Articles about Company

Above the table, nested horizontal scope brackets (widest to narrowest):
- All Information Useful for Investment, Credit, and Similar Decisions (Concepts Statement 1, paragraph 22; partly quoted in footnote 6)
- Financial Reporting (Concepts Statement 1, paragraphs 5-8)
- Area Directly Affected by Existing FASB Standards
- Basic Financial Statements (in AICPA Auditing Standards Literature)
- Scope of Recognition and Measurement Concepts Statement

Components of the Conceptual Framework. The components of the conceptual framework for financial accounting and reporting include objectives, qualitative characteristics, elements, recognition, measurement, financial statements, earnings, funds flow, and liquidity. The relationship between these components is illustrated in the following diagram, also from Financial Statements and Other Means of Financial Reporting, a FASB Invitation to Comment.

In the diagram below, components to the left are more basic and those to the right depend on components to their left. Components are closely related to those above or below them.

Conceptual Framework
For Financial Accounting and Reporting

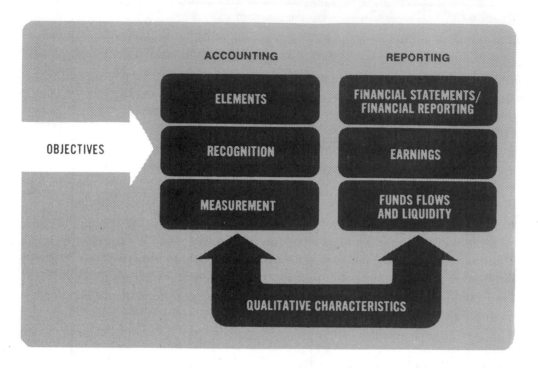

The most basic component of the conceptual framework is the objectives. The objectives underlie the other phases and are derived from the needs of those for whom financial information is intended. The objectives provide a focal point for financial reporting by identifying what types of information are relevant.

The qualitative characteristics also underlie most of the other phases. They are the criteria to be used in choosing and evaluating accounting and reporting policies.

Elements of financial statements are the components from which financial statements are created. They include assets, liabilities, equity, investments by owners, distributions to owners, comprehensive income, revenues, expenses, gains, and losses.

In order to be included in financial statements, an element must meet criteria for recognition and possess an attribute which is relevant and can be reliably measured.

Finally, reporting or displayed considerations are concerned with what information should be provided, who should provide it, and where it should be displayed. How the financial statements (financial position, earnings, and cash flow) are presented is the focal point of this part of the conceptual framework project.

Objectives of Financial Reporting. (See outline of SFAC 1). Remember, objectives of financial reporting underlie the conceptual framework. They are the basis upon which a body of theory is established. The objectives described in SFAC 1 have not been verified by an empirical process, but they are an attempt by the FASB to provide a foundation for a cohesive set of interrelated concepts.

The objectives focus on users of financial information. They are derived from "the needs of external users who lack the authority to prescribe the information they want and must rely on information management communicates to them." The external users who are emphasized in the objectives are actual and potential investors and creditors. These users are particularly interested in the amounts, timing and relative uncertainty of future cash flows, whether they be return of capital, interest, dividends, etc.

Three basic objectives are listed in SFAC 1. The objectives state that financial reporting should provide (1) information useful in investment and credit decisions, (2) information useful in assessing cash flow prospects (amount, timing, and uncertainty), and (3) information about enterprise resources, claims to those resources, and changes therein. A focal point in SFAC 1 is information about earnings and earning power. Earnings are a major cause of changes in resources. Despite the emphasis on cash flows, earnings are to be computed on the accrual basis, because accrual accounting "provides a better indication of an enterprise's present and continuing ability to generate favorable cash flows than information limited to the financial effects of cash receipts and payments."

Qualitative Characteristics. (See outline of SFAC 2). The qualitative characteristics also underlie the conceptual framework, but in a different way. While the objectives provide an overall basis, the qualitative characteristics establish criteria for selecting and evaluating accounting alternatives which will meet the objectives. In other words, information must possess the qualitative characteristics if that information is to fulfill the objectives.

SFAC 2 views these characteristics as a hierarchy of accounting qualities, as represented in the diagram below.

A HIERARCHY OF ACCOUNTING QUALITIES

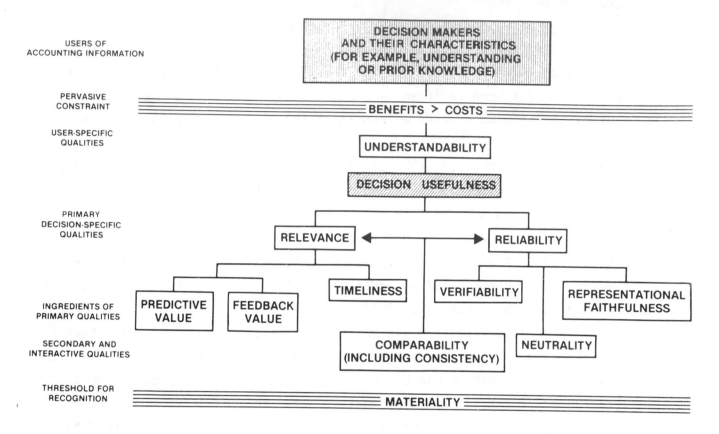

The diagram reveals many important relationships. At the top and bottom are constraints. If information falls outside these constraints, it would not be reported although it may possess some qualitative characteristics. Thus, information is not disclosed if the costs of disclosure outweigh the benefits or if the information is not material enough to influence users.

The first two qualities in the hierarchy (understandability and decision usefulness) are not qualities relating solely to information. They also depend on qualities of particular decision makers. The usefulness and understandability of information depends on the knowledge and ability of those using it. SFAC 1 states that "financial information is a tool, and like most tools, cannot be of direct help to those who are unable or unwilling to use it or who misuse it."

The primary qualities that accounting information should possess are relevance and reliability. As the chart indicates, each of these is broken down into three components. Comparability is a secondary quality which interacts with relevance and reliability to enhance usefulness of information.

Accounting information is relevant if it has the "capacity to make a difference" in a decision. To be relevant in an investment or credit decision, information must help users form predictions about future cash flows (refer to objectives). This can occur through predictive value (improving capacity to predict) or feedback value (confirmation or correction of prior predictions). Of course, in order to be relevant, information must be available before it loses its capacity to affect decisions (timeliness).

Information is reliable if it is reasonably free from error and bias, and faithfully represents what it claims to represent. Reliability consists of verifiability, representational faithfulness, and neutrality.

The secondary qualities of comparability and consistency become important when assessing cash flows of different enterprises or of the same enterprises over different periods. Comparability of information enables users to identify similarities in and differences between two enterprises, while consistency (unchanging policies and procedures from period to period) does the same between periods for each enterprise.

Basic Elements. (See outline of SFAC 6). Elements of financial statements are the ten basic building blocks from which financial statements are constructed. These definitions are based upon the objectives of SFAC 1. They are intended to assure that users will receive decision-useful information about enterprise resources (assets), claims to those resources (liabilities and equity), and changes therein (the other seven elements). In order to be included in the statements, an item must qualify as an element, meet recognition criteria, and be measurable.

The meaning of financial statement elements depends on the conceptual view of earnings which is adopted. Two basic views are the asset-liability view and the revenue-expense view. Under the asset-liability view, earnings are measured by the change (other than investments or withdrawals) in the net economic resources of an enterprise during a period. Therefore, definitions of assets and liabilities are the key under this view, and definitions of revenues, expenses, gains, and losses are secondary and are based on assets and liabilities.

The revenue-expense view holds that earnings are a measure of an enterprise's effectiveness in using its inputs to obtain and sell outputs. Thus, definitions of revenues and expenses are basic to this view, and definitions of assets, liabilities, and other elements are derived from revenues and expenses.

Rather than review the definitions of all ten elements (contained in the outline of SFAC 6), let us examine one definition in more detail. "Assets are probable future economic benefits obtained or controlled by a particular entity as a result of past transactions or events." This definition is based on the objectives and qualities of SFAC 1 and 2. The overall thrust of the objectives--predicting and evaluating future cash flows--is reflected in the phrase "probable future economic benefits." "Control by a particular entity" is crucial if reporting an item as an asset is to have decision usefulness (or relevance). The quality of reliability is assured by the phrase "as a result of past transactions." Information is more verifiable, valid, and neutral (the components of reliability) if based on past transactions. A similar analysis can be applied to liabilities, equity, investments by owners, distributions to owners, comprehensive income, revenues, expenses, gains and losses.

SFAC 6 also defines some other concepts in addition to the ten elements. Especially important among these 11 additional concepts are accrual accounting, realization, recognition, and matching. Realization and recognition are addressed by the FASB in SFAC 5. The definition of accrual accounting is important because SFAC 1 stated that accrual accounting should be used since it provides a better indication of future cash flows than the cash basis. This is true because accrual accounting records transactions with cash consequences (involving future cash flows) as they occur, not when the cash actually moves. Matching is referred to in most accounting literature as a principle, or fundamental law, of accounting.

Some other basic "features" of accounting (also known as assumptions) were defined in APB Statement 4 (see outline). Especially important among these features are accounting entity, going concern, periodicity, monetary unit, and substance over form.

Recognition and Measurement. (See outline of SFAC 5). Recognition principles establish criteria concerning when an element should be included in the statements, while measurement principles govern the valuation of those elements.

SFAC 5 established four fundamental recognition criteria: definitions, measurability, relevance, and reliability. If an item meets the definition of an element, can be reliably measured, is capable of making a difference in user decisions, and is verifiable, neutral, and representationally faithful, it should be included in the financial statements.

Five different attributes are used to measure assets and liabilities in present practice. These are discussed below in an excerpt from SFAC 5.

a. **Historical cost (historical proceeds).** Property, plant, and equipment and most inventories are reported at their historical cost, which is the amount of cash, or its equivalent, paid to acquire an asset, commonly adjusted after acquisition for amortization or other allocations. Liabilities that involve obligations to provide goods or services to customers are generally reported at historical proceeds, which is the amount of cash, or its equivalent, received when the obligation was incurred and may be adjusted after acquisition for amortization or other allocations.

b. **Current cost.** Some inventories are reported at their current (replacement) cost, which is the amount of cash, or its equivalent, that would have to be paid if the same or an equivalent asset were acquired currently.

c. **Current market value.** Some investments in marketable securities are reported at their current market value, which is the amount of cash or its equivalent, that could be obtained by selling an asset in orderly liquidation. Current market value is also generally used for assets expected to be sold at prices lower than previous carrying amounts. Some liabilities that involve marketable commodities and securities, for example, the obligations of writers of options or sellers of common shares who do not own the underlying commodities or securities, are reported at current market value.

d. **Net realizable (settlement) value.** Short-term receivables and some inventories are reported at their net realizable value, which is the nondiscounted amount of cash, or its equivalent, into which an asset is expected to be converted in due course of business less direct costs, if any, necessary to make that conversion. Liabilities that involve known or estimated amounts of money payable at unknown future dates, for example, trade payables or warranty obligations, generally are reported at their net settlement value, which is the nondiscounted amounts of cash, or its equivalent, expected to be paid to liquidate an obligation in the due course of business, including direct costs, if any, necessary to make that payment.

e. **Present (or discounted) value of future cash flows.** Long-term receivables are reported at their present or discounted value (discounted at the implicit or historical rate), which is the present value of future cash inflows into which an asset is expected to be converted in due course of business less present values of cash outflows necessary to obtain those inflows. Long-term payables are similarly reported at their present or discounted value (discounted at the implicit or historical rate), which is the present or discounted value of future cash outflows expected to be required to satisfy the liability in due course of business.

SFAC 5 states that each of these attributes are appropriate in different situations and that all five attributes will continue to be used in the future.

Similarly, SFAC 5 states that nominal units of money will continue to be the measurement unit. However, if inflation increases to a level where the FASB feels that financial statements become too distorted, another unit (such as units of constant purchasing power) could be adopted.

SFAC 5 is based on the concept of financial capital maintenance. Two basic concepts of capital maintenance (financial and physical) can be used to separate return on capital (earnings) from return of capital (capital recovery). Remember, any capital which is "used up" during a period must be returned before earnings can be recognized. In other words, earnings is the amount an entity can distribute to its owners and be as well-off at the end of the year as at the beginning.

One way "well-offness" can be measured is in terms of financial capital. This concept of capital maintenance holds that the capital to be maintained is measured by the amount of cash (possibly restated into constant dollars) invested by owners. Earnings may not be recognized until the dollar investment in net assets, measured in units of money or purchasing power, is returned. The financial capital maintenance concept is the traditional view which is reflected in most present financial statements.

An alternative definition of "well-offness" is expressed in terms of physical capital. This concept holds that the capital to be maintained is the physical productive capacity of the enterprise. Earnings may not be recognized until the current replacement costs of assets with the same productive capabilities of the assets used up are returned. The physical capital maintenance concept supports current cost accounting. Again, the physical productive capacity may be measured in nominal or constant dollars.

A simple example can further clarify the two capital maintenance concepts. Suppose an enterprise invests $10 in an inventory item. At year end, the enterprise sells the item for $15. In order to replace the item at year end, they would have to pay $12 rather than $10. To further simplify, assume the increase in replacement cost is due to specific price changes, and there is no general inflation.

The financial capital concept would maintain that the firm is as well-off once the dollar investment ($10) is returned. At that point, the financial capital is maintained and the remaining $5 is return on capital, or income. The physical capital concept maintains that the firm is not as well-off until the physical capacity (a similar inventory item) is returned. Therefore, the firm must reinvest $12 to be as well-off. Then physical capital is maintained, and only the remaining $3 is return on capital or income.

SFAC 5 also gives specific guidance as to recognition of revenues and gains, and expenses and losses, as indicated below.

Revenues	When realized or realizable (when related assets received or held are readily convertible to known amounts of cash or claims to cash) and earned
Gains	When realized or realizable
Expenses	When economic benefits are consumed in revenue-earning activities, or when future economic benefits are reduced or eliminated
Losses	When future economic benefits are reduced or eliminated

When economic benefits are consumed during a period, the expense may be recognized by matching (such as cost of goods sold), immediate recognition (such as selling and administrative salaries), or systematic and rational allocation (such as depreciation).

Revenues, expenses, gains, and losses are used to compute earnings. Earnings is the extent to which revenues and gains associated with cash-to-cash cycles substantially completed during the period exceed expenses and losses directly or indirectly associated with those cycles. Earnings adjusted for cumulative accounting adjustments and other nonowner changes in equity (such as foreign currency translation adjustments) is comprehensive income. Comprehensive income reflects all changes in the equity of an entity during a period, except investments by owners and distributions to owners.

Reporting or Display. This facet of the conceptual framework is very dependent on the components previously discussed. Once the elements are defined, and it is determined when to recognize them and how to measure them, the FASB must decide how they will be displayed in the financial statements. The concern is with what information will be provided, who should provide it, and where it should be displayed.

The information spectrum discussed earlier describes the available display options. Information can be formally incorporated in the financial statements (financial position, earnings, and cash flow), or in the notes to the financial statements. Other display alternatives are: required supplementary information (either accompanying the financial statements or available on request) or voluntary information.

Many of the important considerations in this area have been discussed in the accounting literature under the topic of disclosure. Most likely, a disclosure principle of some sort will later be adopted by the FASB. Generally, it is felt that full disclosure is satisfied when the financial statements contain information sufficient to make them useful and not misleading. In other words, no relevant accounting information should be omitted. Qualitative characteristics such as relevance and reliability and the constraint of materiality are important in this area.

An example of the types of reporting and display alternatives available to the FASB can be seen in the earnings statement.

    Disclosure of reasons for past changes in revenues
    Disclosure of reasons for past changes in expenses
    Classification of expenses as fixed or variable
    Detail of revenue and expense breakdowns
    Information to be disclosed concerning irregular earnings
    Types of separate supporting schedules
    Restatement of prior year earnings
    Inclusion of tables, graphs, or narration

Highlighting of certain groupings and relationships (e.g., gross margin or contribution margin)
Summarization of past performance
Disclosure of key ratios
Forecasting of future earnings

Similar alternatives can be developed for other forms of financial reporting.

2. Income Determination (See outlines of SFACs 1, 2, 5, and 6)

The primary objective of accounting is to measure income. Income is a measure of management's efficiency in combining the factors of production into desired goods and services.

Efficient firms with prospects of increased efficiency (higher profits) have greater access to financial capital and at lower costs. Their stock usually sells at a higher price-earnings ratio than the stock of a company with less enthusiastic prospects. The credit rating of the prospectively efficient company is probably higher than the prospectively less efficient company. Thus, the "cost of capital" will be lower for the company with the brighter outlook, i.e., lower stock dividend yield rates and/or lower interest rates.

The entire process of acquiring the factors of production, processing them, and selling the resulting goods and services produces revenue. The acquisition of raw materials is part of the revenue-producing process as is providing warranty protection.

Under accrual basis accounting, revenue is generally recognized at the point of sale (ARB 43, Chapter 1A, Rule 1) or as service is performed. The point of sale is when title passes: generally when shipped, if FOB shipping point and when received, FOB destination.

Three exceptions exist to the general revenue recognition rule: during production, at the point where production is complete, and at the point of cash collection. The table below identifies the criteria applicable to each basis, the appropriate accounting method, and the reasons for using that basis.

Recognition basis/source of GAAP	Accounting method	Criteria for use of basis	Reason(s) for departing from sale basis
• Point of sale ARB 43 (Ch 1A, Rule 1)	• Transactions approach (sales basis)	• Exchange has taken place • Earnings process is (virtually) complete	----
• During production basis ARB 45 and AICPA Contractors Guide	• Percentage-of-completion	• Long-term constuction,* property, or service contract • Dependable estimates of extent of progress and cost to complete • Reasonable assurance of collectibility of contract price	• Availability of evidence of ultimate proceeds • Better measure of periodic income • Avoidance of fluctuations in revenues, expenses, and income
• Completion-of-production basis ARB 43 (Ch 4, St. 9)	• Net realizable value	• Immediate marketability at quoted prices • Unit interchangeability • Difficulty of determining costs	• Known or determinable revenues • Inability to determine costs and thereby defer expense recognition until sale
• Cash collection basis APB 10	• Installment and cost recovery method	• Absence of a reasonable basis for estimating degree of collectibility	• Level of uncertainty with respect to collection of the receivable precludes recognition of gross profit before cash is received

*Note that the "completed contract" method for construction contracts is not a departure from the sale basis.

Source: Adapted from Henry R. Jaenicke, Survey of Present Practices in Recognizing Revenues, Expenses, Gains, and Losses, FASB, 1981.

Under accrual accounting, expenses are recognized as related revenues are recognized, i.e., (product) expenses are matched with revenues. Some (period) expenses, however, cannot be associated with particular revenues. These expenses are recognized as incurred.

(1) Product costs are those which can be associated with particular sales, e.g., cost of sales. Product costs attach to a unit of product and become an expense only when the unit to which they attach is sold. This is known as associating "cause and effect."

(2) Period costs are not particularly or conveniently assignable to a product. They become expenses due to the passage of time by

(a) Immediate recognition if the future benefit cannot be measured, e.g., advertising

(b) Systematic and rational allocation if benefits are produced in certain future periods, e.g., asset depreciation

Thus, income is the net effect of inflows of revenue and outflows of expense during a period of time. The period in which revenues and expenses are taken to the income statement (recognized) is determined by the above criteria.

Cash basis accounting, in contrast to accrual basis accounting, recognizes income when cash is received and expenses when cash is disbursed.

Cash basis accounting is subject to manipulation, i.e., cash receipts and expenses can be switched from one year to another by management. Another reason for adopting accrual basis accounting is that economic transactions have become more involved and multi-period. An expenditure for a fixed asset may produce revenue for years and years.

3. Accruals and Deferrals

Accrual--accrual basis recognition precedes (leads) cash receipt/expenditure

      Revenue--recognition of revenue earned, but not received
      Expense--recognition of expense incurred, but not paid

Deferral--cash receipt/expenditure precedes (leads) accrual basis recognition

      Revenue--postponement of recognition of revenue; cash is received, but revenue is not earned
      Expense--postponement of recognition of expense; cash is paid, but expense is not incurred

A deferral postpones recognition of revenue or expense by placing the amount in liability and asset accounts. Two methods are possible for deferring revenues and expenses depending on whether real or nominal accounts are originally used to record the cash transaction.

Deferrals of Expense

	Expense method			Asset method		
When paid	Insurance expense	xx		Prepaid insurance	xx	
	Cash		xx	Cash		xx
Year end	Prepaid insurance	xx		Insurance expense	xx	
	Insurance expense		xx	Prepaid insurance		xx
Reverse	Yes			No		

Deferrals of Revenue

	Revenue method			Liability method		
When received	Cash	xx		Cash	xx	
	Rent revenue		xx	Unearned rent		xx
Year end	Rent revenue	xx		Unearned rent	xx	
	Unearned revenue		xx	Rent revenue		xx
Reverse	Yes			No		

Accruals do not have two methods, but can be complicated by failure to reverse adjusting entries (also true for deferrals initially recorded in nominal accounts).

Accruals

	Expense		Revenue	
Adjustment	Wages expense	xx	Interest receivable	xx
	Wages payable	xx	Interest revenue	xx
Reverse	Yes		Yes	

Entries are reversed for bookkeeping expediency. If accruals are reversed, the subsequent cash transaction is reflected in the associated nominal account. If accruals are not reversed, the subsequent cash transaction must be apportioned between a nominal and real account.

Cash	(amount received)
Revenue	(earned in current period)
Revenue receivable	(accrual at last year end)

4. Cash to Accrual

Many smaller companies use the cash basis of accounting, where revenues are recorded when cash is received and expenses are recorded when cash is paid (except for purchases of fixed assets, which are capitalized and depreciated). Often the accountant is called upon to convert cash basis accounting records to the accrual basis. This type of problem is also found on the CPA examination.

When making journal entries to adjust from the cash basis to the accrual basis, it is important to identify two types of amounts: the current balance in the given account (cash basis) and the correct balance in the account (accrual basis). The journal entries must adjust the account balances from their current amounts to the correct amounts.

It is also important to understand relationships between balance sheet accounts and income statement accounts. When adjusting a balance sheet account from the cash basis to the accrual basis, the other half of the entry will generally be to the related income statement account. Some examples: when adjusting accounts receivable, the related account is sales; for accounts payable, purchases; for prepaid rent, rent expense; and so on.

For example, assume a company adjusts to the accrual basis every 12/31; during the year, they use the cash basis. The 12/31/87 balance in accounts receivable, after adjustment, is $17,000. During 1988, whenever cash is collected, the company debits cash and credits sales. Therefore, the 12/31/88 balance in accounts receivable before adjustment is still $17,000. Suppose the correct 12/31/88 balance in accounts receivable is $28,000. The necessary entry is

Accounts receivable	11,000
Sales	11,000

This entry not only corrects the accounts receivable account, but also
increases sales since unrecorded receivables means that there are also
unrecorded sales. On the other hand, suppose the <u>correct</u> 12/31/88 balance
of accounts receivable is $12,500. The necessary entry is

Sales	4,500
Accounts receivable	4,500

Sales is debited because during 1988, $4,500 more cash was collected on
account than should be reported as sales. When cash is received on account
the transaction is recorded as a credit to sales, not accounts receivable.
This overstates the sales account.

Some problems do not require journal entries, but instead a computation
of accrual amounts from cash basis amounts, as in the example below.

	12/31/87	12/31/88	1988
Rent payable	$4,000	$6,000	
Prepaid rent	8,000	4,500	
Cash paid for rent			$27,000

The rent expense can be computed using either T-accounts or a formula.
T-accounts are shown below.

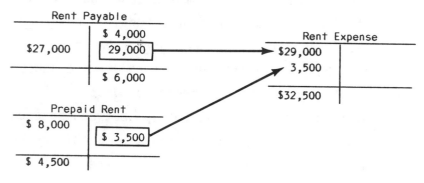

The use of a formula is illustrated next.

$$\text{Payments} + \begin{array}{c}\text{Beginning}\\\text{prepaid}\end{array} + \begin{array}{c}\text{Ending}\\\text{payable}\end{array} - \begin{array}{c}\text{Ending}\\\text{prepaid}\end{array} - \begin{array}{c}\text{Beginning}\\\text{payable}\end{array} = \text{Expense}$$

$$\$27{,}000 + 8{,}000 + 6{,}000 - 4{,}500 - 4{,}000 = \underline{\$32{,}500}$$

Formulas for conversion of various income statement amounts from the
cash basis to the accrual basis are summarized in the following table.

Cash basis	Additions	Deductions	Accrual basis
Collections from sales	+ $\begin{bmatrix} \text{Ending A/R} \\ \text{A/R written off} \end{bmatrix}$	− Beginning A/R	= Sales
Collections from other revenues	+ $\begin{bmatrix} \text{Beginning unearned revenue} \\ \text{Ending revenue receivable} \end{bmatrix}$	− $\begin{bmatrix} \text{Ending unearned revenue} \\ \text{Beginning revenue receivable} \end{bmatrix}$	= Other revenues
Payments for purchases	+ $\begin{bmatrix} \text{Beginning inventory} \\ \text{Ending A/P} \end{bmatrix}$	− $\begin{bmatrix} \text{Ending inventory} \\ \text{Beginning A/P} \end{bmatrix}$	= Cost of goods sold
Payments for expenses	+ $\begin{bmatrix} \text{Beginning prepaid expenses} \\ \text{Ending accrued expenses} \\ \text{payable} \end{bmatrix}$	− $\begin{bmatrix} \text{Ending prepaid expenses} \\ \text{Beginning accrued expenses} \\ \text{payable} \end{bmatrix}$	= Operating expenses*

Provision would also have to be made for depreciation expense and similar write-offs and bad debt expense.

5. Installment Sales

Revenue is recognized as cash is collected. Thus, revenue recognition takes place at the point of cash collection rather than the point of sale. Installment sale accounting can only be used where "collection of the sale price is not reasonably assured" (APB 10, para 12).

Under the installment sales method, gross profit is deferred to future periods and recognized proportionately to collection of the receivables. Installment receivables and deferred gross profit accounts must be kept separate by year, because the gross profit rate usually varies from year to year.

EXAMPLE:

Year	Sales	Cost of sales	Collections of Year 1	Year 3
1	300,000	225,000*	80,000	–
2	0	0	120,000	–
3	200,000	160,000**	100,000	100,000

* 25% gross profit rate   **20% gross profit rate

To record sale	Year 1		Year 2		Year 3	
Install A/R-1	300,000		–		–	
Install A/R-3	–		–		200,000	
Install sales		300,000		–		200,000
To record cash receipt						
Cash	80,000		120,000		200,000	
Install A/R-1		80,000		120,000		100,000
Install A/R-3		–		–		100,000
To record CGS						
Install cost of sales	225,000		–		160,000	
Inventory (or Purchases)		225,000		–		160,000
To defer gross profit						
Install sales	300,000		–		200,000	
Install cost of sales		225,000		–		160,000
Deferred install GP-1		75,000		–		–
Deferred install GP-3		–		–		40,000
To recognize gross profit						
Deferred install GP-1	20,000[a]		30,000[b]		25,000[c]	
Deferred install GP-3	–		–		20,000[d]	
GP realized on install method		20,000		30,000		45,000

[a] (25% x 80,000)   [c] (25% x 100,000)
[b] (25% x 120,000)   [d] (20% x 100,000)

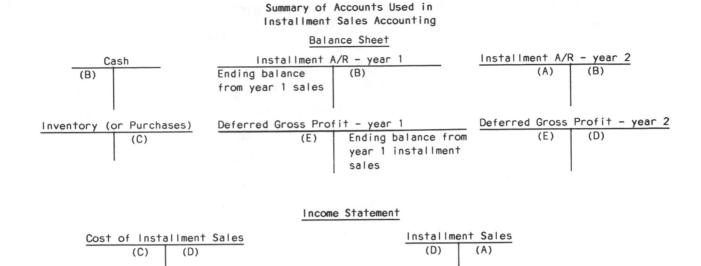

Summary of Accounts Used in
Installment Sales Accounting

Explanation of Journal Entries made in Year 2

(A) To record installment sales
(B) To record cash collected from year 1 and year 2 installment receivables
(C) To record cost of goods sold (perpetual or periodic)
(D) To close installment sales and cost of installment sales accounts
(E) To remove gross profit realized through collections from the deferred gross profit account

    (Gross profit rate for year 1 x cash collections from year 1 receivables)
    (Gross profit rate for year 2 x cash collections from year 2 receivables)

(F) To close realized gross profit at year end

6. Cost Recovery Method

The cost recovery method is similar to the installment sales method in that gross profit on the sale is deferred. The difference is that no profit is recognized until the cumulative receipts exceed the cost of the asset sold. For example, in the installment sales example, the entire profit from year 1 sales ($75,000) would be recognized in year 3. Profit on year 3 sales will be recognized in year 4 to the extent that in year 4 cash collections on year 3 sales exceed $60,000 (160,000 - 100,000). The cost recovery method is used when the uncertainty of collection is so great that even use of the installment method is precluded.

7. Franchise Agreement

SFAS 45 (see outline) provides that the initial franchise fee be recognized as revenue by the franchisor <u>only</u> upon substantial performance of their initial service obligation. The amount and timing of revenue recognized depends upon whether the contract contains bargain purchase agreements, tangible property, and whether the continuing franchise fees are reasonable in relation to future service obligations. Direct franchise costs are deferred until the related revenue is recognized.

8. Sales Basis Criteria for Selected Transactions

Under GAAP, specific rules have been developed which are stated in the form of conditions which must be met before it is acceptable to recognize profit from "a sale in the ordinary course of business." Unfortunately, these rules represent a patchwork set of criteria for applying the sales basis of revenue recognition. This patchwork set of criteria contains many inconsistencies either in the results obtained or in the rationale justifying the criteria. The table below summarizes the criteria which have been devised for applying the sales basis to selected transactions involving the sale of assets.

Recognition issue/ source of GAAP	Factors to be considered before recognizing revenue on the sale basis	Conditions that cause recognition to be delayed beyond time of sale
• Sale with a right of return SFAS 48	• Whether economic substance of the transaction is a sale or a financing arrangement • Determination of sales price • Probability of collection of sales price • Seller's future obligations • Predictability of returns	• Sales price not fixed or determinable • Payment excused until product is sold • Payment excused if property stolen or damaged • Buyer without separate economic substance • Seller's obligation to bring about resale of the property • Inability to predict future returns
• Product financing arrangement SFAS 49	• Whether risks and rewards of ownership are transferred	• Agreement requires repurchase at specified prices or provides compensation for losses
• Real estate sale SFAS 66	• Probability of collection • Seller's continued involvement • Whether economic substance of the transaction is a sale of real estate or another type of transaction, such as a service contract	• Inadequate buyer investment in the property • Seller's continuing obligations, such as participation in future losses, responsibility to obtain financing, construct buildings, or initiate or support operations
• Retail land sale SFAS 66	• Probability of collection • Likelihood of refunds • Likelihood of seller's meeting obligations	• Recision period not over • Inadequate buyer investment • Collection not predictable • Completion of improvements not assured
• Sales-type lease SFAS 13	• Transfer of benefits and risks of ownership • Probability of collection • Predictability of future unreimbursable costs	• Inability to meet conditions specified above for real estate sales • Inability to meet specified conditions (four criteria) indicating transfer of benefits and risks of ownership • Collectibility not predictable • Uncertainty about future unreimbursable costs
• Sale of receivables with recourse SFAS 77	• Control of receivables • Terms under recourse provisions • Predictability of collections and related costs	• Control of receivables not surrendered • Obligation under recourse provisions not reasonably estimable • Repurchase of receivables required by other than recourse provisions
• Nonmonetary exchange APB 29	• Completion of earning process	• Exchanges of similar inventory or productive assets
• Sale-leaseback transaction SFAS 13	• Substance of the transaction • Portion of property leased back • Length of leaseback period	• All sale-leaseback transactions are financing transactions and not sales transactions unless leaseback covers only a small part of the property or is for a short period of time

Source: Adapted from Henry R. Jaenicke, *Survey of Present Practices in Recognizing Revenues, Expenses, Gains, and Losses*, FASB, 1981.

B. Error Correction

Accountants must be in a position to anticipate, locate, and correct errors in their functions of systems and procedures design, controllership, and attestation. Errors which are discovered in the same year that they are made are corrected by

1. Determining the entry that was made
2. Determining the correct entry
3. Reversing the incorrect entry(ies)
4. Making the correct entry

Errors in classification, e.g., sales expense instead of R&D expense, affect only one period. Nonsystematic errors in adjusting entries, e.g., an error in ending inventory of one period, affect two periods and are known as self-correcting (counterbalancing) errors. For example, overstating ending inventory of period A will overstate the income of period A and understate that of period B. Other errors will affect the income of several periods such as misrecording the cost of a long-lived asset, i.e., depreciation will be misstated for all periods.

When an error is discovered in a period subsequent to the period when the error occurred, an entry must be made to correct the accounts as if the error had not been made. For example, assume the entry to accrue wage expense in the amount of $500 is omitted on 12/31/X1. The effects that would be caused by such an omission may be categorized as follows.

	Year 1	Year 2	Year 3
Expense	Understated	Overstated	Correct
Income	Overstated	Understated	Correct
Wages Payable	Understated	Correct	Correct
Retained Earnings	Overstated	Correct	Correct

If the company follows the policy of reversing adjusting entries for accruals, then correction of the error any time during 19X2 will require

Adjustment to correct error	500	
Wage expense		500

The adjustment account, when closed to retained earnings, will correct for the 1/1/X2 overstatement in retained earnings due to the overstatement of 19X1 income. The credit to wage expense will reduce the expense account for 19X2 to an amount equal to 19X2 wages.

If the error was discovered in 19X3, no entry would be required since the error self-corrects during 19X2. The 19X3 balances would be the same with or without the error.

The requirements of error analysis questions vary considerably. When asked for the effect of errors, be careful to determine the effect rather than the correction; they are opposite. The effect of revenue overstatement on income is over or plus, while the correction to income is to minus. Also distinguish between correcting/adjusting entries (which can be made in the accounts to correct the current period) and "worksheet entries" which adjust amounts reported in prior periods, i.e., journal entries are not recorded to correct nominal accounts of prior periods.

Correction of errors meets the criteria for prior period adjustments per SFAS 16. They should be reported as adjustments to beginning retained earnings of single-year statements and to retained earnings of each year presented in comparative statements for the error effects prior to each of the years presented. Note that reporting of prior years' errors is required even if a journal entry is not required because the errors have self-corrected. Adjustments to the comparative years should be made to reflect retroactive application of the prior period adjustments to specific accounts affected.

Format of retained earnings statements showing error corrections or special type accounting changes

	1987	1986	1985
Beginning balance originally reported	XX	XX	XX
Adjustment (Net of tax)	*	*	*
As restated	XX	XX	XX

*The amount will equal the effect of the item from years prior to the year being adjusted net of tax.

The analysis of inventory errors in a periodic inventory system is facilitated by setting up a statement of cost of goods sold. Items which are correct are indicated "OK," while items which are incorrect are listed as overstated (over) or understated (under). In the example below, year X1 will be the error year and year X2 will be the following year assuming the error is not corrected. Case #1 will be an overstatement of the ending inventory and Case #2 will be the understatement of both the ending inventory and purchases.

	Case #1 (Overstatement of EI)		Case #2 (Understatement of EI and PUR)	
	19X1	19X2	19X1	19X2
Beginning inventory	OK	Over	OK	Under
+ Purchases	OK	OK	Under	Over
Goods available for sale	OK	Over	Under	OK
- Ending inventory	Over	OK	Under	OK
Cost of goods sold	Under	Over	OK	OK
Income	Over	Under	OK	OK
Retained earnings	Over	OK	OK	OK
Accounts payable	OK	OK	Under	OK

C. Accounting Changes

1. Changes in Accounting Principle

Changes in accounting principle (or the method of applying them) must be justified by those who (firm's management) make the change unless they are made in order to comply with a FASB position. Study the outline of APB 20 and also see the two tables on pages 701 and 702.

Five special changes require retroactive restatement of all periods presented as if the new method had been used in all prior periods. These five special changes are

1. From LIFO to another inventory method
2. Change in method of accounting for long-term contracts
3. Change to or from the full cost method of accounting for exploration costs in the extractive industries
4. Any change made by a company first issuing financial statements for the purpose of obtaining additional equity capital or effecting a combination or registering securities (APB 20, para 29)
5. Change mandated by an authoritative pronouncement

Retroactive restatement means redoing all statements presented as if they were prepared according to the new accounting principle (or prepared correctly if correction of an error). Also restate statements of changed entities, i.e., changes in accounting entities such as poolings.

All other changes are accounted for by the "cumulative effect" method.

1. <u>Computing</u> the effect of the change on retained earnings at the beginning of the year in which the change is made
2. <u>Using</u> the new principle in the current year
3. <u>Reporting</u> the effect of the new method on beginning retained earnings less tax effects as "cumulative effect on prior years of new accounting method (described), net of tax" to be presented as the last item in the income statements, i.e., after extraordinary items and before net income
4. <u>Presenting</u> comparative years' data as previously reported
5. <u>Recomputing</u> the following income and EPS data for all periods presented <u>as if</u> the new method had been applied retroactively, and disclosing on the face of the income statement after EPS data. These items come after normal EPS disclosures per APB 15.

PRO FORMA AMOUNTS ASSUMING RETROACTIVE APPLICATION OF NEW METHOD

Income before extraordinary items	xxxx	xxxx
PEPS	x	x
FDEPS	x	x
Net income	xxxx	xxxx
PEPS	x	x
FDEPS	x	x

6. The above formats which disclose the effect of retroactive application of the new principle should reflect nondiscretionary items as well as tax effects

   a. Nondiscretionary items, e.g., royalty contracts and executive bonus
       agreements, are those items that would have also changed income
       upon retroactive change to the new accounting method

7. A possible exception is a change in inventory method <u>to</u> LIFO because the
   cumulative effect may not be determinable. For changes to LIFO no recognition is given to any cumulative effect associated with the change.
   The base year inventory for all subsequent LIFO calculations is the
   opening inventory in the year LIFO is adopted.

The following example is adapted from paras 42 and 43 of APB 20. Assume a
change in 1987 from accelerated to straight-line depreciation. The following
figures describe the

   1. Depreciation effect per year (increase in income)
   2. Depreciation (direct) effect net of tax (constant 50%)
   3. Nondiscretionary item effect net of tax, incentive compensation at 10%
      of pretax accounting income (decrease in income)
   4. Pro forma amounts, direct and nondiscretionary items net of tax

Year	*Excess of accelerated depreciation over straight-line depreciation*	*Direct less tax effect*	*Nondiscretionary item, net of tax*	*Pro forma*
Prior to 1983	$ 20,000	$ 10,000	$ 1,000	$ 9,000
1983	80,000	40,000	4,000	36,000
1984	70,000	35,000	3,500	31,500
1985	50,000	25,000	2,500	22,500
1986	30,000	15,000	1,500	13,500
Total at beginning of 1987	$250,000	$125,000	$12,500	$112,500

Example income statements, EPS disclosures, and pro forma retroactive disclosures are presented below for 1987 and 1986.

	1987	1986
Income before extraordinary item and cumulative effect of a change in accounting principle	$1,200,000	$1,100,000
Extraordinary item (description)	(35,000)	100,000
Cumulative effect on prior years (to December 31, 1986) of changing to a different depreciation method	125,000	
Net income	$1,290,000	$1,200,000
Per share amounts--		
Earnings per common share--assuming no dilution:		
Income before extraordinary item and cumulative effect of a change in accounting principle	$ 1.20	$1.10
Extraordinary item	(0.04)	0.10
Cumulative effect on prior years (to December 31, 1986) of changing to a different depreciation method	0.13	
	$ 1.29	$1.20

Earnings per common share--assuming full
dilution:

Income before extraordinary item and cumulative effect of a change in accounting principle	$1.11	$1.02
Extraordinary item	(0.03)	0.09
Cumulative effect on prior years (to December 31, 1986) of changing to a different depreciation method	0.11	
Net income	$1.19	$1.11

Pro forma amounts assuming the new depreciation method is applied retroactively--

Income before extraordinary item	$1,200,000	$1,113,500
Earnings per common share--assuming no dilution	$1.20	$1.11
Earnings per common share--assuming full dilution	$1.11	$1.04
Net income	$1,165,000	$1,213,500
Earnings per common share--assuming no dilution	$1.17	$1.21
Earnings per common share--assuming full dilution	$1.08	$1.13

Special points to note about the preceding example include

1. The 1987 income before extraordinary items of $1,200,000 is the same pro forma as in the income statement, because the new accounting method was used in 1987
2. The 1987 net income differs between the income statement and pro forma by the cumulative effect not included in the pro forma
3. Both the 1986 income figures differ between the income statement and pro forma by $13,500 (depreciation less tax effects and nondiscretionary items)
4. Remember the cumulative effect follows extraordinary items
5. Review the format and title of the pro forma presentation of retroactive application
6. Review the EPS presentation (in compliance with APB 15)

2. Changes in Accounting Estimates

Account for changes in estimates of useful lives, salvage value, collectibility of receivables, etc., prospectively--that is, no retroactive restatement. For example, if the useful life of an asset is increased from 10 years to 15 years during year 6, the remaining depreciable cost is amortized over the years 6 through 15.

SUMMARY OF ACCOUNTING FOR ACCOUNTING CHANGES AND ERROR CORRECTION

	Footnote disclosures	Reporting on financial statements — Effect on income before X-items, NI, EPS		Statement disclosures		Recording in books	
Nature of item	Justification*	Current yr. only	All periods presented	Retroactive treatment: previous financial statements restated	Cumulative effect treatment: pro formas shown for all years	Direct dr./cr. to retained earnings	Cumulative effect account
ACCOUNTING CHANGES							
In Principle							
General-change in principle or method of application from one acceptable GAAP to another. (Change from unacceptable GAAP is correction of error.) — X	X	X			X		X
Special — X	X		X	X		X	
• LIFO to another method							
• Change in method of accounting for long-term construction contracts.							
• Change to or from "full cost" method of accounting in the extractive industries.							
Special Exemptions for closely held corporation when it changes principles before its initial public offering. — X	X			X		X	
FASB Mandated — X			X	X		X	
Examples: equity method, R&D costs, inflation accounting.							
In Estimate**			X***				
Natural occurrence because judgment is used in preparation of statements. New events, more experience, and additional information affect earlier good faith estimates.							
In Reporting Entity*** — X	X		X	X			
Includes consolidated or combined statements in place of individual statements, change in group of subsidiaries for which consolidated statements are prepared, change in companies included in combined statements, and business combination accounted for as a pooling of interests.							
ERROR CORRECTION — X			X	X		X	
Mathematical mistakes, mistakes in applying principles, oversight or misuse of available facts, change from unacceptable to acceptable GAAP.							

*Should clearly explain why the newly adopted accounting principle is preferable.

**Change in estimate effected by a change in principle is accounted for as a change in estimate.

***For _material_ changes affecting more than just the current year.

1. Income and Retained Earnings Statement Formats

Review the outlines of APB 9 and APB 30 before proceeding. Income statements may be prepared using a multiple step or single step form. The multiple step form is illustrated on the previous page for Totman Company. This statement is a combined statement of income and retained earnings. Note that the retained earnings statement begins with prior period adjustments (see outline of SFAS 16).

2. Discontinued Operations

As shown on the above income statement, the "Discontinued operations" section consists of two components. The first one, "Income (Loss) from operations," is disclosed for the current year only if the decision to discontinue operations is made after the beginning of the fiscal year for which the financials are being prepared. In the diagram below, the "Income (Loss) from operations" component is determined for the time period designated by "A"--the period from the beginning of the year to the date the decision is made to discontinue a segment's operations (measurement date). The second component, "Gain (Loss) on disposal" may consist of two elements.

 a. Income (Loss) from operations during the phase-out period (the period between the measurement date and disposal date), and

 b. Gain (Loss) from disposal of segment assets

The "Gain (Loss) on disposal" component is determined for the time period designated "B" in the diagram below.

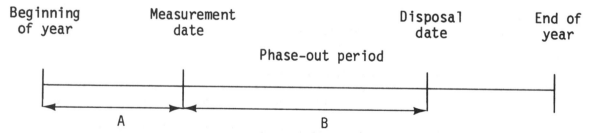

There are special rules for situations in which the disposal date occurs in the year after the measurement date. The problem is one of estimating the unrealized "Gain (Loss) on disposal" for that part of the phase-out period which is in the following year and comparing it to the actual "Gain (loss) on disposal" that has already been realized at the end of the preceding year for which the financials are being prepared. Two rules apply to this situation.

 a. A realized "Loss on disposal" may be increased by an estimated loss or it may be reduced by an estimated gain (but only to zero), or on the CPA exam, questions will ask for the amount of gain (loss) for "discontinued operations" or for the gain (loss) for one of the two

components. You must know these F/S headings and what is included
under each.

b.   A realized "Gain on disposal" may be reduced by an estimated loss
but cannot be increased due to an estimated gain.

The diagram below depicts the relationships discussed above.

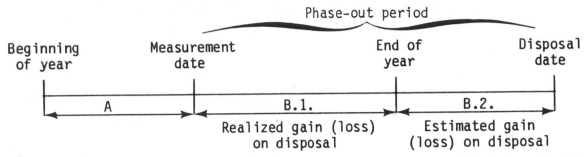

To find the year-end gain (loss), compare the amounts for "B.1." and "B.2."
using the rules stated above.

EXAMPLE

Facts	*Analysis*
A. Loss from Operations from be-ginning of year to the mea-surement date, $699, net of taxes of $466	*Reported as first component of discontinued operations*
B. 1. Realized loss from opera-tions from measurement date to end of current year, $400, net of taxes of $267. 2. Estimated loss from opera-tions from year end to dis-posal date, $200, net of taxes of $133. Estimated gain from disposal of assets during next year, $500, net of taxes of $333.	*Reported as second component of discontinued operations: $400 loss realized during phase-out period minus the $300 estimated <u>net</u> gain to be realized in the next period (estimated gain on disposal less the estimated loss from operations)*

The presentation of this case in the financials is shown in the combined
statement of income and retained earnings illustrated in the Totman
Company example.

When "discontinued operations" are disclosed in a comparative income
statement, the income statement presented for each previous year must be
adjusted retroactively to enhance comparability with the current year's
income statement. Accordingly, the revenues, cost of goods sold, and
operating expenses (including income taxes) for the discontinued segment
are removed from the revenues, cost of goods sold, and operating expenses
of continuing operations and are netted into one figure, i.e., "Income
(Loss) from operations." The following excerpt from a comparative income
statement shows the proper disclosure (19X5 figures assumed).

	19X6	19X5
Discontinued operations:		
Loss from operations of discontinued Division Z net of applicable taxes	$699	$820
Loss on disposal of assets of discontinued Division Z, including loss during phase-out period, net of applicable taxes	$100	-

3. Balance Sheets

Balance sheets or statements of financial position present assets, liabilities, and residual (shareholders' equity). The balance sheet reports the effect of transactions at a point in time, whereas the

    a.   Income statement
    b.   Statement of retained earnings
    c.   Statement of cash flows

report the effect of transactions over a period of time.

Balance sheets are generally presented in one of three formats.

Distinction between current and noncurrent assets and liabilities is almost universal.

Current assets--"cash and other assets or resources commonly identified as those which are reasonably expected to be realized in cash or sold or consumed during the normal operating cycle of the business."
(ARB 43, Chapter 3A, para 4)

Current liabilities--"obligations whose liquidation is reasonably expected to require the use of existing resources properly classifiable as current assets or the creation of other current liabilities" (during the normal operating cycle of the business).
(ARB 43, Chapter 3A, para 7)

Note current assets include those expected to be

    a.   Realized in cash
    b.   Sold
    c.   Consumed

Current liabilities are those expected to

    a.   Use current assets
    b.   Create other current liabilities

The operating cycle is the average time between acquisition of materials and final cash realization. Review the outline of ARB 43, Chapter 3A.

4. Other Financial Statement Concepts

    a. Accounting policies must be set forth as the initial footnote to the statements. Disclosures are required of

        (1) Accounting principles used when alternatives exist
        (2) Principles peculiar to a particular industry
        (3) Unusual or innovative applications of accounting principles

        Turn to the outline of APB 22. Additional disclosures required for specific situations are specified at the end of almost every official pronouncement, e.g., APBs and SFASs. Study these disclosure requirements by assuming you are a financial analyst analyzing the statements: "What would you want disclosed? Note any required disclosures that are not "common sense."

    b. Accounting for development stage enterprises should be per generally accepted accounting principles. The only additional disclosure required is that cumulative amounts from inception of losses, revenues, expenses, and cash flows should be shown in the income statement and statement of cash flows. Furthermore, the stockholders' equity section of the balance sheet should include cumulative net losses termed "deficit accumulated during development stage." These statements should be identified as those of a development stage enterprise. For further discussion, study the outline of SFAS 7 and also see the discussion of development stage enterprises in Module 24, Fixed Assets, section M.

INVENTORY

Inventory is defined in ARB 43 as tangible personal property (1) held for sale in the ordinary course of business, (2) in the process of production for such sale, or (3) to be used currently in the production of items for sale.

Inventory is tested on both the Theory and Practice examinations through the use of multiple choice questions, essays, and problems. The primary topics covered by questions on the exam are

1. Ownership of goods: the determination of which items are to be included in inventory.
2. Cost: the determination of which costs are to be assigned to inventory.
3. Cost flow assumptions: the determination of costs assigned to cost of goods sold and inventory under the various cost flow methods.
4. Valuation: the determination of how and when inventories should reflect their market values.

ARB 43, Chapter 4 is the primary authoritative pronouncement regarding the accounting for inventories. You should review the outline before continuing your study of this module.

A. **Determining Inventory and Cost of Goods Sold**

Inventory cost is a function of two variables

1. The number of units included in inventory, and
2. The costs attached to those units

The units to be included in inventory are those which the firm owns; ownership is usually determined by legal title. There are four areas which create questions in this regard.

1. Goods in transit (discussed in section "D." of this outline)
2. Consignments (discussed in section "E." of this outline)
3. Sales with the right of return (see the outline for SFAS 48)
4. Product financing agreements (see the outline for SFAS 49)

The costs to be included in inventory include all costs necessary to prepare the goods for sale. For a manufacturing entity this would include direct materials, direct labor, and both direct and indirect factory overhead. These costs are then allocated to the work-in-process and finished goods inventory accounts.

For a merchandising concern the costs to be included in inventory include the purchase price of the goods, freight-in, insurance, warehousing, and any other costs incurred in the preparation of these goods for sale. The amount used as a purchase price for the goods will vary depending upon whether the gross or net method is used in the recording of purchases. If the gross method is used to record the purchases, then any subsequent discount taken is shown as purchase discount which is netted against the purchases account in determining cost of goods sold. If the net method is used to record purchases, then any purchase discounts offered are assumed taken and the purchase account reflects the net price. If subsequent to the recording of the purchases the discount is not taken, (i.e., payment is tendered after the discount period has elapsed), a purchase discounts lost account is debited. The balance in the purchase discounts lost account does not enter into the determination of cost of goods sold; this amount is treated as a period expense. Note that regardless of the method used purchases are always recorded net of any allowable trade discounts. These are discounts that are allowed to the entity because of its being a wholesaler, a good customer, or merely the fact that the item is on sale at a reduced price. Also note that interest paid to vendors is not included in the cost of inventory.

The determination of cost of goods sold and inventory under each of the cost flow assumptions depends upon the method used to record the inventory: periodic or perpetual.

Periodic system: inventory is counted periodically and then priced. The ending inventory is usually recorded in the cost of goods sold (CGS) entry.

```
Ending inventory (EI)                        xx
CGS                                       (plug)
        Beginning inventory (BI)                   xx
        Purchases                                  xx
```

CGS = Purchases - (the change in inventory). For example, if ending inventory decreases, all of the purchases and some of the beginning inventory have been sold. If ending inventory increases, all of the purchases have not been sold.

Perpetual system: a running total is kept of the units on hand (and possibly their value) by recording all increases and decreases as they occur. When inventory is purchased, the inventory account, rather than purchases, is debited. As inventory is sold, the following entry is recorded.

```
CGS                     (cost)
        Inventory              (cost)
```

B. **Inventory Valuation and Cost-Flow Methods**

1. Specific identification	10. Dollar-value LIFO
2. Weighted-average	11. Retail dollar-value LIFO
3. Simple average	12. Standard costs
4. Moving average	13. Direct costing
5. Lower of cost or market	14. Market
6. Gross profit	15. Cost apportionment by relative
7. Retail method	sales value
8. First-in, first-out (FIFO)	16. Long-term contracts
9. Last-in, first-out (LIFO)	

1. Specific Identification

    The seller determines which item is sold. For example, a seller has for sale four identical machines costing $260, $260, $180, and $110. Since the machines are identical, a purchaser will have no preference as to which machine s/he receives when purchased. Note that the seller is able to manipulate income as s/he can sell any machine (and charge the appropriate amount to CGS). Significant dollar value items are frequently accounted for by specific identification.

2. Weighted-Average

    The seller averages the cost of all items on hand and purchased during the period. The units in ending inventory and units sold (CGS) are costed at this average cost. For example:

	Cost	Units	
Beginning inventory	$200	100	($2.00 unit)
Purchase 1	315	150	($2.10 unit)
Purchase 2	85	50	($1.70 unit)
	$600	300	

Weighted-average cost $600/300 = $2.00 unit

3. Simple Average

    The seller does not weight the average for units purchased or in beginning inventory, e.g., the above $2.00, $2.10, and $1.70 unit costs would be averaged to $1.93. The method is fairly accurate if all purchases, production runs, and beginning inventory quantities are equal.

4. Moving Average

    The average cost of goods on hand must be recalculated any time additional inventory is purchased at a unit cost different from the previously calculated average cost of goods on hand. For example:

	Dollar cost of units on hand	÷	Units on hand	=	Inventory unit cost
Beginning inventory	$200		100		$2.00
Sale of 50 units @ $2.00 = $100	100		50		2.00
Purchase of 150 units for $320	420		200		2.10
Sale of 50 units @ $2.10 = $105	315		150		2.10
Purchase of 50 units for $109	424		200		2.12

Note that sales do not change the unit price because they are taken out of inventory at the average price. Moving average may only be used with perpetual systems which account for changes in value with each change in inventory (and not with perpetual systems only accounting for changes in the number of units).

5. Lower of Cost or Market

"A departure from the cost basis of pricing the inventory is required when the utility of the goods is no longer as great as its cost." (ARB 43, Chapter 4, para 8)

The following steps should be used to apply the lower of cost or market rule given in Chapter 4 of ARB 43.

a. Determine market

Market is replacement cost limited to

(1) Ceiling--which is net realizable value (selling price less selling costs and costs to complete)
(2) Floor--which is net realizable value less normal profit

Note, if replacement cost is above net realizable value, market is net realizable value. Likewise, market is net realizable value minus normal profit if replacement cost is less than net realizable value minus normal profit.

b. Determine cost

Note that the floor and ceiling have nothing to do with cost

c. Select the lower of cost or market for either each individual item or for inventory as a whole (compute total market and total cost, and select lower)

Lower of Cost or Market Example

Item	Cost	Replacement cost	Selling price	Selling cost	Normal profit
A	$10.50	$10.25	$15.00	$2.50	$2.50
B	5.75	5.25	8.00	1.50	1.00
C	4.25	4.75	5.50	1.00	1.50

Item	Replacement cost	NRV (ceiling)	NRV-Profit (floor)	Designated market value	Cost	LCM
A	$10.25	$12.50	$10.00	$10.25	$10.50	$10.25
B	5.25	6.50	5.50	5.50	5.75	5.50
C	4.75	4.50	3.00	4.50	4.25	4.25

Item A--Market is replacement cost, $10.25, because it is between the floor ($10.00) and the ceiling ($12.50). Lower of cost or market is $10.25.

Item B--Market is limited to the floor, $5.50 ($8.00 - $1.50 - $1.00) because the $5.25 replacement cost is beneath the floor. Lower of cost or market is $5.50.

Item C--Market is limited to the ceiling, $4.50 ($5.50 - $1.00) because the $4.75 replacement cost is above the ceiling. Lower of cost or market is $4.25.

Observations about the ARB 43 rule

(1) The floor limitation on market prevents recognition of more than normal profit in future periods (if market is less than cost)

(2)   The ceiling limitation on market prevents recognition of a loss in future periods (if market is less than cost)

(3)   Cost or market applied to individual items will always be as low as and usually lower than cost or market applied to the inventory as a whole. They will be the same when all items at market or all items at cost are lower.

(4)   Once inventory has been written down there can be no recovery from the write-down until the units are sold. Recall that this differs from marketable securities where recoveries of prior write-downs are required to be taken into the income stream.

Methods of recording the write-down

If market is less than cost at the end of any period, there are two methods available to record the market decline. The entry to establish the ending inventory can be made using the market figure. The difficulty with this procedure is that it forces the loss to be included in the cost of goods sold, thus overstating the cost of goods sold by the amount of the loss. Note that under this method the loss is not separately disclosed.

An alternative treatment is to debit the inventory account for the actual cost (not market) of goods on hand, and then to make the following entry to give separate recognition to the market decline.

Loss due to market decline	xx	
Inventory		xx

6. Gross Profit

Ending inventory is estimated by using the gross profit (GP) percentage to convert sales to cost of goods presumed sold. Since ending inventory is only estimated, the gross profit method is not acceptable for either tax or annual financial reporting purposes. Its major uses are to estimate ending inventory for internal use, for use in interim financial statements, and for establishing the amount of loss due to the destruction of inventory by fire, flood, or other catastrophes.

As an example, suppose the inventory of the Luckless Company has been destroyed by fire and the following information is available from duplicate records stored at a separate facility: beginning inventory of $30,000, purchases for the period of $40,000, sales of $60,000, and an average GP percentage of 25%. The cost of the inventory destroyed is computed as follows.

Beginning inventory	$30,000
+ Purchases	40,000
Goods available	70,000
− Cost of goods sold	45,000*
Inventory destroyed	$25,000

*Cost of goods sold is computed as (1) sales of $60,000 − ($60,000 x 25%) or (2) sales of $60,000 x 75%.

If you need to convert a GP rate on cost to a markup (MU) rate on the selling price, divide the GP rate on cost by 1 plus the GP rate on cost; i.e., if the GP rate on cost is 50%, then .50/(1 + .50) = 33 1/3% is the MU rate on the selling price. If instead you need to convert a MU rate on the selling price to a GP rate on cost, divide the MU rate on the selling price by 1 minus the MU rate on the selling price; i.e., if the MU rate on the selling price is 20%, then .20/(1 - .20) = 25% GP rate on cost. Always be cautious about gross profit rates (on cost or the selling price).

7. Retail Method

Inventory is counted at retail value and then reduced to cost by a COST/RETAIL ratio. A "conservative" retail method adds markups but not markdowns in determining the COST/RETAIL ratio, e.g.:

	Cost	Retail
Beginning inventory	x	x
+ Purchases	x	x
+ Markups	—	x
Goods available	z	zz
− Sales		x
− Markdowns		x
Ending inventory		x

$$\text{EI at retail} \quad \times \quad \frac{\text{COST}}{\text{RETAIL}} \quad \text{ratio} = \text{EI at cost}$$

The goods available ratio (z/zz) provides the COST/RETAIL ratio. The retail inventory method can be calculated to approximate FIFO, FIFO LCM, average, average LCM, LIFO, or LIFO LCM inventory methods. LIFO LCM is not acceptable for tax purposes. Which of these approximations is obtained depends upon the figures which are used to calculate the COST/RETAIL ratio.

To obtain valuations at cost, the goods available at retail should include both markups and markdowns in the calculation of the COST/RETAIL ratio. To obtain LCM valuations, markdowns are excluded from the goods available at retail, thus inflating the denominator of the ratio and making the ratio smaller or more conservative.

The average cost ratio includes the BI in the ratio, while FIFO ratio ignores the BI and includes only the purchases in the calculation. The FIFO and average ratios may be dichotomized as shown below.

	Include BI	Exclude BI
Include markups and markdowns	Average cost	FIFO cost
Include markups but exclude markdowns	Average LCM	FIFO LCM

The FIFO or average retail EI is the EI at retail multiplied by the respective COST/RETAIL percentages. Remember that the average LCM calculation is frequently referred to as the <u>conventional</u> retail inventory method.

The LIFO calculation also uses the FIFO percentages if the inventory is increasing. The percentage is used to calculate the value of the incremental layer only--not the value of the whole inventory. The value of the incremental layer is added to the BI at cost to establish the EI at LIFO. If the EI at retail is less than the BI at retail, then the reduction in the LIFO inventory takes place at the COST/RETAIL ratio of the BI.

The following example, which assumes no additional markups or markdowns, illustrates the LIFO calculations.

	Cost	Retail
BI	$20	$ 40
Purchases	30	90
		$130
Sales		80
EI at retail		$ 50

Since the EI at retail has increased, the BI is still unused under a LIFO assumption and a new layer of $10 at retail has been added to the inventory. Since the layer was established from purchases of the current period, the FIFO percentage of 30/90 is used to convert the $10 retail layer to the new cost layer of $3.33. The EI at LIFO will be $20 + 3.33, or $23.33.

If the EI at retail had been $30, not $50, then the EI at cost would have been $30 x (20/40), or $15. The purchases of the current period would be irrelevant since it is assumed they are all sold and cannot be in inventory.

8. <u>First-in, First-Out (FIFO)</u>

The goods from beginning inventory and the earliest purchases are assumed to be the goods sold first. In a period of rising prices, cost of goods sold is made up of the earlier, lower-priced goods resulting in a larger profit (relative to LIFO). The ending inventory is made up of more recent purchases and thus represents a more current value (relative to LIFO) on the balance sheet. It should be noted that this cost-flow assumption may be used even when it does not match the physical flow of goods.

9. Last-in, First-Out (LIFO)

Under this cost-flow method, the most recent purchases are assumed to be the first goods sold; thus, ending inventory is assumed to be composed of the oldest goods. Therefore, the cost of goods sold contains relatively current costs (resulting in the matching of current costs with sales). Again, this cost-flow assumption usually does not parallel the physical flow of goods.

LIFO is widely adopted because it is acceptable for tax purposes and because in periods of rising prices it reduces tax liability due to the lower reported income (resulting from the higher cost of goods sold). LIFO smoothes out fluctuations in the income stream relative to FIFO, because it matches current costs with current revenues. A primary disadvantage of LIFO is that it results in large profits if inventory decreases and earlier, lower valued layers are included in the cost of goods sold. This is generally known as a LIFO liquidation. Another disadvantage is the cost involved in maintaining separate LIFO records for each item in inventory. If LIFO is used for tax purposes, it must be used for financial reporting purposes. This is known as the LIFO conformity rule. Inventory layers may be added using the (1) earliest acquisition costs, (2) weighted-average unit cost for the period, or (3) latest acquisition costs.

10. Dollar-Value LIFO

Dollar-value LIFO is LIFO applied to pools of inventory items rather than to individual items. Thus, the cost of keeping inventory records is less under dollar-value LIFO than under unit LIFO. Because the LIFO conformity rule (if LIFO is used for tax, it must also be used for external financial statements) also applies to dollar-value LIFO, companies using dollar-value LIFO define their LIFO pools so as to conform with IRS regulations. Under these regulations, a LIFO pool can contain all of the inventory items for a natural business unit, or a multiple pool approach can be elected whereby a business can group similarly used inventory items into several groups or pools.

The advantage of using inventory pools is that an involuntary liquidation of LIFO layers is less likely to occur because of the increased number of items in the pool (if the level of one item decreases it can be offset by increases in the levels of other items) and because the pools can be adjusted for changes in product composition or product mix.

Like unit LIFO, dollar-value LIFO is a layering method. Unlike unit LIFO, dollar-value LIFO determines increases or decreases in ending inventory in terms of dollars of the same purchasing power rather than in terms of units. Dollar-value LIFO seeks to determine the real dollar change in inventory. Therefore, ending inventory is deflated to base-year cost by dividing ending inventory by the current year's conversion price index and comparing the resulting amount with the beginning inventory which has also been stated in base-year dollars.

The difference represents the layer which, after conversion, must be added or subtracted to arrive at the appropriate value of ending inventory. Always remember that the individual layers in a dollar-value LIFO inventory are valued as follows.

$$\begin{array}{ccc} \$ \\ \text{value} \\ \text{LIFO} \end{array} = \begin{array}{c} \text{Inventory at} \\ \text{base-year prices} \end{array} \times \begin{array}{c} \text{Conversion} \\ \text{price index} \end{array}$$

In applying dollar-value LIFO, manufacturers develop their own indexes while retailers and wholesalers use published figures. In computing the conversion price index, the <u>double-extension technique</u> is used, named so because each year the ending inventory is extended at both base-year prices and current-year prices. The index, computed as follows, measures the change in the inventory prices since the base year.

$$\frac{\text{EI at end-of-year prices}}{\text{EI at base-year prices}} = \begin{array}{c} \text{Conversion} \\ \text{price index} \end{array}$$

To illustrate the computation of the index, assume that the base-year price of products A and B is $3 and $5, respectively, and at the end of the year, the price of product A is $3.20 and B, $5.75, with 2,000 and 800 units on hand, respectively. The index for the year is 110%, computed as follows.

	EI at end-of-year prices	÷	EI at base-year prices	= Conversion price index
Product A	2,000 @ $3.20 = $ 6,400		2,000 @ $3 = $ 6,000	
Produce B	800 @ $5.75 = $ 4,600		800 @ $5 = $ 4,000	
	$11,000	÷	$10,000 =	1.10
				(or 110%)

Steps in dollar-value LIFO

Manufacturers	Retailers and Wholesalers
1. Compute the conversion price index	1. Determine index from appropriate published source
2. Compare BI at base-year prices to EI at base-year prices to determine the a) New inventory layer added, or	2. Divide EI by conversion price index to restate to base-year prices 3. Same as "2." opposite

b)   Old inventory layer re-
      moved (LIFO liquidation)
3. If there is an increase at base-   4. Same as "3." opposite
   year prices, value this new
   layer by multiplying the layer
   (stated in base-year dollars) by
   the conversion price index. If
   there is a decrease at base-year
   prices, the remaining layers are
   valued at the index in effect
   when the layer was first added.

For example, assume the following.

	EI at end-of-year prices ÷	Conversion price index =	EI at base-year prices	Change as measured in base-year dollars
Year 1 (base)	$100,000	1.00	$100,000	
Year 2	121,000	1.10	110,000 >	$10,000
Year 3	150,000	1.20	125,000 >	15,000
Year 4	135,000	1.25	108,000 >	(17,000)

In both year 2 and year 3, ending inventory in terms of base-year dollars increased 10,000 and $15,000 base-year dollars, respectively. Since layers are added every year that ending inventory at base-year prices is greater than the previous year's ending inventory at base-year prices, the ending inventory for year 3 would be computed as follows.

Ending inventory, Year 3

	Base-year prices x	Index =	EI at dollar-value LIFO cost
Year 1 (base)	$100,000	1.00	$100,000
Year 2 layer	10,000	1.10	11,000
Year 3 layer	15,000	1.20	18,000
Ending inventory	$125,000		$129,000

Note that each layer added is multiplied by the conversion price index in effect when the layer was added. Thus, the year 2 layer is multiplied by the year 2 index of 1.10 and the year 3 layer is multiplied by the year 3 index of 1.20.

In year 4, ending inventory decreased by 17,000 base-year dollars. Therefore, a LIFO liquidation has occurred whereby 17,000 base-year dollars will have to be removed from the previous year's ending inventory. Because LIFO is being used, the liquidation affects the most recently added layer first and then, if necessary, the next most recently added layer(s). Ending inventory in year 4 is composed of

	Base-year prices x	Index =	EI at dollar-value LIFO cost
Year 1 (base)	$100,000	1.00	$100,000
Year 2 layer	8,000	1.10	8,800
Ending inventory	$108,000		$108,800

Note that the liquidation of 17,000 base year dollars in year 4 caused the entire year 3 layer of 15,000 base-year dollars to be liquidated as well as 2,000 base-year dollars from year 2. Also note that the remaining 8,000 base-year dollars in the year 2 layer is still multiplied by the year 2 index of 1.10.

Link-chain technique. The computations for application of the double-extension technique can become very arduous even if only a few items exist in the inventory. Also, consider the problems that arise when there is a constant change in the inventory mix or in situations in which the breadth of the inventory is large.

The link-chain method was originally developed for (and limited to) those companies that wanted to use LIFO but, because of a substantial change in product lines over time, were unable to recreate or keep the historical records necessary to make accurate use of the double-extension method.

The link-chain method is the process of developing a single cumulative index which is applied to the ending inventory amount priced at the beginning of the year costs. Technological change is allowed for by the method used to calculate each current year index. The index is derived by double extending a representative sample (generally thought to be between 50% and 75% of the dollar value of the pool) at both beginning-of-year prices and end-of-year prices. This annual index is then applied (multiplied) to the previous period's cumulative index to arrive at the new current year cumulative index.

The brief example below illustrates how the links and cumulative index are computed.

End of period	Ratio of end of period prices to beginning prices*	Cumulative index number**
0	--	1.000
1	1.10	1.100
2	1.05	1.155
3	1.07	1.236

$* \dfrac{\text{End of period prices}}{\text{Beginning of period prices}}$ = Index number for this period only

**Multiply the cumulative index number at beginning of the period by the ratio computed with the formula shown above.

11. Retail Dollar-Value LIFO

This method couples the retail method with dollar-value LIFO. The dollar-value LIFO records are counted and maintained at retail with the conversion to cost by a COST/RETAIL ratio being made as a final step.

Retail dollar-value LIFO involves the following five steps.

a. Count the EI at current retail price and convert it to base-year retail prices by dividing by the current year's conversion price index
b. Determine the BI (previous year's ending inventory) at base-year retail prices

c. Compare "b." with "a." to determine the real change in inventory measured in terms of base-year retail prices
d. If the inventory has increased, convert the real change in inventory at base year's retail prices to the real change in inventory at current year's retail prices by multiplying the quantity in "c." by the conversion price index
e. Determine the cost of the new layer by multiplying the quantity in "d." by the COST/RETAIL ratio for the current year

Any increase will form a layer which will be added to the BI at cost to establish the EI at cost. The following example illustrates these steps.

Assume the following information.

		Cost	Retail	COST/RETAIL %	Conversion price index
1)	BI	$24,000	$40,000	60%	1.00

2) EI--counted at ending retail prices = $44,100
3) COST/RETAIL ratio on current year purchases = 80%
4) The price level has increased from 100 to 105 during the year

The previously described steps are as follows for the above data.

	Inventory at retail prices	÷	Conversion price index	=	Inventory at base-year retail prices	Change as measured in base-year retail dollars
BI	$40,000		1.00		$40,000	
EI	44,100		1.05		42,000	> $2,000

Ending inventory at cost

	Base-year retail dollars	x	Conversion price index	x	COST/ RETAIL %	=	Extension
BI layer	$40,000		1.00		60%		$24,000
EI layer	2,000		1.05		80%		1,680
							$25,680 EI at cost

If the EI counted at retail prices had been $31,500 and all other data remained unchanged, the ending inventory would be computed as follows.

	Inventory at retail prices	÷	Conversion price index	=	Inventory at base-year retail prices	Change as measured in base-year retail dollars
BI	$40,000		1.00		$40,000	
EI	31,500		1.05		30,000	> $(10,000)

Ending inventory

Base-year retail dollars	x	Conversion price index	x	COST/ RETAIL %	=	Extension
$30,000		1.00		60%		$18,000

Thus, a LIFO liquidation has occurred, and part of the base-year layer has been removed. The remaining portion of the base-year layer is multiplied by the price index in effect when the layer was established and also by the COST/RETAIL ratio in effect when the layer was first established to arrive at the appropriate EI figure.

12. Standard Costs

Standard costs are predetermined costs in a cost accounting system, generally used for control purposes. Inventory may be costed at standard only if variances are reasonable, i.e., not large. Large debit (unfavorable) variances would indicate inventory (and cost of sales) were undervalued, whereas large credit (favorable) variances would indicate inventory is overvalued. See Module 36 (Standards and Variances) for further discussion of Standard Costs.

13. Direct (Variable) Costing

Direct costing is not an acceptable method for valuing inventory (ARB 43, Chapter 4, para 5). Direct costing considers only variable costs as product costs and fixed production costs as period costs. In contrast, absorption costing considers both variable and fixed manufacturing costs as product costs. See Module 35 (Planning, Control, and Analysis) for further discussion.

14. Market

Inventory is usually valued at market value when market is lower than cost. However, occasionally, inventory will be valued at market even if it is above cost. This usually occurs with

a. Precious metals with a fixed market value
b. Industries such as meatpacking where costs cannot be allocated and

   (1) Quoted market prices exist
   (2) Goods are interchangeable, e.g., agricultural commodities

15. Cost Apportionment By Relative Sales Value

Basket purchases and similar situations require cost allocation based on relative value. For example, a developer may spend $400,000 to acquire land, survey, curb and gutter, pave streets, etc. for a subdivision. Due to location and size, the lots may vary in selling price. If the total of all selling prices were $600,000, the developer could cost each lot at 2/3 (400/600; COST/RETAIL ratio) of its selling price.

16. Long-Term Construction Contracts

The outline of ARB 45 should be reviewed before continuing to study long-term construction contracts. This section also reflects the treatment of these contracts in the AICPA's Construction Contractors Audit and Accounting Guide.

Long-term contracts are accounted for by two methods: completed-contract method and percentage-of-completion method.

a. Completed-contract method--recognition of contract revenue and profit at contract completion. All related costs are deferred until completion and then matched to revenues.

b. Percentage-of-completion--recognition of contract revenue and profit during construction based on expected total profit and estimated progress towards completion in the current period. All related costs are recognized in the period in which they occur.

The use of the percentage-of-completion method depends on the ability to make reasonably dependable estimates of contract revenues, contract costs, and the extent of progress toward completion. For entities which customarily operate under contractual arrangements and for whom contracting represents a significant part of their operations, the presumption is that they have the ability to make estimates that are sufficiently dependable to justify the use of the percentage-of-completion method of accounting.

In Statement of Position 81-1, the Accounting Standards Division states that the percentage-of-completion method is preferable in circumstances in which reasonably dependable estimates can be made and in which all of the following conditions exist:

• Contracts executed by the parties normally include provisions that clearly specify the enforceable rights regarding goods or services to be provided and received by the parties, the consideration to be exchanged, and the manner and terms of settlement.

• The buyer can be expected to satisfy obligations under the contract.

• The contractor can be expected to perform contractual obligation.

The completed-contract method is preferable in circumstances in which estimates cannot meet the criteria for reasonable dependability or one of the above conditions does not exist.

The advantage of percentage-of-completion is periodic recognition of income and the disadvantage is dependence on estimates. The advantage of the completed-contract method is that it is based on results, not estimates, and the disadvantage is that current performance is not reflected and income recognition may be irregular.

General and Administrative Costs. When the percentage-of-completion method is used, general and administrative expenses are normally charged to income in the period in which they occur, the reason being that the financial statements generally are not materially distorted as compared to the deferment and subsequent recognition of these expenses. Similarly, under the completed-contract method, these costs are also immediately expensed when the contractor is engaged in numerous contracts. However, when the contractor is engaged in relatively few contracts, it is preferable to defer these costs as contract costs so as to obtain a better matching of revenues and expenses. In no case should there be any excessive deferring of these costs. In cases where an estimated loss exists, these costs should be immediately expensed, even when the costs were previously being deferred through the use of the completed-contract method.

In practice, various procedures are used to measure the extent of progress toward completion under the percentage-of-completion method, but the most widely used one is <u>cost-to-cost</u> which is based on the assumed relationship between a unit of input and productivity. Under cost-to-cost, either revenue and/or profit to recognize in the current period can be determined by the following formula.

$$\text{Revenue (profit)} = \left(\frac{\text{Cost to date}}{\substack{\text{Total expected} \\ \text{cost based on} \\ \text{latest estimate}}} \times \substack{\text{Contract price} \\ \text{(Expected profit)}} \right) - \substack{\text{Revenue (profit)} \\ \text{recognized in} \\ \text{previous periods}}$$

It is important to note that revenue and profit are two different terms. Profit is calculated by subtracting construction expenses from revenue. Revenue is the contract price. Therefore, pay particular attention to what item the CPA Exam asks you to calculate.

The ledger account titles used in the following discussion are unique to long-term construction contracts. In practice, there are numerous account titles for the same item (e.g., "billings on LT contracts" vs. "partial billings on construction in process") and various methodologies for journalizing the same transactions (e.g., separate revenue and expense control accounts in lieu of an "income on LT contracts" account). The following example has been simplified to highlight the main concepts.

EXAMPLE: Assume a three-year contract at a contract price of $500,000 as well as the following data.

	Year 1	Year 2	Year 3
Cost incurred this year	$135,000	$225,000	$ 45,000
Prior years' costs	-0-	135,000	360,000
Estimated costs to complete	$315,000	40,000	-0-
Total costs	$450,000	$400,000	$405,000
Progress billings made during the year	$200,000	$200,000	$100,000
Collection of billings each year	$175,000	$200,000	$125,000

From the above information, the following may be determined.

Percent of completion (costs to date/total costs)
Year 1: $135,000/$450,000 = 30%
Year 2: $360,000/$400,000 = 90%
Year 3: $405,000/$405,000 = 100%

	Year 1	Year 2	Year 3
Total revenue	$500,000	$500,000	$500,000
x percent of completion	x 30%	x 90%	x 100%
Total revenue to be recognized by end of year	$150,000	$450,000	$500,000
- Revenue recognized in prior periods	-0-	(150,000)	(450,000)
Current year's revenue (to be recognized)	$150,000	$300,000	$ 50,000
Contract price	$500,000	$500,000	$500,000
- Total estimated costs	(450,000)	(400,000)	(405,000)
Estimated profit	$ 50,000	$100,000	$ 95,000
x percent of completion	x 30%	x 90%	x 100%
Total profit to be recognized by end of year	$ 15,000	$ 90,000	$ 95,000
- Profit recognized in prior periods	-0-	(15,000)	(90,000)
Current year's profit (to be recognized)	$ 15,000	$ 75,000	$ 5,000

		Percentage-of-completion	Completed-contract
Year 1 Costs	Construction in progress	135,000	135,000
	Cash	135,000	135,000
Year 1 Progress billings	Accounts receivable	200,000	200,000
	Billings on LT contracts	200,000	200,000
Year 1 Cash collected	Cash	175,000	175,000
	Accounts receivable	175,000	175,000
Year 1 Profit recognition	Construction expenses	135,000	none
	Construction in progress	15,000	
	Construction revenue	150,000	
Year 2 Costs	Construction in progress	225,000	225,000
	Cash	225,000	225,000
Year 2 Progress billings	Accounts receivable	200,000	200,000
	Billings on LT contracts	200,000	200,000
Year 2 Cash collected	Cash	200,000	200,000
	Accounts receivable	200,000	200,000
Year 2 Profit recognition	Construction expenses	225,000	none
	Construction in progress	75,000	
	Construction revenue	300,000	

Year 3 Costs	Construction in progress	45,000	45,000
	Cash	45,000	45,000
Year 3 Progress billings	Accounts receivable	100,000	100,000
	Billings on LT contracts	100,000	100,000
Year 3 Cash collected	Cash	125,000	125,000
	Accounts receivable	125,000	125,000
Year 3 Profit recognition and closing of special accounts	Construction expenses	45,000	
	Construction in progress	5,000	
	Construction revenue	50,000	
	Billings on LT contracts	500,000	
	Const. in progress	500,000	
	Construction expenses		405,000
	Const. in progress		405,000
	Billings on LT contracts		500,000
	Construction revenue		500,000

The "construction in progress" (CIP) account is a cost accumulation account similar to "work in process" for job order costing, except that the percentage-of-completion method includes interim profits in the account. The "billings on LT contracts" account is similar to an unearned revenue account. At each financial statement date, the "construction in progress" account should be netted against the "billings on LT contracts" account on a project-by-project basis, resulting in a net current asset and/or a net current liability. Under the percentage-of-completion method in the above example, a net current asset of $50,000 [($135,000 + $15,000 + $225,000 + $75,000) - ($200,000 + $200,000)] would be reported at the end of year 2. A net current liability of $40,000 would result under the completed-contract method [($200,000 + $200,000) - ($135,000 + $225,000)] for the same year.

SUMMARY OF ACCOUNTS USED IN CONSTRUCTION ACCOUNTING
(NO LOSS EXPECTED OR INCURRED)

Balance Sheet

Construction in Progress
```
(A)  |  (E)
(F)  |  (G)
     |
```

A/P, Materials, etc.
```
     |  (A)
```

Income Statement

Construction Revenue
```
     |  (D)
     |
     |  (F)
```

Accounts Receivable
```
(B)  |  (C)
     |
```

Billings on LT Contracts
```
(D)  |  (B)
(G)  |
     |
```

Construction Expenses
```
(E)  |
(F)  |
```

Cash
```
(C)  |
     |
```

Explanation of Journal Entries

Both Methods
- (A) To record accumulated costs
- (B) To record progress billings
- (C) To record cash collections

Completed-Contract Method
- (D) To record revenue upon completion and to close billings account
- (E) To record expenses upon completion and to close construction in progress account

Percentage-of-Completion Method
- (F) To record recognition of interim revenue and expense
- (G) To close construction in progress and billings accounts at project completion

Balance Sheet Classification*

Current Asset

Projects where CIP at year end** > Billings

Current Liability

Projects where billings > CIP at year end**

Estimated loss on uncompleted contract***

*Evaluate and classify on a project-by-project basis.

**Construction in progress including income (loss) recognized.

***When recognizing and reporting losses, it is acceptable to use a current liability account instead of reducing CIP.

Contract Losses. In any year when a percentage-of-completion contract has an expected loss on the entire contract, the amount of the loss reported in that year is the total expected loss on the entire contract plus all profit previously recognized. For example, if the expected costs yet to be incurred at the end of year 2 were $147,000, the total expected loss is $7,000 [$500,000 - ($135,000 + $225,000 + $147,000)] and the total loss reported in year 2 would be $22,000 ($7,000 + $15,000). Similarly, under the completed-contract method, total expected losses on the entire contract are recognized as soon as they are estimated. The loss recognized is similar to that for percentage-of-completion except the amount is for the expected loss on the entire contract. In the aforementioned example, the loss to be recognized is only $7,000 (the entire loss on the contract expected in year 2) because interim profits have not been recorded. Journal entries and a schedule for profit or loss recognized on the contract under the percentage of completion method follow.

Journal entry at end of year 2	Percentage-of-completion		Completed-contract
Construction expenses	227,000*		
Construction in progress (loss)		22,000	
Construction revenue		205,000**	
Loss on uncompleted LT contracts			7,000
Estimated loss on uncompleted			
contract (a current liability)			7,000
Supporting Calculations:			
*Year 2 costs			$225,000
Loss attributable to year 3:			
Year 3 revenue ($500,000 –			
$150,000 – $205,000)		$145,000	
Year 3 costs (expected)		147,000	2,000
Total			$227,000

** ($360,000/$507,000) (Costs to date/Total estimated costs) = 71% (rounded); (71% x $500,000) – $150,000 = $205,000

Profit or Loss Recognized on Contract
(Percentage-of-Completion Method)

	Year 1	Year 2	Year 3
Contract price:	$500,000	$500,000	$500,000
Estimated total costs:			
Costs incurred this year	$135,000	$225,000	$144,000*
Prior year's costs	–	135,000	360,000
Estimated cost yet to be incurred	315,000	147,000	–
Estimated total costs for the three-year period, actual for year 3	$450,000	$507,000	$504,000
Estimated total income (loss) for three-year period, actual for year 3	$ 15,000	$ (7,000)	$ (4,000)
Income (loss) on entire contract previously recognized	–	15,000	(7,000)
Amount of estimated income (loss) recognized in the current period, actual for year 3	$ 15,000	$ (22,000)	$ 3,000

*Assumed

C. Losses on Purchase Commitments

Purchase commitments (PC) result from legally enforceable contracts to purchase specific quantities of goods at fixed prices in the future. When there is a decline in market value below the contract price at the balance sheet date and the contracts are noncancellable, an unrealized loss has occurred and, if material, should be recorded in the period of decline.

    Estimated loss on PC   (excess of PC over mkt.)
        Accrued loss on PC   (excess of PC over mkt.)

If further declines in market value are estimated to occur before delivery is made, the amount of the loss to be accrued should be increased to include this additional decline in market value per SFAS 5. The loss is taken to the income statement; the accrued loss on PC is a liability account and shown on the balance sheet.

When the goods are subsequently received:

    Purchases   xx
    Accrued loss on PC   xx
        Cash   xx

If a partial or full recovery occurs before the inventory is received, the accrued loss account would be reduced by the amount of the recovery. Likewise, an income statement account, "Recovery on Loss of PC," would be credited.

D. Items to Include in Inventory

Goods shipped FOB shipping point which are in transit should be included in the inventory of the buyer since title passes to the buyer when the carrier receives the goods. Goods shipped FOB destination should be included in the inventory of the seller when the goods are received by the buyer since title passes to the buyer when the goods are received at their final destination. The more complicated UCC rules concerning transfer of title should be used for the law portion, not the practice portion, of the exam.

E. **Consignments**

Consignors consign their goods to consignees who are sales agents of the consignors. Consigned goods remain the property of the consignor until sold. Therefore, any unsold goods (including a proportionate share of freight costs incurred in shipping the goods to the consignee) must be included in the consignor's inventory.

Consignment sales revenue should be recognized by the consignor when the consignee sells the consigned goods to the ultimate customer. Therefore, no revenue is recognized at the time the consignor ships the goods to the consignee. Note that sales commission made by the consignee would be reported as a selling expense by the consignor and would <u>not</u> be netted against the sales revenue recognized by the consignor. The UCC rules concerning consignments should be used for the law portion, not the practice portion, of the exam.

FIXED ASSETS

A. Acquisition Cost

Fixed assets are those expenditures for tangible property which will be used for a period of more than one year. Their cost, therefore, is deferred to future periods in compliance with the matching principle. All of the costs necessary to get the assets in the existing condition and location are capitalized, e.g., cost of negotiations, sales taxes, finders' fees, razing an old building, shipment, installation, breaking in, etc. Charges for self-constructed fixed assets include direct materials, direct labor, variable overhead, and a fair share of fixed overhead.

B. Capitalization of Interest

SFAS 34 (see outline) requires the capitalization of interest as part of the cost of certain assets. Only assets which require a period of time to be prepared for use qualify for interest capitalization. These include assets constructed for sale produced as discrete projects (e.g., ships) and assets constructed for a firm's own use, whether by the entity itself or by an outsider. For example, a building purchased by an entity would not qualify, but one constructed over a period of time would. Other assets that do not qualify include those in use or ready for use and ones not being used in the earnings activities of a firm (e.g., idle land). Inventories routinely manufactured or repetitively produced in large quantities do not qualify, even if a long maturation period is involved (e.g., tobacco and whiskey).

The amount of interest to be capitalized is the amount which could have been avoided if the project had not been undertaken. This amount includes amortization of any discount, premium, or issue costs; but, shall not exceed the actual interest incurred during the period. The amount of "avoidable" interest is computed as

$$\left(\begin{array}{c} \text{Average accumulated expenditures} \\ \text{during construction} \end{array} \right) \times \left(\text{Interest Rate} \right) \times \left(\begin{array}{c} \text{Construction} \\ \text{Period} \end{array} \right)$$

The interest rate used is the rate on specific borrowings for the asset, or a weighted-average of other borrowings when a specific rate is not available. Capitalized interest should be compounded. This is usually accomplished by including the interest capitalized in a previous period in the calculation of average accumulated expenditures of subsequent periods. Furthermore, noninterest bearing payables (e.g., trade payables and accruals) are excluded in determining these expenditures. In practice, both the weighted-average interest rate and the average accumulated expenditures have been computed on the

capitalization period begins when, and continues as long as, all three of the following conditions are met.

1) Expenditures for the asset have been made
2) Activities necessary to get the asset ready for its intended use are in progress
3) Interest cost is being incurred

The period ends when the asset is substantially complete. Brief interruptions and delays do not suspend interest capitalization, while suspension of the activities will. In no case should the amount capitalized exceed the interest actually incurred.

EXAMPLE: Interest Capitalization

Assume the company is constructing an asset which qualifies for interest capitalization. By the beginning of July $3,000,000 had been spent on the asset, an additional $800,000 was spent during July. The following debt was outstanding for the entire month.

1) A loan of $2,000,000, interest of 1% per month, specifically related to the asset.
2) A note payable of $1,500,000, interest of $1\frac{1}{2}$% per month.
3) Bonds payable of $1,000,000, interest of 1% per month.

The amount of interest to be capitalized is computed below.

Average accumulated expenditures (for the month of July)
($3,000,000 + $3,800,000) ÷ 2 = $3,400,000

Avoidable interest			Actual interest		
$2,000,000 x 1%	=	$20,000	$2,000,000 x 1%	=	$20,000
1,400,000 x 1.3%*	=	18,200	1,500,000 x 1.5%	=	22,500
			1,000,000 x 1%	=	10,000
$3,400,000		$38,200	$4,500,000		$52,500

Amount of interest to be capitalized is $38,200

Asset   38,200
        Interest expense   38,200

*The average rate on other borrowings is ($22,500 + $10,000) ÷ ($1,500,000 + $1,000,000) = 1.3%. Notice that a specific rate is used to the extent possible and the average rate is used only on any excess.

Interest on expenditures made to acquire land on which a building is to be constructed qualifies for interest capitalization. The capitalization period begins when activities necessary to construct the building commence and ends when the building is substantially complete. Interest so capitalized becomes part of the cost of the building. Thus, it is charged to expense as the building is depreciated.

Frequently, the funds borrowed to finance the construction project are temporarily invested until needed. Per FASB Technical Bulletin 81-5, the interest earned on these funds must be recognized as revenue and may not be offset against the interest expense to be capitalized.

The diagram below outlines the requirements pertaining to capitalization of interest.

SUMMARY OF ACCOUNTING FOR INTEREST CAPITALIZATION

```
┌─────────────────────────────────────────────────────────────┐
│       Capitalization of Interest During Construction          │
└─────────────────────────────────────────────────────────────┘

┌─────────────────────────────────────────────────────────────┐
│ Qualifying Assets:                                            │
│ a.  Assets constructed for use in operations                 │
│ b.  Assets for sale or lease which are constructed as discrete│
│     projects (ships, real estate), but not inventory         │
└─────────────────────────────────────────────────────────────┘

┌─────────────────────────────────────────────────────────────┐
│ When to Capitalize Interest (All three must be met):         │
│ a.  Expenditures for asset have been made                    │
│ b.  Activities intended to get asset ready are in progress   │
│ c.  Interest cost is being incurred                          │
└─────────────────────────────────────────────────────────────┘

┌─────────────────────────────────────────────────────────────┐
│ Applicable Interest (Net of discounts, premiums, and issue costs):│
│ a.  Interest obligations having explicit rates               │
│ b.  Imputed interest on certain payables/receivables         │
│ c.  Interest related to capital leases                       │
└─────────────────────────────────────────────────────────────┘
```

Amount of Interest to Capitalize

+ Accumulated expenditures at beg. of the period (including any previously capitalized interest)
+ Accumulated expenditures at end of the period (including any previously capitalized interest)
  Total used in averaging calculation
÷ 2
  Average accumulated expenditures

$$\left(\begin{array}{c}\text{Specific borrowings}\\ \text{x Applicable interest rate}\end{array}\right) + \left(\begin{array}{c}\text{Other borrowings}\\ \text{x Weighted-average interest rate*}\end{array}\right)$$

```
┌─────────────────────────────────────────────────────────────┐
│ Qualifications:                                               │
│ a.  Amount of interest to be capitalized cannot              │
│     exceed total interest costs incurred during              │
│     the entire reporting period                              │
│ b.  Interest earned on temporarily invested bor-            │
│     rowings may not be offset against interest to            │
│     be capitalized                                           │
└─────────────────────────────────────────────────────────────┘
```

$$\text{*Weighted-average interest rate} = \frac{\text{Total interest on other borrowings}}{\text{Total principal on other borrowings}}$$

Rationale for interest, capitalization:
a. To properly reflect asset's acquisition cost
b. To properly match asset's cost with revenue of periods that benefit from its use

C. **Nonmonetary Exchanges**

Study the outline of APB 29. Nonmonetary exchanges are generally to be
recorded at fair market value (of asset given up or asset received if "more
clearly evident") with gains (losses) recognized. There are some exceptions.
Accounting for nonmonetary exchanges is summarized in the diagram on the
following page. One important point to note is that under all methods, in all
situations, losses are recognized in full. The special accounting methods apply
only to certain gains.

Situation A-1. Dissimilar assets. When dissimilar assets are exchanged, it
is assumed that the earnings process is complete. Normal accounting procedures
are followed. The asset received is recorded at the fair value of the asset
surrendered, and any gain (loss) is recognized.

*EXAMPLE: Assume a company trades a machine with a fair market value (FMV) of
$12,000 (cost, $10,000; accumulated depreciation, $3,000) for land.*

Land	12,000		*(FMV)*
Accumulated depreciation	3,000		
Machine		10,000	
Gain on exchange		5,000	*(FMV−NBV)*

ACCOUNTING FOR NONMONETARY EXCHANGES

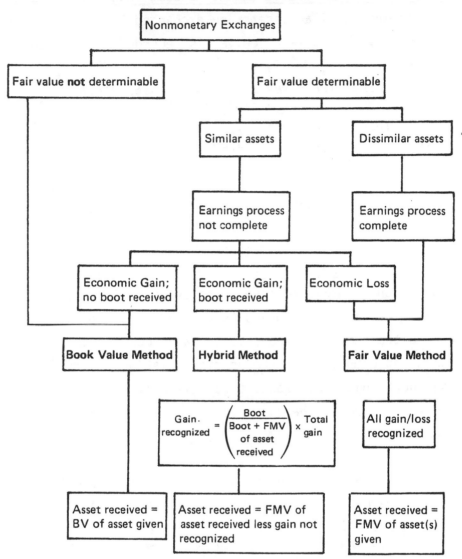

Situation A-2(a). Similar assets (loss). When similar assets are exchanged, it is assumed that the earnings process is <u>not</u> complete, and gains are <u>not</u> recognized. However, a conservative approach is taken and <u>losses are recognized</u> in full. Therefore, in a loss situation, the asset received is recorded at fair value.

EXAMPLE: Assume a machine with a FMV of $5,000 (cost, $10,000; accumulated depreciation, $3,000) is traded for a similar machine.

Machine (new)	5,000	(FMV)
Accumulated depreciation	3,000	
Loss on exchange	2,000	(NBV-FMV)
Machine (old)	10,000	

Situation A-2(b). Similar assets (gain, no boot received). Gains are not generally recognized when similar assets are exchanged because the earnings process is not complete. The asset received is recorded at the book value of the asset relinquished.

EXAMPLE: Assume a machine with a FMV of $12,000 (cost, $10,000; accumulated depreciation, $3,000) is traded for a similar machine.

Machine (new)	7,000	
Accumulated depreciation	3,000	
Machine (old)		10,000

There are two ways to compute the amount at which the new machine is recorded.

1) Net book value of the machine given up ($10,000 - $3,000)
2) FMV of new machine ($12,000) less gain not recognized ($5,000)

Also note that if boot is paid, the same procedure is followed.

Situation A-2(c). Similar assets (gain, boot received). When similar assets are exchanged and boot is received, the exchange is treated as part sale and part exchange. The earnings process is assumed to be complete for the portion relating to the boot received (i.e., "sale" portion). The earnings process is assumed not complete for the portion relating to the asset received (i.e., "exchange" portion). Therefore, a gain is only recognized for that portion relating to the boot. The gain recognized is computed as follows.

$$\left(\frac{\text{Boot}}{\text{Boot} + \text{FMV of Asset Received}}\right) \times \left(\text{Total Gain}\right) = \text{Gain Recognized}$$

If the FMV of the asset received is not given, it may be determined by subtracting the boot received from the FMV of the asset given up.

EXAMPLE: Assume a machine with a FMV of $12,000 (cost, $10,000; accumulated depreciation, $3,000) is traded for a similar machine and $4,000 cash.

Cash	4,000	
Machine (new)	4,667	
Accumulated depreciation	3,000	
Machine (old)		10,000
Gain on exchange		1,667

The total gain realized is $5,000 ($12,000 FMV of old machine less $7,000 NBV given up). However, only the portion relating to the boot is recognized.

$$\left(\frac{\$4,000}{\$4,000 + \$8,000*}\right) \times \left(\$5,000\right) = \underline{\$1,667}$$

*[$12,000 FMV of old machine less $4,000 cash (boot) received]

There are two ways to compute the amount at which the new machine is recorded.

1) Net book value of machine given up, less cash received, plus gain recognized

$7,000 - $4,000 + $1,667 = $4,667

2) FMV of new machine ($8,000) less gain not recognized ($3,333)

Situation B. Fair value not determinable. When the fair values of the assets exchanged are not determinable, a gain (loss) cannot be computed. Therefore, the book value method is used. The asset received is recorded at the book value of the asset relinquished, and no gain (loss) is recognized.

D. **Purchase of Groups of Fixed Assets** (Basket purchase)

Cost should be allocated based on relative market value as in inventory.

$$(\text{Cost of all assets acquired}) \times \frac{\text{Market value of A}}{\text{Market value of all assets acquired}}$$

EXAMPLE: Purchase of Asset 1 with a FMV of $60,000, Asset 2 with a FMV of $120,000, and Asset 3 with a FMV of $20,000 all for $150,000 cash.

	FMV	Relative FMV x	Total Cost =	Allocated Cost
Asset 1	$ 60,000	60/200	$150,000	$45,000
Asset 2	120,000	120/200	150,000	90,000
Asset 3	20,000	20/200	150,000	15,000
Total FMV	$200,000			

Journalized:

Asset 1	$ 45,000	
Asset 2	90,000	
Asset 3	15,000	
Cash		$150,000

E. **Capital Versus Revenue Expenditures**

Capital expenditures and revenue expenditures are charges that are incurred after the acquisition cost has been determined and the related fixed asset is in operation.

Capital expenditures are not normal, recurring expenses; they benefit the operations of more than one period. The cost of major rearrangements of assets to increase efficiency is an example of a capital expenditure.

Revenue expenditures are normal recurring expenditures. However, some expenditures that meet the test for capital expenditures are expensed because they are immaterial, e.g., less than $50.

Expenditures to improve the efficiency or extend the asset life should be capitalized and charged to future periods. A subtle distinction is sometimes made between an improvement in efficiency and an extension of the asset life. Some accountants feel improvements in efficiency should be charged to the asset account, and improvements extending the asset life should be charged to the accumulated depreciation account. The rationale is that improvements extending the asset life will need to be depreciated over an extended period of time, requiring revision of depreciation schedules.

The chart on the following page summarizes the appropriate treatment of expenditures related to fixed assets.

F. **Depreciation**

Depreciation is the annual charge to income for asset use during the period. This is simply a means of spreading asset costs to periods in which the assets produce revenue. Essentially, the "depreciation base" is spread over the asset's useful life (period during which it produces revenue). The objective is to match asset cost with revenue produced. The depreciation base is cost less salvage value (except for the declining balance method which ignores salvage value). The cost of an asset will include any reasonable cost incurred in bringing an asset to an enterprise and getting it ready for its intended use. The useful life can be limited by

1)   Technological change
2)   Normal deterioration
3)   Physical usage

The first two indicate depreciation is a function of time whereas the third indicates depreciation is a function of the level of activity. Other depreciation methods include retirement, replacement, group, composite, etc.

Depreciation methods based on time are

1)   Straight-line
2)   Accelerated

  a) Declining balance (DB)

    1] Most common is double-declining balance (DDB)

  b) Sum-of-the-years' digits (SYD)

3)   Present value

  a) Sinking fund
  b) Annuity

Straight-line and accelerated depreciation are illustrated by the following example: $10,000 asset, 4-year life, $2,000 salvage value.

Year	Straight line	DDB	SYD
1	$2,000	$5,000	$3,200
2	$2,000	$2,500	$2,400
3	$2,000	$ 500	$1,600
4	$2,000	--	$ 800

COSTS SUBSEQUENT TO ACQUISITION OF PROPERTY, PLANT, AND EQUIPMENT

Type of Expenditure / Characteristics	Expense When Incurred	Capitalize — Charge to Asset	Capitalize — Charge to Accum. Deprec.	Other
1. Additions • Extensions, enlargements, or expansions made to an existing asset		X		
2. Repairs and Maintenance				
a. Ordinary • Recurring, relatively small expenditures				
1. Maintain normal operating condition	X			
2. Do **not** add materially to use value	X			
3. Do **not** extend useful life	X			
b. Extraordinary (major) • Not recurring, relatively large expenditures				
1. Primarily increase the use value		X		
2. Primarily extend the useful life			X	
3. Replacements and betterments • Major component of asset is removed and replaced with the same type of component with comparable performance capabilities (replacement) or a different type of component having superior performance capabilities (betterment)				
a. Book value of old component is known				• Remove old asset cost and accum. deprec. • Recognize any loss (or gain) on old asset • Charge asset for replacement component
b. Book value of old component is **not** known		X	X	
4. Reinstallations and Rearrangements • Provide greater efficiency in production or reduce production costs				
1. Material costs, benefits extend into future accounting periods		X		
2. No measurable future benefit	X			

Normal Accounting Treatment

Straight line $\dfrac{\$10,000 - \$2,000}{4}$

DDB   Twice the straight line rate (2 x 25%) times the net book value at beginning of each year, but not below salvage value (salvage value is not deducted for depreciation base).

SYD   4/10*, 3/10, 2/10, 1/10 of ($10,000 - $2,000).

$$\text{*}\dfrac{n(n + 1)}{2} = \dfrac{4 \times 5}{2} = 10$$

<u>Physical usage depreciation</u> is based on activity, e.g., machine hours, or output, e.g., finished widgets.

$$\begin{array}{c}\text{Annual}\\\text{depreciation}\end{array} = \dfrac{\text{Current activity or output}}{\text{total expected activity or output}} \times \text{Depreciation base}$$

EXAMPLE: A machine costs $60,000. The machine's total output is expected to be 500,000 units. If 100,000 units are produced in the first year, $12,000 of depreciation would be incurred (100/500 x $60,000).

Note that physical usage depreciation results in a varying charge, i.e., not constant. Also physical usage depreciation is based on asset activity rather than expiration of time.

<u>Present value depreciation</u> is a depreciation method wherein the rate of return on investment remains constant. Utilities and other rate-regulated industries may benefit by constant rates of return.

$$\dfrac{\text{NI from asset}}{\text{Book value of asset}}$$

Assuming a constant cash flow from the asset, the depreciation charge must be increasing in nature, because the book value of the asset is decreasing. Two methods involving time value of money formulas (annuity and sinking fund) may be used to compute PV depreciation. Both methods result in the same depreciation; one is computed by the present value of annuity formula and the other is computed with the future value of an annuity formula.

Note that increasing depreciation charges is contrary to straight-line and accelerated depreciation as illustrated by the following graph.

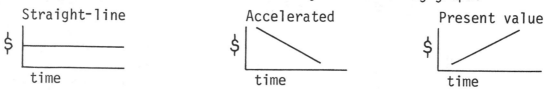

Straight-line   Accelerated   Present value

Accelerated depreciation is justified by

1)   Book value approximates market value
2)   Increased productivity when asset is new
3)   Increasing maintenance charges with age

Little justification, however, can be given for present-value depreciation other than from a capital budgeting and rate regulation viewpoint.

Retirement depreciation is a method wherein the cost of an asset is charged to expense in the period in which it is retired. Replacement depreciation is a method wherein the original cost is carried in the accounts and cost of replacement is expensed in the period of replacement.

Composite (group) depreciation averages the service life of a number of property units and depreciates the group as if it were a single unit. The term "group" is used when the assets are similar; "composite" when they are dissimilar. The depreciation rate is the following ratio.

$$\frac{\text{Sum of annual SL depreciation of individual assets}}{\text{Total asset cost}}$$

Thus composite depreciation is a weighted average of a group of assets -- usually of a similar nature, expected life, etc.

EXAMPLE: Three types of assets (A, B, and C) are depreciated under the composite method.

Asset Type	Asset Cost	Salvage Value	Depreciation Base	Useful Life (Yrs.)	SL Annual Depreciation
A	$ 45,000	$15,000	$ 30,000	5	$ 6,000
B	90,000	50,000	40,000	4	10,000
C	145,000	25,000	120,000	3	40,000
	$280,000	$90,000	$190,000		$56,000

$$\text{Depreciation or composite rate} = \frac{\$56,000}{\$280,000} = 20\%$$

Composite life = 3.39 years ($190,000 ÷ $56,000)

Note that the composite life is the depreciation base divided by the annual depreciation. Depreciation is recorded until the book value of the composite group is depreciated to the salvage value of the then remaining assets. As assets are retired the composite group salvage value is reduced. Also note that gains and losses are not recognized on disposal, i.e., gains and losses are netted into accumulated depreciation. This latter practice also affects the length of time required to reduce the book value (cost less accumulated depreciation) to the group salvage value. The entry to record a retirement is

Cash, other consideration	(amount received)
Accumulated depreciation	(plug)
Asset	(original cost)

Changes in Depreciation. The exam frequently tests changes in depreciation due to changes in expected useful life and salvage value. Make the change

prospectively from the beginning of the year in which the change in estimate is
made. The procedure for straight-line depreciation is

1) Divide the periods remaining (from the beginning of the year of change)
into
2) The remaining depreciation base, i.e., undepreciated cost to date less
revised salvage value

Fractional Year Depreciation. Many conventions exist for accounting for
depreciation for midyear asset acquisitions. They include

1) A whole year's depreciation in year of acquisition and none in year of
disposal
2) One-half year's depreciation in year of acquisition and year of disposal
3) Depreciation to nearest whole month in both year of acquisition and year
of disposal

CPA exam questions generally specify the convention to be followed. If not,
select a convention reasonable in the circumstances and provide an explanation
to the grader.

G. **Other Disposals**

Cash	(amount received)	
Accumulated depreciation	(old asset)	
Old asset		(cost)
Gain or loss	(loss)	(gain)

Do not forget to depreciate disposed assets up to the point of disposal. Also,
recognize the need to write off fully depreciated assets that are retired.

Accumulated depreciation	(cost)	
Old asset		(cost)

In addition, recognize that the carrying (book) value of fixed assets may have
to be either removed or reduced due to an impairment of value resulting from
obsolescence or other economic influences. If technological changes result in
total obsolescence (permanent impairment) of a machine (due to either a change
in technology in the machine itself or in the product it makes if usable only in
making that product), the machine should be removed from the accounts.

Accumulated depreciation	xxx	
Loss due to impairment	xxx	
Obsolete asset		xxx

If technological change results in a partial impairment of the fixed asset, the
machine should be written down by increasing accumulated depreciation.

Loss due to impairment	xxx
Accumulated depreciation	xxx

H. Depletion

Depletion is "depreciation" of natural resources. The depletion base is the total cost of the property providing the natural resources. This includes all development costs such as exploring, drilling, excavating, and other preparatory costs.

The depletion base is usually allocated by the ratio of extracted units over the total expected recoverable units.

$$\frac{\text{Units extracted}}{\text{Total expected recoverable units}} \times \text{(Depletion base)}$$

The unit depletion rate is frequently revised due to the uncertainties surrounding the recovery of natural resources. The revised unit rate in any year takes the following form.

$$\frac{\text{orig. cost + add'l. cost incurred - resid. value - depletion taken in prev. yrs.}}{\text{units withdrawn currently + estimated units recoverable at year end}}$$

Note that the adjustment is being made prospectively, i.e., the remaining undepleted cost is being expensed over the remaining recoverable units.

I. Insurance

Loss Account for Fixed Assets. When an insured loss occurs, an insurance loss account should be set up and charged for all losses. These losses include decreases in asset value, earned insurance premiums, etc. The account should be credited for any payments from the insurance company. The remainder is closed to revenue and expense summary.

Coinsurance. This area is tested on the Business Law section of the exam.

J. Intangible Assets (See the outline of APB 17)

Intangible assets are nonphysical assets. Intangible assets normally include only noncurrent intangibles, e.g., accounts receivable are not considered intangibles. Examples of intangible assets include copyrights, leaseholds, organizational costs, trademarks, franchises, patents, and goodwill. These intangibles may be categorized according to the following characteristics.

1) Identifiability. Separately identifiable or lacking specific identification.
2) Manner of acquisition. Acquired singly, in groups, or in business combinations; or developed internally.
3) Expected period of benefit. Limited by law or contract, related to human or economic factors, or indefinite or indeterminate duration.
4) Separability from enterprise. Rights transferable without title, salable, or inseparable from the entire enterprise.

Acquisition of Intangibles. Purchased intangibles should be recorded at cost, which represents the potential earning power of the intangible at time of acquisition. Internally developed intangibles are recorded at the cost of development, unless the intangible

1) Is not specifically identifiable
2) Has an indeterminate life, or
3) Is not separable from the enterprise (such as goodwill)

If one of the above criteria is present, all costs of development are expensed because measurement of the asset and association of costs with future benefits is difficult. Goodwill is recorded only when an entire business is purchased because internally developed goodwill is not specifically identifiable, has an indeterminate life, and is not separable from the enterprise. Purchase of goodwill as part of acquiring a business is discussed in the Investments and Business Combinations and Consolidation modules.

Amortization of Intangibles. Intangible assets should be amortized by crediting the intangible account directly (contra accounts are not used).

Amortization expense	xx	
Intangible asset		xx

Intangibles are normally amortized on a straight-line basis, although any systematic and rational approach is acceptable. Amortization is over the intangible's useful life, which may be less than its legal life. In no case is the useful life to exceed forty years. Factors to consider in determining useful life are listed in the outline of APB 17. Refer to Present Value module under Leases for discussion and treatment of Leasehold Improvements.

K. **Deferred Charges**

Expenditures of a prepayment nature that benefit several future periods, but are not prepaid expenses, are sometimes categorized as deferred charges rather than as intangibles. Examples are organizational costs and bond issue costs. These types of costs should be amortized over the periods benefited. Even though organizational costs theoretically benefit an indefinite number of future periods, they are usually amortized over a relatively short period of time, e.g., 5 years.

L. **Research and Development Costs (SFASs 2 and 68)**

SFAS 2 (see outline) requires R&D costs to be expensed as incurred except for intangibles or fixed assets purchased from others having alternative future uses. These should be capitalized and amortized over their useful life. Thus, the cost of patents and R&D equipment purchased from third parties may be deferred and amortized over the asset's useful life. Internally developed R&D may not be deferred.

Finally, R&D done under contract for others is not required to be expensed per SFAS 2. The costs incurred would be matched with revenue using the completed-contract or percentage-of-completion method.

M. **Development Stage Enterprises (SFAS 7)**

SFAS 7 (see outline) defines a development stage enterprise as one devoting substantially all of its efforts to establishing a new business and 1) planned principal operations have not commenced or 2) planned principal operations have commenced but there has been no significant revenue. It is important to note that generally accepted accounting principles are to be followed in preparing the financial statements of a development stage enterprise. Therefore, no special treatment is allowed concerning capitalization or deferral of costs. The income statement and statement of cash flows should include cumulative amounts, since inception, of revenues, expenses, losses, and cash flows. The financial statements must be identified as those of a development stage enterprise. It should also be noted that the first fiscal year after the development stage, a disclosure is required in the financial statements stating that the entity was previously in the development stage.

MONETARY CURRENT ASSETS AND CURRENT LIABILITIES

Chapter 3A of ARB 43 defines current assets and current liabilities. This study module reviews the accounting for all monetary current assets (except inventory which is presented in Module 23 and short-term investments which are presented in Module 29). This module also reviews current liabilities.

A. Cash

Per SFAS 95, the definition of cash includes both cash (cash on hand and demand deposits) and cash equivalents (short term, highly liquid investments). Cash equivalents have to be readily convertible into cash and so near maturity that they carry little risk of changing in value due to interest rate changes. Generally this will include only those investments with original maturities of three months or less. Common examples of cash equivalents include Treasury bills, commercial paper, and money market funds. Unrestricted cash and cash equivalents available for general use is presented as the first current asset.

Cash set aside for special uses is usually disclosed separately. The entry to set up a special fund is

    Special cash fund   xx
         Cash   xx

Cash restricted as to use, e.g., not transferable out of a foreign country, should be disclosed separately, but not as a current asset if it cannot be used in the next year (this is true of special funds also).

Imprest (petty) cash funds are generally included in the total cash figure, but unreimbursed expense vouchers are excluded.

1. Bank Reconciliations

Bank reconciliations are prepared by bank depositors when they receive their monthly bank statements. The reconciliation is made to determine any required adjustments to the cash balance. Two types of reconciling items are possible.

a. Reconciling items not requiring adjustment on the books (type A)
b. Reconciling items requiring adjustment on the books (type B)

There are three type A reconciling items. They do not require adjusting journal entries.

    (1) Outstanding checks
    (2) Deposits in transit
    (3) Bank errors

All other reconciling items (type B) require adjusting journal entries.

Examples of type B reconciling items include

(1) Unrecorded returned nonsufficient funds (NSF) checks
(2) Unrecorded bank charges
(3) Errors in the cash account
(4) Unrecorded bank collections of notes receivable

Two types of formats are used in bank reconciliations.

Format 1	Format 2
Balance per bank	Balance per bank
+(-) A adjustments	+(-) A adjustments
Correct cash balance	+(-) B adjustments
	Balance per books
Balance per books	+(-) B adjustments
+(-) B adjustments	Correct cash balance
Correct cash balance	

Type A and B adjustments can be either added or subtracted depending upon the type of format and the nature of the item.

Reconciling items must be analyzed to determine whether they are included in (1) the balance per bank, and/or (2) the balance per books. If they are included in one, but not the other, an adjustment is required. For instance, the $1,800 deposit in transit in the following example is included in the balance per books but not in the balance per bank. Thus, it must be added to the balance per bank to reconcile to the correct cash balance. Deposits in transit do not require an adjusting journal entry. Analyze all reconciling items in this manner, but remember, only journalize type B reconciling items.

Sample Bank Reconciliation (Format 1)

Per bank statement	$ 4,702
Deposits in transit	1,800
Outstanding checks	(1,200)
Bank error	50
Correct cash balance	$ 5,352
Per books	$ 5,332
Service charges	(5)
Note collected by bank	150
Customer's NSF check	(170)
Deposit of July 10 recorded as $749 instead of $794	45
Correct cash balance	$ 5,352

Note that the balance per bank and balance per books each are reconciled directly to the corrected balance.

a. Adjusting Journal Entries
All of the items in the per books section of a bank reconciliation (type B) require adjusting entries. The entries for the above example appear below.

Miscellaneous expense 5		A/R	170
Cash	5	Cash	170
Cash	150	Cash	45
Notes receivable	150	A/R (or sales)	45

b. Four-Column Cash Reconciliation

Unlike the bank reconciliation above, which is as of a specific date, a four-column cash reconciliation, also known as a "proof of cash," reconciles bank and book cash balances over a specified time period. A proof of cash consists of four columns: beginning of the period bank reconciliation, receipts, disbursements, and end of the period bank reconciliation. Thus, the proof of cash cross-foots as well as foots.

Sample Proof of Cash (Format 2)

	Bank reconciliation June 30, 1986	Receipts	Disburse-ments	Bank reconciliation July 31, 1986
Balance per bank statement	$3,402	$25,200	$23,900	$ 4,702
Deposits in transit				
June 30, 1986	1,610	(1,610)		
July 31, 1986		1,800		1,800
Outstanding checks				
June 30, 1986	(450)		(450)	
July 31, 1986			1,200	(1,200)
Service charges			(5)	5
Note collected by bank		(150)		(150)
Customer's NSF check			(170)	170
Deposit of July 10 recorded as $749 instead of $794		(45)		(45)
Bank error			(50)	50
Balance per books	$4,562	$25,195	$24,425	$ 5,332

Note that there are no type B reconciling items in the beginning reconciliation column. This is because the $4,562 has been adjusted when the June bank statement was reconciled. Notice that figures appearing in the center columns have unlike signs if they are adjacent and like signs if they are not adjacent to amounts in the side columns.

The purpose of the proof of cash is to disclose any irregularities, such as unrecorded disbursements and receipts within a month, which would not be detected by a bank reconciliation. For example, if the center two columns each required a negative $1,000 to make the top line reconcile with the bottom line, there may be unrecorded receipts and deposits of $1,000.

B. Receivables

Accounts receivable should be disclosed in the balance sheet at net realizable value (gross amount less estimated uncollectibles) by source, e.g., trade, officer, etc. Officer, employee, and affiliate company receivables should be separately disclosed (ARB 43, Chapter 1A). Unearned interest and finance charges should be deducted from gross receivables (APB 6, para 14).

1. Anticipation of Sales Discounts

Cash discounts are generally recognized as expense when cash payment is received within the discount period. As long as cash discounts to be taken on year-end receivables remain constant from year to year, there is no problem. If, however, discounts on year-end receivables fluctuate, a year-end allowance can be set up or sales can be recorded net of the discounts. The entries to record sales at net are shown below in comparison to the sales recorded gross.

		Sales at net		Sales at gross	
a.	Sale	A/R (net)		A/R (gross)	
		Sales	(net)	Sales	(gross)
b.	Cash receipt within discount period	Cash (net)		Sales disc. (disc.)	
		A/R	(net)	Cash (net)	
				A/R	(gross)
c.	Cash receipt after discount period	Cash (gross)		Cash (gross)	
		A/R	(net)	A/R	(gross)
		Disc. not taken	(disc.)		

If a sales discount allowance method is used, the entry below is made with the gross method entries. The entry should be reversed.

Sales discounts   (expected disc. on year-end A/R)
    Allowance for sales disc.   (expected disc. on year-end A/R)

Similarly, when using the "net method," an entry should be made to pick up discounts not expected to be taken on year-end receivables. Generally, however, these latter adjustments are not made, because they are assumed to be about the same each period.

2. Bad Debts Expense

There are two approaches to bad debts.

    a. Direct write-off method
    b. Allowance method

a. Under the direct write-off method, bad debts are considered expenses in the period in which they are written off. Note that this method is not considered acceptable under GAAP, unless the amounts are immaterial.

        Bad debts expense   (uncollectible A/R)
            A/R   (uncollectible A/R)

b. The allowance method seeks to estimate the amount of uncollectible receivables, and establishes a contra valuation account (allowance for bad debts) for the amount estimated to be uncollectible. The adjusting entry to set up the allowance is

        Bad debts expense   (estimated)
            Allowance for bad debts (estimated)

The entry to write off bad debts is

        Allowance for bad debts   (uncollectible A/R)
            A/R   (uncollectible A/R)

There are two methods to determine the annual charge to bad debts expense.

(1) Annual sales
(2) Year-end A/R

For example, charging bad debts expense for 1% of sales is based on the theory that bad debts are a function of sales; this method emphasizes the income statement.

Charging bad debts on year-end A/R is based on the theory that bad debts are a function of A/R collections during the period; this method emphasizes the balance sheet. A bad debts percentage can be applied to total A/R or subsets of A/R. Often an aging schedule is prepared for this purpose. An A/R aging schedule classifies A/R by their age, e.g., 30, 60, 90, 120, etc., days overdue.

When bad debts expense is estimated as a function of sales, any balance in the allowance account is ignored in making the adjusting entry. Bad debts expense under this method is simply the total amount computed (i.e., sales x percentage). However, when bad debts expense is estimated using outstanding receivables, the expense is the amount needed to adjust the allowance account to the amount computed [i.e., A/R x percentage(s)]. Thus, bad debts expense under this method is the amount computed less any credit balance currently in the allowance account (or plus any debit balance).

Net accounts receivable is the balance in accounts receivable less the allowance for bad debts. Also remember that net receivables <u>do not change</u> when a specific account is written off since both accounts receivable and the allowance account are reduced by the same amount.

3. <u>Pledging, Assigning, Selling A/R</u> (see outline of SFAS 77)

Sometimes businesses cannot wait for the cash flow from the normal collection of A/R. In some cases, A/R may be pledged to secure a loan. The A/R pledged serve as collateral in case of default. At the balance sheet date, the amounts of A/R pledged should be disclosed either parenthetically or in the notes.

Assignment of A/R is a procedure where more formal rights in the A/R are given (assigned) to the lender. The assignor (debtor) still collects on the A/R assigned, but remits the proceeds to the lender. Generally, the amount of A/R assigned is greater than the cash received from the assignee (creditor) so as to cover finance charges and uncollectible accounts. The journal entries for both the assignor and the assignee follow.

		Assignor	Assignee

a.	Cash is advanced for less than total A/R assigned	A/R assigned
		    A/R
			Note receivable
			    Finance revenue
			    Cash

		Cash Finance charge Note payable	
b.	Cash is collected and re-mitted to finance company	Cash A/R assigned	

		Note payable
		    Cash
			Cash
			    Note receivable

c.	A/R are written off	Allowance for doubt-
		    ful accounts
		    A/R assigned	

d.	Additional cash is collected and note paid	Cash A/R assigned	

		Note payable
		Interest expense
		    Cash
			Cash
			    Note receivable
			    Interest revenue

e.	Remainder of A/R are transferred back	A/R A/R assigned	

f.	Financial statement presentation	Current Assets:
		  A/R assigned
		Current Liabilities:
		  Note payable
			Note receivable

Showing the note payable as a liability on the assignor's balance sheet agrees with the SFAS 77 reporting of transfers of A/R with recourse that are handled as borrowings. Due to the contractual connection between the assigned A/R and their obligation, (the note payable), a common practice has been to deduct the note payable from the assigned A/R on the face of the balance sheet. We believe this off-setting treatment is no longer acceptable. The assignee discloses either parenthetically or in a footnote the amount of the assigned A/R securing the loan.

Sales (factoring) of accounts receivable usually result in collection of the receivables by the factor. In most factoring transactions, the factor buys A/R without recourse. The entry for selling A/R without recourse is

    Cash
    Factor's margin
    Loss on sale of A/R
        A/R

The factor's margin provides a margin of protection against sales re-turns, allowances, and disputed accounts. As sales returns and allowances are approved, the following entry is made on the books of the seller.

    Sales returns and allowances
        Factor's margin

The balance in factor's margin is reported as a current asset on the balance sheet. When all of the amounts have been collected by the factor, the balance in the factor's margin account is returned to the seller.

In some cases, A/R may be transferred to a factor with recourse. Per SFAS 77, these conditions must be met for the transfer of A/R with recourse to be considered a sale.

(1) Transferor surrenders control of future economic benefits from A/R
(2) Obligation of transferor under recourse provisions is reasonably estimable (e.g., uncollectible account losses)
(3) Required repurchase of A/R by transferor is limited to recourse provisions

If these are met, the difference between the selling price and the receivables transferred is recognized as a gain (loss). If any of the above conditions are not met, the transaction is viewed as a loan collateralized by A/R, and the amount of the proceeds should be reported as a liability.

4. Discounting Notes Receivable*

Notes are simply formal receivables with a written promise to pay and may be negotiable and/or interest bearing. Traditionally, notes receivable have been accounted for independently of accounts receivable. Aside from accruing interest revenue, etc., the common transaction involving notes receivable is discounting them, i.e., selling them.

Notes receivable are discounted with and without recourse; and, if the note is discounted with recourse, it is accounted for as either a sale or a borrowing. If the discounting is without recourse, it is essentially a sale. For a N/R discounted with recourse to be treated as a sale, the three conditions discussed under factoring of receivables (per SFAS 77, as previously noted) must be met. Otherwise the discounting with recourse is treated as a borrowing.

When a N/R discounted with recourse is treated as a sale, the procedures to calculate cash proceeds, interest revenue, and loss (gain) on sale are as follows.

a. Compute maturity value of the note. Face value plus (face value x contract interest rate for number of days of note).
b. Compute discount, i.e., bank interest. Maturity value x bank interest or discount rate for days remaining to maturity date.
c. Subtract discount from maturity value. Note that the bank is lending the maturity value, i.e., the amount to be collected at the maturity date.

*Other considerations in accounting for notes receivable are covered in Module 26, Section "A.9."

    d.   <u>Compute interest earned prior to discounting</u>. Face value x contract interest rate for number of days prior to discounting.

    e.   <u>Compute loss (gain)</u>. (Face value + prior interest) minus cash proceeds.

EXAMPLE: 60 days, 9%, $1,000 note discounted with the bank when 30 days remain to maturity. Bank interest rate is 11%. The note is discounted with recourse and is appropriately treated as a sale.

a. $\frac{60}{360}$ x 9% x $1,000 + $1,000 = $1,015 Maturity value

b. $\frac{30}{360}$ x 11% x $1,015 = $9.30 Bank discount (interest charge)

c. $1,015 - $9.30 = $1,005.70 Cash proceeds

d. $\frac{30}{360}$ x 9% x $1,000 = $7.50 interest earned

e.   ($1,000 + $7.50) - $1,005.70 = $1.80 loss on sale

The journal entry to record the discounting is

Cash	1,005.70	
Loss on sale of note	1.80	
N/R discounted		1,000.00
Interest revenue		7.50

If the three conditions in SFAS 77 are not met and the discounting is treated as a borrowing, the entry above is modified slightly. "Interest expense (income)" is debited (credited) instead of "Loss (Gain) on sale of note." Also, "Liability on N/R discounted" is credited instead of "N/R discounted." The calculations used to arrive at the amounts are the same. "N/R discounted" is a contra N/R account which discloses the contingent liability. "Liability on N/R discounted" is a current liability. If notes are sold "without recourse," there is no contingent liability; it is essentially a sale and the credit in the entry above would be to "notes receivable." At the maturity date (when the note discounted with recourse is honored or dishonored), the following entry is recorded to recognize that the contingency is resolved.

N/R discounted*	(face)	
N/R		(face)

    *"Liability on N/R discounted" if initially treated as a borrowing

If the note is dishonored

A/R	(maturity value + penalty)	
Cash		(maturity value + penalty)

This entry is made in addition to eliminating the contingent liability (N/R discounted). The A/R is from the maker who dishonored the note.

The contingent liability may also be disclosed by footnote or parenthetically. "N/R" instead of "N/R discounted" would be credited when the
note is discounted (i.e., no contingent liability account is used).

The chart on the following page summarizes the accounting for transfers
of receivables.

C. Current Liabilities

"Obligations whose liquidation is reasonably expected to require the use of
existing resources properly classifiable as current assets, or the creation of
other current liabilities." (ARB 43, Chapter 3, para 7)

1. Examples of Current Liabilities (as they fall within the above definition)

  a. Trade accounts and notes payable
  b. Loan obligations--including current portions of long-term debt. This is
      not true if the current portion of long-term debt will not require the
      use of current assets, e.g., be paid from a sinking fund which is not
      classified as current.
  c. Short-term obligations expected to be refinanced cannot be reclassified
      as noncurrent liabilities unless there is both an intent and an ability
      to refinance. See the outline of SFAS 6.
  d. Dividends payable--cash dividends are a liability when declared. They
      cannot be rescinded.
  e. Accrued liabilities--adjusting entries to reflect our use of goods or
      services before we pay for them. We will pay in future periods even
      though we have incurred the expense in this period, e.g., interest, pay-
      roll, rent expenses.

        Expense account   xx
              Liability (usually current) account   xx

  f. Payroll--there are two entries to record payroll. The first records the
      employee's payment and our deductions on behalf of the employee. The
      second is to record the employer's taxes.

        Payroll expense   xx (gross pay)
              Payroll payable, cash   xx (net pay)
              Income taxes payable   xx
              FICA taxes payable   xx
              Union dues payable   xx
              Medical insurance payable   xx
        Payroll tax expense   xx
              FICA taxes payable   xx
              Federal unemployment tax payable   xx
              State unemployment tax payable   xx

  g. Property taxes. See the outline of ARB 43, Chapter 10A. Generally,
      there is a monthly accrual for property taxes over the fiscal period of
      the taxing authority. If taxes are payable at the end of the tax
      authority's fiscal period, the monthly accrual would be

        Property tax expense   xx
              Property tax payable   xx

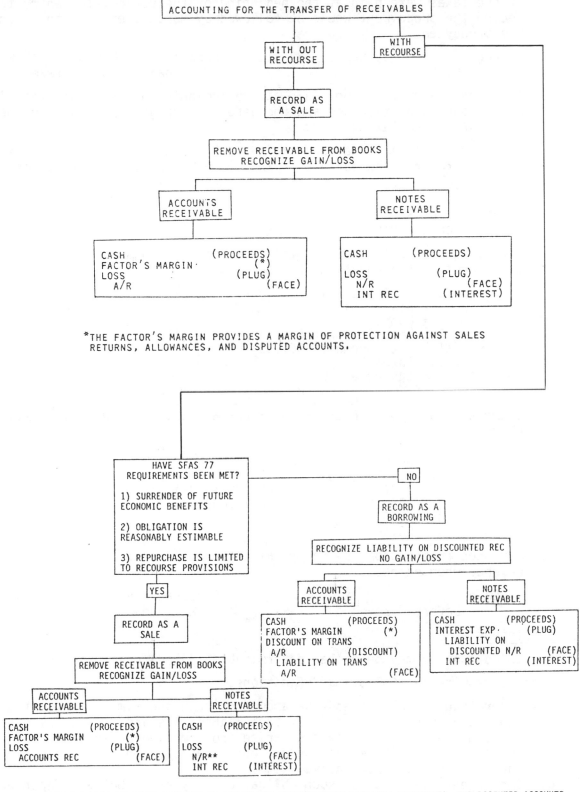

ACCOUNTING FOR THE TRANSFER OF RECEIVABLES

WITH OUT RECOURSE

WITH RECOURSE

RECORD AS A SALE

REMOVE RECEIVABLE FROM BOOKS
RECOGNIZE GAIN/LOSS

ACCOUNTS RECEIVABLE

CASH	(PROCEEDS)
FACTOR'S MARGIN	(*)
LOSS	(PLUG)
A/R	(FACE)

NOTES RECEIVABLE

CASH	(PROCEEDS)
LOSS	(PLUG)
N/R	(FACE)
INT REC	(INTEREST)

*THE FACTOR'S MARGIN PROVIDES A MARGIN OF PROTECTION AGAINST SALES
RETURNS, ALLOWANCES, AND DISPUTED ACCOUNTS.

HAVE SFAS 77
REQUIREMENTS BEEN MET?

1) SURRENDER OF FUTURE
ECONOMIC BENEFITS

2) OBLIGATION IS
REASONABLY ESTIMABLE

3) REPURCHASE IS LIMITED
TO RECOURSE PROVISIONS

NO

RECORD AS A BORROWING

RECOGNIZE LIABILITY ON DISCOUNTED REC
NO GAIN/LOSS

YES

RECORD AS A SALE

REMOVE RECEIVABLE FROM BOOKS
RECOGNIZE GAIN/LOSS

ACCOUNTS RECEIVABLE

CASH	(PROCEEDS)
FACTOR'S MARGIN	(*)
LOSS	(PLUG)
ACCOUNTS REC	(FACE)

NOTES RECEIVABLE

CASH	(PROCEEDS)
LOSS	(PLUG)
N/R**	(FACE)
INT REC	(INTEREST)

ACCOUNTS RECEIVABLE

CASH	(PROCEEDS)
FACTOR'S MARGIN	(*)
DISCOUNT ON TRANS	
A/R	(DISCOUNT)
LIABILITY ON TRANS	
A/R	(FACE)

NOTES RECEIVABLE

CASH	(PROCEEDS)
INTEREST EXP	(PLUG)
LIABILITY ON	
DISCOUNTED N/R	(FACE)
INT REC	(INTEREST)

*THE FACTOR'S MARGIN PROVIDES A MARGIN OF PROTECTION AGAINST SALES RETURNS, ALLOWANCES, AND DISPUTED ACCOUNTS.

**ASSUMES ADEQUATE B/S FOOTNOTE DISCLOSURE. ALTERNATIVELY NOTES RECEIVABLES DISCOUNTED MAY BE
CREDITED AND OFFSET AGAINST NOTES RECEIVABLES ON THE B/S.

If the taxes were paid at the beginning of the period, the entry to record the prepayment would be followed by monthly entries to expense the prepayment.

Prepaid property taxes	xx		Property tax expense	xx
Cash		xx	Prepaid property taxes	xx

If taxes are due, but not paid at the beginning of the year, the liability should be recorded and the deferred charge expensed over the fiscal year of the taxing body.

Deferred property taxes	xx		Property tax expense	xx
Property tax payable		xx	Deferred property taxes	xx

h. Bonus arrangements

Bonus expense	xx
Bonus payable	xx

Set up equations to describe the terms of the bonus agreement. The general forms of the equations follow

$$B = P(NI - B - T)$$
$$T = R(NI - B)$$
$$B = \text{bonus}$$
$$P = \text{bonus or profit sharing rate (10\%)}$$
$$NI = \text{net income (\$150,000)}$$
$$T = \text{taxes}$$
$$R = \text{tax rate (40\%)}$$

EXAMPLE: Work through the above equations using the data in parentheses.

$$T = .40(150,000 - B)$$
$$T = 60,000 - .4B$$
$$B = .10(150,000 - B - T)$$
$$B = .10(150,000 - B - 60,000 + .4B)$$
$$B = 15,000 - .1B - 6,000 + .04B$$
$$1.06B = 9,000$$
$$B = \$8,491$$

i. Advances from customers--record as deferred revenue and recognize as revenue when earned

Cash	xx		Deferred revenue	xx
Deferred revenue		xx	Revenue	xx

2. **Contingencies**

An obligation may be either determinable (fixed) or contingent in accordance with the following definitions.

a. **Determinable Liabilities**--the amount of cash and time of payment are known and reasonably precise. Such liabilities are usually evidenced by written contracts but may also arise from implied agreements or imposed legal statutes. Examples include notes payable and liabilities for various taxes as shown above.

b. **Contingent Liabilities**--such obligations <u>may</u> exist but are dependent on uncertain future events. According to SFAS 5 a contingency is defined as an existing condition, situation, or set of circumstances involving uncertainty as to possible gain or loss to an enterprise that will ultimately be resolved when one or more future events occur or fail to occur.

The accounting problems related to contingencies involve the following issues.

(1)   When is it appropriate to record and report the effects of a contingency in the financial statements? Should the financial impact of the contingency be reported in the period when the contingency is still unresolved or in the period in which the contingency is resolved?

(2)   For contingencies not recorded and reported on the financial statements before they are resolved, what disclosures, if any, are needed in the footnotes to the financial statements?

According to SFAS 5 (see outline), a loss contingency should be accrued if it is <u>probable</u> that an asset has been impaired or a liability has been incurred at the balance sheet date <u>and</u> the amount of the loss is <u>reasonably estimable</u>. When loss contingencies are accrued, a debit should be made to an expense or to a loss account and a credit should be made to either a liability or to a contra-asset account. Note that to accrue a loss contingency means that the financial effects of a contingency are reported in the financial statements <u>before</u> the contingency is resolved.

When making the decision concerning the accrual of a loss contingency, the term <u>probable</u> relates to the likelihood of a future event taking place or failing to take place which would resolve the uncertainty. However, the likelihood of a future event taking place or failing to take place may not always be judged to be probable. The likelihood of the future event taking place or failing to take place may instead be judged to be <u>reasonably possible</u> or <u>remote</u>. In these last two situations, it is <u>not</u> appropriate to accrue the loss contingency as of the balance sheet date, although footnote disclosure may be necessary. Footnote disclosure will be discussed later in this section.

In addition to being probable, the accrual of a loss contingency also requires that the amount of the loss be <u>reasonably estimable</u>. In most situations, a single amount can be estimated, and this represents the loss that is accrued. In other situations, the loss may be estimated in terms of a range, for example, the range of loss may be $100,000 to $500,000. In these situations, the amount of loss to accrue is the best estimate within the range. For example, if the best estimate within the range is $200,000, the loss should be accrued in the amount of $200,000. However, if no number in the range is a better estimate of the loss than any other number in the range, the lower number in the range is accrued as the loss. Thus, $100,000 would be accrued if no other number in the range from $100,000 to $500,000 were a better estimate of the loss than any other number in the range.

Loss contingencies that are usually accrued relate to losses involving

- Collectibility of receivables (Bad Debts Expense/Allowance for Uncollectible Accounts),
- Obligations related to product warranties and product defects (Warranty Expense/Warranty Liability), and
- Premiums offered to customers (Premium Expense/Premium Liability)

These contingencies are usually accrued because it is probable that some receivables will not be collected, that some of the products sold will be defective and may need warranty work, and that some customers will take advantage of premiums offered by the company. In addition, the amounts in each case can usually be estimated because of past experience with each of these situations.

To illustrate the accrual of a loss contingency, let's focus on a product warranty situation. Here are the facts related to the illustration for ABC Company.

Year	Sales	Actual warranty expenditures	Estimated warranty costs related to dollar sales
1988	$500,000	$15,000	Year of sale 4%
1989	$700,000	$47,000	Year after sale 6%

In 1988, ABC should accrue a loss contingency related to product warranties for $50,000 [$500,000 x (4% + 6%)]. The entry would appear as follows.

Warranty expense	50,000	
Liability for product warranty		50,000

The actual warranty expenditures in 1988 would be recorded in the following manner. (Note that the actual expenditures reduce the liability and have no effect on the expense account.)

Liability for product warranty	15,000	
Cash, parts inventory, etc.		15,000

ABC's income statement for 1988 would report an expense for $50,000 related to its product warranty, and its December 31, 1988, balance sheet would report a current liability for product warranty of $35,000 ($50,000 - 15,000). In 1989, ABC should accrue a loss contingency related to product warranties for $70,000 [$700,000 x (4% + 6%)]. The entry would appear as follows.

Warranty expense	70,000	
Liability for product warranty		70,000

The actual warranty expenditures for 1989 would be recorded in the following manner. (Again, note that the actual expenditures only affect the liability account.)

Liability for product warranty	47,000	
Cash, parts inventory, etc.		47,000

ABC's income statement for 1989 should report an expense related to product warranties of $70,000, and its December 31, 1989, balance sheet should report a current liability for product warranty of $58,000 (the 1/1/89 balance of $35,000 + the 1989 expense of $70,000 less the actual warranty expenditures of $47,000 in 1989).

Another example of accrual of a contingent liability involves companies offering premiums, e.g., towels, knives, and other prizes, to promote their products. Such companies often have premium liability for outstanding coupons when it is probable that some of the coupons will be redeemed and the amount can be estimated. The expense should be accrued in the period of sale based on the estimated redemption rate.

```
Premium plan expense              xx
    Premium plan liability                xx
```

As coupons are actually redeemed by customers, the liability is reduced.

```
Premium plan liability            xx
    Premiums                              xx
```

Loss contingencies that may be accrued (depending upon whether or not the two conditions of probable and reasonably estimable are satisfied) include the following events.

- Threat of expropriation of assets
- Pending or threatened litigation
- Actual or possible claims and assessments
- Guarantees of indebtedness of others
- Obligations of commercial banks under "Standby letters of credit," and
- Agreements to repurchase receivables (or the related property) that have been sold

The one event listed above that appears frequently on the exam involves pending litigation. If the loss from litigation is reasonably estimable, and it is probable as of the balance sheet date that the lawsuit will be lost, the loss should be accrued.

To illustrate this point, assume that XYZ Company is presently involved in litigation involving patent infringement that allegedly occurred during 1988. The financial statements for 1989 are being prepared, and XYZ's legal counsel believes it is probable that XYZ will lose the lawsuit and that the damages will be in the range from $500,000 to $800,000 with the most likely amount being $700,000. Based upon XYZ's legal counsel, it should accrue the loss contingency in the following manner at December 31, 1989.

```
Loss from litigation              700,000
    Liability from litigation             700,000
```

The $700,000 loss from litigation should be reported on XYZ's 1989 income statement, and the liability should be reported on the December 31, 1989, balance sheet.

If XYZ settles the litigation in 1990 by paying damages of $600,000, the following journal entry should be made.

Liability from litigation	700,000	
Cash		600,000
Gain from settlement of litigation		100,000

The above entry results in a gain for 1990 because the damages were settled for less than their expected amount. This situation is not unusual because the loss contingency related to the litigation was based upon an estimated amount. Note that it would be incorrect to revise the 1989 financial statements so that the loss contingency reflected the actual damages of $600,000. When the financial statements for 1989 were issued, the best estimate of loss was $700,000. This estimate is not revised subsequent to the issuance of the 1989 financial statements.

Since loss contingencies involving litigation are only accrued if the conditions of probable and reasonably estimable are present, you should be aware of what is reported if either or both of these conditions are not present. For XYZ's case, suppose that its legal counsel believed it was only reasonably possible (not probable) as of the balance sheet date, December 31, 1989, that XYZ would lose its lawsuit. In this situation, it would not be appropriate for XYZ to accrue a loss at December 31, 1989. However, because XYZ's legal counsel believes it is reasonably possible to lose the lawsuit, XYZ should disclose this litigation in its footnotes for its 1989 financial statements. The range of loss, noted before as being from $500,000 to $800,000, would also be disclosed in the footnote. In 1990, when the actual damages of $600,000 are known, XYZ would record a loss of this amount and report it on its 1990 income statement.

If XYZ's legal counsel believed that it was remote as of December 31, 1989, that the lawsuit would be lost, no accrual or disclosure of the litigation would be necessary.

Loss contingencies that are not accrued or even disclosed in the footnotes include the following events.

- Risk of loss or damage of enterprise property by fire, explosion, or other hazards
- General or unspecified business risks
- Risk of loss from catastrophes assumed by property and casualty insurance companies including reinsurance companies

Losses which result from the above events are recorded and reported in the period when the event occurs that causes the loss. For example, if XYZ's factory is destroyed by fire in 1988, the loss from this event should be recorded and reported in 1988. If the damages from the fire amount to $1,000,000, and XYZ's insurance company reimburses XYZ $800,000, XYZ's loss is $200,000. If XYZ does not insure for fire with an insurance company, XYZ's loss for 1988 would be $1,000,000.

The discussion relating to contingencies has focused on the accounting for loss contingencies. On the other hand, contingencies exist that may also result in possible gains. According to SFAS 5, contingencies that might result in gains usually are not reflected in the accounts since to do so might be to recognize revenue prior to its realization. This means that any gains that result from gain contingencies should be recorded and reported in the period during which the contingency is resolved. For example, the plaintiff in a lawsuit should not record or report the expected damages to be received until the lawsuit has been decided.

Knowledge of the conditions that must be present in order to accrue a loss contingency is helpful in the accounting for compensated absences (vacation, sick leave pay, etc.). According to SFAS 43 (see outline), an employer shall accrue a liability for employees' compensation for future absences if all of the following conditions are met.

- The employer's obligation relating to employees' rights to receive compensation for future absences is attributable to employees' services already rendered
- The obligation relates to rights that vest or accumulate
- Payment of the compensation is probable
- The amount can be reasonably estimated

To illustrate the accounting for compensated absences, assume MNO Company employees earn two weeks of paid vacation for each year of employment. Unused vacation time can be accumulated and carried forward to succeeding years, and will be paid at the salary level in effect when the vacation is taken. As of December 31, 1988, when John Baker's salary was $600 per week, John Baker had earned 18 weeks vacation time and had used 12 weeks of accumulated vacation time. At December 31, 1988, MNO should report a liability for John Baker's accumulated vacation time of $3,600 (6 weeks of accumulated vacation time times $600 per week). The journal entry at December 31, 1986, would appear as follows (assume previous year's entry was reversed).

```
Salary and wages expense                        3,600
   Accrued liability for compensated absences           3,600
```

PRESENT VALUE

This module starts off by reviewing the basic concepts related to time value of money. The module then covers four major topics where time value of money applications are used extensively: 1) bonds payable and bond investments, 2) debt restructure, 3) pensions, and 4) leases.

A. Fundamentals

The concepts of time value of money are essential for successful completion of the CPA exam. Time value of money concepts are central to capital budgeting, leases, pensions, bonds, and other topics. You must understand the mechanics as well as the concepts. After studying the next few pages, work the multiple choice questions entitled "Fundamentals." Note that the following abbreviations are used in the text that follows.

> i = interest rate
> n = number of periods or rents

On the CPA exam, you do not have to know the complex formulas that are used to compute time value of money factors (TVMFs). The factors will be given to you or enough information will be given to you so that you can easily compute them (See A.8. TVMF Applications). Your main focus of attention should be centered on understanding which TVMF should be used in a given situation.

1. Future Value (FV) of an Amount (amount of $1)

The future value of an amount is the amount that will be available at some point in the future if an amount is deposited today and earns compound interest for "n" periods. The most common application is savings deposits. For example, if you deposited $100 today at 10%, you would have $110 ($100 x 10%) at the end of the first year, $121 ($110 x 10%) at the end of the second year, etc. The compounding feature allows you to earn interest on interest. In the second year of the example you earn $11 interest: $10 on the original $100 and $1 on the first year's interest of $10.

2. Present Value (PV) of a Future Amount (present value of $1)

The present value of a future amount is the amount you would pay now for an amount to be received "n" periods in the future given an interest rate of "i." A common application would be the money you would lend today for a noninterest-bearing note receivable in the future. For example, if you were lending money at 10%, you would lend $100 for a $110 note due in one year or for a $121 note due in two years.

The present value of $1 is the inverse of the future value of $1. Thus, given a future value of $1 table, you have a present value of $1 by dividing each value into 1.00. Look at the present value of $1 and future value of $1 tables on the next page. The future value of $1 at 10% in 5 years is 1.611. Thus, the present value of $1 in 5 years would be 1.00 ÷ 1.611 which is .621 (check the table). Conversely, the future value of $1 is found by dividing the present value of $1 into 1.00, e.g., 1.00 ÷ .621 = 1.611.

3. Compounding

When interest is compounded more than once a year, two extra steps are needed. First, <u>multiply</u> "n" by the number of times interest is compounded annually. This will give you the total number of interest periods. Second, <u>divide</u> "i" by the number of times interest is compounded annually. This will give you the appropriate interest rate for each interest period. For example, if the 10% were compounded semiannually, the amount of $1.00 at the end of 1 year would be $110.25 [$(1.05)^2$] instead of $110.00. The extra $.25 is 5% of the $5.00 interest earned in the first half of the year.

4. Future Value of an Ordinary Annuity

The future value of an ordinary annuity is the amount available "n" periods in the future as a result of the deposit of an amount (A) at the end of every period 1 through "n." Compound interest is earned at the rate of "i" on the deposits. A common application is a bond sinking fund. A deposit is made at the end of the first period and earns compound interest for n-1 periods (not during the first period, because the deposit is made at the end of the first period). The next to the last payment earns one period's interest, i.e., n - (n-1) = 1. The last payment earns no interest, because it is deposited at the end of the last (nth) period. Remember that in the FUTURE AMOUNT OF AN ORDINARY ANNUITY TABLE, all of the factors for any "n" row are based on one less interest period than the number of payments.

Time Value of Money Factor (TVMF) Tables

Future Value (Amount) of $1

n	6%	8%	10%	12%	15%
1	1.060	1.080	1.100	1.120	1.150
2	1.124	1.166	1.210	1.254	1.323
3	1.191	1.260	1.331	1.405	1.521
4	1.262	1.360	1.464	1.574	1.749
5	1.338	1.469	1.611	1.762	2.011

2
6

Present Value of $1

n	6%	8%	10%	12%	15%
1	.943	.926	.909	.893	.870
2	.890	.857	.826	.797	.756
3	.840	.794	.751	.712	.658
4	.792	.735	.683	.636	.572
5	.747	.681	.621	.567	.497

Future Value (Amount) of an Ordinary Annuity of $1

n	6%	8%	10%	12%	15%
1	1.000	1.000	1.000	1.000	1.000
2	2.060	2.080	2.100	2.120	2.150
3	3.184	3.246	3.310	3.374	3.473
4	4.375	4.506	4.641	4.779	4.993
5	5.637	5.867	6.105	6.353	6.742

Present Value of an Ordinary Annuity of $1

n	6%	8%	10%	12%	15%
1	.943	.926	.909	.893	.870
2	1.833	1.783	1.736	1.690	1.626
3	2.673	2.577	2.487	2.402	2.283
4	3.465	3.312	3.170	3.037	2.855
5	4.212	3.993	3.791	3.605	3.352

5. Present Value of an Ordinary Annuity

The present value of an ordinary annuity is the value today, given a discount rate, of a series of future payments. A common application is the capitalization of lease payments by either lessors or lessees. Payments "1" through "n" are assumed to be made at the end of years "1" through "n," and are discounted back to the present.

> EXAMPLE:
>
> Assume a 5-year lease of equipment requiring payments of $1,000 at the end of each of the five years, which is to be capitalized. If the discount rate is 8%, the present value is $3,993 ($1,000 x 3.993).

6. Distinguishing a Future Value of an Annuity from a Present Value of an Annuity

Sometimes confusion arises in distinguishing between the future value (amount) of an annuity and the present value of an annuity. These two may be distinguished by determining whether the total dollar amount in the problem comes at the beginning (e.g., cost of equipment acquired for leasing) or at the end (e.g., the amount needed to retire bonds) of the series of payments as illustrated below.

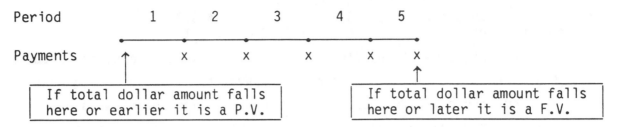

Remember: if the amount given or to be computed comes at the end of the series of payments, it is a <u>future value</u> of annuity situation. If the amount given or to be computed comes at the beginning of the series of payments, it is a <u>present value</u> of annuity situation.

7. Annuities Due

In some cases, the payments or annuities may not conform to the assumptions inherent in the annuity tables. For example, the payments might be made at the beginning of each of the five years instead of at the end of each year. This is an annuity due (annuity in advance) in contrast to an ordinary annuity (annuity in arrears). Both annuity due and ordinary annuity payments are represented by the "x's" in the illustration below.

Period		1	2	3	4	5	
Annuity		x	x	x	x		x
Annuity Due	x	x	x	x	x		

For a future value of annuity due situation, it is necessary to (a) find the TVMF for n + 1 periods and to (b) subtract 1.00. It is necessary to add "1" to "n" because the row of factors for each "n" in the ordinary annuity table has one less interval (interest period) than the number of payments. It is necessary to subtract 1.00 from the factor found on the n + 1 line in the table because the factor will contain one more payment (1.00) than is actually being made. Finding the n + 1 factor and subtracting 1.00 gives a factor which includes compound interest for the additional period.

The TVMF of the present value of an annuity due is found by (a) finding the n - 1 factor in the ordinary annuity table and (b) adding 1.00 to that factor. It is necessary to use the n - 1 factor because the present value of annuity due has one less discount period than the number of payments. It is necessary to add 1.00 to the factor, because there is a payment at the beginning of period 1. If the payments in the 5-period lease example above were made at the beginning of the period, the present value would be calculated as follows:

Annuity due factor: 3.312 + 1.000 =   4.312
Present value: 4.312 x $1,000 = $4,312

The present value of the first payment which is made today is $1,000, i.e.,
the TVMF is 1.00. The remaining four payments comprise an ordinary annuity
for four periods as you can see on the above diagram. Always use time
diagrams to analyze application of annuities. Finally, notice that the
present value of the annuity due in the above example is $319 greater than
the present value of the ordinary annuity because the payments are moved
closer to the present.

8. TVMF Applications

The basic formula to use is

FV or PV = TVMF x Amount

If an annuity is involved, the amount is the periodic payment or deposit; if
not, it is a single sum. Note that FV or PV is determined by 3 variables:
time, interest rate, and payment. TVMF represents two variables: time and
interest rate. The tables usually have the interest rate on the horizontal
axis and time on the vertical axis. The above formula may also be stated as

$$\text{Amount} = \frac{\text{FV or PV}}{\text{TVMF}}$$

For example, if we need to accumulate $12,210 in five years to repay a
loan, we could determine the required annual deposit with the above formula.
If the savings rate were 10%, we would divide the FV ($12,210) by the TVMF
of the future value of annuity, n=5, i=.10 (6.105) and get $2,000. Thus,
$2,000 deposited at the end of each of five years earning 10% will result in
$12,210. This formula may also be used to find future values of an amount,
present values of amounts, and annuities in the same manner.

Another variation of the formula is

$$\text{TVMF} = \frac{\text{FV or PV}}{\text{Amount}}$$

For example, we may be offered a choice between paying $3,312 in cash or
$1,000 a year at the end of each of the next four years. We determine the
interest rate by dividing the annual payment into the present value of the
annuity to obtain the TVMF (3.312) for n=4. We then find the interest rate
which has the same or similar TVMF (in this case 8%).

Alternatively, using the above formula, we may know the interest rate
but not know the number of payments. Given the TVMF, we can determine "n"
by looking in the TVMF table under the known interest rate. Remember the
TVMF reflects two variables: time and interest rate.

9. Notes Receivable and Payable

Notes should be recorded at their present values (see outline of APB 21). Upon receipt or issuance of a note, record the net value of the note receivable or payable (i.e., note plus or minus premium or discount) at

1. Cash received or paid

   a. Assumes no other rights or privileges

2. Established exchange price (fair market value) of property or services received or provided

   a. If not determinable, determine present value with imputed interest rate

Record interest revenue (on notes receivable) or interest expense (on notes payable) as the effective rate of interest times the net receivable or payable during the period.

When a note is exchanged for cash and no other rights or privileges are exchanged, the present value of the note is equivalent to the cash exchanged. The cash exchanged, however, may not be equal to the face amount of the note (the amount paid at maturity). When the face amount of a note does not equal its present value, the difference is either a discount or a premium. A discount results when the face of the note exceeds its present value, and a premium results when the present value of the note exceeds its face (see Section "B.1." in this module for a more detailed discussion of discounts and premiums).

In the preceding discussion, notes were issued solely for cash, and no other rights or privileges were exchanged. The accounting treatment differs, however, when a note is issued for cash and unstated rights and/or privileges are also exchanged. The cash exchanged for such a note consists of two elements: (1) the present value of the note, and (2) the present value of the unstated right or privilege. Proper accounting for this situation requires that one of the two present values above be determined. Once this is done, the remaining present value is simply the difference between the face amount of the note and the present value that was determined.

For example, on January 1, 1986, Zilch Company borrowed $200,000 from its major customer, Martha Corporation. The borrowing is evidenced by a note payable due in 3 years. The note is noninterest bearing. In consideration for the borrowing, Zilch Company agrees to supply Martha Corporation's inventory needs for the loan period at favorable prices. This last feature of the transaction is the unstated right or privilege; that is, the ability of Martha to purchase inventory at less than regular prices.

The present value of the note (assuming it is easier to determine) should be based upon the interest rate Zilch would have to pay in a normal borrowing of $200,000 (that is, in a transaction that did not include unstated rights or privileges). Assume that Zilch would have to pay interest at 12% in a normal borrowing. The present value of $200,000 discounted for 3 years at 12% is $142,400 ($200,000 x .712). The difference between the face amount of the note, $200,000, and its present value of $142,400 represents the present value of the unstated right or privilege. The amount of this present value is $57,600.

The entries below show how both Zilch and Martha should account for this transaction during 1986.

Zilch			Martha		
1/1/86			1/1/86		
Cash	142,400		Note Receivable	200,000	
Discount on Note			Discount on Note		
Payable	57,600		Receivable		57,600
Note Payable		200,000	Cash		142,400
Cash	57,600		Advance Payments on		
Deferred Revenue		57,600	Inventory	57,600	
			Cash		57,600
12/31/86			12/31/86		
Interest Expense	17,088*		Discount on Note Re-		
Discount on Note			ceivable	17,088	
Payable		17,088	Interest Income		17,088

$142,400 x .12 = $17,088

Zilch			Martha		
Deferred Revenue	xx		Inventory (Purchases)	xx	
Sales		xx	Advance Payments		
			on Inventory		xx

The amounts represented by "xx" in the entries above depend upon the amount of goods acquired by Martha during 1986.

On the December 31, 1986, balance sheets of both Zilch and Martha, the above notes should be disclosed in the noncurrent liability (Zilch) and asset (Martha) sections net of the unamortized discount applicable to each note.

In addition to notes issued for cash, a note may also be received or issued in a noncash transaction; that is, for goods, property, or services. The problem created in this situation is how to determine the note's present value in the absence of cash. One way to solve this problem is to assume that the stated or contractual rate stated on the note represents a fair rate of return to the supplier for the use of the related funds. If the interest rate is presumed to be fair, then the face amount of the note is presumed to equal its present value. Interest revenue (expense) is computed by multiplying the interest rate stated on the face of the note by the face of the note. There is no discount or premium to consider because the face of the note is assumed to be equal to its present value.

The assumption that the interest rate on the face of the note is fair is not always valid. According to APB 21, the assumption is not valid if

1) The interest rate is not stated (usually, this means the note is noninterest bearing), or
2) The stated rate is unreasonable (this refers to both unreasonably low and high rates), or
3) The stated face amount of the note is materially different from the current cash sales price for the same or similar items or from the market value of the note at the date of the transaction.

When the interest rate is not fair, the face amount of the note does not equal its present value. In the absence of cash, the present value of a note is determined according to the following priorities.

1) First determine if the goods, property, or services exchanged have a reliable fair market value. If they do, the fair market value is presumed to be the present value of the note.
2) If a reliable fair market value does not exist for the goods, property, or services exchanged, then determine if the note has a market value. If it does, the note's market value is equal to the present value of the note.
3) Finally, if market values do not exist for either the goods, property, or services or for the note, then an interest rate must be imputed. This imputed interest rate is then used to determine the present value of the note. The imputed interest rate represents the debtor's incremental borrowing rate.

To illustrate the situation where the interest rate on a note is not fair, yet the fair market value of the property exchanged is known, assume the following facts: Doink Co. sold a building on January 1, 1986, which originally cost $7,000,000 and which had a book value of $4,000,000 for a $14,000,000 (face amount) noninterest bearing note due in three years. Since zero interest is not considered to be a fair rate of return, the face amount of Doink's note does not equal its present value. In Doink's case, the face of its note is $14,000,000. The present value of the note is the unknown and must be calculated.

To determine the present value of Doink's $14,000,000 noninterest bearing note, you should first see if the building it sold had a reliable fair market value at the date it was sold. Assume that Doink's building could have sold on January 1, 1986, for $10,000,000 in a straight cash transaction. Given the information about the building, its fair market value of

$10,000,000 on January 1, 1986, represents the note's present value. Since
the face of the note is $14,000,000 and its present value is $10,000,000,
the $4,000,000 difference represents the discount. Doink should record this
transaction in the following manner.

Note Receivable	14,000,000	
Accumulated Depreciation	3,000,000	
Building		7,000,000
Gain on Sale of Building		6,000,000
Discount on Note Receivable		4,000,000

It is important that you note how the gain is calculated in the entry
above. The gain is the difference between the present value of the note
($10,000,000) and the book value of the property sold ($4,000,000). The
difference between the face amount of the note ($14,000,000) and its present
value ($10,000,000) represents the discount of $4,000,000. This discount
should be amortized to interest income using the effective interest
method. However, before this discount can be amortized, the interest rate
must be determined. In situations like this, the interest rate is determined by reference to present value tables. In Doink's situation, the
present value of the note, $10,000,000, divided by its face amount,
$14,000,000, results in the number .714. This number represents a factor
from the present value of $1 table. Since Doink's note is for 3 periods,
the factor .712 in the present value of $1 table is under the 12% interest
rate. Thus, Doink's interest rate is approximately 12%.

   If the building sold by Doink did not have a reliable fair market value
on January 1, 1986, the next step would be to determine if the note had a
market value on that date.

   Finally, if the building sold by Doink did not possess a reliable fair
market value on January 1, 1986, and the note did not have a market value on
that date, the present value of Doink's note would have to be determined by
imputation. This means that Doink would determine the present value of its
note by reference to the incremental borrowing rate of the company which
acquired its building.

   The following diagram represents the forementioned relationships and
procedures for determining the present value of a note receivable or payable
(monetary assets and liabilities) and the amount of a discount/premium.

ACCOUNTING FOR MONETARY ASSETS AND LIABILITIES WHICH HAVE MATURITIES GREATER THAN 1 YEAR FROM THE BALANCE SHEET DATE

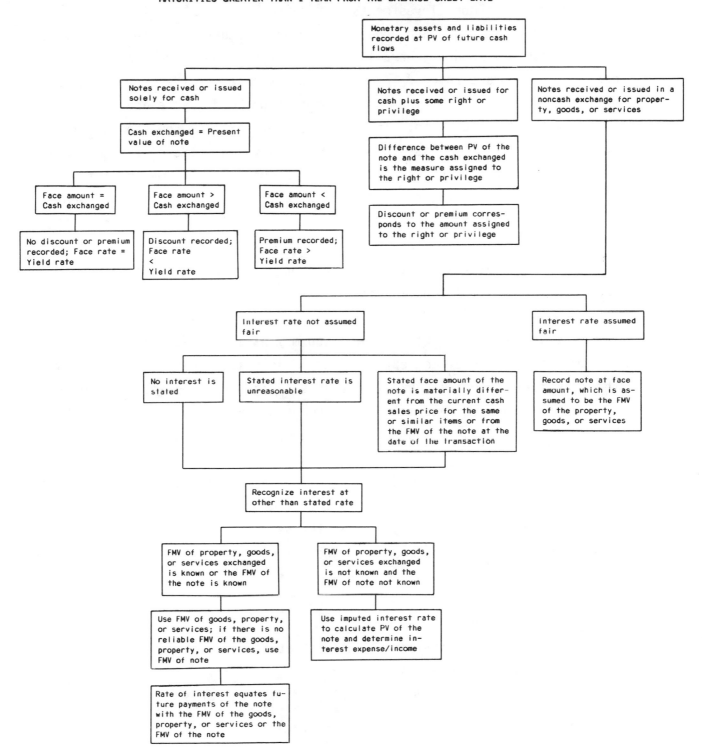

B. Bonds

1. Bonds Payable and Bond Investments

Investment in bonds and bonds payable are discussed together to contrast their treatment. Bonds generally provide for periodic fixed interest payments at a contract rate of interest. At issuance, or thereafter, the market rate of interest for the particular type of bond may be above, the same, or below the contract rate. If the market rate exceeds the contract rate, the bond value will be less than the maturity value. The difference (discount) will make up for the contract rate being below the market rate.

Conversely, when the contract rate exceeds the market rate, the bond will sell for more than maturity value to bring the effective rate to the market rate. This difference (premium) will make up for the contract rate being above the market rate. When the contract rate equals the market rate, the bond will sell for the maturity value.

The market value of a bond is equal to the maturity value and interest payments discounted to the present. You may have to refer to the discussion of time value of money concepts in the previous section before working with the subsequent material. Finally, when solving bond problems, candidates must be careful when determining the number of months to use in the calculation of interest and discount/premium amortization. For example, candidates frequently look at a bond issue with an interest date of September 1 and count three months to December 31. This error is easy to make because candidates focus only on the fact that September is the ninth month instead of also noting whether the date is at the beginning or end of the month. Candidates should also be aware that bond issues that mature on a single date are called term bonds and bond issues that mature in installments are called serial bonds.

2. Bond Valuation Example

$10,000 in bonds, semiannual interest at 6% contract rate, maturing in 6 years, and market rate of 5%.

      1)   Find present value of maturity value. Use present value of $1 factor. Discount $10,000 back 12 periods at 2 1/2% interest (Factor = .7436). (Semiannual compounding is going to be required to discount the semiannual payments so it is also assumed here.)

                $10,000 x .7436 = $7,436

2)   Find the present value of the annuity of twelve $300 interest
     payments. Use present value of an ordinary annuity of $1 factor
     for 12 periods at 2½% interest (Factor = 10.26).

          $300 x 10.26 = $3,078

3)   Today's value is $10,514 (7,436 + 3,078)

The $514 premium is to be recognized over the life of the bond issue.
It is a reduction of interest expense on the books of the issuer and a reduction of interest revenue on the books of the investor. Amortization is
to be by the interest, or present value basis. (See outline of APB 21.)

3. Journal Entries

     The issuer's books will be illustrated at gross (including a premium or
discount account) and the investor's books will be illustrated at net (no
discount or premium account). The investor may record the bonds either net
or gross, but the issuer records at gross. In the past, CPA examination
problems and solutions have followed the net method on the books of the
investor.

		Issuer			Investor		
1)	Issue and Acquisition	Cash	10,514		Bond invest	10,514	
		Bonds pay		10,000	Cash		10,514
		Bonds prem		514			
2)	First int payment	Interest exp	300		Cash	300	
		Cash		300	Interest rev		300
3)	Premium-- Amortization	Bond prem	37.15*		Interest rev	37.15	
		Interest exp		37.15	Bond invest		37.15*

*Interest receipt (payment) minus effective interest = 300 - 262.85 = 37.15
 Effective interest = net book value times effective rate = 10,514 x .025 = 262.85

     Entry 1 assumes that the bonds are issued on the interest payment
date. If bonds are purchased between interest payment dates, the purchaser
will also include accrued interest through the purchase date in the total
cash paid for the bonds. The payment of this accrued interest on the purchase date will serve to reduce the subsequent receipt of interest income
(which covers a time period longer than the time the purchaser held the
bond).

     Subsequent interest payments are recorded the same as entry 2 shown
above. The amount of subsequent amortization (entry 3 above) changes.
Interest to be recorded under the interest method is always computed by

Effective interest rate x Net book value

This formula is true of all applications of the interest method. The effective rate of interest times net book value is the actual interest revenue or expense for the period. The difference between the actual interest and the amount received or paid is the amortization. The amortization table below shows the effective interest amounts and premium amortizations for the first four periods.

Period	3% cash interest	2½% effective interest	Decrease in book value	Book value of bonds
0				$10,514.00
1	$300 (a)	$262.85 (b)	$37.15 (c)	10,476.85 (d)
2	300	261.92	38.08	10,438.77
3	300	260.97	39.03	10,399.74
4	300	259.99	40.01	10,359.73

(a) 3% x $10,000   (c) $300 - $262.85
(b) 2½% x $10,514.00   (d) $10,514.00 - $37.15

Since the interest is paid semiannually, interest (including premium amortization) is recorded every six months. The journal entries for periods 2, 3, and 4 are

	Issuer			Investor	
Period 2	Interest expense	261.92	Cash		300.00
	Bond premium	38.08		Interest rev	261.92
	Cash	300.00		Bond invest	38.08
Period 3	Interest expense	260.97	Cash		300.00
	Bond premium	39.03		Interest rev	260.97
	Cash	300.00		Bond invest	39.03
Period 4	Interest expense	259.99	Cash		300.00
	Bond premium	40.01		Interest rev	259.99
	Cash	300.00		Bond invest	40.01

Notice that the interest (revenue and expense) decreases over time. This is because the net book value (which is also the present value) is decreasing from the maturity value plus premium to the maturity value. Thus, the effective rate is being multiplied by a smaller amount each 6 months.

Also, note that the change in interest each period is the prior period's premium amortization times the effective rate. For example, the interest in period 3 is $.95 less than in period 2, and $38.08 of premium was amortized in period 2. The effective rate of 2.5% (every 6 months) times $38.08 is $.95. Thus, if the interest changes due to the changing level of net book value, the change in interest will be equal to the change in the net book value times the effective rate of interest.

Another complication may arise if the year end does not coincide with the interest dates. In such a case, an adjusting entry must be made. The proportional share of interest payable or receivable should be recognized along with the amortization of discount or premium. The amortization of discount or premium should be straight-line within the amortization period.

> EXAMPLE: Assume that in the above example, both issuer and investor have reporting periods ending 3 months after the issuance of the bonds.

	Issuer		Investor	
Entries on the closing date	Interest expense 150		Interest receivable 150	
	Interest payable	150	Interest revenue	150
	Bond premium 18.57		Interest revenue 18.57	
	Interest expense	18.57	Bond investment	18.57

Reverse at beginning of new period and make regular entry at next interest payment date.

If bonds are sold (bought) between interest dates, premium/discount amortization must be computed for the period between sale (purchase) date and last (next) interest date. This is accomplished by straight-lining the six-month amount which was calculated using the effective interest method.

> EXAMPLE: The investor sold $5,000 of bonds in the above example, two months after issuance, for $5,250 plus interest.
>
> 1. The bond premium which must be amortized to the point of sale ($5,000 for 2 months) is 1/2 x 1/3 x $37.15 or $6.19.
>
>   Interest revenue   6.19
>   Investment   6.19
>
> 2. The sale is recorded. The investment account was $5,257 before amortization of $6.19. The cash received would be $5,250 plus $50 interest (1/2 x 1/3 x $300). The loss is a forced figure.
>
>   Cash   5,300.00
>   Loss   .81
>   Interest revenue   50.00
>   Investment   5,250.81
>
> 3. Check the interest revenue recorded ($50.00 - $6.19) to the interest earned: $5,257 x 2 1/2% x 1/3 (which equals $43.81).

Costs incurred in connection with the issuance of bonds (e.g., printing and engraving, accounting and legal fees, and commissions), according to SFAC 6, may be treated two ways. However, APB Opinion 21 currently allows the treatment of bond issue costs only in one of these ways.

SFAC 6 states that the bond issue costs can be treated as either an expense or a reduction of the related bond liability. Bond issue costs are not considered as assets because they provide no future economic benefit. The argument for treating them as a reduction of the related bond liability is that they reduce bond proceeds thereby increasing the effective interest rate.   Thus, they should be accounted for the same as unamortized discounts.

In practice, however, the only acceptable GAAP for bond issue costs is to treat them as deferred charges and amortize them on a straight-line basis over the life of the bond.

4. Comparison of Effective Interest and Straight-Line Amortization Methods

Although APB 21 requires use of the effective interest method for determining interest on receivables and payables, the straight-line method may be used if the result obtained is not materially different from that obtained using the effective interest method.

Several recent CPA exam questions have asked candidates to compare the dollar amount of interest revenue (expense) and the interest rate obtained under each method.   The table below summarizes the relationships which are obtained under both methods when a note is issued at: (1) a premium and (2) a discount.

	Effective Interest			Straight-Line Method		
Note Issued At:	(a) Effective Interest Rate	x (b) Carrying (Book) Value	= (c) Amount of Interest Income (Expense)	(d) Cash Interest	+ (e) Discount (Premium) Amortization	= (f) Amount of Interest
(1) Discount	Constant	Increasing	Increasing	Constant	Constant	Constant
(2) Premium	Constant	Decreasing	Decreasing	Constant	Constant	Constant

In the above chart, the three columnar headings under each method are written in the form of an equation.   Under the effective interest method, the dollar amount of interest revenue (expense), column (c), is derived by multiplying the effective rate (a constant percentage), column (a), by an increasing (decreasing) carrying value, column (b), resulting in an increasing (decreasing) dollar amount of interest, column (c).

Under the straight-line method, the dollar amount of interest revenue (expense), column (f), is the dollar amount of cash interest (nominal or stated rate times the face of the note), column (d) plus (minus) the discount (premium) amortization, column (e).   When the constant dollar amount of interest revenue (expense) is related to an increasing (decreasing) carrying value the result is a decreasing (increasing) interest rate which is, essentially, an "accounting" or "book" interest rate. This rate is the result of using an arbitrary method (straight-line) which ignores the economic facts of the situation.   The effective inter-

est method gives recognition to the economic facts by using the rate (effective) which resulted from the bargaining of the parties to the note.

When the note is a bond, this may involve many parties (i.e., the
market) and the effective rate is referred to as the "market" or "yield"
rate.

5. Convertible Bonds (See outlines of APB 14 and SFAS 84)

Bonds are frequently issued with the right to convert the bonds into
common stock. When issued, no value is apportioned to the conversion
feature. Two approaches are possible to account for bond conversions:
valuing the transaction at cost (book value of the bonds) or valuing at
market (of the stocks or bonds, whichever is more reliable). At market,
assuming market value exceeds book value, the entries would be

Issuer		Investor	
Loss on redemption	(plug)	Stock invest (mkt)	
Bonds payable	(book value)	Invest in bonds	(carrying value)
Bond premium	(book value)	Gain on conver-	
Common stock	(par)	sion	(plug)
Paid-in excess of par	(mkt-par)		

On the issuer's books, the debit (credit) to the loss (gain) account
(ordinary) would be for the difference between the market value of the
stock (bonds) and the book value of the bonds. The conversion is treated
as the culmination of an earnings process; thus the loss (gain) should be
recognized. The bonds and the related accounts must be written off, and
paid-in excess of par is credited for the excess of the market value of
the stock (bonds) over the stock's par value. On the investor's books,
the gain (loss) would also be the difference between the market value of
the stock (bonds) and the book value of the bonds. Remember in both
cases that the accrued interest and discount or premium amortization must
be recorded prior to the conversion.

Conversion under the cost method would result in debits to bonds
payable and bond premium (or a credit to bond discount) equal to the book
value of the bonds, and credits to common stock and paid-in excess of par
equal to the book value. In practice, conversions are usually recorded
at book value. Note that under this method no gain (loss) is recorded,
as no gain (loss) should result from an equity transaction.

To induce conversion, firms sometimes change the original conversion
privilege or give additional considerations to the bondholders. Per
SFAS 84, the fair market value of these "sweeteners" should be recognized
as an expense (ordinary in nature) upon conversion, determined as the ex-

cess of the FMV of all securities and consideration transferred over the FMV of the securities issuable per the original conversion terms.

6. Debt Issued with Detachable Purchase Warrants

APB 14 (see outline) requires the proceeds of debt issued with detachable stock purchase warrants to be allocated between the debt and stock warrants based on relative market values. Example: units of one bond and one warrant (to buy 10 shares of stock at $50/share) are issued for $1,030. Thereafter, warrants trade at $40 and the bonds at $960. The relative market value of the warrants is 4% (40/1,000) and the relative market value of the bonds is 96% (960/1,000). Thus, $41.20 (.04 x $1,030) of the issue price is assigned to the warrants.

Cash	1,030.00	
Bond discount	11.20	
Bonds payable		1,000.00
Paid-in capital--stock warrants		41.20

If one warrant was subsequently exercised

Cash	500.00	
Paid-in capital--stock warrants	41.20	
Common stock		(par of 10 shs)
Paid-in excess		(plug)

Alternatively, the example above could have indicated the market value of the stock, e.g., $54, rather than the market values of the bonds and warrants. In such a case, one would value the warrants based on the difference between option price and market price, e.g., [$54 (market) - $50 (option)] x 10 shares = $40 value for the warrants.

Notice the effect of requiring allocation of the cash received to the stock warrants. The final effect is to increase interest costs on the bond issue by reducing the premium or increasing the discount.

Note that the allocation to equity shown above is only applicable where the purchase warrants are detachable. In contrast, no allocation is made to equity if the bonds are issued with nondetachable stock purchase warrants. Detachable warrants are often traded separately from the debt and therefore have a readily determinable market value of their own. The inseparability of nondetachable warrants prevents the determination of a separate market value; therefore, no allocation to equity is permitted by APB 14.

7. Extinguishment of Debt (See outlines of APB 26 and SFAS 76)

Debt is considered extinguished whenever the debtor pays the creditor and is relieved of all obligations relating to the debt. Typical exam-

ples of this are the calling of a bond by the debtor, requiring the bond-
holder to sell the bond to the issuing corporation at a certain date and
stated price, and the open market repurchase of a debt issue. Refunding
of debt (replacement of debt with other debt) is also considered an extinguishment. However, troubled debt restructures (situations where
creditors agree to grant relief to debtors) and debt conversions initiated by the debt holders are not. Additionally, when the debtor is
legally released from being the primary obligor of the debt either judicially or by the creditor and it is probable the debtor will make no
further payments on it, the debt is considered extinguished.

All gains (losses) resulting from the extinguishment of debt should
be recognized in the period of extinguishment. The gain (loss) is the
difference between the bond's reacquisition price and its net book value
[face value plus (minus) any unamortized premium (discount) and issue
costs]. The rule is not affected by the reissuance of debt before or
after the refunding. Furthermore, this rule applies to convertible bonds
when reacquired with cash. The gain or loss is extraordinary (see
SFASs 4 and 64).

Loss or gain	xx	xx
Bonds payable	xx	
Bond premium	xx	
Unamortized issue		
costs		xx
Bond discount		xx
Cash		xx

Debt may also be extinguished through defeasance, whereby the debtor
places cash or essentially risk-free monetary assets (e.g., government
and government guaranteed debt obligations) into an irrevocable trust
used solely to service the interest and principal payments of a debt
issue (SFAS 76). The timing and amounts of the cash flows provided by
the monetary assets used must approximately coincide with the scheduled
interest and principal payments of the debt being extinguished. The
entry required is as above, except that "Marketable debt securities" is
credited instead of "Cash" when used. Prior to recording the extinguishment, the securities are revalued to FMV and an ordinary gain (loss) is
recorded. Consequently, two different gains (losses) may be recorded in
a defeasance using securities. The first results from the revaluation of
the securities to FMV (ordinary in nature), and the second from the difference between the FMV of the securities placed in the trust and the net
book value of the debt (extraordinary).

C. Debt Restructure

SFAS 15 (see outline) prescribes accounting for situations where creditors are compelled to grant relief (i.e., restructure debt) to debtors. Two
types of restructure are described. The first is a settlement of the debt at
less than the carrying amount and the second is a continuation of the debt
with a modification of terms; accounting is prescribed for both debtors and
creditors.

Debtors--If the debt is settled by the exchange of assets, an extraordinary gain is recognized for the difference between the carrying amount of the
debt and the consideration given to extinguish the debt. If a noncash asset
is given, a separate, ordinary gain or loss is recorded to revalue the
noncash asset to FMV as the basis of the noncash asset given. Thus, a two-
step process is used: (1) revalue the noncash asset to FMV and (2) determine
the restructuring gain. If stock is issued to settle the liability, record
the stock at FMV.

If the debt is continued with a modification of terms, it is necessary to
compare the total future cash flows of the restructured debt (both principal
and stated interest) with the prestructured carrying value. If the total
amount of future cash flows is greater than the carrying value, no adjustment
is made to the carrying value of the debt; however, a new effective interest
rate must be computed. This rate makes the present value of the total future
cash flows equal to the present carrying value of debt (principal and accrued
interest). If the total future cash flows of the restructured debt are less
than the present carrying value, the current debt should be reduced to the
amount of the future cash flows and an extraordinary gain should be recognized. No interest expense would be recognized in subsequent periods when
only principal is repaid.

If the restructuring consists of part settlement and part modification of
payments, first account for the part settlement per the above, and then account for the modification of payments per the above.

Creditors--The accounting for restructurings is very similar to debtors,
only in reverse or mirror-image form.

1) Assets received in full settlement are recorded at FMV

    a) Excess of receivable over asset FMV is an ordinary loss
    b) Subsequently account for the assets as if purchased for cash

2) Modification of payments results in reduction of future interest revenue. No recognition of loss in current period.

   a) Unless total future interest and principal receipts are less than book value of receivable

      1] Then write receivable down to total cash to be received and recognize no interest revenue in the future

      2] Note that this procedure is in contrast to the general doctrine of recognizing losses when they are evident. The prescribed procedure defers the loss (by not recognizing interest revenue in the future).

3) Part settlement and part modification of payments restructurings are accounted for per the above

   a) First as to the settlement portion
   b) Second as to the modification of terms

The following examples will further illustrate accounting for troubled debt restructures.

Example 1: Settlement of Debt--Debtor company transfers land in full settlement of its loan payable.

Loan Payable (5 years remaining)	$ 90,000
Accrued interest payable on loan	10,000
Land:	
Book value	70,000
Fair value	80,000

Debtor			Creditor		
1. Land	10,000		1. Land	80,000	
Gain on transfer of assets		10,000	Loss on settlement	20,000	
2. Loan	90,000		Loan receivable		90,000
Interest payable	10,000		Interest receivable		10,000*
Land		80,000			
Extraordinary gain on settlement of debt		20,000			

*If the creditor was a bank or other finance company, this amount would be included as part of Loan receivable.

Example 2: Restructure Gain/Loss Recognized--Assume the interest rate on above loan is 5%. Interest rate is reduced to 4%, the accrued interest is forgiven, and the principal at the date of restructure is reduced to $80,000.

Future cash flows (after restructuring):
```
  Principal                                              $80,000
  Interest (5 years x $80,000 x 4%)                      +16,000
  Total cash to be received:                             $96,000
```
Amount prior to restructure:
```
  ($90,000 principal + $10,000 accrued interest) -100,000
```
Gain/Loss to be recognized $ 4,000
  Debtor gain (extraordinary)
  Creditor loss (ordinary)

Debtor		Creditor		
Beginning of Year 1		**Beginning of Year 1**		
Interest payable	10,000	Loan receivable	6,000	
Extraordinary gain		Loss on restructure		
on restructure of		of debt	4,000	
debt	4,000	Interest receivable		10,000
Loan payable	6,000			
End of Year 1-5		**End of Year 1-5**		
Loan payable	3,200	Cash	3,200	
Cash	3,200	Loan receivable		3,200
(Note: No interest expense re-corded in this case)				
End of Year 5		**End of Year 5**		
Loan payable	80,000	Cash	80,000	
Cash	80,000	Loan receivable		80,000

Example 3: Restructure No Gain/Loss Recognized--Assume the $100,000 principal is reduced to $85,000. The interest rate of 5% is reduced to 4%.

Future cash flows (after restructuring):
```
  Principal                                            $ 85,000
  Interest (5 years x $85,000 x 4%)                      17,000
  Total cash to be received                            $102,000
```
Amount prior to restructure:
```
  ($90,000 principal + $10,000 accrued interest) -100,000
  Interest expense/revenue over 5 years          $  2,000
```

In Example 3, a new effective interest rate must be computed so PV of future payments = $100,000. A trial and error approach would be used. For the exam, you need to be prepared to describe this process and the entries, but not to make such a computation.

Debtor		Creditor		
End of Year 1-5		**End of Year 1-5**		
Loan payable	xxxx	Cash	3,400	
Interest expense	xxx	Loan receivable		xxxx
Cash	3,400	Interest revenue		xxx

End of Year 5

Loan payable	85,000	
Cash		85,000

(Note: x's equal different amounts each year based on effective interest rate computed)

End of Year 5

Cash	85,000	
Loan receivable		85,000

(Note: x's equal different amounts each year)

To summarize the two basic situations

1) Settlement of Debt: the debtor transfers assets or grants an equity interest to the creditor in full satisfaction of the claim. Both debtor and creditor account for the fair values of assets transferred and equity interest granted. A gain or loss is recognized on the asset transferred. The debtor recognizes a gain and the creditor recognizes a loss for the difference between the recorded value of the debt and the fair values accounted for.

2) Restructuring of the Debt: the terms of the debt are modified in order to reduce or defer cash payments that the debtor is obligated to make to the creditor, but the debt itself is continued. Both debtor and creditor account for the modification of terms as reductions in interest expense and interest revenue respectively, from the date of restructuring until maturity. Gains and losses will generally not be recognized unless the total future cash payments specified by the new terms are less than the recorded amount of the debt. Then the creditor (debtor) would recognize a loss (gain) for the difference. The creditor's loss is considered ordinary and the debtor's gain extraordinary.

Refer to the outline of SFAS 15 for the disclosure requirements.

D. **Pensions**

Accounting for pensions involves the use of special terminology. Mastery of this terminology is essential both to an understanding of accounting practice problem requirements and to the ability to respond correctly to accounting theory questions. Review the outline of SFAS 87 before proceeding with this pension section of the module, paying particular attention to pension terminology. When you are finished with this section, review the outline of SFAS 88.

In this section the key points covered are as follows:

1. The differences between a defined contribution pension plan and a defined benefit pension plan and the resulting accounting and reporting differences between these two types of plans.

2. The bookkeeping entries made to record an employer's pension cost (expense) and the funding of pension cost.

3. The difference between the accumulated benefits actuarial approach and the benefits/years-of-service approach.

4. The calculation and reporting of the additional minimum liability for employers who sponsor defined benefit pension plans.

5. The six factors which an employer sponsoring a defined benefit pension plan must include in its pension cost (expense) each year. These factors are: (1) service cost, (2) interest cost, (3) actual return on plan assets, (4) amortization of unrecognized prior service cost, (5) gain or loss, and (6) amortization of the unrecognized net obligation or unrecognized net asset existing at the date of initial application of SFAS 87. (We refer to this below as the transition adjustment.)

6. The required disclosures in the financial statements of employers who sponsor pension plans. In our opinion the two most significant disclosures are: (1) the six factors included in pension cost (expense), and (2) a reconciliation of the funded status of the plan and the pension liability (or prepaid pension cost) reported in the employer sponsor's statement of financial position.

In order to understand the accounting and reporting requirements for pension plans, you must keep in mind that there are two accounting entities involved--(1) the employer sponsor of the plan, and (2) the pension plan itself.

The employer sponsor of the plan records in its financial statements (1) pension cost (expense), (2) accrued pension liability (or prepaid pension cost), and (3) in some cases, if required, an intangible asset called deferred pension cost and an additional minimum liability.

You should note as you read the section below that the obligations of the pension plan, the interest on these obligations, the pension plan assets available to meet these obligations, and returns (income) on these plan assets are all economic variables which impact the employer sponsor's yearly calculations of pension cost (expense) and its year-end pension liability (or prepaid pension cost).

In the following presentation, key concepts are underlined to call attention to those terms and phrases that must be clearly understood.

1. An Overview of Employer's Accounting for Pension Plans

Under a defined contribution plan the employer agrees to make a defined contribution as determined by the provisions of the plan. Consequently, plan participants will receive at retirement whatever benefits the contributions can provide. Accounting for a defined contribution plan is relatively straight-forward. Each year the employer records an expense and a related liability for the agreed upon contribution. Payments are charged against the liability with an offsetting reduction in cash. Additional disclosure requirements include: a description of the plan including employee groups covered, the basis for determining contributions, and the nature and effects of events affecting comparability.

Under a defined benefit plan the employer agrees to provide a benefit at retirement that is defined or fixed by a formula. Because the benefits are defined, the employer accepts the risk associated with changes in the variables that determine the amounts needed to meet the obligation to plan participants. This results in the use of estimates that may become very complex. However, these estimates are made by actuaries hired by the management of the employer sponsor. They are not made by the sponsoring company's accountants. The remainder of our pension coverage is devoted to a discussion of the issues that arise under this type of plan.

The changes introduced into pension accounting by SFAS 87 are intended to have the following effects: to improve comparability and understanding by providing more standardization, to alter the accounting for unrecognized pension liabilities, to provide expanded disclosures, and to affirm the use of accrual accounting for pension plans. The accrual accounting objective for pension costs is to recognize the compensation cost of an employee's pension benefits including prior service costs over that employee's service period. Under accrual accounting pension expense should not be determined on the basis of the employer's cash payout (funding) practices. The funding of pension obligation refers to the amount that the employer contributes to an independent trustee for the pension plan (plans where the fund is under the control of the employer are considered unfunded). Many factors including tax considerations, working capital management, and contractual agreements influence funding decisions. Thus, the amount selected for funding should not govern the determination of the amount to be reported as pension expense under accrual accounting; these events should be distinguished. Although both events can be recorded with one entry, we use two entries to provide this distinction.

```
Pension Expense                          xxxx
     Accrued/Prepaid Pension Cost              xxxx
```

This adjusting entry is to record the accrued expense. The optional use of the Accrued/Prepaid Pension Cost account simplifies the accounting. If the account has a net debit balance, it is a prepaid asset account. If the account has a net credit balance, it is a liability.

```
    Accrued/Prepaid Pension Cost        xxxx
        Cash                                    xxxx
```
This entry is to record the funding of the pension obligation by transferring cash to the plan's trustee.

The determination of the amounts to be used in the above entries requires the professional expertise of actuaries who assess the benefits to be provided under the pension formula and the characteristics of the employees covered under the plan (e.g., average age). With these factors as given, the actuaries must estimate the values of the variables that will influence the actual amounts to be paid at retirement by making actuarial assumptions about factors such as longevity, early retirements, turnover rate, and the rates of return to be earned on invested funds.

Of the many methods employed by actuaries to estimate pension related amounts, the methods of particular importance in accounting for pensions are the accumulated benefits approach and the benefits/years-of-service approach. The accumulated benefits approach (also referred to as the unit credit approach) provides estimates of period expenses and end of period pension obligations based on service to date, actuarial assumptions, and current salary levels. The benefits/years-of-service approach (also referred to as the projected unit credit approach) provides these same estimates based on service to date, actuarial assumptions, and projected salary levels that are expected to determine the actual pension payouts to retirees rather than current salary levels. The actuarial present value of the obligation determined under the accumulated benefits method is referred to as the accumulated benefit obligation. The actuarial present value of the obligation determined under the benefits/years-of-service method is referred to as the projected benefit obligation. If the defined benefit formula is not dependent on the amount of a future salary (say a retiree receives a fixed amount for each month worked), then there would be no difference between the two approaches. If the defined benefit formula is pay-related and salaries are assumed to increase over time, then the projected benefit obligation will be a greater amount than the accumulated benefit obligation.

Many of the provisions of SFAS 87 employ the use of amortization procedures that will significantly reduce, over time, the amount of the unrecognized pension liability associated with defined benefit plans. While the FASB conceptually supported immediate recognition of the projected benefit obligation, this position was not adopted because it represented too significant a departure from past practices. The FASB did, however, focus on the accumulated benefit obligation stipulating that independent of the other reporting requirements for defined benefit plans, a <u>minimum liability</u> must be recognized to the extent that the accumulated benefit obligation at year end exceeds the fair value of plan assets at year end. It should be noted that an asset may not be recorded when the fair value of plan assets exceeds the amount of the accumulated benefit obligation.

When the minimum liability requirement applies, the amount of the adjustment (the "Additional Liability") should take into consideration any existing balance in the Accrued/Prepaid Pension Cost account. An existing credit balance in this account will lessen the amount of the adjustment and correspondingly a debit balance will increase the amount of the adjustment. However, for purposes of statement presentation a debit balance representing a prepayment in the Accrued/Prepaid Pension Cost account is netted against the balance in the Additional Liability account. With one exception, the account that offsets the Additional Liability account when an adjustment is required is an intangible asset account termed Deferred Pension Cost. The one exception arises when the tentative value assigned to the Intangible Asset--Deferred Pension Cost account would exceed the amount of unrecognized prior service cost (including any unrecognized net obligation existing at the date SFAS 87 is initially adopted). In this case, the excess should be charged to a contra-equity account entitled Net Loss Not Recognized as Pension Expense. This account is shown as a deduction from total stockholders' equity (see first page of Module 28). It is important to note that the offsetting charge to either of the debit balance accounts is not amortized. Instead, at each statement date the amount of the Additional Liability account and the offsetting account (or accounts) are adjusted upward or downward to reflect the relationship between the accumulated benefit obligation and the fair value of plan assets at that date.

This completes the overview of the accounting required by employers for pension plans. In the next section, the determination of Pension Cost is thoroughly reviewed. While the general term <u>"Pension Cost"</u> is preferred over pension expense because pension cost is included in overhead in the determination of product costs, when permissible the term "Pension Expense" is used instead because it is simpler and clearer. The disclosure of the elements included in pension cost is one of the most significant disclosures

required by SFAS 87 and should be carefully studied. A comprehensive illustration is presented in section 4 below. This illustration integrates the
concepts and calculations that have been introduced in the preceding
discussions. Section 3 below is concerned with the effective date and the
additional disclosure requirements that apply.

2. Determination of Pension Cost

Pension Cost is a net amount calculated by adding together six factors.
These factors are: (1) service cost, (2) interest on the projected benefit
obligation, (3) actual return on plan assets, (4) amortization of unrecognized prior service cost, (5) the effect of gains and losses, and (6) the
amortization of an unrecognized transition adjustment. Each of these
components is discussed below.

a. Service Cost--increases pension expense

Service cost is defined as the actuarial present value of benefits
attributed by the pension benefit formula to employee service during the
current period. Recall that if a defined benefit plan's formula is pay-
related, the actuarial estimate of the service cost would be different
under the benefits/years-of-service approach (the projected benefit
obligation approach) as compared to the accumulated benefits approach.
SFAS 87 requires that future salary levels be taken into consideration
in this calculation (i.e., the benefits/years-of-service approach).

b. Interest on Projected Benefit Obligation--increases expense

The interest on the projected benefit obligation is defined as the
increase in the amount of the projected benefit obligation due to the
passage of time. Since the pension plan's obligation at the beginning
of the year is stated in terms of present value, a provision for
interest is required. By the end of the period the plan's obligation
will increase by the amount of interest that would accrue based on the
discount (settlement) rate selected. The discount rate selected should
be determined by reference to market conditions using such rates as the
return on high quality investments or the implicit rate of return in
retirement annuities as a basis for comparison. Also, the rate selected
must be explicit and an unreasonable rate cannot be justified by an
argument that the unreasonable rate is implicitly valid because of other
offsetting actuarial assumptions. The selected discount rate is referred to as the settlement rate because it is the rate at which the
plan's obligation could be settled.

*EXAMPLE: Compute the "interest" component of net pension cost for 19X4,
if the projected benefit obligation was $4,800,000 on January 1, 19X4
and the settlement rate is 9%. Answer: Net pension cost for 19X4 is
increased by $432,000 (9% x $4,800,000) to provide for interest on the
projected benefit obligation.*

c. Actual Return on Plan Assets,--decreases or possibly increases pension
expense

The actual return on plan assets is defined as the difference in
the fair value of plan assets at the beginning and the end of the period
adjusted for contributions made to the plan and benefit payments made by
the plan during the period.

The formula for determining the actual return is as follows:

Actual return = (End. bal. of plan assets - Beg. bal. of plan assets) + Benefits - Contributions

The <u>fair value or market value</u> of plan assets is defined as the price expected in a sales transaction between a willing buyer and seller. <u>Plan assets</u> typically include marketable securities and other investments such as real estate that are held in trust for the plan participants. Assets that are under the control of the employer are not considered to be plan assets. In calculating the return on plan assets, considerable leeway has been allowed in measuring the fair value of plan assets.

EXAMPLE: Compute the "actual return on plan assets" component of net pension cost, if the fair value of plan assets was $3,100,000 at the beginning of the year and $3,820,000 at year end. The employer sponsor contributed $450,000 to the plan and the plan paid benefits of $200,000 during the year. Answer: Net pension cost is decreased by $470,000 [($3,820,000 - $3,100,000) - $450,000 + $200,000] to report the actual return earned on the fair value of plan assets.

Although the actual return on plan assets is measured and disclosed as one of the components of net pension cost, net pension cost will include only an amount equal to the expected return on plan assets. This is because the difference between the actual return on plan assets and the expected return on plan assets is a cancelling adjustment that is included in the gain or loss calculation to be discussed below.

d. <u>Prior Service Cost--increases or possibly decreases pension expense</u>
   <u>Prior service costs</u> are retroactive adjustments that are granted to recognize services rendered in previous periods. These costs are caused by either an amendment to an existing plan or the initiation of a new plan where a <u>retroactive allowance</u> is made for past services rendered. If as a result of an amendment to an existing plan the benefits are increased, then the amount of the plan's projected benefit obligation will increase. The amount of the prior service costs is measured by the increase in the projected benefit obligation caused by the amendment or the initiation of the plan.
   While the prior service costs are related to the past, it is assumed that the initiation or amendment of the plan was made with the intent of benefiting the employer's future operations rather than its past operations. Because of this assumption, prior service costs should be amortized over the present and future periods affected. Two methods approved for use in determining the assignment of prior service costs are (1) the expected future years of service method, and (2) the straight-line basis over the average remaining service period of active employees method.
   Under the <u>expected future years of service</u> method, the total number of employee service years is calculated by grouping employees according to the time remaining to their retirement, based on actuarial assumptions, and multiplying the number in each group by the number of periods remaining to retirement. For example, eight employees expected to work ten years until retirement would contribute 80 expected future years of service to the total. To calculate the amortization of prior service costs for a given year, the number of employee service years applicable to that period is used as the numerator of the fraction and the

denominator is the total employee service years based on all the
identified groups. This method produces a declining pattern similar to
the amortization applicable to premiums or discounts on serial bonds and
the sum-of-the-years'-digits method of depreciation.

The straight-line basis over the average remaining service period
of active employees is a simpler method. The projected average remaining service period for the affected participants is estimated by the
use of a weighted average method. For example, ten employees with ten
years remaining to retirement and fifteen employees with twenty years
remaining to retirement would have a weighted average service life of 16
years computed as follows: (10 x 10 + 15 x 20)/25. In this example,
the prior service costs would be amortized and included in pension
expense over 16 years. Note by including these prior service costs in
pension expense these costs will also be included in the employer's
Accrued/Prepaid Pension Cost account over the 16 years. Thus, the
employer will gradually record on its balance sheet the liability
associated with these prior service costs.

*EXAMPLE: Compute the "amortization of prior service cost" component of
net pension cost for the first three years after an amendment, based on
the following facts. The prior service cost associated with the
amendment is determined to be $650,000 (the difference between the
projected benefit obligation before and after the amendment). The
employer has 200 employees at the time of the amendment. It is expected
that workers will retire or terminate at the rate of 4% per year, and
the employer will use the "expected future years of service" method of
amortization. Answer: Since the workers will leave at the rate of 8
per year, the denominator of the amortization fraction is computed by
summing 200 + 192 + 184 + ... + 8. This series can be written as 8(25 +
24 + 23 + ... + 1) or 8n(n+1)/2 = 8(25)(26)/2 = 2,600. The calculations
for the first three years and the unamortized balance at year-end are
presented in the table below.*

Year	Amortization fraction	Annual amortization	Unamortized balances
0			$650,000
1	200/2,600	$50,000	600,000
2	192/2,600	48,000	552,000
3	184/2,600	46,000	506,000

e. Gain or Loss--increases or decreases pension expense

Net gain or loss is defined as the change in the amount of the
projected benefit obligation as well as the change in the value of plan
assets (realized and unrealized) resulting from experience being
different from that assumed or from a change in an actuarial assumption. For this calculation plan assets are valued at the market-
related value. The market-related value of plan assets can be either
fair market value or any calculated value that recognizes changes in
fair value in a rational and systematic manner over not more than five
years. For example, the market-related value for a plan's common stocks
might be calculated based on a five-year moving average of the year end
market prices for these shares. The net effect of permitting several
methods of calculating market-related value is to introduce adjustments
that will minimize volatility arising from the use of estimates and
dampen the effects of volatile swings in market value.

The gain or loss component consists of two components: (1) the
current period difference between the actual and expected return

[(average rate of return on plan assets) x (market-related value of plan assets at the beginning of the period)] on plan assets, and (2) the unrecognized net gain or loss from previous periods. The current period difference is reported as a component of the current period net pension cost and the unrecognized net gain or loss is subject to amortization. In the unusual case when a gain or loss arises from an event such as the discontinuation of a business segment, the gain or loss should be recognized immediately and associated with the event that was the cause (e.g., discontinued segment) rather than the pension plan.

When the amortization of the cumulative unrecognized net gain or loss from previous periods is required, the procedure is comparable to the amortization of prior service cost and, in general, it requires the use of a systematic method applied on a consistent basis that is dependent on the average remaining service period for active employees. Unlike past service cost, however, the amount to be amortized is not necessarily the calculated amount of the cumulative unrecognized net gain or loss. Instead, the minimum amount subject to amortization is determined by the use of a method sometimes referred to as the "corridor" approach. The minimum amount of the cumulative unrecognized gain or loss required to be amortized is determined by computing at the beginning of the fiscal year the excess of the cumulative unrecognized gain or loss over 10 percent of the greater of the projected benefit obligation or the market-related asset value. If the cumulative unrecognized gain or loss is equal to or less than the 10% calculated value, no amount need be amortized.

EXAMPLE: Compute the "gain or loss" component of net pension cost and the other elements of pension cost based on the following facts:

At the beginning of the year the cumulative unrecognized net loss was $500,000, the market-related value of plan assets was $3,100,000, and the projected benefit obligation was $4,800,000. The expected return on assets for the year was 9% and the settlement rate was 11%. The fair value of plan assets at year end was $3,400,000. The fair value of plan assets at the beginning of the year was $3,100,000. There were no contributions to the plan during the year. The plan made no benefit payments during the year. Service costs for the year were $400,000. At the beginning of the year the average remaining service period of active employees was 10 years. There are no other factors to be considered in computing pension cost for the year.

Answer: The elements of net pension cost are calculated as follows:

Service cost	$400,000
Interest (.11 x $4,800,000)	528,000
Actual return on plan assets	(300,000) (1)
Amortization of unrecognized net loss	2,000 (2)
Asset gain deferred	21,000 (3)
Net pension cost	$651,000

Note: The above components of pension cost are required to be disclosed in the employer sponsor's financial statements. This would be done in the footnotes to those statements.

(1) $3,400,000 less $3,100,000 less contributions to the plan of $0 plus benefit payments of the plan of $0.

(2)   Amortization of unrecognized net loss is calculated as follows:

"Corridor" 10% x $4,800,000	*$480,000*
Cumulative unrecognized net loss at	
the beginning of the year	*500,000*
Excess to be amortized	*$ 20,000*

Amortization of unrecognized loss is: $20,000/10 years = $2,000.

(3)   The asset gain deferred of $21,000 is calculated as follows: Actual return on plan assets of $300,000 less expected return on plan assets of $279,000.   The expected return on plan assets is determined by multiplying the expected return on plan assets of 9% times the market-related value of plan assets at the beginning of the year of $3,100,000. Note that in the above computation of pension cost actual return on assets of $300,000 is included as required by SFAS 87.   However, the expected return on plan assets of $279,000 ($300,000 - $21,000) is the amount that is actually included in pension cost for the year.

f.   Transition Adjustment--increases or decreases pension expense
        The preceding five components of net periodic pension cost can be viewed as the ongoing elements of net periodic pension cost in that they are not affected by SFAS 87's transition provisions. To address this problem SFAS 87 provides for a separate transition adjustment. The type and extent of the transition adjustment required is determined by first calculating at the transition date the difference between the projected benefit obligation and the fair value of plan assets. This difference represents the funded status of a defined benefit plan. This difference is decreased by any amount previously recorded as an accrued liability in the employer's balance sheet or increased if an amount has previously been recorded as a prepaid asset. In general, this difference should be amortized on a straight-line basis over the average remaining employee service period. An exception is provided when the length of the computed amortization period is less than 15 years. In that case, the employer can elect to use a 15-year period to amortize the transition adjustment.

EXAMPLE: Compute the "amortization of the transition adjustment" component of net pension cost for the first three years after the transition date, based on the following facts.   At the transition date, cumulative pension expense recognized from prior years exceeds prior years' contributions by $50,000.   Also at the transition date, the fair value of plan assets is $2,500,000 and the projected benefit obligation is $4,100,000. As in "d." above, there are 200 employees and the attrition rate is assumed to be 4%.   The "straight-line basis over the average remaining service period" method of amortization will be used.   Answer: The transition amount subject to amortization is $1,600,000 ($4,100,000 - $2,500,000) less $50,000 (the amount already recognized as a liability) = $1,550,000.   From "d." above, the sum of 200 + 192 + 184 ... + 8 is known to be 2,600.   The average remaining service life is found by dividing 2,600 by 200 (the number of employees) = 13 years.   The calculations for the first three years and the unamortized balance at year end are presented in the table below (assuming nonelection of the 15-year amortization period).

Year	Amortization fraction	Annual amortization	Unamortized balance
0			$1,550,000
1	1/13	$119,231	1,430,769
2	1/13	119,231	1,311,538
3	1/13	119,231	1,192,307

3. Effective Date and Disclosures

   With certain exceptions, most notably the minimum liability provision, SFAS 87 is effective for fiscal years beginning after 12/15/86, and earlier application is encouraged. Under SFAS 87, disclosure in the statement of financial position follows the practice of offsetting the financial effects of plan assets and obligations where the plan's assets can be used directly to satisfy its obligations. This practice and the practice of netting the components of pension expense in the income statement, and the complexities inherent in pension accounting put added emphasis on the use of notes to the financial statements to provide disclosure. The required disclosures are as follows.

   a. A description of the plan including the benefit formula, employee groups covered, funding policy, types of assets held, and the nature of all significant matters affecting comparability
   b. The amounts of the components of net period pension cost for the period
   c. A reconciliation schedule relating the funding status of the plan to the amounts reported in the statement of financial position including the following amounts: (1) fair value of plan assets, (2) projected benefit obligation, (3) accumulated benefit obligation, (4) vested benefit obligation, (5) unrecognized prior service cost, (6) unrecognized net gain or loss, (7) unamortized balance of any transition adjustment, (8) additional liability recognized so as to meet minimum liability requirement, and (9) end-of-period prepaid or accrued pension cost balance.

   If an employer sponsors more than one pension plan, the plans should not be netted together unless the assets of one may be used to satisfy the commitments of the other.

4. Comprehensive Illustration

   Schaefer Company sponsors a noncontributory (i.e., employees make no contributions) defined benefit plan for its 100 employees. Within this group of 100 employees, it is expected that workers will retire or terminate at the rate of five per year for the next twenty years. The company has decided to adopt SFAS 87 "Employers' Accounting for Pensions" as of January 1, 1986, the start of their fiscal year. Prior to 1986, cumulative pension expense recognized exceeded cumulative contributions by $30,000 resulting in a $30,000 balance sheet liability. As of January 1, 1987, the company has agreed to an amendment to their plan that includes a retroactive provision to recognize prior service. To illustrate how the provisions of SFAS 87 should be applied, assumptions about the facts relevant to the pension plan for the years 1986 and 1987 are presented in the tables that follow.

	1/1/1986	1/1/1987
Plan assets (at fair value = market-related value)	$400,000	$455,000
Accumulated benefit obligation (ABO; 60% vested)	460,000	640,000*
Projected benefit obligation	550,000	821,500*
Rate of return on assets	9%	10%
Settlement rate	9%	10%
Unrecognized cumulative gain (loss)--due to unexpected decrease in asset value	-0-	(106,000)
Prior service cost amendment		105,000
Accrued pension cost (liability)	30,000	?

*Includes effects of amendment

	12/31/1986	12/31/1987
Service cost	117,000	130,000
Employer's funding contribution	125,000	260,000
Plan assets (at fair value = market-related value)	455,000	760,500
Accumulated benefit obligation (60% vested)	570,000	710,000
Benefits paid by the plan	-0-	-0-
Unrecognized cumulative gain (loss)--due to unexpected decrease in asset value	(106,000)	(103,729)

Schedule of Changes in Plan Assets

	1986	1987
Plan Assets at 12/31	455,000	760,500
Plan assets at 1/1	400,000	455,000
Increase in plan assets	55,000	305,500
Add:		
Benefits Paid	-0-	-0-
Less:		
Funding contributions for the year	<125,000>	<260,000>
Actual return or (loss) on plan assets	< 70,000>	45,500
Expected return on plans assets		
1986: 9% x $400,000	36,000	
1987: 10% x $455,000		45,500
Unrecognized gain (loss)	<106,000>	-0-

Required:

A. Prepare a supporting schedule to determine the amounts to be reported as pension expense for 1986 and 1987. The 1986 transition adjustment is to be amortized over the maximum period allowed. Furthermore, the company has decided to use the "expected future years of service" method to amortize the effects of the amendment.

B. Prepare the journal entries required for 1986 and 1987 with respect to the pension plan including any entry necessary to comply with the minimum liability requirement.

C. Indicate the pension related amounts that should appear in the company's financial statements prepared at the end of 1986 and 1987.

D. Prepare a reconciliation of the funded status of the plan to the liability shown in the company's balance sheet at 1-1-86 and 12-31-86. Include in this reconciliation the amount of the accumulated benefit obligation at 1-1-86 and 12-31-86 and the vested amounts of accumulated benefit obligations on these dates.

(Note: This reconciliation is one of the major disclosures required by SFAS 87 as discussed above.)

Solution
Part A

Pension Expense

		1986	1987
1.	Service cost	$117,000	$130,000
2.	Interest on projected benefit obligation	49,500	82,150
3.	(Actual return) or loss on plan assets	70,000	(45,500)
4.	Prior service cost amortization		10,000
5.	Deferral of gain (loss)	<106,000>	-0-
6.	(Gain) loss amortization	--	2,271
7.	Transition adjustment amortization	8,000	8,000
	Total expense	$138,500	$186,921

Calculations

1. Service cost is given
2. Interest: 9% x $550,000 (1986), and 10% x $821,500 (1987)
3. Actual return: $<70,000> for 1986 and $45,500 (same as expected) for 1987. Note that in 1986, the $70,000 actual loss on plan assets less the $106,000 unrecognized loss equals the expected return ($36,000).
4. Prior service: Compute the denominator of the fraction for amortization by calculating the sum of the estimated remaining service years by adding 100 + 95 + 90 + ... + 10 + 5. This series can be written as 5(20 + 19 + 18 + ... + 2 + 1) or 5n(n+1)/2 = 5(20)(21)/2 = 1,050. For 1987 the amount is (100/1,050) x $105,000 = $10,000.
5. Loss: The $106,000 unrecognized loss that arose in 1986 is not amortized until 1987, because the amortization of the unrecognized net gain or loss should be included as a component of pension expense only if the unrecognized net gain or loss existed as of the beginning of the year and the unrecognized gain or loss exceeded the corridor. 10% of the greater of the projected benefit obligation ($821,500) or the market-related asset value ($455,000) is equal to $82,150. The minimum loss to be amortized is $106,000 - $82,150 or $23,850. The average employee service remaining in 1987 assuming a constant work force of 100 and an attrition rate of 5 workers per year is (100 + 95 + 90 + ... + 10 + 5)/100 or 1,050/100 = 10.5 years. The amount of the loss recognized in 1987 is $23,850/10.5 = $2,271. Since actual and expected returns are equal, no further adjustment is required.
6. Transition adjustment: To calculate the transition amount, first calculate the difference between the projected benefit obligation ($550,000) and the fair value of plan assets ($400,000) at the transition date. This amount is decreased by the amount of the existing balance in the pension liability account ($30,000) on 1/1/86, resulting in a transition adjustment of $120,000. The average remaining service period for a group of 100 employees with an attrition rate of 5 per year was calculated above to be 10.5 years. Because the company desires the maximum amortization period, they will elect to use the 15 year write-off period instead. $120,000/15 years is $8,000 per year.

Part B

Journal Entries

	1986	1987
Pension Expense	138,500	186,921
Accrued/Prepaid Pension Cost	138,500	186,921
(to record pension expense)		
Accrued/Prepaid Pension Cost	125,000	260,000
Cash	125,000	260,000
(to record funding)		

The amount of the <u>minimum liability</u> is the excess, if any, at the balance sheet date of the accumulated benefit obligation over the fair value of plan assets. An adjustment is required to the extent that the liability has not already been reflected. (Note that this adjustment does not impact the determination of pension expense.)

	1986	1987
Intangible Asset--Deferred Pension Cost	71,500	
Additional Liability	71,500	

[to adjust as of 12/31/86 for the minimum liability by increasing the liability from $43,500 (credit balance in the "Accrued/Prepaid Pension Cost" account below) to $115,000 ($570,000 ABO - $455,000 FMV of plan assets)]

	1986	1987
Additional Liability		71,500
Intangible Asset--Deferred Pension Cost		71,500

(to adjust as of 12/31/87 the balance in additional liability account, no balance is required because the FMV of plan assets exceed the ABO)

```
         Pension Expense                         Accrued/Prepaid Pension Cost
1986 138,500   |                       1986 Funding  125,000 | 1/1/86 balance     30,000
---------------|-----------                                  | 1986 accrual      138,500
               |                       -----------------------|-------------------------
1987 186,740   |                       1987 Funding  260,000 | 12/31/86 balance   43,500
                                                             | 1987 accrual      186,921
                                       -----------------------|-------------------------
                                       12/31/87 bal.  29,579 |
```

```
     Intangible Asset--                         Additional
       Def. Pension Cost                      Minimum Liability
1986  71,500 | 71,500  1987           1987  71,500 | 71,500  1986
```

Part C

Financial Statements

	12/31/1986	12/31/1987
Assets		
Prepaid Pension Cost**	--	$ 29,579
Intangible Asset--Deferred Pension Cost	$ 71,500	--
Liabilities		
Pension Liability**	115,000*	--
Income statement		
Pension expense	138,500	186,921

Accrued liability ($43,500) plus adjustment for minimum liability ($71,500)

Although not specifically addressed by SFAS 87, we believe these amounts **should be classified as noncurrent, unless evidence indicates otherwise, in accordance with ARB 43, Chapter 3A (current assets and liabilities).*

Part D

Reconciliation Schedule (Footnote Disclosure)

	1/1/1986	12/31/1986
Accumulated benefit obligation (60% vested)	$(460,000)	$(570,000)
Projected benefit obligation	$(550,000)	$(821,500)
Plan assets at fair value	400,000	455,000
Under-funded status of the plan	$(150,000)	$(366,500)
Unrecognized net (gain) loss	-0-	106,000
Unrecognized prior service cost	-0-	105,000
Unrecognized net obligation at date of initial application	120,000	112,000
Adjustment required to recognize minimum liability	-0-	(71,500)
Accrued pension cost (pension liability) recognized in statement of financial position	$(30,000)	$(115,000)

E. Leases

The major issue in accounting for leases is whether the financial impact of the lease agreement should be included in the main body of the financial statements. A lease is a contract which specifies the terms of an exchange transaction between the contracting parties. When it is deemed that the lease arrangement is in <u>substance</u> an installment sale, the economic impact of the lease contract will be emphasized over the <u>legal form</u> of the agreement. This focus is clearly stated in SFAS 13 as follows:

> "A lease that transfers substantially all of the benefits and risks incident to ownership of property should be accounted for as the acquisition of an asset and the incurrence of an obligation by the lessee and as a sale or financing by the lessor."

The FASB operationalized the economic substance criterion by developing four criteria that apply to both lessors and lessees. These are:

1. The lease <u>transfers title</u> to the lessee
2. The lease contains a <u>bargain purchase</u> option
3. The lease <u>term is 75% or more</u> of useful life and the lease is not first executed within the last 25% of the original useful life
4. The <u>present value</u> of minimum lease payments <u>is 90% or more</u> of the net of the <u>fair market value</u> of the asset reduced by the investment tax credit (when in effect) retained by the lessor and the lease is not executed in the last 25% of the original useful life

Per SFAS 13, if at least one of the four criteria is met the benefits and risks of ownership are deemed to have been passed from the lessor to the lessee. However, for lessors, both of the following criteria must also be satisfied.

1. <u>Collectibility</u> of minimum lease payments is predictable, and
2. There are <u>no important uncertainties</u> concerning costs yet to be incurred by the lessor under the lease

1. Study Program for Leases

1) Begin by reviewing the terms peculiar to leases that appear at the beginning of the outline of SFAS 13 in the pronouncement outlines that begin after Module 33
2) Review the material in this module so that you will be familiar with the major concepts and applications in the leasing area.
3) After you have developed a solid base of understanding, you should review the outline of SFAS 13 (as comprehensively restated).
4) The discussion of accounting for leases is structured to follow the lease classification matrix listed below.

<u>Lessor</u>   <u>Lessee</u>

Operating ················ Operating

Direct Financing ·········::Capital

Sales-type ·········

a. Operating Lease, Lessor and Lessee
    Any lease not meeting the criteria for a direct financing or sales-type lease in the case of a lessor or for a capital lease in the case of a lessee automatically is treated as an operating lease. For accounting purposes, operating leases are regarded as rental agreements which do not affect the reporting of assets and equities in the main body of the financial statements. The lessor would continue to carry the leased property as an asset and rental revenues and related expenses would be included in the lessor's calculation of net income. Similarly, the lessee would not report leased assets or equity claims in the financial statements and rental expense would be included in the lessee's calculation of net income. Rental revenue should be recognized by the lessor and rental expense recognized by the lessee on a straight-line basis unless another method more reasonably reflects the pattern of services rendered. When the pattern of cash flows under the lease agreement is other than straight-line, this will result in the recording of accruals/deferrals. Initial direct costs, such as the real estate broker's fee, should be treated as an asset by a lessor and amortized over the life of the lease on the same basis as rental revenue.
    The summary below lists the elements commonly encountered in operating leases.

Operating Lease F/S Elements

	Lessee	Lessor
Balance Sheet:	• Prepaid rent (asset)	• Unearned rent (liability)
	• Leasehold improvements (net of acc. amort.)	• Leased asset (net of accumulated depreciation)
		• Unamortized initial direct costs (asset)
Income Statement:	• Rent expense	• Rent income
	• Amortization of leasehold improvements	• Depreciation expense
		• Other expenses of maintaining property
		• Amort. of initial direct costs

Knowledge of these is helpful in answering questions that require a determination of lessor's net income or lessee's total expense in connection with an operating lease.

b. Direct Financing Lease, Lessor
    Although most discussions, including SFAS 13, begin with the lessee's accounting for a capital lease, we have chosen to present the lessor's accounting first because the lessor is the party that determines the fixed cash schedule of lease payments that are to be made by the lessee. In this determination, the lessor uses the appropriate time value of money factor(s) (TVMF) that produces the desired rate of return (known as the implicit rate). A direct financing lease is an arrange-

ment whereby the lessor (e.g., bank) agrees to purchase an asset (e.g., airplane) and lease it to the lessee (e.g., airlines). The relationships in a direct financing lease arrangement are shown below:

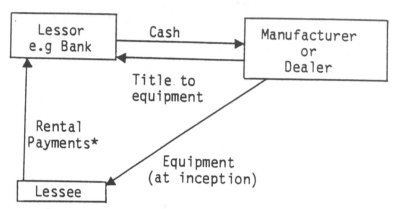

*and equipment at end of lease unless criterion (1) or (2) above, applicable to both parties, is met in which case title would pass to the lessee

A lease is considered to be a direct financing lease from the point of view of the lessor if at least one of the four criteria applicable to both lessors and lessees is met, both of the additional criteria applicable to lessors is met, and the FMV of the leased asset at the inception of the lease is approximately equal to the cost or carrying amount of the asset.

The agreement is initiated because the lessee does not want (or is unable) to purchase the asset outright. The lessor's entry to record the acquisition of the asset to be leased is as follows:

Asset to be leased   (Cost of asset)
    Cash   (Cash paid)

Direct financing leases result in only interest revenue for the lessor. There is no selling or dealer's profit from this type of lease. As noted above, the lessor determines the schedule of lease payments and terms based on its required rate of return. The difference between the asset cost and the total payments to be received by the lessor is interest revenue, earned over the life of the lease. Alternative methods of recording the lease transaction are shown below.

Lease receivable (gross)   Lease receivable (net)
    Asset to be leased   or   Asset to be leased
    Unearned interest revenue

We will follow the gross method in our examples for the lessor because it is consistent with SFAS 13 and the questions on the CPA exam. In addition, SFAS 13 specifies the following considerations and definitions.

- The lease receivable (gross) equals the minimum lease payments (includes periodic rental payments and a guaranteed residual value or bargain purchase option, but excludes executory costs such as property taxes) plus any unguaranteed residual value. No residual value is assumed to accrue to the value of the lessor if the lease transfers ownership or contains a bargain purchase option.

- Unearned revenue must be amortized to produce a constant periodic rate of return on net investment, i.e., the interest method.

- At the termination of the lease, the balance in the receivable should equal the guaranteed or unguaranteed residual value, assuming title is not transferred and there is no bargain purchase option.

Numerical Example 1:

Lease Information

1) A three year lease is initiated on 1/1/X1 for equipment costing $131,858 with an expected useful life of five years. FMV at 1/1/X1 of equipment is $131,858.
2) Three annual payments are due to the lessor beginning 12/31/X1. The property reverts back to the lessor upon termination of the lease.
3) The guaranteed residual value at the end of year 3 is $10,000
4) The lessor is to receive a 10% return (implicit rate)
5) Collectibility of minimum lease payments is predictable, and there are no important uncertainties concerning costs yet to be incurred by the lessor under the lease
6) The cost (FMV) of the asset to the lessor is to be recovered through two components: the annual lease payments and guaranteed residual value using a discount (implicit) rate of 10%.
7) The annual lease payment to the lessor is computed as follows:

> First: Find PV of guaranteed residual value = $10,000 x .7513 = $7,513
> Then: Find PV of annual lease payments = $131,858 - $7,513 = $124,345

$$\text{Annual receipt (payment)} = \frac{\$124,345}{\text{PV3},.10} = \frac{\$124,345}{2.4869} = \$50,000$$

Lease Classification

This is a direct financing lease because the 90% test is satisfied. (Since the residual value is guaranteed the present value of the minimum lease payments is 100% of the FMV). The two additional criteria for the lessor are satisfied and FMV equals cost.

Accounting for Lease

1) The following table illustrates the application of the interest method

Date	Cash receipt	Interest revenue (10%)	Reduction in carrying amount	PV or carrying amount
1/1/X1				$131,858
12/31/X1	$50,000	$13,186	$36,814	95,044
12/31/X2	50,000	9,504	40,496	54,548
12/31/X3	50,000	5,452	44,548	10,000

Note: The current asset and noncurrent asset balance sheet amounts at the end of any year can be taken directly from the amortization table by referring to the next year-end line in the table. For example, at 12/31/X1, the net lease receivable of $95,044 (1/1/X1 balance $131,851 - $36,814, reduction of carrying amount) is $40,496 current and $54,548 noncurrent (last two amounts are from the 12/31/X2 line in the above table). Note that the interest to be received on 12/31/X2 is not part of either the current or noncurrent asset amount because it has not been earned as of 12/31/X1.

2)   The lease should be recorded at the beginning of year 1 by the lessor.

3)   In the amortization table above, the present value or carrying value is the difference between lease receivable (annual rents plus guaranteed residual value) and unearned interest revenue.

4)   The journal entries for the lessor are shown below.

Journal Entries for the Lessor

Initial entries (Beg. of Yr. 1)

Equipment for leasing	131,858	
Cash		131,858
Lease receivable	160,000	
Equipment for leasing		131,858
Unearned interest		28,142

End of Year 1

Cash	50,000	
Lease receivable		50,000
Unearned interest	13,186	
Interest revenue		13,186

End of Year 2

Cash	50,000	
Lease receivable		50,000
Unearned interest	9,504	
Interest revenue		9,504

End of Year 3

Cash	50,000	
Lease receivable		50,000
Unearned interest	5,452	
Interest revenue		5,452

5)   Assume that when the asset is returned at the end of year 3 the asset has a FMV of only $4,000. The lessee will need to make a payment of $6,000 ($10,000 - $4,000) because the residual value was guaranteed. The lessor would make the following entry.

Cash	6,000	
Residual value of equipment	4,000	
Lease receivable		10,000

c. Sales-Type Lease, Lessor

Sales-type leases arise when a manufacturer or dealer (e.g., aircraft manufacturer, car dealership) leases an asset which otherwise might be sold outright for a profit. The relationships in a sales type lease arrangement are illustrated below:

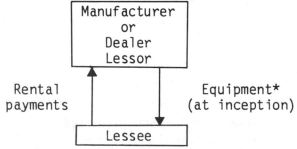

*Title stays with lessor and property will be returned to lessor unless criterion (1) or (2) above, applicable to both parties, is met.

The lessor's profit consists of two components: (1) gross profit in the
period of sale, and (2) unearned interest revenue to be earned over the
lease term using the effective interest method. The diagram below
compares and contrasts direct financing leases with sales-type leases.

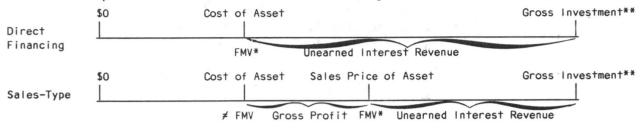

*Also present value of minimum lease payments and unguaranteed residual value, if any, to be received
from lessee
**Minimum lease payments plus unguaranteed residual value, if any, to be received from lessee

Prepared by Professor John R. Simon, Northern Illinois University.

A lease is considered to be a sales-type lease from the viewpoint of the
lessor if the criteria mentioned earlier for direct financing leases are
satisfied. However, in the case of a sales-type lease, the FMV of the
asset, which is the sales price in the ordinary course of the lessor's
business is greater than the cost or carrying value of the leased asset.
Because of this difference, a sales-type lease is more complex than a
direct financing lease. The journal entry to record a sales-type is:

> Lease receivable (Gross)
> Cost of goods sold
> > Sales
> > Inventory
> > Unearned interest

SFAS 13 specifies the following considerations and definitions:

1)   The gross investment (lease receivable) in the lease equals
     the sum of the minimum lease payments (excluding executory
     costs) plus any unguaranteed residual value.
2)   The unearned interest revenue in the lease equals the
     difference between the gross investment and the selling price
     [present value of the two components of gross investment
     (i.e., minimum lease payments and unguaranteed residual
     value)].
3)   Unearned interest must be amortized to produce a constant
     periodic rate of return on investment, i.e., the effective
     interest method.
4)   The cost of goods sold to be charged against income is equal
     to the historic cost or carrying value of the leased asset
     (most likely inventory) less the present value of any unguaran-
     teed residual value. The difference between the selling
     price and the amount computed as cost of goods sold is the
     gross profit recognized by the lessor at the inception of the
     lease.

Numerical Example 2:

Lease Information

Assume same information as in previous example except

1)   The cost of the equipment is $100,000 (either manufactured cost or purchase price paid by dealer)
2)   The normal selling price of the equipment is $131,858 which is greater than the $100,000 cost
3)   The residual value is <u>unguaranteed</u>
4)   The lease payments are $50,000, the same as computed in the previous example, because the lessor treats an <u>unguaranteed</u> residual value in the same way as a guaranteed residual value. However, as mentioned below the present value of the unguaranteed residual value is not included in the 90% test.

Lease Classification

This is a sales-type lease since the 90% test is satisfied; 90% of the $131,858 FMV = $118,672, which is less than $124,345, the present value of the minimum lease payments (see Numerical Example 1); the present value of the residual value is excluded because it is unguaranteed. Additionally, the cost of the asset is less than its fair market value (also the present value of the minimum lease payments plus the unguaranteed residual value). Assume the two additional criteria for the lessor have been satisfied.

Accounting for Lease

1)   The gross investment is: $160,000 [3 payments of $50,000 (same as Numerical Example 1) plus a $10,000 unguaranteed residual value]

The PV of gross investment is: $131,858 [($50,000 x 2.4869) + ($10,000 x .7513)]

The unearned interest revenue is: $28,142 ($160,000 - $131,858)

Sales are: $124,345 [$131,858 - ($10,000 x .7513)]*

CGS is: $92,487 [$100,000 - ($10,000 x .7513)]*

*Note that there is no effect on gross profit of not including the present value of the unguaranteed residual value in either sales or cost of goods sold. If the residual value were guaranteed, this adjustment would not be made.

2)   The entry to record the lease is:

Lease receivable**	160,000	
Cost of goods sold	92,487	
Sales		124,345
Inventory		100,000
Unearned interest		28,142

**On the balance sheet this amount is termed gross investment since it includes an unguaranteed residual value.

At the end of year 1, the following entry(ies) would be made.

Cash	50,000	
Lease receivable		50,000

```
          Unearned interest          13,186
            Interest revenue                      13,186
```

The interest revenue will be recognized at 10% of the outstanding net investment (lease receivable less unearned interest) each period. At termination, the lease receivable will have a balance of $10,000 which is the unguaranteed residual value. If the asset is returned to the lessor and its fair market value is only $4,000, the following entry is made on the lessor's books.

```
     Loss                   6,000
     Residual value of
       equipment            4,000
          Lease receivable              10,000
```

Now that we have completed our discussion of lessors' direct financing and sales-type leases, it should be helpful to review the financial statement elements for the lessor, and before discussing lessee's capital lease to preview the elements that appear on lessee's financial statements. These balance sheet elements are shown below:

	Lessor	Lessee
	Direct Financing Lease	Capital Lease
Balance Sheet:	• Lease payments receivable* (current and noncurrent portion)	• Leased asset (net of accumulated depreciation)
	• Initial Direct costs are added to Net Investment, causing a new implicit rate of interest	• Lease obligation (current and noncurrent portion)
Income Statement:	• Interest revenue	• Depreciation expense
		• Interest expense
		• Other costs of maintaining property
	Sales-Type Lease	Capital Lease
	• Same as preceding except, in year of sale, dealer's profit is reported on the income statement	• Same as preceding
	Initial direct costs charged to expense immediately	

*Gross investment in lease

d. Capital Leases, Lessee
A lease is considered to be a capital lease from the point of view of the lessee if any one of the four criteria of SFAS 13 common to both lessors and lessees is satisfied (i.e., transfer of title, bargain purchase, 75% of useful life, 90% of net FMV). Lease agreements not meeting at least one of the criteria for capital leases are treated as operating leases on the lessee's books. If the lease is classified as a capital lease, the lessee must record an asset and a liability based on the present value of the minimum lease payments as follows.

Leased asset   (PV of payments)
  Lease obligation   (PV of payments)

Note that the above entry reflects recording the transaction "net." If the lease was recorded gross the lease obligation would be credited for the total amount of the minimum lease payments (rental payments excluding executory costs plus any guaranteed residual value) and there would be a debit to "discount on lease obligation."

In addition, SFAS 13 specifies the following considerations and definitions.

1) <u>Minimum lease payments</u> are payments to be made during the lease term including: rental payments, a bargain purchase option payment, guaranteed residual value, penalties for failure to renew, and other similar payments. Note, minimum payments do not include executory costs and contingent rentals (e.g., payments for excessive use of the leased asset. Both of these are treated as expenses in period incurred).

2) The lessee's incremental borrowing rate should be used to determine the present value of the minimum lease payments unless the lessor's implicit rate is lower and is known by the lessee. Leased assets should not be recorded at greater than FMV. If the present value of the minimum lease payments using the lessee's incremental borrowing rate is greater than the FMV of the leased assets, the lease should be recorded at the FMV and a new implicit interest rate calculated to reflect a constant periodic rate applied to the remaining balance of the obligation.

3) The lease term does not extend beyond the date of a bargain purchase option but includes bargain renewal periods, periods when the lessor has the option to renew or extend, periods during which the lessee guarantees the debt of the lessor and periods in which a material penalty exists for failure to renew.

4) The amortization (depreciation) method should be consistent with the lessee's normal depreciation policy. The cost of the leased asset should be depreciated over the lease term to the expected residual value to the lessee unless the lease transfers ownership or contains a bargain purchase option. If either of these is present, then depreciate over the estimated useful life of the asset.

5) In allocating the cash payments to the reduction of the obligation and to interest expense, the interest method should be used.

6) When the lease terminates, the balance in the obligation account should equal the bargain purchase option price or guaranteed residual value.

7) Leased assets and obligations should be disclosed as such in the balance sheet. The obligation should be separated into current and noncurrent components.

Numerical Example 3:

<u>Lease Information</u>

1) Lease is initiated on 1/1/X1 for equipment with an expected useful life of three years. The equipment reverts back to the lessor upon expiration of the lease agreement.

2)   Three payments are due to the lessor in the amount of $50,000 per year beginning 12/31/X1. An additional sum of $1,000 is to be paid annually by the lessee for insurance.

3)   Lessee guarantees a $10,000 residual value on 12/31/X3 to the lessor

4)   Irrespective of the $10,000 residual value guarantee, the leased asset is expected to have only a $7,000 salvage on 12/31/X3. Thus, the asset should be depreciated down to the $7,000 expected residual value.

5)   The lessee's incremental borrowing rate is 10% (same as lessor's implicit rate)

6)   The present value of the lease obligation is

PV of guaranteed residual value = $10,000 x .7513 = $ 7,513
PV of annual payments   = $50,000 x 2.4869 = 124,345
                                                       $131,858

Note that since the lessee's incremental borrowing rate is 10% and the residual value is guaranteed the present value of $131,858 is the same amount used by the lessor in the direct financing lease example (Numerical Example 1) to determine the payments to be made by the lessee. If an incremental borrowing rate different than the lessor's is used and/or the lease contains an unguaranteed residual value, the present value computed by the lessee will differ from the lessor's present value (FMV). These differences account for the fact that many leases are not capitalized by lessee's because they don't meet the 90% test.

Lease Classification

This lease is for the entire economic life of the asset. Since the 75% test is satisfied, the lease is accounted for as a capital lease by the lessee. The 90% test is also met because the present value of the minimum lease payments, $131,858, is 100% of the FMV of the leased asset.

Accounting for Lease

1)   Note that executory costs (e.g., insurance, property taxes, etc.) are not included in the present value calculations

2)   The entry to recognize the lease is

1/1/X1 Leased equipment   131,858
            Lease obligation   131,858

3)   The entries to record the payments and depreciation are

	12/31/X1	12/31/X2	12/31/X3
Insurance expense	1,000	1,000	1,000
Lease obligation*	36,814	40,496	44,548
Interest expense*	13,186	9,504	5,452
Cash	51,000	51,000	51,000
Depreciation expense**	41,619	41,619	41,620
Accumulated depreciation	41,619	41,619	41,620***

Refer to the amortization table in the direct financing lease discussion (Numeric Example 1).
**[($131,858 - 7,000) ÷ 3 years]*
***Rounding error of $1*

4)   The 12/31/X3 entry to record the guaranteed residual value payment (assuming salvage value = estimated residual value = $7,000) and to clear the lease related accounts from the lessee's books is

Lease obligation	10,000
Accumulated Depreciation	124,000
Cash	3,000
Leased Equipment	131,858

If the actual residual value were only $5,000, the credit to "cash" would be $5,000 and a $2,000 loss would be recognized by the lessee.

Remember that leased assets are amortized over the life of the lease unless title transfers or a bargain purchase option exists--then over the useful life of the leased asset. At the end of the lease, the balance of the lease obligation should equal the guaranteed residual value or the bargain purchase option price. To illustrate, consider the example below.

Numerical Example 4:

Lease Information

1)   A three year lease is initiated on 1/1/X1 for equipment with an expected useful life of five years
2)   Three annual $50,000 payments are due the lessor beginning 1/1/X1
3)   The lessee can exercise a bargain purchase option on 12/31/X3 for $10,000. The expected residual value at 12/31/X5 is $1,000.
4)   The lessee's incremental borrowing rate is 10% (lessor's implicit rate is unknown)

Lease Classification

Although the lease term is for only 60% of the asset's useful life, the lessee would account for this as a capital lease because it contains a bargain purchase option.

Accounting for Lease

1)   The present value of the lease obligation is

PV of bargain purchase option = $10,000 x .7513 = $ 7,513
PV of annual payments   = $50,000 x 2.7355 = 136,775
                                                  $144,288

2)   The following table summarizes the liability amortization

Date	Cash payment	Interest expense	Reduction in obligation	Lease obligation
1/1/X1				$144,288
1/1/X1	$50,000		$50,000	94,288
1/1/X2	50,000	$9,429	40,571	53,717
1/1/X3	50,000	5,372	44,628	9,089
12/31/X3		911*		10,000
12/31/X3	10,000		10,000	-0-

*Rounding error of $2

Note: The amortization table reflects the fact that this is an annuity due with cash payments on 1/1 and interest expense accruals on 12/31. Thus, the first payment does not include any interest.

3)   The entry to record the lease is

1/1/X1 Leased equipment   144,288
           Lease obligation   144,288

4)   The entries to record the payments, interest expense, depreciation (amortization) expense, and the exercise of the bargain purchase are

		19X1		19X2		19X3	
1/1	Lease obligation	50,000		40,571		44,628	
	Accrued interest payable						
	or interest expense*			9,429		5,372	
	Cash		50,000		50,000		50,000
12/31	Interest expense	9,429		5,372		911	
	Accrued int. payable		9,429		5,372		
	Lease obligation						911
12/31	Depreciation expense**	28,658		28,658		28,658	
	Accumulated depre-						
	ciation		28,658		28,658		28,658
12/31	Lease obligation					10,000	
	Cash						10,000

*If 12/31 accruals are reversed
**(143,288 ÷ 5 years)

2. Other Considerations

To supplement the review of accounting for leases presented above, the following topics have been selected for further discussion.

- a.   Residual Value
- b.   Initial Direct Costs
- c.   Lessee's Fair Market Value Limitation
- d.   Sale-leaseback
- e.   Disclosure Requirements
- f.   Leasehold Improvements

a. Residual value

Residual value can be unguaranteed or guaranteed. Some lease contracts require lessees to guarantee residual value to lessors. The lessee can either buy the leased asset at the end of the lease term for the guaranteed residual value or allow the lessor to sell the leased asset (with the lessee paying any deficiency or receiving any excess over the guaranteed residual value).

Guaranteed residual value is considered a "minimum lease payment" and is reflected in the lessor's lease receivable account and the lessee's lease payable account. At the end of the lease term, the receivable and payable on the respective lessor and lessee books should be equal to the guaranteed residual value. Both lessor and lessee consider the guaranteed residual value a final lease payment.

The lessee should amortize (depreciate) the asset down to the guaranteed residual value.

The present value of the unguaranteed residual value should be included in the lessor's net investment in the lease unless the lease transfers title to the leased asset or there is a bargain purchase option. The unguaranteed residual value is the estimated residual value of the leased asset at the end of the lease (if a guaranteed residual value exists, the unguaranteed residual value is the excess of estimated value over the guaranteed residual value).

At the end of the lease, the lessor's receivable account should be equal to the unguaranteed residual value. The lessor must review the estimated residual value annually and recognize any decreases as a loss. No upward adjustments of the residual value are permitted.

The lessee should amortize the leased asset over the life of the lease unless the lease transfers title or has a bargain purchase option; no residual value should be assumed. If the lease transfers title or has a bargain purchase option, the lessee should amortize the asset cost less estimated residual value at the end of the asset's useful life over the asset's useful life.

b. Initial direct costs*

Initial direct costs are the lessor's costs directly associated with negotiation and consummation of leases. These costs include commissions, legal fees, credit investigations, document preparation, etc. In operating leases, initial direct costs are capitalized and subsequently amortized to expense in proportion to the recognition of rental revenue (which is usually straight-line).

Initial direct costs of direct financing and sales-type leases are accounted for differently. (1) In sales-type leases, charge initial direct costs to operations in the year the sale is recorded. (2) In direct financing leases add the initial direct costs to the net investment in the lease. Compute a new effective interest rate that equates the minimum lease payments and any unguaranteed residual value with the combined outlay for the leased asset and initial direct costs. Finally, the unearned lease (interest) income and the initial direct costs are to be amortized to income over the lease term so that a constant periodic rate is earned on the net investment.

c. Lessee's fair market value limitation

A lessee would normally record a capital lease (leased asset and related liability) at the present value of the minimum lease payments. In determining present value, the lessee discounts the future payments using the lesser of:

(1) The lessee's incremental borrowing rate, or
(2) The lessor's implicit rate (if known by the lessee). (Note that using a lower interest rate increases the present value.)

The amount recorded by the lessee, however, is limited to the FMV of the leased asset. If the FMV is less than the present value of the minimum lease payments, a new effective rate must be computed.

d. Sale-leaseback

Sale-leaseback describes a transaction where the owner of property (seller-lessee) sells the property, and then immediately leases all or part of it back from the new owner (buyer-lessor). The important consideration in this type of transaction is the recognition of two separate and distinct economic transactions. However, it is important to note that there is not a physical transfer of property. First, there is a sale of property, and second, there is a lease agreement for the same property in which the seller is the lessee and the buyer is the lessor. This is illustrated below:

---

*Application of the accounting for initial direct costs in a direct financing lease on the Accounting Practice Exam is not likely because candidates are not permitted to use calculators. However, a description of the approach may be required on the Accounting Theory Exam.

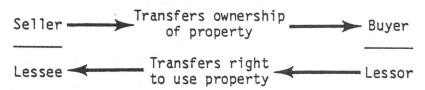

The accounting treatment from the seller-lessee's point of view will depend upon the degree of rights to use retained by the seller-lessee. The degree of rights to use retained may be categorized as follows:

1.   Substantially all
2.   Minor
3.   More than minor but less than substantially all

The guideline for the determination of substantially all is based upon the classification criteria presented for the lease transaction. For example, a test based upon the 90% recovery criterion seems appropriate. That is, if the present value of fair rental payments is equal to 90% or more than the fair value of the sold asset, the seller-lessee is presumed to have retained **substantially all** of the rights to use the sold property. The test for retaining minor rights would be to substitute 10% or less for 90% or more in the preceding sentence.

If substantially all the rights to use the property are retained by the seller-lessee, and the agreement meets at least one of the criteria for capital lease treatment, the seller-lessee should account for the leaseback as a capital lease and any profit on the sale should be deferred and amortized over the life of the property. If the leaseback is classified as an operating lease, any profit on the sale should be deferred and amortized over the lease term in proportion to the related gross rental charged to expense over the lease term. However, any loss on the sale would be recognized immediately.

Although most leases in the "substantially all" category are capital leases, an example of a lease classified as an operating lease is a sale-leaseback that occurs in the last 25% of an asset's economic life.

If only a minor portion of the rights to use are retained by the seller-lessee, the sale and the leaseback should be accounted for separately with immediate recognition of a profit (loss).

If the seller-lessee retains more than a minor portion but less than substantially all the rights to use the property, any excess profit on the sale should be recognized on the date of the sale. For purposes of this paragraph, excess profit is derived as follows:

1.   If the leaseback is classified as an operating lease, the excess profit is the profit which exceeds the present value of the minimum lease payments over the lease term. The seller-lessee should use its incremental borrowing rate to compute the present value of the minimum lease payments. If the implicit rate of interest in the lease is known and lower, it should be used to compute the present value of the minimum lease payments.
2.   If the leaseback is classified as a capital lease, the excess profit is the amount of profit that exceeds the recorded amount of the leased asset.

When the fair value of the property at the time of the leaseback is less than its undepreciated cost, the seller-lessee should immediately recognize a loss for the difference.

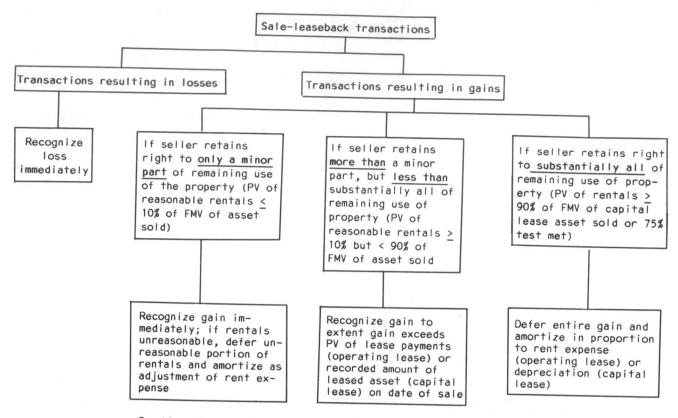

In the above circumstances, when the leased asset is land only, any amortization should be on a straight-line basis over the lease term, regardless of whether the lease is classified as a capital or operating lease.

The buyer-lessor should account for the transaction as a purchase and a direct financing lease if the agreement meets the criteria of **either** a direct financing lease **or** a sales-type lease. Otherwise, the agreement should be accounted for as a purchase and an operating lease.

To illustrate a sale-leaseback transaction, consider the example below.

Numerical Example 5:

Lease Information

   1)   Lessee Corporation sells equipment that has a book value of $80,000 and a fair value of $100,000 to Lessor Corporation, and then immediately leases it back.

   2)   The sale date is January 1, 1986, and the equipment has a fair value of $100,000 on that date and an estimated useful life of 15 years.

   3)   The lease term is 15 years, noncancelable, and requires equal rental payments of $13,109 at the beginning of each year.

   4)   Lessee Corp. has the option to annually renew the lease at the same rental payments upon expiration of the original lease.

   5)   Lessee Corp. has the obligation to pay all executory costs.

   6)   The annual rental payments provide the lessor with a 12% return on investment.

   7)   The incremental borrowing rate of Lessee Corp. is 12%.

   8)   Lessee Corp. depreciates similar equipment on a straight-line basis.

Lease Classification

Lessee Corp. should classify the agreement as a capital lease since the lease term exceeds 75% of the estimated economic life of the equipment, and because the present value of the lease payments is greater than 90% of the fair value of the equipment. Assuming that collectibility of the lease payments is reasonably predictable and that no important uncertainties exist concerning the amount of unreimbursable costs yet to be incurred by the lessor, Lessor Corp. should classify the transaction as a direct financing lease because the present value of the minimum lease payments is equal to the fair market value of $100,000.

Accounting for Lease

Lessee Corp. and Lessor Corp. would normally make the following journal entries during the first year:

Upon Sale of Equipment on January 1, 1986

Lessee Corp.			Lessor Corp.		
Cash	100,000		Equipment	100,000	
Equipment		80,000	Cash		100,000
Unearned profit on					
sale-leaseback		20,000			
Leased equipment	100,000				
Lease obligations		100,000			
			Lease receivable	196,635*	
			Equipment		100,000
			Unearned interest		96,635
			*($13,109 x 15)		

To Record First Payment on January 1, 1986

Lessee Corp.			Lessor Corp.		
Lease obligations	13,109		Cash	13,109	
Cash		13,109	Lease receivable		13,109

To Record Incurrence and Payment of Executory Costs

Lessee Corp.			Lessor Corp.
Insurance, taxes, etc.	xxx		(No entry)
Cash (accounts			
payable)		xxx	

To Record Depreciation Expense on the Equipment, December 31, 1986

Lessee Corp.			Lessor Corp.
Depreciation expense	6,667		(No entry)
Accum. depr. --			
capital leases			
($100,000 ÷ 15)		6,667	

To Amortize Profit on Sale-Leaseback by Lessee Corp., December 31, 1986

Lessee Corp.			Lessor Corp.
Unearned profit on			(No entry)
sale-leaseback	1,333		
Depr. expense			
($20,000 ÷ 15)		1,333	

<u>To Record Interest for 1986, December 31, 1986</u>

Lessee Corp.		Lessor Corp.	
Interest expense	10,427	Unearned interest income	10,427
Accrued interest payable	10,427	Interest income	10,427

(Carrying value $86,891 x .12 = $10,427)

e. <u>Disclosure requirements</u>

The disclosures required of the lessor and lessee are very comprehensive and detailed. In essence, all terms of the leasing arrangement are required (i.e., contingent rentals, subleases, residual values, unearned interest revenue, etc.). For the details see the outline of SFAS 13 ("D.4." and "E.5."). There are, however, a couple of generic disclosure requirements. First, a <u>general description</u> of the leasing arrangement is required. Second, the minimum future payments to be received (paid) by the lessor (lessee) for each of the <u>five succeeding fiscal years</u> should also be disclosed.

f. <u>Leasehold improvements</u>

Frequently the lessee will make improvements to the leased property. Moveable equipment or office furniture that are not attached to the leased property are not considered leasehold improvements. Since the lessee is granted a right to use property owned by the lessor for a <u>specified period of time</u> for a <u>specific periodic cost</u>, leasehold improvements revert to the lessor at the expiration of the lease. Leasehold improvements are properly capitalized and amortized over the remaining life of the lease, or the useful life of the improvement, whichever is shorter. Improvements made in lieu of rent should be expensed in the period incurred. If the lease contains an option to renew and the likelihood of renewal is uncertain, the leasehold improvement should be written off over the life of the initial lease term or useful life of improvement, whichever is shorter.

Tables showing Key Problem Solution Points and Treatment of Selected Items in Accounting for Leases appear below and on the next page.

SUMMARY OF KEY PROBLEM SOLUTION POINTS

- <u>Lessor--direct financing and sales type leases</u>

  - Lease payments Receivable/gross Investment = (Periodic Lease Payments x Number of Rents) + Guar./Unguar. Residual Value

  - Periodic Lease Rental Payments = $\frac{\text{FMV of leased property - residual value*}}{\text{(PV of an annuity factor** using the lessor's implicit rate)}}$

    *Guaranteed/unguaranteed
    **Annuity due or ordinary

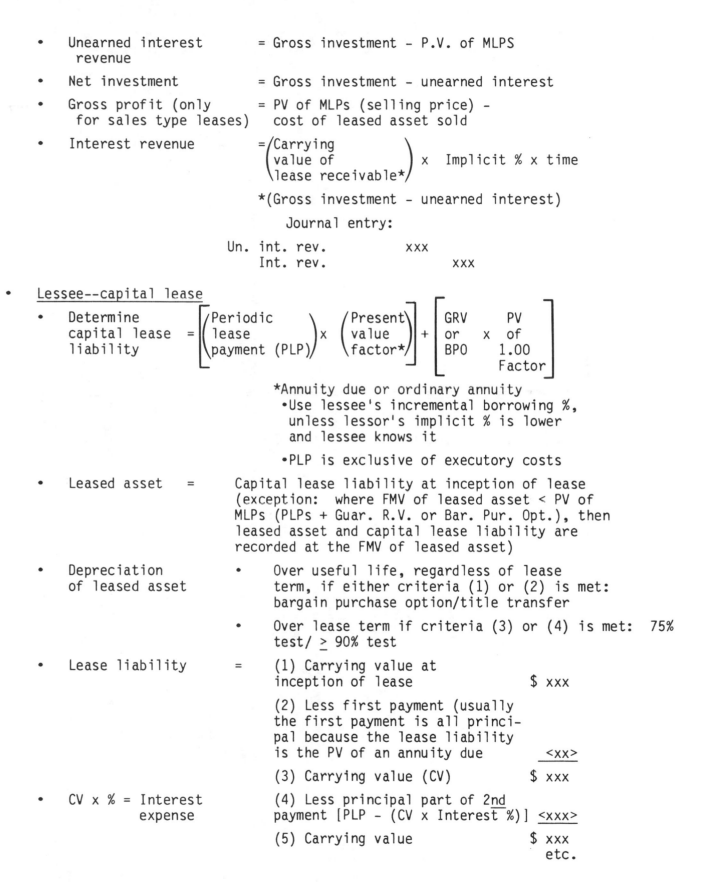

- Unearned interest   = Gross investment - P.V. of MLPS
    revenue

- Net investment   = Gross investment - unearned interest

- Gross profit (only   = PV of MLPs (selling price) -
    for sales type leases)   cost of leased asset sold

- Interest revenue   = $\begin{pmatrix} \text{Carrying} \\ \text{value of} \\ \text{lease receivable*} \end{pmatrix}$ x Implicit % x time

                       *(Gross investment - unearned interest)

                           Journal entry:

              Un. int. rev.   xxx
              Int. rev.   xxx

- Lessee--capital lease

  - Determine $= \begin{bmatrix} \begin{pmatrix} \text{Periodic} \\ \text{lease} \\ \text{payment (PLP)} \end{pmatrix} \text{x} \begin{pmatrix} \text{Present} \\ \text{value} \\ \text{factor*} \end{pmatrix} \end{bmatrix} + \begin{bmatrix} \text{GRV} & \text{PV} \\ \text{or} & \text{x of} \\ \text{BPO} & 1.00 \\ & \text{Factor} \end{bmatrix}$
      capital lease
      liability

                           *Annuity due or ordinary annuity
                           •Use lessee's incremental borrowing %,
                            unless lessor's implicit % is lower
                            and lessee knows it

                           •PLP is exclusive of executory costs

  - Leased asset   =   Capital lease liability at inception of lease
                       (exception: where FMV of leased asset < PV of
                       MLPs (PLPs + Guar. R.V. or Bar. Pur. Opt.), then
                       leased asset and capital lease liability are
                       recorded at the FMV of leased asset)

  - Depreciation   •   Over useful life, regardless of lease
      of leased asset   term, if either criteria (1) or (2) is met:
                           bargain purchase option/title transfer

                       •   Over lease term if criteria (3) or (4) is met: 75%
                           test/ $\geq$ 90% test

  - Lease liability   =   (1) Carrying value at
                           inception of lease $ xxx

                           (2) Less first payment (usually
                           the first payment is all princi-
                           pal because the lease liability
                           is the PV of an annuity due   <xx>

                           (3) Carrying value (CV) $ xxx

  - CV x % = Interest   (4) Less principal part of 2nd
          expense   payment [PLP - (CV x Interest %)] <xxx>

                           (5) Carrying value $ xxx
                                                               etc.

TREATMENT OF SELECTED ITEMS IN ACCOUNTING FOR LEASES

	Lessor		Lessee	
	Operating	Direct Financing and Sales-Type	Operating	Capital
Initial Direct Costs	Capitalize and amortize over lease term in proportion to rent revenue recognized (normally S.L. basis)	Direct financing: Record in separate account. Add to net investment in lease. Compute new effective rate that equates gross amt. of min. lease payments and unguar. residual value with net invest. Amortize so as to produce constant rate of return over lease term. Sales-type: Expense in period incurred	N/A	N/A
Investment Tax Credit Retained by Lessor	N/A	Reduces FMV of leased asset for 90% test	N/A	Reduces FMV of leased asset for 90% test
Bargain Purchase Option	N/A	Include in: Minimum lease payments 90% test	N/A	Include in: Minimum lease payments 90% test
Guaranteed Residual Value	N/A	Include in: Minimum lease payments 90% test. Sales-type: Include PV in sales revenues	N/A	Include in: Minimum lease payments 90% test
Unguaranteed Residual Value	N/A	Include in: "Gross Investment in Lease". Not included in: 90% test. Sales-type: Exclude from sales revenue. Deduct PV from cost of sales	N/A	Not included in: Minimum lease payments 90% test
Contingent Rentals	Revenue in period earned	Not part of minimum lease payments; revenue in period earned	Expense in period incurred	Not part of minimum lease payments; expense in period incurred
Amortization Period	Amortize down to estimated residual value over estimated economic life of asset	N/A	N/A	[b]Amortize down to estimated residual value over lease term or estimated economic life
[a]Revenue (Expense)	Rent revenue (normally S.L. basis); Amortization (depreciation expense)	Direct financing: Interest revenue on net investment in lease (gross investment less unearned interest income); Sales-type: Dealer profit in period of sale (sales revenue less cost of leased asset); Interest revenue on net investment in lease	[c]Rent expense (normally S.L. basis)	Interest Expense and Depreciation Expense

[a]Elements of revenue (expense) listed for the above items are not repeated here (e.g., treatment of initial direct costs).
[b]If lease has automatic passage of title or bargain purchase option, use estimated economic life; otherwise, use the lease term.
[c]If payments are not on a S.L. basis, recognize rent expense on a S.L. basis unless another systematic and rational method is more representative of use benefit obtained from the property, in which case, the other method should be used.

DEFERRED TAXES

In December 1987, the FASB issued SFAS 96, "Accounting for Income Taxes," which requires an asset and liability approach to recognizing deferred taxes. **Coverage of SFAS 96 on the CPA exam is not affected by SFAS 100 that delays effective date in practice to years beginning after 12/15/89.** To understand the basic concepts of deferred taxes study this module and the outlines of SFAS 96 and APB 23.

A. **Differences Between Pretax Financial (Book) and Taxable Income**

The recognition of revenue and expense items for income tax purposes does not always agree with the recognition of these items for financial accounting purposes. A temporary difference is a difference between the tax basis of an asset or liability and its reported amount in the financial statements that will result in taxable or deductible amounts in future years when the reported amount of the asset or liability is recovered or settled, respectively. An example of a temporary difference would be the use of straight-line depreciation for book purposes, but ACRS for tax purposes. A permanent difference occurs when an item affects only financial accounting income or taxable income, but not both. For example, interest income on municipal bonds is included in accounting income, but is not included in taxable income because it is tax exempt.

SFAS 96 does not use the term "permanent difference" when referring to differences that do not result in future taxable or deductible amounts. To ease our explanation and your comprehension, the term "permanent difference" will be used in this module, but remember that it is not part of SFAS 96.

Working a tax allocation problem depends on the candidate's ability to correctly identify the differences between book income and taxable income and to reconcile the two. Common reconciling items between book and taxable income are

1. Permanent differences

    a. State and municipal bond interest income. This amount is included in book income but not included in taxable income.
    b. Amortization of goodwill. This is a deduction for book income but not a deduction for taxable income.
    c. Life insurance premium expense where the corporation is the beneficiary of the policy. This is a deduction for book income but not a deduction for taxable income.
    d. Federal income tax expense. This is a deduction for book income but not a deduction for taxable income.
    e. Payment of penalty or fine. This is a deduction for book income but not for taxable income.
    f. Dividend received deduction (DRD). A corporation's DRD (70%, 80%, 100%) is a deduction for taxable income but not a deduction for book income.

2. Temporary differences

    a. ACRS tax depreciation in excess of book depreciation
    b. Prepaid rental income. This is included in income when received for taxable income and included when earned for book income.

c. Accounting for long-term investments by the equity method for book purposes while using the cost method for tax purposes

d. Estimated accrued liability for warranties. This is deductible when accrued for book income but not deductible for taxable income until the work is actually performed.

e. Use of percentage-of-completion method for accounting purposes and the completed contract method for tax purposes (still acceptable if tax law criteria for a small contract are met)

EXAMPLE 1: A corporation has pretax financial accounting (book) income of $146,000. Additional information is as follows:

1. *Municipal bond interest income is $35,000*
2. *Goodwill amortization expense per books is $4,000*
3. *Accelerated depreciation is used for tax purposes, while straight-line is used for books. Tax depreciation is $10,000; book depreciation is $5,000.*
4. *Estimated warranty expense of $500 is accrued for book purposes.*

Taxable income can be determined as follows:

Income per books before income taxes	*$146,000*
Permanent differences	
* Goodwill amortization*	*4,000*
* Municipal bond interest*	*(35,000)*
	$115,000
Temporary differences	
* Tax depreciation in excess of book*	
* depreciation (10,000 - 5,000)*	*(5,000)*
* Warranty expense included per books*	
* not deducted for tax*	*500*
Taxable income	*$110,500*

The above schedule is known as the reconciliation of book income to taxable income. It is similar to the Schedule M-1 of the U.S. Corporate Income Tax Return (Form 1120) except it starts with pretax financial accounting income instead of net income as Schedule M-1 does.

B. Deferred Tax Liability and Deferred Tax Asset

When <u>temporary differences</u> occur it may be necessary to record a deferred tax liability or deferred tax asset. The objective under the accrual basis is to recognize the tax consequences of an event in the same year that the event is recognized in accounting income. For example, if an item of income is recognized for accounting income in the current year, but not recognized as taxable income until a later year, it is necessary to record the tax consequences of that item in the current year even though the tax on that item will not be paid until a future year. In this case, a deferred tax liability would be recognized at year end to record the tax expected to be paid on that income item in the future.

EXAMPLE 2: Percentage of completion is used for accounting purposes and the completed contract method is used for tax purposes. Percentage of completion income is 40,000 in year 1. Taxable income is zero in year 1. Assume a tax rate of 40%. The taxes payable in year 1 are zero. A deferred tax liability of $16,000 (40,000 x 40%) should be recognized in year one for the tax expected to

be paid in the future on the accounting income recognized in year one.   The
following entry would be made for year one:

Income tax expense--deferred	*$16,000*	
Deferred tax liability		*$16,000*

A <u>deferred tax liability</u>, as shown above, meets the definition of a
liability in SFAC 6. It results from a past event, completion of a portion of
the contract. It is a probable future sacrifice. The timing of the future
payment may be indefinite or the amount may be affected by future events, but
the existence of the liability is definite.

    <u>Permanent differences</u>, unlike temporary differences, do not have future tax
consequences. Therefore, they do not result in deferred tax assets or
liabilities.

    <u>Measurement of Deferred Tax Assets and Liabilities</u>. When measuring the
deferred tax liability or deferred tax asset at year end, it should be assumed
that the only taxable or deductible amounts to be reported in the future are the
results of events recognized in financial statements in the current or preceding
years. That is, it is assumed that the enterprise will just break even from an
accounting or book income standpoint and, therefore, the only elements causing
taxable income (loss) are the temporary differences. Future <u>taxable amounts</u>
result from lower amounts of expense or higher amounts of revenue being reported
on the tax return than will be reported on the books in the future period.
Future <u>deductible amounts</u> result from higher amounts of expense or lower amounts
of revenue being reported on the tax return than will be reported on the books
in the future period. Although it is possible that future profits or losses may
indeed change the tax consequences of the temporary differences, these future
profits or losses should not be assumed at year end. Future income or losses
are future events that should not be recognized in the financial statements of
the current year, no matter how probable. The tax consequences of the future
events will be recognized and reported in the financial statements in the future
years when they actually do occur.

    The table below gives an overview of the treatment of differences between
pretax financial accounting income and taxable income.

Summary of Differences Between Pretax
Financial and Taxable Income

	Current and Prior years	Future years
Pretax Financial Accounting Income	$ XXXX	$ -0-*
• Permanent differences	XXXX	-0-**
	or	
	<XXXX>	-0-**

• Temporary differences
  1. Revenues or Gains
     a. Taxable <u>after</u> recognized
        on the books   (XXXX)   XXXX
     b. Taxable <u>before</u> recognized
        on the books   XXXX   (XXXX)
  2. Expenses or Losses
     a. Deductible <u>after</u> recognized
        on the books   XXXX   (XXXX)
     b. Deductible <u>before</u> recognized
        on the books   (XXXX)   XXXX

Taxable Income $ XXXX $ XXXX

* Because future events (e.g., earning income) may not be assumed
** Because these differences do not have future tax effects

*NOTE: Taxable (Deductible) refers to whether the effect of a temporary
difference is added to (deducted from) pretax financial (book) income in
arriving at taxable income for a given year. This causes much confusion
with respect to 1.b. and 2.b. above. The explanation for these is as
follows:*

*1.b.   Although a revenue or gain item, it is termed <u>deductible</u> in future years
and subtracted from future pretax financial accounting income (assumed to
be -0-) because it was included on the tax return as gross income in an
earlier year.*

*2.b.   Although an expense or loss item, it is termed <u>taxable</u> in future years
and added to future pretax financial accounting income (assumed to be
-0-) because it was deducted on the tax return as an expense in an
earlier year.*

To determine the deferred tax asset/liability at each balance sheet date,

prepare a schedule of future deductible and taxable amounts on an "<u>as if" or pro</u>

<u>forma basis</u>, performing the following steps:

1. Estimate particular future years in which temporary differences will result
   in taxable or deductible amounts
2. Determine the <u>net</u> taxable or deductible amount in each future year arising
   only from events that have been recognized in F/Ss at current year end
3. Deduct <u>operating loss carryforwards for tax purposes</u> (as required or
   permitted by tax law) from <u>net</u> taxable amounts scheduled to occur in the
   future years that fall within the loss carryforward period
4. Carryback or carryforward <u>net</u> deductible amounts occurring in particular
   years just as <u>actual</u> operating losses are treated to offset <u>net</u> taxable
   amounts that are scheduled to occur in prior or subsequent years

*NOTE: You may want to review Section D in this module and Module 43, Section
C.4.j.7. that covers tax law rules for operating losses before proceeding
further*

5. Recognize <u>deferred tax asset</u> for tax benefit of net deductible amounts that could be realized by loss carryback from future years

   a. To reduce a current deferred tax liability (amount to be paid in the next year shown under first future in schedule) as a result of a net taxable amount

   b. To reduce taxes paid in current or prior year

6. Compute amount of tax for remaining <u>net</u> taxable amounts scheduled to occur in each future year

   a. Apply presently enacted tax rates and laws that pertain to each of those years

7. Deduct <u>tax credit carryforwards for tax purposes</u> (e.g., the investment tax credit when it is in effect) from amount of tax for future years that are included in carryforward period

   a. No asset is recognized for any additional amount of tax credit carryforward

8. Recognize a <u>deferred tax liability</u> for remaining amount of taxes payable

As mentioned earlier, the above steps involve preparing a tax return for each affected future year <u>assuming</u> that the only elements of taxable income (loss) are taxable or deductible amounts from temporary differences

EXAMPLE 3:

This example shows the deferred tax accounting in 1987 for the temporary differences included in EXAMPLE 1 earlier in this module. Additional details are:

a. On 1/1/85 the enterprise acquired a depreciable asset for $30,000 that had an estimated life of 6 years and is depreciated on a straight-line basis for book purposes. For tax purposes, the asset is depreciated using the straight-line election under ACRS and qualifies as a three year asset.

b. The enterprise deducts warranty expense of $500 for book purposes in 1987 that is expected to be deductible for tax purposes in 1988.

c. Taxable income was $110,500 in 1987 and -0- in both 1986 and 1985.

d. The applicable tax rate is 40% for all years affected.

e. The deferred component of income tax expense for 1987 is computed as follows. First, a schedule of the <u>temporary depreciation differences</u> for all affected years is prepared:

	1985	1986	1987	1988	1989	1990
Book depreciation	$5,000	$5,000	$5,000	$5,000	$5,000	$5,000
Tax depreciation	5,000*	10,000	10,000	5,000*	–	–
Temporary difference: reversing (originating) amount	$ 0	($5,000)	($5,000)	$ 0	$5,000	$5,000

*Due to ACRS half-year convention

Then, a schedule of <u>future taxable (deductible) amounts</u> is prepared.

	1987	1988	1989	1990
Taxable income (from Example 1)	$110,500			
Scheduled taxable (deductible) amounts				
Depreciation reversals			$5,000	$5,000
Warranty expense reversal		$ (500)		
Net future taxable (deductible amounts)		$ (500)	$5,000	$5,000
"As if" loss carryback	(500)	500		
Amounts after assumed carryback and carryforward	$ (500)	-0-	$5,000	$5,000

The above schedule shows that the future tax benefit of the $500 temporary difference resulting from the warranty expense can be recognized as a deferred tax asset in 1987 because it can be carried back and offset against 1987 taxable income. If there had been taxable income in 1985 and 1986 it would have been necessary to carry the $500 net deductible amount back to 1985 under the tax law NOL carryback election. The deferred tax asset of $200 ($500 x 40%) should be reported as a current asset at 12/31/87 because the temporary difference is expected to reverse in 1988. The amount of future taxes payable associated with the total temporary difference of $10,000 resulting from excess depreciation [$5,000 (1989) + $5,000 (1990)] is $4,000 [($5,000 + 5,000) x 40%]. The $4,000 amount is recognized as a deferred tax liability reported as noncurrent at 12/31/87, because the temporary differences related to depreciation are not expected to reverse until after 1988. If the amount carried back had been larger than the taxable income in 1987, the excess could have been carried forward and offset against the two $5,000 taxable amounts scheduled for reversal in 1989 and 1990.

Once the deferred tax liability has been measured at year end, a journal entry is necessary to adjust the deferred tax account balance to the current year-end amount. As shown below, income tax expense for the year will consist of the taxes currently payable (based on taxable income) plus or minus any change to the deferred tax accounts.

Equation for Determining
Income Tax Expense

Income Tax Expense for Financial Reporting	=	Income Taxes Payable From the Tax Return	±	Change in Deferred Taxes (net)*

*Ending balance of deferred tax liability/asset (net) less beginning balance of deferred tax liability or asset (net)

NOTES:

1. Income tax expense is the sum of the two numbers on the right side of the equation. Each of these two numbers is determined directly using independent calculations. It is not possible to derive income tax expense from pretax financial accounting income adjusted for permanent differences, unless the tax rate is constant for all years affected.
2. The ± refers to whether the change is a credit (+) or a debit (-).
3. Income taxes payable is the amount of taxes calculated on the corporate tax return. It is the amount legally owed the government (after credits).
4. One deferred tax (net) account may be used in practice. If separate accounts are used to conform with balance sheet classification, the changes in each account would all be netted to determine the deferred tax component of income tax expense.

To illustrate, we will use the deferred tax liability computed in Example 3 along with the taxable income derived in Example 1. Note that prior to adjustment, the deferred tax asset account has a zero balance and the deferred tax liability account has a balance of $2,000 ($5,000 x 40%) that was recognized as a result of the depreciation temporary difference that originated in 1986. To focus on the two components of income tax expense, two entries rather than the typical combined entry are used for recording it:

Income tax expense--current	44,200	
Income tax payable		44,200 (a)

     (a) $110,500 taxable income x 40% = $44,200

Income tax expense--deferred (d)	1,800	
Deferred tax asset--current (b)	200	
Deferred tax liability--noncurrent (c)		2,000

     (b) $500 x 40% = $200 Ending balance; $200 Ending balance - (-0-) beginning balance = $200 increase needed in the account

     (c) $10,000 x 40% = $4,000 Ending balance; $4,000 Ending balance - $2,000 Beginning balance = $2,000 increase needed in the account

     (d) $2,000 increase in noncurrent tax liability account - $200 increase in current deferred tax asset account = $1,800

Note that in practice one deferred tax (net) account would typically be used instead of separate asset and liability accounts. However, use of separate accounts on the CPA exam helps to simplify determination of the deferred component of income tax expense and the balance sheet classification of deferred tax assets and liabilities.

The bottom of the income statement would appear as follows:

Income before income tax		$146,000
Income tax expense		
Current	$44,200	
Deferred	1,800	46,000
Net income		$100,000

Changing tax rates. The previous examples assumed a constant tax rate of 40%. Under the liability method, future taxable or deductible amounts must be measured using tax rates expected to be in effect in the reversal periods. However, with respect to net deductible amounts that are carried back to earlier periods under the as if approach, the appropriate rate to use in measuring the deferred income tax asset is the rate applicable to the carryback year. When tax rates change, adjustments to reflect such changes are automatically included in the journal entry amount to increase or decrease deferred taxes on the balance sheet and to recognize the deferred component of income tax expense by comparing the necessary balance of deferred taxes at the end of the period with the beginning of the period and taking the difference.

EXAMPLE 4*:   Dart Corporation has the following temporary differences from its first year of operations:

1. <u>Income on long-term contracts</u>:   future $300 taxable amount in year 2
2. <u>Depreciation</u>: $900 of deductible amount in year 2; taxable amounts, $600 in year 3 and $400 in year 4.
3. <u>Estimated expenses</u>: $200 deductible amount in year 5.
4. <u>Tax rates</u>: Year 1:   40%
                   Year 2:   35%
                   Years 3-5: 30%

In the schedule below which combines the pretax accounting income to taxable income reconciliation with the future taxable (deductible) amounts, taxable income and deferred tax liability (asset) for Year 1 would be determined as follows:

	Current Year		Future Years		
	Year 1	Year 2	Year 3	Year 4	Year 5
Pretax accounting income	$ 900	$	$	$	$
Temporary differences:					
Income on L-T contracts	(300)	300			
Depreciation	(100)	(900)	600	400	
Estimated expenses	200				(200)
Taxable income	$ 700				
Net taxable (deductible) amounts		$(600)	$ 600	$ 400	$(200)
"As if" loss carryback	(500)	500		(200)	200
"As if" loss carryforward		100	(100)		
Amounts after assumed carryback and carry-forward	$(500)	$ 0	$ 500	$ 200	$ 0
Enacted tax rate	40%	35%	30%	30%	30%
Deferred tax liability (asset):					
Current	$(200)				
Noncurrent			$ 150	$ 60	

*Taken directly from SFAS 96, para 42e with modifications.

Income tax expense would be computed as follows:

Income tax expense	=	Income taxes payable	+	Change in deferred taxes (net)	
Income tax expense	=	40% ($700)	+	Ending balance	[(30% x $500) + (30% x $200) - (40% x $500)] - Beg. bal. (-0-)
$290	=	$280	+	$10	

The entry to record income taxes is:

Income tax expense	290	
Income taxes payable		280
Deferred taxes (net)		10

Note that the $900 originating temporary difference from excess tax depreciation in Year 2 is a deductible amount in year 2 because the property was acquired in the current year. Future originating differences on planned future asset acquisitions (a future event) may not be assumed. Also note that since this is the firm's first year of operations, the beginning balance in deferred taxes (net) is -0-.

C. Deferred Tax Related to Business Investments

One additional issue concerns temporary differences from income on long-term investments that are accounted for using the equity method. For investments greater than 50%, SFAS 96 by not superseding APB 23 allows a corporation to assume that the temporary difference (the undistributed income since date of acquisition) will ultimately become taxable in the form of a dividend or in the form of a capital gain--or that it will not become taxable at all. Obviously the tax expense and deferred tax liability recorded when the difference originates will be a function of which of these three assumptions is made.

For long-term investments between 20 and 50 percent, SFAS 96 requires the investor to assume reversal either in the form of a dividend or capital gain. Again the entry to be made will depend upon the assumed form the reversal takes.

To illustrate the application of the requirements of SFAS 96 to these two thresholds of ownership, assume the Parent Company owns 70% of the outstanding common stock of Subsidiary Company and 30% of the outstanding common stock of Investee Company. Additional data for Subsidiary and Investee Companies for the year 1989 are as follows:

	Investee Co.	Subsidiary Co.
Net income	$50,000	$100,000
Dividends paid	20,000	60,000

1. Income Tax Effects from Investee Co.

The pretax accounting income of Parent Company will include equity in investee income equal to $15,000 ($50,000 times 30%). Parent's taxable income, however, will include dividend income of $6,000 ($20,000 times 30%), and a dividends received deduction of 80% of the $6,000, or $4,800, will also be allowed for the dividends received. This 80% dividends received deduction is a permanent difference between pretax accounting and taxable income and is allowed for dividends received from domestic corporations in which the ownership percentage is less than 80% and equal to or greater than 20%. The originating temporary difference results from Parent's equity ($9,000) in Investee's undistributed income of $30,000. The amount by which the deferred tax liability account would increase in 1989 depends upon the expectations of Parent Co. as to the manner in which the $9,000 of undistributed income will be received. If the expectation of receipt is via dividends, then the temporary difference is 20% of $9,000 because 80% of the expected dividend will be excluded from taxable income when received. This temporary difference in 1989 of $1,800, multiplied by the tax rate, will give the amount of the increase in the deferred tax liability.

If the expectation of receipt, however, is through future sale of the investment, then the temporary difference is $9,000, and the change in the deferred tax liability is the capital gains rate (currently the same as ordinary rate) times the $9,000.

The entries below illustrate these alternatives. A tax rate of 34% is used for both ordinary income and capital gains. Note that the amounts in the entries below relate only to Investee Company's incremental impact upon Parent Company's tax accounts.

	Expectations for undistributed income	
	Dividends	Capital gains
Income tax expense	1,020	3,468
Deferred taxes (net)	612[b]	3,060[c]
Income taxes payable	408[a]	408[a]

[a]Computation of income taxes payable

Dividend income--30% ($20,000)	$6,000
Less: 80% dividends received deduction	(4,800)
Amount included in Parent's taxable income	$1,200
Tax liability--34% ($1,200)	$ 408

[b]Computation of deferred tax liability (dividend assumption)

Temporary difference

Parent's share of undistributed income-- 30%($30,000)	$9,000
Less: 80% dividends received deduction	(7,200)
Originating temporary difference	$1,800
Deferred tax liability--34%($1,800)	$ 612

[c]Computation of deferred tax liability (capital gain assumption)

Temporary difference--Parent's share of undistributed income-- 30%($30,000)	$9,000
Deferred tax liability--34%($9,000)	$3,060

2. **Income Tax Effects from Subsidiary Co.**

The pretax accounting income of Parent will also include equity in subsidiary income of $70,000 (70% of $100,000). Note also that this $70,000 will be included in pretax consolidated income if Parent and Subsidiary consolidate. For tax purposes, Parent and Subsidiary cannot file a consolidated tax return because the minimum level of control (80%) is not present. Consequently, the taxable income of Parent will include dividend income of $42,000 (70% of $60,000) and there will be an 80% dividends received deduction of $33,600. The temporary difference results from Parent's equity ($28,000) in Subsidiary's undistributed earnings of $40,000. Remember that the undistributed income of Subsidiary has been recognized for book purposes, but only distributed income (dividends) has been included in taxable income. The amount of the deferred tax liability in 1987 depends upon the expectations of Parent Company as to the manner in which this $28,000 of undistributed income will be received in the future. The same expectations can exist as previously discussed for Parent's equity in Investee's undistributed earnings, i.e., through future dividend distributions or capital gains. Determination of the amounts and the accounts affected for these two assumptions would be similar. However, for stock investments greater than 50% but less than 80%, if the parent can demonstrate that its share of Subsidiary Company's earnings will be permanently reinvested by Subsidiary, APB 23 states that no temporary difference exists, and therefore, no deferred tax liability arises. The entry for this third assumption is shown below. Note that the amount in the entry below relates only to Subsidiary Company's incremental impact upon Parent Company's tax accounts.

Income tax expense	2,856	
Income taxes payable		2,856[a]

[a]Computation of income taxes payable

Dividend income--70% ($60,000)	$42,000
Less: 80% dividends received deduction	(33,600)
Amount included in Parent's taxable income	8,400
Tax liability--34% ($8,400)	$ 2,856

If a parent company owns 80% or more of the voting stock of a subsidiary, and the parent consolidates the subsidiary for both financial and tax reports, then no temporary differences exist between pretax consolidated income and taxable income. If, in the circumstances noted above, consolidated financial statements are prepared but a consolidated tax return is not, then it should be noted that a dividends received deduction of 100% is allowed. Accordingly, the temporary difference between pretax consolidated income and taxable income is zero if the parent assumes the undistributed income will be realized in dividends.

The diagram below illustrates the accounting and income tax treatment of the undistributed investee/subsidiary earnings by corporate investors under different levels of ownership.

SUMMARY OF TEMPORARY DIFFERENCES OF INVESTEES AND SUBSIDIARIES

Level of Ownership Interest

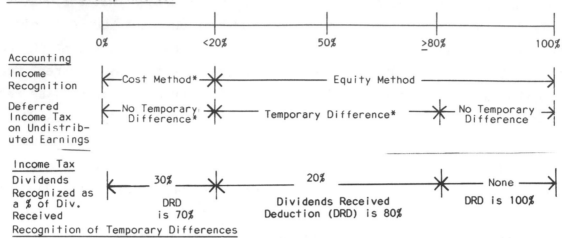

*Both pretax financial accounting and taxable income would include only dividends declared by the investee. If evidence indicates that significant influence exists at an ownership level less than 20%, a temporary difference would be recognized.

Ownership level ≥ 20% < 50%: temporary difference **must** be accounted for.

Ownership level > 50% < 80%: temporary difference must **normally** be accounted for, unless management
   intends to reinvest the subsidiary's earnings indefinitely into the future.

D. Loss Carryforwards and Carrybacks

Operating losses of a particular period can be carried back to the 3 immediate past periods' income resulting in a tax credit. Losses still remaining after carrybacks may also be carried forward for 15 years to offset income if income arises in any of those 15 years. Companies may at the time of the loss elect to use only the carryforward provision.

Loss carrybacks occur when losses in the current period are carried back to periods in which there was income. Loss carrybacks result in tax refunds in the loss period and thus should be recognized in the year of the loss. The entry to record the benefit is:

Tax refund receivable   (based on tax credit due to loss)
      Tax loss benefit(income tax expense)   (same)

The tax loss benefit would be closed to revenue and expense summary in the year of the loss and shown as a reduction of the loss from continuing operations on the face of the income statement as follows:

Loss before income taxes	$(xxxx)
Less: Benefit from operating loss carryback	xxx
Net loss	$ (xxx)

Tax loss carryforwards generally are not recognized in the year the loss
occurs. The carryforward should not be recognized until it is realized; i.e.,
it should be recognized in the subsequent period when income arises and creates
a current receivable from the government. Whether the benefit of the
carryforward, when realized, is an extraordinary item depends on the item which
gave rise to the loss carryforward. If the loss carryforward results from
ordinary operations, then the subsequent benefit of the carryforward will be
treated as a reduction of income tax expense from continuing operations. On the
other hand, if the item which created the carryforward was an extraordinary
loss, then the subsequent benefit will be treated as an extraordinary gain.

The benefit of a net operating loss carryforward can be recognized in the
loss year in only one circumstance: when existing temporary differences are
expected to result in net taxable amounts in the carryforward period. In this
case, realization is assured because the carryforward is assumed to be offset
against those future taxable amounts. Since the future taxable amounts have
caused a deferred tax liability to be previously recorded, that deferred tax
liability is reduced when the tax benefit is recognized in the loss year. The
entry is:

<pre>
            Deferred taxes (net)   xxx
                Tax loss benefit
                (income tax expense)   xxx
</pre>

E. **Financial Statement Presentation of Income Tax**

1. Income Statement

    Continuing Operations. For each year presented, the significant
    components of income tax expense arising from continuing operations shall be
    disclosed on the face of the income statement or in the notes. These
    components would include:

    a. Current tax expense or benefit
    b. Deferred tax expense or benefit, exclusive of (e) below
    c. Investment tax credits and grants
    d. The benefits of operating loss carryforwards
    e. Adjustments of a deferred tax liability or asset for enacted changes in
        tax laws or rates or a change in the tax status of an enterprise; tax
        effects of changes in items reported in stockholders' equity are also
        included with the rate change component of income taxes arising from
        continuing operations

    Other components of Net Income. Income tax expense must be allocated
    within an accounting period between continuing operations and other
    components of net income (i.e., discontinued operations, extraordinary

items, etc.). The amount of income tax expense allocated to continuing operations is equal to the tax on pretax income or loss from continuing operations. This tax on the pretax income or loss is computed exclusive of any other items that occurred during the year. The amount allocated to an item other than continuing operations is equal to the incremental effect on income taxes resulting from that item.

EXAMPLE: $(50,000)   Loss from continuing operations
              90,000   Extraordinary gain
            $ 40,000   Income before taxes

Assume that if the $50,000 loss were carried back it would result in a $15,000 refund of taxes paid in prior years. Assume that the current year's tax rate is 40% and income taxes currently payable are $16,000 on $40,000 of taxable income including the extraordinary gain. Income tax expense would be allocated as follows:

Tax benefit associated with the loss from operations	$(15,000)
Incremental tax consequence attributable to the extraordinary gain	31,000
Total tax liability	$ 16,000

When income tax expense is allocated to two or more items other than continuing operations, the sum of the incremental tax effects of each of the items may not equal the incremental tax effect of all of the items together. This may occur, for example, where a statutory limitation exists on the utilization of tax credits. In this situation the following sequence must be followed.

a. Determine the incremental tax benefit of the total net loss for all net loss categories
b. Apportion that incremental tax benefit ratably to each net loss category
c. Apportion ratably to each net gain category the difference between (1) the incremental tax effect of all categories other than continuing operations and (2) the incremental tax benefit of the total net loss for all net loss categories

EXAMPLE:

Huskie Company has the following components of income before taxes (for both book and tax purposes):

$ 6,000	Income from continuing operations
5,000	Gain from discontinued operations
2,000	Gain from extraordinary item
<1,000>	Loss from cumulative effect of an accounting change
$12,000	

Assume that the tax rate is 40% and the company has $3,000 of tax credits available which are subject to a limitation of 90% of taxes payable. Total income tax expense and income tax allocated to continuing operations are computed as follows:

	Continuing Operations	Total
Taxable income	$6,000	$12,000
Tax at 40%	$2,400	$ 4,800
Tax credits (90% limitation)	2,160	3,000
Tax expense	$ 240	$ 1,800

The aggregate incremental tax effect resulting from all of the other income component items is $1,560 (1,800 - 240). The incremental effect of **each** of these items is computed as follows:

	Gain 1 Discont. Oper.	Gain 2 X-O item	Loss Cum. Effect
Total taxable income	12,000	12,000	12,000
Gain (loss) item	5,000	2,000	(1,000)
Taxable income without the gain (loss) item	7,000	10,000	13,000
Tax at 40%	$ 2,800	$ 4,000	$ 5,200
Tax credits (90% limit)	2,520	3,000	3,000
Tax without the gain (loss)	280	1,000	2,200
Total tax for the year	1,800	1,800	1,800
Incremental tax effect of each item	$ 1,520	$ 800	$ (400)

Since there is only one loss item, the cumulative effect of an accounting change, it is assigned a tax benefit of $400.

The difference between $1,560 incremental tax effect from all of the income statement components other than continuing operations and the $400 loss or $1,960 is apportioned ratably to each of the gain items as follows:

	Individual Amount	Ratable Portion	Apportioned Amount
Gain 1	$1,520	1520/2320 x 1960	$1,284
Gain 2	800	800/2320 x 1960	676
	$2,320		$1,960

Thus, income tax expense is allocated as follows:

	Pretax Income	Tax Expense
Income from continuing operations	$ 6,000	$ 240
Discontinued operations	5,000	1,284
Extraordinary items	2,000	676
Accounting change	<1,000>	< 400>
	$12,000	$1,800

Any income tax effects associated with adjustments of the opening balance of retained earnings for a special type change in accounting principle or correction of an error are to be charged or credited directly to retained earnings. The income tax effects of other stockholders' equity items (e.g., cumulative translation adjustment) are charged or credited to stockholders' equity.

2. Balance Sheet

The classification of deferred tax liabilities and assets is a two-stage process. First, all deferred tax liabilities and assets are classified as current or noncurrent. The liability or asset will be considered current to the extent that the deferred tax liability or asset results from temporary differences that become taxable or deductible in the next year. The liability or asset will be considered noncurrent to the extent that it results from temporary differences that become taxable or deductible in years after next year. Once classification has been determined, all current amounts are netted to get a net current asset or liability and the noncurrent amounts are likewise netted to obtain a net noncurrent amount.

This process is illustrated in Example 4. Example 4 shows that when using the schedule format illustrated, the net current liability or net current asset will already be identified ($200 net current asset in this example). All other items are netted to find the net noncurrent amount. (In this case both amounts are liabilities and the net noncurrent amount is $210 ($150 + 60).

F. **Alternative Minimum Tax (AMT)**

Under current tax law the federal tax liability for each year is the greater of taxes calculated under the regular tax system or the AMT system (see Module 43, Section C.2.c.).

Because SFAS 96 requires computation of deferred taxes as if a tax return were prepared for each future year with future taxable (deductible) amounts as the only elements of taxable income, it is also necessary to perform the deferred tax calculations under both systems.

Due to the complexity of these calculations we have decided not to include an example of the deferred tax calculations using AMT in this module. Additionally, deferred tax questions on the May 1989 exam indicated AMT should either be ignored or assumed to be less than the regular tax.

STOCKHOLDERS' EQUITY

Stockholders' equity is the residual of assets minus liabilities, i.e., net assets. Due to the number of fraudulent manipulations involving stocks, many states have legislated accounting for stockholder equity transactions and they are controlled to some degree, e.g., conditions under which dividends may be paid.

Common stockholders' equity consists of two major categories: contributed capital and retained earnings. Retained earnings are either appropriated or unappropriated. Contributed capital consists of paid-in and donated. Paid-in consists of paid-in excess and legal capital. Legal capital is the par or stated value of stock. An outline of stockholders' equity follows.

Contributed capital

- Paid-in, e.g., common and preferred stock

    - Legal--par, stated, no par
    - Paid-in excess of par or stated value
    - Paid-in from other transactions

        - Treasury stock
        - Retirement of stock
        - Stock dividends recorded at market
        - Stock warrants detachable from bonds
        - Lapse of stock purchase warrants
        - Conversion of convertible bonds recorded at market value of the stock
        - Any other gain on the company's own stock transactions

Donated capital

Retained earnings

- Appropriated
- Unappropriated

Contra stockholders' equity items (deducted after contributed capital and retained earnings above are totaled)

- Treasury stock (cost method)
- Unrealized losses on long-term equity securities (SFAS 12, para 11)
- Deferred compensation costs if by issuance of stock to employees (APB 25, para 14)
- Some unrealized foreign currency translations (see SFAS 52, paras 13, 18, and 19; may also increase S/E)
- Excess of minimum pension liability over unrecognized prior service cost (SFAS 87, para 37)

A. **Common Stock**

The entry to record the issuance of common stock is

Cash	(amount received)
Common stock	(par or stated value)
Paid-in excess	(forced)

If stock is sold for less than par, a discount account is debited.

Very little stock is issued at a discount because of the resulting potential liability to the original purchaser for the difference between the issue price (when less than par) and par which in many states is legal capital. This liability has been avoided by use of stated value and no par stock, but is mainly avoided by establishing par values below market.

Control accounts are occasionally used to control unissued stock. At authorization

```
    Unissued common stock          (total par or stated value)
        Common stock authorized        (same)
```

At issuance

```
    Cash                           (cash received)
        Unissued common stock          (par or stated value)
        Paid-in excess                 (forced)
```

The credit balance in the authorized account is the total available for issuance. The debit balance in the unissued account is the amount not issued. Thus, authorized (cr) - unissued (dr) = issued (cr). The unissued account is an offset account to the authorized account.

No-par stock is occasionally issued, i.e., no par or stated value exists. All of the proceeds from issuance of no-par stock are credited to "common stock."

Stock issued for services or assets should be valued at FMV.

```
    Legal expenses                 (FMV)
    Assets                         (FMV)
        Common stock                   (par)
        Paid-in excess                 (forced)
```

Costs of registering and issuing common stock are generally netted against the proceeds, i.e., reduce "paid-in excess." An alternative method is to consider stock issue costs an organizational cost.

B. **Preferred Stock**

As implied, preferred stock has preferential rights: most commonly the right to receive dividends prior to common stockholders. Generally the dividend payout is specified, e.g., 7% of par. Additional possible features

1. Participating--share with common stockholders in dividend distributions after both preferred and common stockholders receive a specified level of dividend payment

a. Participation with common stockholders in dividends is usually specified in terms of a percentage of legal capital. For example, 7% preferred receive 7% of their par value in dividends before common stockholders receive dividends. Fully participating preferred would receive the same percentage dividend as common stockholders if the common stockholders received over a 7% (of par value) dividend.

2. Cumulative--dividends not paid in any year (dividends in arrears) must be made up before distributions can be made to common stockholders

   a. However, dividends in arrears are not a liability until declared. They should be disclosed parenthetically or in the footnotes.

3. Convertible--preferred stockholders have an option of exchanging their stock for common stock at a specified ratio

   a. Conversion is usually accounted for at book value

Preferred stock	(par converted)
Preferred paid-in accounts	(related balances)
Common stock	(par)
Paid-in excess	(forced)

   b. If market value is used, common stock and paid-in excess are credited for the market value, usually resulting in a large debit to retained earnings. (Plug figure in the journal entry.)

4. Callable--the corporation has the option to repurchase the preferred stock at a specified price

   a. If called, no gain or loss is recognized. Gains are taken to a paid-in capital account; losses are charged to retained earnings

Preferred stock	(par)
Preferred paid-in accounts	(related balances)
Retained earnings	(if dr. needed)
Cash	(amount paid)
Paid-in from preferred	
retirement	(if cr. needed)

Any of the above features present in a preferred stock issuance should be disclosed parenthetically in the balance sheet next to the account title.

C. **Stock Subscriptions**

   Stock (common/preferred) can be subscribed by investors. A receivable is established and "stock subscribed" credited. When the total subscription price is received, the stock (common/preferred) is issued.

   At subscription

Cash	(any cash received)
Subscription receivable	(balance)
Stock subscribed	(par)
Paid-in excess	(subscription price > par)

Cash receipt and issuance

```
        Cash                          (balance)
            Subscriptions receivable    (balance)
        Common stock subscribed      (par)
            Stock*                      (par)
```

     *Unissued common stock, if unissued and authorized accounts are being used.

Upon default of subscription agreements, depending on the agreement, the amount paid to date may be

1. Returned to subscriber
2. Kept by company
3. Held to cover any losses on resale and balance returned

If returned

```
        Stock subscribed
        Paid-in excess
            Cash
            Subscriptions receivable
```

If kept by the company, no cash would be paid and "paid-in from subscription default" credited instead of cash.

    If held to cover any losses on resale, a "refundable subscription deposit" liability would be credited instead of cash. If the stock were resold at less than the original subscription price, the difference would be debited to "refundable subscription deposit."

```
        Cash                             (payment)
        Refundable subscription deposit   (forced)
            Stock                            (par)
            Paid-in excess                   (amount from original sale)
```

The balance in the refundable subscription account would be paid (possibly in an equivalent number of shares) to the original subscriber.

D. **Treasury Stock Transactions**

    A firm's own stock repurchased on the open market is known as treasury stock. Treasury stock is <u>not</u> an asset, as a firm may not own shares of itself. Instead it is treated as a reduction of stockholders' equity. There are two methods for accounting of treasury stock: cost and par value.

1. <u>Cost Method</u>

    Under the <u>cost method</u>, treasury stock is debited for the cost of treasury stock. Any gain (loss) is recognized at the point of resale. However, such gains (losses) are not included in the determination of periodic income. Gains are credited to "paid-in capital from treasury stock transactions." Losses should be charged first to "paid-in capital from treasury stock (TS) transactions" or "paid-in capital from stock retirement" to the extent that either of these exists for that class of stock. The remainder of any loss is to be charged to retained earnings. In essence a one-transaction viewpoint is used, as the firm is treated as a middle "person" for the transfer of stock between two shareholders.

2. Par Value Method

Under the par value method, all capital balances associated with the treasury shares are removed upon acquisition. Any excess of treasury stock cost over par value is accounted for by charging "paid-in capital from common stock" for the amount in excess of par received when the shares were originally issued. Any excess of the cost of acquiring the treasury stock over the original issue cost is charged to retained earnings. If treasury stock is acquired at a cost equal to or less than the original issue cost, "paid-in capital from common stock" is charged (debited) for the original amount in excess of par and "paid-in capital from treasury stock" is credited for the difference between the original issue price and the cost to acquire the treasury stock. When the treasury stock is resold, it is treated as a typical issuance, with the excess of selling price over par credited to "paid-in capital from common stock." Note that the par value method takes on a two-transaction viewpoint. The purchase is treated as a "retirement" of the shares, while the subsequent sale of the shares is treated as a "new" issue.

EXAMPLE: 100 shares ($50 par) are originally sold at $60, reacquired at $70, and subsequently resold at $75.

Cost method			Par value method		
Treasury stock	7,000		Treasury stock	5,000	
Cash		7,000	Paid-in capital--		
			common stock	1,000	
			Retained earnings	1,000	
			Cash		7,000
Cash	7,500				
Treasury stock		7,000	Cash	7,500	
Paid-in capital--			Treasury stock		5,000
treasury stock		500	Paid-in capital--		
			common stock		2,500

If the shares had been resold at $65

Cost method			Par value method		
Cash	6,500		Cash	6,500	
*Retained earnings	500		Treasury stock		5,000
Treasury stock		7,000	Paid-in capital--		
			common stock		1,500

*"Paid-in capital--treasury stock" or "paid-in capital--retired stock" of that issue would be debited first to the extent it exists.

Note that total stockholders' equity is not affected by the method selected; only the allocation among the equity accounts is different.

E. **Retirement of Stock**

Formal retirement or constructive retirement (purchase with no intent of reissue) of stock is handled very similarly to treasury stock. When formally retired

```
    Common stock
   *Paid-in excess
   *Retained earnings
        *Treasury stock
```

*Assuming a loss on the retirement of treasury stock

1. "Paid-in from treasury stock transactions" may be debited to the extent it exists

2. A pro rata portion of all paid-in capital existing for that issue, e.g., if 2% of an issue is retired, up to 2% of all existing paid-in capital for that issue may be debited

Alternatively, the entire or any portion of the loss may be debited to retained earnings. Any gains are credited to a "paid-in from retirement" account.

F. **Dividends**

1. At the date of declaration, an entry is made to record the dividend liability

```
    Retained earnings (Dividends)
        Dividends payable
```

2. No entry is made at the date of record. Those owning stock at the date of record will be paid the previously declared dividends.

a. The stockholder records consist of

(1) General ledger account
(2) Subsidiary ledger

(a) Contains names and addresses of stockholders

(3) Stock certificate book

b. Outside services: usually banks

(1) Transfer agent issues new certificates, cancelling old, and maintains stockholder ledger
(2) Registrar validates new certificates and controls against over-issuance
(3) Functions are now becoming combined

3. At the payment date, the liability is paid

```
    Dividend payable
        Cash
```

4. Property dividends are accounted for as cash dividends. They are recorded at FMV of the asset transferred with a gain (loss) recognized on the difference between the asset's BV and FMV at disposition (see APB 29).

    a. Except for rescission of prior business combinations

5. Liquidation dividends (dividends based on other than earnings) are a return of capital to stockholders and should be so disclosed. Paid-in capital is usually debited rather than retained earnings. Common stock cannot be debited because it is the legal capital which can only be eliminated upon corporate dissolution.

6. Scrip dividends are issuance of promises to pay dividends in the future (and may bear interest) instead of cash

        Retained earnings   xx
            Scrip dividends payable   xx

    Scrip dividends are a liability which is extinguished by payment

        Scrip dividends payable   xx
        Interest expense (maybe)   xx
            Cash   xx

7. Unlike cash and property dividends, stock dividends are not a liability when declared. They can be rescinded as nothing is actually being distributed to stockholders except more stock certificates. Current assets are not used to "pay" the dividend.

    a. After stock dividends, shareholders continue to own the same proportion of the corporation
    b. At declaration

        Retained earnings   (FMV of shares)
            Stock dividend distributable   (par)
            Paid-in excess of par   (plug)

    c. At issuance

        Stock dividend distributable   xx
            Common stock   xx

    d. Charge retained earnings for FMV of stock dividend if less than 20%-25% increase in stock outstanding

        (1) Not required if closely-held company

G. **Stock Splits**

    Stock splits change the number of shares outstanding and the par value per share. Par value is reduced in proportion to the increase in the number of shares. The total par value outstanding does not change and no charge is made to retained earnings. If legal requirements preclude changing the par or stated value, charge retained earnings only for the par or stated value issued.

STOCK DIVIDENDS AND SPLITS: SUMMARY OF EFFECTS

	Total S.E.	Par value per share	Total par outstanding	R.E.	Legal capital	Additional paid-in capital	No. of shares outstanding
Stock dividend < 20-25% of shares outstanding	N/C	N/C	+	Decrease by market value of shares issued	+	+	+
Stock split effected in form of dividend > 20 - 25% of shares outstanding	N/C	N/C	+	Decrease by par value of shares issued	+	N/C	+
Stock split	N/C	Decrease proportionately	N/C	N/C	N/C	N/C	+

N/C = No Change
 + = Increase

Prepared by Professor John R. Simon, Northern Illinois University

H. Appropriations of Retained Earnings (Reserves)

An entry to appropriate retained earnings restricts the amount of retained earnings that is available for dividends.

RE (or Unappropriated RE)
    Reserve for RE (or Appropriated RE)

It is important to note, however, that the restriction of retained earnings does not necessarily provide cash for any intended purpose. The purpose is to show that assets in the amount of the appropriation are not available for dividends. SFAS 5 requires that when a reserve is no longer needed it must be returned directly to unappropriated retained earnings by reversing the entry that created it.

I. Stock Options

Study ARB 43, Chapter 13B, and APB 25 before studying this section.

Compensation is generally measured by the dollar value difference between the option price and the market price if the option price is below the market price.

For financial reporting purposes, compensation is measured on the measurement date--that date on which both the number of shares the individual employee is entitled to and the option or purchase price are known. The measurement date is usually, though not always, the grant date.

Many options are granted at a price equal to or greater than the market price when the option is granted for a fixed number of shares. Thus, there is no compensation expense and no journal entry involving compensation expense is recorded. Disclosure, however, as to the options outstanding, is required. When the employee acquires stock under these circumstances, the corporation debits cash for the option price, and credits common stock for par and paid-in capital for the excess.

If the measurement date is the grant date and deferred compensation is recorded, it is amortized over the periods in which the employee provides the services for which the option contract is the reward. For example, an option is granted to a corporate officer to purchase 100 shares of $1 par common at $52 when the market price is $58. The entry to record the granting of the option is

```
Deferred compensation expense   600    (a contra paid-in capital account)
     Stock options outstanding        600    (a paid-in capital account)
```

Deferred compensation is subtracted from stock options outstanding in the paid-in capital section of owners' equity to indicate the net contributed services on any date--i.e., on the grant date nothing has yet been contributed by the option holder, and this would be measured by ($600 - $600 = 0). As the employee provides services to earn the option, an entry is made assigning compensation expense to periods (assume a 5-year period).

```
Compensation expense                120
     Deferred compensation exp.           120
```

When the option is exercised, cash is received and stock is issued as reflected in the following entry (assume exercise after the 5-year period).

```
Cash                              5,200     (option price)
Stock options outstanding           600
     Common stock                        100     (par)
     Additional paid-in capital       5,700     (plug)
```

If the options are forfeited due to the employee(s) failing to fulfill an obligation, e.g., staying with the company, compensation expense is credited in the year of forfeiture. The amount credited reflects the total compensation expense previously charged to the income statement for the employee(s) who forfeited the options. In the example, assume the officer leaves the company in year 3, two years before the options can be exercised. The following entry is made in year 3.

```
Stock options outstanding             600
     Deferred compensation expense         360
     Compensation expense                  240
```

In the example above, the grant date and the measurement date coincide. If the measurement date follows the grant date, it is necessary to assume compensation expense based on the market values of the common stock that exist at the end of each period until the measurement date is reached. For example, assume that on 1/1/85, a company grants an option to purchase 100 shares of common stock at 90% of the market price at 12/31/87 and that the compensation period is 4 years. Note that at 1/1/85, the number of shares is determinable, but the option price is unknown. The market values and option prices of the common are as follows.

12/31/85	$10 x 90% = $ 9.00
12/31/86	13 x 90% = 11.70
12/31/87	15 x 90% = 13.50

The following entries for compensation expense are recorded.

	1985	1986	1987	1988
Compensation expense	25	40*	47.50*	37.50
Stock options outstanding		25	40	47.50	37.50

1985: [($10 - 9.00) x 100 shares x 1/4)] = $25
1986: [($13 - 11.70) x 100 shares x 2/4)] - expense recognized to date = $40
1987: [($15 - 13.50) x 100 shares x 3/4)] - expense recognized to date = $47.50
1988: [($15 - 13.50) x 100 shares x 4/4)] - expense recognized to date = $37.50

Note that the market value of the stock at the end of 1985 and 1986 is used as an estimate of the market price of the stock at 12/31/87. Also, in accordance with FASB Interpretation No. 28, changes in the market value of the stock between the date of grant and the measurement date are adjustments to compensation expense <u>in the period the market value of the stock changes</u>. The effect of such changes are not spread over future periods.

A time line depicting the actual and estimated compensation expense would appear as follows.

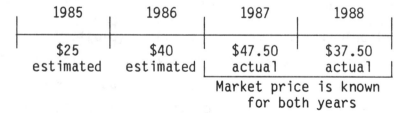

J. **Stock Appreciation Rights**

Study the summary of FASB Interpretation No. 28 in conjunction with study of this section.

Stock appreciation rights (SARs) allow employees to receive stock or cash equal in amount to the difference between the market value and some predetermined amount per share for a certain number of shares. SARs allow employees to receive share appreciation without having to make a cash outlay as is common in stock option plans.

*Results from change in estimate

For financial reporting purposes, compensation expense is the excess of market value over a predetermined amount. Compensation expense is recorded in each period prior to exercise based on the excess of market value at the end of each period over a predetermined amount. Compensation expense is adjusted up or down as the market value of stock changes before the measurement date (which is the exercise date). Therefore, compensation expense could be credited if the stock's market value drops from one period to the next.

For example, assume a company grants 100 SARs, payable in cash, to an employee on 1/1/85. The predetermined amount for the SAR plan is $50 per right, and the market value of the stock is $55 on 12/31/85, $53 on 12/31/86, and $61 on 12/31/87. Compensation expense recorded in each year would be

	Total expense	– Exp. previously accrued	= Current expense
1985	100 ($55-$50) = $ 500	– $ 0	= $500
1986	100 ($53-$50) = $ 300	– $500	= ($200)
1987	100 ($61-$50) = $1,100	– $300	= $800

The total expense recognized over the 3-year period is $1,100 [100($61-$50)].

Journal entries would be

1985 and 1987		1986	
Compensation expense $500/$800		Liability under SAR plan $200	
Liability under SAR plan $500/$800		Compensation expense $200	

If the SARs were to be redeemed in common stock, Stock Rights Outstanding (a paid-in capital account) would replace the liability account in the above entries.

The above example assumes no service or vesting period, which is a period of time until the SARs become exercisable. If the above plan had a 2-year service period, 50% of the total expense would be recognized at the end of the first year, and 100% at the end of the second year and thereafter until exercise. The compensation would be accrued as follows.

1985   ($ 500)(50%)   = $ 250 – $ 0 = $250

1986   ($ 300)(100%) = $ 300 – $250 = $ 50

1987   ($1,100)(100%) = $1,100 – $300 = $800

K. Earnings Per Share for Simple Capital Structures

In reviewing earnings per share, we recommend that candidates work through this section before reading the outline of APB 15.

A corporation is said to have a simple capital structure when (1) there are no potentially dilutive securities, or (2) if potentially dilutive securities are present, their aggregate effect on earnings per share (EPS) based upon weighted average common shares outstanding is less than (<) 3%. In this calculation, all antidilutive securities (those that would individually increase EPS based upon outstanding common shares) are disregarded.

In the simple capital structure situation, the calculation of EPS can be stated as follows.

$$\text{Earnings per common share} = \frac{\text{Net income - Applicable preferred dividends}}{\text{Weighted average number of common shares outstanding}}$$

The following example will illustrate the application of this formula.

Numerator information

a.   Net income $100,000

b.   Extraordinary loss
     (net of tax)   30,000

c.   6% preferred stock,
     $100 par, 1,000 shares
     issued and outstanding
     ($100,000 x .06)   6,000

Denominator information

a.   Common shares outstanding   100,000
     1-1-86

b.   Shares issued for cash 4-1   20,000

c.   Shares issued in 10% stock
     dividend declared in July   12,000

d.   Shares of treasury stock
     purchased 10-1   10,000

When a corporation reports discontinued operations, an extraordinary item and/or cumulative effect of an accounting principles change, earnings per share information is required for the following income elements.

1.   Income from continuing operations

2.   Income before extraordinary item

3.   The cumulative effect of the change in principle (net of tax) and

4.   Net income

Reporting EPS on these four income elements is required regardless of whether the capital structure is simple or complex. In the example, earnings per share information is required for the second and fourth income elements.

When calculating the amount of the numerator the claims of senior securities (i.e., preferred stock) should be deducted to arrive at the earnings attributable to common shareholders. In the example, the preferred stock is cumulative. Thus, regardless of whether or not the board of directors declares a preferred dividend, holders of the preferred stock have a claim of $6,000 (1,000 shares x $6 per share) against 1986 earnings. Therefore $6,000 is deducted from the numerator to arrive at the net income attributable to common shareholders. Note that this $6,000 would have been deducted for noncumulative preferred only if a dividend of this amount had been declared.

To summarize, at this point, the EPS calculations look as follows.

Earnings per common share:

On income before extraordinary item = $\dfrac{\$130,000 - 6,000}{\text{Common shares outstanding}}$

On net income = $\dfrac{\$100,000 - 6,000}{\text{Common shares outstanding}}$

The numerator of the EPS calculation covers a particular time period such as a month, a quarter, or a year. It is, therefore, consistent to calculate the average number of common shares which were outstanding during this same time period. The calculation below in Table I illustrates the determination of weighted average common shares outstanding. Note that for stock dividends the number of shares is adjusted retroactively for the shares which where outstanding prior to the stock dividend. Since the stock dividend was issued <u>after</u> the issuance of additional shares for cash on 4/1, the shareholders of those additional shares and the shareholders of the shares outstanding at the beginning of the year will receive the stock dividend. However, if the stock dividend had been issued <u>before</u> the issuance of additional shares of stock for cash on 4/1, only the shareholders who own the shares outstanding at the beginning of the period would have received the stock dividend. Stock splits are handled in identical fashion.

TABLE I

Dates	Number common shares outstanding	Months outstanding	Fraction of year	Shares x Fraction of year
1/1 to 4/1	100,000 + 10% (100,000) = 110,000	3	1/4	27,500
4/1 to 10/1	110,000 + 20,000 + 10% (20,000) = 132,000	6	1/2	66,000
10/1 to 12/31	132,000 - 10,000 = 122,000	3	1/4	30,500
Weighted average of common shares outstanding				124,000

In the weighted average computation, an additional problem is created if common shares are issued in a business combination during the year. If the combination is accounted for as a purchase, the common shares are weighted from the date of issuance. If the pooling method is used the shares are considered to be outstanding for the entire year, regardless of the date the pooling was consummated. Other complications in the weighted average calculation are posed by actual conversions of debt and preferred stock to common during the year and by exercise of warrants and options. These situations are introduced in the example presented for a complex capital structure in the next section.

To complete the simple capital structure EPS example, the weighted average number of common shares determined in Table I is divided into the income elements previously computed to arrive at the following.

Earnings per common share:

On income before extraordinary items $\dfrac{\$130,000 - 6,000}{124,000 \text{ common shares}} = \$1.00$

On net income $\dfrac{\$100,000 - 6,000}{124,000 \text{ common shares}} = \$ .76$

Reporting a $.24 loss per share due to the extraordinary item is optional. These EPS numbers should be presented on the face of the income statement.

L. **Earnings Per Share for Complex Capital Structures**

By definition, complex capital structures are those which contain securities which have the potential if assumed converted, if assumed exercised, etc. to reduce or dilute earnings per share. If the aggregate reduction in EPS based upon the weighted average of common shares outstanding is $\geq$ 3%, then a dual presentation of EPS is mandated by APB 15--both primary EPS and fully diluted EPS must be disclosed. Primary EPS is based upon outstanding common shares and dilutive common stock equivalents (CSE), while fully diluted EPS is based upon outstanding common shares, dilutive CSEs, and dilutive securities which are not CSEs. A CSE is a security which, in form, is not a common stock but which, in substance, is accounted for as if it were a common stock.

It is very important to note that in order to determine if dilution is $\geq$ 3%, EPS based upon the weighted average number of common shares outstanding must be calculated. If the dilution is immaterial (< 3%), then EPS based upon common shares outstanding is reported on the face of the income statement as if the capital structure were simple. Otherwise, if the dilution is material, ($\geq$ 3%), then the dual presentation noted above is required.

The following two independent examples will illustrate the procedures necessary to calculate primary and fully diluted EPS. For both examples, assume net income is $50,000, and the weighted average of common shares outstanding is 10,000.

In the first example, assume the following additional information with respect to the capital structure.

1. 4% nonconvertible, cumulative preferred stock, par $100, 1,000 shares issued and outstanding the entire year
2. Options and warrants to purchase 1,000 shares of common stock at $8 per share. The average market price of common stock during the year was $10 and the closing market price was $12 per share. The options and warrants were outstanding all year.

The capital structure in the example is complex because of the presence of the options and warrants. The preferred stock is not convertible; therefore, it is not a potentially dilutive security.

The first step in the solution of this problem is the determination of the EPS on the weighted average of common shares outstanding. This calculation appears as follows.

$$\frac{\text{Net income} - \text{Preferred dividends}}{\text{Weighted average of common shares outstanding}} = \frac{\$50,000 - 4,000}{10,000 \text{ shares}} = \$4.60$$

For purposes of this discussion, the EPS on weighted average common shares is referred to as the "benchmark" EPS. The "benchmark" EPS is used to determine if the 3% test is satisfied. In other words, if either primary or fully diluted EPS is $\leq$ \$4.46 (\$4.60 x 97%), a dual presentation of EPS is required. Note, also, that preferred dividends are deducted to arrive at net income applicable to common stock. When preferred is cumulative, this deduction is made whether or not dividends have been declared.

The calculation of primary EPS is based upon outstanding common stock and dilutive common stock equivalents. In the example, the options and warrants are the only potentially dilutive security. Options and warrants are considered to be common stock equivalents at all times. Consequently, the only question that must be resolved is whether or not the options and warrants are dilutive. For the primary computation, this question is resolved by comparing the average market price per common share of \$10 with the exercise price of \$8. If the average market price is > the exercise price, the effect of assuming the exercise of options and warrants is dilutive. However, if the average market price is $\leq$ the exercise price, the effect of assuming the exercise of options and warrants would be antidilutive, i.e., EPS would stay the same or increase. In the example, the options and warrants are dilutive (\$10 > \$8).

The method used to determine the dilutive effects of options and warrants is called the "treasury stock" method. In this example, all of the options and warrants are assumed to be exercised at the beginning of the year (the options and warrants were outstanding the entire year) and that the cash received is used to reacquire shares (treasury stock) at the average market price. The computation below illustrates the "treasury stock" method in the primary computation.

Proceeds from assumed exercise of
options and warrants (1,000 shares x $8) $8,000
Number of shares issued   1,000
Number of shares reacquired ($8,000 ÷ $10)   800
Number of shares assumed issued and not
reacquired   200 *

Primary EPS can now be calculated, as follows, including the effects of applying the "treasury stock" method.

$$\frac{\text{Net income - Preferred dividends}}{\substack{\text{Weighted average of common shares} \\ \text{outstanding + Number of shares not} \\ \text{acquired with proceeds from} \\ \text{options and warrants}}} = \frac{\$50,000 - 4,000}{10,200 \text{ shares}} = \$4.51$$

Note the incremental effects of the treasury stock method; there was no effect on the numerator of the EPS calculation while there were 200 shares added to the denominator. Note also that the options and warrants are dilutive. EPS is reduced from $4.60 to $4.51.

The calculation of fully diluted EPS is based upon outstanding common stock, dilutive CSEs, and other dilutive securities. This example does not contain any other dilutive securities. The options and warrants are the only potentially dilutive security in the example, and it has been shown that these securities are dilutive CSEs. However, the application of the "treasury stock" method differs for fully diluted EPS if the closing market price is higher than the average market price. When this occurs, use the closing market price in applying the "treasury stock" method.

The computation below illustrates this difference.

Proceeds from assumed exercise
of options and warrants (1,000 shares x $8) $8,000
Number of shares issued   1,000
Number of shares reacquired ($8,000 ÷ $12)   667
Number of shares assumed issued and
not reacquired   333

---

*An alternative approach that can be used to calculate this number for primary EPS is demonstrated below.

$$\frac{\text{Ave. mar. price - Exer. price}}{\text{Average market price}} \times \substack{\text{Number of} \\ \text{Shares under} \\ \text{options/warrants}} = \text{Shares not reacquired}$$

$$\frac{\$10 - 8}{\$10} \times 1,000 \text{ shares} = 200 \text{ shares}$$

Fully diluted EPS can now be calculated, as follows.

$$\frac{\text{Net income} - \text{Preferred dividends}}{\substack{\text{Weighted average of common shares} \\ \text{outstanding} + \text{Number of shares not} \\ \text{acquired with proceeds of} \\ \text{options and warrants}}} = \frac{\$50,000 - 4,000}{10,333 \text{ shares}} = \$4.45$$

Since fully diluted EPS satisfies the 3% test (the "benchmark" $4.60 x 97% = $4.46), a dual presentation of EPS is required (primary EPS = $4.51 and fully diluted = $4.45).   Table II summarizes the calculations made for the first example involving complex capital structures.

TABLE II

Computations of Primary and Fully Diluted Earnings Per Share

Items	EPS on outstanding common stock (the "benchmark" EPS)		Primary		Fully diluted	
	Numerator	Denominator	Numerator	Denominator	Numerator	Denominator
Net income	$50,000		$50,000		$50,000	
Preferred div.	(4,000)		(4,000)		(4,000)	
Common shares outstanding		10,000 shs.		10,000 shs.		10,000 shs.
Options and warrants				200		333
Totals	$46,000 ÷	10,000 shs.	$46,000 ÷	10,200 shs.	$46,000 ÷	10,333 shs.
EPS	$4.60		$4.51		$4.45	

Before proceeding to the second example, note that the alternative approach to the calculation of the number of shares for the "treasury stock" method described on the previous page may also be used in the fully diluted calculation. The 333 shares that could not be reacquired are computed as follows.

$$\frac{\substack{\text{End of period market price (if higher)} \\ - \text{ Exercise price}}}{\text{End of period market price (if higher)}} \times \substack{\text{Number of option/} \\ \text{warrant shares}} = \substack{\text{Shares not} \\ \text{reacquired}}$$

$$\frac{\$12 - 8}{\$12} \times 1,000 \text{ shares} = 333 \text{ shares}$$

For the second example, assume the following additional information about the capital structure (net income of $50,000 and common shares of 10,000 as in previous example).

1. 8% convertible debt, 200 bonds each convertible into 40 common shares. The bonds were outstanding the entire year. The average Aa corporate bond yield was 10% at the date the bonds were issued. The income tax rate is 40%. The bonds were issued at par ($1,000 per bond). No bonds were converted during the year.

2. 4% convertible, cumulative preferred stock, par $100, 1,000 shares issued
    and outstanding. Each preferred share is convertible into 2 common shares.
    The preferred was outstanding the entire year, and the average Aa corporate
    bond yield at the date the preferred was issued was 10%. The preferred was
    issued at par. No preferred stock was converted during the year.

The capital structure is complex in this example because of the presence of the
two convertible securities.

The first step in the solution of this example is the calculation of EPS
based upon weighted average of common shares outstanding. This "benchmark" EPS
is the same as it was for the first example, i.e., $4.60. Again, a dual presen-
tation of EPS will be required if either primary or fully diluted EPS $\leq$ $4.46
($4.60 x 97%).

The next step is the computation of primary EPS. Unlike options and warrants, convertible securities are not automatically CSEs. A yield test must be
performed on each convertible security to determine its CSE status. For securities issued prior to April 1, 1985, a "cash" yield test is applied. If the
"cash" yield (cash to be received annually divided by the issue price) is < 2/3
of the average Aa corporate bond yield (SFAS 55), the convertible security is a
CSE; otherwise it is not a CSE. For securities issued on April 1, 1985 or
later, an "effective" yield test is applied (SFAS 85). The "effective" yield
test more properly reflects the nature of "zero-coupon" securities. Under the
cash yield test prescribed by APB 15 zero-coupons were always CSEs. The effective yield rate is the implicit or market rate reflected in the transaction at
the date of issuance.

The formula to compute the effective yield is

$$MP = \left[\frac{1}{(1+i)^y} \times FV \right] + \left[\frac{1 - \frac{1}{(1+i)^y}}{i} \times CR \right]$$

Where: MP = Market price of security
           y = Life of security
          FV = Face value of security
          CR = Coupon rate of security
solve for i = Effective rate of interest

EXAMPLE: *Nolan Corp. purchased a ten-year convertible bond (face amount $1,000)*
with a coupon rate of 14% and a market price of $1,245. It would have an
effective yield to the purchaser of 10%.

$$\$1245 = \frac{1}{(1+i)^{10}} \times \$1,000 + \frac{1 - \frac{1}{(1+i)^{10}}}{i} \times \$140$$

The lower of the effective yield to a call date or the effective yield to
maturity should be used. For securities without a stated maturity date (e.g.,
convertible preferred stock), the effective yield test is the same as the cash

yield test (the ratio of the security's stated annual interest or dividend payments over the market price at issuance). Keep in mind that securities which fail the "effective" yield test can still affect the fully diluted EPS.

In the present example, the convertible bonds are not common stock equivalents because the effective yield at date of issuance of 8% is larger than 6.7% (2/3 x 10%). On the other hand, the convertible preferred is a CSE because its effective yield of 4% is less than 6.7%. The primary computation will include the convertible preferred if it is dilutive.

To determine the dilutive effect of the preferred stock, an assumption (called the "if converted" method) is made that all of the preferred stock is converted at the earliest date that it could have occurred during the year. In this example, the date would be January 1. The effects of this assumption are twofold. One, if the preferred is converted, there will be no preferred dividend of $4,000 for the year; and, two, there will be an additional 2,000 shares of common outstanding during the year (the conversion rate is 2 common for 1 preferred). Primary EPS is computed, as follows, reflecting these two assumptions.

$$\frac{\text{Net income}}{\substack{\text{Weighted average of common shares} \\ \text{outstanding + Shares issued upon} \\ \text{conversion of preferred}}} = \frac{\$50,000}{12,000 \text{ shares}} = \$4.17$$

The convertible preferred is dilutive because it reduced EPS from $4.60 to $4.17. Furthermore, primary EPS is lower than $4.46 ($4.60 x 97%). This means that a dual presentation of EPS is required.

Fully diluted EPS includes the dilutive effects of CSEs and other dilutive securities. In the example, the convertible bonds are assumed to have been converted at the beginning of the year. The effects of this assumption are twofold. One, if the bonds are converted, there will be no interest expense of $16,000 (8% x $200,000 face value); and, two, there will be an additional 8,000 shares (200 bonds x 40 shares) of common stock outstanding during the year. One note of caution, however, must be mentioned; namely, the effect of not having $16,000 of interest expense will increase income, but it will also increase tax expense. Consequently, the net effect of not having interest expense is $9,600 [$16,000 - (40% x $16,000)]. Fully diluted EPS is computed, as follows, reflecting the dilutive preferred and the effects noted above for the convertible bonds.

$$\frac{\text{Net income + Interest expense (net of tax)}}{\substack{\text{Weighted average of common shares} \\ \text{outstanding + Shares issued upon} \\ \text{conversion of preferred and} \\ \text{conversion of bonds}}} = \frac{\$50,000 + 9,600}{20,000 \text{ shares}} = \$2.98$$

The convertible debt is dilutive. Both the convertible bonds and preferred reduced EPS from $4.60 to $2.98. Table III summarizes the computations made for the second example.

The income statement disclosures for EPS, as a result of the second example, would be as follows.

Earnings per common and common equivalent shares (see Note X) . $4.17
Earnings per share assuming full dilution   2.98

Note X would state the assumptions made in determining both primary and fully diluted EPS numbers.

TABLE III

Computations of Primary and Fully Diluted Earnings Per Share

Items	EPS on outstanding common stock (the "benchmark" EPS) Numerator	Denominator	Primary Numerator	Denominator	Fully diluted Numerator	Denominator
Net income	$50,000		$50,000		$50,000	
Preferred div.	(4,000)					
Common shares outstanding		10,000 shs.		10,000 shs.		10,000 shs.
Conversion of preferred				2,000		2,000
Conversion of bonds					9,600	8,000
Totals	$46,000 ÷	10,000 shs.	$50,000 ÷	12,000 shs.	$59,600 ÷	20,000 shs.
EPS	$4.60		$4.17		$2.98	

In the two examples, all of the potentially dilutive securities were outstanding the entire year and no conversions or exercises were made during the year. If a potentially dilutive security were not outstanding the entire year, then the numerator and denominator effects would have to be "time-weighted." For instance, suppose the convertible bonds in the second example were issued during the current year on July 1. If all other facts remain unchanged, fully diluted EPS would be computed as follows.

$$\frac{\text{Net income + Interest expense (net of tax)}}{\begin{array}{c}\text{Weighted average of common shares}\\\text{outstanding + Shares issued upon}\\\text{conversion of preferred and}\\\text{conversion of bonds}\end{array}} = \frac{\$50,000 + \frac{1}{2}(9,600)}{10,000 + 2,000 + \frac{1}{2}(8,000)} = \$3.43$$

The convertible debt is dilutive whether or not it is outstanding the entire year or for part of a year.

If actual conversions or exercises take place during a period, the common shares issued will be outstanding from their date of issuance and, therefore, will be in the weighted average of common shares outstanding. These shares are then weighted from their respective times of issuance. For example, assume that all the bonds in the second example are converted on July 1 into 8,000 common shares. Several important effects should be noted, as follows.

    (1)   The weighted average of common shares outstanding will be increased by (8,000)(.5) or 4,000. Income will increase \$4,800 net of tax, because the bonds are no longer outstanding.

    (2)   The "if converted" method is applied to the period January 1 to July 1 because it was during this period that the bonds were potentially dilutive. The interest expense, net of tax, of \$4,800 is added to the income, and 4,000 shares (.5 of 8,000) are added to the denominator.

    (3)   Interestingly, the net effect of items 1 and 2 is the same for the period whether these dilutive bonds were outstanding the entire period or converted during the period.

It is also important to note that, in the second example, the preferred stock and bonds were both issued at par. This was done to facilitate the determination of effective yield. If, however, the convertible preferred and/or the convertible bonds were issued at amounts other than par, then effective yield would be determined at issuance as follows.

    (1) $\dfrac{\text{Preferred}}{\text{stock}} = \dfrac{\text{Annual dividend}}{\text{Amount received at issuance}} = \dfrac{\text{Effective}}{\text{yield \%}}$

    (2)   Bonds: Effective yield is their market rate of interest at date of issuance (see Module 26, "B.")

The effective yield for each issue is then compared with 2/3 of the average Aa corporate bond yield rate at date of issue to determine if the security is a CSE. Also, when convertible debt is issued for a premium or a discount the interest expense net of taxes must be computed after giving effect to premium or discount amortization.

The topics discussed in the calculation of EPS for simple and complex capital structures have touched upon the major issues which should be understood. For topics or issues not explained in the example, e.g., the 20% limitation on purchase of shares in the treasury stock method, antidilutive conversions, etc., the reader is advised to study an intermediate accounting textbook and to examine the interpretation of APB 15.

M. **Corporate Bankruptcy**

The going concern assumption is one of the basic principles underlying the primary financial statements (Balance Sheet, Income Statement and Statement of Cash Flows). However, this assumption of continued existence is threatened in corporations that are in severe financial trouble. A range of alternative actions is available to a company before it enters bankruptcy such as seeking extensions on due dates of debt, restructuring its debt, or allowing a court-appointed trustee to manage the corporation. These pre-bankruptcy options are presented in the following modules.

Creditor's agreements--Module 11, Bankruptcy
Troubled debt restructurings--Module 26, Present Value, Section C

Bankruptcy is the final legal act for a company. In bankruptcy, the accounting and financial reporting must present the information necessary for the liquidation of the business. The Statement of Affairs is prepared to present the current market values of the assets and the status of the various categories of the equity interests of the corporation.

The accountant must provide a prioritization of the creditors' claims against the net assets of the corporation. The legal rights of each creditor are determined by the terms of the credit agreement it has with the company and by the National Bankruptcy Act.

The Statement of Affairs classifies assets in the following order of priority (highest to lowest).

(1) Assets pledged with fully secured creditors--assets having a fair valuation equal to or greater than the debts they serve as collateral for
(2) Assets pledged with partially secured creditors--assets having a fair valuation less than their associated debts
(3) Free assets--uncommitted assets available for remaining equity interests

The equity interests are classified in the following order (highest to lowest).

(1) Preferred claims--these claims have priority as specified in the Bankruptcy Act
(2) Fully secured creditors--these are claims which should be fully covered with the realizations from the assets pledged to the claims
(3) Partially secured creditors--these are claims which may not be fully covered by the realizations of the pledged assets for these claims; the amount of the uncovered claims goes to the unsecured creditors category
(4) Unsecured creditors--these are claims that have no priority and do not have any collateral claims to any specific assets
(5) Stockholders' Equity--this represents any residual claim

The historical cost valuation principles used in a balance sheet assume a going concern assumption. As a business enters bankruptcy, the liquidation values of the assets become the most relevant measures. In addition, anticipated costs of liquidation should be recognized. The Statement of Affairs begins with the present book values of the company's assets in order to articulate with the balance sheet. After relating the projected proceeds from the liquidation of the assets to the various equity interests, the statement concludes with the estimated dollar amount of unsecured claims that cannot be paid (estimated deficiency).

EXAMPLE: The Vann Corporation's Balance Sheet for December 31, 1986 is shown below. The corporation is entering bankruptcy and expects to incur $8,000 of costs for the liquidation process. The estimated current values of the assets are determined and the various equity claims are prioritized. The Statement of Affairs for Vann Corporation is presented on the following page.

The Vann Corporation
Balance Sheet
December 31, 1986

Assets

Cash	$ 1,500
Marketable securities	10,000
Accounts receivable (net)	18,000
Merchandise inventory	41,000
Prepaid expenses	2,000
Land	6,000
Building (net of depreciation)	65,000
Machinery (net of depreciation)	21,000
Goodwill	10,000
	$174,500

Equities

Accounts payable	$ 30,000
Notes payable	37,000
Accrued wages	6,500
Mortgages payable	45,000
Capital stock ($10 par)	100,000
Retained earnings (deficit)	(44,000)
	$174,500

N. Stock Rights

Generally, before additional stock is offered to the public, stock rights are issued to existing shareholders to prevent involuntary dilution of their voting rights (e.g., the preemptive privilege). The stock rights, evidenced by warrants, indicate the number and price at which the shares may be purchased.

At issuance, the issuer makes only a memorandum entry. Upon exercise, the following entry is made.

```
    Cash                            (proceeds)
        Common stock                    (par)
        Paid-in capital                 (plug)
```

Information relating to stock rights outstanding must be disclosed. Detachable stock rights issued with preferred stock are treated like those on bonds (see Module 26, section "B.6."). Treatment of stock rights by recipients is discussed in Module 29, Section "F.".

The Vann Corporation
Statement of Affairs
December 31, 1986

ASSETS

Book Values		Estimated Current Values	Amount Available to Unsecured Claims
	(1) Assets Pledged with Fully Secured Creditors:		
$ 6,000	Land	$12,000	
65,000	Building	41,000	
		$53,000	
	Less Mortgages Payable	45,000	$ 8,000
	(2) Assets Pledged with Partially Secured Creditors:		
10,000	Marketable Securities	$12,000	
	Notes Payable	37,000	
	(3) Free Assets		
1,500	Cash	1,500	
18,000	Accounts Receivable (net)	14,000	
41,000	Merchandise Inventory	22,500	
2,000	Prepaid Expenses	0	
21,000	Machinery	13,200	
10,000	Goodwill	0	
			51,200
	Estimated amount available		59,200
	Less: creditors with priority		(14,500)
	Net Estimated amount available to unsecured creditors (81 cents on the dollar)		44,700
	Estimated deficiency to unsecured creditors		10,300
$174,500			$55,000

EQUITIES

Book Values		Amount Unsecured
	(1) Creditors with Priority	
	Estimated Liquidation Expenses (accounting, legal and other costs of liquidation process)	$ 8,000
$ 0		
6,500	Accrued Wages	6,500
		$14,500
	(2) Fully Secured Creditors	
45,000	Mortgages Payable	45,000
	(3) Partially Secured Creditors	
37,000	Notes Payable	37,000
	Less Marketable Securities	12,000
		25,000
	(4) Unsecured Creditors	
30,000	Accounts Payable	30,000
	(5) Stockholders' Equity	
100,000	Capital Stock	
(44,000)	Retained Earnings (deficit)	
$174,500		$55,000

INVESTMENTS

A. **Concepts of Accounting and Investment Percentage**

The accounting rules for investments in the stock of another corporation are generally based on the percentage of the voting stock obtained.

1. Investments of less than 20% of the outstanding stock

SFAS 12 requires that "small" investments in marketable equity securities be carried at the lower of aggregate cost or market. Income is realized under the cost method when dividends are received. Discussion of these smaller investments is presented in section "B."

2. Investments between 20% and 50% of the outstanding stock

At 20% or more ownership, the investor is presumed to be able to significantly influence the operating or financial decisions of the investee. Most investments in this range will result in significant influence; however, the 20% level is just a guide. FASB Interpretation 35 presents several examples in which an investor owning between 20% and 50% may not be able to exercise influence over the investee. An example of this is a situation in which the majority ownership is concentrated among a small group of investors who ignore the views of the minority investor. Additional examples are included in the summary of Interpretation 35, page 789. The equity method of accounting is used for investments resulting in significant influence. The few cases of investments in this range that do not provide significant influence are generally accounted for under the lower of aggregate cost or market method per SFAS 12. Investments where significant influence does exist are discussed in section "C."

3. Investments of more than 50% of the outstanding stock

At more than 50% ownership, the investor has control because of its majority ownership of the voting stock. Most of these investments will require the preparation of consolidated financial statements. Consolidations are discussed in Module 31.

The exhibit below illustrates the major concepts of accounting for investments.

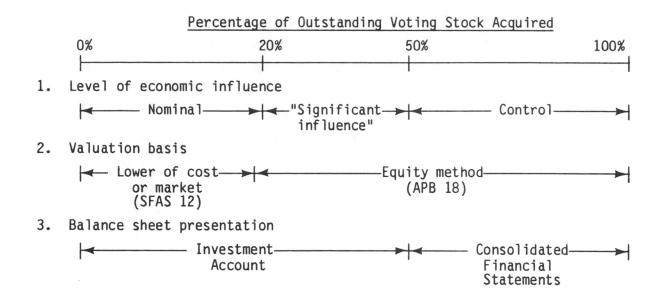

Several exceptions to these general concepts exist. These exceptions are noted in the following discussions.

B. **Investments Where Significant Influence Does <u>Not</u> Exist**

Short-term or temporary investments, a current asset, ordinarily consists of marketable debt securities and marketable equity securities. To be considered a temporary investment a security must be both <u>readily marketable</u> and <u>intended</u> to be <u>converted into cash</u> within one year or the operating cycle, whichever is longer.

Securities held for control, to maintain a business relationship, or for long-term price appreciation are specifically excluded from this category.

The cost of debt securities includes brokerage fees and taxes, but accrued interest (on debt securities) at the date of purchase must be segregated as a separate asset. The selling price is considered net of brokerage fees, etc. Premiums and discounts on short-term debt investments are not amortized as they are for long-term investments.

If there have been numerous purchases of the same security, then some flow assumption is necessary at the time of sale. Specific identification, FIFO, and weighted average are acceptable for financial reporting. For tax purposes, FIFO is required unless specific identification has been used.

1. <u>Marketable Equity Securities</u>

The accounting for marketable equity securities is governed by SFAS 12 (see the outline and related FASB Interpretations). Equity securities so covered include common, preferred, and other capital stock warrants, rights, and call options. Treasury stock, redeemable preferred stock, and convertible bonds are <u>excluded</u>.

The cost of an equity security includes the purchase price and all costs incidental to acquisition such as brokerage commissions and taxes. Subsequent to acquisition, SFAS 12 specifies that the carrying value of these securities must be the <u>lower</u> of the aggregate cost or market value of the portfolio as determined on the balance sheet date.

SFAS 12 specifies that the excess of aggregate cost over aggregate market value must be carried in a separate "valuation allowance" account. The purpose of this account is to allow the securities to be adjusted to their net realizable value at the balance sheet date. SFAS 12 requires that realized gains and losses, as well as changes in the valuation allowance for <u>short-term marketable equity securities</u>, be used in the calculation of net income. Thus, unrealized losses and their recoveries due to the year-end adjustment of the valuation allowance account are to be reported in net income. In <u>no</u> case may the recovery exceed the balance in the allowance account. In other words, the recovery is limited to the extent to which previous losses were recognized.

At the end of the year an adjusting entry is made to change the balance in the valuation allowance account to the balance dictated by the aggregate cost/aggregate market comparison.

For example, consider the three-security portfolio (current) below for the years 1985 and 1986.

| Security | 1985 (Yr. of purchase) | | | 1986 | | |
	Cost	Market	Allowance	Cost	Market	Allowance
A	8,000	10,000	2,000	8,000	6,000	(2,000)
B	20,000	16,000	(4,000)	20,000	25,000	5,000
C	30,000	12,000	(18,000)	30,000	15,000	(15,000)
Total	58,000	38,000	(20,000)	58,000	46,000	(12,000)

Since the aggregate cost exceeds market in 1985, the year-end adjustment is as follows.

Unrealized loss on marketable securities   20,000
    Allowance for excess of cost over market   20,000

The unrealized loss would appear as other expense on the income statement and ultimately be closed out to retained earnings. The allowance account (not closed out) would be deducted from the securities account on the balance sheet date and remain unchanged until the next balance sheet date.

In 1986, two items should be noted. First, aggregate cost still exceeds market, so the allowance account is still necessary. Second, the allowance balance needed is $12,000, while the present balance of $20,000 remains in

the general ledger from last year. Thus, a recovery of an unrealized loss
of $8,000 is recorded to reduce the allowance account to $12,000. The
securities would be presented in the 1986 balance sheet at their fair market
value of $46,000.

Allowance for excess of cost over market	8,000
Recovery of unrealized loss on	
marketable securities	8,000

Note that the reversal of the writedown ($8,000) is treated as a recovery,
instead of as an unrealized gain, since it is considered a change in the estimate of an unrealized loss. It would appear on the income statement in
other revenues, while the allowance account would appear as before.

If instead the aggregate market value had been $62,000 (i.e., greater
than cost), the above entry would have been for $20,000, the entire balance
in the allowance account. This would reduce its balance to zero, and the
securities would be shown on the balance sheet at cost.

Realized gains (losses) result from the actual sale of the securities
and are treated in the traditional manner, with the gain (loss) as the difference between the cost of the security and its selling price. Disposition
of securities does not affect the valuation account. At the end of the
year, the aggregate cost and market values of the remaining securities are
compared in determining the valuation balance.

For classified balance sheets, equity securities should be grouped into
two portfolios--a current and a noncurrent portfolio. If unclassified
balance sheets are prepared, all marketable equity securities are treated as
noncurrent.

For noncurrent marketable equity securities, a separate comparison of
aggregate cost and aggregate market is also made each year in the same
manner as for current securities. It is important to note, however, that
the unrealized losses or their recoveries due to the adjustment of the
valuation allowance for noncurrent assets do not go to the income
statement. Instead, the balance in the unrealized loss account appears in
the equity section of the balance sheet reducing owner's equity (similar to
the treatment accorded to treasury stock). The unrealized loss account is
reduced only as the balance needed in the allowance account becomes
smaller. Thus, as the market value of the noncurrent portfolio increases to
cost, the allowance is debited and the unrealized loss account is
credited. Changes in value of noncurrent marketable equity securities do

<u>not</u> appear in income until actually realized. The reason for this treatment is that a decline in market value of a noncurrent equity security can be viewed as temporary and is therefore not reflected in income since the probability of realization of the loss is small.

If a decline in value takes place for long-term equity securities and the decline is viewed as not being temporary, then the cost basis of the security is written down to a new cost basis. The write-down is permanent and is considered realized.

SFAS 12 also provides that if a security is moved from the current to the noncurrent portfolio, or vice versa, when its market value is less than cost, the market value becomes the new cost at the time of transfer and the loss is considered realized.

2. <u>Marketable Debt Securities</u>

SFAS 12 is not applicable to debt securities. ARB 43 prescribes cost as the carrying value for debt securities unless two conditions have occurred. The two conditions which necessitate a switch to lower of cost or market are when

- The decline in the value of debt securities is substantial, <u>and</u>
- The decline in market value is not due to a temporary condition

Thus, debt securities are carried at cost or at lower of cost or market depending upon whether the conditions specified above have occurred. Note that the lower of cost or market treatment is not automatically applied as it is for marketable equity securities.

The premium or discount on <u>long-term debt securities</u> is amortized. However, amortization on <u>short-term debt securities</u> is generally ignored. Investor accounting for debt securities is discussed in Module 26, Section "B."

C. **Investments Where Significant Influence <u>Does</u> Exist**

APB 18 requires the use of the **equity method** when accounting for investments in which the investor has the ability to exercise significant influence over the operating and financial policies of the investee. APB 18 assumes that ownership of 20% or more of the outstanding stock will result in that ability. Exceptions to the use of the equity method (i.e., use the cost method) are related to an assessment of the investor's level of influence over the investee. The cost method should be used if the investment of more than 20% is judged to be temporary, if the investment is in a company operating in a foreign country which has severe restrictions on the operations of companies and on the transfer

of monies to outside the country, and for other investments of more than 20%
that do not result in significant influence.

The cost and equity methods differ in the treatment of the investment
account and in the recognition of earnings from the investment. The cost method
begins with recording the cost of the investment in the investment account.
Income is recognized for the dividends which are distributed from earnings of
the investee earned since the date the investor acquired the stock. Any
dividends distributed by the investee which exceed the earnings since the
acquisition date are classified as return of capital and recorded as a reduction
of the investment account. No periodic amortizations or accruals are made to
the investment account under the cost method.

The equity method also begins with recording the cost of the investment in
the investment account but the cost and equity methods differ from this point
on. A basic concept of the equity method is the reciprocal relationship formed
between the investment account on the investor's books and the book values of
the net assets on the investee's books. As changes in the investee's net assets
occur (e.g., earnings, dividends, etc.), the investor will recognize the
percentage of ownership share of that change in the investment account.

Another aspect of the equity method is the computation and eventual
amortization of the difference between the cost of the investment and the book
value of the acquired asset share at the investment date. The abundance of
advanced accounting texts currently in print use an assortment of terms to
describe the characteristics of this concept. For purposes of uniformity, the
following underlined terms shall be used throughout this module.

Differential: the difference between the cost of the investment and the
                 underlying book value of the net assets of the investee. This
                 difference can be either positive or negative, as follows:

1. Excess of Cost over Book Value, which is generally attributable to

    a. Excess of fair value over book value, when the fair values of the
        investee's assets are greater than their book values, and
    b. Goodwill, when the investee has high earnings potential for which
        the investor has paid more than the fair values of the other net
        assets

2. Excess of Book Value over Cost, which is generally attributable to

    a. Excess of book value over fair value, when the book values of the
        net assets of the investee are greater than their fair values, and
    b. Excess of fair value over cost, when the cost of the investment is
        less than even the fair values of the investee's net assets. Some
        authors term this "negative goodwill."

The differential will be amortized to the investment account. Thus, similar
to the amortization of bond investment premium or discount, the original

investment in stock will approach the underlying book values of the investee's net assets held at the investment date.

> EXAMPLE: Company A purchased 20 shares of B Company's 100 shares of common outstanding for $25,000. The book value of B's total net worth (i.e., stockholders' equity) at the date of the investment was $120,000. Any excess of cost over book value is due to goodwill to be amortized over 40 years.

Investment cost		$25,000
Book value of B Company	$120,000	
Percentage owned	20%	
Investor's share		24,000
Excess of cost over book value (due to goodwill)		$ 1,000

> Amortization over 40 years
> $1,000 ÷ 40 years = $25

An illustration of accounting just for the amortization is shown below. Other adjustments to the investment account which are normally required are discussed later in this module.

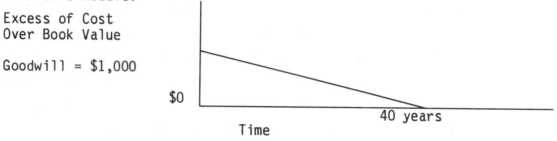

Excess of Cost
Over Book Value

Goodwill = $1,000

$0

40 years

Time

Under the equity method, the "Income from investment" account is a parallel income statement account to the "Investment in stock" balance sheet account. These two accounts should include all the income recognitions and amortizations resulting from the investment. Note that under the equity method, dividends received from the investee are a reduction in the balance sheet account and are not part of the "Income from Investment" account.

Alternative levels of recording the results of intercompany transactions and amortizations in both the investment and investment income accounts are used in accounting practice. The alternatives are presented below.

1) Cost method--No intercompany transactions or amortizations are recognized in either the investment account or investment income account under this method.

2) "Partial" equity--Includes recognition of percentage share of income or loss, dividends, and any changes in the investment percentage. This method is often used for investments that will be consolidated. Thus, amortizations and other adjustments are made on the work sheets, not in the investment account.

3) "Full" equity--In addition to the factors above, this level includes the amortization of the differential between the investment cost and book value of the investment. This level also recognizes the effects of any intercompany transactions (e.g., inventory, fixed assets, and bonds)

between the investor and investee corporations. APB 18 requires that all unconsolidated investments be reported in the financial statements using the "full" equity method.

EXTENDED EXAMPLE: Assume the same facts for A Company and B Company as stated above. In addition, B Company earned $10,000 income for the year and paid $6,000 in dividends. There were no intercompany transactions. If A Company does not have significant influence over B Company, the investment would be accounted for by the cost method. If A Company can significantly influence B Company, the equity method is used to account for and report the investment. The appropriate entries are

<u>Cost Method</u>   <u>Equity Method</u>

1. To record purchase of 20% interest

    Investment in Stock of B   25,000   Investment in Stock of B   25,000
        Cash   25,000   Cash   25,000

2. To record percentage share of investee's reported income

    No Entry   Investment in Stock of B   2,000
                                              Income from Investment   2,000
                                                  (20% x $10,000)

3. To record percentage share of dividend received as distribution of income

    Cash   1,200   Cash   1,200
        Dividend Income from   Investment in Stock of B   1,200
          Investment   1,200
          (20% x $6,000)

4. To record amortizations of goodwill in accordance with APB 18 using maximum period allowed by APB 17

    No Entry   Income from Investment   25
                                              Investment in Stock of B   25

The differences in the account balances under the equity vs. cost methods reflect the different income recognition processes and underlying asset valuation concepts of the two methods. The investment account balance under the cost method remains at the investment cost of $25,000, while under the equity method, the investment balance increases to $25,775. The $775 difference is the investor's share of the increase in the investee's undistributed earnings less the investor's amortization of the differential (excess of cost over the book value of the investment).

The amount of the investment income to be recognized by the investor is also dependent upon the length of time during the year the investment is owned. For example, assume that A Company acquired the 20% interest on July 1, 1986, and B Company earned $10,000 of income ratably over the period from January 1, to December 31, 1986. The entry to record A Company's percentage share of B Company's income for the period of July 1 to December 31, 1986, would be

Cost Method	Equity Method		
No Entry	Investment in Stock of B	1,000	
	Income from Investment		1,000
	(20% x $10,000 x 6/12)		

The receipt of the $1,200 of dividends after the acquisition date would require additional analysis since the $1,200 dividend received is greater than the investor's share of the investee's income ($1,000) since acquisition. The difference of $200 ($1,200 - $1,000) is a return of capital under the cost method, and is recorded as follows.

Cost Method		Equity Method	
Cash	1,200	Cash	1,200
Dividend Income		Investment in	
from Investment	1,000	Stock of B	1,200
Investment in			
Stock of B	200		

The amortization of goodwill will also be pro-rated to the time period the investment was held. The entry to record the partial year's amortization since the date of acquisition is

Cost Method	Equity Method	
No Entry	Income from Investment	12.50
	Investment in Stock	
	of B	12.50
	($1,000 ÷ 40 years = $25.00)	
	($25 x 6/12 = $12.50)	

When an investor changes from the cost to the equity method, the investment account must be adjusted retroactively and prior years' income and retained earnings must be retroactively restated. A change to the equity method would be made if an investor made additional purchases of stock and, for the first time, is able to exercise significant influence over the operating and financial decisions of the investee. Remember that APB 18 states that investments of 20% or more of the investee's outstanding stock carry the "presumption" that the investor has the ability to exercise significant influence. Therefore, in most cases, when an investment below 20% increases to above 20%, the investor will retroactively change from the cost method to the equity method.

The retroactive change to the equity method requires a prior period adjustment for the difference in the investment account and retained earnings account between the amounts that were recognized in prior periods under the cost method and the amounts that would have been recognized if the equity method had been used. In the full-year investment example earlier, if A Company had previously accounted for its investment in B Company using the cost method and now begins applying the equity method because of the increased ability to significantly influence B Company, the change entry would be

```
Investment in B Company            775
    Retained earnings                      775
    ($775 = $2,000 - $1,200 - $25)
```

If the change is made at any time point other than the beginning of the fiscal period, the change entry would also include an adjustment to the period's "Income from Investment" account to record the difference between the cost and equity methods for the current period.

When an investor discontinues using the equity method because of an inability to influence the investee's financial and operating policies, no retroactive restatement is allowed. An example of this would be a disposal of stock resulting in a decrease in the percentage of stock owned from above 20% to below 20%. The earnings or losses that relate to the shares retained by the investor that were previously recognized by the investor should remain as a part of the carrying amount. However, if dividends received by the investor in subsequent periods exceed the investor's share of the investee's earnings for such periods, the excess should be accounted for as a return of capital and recorded as a reduction in the investment carrying amount.

A T-account is used to exhibit the major changes in the "Investment in Stock" account.

Investments in Stock	
Original cost of investment	
Percentage share of investee's income since acquisition	Percentage share of investee's losses since acquisition
	Percentage share of dividends received
	Amortizations of excess of cost over book value
Amortizations of excess of book value over cost	
Increase above "significant influence" ownership - retroactive adjustment for change to equity	Disposals or sales of investment in stock

In addition to the above, several adjustments may be added if the "full equity" method is used. This method eliminates the effects of intercompany profits from transactions such as sales of inventory between the investor and investee corporations. This method is rarely required on the exam but candidates should briefly review these additions in association with the discussion of the elimination entries required for consolidated working papers presented later in this module.

Investments in Stock (continued)	
Realized portion of intercompany profit from last period confirmed this period	Elimination of unrealized portion of intercompany profit transactions from current period

D. Equity Method and Interperiod Tax Allocation

Interperiod tax allocation may be required when the equity method is used. The difference between the income recognized using the equity method and the dividends received from the investee normally represent a timing difference item for which interperiod allocation is necessary. Note that companies are allowed to exclude 80% of the dividend income from investees. If an investor owns 80% or more of the investee's stock, the dividend exclusion is increased to 100%, i.e., no taxes are due on investee dividend distributions. The dividend exclusion (dividend received deduction) is a permanent difference.

APB 23 discusses the tax allocation criteria for investments of more than 50% of the outstanding stock and APB 24 presents the criteria for investments of less than 50% which are accounted for by the equity method. A discussion of tax allocation concepts and several examples are provided in Module 27, Deferred Taxes.

E. Stock Dividends and Splits

Do not record as income. The recipient continues to own the same proportion of the investee as before the stock split or dividend. The investor should make a memo entry to record the receipt of the additional shares and recompute the per-share cost of the stock.

F. Stock Rights

Investors in common stocks occasionally receive stock rights to purchase additional common stock below the existing market price. The investee company has probably issued the stock rights to satisfy the investor's preemptive right to maintain an existing level of ownership of the investee. It is possible to waive these preemptive rights in some jurisdictions.

Rights are issued below the existing market price to encourage the exercise of the rights, i.e., investor's use thereof resulting in acquisitions of additional shares of stock. The rights represent a possible dilution of investor ownership and should be recorded by allocating the cost of the stock between the market value of the rights and the market value of the stock. This is accomplished by applying the following ratio to the cost basis of the stock.

$$\frac{\text{Market value of right}}{\text{Market value of right + Market value of stock}}$$

The following entry is made to record the receipt of the rights.

Investment in stock rights	xx	
Investment in common stock		xx

The rights can be sold or exercised. The entry for exercise is

Investment in common stock	xx	
Investment in stock rights		xx
Cash		xx

If the stock rights lapse

Loss on expiration of stock rights	xx	
Investment in stock rights		xx

EXAMPLE: A Company acquired 1,000 shares of common stock in B Company for $12,000. A Company subsequently received two stock rights for every share owned in B Company. Four rights and $12 are required to purchase one new share of common stock. At the date of issuance the market value of the stock rights and the common stock is $5 and $20, respectively. The entry to record the receipt of the rights is as follows.

Investment in stock rights	4,000	
Investment in common stock		4,000

The $4,000 above was computed as follows.

Total market value of rights	2,000 rights x $5 =	$10,000
Total market value of shares	1,000 shares x $20 =	$20,000
Combined market value		$30,000

$$\text{Cost allocated to stock rights} \quad \frac{\$10,000}{\$30,000} \times \$12,000 = \$4,000$$

$$\text{Cost allocated to common stock} \quad \frac{\$20,000}{\$30,000} \times \$12,000 = \$8,000$$

Note that $2 ($4,000 ÷ 2,000 rights) of cost is assigned to each stock right and $8 ($8,000 ÷ 1,000 shares) of cost to each share of stock.

If A uses 800 rights to purchase 200 additional shares of stock, the following entry would be made to record the transaction.

Investment in common stock	4,000	
Investment in stock rights		1,600*
Cash		2,400**

* (800 rights x $2/right)
** (200 shares x $12/share)

If 1,000 stock rights are sold outright for $5 per right, the following entry would be made to record the transaction.

Cash	5,000*	
Investment in stock rights		2,000**
Gain on sale of investments		3,000

* (1,000 rights x $5/right)
** (1,000 rights x $2/right)

If the 200 remaining stock rights are permitted to expire, the following entry would be made.

```
Loss on expiration of stock rights        400*
    Investment in stock rights                    400*
*   (200 rights x $2/right)
```

The journal entries above can be summarized as follows:

	Investment in Common Stock				Investment in Stock Rights	
Purchase, 1,000 shares @ $12	$12,000	$4,000 ←—Cost allocated to stock rights—→	$4,000			
					$1,600	Exercise of 800 rights
Purchase, 200 shares by exercise of rights	$ 4,000				$2,000	Sale of 1,000 rights
	$12,000				$400	Expiration of 200 rights
					-0-	

G. Cash Surrender Value of Life Insurance

Another noncurrent investment is cash surrender value of life insurance policies when the company is beneficiary (rather than insured employees). The entry to record insurance premiums that increase cash surrender value is

```
Insurance expense                    (plug)
Cash surrender value                 (increase in CSV)
    Cash                                          (total premium)
```

Cash surrender value is then a noncurrent asset unless the company plans to cash the policy, e.g., next period the policy is going to be cashed in.

During the first few years of a policy, no cash surrender value may attach to the policy. If so, all of the insurance premium would be expense. Also note that any dividends received from the life insurance policy are **not** recorded as revenue but instead are offset against insurance expense.

STATEMENT OF CASH FLOWS

A. **Objectives of the Statement of Cash Flows** (See outline of SFAS 95 also)

The primary purposes of this statement are to provide information about an entity's cash receipts and cash payments and to disclose information about the financing and investing activities of an entity. This statement should help the users of the statement assess: 1) an entity's ability to generate positive future cash flows; 2) an entity's ability to meet its obligations and pay dividends; 3) the reasons for differences between income and associated cash receipts and payments; and 4) the cash and noncash aspects of an entity's investing and financing transactions.

In order to facilitate the users in making those assessments, a statement of cash flows shall report cash receipts and cash payments of an entity's operations, its investing transactions, and its financing transactions. A separate schedule accompanying the statement should also report the effects of investing and financing transactions that do not affect cash.

The statement of cash flows is required to be prepared based on changes during the period in cash and cash equivalents. Cash equivalents include short-term, highly liquid investments that (a) are readily convertible to known amounts of cash and (b) are so near their maturity (original maturity of three months or less) that they present negligible risk of changes in value because of changes in interest rates. Treasury bills, commercial paper, and money market funds are all examples of cash equivalents.

B. **Statement of Cash Flows Classification**

Cash receipts and cash payments are to be classified into operating, financing, and investing activities.

Operating activities include delivering or producing goods for sale and providing services. Operating activities include all transactions that are not investing and financing activities. More specifically, cash flows from operations should not include cash flows from transactions whose effects are included in income but are investing and financing activities. For example, a gain (loss) on extinguishment of debt should properly be classified as a financing activity, and a gain (loss) from disposal of property should be classified as an investing activity.

Investing activities include the acquisition and disposition of long-term productive assets or securities that are not considered cash equivalents. Investing activities also include the lending of money and collection on loans.

Financing activities include obtaining resources from owners and returning the investment. Also included is obtaining resources from creditors and repaying the amount borrowed.

The FASB has listed the following as examples of classifications of transactions.

Operating Activities

Cash Inflows
*   Receipts from sale of goods or services
*   Returns on loans (interest)
*   Returns on equity securities (dividends)

Cash Outflows
*   Payments for inventory
*   Payments to employees
*   Payments of taxes
*   Payments to suppliers for other expenses
*   Payments for interest

Investing Activities

Cash Inflows
*   Principal collections from loans
*   Sale of loans made by the entity
*   Sale of long-term debt or equity securities
*   Sale of property, plant, and equipment
*   Sale of a business unit

Cash Outflows
*   Loans made
*   Purchase of long-term debt or equity securities
*   Purchase of property, plant, and equipment
*   Purchase of a business
*   Purchase loans from another entity

Financing Activities

Cash Inflows
*   Proceeds from issuing stock
*   Proceeds from issuing debt (short-term or long-term)

Cash Outflows
*   Payment of dividends
*   Repurchase of entity's own stock
*   Repayment of debt principal (short-term or long-term)

Note that noncash investing and financing activities should be excluded from the statement itself and reported in a separate schedule. Examples of noncash investing activities include conversion of debt to equity, acquisition of assets by assuming liabilities (includes capital lease obligations), and exchanges of assets or liabilities. These transactions involve no cash inflows and outflows, but they have a significant effect on the prospective cash flows of a company. Therefore, they must be distinguished from activities that involved cash receipts and payments and must be reported in a separate schedule. As was the case with APB 19 which SFAS 95 superseded, both stock dividends and stock splits should be excluded from the statement because they are not significant financing activities.

In the statement, the inflows and outflows for each category (operating, investing, and financing) should be shown separately, and the net cash flows (the difference between the inflows and outflows) should be reported.

C. **Direct or Indirect Presentation in Reporting Operating Activities**

The FASB decided that the preferable method of presenting net cash flows from operating activities is by directly showing major classes of operating cash receipts and payments. However, the indirect (reconciliation) method is also permitted. When the direct method is used, it is necessary to also present a separate accompanying schedule showing the indirect method. The direct method is discussed first followed by a discussion of the indirect method.

Under the direct approach, cash flow elements of operating activities are derived from the accrual basis components of net income. In converting to the cash basis, accounts that should be analyzed under operating activities are those which are debited or credited when recording transactions that affect the income statement. These transactions include transactions with outsiders, and adjusting entries. For example, these accounts include sales, cost of sales, operating expenses, and tax expense, as well as assets and liabilities which are related to them, such as accounts receivable, inventory, accounts payable, accrued expenses, and prepaid expenses. Note that interest expense and interest revenue are included within operating activities. Formulas for conversion of various income statement amounts from the accrual basis to the cash basis are summarized in the following table.

Accrual basis	Additions	Deductions	Cash basis
Net sales	+ Beginning A/R	− [Ending A/R / A/R written off]	= Cash received from customers
Cost of goods sold	+ [Ending inventory / Beginning A/P]	− [Depreciation and amortization[1] / Beginning inventory / Ending A/P]	= Cash paid to suppliers
Operating expenses	+ [Ending prepaid expenses / Beginning accrued expenses payable]	− [Depreciation and amortization / Beginning prepaid expenses / Ending accrued expenses]	= Cash paid for operating expenses

[1]Applies to a manufacturing entity

A T-account analysis method may be used instead of the above formulas to determine cash received and cash paid. T-account analysis provides a quick, systematic way to accumulate the information needed to prepare the statement.

The direct approach would be presented in the statement of cash flows as follows

Cash flows from operating activities:

Cash received from dividends	$ 500	
Cash received from sale of goods	10,000	
Cash provided by operating activities		$10,500
Cash paid to suppliers	5,000	
Cash paid for operating expenses	500	
Cash paid for interest	500	
Cash paid for taxes	500	
Cash disbursed from operating activities		6,500
Net cash flows from operating activities		$ 4,000

The other way of reporting net cash flows from operations is known as the indirect method. This is done by starting with income from continuing operations and adjusting for changes in operating related accounts (e.g., inventory and accounts payable) and noncash expenses, revenues, losses, and gains.

Noncash items that were subtracted in determining income must be added back in determining net cash flows from operations. Each of these noncash items is a charge against income but does not decrease cash.

Items to be added back include depreciation, amortization of intangibles, amortization of discount on bonds payable, bad debt expense, and any increase in the deferred tax liability. Note each of these items is charged against income but does not decrease cash.

Noncash items that were added in determining income must be subtracted from net income in determining net cash flows from operations. Each of these noncash items is an increase to income but does not increase cash.

Items to be deducted from income include decreases in the deferred tax liability and amortization of the premium on bonds payable.

Finally, gains (losses) on fixed assets require adjustment, since the cash received is not measured by the gain (loss), i.e., a fixed asset with a book value of $10, sold for $15 in cash, provides $15 in cash but is reported as only a $5 gain on the income statement. The $15 is shown as a separate item on the cash flow statement under investing activities and the $5 gain is subtracted from income. Losses on asset disposals are added back to income.

When preparing the cash flows from operating activities section of a Statement of Cash Flows under the indirect method, reconstructing journal entries may help in determining if an item should be added or subtracted to net income.

For example, if accounts receivable increased by $20,000 over the year, the journal entry that would result in an increase to accounts receivable would be:

Accounts receivable	xx	
Sales		xx

This entry results in an increase to net income (through sales), but cash is not affected. Therefore, the amount of the increase is deducted from net income in determining cash flows from operating activities.

If accounts payable decreased by $35,000, the entry for a decrease in accounts payable would be:

Accounts payable	xx	
Cash		xx

Since the corresponding credit results in a decrease to cash, the amount of this decrease should be deducted from net income in determining cash flows from operating activities.

When the indirect method is used, SFAS 95 permits, but does not require, separate disclosure of cash flows related to extraordinary items and discontinued operations. If an entity chooses to disclose this information, disclosure must be consistent for all periods affected. Extraordinary items, if disclosed, should be added to (or subtracted from) operating activities (adjustment to net income) at the gross amount, not the net-of-tax amount. Under either method the extraordinary item should be included in financing or investing activities, whichever is appropriate.

The direct and indirect approaches will both be illustrated throughout the remainder of this module.

D. **Example of Statement of Cash Flows**

The illustration is based on information concerning the Haner Company.

- Fixed assets costing $5,000 with a book value of $2,000 were sold for $4,000
- Three-year insurance policy was purchased in 19X1
- Long-term investments costing $5,000 were used to retire $5,000 of bonds outstanding
- Other expenses and losses consist of $1,000 interest paid
- Comparative balance sheets for 19X1 and 19X2 are as follows

	19X2	19X1	Net change
Cash	$9,000	$ 8,000	$ 1,000
Treasury bills	4,000	3,000	1,000
Accounts receivable	4,000	5,000	(1,000)
Inventory	1,000	2,000	(1,000)
Prepaid insurance	2,000	3,000	(1,000)
Long-term investment in ABC Co.	17,000	22,000	(5,000)
Fixed assets	22,000	17,000	5,000
Accumulated depreciation	(5,000)	(4,000)	(1,000)
	$54,000	$56,000	$(2,000)

	19X2	19X1	
Accounts payable	$ 4,000	$ 7,000	$(3,000)
Income tax payable	3,000	1,000	2,000
Deferred tax liability	5,000	3,000	2,000
Bonds payable	5,000	10,000	(5,000)
Common stock	20,000	20,000	-0-
Retained earnings	17,000	15,000	2,000
	$54,000	$56,000	(2,000)

- The income statement for 19X2 is as follows

Net sales		$50,000
Cost of goods sold		(20,000)
Gross profit		30,000
Operating expenses		(17,000)
Income from operations		13,000
Other revenue and gains		2,000
Other expenses and losses		(1,000)
Income before tax		$14,000
Income tax expense:		
Current portion	$5,000	
Deferred portion	2,000	7,000
Net income		$ 7,000

1. **Procedural Steps**

a. The first step is to calculate the change in cash and cash equivalents. This is the number that all other changes "must net out to" when the statement is finished.

	19X2	19X1	Change
Cash	$9,000	$8,000	+$1,000
Treasury bills	4,000	3,000	+ 1,000
Net change in cash and cash equivalents			+$2,000

b. Calculate net cash flows from operating activities

   (1) Indirect approach

Net income	$ 7,000	
Decrease in accounts receivable	1,000	(a)
Decrease in inventory	1,000	(b)
Decrease in prepaid insurance	1,000	(c)
Decrease in accounts payable	(3,000)	(d)
Increase in income tax payable	2,000	(e)
Increase in deferred tax liability	2,000	(f)
Gain on sale of fixed assets	(2,000)	(g)
Depreciation expense	4,000	(h)
Net cash flows from operating activities		$13,000

Reconstructing journal entries may serve to explain the effect on net income of an increase or decrease of a particular account.

(a) Accounts Receivable. For accounts receivable to decrease, the journal entry must have been:

Cash	xx	
Accounts receivable		xx

Cash increased as a result of the collection of accounts receivable. The amount of the decrease in accounts receivable should be added to net income.

(b) Inventory. For inventory to decrease, the entry must have been:

Cost of goods sold	xx	
Inventory		xx

Expenses (COGS) increased without an additional cash outlay for inventory, so the decrease is added back to net income

(c) Prepaid Insurance. For prepaid insurance to decrease, the entry must have been:

Insurance expense	xx	
Prepaid insurance		xx

Because expenses increased without a corresponding cash outlay, the amount of the decrease in prepaid insurance should be added to net income

(d) Accounts Payable. For accounts payable to decrease, the entry must have been:

Accounts payable	xx	
Cash		xx

The entry involves a cash outlay, so the decrease in accounts payable is deducted from net income

(e) Income Tax Payable. For income tax payable to increase, the entry must have been:

Income tax expense	xx	
Income tax payable		xx

Expenses increased without an actual cash outlay; therefore the amount of the increase in the liability is added back to net income

(f) Deferred Tax Liability. For deferred tax liability to increase, the entry must have been:

Income tax expense	xx	
Income tax payable		xx
Deferred tax liability		xx

Because the tax expense is greater than the amount of tax payable for this year, the difference between the two, the amount of the increase in the deferred tax liability, should be added back to net income

(g) Gain on Sale. The entry to record the sale would have been:

Cash	xx	
Accumulated depreciation	xx	
Gain on sale		xx
Asset		xx

The amount of cash received in payment for the asset represents the cash inflow, not only the amount of the gain. Since cash inflow from the sale (including the amount of the gain) appears in the investing section, the gain should be subtracted from net income.

(h) Depreciation expense. The entry to record depreciation is:

Depreciation expense	xx	
Accumulated depreciation		xx

Because expenses increased without a corresponding cash outlay, the amount recorded for depreciation expense should be added to net income. In this case, the increase in accumulated depreciation must take into consideration the accumulated depreciation removed with the sale of the asset.

```
                                     A/D
A/D of sold asset    3,000*  |  4,000   Beg. bal
                             |  4,000   Depreciation (plug)
                             |  5,000   End. bal.
```

*$5,000 Cost - 2,000 book value

(2) Direct approach

Cash received from customers	$51,000(a)	
Cash provided by operating activities		$51,000
Cash paid to suppliers	22,000(b)	
Cash paid for operating expenses	12,000(c)	
Cash paid for interest	1,000(d)	
Cash paid for income taxes	3,000(e)	
Cash disbursed for operating activities		38,000
Net cash flows from operating activities		$13,000

    (a) Net sales + Beginning A/R - Ending A/R = Cash received from customers
        $50,000 + $5,000 - $4,000 = $51,000

Cash received from customers also may be calculated by analyzing T-accounts.

Accounts Receivable

Beg. bal	5,000		
Sales	50,000		
		51,000	Cash collected
End. bal	4,000		

(b) Cost of goods sold + Beginning A/P - Ending A/P + Ending inventory - Beginning inventory = Cash paid to suppliers $20,000 + $7,000 - $4,000 + $1,000 - $2,000 = $22,000 Cash paid to suppliers. This is a two-account analysis. The amount for cash paid to suppliers is the debit to accounts payable, but to solve for that amount, you must first determine purchases. To calculate purchases you must analyze the inventory account

Step #1 Calculate purchases:

Inventory

Beg. bal	2,000		
		20,000	COGS
Purchases	19,000		
End. bal	1,000		

Step #2 Calculate cash payments to suppliers:

Accounts Payable

		7,000	Beg. bal
		19,000	Purchases
Cash paid to suppliers	22,000		
		4,000	End. bal

(c) Operating expenses + Ending prepaid expenses - Beginning prepaid expenses - Depreciation expense (and other noncash operating expenses) = Cash paid for operating expenses $17,000 + $2,000 - $3,000 - $4,000 = $12,000

Cash paid for operating expenses. The two accounts in this problem that relate to operating expenses are accumulated depreciation and prepaid insurance.

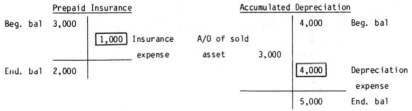

Since neither the expiration of prepaid insurance nor depreciation expense required a cash outlay, cash basis operating expenses are accrual expenses of $17,000 less depreciation ($4,000) and insurance expense ($1,000), or $12,000.

(d) Cash paid for interest. No analysis needed; amount was given in problem

(e) Current portion of income tax expense + Beginning income tax payable - Ending income tax payable = Cash paid for income taxes

$5,000 + $1,000 - $3,000 = $3,000 income taxes. The journal entry for income tax expense (see 19X2 income statement for figures) is:

Income tax expense	7,000	
Income tax payable (current portion)		5,000
Deferred tax liability		2,000

Therefore, taxes paid are $3,000, as shown in the T-account below:

```
                    Income Tax Payable
                          | 1,000   Beg. bal
 Income taxes             | 5,000   Current portion
 paid        | 3,000 |
                          | 3,000   End. bal
```

c. Analyze other accounts and determine whether the change is a cash inflow or outflow and whether it is a financing, an investing, or a noncash investing and financing activity

(1) Investments in ABC Co. decreased by $5,000 as they were exchanged for bonds outstanding (noncash investing and financing activity)

(2) Fixed assets increased by $5,000 after $5,000 of assets were sold for $4,000 (cash inflow, investing activity). Thus, $10,000 of fixed assets were purchased (cash outflow, investing activity).

```
                       Fixed Assets
 Beg. bal    $17,000 |
                     |  5,000 Sold asset
 Purchase of         |
 new assets  | 10,000 |
 End. bal     22,000 |
```

(3) Bonds payable decreased by $5,000 as they were retired as explained in (1) (noncash investing and financing activity)

(4) Common stock had no change

(5) Retained earnings increased $2,000 after net income of $7,000, indicating a dividend of $5,000 (cash outflow, financing activity)

```
                 Retained Earnings
                       | 15,000   Beg. bal
                       |  7,000   Net income
 Cash
 dividend  | 5,000 |
                       | 17,000   End. bal
```

d. Prepare formal statement

Haner Company
Statement of Cash Flows
For the Year Ended December 31, 19X2

Cash flows from operating activities:

Cash received from customers	$51,000	
Cash provided by operating activities		$51,000
Cash paid to suppliers	22,000	
Cash paid for operating expenses	12,000	
Cash paid for income taxes	3,000	
Cash paid for interest expense	1,000	
Cash disbursed for operating activities		38,000
Net cash flows from operating activities		$13,000
Cash flows from investing activities:		
Proceeds from sale of fixed assets	4,000	
Acquisition of fixed assets	(10,000)	
Net cash used by investing activities		(6,000)
Cash flows from financing activities:		
Dividends paid	(5,000)	
Net cash used by financing activities		(5,000)
Net increase in cash and cash equivalents		$ 2,000
Cash and cash equivalents at beginning of year		11,000
Cash and cash equivalents at end of year		$13,000

Reconciliation of net income to cash provided by operating activities:

(This schedule would include the amounts from "b.(1)." (near the beginning of this example) starting with "net income" and ending with Net cash flows from operating activities of $13,000.)

Schedule of noncash investing and financing activities:
Exchange of investments to retire bonds payable $ 5,000

Disclosure of accounting policy:

For purposes of the statement of cash flows, the Company considers all highly liquid debt instruments purchased with a maturity of three months or less to be cash equivalents.

Note that if the reconciliation approach for operating activities had been shown in the body of the statement instead of the direct approach, an additional schedule showing interest paid and income taxes paid would be necessary.

E. Accounts Receivable Write-Offs

In the examples we assumed that there were no write-offs of uncollectible receivables. When write-offs occur, the indirect approach is modified only to the extent that the adjustment made to net income is for accounts receivable "(net)". However, when using the direct approach, the write-offs must be deducted when computing the amount of cash collected and operating expenses must be reduced by the amount of bad debt expense recorded in the period because such expense is a noncash item.

For example, assume a company has the following data available in its records.

```
        Accounts receivable                      Allowance for bad debts
Beg. bal    15                                                    2  Beg. bal
Charge              5 Write-off           Write-off   5           4  Est. exp.
Sales      100     98 Cash collected                             1  End. bal
End. bal    12
```

```
                    Bad debts expense
              Est. exp.    4
```

Cash flows would be computed under the indirect and the direct approach as follows:

Indirect Approach		Direct Approach	
Net Income	$96	Sales	$100
($100 sales – $4 bad		+ Beg. A/R	15
debt expenses)			$115
		– End. A/R	12
			103
Add: Decrease in			
A/R (Net)	2*	– Less write-offs	5
Cash collected		Cash collected	
from customers	$98	from customers	$ 98
		Operating exp.	$ xx
		Bad debts exp.	– 4
		Cash paid for op-	
		erating exp.	xx

*[A/R (net) beg. bal. $13 – end. bal. $11]

Under the indirect approach, net income is adjusted for net accounts receivable. When an account is written-off, both "accounts receivable" and "allowance for doubtful accounts" are reduced, which has no net effect on accounts receivable, and no cash flow effect. Therefore, there is no modification to the calculation for the written-off account.

Under the direct method, accounts receivable (net) is not used as in the case of the indirect method. Rather the gross accounts receivable are used. The change in gross "accounts receivable" is $3 ($15 beg. bal – $12 end. bal) and includes the $5 write-off of the bad debt. Though the accounts receivable is reduced by $3, $5 of this reduction represents a write-off, not a collection. Therefore, the $5 write-off needs to be deducted from $103 ($100 Sales + 3 decrease in A/R) to calculate the amount of cash collected of $98 ($103 – $5 write-off).

F. Solutions Approach Example

The following problem concerning the Sodium Company is presented as an example of the solutions approach applied to a statement of cash flows. To obtain the maximum benefit, study the problem, ignoring the felt tip pen markings. As you reread the problem, work through the solutions approach as illustrated.

First, glance over the problem. Note that the changes in balance sheet accounts during the calendar year 1987 are presented, not beginning and ending balances. Six paragraphs of additional information regarding transactions during 1987 are also presented.

Second, study the requirement. It is very straightforward: a Statement of Cash Flows for 1987.

Next, visualize the solution format. The statement of cash flows is a listing of the net cash flows from operating, investing, and financing activities and the aggregate effect of those flows on cash and cash equivalents. Also, a separate schedule of noncash investing and financing activities is required.

Third, determine the steps to your solution. One approach is to compute the change in cash and cash equivalents for the year (the figure you are working to in the statement of cash flows, i.e., your check figure). Next you need to determine the net cash flows from operations. Then, analyze the changes in each of the other accounts in the balance sheet during 1987 to determine the cash inflows and outflows from financing and investing activities in order to ultimately determine the net cash flows from investing and financing activities. You should also note any noncash financing and investing activities because these activities must be reported in a separate schedule. Upon completion of these analyses, you will be able to prepare the final solution.

As part of this solution step, you should do a quick mental review of accounting principles and procedures applicable to the statement of cash flows.

You may wish to refresh your understanding of the statement of cash flows. It explains the change in cash and cash equivalents during the period in terms of changes in all of the other accounts.

Fourth, study the text of the problem preparing intermediary solutions as you proceed.

Illustration of Solutions Approach

The following schedule showing net changes in balance-sheet accounts at December 31, 1987, compared to December 31, 1986, was prepared from the records of The Sodium Company. The income statement for the year ended December 31, 1987 follows after the schedule of net changes in balance sheet accounts. The Statement of Cash Flows for the year ended December 31, 1987, has not yet been prepared.

Assets	Net change increase (decrease)
Cash	$ 40,000
Treasury bills	10,000
Accounts receivable	76,000
Inventories	37,000
Prepaid expenses	1,000
Property, plant, and equipment net	64,000
Total assets	$228,000

Liabilities	
Accounts payable	$(55,500)
Notes payable--current	(15,000)
Accrued expenses	33,000*
Bonds payable	(28,000)
Less: Unamortized bond discount	1,200
Total liabilities	(64,300)

*None for interest

Stockholders' Equity	
Common stock, $10 par value	500,000
Capital contributed in excess of par value	200,000
Retained earnings	(437,700)
Appropriation of retained earnings for possible future inventory price decline	30,000
Total stockholders' equity	292,300
Total liabilities and stockholders' equity	$228,000

Sodium Company
Income Statement
For the Year Ended December 31, 1987

Sales	$ 683,000
Cost of sales	(201,000)
Gross profit	482,000
Operating expenses	(241,900)
Income from operations	240,100
Other expenses and losses	(37,800)*
Income before income taxes	$ 202,300
Income tax expense	30,000
Net income	$ 172,300

*Includes interest expense

Additional Information:

1. A comparison of property, plant, and equipment as of the end of each year follows:

	December 31, 1987	December 31, 1986	Net increase (decrease)
Property, plant, and equipment	$570,500	$510,000	$60,500
Less: Accumulated depreciation	224,500	228,000	(3,500)
Property, plant, and equipment, net	$346,000	$282,000	$64,000

During 1987, machinery was purchased at a cost of $45,000. In addition, machinery that was acquired in 1980 at a cost of $48,000 was sold for $3,600. At the date of sale, the machinery had an undepreciated cost of $4,200. The remaining increase in property, plant, and equipment resulted from the acquisition of a tract of land for a new plant site.

2. The bonds payable mature at the rate of $28,000 every year.

3. In January 1987, the Company issued an additional 10,000 shares of its common stock at $14 per share upon the exercise of outstanding stock options held by key employees. In May 1987, the Company declared and issued a 5% stock dividend on its outstanding stock. During the year, a cash dividend was paid on the common stock. On December 31, 1987, there were 840,000 shares of common stock outstanding.

4. The appropriation of retained earnings for possible future inventory price decline was provided by a charge against retained earnings, in anticipation of an expected future drop in the market related to goods in inventory.

Required:

Prepare a Statement of Cash Flows using the direct method for operating activities for the year ended December 31, 1987, based upon the information presented above.

a. Note the change in cash and cash equivalents for 1987, $50,000. This is the "bottom line" amount you are working towards.

Cash	$40,000
Treasury bills	10,000
	50,000

b. Become conversant with each of the other accounts before reading the additional information. This makes you more efficient in analyzing the additional information.

c. Read through each of the six paragraphs of additional information noting their effect on the statement of cash flows. Although beginning and ending balances are not given for most of the accounts, it is still possible to use the T-account analysis approach by assuming either a zero ending or beginning balance and adjusting the account to reflect the increase to decrease.

(1) When presenting cash flows from operating activities using the direct approach, accrual sales must be converted to sales on a cash basis. To do this, accrual sales will be increased (or decreased) by the decrease (or increase) in net accounts receivable. Accounts receivable increased by $76,000, implying sales have been made and recorded as sales revenue in excess of amounts received from customer. This amount, therefore, is subtracted from sales to arrive at cash received from customers $607,000 ($683,000 - $76,000). Accounts receivable can also be analyzed using the T-account approach to determine cash collected from customers (cash basis sales). Since accounts receivable increased by $76,000, the beginning balance can be set at zero and the ending balance at $76,000. Since sales were $683,000, the T-account could be set up as follows:

	Accounts Receivable	
Beg. bal (assumed)	0	
Sales	683,000	
		607,000 Cash collected
End. bal (assumed)	76,000	

(2) Cash paid to suppliers is computed by adjusting cost of sales for changes in inventories and accounts payable. Accounts payable has decreased by $55,500. This means the company spent funds for purchases in excess of what has been recorded as cost of sales on the income statement. Therefore, cost of sales is increased by this amount. Inventories increased during the year, thus necessitating an addition to cost of sales. Even though $37,000 additional cash was expended to increase inventories, these expenditures have not been reflected in the accrual-based cost of sales. Cash paid to suppliers is $293,500 ($201,000 + 55,500 + 37,000).

Using the T-account approach, assume a zero beginning inventory and $37,000 ending inventory (thus, allowing for the $37,000 increase). Also assume beginning accounts payable of $55,500 and ending accounts payable of zero (thus allowing for the $55,500 decrease). Now solve for purchases and cash payments for purchases. Since COGS is given in the problem, we can solve for pur-

chases, the unknown element in the inventory T-account.   Purchases
result in a credit to accts. payable, and after inserting the
purchases amount in the accounts payable account we can solve for
cash payments to suppliers.

	Inventory				Accounts Payable	
Beg. bal (assume)	0				55,500	Beg. bal (assume)
		201,000	COGS		238,000	Purchases
Purchases	238,000		(given)			
End. bal (assume)	37,000		Cash payments to suppliers	293,500		
					0	End. bal (assume)

(3)   Cash paid for operating expenses must be computed by adjusting
accrual-based operating expenses for noncash expenses, accrued
expenses, and deferred expenses.   The T-account analysis in (6)
indicates 1987 depreciation of $40,300.   This amount was included
in operating expenses, but did not require a cash outlay.   Therefore, this amount is subtracted from accrual-based operating
expenses.   Accrued expenses have increased by $33,000, implying
that charges to operating expenses have been made for which the
actual cash expenditure has not been made.   This amount must be
subtracted from operating expenses to properly reflect the nonex-
penditure of cash.
     The prepaid expenses account has increased by $1,000.   This
indicates the company has expended cash which has not been included
on the income statement due to its prepaid nature.   Thus, operating
expenses must be increased by $1,000.   Cash paid for operating
expenses is $169,600 ($241,900 - $40,300 - $33,000 + $1,000).

(4)   There were no cash outlays for amortization of bond discount or the
loss on sale of asset; cash paid for interest is $36,000 ($37,800
other expenses and losses - 1,200 amortization - 600 loss on
equipment.)

(5)   Income taxes paid is the same as income tax expense because there
is no income taxes payable account among the liabilities.

(6)   The fixed asset and accumulated depreciation accounts need to be
analyzed separately.   The T-account analysis below, of the fixed
asset account, indicates Sodium purchased a $45,000 machine and
land for $63,500.   This is a cash outflow which will be classified
as an investing activity.   The sale of the old machine for $3,600
was a cash inflow investing activity.   The T-account analysis of
the accumulated depreciation account indicates 1987 depreciation of
$40,300.

	Fixed Assets				Acc. Dep.		
New machine	45,000			Old machine	43,800*		
		48,000	Sale of old machine			40,300	1987 deprec.
Land	63,500			Net decrease	3,500		
Net increase	60,500						

*48,000 cost - 4,200 undepreciated cost

(7)   The bonds payable decreased by $28,000, indicating a cash outflow
on the repayment of principal (financing activity).

(8)   T-account analysis should be used to analyze the changes in common
      stock, paid-in capital, and retained earnings accounts. In Janu-
      ary, stock with a par value of $100,000 was sold (10,000 shares x
      $10 par). Since the only other stock transaction during the year
      was the stock dividend in May, the remaining $400,000 increase in
      the common stock account must be due to the 5% stock dividend
      $400,000/$10 par = 40,000 shares issued for the stock dividend.
      This number represents 5% of the shares outstanding prior to the
      stock dividend, so $40,000/.05 = 800,000 shares before the stock
      dividend (800,000 shares + 40,000 shares in the stock dividend =
      840,000 shares, the number of shares outstanding at 12/31/87, given
      in the problem). The increase of $200,000 in the premium account is
      made up of $40,000 in excess of par value from the sale of 10,000
      shares and $160,000 from the stock dividend. The $140,000 proceeds
      from the exercise of the common stock options is considered a cash
      inflow and classified as a financing transaction. The stock
      dividend would not be included in the statement as it was not an
      operating, financing, or investing activity.

Stock		Paid-in Capital		Retained Earnings		
100,000	Stock sale	40,000	Stock sale	Stock dividend 560,000	172,300	1987 income
400,000	Stock dividend	160,000	Stock dividend	Appropriation 30,000		
500,000	1987 increase	200,000	1987 increase	Dividend 20,000		
				1987 decrease 437,700		

(9)   The stock dividend resulted in a $560,000 debit to retained earn-
      ings. The appropriation of retained earnings (also not a financing
      or investment transaction) resulted in a debit of $30,000. If the
      $172,300 of 1987 income is subtracted from the $590,000 ($560,000 +
      $30,000) of debits, only a $417,700 decrease is obtained and a
      $437,700 decrease in retained earnings occurred. Thus, the differ-
      ence of $20,000 is a cash dividend, as is implied in paragraph (5)
      of the problem. The cash dividend is a cash outflow classified as
      a financing activity.
(10) The company reduced its notes payable by $15,000. This outflow
      should be classified under financing activities.

Fifth, prepare the solution. Remember that the statement should begin with
a three-line heading: company name, statement title, and period covered. When
using the direct approach in determining net cash flows from operations, remember to only include all transactions and other events that are not financing and
investing activities. Next, list all investing inflows and outflows of cash to
arrive at net cash provided or used by investing activities. And then, list all
financing inflows and outflows of cash to arrive at net cash provided or used by
financing activities.

Sixth, when the changes per the statement of cash flows equal the change in
cash, you probably have a substantially correct solution. You should also include the T-account analyses prepared above as part of your supporting schedules
for the solution.

If on the other hand, your change in cash per the statement of cash flows does not equal the change in cash, rework the statement of cash flows as time permits. Remember, do not go beyond the maximum time allowed. Also, you may find it better to go on and work another problem and come back and get a fresh start if time permits. If you are forced to turn in an incomplete or incorrect solution you probably are missing only one or two items (or you made a math error). Thus, you probably still scored 75% or better on the problem.

The Sodium Company
Statement of Cash Flows
For the Year Ended December 31, 1987

Cash flows from operating activities:		
Cash received from customers	$607,000	
Cash provided by operating activities		$607,000
Cash paid to suppliers	293,500	
Cash paid for operating expenses	169,600	
Cash paid for interest	36,000	
Cash paid for income taxes	30,000	
Cash disbursed for operating activities		529,100
Net cash flows from operating activities		$ 77,900
Cash flows from investing activities:		
Purchase of machinery	(45,000)	
Purchase of land	(63,500)	
Proceeds from sale of machinery	3,600	
Net cash used by investing activities		(104,900)
Cash flows from financing activities:		
Proceeds from stock options	140,000	
Payment of dividends	(20,000)	
Repayment of bonds payable	(28,000)	
Repayment of notes payable	(15,000)	
Net cash provided for financing activities		77,000
Net increase in cash and cash equivalents		50,000
Cash and cash equivalents at beginning of year		xxxxxx*
Cash and cash equivalents at end of year		$xxxxxx*

    *Not given in this example problem.

(See required supplementary schedule and required disclosure below)

Reconciliation of net income to net cash provided by operating activities:

Net income	$172,300
Noncash items included in income:	
Depreciation	40,300
Amortization of bond discount	1,200
Loss on sale of machinery	600
Increase in receivable	(76,000)
Increase in inventories	(37,000)
Increase in prepaid expenses	(1,000)
Decrease in accounts payable	(55,500)
Increase in accrued expenses	33,000
Net cash flows from operating activities	$77,900

Disclosure of accounting policy:

For purposes of the statement of cash flows, the Company considers all highly liquid debt instruments purchased with a maturity of three months or less to be cash equivalents.

Explanation of Reconciliation (Indirect Method)

(1) The $172,300 of net income is a base figure for computing net cash flows from operations when interest expense, interest revenue, and dividend revenue do not exist. Add income statement items not using cash or cash equivalents, e.g., depreciation, and deduct income statement items not producing cash or cash equivalents, e.g., amortization of deferred revenues.

(2) Since $3,600 is included as a cash inflow investing activity, the $600 loss, i.e., the book value was $4,200, must be added to income so as not to include the transaction twice.

(3) The related bond amortization of $1,200, for the bond must be added back to net income in the process of determining net cash flows from operations.

(4) Accounts receivable increased by $76,000, implying sales have been made and recorded as income in 1987 in excess of amounts received from customers. Income from operations must therefore be reduced by this amount.

(5) Inventories also increased during the year, thus necessitating a deduction from net income. Even though $37,000 additional cash was expended to increase inventories, these expenditures have not been reflected in the accrual-based cost of goods sold.

(6) The prepaid expenses account has increased by $1,000. This indicates the company has expended cash which has not been included on the income statement due to its prepaid nature. Thus, income from operations must be decreased by $1,000.

(7) Accounts payable has decreased by $55,500. This means the company spent funds for purchases in excess of what has been recorded as expenses on the income statement. Therefore, a charge (decrease) to income is necessary to reflect the additional cash expended which reduced the payable.

(8) Accrued expenses have increased by $33,000, implying that charges to net income have been made for this amount for which the actual cash expenditure has not yet occurred. This amount must thus be added back to net income to properly reflect the nonexpenditure of cash.

BUSINESS COMBINATIONS AND CONSOLIDATIONS

Many companies expand their operations by acquiring other businesses. The
acquiring company may be seeking diversification of its business, a more stable
supply of raw materials for its production, an increase in the range of products or
services it offers, or any one of many other business reasons. The accounting
issues of business combinations begin with properly recording and reporting the
economic events of the date of business combination. Accounting subsequent to the
combination is dependent on the alternatives selected at the combination date.
Thus, as you study this section, you should fully understand how the combination is
first recorded and reported before proceeding to events occurring after the combination date.

From a legal perspective, business combinations are classified into three
categories as follows.

1. Merger--One company acquires the assets and liabilities of one or more other
    companies in exchange for stock, cash, or other consideration. The acquiring
    company continues to exist as a separate legal entity, but the acquired company
    ceases to exist as a separate legal entity, its stock is cancelled, and its
    books are closed. The separate assets and liabilities are recorded on the
    acquiring firm's books. (A Corp. + B Corp. = A Corp.)

2. Consolidation--A new firm is formed to issue stock in exchange for the stock of
    two or more combining or consolidating companies. The acquired firms normally
    cease to continue as separate legal entities; therefore, the new (acquiring)
    firm will record the separate assets and liabilities of the acquired firms. (A
    Corp. + B Corp. = C Corp.)

3. Acquisition--A company acquires a majority (> 50%) of the common stock of
    another company and each company continues its legal existence. The acquiring
    company (parent) will record an "Investment in Acquired Company's Stock" in the
    combination entry. (A Corp. + B Corp. = Consolidated Financial Statements of A
    and B)

Mergers and consolidations require 100% ownership of the acquired company but the
acquisition business combination requires only a majority ownership of the
outstanding stock. In addition, by maintaining the separate legal existence of the
acquired company (B Corp.) and not cancelling its stock, the parent company (A
Corp.) can retain greater flexibility in raising additional capital by using B Corp.
shares as collateral for a loan or through the issuance of new shares of B Corp.

Financial statements for combinations which are in the legal forms of mergers and consolidations are prepared in the normal accounting process since all assets and liabilities are recorded on just one set of books. Accounting for an acquisition, however, results in an investment account on the acquiring company's books while the assets and liabilities are still recorded and shown on the books of the acquired company. Financial reporting for this combination generally requires the bringing together, or accounting consolidation, of the accounts from these two sets of books to prepare financial reports for the economic entity now formed between the parent and subsidiary companies.

A. **Accounting for the Combination**

Regardless of the legal form, there are only two accounting methods applied to any business combination--purchase or pooling. These two methods are mutually exclusive and the selection of the accounting method is determined by specific aspects of the facts surrounding the combination.

1. Purchase Accounting

Purchase accounting for a combination is similar to the accounting treatment used in the acquisition of any asset group. The fair market value of the consideration (cash, stock, debt securities, etc.) given by the acquiring firm is used as the valuation basis of the combination. The assets and liabilities of the acquired firm are revalued to their respective fair market values at the combination date. The accounting for a preacquisition contingency of an acquired enterprise under the purchase method is covered by SFAS 38 (see outline). Any difference between the value of the consideration given and the fair market values of the net assets obtained is normally recorded as goodwill. The financial statements of the acquiring company reflect the combined operations from the date of combination.

2. The Pooling Method

The pooling method assumes a combining of stockholders' interests. The basis of valuation in pooling is the book value of the net assets on the books of the acquired company. Therefore, goodwill may not be created at the date of combination in a pooling combination. The financial statements of the acquiring company will include a restatement of all prior years' presented to include the operations and financial position of the pooled companies for all years presented.

APB 16 specified twelve criteria which must be met before a combination may be accounted for as a pooling of interests. Failure to meet any one of these twelve criteria will preclude a pooling treatment. A complete list of

the criteria is provided in the outline of APB 16. The major criteria
are: (a) the combining companies have ownership interests independent of
each other and were not recently a subsidiary or division of any other
company; (b) the combination is effected by a single transaction or in
accord with a plan lasting not more than one year; (c) at least 90% of the
voting ownership interests of the combinee company are acquired in exchange
for the issuance of the combinor company's voting shares, and all shareholders have the same equity rights; and (d) no planned intent exists to
segment the operations or acquired stockholders' interests after the combination date.

A recent issue of Accounting Trends and Techniques indicates that
slightly less than 20% of the combinations made by its sample companies used
the pooling method. Although its use has been declining, pooling accounting
is still an accounting alternative for business combinations and has been
tested on recent CPA exams.

B.   A Company and B Company--Date of Combination

A presentation of the date of combination entries for purchase and pooling
will be made in the next two sections of this module. We will be using a
comprehensive example for these sections and the remaining parts of the discussion on consolidation accounting. The following balance sheets of A Company
and B Company provide the foundation for further discussion. As you study the
remainder of this module, be sure you understand where the numbers are being
derived from.

A Company and B Company
Balance Sheets 1/1/86
(Immediately Before Combination)

	A Company	B Company
Assets		
Cash	$ 30,900	$ 37,400
Accounts receivable	34,200	9,100
Inventories	22,900	16,100
Equipment	200,000	50,000
Less: Accumulated depreciation	(21,000)	(10,000)
Patents	-0-	10,000
Total assets	$267,000	$112,600
Liabilities and Equity		
Accounts payable	$ 4,000	$ 6,600
Bonds payable	100,000	-0-
Capital stock ($10 par)	100,000	50,000
Additional paid-in capital	15,000	15,000
Retained earnings	48,000	41,000
Total liabilities and equity	$267,000	$112,600

The concept of book value of the investment is a basic principle of accounting for business combinations and will be used in many different computations. Note that the book value of the net assets of B Company may be computed by two different methods.

1. Subtract the book value of the liabilities from the book values of the assets

$$\$112,600 - \$6,600 = \$106,000$$

2. Add the book values of the components of B Company stockholders' equity

$$\$50,000 + \$15,000 + \$41,000 = \$106,000$$

C. Date of Combination--Purchase Accounting

Purchase accounting uses fair market values of the net assets as the valuation basis for the combination. The difference between the value of the consideration given by the acquiring firm and the book value of the net assets obtained is the excess of cost over book value, or excess of book value over cost (referred to here as differential) of the net assets obtained. As discussed earlier, this differential has two components, as follows.

1. An amount representing an adjustment of the book values of the net assets up (or down) to their respective fair market values, and

2. An amount representing goodwill

Assume that our Company A purchased all the net assets of B Company. At the date of combination, the fair values of all the assets and liabilities were determined by appraisal, as follows.

B Company item	Book value (BV)	Fair market value (FMV)	Difference between BV and FMV
Cash	$ 37,400	$ 37,400	$ -0-
Accounts rec. (net)	9,100	9,100	-0-
Inventories	16,100	17,100	1,000
Equipment (net)	40,000	48,000	8,000
Patents	10,000	13,000	3,000
Accounts payable	(6,600)	(6,600)	-0-
Totals	$106,000	$118,000	$12,000

The $12,000 is the difference between the book value and fair market values of B Company and is one component of the differential.

Four different cases displaying a range of total acquisition costs are presented below. The form of consideration paid to B Company by A Company is assumed to be cash but, under purchase accounting, it could be stock, cash, debentures, or any other form of payment.

The allocation of the difference between cost and book value is a two-step process. First, the assets and liabilities must be valued at their respective fair market values and then any remainder is allocated to goodwill. Note that the differential may be positive or negative and that the net assets could have fair market values less than book values.

Case:	Case A	Case B	Case C	Case D
Consideration paid	$134,000	$118,000	$106,000	$100,000
Notes:	(> FMV)	(= FMV)	(< FMV)	(< FMV)
	(> BV)	(> BV)	(= BV)	(< BV)

Step 1. Compute the Differential

	Case A	Case B	Case C	Case D
Book value	$106,000	$106,000	$106,000	$106,000
Investment cost	134,000	118,000	106,000	100,000
Differential	$ 28,000	$ 12,000	-0-	($ 6,000)

Step 2. Allocation of Differential

a. Revaluation of net assets to fair market value

	Case A	Case B	Case C	Case D
FMV, net assets	$118,000	$118,000	$118,000	$118,000
Less BV	106,000	106,000	106,000	106,000
Portion to net assets	$ 12,000	$ 12,000	$ 12,000	$ 12,000

b. Remainder (Excess of cost greater than fair value, or fair value greater than cost)

	Case A	Case B	Case C	Case D
FMV, net assets	$118,000	$118,000	$118,000	$118,000
Less Investment cost	134,000	118,000	106,000	100,000
Goodwill	$ 16,000	-0-	($ 12,000)	($ 18,000)

Step 3. Accounting for Goodwill and the Excess of fair value greater than cost.

APB 16 assumes the excess of cost greater than fair value is goodwill (Case A). This would be amortized in accordance with APB 17. If the fair value of the assets is greater than the investment cost (Cases C and D), then APB 16 requires this excess to be proportionally applied to reduce the assigned values of the noncurrent assets acquired (except long-term investments in marketable securities). If these assets are reduced to zero value, any remaining excess of fair value over cost shall be established as a deferred credit.

Reallocations are required in Cases C and D because the fair values of the net assets are greater than costs, as follows.

	Item	Assigned values of noncurrent assets acquired	Proportion	Excess of fair value over cost	Reallocation	New assigned value
Case C:	Equipment	$48,000	$48,000/$61,000	($12,000)	($ 9,443)	$38,557
	Patents	$13,000	$13,000/$61,000	($12,000)	($ 2,557)	$10,443
		$61,000			($12,000)	
Case D:	Equipment	$48,000	$48,000/$61,000	($18,000)	($14,164)	$33,836
	Patents	$13,000	$13,000/$61,000	($18,000)	($ 3,836)	$ 9,164
		$61,000			($18,000)	

Date of combination entries on A Company's books for the purchase-merger are

	Case A	Case B	Case C	Case D
Cash	$37,400	$37,400	$37,400	$37,400
A/R	9,100	9,100	9,100	9,100
Inventories	17,100	17,100	17,100	17,100
Equipment (net)	48,000	48,000	38,557	33,836
Patents	13,000	13,000	10,443	9,164
Goodwill	16,000	-0-	-0-	-0-
A/P	$ 6,600	$ 6,600	$ 6,600	$ 6,600
Cash	134,000	118,000	106,000	100,000

B Company would close its books and cease to operate as a separate entity.

If B Company maintained its separate legal status, the combination would be accounted for as a 100% acquisition. The date of combination entries on A Company's books for each of the four cases would be

Investment in				
B Company	$134,000	$118,000	$106,000	$100,000
Cash	$134,000	$118,000	$106,000	$100,000

Consolidated financial statements would normally be prepared when acquisitions of more than 50% of outstanding stock are made. Consolidated statements are discussed later in this module.

Some candidates find that using value lines to display the features of purchase accounting helps to sort out the various concepts. Value lines are provided below for Cases A and D. You might want to do the value lines for Cases B and C.

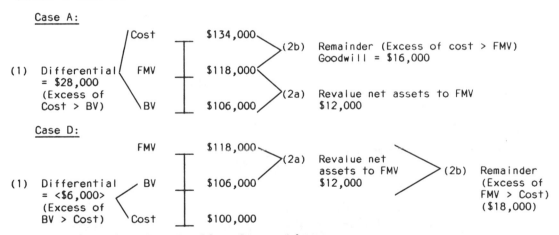

D. Date of Combination-Pooling Accounting

Pooling accounting requires a uniting of the stockholders' equities of the combining firms. A comparison of the par or stated value of the surviving company's common stock must be made with the total par or stated value of the common stock capital of the combining companies before combination. This process is often referred to as determining the "mix" of the pooled stockholders' equity and must be performed prior to making the date of combination entries. In determining the "mix" of pooled stockholders' equity, it is necessary to remember that under pooling the book value of the net assets is used to record the combination.

To illustrate this process, we will use the information from our comprehensive example of A Company and B Company. Note the companies have the following equity accounts immediately before the combination.

	A	B
Capital stock ($10 par)	$100,000	$ 50,000
Additional paid-in capital	15,000	15,000
Retained earnings	48,000	41,000
Totals	$163,000	$106,000

Pooling requires the continuation of at least $65,000 of contributed capital from B Company ($50,000 Capital Stock + $15,000 Additional Paid-in Capital). The "mix" of the contributed capital items in A Company's date of combination entry will be based on the par of the stock given up by A Company.

If the par of the stock issued by the issuer (Company A) is greater than the present par on the books of the combinee company (Company B), the following sequence should be used as each item is fully extinguished.

1.   Total par value outstanding of combinee (Company B)
2.   Additional paid-in capital of combinee (Company B)
3.   Additonal paid-in capital of issuer (Company A)
4.   Retained earnings of combinee (Company B)
5.   Retained earnings of issuer (Company A)

If the par issued is less than the present par on the books of the combinee, the excess of the prior par over the new par is added to Additional Paid-in Capital.

The company name in parentheses provides the company source for determining the amount of the entry.

1. Merger and consolidation legal forms

     Case 1: Par value of common stock issued by A Company is $30,000. The entry on A's books would be as follows.

*Net assets of B	106,000	
Capital stock (Co. A)		30,000
Additional paid-in capital (Co. B)		35,000
Retained earnings (Co. B)		41,000

     *Note: The book values of B's specific assets and liabilities would be listed separately.

     Case 2: Par value of common stock issued by A Company is $60,000. The entry on A's books would be as follows.

Net assets of B	106,000	
Capital stock (Co. A)		60,000
Additional paid-in capital (Co. B)		5,000
Retained earnings (Co. B)		41,000

Case 3:   Par value of common stock issued by A Company is $75,000. The
entry on A's books would be as follows.

Net assets of B	106,000	
*Paid-in capital (Co. A)	10,000	
Capital stock (Co. A)		75,000
Retained earnings (Co. B)		41,000

*Note: This represents paid-in capital formerly associated with A
Company's stockholders. If the par of the stock issued by A was >
$80,000, the retained earnings credit above would have been
reduced.

2. Acquisition legal form

If Company B is maintained as a separate legal entity, consolidated
financial statements will have to be prepared. The combination entries will
include an "Investment in B Stock" account rather than the specific net
assets of Company B. The combination entry on A's books for Case 1 on the
preceding page would be as follows.

Investment in Company B's common stock	106,000	
Capital stock (Co. A)		30,000
Additional paid-in capital (Co. B)		35,000
Retained earnings (Co. B)		41,000

Subsequent cases would be treated similarly based on the par of the stock
issued. It is important to note that in 100% acquisitions, all of the final
amounts and accounts in the consolidated financial statements would be the
same as if the business combination were treated as a merger or consolidation.

APB 16 requires that pooled operations be reported for the first
complete period reported. Thus, if the pooling took place in mid-period,
the pooling method will have to be applied retroactively from the point of
pooling to the beginning of the period. In addition, if comparative statements are presented, they must be restated on a combined basis to reflect
the pooled firms. Intercompany transactions occurring before the date of
combination should be eliminated when the pooling method is applied retroactively. Intercompany eliminations are explained later in this module.

E. **Purchase and Pooling Combination Entries Reviewed**

The following matrix provides a review of the combination entries of the
surviving or investing firm for the three legal forms of combination (merger,
consolidation, and acquisition) for which stock is given. The legal form is
primarily dependent on whether the combined company, Company B in our examples,
retains a separate, legal existence or transfers its assets and liabilities to
Company A and cancels any remaining stock of Company B. The purchase versus

pooling choice is independent of the legal form. Accounting for the combination (purchase or pooling) will be determined by the specific aspects of the combination transaction that are specified in APB 16. The items in the parentheses are valuation bases or the company source for determining the dollar amount for the entry.

Purchase-Pooling Matrix

	Accounting method	
Legal form	Purchase	Pooling
1. Merger (A Co. + B Co. = A. Co.)	Assets (FMV of B) Liabilities (FMV of B) Capital stock (Co. A) Add'l. PIC (Co. A)	Assets (BV of B) Liabilities (BV of B) Capital stock (Co. A) Add'l PIC (Co. B) Retained earnings (Co. B)
2. Consolidation (A Co. + B Co. = C Co.)	Assets (FMV of both A and B) Liabilities (FMV of A and B) Capital stock (Co. C) Add'l. PIC (Co. C)	Assets (BV of both A and B) Liabilities (BV of A and B) Capital stock (Co. C) Add'l. PIC (both A and B) Retained earnings (both A and B)
3. Acquisition (A Co. + B Co. = Consolidated statements of A and B)	Investment in B (FMV) Capital stock (Co. A) Add'l PIC (Co. A)	Investment in B (BV) Capital Stock (Co. A) Add'l. PIC (Co. B) Retained earnings (Co. B)

F. Consolidated Financial Statements

An investment of more than 50% of the outstanding voting stock will normally require the preparation of consolidated financial statements. The complete consolidation process is presented in the next section of this module. The investment account will be eliminated in the consolidation working papers and will be replaced with the specific assets and liabilities of the investee corporation. Consolidation is generally required for investments of more than 50% of the outstanding voting stock except when

1. The control is likely to be temporary
2. Control is not held by the majority owner

    a. The investee is in legal reorganization or bankruptcy
    b. The investee operates in a foreign country which has severe restrictions on the financial transactions of its business firms or is subject to material political or economic uncertainty that casts significant doubt on the parent's ability to control the subsidiary

In these limited cases, the investment will be reported as a long-term investment in an unconsolidated subsidiary on the investor's balance sheet with its balance determined by using the cost method unless the parent can demonstrate that it has significant influence in which case the equity method shall be used.

The concept of consolidated statements is that the resources of two or more companies are under the control of the parent company. Consolidated statements are prepared as if the group of legal entities were one economic entity group. Consolidated statements are presumed to be more meaningful for management, owners, and creditors of the parent company and they are required for fair presentation of the financially-related companies. Individual company statements should continue to be prepared for minority ownership and creditors of the subsidiary companies.

The accounting principles used to record and report events for a single legal entity are also applicable to a consolidated economic entity of two or more companies. The concept of the reporting entity is expanded to include more than one company, but all other accounting principles are applied in the same way as for an individual company. The consolidation process eliminates reciprocal items that are shown on both the parent's and subsidiary's books. These eliminations are necessary to avoid double-counting the same items which would misstate the financials of the combined economic entity.

Consolidated financial statements are prepared from worksheets which begin with the trial balances of the parent and subsidiary companies. Eliminating worksheet entries are made to reflect the two separate companies' results of operations and financial position as one combined economic entity. The entire consolidation process takes place only on a worksheet; no consolidation elimination entries are ever recorded on either the parent's or subsidiary's books.

Consolidated balance sheets are typically prepared at the date of combination to determine the initial financial position of the economic entity. Any intercompany accounts between the parent and subsidiary must be eliminated against each other. In addition, the "Investment in subsidiary's stock" account from the parent's books will be eliminated against the reciprocal accounts of the subsidiary's stockholders' equity. The remaining accounts are then combined to prepare the consolidated balance sheet. The preparation of consolidated statements after the date of combination becomes a little more complex because the parent's and subsidiary's income statements may include reciprocal intercompany accounts which must be eliminated. The next section of the module will present an example of the preparation of a consolidated balance sheet at the date of combination for both purchase and pooling accounting. You should carefully review the date of combination consolidation process before proceeding to the preparation of consolidation statements subsequent to combination.

G. **Date of Combination Consolidated Balance Sheet--Purchase Accounting**

This example uses the numbers from the A Company and B Company presented on page 613. The discussion in the preceding sections assumed a 100% combination in which the parent acquired control of all the subsidiary's stock or net assets. For the remainder of the module, we will assume that the parent company (A Company) acquired a 90% interest in the net assets of the subsidiary company (B Company). The remaining 10% of the outstanding stock is held by third party investors referred to as the minority interest. In the illustrated problem, you will be able to review the determination of how minority interest is computed and disclosed on the consolidated financial statements. Note that only the "acquisition" legal form leads to the preparation of consolidated statements and includes less than 100% business combinations.

The assumptions for this illustration are

1. On January 1, 1986, A Company acquires a 90% interest in B Company in exchange for 5,400 shares of $10 par stock having a total market value of $120,600
2. The purchase method of accounting is used for the combination
3. Any goodwill resulting from the combination will be amortized over a period of 10 years

The workpaper for a consolidated balance sheet at the date of acquisition is presented on page 622. The first two columns are the trial balances from the books of A Company and B Company immediately following the acquisition.

1. Investment Entry on A Company's books

The entry to record the 90% purchase-acquisition on A Company's books was

Investment in Stock of B Company	120,600	
Capital Stock		54,000
Additional Paid-in Capital		66,600

(To record the issuance of 5,400 shares of $10 par stock to acquire a 90% interest in B Company.)

Although common stock is used for the consideration in our example, A Company could have used debentures, cash, or any other form of consideration acceptable to B Company's stockholders to make the purchase combination.

A COMPANY AND B COMPANY CONSOLIDATED WORKING PAPERS
For Date of Combination – 1/1/86

Purchase Accounting
90% Interest

	A Company	B Company	Adjustments and Eliminations Debit	Adjustments and Eliminations Credit	Minority Interest	Consolidated Balances
Balance sheet 1/1/86						
Cash	30,900	37,400				68,300
Accounts Receivable	34,200	9,100				43,300
Inventories	22,900	16,100	(b) 900			39,900
Equipment	200,000	50,000	(b) 9,000			259,000
Accumulated Depreciation	(21,000)	(10,000)		(b) 1,800		(32,800)
Investment in Stock of B Company	120,600			(a) 120,600		
Difference Between Cost and Book Value			(a) 25,200	(b) 25,200		
Excess of Cost over Fair Value (Goodwill)			(b) 14,400			14,400
Patents		10,000	(b) 2,700			12,700
Total Assets	387,600	112,600				404,800
Accounts Payable	4,000	6,600				10,600
Bonds Payable	100,000					100,000
Capital Stock	154,000	50,000	(a) 45,000		5,000	154,000
Additional Paid-in Capital	81,600	15,000	(a) 13,500		1,500	81,600
Retained Earnings	48,000	41,000	(a) 36,900		4,100	48,000
Minority Interest					10,600	10,600 MI
Total Liabilities and Equity	387,600	112,600	147,600	147,600		404,800

2. Difference between Investment Cost and Book Value

The difference between the investment cost and the parent company's equity in the net assets of the subsidiary is computed as follows.

Investment cost		$120,600
– Book Value % at date of combination		
B Company's:		
Capital Stock	$ 50,000	
Additional Paid-in Capital	15,000	
Retained Earnings	41,000	
Total	$106,000	
Parent's share of ownership	x 90%	
Parent's share of book value		95,400
Excess of Cost over Book Value		$ 25,200

This difference is due to several undervalued assets and to unrecorded goodwill. The allocation procedure is similar to that shown on page 603 for a 100% purchase; however, in this case, the parent company obtained a 90% interest and thus will recognize 90% of the difference between the fair market values and book values of the subsidiary's assets, not 100%. The allocation is presented as

Item	Book Value (B.V.)	Fair Market Value (F.M.V.)	Difference Between B.V. and F.M.V.	Ownership Percentage	Percentage Share of Difference Between B.V. and F.M.V.
Cash	$ 37,400	$ 37,400	$ -0-		
Accounts Receivable (net)	9,100	9,100	-0-		
Inventories	16,100	17,100	1,000	90%	$ 900
Equipment	50,000	60,000	10,000	90%	9,000
Accumulated Depreciation	(10,000)	(12,000)	(2,000)	90%	(1,800)
Patents	10,000	13,000	3,000	90%	2,700
Accounts Payable	(6,600)	(6,600)	-0-		
Total	$106,000	$118,000	$12,000		

Amount of difference between cost and book value share allocated to
  revaluation of net assets $10,800
Total differential   25,200
    Remainder allocated to goodwill $14,400

The equipment has a book value of $40,000 ($50,000 less 20% depreciation of $10,000). An appraisal concluded with a judgment that the equipment's replacement cost was $60,000 less 20% accumulated depreciation of $12,000 resulting in a net fair value of $48,000.

3. Elimination entries on workpaper

The basic reciprocal accounts are the investment in subsidiary account on the parent's books and the subsidiary's stockholder equity accounts. Only the parent's share of the subsidiary's accounts may be eliminated as reciprocal accounts. The remaining 10% portion is allocated to the minority interest. The entries below include documentation showing the company source for the information. Those aids will help you trace the numbers. The workpaper entry to eliminate the basic reciprocal accounts is

(a) Capital stock--B Co.   45,000
     Additional Paid-in Capital--B Co.   13,500
     Retained Earnings--B Co.   36,900*
     Differential   25,200
          Investment in Stock of B Co.--A Co.   120,600
*($36,900 = 90% x $41,000)

Note that only 90% of B Company's stockholders' equity accounts are eliminated. Also, an account called "Differential" is debited in the workpaper entry. The differential account is a temporary account to record the difference between the cost of the investment in B Company from the parent's books and the book value of the parent's interest (90% in our case) from the subsidiary's books.

The next step is to allocate the differential to the specific accounts by making the following workpaper entry

(b)	Inventories	900	
	Equipment	9,000	
	Patents	2,700	
	Goodwill	14,400	
	Accumulated depreciation		1,800
	Differential		25,200

This entry reflects the allocations prepared in step 2 on the previous page and recognizes the parent's share of the asset revaluations.

The minority interest column is the 10% interest of B Company's net assets owned by outside, third parties. Minority interest must be disclosed because 100% of the book values of B Company are included in the consolidated statements although A Company controls only 90% of the net assets. An alternative method to "prove" minority interest is to multiply the net assets of the subsidiary by the minority interest share, as follows.

$$\frac{\text{Stockholders' Equity of B Company}}{\$106,000} \times \frac{\text{Minority Interest \%}}{10\%} = \$10,600$$

The $10,600 would be reported on the credit side of the consolidated balance sheet between liabilities and stockholders' equity.

The principle used to prepare the consolidated balance sheet is called the parent company concept. This is the method used most often on the CPA exam and also used in about ninety percent of actual cases of consolidations. An alternative approach is known as the entity concept. The two differ in the amount of the asset revaluations recognized on the consolidated balance sheet. Under the parent company concept, just the parent's share of the revaluation is shown and the minority interest is reported at its share of the subsidiary's book value. If the entity concept were used, the net assets of B Company would be included in the consolidated balance sheet at 100% of their fair values at the date of acquisition and minority interest would be reported at its share of the fair value of the subsidiary. In our example, minority interest under the entity concept would have been

$$\frac{\text{Total Fair Market Value}}{\frac{\text{of Net Assets of B Company}}{\$118,000}} \times \frac{\text{Minority}}{\frac{\text{Percentage}}{10\%}} = \$11,800$$

Our example does not include any other intercompany accounts as of the date of combination. If any existed, they would be eliminated to fairly present the consolidated entity. Several examples of other reciprocal accounts will be shown later in this module for the preparation of consolidated financial statements subsequent to the date of acquisition.

H. **Date of Combination Consolidated Balance Sheet--Pooling Accounting**

The preparation of a consolidated balance sheet for a pooling acquisition follows the basic principles discussed in the section on recording the pooling combination. Book values are reported as the basis of the net assets of the combined companies and the continuity of the acquired stockholders' equity is reflected in the carryforward of the capital "mix" from the values shown on the acquired company's books.

For purposes of this section, the following assumptions will be made.

1. On January 1, 1986, A Company acquired a 90% interest in B Company in exchange for 5,400 shares of $10 par value stock of A Company
2. All criteria for a pooling have been met and the combination is treated as a pooling of interests.

The workpaper for a consolidated balance sheet at the date of combination is presented below. Note that the first two columns are trial balances of A Company and B Company immediately after the combination was recorded by A Company.

1. Investment entry recorded on A Company's books

The following entry was made by A Company to record its 90% acquisition-pooling of B Company.

Investment in Stock of B Company	95,400	
Capital Stock, $10 par		54,000
Additional Paid-in Capital		4,500
Retained Earnings		36,900

A COMPANY AND B COMPANY CONSOLIDATED WORKING PAPERS
For Date of Combination - 1/1/86

Pooling Accounting
90% Interest

	A Company	B Company	Adjustments and Eliminations Debit	Credit	Minority Interest	Consolidated Balances
Balance Sheet 1/1/86						
Cash	30,900	37,400				68,300
Accounts Receivable	34,200	9,100				43,300
Inventories	22,900	16,100				39,000
Equipment	200,000	50,000				250,000
Less Accumulated Depreciation	(21,000)	(10,000)				(31,000)
Investment in Stock of B Company	95,400			(a) 95,400		
Patents		10,000				10,000
Total Assets	362,400	112,600				379,600
Accounts Payable	4,000	6,600				10,600
Bonds Payable	100,000					100,000
Capital Stock	154,000	50,000	(a) 45,000		5,000	154,000
Additional Paid-in Capital	19,500	15,000	(a) 13,500		1,500	19,500
Retained Earnings	84,900	41,000	(a) 36,900		4,100	84,900
Minority Interest					10,600	10,600
Total Liabilities and Equity	362,400	112,600	95,400	95,400		379,600

The investment entry reflects the capital "mix" for a pooling of less than a 100% investment. The following schedule shows the mix for our 90% combination accomplished by the issuance of 5,400 shares of A Company's $10 par stock.

	B Company	A Company's Percentage Share	A's Share of B's Equity
Capital Stock	$ 50,000	90%	$45,000
Additional Paid-in Capital	15,000	90%	13,500
Retained Earnings	41,000	90%	36,900
	$106,000		$95,400

The $54,000 (5,400 shares x $10 par) in new capital issued by A Company represents $45,000 from B Company's Capital Stock and $9,000 of the $13,500 share of B Company's Additional Paid-in Capital. Note the remaining $4,500 of capital and $36,900 of B Company's Retained Earnings are carried over to A Company's books in the combination date entry. The $10,600 of B's capital that is not carried over to A will eventually be shown as Minority Interest on the Consolidated Balance Sheet.

2. Elimination entry on workpaper

Pooling accounting uses book values as a basis of valuation; therefore, no "differential" will ever occur in a pooling. The reciprocal accounts in a pooling consolidated balance sheet are the "Investment in Stock of B Company" account from the parent's books and the stockholders' equity accounts from the subsidiary's books. Again, note that only 90% of the equity of B Company is being eliminated; the 10% remainder will be recognized as minority interest. The workpaper elimination entry is

(a)	Capital Stock--B Co.	45,000
	Additional Paid-in Capital--B Co.	13,500
	Retained Earnings--B Co.	36,900*
	Investment in Stock of B Company--A Co.	95,400

(*36,900 = 90% x $41,000)

The next section of the module will cover the preparation of consolidated financial statements subsequent to the date of acquisition. You should be sure you fully understand date of combination consolidations before proceeding.

I. **Consolidated Financial Statements Subsequent to Acquisition**

The concepts used to prepare subsequent consolidated statements are essentially the same as used to prepare the consolidated balance sheet at the acquisition date. The income statement and statement of retained earnings are added to reflect the results of operations since the acquisition date. Furthermore, some additional reciprocal accounts may have to be eliminated because of intercompany transactions between the parent and subsidiary corporations. Please note that the financial statements of a consolidated entity are prepared using the same accounting principles that would be employed by a single, unconsolidated enterprise. The only difference is that some reciprocal accounts appearing on both companies' books must be eliminated against each other before the two corporations may be presented as one consolidated economic entity. Your review should concentrate on the accounts and amounts appearing on the consolidated statements (amounts in the last column of the worksheet). This "end-result" focus will help provide the understanding of why certain elimination entries are necessary.

An expanded version of the consolidated worksheet is necessary if the income statement and retained earnings statement must also be prepared. A comprehensive format often called "the three statement layout" is an integrated vertical array of the income statement, the retained earnings statement, and the balance sheet. The net income of the period is carried to the retained earnings statement and the ending retained earnings is carried down to the balance sheet. If you are required to prepare just the consolidated balance sheet, then eliminating entries involving nominal accounts (income statement accounts and "Dividends declared" account) would be made directly against the ending balance of retained earnings presented on the balance sheet.

The following discussion assumes the parent is using the partial equity method to account for the majority investment. Some firms may use the cost method during the period to record investment income because it requires fewer book adjustments to the investment account. In cases where the cost method is used during the period, one approach is to adjust the investment and investment income accounts to the equity method through an entry on the workpaper and the consolidation process may then be continued. Assuming that an income statement and retained earnings statement are being prepared in addition to the balance sheet, the general form of this entry is made on the workpapers.

Dividend income (for income recognized using cost method)
Investment in sub (% of undistributed income of sub)
　　Equity in subsidiary's income (for income recognized using equity
　　　　　method)

Additional entries would be required to recognize the equity income in prior periods if the investment were owned for more than one period and to recognize the amortizations of any differential for all periods the investment was held. After these entries are made, the investment and equity in subsidiary's income accounts would be stated at equity and the consolidation process may continue. It is important to note that the formal consolidated statements will be the same regardless of the method used by the parent to account for the investment on its books. The concept of measurement used in the preparation of the consolidated statements is equivalent to the full equity method and the elimination process will result in statements presented under that concept.

J. **Intercompany Transactions and Profit Confirmation**

Three general types of intercompany transactions may occur between the parent and subsidiary companies. Intercompany transactions require special handling because the profit or loss from these events must be properly presented on the consolidated financial statements. The three types of intercompany transactions are: intercompany sales of merchandise; transactions in fixed assets; and intercompany debt/equity transactions. These events may generate "unrealized profit" (also referred to as unconfirmed profit) which is a profit or gain shown in the trial balance from one of the company's books, but should not be shown in the consolidated financial statements. Intercompany bond transaction may require recognition of a gain or loss on the consolidated financials which is not in the trial balances of either the parent or subsidiary companies.

1. Intercompany inventory transactions

Unrealized profit in ending inventory arises through intercompany sales above cost that are not resold to third parties prior to year end. Thus, the profit on the selling corporation's books is overstated, because an arm's length transaction has not yet taken place. The inventory is overstated on the purchaser's books for the amount of the unrealized intercompany profit. An exhibit of the relationships is shown below.

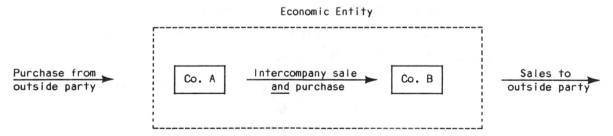

Companies A and B are two separate legal entities and will each record the sale or purchase of goods. From a consolidated or economic entity viewpoint, however, the intercompany transaction is a transfer of assets which cannot result in revenue recognition until these goods are sold to a third party. Assuming a sale from Company A to Company B (a "downstream"

intercompany sale), the sale income of Company A cannot be recognized until the goods are sold to third parties by Company B. In addition, the ending inventory of Company B is overstated by the amount of profit in the inventory acquired from Company A. Once intercompany sales have been sold to third parties, the earning process has been verified by an arm's-length transaction with third parties. Thus, recognition of previously unrecognized profit must be made at that time.

2. Intercompany fixed asset transactions

Unrealized profits on fixed assets arise through intercompany sales of fixed assets above undepreciated cost. From a consolidated viewpoint, the transaction represents the internal transfer of assets and no gain (loss) should be recognized. Therefore, any gain (loss) must be eliminated and the carrying value of the transferred asset must be returned to its initial book value basis. In subsequent periods, depreciation expense is overstated, because an overvalued asset is being depreciated on the books of the company showing the asset. This overstatement of depreciation must also be eliminated in the consolidation process.

3. Intercompany bond transactions

When one consolidated company buys bonds of another consolidated company, there are several reciprocal items to eliminate: investment in bonds and bonds payable, interest income and interest expense, and interest payable and interest receivable. Intercompany gains and losses cannot arise from direct intercompany bond purchases. The book value would be the same on both books and the interest accounts would be reciprocal. Note that APB 21 does not require the use of the effective interest method for debt transactions between parent and subsidiary companies. Straight-line amortizations of premiums or discounts are often used in these instances.

Gains and losses on intercompany bond holdings may occur when
a. Already outstanding bonds are purchased by a parent or subsidiary
b. From a third party
c. For an amount different from the carrying value of the issuer
However, the bonds are still recorded as liabilities on the issuer's separate books and as investment in bonds on the purchasing corporation's books. It is only from the consolidated position that these bonds may be viewed as being "retired." The eliminating entry is to recognize the gain (loss) on the consolidated "retirement of debt" in the year of intercompany

bond purchase. This gain (loss) would normally be an extraordinary item in accordance with SFAS 4.

K. **Example of Subsequent Consolidated Financial Statements**

The following information extends the basic example of A Company and B Company begun earlier in this module. The example illustrates the major consolidation concepts and procedures most likely to appear on the exam.

EXTENDED EXAMPLE

On January 1, 1986, A Company acquired 90% of the stock of B Company in exchange for 5,400 shares of $10 par stock having a total market value of $120,600.

The purchase method of accounting is used for the combination.

On January 1, 1986, B Company's assets and liabilities had the following book and fair values.

	Book Value	Fair Value
Cash	$ 37,400	$ 37,400
Accounts Receivable (net)	9,100	9,100
Inventories	16,100	17,100
Equipment	50,000	60,000
Accumulated Depreciation	(10,000)	(12,000)
Patents	10,000	13,000
Accounts Payable	(6,600)	(6,600)
	$106,000	$118,000

Any cost in excess of the fair values of the net assets of B Company was attributable to expected future earnings of B Company and will be amortized over a period of 10 years.

Financial statement data of the two companies as of December 31, 1986 (the end of the first year after combination) are presented below.

During 1986, A Company sold merchandise to B Company that originally cost A Company $15,000 and the sale was made for $20,000. On December 31, 1986, B Company's inventory included merchandise purchased from A Company at a cost to B Company of $12,000.

Also during 1986, A Company acquired $18,000 of merchandise from B Company. B Company uses a normal markup of 25% above its cost. A Company's ending inventory includes $10,000 of the merchandise acquired from B Company.

B Company reduced its intercompany account payable to A Company to a balance of $4,000 as of December 31, 1986, by making a payment of $1,000 on December 30. This $1,000 payment was still in transit on December 31, 1986.

On January 2, 1986, B Company acquired equipment from A Company for $7,000. The equipment was originally purchased by A Company for $5,000 and had a book value of $4,000 at the date of sale to B Company. The equipment had an estimated remaining life of 4 years as of January 2, 1986.

On December 31, 1986, B Company purchased for $44,000, 50% of the outstanding bonds issued by A Company. The bonds mature on December 31, 1991 and were originally issued at par. The bonds pay interest annually on

December 31 of each year and the interest was paid to the prior investor immediately before B Company's purchase of the bonds.

The consolidated worksheet for the preparation of consolidated financial statements as of December 31, 1986, is presented on the next page.

The investment account balance at the statement date should be reconciled to ensure the parent company made the proper entries under the method of accounting used to account for the investment. As noted earlier, A Company is using the partial equity method, without amortizations. The amortizations of the excess of cost over book value will be recognized only on the worksheets. This method is the one typically followed on the CPA exam; however, be sure you determine the method used in the exam problem--don't assume! The "proof" of the investment account of A Company is

Investment in Stock of B Company

Original cost	120,600		
% of B Company's income (90% x $9,400)	8,460	3,600	% of B Company's dividends declared (90% x $4,000)
Bal (12/31/86)	125,460		

Any errors will require correcting entries before the consolidation process is continued. Correcting entries will be posted to the books of the appropriate company; eliminating entries are <u>not</u> posted to either company's books.

The difference between the investment cost and the book value of the net assets acquired was determined and allocated in the preparation of the date of combination consolidated statements presented on page 622. For purposes of brevity, that process will not be duplicated here since the same computations are used in preparing financial statements for as long as the investment is owned.

A COMPANY AND B COMPANY CONSOLIDATED WORKING PAPERS
Year Ended December 31, 1986

Purchase Accounting
90% Owned
Subsequent, Partial Equity

	A Company	B Company	Adjustments and Eliminations Debit	Adjustments and Eliminations Credit	Minority Interest	Consolidated Balances
Income Statement For Year Ended 12/31/86						
Sales	750,000	420,000	(a) 38,000			1,132,000
Cost of Sales	581,000	266,000	(b) 5,000 (i) 900	(a) 38,000		814,900
Gross Margin	169,000	154,000				317,100
Depreciation and interest expense	28,400	16,200	(i) 1,800	(d) 750		45,650
Other operating expenses	117,000	128,400	(i) 1,710			247,110
Net income from operations	23,600	9,400				24,340
Gain on sale of equipment	3,000		(d) 3,000			
Gain on bonds				(e) 6,000		6,000
Equity in Subsidiary's Income	8,460		(f) 8,460			
Minority Income (.10 x $7,400)					740	(740)
Net Income	35,060	9,400	58,870	44,750	740	29,600
Statement of Retained Earnings for Year Ended 12/31/86						
1/1/86 Retained Earnings						
A Company	48,000					48,000
B Company		41,000	(g) 36,900		4,100	
Add Net Income (from above)	35,060	9,400	58,870	44,750	740	29,600
Total	83,060	50,400			4,840	77,600
Deduct Dividends	15,000	4,000		(f) 3,600	400	15,000
Balance December 31, 1986	68,060	46,400	95,770	48,350	4,440	62,600
Balance Sheet 12/31/86						
Cash	45,300	6,400	(1) 1,000			52,700
Accounts Receivable (net)	43,700	12,100		(1) 1,000 (c) 4,000		50,800
Inventories	38,300	20,750	(h) 900	(b) 5,000 (i) 900		54,050
Equipment	195,000	57,000	(h) 9,000	(d) 2,000		259,000
Accumulated Depreciation	(35,200)	(18,900)		(d) 250 (h) 1,800 (i) 1,800		(57,950)
Investment in Stock of B Company	125,460			(f) 4,860 (g) 120,600		
Differential			(g) 25,200	(h) 25,200		
Goodwill			(h) 14,400	(i) 1,440		12,960
Investment in Bonds of A Company		44,000		(e) 44,000		
Patents		9,000	(h) 2,700	(i) 270		11,430
Total assets	412,560	130,350				382,990
Accounts Payable	8,900	18,950	(c) 4,000			23,850
Bonds Payable	100,000		(e) 50,000			50,000
Capital Stock	154,000	50,000	(g) 45,000	5,000		154,000
Additional Paid-in Capital	81,600	15,000	(g) 13,500	1,500		81,600
Retained Earnings (from above)	68,060	46,400	95,770	48,350	4,440	62,600
Minority Interest					10,940	10,940
Total liabilities and equity	412,560	130,350	261,470	261,470		382,990

The following adjusting and eliminating entries will be required to prepare consolidated financials as of December 31, 1986. Note that a consolidated income statement is required and, therefore, the nominal accounts are still "open." The number or letter in parentheses to the left of the entry corresponds to the key used on the work sheet.

Step 1: Complete the transaction for any intercompany items in transit at the end of the year.

   (1)   Cash   1,000
             Accounts Receivable   1,000

   This adjusting entry will now properly present the financial positions of both companies and the consolidation process may be continued.

Step 2: Prepare the eliminating entries.

   (a)   Sales   38,000
             Cost of Goods Sold   38,000

   Total intercompany sales of $38,000 include $20,000 in a downstream transaction from A Company to B Company and $18,000 in an upstream transaction from B Company to A Company.

   (b)   Cost of Goods Sold   5,000
             Inventories   5,000

   The ending inventories are overstated because of the unrealized profit from the intercompany sales. The debit to cost of goods sold is required because a decrease in ending inventory will increase cost of goods sold to be deducted on the income statement. Supporting computations for the entry are

	In Ending Inventory of	
	A Company	B Company
Intercompany sales not resold, at selling price	$10,000	$12,000
Cost basis of remaining inter-company merchandise		
From B to A (÷ 125%)	(8,000)	
From A to B (÷ 133 1/3%)		(9,000)
Unrealized profit	$ 2,000	$ 3,000

When preparing consolidated work papers for 1987 (the next fiscal period), an additional eliminating entry will be required if the goods in 1986's ending inventory are sold to outsiders during 1987. The additional entry will recognize the profit for 1987 that was eliminated as unrealized in 1986. This entry is necessary since the entry at the end of 1986 was made only on the worksheet. The 1987 entry will be

   Retained Earnings--B Comp. (1/1/87)   2,000
   Retained Earnings--A Comp. (1/1/87)   3,000
        Cost of Goods Sold (1987)   5,000

(c) Accounts Payable   4,000
         Accounts Receivable   4,000

This eliminates the remaining intercompany receivable/payable owed by B Company to A Company. This eliminating entry is necessary to avoid overstating the consolidated entity's balance sheet. The receivable/payable is not extinguished and B Company must still transfer $4,000 to A Company in the future.

(d) Gain on Sale of Equipment   3,000
         Equipment   2,000
         Accumulated Depreciation   250
         Depreciation Expense   750

Eliminates the gain on the intercompany sale of the equipment, eliminates the overstatement of equipment, and removes the excess depreciation taken on the gain. Supporting computations for the entry are

	Cost	At date of intercompany sale accum. depr.	1986 depreciation expense	End-of-period accum. depr.
Original basis (to seller–A Co.)	$5,000	($1,000)	$1,000	($2,000)
New basis (to buyer–B Co.)	7,000	-0-	1,750	(1,750)
Difference	($2,000)		($ 750)	$ 250

If the intercompany sale had not occurred, A Company would have depreciated the remaining book value of $4,000 over the estimated remaining life of 4 years. However, since B Company's acquisition price ($7,000) was more than A Company's basis in the asset ($4,000), the depreciation recorded on the books of B Company will include part of the intercompany unrealized profit. The equipment must be reflected on the consolidated statements at the original cost to the consolidated entity. Therefore, the "write-up" of $2,000 in the equipment, the excess depreciation of $750, and the gain of $3,000 must be eliminated and the ending balance of accumulated depreciation must be shown at what it would have been if the intercompany equipment transaction had not occurred. In future periods, a retained earnings account will be used instead of the gain account; however, the other concepts will be extended to include the additional periods.

(e) Bonds Payable   50,000
         Investment in Bonds of A Company   44,000
         Gain on Extinguishment of Debt   6,000

This entry eliminates the book value of A Company's debt against the bond investment account of B Company. To the consolidated entity, this transaction must be shown as a retirement of debt even though A Company has the outstanding intercompany debt to B Company. SFAS 4 specifies gains or losses on debt extinguishment, if material, should be shown as an extraordinary item. In future periods, B Company will amortize the discount, thereby bringing the investment account up to par value and a retained earnings account will be used in the eliminating entry instead of the gain account.

(f)   Equity in Subsidiary's Income--A Co.   8,460
          Dividends Declared--B Co.   3,600
          Investment in stock of B Company   4,860

This elimination entry adjusts the investment account back to its
balance at the beginning of the period and also eliminates the
subsidiary income account.

(g)   Capital Stock--B Co.   45,000
       Additional Paid-in Capital--B Co.   13,500
       Retained Earnings--B Co.   36,900
       Differential   25,200
          Investment in Stock of B Co.--A Co.   120,600

This entry eliminates 90% of B Company's stockholders' equity at
the beginning of the year, 1/1/86. Note that the changes <u>during</u>
the year were eliminated in entry (f) above. The differential
account reflects the excess of investment cost greater than the
book value of the assets acquired.

(h)   Inventories   900
       Equipment   9,000
       Patents   2,700
       Goodwill   14,400
          Accumulated Depreciation   1,800
          Differential   25,200

This entry allocates the differential (excess of investment cost
over the book values of the assets acquired). Note that this
entry is the same as the allocation entry made to prepare consolidated financial statements for January 1, 1986, the date of
acquisition.

(i)   Cost of Goods Sold   900
       Depreciation Expense   1,800
       Other Operating Expenses--
         Patent Amortization   270
       Other Operating Expenses--
         Goodwill Amortization   1,440
          Inventories   900
          Accumulated Depreciation   1,800
          Patents   270
          Goodwill   1,440

This elimination entry amortizes the revaluations to fair market
value made in entry (h). The inventory has been sold and therefore becomes part of the cost of goods sold. The remaining revaluation will be amortized as follows.

	Revaluation	Amortization Period	Annual Amortization
Equipment (net)	$ 7,200	4 years	$1,800
Patents	2,700	10 years	270
Goodwill	14,400	10 years	1,440

The amortizations will continue to be made on future work
sheets. For example, at the end of the next year (1987), the
amortization entry (i) would be as follows.

Differential	4,410	
Depreciation Expense	1,800	
Other Operating Expenses--		
Patent Amortization	270	
Other Operating Expenses--		
Goodwill Amortization	1,440	
Inventories		900
Accumulated Depreciation		3,600
Patents		540
Goodwill		2,880

The initial debit of $4,410 to differential is an aggregation of the prior period's charges to income statement accounts ($900 + $1,800 + $270 + $1,440). During subsequent years, some authors prefer reducing the allocated amounts in entry (h) for prior period's charges. In this case, the amortization entry in future periods would reflect just that period's amortizations.

This extended example has assumed the purchase method was used to account for the combination of A Company and B Company. As a result, the consolidated financial statements will include the parent company's share of the revaluations to fair market values of the subsidiary's net assets. A pooling, however, is based on book values. No differential exists in pooling accounting and, thus, entry (g) above would be different while entries (h) and (i) would not be made for a pooling. All other eliminating entries would be the same. The basic elimination entry (g) for a pooling, using the equity method of accounting for the investment, would be

Capital Stock--B Co.	45,000	
Additional Paid-in Capital--B Co.	13,500	
Retained Earnings--B Co.	36,900	
Investment in Stock of B Company		95,400

L. Minority Interest

The parent company often acquires less than 100% (but more than 50%) of the subsidiary's outstanding stock. Under either the purchase or pooling method the consolidated financial statements will include all of the assets, liabilities, revenues, and expenses of these less than wholly-owned subsidiaries. The percentage of the stock not owned by the parent company represents the minority interest's share of the net assets of the subsidiary. Minority interest will be a line item deduction on the income statement for its portion of the subsidiary's income and, under the parent company concept, will be shown on the consolidated balance sheet after long-term debt but before stockholders' equity. The following procedures apply to cases of less than wholly-owned subsidiaries.

1) Only the parent's share of the sub's shareholders' equity is eliminated in the basic eliminating entry. The minority interest's share is presented separately.

2) The entire amount of intercompany reciprocal items is eliminated. For example, all receivables/payables and sales/cost of sales with a 90% subsidiary are eliminated.
3) For intercompany transactions in inventory and fixed assets, the possible effect on minority interest depends on whether the original transaction affected the subsidiary's income statement. Minority interest is adjusted only if the subsidiary is the selling entity. In this case, the minority interest is adjusted for its percentage ownership of the common stock of the subsidiary. The minority interest is not adjusted for unrealized profits on downstream sales. The effects of downstream transactions are confined solely to the parent's (i.e., controlling) ownership interests.

The minority interest's share of the subsidiary's income is shown as a deduction on the consolidated income statement since 100% of the subsidiary's revenues and expenses are combined although the parent company owns less than a 100% interest. For our example, the minority interest deduction on the income statement is computed as follows.

B Company's reported income	$9,400
Less: unrealized profit on an	
upstream inventory sale	(2,000)
B Company's income for con-	
solidated financial purposes	$7,400
Minority interest share	10%
Minority interest on	
Income Statement	$ 740

The minority interest's share of the net assets of B Company is shown on the Consolidated Balance Sheet between liabilities and controlling interest's equity. The computation for the minority interest shown in the balance sheet for our example is

B Company's capital stock, 12/31/86	$50,000	
Minority interest share	10%	$ 5,000
B Company's additional paid-in capital, 12/31/86	$15,000	
Minority interest share	10%	1,500
B Company's retained earnings, 1/1/86	$41,000	
Minority interest share	10%	4,100
B Company's 1986 income for consolidated purposes	$ 7,400	
Minority interest share	10%	740
B Company's dividends during 1986	$ 4,000	
Minority interest share	10%	(400)
Total minority interest, 12/31/86		$10,940

The remainder of the consolidation process is just work sheet techniques, as follows.

a. Take all income items across horizontally and foot the adjustments, minority interest, and consolidated columns down to the net income line.
b. Take the amounts on the net income line (on income statement) in the adjustments, minority interest, and consolidated balances columns down

to retained earnings items across the consolidated balances column. Foot and crossfoot the retained earnings statement.

c. Take the amounts of ending retained earnings in each of the four columns down to the ending retained earnings line in the balance sheet. Foot the minority interest column and place its total in the consolidated balances column. Take all the balance sheet items across to consolidated balances column.

M. Subsequent Consolidated Balance Sheet Only

Consolidation exam problems generally require only the Consolidated Balance Sheet. In this case, the effects of all the income statement account balances will have been closed to the retained earnings accounts. You should carefully review the adjustments and eliminations that were made noting that the nominal accounts (income statement accounts and Dividends Declared account) would be replaced with the account "Retained Earnings." Thus, elimination entry "(a)" would not be required; entry "(b)" would be

(b) Retained earnings	5,000	
Inventories		5,000

Retained earnings would be substituted for the nominal accounts in all other eliminating entries. A shortcut alternative to eliminating entries "(f)" and "(g)" is to use the ending balance of B Company's Retained earnings as follows.

(f & g) Capital stock--B Co.	45,000	
Additional paid-in capital--B Co.	13,500	
*Retained earnings--B Co.	41,760	
Differential	25,200	
Investment in stock of B Co.--A Co.		125,460

($41,760 = 90% x $46,400 ending balance of B Company's Retained earnings)

A worksheet for just the Consolidated Balance Sheet is presented on the next page. The adjusting and eliminating entries are keyed to the entries and entry explanations for the three-statement layout presented earlier. Several elimination entries have been combined and are shown as "(f/g)" or "(h/i)." Note that the final Consolidated Balance Sheet amounts are the same when only the balance sheet is being prepared as well as when all three statements are being prepared.

N. Consolidated Net Income and Consolidated Retained Earnings

In some cases, you may be asked just to determine the Consolidated Net Income (CNI) of the parent and subsidiary companies. A shorter, analytical approach may be used instead of the worksheet method. An analytical definition of CNI is exhibited for our example on the following page.

If the "full" equity method had been used to account for the investment, all the adjustments to the parent company's income (see following page) would

A COMPANY AND B COMPANY CONSOLIDATED WORKING PAPERS
CONSOLIDATED BALANCE SHEET ONLY
December 31, 1986

Purchase accounting
90% Owned
Subsequent, Partial Equity

	A Company	B Company	Adjustments and Eliminations Debit		Adjustments and Eliminations Credit		Minority Interest	Consolidated Balance
Assets								
Cash	45,300	6,400	(1)	1,000				52,700
Accounts receivable (net)	43,700	12,100			(1) (c)	1,000 4,000		50,800
Inventories	38,300	20,750	(h/i)	900	(b) (h/i)	5,000 900		54,050
Equipment	195,000	57,000	(h/i)	9,000	(d)	2,000		259,000
Accumulated Depreciation	(35,200)	(18,900)			(d) (h/i)	250 3,600		(57,950)
Investment in Stock of B Company	125,460				(f/g)	125,460		
Differential			(f/g)	25,200	(h/i)	25,200		
Goodwill			(h/i)	12,960				12,960
Investment in Bonds of A Company		44,000			(e)	44,000		
Patents		9,000	(h/i)	2,430				11,430
Total	412,560	130,350						382,990
Liabilities and Stockholder's Equity								
Accounts payable	8,900	18,950	(c)	4,000				23,850
Bonds Payable	100,000		(e)	50,000				50,000
Capital Stock	154,000	50,000	(f/g)	45,000			5,000	154,000
Additional Paid-in Capital	81,600	15,000	(f/g)	13,500			1,500	81,600
Retained Earnings	68,060	46,400	(b) (d) (f/g) (h/i)	5,000 2,250 41,760 4,410	(e)	6,000	4,440	62,600
Minority Interest							10,940	10,940
Total	412,560	130,350		217,410		217,410		382,990

Parent company's net income from <u>independent</u> operations		$26,600
± Parent company's share of subsidiary's equity income (loss) (equity accrual) (90% x $9,400--reported income of B Co.)	+	8,460
± Period's amortization of difference between cost and book value ($900--inventories; $1,800--equip.; $270--patent; $1,440--goodwill)	-	4,410
- Parent company's share of <u>unrealized</u> profit on intercompany transactions ($3,000--merchandise sale of A to B; $1,800--90% of sale of goods from B to A; $3,000--sale of equipment)	-	7,800
+ Parent company's share of <u>realized</u> profit on intercompany transactions ($6,000--bonds; $750--from elimination of excessive depr. on equip. sale from A to B)	+	6,750
CNI		$29,600

have been reflected in the "Equity in Subsidiary's Income" account on the parent company's books. Under the "partial" equity method, only the equity accrual of $8,460 is shown in the Equity in Subsidiary's Income account. All other adjustments are made only on the consolidated worksheet.

Consolidated Retained Earnings (CRE) may be determined once CNI is found. An analytical definition of CRE for our example is

Parent company's beginning Retained Earnings (1/1/86)		$48,000
+ Consolidated net income for period	+	29,600
- Parent company's dividends to its shareholders (note: subsidiary's dividends to outside parties are a component of minority interest, not CRE)	-	15,000
CRE		$62,600

Make special note that under the "full" equity method of accounting, consolidated retained earnings will equal the retained earnings of the parent company. This is true because consolidated retained earnings under the equity method equals beginning of the year consolidated retained earnings plus consolidated net income (which is identical to parent company net income), minus dividends declared during the year by the parent company only.

O. **Changes in Ownership**

Changes in the level of ownership of subsidiaries frequently occur through purchase or sale of the subsidiary's stock by the parent or changes in the sub's shares outstanding. If the subsidiary changes the number of shares outstanding (for example, through treasury stock transactions), the transaction may require an entry on the parent's books to maintain the parent's reciprocity in the net assets of the subsidiary.

For example, if the subsidiary, through treasury stock transactions, increases the relative book value owned by the parent, the increase must be recorded to maintain reciprocity between the investment account on the parent's accounting records and its equivalent stockholders' equity accounts in the subsidiary's books.

Investment in subsidiary	xx	
Paid-in capital		xx

On the other hand, if the subsidiary's treasury stock transactions decrease the parent's equity

Paid-in capital	xx	
Investment in subsidiary		xx

When the parent's share of ownership increases through a purchase of additional stock, simply debit investment and credit cash for cost. A problem occurs with consolidated income statements when the change in ownership takes place in mid-period. Consolidated statements should be prepared based on the ending ownership level. For example, assume that A Company increased its ownership of B Company from 90% to 95% on October 1, 1986. The investment was acquired at book value of $5,452.50 (5% X [$50,000 C.S. + $15,000 A.P.I.C. + $44,050 R.E. at 10-1-86]). If the subsidiary earned its income of $9,400 evenly over the year, the consolidated net income should reflect a net of

```
   90% x $9,400 x 12/12    = $8,460.00
 +  5% x $9,400 x  3/12    = $  117.50
   95%                       $8,577.50
```

The interim stock purchase will result in a new account being shown on the Consolidated Income Statement. The account is <u>Purchased Preacquisition Earnings</u> which represents the percentage of the subsidiary's earnings earned, in this case, on the 5% stock interest from January 1, 1986, to October 1, 1986. The basic eliminating entries would be based on the 95% ownership as follows.

```
Equity in Subsidiary's Income--A Co.     8,577.50
     Dividends Declared--B Co.                          3,600.00
     Investment in Stock of B Company                   4,977.50
Capital Stock--B Co.                    47,500.00
Additional Paid-in Capital--B Co.       14,250.00
Retained Earnings--B Co.                38,750.00*
Purchased Preacquisition earnings          352.50**
Differential                            25,200.00
     Investment in stock of B Co.--A Co.              126,052.50
```

```
 *[95% x $41,000 beginning 1986 balance      = $38,950 ]
  [Less preacquisition dividend of 5% x $4,000 =   ($200)]
  [Retained earnings available, as adjusted   = $38,750 ]
**($352.50 = 5% x $9,400 x 9/12)
```

Purchased Preacquisition Earnings is shown as a deduction along with Minority Interest to arrive at Consolidated Net Income. You should note that purchased preacquisition earnings are used only with interim acquisitions under the purchase accounting method; all poolings are assumed to take place at the beginning of the period regardless of when, during the period, the acquisition was actually made.

P. **Combined Financial Statements**

Combined financial statements is the term used to describe financial statements prepared for companies that are owned by the same parent company or individual. These statements are often prepared when several subsidiaries of a common parent are not consolidated. Combined financial statements are prepared by combining all of the separate companies' financial statement classifications. Intercompany transactions, balances, and profit (loss) should be eliminated in the same way as in consolidated statements.

CHANGING PRICES AND FOREIGN CURRENCY TRANSLATION

Alternative reporting models which could provide a solution to the changing price dilemma are constant dollar accounting, current cost accounting, and current cost/constant dollar accounting. It is recommended that candidates work through this section before studying the outline of SFAS 89.*

A. Constant Dollar Accounting

Constant dollar accounting is a method of reporting financial statement elements in dollars which have the same purchasing power. This method is often described as accounting in units of current purchasing power.

Purchasing power indicates the ability of a dollar to command goods and services. If the inflation rate during a given year for a group of items is 10%, then 110 end-of-year dollars are needed to purchase the same group of items which cost $100 at the beginning of the year. Similarly, a machine purchased at the beginning of that year for $1,000 would be presented in a year-end constant dollar balance sheet at a restated cost of $1,100. This represents the basic thrust of constant dollar accounting: the adjustment of historical data (nominal dollars) for changes in the general price level.

The adjustment of nominal dollar data is facilitated by the use of the Consumer Price Index, which reflects the average change in the retail prices of a wide variety of consumer goods. The adjustment is made by multiplying historical cost by the TO/FROM ratio.

$$\text{Historical cost (nominal dollars)} \times \frac{\text{Price level adjusting to}}{\text{Price level adjusting from}} = \text{Restated historical cost (constant dollar)}$$

For example, an asset was purchased on 12/31/85 for $20,000 and the Consumer Price Index was 100 on 12/31/85, 110 on 12/31/86, and 120 on 12/31/87. Restatement for end-of-year balance sheets would be

$$12/31/85 \quad \$20,000 \times \frac{100}{100} \quad = \quad \$20,000$$

$$12/31/86 \quad \$20,000 \times \frac{110}{100} \quad = \quad \$22,000$$

$$12/31/87 \quad \$20,000 \times \frac{120}{100} \quad = \quad \$24,000$$

$$\text{or}$$

$$\$22,000 \times \frac{120}{110} \quad = \quad \$24,000$$

---

*Although SFAS 89 made reporting of supplementary information concerning changing prices voluntary, rather than required, candidates should be prepared to answer several questions on this area in both the Theory and Practice Exams.

The preparation of constant dollar financial statements requires the classification of balance sheet items as either monetary or nonmonetary. Items are monetary if their amounts are fixed by statute or contract in terms of numbers of dollars. Examples include cash, accounts and notes receivable, accounts and notes payable, and bonds payable. By contract or statute these items are already stated in current dollars and require no restatement. Nonmonetary items, on the other hand, do require restatement to current dollars. Inventory, property, plant and equipment, and unearned service revenue are examples of nonmonetary items. Under some increasingly popular loan arrangements when the repayment of loan principal is adjusted by an index, the receivable/payable is classified as a nonmonetary item.

The holding of a nonmonetary asset such as land during a period of inflation need not result in a loss of purchasing power because the value of that land can "flow" with the price level (hence, the need for restatement). However, if a monetary asset such as cash is held during a period of inflation with no interest, purchasing power is lost because the cash will be able to purchase less goods and services at year end than at the beginning of the year. This type of loss is simply called a "purchasing power loss." If a firm's balance sheet included more monetary liabilities than monetary assets throughout a given year, a purchasing power gain would result, since the firm could pay its liabilities using cash which is 'worth less' than the cash they borrowed.

A simple example can illustrate both the restatement process and the effect of holding monetary assets. Assume that the Static Company has the following balance sheet at the beginning of period 1.

Static Co.
Beginning of Period 1
Consumer Price Index = 100

Cash	$1,000	Common Stock	$2,000
Land	1,000		
	$2,000		$2,000

If the index increases to 110 by the end of year 1 and no transactions have taken place, both the land and common stock would be restated to end-of-year dollars. But in order to maintain the same level of purchasing power that was present at the beginning of the year, Static Co. should also have cash of $1,100 at year end. The fact that the company held $1,000 cash throughout the year has resulted in a $100 purchasing power loss. The balance sheet at the end of period 1 would therefore be

Static Co.
End of Period 1
Consumer Price Index = 110

Cash	$1,000	Common Stock	$2,200[b]
Land	1,100[a]	Retained Earnings	(100)[c]
	$2,100		$2,100

[a]$1,000 \times \dfrac{110}{100}$ [b]$2,000 \times \dfrac{110}{100}$ [c]Purchasing power loss $1,000 - ($1,000 \times \dfrac{110}{100})$

1. Constant Dollar Balance Sheet

Preparation of a constant dollar balance sheet is an OBJECTIVE process. Monetary assets and liabilities need not be restated because they are already reported in end-of-year dollars. All other assets, liabilities, and owners' equity accounts (other than retained earnings) are restated in the same manner as were land and common stock in the Static Company example. Retained earnings is computed by adding constant dollar net income including purchasing power gains/losses less any dividends (converted to end-of-year dollars) to the beginning balance of retained earnings.

The following data will serve to better illustrate a more complex balance sheet restatement.

Equipment purchased 1/1/81	$60,000	Accumulated depreciation	$21,000
Equipment purchased 1/1/84	20,000	Accumulated depreciation	5,000
	$80,000		$26,000

Price indexes: 1/1/81, 100; 1/1/84, 120; 12/31/87, 150.

Adjustment to end-of-year dollars for a 12/31/87 balance sheet is as follows.

Equipment: $60,000 \times \dfrac{150}{100} = \$90,000$ Accumulated Depreciation: $21,000 \times \dfrac{150}{100} = \$31,500$

$20,000 \times \dfrac{150}{120} = \dfrac{25,000}{\$115,000}$ $5,000 \times \dfrac{150}{120} = \dfrac{6,250}{\$37,750}$

2. Constant Dollar Income Statement

Income statement items must also be restated to end-of-year dollars when constant dollar statements are prepared. For example, the depreciation expense related to the equipment purchased on 1/1/81 in the previous illustration would have to be multiplied by 150/100 in order to be properly stated on a constant dollar income statement for 1987. Similarly, all other revenue and expense items must be adjusted, as the following example illustrates.

Huskie Company
Historical Cost Income Statement
1987

Sales	$100,000
less Cost of Goods Sold	(50,000)
Gross Margin	50,000
less Depr. Expense	(10,000)
Other Operating Expenses	(25,000)
Net Income	$ 15,000

Sales and operating expenses incurred evenly throughout the year. Inventory sold during year purchased in first quarter. Depreciation expense related to building purchased 1/1/77. Indexes

1/1/77	100
First quarter, 87	180
1987 average	190
12/31/87	200

Huskie Company
Constant Dollar Income Statement
1987

Sales	$(100,000 \times \frac{200}{190})$	$105,263
less Cost of Goods Sold	$(50,000 \times \frac{200}{180})$	(55,556)
Gross Margin		49,707
less Depr. Expense	$(10,000 \times \frac{200}{100})$	(20,000)
Other Operating Expenses	$(25,000 \times \frac{200}{190})$	(26,316)
Income before Purchasing Power Gain (Loss)		$ 3,391

Notice that before the above income statement would be complete, the purchasing power gain or loss on net monetary items would have to be computed and included in the statement.

The computation of purchasing power loss in the Static Company example was rather simple since only one monetary item and no transactions were involved. The calculations become a little more difficult in more complex situtations. The basic format is as follows.

1) Determine all monetary items at the beginning and end of the year
2) Subtract monetary liabilities from monetary assets to determine "net monetary items"
3) Determine what the amount of year-end net monetary items would be if they were nonmonetary items

   a) Restate beginning net monetary items to year-end dollars
   b) Add all sources of monetary items (restated)
   c) Deduct all uses of monetary items (restated)

4) Compare the "as if" amount from (3) with the actual year-end net monetary items

   a) "As if" > actual ---- Purchasing power loss
   b) "As if" < actual ---- Purchasing power gain

Notice that if a firm has more monetary liabilities than monetary assets, the amount of net monetary items would be negative. Step 4, above, would still apply. For example, assume "as if" = ($10,000), and "actual" = ($20,000). A purchasing power loss would result because ($10,000) > ($20,000).

The following example illustrates the calculation of purchasing power gain or loss.

	Historical 12/31/86	To/From index	Constant dollar 12/31/86
Net monetary items - 1/1/86			
Cash, receivables, and other monetary assets	$300,000		
Current liabilities (all monetary)	(100,000)		
Long-term liabilities (all monetary)	(50,000) $ 150,000	110/100	$ 165,000
Add (sources of monetary items): Sales	1,290,000	110/106	1,338,680
	$1,440,000		$1,503,680
Deduct (uses of monetary items): Purchases	1,100,000		
Selling Expenses	570,000		
Interest Expense	20,000		
Cash Dividends	75,000		
Income Taxes	57,000		
	1,822,000	110/106	1,890,755
Net monetary items-historical	$ (382,000)		
Net monetary items-historical restated to 12/31/86 ("as if")			(387,075)
Net monetary items-12/31/86 (actual)			(382,000)
Purchasing power gain ("as if" < actual)			$ (5,075)

The following CPI-U indexes were assumed for the above illustration.

1/1/86	100	
1986	106	(Average)
12/31/86	110	

Note that the left hand column of numbers is a funds flow statement where funds are defined as <u>net</u> monetary items. It includes some items from the income statement which affect net monetary assets (such as sales) but not others (e.g., depreciation) which have no effect on net monetary items. Also note that this example is simplified--all sources and uses occurred evenly throughout the year (same restatement ratio used). A more realistic example might have some changes occurring evenly throughout the year, and some occurring at specific points during the year (requiring different restatement ratios).

B. **Current Cost Accounting**

Current cost accounting is a method of valuing and reporting assets, liabilities, revenues, and expenses at their current cost at the balance sheet date or at the date of their use or sale.

It is important to distinguish between constant dollar and current cost accounting. Constant dollar accounting is concerned only with changes in the unit of measure--from nominal dollars to units of general purchasing power. Current cost accounting discards historical cost as a reporting model. The following matrix from APB Statement No. 3, Appendix D, illustrates the different reporting options.

	Unit of Measure	
Relationship measured	Nominal (Unadjusted) Dollars	Constant Dollars
Historical Cost	1	2
Current Cost	3	4

1) <u>Historical Cost/Nominal Dollars</u>. The original cost of the asset or liability and generally no changes in specific prices or the general price level are recorded.

2) <u>Historical Cost/Constant Dollars</u>. Original cost is reported but measured in dollars of equal purchasing power. Changes in specific prices are generally not recorded.

3) <u>Current Cost/Nominal Dollars</u>. The relationship measured is no longer historical cost, but current cost. The effect of changes in the general price level is not separated from the effect of changes in specific value.

4) <u>Current Cost/Constant Dollar</u>. The relationship measured is current cost, but the measuring unit is restated dollars. Changes in both the general and specific price levels are separately recorded.

Both constant dollar and current cost accounting are based in part on the theory of <u>capital maintenance</u>, which measures income by the difference in net assets (adjusted for owner investments and withdrawals) at two points in time. In other words, income is not recognized unless net assets are maintained.

Two basic concepts of capital maintenance (financial and physical) can be used to separate return on capital (earnings) from return of capital (capital recovery). Remember, any capital which is "used up" during a period must be returned before earnings can be recognized. In other words, earnings is the amount an entity can distribute to its owners and be as well-off at the end of the year as at the beginning.

One way "well-offness" can be measured is in terms of financial capital. This concept of capital maintenance holds that the capital to be maintained is measured by the amount of cash (possibly restated into constant dollars) invested by owners. Earnings may not be recognized until the dollar investment in net assets, measured in units of money or purchasing power, is returned. The financial capital maintenance concept is the traditional view which is reflected in most present financial statements.

An alternative definition of well-offness is expressed in terms of physical capital. This concept holds that the capital to be maintained is the physical productive capacity of the enterprise. Earnings may not be recognized until the current replacement costs of assets with the same productive capabilities as the assets used up are returned. The physical capital maintenance concept supports current cost accounting which must be reported in some disclosures by certain entities (see SFAS 33). Again, the physical productive capacity may be measured in nominal or constant dollars.

A simple example can further clarify the two capital maintenance concepts. Suppose an enterprise invests $10 in an inventory item. At year end, the enterprise sells the item for $15. In order to replace the item at year end, it would have to pay $12 rather than $10. To further simplify, assume the increase in replacement cost is due to specific price changes, and there is no general inflation.

The financial capital concept would maintain that the firm is as well-off once the dollar investment ($10) is returned. At that point, the financial capital is maintained and the remaining $5 is return on capital, or income. The physical capital concept maintains that the firm is not as well-off until the physical capacity (a similar inventory item) is returned. Therefore, the firm must reinvest $12 to be as well-off. Then physical capital is maintained and only the remaining $3 is return on capital, or income.

1. Current Cost/Nominal Dollar Balance Sheet

Preparation of a current cost/nominal dollar balance sheet is fairly simple--for each item, the current cost is reported. Common stock is reported at the same amount as in conventional historical cost statements, and retained earnings is computed by adding to the beginning balance current cost net income less any dividends (already stated at current cost) declared during the year. No constant dollar adjustments are made.

2. Current Cost/Nominal Dollar Income Statement

Preparation of a current cost/nominal dollar income statement is more complicated, and an understanding of certain basic current cost concepts is necessary. Current cost income from continuing operations is sales revenue less expenses on a current cost basis. Realized holding gains (the difference between current cost and historical cost of assets consumed) are then added to arrive at realized income, which will always be equal to historical cost net income. Finally, unrealized holding gains (increases in the current cost of assets held throughout the year) are included to result in current cost net income.

An example should help clarify these terms. Bell Co. went into business on 1/1/87. 1987 sales revenue was $200,000 and purchases totaled $150,000. Inventory with a historical cost of $100,000 was sold when its current cost was $160,000. Ending inventory (historical cost, $50,000) had a year-end current cost of $80,000. No other revenue was realized or expenses incurred during 1987. Historical and current cost income statements for 1987 are presented below.

Bell Company
Income Statements

Historical cost/
nominal dollar basis

Sales	$200,000
less C.G.S.	(100,000)
Net Income	$100,000

Current cost/Nominal dollar basis

Sales	$200,000
less C.G.S.	(160,000)
Cur. Cost Income from Cont. Oper.	40,000
Realized Holding Gains (160,000 - 100,000)	60,000
Realized Income	100,000
Unrealized Holding Gains (80,000 - 50,000)	30,000
Current Cost Net Income	$130,000

(Net Income $100,000 ←→ Realized Income)

1987 journal entries for Bell Company in current cost system would be as follows.

a) Inventory   150,000
       Cash   150,000

b) Inventory   90,000
       Realizable
         Holding Gain   90,000

c) Cash   200,000
       Sales Revenue   200,000

d) Cost of Goods Sold   160,000
       Inventory   160,000

e) Realizable Holding Gain   90,000
       Realized Holding Gain   60,000
       Unrealized Holding Gain   30,000

In general, sales and some expense amounts (salaries, rent, etc.) will be the same under historical and current cost systems. However, whenever an expense represents the use or consumption of an asset whose current cost has changed since its acquisition (as with the inventory in the Bell Co. example), that expense must be expressed at the current cost of the asset when used. Realized holding gains are computed by comparing the current cost of assets when used or consumed with their historical cost. Unrealized holding gains for the period are determined by identifying changes in the current cost of assets held throughout the year (not used or consumed). Notice that the holding gains do not reflect changes in the general purchasing power. In other words, the holding gains are not reported net of general inflation when the reporting model is current cost/nominal dollar.

C. **Current Cost/Constant Dollar Accounting**

Current cost/constant dollar accounting is a method of accounting based on measures of current cost in terms of dollars which have the same general purchasing power. This method discards both historical cost (in favor of current cost) and nominal dollars as the unit of measurement (in favor of units of general purchasing power). One key point concerning current cost/constant dollar accounting: it attempts to separate both the effects of general inflation and changes in specific prices (measuring holding gains net of inflation).

The following two cases highlight differences in the various reporting models.

CASE FACTS

Date	Event	Historical cost	Current cost	Case 1 Price index	Case 2 Price index
1/1/87	Purchase of marketable security	$1,000	$1,000	100	100
12/31/87	Preparation of financial statements (Information pertains to marketable security)	1,000	1,600	120	180

Comparative Analysis

Reporting model	Income statement Case		Balance sheet Case	
	1	2	1	2
Historical Cost/Nominal Dollar	-0-	-0-	$1,000	$1,000
Historical Cost/Constant Dollar (a)	-0-	-0-	$1,200	$1,800
Current Cost/Nominal Dollar (b)	$600	$600	$1,600	$1,600
Current Cost/Constant Dollar (c)	$400	($200)	$1,600	$1,600

Supporting Computations

Case 1

Case 2

(a) $\$1,000 \times \dfrac{120}{100}$ $\$1,000 \times \dfrac{180}{100}$

(b) $\$1,600 - \$1,000$ $\$1,600 - \$1,000$

(c) $\$1,600 - \left(\$1,000 \times \dfrac{120}{100}\right)$ $\$1,600 - \left(\$1,000 \times \dfrac{180}{100}\right)$

1) Generally, no gains or losses are recognized under historical cost/nominal dollar or historical cost/constant dollar because the securities have not been sold; changes in current cost ignored (except in lower of cost or market)
2) Balance sheet amounts for historical cost/nominal dollar and historical cost/constant dollar are both historical cost; only difference is restatement into constant dollar
3) Gains and losses recognized in the last two alternatives due to changes in current cost. Amounts differ when nominal or constant dollars are used as measuring unit
4) All balance sheet amounts are expressed at current cost under the last two alternatives.

1. Current Cost/Constant Dollar Balance Sheet

All assets and liabilities are stated at current cost, as in a current cost balance sheet. Common stock would be adjusted to end-of-year dollars, while retained earnings will be equal to the beginning balance plus current cost/constant dollar net income less any dividend restated to end-of-year dollars.

2. Current Cost/Constant Dollar Income Statement

First, the current cost income statement is restated to end-of-year dollars. Then, both realized and unrealized holding gains must be computed net of inflation (as shown previously in Cases 1 and 2). Finally, a purchasing power gain or loss on net monetary items is computed in the same fashion as was done in constant dollar accounting.

D. SFAS 89

SFAS 89 supersedes SFAS 33 and its subsequent amendments. SFAS 89 <u>encourages</u>, but does not require, a business enterprise that prepares its financial statements in U.S. dollars and in accordance with U.S. generally accepted accounting principles to disclose supplementary information on the effects of changing prices. This statement consolidates prior requirements of SFAS 33, as amended, and presents them as <u>requirements</u> to be followed by enterprises that <u>voluntarily</u> elect to disclose this information. (See the outline of SFAS 89.) Disclosure requirements include

1. Net sales and other operating revenues
2. Income from continuing operations on a current cost basis
3. Purchasing power gain or loss on net monetary items
4. Increase or decrease in the current cost or lower recoverable amount of inventory and property, plant, and equipment, net of inflation
5. The aggregate foreign currency translation adjustment on a current cost basis, if applicable
6. Net assets at year end on a current cost basis
7. Income from continuing operations on a current cost basis per common share
8. Cash dividends per common share
9. Market price per common share at year end

The above information should be disclosed for each of the five most recent years. The five-year summary should be stated as either of the following

a. In average-for-the-year or end-of-year units of constant purchasing power
b. In dollars having a purchasing power equal to that of dollars of the base period

These disclosures are explained and illustrated in the following pages using the Moore Corporation as an example.

1. <u>Net sales and other operating revenues</u>

Revenues are stated at their current cost when sold and, therefore, their amount is the same on a historical cost or current cost system. Assume that net sales and other operating revenues for Moore Corporation are $253,000 for 1987.

2. <u>Income from continuing operations on a current cost basis</u>

The FASB requires only cost of goods sold and depreciation, depletion, and amortization expense of property, plant, and equipment be expressed on a current cost basis. Other revenues, expenses, gains, and losses may be measured at the amounts included in the primary income statement. Assume information with respect to Moore Corporation cost of goods sold was as follows

	Historical Cost	Units
Inventory, 1/1/87	$200,000	20,000
Production during 1987	107,000	10,700
Goods available	307,000	30,700
Inventory, 12/31/87	110,000	11,000
Cost of goods sold	$197,000	19,700

Moore estimates that the current cost per unit of inventory was $8.34 at 1/1/87 and $12.52 at 12/31/87. The average current cost of cost of goods sold as adjusted for changing prices would be [($8.34 + $12.52) ÷ 2 = $10.43], 19,700 units x $10.43 = $205,471.

Assume information with respect to Moore Corporation's depreciation, depletion, and amortization expense for PP&E was as follows.

	Historical Cost	Current Cost	Useful Life
Asset 1	$10,000	$11,050	5 years
Asset 2	$20,700	$22,000	5 years
Asset 3	$ 7,800	$ 8,100	5 years
Asset 4	$ 5,100	$10,850	5 years
	$43,600	$52,000	

Current cost depreciation, depletion, and amortization expense is [($43,600 + $52,000) ÷ 2 = $47,800 ÷ 5 = $9,560]. Depreciation, depletion, and amortization as reported on the primary statements is $8,720 ($43,600 ÷ 5 years).

Assume other operating expenses, interest expense, and the provision for income taxes as reported on the primary statements are $20,835, $7,165, and $9,000, respectively.

Income from continuing operations adjusted for changing prices is illustrated on page 685.

3. Purchasing power gain or loss on net monetary items

Purchasing power gain or loss is computed using the same process described earlier for constant dollar statements. Average-for-the-year dollars are used to illustrate the purchasing power gain or loss on net monetary items. Assume price indexes are as follows

1/1/87 price index	100
1987 average index	110
12/31/87 price index	115

Moore Corporation has the following information for net monetary items.

	Nominal dollars	Index	Average 1987 dollars
Balance--1/1/87	$70,500	110/100	$77,550
Decrease in net monetary liabilities during the year	(6,000)	*	(6,000)
Balance--12/31/87	$64,500	110/115	(61,696)
Purchasing power gain on net monetary items			$ 9,854

Assumed to be in average 1987 dollars.

4. Increase or decrease in the current cost or lower recoverable amount of inventory and property, plant, and equipment, net of inflation

    Assume that Moore Corporation's increase in current cost of inventory and property, plant, and equipment for 1987 is $24,608. The effect of increase in the general price level was $18,959. Therefore, the net of inflation amount, i.e., the excess of the increase in specific prices over the increase in general price level, is $5,649.

5. The aggregate foreign currency translation adjustment on a current cost basis

    Assume that Moore Corporation did not have any foreign operations.

6. Net assets at year end on a current cost basis

    Net assets include inventory and property, plant, and equipment at current cost and all other items as reported in the primary financial statements (restated into average-for-1987-dollars). Assume this amount is $97,070.

7. Income from continuing operations on a current cost basis per common share

    Assume that Moore Corporation has 200,000 shares of common outstanding at 12/31/87. Income from continuing operations on a current cost basis for 1987 is $969,000. Therefore, this disclosure requirement is $4.85 ($969,000 ÷ 200,000).

8./9. Cash dividends per common share and market price per common share at year end

    Assume that these amounts were $2.00 and $36.00, respectively. Moore Corporation would report these disclosures in a schedule of annual information (this format is shown; however, 6., 7., 8., and 9. would not be included, but they would be included in the five-year summary), in a five-year summary, and in notes to those schedules.

MOORE CORPORATION
STATEMENT OF INCOME FROM CONTINUING OPERATIONS ADJUSTED FOR CHANGING PRICES
For the Year Ended December 31, 1987

	As reported in the primary statements	Adjusted for changes in specific prices (current costs)
1. Net sales and other operating revenues	$253,000	$253,000
Cost of goods sold	197,000	205,471
Depreciation and amortization expense	8,720	9,560
Other operating expenses	20,835	20,835
Interest expense	7,165	7,165
Provision for income taxes	9,000	9,000
	242,720	252,031
2. Income from continuing operations on a current cost basis	$ 10,280	$ 969
3. Purchasing power gain or loss on net monetary items		$ 9,854
4. Increase or decrease in the current cost or lower recoverable amount of inventory and property, plant, and equipment, net of accumulated depreciation		$ 24,608
Effect of increase in general price level		18,959
Excess of increase in specific prices over increase in the general price level		$ 5,649
5. The aggregate foreign currency translation adjustment on a currenct cost basis		
6. Net assets at year end on a current cost basis		$ 97,070
7. Income from continuing operations on a current cost basis per common share		4.85
8. Cash dividends per common share		2.00
9. Market price per common share at year end		36.00

CLASSIFICATION OF MONETARY VS. NONMONETARY ITEMS
Assets

Item	Monetary	Nonmonetary	Requires analysis
Cash on hand, demand deposits, time deposits	X		
Foreign currency and claims to foreign currency	X		
Securities:			
Common stock (equity method not used)		X	
Preferred stock (convertible or participating), convertible bonds			X[a]
Other preferred stock or bonds	X		
Accounts and notes receivable, allowance for doubtful accounts	X		
Mortgage loans	X		
Inventories		X	
Loans to employees	X		
Prepaid expenses			X[b]
Long-term receivables	X		

Item	Monetary	Nonmonetary	Requires analysis
Refundable deposits	X		
Advances to unconsolidated subsidiaries	X		
Equity in unconsolidated subsidiaries		X	
Pension and other funds			X[c]
Property, plant and equipment and accumulated depreciation		X	
Cash surrender value of life insurance	X		
Purchase commitments (portion paid on fixed price contracts)		X	
Advances to supplier (not on fixed price contracts)	X		
Deferred tax assets	X		
Patents, trademarks, goodwill, and other intangible assets		X	
Deferred life insurance policy acquisition costs	X		
Deferred property and casualty insurance policy acquisition costs		X	

Liabilities

Item	Monetary	Nonmonetary	Requires analysis
Accounts and notes payable, accrued expenses payable	X		
Accrued vacation pay			X[d]
Cash dividends payable	X		
Obligations payable in foreign currency	X		
Sales commitments (portion collected on fixed price contracts)		X	
Advances from customers (not on fixed price contracts)	X		
Accrued losses on purchase commitments	X		
Deferred revenue			X[e]
Refundable deposits	X		
Bonds payable, other long-term debt, and related discount or premium	X		
Accrued pension obligations			X[f]
Obligations under warranties		X	
Deferred tax liabilities	X		
Deferred investment tax credits		X	
Life or property and casualty insurance policy reserves	X		
Unearned insurance premiums		X	
Deposit liabilities of financial institutions	X		

[a] If the market values the security primarily as a bond, it is monetary; if it values the security primarily as stock, it is nonmonetary.

[b] Claims to future services are nonmonetary. Prepayments that are deposits, advance payments, or receivables are monetary because the prepayment does not involve a given quantity of future services, but rather is a fixed-money offset.

[c] The specific assets in the fund should be classified as monetary or nonmonetary.

[d] If to be paid at the wage rates as of the vacation dates and if those rates may vary, it is nonmonetary.

[e] If an obligation to furnish goods or services is involved, deferred revenue is nonmonetary. Certain "deferred income" of savings and loan associations are monetary.

[f] Fixed amounts payable to a fund are monetary; all other amounts are nonmonetary.

E. **Foreign Currency Translation**

The rules for the translation of foreign currency into U.S. dollars apply to two major areas.

1) Foreign currency transactions which are denominated in other than a company's functional currency (e.g., exports, imports, loans) and
2) Foreign currency financial statements of branches, divisions, subsidiaries, and other investees which are incorporated with the financial statements of a U.S. company by combination, consolidation, or the equity method

The objectives of translation are

1) To provide information relative to the expected economic effects of rate changes on an enterprise's cash flows and equity and
2) To provide information in consolidated statements relative to the financial results and relationships of each individual foreign consolidated entity as reflected by the functional currency of each reporting entity

The first objective influences the rules for the translation of foreign currency transactions, while both objectives influence the rules for the translation of foreign currency financial statements. After working through this module, read through the outline of SFAS 52.

F. **Translation of Foreign Currency Statements**

Assume that a U.S. company has a 100% owned subsidiary in West Germany. The subsidiary's operations consist of leasing space in an office building. Its balance sheet at December 31, 1987 and its income statement for 1987 are presented below.

West German Company
Balance Sheet
December 31, 1987

Assets	Deutsche marks	Liabilities and owners' equity	Deutsche marks
Cash	60	Accounts Payable	100
Accounts Receivable (Net)	100	Mortgage Payable	200
Land	200	Common Stock	100
Building	500	Retained Earnings	360
Less Accumulated Depr.	(100)		
Total Assets	DM 760	Total Liabilities and Owners' Equity	DM 760

West German Company
Income Statement
For Year Ended December 31, 1987

Revenues	DM 260
Operating Expenses (includes depreciation expense of 20 DM)	160
Net Income	DM 100

In addition to the information above, the following data are also needed for the translation process.

1) Transactions involving land, building, mortgage payable, and common stock all occurred in 1982.
2) No dividends were paid during 1987.
3) Exchange rates for various dates follow.

    1DM = $.30 in 1982
    1DM = $.40 average for 1982 to 1987
    1DM = $.50 at beginning of 1987
    1DM = $.55 at end of 1987
    1DM = $.53 weighted average for 1987

If the U.S. company wants to present consolidated financial statements which include the results of its West German subsidiary, the financial statements of the West German company must be translated into U.S. dollars. However, before this can be accomplished, the management of the U.S. company must determine the functional currency of its West German subsidiary. SFAS 52 defines an entity's functional currency as ". . .the currency of the primary economic environment in which the entity operates; normally, that is the currency of the environment in which an entity primarily generates and expends cash." The decision concerning the functional currency is important because, once determined, it should be used consistently, unless it is clear that economic facts and circumstances have changed. The selection of the functional currency is dependent upon an evaluation of several factors. These factors include the following.

1) Cash flows (Do the foreign entity's cash flows directly affect the parent's cash flows and are they immediately available for remittance to the parent?)
2) Sales prices (Are the foreign entity's sales prices responsive to exchange rate changes and to international competition?)
3) Sales markets (Is the foreign entity's sales market the parent's country or are sales denominated in the parent's currency?)
4) Expenses (Are the foreign entity's expenses incurred in the parent's country?)
5) Financing (Is the foreign entity's financing primarily from the parent or is it denominated in the parent's currency?)
6) Intercompany transactions (Is there a high volume of intercompany transactions between the parent and foreign entity?)

If the answers to the questions above are predominantly yes, the functional currency would be the reporting currency of the parent, i.e., the U.S. dollar. On the other hand, if the answers to the questions were predominantly no, the functional currency would be the foreign currency. In the example described previously, the DM would be the functional currency if the answers were no. Note that the functional currency does not necessarily have to be the local currency of the foreign country when the answers to the questions are negative. In other words, it is possible for a foreign currency other than deutsche marks to be the functional currency of our West German company, e.g., Swiss francs or Italian lira could be the functional currency. However, assume these other possibilities are not alternatives in the example mentioned previously.

If the circumstances indicate the DM to be the functional currency, SFAS 52 mandates the current rate method for the translation of the foreign currency financial statements. This technique is illustrated below for the West German financial statements shown previously.

Balance Sheet
(Deutsche mark is Functional Currency)

	DM	Exchange rates	U.S. dollars
Assets:			
Cash	60	.55	33
Accounts Receivable (Net)	100	.55	55
Land	200	.55	110
Building (Net)	400	.55	220
Totals	DM 760		$418
Liabilities and Owners' Equity:			
Accounts Payable	100	.55	55
Mortgage Payable	200	.55	110
Common Stock	100	.30	30
Retained Earnings	360	see income statement	157
Translation Adjustments	--		66
Totals	DM 760		$418

Combined Income and Retained Earnings Statement

	DM	Exchange rates	U.S. dollars
Revenues	260	.53	$137.80
Operating Expenses (including 20 DM of depreciation expense)	160	.53	84.80
Net Income	100		53.00
Retained Earnings at 1/1/87	260	.40	104.00
Retained Earnings at 12/31/87	DM 360		$157.00

The following points should be noted from the illustration of the translation process.

a) All assets and liabilities are translated using the current rate at the balance sheet date. All revenues and expenses should be translated at the rates in effect when these items are recognized during the period. Due to practical considerations, however, weighted average rates can be used to translate revenues and expenses.

b) Owners' equity accounts are translated by using historical exchange rates. Common stock was issued in 1982 when the exchange rate was

1DM = $.30. The beginning balance of retained earnings for 1987 was accumulated when the weighted average exchange rate was 1DM = $.40.

c) Translation adjustments result from translating all assets and liabilities at the current rate, while owners' equity is translated by using historical rates and income statement items are translated by using weighted average rates. The translation adjustments balance is reported in the owners' equity section of the consolidated balance sheet.

d) The translation adjustments credit of $66 is calculated as follows (note the items below are the only ones not translated at the current rate).

Common Stock	100 DM (.55 - .30) =	$25
Retained Earnings 1/1/87	260 DM (.55 - .40) =	39
Net Income for 1987	100 DM (.55 - .53) =	2
	Translation Adjustment	$66

The illustration of the current rate technique assumed the DM to be the functional currency. Assume, however, that the circumstances were evaluated by the U.S. company, and the U.S. dollar was chosen as the functional currency. Under this alternative, SFAS 52 requires the foreign currency financial statements to be remeasured into U.S. dollars. According to SFAS 52, the ". . . remeasurement process is intended to produce the same result as if the entity's books of record had been maintained in the functional currency." If the U.S. dollar is the functional currency, the remeasurement of foreign currency financial statements into U.S. dollars makes translation adjustments unnecessary. The remeasurement process is illustrated below for the West German subsidiary. Note that the remeasurement process is similar to the temporal method of translation which was recommended in SFAS 8, the predecessor of SFAS 52.

Balance Sheet
(U.S. Dollar is Functional Currency)

	DM	Exchange rates	U.S. dollars
Assets:			
Cash	60	.55	33
Accounts Receivable (Net)	100	.55	55
Land	200	.30	60
Building (Net)	400	.30	120
Totals	DM 760		$268
Liabilities and Owners' Equity:			
Accounts Payable	100	.55	55
Mortgage Payable	200	.55	110
Common Stock	100	.30	30
Retained Earnings	360	see income statement	73
Totals	DM 760		$268

One significant difference between remeasurement and the temporal method is the translation of deferred taxes. Deferred taxes are now considered monetary and would be translated by using the current rate. Under SFAS 8, they were considered nonmonetary and were translated by using historical rates.

Combined Income and Retained Earnings Statement

	DM	Exchange rates	U.S. Dollars
Revenues	260	.53	$137.80
Expenses (exclusive of depreciation)	140	.53	$ 74.20
Depreciation	20	.30	6.00
Total Expenses	160		$ 80.20
Foreign Exchange Loss	--	--	10.60
Net Income (Loss)	100		$ 47.00
Retained Earnings at 1/1/87	260		26.00
Retained Earnings at 12/31/87	DM 360		$ 73.00

The following observations should be noted about the remeasurement process.

a) Assets and liabilities which have historical cost balances are translated by using historical exchange rates. Monetary assets and monetary liabilities, on the other hand, are translated by using the current rate at the balance sheet date.

b) Revenues and expenses that occur during a period are translated, for practical purposes, by using the weighted average exchange rate for the period. Revenues and expenses that represent allocations of historical balances (e.g., depreciation) are translated by using historical exchange rates.

c) The foreign exchange loss of $10.60 is reported on the consolidated income statement. The loss is the result of the remeasurement process which assumes the U.S. dollar is the functional currency.

d) The calculation of the loss is the result of the rules employed in the remeasurement process. In mechanical terms, the foreign exchange loss is the amount needed to make the debits equal the credits in the West German Company's U.S. dollar trial balance. Note this technique below.

	DM		Exchange rates	U.S. dollars	
	DR	CR		DR	CR
Cash	60		.55	33	
Accounts Rec. (Net)	100		.55	55	
Land	200		.30	60	
Building (Net)	400		.30	120	
Accounts Payable		100	.55		55
Mortgage Payable		200	.55		110
Common Stock		100	.30		30
Retained Earnings (1/1/87)		260			26
Revenues		260	.53		137.80
Expenses	140		.53	74.20	
Depreciation Exp.	20		.30	6	
Totals	DM 920	DM 920		$348.20	$358.80
Foreign Exchange Loss				10.60	
Totals				$358.80	$358.80

e) To fully understand the remeasurement proceeds when the U.S. dollar
    is the functional currency, the beginning balance in Retained
    earnings (1/1/87) should be examined. The exchange rate for the
    beginning balance in retained earnings is a combination of exchange
    rates from the remeasurement of the prior year's balance sheet. The
    schedule below shows the balance sheet at 1/1/87 and the calculation
    of the beginning balance of retained earnings.

Calculation of Balance Sheet - 1/1/87

	12/31/87 DM	Adjustments to get back to 1/1/87 DM	1/1/87 DM	1/1/87 Rates	1/1/87 $
Assets:					
Cash	60 }	{ + 140 Exp. }	40	.50	$ 20
Accounts Receivable (Net)	100 }	{ - 260 Rev. }			
Land	200		200	.30	60
Building (Net)	400	+ 20 Depr.	420	.30	126
Totals	DM 760				$206
Liabilities and Owners' Equity:					
Accounts Payable	100		100	.50	$ 50
Mortgage Payable	200		200	.50	100
Common Stock	100		100	.30	30
Retained Earnings	360	- 100 NI	260		26*
Totals	DM 760				$206

        * $206 - 180 = $26 plug

NOTE: Work backwards to get the 1/1/87 DM by taking out 1987 revenues and
        expenses (net them out against cash and receivables). Then, remeasure
        all accounts except retained earnings, which is plugged.

        The significant points to remember about the West German illustration are
summarized on the following page.

1) Before foreign currency financial statements can be translated into U.S. dollars, a decision has to be made regarding the functional currency.

2) If the functional currency is the foreign currency, the current rate method is used to translate to U.S. dollars. All assets and liabilities are translated by using the current rate at the balance sheet date. Owners' equity is translated by using historical rates while revenues (and gains) and expenses (and losses) are translated at the rates in existence during the period when the transactions occurred. A weighted average rate can be used for items occurring numerous times throughout the period. The translation adjustments (debit or credit) which result from the application of these rules are reported in owners' equity.

3) If the functional currency is the reporting currency (the U.S. dollar), the foreign currency financial statements are remeasured into U.S. dollars. All foreign currency balances are restated to U.S. dollars using both historical and current exchange rates. Foreign currency balances which reflect prices from past transactions (e.g., inventories carried at cost, prepaid insurance, property, plant, and equipment, etc.) are translated by using historical rates while foreign currency balances which reflect prices from current transactions (e.g., inventories and marketable equity securities carried at market, etc.,) are translated by using the current rate. Monetary assets and liabilities are translated by using the current rate. (Deferred taxes are translated by using the current rate.) Foreign exchange gains/losses that result from the remeasurement process are reported on the income statement under "Other Income (Expense)."

The above summary can be arranged in tabular form as shown below.

Functional currency	Functional currency determinants	Translation method	Reporting
Local currency of foreign company[a]	a. Operations not integrated with parent's operations b. Buying and selling activities primarily in local currency c. Cash flows not immediately available for remittance to parent	Current Rate (All assets/liabilities translated using current rate; revenues/expenses use weighted average rate; equity accounts use historical rates)	Translation adjustments are reported in equity section of consolidated balance sheet. Analysis of changes in accumulated translation adjustments disclosed via footnote.
U.S. Dollar	a. Operations integrated with parent's operations b. Buying and selling activities primarily in U.S. and/or U.S. dollars c. Cash flows immediately available for remittance to parent	Remeasurement (Monetary assets/liabilities use current rate; historical cost balances use historical rates; revenues/expenses use weighted average rates and historical rates, the latter for allocations like depr. exp.).	Foreign exchange gain/loss is reported on the consolidated income statement

[a]The functional currency could be a foreign currency other than the local currency. If this is the case, the foreign currency statements are first remeasured in the functional currency before they are translated to U.S. dollars using the current rate method.

Before proceeding to foreign currency transactions, a few comments concerning the translation of foreign currency financial statements in highly inflationary economies should be made. If the cumulative inflation rate is $\geq$ 100% over a three year period in a foreign country, the foreign currency statements of a company located in that country are remeasured into the reporting currency, i.e., the U.S. dollar. In other words, it is assumed the reporting currency is the functional currency. The flowchart on the next page summarizes the requirements of SFAS 52 with respect to foreign currency financial statements.

FOREIGN CURRENCY FINANCIAL STATEMENTS

Functional Currency = Local Currency	Functional Currency = Reporting Currency	Functional Currency ≠ Local Currency or Reporting Currency

```
                                    ┌─────────┐
                                    │  Start  │
                                    └────┬────┘
                                         │
                                         ▼
        ◇ Is functional currency      ◇ Is functional currency        ┌─────────────────┐
          the local currency? ──No──►   the reporting currency? ──No──►│ First remeasure  │
                                                                        │ into functional  │
                                                                        │ foreign currency │
              │ Yes                          │ Yes                      └────────┬─────────┘
              ▼                              ▼                                   ▼
     ┌──────────────┐              ┌──────────────┐              ┌──────────────┐
     │ Translate into│             │ Remeasure into│             │ Translate into│
     │ U.S. dollars  │             │ U.S. dollars  │             │ U.S. dollars  │
     │ using current │             │               │             │ using current │
     │ rate method   │             │               │             │ rate method   │
     └──────┬───────┘              └──────┬───────┘              └──────┬───────┘
            │                             │                             │
            ▼                             │                             │
      ┌─────────┐                         │                             │
      │   End   │◄────────────────────────┴─────────────────────────────┘
      └─────────┘
```

G. Translation of Foreign Currency Transactions

A foreign currency transaction, according to SFAS 52, is a transaction ". . . denominated in a currency other than the entity's functional currency." Denominated means that the balance is fixed in terms of the number of units of a foreign currency regardless of changes in the exchange rate. When a U.S. company buys or sells to an unrelated foreign company, and the U.S. company agrees either to pay for goods or receive payment for the goods in foreign currency units, this is a foreign currency transaction from the point of view of the U.S. company (the functional currency is the U.S. dollar). In these situations, the U.S. company has "crossed currencies" and directly assumes the risk of fluctuating foreign exchange rates of the foreign currency units. This exposed foreign currency risk may lead to recognition of foreign exchange gains or losses in the income statement of the U.S. company, as defined in SFAS 52. If the U.S. company pays or receives U.S. dollars in import and export transactions, the risk which occurs as the result of fluctuating foreign exchange rates is borne by the foreign supplier or customer, and there is no need to apply the procedures outlined in SFAS 52 to the transaction reported in U.S. dollars on the U.S. company's books, i.e., as part of stockholders' equity.

The following example will illustrate the terminology and procedures applicable to the translation of foreign currency transactions. Assume that U.S. Company, an exporter, sells merchandise to a customer in West Germany on December 1, 1986, for 10,000 deutsche marks (DM). Receipt is due on January 31, 1987, and U.S. Company prepares financial statements on December 31, 1986. At the transaction date (December 1, 1986), the spot rate for immediate exchange of foreign currencies indicates that 1 DM is equivalent to $.50. This quotation is referred to as a direct quotation since the exchange is stated in terms of a direct translation of the currency in which the debt is measured. To find the U.S. dollar equivalent of this transaction, simply multiply the foreign currency amount, 10,000 DM, by $.50 to get $5,000. Occasionally, spot rates are quoted indirectly (e.g., $1 is equivalent to 2 DM). In the example used, since $1 is equivalent to 2 DM, the foreign currency amount would be divided by 2 to get the U.S. dollar amount of $5,000 if an indirect quotation were used.

At December 1, 1986, the foreign currency transaction should be recorded by U.S. Company in the following manner.

Accounts receivable--West Germany	5,000	
Sales		5,000

The accounts receivable and sales are measured in U.S. dollars at the transaction date using the spot rate at the time of the transaction. While the accounts receivable is measured and reported in U.S. dollars, the receivable is denominated or fixed in DM. This characteristic can result in foreign exchange gains or losses if the spot rate for DM changes between the transaction date and the date the transaction is settled.

If financial statements are prepared between the transaction date and the settlement date, the FASB requires that receivables and liabilities denominated in a currency other than the functional currency be restated to reflect the spot rates in existence at the balance sheet date. Assume that, on December 31, 1986, the spot rate for DM is 1 DM = $.52. This means that 10,000 DM are worth $5,200, and that the accounts receivable denominated in DM are increased by $200. The following journal entry should be recorded as of December 31, 1986.

Accounts receivable--West Germany	200	
Foreign currency transaction gain		200

Note that the sales account, which was credited on the transaction date for $5,000, is not affected by changes in the spot rate. This treatment exemplifies the "two-transaction" viewpoint adopted by the FASB. In other words, making the sale is the result of an operating decision, while bearing the risk of fluctuating spot rates is the result of a financing decision. Therefore, the amount determined as sales revenue at the transaction date should not be altered because of a financing decision to wait until January 31, 1987, for payment of the account. The risk of a foreign exchange loss can be avoided either by demanding immediate payment on December 1 or by entering into a forward exchange contract to hedge the exposed asset (accounts receivable). The fact that U.S. Company, in the example, did not act in either of these two ways is reflected by requiring the recognition of foreign currency transaction gains or losses on this type of transaction. These gains or losses are reported on the U.S. Company's income statement as financial (nonoperating) items in the period during which the exchange rates changed.

It is also important to note that reporting transaction gains or losses before the transaction is settled results in reporting unrealized gains or losses. This is an exception to the conventional realization principle which normally applies. This practice also results in a timing (temporary) difference between pretax accounting income and taxable income. This is due to the fact that foreign exchange gains and losses do not enter into the determination of taxable income until the year they are realized. Thus, interperiod tax allocation adjustments are required.

To complete the previous illustration, assume that on January 31, 1987, the foreign currency transaction is settled when the spot rate is 1 DM = $.51. Note that the account receivable is valued at $5,200 at this point. The receipt of DM and their conversion into dollars should be journalized as follows.

Foreign currency	5,100	
Foreign currency transaction loss	100	
Accounts receivable--West Germany		5,200
Cash	5,100	
Foreign currency		5,100

The net effect of this foreign currency transaction was to receive $5,100 from a sale which was measured originally at $5,000. This realized net foreign currency transaction gain of $100 is reported on two income statements--a $200 gain in 1986 and a $100 loss in 1987.

It was stated previously that foreign currency transaction gains and losses on assets and liabilities, which are denominated in a currency other than the functional currency, can be hedged if the U.S. Company enters into a forward exchange contract. In the example, the U.S. Company could enter into a forward exchange contract on December 1 to sell 10,000 DM for a negotiated amount to a foreign exchange broker for future delivery on January 31, 1987. This forward contract is a hedge against the exposed asset position created by having accounts receivable denominated in DM.

The negotiated rate referred to above is called a futures or forward rate. In most cases, this futures rate is not identical to the spot rate at the date of the forward contract. The difference between the futures rate and the spot rate at the date of the forward contract is referred to as a discount or a premium. Any discount or premium must be amortized over the term of the forward contract, generally on a straight-line basis. The amortization of discount or premium is reflected in a separate revenue or expense account, not as an addition or subtraction to the foreign exchange gain or loss amount. Under this treatment it is important to observe that no net foreign exchange gains or losses result if assets and liabilities denominated in foreign currency are completely hedged at the transaction date.

To illustrate the preceding discussion, consider the following additional information for the example previously covered.

> On December 1, 1986, U.S. Company entered into a forward exchange contract to sell 10,000 DM on January 31, 1987 at $.505 per DM. The spot rate on December 1 is $.50 per DM.

The transactions which reflect the sale of goods and the forward exchange contract appear as follows.

Sale transaction entries		Forward exchange contract entries		
		(Futures Rate 1 DM = $.505)		

12/1/86 (spot rate 1 DM = $.50)

Accounts receivable –		Due from exchange broker	5,050	
West Germany 5,000		Due to exchange broker		5,000
Sales	5,000	Premium on forward		
		contract		50

12/31/86 (spot rate 1 DM = $.52)

Accounts receivable –		Foreign cur. trans. loss	200	
West Germany 200		Due to exchange broker		200
Foreign currency		Premium on forward contract	25	
transaction gain	200	Financial revenue		25
		($25 = $50/2 months)		

01/31/87 (spot rate 1 DM = $.51)

Foreign currency	5,100	Due to exchange broker	5,200	
Foreign cur. trans. loss 100		Foreign currency		5,100
Accounts receivable –		Foreign cur. trans. gain		100
West Germany	5,200			
		Cash	5,050	
		Due from exchange broker		5,050
		Premium on contract	25	
		Financial revenue		25

The following points should be noted from the entries above.

1) The net foreign currency transaction gain/loss is zero. The account "Due from Exchange Broker" is fixed in terms of U.S. dollars and this amount is not affected by changes in spot rates between the transaction and settlement dates. The account "Due to Exchange Broker" is fixed or denominated in DM. The U.S. Company owes the exchange broker 10,000 DM, and these must be delivered on January 31, 1987. Because this liability is denominated in DM, its amount is determined by spot rates. Since spot rates change, this liability changes in amount equal to the changes in accounts receivable because both of the amounts are based on the same spot rates. These changes are reflected as foreign currency transaction gains and losses which net out to zero.

2) The "Premium on Forward Contract" is fixed in terms of U.S. dollars. This amount is amortized to a financial revenue account over the life of the forward contract on a straight-line basis.

3) The net effect of this transaction is that $5,050 was received on January 31, 1987, for a sale originally recorded at $5,000. The $50 difference was taken into income via amortization.

SFAS 52 does not require a forward exchange contract in order for a hedge to take place. For example, it is possible for a foreign currency transaction to act as an economic hedge against a parent's net investment in a foreign entity. Assume that an American parent company has a wholly owned British subsidiary which has net assets of 2 million pounds. The parent company can borrow 2 million pounds to hedge its net investment in the

British subsidiary. Fluctuations in the exchange rate for pounds will have no effect on the parent company because of the foreign currency transaction. Note that SFAS 52 requires that transaction gains/losses resulting from hedging net investments in foreign entities be reported on the balance sheet in the same way that translation adjustments are reported.

The financial statement disclosures required by SFAS 52 consist of the following.

1) Aggregate transaction gain (loss) that is included in the entity's net income
2) Analysis of changes in accumulated translation adjustments which are reported as part of the entity's owners' equity
3) Significant rate changes subsequent to the date of the financial statements including effects on unsettled foreign currency transactions

H. Glossary

Discount or Premium on a Forward Contract

"The foreign currency amount of the contract multiplied by the difference between the contracted forward rate and the spot rate at the date of inception of the contract."

Foreign Currency Statements

"Financial statements that employ as the unit of measure a functional currency that is not the reporting currency of the enterprise."

Foreign Currency Transactions

"Transactions whose terms are denominated in a currency other than the entity's functional currency. Foreign currency transactions arise when an enterprise (a) buys or sells on credit goods or services whose prices are denominated in foreign currency, (b) borrows or lends funds and the amounts payable or receivable are denominated in foreign currency, (c) is a party to an unperformed forward exchange contract, or (d) for other reasons, acquires or disposes of assets, or incurs or settles liabilities denominated in foreign currency."

Foreign Currency Translation

"The process of expressing in the reporting currency of the enterprise those amounts that are denominated or measured in a different currency."

Forward Exchange Contract

"An agreement to exchange at a specified future date currencies of different countries at a specified rate (forward rate)."

Functional Currency

"An entity's functional currency is the currency of the primary economic environment in which the entity operates; normally, that is the currency of the environment in which an entity primarily generates and expends cash."

Local Currency

"The currency of a particular country being referred to."

Remeasurement

"If an entity's books and records are not kept in its functional currency, remeasurement into the functional currency is required. Monetary balances are translated by using the current exchange rate and nonmonetary balances are translated by using historical exchange rates. If the U.S. dollar is the functional currency, remeasurement into the reporting currency (the U.S. dollar) obviates translation."

Reporting Currency

"The currency in which an enterprise prepares its financial statements."

Transaction Gain or Loss

"Transaction gains or losses result from a change in exchange rates between the functional currency and the currency in which a foreign currency transaction is denominated. They represent an increase or decrease in (a) the actual functional currency cash flows realized upon settlement of foreign currency transactions and (b) the expected functional currency cash flows on unsettled foreign currency transactions."

Translation Adjustments

"Translation adjustments result from the process of translating financial statements from the entity's functional currency into the reporting currency."

MISCELLANEOUS

A. Personal Financial Statements*

Personal financial statements may be prepared for an individual, husband and wife, or family. Personal financial statements (PFS) consist of

1. Statement of financial condition--presents estimated current values of assets, estimated current amounts of liabilities, estimated income taxes and net worth at a specified date
2. Statement of changes in net worth--presents main sources of increases (decreases) in net worth (optional when a statement of financial condition is prepared)

Assets and liabilities, including changes therein, should be recognized using the accrual basis of accounting. Assets and liabilities should be listed by order of liquidity and maturity, not a current/noncurrent basis.

In PFSs, <u>assets</u> should be presented at their estimated current value. This is an amount at which the item could be exchanged assuming both parties are well informed, neither party is compelled to buy or sell, and material disposal costs are deducted to arrive at current values. <u>Liabilities</u> should be presented at the lesser of the discounted amount of cash to be paid or the current cash settlement amount. Income taxes payable should include unpaid income taxes for completed tax years and the estimated amount for the elapsed portion of the current tax year. Also, PFSs should include the estimated income tax on the difference between the current value (amount) of assets (liabilities) and their respective tax bases as if they had been realized or liquidated. The table below summarizes the methods of determining "estimated current values" for assets and "estimated current amounts" for liabilities.

Business interests which comprise a large portion of a person's total assets should be shown separately from other investments. An investment in a separate entity which is marketable as a going concern (e.g., closely held corporation) should be presented as one amount. If the investment is a limited business activity, not conducted in a separate business entity, separate asset and liability amounts should be shown (e.g., investment in real estate and related mortgage). Of course, only the person's beneficial interest in the investment is included in their PFS.

---

*The source of GAAP for personal financial statements is AICPA Statement of Position 82-1 which has been summarized in this module. (These are not outlined in this text)

Assets and liabilities	Discounted cash flow	Market price	Appraised value	Other
• Receivables	X			
• Marketable securities		X		
• Options		X		
‐ Investment in life insurance				Cash value less outstanding loans
• Investment in closely held business	X		X	Liquidation value, multiple of earnings, reproduction value, adjustment of book value or cost
• Real estate	X		X	Sales of similar property
• Intangible assets	X			
• Future interests (non-forfeitable rights)	X			
• Payables and other liabilities	X			Discharge amount if lower than discounted amount
• Noncancellable commitments	X			
• Income taxes payable				Unpaid income tax for completed tax years and estimated income tax for elapsed portion of current tax year to date of financial statements
• Estimated income tax on difference between current values of assets and current amounts of liabilities and their respective tax bases				Computed as if current value of assets and liabilities had been respectively realized or liquidated considering applicable tax laws and regulations, recapture provisions and carryovers

B. Interim Reporting

The term interim reporting is used to describe financial reporting for periods of less than one year, generally quarterly financial statements. The primary purposes of interim reporting are to provide information which is more timely than is available in annual reports, and to highlight business turning points which could be "buried" in annual reports.

There are two basic conceptual approaches to interim reporting: the discrete view and the integral view.

Discrete view--each interim period is a separate accounting period; interim period must stand on its own; same principles and procedures as for annual reports; no special accruals or deferrals.

Integral view--each interim period is an integral part of an annual period; expectations for annual period must be reflected in interim reports; special accruals, deferrals, and allocations utilized.

APB 28 (see outline) adopted the integral view.

APB 28 consists of two parts. Part one does not require issuance of interim financial statements, but does prescribe accounting standards to be used in preparing such statements. Part two sets forth minimum disclosures to be included in interim financial reports.

The table below summarizes the accounting standards set forth in part one of APB 28.

Income statement item	General rule	Exceptions
Revenues	Same basis as annual reports	None
Cost of goods sold	Same basis as annual reports	1. Gross profit method may be used to estimate CGS and ending inventory for each interim period 2. Liquidation of LIFO base-period inventory, if expected to be replaced by year end, should not affect interim CGS 3. Temporary declines in inventory market value need not be recognized 4. Planned manufacturing variances should be deferred if expected to be absorbed by year end
All other costs and expenses	Same basis as annual reports	Expenditures which **clearly benefit** more than one interim period may be allocated among periods benefitted, e.g., annual repairs, property taxes
Income taxes	(Year-to-date income) x (estimated annual tax rate), less (expense recognized in previous quarters)	None
Discontinued operations	Recognized in interim period as incurred	None
Extraordinary items	Recognized in interim period as incurred. Materiality is evaluated based upon expected annual results	None
Change in accounting principle	Retroactive—same as annual reports. Cumulative effect—if change made in first quarter, report cumulative effect in first quarter's results. If change made in 2nd or 3rd quarter, report cumulative effect only in 6 or 9 month summary	None

The disclosures required in part two of APB 28 are summarized in the pronouncement outline. A key disclosure item for interim reporting is the seasonal nature of the firm's operations. This disclosure helps prevent misleading inferences and predictions about annual results.

APB 28 as interpreted by FASB Interpretation 18 requires that income tax expense be estimated each period using an estimated annual effective tax rate (see FASB Interpretation 18). The example below illustrates the application of this requirement.

	(a)	(b)	(c)	(d) = (b)x(c)	(e)	(f) = (d)-(e)
Qtr.	Quarterly income before income taxes	Year-to-date income before income taxes	Estimated annual effective tax rate	Year-to-date income tax expense	Previous quarters' expense	Current quarter's expense
1	$100,000	$100,000	30%	$ 30,000	$ 0	$ 30,000
2	150,000	250,000	32%	80,000	30,000	50,000
3	300,000	550,000	36%	198,000	80,000	118,000
4	200,000	750,000	35%	262,500	198,000	64,500

In the above chart, columns (a) and (c) are assumed to be given. Column (b) is obtained by accumulating column (a) figures. Column (e) is either the preceding quarter's entry in column (d) or the cumulative total of previous quarters in column (f).

C. **Segment Reporting**

SFAS 14 (see outline) sets forth financial reporting standards for segments of a business enterprise. Four different types of segment information must be disclosed.

1. Different industries
2. Foreign operations and geographic areas
3. Export sales
4. Major customers

The purpose of segment disclosure is to assist investors and lenders in assessing the future potential of an enterprise. Consolidated statements give the user the overall view (results of operations, financial position, cash flows). However, trends, opportunities, risk factors, etc., can get lost when data for a diversified company are merged into consolidated statements. Additionally, most intersegment transactions that are eliminated from consolidated financial information are included in segment information. Consolidated statements refer to the primary statements of the reporting entity. They are not limited to the statements of parent and subsidiaries (the conventional meaning of the term consolidated statements). Note that segment information pertaining to unconsolidated subsidiaries or other unconsolidated investees (i.e., corporate joint venture or 50 percent or less owned investee) should be reported if it satisfies the tests of SFAS 14. Segment disclosure, as required by SFAS 14, breaks out this useful, more detailed information from the consolidated statements.

Different industries. Certain disclosures must be made for significant industry segments. An industry segment sells a related group of products primarily to unaffiliated customers for a profit. An industry segment is significant (reportable) if it satisfies at least one of the following three 10% tests.

Revenues--10% or more of combined segment revenue (including intersegment revenue)

Operating profit or loss--10% or more of the greater of combined profit of segments reporting profit, or combined loss of segments reporting loss

Identifiable assets--10% or more of combined segment identifiable assets

The key disclosures for reportable segments are sales to unaffiliated customers, intersegment sales, operating profit or loss, and identifiable assets, all reconciled to consolidated amounts. Other disclosures include depreciation, depletion and amortization expense, and capital expenditures.

Operating profit or loss is unaffiliated revenue and intersegment revenue, less all operating expenses, including common costs (operating expenses incurred for the benefit of more than one segment). Common costs are generally allocated based on relative revenue or profit before allocation. General corporate revenues and expenses (interest, taxes, X/O items, etc.) are not allocated. Similarly, identifiable assets used by more than one segment are allocated to those segments, but general corporate assets (cash and marketable securities) are not allocated.

There are some limitations to the number of segments which are to be reported. There must be enough segments reported so that at least 75% of unaffiliated revenues is shown by reportable segments (75% test). Also, the number of reportable segments should not be so large (10 is a rule of thumb) as to make the information less useful. When a reportable segment is excluded or a nonreportable segment included, appropriate disclosure must be made.

The following example illustrates the three 10% tests (revenues, operating profit or loss, and identifiable assets) and the 75% test.

Segment	Unaffiliated revenue	Intersegment revenue	Total revenue	Operating profit (loss)	Identifiable assets
A	$ 90	$ 90	$ 180	$ 20	$ 70
B	120		120	10	50
C	110	20	130	(40)	90
D	200		200	0	140
E	330	110	440	(100)	230
F	380		380	60	260
Total	$1,230	$220	$1,450	$ (50)	$840

Revenues test: (10%)($1,450) = $145
   Reportable segments: A, D, E, F

Operating profit or loss test: (10%)($140) = $14
   Reportable segments: A, C, E, F
   [Note: Operating loss ($140) is greater than operating profit, $90]

Identifiable assets test: (10%)($840) = $84
   Reportable segments: C, D, E, F

Reportable segments: Those segments which pass at least one of the 10% tests.
   Segments A, C, D, E, and F are reportable in this example.

75% test: (75%)($1,230) = $922.50
   Segments A, C, D, E, and F have total unaffiliated revenue of $1,110, which is greater than $922.50. The 75% test is satisfied; no additional segments need be reported

Foreign operations, geographic areas, and export sales. Information must be disclosed for foreign operations in general, or geographic areas specifically, if at least one of the following two 10% tests are met.

Revenues (unaffiliated): 10% or more of consolidated revenue
Identifiable assets: 10% or more of consolidated total assets

The key disclosures are sales to unaffiliated customers, inter-area sales, operating profit or loss, and identifiable assets, all reconciled to consolidated amounts. This information is disclosed for foreign operations in total if there are no reportable geographic areas, or for each reportable geographic area. Domestic operations are also disclosed.

Disclosure is also required if sales to unaffiliated customers outside the U.S. are equal to or exceed 10% of consolidated revenue. Note this disclosure is required independently of that for foreign operations and geographic areas.

Major customers. Certain disclosures are made concerning major customers if the following 10% test is met. If 10% or more of consolidated revenue comes from a single customer, the enterprise must disclose this fact in addition to the amount of such revenues, and the industry segment making the sales.

Practice and theory multiple choice questions on segment reporting have emphasized industry segments (more specifically, operating profit or loss, the 10% tests, and allocation of common costs). Essay questions have emphasized definitions (industry segment, revenue, operating profit and loss, identifiable assets), the 10% tests, the 75% test, and the rule of thumb for maximum number of segments. There have been no segment reporting practice problems.

D. **Ratio Analysis**

Ratio analysis familiarity is often required on the CPA examination, especially on objective questions. Financial ratios are used to evaluate a particular firm against industry norms, e.g., a current ratio of 1:1 may be indicative of solvency problems for a company in an industry where experience has determined 2.5:1 to be a reasonable current ratio.

Financial ratios generally relate to solvency, operational efficiency, and also to profitability.

1. Solvency (Short-Term Viability)

    a. Acid, quick--measures ability to pay current liabilities from cash and near-cash items

$$\frac{\text{Cash, Net receivables, Marketable securities}}{\text{Current liabilities}}$$

b. Current--measures ability to pay current liabilities from cash, near-cash and cash-flow items

$$\frac{\text{Current assets}}{\text{Current liabilities}}$$

2. Operational Efficiency

a. Asset turnover--indicates how efficiently an enterprise utilizes its assets

$$\frac{\text{Net sales}}{\text{Total assets}}$$

b. Inventory turnover--measures the number of times inventory was sold and reflects inventory order and investment policies

$$\frac{\text{Cost of goods sold}}{\text{Average inventory}}$$

c. Number of days supply in average inventory--number of days inventory is held before sale; reflects on efficiency of inventory policies

$$\frac{365*}{\text{Inventory turnover}}$$

d. Receivable turnover

$$\frac{\text{Net credit sales}}{\text{Average net receivables}}$$

e. Number of days sales in average receivables--average length of outstanding receivables which reflects on credit and collection policies

$$\frac{365*}{\text{Receivable turnover}}$$

f. Length of operating cycle--measures length of time from purchase of inventory to collection of cash

$$
\begin{array}{c}
\text{Number of days} \\
\text{supply in average} \\
\text{inventory}
\end{array}
+
\begin{array}{c}
\text{Number of days} \\
\text{sales in average} \\
\text{receivables}
\end{array}
$$

3. Leverage (Long-Term Risk)

a. Times interest earned--measure of ability to pay interest costs

$$\frac{\text{Net income + Interest expense + Income taxes}}{\text{Interest expense}}$$

b. Debt ratio--percent of assets financed by creditors. One minus the debt ratio equals the percent of assets financed by stockholders.

$$\frac{\text{Total liabilities}}{\text{Total assets}}$$

c. Debt to equity--measures leverage

$$\frac{\text{Total liabilities}}{\text{Common stockholders' equity}}$$

d. Leverage is the common stockholders' ability to profit from rates of return on assets which exceed the cost of liabilities. Conversely, rates of return below cost of liabilities magnify stockholders' losses.

*Alternatively 300 or 360 may be considered the number of days in a year.

EXAMPLE:

Leverage

Total assets	$100,000	Total liabilities	$90,000
		Shareholders' equity	10,000

Assume 5% average interest cost on all liabilities, i.e., interest expense is $4,500.

If net income, before interest expense, is $10,000 (10% return on assets), the return on shareholder equity is $5,500 (55%).

If net income, before interest expense, is $2,000 (2% return on assets), the return on shareholder equity is -$2,500 (-25%).

4. Profitability

    a. EPS--measures income per share of ownership

    Net income available to common stockholders, e.g., less pref. div.
    Average shares outstanding

    b. Profit margin--measures the percent of profit on each dollar of sales

    $$\frac{\text{Net income}}{\text{Net sales}}$$

    c. Rate of return on assets--permits analysis of the components of return of assets (i.e., profit margin and asset turnover)

    Profit margin x Asset turnover

    d. Common stock yield--measures cash flow return on investment in common stock

    $$\frac{\text{Dividend per share}}{\text{Market value per share}}$$

    e. Book value of common stock (at a point in time)--not a meaningful measure as assets are carried at historical costs

    $$\frac{\text{Common stockholders' equity}}{\text{Shares outstanding}}$$

    f. Rate of return on common stockholders' equity--measures the return earned on the stockholders' investment in the firm

    $$\frac{\text{Net income available to common stockholders}}{\text{Common stockholders' equity}}$$

5. Common size financial statements are set forth as percentages in place of the traditional dollar amounts, e.g., every item in the statements expressed as a percent of sales. Common size statements permit relative efficiency of different sized companies to be compared and evaluated.

6. Other

    Many ratios exist. You should be able to identify numerator and denominator by their title, e.g., sales to fixed assets.

    a. Price-earnings (an important ratio which determines the amount of capital available through stock issuances)
    b. Sales to fixed assets

   c. Sales to owners' equity
   d. Owners' equity to total liabilities
   e. Fixed assets to long-term debt
   f. Dividend payout ratio
   g. Cash flow per share
   h. Book value per preferred share (using the stock's liquidation value)

Caution: Be careful to determine the appropriate dollar figure to use as numerator or denominator after you understand the concept, e.g., accounts receivable, shares outstanding, etc. Consider the following before settling on the amount.

   1. Average or year end (e.g., shares outstanding)
   2. Net or gross (e.g., receivables)
   3. Before or after adjusting items (e.g., taxes, preferred dividends, etc.)

Evaluate the purpose and usefulness of ratios in terms of the following categories.

   1. Solvency
   2. Operational efficiency
   3. Leverage
   4. Overall profitability, value

E. Partnership Accounting

There are no authoritative pronouncements concerning the accounting for partnerships; thus, all of the principles described below have evolved through accounting practice.

Partnership accounting typically is tested through a few multiple choice questions on the accounting practice exam. Occasionally, the material is tested through a problem.

1. Partnership Formation

The partnership is a separate <u>accounting entity</u> (not to be confused with a separate legal entity), and therefore its assets and liabilities should remain separate and distinct from the individual partners' personal assets and liabilities.

Thus, all assets contributed to the partnership are recorded by the partnership at their <u>fair market values</u>. All liabilities assumed by the partnership are recorded at their <u>present values</u>.

Upon formation, the amount credited to each partner's capital account is the difference between the fair market value of the assets contributed and the present value of the liabilities assumed from that partner. The capital accounts represent the residual equity of the partnership. The capital account of each partner reflects all of the activity of an individual partner: contributions, withdrawals, and the distributive share of net income (loss). In some cases, a <u>drawing</u> account is used as a clearing account for each partner's transactions with only the net effect of each period's activity shown in the capital account.

EXAMPLE: Partnership Formation

A and B form a partnership. A contributes cash of $50,000, while B contributed land with a fair market value of $50,000 and the partnership assumes a liability on the land of $25,000.

The entry to record the formation of the partnership is

Cash	*50,000*	
Land	*50,000*	
Liabilities		*25,000*
A Capital		*50,000*
B Capital		*25,000*

2. Allocation of Partnership Income (Loss)

The partners should have a written agreement (articles of co-partnership) specifying the manner in which partnership income (loss) is to be distributed. Note that in the absence of a predetermined agreement, the profit and loss (P&L) is divided equally among the partners.

It is important to remember that P&L should <u>not</u> be distributed using a ratio based on the partners' capital balances unless this is the ratio specified in the articles of co-partnership. A number of issues arise which complicate the allocation of partnership income (loss).

a. Partners may receive interest on their capital balances. If so, it must be determined what will constitute the capital balance (e.g., the year-end amount or some type of weighted-average).

b. Some of the partners may receive a salary

c. Some of the partners may receive a bonus on distributable net income. If so, you need to determine if the bonus should be computed before or after salary and interest allocations.

d. A formula needs to be determined for allocating the remaining income. The formula agreed upon is usually termed the <u>residual</u>, <u>remainder</u>, or <u>profit (loss) sharing ratio</u>.

e. Finally, the partners should decide upon how income is to be allocated if net income is insufficient to cover partners' salaries, bonuses, and interest allocations. These allocations are usually made even if the effect is to create a negative remainder. This remainder is usually allocated in accordance with the profit (loss) ratio. However, it is important to note that partners may choose to allocate losses (or a negative remainder) in a different manner than income.

EXAMPLE: Partnership P&L Distribution

Partners receive 5% interest on beginning capital balances
Partner B receives a $6,000 salary
Partner C receives a 10% bonus after interest and salaries
The P&L ratios are A -- 50%, B -- 30%, C -- 20%

Assuming partnership net income of $18,250, the following distribution schedule would be prepared.

		A	B	C
P&L ratio		50%	30%	20%
Beginning capital balance		30,000	10,000	5,000
	Cumulative distribution			
5% interest	2,250	1,500	500	250
Salary	8,250		6,000	
Bonus	9,250			1,000*
Remaining dist.	18,250	4,500	2,700	1,800
P&L dist.		6,000	9,200	3,050
Ending capital balances		36,000	19,200	8,050

*($18,250 - $8,250) x .10 = $1,000

Note that if the interest, salary, and bonus allocation had exceeded net income, the excess would have been deducted on the distribution schedule in the P&L ratio.

3. Partnership Dissolution (Changes in Ownership)

Partnership dissolution occurs whenever there is a change in ownership (e.g., the addition of a new partner, or the retirement or death of an existing partner). This is not to be confused with partnership liquidation which is the winding up of partnership affairs and termination of the business. Under dissolution the partnership business continues, but under different ownership.

When partnership dissolution occurs a new accounting entity results. The partnership should first adjust its records so that all accounts are properly stated at the date of dissolution. After the income (loss) has been properly allocated to the existing partners' capital accounts, all assets and liabilities should be adjusted to their fair market value and their present values, respectively. The latter step is performed because the dissolution results in a new accounting entity.

After all adjustments have been made, the accounting for dissolution depends on the type of transaction that caused the dissolution. These transactions can be broken down into two types.

•   Transactions between the partnership and a partner (e.g., a new partner contributes assets, or a retiring partner withdraws assets)
•   Transactions between partners (e.g., a new partner purchases an interest from one or more existing partners, or a retiring partner sells his/her interest to one or more existing partners)

a. Transactions Between a Partner and the Partnership

(1) Admission of a New Partner

When a new partner is admitted to the partnership essentially three cases can result. The new partner can invest assets into the partnership and receive a capital balance

(a) Equal to his/her purchase price
(b) Greater than his/her purchase price
(c) Less than his/her purchase price

If the new partner's capital balance is equal to the assets invested, then the entry debits the asset(s) contributed and credits the new partner's capital account for the fair value of the asset(s) contributed.

If the new partner's capital balance is not equal to the assets invested (as in situation 2 and 3 above), then either the bonus or goodwill method must be used to account for the difference.

> Bonus Method - The old partnership capital plus the new partner's asset contribution is equal to the new partnership capital. The new partner's capital is allocated his purchase share (e.g., 40%) and the old partner's capital accounts are adjusted as if they had been paid (or as if they paid) a bonus. The adjustment to the old partners' capital accounts is made in accordance with their profit (loss) sharing ratio.

The bonus method implies that the old partners either received a bonus from the new partner, or they paid a bonus to the new partner. As a result the old partners' capital accounts are either debited to reflect a bonus paid, or credited to reflect a bonus received. The new partner's capital account is never equal to the amount of assets contributed in a case where the bonus method is used.

> Goodwill Method - The old partnership capital plus the new partner's asset contribution is not equal to the new partnership capital. This is because goodwill is recorded on the partnership books for the difference between the total identifiable assets of the partnership (not including goodwill) and the deemed value of the partnership entity (which includes goodwill). An adjustment is made to the capital accounts of the existing partners to reflect the goodwill (whether acquired or given) in their profit (loss) sharing ratio. Under the goodwill method, valuation of the partnership is the objective.

How the value of the partnership is determined depends on whether the book value acquired is greater or less than the asset(s) invested. If the book value acquired is less than the asset(s) invested, the value is determined based upon the new partner's contribution, and goodwill is allocated to the old partners' accounts. If the book value acquired is greater than the asset(s) contributed, the value is based upon the existing capital accounts, and goodwill is attributed to the new partner.

The decision as to whether the bonus or goodwill method should be used rests with the partners involved. In other words, the bonus and goodwill methods are alternative solutions to the same problem.

EXAMPLE: Partnership Dissolution--Bonus Method

Total old capital for ABC Partnership is $60,000

Partner	A	B	C
Capital	$10,000	$20,000	$30,000
P&L Ratio	40%	40%	20%

Case 1

   D is admitted to the partnership and is given a 20% interest
   in the capital in return for a cash contribution of $30,000.

Cash	30,000	
D Capital		18,000
A Capital		4,800
B Capital		4,800
C Capital		2,400

   The total partnership capital to be shown on the books is
   $90,000 ($60,000 + $30,000) of which D is entitled to a 20%
   interest, or a capital balance of $18,000.   The remaining
   $12,000 is treated as a bonus to the old partners and is al-
   located to their capital accounts in accordance with their P&L
   ratio.

Case 2

   D is admitted to the partnership and is given a 20% interest
   in the capital in return for a cash contribution of $10,000.

Cash	10,000	
A Capital	1,600	
B Capital	1,600	
C Capital	800	
D Capital		14,000

   The total partnership capital to be shown on the books is
   $70,000 ($60,000 + $10,000) of which D is entitled to a 20%
   interest, or a capital balance of $14,000.   The difference of
   $4,000 ($10,000 - $14,000) is allocated to the old partners'
   accounts as if they had paid a bonus to the new partner.

EXAMPLE: Partnership Dissolution--Goodwill Method

   Use the same original data as given above

Case 1

   D is admitted to the partnership and is given a 20% interest
   in the capital in return for a cash contribution of $20,000.
   The partners elect to record goodwill.   The book value
   acquired [($60,000 + $20,000) x 20% = $16,000] is less than
   the asset contributed.

   The value of the partnership is determined based upon the contribution of the new partner.   In this case it is assumed that
   the partnership value is $100,000 ($20,000/20%).   The
   resulting goodwill is $20,000 ($100,000 - $80,000).   The
   $80,000 represents the total current capital, exclusive of
   goodwill, $60,000 of which is attributable to the old partners
   and $20,000 of which is attributable to the new partner.

Goodwill	20,000	
A Capital		8,000
B Capital		8,000
C Capital		4,000
Cash	20,000	
D Capital		20,000

Goodwill was allocated to the old partners in their P&L ratio. Also note that the capital balance of D represents 20% of the total capital of the partnership.

Case 2

D is admitted to the partnership and is given a 20% interest in the capital in return for a cash contribution of $10,000. The partners elect to record goodwill. The book value acquired [($60,000 + $10,000) x 20% = $14,000] is greater than the asset contributed.

The partnership value is based upon the capital accounts of the existing partners. Because D is entitled to a 20% interest, the $60,000 capital of the old partners must represent 80% of the capital. This means that the total value of the partnership is $75,000 ($60,000/80%). D's total contribution consists of the $10,000 in cash and $5,000 of goodwill. The goodwill is determined as the difference between the cash contribution and the 20% of the partnership capital.

Cash	10,000	
Goodwill	5,000	
D Capital		15,000

Note that in this last case no adjustment is made to the capital accounts of partners A, B, and C.

The table below summarizes the bonus and goodwill situations discussed above.

When to Apply Bonus Method

New Partnership Capital $=$ Old Partners' Capital $+$ New Partner's Asset Investment

Which Partner(s) Receive Bonus

- **New Partner**

    New Partner's Capital Credit $>$ New Partner's Asset Investment

    (The difference represents the bonus)

- **Old Partners**

    New Partner's Capital Credit $<$ New Partner's Asset Investment

    (The difference represents the bonus allocated to old partners in their P/L Ratio)

When to Apply Goodwill Method

New Partnership Capital $>$ Old Partners' Capital $+$ New Partner's Asset Investment

Which Partner(s) Goodwill is Recognized

- **New Partner's Goodwill**

    New Partner's Capital Credit $>$ New Partner's Asset Investment

    (The difference represents goodwill)

- **Old Partner's Goodwill**

    New Partner's Capital Credit $=$ New Partner's Asset Investment

    (Goodwill is allocated to old partners in their P/L Ratio)

(2)   Partner Death or Withdrawal

The death or withdrawal of a partner is treated in much the same manner as the admission of a new partner. However, there is no new capital account to be recorded; we are dealing only with the capital accounts of the original partners. Either the bonus or goodwill method may be used. The key thing to remember in regard to a partner's withdrawal from the partnership is that the withdrawing partner's capital account must be adjusted to the amount that the withdrawing partner is expected to receive.

EXAMPLE: Partner Withdrawal

Assume the same partnership data as given for the ABC partnership earlier.

Case 1

Assume that A withdraws from the partnership after reaching an agreement with partners B & C that would pay him $16,000. The remaining partners elect not to record goodwill.

B Capital	4,000	
C Capital	2,000	
A Capital		6,000
A Capital	16,000	
Cash		16,000

The $6,000 bonus is determined as the difference between the current balance of A's capital account and the amount of his buyout agreement. This "bonus" is then allocated between the remaining partners' capital accounts in proportion to their P&L ratios.

Case 2

Assume again that A withdraws from the partnership pursuant to the same agreement except that this time the partners elect to record goodwill.

The first step is to determine the amount of goodwill to be recorded. In this case we know that A's capital account must have a balance of $16,000, the agreed buyout payment he is to receive. In order to accomplish this the total partnership assets must be increased by some amount of which $6,000 represents 40%, A's P&L ratio. Therefore, the amount of goodwill to be recorded is $15,000 ($6,000/40%).

Goodwill	15,000	
A Capital		6,000
B Capital		6,000
C Capital		3,000
A Capital	16,000	
Cash		16,000

Note that in this case all of the partner's capital accounts are adjusted to record the goodwill in accordance with their P&L ratios.

b. Transactions between Partners

The sale of a partnership interest is a transaction only between the partners. Thus, the treatment accorded the transaction is determined by the partners involved.

There are two means of dealing with such a transaction. The first is to simply transfer a portion of the existing partners' capital to a new capital account for the buying partner.

EXAMPLE: Sale of a Partnership Interest--No Goodwill Recorded

Assume the following for the AB partnership:

Partner	A	B
Capital	$50,000	$50,000
P&L Ratio	60%	40%

Case 1

Assume that C wishes to enter the partnership by buying 50% of the partnership interest from both A and B for a total of $80,000. It is important to note that the $80,000 is being paid to the individual partners and _not_ to the partnership. Thus, we are only concerned with the proper adjustment between the capital accounts, _not_ the recording of the cash. This approach ignores the price that C paid for the partnership interest.

A Capital	25,000	
B Capital	25,000	
C Capital		50,000

The other method available for recording a transaction between partners is the recording of implied goodwill.

EXAMPLE: Sale of Partnership Interest--Recording Goodwill

Assume the same facts presented above for the sale of the partnership interest except that in this case the partners elect to record goodwill.

Case 1

Assuming that C paid $80,000 for a 50% interest in the partnership the implied value of the partnership assets is $160,000 ($80,000/50%). Because total capital prior to the purchase is only $100,000, the amount of goodwill that must be recorded is $60,000. The goodwill is allocated to the partners' accounts in proportion to their P&L ratios. Note that this entry is made _before_ an adjustment is made to reflect C's admission to the partnership.

Goodwill	60,000	
A Capital		36,000
B Capital		24,000

Now we can record the sale of the partnership interest to C. The capital balance of A is now $86,000 ($50,000 + $36,000) while the capital balance of B is $74,000 ($50,000 + $24,000). Recall that C is to receive 50% of each balance.

A Capital	43,000	
B Capital	37,000	
C Capital		80,000

Notice that in this situation the capital balance of C after the purchase is equal to the amount of the purchase price. Again no entry is made to record the receipt of cash because the cash goes directly to the individual partners, A and B.

4. Partnership Liquidation

A liquidation is the winding up of the partnership business. That is, it sells all of its noncash assets, pays its liabilities, and makes a final liquidating distribution to the remaining partners.

There are four basic steps to a partnership liquidation.

1. Any operating income or loss up to the date of the liquidation should be computed and allocated to the partners' capital accounts on the basis of their P&L ratio
2. All noncash assets are sold and converted to cash. The gain (loss) realized on the sale of such assets is allocated to the partners' capital accounts on the basis of their P&L ratio.
3. Any creditors' claims, including liquidation expenses or antici- pated future claims, are satisfied through the payment or reserve of cash
4. The remaining unreserved cash is distributed to the remaining partners in accordance with the balance in their capital accounts. Note that this is not necessarily the P&L ratio.

Two factors that may complicate the liquidation process are the exis- tence of loans or advances between the partnership and one or more of the partners, or the creation of a deficit in a partner's capital account be- cause of the allocation of a loss. When loans exist between the partnership and a partner, the capital account and the loan(s) are combined to give a net amount. This is often referred to as the right of offset. When a deficit exists, the amount of the deficit is allocated to the remaining solvent partners' capital accounts on the basis of their relative P&L ratio. Note here that if the partner with the capital deficit is personally solvent, he has a liability to the remaining partners for the amount of the deficit.

There are two topics that appear with regularity on the CPA examination in regard to the liquidation of a partnership. They are the statement of partnership liquidation and the determination of a "safe payment" in an in- stallment liquidation.

a. Statement of Partnership Liquidation

The statement of partnership liquidation shows in detail all of the transactions associated with the liquidation of the partnership. It should be noted here that the liquidation of a partnership can take one of two forms: simple or installment. A simple liquidation (illustrated below) is one in which all of the assets are sold in bulk and all of the creditors' claims are satisfied before a single liquidating distribution is made to the partners. Because the assets are sold in bulk there is a tendency to realize greater losses than if the assets were sold over a

period of time. As a result, many partnerships liquidate on an installment basis. In an installment liquidation the assets are sold over a
period of time and the cash is distributed to the partners as it becomes
available.

EXAMPLE: *Statement of Partnership Liquidation - Simple Liquidation*

Assume the following:

The capital balances are as given below.
The P&L ratio is 5:3:2 for A, B, and C, respectively.

Statement of Partnership Liquidation

	Cash	Other assets	Liabilities	Capital A	B	C
Balances	5,000	75,000	45,000	12,000	17,000	6,000
Sale of assets	40,000	(60,000)		(10,000)	(6,000)	(4,000)
	45,000	15,000	45,000	2,000	11,000	2,000
Payment of liabilities	(45,000)		(45,000)			
	0	15,000	0	2,000	11,000	2,000
Sale of assets	10,000	(15,000)		(2,500)	(1,500)	(1,000)
	10,000	0	0	(500)	9,500	1,000
Distribution of A's deficit				500	(300)	(200)
	10,000	0	0	0	9,200	800
Final distribution of cash	(10,000)				(9,200)	(800)

Notice that after the noncash assets have been sold and the
creditors satisfied, a $500 deficit remains in A's capital account. The
deficit is allocated to the remaining solvent partners on the basis of
their relative P&L ratios, in this case, 3:2. A is liable to the partnership for the $500. If A is personally solvent and repays the $500,
then $300 will go to B and $200 will go to C.

If in the above example there had been liquidation expenses or loans
between the partnership and partners these would have to be recognized
in the statement prior to any distribution to partners.

b.   Installment Method of Cash Distribution

There are two keys to preparing a statement of partnership
liquidation under the installment method: the determination of the
available cash balance at any given point in time and the determination
of which partner(s) is (are) to receive the payment of that cash. The
reason that the cash is not distributed in accordance with the P&L ratio
is twofold: first, the final cash distribution is based upon the
balance in each partner's capital account, not the P&L ratio, and
second, there will be situations, as illustrated in the previous

example, where one or more partners will have deficit balances in their capital accounts. If this is the case, they should never receive a cash distribution, even if the deficit does not arise until late in the liquidation process.

The determination of the available cash balance is generally very straightforward. The beginning cash balance (cash on hand at the start of the liquidation process) is adjusted for the cash receipts from receivables, sale of noncash assets, payment to creditors, and liquidation expenses incurred. A situation may occur where a certain amount of cash is to be reserved for payment of future liabilities that may arise. If this is the case, this cash should be treated as a noncash asset which makes it unavailable for current distribution to the partners.

The determination of which partner(s) is (are) to receive the available cash is somewhat more difficult. There are a number of ways to make this computation, all of which are equally correct in the eyes of the examiners. This determination can be made at the beginning of the liquidation process or at the time of each payment. In making this determination there are two key assumptions that must be made: (1) the individual partners are assumed to be personally insolvent, and (2) the remaining noncash assets are deemed to be worthless (thus creating a maximum possible amount of loss).

One method of determining the amount of the "safe payment" is the use of an Installment Cash Distribution Schedule. This schedule is prepared by determining the amount of loss required to eliminate each partner's capital account. As noted above, all of the remaining noncash assets are to be considered worthless at the time a safe payment is determined. Thus, if we determine the amount of loss required to eliminate each partner's capital balance, we can determine the order in which the partners should receive the cash payments.

When preparing this schedule it is important to make sure that the proper capital balance is used. The capital balance used must be inclusive of any loans or advances between the partnership and partners. Thus, the capital balance at the beginning of the liquidation process is increased by any amount owed to the partner by the partnership, and decreased by any amount owed to the partnership by the partner.

EXAMPLE: *Schedule of Possible Losses and Installment Cash Distribution*

Assume the same data as used for the previous example.

Schedule of Possible Losses

	Total	A	B	C
Capital balances	$35,000	$ 12,000	$17,000	$ 6,000
Loss to eliminate A	24,000	(12,000)	(7,200)	(4,800)
		0	$ 9,800	$ 1,200
Additional loss to eliminate C	3,000*		(1,800)	(1,200)
			8,000	0
Additional loss to eliminate B			(8,000)	
	8,000		0	
	$35,000			

*Allocated 60:40

The total capital balance of $35,000 indicates that if the noncash assets are sold for $35,000 less than their book value, then none of the partners will receive a cash distribution. The purpose of this schedule is to determine how much of a loss each partner's capital account can withstand based on that partner's P&L ratio. In this example A's capital would be eliminated if the partnership incurred a $24,000 ($12,000/50%) loss, B's would be eliminated by a $56,667 ($17,000/30%) loss, and C's by a $30,000 ($6,000/20%) loss. A is assumed to be eliminated first because it would take the smallest amount of loss to eliminate his account. Once A is eliminated as a partner, the P&L ratios change to reflect the relative P&L ratio of the remaining partners, in this case B and C. Based on the remaining capital balances and the relative P&L ratio, it would take a $16,333 ($9,800/60%) loss to eliminate B and a $3,000 ($1,200/40%) loss to eliminate C. Now that C is eliminated B will share all of the profits and losses as a sole partner (i.e., 100%). It will now take an $8,000 loss to eliminate B's capital. The resulting installment cash distribution schedule would appear as follows (this schedule assumes that all creditors have already received full payment; thus, the cash amount represents available cash):

Installment Cash Distribution Schedule

Partner		A	B	C
First	$ 8,000		100%	
Next	3,000		60%	40%
Next	24,000	50%	30%	20%
Any other		50%	30%	20%

While the example shown in the previous section was not an installment liquidation, the Installment Cash Distribution Schedule shown above could still be used to determine how the available cash of $10,000 is to be distributed. This is illustrated below.

Partner		A	B	C
First	$ 8,000		$8,000	
Next	$ 2,000		$1,200	$800
Total	$10,000	-	$9,200	$800

It is important to note that this method is acceptable for most all purposes; however, a CPA exam problem may require the "safe payment" approach where the amount of the safe payment is computed at a specific point in time. This particular instance is illustrated in the partnership problem from the November 1982 practice exam. We suggest that you use this problem (in the problem section for this module) as part of your study plan.

5. Incorporation of a Partnership

The incorporation of a partnership results in the formation of a new accounting (and legal) entity. This means that the partnership must adjust its records up to the date of incorporation. First, the partnership closes its books and recognizes any income or loss up to the date of incorporation. Second, the books of the partnership are adjusted to reflect the fair market value of the partnership assets and the present value of partnership liabilities. A corresponding adjustment is made to the capital accounts in

accordance with the partners' P&L ratio. Third, common stock is distributed
to the partners in accordance with the amounts in their capital accounts.
Note that the entries to record the receipt of stock by the corporation are
different depending upon whether the corporation retains the partnership
books or establishes new books.

Retention of the partnership books means that the issuance of common
stock results in the closing of the partners' capital accounts with credits
going to common stock and additional paid-in capital.

Establishing new books means that the assets and liabilities are closed
out and the difference between their net value and the value of the
corporate stock is debited to an asset "capital stock from corporation."
This account is then credited and the partners' capital accounts debited to
record the distribution of stock.

ARB, APB, AND FASB PRONOUNCEMENTS

The AICPA was formed as the American Association of Public Accountants in 1887, changing its name to American Institute of Accountants in 1917. The name was again changed to American Institute of Certified Public Accountants in 1957. The Institute is a voluntary professional association which regulates the public accounting profession internally and represents the profession to the business community, government, and society in general.

The Institute's first "pronouncement" effort came in reaction to the threat of punitive federal legislation after the 1929 stock market crash. The Institute formed the Committee on Cooperation with Stock Exchanges, which sought ways to improve corporate reporting. The Committee's report, Audits of Corporate Accounts, coined the term "accounting principles" and a standard short-form report. The Committee also recommended 5 accounting principles which were adopted by the Institute's membership. They appear in Chapter 1A of ARB 43.

The Securities Acts of 1933 and 1934 resulted in the SEC and its power to specify the form and content of financial statements (i.e., accounting principles). The SEC, noting tremendous lack of uniformity in accounting principles, threatened to promulgate accounting rules if the Institute failed to exercise leadership in narrowing areas of inconsistency in accounting practices. The Committee on Accounting Procedure was formed by the Institute in 1939 to perform this function.

The Committee on Accounting Procedure (CAP) promulgated 51 Accounting Research Bulletins (ARBs). ARB 43 is a rewrite of ARBs 1-42. The Committee on Accounting Procedure was superseded in 1959 by the Accounting Principles Board (APB) which issued 31 Opinions and 4 Statements. The APB was an Institute committee as was the Committee on Accounting Procedure.

APB Opinions constitute generally accepted accounting principles and must be complied with by companies in their financial statements. APB Statements are more advisory in nature and do not carry the official status of Opinions. In 1973, the APB was superseded by the Financial Accounting Standards Board.

The Financial Accounting Standards Board (FASB) is an independent agency comprised of seven full-time board members and a substantial research staff. The FASB

issues Statements of Financial Accounting Standards (SFAS) and also interpretations
of existing ARBs, APBs, and FASBs. In 1978, a new series of pronouncements, Statements of Financial Accounting Concepts (SFAC), which are similar in nature and scope
to APB Statements, was initiated. SFACs do not establish GAAP.

As implied above, the Institute's efforts in the promulgation of accounting principles, rules, etc., has come from government impetus. Six periods of public criticism of accounting principles and their promulgation are evident.

1. Post-1929 market crash resulting in the Committee on Cooperation with Stock
   Exchanges
2. Latter 1930s when multitudes of alternative practices were discovered through
   SEC disclosure requirements resulting in the Committee on Accounting
   Procedure
3. Post World War II when rapid inflation was not reflected in the accounts
   resulting in the rewrite of ARBs 1-42 into ARB 43
4. Mid-50s when a general dissatisfaction with the acceptability of alternative
   accounting practices resulted in the APB
5. Late 60s when the APB came under intense criticism for its compromise
   positions on controversial topics resulting in the FASB
6. Mid-70s when the U.S. Senate Subcommittee on Reports, Accounting and management (Metcalf Committee) issued its staff report, "The Accounting Establishment"
7. Mid-80s when the U.S. House Sub-Committee on Oversights and Investigations
   (Dingell Committee) has been conducting its public hearings

References to FASB Materials

Each of the outlines in the last part of this chapter is referenced to the section where it is found in the FASB's Accounting Standards--Current Texts: General/
Industry Standards, McGraw-Hill Book Company. These references appear in parentheses
right after the original pronouncement reference in the heading of each pronouncement
outlined. When using either the FASB's Current Text or Original Pronouncements to
supplement your study, be sure you have a recent edition (not more than 2 years old).

In studying the outlines, you might notice that parts of some pronouncements have
not been outlined. The reason some sections of the pronouncements are excluded from
the outlines is that they have never been tested on the exam. Also, outlines for
very specialized pronouncements (e.g., SFAS 50, Financial Reporting in the Record and
Music Industry) are not included in this manual. Several others are outlined more
generally. Only those FASB Interpretations and Technical Bulletins having widespread
applicability are included in this chapter. They are set apart with solid lines only
to distinguish them from the SFASs.

Study Program for the Accounting Pronouncements

Outlines of the unsuperseded official accounting pronouncements are presented in
chronological order in this chapter. Effective dates of pronouncements are omitted
unless they are a current implementation problem. You should

1. Study through the outlines as you are referred to them in the modules in this chapter

    a. The outlines presume prior study of the pronouncements
    b. If the outlines are your first contact with the pronouncements

        (1) Read the outline for an overview of the pronouncement
        (2) Read the pronouncement
        (3) Study the outline

    c. Note that additional comments have been added to some outlines, relating to the rationale or justification for these standards

2. As you study this chapter

    a. Each study module contains references back to relevant pronouncements
    b. Return to this section of the chapter to review appropriate pronouncements
    c. SFASs that deal only with disclosure requirements are not covered in the modules; you should read through these before the theory exam

3. Required disclosures. It is almost impossible to memorize all the required disclosures. A good approach is to take the position of a financial analyst: What data would you want to know? Utilizing this approach, you only have to memorize any exceptions, i.e., items you would not normally think a financial analyst would be interested in

Accounting Research Bulletins

ARB 43--Chapter 1A (A31, B50, C08, C23, R36, R70, R75)* Rules Adopted by Membership

Five rules recommended by the Committee on Cooperation with Stock Exchanges in 1934. The last rule is from another 1934 Institute committee.

1. Profit is realized at the point of sale unless collection is not reasonably assured.
2. Capital (paid-in) surplus should not be charged with losses or expenses, except in quasi-reorganizations.
3. Retained earnings of subsidiary created prior to acquisition is not part of consolidated retained earnings. This does not apply to poolings.
4. Receivables from officers, employees, and affiliates must be separately disclosed.
5. Par value of stock issued for assets cannot be used to value the assets if some of the stock is subsequently donated back to the corporation.

Chapter 1B (C23) Profits or Losses on Treasury Stock (Revised by APB 6, para 12)

Profits on treasury stock are not income and should be reflected in capital surplus.

Chapter 2A (F43) Comparative Financial Statements (Cross-referenced to APB 20)

Comparative statements enhance the usefulness of financial statements and should be presented.

---

*The references in parentheses are from the FASB Accounting Standards - Current Texts, General/Industry, Richard D. Irwin, Inc.

Chapter 3A (B05) Current Assets and Current Liabilities
(Amended by APBs 6, 21 and SFAS 6)

Chapter 3A contains the definitions and examples of current assets and liabilities. See SFAS 6 for refinancing short-term debt.

A. Current assets are "cash and other assets or resources commonly identified as those which are reasonably expected to be (1) realized in cash, (2) sold, or (3) consumed during the ordinary operating cycle of the business."

 1. Cash available for current operations (para 4)

 2. Inventories

 3. Trade receivables

 4. Other receivables collectible in one year

 5. Installment, deferred accounts, and notes receivable

 6. Marketable securities available for current operations

 7. Prepaid expenses

B. Current liabilities are "obligations whose liquidation is reasonably expected to require the use of existing resources properly classifiable as current assets or the creation of other current liabilities during the ordinary operating cycle of the business."

 1. Trade payables

 2. Collections received in advance of services

 3. Accruals of expenses

 4. Other liabilities coming due in one year

 5. Note that liabilities not using current assets for liquidation are not current liabilities, e.g., bonds being repaid from a sinking fund

C. Operating cycle is "average time intervening between the acquisition of materials or services entering this process and the final cash realization."

Chapter 4 (I78) Inventory Pricing
Contains 10 statements outlining inventory valuation

 1. Inventory consists of tangible personal property

     a. Held for sale in ordinary course of business
     b. In process of production for such sale
     c. To be currently consumed in the production of such goods

 2. Major objective of inventory valuation is proper income determination

     a. Matching of costs and revenues

 3. Primary basis is cost. Cost includes all reasonable and necessary costs of preparing inventory for sale. These costs would include expenditures to bring inventory to existing condition and location

     a. Direct or variable costing is not acceptable (use absorption costing)

4. Cost may be determined under any flow assumption. Use method which most clearly reflects income

5. Departure from cost to market required when utility of goods, in their disposal in the ordinary course of business, is not as great as cost

    a. Write-down recognized as a loss of the current period
    b. Use of lower of cost or market method more fairly reflects income of the period than would the cost method
    c. Results in a more realistic estimate of future cash flows to be realized from the assets
    d. Supported by doctrine of conservatism

6. Market means current replacement cost subject to

    a. Market should not exceed net realizable value (sales price less selling and completion costs)
    b. Market should not be less than net realizable value less normal profit

7. Lower of cost or market may be applied to individual items or the inventory as a whole. Use method which most clearly reflects income

8. Basis for stating inventories and changes therein should be consistent and disclosed

9. Inventories may be stated above cost in exceptional cases

    a. No basis for cost allocation, e.g, meatpacking
    b. Disposal assured and price known, e.g, precious metals

10. Purchase commitment loss should be recognized in the same manner as inventory losses

Chapter 7B (C20) Stock Dividends and Stock Splits

A. Dividend--evidence given to shareholders of their share of accumulated earnings which are going to be retained in the business

B. Split--stock issued to increase number of outstanding shares to reduce market price and/or to obtain a wider distribution of ownership

C. To the recipient, splits and dividends are not income. Dividends and splits take nothing from the property of the corporation and add nothing to the property of the recipient

1. Upon receipt of stock dividend or split, recipient should reallocate cost of shares previously held to all shares held

D. Issuer of a stock dividend (issuance is small in relation to shares outstanding and consequently has no apparent effect on market price) should capitalize retained earnings equal to the fair market value of shares issued

1. Unless retained earnings are capitalized, retained earnings thought to be distributed by the recipient will be available for subsequent distribution

2. Issuances less than 20-25% of previously outstanding shares are dividends. Issuances greater than 20-25% of previously outstanding shares are splits

3. Where stock dividend is so large it may materially affect price (a split effected in the form of a dividend), no capitalization is necessary other than that required by law

   a. Some jurisdictions require that the par value of splits be capitalized, i.e., changes in par value are not permitted

4. For closely held corporations, there is no need to capitalize retained earnings other than to meet legal requirements

Chapter 10A (T10) Real and Personal Property Taxes

Accounting for personal and real property taxes which vary in time of determination and collection from state to state

A. In practice, the dates below have been used to apportion taxes between accounting periods

   1. Assessment date
   2. Beginning of fiscal period of taxing authority
   3. End of fiscal period of taxing authority
   4. Lien date
   5. Date of tax levy
   6. Date tax is payable
   7. Date tax is delinquent
   8. Period appearing on tax bill

B. The most acceptable basis is a monthly accrual on the taxpayer's books during the fiscal period of the taxing authority

   1. At year end, the books will show the appropriate prepayment or accrual
   2. An accrued liability, whether known or estimated, should be shown as a current liability
   3. On income statement, property taxes may be charged to operating expense, deducted separately from income, prorated among accounts to which they apply, or combined with other taxes (but not with income taxes)

Chapter 11A (C05) Cost-Plus-Fixed-Fee Contracts (CPFF)

A. When should CPFF revenues be included in the contractor's income statement?

   1. Revenue may be credited to income based on partial performance if realization is reasonably assured

      a. Based on delivery of finished units is generally acceptable
      b. Per contract terms if representative of performance

B. What amounts are included in sales?

1. Reimbursable costs for manufacture and delivery of products

2. Fees for contracts involving services

C. What is proper balance sheet classification?

1. Unbilled costs and fees are receivables rather than inventory but should be shown separately

D. What is proper balance sheet disclosure of items related to CPFF?

1. Offsetting advances on CPFF contracts against CPFF receivables is acceptable only if provided by contract and that treatment is expected in the normal course of transactions. Offsets should be clearly disclosed

Chapter 13B (C47) Stock Option Compensation Plans (Also see APB 25)

Cost of services received for compensation paid in stock options should be included in operations

A. Compensation may arise when the corporation agrees to issue common stock to an employee at a stated price

1. Other options may result in employee obligations such as continued employment

B. Stock options do not result in compensation if

1. Stock options are offered at a reasonable amount to raise capital

2. Stock options are offered at a reasonable amount to induce wider holdings by employees

C. Alternative dates of measurement are when

1. Option plan is adopted

2. Option is granted

3. Grantee performs required conditions

4. Grantee may first exercise option

5. Grantee exercises option

6. Grantee disposes of stock

D. Date of grant should be used

1. Considering the date of grant as a contract, it is the date value is determined

2. Date of grant is date corporation foregoes alternative use

3. In "C." above, "1." and "6." are not relevant

E. Compensation is excess of <u>fair value over option price</u>. APB 25 states the quoted market price or best estimate of fair market value is fair value

F. Compensation cost should be spread over the period of service covered by the option contract

1. Cash and compensation are equal to consideration for the stock when exercised (amount credited to stock and paid-in capital)

G. Disclosure should be made annually of

1. Number of shares under option

2. Option price

3. Number of shares exercisable

4. Number of shares and price of options exercised

ARB 45 (Co4) Long-Term Construction Contracts

Discusses accounting for multiple period projects

A. The percentage-of-completion method recognizes income as work progresses

1. Recognized income based upon a percentage of estimated total income

   a. (Incurred costs to date)/(Total expected costs) known as cost-to-cost measure

   b. Other measure of progress based on work performed, e.g., engineering or architectural estimate

2. Costs, for percentage-of-completion estimate, might exclude materials and subcontracts, especially in the early stages of a contract

   a. Avoids overstating the percentage-of-completion

3. If a loss is estimated on the contract, the <u>entire loss</u> should be recognized currently

4. Current assets include costs and income (loss) in excess of billings. Current liabilities include billings in excess of costs and income (loss)

   a. Contracts should be separated into net assets and net liabilities
   b. Contracts should not be offset on the balance sheet

5. Advantages of percentage-of-completion are periodic recognition of income and reflection of the status of the contract

   a. Results in appropriate matching of costs and revenues
   b. Avoids distortions in income from year to year and thus provides more relevant information to financial statement users

6. The principal disadvantage is the reliance on estimates

B. The completed-contract method recognizes income when the contract is complete

1. General and administrative expenses can be allocated to contracts

   a. Not necessary if many projects are in process
   b. No excessive deferring of costs

2. Provision should be made for <u>entire amount of any expected loss</u> prior to job completion

   a. I.e., losses are recognized immediately in their entirety--conservative treatment

3. An excess of accumulated costs over related billings is a current asset. An excess of accumulated billings over related costs is a liability (current in most cases)

   a. Balance sheet accounts are determined as in "A.4.a." & "b."
   b. Recognized losses "B.2." reduce accumulated costs

4. The advantage of the completed-contract method is that it is based on final results, and its primary disadvantage is that it does not reflect current performance

   a. Overall, the completed contract method represents a conservative approach

C. The percentage-of-completion method is recommended when total costs and percent of completion can be reasonably estimated

ARB 51 (B50, C20, C51, R70) Consolidated Financial Statements (Also see APB 16) (Amended by SFAS 94)

A. Consolidated statements present financial statements of a parent and subsidiaries, as if the group were a single company for the benefit of the parent's stockholders and creditors

1. Substance (effectively a single entity) takes precedence over legal form (legally separate entities)

2. Consolidated financial statements result in more meaningful presentation of financial position and operating results than if separate statements were presented for the parent and subsidiary

B. The general condition for consolidation is over 50% ownership of subsidiaries

1. Theoretical condition is control of the subsidiaries

   a. This is generally implicit in greater than 50% ownership

2. Subsidiaries which are a temporary investment (in reorganization, in bankruptcy, etc.) should not be consolidated

3. Large indebtedness to bondholders should not preclude consolidation

C. A difference in fiscal periods should not preclude consolidation

1. Differences of 3 months are acceptable if one discloses material intervening events

2. Differences in excess of 3 months should be consolidated on the basis of interim statements of the subsidiary

D. Consolidation policy should be disclosed by headings or footnotes

E. Intercompany balances and transactions should be eliminated in consolidated statements

1. Intercompany gains and losses on assets remaining in the group should be eliminated (eliminate entire gross profit or loss even on transactions with minority interest subsidiaries)

F. Retained earnings of subsidiaries at the acquisition date should not appear in the consolidated statements

G. When a parent purchases a subsidiary in several blocks of stock, the subsidiary's retained earnings should be determined by the step method (apply equity method to subsidiary retroactively)

H. When a subsidiary is purchased in midyear, subsidiary operations may be included in the consolidated income statement for the year and then the operating results prior to acquisition would be deducted

1. As an alternative for a subsidiary purchased in midyear, post acquisition operations can be included in the consolidated income statement

2. For midyear disposals, omit operations from the consolidated income statement and include equity in subsidiary's operations up to disposal date as a separate item in the income statement

Note: "F." through "H." pertain only to acquisitions accounted for as purchases per APB 16.

I. Subsidiaries' stock held by the parent should not be treated as outstanding in the consolidated balance sheet

J. If subsidiary losses eliminate the minority interest, charge any further minority interest losses to the parent's interest. If subsequent earnings arise, give parent's interest credit for minority interest losses previously absorbed

K. Summarized information about the assets, liabilities, and results of operations (or separate statements) for subsidiaries not consolidated for F/Y 1986 or 1987 under pre-SFAS 94 criteria shall be provided in consolidated FSs or notes

L. Sometimes combined, as distinguished from consolidated, financial statements are appropriate for commonly owned companies and are prepared when consolidated statements are not appropriate

M. Parent company statements are sometimes required to adequately inform creditors and preferred stockholders. Dual column presentation of parent and consolidated statements is possible

Accounting Principles Board Opinions

APB 2 (I32) and 4 (I32) Accounting for the Investment Credit

The investment credit, a tax credit, is equal to a specified percentage of certain assets purchased. The tax credit, subject to limitations, reduces income tax payable during the year of purchase

A. The APB considered three alternative accounting treatments

1. Subsidy to taxpayer's capital which was rejected, because the investment credit was thought to be an income item

2. Tax expense reduction (flow through) in year of asset purchase which was rejected in APB 2

   a. It was accepted in APB 4, because many firms and the SEC accepted this method after APB 2
   b. The argument for this treatment is that the tax savings is in year of purchase, because of the decision to purchase in that year

3. Cost reduction (deferral) which was accepted in APB 2 and APB 4. The APB supported the original adoption of this method because

   a. Earnings arise from use of facilities, not acquisition
   b. And ultimate realization is dependent on future use (otherwise it is recapturable)

B. The credit can be netted against the asset or shown as a deferred credit account. Carryforwards and carrybacks are allowable due to maximum annual credits, permitted by IRS

1. Carrybacks should be shown as a receivable

2. Carryforwards should not be shown in the accounts until the credit becomes allowable, i.e., income is earned

APB 6 (B05, C23, D40, I60) Status of Accounting Research Bulletins

A. ARB 43, Chapter 1B Treasury Stock

1. An excess of purchase price of treasury stock, purchased for retirement or constructive retirement, over par or stated value may be allocated between paid-in capital and retained earnings

   a. The charge to paid-in capital is limited to all paid-in capital from treasury stock transactions and retirements of the same issue and a pro rata portion of all other paid-in capital of that issue
   b. Also, paid-in capital applicable to fully retired issues may be charged

2. Alternatively, losses may be charged entirely to retained earnings

3. All gains on retirement of treasury stock go to paid-in capital

4. When the decision to retire treasury stock has not been made, the cost of such is a contra shareholders' equity item. Losses may only be charged to paid-in capital from treasury transactions and retirements of the same issue

5. Some state laws prescribe accounting for treasury stock. The laws are to be followed where they are at variance with this APB. Disclose all statutory requirements concerning treasury stock such as dividend restrictions

B. ARB 43, Chapter 3A Current Assets and Liabilities
Unearned interest, finance charges, etc. included in receivables should be deducted from the related receivable

C. ARB 43, Chapter 7B Stock Dividends and Splits
States "the shareholder has no income solely as a result of the fact that the corporation has income," but does not preclude use of the equity method

APB 9 (I17, CO8) Reporting the Results of Operations (Part II superseded by APB 15)

A. Designates a new format for income statement in which all normal operating items would be presented at the top of the income statement resulting in "net income before extraordinary items"
   1. "Net income before extraordinary items" is followed by extraordinary items resulting in "net income"

B. "Prior period adjustments" are excluded from the income statement and constitute adjustments of beginning retained earnings disclosed at the top of the retained earnings statement
   1. Beginning retained earnings are adjusted by "prior period adjustments" resulting in "restated beginning retained earnings"
   2. "Restated retained earnings" is then adjusted for net income and dividends which results in ending retained earnings

C. See SFAS 16 for description of prior period adjustments

D. Prior period adjustments should be disclosed in the period of adjustment
   1. The effect on each prior period presented should be disclosed including restated income taxes
   2. Disclosure in subsequent periods is not normally required
   3. Historical summary data should also be restated and disclosed in the period of adjustment

E. The APB also reaffirmed earlier positions that the following should not affect determination of net income
   1. Transactions in the company's own stock
   2. Transfers to or from retained earnings
   3. Quasi-reorganization adjustments

APB 10 (A35, C16, I24, I28, R75) Omnibus Opinion--1966

A. ARB 43, Chapter 3B Working Capital

1. Offsetting of liabilities and assets in the balance sheet is not acceptable unless a right of offset exists

2. Most government securities are not designed to be prepayment of taxes and thus may not be offset against tax liabilities. Only where an explicit pre-payment exists may an offset be used

B. Liquidation preference of preferred stock
For preferred stock, disclose

1. Involuntary liquidation value when it considerably exceeds par value

2. Aggregate or per share amounts to call or redeem

3. Aggregate <u>and</u> per share dividend arrearages when cumulative

C. Installment method of accounting
Revenues should be recognized at the point of sale unless receivables are in doubt. The installment or cost recovery method may be used

APB 12 (C08, C38, D40, I69, V18) Omnibus Opinion--1967

A. Allowance or contra accounts (allowance for bad debts, accumulated depreciation, etc.) should be deducted from assets or groups of assets with appropriate disclosure

B. Disclosure of depreciable assets should include

1. Depreciation expense for the period

2. Balances of major classes of depreciable assets by nature or function

3. Accumulated depreciation either by major class or in total

4. Description of method(s) of depreciation by major classes of assets

C. Deferred compensation contracts should be accounted for in compliance with APB 8
<u>Accounting for the Cost of Pension Plans</u>

1. The cost of these plans should be accrued over the period of active employment from the time the contract is entered into or the effective date of APB 12

2. When a plan calls for the option of a deferred annuity or minimum payment at death, the cost should be based on the deferred annuity

D. Changes in the separate shareholder equity accounts in addition to retained earnings and changes in number of equity securities must be disclosed in the year of change

1. In separate statements

2. Or the financial statements

3. Or the notes

APB 14 (D10, C08) Convertible Debt and Debt Issued with Stock Warrants

A. Convertible debt constitutes securities which are convertible into common stock
    of the user or affiliate. Terms generally include

    1. Lower interest rate than on ordinary debt

    2. Initial conversion price greater than the common price at time of issuance

    3. A conversion price which does not decrease except to protect against
        dilution

B. While there are arguments to account for the debt and equity characteristics
    separately, the APB has concluded no proceeds of a convertible issue should be
    attributed to the conversion factor

    1. Primary reasons are

        a. The inseparability of the debt and conversion features
        b. The practical difficulties of valuing the conversion feature

C. When debt is issued with detachable purchase warrants, the debt and warrants
    generally trade separately and should be treated separately

    1. The allocation of proceeds should be based on relative market value at date
        of issuance

    2. Any resulting debt discount or premium should be accounted for as such

D. Separate valuation of debt and warrants is applicable where the debt may be used
    as consideration when exercising the warrants. Separate valuation is not
    acceptable where the debt must be tendered to exercise the warrants (i.e., the
    warrants are, in essence, nondetachable)

APB 15 (E09, C16) Earnings per Share (only applies to publicly held companies per
SFAS 21)

A. Earnings per share information must be presented on the face of the income
    statement for the following income elements

    1. Income from continuing operations (APB 30)

    2. Income before extraordinary items and/or cumulative effect of an accounting
        change

    3. Cumulative effect of change in accounting principle (APB 20)

    4. Net income

    5. It is desirable, but not required, for

        a. Discontinued operations (APB 30)
        b. Extraordinary items

B. Simple capital structures

    1. No potentially dilutive securities exist, e.g., no convertible bonds or
        preferred, no options or warrants, no contingent share agreements, etc.

2. If potentially dilutive securities exist, then dilution from these securities is less than 3% in the aggregate

    a. Dilution is defined as a reduction of EPS on outstanding weighted-average common shares

    b. Antidilutive securities are not figured in the 3% test above because these securities either increase EPS on weighted-average common shares outstanding or a loss per these shares is reduced

C. Complex capital structures

1. Contain potentially dilutive securities, e.g., convertible debt and preferred, options, contingent shares, e.g., which in the aggregate dilute EPS based upon outstanding common shares by 3% or more and require a dual presentation of EPS

2. <u>Primary Earnings Per Share</u> (PEPS) is based upon outstanding common and those securities substantially equivalent to common stock having a dilutive effect

    a. Common stock equivalents (CSE) are defined as, "a security which is not, in form, a common stock, but which usually contains provisions to enable its holder to become a common stockholder and which, because of its terms and the circumstances under which it was issued, is in substance equivalent to a common stock." (Para 25) Securities which either are CSE or have the potential to be are

        (1) Convertible debt and convertible preferred stock
        (2) Stock options and warrants
        (3) Participating securities and two class common
        (4) Contingent issuances

    b. Convertible securities are determined to be or not to be CSE at issuance

        (1) Convertible securities are CSE if their effective yield rate, at issuance, is less than 2/3 of the then existing average Aa corporate bond yield
        (2) Convertible securities subsequently issued or outstanding with the same terms as other CSE are CSE

    c. Options and warrants are CSE at all times. The assumption of exercise, however, is not made until the exercise price is below the market price for substantially all of the last 3 months of the year

    d. Contingent issuances are CSE if shares issued depend merely upon the passage of time or, if contingency is based upon maintenance or attainment of earnings levels and the earnings level is currently attained

3. <u>Fully diluted earnings per share</u> (FDEPS) is a pro forma presentation of the maximum dilution of EPS based upon outstanding common shares by including all contingent issuances individually having a dilutive effect as of the beginning of the period

    a. FDEPS includes dilutive CSE, and
    b. FDEPS also includes the dilutive effects of securities which are not CSE

D. Computational guidelines

1. For both simple and complex capital structures, the following procedures apply

a. Compute the weighted-average of common shares outstanding. Treasury shares should be excluded as of date of repurchase

b. EPS data for all periods presented should be retroactively adjusted for all splits and dividends, even those subsequent to the period being presented

c. For stock issued in purchase combinations, use weighted-average from date of combination. For pooling combination, shares assumed outstanding the entire period regardless of when issued

d. The claims of senior securities (nonconvertible preferred dividends) should be deducted from income prior to computing EPS. Dividends on cumulative preferred are deducted whether or not declared, while dividends on noncumulative preferred are deducted only if declared

e. EPS figures should be based upon consolidated income figures after consolidating adjustments and eliminations

2. For complex capital structures, these additional procedures apply for PEPS and FDEPS

a. The "if converted" method is used to adjust EPS on outstanding common shares for dilutive convertible securities

  (1) The convertible securities are considered to have been converted at the beginning of the period (or at issuance if later) increasing the denominator of EPS

  (2) For convertible bonds, the interest savings net of tax is added to the numerator of EPS

  (3) For convertible preferred, the preferred dividends deducted in arriving at EPS are not deducted, thereby, increasing the numerator. There is no tax effect because dividends are not an expense

b. The "treasury stock" method is used to adjust EPS on outstanding common shares for dilutive options and warrants, i.e., those for which the exercise price is below the market price

  (1) The options and warrants are assumed to be exercised at the beginning of the period (or the date the options and warrants were issued if later). The shares assumed issued increase the denominator of EPS

  (2) The hypothetical proceeds are used to purchase treasury stock at the average price over the year for PEPS and at the end of year price, if higher, for FDEPS. This has the effect of decreasing the denominator but not to the extent increased in "(1)" directly above

    (a) No more than 20% of the common stock outstanding at the end of the period may be treated as repurchased. The shares over 20% are added to the denominator

    (b) If options and warrants for more than 20% of the common shares exist, then the excess hypothetical funds are due to the 20% limitation should be considered to reduce long-term debt or to be invested in interest bearing securities. The resulting interest savings (on debt) or earnings (on securities) are added to the numerator net of tax

  (3) No retroactive adjustment should be made to EPS figures for options and warrants as a result of market price changes

c. When convertible securities require payment of cash at conversion, they are considered options. The "if converted" method is used for the conversion and the "treasury stock" method is applied to the cash proceeds

d. Contingent issuances depend on certain conditions being met

    (1) Maintenance or attainment of earning levels

        (a) If level is currently attained, include shares in both PEPS and FDEPS

        (b) If earnings level is not currently attained, do not include shares in PEPS calculation, but do include them in FDEPS, if dilutive, after adjusting numerator to specified earnings level

        (c) If the contingency agreement expires without issuance of additional stock, the contingency should be excluded from the last period and the contingency should be retroactively removed from earlier periods

    (2) Market price of stock at future date (applies to both PEPS and FDEPS)

        (a) EPS should reflect number of shares issuable at year-end price
        (b) Prior EPS figures should be retroactively adjusted for changes in shares issuable due to market price changes

    (3) If contingent stock issuances are contingent on both market price and earnings levels, EPS adjustments should be based on both conditions

e. Computation guidelines for participating services and two class common are not presented because of their relative unimportance insofar as the CPA exam is concerned

f. Antidilutive securities should not be included in either PEPS and FDEPS

E. Disclosure guidelines

1. Captions for the income statement

    a. For simple capital structures--Earnings Per Common Share
    b. For complex capital structures

        (1) Primary--Earnings per common and common equivalent share
        (2) Fully diluted--Earnings per share assuming full dilution

2. Additional disclosures for complex capital structure EPS

    a. A schedule explaining the EPS figures should be presented disclosing common stock equivalents, underlying assumptions, and number of shares issued upon conversion, warrants, etc.

    b. If potential dilution exists in any of the periods, both PEPS and FDEPS should be presented for all periods

        (1) Gives the reader understanding of the trend in potential dilution
        (2) If earnings of a prior period presented have been restated, the EPS data should be revised and effect of restatement in EPS should be disclosed in year of restatement

3. For both simple and complex capital structures, as the case may be, the financial statements should summarize the rights or equity issues outstanding

    a. Dividend and liquidation preferences
    b. Participation rights
    c. Call prices and dates
    d. Conversion or exercise prices and dates
    e. Sinking fund requirements
    f. Unusual voting rights

APB 16 (B50) Business Combinations

(Para 96 amended by SFAS 79)

Both pooling and purchase accounting are applicable to business combinations but not as alternatives. No part purchase, part pooling

A. A combination meeting all of the following criteria is a pooling; all others are purchases

1. <u>Combining companies</u>. Independent ownerships are combined to continue previously separate operations (para 46)

   a. "Each of the combining companies is autonomous and has not been a subsidiary or division of another corporation within two years before the plan of combination is initiated."

      (1) Plan is initiated when announced publicly to stockholders
      (2) A new company meets criterion as long as it is not a successor to a nonindependent company
      (3) A previously owned company divested due to government order is exempted from this criterion

   b. "Each of the combining companies is independent of the other combining companies."

      (1) No more than 10% of any combining company is held by any other combining company(ies)

2. <u>Combining of interest</u>. Combination by exchange of stock (para 47)

   a. "The combination is effected in a single transaction or is completed in accordance with a specific plan within one year after the plan is initiated."

      (1) Must be completed in a year unless governmental proceeding or litigation prevents completion in one year

   b. "A corporation offers and issues only common stock with rights identical to those of the majority of its outstanding voting common stock in exchange for substantially all of the voting common stock interest of another company at the date the plan of combination is consummated."

      (1) Cash may be distributed for partial shares but not pro rata to all stockholders
      (2) 90% of stock outstanding at consummation must be acquired by issuing corporation. The following shares are excluded from the shares considered acquired at consummation

         (a) Stock acquired before plan was initiated and still owned
         (b) Stock acquired between initiation and consummation

      (3) When more than 2 companies are combined, the criteria must be met for each of them
      (4) An issuing company may acquire equity securities of the combining company other than common by any means <u>except those</u> issued for the combining company's stock within the prior two years (which must be acquired with common stock)

   c. "None of the combining companies changes the equity interest of the voting common stock in contemplation of effecting the combination either within two years before the plan of combination is initiated or between the dates the combination is initiated and consummated; changes in contemplation of effecting the combination may include distributions to stockholders and additional issues, exchanges, and retirements of securities."

  (1) Normal dividend distributions (as determined by past dividends) are permitted

 d. "Each of the combining companies reacquires shares of voting common stock only for purposes other than business combinations, and no company reacquires more than a normal number of shares between the dates the plan of combination is initiated and consummated."

  (1) Normal treasury stock acquisitions (as determined by past acquisitions) are permitted
  (2) Acquisition by other combining companies is the same as treasury stock acquisition

 e. "The ratio of the interest of an individual common stockholder to those of other common stockholders in a combining company remains the same as a result of the exchange of stock to effect the combination."

  (1) No stockholder denies or surrenders his/her potential share in the issuing corporation

 f. "The voting rights to which the common stock ownership interests in the resulting combined corporation are entitled are exercisable by the stockholders; the stockholders are neither deprived of nor restricted in exercising those rights for a period."

  (1) For example, stock cannot be put in a voting trust

 g. "The combination is resolved at the date the plan is consummated and no provisions of the plan relating to the issue of securities or other consideration are pending."

  (1) No contingent future issuances or other consideration (including through a trustee)
  (2) Later settlement of contingencies at the date of consummation is permitted

3. Absence of planned transactions (para 48)

 a. "The combined corporation does not agree directly or indirectly to retire or reacquire all or part of the common stock issued to effect the combination."
 b. "The combined corporation does not enter into other financial arrangements for the benefit of the former stockholders of a combining company, such as a guaranty of loans secured by stock issued in the combination, which in effect negates the exchange of equity securities."
 c. "The combined corporation does not intend or plan to dispose of a significant part of the assets of the combining companies within two years after the combination other than disposals in the ordinary course of business of the formerly separate companies and to eliminate duplicate facilities or excess capacity."

B. Application of pooling method

1. Assets and liabilities are aggregated after adjusting all the accounts to conform to a uniform set of methods. The accounting changes are made retroactively, and prior periods statements restated

2. Stockholder equities are also combined. If the par or stated value of the new corporation exceeds that of all the combining companies, the excess should be taken first from combined paid-in capital, and then from retained earnings

   a. If a combining corporation has a deficit, it should not be eliminated before the combination but rather netted against the combined retained earnings
   b. An issuing corporation using its treasury stock to effect a combination should account for its first as retired and then reissued

3. The first combined income statement should be reported as if the pooling had taken place at the beginning of the period, i.e., restate pooling to beginning of period to report a year of combined operations

   a. The effects of intercompany transactions on current assets and liabilities, revenues, and cost of sales during the interim period prior to the combination should be eliminated

      (1) Per share effects of nonrecurring transactions on long-term assets and liabilities should be disclosed (they need not be eliminated)

   b. The balance sheet and other statements restated at the beginning of the period should be disclosed as being retroactively combined individual company statements
   c. Revenue, extraordinary items, and net income of each of the combining companies for the interim period prior to the pooling should be disclosed in the notes to the financial statements

4. The costs of a pooling are expensed as incurred

5. The notes of a combined company in the period of pooling should disclose

   a. Name and description of pooled companies
   b. Pooling accounting was used
   c. Description and number of shares issued
   d. Details of operations of separate companies for period prior to pooling included in first year's operation
   e. Accounting adjustments to achieve uniform accounting methods
   f. Explanation of change in retained earnings caused by change in fiscal year
   g. Reconciliation of individual company operating results to combined results

6. The rationale for pooling of interests is that it represents a combination of ownership interests in companies that previously were operated separately. It is regarded as an arrangement among stockholder groups. Because of this, under pooling of interests the existing basis of accounting continues

C. Application of the purchase method

   1. The standard historical cost principle is applied to purchase accounting

      a. Use fair value of property given or fair value of property received, whichever is more clearly evident

2. The cost of a company includes direct costs of acquisition but not indirect general expenses

3. Additional payments to be made, contingent on future earnings and/or security prices, should be disclosed but not recorded as a liability

    a. If contingency payments are made because of attainment of specified earnings levels, the additional payment is considered an increase in the cost of the subsidiary (usually results in debit to goodwill)
    b. If contingency payments are made due to attainment of specified security price levels, the cost of the acquired company is not affected. Rather the amount originally recorded as consideration in acquisition should be reduced by the contingency payment (usually results in decreasing paid-in capital)
    c. The contingency payments are based on both security prices and earnings, the payment should be separated and accounted as in "a." and "b."

4. The acquiring corporation should allocate the cost of the acquired company to assets and liabilities acquired. Independent appraisals may be used

    a. Marketable securities--net realizable value
    b. Receivables--present value after allowance and collection costs
    c. Finished goods and work-in-process inventories--net realizable value less normal profit
    d. Raw materials--replacement costs
    e. Plant--replacement cost if to be used and at net realizable value if to be sold
    f. Intangible assets (identifiable)--appraisal values
    g. Other assets--appraisal values
    h. Payables--present values
    i. Accruals (pensions, warranties, etc.)--present values

5. The acquiring company should recognize the accrual of interest on assets and liabilities recorded at present values

    a. Previously recorded goodwill of the acquired company should not be recorded by the acquiring company
    b. The acquiring company should retroactively adjust goodwill for unrecognized tax loss carryforwards of an acquired company as they are recognized

6. SFAS 96 addresses accounting for deferred tax consequences of differences between assigned values and tax bases of assets and liabilities of enterprise acquired in purchase business combination

7. The value assigned to net assets should not exceed cost

    a. If the cost of the net assets acquired exceeds the net revised asset values, the excess should be recorded as goodwill
    b. If the net revised asset value exceeds cost, the excess should be credited, pro rata, to all noncurrent assets except marketable securities

        (1) If a credit (negative goodwill) continues to exist after all noncurrent assets except marketable securities are written down to zero, the excess is a deferred credit and should be taken to income systematically and rationally

(2) Negative goodwill should not be added directly to shareholders' equity at acquisition

8. The date of acquisition is the date assets are received and securities issued

9. The notes of the acquiring company in the year of purchase should include

   a. Name and description of acquired company
   b. Acquisition was a purchase
   c. Period that acquired results of operations are consolidated
   d. Cost of acquired company and shares issued
   e. Plan of amortization and goodwill
   f. Contingent payments

10. Pro forma results of operations of the current and immediate prior period (no other prior periods) should reflect operations of the combination including*

    a. Revenue
    b. Income before extraordinary items
    c. Net income
    d. EPS

11. The rationale for purchase accounting is that the business combination represents a bargained or arm's length transaction. The purchased company is treated as an acquired asset. Because of this, a new basis of accounting for the net assets of the acquired company is established under purchase accounting

APB 17 (I60) Intangible Assets

(R&D references amended by SFAS 2)

A. Costs of intangible assets acquired from others should be recorded as assets

   1. Expenditures to develop or maintain goodwill should be expensed when the intangibles

      a. Are not specifically identifiable
      b. Have indeterminate lives
      c. Are related to the enterprise as a whole

   2. Cost of an unidentifiable intangible is cash or fair value disbursed, or present value of liabilities assumed

   3. Cost of an unidentifiable intangible (acquired with a group of assets) should be determined per APB 16

B. Intangibles should be amortized systematically over years benefited in view of the following factors

   1. Legal, regulatory, or contractual provisions
   2. Provisions for renewal or extension

*Pro forma results in financial statements no longer required of nonpublic enterprises per SFAS 79.

3. Obsolescence, demand, competition, etc.

4. Life expectancies of employees

5. Expected actions of competitors

6. Benefits may not be reasonably projected

7. Composite of many individual factors

C. Straight line amortization should be used unless another method is more appropriate

1. Cost should be amortized over the life of each individual asset

2. Period of amortization should not exceed forty years

3. The method and period should be disclosed

D. Periodic review of amortization policies should be undertaken, and required changes should be made prospectively but not to exceed forty years after acquisition

APB 18 (I82) The Equity Method for Investments

A. The equity method should be used for corporate joint ventures

B. The equity method should be applied to investments where less than 50% ownership is held but the investor can exercise significant influence over operating and financing policies of the investee

1. Twenty percent (20%) or more ownership should lead to presumption of substantial influence, unless there is evidence to the contrary

2. Conversely, less than 20% ownership leads to the presumption of no substantial influence unless there is evidence to the contrary

3. The 20% test should be based on voting stock outstanding and disregard common stock equivalents

4. The following procedures should be used in applying the equity method

a. Intercompany profits should be eliminated
b. Difference between cost and book value of net assets acquired should be accounted for per APB 16 and APB 17
c. The investment account and investor's share of investee income should be presented as single amounts in investor statements with the exception of "d." below
d. Investor's share of discontinued operations, extraordinary items, cumulative effects of accounting changes, and prior period adjustments of investee should be so presented in statements of investor
e. Investee capital transactions should be accounted for as are subsidiary capital transactions in consolidated statements
f. Gains on sale of investment are the difference between selling price and carrying value of investment
g. When investee and investor fiscal periods do not coincide, use most recent investee statement and have consistent time lag
h. Losses, not temporary in nature, of investment value should be recognized by investor

      i. Investor's share of investee loss should not be recorded once investment account is written to zero. Subsequent income should be recognized after losses not recognized are made up

      j. Investor's share of investee's earnings should be computed after deducting investee's cumulative preferred dividends whether declared or not

      k. If an investor's holding falls below 20%, discontinue applying the equity method but make no retroactive adjustment

      l. When an investor's holding increases from a level less than 20% to a level equal to or greater than 20%, the investment account and retained earnings of the investor should be adjusted retroactively to reflect balances as if the equity account had been used. This is a prior period adjustment

5. Statements of investors applying the equity method should disclose

    a. Investees and percentages held

      (1) Accounting policies followed
      (2) Treatment of goodwill, if any

    b. Aggregate market value of investment (not for subsidiaries)

    c. When investments are material to investor, summarized information of assets, liabilities, and results of operations of investee may be necessary

    d. Conversion of securities, exercise of warrants, or issuances of investee's common stock which significantly affects investor's share of investee's income

---

FASB INTERPRETATION NO. 35 CRITERIA FOR APPLYING THE EQUITY METHOD OF ACCOUNTING FOR INVESTMENTS IN COMMON STOCK. Interprets APB 18.

    Investors owning between 20 and 50 percent of an investee may <u>not</u> be able to exercise significant influence over the investee's operating and financial policies. The presumption of significant influence stands until overcome by evidence to the contrary, such as: (1) opposition by the investee, (2) agreements under which the investor surrenders shareholder rights, (3) majority ownership by a small group of shareholders, (4) inability to obtain desired information from the investee, (5) inability to obtain representation on investee board of directors, etc. Whether contrary evidence is sufficient to negate the presumption of significant influence is a matter of judgment requiring a careful evaluation of all pertinent facts and circumstances, in some cases over an extended period of time. Application of this interpretation resulting in changes to or from the equity method shall be treated per APB 18, para 19l and 19m.

APB 20 (A06, A35) Accounting Changes

Prescribes accounting for three types of accounting changes and correction of an error in prior periods' financial statements. Both should be reported to facilitate analysis and understanding of the financial statements

A. Changes in principle

    1. Changes of principles should not be made unless to a preferable principle

      a. When the APB expresses a preference or rejects a principle, this is a justification for change

      b. Burden of justification for other changes rests on entity proposing change

2. Special changes require retroactive adjustment of prior period statements

    a. Special changes include

        (1) From LIFO to any other inventory method
        (2) Change in accounting for long-term contracts
        (3) Change to or from full cost method in extractive industries

    b. Nature and justification for change should be disclosed. Also, disclose effect on income before extraordinary items, net income, and per share amounts for all periods presented. The purpose of the disclosure is to avoid misleading financial statement users

3. For all other changes do not retroactively adjust prior periods

    a. Apply new method to current year
    b. The cumulative effect of the change on beginning retained earnings, as if the new principle had always been followed, should be presented on the income statement between extraordinary items and net income

        (1) The cumulative effect should be net of tax effects

    c. The effect of the change in principle, on income before extraordinary items and net income, should be disclosed for the period of change
    d. The pro forma effect of retroactive application of the change should be shown on the face of the income statement as a separate section

        (1) Net income before extraordinary items and net income should be retroactively computed
        (2) PEPS and FDEPS should be presented for each income figure
        (3) The restatement should be net of tax effects and nondiscretionary items (bonuses, royalties, etc.)

    e. A change in amortization method of assets is not considered a change in principle if only applied to new assets

        (1) Disclose change and effect on income figures in year of change
        (2) If new method is applied to old assets, it is a change in principle

    f. If pro forma amounts cannot be calculated, disclose reasons
    g. If the cumulative effect cannot be computed, disclose reasons and effect of change on current year's income figures

B. Changes in estimate

    1. A change in estimate should be disclosed in the period of change if it affects that period only

        a. Disclosure should be made in year of change if it affects future periods (e.g., change in useful life of depreciable assets)
        b. A change in estimate that is recognized by a change in principle should be accounted for as a change in estimate

            (1) For example, change from capitalizing a cost to immediately expensing it

    2. Disclosure of changes in estimates should include effect on

        a. Income before extraordinary items
        b. Net income
        c. Related per share amounts

C. Change in accounting entity (e.g., a business combination accounted for as a pooling)

1. Financial statements should be restated for all prior periods

2. The nature and reasons of change should be explained in year of change

3. Effect of changes on income figures and per share amounts should be disclosed for all periods presented

D. Correction of an error in prior statements

1. Prior period adjustment

2. Nature of error and effect on the income figures and per share amounts should be disclosed in the period the error is discovered

E. Methods of accounting for and disclosing accounting changes and error correction are designed to facilitate <u>consistency</u> in reporting by the entity from period to period, and <u>comparability</u> of reporting with that of other entities

---

FASB INTERPRETATION NO. 1   ACCOUNTING CHANGES RELATED TO THE COST OF INVENTORY
    Changes in the cost composition of inventory is an accounting change and must conform to APB Opinion 20, including justification for the change. Preferably should be based on financial reporting objectives rather than tax-related benefits.

FASB INTERPRETATION NO. 20   REPORTING ACCOUNTING CHANGES UNDER AICPA STATEMENTS OF POSITION
    Accounting changes, to comply with an AICPA Statement of Position (SOP), should be accounted for as specified by the SOP. If the SOP does not specify a method of change, the entity must follow APB Opinion 20.

APB 21 (I69) Interest on Receivables and Payables

Accounting for receivables and payables whose face value does not approximate their present value

A. Applies to receivables and payables except

1. Normal course of business receivables and payables maturing in less than one year

2. Amounts not requiring repayment in the future (will be applied to future purchases or sales)

3. Security deposits and retainages

4. Customary transactions of those whose primary business is lending money

5. Transactions where interest rates are tax affected or legally prescribed, e.g., municipal bonds and tax settlements

6. Parent-subsidiary transactions

7. Estimates of contractual obligations such as warranties

B. Notes exchanged for cash are recorded at their present value. Present value equals the cash paid/received. If face value of note ≠ cash paid/received, difference is a discount/premium

1. If <u>unstated rights or privileges</u> are exchanged in issuance of note for cash, adjust cash payment to obtain present value of the note and unstated rights

C. Notes exchanged for <u>goods or services</u> in arm's-length transaction are recorded at face amount (presumption that face amount = present value)

1. Presumption not valid if note is

a. Noninterest bearing
b. Stated interest rate is unreasonable
c. Face amount of the note differs materially from sales price of goods or services

2. When presumption not valid, record note at fair value of goods or services

a. Compute <u>implicit</u> rate [rate that discounts the future value (face of note plus cash interest, if any) to fair value of goods and services] for interest expense/revenue recognition

3. When no established market price for goods and services exists, record note at its fair market value

a. Compute <u>implicit</u> rate [rate that discounts the future value (face of note plus cash interest, if any) to fair value of note] for interest expense/revenue recognition

4. When no fair market value exists for either the goods and services or the note, record note at approximation of market value

a. Use <u>imputed</u> rate to compute present value of (and discount on) note
b. Imputed rate should approximate the rate an independent borrower and lender would negotiate in a similar transaction. Consider

(1) Credit standing of issuer
(2) Restrictive covenants
(3) Collateral
(4) Payment and other terms
(5) Tax consequences to buyer and seller
(6) Market rate for sale or assignment
(7) Prime rate
(8) Published rates of similar bonds
(9) Current rates charged for mortgages on similar property

D. Discount or premium should be amortized by the interest method (constant rate of interest on the amount outstanding)

1. Other methods (e.g., straight-line) may be used if the results are not materially different from those of the interest method

E. Discount or premium should be netted with the related asset or liability and <u>not</u> shown as separate asset or liability

1. Issue costs should be reported as deferred charges

APB 22 (A10) Disclosure of Accounting Policies

A. Accounting policies can affect reported results significantly and the usefulness
   of the financial statements depends on the user's understanding of the accounting policies adopted by the reporting entity. Disclosure of accounting policies
   are

   1. Essential to users

   2. Integral part of financial statements

   3. Required for one or more financial statements

   4. Required for not-for-profit entities

   5. Not required for unaudited interim statements

      a. If no change in accounting policy has occurred

B. Disclosure should include accounting principles and methods of applying them if
   material to reported amounts

   1. Generally, disclosure pertinent to principles involving recognition of
      revenue and expense

   2. Specifically, disclosure pertinent to

      a. Selection from existing alternatives
      b. Principles peculiar to a particular industry
      c. Unusual or innovative applications

   3. Examples

      a. Consolidation method
      b. Depreciation method
      c. Amortization of intangibles
      d. Inventory pricing
      e. R&D references amended by SFAS 2
      f. Translation of foreign currencies
      g. Long-term contract accounting
      h. Franchising and leasing activities

   4. Accounting policy disclosure should not duplicate disclosures elsewhere in
      the statements

      a. The disclosure of accounting policies may refer to details elsewhere,
         e.g., footnotes

C. Particularly useful is a separate <u>Summary of Significant Accounting Policies</u>
   preceding the notes

   1. Or as the initial note

APB 23 (I42) Accounting for Income Taxes--Special Areas

A. Undistributed earnings of subsidiaries

   1. Undistributed earnings should be presumed to be distributed in the future

      a. Tax effect may be based on assumptions such as the earnings were dis-
         tributed currently and all tax benefits <u>were</u> taken
      b. Operating loss tax effects should be recognized in accordance with
         SFAS 96

2. No tax need be accrued when sufficient evidence exists that the subsidiary
will reinvest the undistributed earnings indefinitely or remit them tax free

   a. Parent should have specific evidence of the above, such as past experience and definite future programs

3. If taxes have been accrued on undistributed earnings and it becomes apparent
the earnings will not be remitted, adjust the deferred income taxes account,
and adjust current tax expense (not an extraordinary item)

   a. If taxes have not been accrued and it becomes apparent the earnings will
   be distributed, accrue taxes as a current expense (not extraordinary)

4. If a change in the investment results in

   a. Change from subsidiary status to APB 18 status, follow SFAS 96

      (1) If taxes on the subsidiary's undistributed earnings have not been
      accrued, accrue them when investee ceases to be a subsidiary

   b. Accrued taxes on undistributed earnings should be recognized upon
   disposition of a subsidiary or part thereof

5. If a parent does not accrue taxes on subsidiaries' undistributed earnings

   a. The intention to reinvest permanently or receive tax free should be
   declared

   b. The cumulative amount of undistributed earnings on which taxes were not
   accrued should be disclosed

B. Investments in long-term corporate joint ventures follow the same rules for tax
accruals on undistributed earnings for subsidiaries in "A." above, including
required disclosures

APB 25 (C47) Accounting for Stock Issued to Employees

Redefines "measure of compensation" in ARB 43, Chapter 13B and prescribes accounting
for "variable factor" plans and tax benefits related to stock issue plans

A. No compensation is recognized for noncompensatory plans. Four noncompensation
characteristics must be present

1. Substantially all full-time employees may participate

2. Stock is offered to employees equally or based on salary

3. Time permitted for exercise of option is reasonable

4. Discount from market is not greater than would be in an offer to sell stock
to shareholders

B. All other plans are compensatory

1. Compensation is the quoted market price less the amount the employee is required to pay

   a. If unavailable, use best estimate of market value

2. The measurement date for determining compensation is the first date on which
both of the following are known

   a. Number of shares the individual may receive

b. Option price, if any

3. Note that the corporation recognizes compensation cost unless the employee must pay at least the market price (at measurement date)

C. Special rules in applying the measurement principle

1. Cost of treasury stock distributed in an option plan does not determine compensation cost. Use market value unless

   a. Treasury stock is acquired during period, and
   b. Is awarded to employees shortly thereafter

2. Measurement date is not changed because of provision that termination of employment reduces shares available

3. Measurement date may be year end rather than date of individual award if

   a. Award is provided by formal plan and
   b. Plan designates factors to determine award and
   c. Award pertains to current service

4. Measurement date for convertible securities is date the ratio of conversion is known

   a. Compensation is based on the higher value of

      (1) Original security, or
      (2) Security into which original is convertible

5. If option plans are combination of more than one plan, compensation should be measured for each of the parts

   a. If employee has a selection of alternatives, compensation on cost should be measured for the alternative most likely to be chosen

D. Compensation expense should be recognized as an expense in periods employee performs services

1. If an employee performs services for several periods prior to stock issuance, compensation expense should be accrued

   a. If the measurement date is after the grant date, the compensation should be accrued based on the current market price of stock

2. If stock is issued prior to when some of the services are performed, compensation expense should be deferred to those periods as a contra shareholder's equity item

3. Any adjustments of estimates regarding option plans should be done currently and prospectively

   a. If an employee fails to exercise an option, compensation expense recognized in earlier periods should reduce compensation expense of the present period

---

FASB INTERPRETATION NO. 28 ACCOUNTING FOR STOCK APPRECIATION RIGHTS AND OTHER
VARIABLE STOCK OPTION OR AWARD PLANS
Changes in the market value of stock between the date of the grant and the measurement date (the date both the number of shares and the option price are
known) are adjustments to compensation expense in the period the market value of
the stock changes. Stock appreciation rights are common stock equivalents for
computing EPS, unless they are payable only in cash.

APB 26 (D14) Early Extinguishment of Debt
(Amended by SFAS 76 and 84)

*Note: SFAS 76 has expanded coverage of APB 26 to all extinguishments of debt other
than debt conversions (including those induced by use of "sweeteners") and troubled
debt restructurings whether early or not. Consequently, in this outline, references
to the term "early" have been deleted.*

A. Definitions (para 3)

1. Extinguishment of debt. SFAS 76 defines transactions that should be recog-
    nized as an extinguishment of debt by the debtor

2. Net carrying amount. "Amount due at maturity, adjusted for unamortized pre-
    mium, discount, and cost of issuance."

3. Reacquisition price. "Amount paid on extinguishment, including a call pre-
    mium and miscellaneous costs of reacquisition. If early extinguishment is
    achieved by a direct exchange of new securities, the reacquisition price is
    the total present value of the new securities."

4. Refunding. Replacement of debt with other debt

B. Retirement is usually achieved by use of liquid assets

1. Currently in existence

2. From sale of equity securities

3. From sale of debt securities

4. Creation of an irrevocable trust (see outline of SFAS 76)

C. Prior to APB 26

1. Nonrefunding extinguishments were current losses and gains

2. Gains and losses on refunding transactions were

    a. Amortized over the life of the old issue (no longer permissible)
    b. Amortized over the life of the new issue (no longer permissible)
    c. Currently recognized in income

D. A difference between reacquisition price and net carrying amount of the extin-
    guished debt should be recognized in the year of extinguishment as a separate
    item

1. Gains and losses should not be amortized to future years

2. Gains and losses are extraordinary (except on purchases to satisfy sinking
    fund requirements that an enterprise would have to meet within one year of
    extinguishment date). See SFAS 4 and 64

E. The gains and losses on extinguishment of convertible debt should also be recognized currently. See "D." above

APB 28 (I73) Interim Financial Reporting
(Amended by SFAS 3, FASB Interpretation 18)

PART I Application of GAAP to Interim Periods
A. APB faced basic question about interim periods
  1. Are interim periods basic accounting periods?
  2. Are interim periods integral parts of the annual period?
B. The APB decided interim periods are an <u>integral part of an annual period</u>
  1. Certain GAAP must be modified for interim reporting to better relate the interim period to the annual period
C. Revenue should be recognized on the same basis as for the annual period
D. Costs directly associated with revenue should be reported as in annual periods with the following <u>exceptions</u>
  1. Estimated gross profit rates may be used to estimate inventory. Disclose method used and significant adjustments to reconcile to later physical inventory
  2. When LIFO base period inventories are liquidated during the interim period but are expected to be replaced by the end of the annual period, cost of sales should be priced at replacement costs rather than at base period costs
  3. Declines in inventory market values, unless temporary, should be recognized. Subsequent recovery of market value should be recognized as a cost recovery in the subsequent period
  4. Unanticipated and unplanned standard cost variances should be recognized in the respective interim period
E. The objective of reporting all other costs is to obtain fair measure of operations for the annual period. These expenses include
  1. Direct expenditures--salaries
  2. Accruals--vacation pay
  3. Amortization of deferrals--insurance
F. These costs should be applied in interim statements as follows
  1. Charge to income as incurred, or based on time expiration, benefit received, etc. Follow procedures used in annual reports
  2. Items not identified with specific period are charged as incurred
  3. No arbitrary assignment

     4. Gains and losses of any interim period that would not be deferred at year end cannot be deferred in the interim period

     5. Costs frequently subjected to year-end adjustments should be anticipated in the interim periods

        a. Inventory shrinkage
        b. Allowance for uncollectibles, quantity discounts
        c. Discretionary year-end bonuses

G. Seasonal variations in above items require disclosure and one may add twelve-month reports ending at the interim date for current and preceding years

H. The best estimate of the annual tax rate should be used to provide taxes on a year-to-date basis (also see FASB Interpretation 18)

     1. The best estimate should take investment credits, capital gains, etc. into account, but not extraordinary items

     2. Tax effects of losses in early portion of the year should not be recognized unless realization in subsequent interim periods is assured beyond a reasonable doubt, e.g., an established pattern of loss in early periods

        a. When tax effects of losses in early periods are not recognized, no taxes should be accrued in later periods until loss credit has been used

I. Extraordinary items should be disclosed separately and recognized in the interim period in which they occur

     1. The materiality of extraordinary items should be determined in relation to expected annual income

     2. Effects of disposals of a segment of a business are not extraordinary items, but should be disclosed separately

     3. Extraordinary items should not be prorated over remainder of the year

     4. Contingencies should be disclosed in the same manner as required in annual reports

J. Each interim report should disclose any change in accounting principle from

     1. Comparable period of prior year

     2. Preceding periods of current year

     3. Prior annual report

K. Reporting these changes

     1. APB 20 should be complied with, including restatement provisions

     2. A change in accounting estimate (including effect on estimated tax rate) should be accounted for in period of change and disclosed in subsequent periods of material

     3. Changes in principle, requiring cumulative effect, should be calculated for the effect on beginning annual retained earnings

a.   The cumulative effect should be reported in the first interim period (by restatement if necessary, see SFAS 3)
b.   Previously reported interim information should be restated
c.   Changes should be made in first period whenever possible
d.   Items not material to annual results, but material to interim results, should be disclosed separately in the interim reports

PART II Required Interim Disclosures by Publicly Traded Companies

A.   Minimum disclosure includes

1.   Sales, provision for taxes, extraordinary items, cumulative effect of principle changes, and net income

2.   PEPS and FDEPS

3.   Seasonal revenue, costs, and expenses

4.   Significant changes in estimates of taxes

5.   Disposal of a business segment and extraordinary items

6.   Contingent items

7.   Changes in accounting principles and estimates

8.   Significant changes in financial position

B.   When summarized interim data are reported regularly, the above should be reported for the

1.   Current quarter

2.   Current year-to-date or last 12 months with comparable data for the preceding year

C.   If fourth quarter data are not separately reported, disclose in annual report

1.   Disposal of business segment

2.   Extraordinary, unusual, and infrequent items

3.   Aggregate year-end adjustments

D.   The APB encourages interim disclosure of financial position and funds flow data

1.   If not disclosed, significant changes therein should be disclosed

---

FASB INTERPRETATION NO. 18 ACCOUNTING FOR INCOME TAXES IN INTERIM PERIODS
    Tax on income from continuing operations for an interim period is based on estimated annual effective rate, which reflects anticipated tax planning alternatives. Expense of interim period is (year-to-date income) x (estimated rate) less (expense recognized in prior interim periods). Tax effect of special items (below continuing operations) computed as they occur.

APB 29 (N35, C11) Accounting for Nonmonetary Transactions

A.   Definitions (para 3)

1.   Monetary assets and liabilities. "Assets and liabilities whose amounts are fixed in terms of units of currency by contract or otherwise. Examples are

cash, short or long-term accounts and notes receivable in cash, and short or long-term accounts and notes payable in cash."

2. <u>Nonmonetary assets and liabilities</u>. "Assets and liabilities other than monetary ones. Examples are inventories; investments in common stocks; property, plant and equipment; and liabilities for rent collected in advance."

3. <u>Exchange</u>. "A reciprocal transfer between an enterprise and another entity that results in the enterprise's acquiring assets or services or satisfying liabilities by surrendering other assets or services or incurring other obligations."

4. <u>Nonreciprocal transfer</u>. "Transfer of assets or services in one direction, either from an enterprise to its owners (whether or not in exchange for their ownership interests) or another entity or from owners or another entity to enterprise. An entity's reacquisition of its outstanding stock is an example of a nonreciprocal transfer."

5. <u>Productive assets</u>. "Assets held for or used in the production of goods or services by the enterprise. Productive assets include an investment in another entity if the investment is accounted for by the equity method but exclude an investment not accounted for by that method. <u>Similar productive assets</u> are productive assets that are of the same general type, that perform the same function or that are employed in the same line of business."

B. APB 29 does <u>not</u> apply to

1. Business combinations

2. Transfer of nonmonetary assets between companies under common control

3. Acquisition of nonmonetary assets with capital stock of an enterprise

4. Stock dividends and splits, issued or received

C. APB 29 does apply to

1. Nonreciprocal transfers with owners. Examples are distributions to stockholders

   a. Dividends
   b. To redeem capital stock
   c. In liquidation
   d. To settle rescission of a business combination

2. Nonreciprocal transfer with other than owners. Examples are

   a. Contribution to charitable institutions
   b. Contribution of land by governmental unit to a business

3. Nonmonetary exchange. Examples are exchanges of

   a. Property exchanged for dissimilar property
   b. Property exchanged for similar property

D. Nonmonetary transactions should generally be accounted for as are monetary transactions

    1. Cost of a nonmonetary asset is the fair value of the asset surrendered to obtain it

        a. The difference between fair value and book value is a gain or loss

        b. Fair value of asset received, if clearer than that of asset given, should value transaction

    2. Fair value should <u>not</u> be used to recognize gains unless fair value is determinable within reasonable limits

    3. Fair value should <u>not</u> be used to recognize gains when exchange is not the culmination of an earnings process, e.g.

        a. Exchange of property held for sale for similar property

        b. Exchange of similar productive assets

E. If a nonmonetary exchange, which is not a culmination of the earnings process, contains boot, the gain should be limited to the ratio (boot ÷ total consideration received) times the gain (total consideration received minus total consideration given)

    1. Firm paying boot should <u>not</u> recognize any gain

F. Liquidation distributions to owners should <u>not</u> be accounted for at fair value if a gain results (loss may be recognized)

    1. Use historical cost

    2. Other nonreciprocal distributions to owners should be accounted for at fair value if fair value

        a. Is objectively measurable

        b. Would be clearly realizable if sold

G. Fair value should be determined in reference to

    1. Estimated realizable values in cash transactions of similar assets

    2. Quoted market prices

    3. Independent appraisals

    4. Estimated fair value of that received in exchange

    5. Other evidence

H. Nonmonetary transaction disclosures should include

    1. Nature of the transactions

    2. Basis of accounting

    3. Gains and losses recognized

FASB INTERPRETATION NO. 30 ACCOUNTING FOR INVOLUNTARY CONVERSIONS OF NONMONE-
TARY ASSETS TO MONETARY ASSETS
    When involuntary conversions of nonmonetary assets (e.g., fixed assets) to
monetary assets (e.g., insurance proceeds) occur, the difference between the
assets' cost and the monetary assets received should be reported as a gain or
loss. If an unknown amount of monetary assets are to be received in a later
period, gain (loss) is estimated per SFAS 5. Could be extraordinary per APB 30.

APB 30 (E09, I13, I17, I22) Reporting the Results of Operations
(Amended by SFAS 4)

A. Discontinued operations definitions

 1. Segment of a business. "A component of an entity whose activities represent
     a separate major line of business or class of customer. A segment may be in
     the form of a subsidiary, a division or a department, and in some cases a
     joint venture or other nonsubsidiary investee, provided that its assets,
     results of operations, and activities can be clearly distinguished, physi-
     cally and operationally and for financial reporting purposes, from the other
     assets, results of operations, and activities of the entity."   (para 13)

 2. Measurement date. "Date on which the management having authority to approve
     the action commits itself to a formal plan to dispose of a segment of the
     business, whether by sale or abandonment."   (para 14)

 3. Disposal date. "Date of closing the sale if the disposal is by sale or the
     date that operations cease if the disposal is by abandonment." (para 14)

B. The results of discontinued operations should be disclosed separately after
    income from continuing operations and before extraordinary items

 1. Any estimated loss from disposal of discontinued operations should be
     reported with the results of discontinued operations

 2. A gain on disposal should be recognized when realized

 3. An example from APB 30 follows

```
Income from continuing operations before
  income taxes................................. $XXXX
Provision for income taxes....................   XXX
      Income from continuing operations.......                $XXXX
Discontinued operations (Note ____):
    Income (loss) from operations
     of discontinued Division X
     (less applicable income
     taxes of $____)......................... $XXXX
    Loss on disposal of Division X,
     including provision of $____ for
     operating losses during phase-out
     period (less applicable income
     taxes of $____).........................   XXXX              XXXX
                         Net income                            $XXXX
```

C. "Income (loss) from operations" is calculated from beginning of period to measurement date

D. "Gain (loss) on disposal" is calculated on the measurement date based on

1. Net realizable value

2. Less costs directly associated with disposal

   a. Includes adjustments directly related to the disposal (e.g., severance pay, additional pension expenses, relocation expenses)

   b. Does not include costs of normal business activities (e.g., write-down of A/R or inventories)

3. Plus (minus) income (loss) from operations subsequent to measurement date (i.e., during phase-out period). If disposal date is in a subsequent period, remaining phase-out income (loss) must be estimated

   a. Income limited to amount of loss otherwise recognizable from the disposal

   b. Limited to those estimates which can be projected with reasonable accuracy

   c. Limited, in the usual case, to disposals to be completed in less than one year

E. Additional disclosures for disposal of a segment

1. Identity of segment

2. Expected disposal date

3. Expected manner of disposal

4. Description of assets and liabilities remaining at balance sheet date

5. Income or loss from operations and proceeds

F. Extraordinary items are <u>both</u> unusual and infrequent

1. <u>Unusual nature</u>. "The underlying event or transaction should possess a high degree of abnormality and be of a type clearly unrelated to, or only incidentally related to, the ordinary and typical activities of the entity, taking into account the environment in which the entity operates."
(para 20)

   a. Special characteristics of the entity

      (1) Type and scope of operations
      (2) Lines of business
      (3) Operating policies

2. <u>Infrequency of occurrence</u>. "The underlying event or transaction should be of a type that would not reasonably be expected to recur in the foreseeable future, taking into account the environment in which the entity operates."
(para 20)

3. Example of extraordinary presentation (para 11)

Income before extraordinary items...................... $XXX
Extraordinary items (less applicable income
  taxes of $____) (Note _____).......................... XXX
Net income.. $XXX

4. Examples of gains and losses that are not generally extraordinary

   a. Write-downs or -offs of receivables, inventories, R&D, etc.
   b. Translation of foreign exchange including major devaluations
   c. Disposal of a segment of a business
   d. Sale of productive assets
   e. Effects of strikes
   f. Accruals on long-term contracts

5. Extraordinary items should be classified separately if material on an individual basis

6. Gains or losses which are unusual or infrequent but not both should be disclosed separately (but not net of tax) in the income statement or notes

7. See outline of SFAS 4 for treatment of gains (losses) on early extinguishment of debt

APB Statements

Statements are not Opinions and are issued as special reports for the information and assistance of interested parties

APB Statement 4

A. Purpose and nature

1. Provides a basis for better understanding of the broad fundamentals of financial accounting

2. Provides a basis for guiding the future development of financial accounting

3. The statement

   a. Discusses nature, environment, limitations, etc. of financial accounting
   b. Lists the objectives of financial accounting
   c. Describes GAAP

4. The nature is descriptive rather than prescriptive

B. The environment of financial accounting

1. Accounting "is a service activity. Its function is to provide quantitative information, primarily financial in nature, about economic entities that is intended to be useful in making economic decisions." (para 9)

2. Uses and users of financial accounting

   a. Users with direct interests

     (1) Owners
     (2) Creditors and suppliers
     (3) Potential owners, creditors, and suppliers

        (4) Management
        (5) Taxing authorities
        (6) Employees
        (7) Customers

    b. Users with indirect interests

        (1) Financial analysts and advisors
        (2) Stock exchanges
        (3) Lawyers
        (4) Regulatory and registration authorities
        (5) Financial press
        (6) Trade associations
        (7) Labor unions

    c. Financial accounting data may be prepared for common or special needs of
        users

3. Individual business enterprise

    a. Economic resources

        (1) Productive resources owned by enterprise
        (2) Contractual rights to productive resources
        (3) Products: finished and in-process
        (4) Money
        (5) Claims to receive money
        (6) Ownership interests in other enterprises

    b. Economic obligations

        (1) To pay money
        (2) To provide goods and services

    c. Residual interest = Resources - Obligations
    d. Classification of events

        (1) External events

            (a) Transfers of resources or obligations

                1] Exchanges
                2] Nonreciprocal transfers between

                    a] Enterprise and owners
                    b] Enterprise and nonowners

            (b) Other external events, changes in market values, etc.

        (2) Internal events

            (a) Production
            (b) Casualties

4. Measuring economic activity

    a. Historical cost
    b. Current replacement cost
    c. Current selling price
    d. Present value basis
    e. Note each of the above has at least some current usage

C. Objectives of financial accounting and financial statements

    1. General objectives (supplanted by SFAC 1; see outline at end of this chapter)

    2. Qualitative objectives (supplanted by SFAC 2; see outline at end of this chapter)

D. Basic features and basic elements

    1. Basic features

        a. Accounting entity--circumscribed area of interest
        b. Going concern--entity is viewed as continuing operations
        c. Measurement of economic resources and obligations--primary objective
        d. Time periods--specified periods shorter than business life
        e. Measurement in terms of money--monetary attributes
        f. Accrual--measurement as incurred, not on receipts and payments
        g. Exchange price--measurements primarily based thereon
        h. Approximation--required by complex and joint activities
        i. Judgment--necessarily involved
        j. General purpose financial information--accounting serves many users
        k. Fundamentally related financial statement--based on the same data
        l. Substance over form--legal form may differ from economic substance
        m. Materiality--only concerned with significant items

    2. Basic elements (supplanted by SFAC 6; see outline at end of this chapter)

E. Pervasive principles (supplanted by SFAC 5; see outline at end of this chapter)

Statements of Financial Accounting Standards

SFAS 2 (R50) Accounting for Research and Development Costs (R&D)

A. Establishes accounting standards for R&D costs with objective of reducing alternative practices. In summary, all R&D costs are expensed except intangible assets purchased from others and tangible assets that have alternative future uses (which are capitalized and depreciated or amortized as R&D expense)

    1. SFAS 2 specifies

        a. R&D activities
        b. Elements of R&D costs
        c. Accounting for R&D costs
        d. Required disclosures for R&D

    2. SFAS 2 does not cover

        a. R&D conducted for others under contract
        b. Activities unique to extractive industries

    3. Amends APB 17 to exclude R&D

        a. APB 22 is amended so as not to state that R&D accounting disclosure is commonly required

B. R&D activities

    1. Research is "planned search or critical investigation aimed at discovery of new knowledge with the hope that such knowledge will be useful in developing

a new product or service or a new process or technique in bringing about a significant improvement to an existing product or process."

2. Development is "the translation of research findings or other knowledge into a plan or design for a new product or process or for a significant improvement to an existing product or process whether intended for sale or use."

3. R&D examples

 a. Laboratory research to discover new knowledge

   (1) Seeking applications for new research findings

 b. Formulation and design of product alternatives

   (1) Testing for product alternatives
   (2) Modification of products or processes

 c. Preproduction prototypes and models

   (1) Tools, dies, etc. for new technology
   (2) Pilot plants not capable of commercial production

 d. Engineering activity until product is ready for manufacture

4. Exclusions from R&D

 a. Engineering during an early phase of commercial production
 b. Quality control for commercial production
 c. Troubleshooting during commercial production breakdowns
 d. Routine, ongoing efforts to improve products
 e. Adaption of existing capability for a specific customer or other requirements
 f. Seasonal design changes to products
 g. Routine design of tools, dies, etc.
 h. Design, construction, startup, etc. of equipment except that used solely for R&D
 i. Legal work for patents or litigation
 j. Items "a. - h." above are normally expensed but not as R&D; "i." is capitalized

C. Elements of R&D costs

 1. Materials, equipment, and facilities

  a. If acquired for a specific R&D project and have no alternative use
  b. If there are alternative uses, costs should be capitalized

   (1) Charge to R&D as these materials, etc., are used

 2. Salaries, wages, and related costs

 3. Intangibles purchased from others are treated as materials, etc. in "1." above

  a. If capitalized, amortization is covered by APB 17

 4. R&D services performed by others

 5. A reasonable allocation of indirect costs

  a. Exclude general and administrative costs not clearly related to R&D

D. Accounting for R&D

  1. Expense R&D as incurred

E. Disclosure requirement

  1. Total R&D expensed per period

FASB INTERPRETATION NO. 4 APPLICABILITY OF SFAS 2 TO BUSINESS COMBINATIONS
ACCOUNTED FOR BY THE PURCHASE METHOD
     Acquisition cost should be assigned to all identifiable assets including
intangibles which were the result from R&D. Subsequent to purchase, account for
assets related to R&D per SFAS 2 including write-off of those intangibles having
no alternative future use.

FASB INTERPRETATION NO. 6 APPLICABILITY OF SFAS 2 TO COMPUTER SOFTWARE
     Computer software costs, if incurred for internal use in R&D, are treated
as any other R&D costs.

SFAS 3 (I73) Reporting Accounting Changes in Interim Financial Statements
(Supersedes para 27 of APB 28)

(Amends para 31 of APB 28)

A. For cumulative effect changes made during the first interim period, include the
cumulative effect of the change on beginning retained earnings in income of the
first interim period

  1. The new principle is used in the first period

B. For cumulative effect changes made in other interim periods, restate the
previous interim periods using the newly adopted principle

  1. Also include the cumulative effect on beginning (of the fiscal year)
retained earnings in the restated results of the first interim period

    a. When prechange interim periods are subsequently presented (e.g., for
comparative purposes), use restated figures

C. Required disclosures for cumulative changes in interim reports

  1. Nature and justification of change in interim period of change

  2. The effect of the change on income from operations and net income (and
related per share amounts) in period of change

    a. Also for prechange interim periods

  3. EPS figures on a pro forma retroactively adjusted basis as in para 19-25 of
APB 20 in period of change

    a. To provide comparability with prior years' interim periods

  4. The same disclosures described in "2." and "3." above in period of change

         a. For year-to-date statements
         b. For 12 months-to-date statements

    5. For subsequent interim periods (after the change), the effect of the change on the earnings and EPS figures for that period

D. For changes (principally to LIFO) where the effect on beginning retained earnings and pro forma amounts <u>cannot</u> be determined, explain reason for omitting such (See para 11 of SFAS 3)

    1. If change is made in other than first interim period, restate prior interim periods

E. If a publicly traded company made a fourth quarter change and does not issue a fourth quarter report or explain the change in the annual report, the required disclosures shall be made in a footnote to the financial statements

SFAS 4 (D14, I17) Reporting Gains and Losses from Extinguishment of Debt

(Amends APB 30)

(Amended by SFAS 64)

A. Gains and losses from debt extinguishment are to be classified as extraordinary items (net of tax effect)

    1. Does not apply to purchases of debt to satisfy sinking fund requirements that an enterprise would have to meet within one year of extinguishment date (See also SFAS 64)

         a. Such gains and losses must be disclosed as a separate item

B. Disclosures required in statements or notes

    1. Description of transaction and source of funds

    2. Tax effect

    3. Per share amount of gain or loss (net of tax)

SFAS 5 (C59, I50, R70) Accounting for Contingencies (Supersedes Chapter 6, ARB 43)

(Supersedes ARB 50)

A. Contingency is "an existing condition, situation, or set of circumstances involving uncertainty as to possible gain or loss to an enterprise that will ultimately be resolved when one or more future events occur or fail to occur."

    1. Definitions

         a. Probable--future events are likely to occur
         b. Reasonably possible--chance of occurrence is more than remote, but less than likely
         c. Remote--chance of occurrence is slight

    2. Loss contingency examples

         a. Receivable collection
         b. Product warranty obligations
         c. Risk of property losses by fire, explosion, etc.

   d. Asset expropriation threat
   e. Pending, threatened, etc., litigation
   f. Actual or possible claims and assessments
   g. Catastrophe losses faced by insurance companies

      (1) Including reinsurance companies

   h. Guarantees of indebtedness of others
   i. Banks' obligations under "standby letters of credit"
   j. Agreements to repurchase receivables, related property, etc. that have
       been sold

B. Estimated loss from contingencies shall be accrued and charged to income when

   1. It is probable (at balance sheet date) that an asset has been impaired or
       liability incurred

   2. And the amount of loss can be reasonably estimated

      a. Difference between estimate recorded and actual amount determined in
          subsequent period is a change in accounting estimate

C. Loss contingency disclosures

   1. Nature and amount of material items

   2. Nonaccrued loss contingencies for which a reasonable possibility of loss
       exists

      a. Disclose nature of contingency
      b. Estimate possible range of loss

         (1) Or state estimate cannot be made

   3. If a loss contingency develops after year end, but before statements are
       issued, disclosure of the nature of the contingency and amount may be
       necessary

      a. If a year-end contingency results in a loss before issuance of the
          statements, disclosure (possibly pro forma amounts) may be necessary

   4. Disclose nature and amount of the following loss contingencies (even if
       remote)

      a. Guarantees of others' debts
      b. Standby letters of credit by banks
      c. Agreements to repurchase receivables

D. General, unspecified risks are not contingencies

E. Appropriation of RE for contingencies shown within shareholders' equity is not
    prohibited

   1. Cannot be shown outside shareholders' equity

   2. Contingency costs and losses cannot be charged to appropriation

F. Gain contingency accounting remains in effect as stated in ARB 50

   1. Normally not reflected in accounts until realized

   2. Adequate disclosure should be made without misleading implications of
       likelihood of realization

G. Overall, accounting for contingencies reflects <u>conservatism</u>--recognize losses immediately (if probable and reasonably estimable), but recognize gains only when realized

H. Also results in better matching--contingent losses are recognized in time period of origin

I. Other required disclosures per ARB and APB pronouncements remain in effect

---

FASB INTERPRETATION NO. 14 REASONABLE ESTIMATION OF THE AMOUNT OF LOSS
   A range of the amount of a loss is sufficient to meet the criteria of SFAS 5 that the amount of loss be "subject to reasonable estimate." When one amount in the range is a better estimate, use it; otherwise, use the minimum of the range and disclose range.

FASB INTERPRETATION NO. 34 DISCLOSURE OF INDIRECT GUARANTEES OF INDEBTEDNESS OF OTHERS
   Interprets SFAS 5 by defining the meaning of "indirect guarantee of the indebtedness of another." These are agreements which obligate one entity under conditions in which the funds are legally available to the second entity's creditors and these creditors may enforce the second entity's claims against the first entity.

SFAS 6 (B05) Classification of Short-Term Obligations Expected to be Refinanced
Modifies para 8 of Chapter 3A, ARB 43

A. Short-term obligations per para 8 of ARB 43, Chapter 3A, shall be classified as a current liability unless

  1. Enterprise intends to refinance the obligation on a long-term basis
  2. AND the intent is supported by ability to refinance (either "a." or "b.")
     a. Post balance sheet issuance of long-term debt or equity securities
     b. Financing agreement that clearly permits refinancing on a long-term basis
        (1) Does not expire or is not callable for one year
        (2) No violation of the agreement exists at the balance sheet date or has occurred to date
  3. The amount of the short-term obligation excluded from current liability status should not exceed the
     a. Net proceeds of debt or securities issued
     b. Net amounts available under refinancing agreements
        (1) The enterprise must intend to exercise the financing agreement when the short-term obligation becomes due
  4. Refinancing of short-term obligations is a F/S <u>classification</u> issue, <u>not</u> a <u>recognition</u> and <u>measurement</u> issue

FASB INTERPRETATION NO. 8   CLASSIFICATION OF A SHORT-TERM OBLIGATION REPAID
PRIOR TO BEING REPLACED BY A LONG-TERM SECURITY
        Short-term obligations that are repaid after the balance sheet date but
<u>before</u> funds are obtained from long-term financing are to be classified as
current liabilities at the balance sheet date.

EXAMPLES:

        In situation 1 below, the obligation will be classified as a noncurrent liability at the
balance sheet date. Why? Proceeds from refinancing were obtained <u>prior</u> to the due date of the
obligation.

Situation 1: Classify as noncurrent liability at balance sheet date

        In situation 2 below, the short-term obligation will be classified as a current liability.

Why? Proceeds from the issuance of stock or long-term debt were not obtained until <u>after</u> the due

date of the short-term obligation. Therefore, current assets must have been used to pay the

short-term obligation.

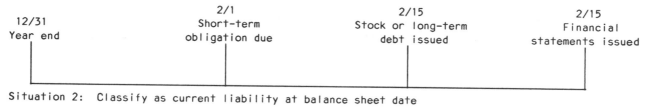

Situation 2: Classify as current liability at balance sheet date

SFAS 7 (De4) Accounting and Reporting by Development Stage Companies
A. A company, division, component, etc., is in the development stage if
    1. Substantially all efforts are devoted toward establishing the business, or
    2. Principal operations are underway but have not produced significant revenues
B. Example activities of development stage companies
    1. Financial planning
    2. Raising capital
    3. Exploring or developing natural resources
    4. R&D
    5. Establishing sources of supply
    6. Acquiring property, plant, equipment, etc.
    7. Personnel recruitment and training
    8. Developing markets
    9. Production start-up

C. No special accounting standards apply to development stage companies

1. Report revenue in the income statement as in normal operations

2. Expense costs as one would for a company in normal operations

3. Capitalize costs as one would for a company in normal operations

   a. Determine cost recoverability within entity for which statements are being prepared

D. Development stage company statements include

1. A balance sheet

   a. With cumulative net losses termed "deficit accumulated during development stage"

2. An income statement with revenues and expenses

   a. Also disclose cumulative expenses and revenues from the inception of the development stage

3. A statement of changes in financial position

   a. Also disclose cumulative amounts from inception

4. Statement of owner's investment including

   a. Dates of issuance and number of shares, warrants, etc.
   b. Dollar amounts must be assigned to each issuance

      (1) Dollar amounts must be assigned for noncash consideration

   c. Dollar amounts received for each issuance or basis for valuing noncash consideration

5. Identification of statements as those of a development stage company

6. During the first period of normal operations, notes to statements should disclose that company was, but is no longer, in the development stage

---

FASB INTERPRETATION NO. 7 APPLYING SFAS 7 IN FINANCIAL STATEMENTS OF ESTAB-
LISHED OPERATING ENTERPRISES
     Allows parent or equity method investor companies to defer some development stage company costs which would have to be expensed by the development stage company. Costs may be deferred if recoverable within the entire entity.

SFAS 12 (I89) Accounting for Certain Marketable Securities

A. Marketable equity securities shall be carried at the lower of aggregate cost or market

1. Determined at the balance sheet date

2. An excess of aggregate cost over market is carried in a valuation (contra) allowance account

3. "Marketable" means prices are readily available on a national market or in the over-the-counter market (quotations included from at least 3 dealers) but not restricted stock

4. "Equity" means ownership shares or right to acquire (sell) common or preferred shares, e.g., put and call options

    a. Does not include treasury stock, convertible bonds, or redeemable preferred stock

B. The carrying amount (lower of aggregate cost or market) of current and noncurrent portfolios shall be determined separately

  1. In an unclassified balance sheet, marketable equity securities shall be considered noncurrent

  2. Portfolios (current and noncurrent) of consolidated entities not following specialized accounting practices for marketable securities shall be consolidated to determine carrying amount

    a. Portfolios of investees accounted by the equity method shall not be consolidated

  3. If the classification (current vs. noncurrent) changes, security is transferred at the lower of cost or market

    a. If market is lower, the write-down is considered a realized loss
    b. And the market value becomes the new cost basis

C. Realized gains and losses are included in income in the period they occur

  1. Changes in the valuation account for the current portfolio are also included in income each year

  2. The accumulated changes in the valuation account for the noncurrent portfolio are separately disclosed in the equity section of the balance sheet, i.e., not taken to income until realized

    a. The debit is titled "Net unrealized loss in noncurrent marketable equity securities" and its balance sheet presentation is similar to treasury stock under the cost method

D. Lower of cost or market method reflects conservatism

E. Difference in treatment of current vs. noncurrent portfolios

  1. Inclusion of unrealized gains (recoveries) or losses from current portfolio in income justified because any gains (losses) on these securities are expected to be realized within one year or operating cycle in any case

F. Required disclosures for marketable equity securities

  1. As of each balance sheet, aggregate cost and market value of marketable securities

    a. Each segregated as to current and noncurrent when so presented on the balance sheet
    b. Identification of which is the carrying amount

  2. As of the latest balance sheet (segregated as to current and noncurrent)

    a. Gross unrealized gains for all marketable securities

b. Gross unrealized losses for all marketable securities

3. For each period an income statement is presented

   a. Net realized gain or loss
   b. Basis on which cost was computed to determine the gain or loss
   c. The change in the valuation allowance account included in income (pertains to the current portfolio)
   d. The change in the valuation account included in the equity section of the balance sheet (pertains to the noncurrent portfolio)

4. Financial statements are not adjusted for realized gains or losses occurring after the balance sheet date

   a. Significant net realized and net unrealized gains or losses occurring after the balance sheet should be disclosed

G. A permanent decline in market value is a realized loss (even for entities with no current-noncurrent classification)

  1. No write-up for subsequent cost recoveries

H. Unrealized gains and losses, whether realized in income or included in the equity section, are temporary differences

Part II Industries having specialized accounting practices with respect to marketable equity securities. (This section is not included because the authors feel that it is too specialized for the CPA exam.)

FASB INTERPRETATION NO. 11 CHANGES IN MARKET VALUE AFTER THE BALANCE SHEET DATE
    Post-balance-sheet-date market value declines in marketable equity securities may indicate a permanent decline had occurred at the balance sheet date. Any such permanent decline is recognized as loss in period it occurs. Loss measured by difference between cost and market value at balance sheet date. New adjusted cost not to be increased if market value increases.

FASB INTERPRETATION NO. 13 CONSOLIDATION OF A PARENT AND ITS SUBSIDIARIES HAVING DIFFERENT BALANCE SHEET DATES
    Aggregate each subsidiary's marketable equity securities' cost and market value existing at the subsidiaries' balance sheet dates and combine them with the parent's aggregate cost and aggregate market value. Disclose net realized and unrealized gains or losses of both parent and subsidiaries arising between balance sheet dates and the date consolidated statements are issued.

SFAS 13 (L10, C51) Accounting for Leases (Supersedes APB 5, 7, 27, 31, and para 15 of APB 18; para 18 and 23 amended by SFAS 91)

[The outline below is based on the comprehensive restatement as of May 1980 which includes SFAS 17 (rescinded by SFAS 91), 22, 23, 26, 27, 28, and 29 and Interpretations 19, 21, 23, 24, 26, and 27.]

Applies to agreements for use of property, plant, and equipment, but not natural resources and not for licensing agreements such as patents and copyrights.

The major issue in accounting for leases is whether the benefits and risks incident to ownership have been transferred from lessor to lessee. If so, the lessor treats the lease as a sale or financing transaction and the lessee treats it as a purchase. Otherwise, the lease is accounted for as a rental agreement. These different treatments recognize the substance of a transaction rather than its form; that is, what is legally a lease may be effectively the same as or similar to an installment purchase.

The following terms are given specific definitions for the purpose of SFAS 13.

Bargain purchase option--a provision allowing the lessee the option of purchasing the leased property for an amount which is sufficiently lower than the expected fair value of the property at the date the option becomes exercisable. Exercise of the option must appear reasonably assured at the inception of the lease.

Contingent rentals--rentals that represent the increases or decreases in lease payments which result from changes in the factors on which the lease payments are based occurring subsequent to the inception of the lease. However, changes due to the passthrough of increases in the construction or acquisition cost of the leased property or for increases in some measure of cost during the construction or preconstruction period should be excluded from contingent rentals. Also, provisions that are dependent only upon the passage of time should be excluded from contingent rentals. A lease payment that is based upon an existing index or rate, such as the consumer price index or the prime rate, is a contingent payment, and the computation of the minimum lease payments should be based upon the index or rate applicable at the inception of the lease.

Estimated economic life of lease property--the estimated remaining time which the property is expected to be economically usable by one or more users, with normal maintenance and repairs, for its intended purpose at the inception of the lease. This estimated time period should not be limited by the lease term.

Estimated residual value of leased property--the estimated fair value of the leased property at the end of the lease term.

Executory costs--those costs such as insurance, maintenance, and taxes incurred for leased property, whether paid by the lessor or lessee. Amounts paid by a lessee in consideration for a guarantee from an unrelated third party of the residual value are also executory costs. If executory costs are paid by the lessor, any lessor's profit on those costs is considered the same as executory costs.

Fair value of leased property--the property's selling price in an arm's length transaction between unrelated parties.

When the lessor is a **manufacturer or dealer**, the fair value of the property at the inception of the lease will ordinarily be its normal selling price net of volume or trade discounts. In some cases, due to market conditions, fair value may be less than the normal selling price or even the cost of the property.

When the lessor is **not a manufacturer or dealer**, the fair value of the property at the inception of the lease will ordinarily be its costs net of volume or trade discounts. However, if a significant amount of time has lapsed between the acquisition of the property by the lessor and the inception of the lease, fair value should be determined in light of market conditions prevailing at the inception of the lease. Thus, fair value may be greater or less than the cost or carrying amount of the property.

<u>Implicit interest rate</u>--the discount rate that, when applied to the minimum lease payments, excluding that portion of the payments representing executory costs to be paid by the lessor, together with any profit thereon, and the unguaranteed residual value accruing to the benefit of the lessor, causes the aggregate present value at the beginning of the lease term to be equal to the fair value of the leased property to the lessor at the inception of the lease, minus any investment tax credit retained and expected to be realized by the lesor (and plus initial direct costs in the case of direct financing leases)

<u>Inception of the lease</u>--the date of the written lease agreement or committment (if earlier) wherein all principal provisions are fixed and no principal provisions remain to be negotiated

<u>Incremental borrowing rate</u>--the rate that, at the inception of the lease, the lessee would have incurred to borrow over a similar term (i.e., a loan term equal to the lease term) the funds necessary to purchase the leased asset

<u>Initial direct costs</u>--(see outline of SFAS 91 Section E.2.)

<u>Lease term</u>--the fixed, noncancelable term of the lease plus all renewal terms when renewal is reasonably assured. Note: The lease term should not extend beyond the date of a bargain purchase option. (See expanded definition in the outline of SFAS 98)

<u>Minimum lease payments</u>--for the **lessee:** The payments that the lessee is or can be required to make in connection with the leased property. Contingent rental guarantees by the lessee of the lessor's debt, and the lessee's obligation to pay executory costs are excluded from minimum lease payments. If the lease contains a bargain purchase option, only the minimum rental payments over the lease term and the payment called for in the bargain purchase option are included in minimum lease payments. Otherwise, minimum lease payments include the following:

1. The minimum rental payments called for by the lease over the lease term

2. Any guarantee of residual value at the expiration of the lease term made by the lessee (or any party related to the lessee), whether or not the guarantee payment constitutes a purchase of the leased property. When the lessor has the right to require the lessee to purchase the property at termination of the lease for a certain or determinable amount, that amount shall be considered a lessee guarantee. When the lessee agrees to make up any deficiency below a stated amount in the lessor's realization of the residual value, the guarantee to be included in the MLP is the stated amount rather than an estimate of the deficiency to be made up.

3. Any payment that the lessee must or can be required to make upon **failure to renew or extend** the lease at the expiration of the lease term, whether or not the payment would constitute a purchase of the leased property

For the **lessor:** The payments described above plus any guarantee of the residual value or of the rental payments beyond the lease term by a third party unrelated to either the lessee or lessor (provided the third party is financially capable of discharging the guaranteed obligation).

<u>Unguaranteed residual value</u>--the estimated residual value of the leased property exclusive of any portion guaranteed by the lessee, by any party related to the lessee, or any party unrelated to the lessee. If the guarantor is related to the lessor, the residual value shall be considered as unguaranteed.

A. Classification of leases by lessees. Leases that meet one or more of the following criteria are capital leases; all other leases are operating leases

1. Lease transfers ownership (title) to lessee during lease term

2. Lease contains a bargain purchase option

Note: "3." and "4." do not apply if lease begins in last 25% of asset's life.

3. Lease term is 75% or more of economic useful life of property

4. Present value of minimum lease payments equals 90% or more of FMV of the leased property less lessor investment tax credit (when in effect)

a. Present value is computed with lessee's incremental borrowing rate, unless lessor's implicit rate is known and is less than lessee's incremental rate (then use lessor's implicit rate)

b. FMV is cash selling price for sales-type lease; lessor's cost for direct financing of lease (If not recently purchased, estimate FMV)

B. Classification of leases by lessors

1. Sales-type leases provide for a manufacturer or dealer profit, i.e., FMV of leased property is greater than lessor cost or carrying value

a. Sales-type leases must meet one of the four criteria for lessee capital leases ("A.1." to "A.4." above) and <u>both</u> of the following two criteria

(1) Collectibility is reasonably predictable, and

(2) No important uncertainties regarding costs to be incurred by lessor exist, such as unusual guarantees of performance. Note estimation of executory expense such as insurance, maintenance, etc., is not considered

2. Direct financing leases must meet same criteria as sales-type leases (just above) but do not include a manufacturer's or dealer's profit

3. Leveraged leases are described below in "J."

4. Operating leases are all other leases which have not been classified as sales-type, direct financing, or leveraged

C. Lease classification is determined at the inception of the lease

1. If changes in the lease are subsequently made which change the classification, the lease should be considered a new agreement and reclassified and accounted for as a new lease. Exercise of renewal options, etc., are not changes in the lease

2. Changes in estimates (e.g., economic life or residual value) or other circumstances (e.g., default) do not result in a new agreement but accounts should be adjusted and gains or losses recognized

3. At the time of inception, sales-type leases involving real estate are subject to the additional requirements that a sale of the same property would have to meet for full and immediate profit recognition under the AICPA Industry Accounting Guide applicable to sales of real estate. If these additional requirements are not satisfied, the lease that would otherwise have been accounted for as a sales-type lease will be classified as an operating lease

4. Lease classification shall not be changed as a result of a business combination

5. An important goal of SFAS 13 was to achieve symmetry in lease accounting-- i.e., an operating lease for the lessee will be an operating lease for the lessor, and likewise for capital leases

D. Accounting and reporting by lessees

1. Record capital leases as an asset and liability

    a. Leased asset shall not be recorded in excess of FMV. If the present value of the lease payments is greater than the FMV, the leased asset and related liability are recorded at FMV and the effective interest rate is thereby increased

    b. Recognize interest expense using the effective interest method

    c. If there is a transfer of ownership or a bargain purchase option, the amortization period is the economic life of the asset. Otherwise, amortize assets to the expected residual value at the end of the lease term

2. Rent on operating leases should be expensed on a straight-line basis unless another method is better suited to the particular benefits and costs associated with the lease

3. When a lessee purchases a leased asset that has been capitalized, any difference between the purchase price and the lease obligation is an adjustment to the asset carrying value but immediate recognition of a loss is not prohibited

4. Disclosures by lessees include

    a. General description of leasing arrangement including

      (1) Basis of computing contingent payments

      (2) Existence and terms of renewal or purchase options and escalation clauses

      (3) Restrictions imposed by the lease agreement such as limitations on dividends and further leasing arrangements

    b. Capital lease requirements

      (1) Usual current/noncurrent classifications

      (2) Depreciation should be separately disclosed

      (3) Future minimum lease payments in the aggregate and for each of the five succeeding fiscal years with separate deductions being made to show the amounts representing executory cost and imputed interest

        (4) Total minimum sublease rentals to be received in the future under noncancelable subleases

        (5) Total contingent rental actually incurred for each period for which an income statement is presented

    c. Operating lease--remaining noncancelable term in excess of one year requirements

        (1) Future minimum lease payments in the aggregate and for each of the five succeeding fiscal years

        (2) Total minimum sublease rentals to be received in the future under noncancelable subleases

    d. All operating leases

        (1) Present separate amounts for minimum rentals, contingent rentals and sublease rentals

        (2) Rental payments for leases with a term of a month or less may be excluded

E. Accounting and reporting by lessors

    1. Sales-type leases

        a. Lease receivable is charged for the gross investment in the lease (the total net minimum lease payments plus the unguaranteed residual value). Sales is credited for the present value of the minimum lease payments

        b. Cost of sales is the carrying value of the leased asset plus any initial direct costs less the present value of the unguaranteed residual value. Note that in a sales-type lease, initial direct costs are deducted in full in the period when the sale is recorded. Unearned Interest Income is credited for the difference between the gross investment and the sales price

        c. Recognize interest revenue using the effective interest method

        d. At the end of the lease term, the balance in the receivable account should equal the amount of residual value guaranteed if any

        e. Contingent rental payments are reported as income in the period earned

    2. Direct financing leases

        a. Accounting is similar to sales-type lease except that no manufacturer's or dealer's profit is recognized

        b. Lease receivable is charged for the gross investment in the lease, the asset account is credited for the net investment in the lease (cost to be acquired for purpose of leasing) and the difference is recorded as unearned income. Neither sales nor cost of goods sold is reported

        c. Initial direct costs are recorded in a separate account. A new effective interest rate is computed that equates the minimum lease payments and any unguaranteed residual value with the combined outlay for the leased asset and initial direct costs. The initial direct costs and unearned lease revenue are both amortized so as to produce a constant rate of return over the life of the lease

        d. The remaining requirements are the same as those for the sales-type lease

    3. Operating leases

        a. Leased property is to be included with or near property, plant and equipment on the balance sheet, and lessor's normal depreciation policies should be applied

  b. Rental revenue should be reported on a straight-line basis unless another method is better suited to the particular benefits and costs associated with the lease

  c. Initial direct costs should be deferred and allocated over the lease term in proportion to the recognition of rental income

 4. Participation by third parties

  a. The sale (or assignment) of a lease (or property leased) accounted for as a sales-type or direct financing lease does not affect original accounting classification

   (1) Profit (loss) is recognized at sale of assignment

   (2) If sale is with recourse, recognized profit (loss) is deferred and spread over lease term in a systematic manner

  b. Sale of property subject to an operating lease is not treated as a sale if substantial ownership risks are retained, e.g., in case of default, a commitment to acquire the leased property

  c. If sale of property subject to an operating lease is not recorded as a sale, transaction is accounted for as a borrowing, i.e., proceeds received are accounted for as a liability

 5. Lessor disclosures when leasing is a predominant activity

  a. A general description of leasing arrangements

  b. Sales-type and direct financing lease disclosure

   (1) Components of net investment in leases

    (a) Future minimum lease payments with separate deductions for executory costs and allowance for bad debts

    (b) Unguaranteed residual values

    (c) For direct financing lease only, initial direct costs

    (d) Unearned income

   (2) Future minimum lease payments for each of next five years

   (3) Contingent rentals earned for each period presented

  c. Operating lease disclosures

   (1) Cost of property in total and by major property category and total accumulated depreciation

   (2) Minimum noncancelable rentals in aggregate and for each of the five succeeding years

   (3) Total contingent rentals for each income statement presented

F. Real estate leases

 1. If land lease only--determine whether capital or operating using only the transfer of ownership and bargain purchase option criteria

 2. Leases involving both land and buildings

  a. If the lease transfers title or has bargain purchase option

   (1) Lessee apportions present value of payments between land and building based on relative fair market values (considered separate leases)

    (a) Building amortized per normal policy

    (b) No amortization of land

       (2) Lessor accounts as single lease--sales-type, direct financing--as appropriate

   b. If the lease does <u>not</u> transfer title or have bargain purchase option

       (1) And land is less than 25% of total FMV, both lessor and lessee account for lease as a single unit per all of the above rules

          (a) Including capitalization if 75% economic life based on the building or the 90% FMV criterion is met

       (2) And land is more than 25% of total FMV, both lessor and lessee shall account for the land and building portion of the lease separately per basic lease rules

3. If land-with-building lease also includes equipment, account for equipment portion separately

4. When costs and FMV are determinable for leases involving only part of a building, account in same manner as entire building

   a. If FMV is not determinable for lessee, use only "75% of economic life" criterion to determine whether to capitalize and amortize

   b. If cost or FMV is not determinable for lessor, then treat as operating

G. Related party leases shall be accounted for as unrelated party leases except when terms have been significantly affected by relationship

1. Nature and extent of related party leasing must be disclosed

2. See ARB 51 and APB 18 for consolidated or investor-investee transactions

3. Leasing subsidiaries must be consolidated

H. Sale-leasebacks

1. Lessee (seller) accounts for the gain (loss) as follows

   a. Any loss (when FMV < Book value) on the sale should be recognized immediately

   b. Gain is deferred unless

       (1) Seller relinquishes the right to substantially all (PV of reasonable rentals ≤ 10% of fair value of asset sold) of the remaining use of the property sold--then separate transactions, and entire gain is recognized

       (2) Seller retains more than a minor part, but less than substantially all (PV of reasonable rentals are > 10% but < 90% of fair value of asset sold) of the remaining use--then gain on sale is recognized to the extent of the excess of gain over the present value of minimum lease payments (operating) or the recorded amount of the leased asset (capital)

   c. If the gain is deferred and lease is accounted for as

       (1) Capital lease--defer and amortize gain over lease term using same method and life used for amortizing cost of leased asset

          (a) Deferral and amortization of the gain are required because the sale and leaseback are components of a single transaction and are interdependent

       (2) Operating lease--recognize on same bases as rental income, ordinarily straight-line

2. Lessor records as a purchase and a direct financing or operating lease

---

FASB TECHNICAL BULLETIN 85-3 ACCOUNTING FOR OPERATING LEASES WITH SCHEDULED RENT INCREASES

SFAS 13 requires lessees or lessors to recognize rent expense or rental income for an operating lease on a straight-line basis. Certain operating lease agreements specify scheduled rent increases over the lease term. The effects of these scheduled rent increases, which are included in minimum lease payments under Statement 13, should also be recognized by lessors and lessees on a straight-line basis over the lease term.

---

*SFAS 14 (S20) Financial Reporting for Segments of a Business Enterprise

(Cross-referenced to SFAS 18, 24, and 30.)

A. This SFAS requires disclosures about

- Enterprise operations in different industries
- Foreign operations and export sales
- Major customers

1. The disclosures are required for all complete annual statements per GAAP including comparative presentations

a. Applies only to publicly-held companies per SFAS 21
b. Does not apply to interim statements per SFAS 18

2. The purpose of the disclosures is to assist statement users in appraising past and future performance of the enterprise

B. Segment information shall be based on the accounting bases used in consolidated rather than separate company statements

1. For example, a segment, if a consolidated subsidiary, may have assets valued differently (because of goodwill allocation) for consolidation purposes than for separate company statements

2. Segment data is not required for unconsolidated subsidiaries and equity method investees. However, disclose industries and geographic areas

3. Certain intercompany eliminations, normally eliminated for consolidation purposes are included (not eliminated) in segment reporting, e.g., intersegment sales and cost of sales

C. Definitions

1. Industry segment "component of a business enterprise engaged in providing a product or service... primarily to unaffiliated customers"
2. Segment revenue includes revenue from unaffiliated customers and intersegment sales (use company transfer prices to determine intersegment sales)
3. Operating profit (loss) segment revenue less all operating expenses
    a. Operating expenses include expenses relating to both unaffiliated customer and segment revenue
    b. Operating expenses not directly traceable to segments shall be allocated thereto on a reasonable basis

*Refer to diagrams on pages 1028 and 1030 as you study this outline.

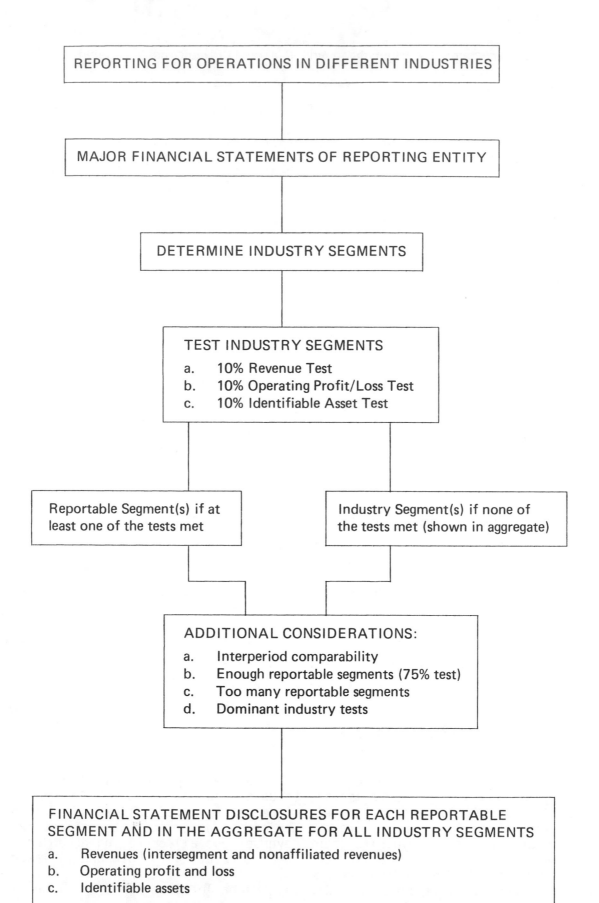

REPORTING FOR OPERATIONS IN DIFFERENT INDUSTRIES

MAJOR FINANCIAL STATEMENTS OF REPORTING ENTITY

DETERMINE INDUSTRY SEGMENTS

TEST INDUSTRY SEGMENTS

a.   10% Revenue Test
b.   10% Operating Profit/Loss Test
c.   10% Identifiable Asset Test

Reportable Segment(s) if at least one of the tests met

Industry Segment(s) if none of the tests met (shown in aggregate)

ADDITIONAL CONSIDERATIONS:

a.   Interperiod comparability
b.   Enough reportable segments (75% test)
c.   Too many reportable segments
d.   Dominant industry tests

FINANCIAL STATEMENT DISCLOSURES FOR EACH REPORTABLE SEGMENT AND IN THE AGGREGATE FOR ALL INDUSTRY SEGMENTS

a.   Revenues (intersegment and nonaffiliated revenues)
b.   Operating profit and loss
c.   Identifiable assets

      c. Intersegment purchases are priced at company transfer price

      d. Excludes general corporate revenues and expenses, income taxes, extraordinary items, interest expense, etc.

  4. <u>Identifiable assets</u> those directly associable or used by the segment

      a. Includes an allocated portion of assets used jointly with other segments, goodwill, asset valuation accounts

      b. Excludes assets used by central administration

      c. Exclude investments (loans) in other segments

         (1) Exception: not excluded from financial segments

D. To determine reportable segments

  1. Identify individual products and services

  2. Group products and services into segments

  3. Select segments significant to enterprise

E. Each industry segment is significant if one or more of the following is true for the latest period

      a. Revenue is 10% or more of combined revenue (revenue includes intersegment revenue)

      b. Operating profit or loss is 10% or more of the greater of

         (1) Combined profit of all segments with profit, or

         (2) Combined loss of all segments with loss

      c. Identifiable assets exceed 10% or more of combined identifiable assets of all segments

  1. A segment, not normally reported separately, may have abnormally high operating profit (loss) or revenue in one period

      a. If useful, report separately

      b. If not useful, report as in past and disclose

  2. The combined sales to nonaffiliated customers of segments reporting separately must be at least 75% of total sales to nonaffiliated customers

      a. If not, additional segments must be identified as reportable segments

  3. The number of reportable segments probably should not exceed 10

      a. Combine closely related segments if number of segments becomes impracticable

  4. No segment information need be disclosed if 90% of revenue, operating profit (loss), and identifiable assets are in a single industry, and

      a. No other segment meets any of the 10% tests

F. Information is to be presented for each reportable segment and in aggregate for the remaining segments not reported separately; disclose effect of any changes

  1. Sales to unaffiliated customers and intersegment sales separately for each income statement presented

      a. Use company transfer prices to price sales

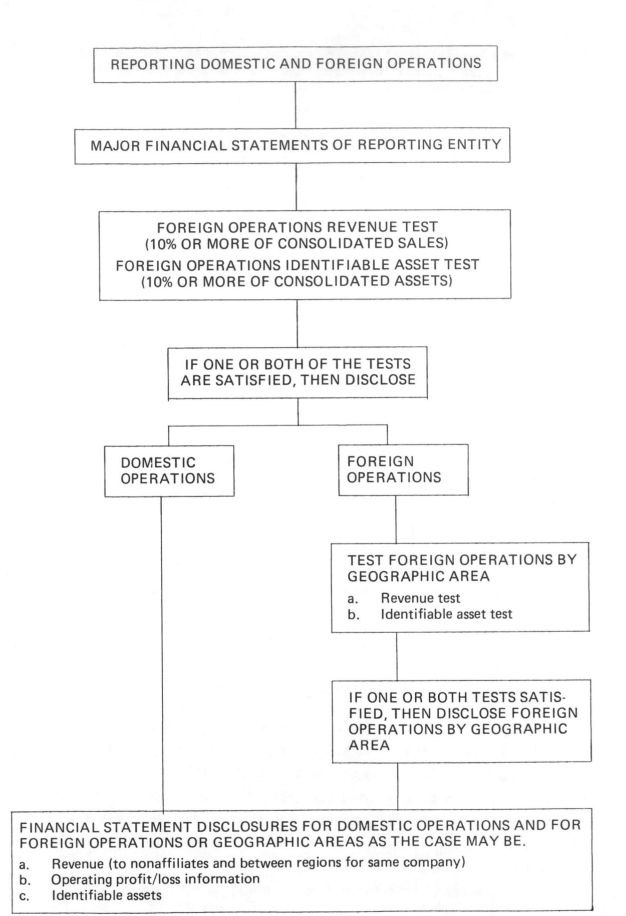

2. Operating profit (loss) for each income statement presented (see "C.3." above)

    a. Disclose unusual or infrequently occurring items
    b. Additional measures of income may be disclosed consistently

3. Carrying amount of identifiable assets. Also for each segment

    a. Aggregate depreciation, depletion, and amortization
    b. Capital expenditures
    c. Equity in vertically integrated unconsolidated subsidiaries and equity method investees

G. Segment information may be presented

    a. In the body of the statements (with appropriate explanatory disclosure)
    b. Entirely in the notes
    c. In a separate schedule to the statements (references as a part of the statements)

1. Segment revenue, profit, and asset data should be reconciled to overall consolidated figures

H. Foreign operations and export sales

1. Foreign operation revenue, operating profit, and identifiable assets (as per segments) shall be disclosed if either

    a. Foreign operation revenue to unaffiliated customers is 10% or more of consolidated revenue
    b. Foreign operation identifiable assets are 10% or more of consolidated assets

2. The foreign operation disclosures shall be further broken down by significant foreign geographic areas and in aggregate for insignificant areas

3. Disclose export sales in aggregate and by geographic area if sales to unaffiliated customers are 10% or more of consolidated sales

I. Disclose amount of revenue to each customer accounting for 10% or more of revenue

1. Disclose similarly if 10% or more revenue is derived from sales to domestic government agencies or foreign governments

2. Identify segment making sales

3. Required even if segmented data or foreign operation data are not required

SFAS 15 (D22) Accounting by Debtors and Creditors for Troubled Debt Restructurings

(Supersedes FASB Interpretation No. 2 and amends APB 26 to exclude troubled debt restructurings from APB 26)

A. Troubled debt restructurings occur when a creditor is compelled to grant relief to a debtor due to the debtor's inability to service the debt. This SFAS prescribes accounting for such debt restructurings if

1. By creditor-debtor agreement

2. Imposed by a court

3. Also includes repossessions and foreclosures

4. But not changes in lease agreements

    a. Nor legal actions to collect receivables
    b. Nor quasi-reorganizations

PART I Accounting by Debtors

A. If a debtor transfers assets to settle fully a payable, recognize a gain on restructuring equal to the book value of the payable less FMV of assets transferred

1. Estimate asset value by cash flows and risk if FMV cannot be determined

2. The difference between set FMV and carrying value of the assets transferred is a gain or loss in disposition of assets per APB 30

B. If a debtor issues an equity interest to settle fully a payable, account for equity issued at FMV

1. Excess of carrying value of payable over equity FMV is a gain on restructuring

C. A debtor having the terms of troubled debt modified should account for the re-structure prospectively, i.e., no adjustment of the payable

1. Recompute the new effective rate of interest based on the new terms

    a. Total cash payments to be paid, less carrying value of payable is the interest
    b. Amortize the payable by the interest method (APB 21) using the new interest rate

2. Exception is if restructured terms require total cash payments (including interest) which are less than the carrying value of the payable, write down the payable to the total cash to be paid

    a. Include contingent payments in calculation; this precludes recognizing a gain currently and interest expense later
    b. Recognize gain on the write-down
    c. All future cash payments reduce the payable, i.e., no interest expense is recognized

D. If restructured by partial settlement (assets and/or equity issuance) and modified terms

1. First account for asset and/or equity issuance per above

2. Then account for modified terms per above

E. Related matters

1. A repossession or foreclosure is accounted for per the above

2. Gains from restructuring debt are aggregated and, if material, are an extraordinary item (see SFAS 4)

3. Contingent payments on restructured debt shall be recognized per SFAS 5
    (i.e., its payment is probable and subject to reasonable estimate)
4. Legal fees on debt restructuring involving equity issuance reduce the
    amounts credited to the equity accounts
    a. All other direct costs of debt restructuring reduce gain or are expenses
        of the period if there is no gain

F. Disclosures by debtors
    1. Description of major changes in debt of each restructuring
    2. Aggregate gain on debt restructuring and related tax effect
    3. Aggregate net gain or loss in asset transfers due to restructuring
    4. EPS amount of aggregate gain in restructuring net of tax effect

PART II Accounting by Creditors (not applicable to receivables at market per
specialized industry practices, e.g., bonds held by a mutual fund)

A. Assets (including equity interest in debtor) received as full payment are
    recorded at FMV
    1. Loss recognized (per APB 30) for excess of carrying value of receivable over
        asset FMV
    2. Account for assets received, e.g., depreciation, etc., as if purchased for
        cash

B. Creditors having terms of receivable modified, account for the modification
    prospectively, i.e., no adjustment of the receivable
    1. Recognize excess of total cash to be received over carrying value of the
        receivable as interest per the interest method (APB 21)
    2. Exception is if total payments to be received (including interest) are less
        than the carrying value of the receivable
        a. Write receivable down to total cash to be received and recognize the
            loss
            (1) Consider contingency payments to be received if probable and
                 subject to estimate
            (2) If interest rates can fluctuate, use rate at time of restructuring
                 to determine total cash to be received
        b. All future cash payments reduce carrying value of the receivable, i.e.,
            no interest income

C. If a creditor's receivable is restructured by both receipt of assets and
    modification of terms, account for each portion of the restructure per the above
    1. First, receivable is reduced by FMV of assets received
    2. Then account for the modification of term

D. Related matters
    1. A repossession or foreclosure is accounted for per the above

2. If an adequate valuation account has already been established for the receivable being restructured, the loss can be charged to the valuation account

3. Contingent interest is not recognized until both the contingency is removed and it is earned

   a. Not recognized, however, if it reduced loss as in "B.2.a.(1)" above

4. Legal fees and other direct costs of restructuring are expensed as incurred

5. Receivables from sale of assets arising from debt restructure are accounted for per APB 21

   a. Difference between the carrying value of the receivable and the FMV of the assets received is a gain or loss

E. Disclosures by creditors for each category of restructured "reduced earnings" receivables

1. Aggregate recorded investment, and

   a. Gross interest income per original terms
   b. Interest income recognized during period
   c. Required only if currently yielding less than "market"

SFAS 16 (A35, C59, I17, I73) Prior Period Adjustments (Supersedes paras 23 and 24 of APB 9)

(Amends inconsistent references to APB 9 in APBs 20, 30, and SFAS 5)

A. All P&L items are included in the determination of net income except the correction of an error in statements of a prior period

1. Account for and report as a prior period adjustment to beginning retained earnings

B. An exception exists for interim reporting regarding certain adjustments relating to prior interim periods of the current year

1. These "adjustments" (affecting prior interim periods of the current fiscal year) are settlements or adjustments of

   a. Litigation or similar claims
   b. Income taxes
   c. Renegotiation proceedings
   d. Utility revenue per the rate-making process

2. These "adjustments" must also

   a. Be material to operating income, trends in income, etc.
   b. All or part of the adjustment is specifically identified with specified prior interim periods of the current fiscal year
   c. Not subject to reasonable estimation prior to the current interim period, e.g, new retroactive tax legislation

SFAS 18 (S20) Financial Reporting for Segments of a Business Enterprise-- Interim Financial Statements

Deletes para 4 of SFAS 14

A. Para 4 of SFAS 14 required interim financial statements (prepared per GAAP) to report segment information that is required in annual statements

B. This SFAS eliminated the required reporting of segment information in interim statements as required by SFAS 14

   1. If interim segment information is presented, it should be per SFAS 14

   2. The FASB has interim financial reporting on its agenda as a major project

SFAS 21 (E09, S20) Suspension of the Reporting of EPS and Segment Data by Nonpublic Enterprises

A. This Statement suspends APB 15 and SFAS 14 applicability to nonpublic companies

   1. APB 15 requires EPS presentations and disclosures

   2. SFAS 14 requires segment data disclosures

   3. Nonpublic companies are those whose securities do not trade in a public market

      a. Companies are considered public when they have to file registration statements on initial offerings
      b. Mutuals and cooperatives are considered nonpublic

B. If EPS and/or segment data are presented

      a. APB 15 and/or SFAS 14 must be complied with

SFAS 24 (S20) Reporting Segment Information in Financial Statements That Are Presented in Another Enterprise's Financial Report

(Amends para 7 of SFAS 14)

A. SFAS 14 "Financial Reporting for Segments of a Business Enterprise" required segment information for investees (subsidiaries, joint ventures, and equity method investees) when their complete set of statements was presented with consolidated statements

   1. SFAS 21 "Suspension of the Reporting of Earnings Per Share and Segment Information by Nonpublic Enterprises" suspended the requirement with respect to separately issued statements of nonpublic investees

B. This SFAS deletes the requirement of segment information for financial statements of consolidated investees which are issued with the consolidated statements

   1. SFAS 14 still applies to statements of unconsolidated investees which are presented in the same financial report and are not exempted by SFAS 21

SFAS 30 (S20) Disclosure of Information about Major Customers

(Amends para 39 of SFAS 14)

A. SFAS 14 required disclosure of sales to domestic government agencies in aggregate and sales to foreign government agencies in aggregate if either exceeded 10% of total sales

1. Identity of customer need not be disclosed, but segment making sales should be disclosed

B. This SFAS changes the disclosure requirement to apply to the federal government, a state government, a local government, or a foreign government

1. Rather than domestic or foreign government sales in aggregate

2. I.e., each governmental unit is treated as a separate customer as are commercial enterprises

3. The 10% of total sales criteria continues

SFAS 32 (A06) Specialized Accounting and Reporting Principles and Practices in AICPA Statements of Position and Guides on Accounting and Auditing Matters

(Amends para 16 of APB 20)

A. The FASB has agreed to take over responsibility for specialized accounting and reporting practices in AICPA Statements of Position, Accounting Guides, and Auditing Guides

1. The plan is to review the SOPs and Guides and to expose and issue SFASs

    a. Following the FASB's "due process" procedures

2. Until each is reviewed, some may consider the SOPs and Guides "without force"

3. Accordingly, the FASB has designated certain SOPs and Guides as "preferable" for justifying an accounting change per APB 20

    a. Thus, the FASB has given the SOPs and Guides status without establishing them as standards per Ethics Rule 203

        (1) I.e., they are considered within GAAP

    b. The FASB excluded coverage of the Guide "Audits of State and Local Governmental Units" and related SOPs as the jurisdiction over governmental accounting is the responsibility of the GASB

    c. Also excluded were a few Guides and an SOP not covering financial reporting topics

SFAS 34 (I67, I69) Capitalization of Interest Cost

(Paras 8 and 9 amended by SFAS 42)
(Paras 9, 10, and 20 amended by SFAS 58)

A. Interest costs, when material, incurred in acquiring the following types of assets, shall be capitalized

1. Assets constructed or produced for a firm's own use

    a. Including construction by others requiring progress payments

2. Assets intended for lease or sale that are produced as discrete projects

    a. E.g., ships and real estate developments

3. But not on

   a. Routinely produced inventories
   b. Assets ready for their intended use
   c. Assets not being used nor being readied for use
   d. Land, unless it is being developed, e.g., as a plant site, real estate development, etc.

4. The objective of interest capitalization is to

   a. Better reflect the acquisition cost of assets
   b. Better match costs to revenues in the period benefited

5. Capitalized interest shall be treated as any other asset cost for depreciation and other purposes

6. Required interest cost disclosures

   a. Total interest cost incurred
   b. Interest capitalized, if any

B. Amount of interest to be capitalized

1. Conceptually, the interest that would have been avoided if the expenditures had not been made

2. Based on the average accumulated expenditures on the asset for the period

   a. Includes payment of cash, transfer of other assets, and incurring interest-bearing liabilities
   b. Reasonable approximations are permitted

3. Use the interest rates incurred during period

   a. First, the rates on specific new borrowings for the asset
   b. Second, a weighted-average of other borrowings

     (1) Use judgment to identify borrowings

4. Interest cost capitalized in any period cannot exceed interest cost incurred in that period

   a. On a consolidated basis for consolidated statements
   b. On an individual company basis for individual company statements

5. Capitalized interest should be compounded

C. Interest capitalization period

1. Begins when all the following three conditions are present

   a. Asset expenditures have been made
   b. Activities to ready asset for intended use are in progress

     (1) Includes planning stages

   c. Interest cost is being incurred

2. If activities to ready asset for intended use cease, interest capitalization ceases

   a. Not for brief interruptions that are externally imposed

3. Capitalization period ends when asset is substantially complete

     a. For assets completed in parts, interest capitalization on a part of the asset ends when that part is complete

     b. Capitalize all interest on assets required to be completed in entirety until entire project is finished

4. Interest capitalization continues if capitalized interest raises cost above market values

     a. Reduction of asset cost to market value is a separate accounting transaction

SFAS 38 (C47, E09) Accounting for Preacquisition Contingencies of Purchased Enterprises

(Amends para 88 of APB 16)

A. This statement describes accounting for contingencies of an acquired enterprise that existed _prior_ to the date on which a business combination accounted for as a _purchase_ was consummated

1. In essence, the acquiring entity may assign final valuations to the acquired assets and liabilities up to one year after the combination occurs

B. Definitions

1. _Preacquisition contingency_--Contingency (asset, asset impairment, or liability) which is acquired from another enterprise in a business combination accounted for by the purchase method

2. _Allocation period_--Period of time necessary to identify and measure the assets purchased and liabilities assumed. This period ends when the acquiror has secured all known and available information. Typically, this period should not extend beyond one year of the date the combination was consummated

C. Portion of total purchase price allocated to a preacquisition contingency other than the potential tax benefit of a loss carryforward (SFAS 96) is measured as follows

1. If fair value is determinable during the "allocation period," use fair value as the basis of allocation

2. If fair value is _not_ determinable during the "allocation period," use criteria of SFAS 5 and FASB Interpretation 14

D. Adjustment resulting from a preacquisition contingency made subsequent to the "allocation period" is a determinant of net income in the later period

SFAS 43 (C44) Accounting for Compensated Absences

A. This statement addresses the accounting for future sick pay benefits, holidays, vacation benefits and other like compensated absences

B. Accrual of a liability for future compensated absences is required if <u>all</u> of the conditions listed below exist

    1. Obligation of employer to compensate employees arises from services already performed

    2. Obligation arises from vesting or accumulation of rights

    3. Probable payment of compensation

    4. Amount can be reasonably estimated

C. Above criteria require accrual of a liability for vacation benefits; however, other compensated absences typically do not require accrual of a liability

    1. In spite of the above criteria, accrual of a liability is not required for accumulating nonvesting rights to receive sick pay benefits because amounts are typically not large enough to justify cost

SFAS 45 (Fr3) Accounting for Franchise Fee Revenue

A. Definitions

    1. <u>Franchisee</u>--party who has been granted business rights

    2. <u>Franchisor</u>--party who grants business rights

    3. <u>Area franchise</u>--agreement transferring franchise rights within a geographical area permitting the opening of a number of franchise outlets

    4. <u>Bargain purchase</u>--franchisee is permitted to purchase equipment or supplies at a price significantly lower than fair value

    5. <u>Continuing franchise fee</u>--consideration for continuing rights granted by the agreement (general or specific) during its life

    6. <u>Franchise agreement</u>--essential criteria

        a. Contractual relation between franchisee and franchisor

        b. Purpose is distribution of a product, service, or entire business concept

        c. Resources contributed by both franchisor and franchisee in establishing and maintaining the franchise

        d. Outline of specific marketing practices to be followed

        e. Creation of an establishment that will require and support the full-time business activity of the franchisee

        f. Both franchisee and franchisor have a common public identity

    7. <u>Initial franchise fee</u>--consideration for establishing the relationship and providing some initial services

    8. <u>Initial services</u>--variety of services and advice; e.g., site selection, financing and engineering services, advertising assistance, training of personnel, manuals for operations, administration and recordkeeping, bookkeeping and advisory services, quality control programs

B. Franchise fee revenue from individual sales shall be recognized when all
    material services or conditions relating to the sale have been substantially
    performed or satisfied by the franchisor
    1. Substantial performance means
        a. Franchisor has no remaining obligation or intent to refund money or
            forgive unpaid debt
        b. Substantially all initial services have been performed
        c. No other material conditions or obligations exist
    2. If a large initial franchise fee is required and continuing franchise fees
        are small in relation to future services, then a portion of the initial
        franchise fee shall be deferred and amortized over the life of the franchise
C. If franchise fee includes a portion for tangible property, portion applicable to
    tangible assets shall be based on the fair value of the assets, and may be
    recognized before or after the revenue from initial services
D. Continuing franchise fees shall be reported as revenue as the fees are earned
    and become receivable from the franchise. Related costs shall be expensed as
    incurred
E. If franchisee is given right to make bargain purchases, then a portion of the
    initial franchise fee shall be deferred and accounted for as an adjustment of
    the selling price when franchisee purchases equipment or supplies
F. Direct franchise costs shall be deferred until related revenue is recognized
    1. These costs should not exceed anticipated revenue less estimated additional
        related costs
G. Accounting for repossessed franchises
    1. If franchisor refunds fee, previously recognized revenue is accounted for as
        a reduction of revenue in current period
    2. If franchisor does not refund fee, previously recognized revenue is not
        adjusted
        a. Provide for estimated uncollectible amount
        b. Consideration retained for which revenue was not previously recognized
            should be recognized as revenue in current period
H. Disclosure of all significant commitments and obligations that have not yet been
    substantially performed are required
    1. Notes to the financial statements should disclose whether the installment or
        cost recovery method is used
    2. Initial franchise fees shall be segregated from other franchise fee revenue
        if significant

SFAS 47 (C32) Disclosure of Long-Term Obligations

A. This statement requires that a firm disclose

1. Commitments under unconditional purchase obligations that are associated with suppliers (financing arrangements)

2. Future payments on long-term borrowings and redeemable stock

B. Unconditional purchase obligations are obligations to transfer funds in the future for fixed or minimum amounts of goods or services at fixed or minimum prices

C. Unconditional purchase obligations that have all the following characteristics must be disclosed; they are not recorded on the balance sheet

1. Is noncancelable or cancelable only

a. Upon occurrence of a remote contingency, or
b. With permission of another party, or
c. If a replacement agreement is signed between same parties
d. Upon penalty payment such that continuation appears reasonably assured

2. Was negotiated as part of arranging financing for the facilities that will provide the contracted goods

3. Has a remaining term greater than one year

D. Disclosure of those unconditional purchase obligations not recorded on the balance sheet shall include

1. Nature and term of the obligation

2. Amount of the fixed and determinable portion of the obligation as of the most recent balance sheet in the aggregate and if determinable for each of the next 5 years

3. Description of any variable elements of the obligation

4. Amounts purchased under the obligation(s) for each year an income statement is presented

5. Encourages disclosing imputed interest to reduce the obligation to present value using

a. Effective interest rate, or if unknown
b. Purchaser's incremental borrowing rate at the date the obligation was entered into

E. This statement does not change the accounting for obligations that are recorded on the balance sheet, nor does it suggest that disclosure is a substitute for accounting recognition. For recorded obligations, the following information should be disclosed for each of the next five years

1. Aggregate amount of payments for unconditional obligations that meet criteria for balance sheet recognition

2. Combined aggregate amount of maturities and sinking fund requirements for all long-term borrowings

3. Amount of redemption requirements for all issues of capital stock that are redeemable at fixed or determinable prices on fixed or determinable dates

SFAS 48 (R75) Revenue Recognition When Right of Return Exists

(Extracts from AICPA Statement of Position (SOP) 75-1)

A. Specifies accounting for sales in which a product may be returned for refund, credit applied to amounts owed, or in exchange for other products

1. Right is specified by contract or is a matter of existing practice

2. Right may be exercised by ultimate customer or party who resells product to others

3. Not applicable to service revenue, real estate or lease transactions, or return of defective goods

B. Recognize revenue from right of return sales only if all of the following conditions are met

1. Price is substantially fixed or determinable at date of sale

2. Buyer has paid or is unconditionally obligated to pay

3. Obligation is not changed by theft, destruction, or damage of product

4. Buyer has "economic substance" apart from seller (i.e., sale is not with a party established mainly for purpose of recognizing sales revenue)

5. Seller has no significant obligation for performance to directly cause resale of product

6. Amount of future returns can be reasonably estimated

C. If all of the conditions in "B." above are met, record sales and cost of sales and

1. Reduce sales revenue and cost of sales to reflect estimated returns

2. Accrue expected costs or losses in accordance with SFAS 5

D. If any condition in "B." above is not met, do not recognize sales and cost of sales until either

1. All conditions are subsequently met, or

2. Return privilege has substantially expired

E. Factors which may impair ability to make a reasonable estimate of returns include

1. Susceptibility of product to significant external factors (e.g., obsolescence or changes in demand)

2. Long period of return privilege

3. Absence of experience with similar products or inability to apply such experience due to changing circumstances (e.g., marketing policies or customer relationships)

4. Absence of large volume of similar transactions

SFAS 49 (D18) Accounting for Product Financing Arrangements
(Extracts from AICPA Statement of Position (SOP) 78-8)

A. Establishes accounting and reporting standards for product financing arrangements by requiring treatment as a borrowing rather than as a sale

1. This statement does not alter any requirement of SFAS 48, nor does it apply to transactions for which sales revenue shall be accorded current recognition in accordance with that statement

B. In product financing arrangements, a sponsor (entity which is financing its inventory)

1. Sells product to another entity and agrees to repurchase the product, <u>or</u>

2. Arranges for another entity to purchase product on a sponsor's behalf and agrees to purchase product, <u>or</u>

3. Controls disposition of product that has been purchased by another entity using the type of arrangement in either "1." or "2." above

C. Other typical, but not necessary, characteristics of such agreements are

1. Entity that purchases product was established for that purpose or is an existing trust, nonbusiness organization, or credit grantor

2. Financed product is to be used or sold by sponsor

3. Financed product is stored in sponsor's premises

4. Debt of purchasing entity is guaranteed by sponsor

D. The standards established (see "E." below) apply to agreements described in "B." above which meet <u>both</u> of the following criteria

1. Sponsor is required to purchase product at specified prices; a predetermined sponsor price is present in agreements that

   a. Include resale price guarantees for products sold to third parties
   b. Give sponsor option to purchase with significant penalty if option is not exercised
   c. Provide option for other entity to require sponsor purchase

2. Payments to other entity are set by the financing agreement and sponsor's payments will be modified, as necessary, to cover fluctuations in purchasing and holding costs (including interest) incurred by other entity

E. Standards of accounting and reporting for sponsors

1. If agreement meets description of "B.1."

   a. Liability is recorded when proceeds received

    b. No sale is recorded

    c. Financed inventory is not removed from balance sheet

2. If agreement meets description of "B.2."

    a. Asset (inventory) and related liability are recorded when purchased by other entity

3. Shall account for financing and holding costs as they are incurred by the other entity in the same manner as such costs are normally accounted for

    a. Interest costs shall be treated separately in accordance with SFAS 34

SFAS 52 Foreign Currency Translation (Supersedes SFAS 8, SFAS 20, and SFAS Interpretations 15 and 17)

A. Primary objectives of foreign currency translation

1. Should provide information disclosing effects of rate changes on enterprise cash flows and equity

2. Should also provide information in consolidated statements as to financial results and relationships of individual consolidated entities measured in their respective functional currencies in accordance with U.S. GAAP

B. <u>Functional currency</u> is the currency of the primary economic environment in which a foreign entity operates (i.e., the environment in which the entity generates and spends cash)

1. A foreign entity's assets, liabilities, revenues, expenses, gains, and losses shall be measured in that entity's functional currency

2. The functional currency could be the currency of the country in which the entity operates if the entity is a self-contained unit operating in a foreign country

EXAMPLE: An entity (1) whose operations are not integrated with those of the parent, (2) whose buying and selling activities are primarily local, and (3) whose cash flows are primarily in the foreign currency.

3. There may be several functional currencies if there are many self-contained entities operating in different countries

4. The functional currency might be the U.S. dollar if the foreign entity's operations are considered to be a direct and integral part of the U.S. parent's operations

EXAMPLE: An entity (1) whose operations are integrated with those of the parent, (2) whose buying and selling activities are primarily in the parent's country and/or the parent's currency, and (3) whose cash flows are available for remittance to the parent.

5. Functional currency for a foreign entity, once determined, shall be used consistently unless it is clear that economic facts and circumstances have changed

   a. If a change is made, do not restate previously issued financial
       statements

6. If a foreign entity's bookkeeping is not done in the functional currency,
   the process of converting from the currency used for the books and records
   to the functional currency is called remeasurement

   a. Remeasurement is intended to produce the same result (e.g., balances for
       assets, expenses, liabilities, etc.) as if the functional currency had
       been used for bookkeeping purposes (to understand the measurement
       process, you should read the foreign currency section in Module 32)
   b. In highly inflationary economies (cumulative inflation over a 3-year
       period is $\geq$ 100%), the remeasurement of a foreign entity's financial
       statements shall be done as if the functional currency were the report-
       ing currency (i.e., the U.S. dollar)

7. The functional currency (if not the U.S. dollar) is translated to the
   reporting currency (assumed to be the U.S. dollar) by using appropriate
   exchange rates (see item "C." below)

   a. If the functional currency is the U.S. dollar, there is no need to
       translate (if the books and records are maintained in U.S. dollars)

C. The translation of foreign currency financial statements (those incorporated in
   the financial statements of a reporting enterprise by consolidation, combination
   or the equity method of accounting) should use a current exchange rate if the
   foreign currency is the functional currency

   1. Assets and liabilities--exchange rate at the balance sheet date is used to
      translate the functional currency to the reporting currency

   2. Revenues (expenses) and gains (losses)--exchange rates when the transactions
      were recorded shall be used to translate from the functional currency to the
      reporting currency

      a. Weighted-averages for exchange rates may be used for items occurring
          numerous times during the period

   3. Translation adjustments will result from the translation process if the
      functional currency is a foreign currency

      a. Translation adjustments are not an element of net income of the
          reporting entity
      b. Translation adjustments are accumulated and reported as part of the
          reporting entity's owners' equity
      c. Accumulated translation adjustments remain part of the owners' equity
          until the reporting entity disposes of the foreign entity

          (1) In period of disposal, these adjustments are reported as part of
               the gain (loss) on sale or liquidation

D. Foreign currency transactions are those which are denominated (fixed) in other
   than the entity's functional currency

1. Receivables and/or payables, which are fixed in a currency other than the functional currency, may result in transaction gains (losses) due to changes in exchange rates after the transaction date

2. Transaction gains or losses generally are reported on the income statement in the period during which the exchange rates change

3. Deferred taxes may have to be provided for transaction gains or losses which are realized for income tax purposes in a time period different than that for financial reporting

E. A forward exchange contract represents an agreement to exchange different currencies at a specified future rate and at a specified future date

1. A forward exchange contract is accounted for like a foreign currency transaction

2. Gains (losses) on forward contracts (except those noted in "4." below) are disclosed on the income statement during the period in which the spot rates change

   a. Spot rate is the rate for immediate delivery of the currencies exchanged

3. Discounts (premiums) on forward contracts are accounted for separately from the gains or losses noted in "2." above

   a. Discounts (premiums) generally are amortized and charged to income during the life of the forward contract

4. Gains (losses) on a forward contract that is intended to hedge an identifiable foreign currency commitment should be deferred until the transaction date

   a. Losses should not be deferred if deferral leads to the recognition of losses in later periods

F. Financial statement disclosures required

1. Aggregate transaction gain (loss) that is included in the entity's net income

2. Analysis of changes in accumulated transaction adjustments which are reported as part of the entity's owners' equity

3. Significant rate changes subsequent to the date of the financial statements including effects on unsettled foreign currency transactions

---

FASB INTERPRETATION NO. 37 ACCOUNTING FOR TRANSLATION ADJUSTMENTS UPON SALE OF PART OF AN INVESTMENT IN A FOREIGN ENTITY

If an enterprise sells part of its ownership interest in a foreign entity, a pro rata portion of the accumulated translation adjustment component of equity attributable to that investment shall be recognized in measuring the gain (loss) on the sale.

SFAS 55 (E09) Determining Whether a Convertible Security is a Common Stock Equivalent

(Amends para 33 of APB 15)

A. APB 15 used bank prime interest rate in cash yield test for determining common stock equivalents (CSEs)

    1. Convertible securities were CSEs if cash yield was less than two-thirds of bank prime interest rate at time of issuance

B. Recent bank prime interest rates have been volatile and often higher than long-term interest rates

    1. Classification of some convertible securities as CSEs was contrary to the intent of APB 15

C. Therefore, in the cash yield test, "bank prime interest rate" is replaced by "average Aa corporate bond yield" (see outline of SFAS 85)

SFAS 56 (A06, Co4) Designation of AICPA Guide and Statement of Position (SOP) 81-1 on Contractor Accounting and SOP 81-2 Concerning Hospital-Related Organizations as Preferable for Purposes of Applying APB Opinion 20

(Amends SFAS 32)

A. SFAS 32 designates, as "preferable," those accounting principles which are contained in the AICPA Statements of Position (SOPs) and AICPA Guides (Accounting and Auditing) listed in Appendix A of SFAS 32

B. The guide and SOPs listed below are added to the list of Appendix A of SFAS 32

    1. Audit and Accounting Guide for Construction Contractors

    2. SOP 81-1, Accounting for Performance of Construction-Type and Certain Production-Type Contracts

    3. SOP 81-2, Reporting Practices concerning Hospital-Related Organizations

SFAS 57 (R36) Related Party Disclosures

A. Definitions

    1. _Affiliate_--Party is controlled by another enterprise, that controls, or is under common control with another enterprise, directly or indirectly

    2. _Control_--Power to direct or cause direction of management through ownerships contract, or other means

    3. _Immediate family_--Family members whom principal owners or management might control/influence or be controlled/influenced by

    4. _Management_--Persons responsible for enterprise objectives who have policy-making and decision-making authority

        a. E.g., board of directors, chief executive and operating officers, and vice-presidents

        b. Includes persons without formal titles

5. Principal owners--Owners of more than 10% of a firm's voting interests
    a. Includes known beneficial owners
6. Related parties--Affiliates, equity method investees, employee benefit trusts, principal owners, management or any party that can significantly influence a transaction

B. Financial statements shall include disclosures of material transactions between related parties except
    1. Compensation agreements, expense allowances, and other similar items in the ordinary course of business
    2. Transactions which are eliminated in the preparation of consolidated/ combined financial statements

C. Disclosures of material transactions shall include
    1. Nature of relationship(s)
    2. Description of transaction(s), including those assigned zero or nominal amounts
    3. Dollar amounts of transactions for each income statement period and effect of any change in method of establishing terms
    4. Amounts due to/from related parties, including terms and manner of settlement

D. Representations concerning related party transactions shall not imply that terms were equivalent to those resulting in arm's length bargaining unless such statement can be substantiated

E. When a control relationship exists, disclose such relationship even though no transactions have occurred

SFAS 64 (D14) Extinguishments of Debt Made to Satisfy Sinking-Fund Requirements
(Amends para 8 and footnote 2 of SFAS 4)

A. Gains (losses) on extinguishment of debt made to satisfy sinking-fund require- ments which would need to be met within one year of extinguishment date do not require extraordinary item classification

B. Means used to achieve the extinguishment (cash, noncash) does not affect the resultant classification of gains (losses)

SFAS 66 (Re1) Accounting for Sales of Real Estate

A. Other than retail land sales
    1. Use the full accrual method if the following criteria are satisfied
        a. Sale is consummated
        b. Buyer's initial and continuing investments demonstrate a commitment to pay for the property
        c. Seller's receivable is not subject to future subordination

      d. Risks and rewards of ownership have been transferred

   2. When the criteria are not met and dependent upon the particular circumstance, use one of the following methods

      a. Installment method
      b. Cost recovery method
      c. Deposit method
      d. Reduced profit method
      e. Financing, leasing, or profit-sharing arrangement rather than a sale

B. Retail land sales (not outlined due to specialized nature)

SFAS 68 (R55) Research and Development Arrangements

A. Establishes accounting for enterprise's obligation under arrangement in which R&D is funded by others

B. Obligation to repay any of the funds provided by other parties <u>regardless of the outcome</u> of the R&D is a liability which shall be estimated and recognized

   1. Obligation may be written, contractual, or presumed (because of surrounding conditions)

   2. Charge R&D costs to expense as incurred

C. Obligation for contract to perform R&D for others arises (no liability recorded) when financial risk associated with R&D has been transferred because repayment of any funds provided by other parties depends <u>solely</u> on the results

D. Loan or advance made by enterprise to other parties should be expensed if repayment depends solely on R&D results having future economic benefits

   1. Classify as R&D expense unless related to some other function (advertising, marketing, etc.)

E. Financial statement disclosure

   1. For arrangements in "B." and "D." above, follow SFAS 2 disclosure

   2. For arrangements in "C." above

      a. Terms of significant agreements under R&D arrangements as of the date of each balance sheet presented
      b. Amount of compensation earned and costs incurred under R&D arrangements for each period for which income statement is presented

SFAS 76 (D14, L10) Extinguishment of Debt
(Amends APB 26)

A. Statement provides guidance to debtors as to what shall be considered an extinguishment of debt for financial reporting purposes

   1. Amends APB 26 by

      a. Referring to standards in this statement
      b. Making it apply to all extinguishments of debt, whether early or not, except for

         (1) Convertible debt

(2) Troubled debt restructurings

2. Other situations excluded from scope of statement

    a. Redeemable preferred stock
    b. Debt with variable terms

B. Debt shall be <u>considered extinguished</u> for financial reporting purposes in following circumstances

1. Debtor pays creditor and is relieved of all obligations relative to that debt

    a. Includes reacquisition of outstanding debt securities in securities markets, regardless of whether securities are cancelled or held as treasury bonds

2. Debtor is legally released from being primary obligor under the debt either judicially or by creditor <u>and</u> it is probable that debtor will not be required to make future payments relative to that debt under any guarantees

3. Debtor places cash or other assets in irrevocable trust

    a. Trust is to be used for sole purpose of satisfying scheduled payments of both interest and principal of a specific obligation
    b. Only remote possibility exists that debtor will be required to make future payments with respect to that debt
    c. In this situation, debt is extinguished even though debtor is <u>not</u> legally released from being primary obligor

C. Requirements regarding nature of assets held by irrevocable trust

1. Trust is restricted to owning only monetary assets that are essentially risk-free as to amount, timing, and collection of interest and principal

2. Monetary assets must be denominated in currency in which debt is payable. For debt denominated in U.S. dollars, essentially risk-free monetary assets are limited to

    a. Direct obligations of U.S. government
    b. Obligations guaranteed by U.S. government
    c. Securities backed by U.S. government obligations as collateral under arrangement by which interest and principal payments on collateral flow to holder (the trust) of security

        (1) Securities that can be paid prior to scheduled maturity are not essentially risk free as to the timing of collection of interest and payment; they do not qualify for ownership

3. Monetary assets held by trust must provide cash flows that approximately coincide with the timing and amount of scheduled interest and principal payments on debt being extinguished

D. Accounting for costs related to placing assets in trust

1. If trust assets will be used to pay any related costs, those costs should be considered in determining amount of funds required by trust

2. If debtor incurs obligation to pay any related costs, debtor shall accrue liability for those probable payments in period debt recognized as extinguished

E. If debt is considered extinguished under provisions of "B.3.," following shall be disclosed so long as debt remains outstanding
   1. General description of transaction
   2. Amount considered extinguished at end of period

SFAS 77 (L10, R20) Reporting by Transferors for Transfers of Receivables with Recourse

(Amends SFAS 13 and 32)

A. Statement establishes financial accounting reporting standards by transferors for transfers of receivables with recourse that purport to be sales of receivables
   1. Also applies to
      a. Transfers of specified interests in particular receivable or pool of receivables that provide for recourse (participation agreement)
      b. Factoring agreements that provide for recourse
      c. Sales or assignments with recourse of leases or property subject to leases accounted for as sales-type or direct financing leases
   2. Does not address accounting and reporting
      a. By transferees
      b. Of loans collateralized by receivables for which receivables and loans are reported on borrower's balance sheet
      c. For exchanges of substantially identical receivables or other assets

B. Definitions
   1. Current (normal) servicing fee rate--rate charged for comparable agreements covering like receivables
   2. Net receivables--gross amount of receivables, including finance and service charges and fees owed by debtor included in recorded receivables, less related unearned finance and service charges and fees
   3. Probable adjustments--adjustments for (a) estimated bad debt losses and related costs of collections and repossessions per SFAS 5, (b) estimated effects of prepayments, (c) defects in eligibility of transferred receivables (e.g., defects in legal title)
   4. Recourse--right of transferee to receive payment from transferor (a) nonpayment of debtors when due (b) effects of prepayments (c) adjustments from defects in eligibility of transferred receivables

C. Transfer of receivables with recourse is recognized as sale if all three of following are met

1. Transferor surrenders control of future economic benefits embodied in receivables
2. Transferor's obligation under recourse provisions can be reasonably estimated
3. Transferee cannot require transferor to repurchase receivables except pursuant to recourse provisions

D. If transfer qualifies as recognizable sale
1. All probable adjustments in connection with recourse obligations to transferor shall be accrued in accordance with SFAS 5
2. Gain (loss) shall be recognized, measured by difference between
    a. Sales price, adjusted for accrual for probable adjustments, and
    b. Net receivables
3. If receivables are sold with servicing retained by transferor, the sales price shall be adjusted to provide for normal servicing fee in each subsequent period in those cases in which either
    a. Stated servicing fee rate differs materially from normal servicing fee rate, or
    b. No servicing fee is specified

E. If any of the conditions in "C." are not met, the amount of proceeds from transfer of receivables shall be reported as liability

F. For transfers of receivables with recourse reported as sale, transferor shall disclose
1. Proceeds received during each period for which income statement is presented
2. Balance of receivables transferred that remain uncollected at date of each balance sheet presented (if available)

SFAS 78 (B05) Classification of Obligations That Are Callable by the Creditor
(Amends ARB 43, Chapter 3A)

A. Statement specifies that the current liability classification is also intended to include
1. Obligations that, by their terms, are due on demand or will be due on demand within one year (or operating cycle, if longer) from balance sheet date, even though liquidation may not be expected within that period
2. Long-term obligations that are or will be callable by creditor either because
    a. Debtor's violation of debt agreement provision at balance sheet date makes obligation callable or
    b. Violation, if not cured within grace period, will make obligation callable

B. Callable obligations in "A.2." should be classified current unless one of the following conditions is met
   1. Creditor has waived or subsequently lost the right to demand repayment for more than one year (or operating cycle, if longer) from balance sheet date
   2. For long-term obligations containing grace period within which debtor may cure violation, it is probable violation will be cured within that period
      a. If obligation meets this condition, the circumstances shall be disclosed
C. This statement does not modify SFAS 6 or 47

SFAS 79 (B50) Elimination of Certain Disclosures for Business Combinations by Non-Public Enterprises

(Amends APB 16, para 96)

A. Disclosures of pro forma results of operations for business combinations accounted for using purchase method no longer required for nonpublic enterprises

SFAS 80 (F80) Accounting for Futures Contracts

A. Statement establishes standards of accounting for exchange-traded futures contracts
   1. Does not cover contracts for foreign currencies
B. Requires that change in market value of an open futures contract be recognized as gain (loss) in period of change unless contract qualifies as hedge of certain exposures to price or interest rate risk
   1. Immediate gain (loss) recognition also required if item hedged by futures contract is reported at FMV (e.g., futures contracts used as hedges by broker-dealers)
C. If contract qualifies as hedge, a change in market value contract is either reported as an adjustment of carrying amount of hedged item or included in measurement of a related subsequent transaction
   1. If high correlation of changes in market value of contract and effects of price or interest rate changes on hedged item has not occurred, enterprise should discontinue treating contract as hedge

SFAS 81 (P50) Disclosure of Postretirement Health Care and Life Insurance Benefits

A. Statement establishes required disclosures for health care and life insurance benefits provided by individual employers to retirees, their dependents or survivors
   1. Health benefits include all health-related aid, such as dental, hearing, and vision benefits
   2. Does not apply to

a.   Death benefits that are presently accrued and disclosed as part of pension costs
b.   Benefits provided by multiemployer-sponsored plans
c.   Government-required employer contributions to a national health plan

B.   Employer providing such retiree benefits is required, at a minimum, to make following disclosures

1.   Description of benefits provided and employee groups covered

2.   Description of accounting and funding policies followed for those benefits

3.   Cost of those benefits recognized for the period, unless they cannot be separated from the benefits for active employees or cannot be reasonably approximated (see "D.")

4.   Effect of significant matters affecting comparability of costs recognized for all periods presented

C.   Statement encourages employers to use reasonable methods to approximate costs of postretirement health care and life insurance benefits

1.   May disclose separately for each type of benefit or for all benefits in total

D.   If employer cannot separate costs for retirees from those for active employees, must disclose

1.   Cost of providing those benefits to both active employees and retirees

2.   Number of people in each category covered by plan

SFAS 84 (D10, D14) Induced Conversions of Convertible Debt

(Amends APB 26, para 2)

A.   Establishes accounting and reporting standards for conversion of convertible debt to equity securities when debtor induces conversion of the debt

1.   Applies only to conversions that both

a.   Occur pursuant to changed conversion privileges exercisable only for limited period of time
b.   Include issuance of all of the equity securities issuable pursuant to the original conversion privileges for each instrument that is converted

2.   Examples of changed terms to induce conversion

a.   Reduction of original conversion price
b.   Issuance of warrants or other securities not included in original conversion terms
c.   Payment of cash or other consideration to debt holders who convert during the specified time period

B.   Debtor enterprise shall recognize expense equal to excess of fair value of all securities and other consideration transferred in the transaction over fair value of securities issuable pursuant to the original conversion terms

1.   Expense is not an extraordinary item

    2. Fair value of securities/other consideration measured as of inducement date

       a. Typically date converted by debt holder or binding agreement entered into

SFAS 85 (E09) Yield Test for Determining Whether a Convertible Security is a Common Stock Equivalent

(Amends APB 15, para 33)

A. Statement establishes "effective yield test" to replace the "cash yield test" for all convertible securities

    1. Established to cover "zero coupon" convertible securities and "deep discount" convertible securities

B. Convertible securities are CSEs if at time of issuance they have an effective yield of less than 66 2/3% of the current average Aa corporate bond yield

C. "Effective yield" is based on securities' stated annual interest or dividend payments, premium or discount, and any call premium or discount

    1. If there is no stated maturity date (e.g., convertible preferred stock), effective yield is computed as stated annual interest or dividend divided by the market price of the security at issuance

D. Effective yield shall be lowest of yield to maturity and yields to all call dates

SFAS 87 (P16) Employers' Accounting for Pensions

(Supersedes ARB 8 and SFAS 36)

Applies to any arrangement that is similar in substance to pension plan regardless of form or means of financing. Applies to written plan and to plan whose existence may be implied from well-defined, although perhaps unwritten, practice of paying postretirement benefits. Does not apply to plan that provides only life insurance benefits or health insurance benefits, or both, to retirees. Does not apply to postemployment health care benefits.

The following terms are given specific definitions for the purposes of SFAS 87.

Accumulated benefit obligation--actuarial present value of benefits (whether vested or nonvested) attributed by the pension benefit formula to employee service rendered before a specified date and based on employee service and compensation (if applicable) prior to that date. The accumulated benefit obligation differs from the projected benefit obligation in that it includes no assumption about future compensation levels. For plans with flat-benefit or non-pay-related pension benefit formulas, the accumulated benefit obligation and the projected benefit obligation are the same.

Actual return on plan assets component (of net periodic pension cost)--difference between fair value of plan assets at the end of the period and the fair value at the beginning of the period, adjusted for contributions and payments of benefits during the period.

Actuarial present value--value, as of a specified date, of an amount or series of amounts payable or receivable thereafter, with each amount adjusted to reflect (a) the time value of money (through discounts for interest) and (b) the probability of payment (by means of decrements for events such as death, disability, withdrawal, or retirement) between the specified date and the expected date of payment.

Amortization--usually refers to the process of reducing a recognized liability systematically by recognizing revenues or reducing a recognized asset systematically by recognizing expenses or costs. In pension accounting, amortization is also used to refer to the systematic recognition in net pension cost over several periods of previously unrecognized amounts, including unrecognized prior service cost and unrecognized net gain or loss.

Assumptions--estimates of the occurrence of future events affecting pension costs, such as mortality, withdrawal, disablement and retirement, changes in compensation and national pension benefits, and discount rates to reflect the time value of money.

Attribution--process of assigning pension benefits or cost to periods of employee service.

Career-average-pay formula (Career-average-pay plan)--benefit formula that bases benefits on the employee's compensation over the entire period of service with the employer. A career-average-pay plan is a plan with such a formula.

Contributory plan--pension plan under which employees contribute part of the cost. In some contributory plans, employees wishing to be covered must contribute; in other contributory plans, employee contributions result in increased benefits.

Defined benefit pension plan--pension plan that defines an amount of pension benefit to be provided, usually as a function of one or more factors such as age, years of service, or compensation. Any pension plan that is not a defined contribution pension plan is, for purposes of SFAS 87, a defined benefit pension plan.

Defined contribution pension plan--plan that provides pension benefits in return for services rendered, provides an individual account for each participant, and specifies how contributions to the individual's account are to be determined instead of specifying the amount of benefits the individual is to receive. Under a defined contribution pension plan, the benefits a participant will receive depend solely on the amount contributed to the participant's account, the returns earned on investments of those contributions, and forfeitures of other participants' benefits that may be allocated to such participant's account.

Expected long-term rate of return on plan assets--assumption as to the rate of return on plan assets reflecting the average rate of earnings expected on the funds invested or to be invested to provide for the benefits included in the projected benefit obligation.

Expected return on plan assets--amount calculated as a basis for determining the extent of delayed recognition of the effects of changes in the fair value of assets. The expected return on plan assets is determined based on the expected long-term rate of return on plan assets and the market-related value of plan assets.

Explicit approach to assumptions--approach under which each significant assumption used reflects the best estimate of the plan's future experience solely with respect to that assumption.

Fair value--amount that a pension plan could reasonably expect to receive for an investment in a current sale between a willing buyer and a willing seller, that is, other than in a forced or liquidation sale.

Final-pay formula (Final-pay plan)--benefit formula that bases benefits on the employee's compensation over a specified number of years near the end of the employee's service period or on the employee's highest compensation periods. For example, a plan might provide annual pension benefits equal to 1 percent of the employee's average salary for the last five years (or the highest consecutive five years) for each year of service. A final-pay plan is a plan with such a formula.

Flat-benefit formula (Flat-benefit plan)--benefit formula that bases benefits on a fixed amount per year of service, such as $20 of monthly retirement income for each year of credited service. A flat-benefit plan is a plan with such a formula.

Fund--used as a verb, to pay over to a funding agency (as to fund future pension benefits or to fund pension cost). Used as a noun, assets accumulated in the hands of a funding agency for the purpose of meeting pension benefits when they become due.

Funding policy--program regarding the amounts and timing of contributions by the employer(s), participants, and any other sources (for example, state subsidies or federal grants) to provide the benefits a pension plan specifies.

Gain or loss--change in the value of either the projected benefit obligation or the plan assets resulting from experience different from that assumed or from a change in an actuarial assumption. See also "Unrecognized net gain or loss".

Gain or loss component (of net periodic pension cost)--sum of (a) the difference between the actual return on plan assets and the expected return on plan assets and (b) the amortization of the unrecognized net gain or loss from previous periods. The gain or loss component is the net effect of delayed recognition of gains and losses (the net change in the unrecognized net gain or loss) except that it does not include changes in the projected benefit obligation occurring during the period and deferred for later recognition.

Interest cost component (of net periodic pension cost)--increase in the projected benefit obligation due to passage of time.

Market-related value of plan assets--balance used to calculate the expected return on plan assets. Market-related value can be either fair market value or a calculated value that recognizes changes in fair value in a systematic and rational manner over not more than five years. Different ways of calculating market-related value may be used for different classes of assets, but the manner of determining market-related value shall be applied consistently from year to year for each asset class.

Measurement date--date as of which plan assets and obligations are measured.

Mortality rate--proportion of the number of deaths in a specified group to the number living at the beginning of the period in which the deaths occur. Actuaries use mortality tables, which show death rates for each age, in estimating the amount of pension benefits that will become payable.

Net periodic pension cost--amount recognized in an employer's financial statements as the cost of a pension plan for a period. Components of net periodic pension cost are service cost, interest cost, actual return on plan assets, gain or loss, amortization of unrecognized prior service cost, and amortization of the unrecognized net obligation or asset existing at the date of initial application of SFAS 87. SFAS 87 uses the term net periodic pension cost instead of net pension expense because part of the cost recognized in a period may be capitalized along with other costs as part of an asset such as inventory.

Plan amendment--change in the terms of an existing plan or the initiation of a new plan. A plan amendment may increase benefits, including those attributed to years of service already rendered. See also "Retroactive benefits".

Prepaid pension cost--cumulative employer contributions in excess of accrued net pension cost.

Prior service cost--cost of retroactive benefits granted in a plan amendment. See also "Unrecognized prior service cost".

Projected benefit obligation--actuarial present value as of a date of all benefits attributed by the pension benefit formula to employee service rendered prior to that date. The projected benefit obligation is measured using assumptions as to future compensation levels if the pension benefit formula is based on those future compensation levels (pay-related, final-pay, final-average-pay, or career-average-pay plans).

Retroactive benefits--benefits granted in a plan amendment (or initiation) that are attributed by the pension benefit formula to employee services rendered in periods prior to the amendment. The cost of the retroactive benefits is referred to as prior service cost.

Service--employment taken into consideration under a pension plan. Years of employment before the inception of a plan constitute an employee's past service; years thereafter are classified in relation to the particular actuarial valuation being made or discussed. Years of employment (including past service) prior to the date of a particular valuation constitute prior service.

Service cost component (of net periodic pension cost)--actuarial present value of benefits attributed by the pension benefit formula to services rendered by employees during the period. The service cost component is a portion of the projected benefit obligation and is unaffected by the funded status of the plan.

Unfunded accrued pension cost--cumulative net pension cost accrued in excess of the employer's contributions (usually used without word "unfunded").

Unfunded accumulated benefit obligation--excess of the accumulated benefit obligation over plan assets.

Unrecognized net gain or loss--cumulative net gain (loss) that has not been recognized as a part of net periodic pension cost. See "Gain or loss".

Unrecognized prior service cost--portion of prior service cost that has not been recognized as a part of net periodic pension cost.

A. Single-Employer Defined Benefit Plans

   1. Pension benefits are part of compensation paid to employees for services

      a. Amount of benefits to be paid depends on a number of future events specified in the plan's benefit formula

   2. Any method of pension accounting that recognizes cost before payment of benefits to retirees must deal with two problems

      a. Assumptions must be made concerning future events that will determine amount and timing of benefits

      b. Approach to attributing cost of pension benefits to individual years of service must be selected

B. Basic Elements of Pension Accounting

   1. Prior service cost

      a. Except as specified otherwise, prior service cost shall be amortized by assigning an equal amount to each future service period of each employee active at the date of a plan amendment who is expected to receive benefits under plan

      b. If all/almost all of plan's participants are inactive, cost of retroactive plan benefits should be amortized over remaining life expectancy of those participants

   c. Consistent use of alternative amortization approach that more rapidly reduces unrecognized cost of retroactive amendments is acceptable

     (1) Alternative method used should be disclosed

   d. When period during which employer expects to realize economic benefits from amendment granting retroactive benefits is shorter than entire remaining service period of active employees, amortization of prior service cost should be accelerated

   e. Plan amendment can reduce, rather than increase, the projected benefit obligation

     (1) Reduction should be used to reduce any existing unrecognized prior service cost

     (2) Excess should be amortized on same basis as cost of benefit increases

2. Gains and losses

   a. Gains (losses)

     (1) Result from changes in amount of either projected benefit obligation or plan assets due to experience different than assumed and changes in assumptions

     (2) Include both realized and unrealized amounts

   b. Asset gains (losses) include both (a) changes reflected in the market-related value of assets and (b) changes not yet reflected in the market-related value

     (1) Asset gains (losses) not yet reflected in market-related value are not required to be amortized as "B.2.c." below

   c. As a minimum, amortization of unrecognized net gain (loss) should be included as a component of net pension cost for a year if, as of the beginning of the year, that unrecognized net gain (loss) $\geq$ .10 of the larger of the projected benefit obligation or the market-related value of plan assets

     (1) Minimum amortization should be the excess divided by the average remaining service period of active employees expected to receive benefits under the plan

       (a) Amortization must always reduce beginning of the year balance

       (b) Amortization of a net unrecognized gain (loss) results in a decrease (increase) in net periodic pension cost

     (2) If all/or almost all of plan's participants are inactive, average remaining life expectancy of inactive participants should be used instead of average remaining service

   d. Any systematic method of amortization of unrecognized gains (losses) may be used in lieu of the minimum specified above provided that

     (1) Minimum is used in any period in which minimum amortization is greater (reduces the net balance by more)

     (2) Method is applied consistently and disclosed

3. Recognition of liabilities and assets

   a. Liability (asset) is recognized if net periodic pension cost recognized exceeds (is less than) amounts the employer has contributed to the plan

    b. Recognition of "additional minimum liability" is required if accumulated benefit obligation is greater than the fair market value of plan assets and

        (1) An asset has been recognized as prepaid pension cost,
        (2) The liability already recognized as unfunded accrued pension cost is less than the unfunded accumulated benefit obligation, or
        (3) No accrued or prepaid pension cost has been recognized

    c. If "additional minimum liability" must be recognized, recognize an equal amount as an "intangible asset," provided that asset recognized should not exceed amount of unrecognized prior service cost

        (1) If "additional liability" required to be recognized exceeds unrecognized prior service cost, excess should be reported as a separate component (a reduction) of equity
        (2) Each time a new determination of required additional liability is made, related intangible asset and separate component of equity should be eliminated or adjusted as necessary

C. Attribution

1. Pension benefits should be attributed to periods of employee service based on plan's benefit formula

2. When employer has a present commitment to make future amendments and substance of plan is to provide benefits attributable to prior service that are greater than benefits defined by written terms of the plan

    a. The substantive commitment should be basis for accounting, and
    b. Existence and nature of the commitment to make future amendments should be disclosed

3. Assumptions

    a. Assumed discount rates reflect rates at which pension benefits could be effectively settled

        (1) Used in measurements of projected and accumulated benefit obligations and the service and interest cost components of net periodic pension cost

    b. Assumed compensation levels (when measuring service cost and the projected benefit obligation) should reflect an estimate of the actual future compensation levels of employees involved, including future changes attributed to general price levels, productivity, seniority, promotion, and other factors
    c. Accumulated benefit obligation shall be measured based on employees' history of service and compensation without estimate of future compensation levels
    d. Automatic benefit increases specified by plan that are expected to occur should be included in measurements of projected and accumulated benefit obligations and the service cost component
    e. Retroactive plan amendments should be included in computations of projected and accumulated benefit obligations

        (1) Once they have been contractually agreed to
        (2) Even if some provisions take effect only in future periods

D. Measurement of Plan Assets

1. For purposes of measuring minimum liability and required disclosures, plan investments, whether equity or debt securities, real estate, or other, should be measured at their fair value as of measurement date

2. Market-related asset value is used for purposes of determining the expected return on plan assets and accounting for asset gains and losses

E. Acceptable Measurement Dates

1. As of date of financial statements or,

2. If used consistently from year to year, as of a date $\leq$ 3 months prior to that date

3. Measurement date is not intended to require that all procedures be performed after that date

4. Information for items requiring estimates can be prepared as of an earlier date and projected forward to account for subsequent events (e.g., employee service)

5. The "additional minimum liability" reported in interim financial statements should be the same "additional minimum liability" recognized in previous year-end balance sheet

   a. Adjusted for subsequent accruals and contributions unless measures of both the obligation and plan assets are available as of a current date or a significant event occurs, such as plan amendment, that would call for such measurements

6. Measurements of net periodic pension cost for both interim and annual financial statements should be based on assumptions used for previous year-end measurements

   a. If more recent measurements are available or a significant event occurs, use these more recent measurements

F. Disclosures

1. Description of plan

   a. Employee groups covered
   b. Type of benefit formula
   c. Funding policy
   d. Type of assets held and significant nonbenefit liabilities
   e. Nature and effect of significant matters affecting comparability

2. Amount of net periodic pension cost, showing separately

   a. Service cost component
   b. Interest cost component
   c. Actual return on assets
   d. Net total of other components

3. Schedule reconciling the funded status of plan with amounts reported in employer's statement of financial position, showing separately

    a. Fair value of plan assets
    b. Projected benefit obligation identifying the accumulated benefit obligation and the vested benefit obligation
    c. Amount of unrecognized prior service cost
    d. Amount of unrecognized net gain or loss (including asset gains and losses not yet reflected in market-related value)
    e. Amount of any remaining unrecognized net obligation or net asset existing at the date of initial application of this Statement
    f. Amount of any additional liability
    g. Amount of net pension asset or liability

        (1) Net result of "a.-f." above

4. Weighted-average discount rate and rate of compensation increase used to measure the projected benefit obligation and the weighted-average expected long-term rate of return on plan assets

5. Amounts and types of any securities of the employer and related parties included in plan assets

6. Approximate amount of annual benefits of employees and retirees covered by annuity contracts issued by employer and related parties

7. Alternative amortization method used

8. Existence and nature of commitment to make future amendments

SFAS 88 (P16) Employers' Accounting for Settlements and Curtailments of Defined Benefit Pension Plans and for Termination Benefits (Supersedes SFAS 74)

Statement applies to an employer that sponsors a defined benefit pension plan accounted for under the provisions of SFAS 87 if all or part of the plan's pension benefit obligation is settled or the plan is curtailed. It also applies to an employer that offers benefits to employees in connection with their termination of employment.

The following terms are given specific definitions for the purposes of SFAS 88.

Settlement--transaction that (a) is an irrevocable action, (b) relieves the employer (or the plan) of primary responsibility for a pension benefit obligation, and (c) eliminates significant risks related to the obligation and the assets used to effect the settlement. Examples include making lump-sum cash payments to plan participants in exchange for their rights to receive specified pension benefits and purchasing nonparticipating annuity contracts to cover vested benefits. A transaction must meet all of the above three criteria to constitute a settlement for purposes of this statement.

Annuity contract--irrevocable contract in which an insurance company* uncondi-tionally undertakes a legal obligation to provide specified benefits to specific individuals in return for a fixed consideration or premium. It involves the transfer of significant risk from the employer to the insurance company. Partici-

---

*If the insurance company is controlled by the employer or there is any reasonable doubt that the insurance company will meet its obligation under the contract, the purchase of the contract does not constitute a settlement for purposes of this statement.

pating annuity contracts provide that the purchaser (either the plan or the employer) may participate in the experience of the insurance company. The insurance company ordinarily pays dividends to the purchaser. If the substance of a participating annuity contract is such that the employer remains subject to all or most of the risks and rewards associated with the benefit obligation covered or the assets transferred to the insurance company, the purchase of the contract does not constitute a settlement.

Curtailment--event that significantly reduces the expected years of future service of present employees or eliminates for a significant number of employees the accrual of defined benefits for some or all of their future services. Curtailments include (a) termination of employee's services earlier than expected, which may or may not involve closing a facility or discontinuing a segment of a business and (b) termination or suspension of a plan so that employees do not earn additional defined benefits for future services. In the latter situation, future service may be counted toward vesting of benefits accumulated based on past services.

A. Relationship of Settlements and Curtailments to Other Events

    1. Settlement and curtailment may occur separately or together

        a. If benefits to be accumulated in future periods are reduced but the plan remains in existence and continues to pay benefits, to invest assets, and to receive contributions, a curtailment has occurred but not a settlement

        b. If employer purchases nonparticipating annuity contracts for vested benefits and continues to provide defined benefits for future services, either in the same plan or in a successor plan, a settlement has occurred but not a curtailment

        c. If a plan is terminated (that is, the obligation is settled and the plan ceases to exist) and not replaced by a successor defined benefit plan, both a settlement and a curtailment have occurred

B. Accounting for Settlement of Pension Obligation

    1. For purposes of this Statement, when a pension obligation is settled, the maximum gain or loss subject to recognition is the unrecognized gain or loss defined in SFAS 87 plus any remaining unrecognized net asset existing at the date of initial application of SFAS 87. (See definition of gains and losses in the outline of SFAS 87.)

        a. Maximum amount includes any gain or loss first measured at the time of settlement

        b. Maximum amount should be recognized if the entire projected benefit is settled

            (1) If only part of the projected benefit is settled, recognize a pro rata portion of the maximum amount equal to the percentage reduction in the projected benefit obligation

    2. If the purchase of a participating annuity contract constitutes a settlement, the maximum gain (but not the maximum loss) should be reduced by the cost of the participation right before determining the amount to be recognized in earnings

3. If the cost of all settlements in a year is less than or equal to the sum of the service cost and interest cost components of net periodic pension cost for the plan for the year, gain or loss recognition is permitted but not required for those settlements

    a. Accounting policy adopted should be consistently applied
    b. For the following types of settlements, the cost of the settlement is

        (1) Cash settlement: amount of cash paid to employees
        (2) Settlement using non-participating annuity contracts: cost of the contracts
        (3) Settlement using participating annuity contracts: cost of the contracts less amount attributed to participation rights

C. Accounting for Plan Curtailment

1. Unrecognized prior service cost is a loss

    a. Cost must be associated with years of service no longer expected to be rendered as result of curtailment
    b. Costs include cost of retroactive plan amendments (refer to outline of SFAS 87) and any remaining unrecognized net obligation existing at the date of initial application of SFAS 87 (refer to outline of SFAS 87)

2. The projected benefit obligation may be decreased (a gain) or increased (a loss) by a curtailment*

    a. To the extent that such a gain exceeds any unrecognized net loss (or entire gain, if unrecognized net gain exists), it is a <u>curtailment gain</u>
    b. To the extent that such a loss exceeds any unrecognized net gain (or the entire loss, if an unrecognized net loss exists), it is a <u>curtailment loss</u>
    c. Any remaining unrecognized net asset existing at the date of initial application of SFAS 87 should be treated as an unrecognized net gain and should be combined with the unrecognized net gain or loss arising subsequent to the transition to SFAS 87

3. If the sum of the effects identified in "C.1." and "C.2." is a net loss

    a. Recognize in earnings when it is probable that a curtailment will occur and
    b. Effects are reasonably estimable

4. If the sum of those effects identified in "C.1." and "C.2." is a net gain

    a. Recognize in earnings when related employees terminate or plan suspension or amendment is adopted

D. Termination Benefits

1. Employer may provide benefits to employees in connection with their termination of employment

    a. Special termination benefits--offered for a short period of time or

        (1) Recognize a liability and a loss when the employee accepts the offer and the amount can be reasonably estimable

*Increases in the projected benefit obligation that reflect termination benefits are excluded from the scope of this paragraph.

   b. Contractual termination benefits--required by terms of plan only if
       specified event occurs

       (1) Recognize a liability and a loss when it is probable that employees
            will be entitled to benefits and amount can be reasonably estimable

   2. Termination benefits may take many forms consisting of

       a. Lump sum payments
       b. Periodic future payments

   3. The cost of termination benefits recognized as a liability and a loss shall
       include the amount of any lump-sum payments and present value of any
       expected future payments

E. Disposal of a Segment

   1. If gain (loss) measured in accordance with "B.", "C.", and "D." above is
       directly related to a disposal of a segment of a business, include it in
       determining gain (loss) with that event and recognize per APB 30

F. Disclosure and Presentation

   1. Employer that recognizes gain (loss) under provisions of this Statement,
       whether directly related to the disposal of a segment of a business or
       otherwise, should disclose the following

       a. Description of the nature of event(s)
       b. Amount of gain or loss recognized

SFAS 89 (C28) Financial Reporting and Changing Prices

This statement encourages but does not require a business enterprise that prepares
its financial statements in U.S. dollars and in accordance with U.S. generally
accepted accounting principles to disclose supplementary information on changing
prices

A. Disclosures

   1. Five-year summary of selected financial data

       a. Net sales and other operating revenues
       b. Income from continuing operations on current cost basis
       c. Purchasing power gain or loss on net monetary items
       d. Increase or decrease in the current cost or lower recoverable amount of
           inventory and property, plant, and equipment, net of inflation
       e. The aggregate foreign currency translation adjustment on current cost
           basis, if applicable
       f. Net assets at year end on current cost basis
       g. Income per common share from continuing operations on current cost basis
       h. Cash dividends declared per common share
       i. Market price per common share at year end

   2. Information presented should be stated as follows

       a. In average-for-the-year or end-of-year units of constant purchasing
           power
       b. In dollars having a purchasing power equal to that of dollars of the
           base period used by the Bureau of Labor Statistics in calculating the
           Consumer Price Index for All Urban Consumers (CPI-U) (currently 1967)

3. Level of CPI-U used for each of the five most recent years should also be presented

4. Significant foreign operations measured in a functional currency other than the U.S. dollar

    a. Disclosure of effects of general inflation based on the U.S. general price level index (translate-restate) or

    b. On a functional currency general price level index (restate-translate)

5. Explanation of disclosures required

B. Additional Disclosures Needed

1. If income from continuing operations (IFCO) on a current cost/constant purchasing power basis would differ significantly from IFCO on a historical cost basis information may be presented

    a. In a statement format,
    b. In a reconciliation format, or
    c. Notes to the five-year summary

2. Disclose the difference between the amount in the primary statements and the current cost amount for

    a. Cost of goods sold
    b. Depreciation, depletion, and amortization expense

       (1) If depreciation allocated among various expense categories, aggregate amount of depreciation should be included in the notes

3. In addition to information about income from continuing operations

    a. Purchasing power gain or loss on net monetary assets
    b. Increase or decrease in the current cost or lower recoverable amount of inventory and property, plant, and equipment, net of inflation
    c. Translation adjustment
    d. Separate amounts for current cost or lower recoverable amount at the end of the current year of inventory and property, plant, and equipment
    e. Increase or decrease in current cost or lower recoverable amount before and after adjusting for the effects of inflation of inventory and property, plant, and equipment
    f. The principal types of information used to calculate the current cost of inventory; property, plant, and equipment; cost of goods sold; and depreciation, depletion, and amortization expense
    g. Any differences between (1) the depreciation methods, estimates of useful lives, and salvage values of assets used for calculations of current cost/constant purchasing power depreciation and (2) the methods and estimates used for calculations of depreciation in the primary financial statements

C. Measurement

1. Inventory

    a. Current cost is the current cost of purchasing or manufacturing, whichever is applicable

       (1) Or recoverable amount if lower

2. Property, plant, and equipment

    a. Current cost is current cost of acquiring same service potential (or recoverable amount if lower)

        (1) I.e., the same operating costs and output
        (2) Three valuation methods

            (a) Current cost of new asset less depreciation
            (b) Cost of comparable used asset
            (c) Adjusting new asset cost for differences in
                1] Useful life
                2] Output capacity
                3] Nature of service
                4] Operating costs

3. In summary, there are several approaches to determine current costs

    a. Indexation (application of price indices to original cost)

        (1) Externally generated by class of goods
        (2) Internally generated by class of goods

    b. Direct pricing

        (1) Current invoices
        (2) Vendors' price quotations
        (3) Current standard manufacturing costs

4. Historical cost amounts adjusted by historical cost/constant purchasing power may be substituted for current cost amounts

    a. If numbers are not significantly different
    b. Then, disclosure "B.4.b." is not required; however, "B.4.d.,e., and g." are required

5. Foreign operations

    a. If measures current cost in a currency other than its functional currency
    b. That amount should be translated into the functional currency at the current exchange rate

6. Specialized assets

    a. Mineral resource assets

        (1) Current cost is current market buying prices or current cost of finding and developing
        (2) If (1) fails to yield a close approximation, use

            (a) Specific price indexes
            (b) Direct information about market buying prices
            (c) Other statistical evidence of the cost of acquisition

    b. Timberlands and growing timber, income-producing real estate, and motion picture films

        (1) May disclose historical cost/constant purchasing power

7. Net assets

    a. Amount of net assets reported in primary financial statements, adjusted for

(1)   Difference between the historical cost amounts and current cost or lower recoverable amounts of inventory and PP&E

8. Recoverable amount

    a. Current worth of net amount of cash expected to be recoverable from the use or sale of an asset

9. Income from continuing operations

    a. At a minimum, the following shall be reflected at current cost (or recoverable amount if related assets are also reflected at recoverable amount)

        (1)   Cost of goods sold
        (2)   Depreciation/amortization

    b. Other revenues, expenses, gains, and losses measured at amounts included in the primary income statement
    c. The income tax expense for current cost/constant dollar statements should be the same as income tax expense on the primary statements, i.e., no adjustment is made

        (1)   No allocation of income tax expense is made between income from continuing operations and changes in the current cost of inventory and PP&E

10. Increase or decrease in current cost amounts of inventory and PP&E, net of inflation

    a. Differences between current cost at entry dates and exit dates

        (1)   Entry dates are the later of the beginning of the year or date of acquisition
        (2)   Exit dates are the earlier of date of use, sale, etc., or year end

    b. In five year summary current costs are to be reported before and after eliminating the effects of inflation

        (1)   Use average-for-year CPI-U
        (2)   Difference between current cost (nominal dollars) and current cost (constant dollars)

11. Restatement of current cost information into units of constant purchasing power

    a. Use CPI-U to restate

12. Translation adjustment

    a. Functional currency other than the dollar

        (1)   Translate-restate method

13. Purchasing power gain or loss on net monetary items

    a. Average-for-year dollars: convert beginning, ending, and changes in net monetary items to average-for-year dollars

        (1)   Compare beginning, adjusted for changes, with ending for gain or loss

    b. End-of-year dollars: restate beginning net monetary items and increase or decrease in net monetary items to end-of-year dollars

SFAS 91 (L20) Accounting for Nonrefundable Fees and Costs Associated with Originating or Acquiring Loans and Initial Direct Costs of Leases (Rescinds SFAS 17, Amends SFAS 13, 60, and 65)

Establishes the accounting for nonrefundable fees and costs associated with lending, committing to lend, or purchasing a loan or group of loans. Applies to all types of loans.

A. Loan origination fees shall be recognized over life of related loan as adjustment of yield

B. Certain direct loan origination costs shall be deferred over the life of the related loan as a reduction of the loan's yield

C. All loan commitment fees shall be deferred except for certain retrospectively determined fees

   1. Those commitment fees meeting specified criteria shall be recognized over the loan commitment period

   2. All other commitment fees shall be recognized as an adjustment of yield over the related loan's life

   3. If commitment expires unexercised, then recognize in income upon expiration of the commitment

D. Loan fees, certain direct loan origination costs, and purchase premiums and discounts on loans shall be recognized as an adjustment of yield generally by the interest method based on contractual terms of the loan

   1. Prepayments by debtors may be anticipated in certain specified circumstances

E. Application to Leasing Activities

   1. Lessors shall account for initial direct costs as part of the net investment in a direct financing lease

   2. Initial direct costs are those costs incurred by the lessor that are

      a. Costs to originate a lease incurred in transactions with independent third parties that

         (1) Result directly from and are essential to acquire that lease and
         (2) Would not have been incurred had that leasing transaction not occurred and

      b. Certain costs directly related to specified activities performed by the lessor for that lease including

         (1) Evaluating the prospective lessee's financial condition
         (2) Evaluating and recording guarantees, collateral, and other security arrangements
         (3) Negotiating lease terms
         (4) Preparing and processing lease documents
         (5) Closing the transaction
         (6) Costs directly related to those activities shall include only that portion of the employees' total compensation and payroll-related fringe benefits directly related to time spent performing those activities for that lease and other costs related to those activities that would not have been incurred but for that lease

SFAS 94 Consolidation of All Majority-owned Subsidiaries (Amends ARB 51 with related amendments of APB 18 and ARB 43, Chapter 12)

A. Precludes use of parent-company FSs prepared for issuance to stockholders as FSs of primary reporting entity

B. Requires consolidation of all majority-owned (ownerships, directly or indirectly, of more than 50% of outstanding voting shares of another company) subsidiaries

   1. Unless control

      a. Temporary
      b. Not held by majority owner. E.g., Subsidiary

         (1) Is in legal reorganization or bankruptcy
         (2) Operates under foreign exchange restrictions, controls, or other governmentally imposed uncertainties

   2. Even if

      a. Sub's operations nonhomogeneous

         (1) Main thrust of this SFAS was to eliminate this exception from criteria of ARB 51

      b. Large minority interest exists
      c. Sub located in foreign country

C. Requires summarized information about assets, liabilities, and results of operations (or separate statements) for majority owned subsidiaries not consolidated in FSs for F/Y 1986 or 1987 under old ARB 51 criteria

SFAS 95 Statement of Cash Flows
(Supersedes APB 19)

A. Statement of Cash Flows in General

   1. Required for each period results of operation are provided
   2. Purpose

      a. Provide information about cash receipts and cash payments
      b. Provide information about investing and financing activities

   3. Helps users to assess

      a. Ability to generate future net cash flows
      b. Ability to meet obligations and pay dividends
      c. Reasons for differences between income and associated cash receipts and payments
      d. Both cash and noncash aspects of entity's investing and financing activities

   4. Shall report

      a. Cash effects during a period from

         (1) Operating activities
         (2) Investing activities

(3) Financing activities

    b. Noncash financing and investing activities in supplemental schedule

B. Gross and Net Cash Flows

    1. Gross amount of cash receipts and payments is relevant

        a. E.g., show issuance of bonds and retirement of bonds separately

    2. Statement should explain change during the period in <u>cash and cash</u> <u>equivalents</u>

        a. Cash equivalents

            (1) Short-term, highly liquid investments that are

                (a) Readily convertible into known amounts of cash
                (b) Near maturity (3 months or less) and present negligible risk of changes in value

            (2) Examples

                (a) Treasury bills
                (b) Commercial paper
                (c) Money market funds

C. Classification

    1. Investing activities

        a. Include

            (1) Lending money and collecting on those loans
            (2) Acquiring and selling, or disposing

                (a) Securities that are not cash equivalents
                (b) Productive assets expected to generate revenue over long periods of time

            (3) Cash inflows

                (a) Receipts from loans by

                    1] Principal repayments
                    2] Sale of loans made by the entity

                (b) Receipts from sale of

                    1] Debt or equity securities of other entities
                    2] Property, plant, and equipment

            (4) Cash outflows

                (a) Loans made or purchased by the entity
                (b) Payments to acquire assets

                    1] Debt or equity of other entities
                    2] Property, plant, and equipment

    2. Financing activities

        a. Include

            (1) Obtaining resources from owners and providing them with a return on, and a return of, their investment
            (2) Obtaining resources from creditors and repaying the amounts borrowed

        b. Cash inflows

(1) Proceeds from the issuance of

    (a) Equity securities
    (b) Bonds
    (c) Mortgages
    (d) Notes
    (e) Other short- or long-term borrowing

c. Cash outflows

(1) Payments of dividends
(2) Outlays to repurchase entity's shares
(3) Repayments from amounts borrowed

3. Operating activities

a. Include

(1) All transactions and other events that are not investing and financing
(2) Delivering or producing goods for sale and providing services
(3) Cash effects of transactions and other events that enter into the determination of income

b. Cash inflows

(1) Cash receipts from sale of goods or services
(2) Interest and dividends received
(3) Other operating cash receipts

c. Cash outflows

(1) Payments to employees and other suppliers of goods or services
(2) Income taxes paid
(3) Interest paid
(4) Other operating cash payments

D. Exchange Rate Effects

1. Report the reporting currency equivalent of foreign currency cash flows using exchange rates in effect at time of cash flows

a. Weighted-average exchange rate may be used if result substantially same

E. Content and Form

1. Report net cash provided or used by operating, investing, and financing activities

2. At end of statement, reconcile beginning and ending cash and cash equivalents by showing net increase or decrease for period as addition to beginning balance to obtain ending balance

3. Cash flow from operating activities

a. Direct presentation (encouraged by FASB)

(1) Report major classes of operating receipts and payments (C.3.b.-c. above)
(2) Difference between cash receipts and payments--net cash flow from operating activities
(3) Supplemental schedule using indirect presentation must be presented when direct method used in body of statement

b. Indirect presentation (acceptable format)

   (1) Shall separately report all major classes of reconciling items

      (a) Deferrals of past operating cash receipts and cash payments such as depreciation and changes during the period in inventory and deferred income

      (b) Accruals of expected future operating cash receipts and cash payments such as changes during the period in receivables and payables

   (2) Interest paid (net of amounts capitalized) and income taxes paid must appear in related disclosures

c. Does not include cash flows from transactions or events whose effects are included in income, but which are not operating activities; E.g.

   (1) Gain or loss on extinguishment of debt--financing activities

   (2) Gain or loss on sale of assets or from disposal of discontinued operations--investing activities

4. Inflows and outflows of cash from investing and financing activities

  a. Noncash aspects should be clearly identified in separate schedule; E.g.

    (1) Conversion of debt to equity

    (2) Acquisition of assets by assuming liabilities

      (a) Includes capital lease obligations

    (3) Exchanges of assets or of liabilities

5. Enterprise shall disclose policy for determining items included in cash equivalent

  a. Change in policy is change in accounting principle requiring restatement of comparative FSs

F. Cash flow per share should not be reported

G. Effective for annual financial statements for F/Ys ending after 7/15/88

SFAS 96 Accounting for Income Taxes (Supersedes ARB 44; APBs 1, 11, and 24; and SFASs 31 and 37)

A. Major Changes

  1. Adopts balance sheet oriented liability method

  2. Replaces income statement oriented deferred method under which deferred taxes were measured by rates in effect in year temporary differences arose

  3. Change foretold with SFAC 6

    a. Defined assets and liabilities as to preclude deferred assets and liabilities as computed in accordance with deferred method per APB 11

  4. Prohibits presenting deferred tax benefits beyond certain limitations

B. Liability Method

  1. General concept

    a. Deferred tax liabilities or assets are presented in the balance sheet at amounts expected to be ultimately payable or refundable

        (1) Example--If tax rate changes after temporary differences originate but before reversal, then the deferred tax liability or asset must be adjusted in period of change

          (a) Increase or decrease flows through current period tax expense

        (2) Contrast--Deferred method required that deferred taxes, once recorded, are not adjusted until temporary differences to which they relate reverse

C. Measurement of Deferred Taxes

    1. Temporary differences (timing differences per APB 11)

      a. Defined more broadly and include

        (1) All timing differences plus
        (2) Tax-book differences in assets' bases (due to basis reduction for ITC when law provides or basis increases for inflationary indexing under a potential future law)

      b. Future effects

        (1) <u>Taxable amounts</u> are from temporary differences that will result in lower amounts of expense or higher amounts of revenue being reported on the tax return than are reported on the books in the future period.
        (2) <u>Deductible amounts</u> are from temporary differences that will result in higher amounts of expense or lower amounts of revenue being reported on the tax return than are reported on the books in the future period

    2. Deferred tax liability or asset measured each balance sheet date

      a. Estimate particular future years in which temporary differences will result in taxable or deductible amounts
      b. Determine **net** taxable or deductible amount in each future year
      c. Deduct <u>operating loss carryforwards for tax purposes</u> (as required or permitted by tax law) from **net** taxable amounts scheduled to occur in the future years included in loss carryforward period
      d. Carryback or carryforward (as permitted or required by law) **net** deductible amounts occurring in particular years to offset **net** taxable amounts that are scheduled to occur in prior or subsequent years

        (1) Assumes no taxable or deductible amounts in future years arising from events that have not been recognized in F/Ss at end of current year

      e. Recognize <u>deferred tax asset</u> for tax benefit of deductible amounts that could be realized by loss carryback from future years

        (1) To reduce a current deferred tax liability
        (2) To reduce taxes paid in current or prior year

      f. Compute amount of tax for remaining **net** taxable amounts scheduled to occur in each future year

        (1) Apply presently enacted tax rates and laws for each of those years

      g. Deduct <u>tax credit carryforwards for tax purposes</u> from amount of tax for future years that are included in carryforward period

        (1) No asset is recognized for any additional amount of tax credit carryforward

   h. Recognize a <u>deferred tax liability</u> for remaining amount of taxes payable for each future year

   i. Tax-planning strategies are used for estimating the years in which temporary differences will result in taxable or deductible amounts [step (a) above]

        (1) Application of a strategy may result in

            (a) Amounts becoming deductible in a different year thereby providing tax benefit by offsetting [step (d)] or loss carryback [step (e)]

            (b) Amounts becoming taxable in a different year before a loss or tax credit carryforward expires [steps (c) and (g)] or in particular year that maximizes benefits of tax credits [steps (f) or (g)]

        (2) Criteria for tax-planning strategies

            (a) Strategy must be prudent and feasible one over which management has control

            (b) Strategy cannot involve significant cost to the enterprise

D. Changes in Tax Rates or Status

   1. Change in rates

      a. Change previously recorded amounts of deferred tax liabilities or assets,

      b. Net adjustments shall be reflected in tax expense in period that includes enactment date, <u>and</u>

      c. Is not an extraordinary item

   2. Change in status

      a. Change from nontaxable (partnership or S Corporation) to taxable (C Corporation) would result in

        (1) Recording deferred taxes if temporary differences exist at that date

        (2) Effect of change flows through current tax expense

      b. Change to nontaxable from taxable would result in reversal of deferred taxes with effect of reversal treated as an adjustment of current tax expense

E. Tax Effects on Undistributed Earnings of Subsidiaries under APB 23

   1. If parent company has evidence of specific plans for reinvestment of such earnings so that remittance indefinitely postponed, no deferred taxes need to be accrued

   2. SFAS 96 accounting continues this exception (APB 23 remains in effect)

F. Business Combinations

   1. Recognize deferred tax liability or asset in accordance with provisions of SFAS 96 for differences between assigned values and tax bases of assets and liabilities

       a. Except goodwill, unallocated negative goodwill, and leveraged leases

   2. Tax benefits of <u>operating loss or tax credit carryforward for financial reporting</u> recognized after acquisition date shall be

       a. First applied to reduce to zero any goodwill and other noncurrent intangible assets related to acquisition

       b. Next be recognized as reduction of income tax expense

G. Financial Statement Presentation

   1. Balance sheet

       a. Current amount of deferred tax liability or asset shall be net deferred tax consequences of

          (1) Temporary differences that will result in net taxable or deductible amounts during the following year

          (2) Temporary differences related to an asset or liability that is classified for financial reporting as current because of operating cycle > 1 year

          (3) Temporary differences for which there is no related, identifiable asset or liability for financial reporting whenever **other** related assets and liabilities are classified as current due to operating cycle > 1 year

       b. Noncurrent if not included in (1)-(3) above

   2. Income statement

       a. Components of tax expense attributable to continuing operations shall be disclosed in F/Ss or notes. For example:

          (1) Current tax expense or benefit

          (2) Deferred tax expense or benefit, exclusive of (6) below

          (3) Investment tax credit

          (4) Government grants (to the extent recognized as a reduction of income tax expense)

          (5) Benefits of operating loss carryforwards (no longer extraordinary)

          (6) Adjustments of a deferred tax liability or asset resulting from enacted changes in tax laws, rates, or status

       b. Variances between statutory and effective tax rates must be disclosed

          (1) Non-publicly held companies must disclose nature of significant reconciling items but may omit numerical reconciliation dollar amounts

       c. Amounts and expiration dates of operating loss and tax credit carryforwards

H. Effective for F/Ys beginning after 12/15/88

SFAS 98 Accounting for Leases (Amends FASB 13, 66, and 91. Rescinds FASB 26 and Technical Bulletin 79-11)

    Authors' note: The outline below includes those changes that relate to all leases. The remainder of SFAS 98 deals with real estate leases which is not outlined since it is not expected to be tested on the exam.

A. Lease term, as redefined, includes

   1. All periods covered by bargain renewal options,

2. All periods for which failure to renew the lease imposes a penalty,

3. All periods during which a loan, directly or indirectly related to the leased property, is outstanding,

4. All periods covered by ordinary renewal options preceeding the exercisable date of a bargain purchase option

5. All periods representing renewals or extensions of the lease at the lessor's option

B. Definition of penalty

1. Any requirement that can be imposed on lessee that would cause lessee to forego economic benefit or suffer economic detriment

2. Requirement can be imposed by lease agreement or by factors outside lease agreement

SFAS 100 Accounting for Income Taxes-Deferral of the Effective Date of SFAS 96 (Amends SFAS 96)

A. Defers the effective date of SFAS 96 to fiscal years beginning after December 15, 1989

Authors' Note: SFAS 100 will not affect the coverage of SFAS 96 on the CPA Exam. Since SFAS 96 was issued in December 1987, its subject matter is "fair game" for the May 1989 CPA Exam.

SFAS 102 Statement of Cash Flows - Exemption of Certain Enterprises and Classification of Cash Flows from Certain Securities Acquired for Resale

As in the case of other SFASs not outlined in this volume, the authors believe that its contents are too specialized for coverage on the CPA exam.

Statements Of Financial Accounting Concepts (SFAC)

Statements of Financial Accounting Concepts (SFACs) set forth financial accounting and reporting objectives and fundamentals that will be used by the FASB in developing standards. Practitioners may also use SFACs in areas where promulgated GAAP does not exist (see SAS 43). SFACs do not establish GAAP as indicated by Rule 203 of the AICPA Code of Professional Ethics.

SFAC 1 Objectives of Financial Reporting by Business Enterprises

A. Financial accounting concepts are fundamentals on which standards of financial accounting and reporting are based

1. I.e., do not establish GAAP

a. And do not come under AICPA Ethics Rule 203

2. Defines financial accounting concepts broader than financial statements and other data

B. Environmental context of objectives

1. Financial reporting provides information for making business and economic decisions

    2. The United States is a market economy

        a. Dominated by investor owned enterprises

        b. Even though the government generates economic statistics

C. Characteristics and limitations of information

    1. Primarily financial (quantitative) in nature

    2. Limited to individual business enterprises

    3. Based on approximated measures, i.e., estimates

    4. Largely limited to past transactions, i.e., historically based

    5. Just one source of users' data base

    6. Must conform to cost-benefit rationale

D. Potential users and their interests

    1. "Owners, lenders, potential investors, suppliers, creditors, employees, management, directors, customers, financial analysts and advisors, brokers, underwriters, stock exchanges, lawyers, economists, taxing authorities, regulatory authorities, legislators, financial press and reporting agencies, labor unions, trade associations, business researchers, teachers and students, and the public."

    2. Users are generally interested in cash flow generation

        a. Amounts, timing, and uncertainties

    3. Many external users lack authority to prescribe information

        a. E.g., absentee owners, customers, etc.

E. General purpose external financial reporting

    1. To satisfy informational needs of external users who lack authority to prescribe data they desire

    2. Focuses on external users

        a. Management may prescribe data for their needs

    3. Directed primarily at investors and creditors

        a. Which results in data of likely usefulness to others

F. Objectives of financial reporting

    1. "Financial reporting should provide information that is useful to present and potential investors and creditors and other users in making rational investment, credit, and similar decisions."

    2. "Financial reporting should provide information to help present and potential investors and creditors and other users in assessing the amounts, timing, and uncertainty of prospective cash receipts from dividends or interest and the proceeds from the sale, redemption, or maturity of securities or loans."

3. "Financial reporting should provide information about the economic resources
   of an enterprise, the claims to those resources (obligations of the
   enterprise to transfer resources to other entities and owner's equity), and
   the effects of transactions, events, and circumstances that change resources
   and claims to those resources."

   a. Economic resource, obligation, and owners' equity data permit assessment
      of

      (1) Liquidity and solvency
      (2) Financial strength

   b. Funds flow data is important
   c. Earnings performance data permit assessment of future performance

      (1) Thus, primary focus of reporting is on earnings

   d. Management stewardship and performance is reported on
   e. Management explanation and interpretation is important

SFAC 2 Qualitative Characteristics of Accounting Information

(Para 4 superseded by SFAC 6)

A. Purpose is to examine the characteristics that make accounting information
   useful and establish criteria for selecting and evaluating accounting alternatives

   1. Guidance needed by both FASB and individual accountants

   2. The usefulness of accounting information must be evaluated in relation to
      decision making

   3. Based on objectives of financial reporting (SFAC 1)

   4. Applies to financial information reported by business enterprises and not-
      for-profit organizations

B. The hierarchy of accounting qualities

   1. User-specific qualities (not inherent in information)

      a. Understandability
      b. Newness

   2. Decision-specific qualities (necessary for usefulness)

      a. Relevance--"capacity" of information to "make a difference" in a
         decision

         (1) Timeliness--being available while able to influence decisions
         (2) Predictive value--improves decision makers' capacity to predict
         (3) Feedback value--enables users to confirm or correct prior
             expectations

      b. Reliability--freedom from error and bias and faithful representation of
         what is claimed to be represented

         (1) Verifiability--secures a high degree of consensus among independent
             measurers
         (2) Representative faithfulness--agreement between data and resources
             or events represented (validity)

(3) <u>Neutrality</u>--freedom from bias toward a predetermined result

3. Secondary and interactive qualities

    a. Comparability between enterprises
    b. Consistency in application over time

4. Constraints

    a. <u>Materiality</u>--information should not be provided if below the user's threshold for recognition
    b. <u>Costs and benefits</u>--benefits derived from disclosure must exceed associated costs

SFAC 5 Recognition and Measurement in Financial Statements of Business Enterprises

A. Statement addresses principal items that a full set of financial statements should show and provides fundamental recognition criteria to use in deciding which items to include in financial statements

1. Recognition criteria presented are not radical change from current practice

2. Only applies to business enterprises

B. Financial statements

1. A principal means of communicating financial information to those outside an entity

2. Some useful information is better provided by other means of financial reporting, such as notes to the statements or supplementary information (SFAC 1)

3. Objectives of financial reporting (which encompasses financial statements) are detailed in SFAC 1

4. Full set of financial statements should show

    a. Financial position at end of period
    b. Earnings for period
    c. Comprehensive income for period
    d. Cash flows for period
    e. Investments by and distributions to owners during period

5. Are intended as "general purpose" statements and, therefore, do not necessarily satisfy all users equally well

6. Simplifications, condensations, and aggregations are necessary and useful, but focusing on one figure (i.e., "the bottom line") exclusively should be avoided

7. Financial statements interrelate and complement each other

8. Information detailed in "4." above is provided by the following individual financial statements

    a. <u>Statement of Financial Position</u>

        (1) Provides information about entity's assets, liabilities, and **equity** and their relationships to each other at a particular point in time
        (2) Does not purport to show the value of an entity

b. Statements of Earnings and Comprehensive Income

(1) Shows how the equity of an entity increased or decreased from all sources (other than from transactions with owners) during period

(2) Item "earnings" is similar to present net income term but does not include certain accounting adjustments recognized in current period (i.e., change in accounting principle)

(3) Earnings is a performance measure concerned primarily with cash-to-cash cycles

(4) Comprehensive income includes all recognized changes in equity except those from transactions with owners (SFAC 6)

(5) The terms "gains" and "losses" are used for those items included in earnings

(6) The terms "cumulative accounting adjustments" and "other nonowner changes in equity" are used for those items excluded from earnings but included in comprehensive income

c. Statement of Cash Flows

(1) Shows entity's cash flows from operating, investing, and financing activities during a period

d. Statement of Investments by and Distributions to Owners

(1) Shows capital transactions of entity which are increases and decreases in equity from transactions with owners during period

9. Financial statements help users assess entity's liquidity, financial flexibility, profitability, and risk

10. Full set of financial statements based on concept of financial capital maintenance--a return is achieved only after capital has been maintained or recovered

C. Recognition criteria

1. Recognition is presentation of item in both words and numbers that is included in the totals of the financial statements (SFAC 6)

2. Item should meet four fundamental recognition criteria to be recognized

a. Definitions--item is element of financial statements as defined by SFAC 6

b. Measurability--item has a relevant attribute that is measurable with sufficient reliability

(1) Five measurement attributes are used in current practice

(a) Historical cost (historical proceeds)
(b) Current (replacement) cost
(c) Current market value
(d) Net realizable (settlement) value
(e) Present (discounted) value of future cash flows

(2) Statement suggests that use of different attributes will continue

(3) The monetary unit of measurement of nominal units of money is expected to continue to be used

c. Relevance--item has capacity to make a difference in users' decisions (SFAC 2)

   d. Reliability--item is representationally faithful, verifiable, and
       neutral (SFAC 2)

       (1) Reliability may affect timing of recognition due to excessive
            uncertainties
       (2) A trade-off may sometimes be needed between relevance and
            reliability because waiting for complete reliability may make
            information untimely

D. Guidance in applying recognition criteria

   1. Need to identify which cash-to-cash cycles are substantially complete

   2. Degree of skepticism is needed (SFAS 2, para 97)

   3. Revenues and gains

       a. Generally not recognized until realizable (SFAC 6, para 83)

           (1) Realizable means assets received or held are readily convertible to
                known amounts of cash or claims to cash

       b. Not recognized until earned (APB Statement 4, para 149 or SFAC 6,
           para 64)

   4. Expenses and losses

       a. Generally recognized when economic benefits are consumed or assets lose
           future benefits
       b. Some expenses are recognized when associated revenues are recognized
           (e.g., cost of goods sold)
       c. Some expenses are recognized when cash is spent or liability incurred
           (e.g., selling and administrative salaries)
       d. Some expenses are allocated by systematic and rational procedures to
           periods benefited (e.g., depreciation and insurance)

E. Recognition of changes in assets and liabilities

   1. Initial recognition generally based on current exchange prices at date of
       recognition

   2. Changes can result from two types of events

       a. Inflows and outflows
       b. Changes in amounts which can be a change in utility or substance (e.g.,
           depreciation) or changes in price

   3. Current price information may only be used if it is reliable, cost
       justified, and more relevant than alternative information

SFAC 6 Elements of Financial Statements

(Replaces SFAC 3)

A. Statement contains definitions of financial statement elements

   1. Definitions provide a significant first screen in determining content of
       financial statements

       a. Possessing characteristics of a definition of an element is necessary
           but not sufficient condition for including an item in financial state-
           ments
       b. To qualify for inclusion in financial statements an item must

(1) Meet recognition criteria, e.g., revenue recognition tests
(2) Possess a relevant attribute which can be measured reliably, e.g., historical cost/historical proceeds

B. Elements of financial statements of both business enterprises and not-for-profit organizations

1. <u>Assets</u> are probable future economic benefits controlled by a particular entity as a result of past transactions or events

   a. Characteristics of assets

      (1) Probable future benefit by contribution to future net cash inflows
      (2) Entity can obtain and control access to benefit
      (3) Transaction or event leading to control has already occurred

   b. Asset continues as an asset until collected, transferred, used, or destroyed
   c. Valuation accounts are part of related asset

2. <u>Liabilities</u> are probable future sacrifices of economic benefits, arising from present obligations of a particular entity which result from past transactions or events

   a. Characteristics of liabilities

      (1) Legal, equitable, or constructive duty to transfer assets in future
      (2) Little or no discretion to avoid future sacrifice
      (3) Transaction or event obligating enterprise has already occurred

   b. Liability remains a liability until settled or discharged
   c. Valuation accounts are part of related liability

3. <u>Equity</u> (net assets) is the owner's residual interest in the assets of an entity that remains after deducting liabilities

   a. Business enterprises

      (1) Characteristics of equity

         (a) The source of distributions by enterprise to its owners
         (b) No unconditional right to receive future transfer of assets; depends on future profitability
         (c) Inevitably affected by enterprise's operations and circumstances affecting enterprise

      (2) Transactions or events that change owners' equity include revenues and expenses; gains and losses; investments by owners; distributions to owners; and changes within owners' equity (does not change total amount)

   b. Not-for-profit organizations

      (1) Characteristics of net assets (equity)

         (a) Absence of ownership interest
         (b) Operating purposes not centered on profit
         (c) Significant receipt of contributions, many involving donor-imposed restrictions

      (2) Classes of net assets

(a) <u>Permanently restricted net assets</u> is the part of net assets of a not-for-profit organization resulting from

   1] Contributions and other inflows of assets whose use by the organization is limited by donor-imposed stipulations that neither expire by passage of time nor can be fulfilled or otherwise removed by actions of the organization
   2] Other asset enhancements and diminishments subject to same kinds of stipulations
   3] Reclassifications from (or to) other classes of net assets as a consequence of donor-imposed stipulations

(b) <u>Temporarily restricted net assets</u> is the part of net assets of a not-for-profit organization resulting from

   1] Contribution and other inflows of assets whose use by the organization is limited by donor-imposed stipulations that either expire by passage of time or can be fulfilled and removed by actions of the organization pursuant to those stipulations
   2] Other asset enhancements and diminishments subject to same kinds of stipulations
   3] Reclassifications to (or from) other classes of net assets as a consequence of donor-imposed stipulations, their expiration by passage of time, or their fulfillment and removal by actions of the organization pursuant to those stipulations

(c) <u>Unrestricted net assets</u> is the part of net assets of a not-for-profit organization that is neither permanently restricted nor temporarily restricted by donor-imposed stipulations. They result from

   1] All revenues, expenses, gains, and losses that are not changes in permanently or temporarily restricted net assets and
   2] Reclassifications from (or to) other classes of net assets as a consequence of donor-imposed stipulations, their expiration by passage of time, or their fulfillment and removal by actions of the organization pursuant to those stipulations

(3) Transactions and events that change net assets include revenues and expenses; gains and losses; and changes within net assets that do not affect assets or liabilities (including reclassifications between classes of net assets)

(4) Changes in classes of net assets of not-for-profit organizations may be significant because donor-imposed restrictions may affect the types and levels of services that a not-for-profit organization can provide

(a) Characteristics of change in permanently restricted net assets

   1] Most increases in permanently restricted net assets are from accepting contributions of assets that donors stipulate must be maintained in perpetuity. Only assets that are not by their nature used up in carrying out the organization's activities are capable of providing economic benefits indefinitely. Gifts of cash, securities, and nonexhaustible property are examples

        (b) Characteristics of change in temporarily restricted net assets

           1] Most increases in temporarily restricted net assets are from accepting contributions of assets that donors limit to use after specified future time or for specified purpose. Temporary restrictions pertain to contributions with donor stipulations that expire or can be fulfilled and removed by using assets as specified

        (c) Characteristics of change in unrestricted net assets

           1] Change in unrestricted net assets for a period indicates whether organization has maintained the part of its net assets that is fully available (free of donor-imposed restrictions) to support the organization's services to beneficiaries in the next period

4. <u>Revenues</u> are increases in assets or decreases in liabilities during a period from delivering goods, rendering services, or other activities constituting the entity's major or central operations

    a. Characteristics of revenues

        (1) Accomplishments of the earning process
        (2) Actual or expected cash inflows resulting from central operations
        (3) Inflows reported gross

5. <u>Expenses</u> are decreases in assets or increases in liabilities during a period from delivery of goods, rendering of services, or other activities constituting the entity's major or central operations

    a. Characteristics of expenses

        (1) Sacrifices involved in carrying out earnings process
        (2) Actual or expected cash outflows resulting from central operations
        (3) Outflows reported gross

6. <u>Gains (losses)</u> are increases (decreases) in equity from peripheral transactions of entity excluding revenues (expenses) and investment by owners (distribution to owners)

    a. Characteristics of gains and losses

        (1) Result from peripheral transactions and circumstances which may be beyond control
        (2) May be classified according to sources or as operating and nonoperating
        (3) Change in equity reported net

7. <u>Accrual accounting</u> and <u>related concepts</u> include

    a. <u>Transaction</u>--external event involving transfer of something of value between two or more entities
    b. <u>Event</u>--a happening of consequence to an entity (internal or external)
    c. <u>Circumstances</u>--a set of conditions developed from events which may occur imperceptibly and create possibly unanticipated situations
    d. <u>Accrual accounting</u>--recording "cash consequence" transactions as they occur rather than with movement of cash; deals with process of cash movement instead of beginning or end of process (per para 44 of SFAC 1)

(1) Based on cash and credit transactions, exchanges, price changes, changes in form of assets and liabilities

e. Accrual--recognizing revenues and related asset increases and expenses and related liability increases as they occur; expected future cash receipt or payment

f. Deferral--recognizing liability for cash receipt with expected future revenue or recognizing asset for cash payment with expected future expense; cash receipt (payment) precedes recognition of revenues (expenses)

g. Allocation--process of assigning or distributing an amount according to a plan or formula

   (1) Includes amortization

h. Amortization--process of systematically reducing an amount by periodic payments or write-downs

i. Realization--process of converting noncash resources and rights into money; refers to sales of assets for cash or claims to cash

   (1) Realized--identifies revenues or gains or losses on assets sold
   (2) Unrealized--identifies revenues or gains or losses on assets unsold

j. Recognition--process of formally recording an item in financial statements

   (1) Major differences between accrual and cash basis accounting is timing of recognition of income items

k. Matching--simultaneous recognition of revenues with expenses which are related directly or jointly to the same transaction or events

C. Elements of financial statement exclusive to business enterprises

1. Investments by owners are increases in net assets resulting from transfers by other entities of something of value to obtain ownership

2. Distributions to owners are decreases in net assets resulting from transferring assets, rendering services, or incurring liabilities by the enterprise to owners

3. Comprehensive income is the change in equity of an entity during a period from transactions and other events of nonowner sources, i.e., all equity amount changes except investment and distributions

a. Term "comprehensive" income is used instead of earnings because the board is reserving "earnings" for a component part of comprehensive income yet to be determined

b. Concept of capital maintenance or recovery of cost is needed in order to separate return on capital from return of capital

c. Financial capital maintenance concept vs. physical capital maintenance concept

   (1) Financial capital maintenance--objective is to maintain purchasing power
   (2) Physical capital maintenance--objective is to maintain operating capacity

d. Comprehensive income is return on financial capital

e. Characteristics, sources and components of comprehensive income include

(1) Cash receipts (excluding owner investments) less cash outlays
     (excluding distributions to owners) over life of enterprise

     (a) Recognition criteria and choice of attributes to be measured
          affect timing, not amount

(2) Specific sources of income are

     (a) Transactions between enterprise and nonowners
     (b) Enterprise's productive efforts
     (c) Price changes, casualties, and other interactions with en-
          vironment

(3) Earnings process is the production and distribution of goods or
     services so firm can pay for goods and services it uses and provide
     return to owners
(4) Peripheral activities may also provide income
(5) Components of comprehensive income

     (a) Basic components--revenues, expenses, gains and losses
     (b) Intermediate components result from combining basic components

(6) Display considerations (e.g., items included in operating income)
     are the subject of another SFAC

CHAPTER NINE
COST ACCOUNTING

Cost and managerial accounting, as contrasted to financial accounting, produce data primarily for management decision making. Management needs data for

1. Planning and controlling day-to-day operations, e.g., use of standard costs to evaluate production efficiency
2. Long-range planning and decision making, e.g., use of capital budgeting techniques in making decisions concerning investment projects

Another function is to determine inventory costs for financial reporting purposes. Determining inventory costs is the more traditional role of cost accounting.

The AICPA Content Specification Outline of the coverage of cost-managerial accounting in the Accounting Practice and Accounting Theory exams, including the authors' frequency analysis thereof (last nine exams), appears on the next page. Be sure to note the number of topics that are tested with about the same frequency on every exam.

Immediately following the frequency analysis is a summary of accounting practice problems referenced to our study modules. The following symbols are used:

Q = Practice II Exam Problem

BASIC COST ACCOUNTING TERMINOLOGY

1. Managerial Accounting emphasizes data for managerial decisions in contrast to cost accounting which emphasizes determination of inventory costs

2. Planning is selecting goals, and choosing methods to attain the goals. Control is the implementation of the plans.

3. Line personnel have direct responsibility for attaining objectives, e.g., plant supervisor, foremen, and production workers. Staff personnel provide service to line functions, e.g., purchasing agents and maintenance personnel.

4. A budget is a quantification of the plan for operations. A flexible budget is a budget which is adjusted for changes in volume. Performance reports compare budgeted and actual performance.

5. Management by exception emphasizes material deviations from plans, e.g., variances in a performance report

6. Responsibility accounting assigns costs and/or revenues to responsibility centers

7. Controller generally implies a financial officer having responsibility for internal operations such as budgeting and the system of internal control. Treasurer generally implies a financial officer having responsibility for obtaining investment capital and cash management.

8. Product costs are those that can be associated with the production of specific revenues, e.g., cost of sales. Product costs attach to a physical unit and become an expense in the period in which the unit to which they attach is sold. Product costs normally include direct labor, direct material, and factory overhead. Period costs cannot be associated (or matched) with specific revenues, e.g., advertising expenditures. Period costs become expenses as time passes.

AICPA CONTENT SPECIFICATION OUTLINE/FREQUENCY ANALYSIS*
Cost Accumulation, Planning, and Control

	Practice									Theory								
	M 85	N 85	M 86	N 86	M 87	N 87	M 88	N 88	M 89	M 85	N 85	M 86	N 86	M 87	N 87	M 88	N 88	M 89
A. Nature of Cost Elements																		
1. Direct Materials	–	1	–	–	1	–	–	–	–	–	–	–	–	–	1	–	–	1
2. Direct Labor	–	1	–	–	1	–	–	–	–	–	–	–	1	1	–	1	–	–
3. Overhead	–	1	–	1	–	–	–	–	–	2	2	1	–	1	–	–	1	1
								[.6]										
B. Process and Job Order Costing	2	–	2	3	3	–	–	–	–	2	2	1	1	–	1	1	1	–
						[.5]												
C. Standard Costing	–	1	3	1	2	–	–	–	–	2	2	1	1	1	1	1	1	1
						[.5]		[.5]										
D. Joint and Byproduct Costing, Spoilage, Waste, and Scrap	–	3	3	2	1	–	–	–	–	1	1	1	1	1	1	1	1	1
E. Absorption and Variable Costing	–	–	1	–	1	–	–	–	–	1	1	1	1	1	1	1	1	1
F. Budgeting and Flexible Budgeting	–	–	–	1	–	–	–	–	–	1	1	1	1	1	1	1	1	1
	[1]							[.5]										
G. Breakeven and Cost-Volume-Profit Analysis	–	1	3	3	1	–	–	–	–	1	1	1	1	1	1	1	1	1
							[1]											
H. Capital Budgeting Techniques																		
1. Net Present Value	1	1	–	1	–	–	–	–	–	2	1	1	–	1	–	–	1	–
		[.25]																
2. Internal Rate of Return	–	–	1	1	–	–	–	–	–	–	–	–	1	–	–	1	–	–
3. Payback Period	–	1	1	–	1	–	–	–	–	–	1	–	–	–	–	–	–	1
4. Accounting Rate of Return	–	–	1	1	1	–	–	–	–	–	–	–	–	–	1	–	–	–
I. Performance Analysis																		
1. Return on Investment	1	–	1	1	1	–	–	–	–	1	1	1	1	1	–	–	1	–
		[.50]																
2. Residual Income	1	–	1	1	1	–	–	–	–	–	–	–	–	–	–	1	–	1
3. Controllable Revenue and Costs	–	–	–	–	–	–	–	–	–	–	–	–	–	–	–	1	–	–
J. Other																		
1. Regression and Correlation Analysis	1	–	–	–	1	–	–	–	–	1	–	–	1	–	–	–	1	–
2. Economic Order Quantity	1	–	–	–	1	–	–	–	–	1	–	–	–	1	–	–	–	1
3. Probability Analysis	1	–	–	2	1	–	–	–	–	–	1	–	–	–	–	1	–	–
		[.25]																
4. Variance Analysis			(See "C." above)									(See "C." above)						
5. Differential Cost Analysis	1	–	1	–	1	–	–	–	–	–	–	–	–	–	–	1	–	–
								[.4]										
6. Product Pricing	–	–	1	1	1	–	–	–	–	–	–	1	–	–	–	–	–	–
Areas No Longer Tested	1	–	1	1	1	–	–	–	–	–	1	–	–	–	–	–	–	–
Total Multiple Choice Questions	10	10	20	20	20	–	–	–	–	15	15	10	10	10	10	10	10	10
Total Problems/Essays	1	1	–	–	–	1	1	1	1	–	–	–	–	–	–	–	–	–
Actual Percentage**	15	15	10	10	10	10	10	10	10	15	15	10	10	10	10	10	10	10

(AICPA 10%; was 15% prior to 5/86)   (AICPA 10%; was 15% prior to 5/86)

*Except where noted, the line items in the outline are the AICPA's; the frequencies, tabulations, and actual percentages are the authors'.

**The "actual percentage" is a measure of the relative coverage of the specific cost topic on each Accounting Practice or Theory exam. This percentage includes both multiple choice questions and essays/problems based on the point allocation used by the AICPA (i.e., multiple choice are assigned ½ point each in Practice and 1 point each in Theory; essays/problems are 10 points each; note that the number of essays/problems, or portion thereof, for each topic is shown in brackets right below the multiple choice questions for that topic).

(Q) - Practice II Exam

MANAGERIAL ACCOUNTING
Problem Summary

Date	Mod 34 Costing Systems	Mod 35 Planning and Control	Mod 36 Standards	Mod 37 Nonroutine Decisions
5/89		Budget of costs for pricing function (other half of problem is in next box) (Q)		
11/88		Allocation of overhead (Q)	Schedule of standard delivery cost per unit (Q)	
5/88		Breakeven analysis for wholesale company (Q)		
11/87	Process costing and variances (Q)		(See Mod 34 on this line)	
5/87				
11/86				
5/86				
11/85				Contribution margin, capital budgeting (Q)
5/85		Cash budget (Q)		

9. <u>Direct (prime) costs</u> are easily traceable to specific units of production, e.g., direct labor and direct material. <u>Indirect costs</u> are not easily traceable to specific units of production, e.g., factory overhead.

10. <u>Direct material</u> is the cost of material directly and conveniently traceable to a product. Minor material items (nails, glue) are not deemed conveniently traceable. These items are treated as indirect material along with production supplies.

11. <u>Direct labor</u> is the cost of labor directly transforming a product. This theoretically should include fringe benefits, but frequently does not. This is contrasted with <u>indirect labor</u> which is the cost of supporting labor (e.g., material handling labor).

12. <u>Factory (manufacturing) overhead</u> normally includes indirect labor costs, supplies cost, and other production facility costs such as plant depreciation, taxes, plant supervisors' salaries, etc. It is comprised of all manufacturing costs that are not direct material or direct labor.

13. <u>Conversion costs</u> include direct labor and manufacturing overhead. They're the costs of converting direct material into finished product.

14. <u>Direct (variable) costing</u> considers all fixed manufacturing overhead as a period cost rather than a product cost. This system is contrasted with <u>absorption (full) costing</u> which considers fixed manufacturing overhead as a product cost. The treatment of fixed manufacturing cost as a period cost rather than a product cost is the only difference between direct costing and absorption costing. All other costs (i.e., variable manufacturing, fixed selling and variable selling) are treated the same under both systems. Direct costing is not acceptable for external reporting per GAAP.

15. <u>Cost behavior patterns</u> are functional relationships between costs and the level of activity. The independent variable, activity level, is on the horizontal axis. The dependent variable, cost, is on the vertical axis.

16. <u>Fixed costs</u> do not vary with the level of activity within the relevant range for a given period of time (usually 1 year), e.g., plant depreciation

17. <u>Variable costs</u> vary proportionately <u>in total</u> with the activity level throughout the relevant range, e.g., direct material

18. <u>Stepped costs (or semi-fixed costs)</u> are fixed over relatively short ranges of production levels, e.g., supervisors' salaries. Fixed, variable, and semi-fixed costs are diagrammed below.

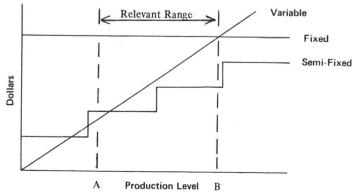

19. Mixed costs (semi-variable) are costs which have a fixed component and a variable component. These components are separated by using the scattergraph, high-low, or linear regression methods.

20. Relevant range is the operating range of activity in which cost behavior patterns are valid (A to B in the preceding illustration). Thus, it is the production range for which fixed costs are fixed, i.e., if production doubles, an additional shift of salaried foremen would be added.

21. Average cost is the total cost divided by the number of units produced. Average variable cost remains constant within the relevant range. Average fixed cost decreases (increases) with increases (decreases) in the level of production as diagrammed below.

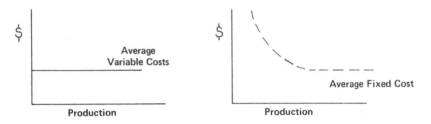

22. Job-order costing is a system for allocating costs to groups of unique products made to customer specification. Process costing is a system for allocating costs to homogeneous units of a mass-produced product.

23. Direct materials inventory includes cost of materials awaiting entry into the production system. Work-in-process inventory includes the cost of units being produced but are not yet completed. Finished goods inventory includes the cost of units completed but unsold.

24. Joint costs are costs common to multiple products that emerge at a split-off point. Joint costing is a system of assigning joint costs to joint products whose sales values are relatively similar. When a joint product has insignificant sales value relative to the other products, it is called a by-product.

25. Standard costs are predetermined target costs. Variances are differences between standards and actual results.

26. Controllable costs can be affected by an individual or level of supervision during the current period, e.g., amount of direct labor per unit of production is usually under the control of a production supervisor. Uncontrollable costs are those which cannot be affected by the individual in question, e.g., depreciation is not usually subject to the production supervisor control.

27. Cost-volume-profit (CVP) analysis is a planning tool used to analyze the effects of changes in volume, sales mix, selling price, variable expense, fixed expense, and profit

28. Contribution margin is revenue less all variable costs

29. Nonroutine decisions include contraction or expansion, make or buy, special orders, capital budgeting, etc. The following terminology is encountered in nonroutine decisions.

a. <u>Sunk, past, or unavoidable costs</u> are committed costs which are not avoidable and are, therefore, irrelevant to the decision process
b. <u>Avoidable costs</u> are costs which will <u>not</u> continue if a department (or product) is terminated
c. <u>Shutdown (committed) costs</u> are fixed costs that cannot be controlled by management within a 1 year time period
d. <u>Discretionary (managed) costs</u> are fixed costs whose level is set by current (within a 1 year time period) management decisions (e.g., advertising, research and development)
e. <u>Relevant costs</u> are future costs that will change as a result of a specific decision
f. <u>Differential (incremental) cost</u> is the difference in cost between two alternatives
g. <u>Opportunity cost</u> is the maximum income (savings) obtainable from the alternative use of a resource
h. <u>Outlay (out-of-pocket) cost</u> is the cash disbursement associated with a specific project

30. <u>Capital budgeting</u> is the planning and controlling of long-term capital outlays

COSTING SYSTEMS

The basic purpose of any costing system is to allocate the costs of production (direct materials, direct labor, and manufacturing overhead) to the units produced. This basic purpose of costing systems (job order, process) is discussed in this module.

A. **Cost of Goods Manufactured**

Regardless of which costing system is used, a cost of goods manufactured (CGM) statement is prepared to summarize the manufacturing activity of the period. CGM for a manufacturing firm is equivalent to purchases for a merchandising firm. Although it may take different forms, essentially the CGM statement is a summary of the direct materials and work-in-process (WIP) account.

$$BWIP + DM + DL + MOH - EWIP = CGM$$

A typical CGM statement is presented below.

Uddin Company
Cost of Goods Manufactured
Year Ended December 31, 1986

Direct materials:		
Inventory, Jan. 1	$ 23,000	
Purchases	98,000	
Materials available for use	121,000	
Inventory, Dec. 31	16,000	
Direct materials used		$105,000
Direct labor		72,000
Factory overhead:		
Indirect labor	$ 14,000	
Supplies	4,000	
Utilities	8,000	
Depreciation	13,000	
Other	3,000	42,000
Manufacturing costs incurred, 1986		219,000
Add work-in-process inventory, Jan. 1		25,000
Manufacturing costs to account for		244,000
Deduct work-in-process inventory, Dec. 31		30,000
Cost of goods manufactured (completed)		$214,000

The result of the CGM statement is used in the cost of goods sold (CGS) statement or cost of goods sold section of the income statement, as indicated below.

Uddin Company
Cost of Goods Sold
Year Ended December 31, 1986

Finished goods, Jan. 1	$ 40,000
Add cost of goods manufactured (completed), per statement above	214,000
Cost of goods available for sale	254,000
Deduct finished goods, Dec. 31	53,000
Cost of goods sold	$201,000

B. Cost Flows

Before discussing any particular costing system, it is important to understand the flow of costs through the accounts, as summarized in the diagram below.

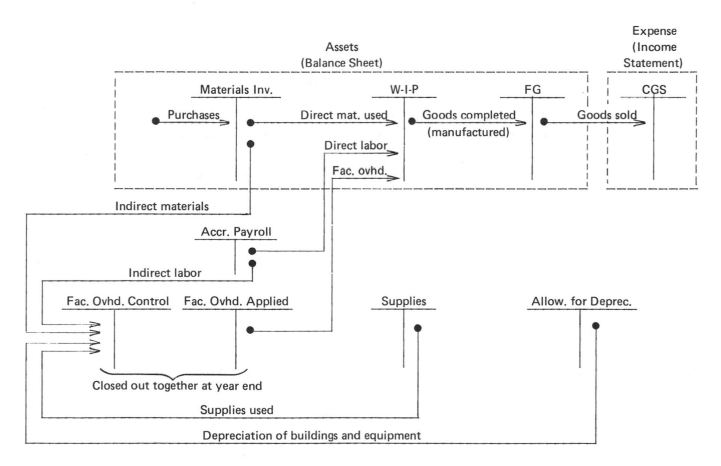

Analyze the diagram carefully before proceeding. The details will be explained further in the next few pages.

C. Job-Order Costing

Job-order costing is a system for allocating costs to groups of unique products. It is applicable to the production of customer-specified products such as the manufacture of special machines. Each job becomes a cost center for which costs are accumulated. A subsidiary record (job cost sheet) is needed to keep track of all unfinished jobs (work in process) and finished jobs (finished goods). Note that the total of unfinished job cost sheets will equal the work-in-process balance.

```
┌─────────────────┐   ┌─────────────────┐
│  Cost Sheet     │   │  Cost Sheet     │        Work in Process
│    Job 1        │   │    Job 2        │   ┌────────────────────────┐
│ DM       800    │   │ DM     1,000    │   │ DM    1,800 │          │
│ DL       600    │   │ DL       500    │   │ DL    1,100 │          │
│ MOH      900    │   │ MOH      750    │   │ MOH   1,650 │          │
│ Total  2,300    │   │ Total  2,250    │   │ Bal.  4,550 │          │
└─────────────────┘   └─────────────────┘   └────────────────────────┘
```

Job-order costing journal entries are presented below. The entries are similar to those made for process costing, which is also discussed in this module.

1. Materials and supplies are purchased.

Materials inventory	xx	
Accounts payable		xx

2. Materials and supplies are used.

Work in process (direct)	xx	
Factory overhead control (indirect)	xx	
Materials inventory		xx

3. The factory payroll is recorded.

Work in process (direct)	xx	
Factory overhead control (indirect)	xx	
Accrued payroll		xx

4. Other actual overhead costs are incurred.

Factory overhead control	xx	
Various accounts		xx

5. Overhead is applied to production.

Work in process	xx	
Factory overhead applied		xx

6. Specific jobs are completed.

Finished goods inventory	xx	
Work in process		xx

7. Specific jobs are sold.

Accounts receivable	xx	
Sales (sales price)		xx
Cost of goods sold	xx	
Finished goods inventory (cost)		xx

Note that whenever work in process is debited or credited in the above entries, the amount of the entry is the sum of the postings on the job-order cost sheets. The balances on the job-order cost sheets are also the basis for the entries transferring completed goods to finished goods inventory and transferring goods shipped to customers to cost of goods sold.

The work-in-process account is analyzed below.

Work in Process	
1. Beginning balance	
2. Direct materials used	
3. Direct labor used	5. Cost of goods manufactured (CGM)
4. Overhead applied	
6. Ending balance	

The total of items 1, 2, 3, and 4 ends up as either CGM (#5) or ending work in process (#6). A similar analysis can be performed on the finished goods account.

Finished Goods	
1. Beginning balance	
2. Cost of goods manufactured	3. Cost of goods sold (CGS)
4. Ending balance	

The total of items 1 and 2 ends up as either CGS (#3) or ending finished goods (#4). Again we see the overall objective of the costing system--to allocate the costs of production to CGS (expense) and ending inventories (assets).

D. **Accounting for Overhead**

Accounting for manufacturing overhead is an important part of job-order costing and any other costing system. Overhead consists of all manufacturing costs other than direct materials and direct labor. The distinguishing feature of manufacturing overhead is that while it must be incurred in order to produce goods, it cannot be directly traced to the final product as can direct materials and direct labor. Therefore, overhead must be applied, rather than directly charged, to goods produced. The overhead application process is described below.

1) Overhead items are grouped by cost behavior, such as fixed and variable
2) The fixed and variable overhead costs are estimated for the forthcoming year (e.g., $500,000)
3) A denominator (activity) base is chosen (see discussion below). A common choice is direct labor hours.
4) The activity level is estimated for the forthcoming year (e.g., 80,000 hours)
5) A predetermined overhead rate is computed

$$\frac{\text{Estimated overhead costs}}{\text{Estimated activity level}} = \frac{\$500,000}{80,000 \text{ hours}} = \$6.25/\text{hour}$$

6) As actual overhead costs are incurred, they are debited to factory overhead control (e.g., $400)

Factory overhead control (actual)   400
      Various accounts   400

7) As jobs are completed, the predetermined overhead rate is used to apply overhead to these jobs. For example, if job 17 used 52 direct labor hours, $325 of overhead (52 x $6.25) would be charged to work in process and entered on the job cost sheet.

Work in process	325	
Factory overhead applied		325

A topic tested sometimes on the CPA exam is the treatment of spoilage costs and rework on defective units. In a job-order system, the costs of spoilage and defective units can be handled in two different ways. When spoilage is attributable to general factory conditions, net spoilage costs are spread over all jobs by including an "allowance for spoiled goods" in the predetermined overhead rate (i.e., estimated spoilage costs are included in the numerator of the computation to derive the predetermined overhead rate). Alternatively, when spoilage is attributable to exacting job specifications, net spoilage costs are charged to the specific jobs involved. With this approach, spoilage is not reflected in the predetermined overhead rate. Under either method, the proceeds from spoiled goods sold should be offset against the total cost of goods produced leaving the net cost to be charged to factory overhead.

To compute the unit cost of goods produced on a given job, spoiled units would be excluded from output. However, defective units that have been re-worked are included in good output. For example, assume final inspection of Job 606 resulted in the production of 2,000 good units, 150 spoiled units, and 40 defective units. The defective units were reworked and the spoiled units were sold. Output for the job would be 2,040 units (2,000 good units plus 40 units reworked). Spoiled units are ignored.

The activity base should be chosen so that there is a causal relationship between the base and overhead costs. Examples of activity bases are

1) Direct labor hours   3) Machine hours
2) Direct labor cost   4) Material cost

For example, overhead may result from (be a function of) hours worked regardless of who works, which would mean that direct labor hours should be the activity base. If, on the other hand, more overhead costs were incurred because of higher paid employees, e.g., higher workers' compensation costs, direct labor dollars might be a more appropriate activity base.

When the activity level is estimated (step "D.4" above), a number of approaches can be used, as illustrated in the diagram below.

Approach	Definition	Support
Theoretical capacity	Output is produced efficiently 100% of the time.	Little
Practical capacity	ADJUSTED FOR: noncontrollable factors such as days off, down time, etc. Output is produced efficiently maximum percentage of time practical (75-85%).	Good guide for competitive pricing; highlights effect of idle capacity
Normal volume	ADJUSTED FOR: long-run product demand. Average annual output necessary to meet sales and inventory fluctuations over 4-5 year period.	Based on expected results; stabilizes product costs from year to year
Expected annual capacity	ADJUSTED FOR: current year fluctuations. Expected output for current year.	Based on expected results, aids current planning and control; costs product at close to actual costs

Note that theoretical capacity is larger than practical capacity, which is larger than normal volume. Expected annual capacity fluctuates above and below normal volume. Most firms use expected annual capacity which minimizes under- or overapplied overhead. Use of normal volume results in more under- or overapplied overhead, but these amounts balance out over a multi-year period. Use of practical capacity results in consistently underapplied overhead.

At year end overhead may be

1) Overapplied--more is applied than incurred (i.e., credit balance in applied account exceeds debit balance in control account) because

    a)   Overhead costs were overestimated,
    b)   More than expected activity took place, and/or
    c)   Actual production costs were less than expected

2) Underapplied--less overhead is applied than incurred (i.e., debit balance in control account exceeds credit balance in applied account) because

    a)   Overhead costs were underestimated,
    b)   Less than expected activity took place, and/or
    c)   Actual production costs were more than expected

E. **Disposition of Under- and Overapplied Overhead**

    1) If the under- or overapplied overhead is immaterial, it is frequently written off to cost of goods sold on grounds of expediency

```
Overhead applied (debit for balance)        xx
Cost of goods sold (debit or credit
  to balance entry)                         xx
    Overhead control (credit for balance)        xx
```

    2) If the balance is material, then an adjustment must be made to all goods which were costed at the erroneous application rate during the current period. The goods with the incorrect costs will be in three accounts: Work-in-Process Inventory, Finished Goods Inventory, and Cost of Goods Sold.

The amount of adjustment to WIP will be calculated as follows

$$\frac{\text{Overhead applied this period in WIP ending inventory}}{\text{Total overhead applied this period}} \times \begin{array}{c}\text{Under- or over-}\\ \text{applied overhead}\end{array}$$

Similar calculations will be made for FG and CGS by substituting the overhead applied to these amounts in the numerator above.

The entry, then, to close the overhead accounts when overhead has been underapplied will be as follows

Cost of goods sold	xx	
Finished goods inventory	xx	
Work-in-process inventory	xx	
Factory overhead applied	xx	
Factory overhead control		xx

The effect of this entry is to close the overhead accounts and to accurately state the cost of the units worked on during the current period.

Another topic often tested on the CPA exam is determining whether a cost is direct material or labor, or an overhead item. In general, if it is feasible to physically trace a production cost to the final product, it is direct. Otherwise, it is an indirect cost included in overhead. The table below shows some specific examples.

Production costs		Nonproduction costs
Direct (prime) costs	**Indirect (overhead) costs**	
Direct materials:	Indirect materials:	Supplies:
Steel	Factory supplies	Office supplies
Lumber	Machine oil	Advertising supplies
Automobile subassemblies		
Direct labor:	Indirect labor:	Payroll:
Machine operator	Factory janitor	Sales Representatives' salaries
Assembly line worker	Forklift operator	Administrative salaries
	Overtime and fringe benefits	
	Other:	Other:
	Factory depreciation	Warehouse depreciation
	Factory power	Office utilities
	Factory rent	Office rent
	Factory insurance	General insurance

F. Process Costing

Process costing, in contrast to job-order costing, is applicable to a continuous process of production of the same or similar goods, e.g., oil refining and chemical production. Since there is no need to determine the costs of different groups of products because the product is uniform, each processing department becomes a cost center.

Process costing computations can be broken down into the 5 steps listed below.

1) Visualize the <u>physical flow of units</u>
2) Compute the <u>equivalent units of production</u>
3) Determine <u>costs to allocate</u>
4) Compute <u>unit costs</u>
5) <u>Allocate total costs</u> to

    a. Goods manufactured (completed)
    b. Ending work in process

Note that the five steps above can be memorized using the acronym: PECUA (<u>P</u>hysical Flow, <u>E</u>quivalent Units of Production, <u>C</u>osts to Allocate, <u>U</u>nit Costs, <u>A</u>llocate Costs).

1. Flow of Units

    The cost flow diagram shown under "B." in this module is the same for process costing except there will typically be several WIP accounts (i.e., one for every department). When solving a process costing problem, it is helpful to visualize the physical flow of units, as illustrated in the diagram below.

    Beginning WIP ——————————→ Good output and spoilage
    Units started ——————————→ Ending WIP

The units in BWIP are either completed or become spoiled. The arrow from units started to good output and spoilage is commonly called "units started and completed." Units started but not completed become EWIP. Good output and spoilage can include units completed, normal spoilage, and/or abnormal spoilage.

2. Equivalent Units of Production (EUP)

    An EUP is the amount of work equivalent to completing one unit from start to finish. In a process costing system, products are assigned costs periodically (usually monthly). At any one moment some units are incomplete which makes the EUP calculations necessary to allocate manufacturing costs between

1) Goods finished during the period (cost of goods manufactured)
2) Ending work in process

The two primary EUP methods used for process costing are first-in, first-out (FIFO) and weighted-average (WA). In FIFO, beginning WIP is handled separately; equivalent units refer only to the work done in the <u>current period</u>. The weighted-average method "averages" work done last period (on this period's beginning WIP) and the current period's work when computing EUP. The EUP calculations are

<u>FIFO</u>
Work to complete BWIP
+ Units started and completed
+ Work to date on EWIP
 Equivalent units (FIFO)

<u>WEIGHTED-AVERAGE</u>
All units completed

+ Work to date on EWIP
 Equivalent units (WA)

Note that the FIFO computation includes only what is done <u>this</u> period on the beginning WIP, while the WA computation includes <u>all</u> work done on the beginning WIP. That is the <u>only</u> difference.

The computation of equivalent units and its interrelationship with the last three steps of the PECUA acronym are diagrammed below.

FIFO Method

<u>Equivalent Units:</u>

    BWIP
    Started and completed
    EWIP
       Total equivalent units

<u>Costs to Allocate:</u>

    In BWIP
    Current costs

<u>Unit Costs:</u>
<u>Allocate Costs:</u>
    In BWIP
    To complete BWIP

    To started and completed
    To EWIP

Materials
EU, Beg
+   S&C
+ EU, End
=   EUP

Labor
& Overhead
EU, Beg
+   S&C
+ EU, End
=   EUP

$$$
÷ EUP
= $.$$

$$$
÷ EUP
= $.$$

Total
$$$
$$$
$$$
$.$$

$$$

$$\left(\begin{array}{c}\text{Mat. EU}\\\text{in beg.}\end{array} \times \$.\$\$\right) + \left(\begin{array}{c}\text{L\&OH EU}\\\text{in beg.}\end{array} \times \$.\$\$\right)$$

$$\left(\begin{array}{c}\text{Mat. EU}\\\text{in end.}\end{array} \times \$.\$\$\right) + \left(\begin{array}{c}\text{L\&OH EU}\\\text{in end.}\end{array} \times \$.\$\$\right) \quad (\text{S\&C} \times \$.\$\$)$$

Weighted-Average Method

Equivalent Units:

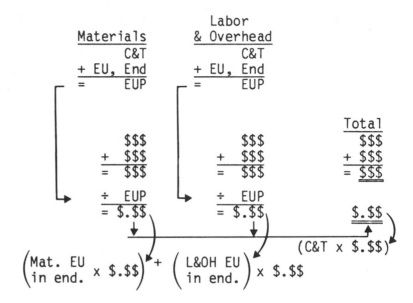

3.   Simple Process Costing Example

Assume we begin with 800 units 25% complete for labor and overhead, and 100% complete for materials because they are introduced at the start of the process. We start 4,200 units. 4,000 units are completed, while 1,000 remain in EWIP (20% complete for labor and overhead and 100% complete for materials). There is no spoilage. The costs are summarized in the following T-account.

Work in Process			
BWIP			
materials	$ 900		Goods finished ???
labor + OH	532	$ 1,432	
Current			
materials	4,200		
labor + OH	14,000	18,200	
EWIP		???	

First, the physical flow of units is diagrammed.

```
BWIP               800 ——— 800 ——————→ 4,000 Completed
                          ╱3,200╱
Started          4,200 ——— 1,000 ——————→ 1,000 EWIP
To Account for   5,000                    5,000 Accounted for
```

Second, equivalent units are computed. Both FIFO and WA are illustrated.

Materials

FIFO		WA	
Work to complete BWIP	0	Units completed	4,000
Started and completed	3,200		
Work on EWIP (1,000 x 100%)	1,000	Work on EWIP (1,000 x 100%)	1,000
EUP (FIFO)	4,200	EUP (WA)	5,000

Labor and Overhead

FIFO		WA	
Work to complete BWIP (800 x 75%)	600	Units completed	4,000
Started and completed	3,200		
Work on EWIP (1,000 x 20%)	200	Work on EWIP (1,000 x 20%)	200
EUP (FIFO)	4,000		4,200

The next step is the computation of unit costs. FIFO is current costs divided by current work, while WA is all costs divided by all work.

FIFO

Current costs
EUP (FIFO)

Materials:
$$\frac{\$4,200}{4,200} = \$1.00$$

Labor and overhead:
$$\frac{\$14,000}{4,000} = \$3.50$$

Total $4.50

WA

All costs
EUP (WA)

Materials:
$$\frac{\$900 + \$4,200}{5,000} = \$1.02$$

Labor and overhead:
$$\frac{\$532 + \$14,000}{4,200} = \$3.46$$

Total $4.48

The final step is to allocate total costs to units completed (4,000) and to EWIP (1,000). Remember, in FIFO, BWIP is handled separately.

FIFO

Cost of units completed:	
Cost of BWIP	$ 1,432
Cost to complete BWIP (800 x 75% x $3.50)	2,100
Cost of units started and completed (3,200 x $4.50)	14,400
	$17,932
Cost of EWIP	
Materials (1,000 x $1.00)	$ 1,000
Labor + OH (200 x $3.50)	700
	$ 1,700

WA

Cost of units completed:	
4,000 x $4.48 =	$17,920
Cost of EWIP	
Materials (1,000 x $1.02)	$1,020
Labor + OH (200 x $3.46)	692
	$1,712

Now the T-account can be filled in.

WIP (FIFO)			WIP (WA)	
1,432			1,432	
18,200	17,932		18,200	17,920
1,700			1,712	

4. EUP for Material

In the above example, material was assumed to be added at the beginning of the production process. Material can also be added at different points in the process, e.g., 10%, 70%, or gradually during the process. Also note that the costs associated with units transferred between departments are treated the same as material added at the beginning of the production process.

5. FIFO Work-in-Process Assumption

Notice that two groups of finished product are transferred out of work in process in the above FIFO example.

1) Product started last period and finished this period
2) Product started and finished this period

In many cases, however, there are multiple processing departments which require the FIFO assumption to be modified. If FIFO were strictly followed, the second processing department would have three groups of finished product.

1) Product started last period and finished this period
2) Product in the first incoming FIFO batch from the prior process
3) Product in the second incoming FIFO batch from the prior process

The third in a series of processing departments might have four groups of finished product priced differently; the fourth department five groups, etc. To overcome this potential bookkeeping nightmare, incoming material from a prior processing department is considered to be one batch (at one average cost).

6. Spoilage and Similar Items

The following terms are commonly used

(1) Spoilage--inferior goods either discarded or sold for disposal value
(2) Defective units--inferior goods reworked and sold as normal product
(3) Waste--materials lost in the manufacturing process
(4) Scrap--material residue which has some salvage value

A major distinction is made between normal and abnormal spoilage.

a. Normal spoilage is the cost of spoiled units which are due to the nature of the manufacturing process, i.e., which occur under efficient operating conditions

(1) Normal spoilage is a necessary cost in the production process and is, therefore, a <u>product cost</u>

b. Abnormal spoilage is the cost of spoiled units which were spoiled through some unnecessary act, event, or condition

(1) Abnormal spoilage is a <u>period cost</u>, e.g., "loss on abnormal spoilage"

(2) Abnormal spoilage costs should not be included in cost of goods sold

When abnormal spoilage occurs and some salvage value exists, the following entry is made.

Loss on abnormal spoilage	(forced)
Spoiled goods	(net realizable value)
Work in process	(costs applicable to the spoiled goods at point of removal)

If no salvage value exists, all of the applicable costs would be charged to the loss account.

If spoilage is normal and consistent, no special entry is needed for the spoilage. Total costs incurred are simply allocated to FG and EWIP, based on relative EUP in FG and EWIP. If the spoilage were not consistent from period to period, unit costs would vary unless spoilage costs were accounted for separately and run through the overhead account when spoilage did occur, e.g.

Overhead	(cost of spoiled goods)
EWIP	(same)

Thus, the cost of this spoilage, even though occurring irregularly, would be spread across a whole year's production.

Note, spoilage must be considered in EUP calculations if a separate entry is going to be made to remove spoilage costs (whether normal or abnormal) from the work-in-process account. For example, if spoilage is discovered at the 60% point in processing and 100 units of abnormal spoilage are discovered, 60 EUP have occurred. The amount of abnormal loss would be the cost of 60 EUP (processing) plus the materials added to 100 units of production up to the 60% point. Spoilage would not include the cost of materials added at the 75% point of production.

All of the process costing examples in this Module and in the solutions to the process costing problems show EUP calculations for spoilage. Some cost textbooks do not recognize showing EUP computations for normal spoilage. The reasoning under this approach is that normal spoilage will automatically be charged to good output through the use of a higher cost per equivalent unit (i.e., same amount of cost with less equivalent units). On the CPA exam, use the method you are most comfortable with unless you are instructed otherwise.

7. Process Cost Example Problem

The BW Toy Company uses a process cost system to collect costs related to its production of plastic sleds. Data relevant to 1986 sled production is given below.

> Material (plastic) is added at the beginning of the process
> Labor and overhead (conversion) costs are added continuously
> Work in process, January 1, 8,000 units; 20% complete
> Work in process, December 31, 12,000 units; 60% complete
> 82,000 units were started into production
> Units spoiled, considered normal, 600 units
> Units spoiled, considered abnormal, 400 units
> Assume spoilage is discovered at the end of the production process
> Material cost for 1986 = $62,320
> Conversion cost for 1986 = $10,868
> Work in process on January 1 has a cost of $11,352 ($5,180 material cost, $6,172 conversion cost)

a. FIFO solution

Step 1 Visualize the physical flow of units.

```
BWIP              8,000——8,000——>78,000  Good output and spoilage
                        70,000——
Started           82,000—12,000——>12,000  EWIP
To account for    90,000          90,000  Accounted for
```

Breakdown of good output and spoilage:

```
                          ——————> 77,000  Good units completed
78,000 ===================——————>   600   Normal spoilage
                          ——————>   400   Abnormal spoilage
```

Step 2 Calculate EUP.

	Material	Conversion	
Work to complete BWIP	0	6,400	(8,000 x 80%)
Started and completed (includes normal spoilage)	69,600[a]	69,600	
Abnormal spoilage	400	400	
Work to date on EWIP	12,000	7,200	(12,000 x 60%)
EUP (FIFO)	82,000	83,600	

[a]77,000 completed + 600 normal spoilage - 8,000 BWIP

Step 3 Determine costs to allocate.

Beginning work in process:		
Material cost	$ 5,180	
Conversion cost	6,172	$11,352
Current period costs:		
Material cost	$62,320	
Conversion cost	10,868	73,188
Total costs to allocate		$84,540

Step 4 Calculate <u>unit costs</u>.

Material cost	$62,320 ÷ 82,000	=	$.76
Conversion cost	$10,868 ÷ 83,600	=	.13
Total unit cost			$.89

Step 5 <u>Allocate costs</u> to finished goods, spoilage, and EWIP.

Goods finished
BWIP
   Previous cost $11,352
   Conversion added (6,400 @ $.13)   832
Started and completed (69,600 @ $.89)
(Includes normal spoilage)   61,944
                                   $74,128   CGM; transferred to finished goods (77,000 units will be recorded in finished goods)

Abnormal Spoilage (400 @ $.89)   356   recognized as loss
EWIP
   Material (12,000 @ $.76) $9,120
   Conversion (7,200 @ $.13)   936   10,056   remains in WIP account
Costs allocated $84,540

The FIFO cost of production report appears on page 1063.

b. <u>Weighted-average solution</u>

Step 1 Visualize the <u>physical flow</u> of units (same as Step 1 on page 1060).

Step 2 Calculate EUP.

	Material	Conversion	
All units completed (includes normal spoilage)	77,600	77,600	
Abnormal spoilage	400	400	
Work to date on EWIP	12,000	7,200	(12,000 x 60%)
EUP (WA)	90,000	85,200	

Step 3 Determine <u>costs to allocate</u> (same as Step 3 on page 1060).

Step 4 Calculate <u>unit costs</u>.

Material cost	($5,180 + $62,320) ÷ 90,000	=	$ .75
Conversion cost	($6,172 + $10,868) ÷ 85,200	=	.20
Total unit cost			$ .95

Step 5 <u>Allocate costs</u> to finished goods, spoilage, and EWIP.

Goods finished (77,600 @ $.95)		$73,720
Abnormal spoilage (400 @ $.95)		380
EWIP		
Material (12,000 @ $.75)	$9,000	
Conversion (7,200 @ $.20)	<u>1,440</u>	<u>10,440</u>
Costs allocated		<u>$84,540</u>

The weighted-average method resulted in more costs remaining in EWIP, because BWIP costs were proportionally greater than the current period costs.

The weighted-average cost of production report appears on page 1064.

BW Toy Company
Costs of Production Report, FIFO Method
For the Year Ended December 31, 1986

Description	Total	Direct Mtls.	Conv.
Physical units to account for			
Beginning inventory	8,000		
Units started	82,000		
Units to be accounted for	90,000		
Equivalent units of production			
Abnormal spoilage	400	400	400
Normal spoilage	600	600	600
Good units completed and transferred out:			
From beg. work in process	8,000	-0-	6,400
Started and completed[a]	69,000	69,000	69,000
Ending work in process:	12,000		
Mat. (12,000 x 100%)		12,000	
Conv. (12,000 x 60%)			7,200
Units Accounted for	90,000		
Work completed during year in equivalent units		82,000	83,600
Manufacturing costs			
Beginning inventory	$11,352		
Current costs	73,188	$62,320	$10,868
Total costs to account for	$84,540		
Cost per equivalent unit[b]	$ .89	$ .76	$ .13

Allocation of costs	Total	Direct Mtls.	Conv.
Abnormal spoilage (400 x eq. unit costs)	$ 356	$ 304	$ 52
Units completed			
Beginning WIP	11,352	5,180	6,172
To finish beg. WIP (Conv: 6,400 x .13)[c]	832	-0-	832
Started & completed[d] (69,600 x unit costs)	61,944	52,896	9,048
Total cost of units completed	$74,128	$58,076	$16,052
Ending work in process	10,056		
(Mat: 12,000 x .76)		9,120	
(Conv: 7,200 x .13)			936
Total costs accounted for	$84,540	$67,500	$17,040

---

[a]Started and completed this period (77,000 good units completed less 8,000 BWIP).

[b]<u>Current</u> costs only ÷ <u>current</u> period equivalent units.

[c]Beginning work in process was 20% complete. Thus, 80% of processing is added this period which is 3,200 equivalent units x equivalent unit costs.

[d]The cost of units started and completed includes normal spoilage cost of the 600 bad units; 77,000 units will be recorded as finished goods. If there were another department, 77,000 units would be recorded as received by the next department.

BW Toy Company
Costs of Production Report, Weighted-Average Method
For the Year Ended December 31, 1986

Description	Total	Direct Mtls.	Conv.
Physical units to account for			
Beginning inventory	8,000		
Units started	82,000		
Units to be accounted for	90,000		
Equivalent units of production			
Abnormal spoilage	400	400	400
Normal spoilage	600	600	600
Good units completed and transferred out	77,000	77,000	77,000
Ending work in process:	12,000		
Mat. (12,000 x 100%)		12,000	
Conv. (12,000 x 60%)			7,200
Units accounted for	90,000		
Work completed during year in equivalent units		90,000	85,200
Manufacturing costs			
Beginning inventory	$11,352	$ 5,180	$ 6,172
Current costs	73,188	62,320	10,868
Total costs to account for	$84,540	$67,500	$17,040
Cost per equivalent unit	$ .95	$ .75	$ .20

Allocation of costs	Total	Direct Mtls.	Conv.
Abnormal spoilage (Loss) (400 x eq. unit costs)	$ 380	$ 300	$ 80
Units completed[a] (77,600 x unit costs)	73,720	58,200	15,520
Ending work in process:	10,440		
(Mat. 12,000 x .75)		9,000	
(Conv. 7,200 x .20)			1,440
Total costs accounted for	$84,540	$67,500	$17,040

[a]The cost of units completed (77,000) includes normal spoilage cost of the 600 bad units; 77,000 units will be recorded as finished goods. If there were another department, 77,000 units would be recorded as received by the next department.

G. Hybrid Costing

Many manufacturing firms have production systems which are not suited for strictly job-order costing or process costing, but instead require a costing system which incorporates ideas from both. This blending of ideas is known as hybrid costing. The continuum below demonstrates the relationship between these costing systems.

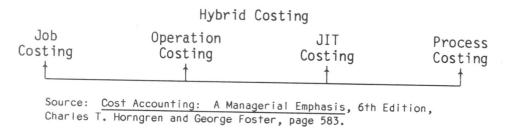

Source: Cost Accounting: A Managerial Emphasis, 6th Edition,
Charles T. Horngren and George Foster, page 583.

The costing system an organization selects will mainly depend on its underlying production system.

Operation costing, also known as specification costing, is used in batch manufacturing environments when products produced have common, as well as distinguishing, characteristics. For example, in the manufacture of clothing, basic suits can be assembled in one operation. These suits can then move on to the next operation and have a regular lining inserted, or they can move on to a different operation and have a deluxe lining added. Based on the variations, the products and the related costs are identified by batches or by production runs.

JIT (Just In Time) costing is used in a constant flow manufacturing system, whereby each unit of product is produced only upon request. This results in minimal inventory levels of finished goods and work in process. Material inventories are also kept to a minimum because materials are usually moved directly into production. Because of this unique feature, material cost is combined with work in process into a single "resources in process" type account.

H. **Joint Products**

Joint products are two or more products produced together up to a split-off point where they become separately identifiable. They cannot be produced by themselves. For example, a steak cannot be produced by itself. Roasts, ribs, liver, hamburger, etc. are produced with steak. Other industries which produce joint products include

1) Chemicals   3) Mining
2) Lumber   4) Petroleum

Joint products are said to have common, or joint costs until the split-off point. The split-off point is the point of production when the joint products can be individually identified and removed from the joint, or common process, i.e., they can be sold, processed further in alternative ways, etc. Costs incurred after the split-off point for any one of the joint products are called separable costs.

Common costs are allocated to the joint products at the split-off point, usually on the basis of sales value at the split-off point, hypothetical sales value less separable costs after further processing (net realizable value), or some physical measure. The following example illustrates the sales value at split-off and hypothetical sales value after further processing methods. The sales value at split-off method must be used if a value at split-off point exists.

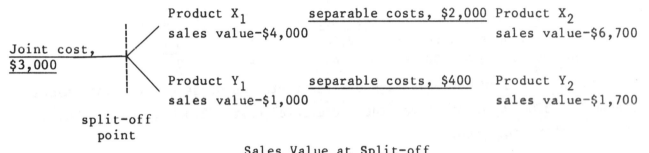

Product X_1 separable costs, $2,000 Product X_2
sales value-$4,000   sales value-$6,700

Joint cost,
$3,000

Product Y_1 separable costs, $400   Product Y_2
sales value-$1,000   sales value-$1,700

split-off
point

Sales Value at Split-off

Product	Sales Value @ Split	Ratio	x	Joint Costs	=	Allocated Joint Costs
X_1	$4,000	$\frac{\$4,000}{\$5,000}$	x	$3,000	=	$2,400
Y_1	$1,000	$\frac{\$1,000}{\$5,000}$	x	$3,000	=	$ 600
Total	$5,000					$3,000

If the sales value at split-off were not available or one did not exist, we must use the hypothetical sales value after further processing method (NRV):

Hypothetical Sales Value After Further Processing (NRV)

Product	Final Sales Value	-	Separable Costs	=	Hypothetical Sales Value	Ratio	x	Joint Costs	=	Allocated Joint Costs
X_2	$6,700	-	$2,000	=	$4,700	$\frac{\$4,700}{\$6,000}$	x	$3,000	=	$2,350
Y_2	$1,700	-	$ 400	=	$1,300	$\frac{\$1,300}{\$6,000}$	x	$3,000	=	$ 650
Total					$6,000					$3,000

Physical measures (units, pounds, etc.) generally are not used because of the misleading income statement effect. With an allocation based on pounds, steak would show a big profit while ground beef would be a consistent loser; each pound would carry the same cost although steak sells for more per pound.

Joint cost allocation is performed for the purpose of inventory valuation and income determination. However, joint costs should be ignored for any internal decisions including the decision on whether to process a joint product further beyond the split-off point. The sell or process further decision should be based on incremental revenues and costs. If incremental revenue from further processing exceeds incremental costs, then process further. If incremental costs exceed incremental revenues, then sell without further processing. In the previous example in which we assumed a sales value at the split-off point both X_1 and Y_1 should be further processed.

Incremental revenue	-	Incremental cost	=	Advantage of Further Processing
X_1: \$6,700 - \$4,000 = \$2,700	-	\$2,000	=	\$700
Y_1: \$1,700 - \$1,000 = \$ 700	-	\$ 400	=	\$300

If X_1 could have sold for only \$5,500 after further processing, the incremental revenue (\$1,500) would not cover the incremental cost (\$2,000), and X_1 should not be further processed.

I. By-Products

By-products, in contrast to joint products, have little market value relative to the overall value of the product(s) being produced. Joint (common) costs are usually not allocated to a by-product. Instead, they are frequently valued at market or net realizable value (NRV) and accounted for as a contra production cost.

    By-product inventory   (Market value/NRV)
        Work in process   (Same)

Additional costs may be incurred to ready the by-product for sale. If incurred, these costs would also be inventoried.

Rather than recognizing by-product market value as a reduction of production cost, it is sometimes recognized when sold and disclosed as

1) Ordinary sales
2) Other income
3) Contra to cost of sales

PLANNING, CONTROL, AND ANALYSIS

This module discusses a number of tools used internally for financial planning, control, and analysis.

A. **Analyzing Cost Behavior**

Many of the tools discussed later require the separation of costs into their fixed and variable components (refer to the definitions of fixed, variable, and mixed costs under "Basic Cost Accounting Terminology" beginning on the second page of this chapter).

1. High-Low Method

The high-low method computes the slope on variable rate based on the highest and lowest observations.

$$\text{Slope} = \frac{\text{Change in cost between high and low points}}{\text{Change in activity between high and low points}}$$

This method is illustrated using the following observations for factory maintenance costs (DLH = Direct labor hours).

Month	DLH	Factory Maintenance Cost
1	45,000	$110,000 (low)
2	50,000	115,000
3	70,000	158,000
4	60,000	135,000
5	75,000	170,000 (high)
6	65,000	145,000

The difference in cost is divided by the difference in activity to obtain the variable cost. The fixed cost can then be computed by using either the high observation or the low observation. You will get the same result with either one. The computation for separating factory maintenance cost is detailed below.

Variable Rate Computation

$$\frac{\$170,000 - \$110,000}{75,000 - 45,000} = \underline{\underline{\$2/DLH}}$$

Fixed Rate Computation

$\$170,000 - (75,000 \times \$2) = \underline{\$20,000}$
or
$\$110,000 - (45,000 \times \$2) = \underline{\$20,000}$

In cases where the highest and lowest cost observations do not correspond with the highest and lowest activity observations, there are conflicting viewpoints among authors as to which observations should be selected for the high-low method. When working a given problem, the candidate should compute the answer using both the cost and activity observations and check the alternatives for agreement. It is unlikely that the Board of Examiners would provide both answers as alternatives which forces the candidate to select between them.

The high-low method is a rather crude technique compared to regression analysis. For example, this method may be inaccurate if the high and low points are not representative as illustrated in the following chart by the solid line.

2. Scattergraph Method. The scattergraph method is a graphical approach to computing the relationship between two variables. The dependent variable is plotted on the vertical axis and the independent variable on the horizontal axis. A straight line is then drawn through the observation points which best describes the relationship between the two variables. In the graph above, the broken line illustrates the relationship. This method lacks precision, because by freely drawing the line through the points, it is possible to obtain a line that does not minimize the deviations of the points from the line.

3. Regression Analysis. Regression (least squares) analysis determines the functional relationship between variables with a measure of probable error. For example, you may wish to determine the relationship of electricity cost to level of activity. Based on activity levels and electricity charges of past months, the following chart (scattergram) might be prepared.

As production increases, electric costs increase. The relationship appears linear. Linearity is an assumption underlying regression. If the power costs begin to fall after 3,000 units of production, the relationship between electricity and production would not be linear, and linear regression would not be appropriate.

The method of least squares fits a regression line between the observation points such that the sum of the squared vertical differences between the regression line and the individual observations is minimized. For example, in the above scattergram, there are 15 observations, and the sum of the squares of vertical differences between each observation and the regression line is minimized. The regression line, Y = a + bx, is determined by the following "normal" equations

$$\sum Y = na + b\sum X$$

$$\sum XY = a\sum X + b\sum X^2$$

Y = dependent variable, e.g., electricity costs
X = independent variable, e.g., level of production
a = Y intercept (where the regression line intersects the vertical axis)
b = slope of the regression line
n = number of observations, e.g., 15 in above example

The goodness of the least squares fit, i.e., how well the regression line fits the observed data, is measured by the coefficient of determination (r^2); the proportion of squared variation between observed data. The better the line fits the observed data points, i.e., the closer the observed data points are to the line, the closer r^2 will be to 1.00 -- r^2s of 90-99% are considered very good (small r^2 is used for simple regression; capital R^2 for multiple regression).

If there is only one independent variable, the analysis is known as simple regression (as in the above example). <u>Multiple regression</u> consists of a functional relationship with multiple independent variables, e.g., cost may be a function of several variables.

4. <u>Correlation Analysis</u>. Correlation is the relationship between variables. If the variables move with each other, they have a direct relationship (positive correlation) as in A. If the variables move in opposite directions, they have an inverse relationship (negative correlation) as in B.

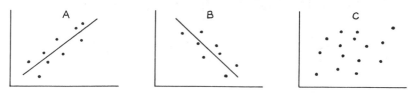

The degree and direction of correlation is measured from -1 to 1. The sign (negative or positive) describes whether the relationship is inverse or direct. The coefficient of correlation is measured by

$$\sqrt{\frac{\text{Amount of variation explained}}{\text{Total variation}}}$$

If all of the observations were in a straight line, all of the variation would be explained and the coefficient of correlation would be 1 or -1 depending upon whether the relationship is positive or negative. If there is no correlation, as in C above, the coefficient of correlation is 0.

Note that the coefficient of correlation is similar in concept to the coefficient of determination discussed above in "method of least squares". The coefficient of determination cannot have a negative value, as can the coefficient of correlation, because the coefficient of determination is based on squared deviations, i.e., if you square a negative number, the result is positive.

B. **Cost-Volume-Profit (CVP) Analysis**

1. <u>Overview</u>

Breakeven (CVP) analysis provides management with profitability esti-mates at all levels of production in the relevant range (the normal oper-ating range). Breakeven or CVP analysis is based on the firm's profit function. Profit is a function of sales, variable costs, and fixed costs.

Profit (NI) = Sales (S) - Fixed Costs (FC) - Variable Costs(VC)
When profit is zero   0 = S - FC - VC
                             S = FC + VC

Fixed costs are constant in the relevant range, but both sales and variable costs are a function of the level of activity, i.e., production and sales. For example, if widgets are sold at $2.00/unit, variable costs are $.40/unit, and fixed costs are $20,000, breakeven is 12,500 units.

$$X = \text{Units of production and sales to breakeven}$$
$$\$2.00X = \$.40X + \$20,000$$
$$\$1.60X = \$20,000$$
$$X = 12,500 \text{ units (breakeven point)}$$

The cost-volume-profit relationship is diagrammed below.

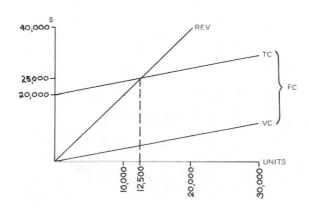

The breakeven point can be thought of as the amount of contribution margin (sales minus variable costs) required to cover the fixed costs. In the previous example, the unit contribution margin (CM) is $1.60 ($2.00 - $.40). Thus, sales of 12,500 units are required to cover the $20,000 of fixed costs. This illustrates the possibility of two shortcut approaches.

Shortcut 1

$$\text{Units to breakeven} = \frac{\text{Fixed costs}}{\text{Unit CM}} = \frac{\$20,000}{\$1.60} = \underline{12,500 \text{ units}}$$

Shortcut 2

$$\text{Dollars to breakeven} = \frac{\text{Fixed costs}}{\substack{\text{CM percentage} \\ \text{(ratio)}}} = \frac{\text{Fixed costs}}{\substack{\text{CM per unit} \\ \text{Selling price} \\ \text{per unit}}} = \frac{\$20,000}{\frac{\$1.60}{\$2.00}} = \frac{\$20,000}{80\%} = \underline{\$25,000 \text{ sales dollars}}$$

A number of variations on the basic CVP calculation are found on the CPA Exam. These are illustrated in the following paragraphs.

a. Target net income. Selling price is $2, variable cost per unit is $.40, fixed costs are $20,000, and desired net income is $5,000. What is the level of sales in units?

Equation $\longrightarrow$ Sales = VC + FC + NI
  $\$2X = \$.4X + \$20,000 + \$5,000$

Shortcut $\longrightarrow$ $\dfrac{\text{FC + NI}}{\text{CM}} = \dfrac{\$20,000 + \$5,000}{\$1.60}$

Solution $\longrightarrow$ $\underline{15,625 \text{ units}}$

b. Target net income-percentage of sales. Same facts, except desired net income is 30% of sales. What is the level of sales in units?

Equation $\longrightarrow$ Sales = VC + FC + NI

  $\$2X = \$.4x + \$20,000 + .30(\$2X)$

Solution $\longrightarrow$ $\underline{20,000 \text{ units}}$

c. No per unit information given. Fixed costs are $20,000, and variable expenses are 20% of sales. What is the level of sales in dollars?

Equation $\longrightarrow$ Sales = VC + FC

  $S = .2(S) + \$20,000$

Shortcut $\longrightarrow$ $\dfrac{\text{FC}}{\text{CM\%}} = \dfrac{20,000}{.8}$

Solution $\longrightarrow$ $\underline{\$25,000 \text{ sales dollars}}$

d. Decision making. Selling price is $2, variable cost per unit is .40, and fixed costs are $20,000. Purchasing a new machine will increase fixed costs by $5,000, but variable costs will be cut by 20%. If the selling price is cut by 10%, what is the breakeven point in units?

$$\text{Equation} \longrightarrow \quad \text{Sales} = VC + FC$$

$$\$1.8X = \$.32X + \$25,000$$

$$\text{Shortcut} \longrightarrow \quad \frac{FC}{CM} = \frac{\$25,000}{\$1.48}$$

$$\text{Solution} \longrightarrow \quad \underline{16,892 \text{ units}}$$

2. Breakeven: Multi-Product Firm

    If a firm makes more than one product, it is necessary to use "composite" units to find the number of units of each product to breakeven. A "composite" unit consists of the proportionate number of units which make up the firm's sales mix. For example, assume that a firm has two products with the following selling prices and variable costs.

Product	Selling price	Variable costs	Contribution margin
A	$.60	$.20	$.40
B	$.40	$.15	$.25

Also assume that the sales mix consists of 3 units of A for every 2 units of B (3:2) and fixed costs are $34,000.

The first step is to find the "composite" contribution margin.

    Composite contribution margin = 3($.40) + 2($.25) = $1.70

Next compute the number of composite units to breakeven.

$$\frac{\$34,000 \text{ fixed costs}}{\$1.70 \text{ composite contribution margin}} = \underline{20,000} \text{ composite units}$$

Finally, determine the number of units of A and B at the breakeven point by multiplying the composite units by the number of units of A (i.e., 3) and the number of units of B (i.e., 2) in the mix.

$$\text{A: } 20,000 \times 3 = \underline{60,000} \text{ units}$$
$$\text{B: } 20,000 \times 2 = \underline{40,000} \text{ units}$$

3. Assumptions of CVP Analysis

    When applying CVP to a specific case and in interpreting the results therefrom, it is important to keep in mind the assumptions underlying CVP which are listed below.

    a. Selling price does not change with the activity level
    b. The sales mix remains constant
    c. Costs can be separated into fixed and variable elements
    d. Variable costs per unit are constant
    e. Total fixed costs are constant over the relevant range
    f. Material, labor, and overhead prices are unchanged
    g. Productivity and efficiency are constant
    h. Volume is the only factor which causes changes in cost
    i. Activity will be in the relevant range where all assumptions are valid
    j. Units produced = Units sold

C. Direct (Variable) and Absorption (Full) Costing

Direct (variable) costing is a form of relevant costing. Direct costing considers fixed manufacturing costs as period rather than product costs. It is advocated because, in the short run, fixed costs are sunk costs and should be disregarded. Therefore, only variable manufacturing costs are inventoried. It is important to note that direct costing is not acceptable as GAAP for external reporting, however.

Direct and absorption costing methods of accounting for fixed manufacturing overhead result in different levels of net income in most cases. The differences are timing differences, i.e., when to recognize the fixed manufacturing overhead as an expense.

1. In the period incurred--direct costing
2. In the period in which the units to which fixed overhead has been related are sold--absorption costing

The relationship between direct costing (DC) income and absorption costing (AC) income follows.

Sales = Production (no change in inventory)	No difference in income
Sales > Production (inventory decreases)	DC income greater than AC income
Sales < Production (inventory increases)	DC income less than AC income

EXAMPLE: Production begins in period A with 5,000 units. Fixed manufacturing costs equal $5,000 and variable manufacturing costs are $1/unit. Sales were 4,000 units at $3/unit. In period B, units produced and production costs were the same as in period A. Sales were 6,000 units at $3/unit.

	Direct costing		Absorption costing	
	Period A	*Period B*	*Period A*	*Period B*
Sales	$12,000	$18,000	$12,000	$18,000
Less costs	9,000	11,000	8,000	12,000
Profit	$ 3,000	$ 7,000	$ 4,000	$ 6,000

(a) $\dfrac{\$5,000\ Fixed\ costs}{5,000\ Units}$ x (1,000 Units E.I. - 0 Units B.I.)

(b) $\dfrac{\$5,000\ Fixed\ costs}{5,000\ Units}$ x (0 Units E.I. - 1,000 Units B.I.)

Both direct and absorption costing recognized $10,000 profit in periods A + B. Direct costing income in period A was less than absorption income, because production exceeded sales which resulted in $1,000 of fixed costs being <u>inventoried</u> under AC that were <u>expensed</u> under DC.

	Fixed costs expensed Period A	Fixed costs expensed Period B	Variable costs expensed Period A	Variable costs expensed Period B	Total costs expensed Period A	Total costs expensed Period B
Direct	$5,000*	$5,000*	$4,000	$6,000	$9,000	$11,000
Absorption	4,000	6,000	4,000	6,000	$8,000	12,000

*The same every period.

If the example above included either variable or fixed selling costs, they would be handled the same under either method--deducted in total on the income statement in the period in which they were incurred.

Note that the format of the income statement changes under direct costing to reflect the alternate treatment given the fixed manufacturing costs and to emphasize contribution margin. The recommended format under direct costing follows.

     Sales
   - Variable manufacturing costs
   = Manufacturing contribution margin
   - Variable selling and administrative expenses
   = Contribution margin
   - Fixed manufacturing, selling, and administrative expenses
   = Net income

Absorption costing can lead to two categories of errors in managerial decision making.

1. Absorption costing overstates the short-run costs of production by including fixed costs (the short-run costs of production may consist of only variable costs). Thus, management may choose not to produce when they should.

2. On the other hand, absorption costing defers fixed costs of production which decreases losses or increases income in periods when production exceeds sales. The result is that management may wish to produce at full capacity when demand is less than capacity to maximize absorption costing income. Remember, only absorption costing is acceptable GAAP.

In summary, variable costs are the only relevant costs in the short run.

D. **Budgeting**

Budgeting is a plan of action for future operations. The most important functions of a budget are to coordinate the various functional activities of the firm and to provide a basis for control of the activities. The budget process begins with an estimate of sales and then proceeds systematically as outlined below.

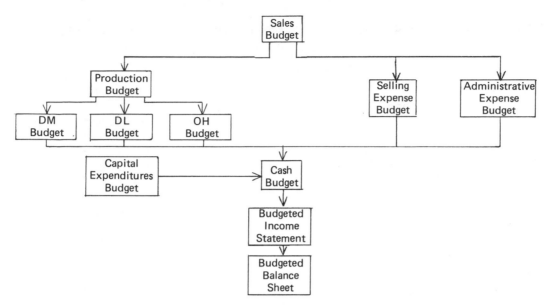

The basic formats of some of the key budgets are presented below.

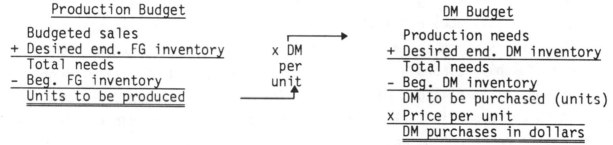

Production Budget		DM Budget

Note that before proceeding to the cash budget, DM purchases would have to be converted to <u>payments</u> for DM purchases, based on some payment schedule (e.g., 70% in month of purchase, 30% in month following).

Cash Budget

Beginning cash balance
+ <u>Receipts</u> (collections from customers, etc.)
  Cash available
- <u>Payments</u> (materials, expenses, payroll, etc.)
  Estimated cash balance before financing
± <u>Financing</u> (planned borrowing or short-term investing to bring cash to
          desired balance)
= <u>Ending cash balance</u>

E. **Flexible Budgets**

A flexible budget is a budget adjusted for changes in volume. In the planning phase, a flexible budget is used to compare the effects of various activity levels on costs and revenues. In the controlling phase, the flexible budget is used to help analyze actual results by comparing actual results with a flexible budget for the level of activity achieved in the period (see Module 36, Standards and Variances).

Presented below is a sample flexible budget for overhead costs.

Factory Overhead
Flexible Budget

	18,000	20,000	22,000
Direct labor hours			
Variable factory overhead			
Supplies	$ 18,000	$ 20,000	$ 22,000
Power	99,000	110,000	121,000
Idle time	3,600	4,000	4,400
Overtime premium	1,800	2,000	2,200
Total ($6.80 per DLH)	$122,400	$136,000	$149,600
Fixed factory overhead			
Supervision	$ 15,000	$ 15,000	$ 15,000
Depreciation	32,000	32,000	32,000
Power	8,000	8,000	8,000
Property taxes	5,000	5,000	5,000
Insurance	1,500	1,500	1,500
Total	$ 61,500	$ 61,500	$ 61,500
Total overhead	$183,900	$197,500	$211,100

F. Responsibility Accounting

Responsibility accounting allocates those revenues and/or assets to responsibility centers which the manager of the responsibility center can control. If a manager is only responsible for costs, the area of responsibility under his/her control is called a cost center. Cost centers represent the most basic activities or responsibilities. Both production and service departments are cost centers representing activities and responsibilities (even though there may be more basic cost centers within production and service departments). The objective of responsibility accounting is to use cost data to evaluate those deemed responsible for the activities and/or decisions of a given cost center.

If the manager is responsible for both revenues and costs, the area of responsibility under his/her control is called a profit center. A contribution income statement similar to the one shown below would be prepared for each profit center. Finally, if the manager is responsible for revenues, costs, and investment, the area of responsibility under his/her control is called an investment center.

G. Segmented Reporting and Controllability

The direct costing income statement shown in "C." Direct (Variable) Costing and Absorption (Full) Costing can be broken into further detail to emphasize controllability.

1. Variable manufacturing costs are deducted from sales to obtain manufacturing contribution margin
2. Variable selling and administrative expenses are deducted from manufacturing contribution margin to obtain contribution margin
3. Controllable and uncontrollable fixed costs of various levels, e.g., division, department, etc., are deducted from contribution margin to obtain the segment contribution at that level

4. Costs common to all operations are finally deducted to obtain <u>income before taxes</u>

Example Contribution Approach Income Statement

	Total	*Segment 1*	*Segment 2*
Sales	*$600*	*$350*	*$250*
- Variable manufacturing costs	*220*	*115*	*105*
Manufacturing contribution margin	*380*	*235*	*145*
- Variable selling and admin. exp.	*100*	*70*	*30*
Contribution margin	*280*	*165*	*115*
- Controllable fixed costs	*80*	*35*	*45*
Controllable contribution	*200*	*130*	*70*
- Uncontrollable fixed costs	*90*	*60*	*30*
Segment contribution	*110*	*$ 70*	*$ 40*
- Unallocable common costs	*60**		
Income before taxes	*$ 50*		

*Not allocated to any segment of the firm. Examples include corporate office salaries and advertising for firm name.

If costs are not controllable by a subdivision (cost or profit center) of a firm, costs should not be allocated to the subdivision for evaluation or decision-making purposes (see "F." Responsibility Accounting).

Contribution margin data can be used in a variety of situations, including

1. Determination of which products to emphasize (see also Scarce Resources in Module 37)
2. Determination of which products should be retained and which should be eliminated (see also Nonroutine Decisions in Module 37)
3. Evaluation of mutually exclusive alternatives such as special orders, sales promotion plans, etc. (see also Nonroutine Decisions in Module 37)
4. Determination of sales level necessary to achieve desired profit (see CVP Analysis above)
5. Establishment of product prices (see also Product Pricing later in this module)
6. Evaluation of the effects of changes in revenues, costs and volume upon profit (see CVP Analysis above)
7. Understanding of the basic profit relationships of the firm (see CVP Analysis above)

H. **Performance Analysis**

As entities become more decentralized, it becomes necessary to evaluate each department or division in terms of profitability. The most popular measure for analyzing the profitability of a division is <u>return on investment</u> (ROI). ROI measures the relationship between a division's profit and the capital invested in the division.

$$\text{ROI} = \frac{\text{Net income of division}}{\text{Sales of division}} \times \frac{\text{Sales of division}}{\text{Invested capital of division}}$$

$$= \frac{\text{Net income of division}}{\text{Invested capital of division}}$$

A division may improve ROI by lowering its asset base while keeping income and sales constant, lowering expenses while keeping sales and assets constant or increasing sales while keeping assets and net profit as a proportion of sales constant. Although ROI is quite popular as a performance evaluation measure, it can, at times, motivate a manager to reject a project which is profitable from the entire company's point of view, because it may lower the division's ROI and thus adversely affect the manager's performance evaluation.

> *EXAMPLE: Borke Company's cost of capital is 10%. One of Borke Company's division managers has the opportunity of investing in a project that will generate $45,000 of net income per year for eight years on an initial investment of $300,000. The division's current income is $250,000 from a total divisional asset base of $1,000,000. The manager should accept the project since it offers a 15% return and the company's cost of capital is 10%. Chances are the manager will reject the project since it will lower the division current ROI from*

$$\frac{250,000}{1,000,000} = 25\% \text{ to } \frac{250,000 \ + \ 45,000}{1,000,000 \ + \ 300,000} = 22.7\%$$

> *In this case the use of ROI has led to an incorrect decision.*

An alternative method for evaluating divisional performance is the residual income method. Residual income is the net income of a division less the cost of capital on the division's assets. The division's residual income before the project would be $250,000 - (.10 x $1,000,000) = $150,000. Under the residual income approach a manager would be evaluated on how well s/he maximizes dollars of residual income instead of maximizing a profit percentage. Using the example above, the manager would have accepted the project under consideration since it would raise his/her residual income by [$45,000 - (.10 x $300,000)] = $15,000 per year.

I. **Product Pricing**

Product pricing requires the use of judgment by the cost accountant and the manager in order to maximize the entity's profits and increase shareholders' wealth. In order to find the combination of sales price and volume yielding the greatest profits, management needs to make many assumptions regarding customer preferences, competitors' reactions, economic conditions, cost structures, etc. Additionally, management must also look at their cost of capital in determining a desired rate of return. This rate of return will represent the desired minimum markup on the cost of goods. This concept is useful in that it recognizes the cost of funds; however, it ignores the complexity of pricing and the effect of changing prices on the amount of capital employed.

In maximizing shareholders' wealth, management must consider not only product costs but must also react to external changes, e.g., a competitor's price on a relatively undifferentiated product. However, costs usually are the starting point in determining prices. In the long-run, all costs, including fixed costs, must be considered. However, decisions involving short-range pricing, such as a special order, may be evaluated on the basis of contribution margin. The contribution margin approach considers all relevant variable costs plus any additional fixed costs needed for the new production level. (Other fixed costs are included in the costs of existing long-range products.)

Cost-plus pricing is a starting point for the pricing decision; prices are set at variable costs plus a percentage markup, or at full manufacturing cost plus a percentage markup. The percentage markup must cover fixed costs and profit (variable approach), or operating expenses and a profit (full cost approach). Consider the following example.

Annual sales--10,000 units

Manufacturing costs		Operating costs	
Fixed	$20,000	Fixed	$10,000
Variable	$3/unit	Variable	$2.50/unit

If price is set at variable cost plus 60% ($5.50 x 160%), or full manufacturing cost plus 76% ($5.00 x 176%), the selling price would be $8.80.

Finally, the use of "standard costs" that are attainable eliminates the effect of unusual efficiency/inefficiency on price. Implementing standard costs can also reduce clerical time and speed up the availability of cost figures for the pricing decision.

J. **Inventory Models**

A basic inventory model exists to assist in two inventory questions.

1. How much to order
2. When to reorder

How Much to Order. The amount to be ordered is known as the economic order quantity (EOQ). The EOQ minimizes the sum of the ordering and carrying costs. The total inventory cost function includes

1. <u>Carrying costs</u> (which increase with order size)
   a. Storage costs
   b. Interest costs
   c. Spoilage, etc.
   d. Insurance

   If x is the number of units received in each shipment, x ÷ 2 would be the average inventory. If k is the unit cost of holding one unit of inventory for one year, kx ÷ 2 is the annual inventory carrying cost.

2. <u>Ordering costs</u> (which decrease with order size)
   a. Transportation costs (carload rates)
   b. Administrative costs of purchasing and accounts payable costs of receiving and inspecting goods

   If a is the fixed cost of an inventory order, b is the variable cost of ordering, D is total demand per year, and (D/x) is the number of orders, the reorder cost is (a + bx) (D/x).

$$\text{Total cost (TC)} = kx/2 + (a + bx)\,(D/x)$$
$$TC = kx/2 + a\,D/x + bD$$

The EOQ formula is a common approach to determine order quantity. The formula is derived by setting the annual carrying cost equal to annual purchase cost or by differentiating the cost function with respect to order size. The formula is

$$EOQ = \sqrt{\frac{2aD}{k}}$$

a = cost of placing one order
D = annual demand in units
k = cost of carrying one unit in inventory for one year
    (cost per unit of material x carrying cost percentage)

The EOQ can also be depicted in a graph as shown below. The EOQ is where the annual carrying costs and annual ordering costs intersect.

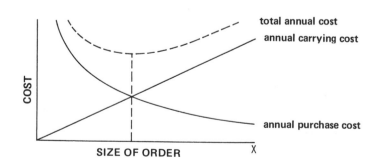

EXAMPLE: The following information relates to Huskie Company.

Units required per year	3,000
Cost of placing an order	$ 40
Unit carrying cost per year	$ 6

Assuming that the units will be used evenly throughout the year, what is the economic order quantity?

      A.   200
      B.   300
      C.   400
      D.   500

Solution:

$$EOQ = \sqrt{\frac{2\ x\ a\ x\ D}{k}} = \sqrt{\frac{2\ x\ \$40\ x\ 3{,}000}{\$6}} = 200\ units$$

The formula for the EOQ model can also be used to determine the optimal size of a production run. In these applications, "a" is the setup cost; "D" is the annual demand for the finished product and "k" is the variable manufacturing cost per unit times the carrying cost percentage.

<u>Assumptions of the EOQ Model</u>. The EOQ model was developed on the basis of several assumptions regarding the acquisition and use of inventory items. The assumptions which underlie the EOQ model are*

1. Demand occurs at a constant rate throughout the year
2. Lead time on the receipt of orders is constant
3. The entire quantity ordered is received at one time
4. The unit costs of the items ordered are constant; thus there can be no quantity discounts
5. There are no limitations on the size of the inventory

The model is insensitive to minor violations of these assumptions. The square root sign makes the EOQ model relatively insensitive to input estimation errors. However, when there are serious violations, the EOQ model should be adapted or not used.

<u>When to Reorder</u>. When to reorder is a stockout problem, i.e., the objective is to order at a point in time so as not to run out of stock before receiving the inventory ordered but not so early that an excessive quantity of "safety" stock is maintained. The stockout problem is diagrammed below.

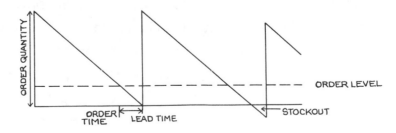

*Taken with permission from "Making EOQ Operational," unpublished manuscript by James A. Hendricks, Northern Illinois University and Cynthia D. Dailey, Peat, Marwick, Main & Co.

The vertical distance is the <u>order size</u> determined by the EOQ formula. The line sloping downward to the right represents the inventory as it is being used or sold. The horizontal broken line is the <u>order point</u>. The horizontal difference between the time the order is placed and received is the order <u>lead time</u>. Theoretically, it is desirable to have zero inventory when the inventory shipment is received. If the order point is so computed, there may be a <u>stockout</u> situation if

1. Demand is greater than expected during the lead time or
2. The order time exceeds the lead time

A <u>stockout</u> is illustrated in the above graph on the second purchase. <u>Safety stocks</u> may be used to guard against stockout. <u>Safety stocks</u> are maintained by increasing the lead time. Both stockouts and safety stocks have costs associated with them. The typical cost elements comprising carrying costs of safety stock and stockout costs are listed below.

Carrying Costs of Safety Stock
1. Storage
2. Interest
3. Spoilage
4. Insurance
5. Property taxes

Stockout Costs
1. Profit on lost sales
2. Customer ill will
3. Idle equipment
4. Work stoppages

<u>Safety stocks</u> decrease <u>stockout costs</u> but increase <u>carrying costs</u>. The amount of safety stock should be such as to minimize the sum of stockout and carrying costs as illustrated below.

Units of Safety Stock

With a larger safety stock, the stockout costs will be smaller, but the carrying costs associated with the safety stock will be larger. The most common approach to setting the optimum safety-stock level is the probabilistic approach which looks at previous lead-time periods to see what the probabilities of running out of stock (a stockout) are for different assessed levels of safety stock. The following example illustrates this approach and shows how the carrying costs and stockout costs behave as units of safety stock are increased.

EXAMPLE: The Polly Company wishes to determine the amount of safety stock to maintain for product D in order to minimize the sum of stockout costs and carrying costs.   The following information is available.

Stockout cost	$80 per occurrence
Carrying cost of safety stock	$ 3 per unit
Number of purchase orders	5 per year

What is the number of units of safety stock that will result in the lowest cost, given the four levels of safety stock and their related probability of being out of stock (columns 1 and 2 below)?

Solution: In order to answer the question it is necessary to compute the stockout costs and carrying costs for each of the four alternatives.

Unit levels of safety stock	Probability of being out of stock	Cost of stockout	# of orders per year	Stockout cost[a]	Carrying cost[b]	Total cost[c]
20	.40	x $80	x 5 =	$160	+ $ 60 =	$220
40	.20	x $80	x 5 =	80	+ 120 =	200
50	.10	x $80	x 5 =	40	+ 150 =	190
60	.05	x $80	x 5 =	20	+ 180 =	200

Computations

[a]Probability of being out of stock x Cost of stockout x Number of orders per year

[b]Safety stock x Cost ($3) of carrying one unit for one year

[c]Carrying cost + Stockout cost

A safety stock of 50 units is optimal since it results in the lowest total cost.

When a safety stock is maintained, the order point is computed as follows:

Order point = (Daily demand x Days in lead time) + Safety stock

If we assume in the Polly example that the average usage is 20 units per day and the lead time is 6 days, the order point would be computed as follows.

Order point = (20 x 6) + 50 = 170 units

STANDARDS AND VARIANCES

Standard costs are predetermined target costs which should be attainable under efficient conditions. The tightness, or attainment difficulty, of standard costs should be determined by the principles of motivation (e.g., excessively tight standards may result in employees feeling the standards are impossible to achieve; consequently, they may ignore the standards). Standard costs are used to aid in the budget process, pinpoint trouble areas, and evaluate performance. Standard costing will often result in lower bookkeeping costs than actual costing, because standard costing does not require actual department costs to be allocated to each unit produced in that department.

The tightness of standards are generally described by one of two terms. <u>Ideal</u> standards reflect the absolute minimum costs which could be achieved under perfect operating conditions. <u>Currently attainable</u> standards should be achieved under efficient operating conditions. Generally, currently attainable standards are set so they will be difficult, but not impossible, to achieve. Currently attainable standards are most often used since they are more realistic for budgeting purposes and are a better motivational tool than ideal standards.

Variances are differences between actual and standard costs. The total variance is generally broken down into subvariances to further pinpoint the causes of the variance.

A. Variance Analysis

In calculating the variances for direct material and direct labor the following symbols will be employed as defined.

AP: Actual price paid per unit of input, e.g., price per foot of lumber, per hour of labor, per ton of steel, etc.
SP: Standard price per unit of input
AQ: The actual quantity of input (feet, hours, tons, etc.) used in production
SQ: The standard quantity of input that should have been used for the good units produced

Variances can be computed using either the diagram approach (facilitates understanding), or the equation approach (quicker problem solving). Both approaches are discussed below.

B. Material Variances

The diagram for computing material variances is

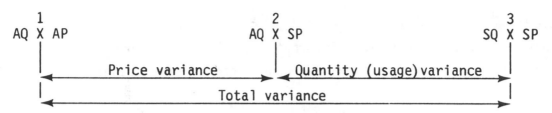

If 1 > 2 or 2 > 3, unfavorable (U) variances result. If 1 < 2 or 2 < 3, a favorable (F) variance is the result. The equation approach is

Price variance = (AP - SP) x AQ
Quantity variance = (AQ - SQ) x SP

The only alternative allowed on the variances above concerns the material price variance. The price variance can be recognized when material is placed in production (as assumed in the previous discussion) or when material is purchased (which is desirable for early identification and control). If the price variance is to be recognized at the time of purchase, AQ (for the price variance only) becomes quantity purchased rather than quantity used.

The materials price variance is generally considered to be the responsibility of the purchasing department, while the materials quantity variance is the responsibility of the production department.

C. **Labor Variances**

The computational form of the labor variances is similar to the calculation of material variances--all that changes is that the price being used changes from price per pound of material to price per hour of labor, and the quantity changes from pounds, yards, etc., to hours. Therefore, the diagrams and equations are the same, although the terminology differs.

Material variance   Labor variance

    Price   ————————————————————>   Rate
    Quantity   ————————————————————>   Efficiency

Both labor variances are usually considered to be the responsibility of the production department.

D. **Overhead Variances**

Overhead variances can be computed at different levels of sophistication. These levels are called 2-way, and 3-way analysis. Overhead variance analysis can be performed on a combined basis (2-way analysis or 3-way analysis), or separately on fixed and variable overhead. The combined basis is more frequently seen on the CPA exam.

E. **Overhead Analysis: 2-Way**

2-way analysis provides more information as to why overhead was under- or overapplied by bringing the flexible budget into consideration.

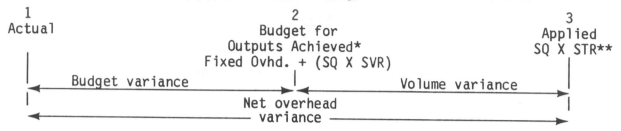

```
1                              2                              3
Actual                    Budget for                     Applied
                       Outputs Achieved*                 SQ X STR**
                      Fixed Ovhd. + (SQ X SVR)
  |                             |                              |
  |<----- Budget variance ----->|<------ Volume variance ----->|
  |                             |                              |
  |<------------------------ Net overhead ---------------------->|
                           ---- variance ----
```

*Based on standard inputs allowed for good units of output.

**Standard total rate (STR) = standard variable rate (SVR) + standard fixed rate (SFR).

Again, if 1 > 2 or 2 > 3, the variances are unfavorable (U); if 1 < 2 or 2 < 3, the variances are favorable (F). When the overhead rate is based on direct labor hours, item 2 is simply the budgeted overhead based on <u>standard</u> direct labor hours (fixed cost, plus standard hours x standard variable rate). It is important to note that the standard variable rate for overhead is the variable rate computed for the flexible budget (by the high-low method, regression analysis, etc.). See the first page of Module 35, PLAN.

The budget variance (also called the flexible-budget or controllable variance) arises when the amount spent on both fixed and variable overhead differs from the amount budgeted for the output achieved.

The volume variance (also called the noncontrollable, activity, capacity, or denominator variance) is solely a <u>fixed</u> overhead variance. It is caused by under- or over utilization of capacity. If actual output is less than (more than) denominator activity, an unfavorable (favorable) volume variance results. A shortcut for computing the volume variance is

$$\text{Standard Fixed Overhead Rate} \times \left(\text{Denominator Volume} - \text{Standard Volume for Output} \right)$$

The denominator volume in the above formula would be the activity level (see Module 34, Section "D.") that is selected for determining the standard fixed overhead cost per unit (to be used in assigning fixed overhead costs to units produced). In other words, the denominator volume is the activity level used to set the predetermined fixed overhead rate for product-costing purposes.

F. **Overhead Analysis: 3-Way**

3-way analysis goes one step further by introducing the flexible budget for actual volume.

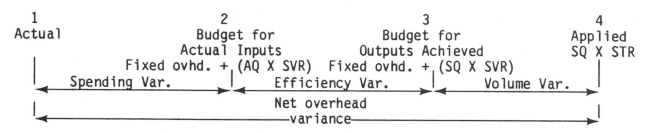

Again, smaller numbers to the left mean favorable variances, while smaller numbers to the right mean unfavorable variances.

The difference between 2 and 3 is that 2 is the flexible budget for <u>actual</u> direct labor hours, and 3 is the flexible budget for <u>standard</u> direct labor hours.

3-way analysis takes the budget variance and breaks it down into the spending and efficiency variances. The spending variance (also called the price variance) is caused by differences between the actual amount spent for fixed and variable overhead items, and the amounts budgeted based on actual direct labor hours.

The efficiency variance is solely a variable overhead variance. It is caused by more (less) variable overhead being incurred due to inefficient (efficient) use of labor hours.

G. **Overhead Analysis by Cost Behavior**

Often, CPA questions on overhead analysis concentrate on either fixed or variable overhead. 2-way and 3-way analysis can be summarized by cost behavior as follows.

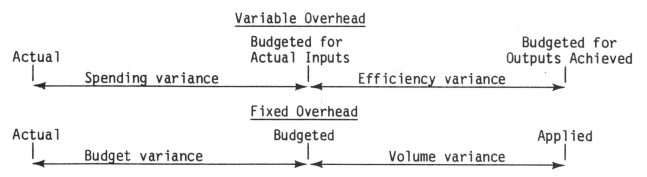

The diagrams below illustrate the relationships among the various overhead variance methods.

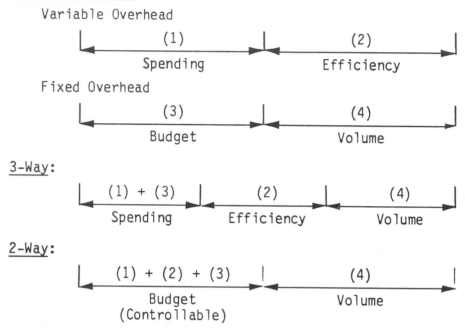

By Cost Behavior:

Variable Overhead

|← ——————— (1) ——————— →|← ——————— (2) ——————— →|
          Spending   Efficiency

Fixed Overhead

|← ——————— (3) ——————— →|← ——————— (4) ——————— →|
           Budget   Volume

3-Way:

|← (1) + (3) →|← —— (2) —— →|← ——— (4) ——— →|
   Spending   Efficiency   Volume

2-Way:

|← (1) + (2) + (3) →|← ——————— (4) ——————— →|
       Budget   Volume
    (Controllable)

Note that the sum of (1), (2), (3), and (4) equals the under- or overapplied overhead. A good way of determining whether overhead is under- or overapplied is to remember the following rule: if the sum is a net UNfavorable variance, overhead is UNderapplied, and vice versa.

H. **4-Way Variances**

A 4-way variance analysis may be undertaken by computing a fixed overhead efficiency variance, but generally it is felt this variance has little or no meaning. It would be computed by (AH - SH) X SFR.

I. **Journal Entries for Variances**

Variances are often computed and analyzed, but not entered into the accounts. If incorporated into the accounts, the standard amounts are entered into the inventory accounts. For example, when materials are purchased, SP is known but SQ is not known. Therefore, the materials account is debited for AQ X SP. When materials are used, SQ is also known, so work in process is debited for SQ X SP. Entries for materials and labor are presented below.

```
Materials                AQxSP
Price variance           XXX(U)    or    XXX(F)
    Accounts payable                     AQxAP

WIP inventory            SQxSP
Quantity variance        XXX(U)    or    XXX(F)
    Materials                            AQxSP
```

```
WIP inventory                 SQxSP
Rate variance                 XXX(U)   or   XXX(F)
Efficiency variance           XXX(U)   or   XXX(F)
    Accrued payroll                         AQxAP
```

A(n) unfavorable (favorable) variance is recorded as a debit (credit) to the variance account. Overhead variances, while computed and analyzed monthly, would not normally be entered in the accounts. The total overhead variance, of course, is the difference between the balances in the Control and Applied accounts.

J. **Disposition of Variances**

If immaterial, variances are frequently written off to cost of goods sold on grounds of expediency (ARB 43 states that you may report inventories using standard costs if they are based on currently attainable standards). If material, the variances must be allocated among the inventories and cost of goods sold, usually in proportion to the ending balances.

K. **Analysis of Variance Example**

Standard costs and actual costs for direct materials, direct labor, and factory overhead incurred for the manufacture of 5,000 units of product were as follows.

Standard costs	Standard cost per unit	Actual costs
Direct materials: 2 lbs. @ $1.60 per lb.	$ 3.20	Materials: 10,100 lbs.
Direct labor: 3 hours @ $2.50 per hour	7.50	purchased @ $1.65 per
Factory overhead on "normal capacity"		lb., 9,500 lbs. used
of 16,000 direct labor hours		in production
Variable: 3 hours @ $1.50	4.50	Labor: 15,400 hours
Fixed: 3 hours @ $ .50*	1.50	worked @ $2.60 per
	$16.70	hour
		Overhead Cost
		Variable $22,800
		Fixed $ 8,100

*$8,000 budgeted fixed overhead costs ÷ by 16,000 direct labor hours

1. **Material Variances**

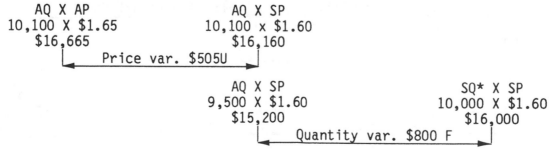

```
      AQ X AP                    AQ X SP
  10,100 X $1.65            10,100 x $1.60
     $16,665                   $16,160
           |___ Price var. $505U ___|

                              AQ X SP                 SQ* X SP
                          9,500 X $1.60            10,000 X $1.60
                             $15,200                  $16,000
                                |___ Quantity var. $800 F ___|
```

*SQ = 5,000 units X 2 lbs. per unit = 10,000 lbs.

2. Labor Variances

AH X AR	AH X SR	SH* X SR
15,400 X $2.60	15,400 X $2.50	15,000 X $2.50
$40,040	$38,500	$37,500

```
        └──── Rate var. $1,540 U ────┘└──── Efficiency var. $1,000 U ────┘
```

*SH = 5,000 units X 3 hours = 15,000 hours

3. Journal Entries

Raw Materials Inventory	16,160	
Materials Price Variance	505	
A/P		16,665
WIP Inventory	16,000	
Materials Quantity Variance		800
Raw Materials		15,200
WIP Inventory	37,500	
Labor Rate Variance	1,540	
Labor Efficiency Variance	1,000	
Wages Payable		40,040

4. Overhead Variances (2-way and 3-way)

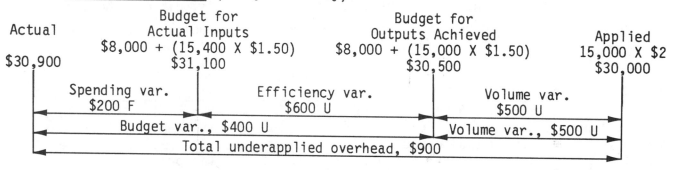

Actual	Budget for Actual Inputs $8,000 + (15,400 X $1.50)	Budget for Outputs Achieved $8,000 + (15,000 X $1.50)	Applied 15,000 X $2
$30,900	$31,100	$30,500	$30,000

```
    ├── Spending var. ──┤├──── Efficiency var. ────┤├──── Volume var. ────┤
    │     $200 F        ││        $600 U            ││        $500 U        │
    ├────── Budget var., $400 U ──────┤            ├──── Volume var., $500 U ────┤
    ├──────────────── Total underapplied overhead, $900 ─────────────────┤
```

If the overhead variances are broken down by cost behavior, they are analyzed as follows.

5. Variable Overhead

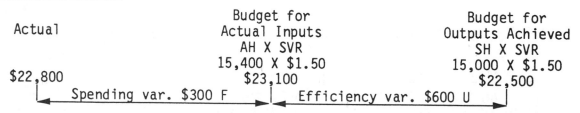

Actual	Budget for Actual Inputs AH X SVR 15,400 X $1.50	Budget for Outputs Achieved SH X SVR 15,000 X $1.50
$22,800	$23,100	$22,500

```
        └── Spending var. $300 F ──┘└── Efficiency var. $600 U ──┘
```

6. Fixed Overhead

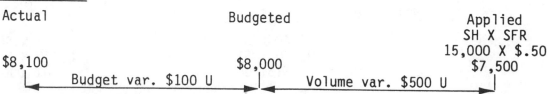

Actual	Budgeted	Applied SH X SFR 15,000 X $.50
$8,100	$8,000	$7,500

```
        └── Budget var. $100 U ──┘└── Volume var. $500 U ──┘
```

L. **Standard Process Costing**

The discussion and examples in this module have assumed the use of standards and variances with a job-order costing system. When standards and variances are used with a process costing system, the allowable quantities of inputs (e.g., direct labor hours) are based on the equivalent units of output achieved during the current period. Therefore, the computation of equivalent units under standard process costing is the same as under FIFO.

NONROUTINE DECISIONS

The focus of this module is nonroutine decision making, which can be broken down into two broad categories, referred to here as short-term differential (relevant) cost analysis and capital budgeting decisions (or long-term differential cost analysis). The basic difference between these two categories is that capital budgeting decisions involve a large initial investment to be returned over a long-term period, while short-term differential cost decisions do not involve such an investment or such a long-term for the returns.

A. **Short-Term Differential Cost Analysis**

Differential cost decisions include

1) Sell or process further (see also Section H., Module 34)
2) Special order
3) Make or buy
4) Closing a department or segment
5) Sale of obsolete inventory
6) Scarce resources

These decisions would better be described as differential cost and revenue decisions, since basically the decision maker must consider differences in costs and revenues over various alternatives. All other things being equal, the alternative providing the greatest profits (or cost savings) should be chosen.

Three concepts are found in most differential cost decisions.

1) The only relevant costs or revenues are those expected future costs and revenues that differ across alternatives
2) All costs incurred in the past (past or sunk costs) are irrelevant, unless they have future tax ramifications
3) Opportunity cost, the income obtainable from an alternative use of a resource, must be considered

The table presented below summarizes the various differential cost decisions, and includes only quantitative factors. Qualitative factors may be equally important. For example, in the make or buy decision, qualitative factors include

1) Quality of purchased part compared to manufactured part
2) Relationships with suppliers
3) Quickness in obtaining needed parts

Uncertainty also affects decision making. See the probability section at the end of this module for further discussion.

Decision	Description	Decision guideline
1. Sell or process further	Should joint products be sold at split-off or processed further?	Ignore joint costs. Process further if incremental revenue exceeds incremental cost.
2. Special order	Should a discount-priced order be accepted when there is idle capacity?	If regular sales are not affected, accept order when the revenue from the order exceeds the incremental cost. Fixed production costs are usually irrelevant.
3. Make or buy	Should a part be manufactured or bought from a supplier?	Choose lower-cost option. Fixed costs usually are irrelevant. Often opportunity costs are present.
4. Closing a department or segment	Should a segment of the company, such as a product line, be terminated?	Compare existing contribution margin with alternative. Consider any changes in future fixed costs.
5. Sale of obsolete inventory	Should obsolete inventory be re-worked or junked?	Cost of inventory is ignored. Choose alternative with greatest excess of future revenue over future cost.
6. Scarce resources	Which products should be emphasized when capacity is limited?	Determine scarce resource (e.g., machine-hours). Emphasize products with greatest contribution margin per unit of scarce resource.

An example of a differential cost decision (special order) is presented below, comparing the simpler, more efficient <u>incremental</u> approach with the equally effective but more cumbersome <u>total</u> approach. Unless a problem requires the total approach, use of the incremental approach will save valuable exam time.

> *EXAMPLE: Potts Co. manufactures cookware. Expected annual volume of 100,000 sets per year is well below full capacity of 150,000. Normal selling price is $40/set. Manufacturing cost is $30/set ($20 variable and $10 fixed). Total fixed manufacturing cost is $1,000,000. Selling and administrative expenses are expected to be $500,000 ($300,000 fixed and $200,000 variable). A catalog company offers to buy 25,000 sets for $27/set. No extra selling and administrative costs would be caused by the order, and acceptance will not affect regular sales. Should the offer be accepted?*

Incremental approach

Incremental revenue (25,000 x $27)	$675,000
Incremental cost (25,000 x $20)	(500,000)
Benefit of accepting order	$175,000

Total approach

		Without order		With order
Sales (100,000 x $40)		$4,000,000	[+(25,000 x $27)]	$4,675,000
less Variable costs:				
Man.	(100,000 x $20)	(2,000,000)	[+(25,000 x $20)]	(2,500,000)
Sell. and admin.	(100,000 x $2)	(200,000)		(200,000)
Contribution margin		1,800,000		1,975,000
less Fixed costs:				
Manufacturing		(1,000,000)		(1,000,000)
Sell. and admin.		(300,000)		(300,000)
Operating income		$ 500,000		$ 675,000

With either approach, operating income is increased by $175,000. Therefore, the order should be accepted.

B. **Capital Budgeting**

Capital budgeting is a technique to evaluate long-term investments. The capital budgeting decision involves evaluation of an investment today in terms of the present value of future cash returns from the investment. The objective is to identify the most profitable or best investment alternative. The cash returns can take two forms depending on the nature of the project. If the project will produce revenue, the return is the difference between the cash revenues (inflows) and cash expenses (outflows). The return from projects which result in cost savings takes the form of negative cash outflows (e.g., cash outflows for labor that are not made because a new machine is more efficient). Conceptually, the results of both types of projects are the same. The entity ends up with more cash by making the initial capital investment.

Two terms frequently used on the CPA exam are net cash flow (difference between future annual cash inflows and outflows) and after-tax net cash flow (net cash flow after tax expense).

The choice among alternative investing decisions can be made on the basis of several capital budgeting models: 1) Payback, 2) Net present value, 3) Internal (time-adjusted) rate of return, and 4) Accounting rate of return.

The <u>payback</u> method evaluates investments on the length of time until re-capture (return) of the investment. For example, if a $10,000 investment were to return a cash flow of $2,500 a year, the payback period would be 4 years. If the payback period is to be computed after income taxes, it is necessary to deduct depreciation from the $2,500 cash flow to determine net income and income taxes. Assuming a five-year life with no salvage value and a 40% income tax rate, the after-tax payback period would be computed as follows.

$2,500 - (40%)($2,500 - $2,000) = <u>$2,300</u>

$10,000 ÷ $2,300 = <u>4.35 years</u>

Note that the depreciation is <u>not</u> subtracted from the $2,500; only the income taxes which are affected by the depreciation deduction are subtracted.

This method ignores project profitability and the time value of money. The only redeeming aspects of the payback method are that it is an indicator of risk and liquidity. The shorter the payback period, the faster the investment is returned (liquidity) and the shorter the time the funds are at risk to changes in the environment.

The <u>net present value</u> method (NPV) calculates the present value of the future cash flows of a project and compares the present value of the cash flows with the investment outlay required to implement the project. The net present value of a project is defined as:

(The present value of future cash flows) minus (The required investment)

The calculation of the present value of the cash flows requires the selection of a discount rate (also referred to as the target or hurdle rate). The rate used should be the minimum rate of return that management is willing to accept on capital investment projects. The rate used should be no less than the cost of capital--the rate management currently must pay to obtain funds. A project which earns exactly the desired rate of return will have a net present value of 0. A positive net present value identifies projects which will earn in excess of the minimum rate. For example, in a company desiring a minimum return of 6%, on an investment of $10,000, that has an expected return of $2,500 for five years, the present value of the cash flows is $10,530 ($2,500 x 4.212: 4.212 is the TVMF for the present value of an annuity, n = 5, i = 6%; see Module 26, Present Value, Fundamentals). The net present value of $530 ($10,530 - $10,000) indicates the project will earn a return in excess of the 6% minimum desired. If the requirement were for a net-of-tax return of 6%, the net-of-tax cash flow of $2,300 computed in the previous section for the payback method would be multiplied by 4.212. This would result in a present value of $9,687.60 for the cash inflows, which is less than the $10,000 initial outlay. Therefore, this investment should not be made.

The <u>internal (time-adjusted) rate of return</u> method (IRR) determines the rate of discount at which the present value of the future cash flows will exactly equal the investment outlay. This rate is compared with the minimum desired rate to determine if the investment should be made. The internal rate of return is determined by setting the investment today equal to the discounted value of future cash flows. The discounting factor (rate of return) is the unknown. Using the example below,

$$PV \text{ (investment today)} = TVMF \times Cash Flows$$
$$\$10,000 = TVMF \times \$2,500$$
$$TVMF = 4.00$$

The interest rate of a TVMF of 4.00 where n = 5 is approximately 8%. The after-tax rate of return is determined using the $2,300 after-tax cash inflow amount as follows.

$$\$10,000 = TVMF \times \$2,300$$
$$TVMF = 4.35$$

The interest rate of a TVMF of 4.35 where n = 5 is approximately 5%. CPA exam multiple choice questions in this area do not require finding the exact rate of return if the exact TVMF falls between two TVMFs given in a table. The answers are worded "less than 5%, but greater than 0%," "less than 7%, but greater than 5%," etc.

The relationship between the NPV method and the IRR method can be summarized as follows.

NPV	IRR
NPV > 0	IRR > Discount Rate
NPV = 0	IRR = Discount Rate
NPV < 0	IRR < Discount Rate

The internal rate of return method is based upon an important assumption when comparing investments of different lengths. The method implicitly assumes that the cash inflows from the investment with the shorter life can be reinvested at the same internal rate of return. For example, when comparing an investment in serial bonds yielding 9%, and single, fixed-maturity bonds yielding 8%, the internal rate of return method assumes that the serial bond repayments can be reinvested at 9%. If the serial bond repayments can only be reinvested at 6%, the 8% fixed-maturity bonds might be the better alternative.

The <u>accounting rate of return</u> method (ARR) computes an approximate rate of return which ignores the time value of money. It is computed as follows.

ARR = Expected increase in annual net income ÷ Average investment

Using the same example, the ARR before taxes is

($2,500 - $2,000) ÷ ($10,000 ÷ 2) = 10%

The ARR after taxes is

($2,300 - $2,000) ÷ ($10,000 ÷ 2) = 6%

Note that the numerator is the increase in <u>net income</u>, not <u>cash flows</u>, so depreciation is subtracted. The average investment is one-half the initial investment because the initial investment is depreciated down to zero by the end of the project. If a problem asked for ARR based on <u>initial</u> investment, you would not divide the investment by 2.

Two complicating factors often found on the CPA exam are <u>salvage value</u> and <u>uneven cash flows</u>. Salvage value affects all methods by changing the depreciation tax deduction. Also, in the NPV and IRR methods, the salvage value is a future cash inflow which must be considered.

Uneven cash flows mean that the payback formula cannot be used; net cash inflows must be accumulated until the investment is returned. For the NPV and

IRR methods, each year's net cash inflow must be discounted separately using the present value of $1 table. Finally, when computing ARR the numerator becomes the <u>average</u> expected increase in annual net income.

The following chart summarizes the strengths and weaknesses of the capital budgeting methods.

Method	Strengths	Weaknesses**
Payback	1. Easy to understand and use 2. Emphasizes liquidity	1. Ignores time value of money 2. Ignores cash flows after payback period 3. Does not measure profitability
Net Present Value (NPV)	1. Emphasizes cash flows 2. Recognizes time value of money 3. Assumes discount rate is reinvestment rate* 4. Easy to apply	1. Favors larger, longer projects 2. Assumes no change in required rate of return
Internal Rate of Return (IRR)	1. Emphasizes cash flows 2. Recognizes time value of money 3. Computes true return of projects	1. Assumes IRR is the reinvestment rate* 2. Favors shorter projects
Accounting Rate of Return (ARR)	1. Easy to understand and use 2. Ties in with income statement and performance evaluation	1. Does not emphasize cash flows 2. Ignores time value of money 3. Misstates the true return of projects

*Note that assuming the discount rate is the reinvestment rate results in using the <u>same</u> reinvestment rate for projects of similar risk, while assuming the IRR is the reinvestment rate assumes higher reinvestment rates for projects with higher true returns, regardless of the risk involved.

**All methods share the weakness of assuming future cash flows are certain.

C. Probability Analysis

Because it is not always possible to make decisions under conditions of total certainty, decision makers must have a method of determining the best estimate or course of action where uncertainty exists. One method is probability analysis. This is used where there are a number of possible outcomes for a single action for which the probability of occurrence of each outcome can be estimated by the decision maker, but the actual outcome of the action is unknown.

For example, assume the life of an asset is unknown; however, the decision maker estimates that there is a 30% probability of a 4-year life, a 50% probability of a 5-year life, and a 20% probability of a 6-year life. By multiplying the probability by the number of years for each possible outcome and then summing the results, the expected (weighted-average) life of the asset can be determined as follows.

Years of Life	x	Probability	=	Expected Value
4		.3		1.2
5		.5		2.5
6		.2		1.2
				4.9 years

Thus, the expected life of the asset is found to be 4.9 years. Notice that, because the expected life or value is the weighted-average of the 3 possible outcomes, it represents the best available estimate.

Another application of probability analysis can be found in question number 35 from Part II of the November 1986 Practice Exam as shown below.

> Clay Co. operated three shipping termi-
> nals, referred to as X, Y, and Z. Of the
> total cargo shipped, terminals X, Y, and Z
> handle approximately 60%, 30%, and 10%, re-
> spectively, with error rates of 3%, 4%, and
> 6%, respectively. Clay's internal auditor
> randomly selects one shipping document, ascer-
> taining that this document contains an error.
> The probability that the error occurred in
> terminal X is
>   a.   60%
>   b.   50%
>   c.   23%
>   d.   3%

A good solutions approach to this question is to set it up as follows.

Terminal	% of Volume	x	Rate of Error	=	Expected Value
X	60%		3%		1.8%
Y	30		4		1.2
Z	10		6		0.6
					3.6%

Here, the expected value of 3.6% represents the rate of error of all the shipping documents combined. The problem states that an error has been found. You must determine the probability that this error occurred in terminal X. Since the 1.8% expected value for terminal X is equal to 50% of the total expected value (1.8% ÷ 3.6%), the probability that the error occurred at terminal X is 50% which is answer (b).

It should be noted that the applications of probability analysis are numerous and the situations may differ greatly. However, the basic character-istics are always the same.

(1) A decision related to a single action must be made.
(2) Conditions of uncertainty exist resulting in two or more possible outcomes for the single action.
(3) A probability or rate of occurrence can be estimated for each possible outcome.
(4) The final outcome is unknown.

CHAPTER TEN
GOVERNMENTAL AND NONPROFIT ACCOUNTING

Module 38/Governmental Accounting (GOV)

Module 39/Nonprofit Accounting (NPF)

Questions on governmental and other nonprofit entities have appeared on all recent examinations. Questions have dealt with local government and various nonprofit organizations. These questions have fallen into four categories.

1) Multiple choice questions on the Practice exam requiring simple calculations of amounts to be reported in various funds or in accounts within such funds for both governmental and nonprofit entities
2) Problems on the Practice exam involving journal entries in one or several local government funds
3) Problems on the Practice exam requiring the preparation of journal entries and/or operating statements for nonprofit organizations
4) Multiple choice questions on the Theory exam requiring identification of the local government fund or nonprofit organization fund in which to account for a specific type of transaction and identifying the required financial statements (including funds and accounts used) for these organizations
5) Essay questions on the Theory exam requiring description of and rationale for various accounting concepts and practices

The AICPA Content Specification Outline of the coverage of governmental and nonprofit accounting in the Practice and Theory exams, including the authors' frequency analysis (last nine exams), appears on the next page.

Immediately following the frequency analysis is a summary of accounting practice problems referenced to our study modules. The following symbols are used:

Q = Practice II Exam Problem

AICPA CONTENT SPECIFICATION OUTLINE/FREQUENCY ANALYSIS*
Not-for-Profit and Governmental Accounting

	Practice									Theory								
	M 85	N 85	M 86	N 86	M 87	N 87	M 88	N 88	M 89	M 85	N 85	M 86	N 86	M 87	N 87	M 88	N 88	M 89
A. Conceptual Framework (Theory Only)										–	–	–	–	–	–	–	–	–
B. Fund Accounting																		
1. Fund Balance	–	–	–	–	–	–	1	–	1	–	–	–	1	–	–	–	1	–
2. Estimated Revenues	–	–	–	–	–	–	1	–	1	–	1	1	–	–	1	–	1	–
3. Appropriations	–	–	–	–	–	–	1	–	1	1	–	–	–	1	–	–	1	–
4. Encumbrances	–	–	–	–	–	–	1	–	1									
5. Fund Bal. Reserved										1	–	1	–	–	1	–	–	1
for Encumb.	–	–	–	–	–	–	1	–	–	–	–	–	1	–	–	1	–	–
6. Revenues	–	–	–	–	–	–	1	–	1	1	1	1	–	1	1	1	–	2
7. Expenditures	–	–	–	–	–	–	1	–	2	–	–	–	–	1	–	–	–	1
C. Types of Funds and Fund Accounts [.5]**																		
1. General Fund	–	–	–	–	–	1	–	–	–	–	1	–	–	–	–	1	1	–
2. Special Revenue Funds	–	–	–	–	1	–	1	–	–	1	–	–	1	–	–	1	–	–
3. Debt Service Funds	–	–	–	–	1	–	1	–	–	–	1	–	–	–	1	–	–	1
4. Capital Projects Funds	–	–	–	–	1	–	2	1	–	–	1	–	–	1	–	–	1	–
5. Enterprise Funds	–	–	–	–	1	1	1	–	–	1	–	1	1	–	1	–	–	–
6. Internal Service Funds	–	–	–	–	1	–	1	–	–	–	1	–	1	1	1	–	2	–
7. Trust and Agency Funds	–	–	–	–	–	1	1	1	–	–	1	–	1	–	–	1	–	–
8. Special Assessment Funds***	–	–	–	[1]	–	1	–	1	–	1	–	1	1	–	–	–	–	–
9. General Fixed Assets Account Group	–	–	–	–	1	–	1	–	–	1	–	1	–	–	–	–	1	1
10. General Long-Term Debt Account Group	–	–	–	–	1	–	1	2	–	–	1	–	1	–	–	–	–	1
11. Endowment and Quasi-Endowment Funds	–	–	–	–	–	–	–	–	–	–	–	–	–	–	–	–	–	–
12. Restricted and Unrestricted Funds	–	–	–	–	–	–	–	–	–	–	–	–	–	–	–	–	1	–
13. Property Funds	–	–	–	–	–	–	–	–	–	–	–	–	–	–	–	–	–	–
D. Presentation of Financial Statements for Various Not-for-Profit and Governmental Organizations	[1]	[1]	–	–	–	–	–	–	–	1	1	1	1	1	1	1	1	1
E. Various Types of Not-For-Profit and Governmental Organizations																		
1. Local and State Governments	–	–	–	–	–	–	–	–	–	–	–	–	–	–	–	–	–	–
2. Educational Institutions	–	–	–	–	–	4	3	3	3	1	–	1	1	1	2	1	–	2
3. Hospitals	–	–	–	–	[1]	5	4	3	3	1	1	–	1	1	–	1	1	–
4. Charitable, Religious, and Other Organizations	–	–	[.5]	–	–	3	3	4	3	–	1	1	–	1	–	–	2	–
Total Multiple Choice Questions	–	–	–	–	–	–	20	20	20	10	10	10	10	10	10	10	10	10
Total Problems/Essays	1	1	1	1	1	–	–	–	–	–	–	–	–	–	–	–	–	–
Actual Percentage****	10	10	10	10	10	10	10	10	10	10	10	10	10	10	10	10	10	10
				(AICPA 10%)										(AICPA 10%)				

*Except where noted, the line items in the outline are the AICPA's; the frequencies, tabulations, and actual percentages are the authors'.

**Included entries involving several funds.

***No longer a separate fund per GASB 6.

****The "actual percentage" is a measure of the relative coverage of the specific Not-for-Profit/Governmental topic on each Accounting Practice or Theory exam. This percentage includes both multiple choice questions and essays/problems based on the point allocation used by the AICPA (i.e., multiple choice are assigned ½ point each in Practice and 1 point each in Theory; essays/problems are 10 points each; note that the number of essays, or portion thereof, for each topic is shown in brackets).

(Q) - Practice II Exam
  * - Part of one problem

NONPROFIT AND GOVERNMENTAL ACCOUNTING
Problem Summary

Date	Mod 38 Governmental	Mod 39 Nonprofit
5/89		
11/88		
5/88		
11/87		
5/87		Allocate amounts to proper funds in a hospital (Q)
11/86	Journal entries for special assessment fund (Q)	
5/86	Journal entries for trust funds (Q)*	Journal entries for Voluntary Health & Welfare (Q)*
11/85		Statement of changes in working capital for a foundation (Q)
5/85		Voluntary Health & Welfare statements (Q)

GOVERNMENTAL (STATE AND LOCAL) ACCOUNTING

Governmental accounting has many similarities to commercial accounting. For example, governmental accounting uses the double-entry system, journals, ledgers, trial balances, financial statements, internal control, etc. Differences arise due to the objectives and environment of government. The major differences include

1) The absence of a profit motive, except for governmental enterprises, such as utilities
2) A legal emphasis which involves restrictions both in the raising and spending of revenues
3) An inability to "match" revenues with expenses, as revenues are often provided by persons other than those receiving the services
4) An emphasis on accountability or stewardship of resources entrusted to public officials
5) The use of fund accounting
6) The recording of the budget in some funds
7) The use of modified accrual accounting rather than full accrual accounting in some funds

The Governmental Accounting Standards Board (GASB) now has the authority to establish standards of financial reporting for all units of state and local government. In the absence of a standard issued by the GASB, the standards issued by the FASB are assumed to apply. When the GASB was formed by the Financial Accounting Foundation in 1984, its first act was to pass Statement 1: Authoritative Status of NCGA Pronouncements and AICPA Industry Audit Guide. In effect, the past pronouncements of the predecessor organization, the National Council on Governmental Accounting (NCGA), and information in the AICPA Audits of State and Local Governmental Units were continued until modified by subsequent Statements issued by the GASB. The GASB then issued a Codification of Governmental Accounting and Financial Reporting Standards, which contained a summary of those past pronouncements.

Since then, the GASB has issued (as of this writing) eight Statements, several interpretations, and a Revised Codification (as of June 15, 1987). The GASB has authority under the AICPA Ethics Rule 203, Accounting Principles.

A. Fund Accounting

The GASB Codification contains twelve basic principles of accounting and reporting for governmental entities. Three of these principles deal specifically with fund accounting. These principles cover the

1) Definition of a fund
2) Types of funds
3) Number of funds

Governmental financial activities should be carried out and accounted for through funds. A fund is defined in the GASB Codification as:

> A fiscal and accounting entity with a self-balancing set of accounts recording cash and other financial resources, together with all related liabilities and residual equities and balances, and changes therein, which are segregated for the purpose of carrying on specific activities or attaining certain objectives in accordance with special regulations, restrictions, or limitations.

There are now seven funds which are classified into three general types.

Governmental Funds
1) General
2) Special Revenue
3) Capital Projects
4) Debt Service

Proprietary Funds
5) Internal Service
6) Enterprise

Fiduciary Funds
7) Trust and Agency

Until recently, a fifth governmental fund type existed: Special Assessment Funds. The Special Assessment Fund type was eliminated by GASB Statement 6. Additionally, there are two account groups: the General Fixed Asset Account Group and the General Long-Term Debt Account Group. These account groups are not funds because they do not have fiscal authority over resource inflows or outflows. The Codification contains three additional principles (discussed later) which cover accounting for fixed assets and long-term debt.

The major peculiarities of governmental accounting are reflected in the governmental funds rather than the proprietary funds or the fiduciary funds. In the governmental funds, the objective is providing services to the public. All of these funds are expendable, i.e., they are not concerned with preserving capital (capital maintenance) or measuring "net income" (matching). Rather, governmental funds are concerned with the availability of resources to provide services, and the emphasis is on working capital flows. Usually, only current assets and current liabilities are accounted for in the expendable funds (four governmental funds plus expendable Trust and Agency funds). Fixed assets and long-term liabilities of governmental funds are mostly accounted for in separate self-balancing account groups.

The proprietary funds use accounting and reporting techniques similar to commercial enterprises. The accounting and reporting techniques of fiduciary funds depend on whether the fund is expendable or nonexpendable. Expendable Trust and Agency Funds are accounted for like governmental funds, while Nonexpendable and Pension Trust Funds are accounted for like proprietary funds.

A basic principle in the <u>Codification</u> dealing with fund accounting states that each governmental unit

> should establish and maintain those funds required by law and sound financial administration. Only the minimum number of funds consistent with legal and operating requirements should be established, however, since unnecessary funds result in inflexibility, undue complexity, and inefficient financial administration.

B. **Budgets and Their Impact upon the Accounting System**

The GASB, in one of its basic principles, states

1) An annual budget(s) should be adopted by every governmental unit
2) The accounting system should provide the basis for appropriate budgetary control
3) A common terminology and classification should be used consistently throughout the budget, the accounts, and the financial reports of each fund

In accordance with the principle above, budgets should be prepared for each of the seven fund types used by governmental units. This directive, by itself, does not differentiate governmental from commercial enterprises. What is different, however, is the inclusion of budgetary accounts in the formal accounting system for the governmental funds. Inclusion of the budgetary accounts facilitates a budget-actual comparison as one of the basic financial statements. The budget-actual comparison is required for the General Fund and all other governmental funds that have a legally adopted annual budget. Budgetary accounts are generally used in those funds for which the budget-actual comparison is made. As a result, the CPA Examination questions always include budgetary accounts for the General Fund and sometimes, but not always, include budgetary accounts for Special Revenue, Debit Service, and Capital Projects Fund.

Budgetary accounts (Estimated Revenues, Appropriations, Estimated Other Financing Sources, Estimated Other Financing Uses) are incorporated into the governmental accounting systems to provide legislative control over revenues and other resource inflows and expenditures and other resource outflows. Recording the budget also provides an assessment of management's stewardship by facilitating a comparison of budget vs. actual. These budgetary accounts are <u>anticipatory asset</u> and <u>anticipatory liability</u> accounts even though they are temporary (nominal) accounts. The journal entries which follow illustrate the budgetary accounts used by the General and Special Revenue Funds.

Upon adoption of the estimated revenues and appropriations budgets (at the beginning of the period), the following entry is made and posted to the general ledger.

Estimated Revenues	1,000,000	
(individual items are posted to subsidiary revenues ledger)		(anticipated resources/ revenues)
Appropriations		980,000
(individual items are posted to subsidiary appropriations expenditure ledger)		(anticipated expenditures/ liabilities)
Budgetary Fund Balance		20,000
		(surplus is anticipated)

"Budgetary Fund Balance" is a budgetary account. This budgetary entry is reversed at year end.

As actual resource inflows and outflows occur during the year, they are recorded in "Revenues" and "Expenditures" accounts, and the detail is posted to the revenues and appropriations subsidiary ledgers in order to facilitate budget vs. actual comparisons. In order to prevent the overspending of an item in the appropriations budget, an additional budgetary account is maintained during the year. This budgetary account is called "Encumbrances." When goods or services are ordered, appropriations (specific items in the subsidiary ledger) are encumbered (restricted) with the following entry.

Encumbrances (detail posted to the subsidiary appropriations ledger)	5,000 (cost estimate)	
Fund Balance Reserved for Encumbrances		5,000 (cost estimate)

"Fund Balance Reserved for Encumbrances" is a fund equity account. When the debit in the entry is posted, the amount that can still be spent (technically known as "Unencumbered Appropriations") for an individual item is reduced. Thereafter, when the goods or services ordered are received, the encumbrance entry is reversed and the actual resource outflow (Expenditures) is recorded.

Fund Balance Reserved for Encumbrances	5,000	
Encumbrances (detail posted to subsidiary ledger)		5,000
Expenditures (detail posted to subsidiary ledger)	5,200 (actual cost)	
Vouchers Payable		5,200 (actual cost)

The "Encumbrances" account does not represent an expenditure; it is a budgetary account which represents the estimated cost of goods or services which have yet to be received. In effect, the recording of encumbrances represents the recording of executory contracts, which is essential to prevent overspending of an appropriation (normally, an illegal act). Likewise, the account "Fund Balance Reserved for Encumbrances" is not a liability account; it is a reservation (restriction) of fund balance. If encumbrances are outstanding at the end of a period, the fund balance reserved for encumbrances is reported in the fund balance section of the balance sheet (similar to an appropriation of retained earnings on a corporation's balance sheet).

At the end of the year, the following closing entries would be recorded, assuming actual revenues for the year totaled $1,005,000, actual expenditures for the year were $950,000, and encumbrances outstanding at year end were $10,000.

1. Budgetary Fund Balance   20,000
    Appropriations   980,000
        Estimated Revenues   1,000,000

    (to reverse the budgetary entry and close the budgetary accounts)
2. Revenues   1,005,000
        Expenditures   950,000
        Encumbrances   10,000
        Fund Balance--Unreserved   45,000

    (If Expenditures and Encumbrances had exceeded Revenues, Fund Balance-- Unreserved, an equity account, would have been debited in this closing entry).

C. The Reporting Entity

The GASB carefully defines the <u>reporting entity</u> in an effort to ensure that all boards, commissions, agencies, etc. that are under the control of the reporting entity are included. Each board, agency, etc. within the reporting entity is called a <u>component unit</u>. The <u>oversight unit</u> is that "component unit that has the ability to exercise the basic criterion of oversight responsibility over component units. Typically, the oversight unit is the primary unit of government directly responsible to the chief executive and the elected legislative body." Thus, the <u>oversight unit</u> and several additional <u>component units</u> may be combined to constitute the <u>reporting entity</u>.

Separately issued financial reports, when issued, are called Component Unit Financial Statements (CUFRs).

D. Financial Statements for State and Local Governments

The GASB <u>Codification</u> provides for two types of annual reports, the <u>General Purpose Financial Statements</u>, which include the minimum statements required for GAAP and a clean opinion, and the <u>Comprehensive Annual Financial Report</u>, which contains a great deal of detail that is helpful for many users. According to the <u>Codification</u>, the Comprehensive Annual Financial Report (CAFR) includes the following.

A. Introductory Section (table of contents, letter of transmittal, etc.)
B. Financial Section
    1. Auditor's Report
    2. General Purpose Financial Statements
        a. Combined Balance Sheet--All Fund Types and Account Groups

       b. Combined Statement of Revenues, Expenditures, and Changes in Fund Balances--All Governmental Fund Types and Expendable Trust Funds

       c. Combined Statement of Revenues, Expenditures, and Changes in Fund Balances--Budget and Actual--General and Special Revenue Fund Types (and similar governmental fund types for which annual budgets have been legally adopted)

       d. Combined Statement of Revenues, Expenses, and Changes in Retained Earnings (or Equity)--All Proprietary Fund Types and Similar Trust Funds

       e. Combined Statement of Changes in Financial Position--All Proprietary Fund Types and Similar Trust Funds

       f. Notes to the Financial Statements

       g. Required Supplementary Information (primarily pensions)

    3. Combining and Individual Fund and Account Group Statements and Schedules

  C. Statistical Tables

  D. Component Unit Financial Reports or Statements (Optional)

The following page reflects the sample "Combined Statement of Revenues, Expenditures, and Changes in Fund Balances--All Governmental Fund Types and Expendable Trust Funds" that is displayed in the GASB Codification. This statement is to be prepared in accordance with generally accepted accounting principles, even if the budget is prepared on a non GAAP basis (such as the cash basis). The "Expenditures" in this statement do not include the amounts encumbered but not yet received. On the other hand, the Combined Statement of Revenues, Expenditures, and Changes in Fund Balances--Budget and Actual ("2.c." above) is to be prepared on the budgetary basis. The budgetary basis may differ from the GAAP basis in various ways. For example, the cash basis of accounting may be assumed in the budget, and it is possible that encumbrances will be included in the expenditures column, especially if outstanding encumbrances do not lapse (carry over to the next fiscal year). If differences exist between the budgetary and GAAP bases, a reconciliation must be provided either on this statement or in the notes.

E. **Governmental Funds and Related Account Groups**

The 7 funds and 2 account groups listed previously are discussed in this section. First, a complete explanation is provided of the General Fund. Second, the distinguishing accounts, entries, etc., of the other funds and account groups are presented. Before sitting for the exam, you need to obtain a thorough understanding of the General Fund and also learn the peculiarities of the other funds. Emphasis should be put on

    1) The purpose and nature of each fund

    2) Account titles of the budgetary accounts

    3) Other peculiar account titles and transactions

    4) Fixed asset and long-term debt accounting

    5) Accrual vs. modified accrual basis accounting

    6) Interfund transactions and transfers

Name of Governmental Unit

Combined Statement of Revenues, Expenditures, and Changes in Fund Balances--
All Governmental Fund Types and Expendable Trust Funds
for the Fiscal Year Ended December 31, 19X2

	Governmental Fund Types				Fiduciary Fund Type	Totals (Memorandum Only) Year Ended	
	General	Special Revenue	Debt Service	Capital Projects	Expend-able Trust	December 31, 19X2	December 31, 19X1
Revenues:							
Taxes	$ 881,300	$ 189,300	$ 79,177	$ --	$ --	$1,149,777	$1,137,900
Special Assessments	--	--	55,500	$ --	$ --	55,500	250,400
Licenses and permits	103,000	--	--	--	--	103,000	96,500
Intergovernmental revenues	186,500	831,100	41,500	1,250,000	--	2,309,100	1,258,800
Charges for services	91,000	79,100	--	--	--	170,100	160,400
Fines and forfeits	33,200	--	--	--	--	33,200	26,300
Miscellaneous revenues	19,500	71,625	36,235	3,750	200	131,310	111,500
Total Revenues	$1,314,500	$1,171,125	$212,412	$1,253,750	$ 200	$3,951,987	$3,041,800
Expenditures:							
Current:							
General government	$ 121,805	$ --	$ --	$ --	$ --	$ 121,805	$ 134,200
Public safety	258,395	480,000	--	--	--	738,395	671,300
Highways and streets	85,400	417,000	--	--	--	502,400	408,700
Sanitation	56,250	--	--	--	--	56,250	44,100
Health	44,500	--	--	--	--	44,500	36,600
Welfare	46,800	--	--	--	--	46,800	41,400
Culture and recreation	40,900	256,450	--	--	--	297,350	286,400
Education	509,150	--	--	--	2,420	511,570	512,000
Capital outlay	--	--	--	1,939,100	--	1,939,100	803,000
Debt service:							
Principal retirement	--	--	115,500	--	--	115,500	52,100
Interest and fiscal charges	--	--	68,420	--	--	68,420	50,000
Total Expenditures	$1,163,200	$1,153,450	$183,920	$1,939,100	$ 2,420	$4,442,090	$3,039,800
Excess of Revenues over (under) Expenditures	$ 151,300	$ 17,675	$ 28,492	$ (685,350)	$ (2,220)	$ (490,103)	$ 2,000
Other Financing Sources (Uses):							
Proceeds of general obligation bonds	$ --	$ --	$ --	$ 900,000	$ --	$ 900,000	$ --
Proceeds of special assessment debt	--	--	--	190,500	--	190,500	--
Operating transfers in	--	--	--	74,500	2,530	77,030	89,120
Operating transfers out	(74,500)	--	--	--	--	(74,500)	(87,000)
Total Other Financing Sources (Uses)	$ (74,500)	$ --	$ --	$1,165,000	$ 2,530	$1,093,030	$ 2,120
Excess of Revenues and Other Sources over (under) Expenditures and Other Uses	$ 76,800	$ 17,675	$ 28,492	$ 479,650	$ 310	$ 602,927	$ 4,120
Fund balances-- January 1	202,500	151,035	227,788	605,450	26,555	1,213,328	1,209,208
Fund balances-- December 31	$ 279,300	$ 168,710	$256,280	$1,085,100	$26,865	$1,816,255	$1,213,328

The notes to the financial statements are an integral part of this statement.

Source: Governmental Accounting Standards Board, Codification of Governmental Accounting and Financial Reporting Standards, pp. 154-55.

Before individual funds are discussed, it is important to understand what is meant by accrual and the modified accrual basis of accounting. One of the basic GASB principles states, "The modified accrual or accrual basis of accounting, as appropriate, should be used in measuring financial position and operating results." Accrual basis accounting is recognition of revenues in the accounting period the revenues are earned and recognition of expenses in the accounting period the expenses are incurred. In addition, revenues and expenses have to be measurable in order to be reported. The following funds should use full accrual accounting.

Proprietary Funds	Fiduciary Funds
Enterprise	Nonexpendable and
Internal Service	Pension Trust Funds

All of the funds which use accrual accounting (except Pension Trust Funds) are nonexpendable; i.e., an objective of each of the funds is to maintain capital. The modified accrual basis of accounting, on the other hand, recognizes

1) Revenues in the accounting period in which they are both measurable and available to finance expenditures made during the current fiscal period
2) Expenditures in the accounting period in which the liabilities are both measurable and incurred*

Revenues normally recognized on the accrual basis include property taxes (when available to finance current expenditures),** firm intergovernmental grants and revenues, interest on investments and delinquent taxes, other taxes collected and not yet released by intermediary governments (such as state-collected local option sales taxes), and regularly billed charges for services. Revenues normally recognized on the cash basis include income taxes, licenses and permits, fines and forfeits, parking meter receipts, etc.

There are three major exceptions to recognition of expenditures as they are incurred.

1) In Debt Service Funds, expenditures for interest on general long-term debt should represent that which is matured (due) and payable during the fiscal period. Expenditures (and the related liability) for unmatured interest (accrued interest) at the end of the year are not recorded.
2) Inventories of materials and supplies may be considered expenditures either when purchased (purchases method) or when used (consumption method)

*In those expendable funds in which the modified accrual basis is used, the term expenditures (an outflow of current resources) is used in lieu of expenses. This is because matching is not an objective of accounting in these funds.

**The GASB indicates that property tax revenue generally is available to finance current expenditures if collected during the current period or will be collected within 60 days after the end of the current period. The GASB is considering a change in this rule.

3) Expenditures for insurance and similar prepaid items may be recognized in the period of acquisition

The modified accrual basis is used in the following funds.

Governmental Funds	Fiduciary Funds
General	Expendable Trust Funds
Special Revenue	Agency Funds
Capital Projects	
Debt Service	

All of the funds which use the modified accrual basis are expendable and do not, therefore, have a capital maintenance objective. Additional description of the modified accrual basis is provided in the discussion of specific funds.

1. The General Fund

The General Fund is the most significant Governmental Fund. It accounts for all transactions not accounted for in any other fund. Revenues come from many sources (taxes, licenses and permits, fines and forfeits, charges for services, etc.), and the expenditures cover the major functions of government (public safety, highways and streets, education, etc.). The illustration on the following page presents an overview of the General Fund Account Structure.

The following represents an accounting cycle problem for the General Fund. Some of these entries have been illustrated previously.

a. Adoption of a budget where estimated revenues exceed appropriations and planned transfers by $10,000. (First year of existence for this governmental unit.)

Estimated Revenues (detail posted to subsidiary ledger)	300,000	
Appropriations (detail posted to subsidiary ledger)		240,000
Estimated Other Financing Uses		50,000
Budgetary Fund Balance		10,000

b. Transfers to a Debt Service Fund (for general long-term debt payments) amount to $50,000.

Operating Transfers Out	50,000	
Due to Debt Service Fund		50,000

According to the GASB, transfers should be recognized in the accounting period in which the interfund receivable and payable arises. The account "Operating Transfers Out" is a temporary account which is compared with the budgetary account "Estimated Operating Transfers Out." The accounts "Due to--Fund" are current liabilities. Note that the Debt Service Fund would record a receivable as follows.

Debt Service

Due from General Fund	50,000	
Operating Transfers In		50,000

General Fund Account Structure

Real Accounts

Current Assets (DR)

Current Liabilities (CR)

Fund Balance (Fund Equity) (CR)

  Reserved (Encumbrances, Inventories, etc.)

  Unreserved

    Designated

    Undesignated

Nominal Accounts	Budgetary Accounts
Revenues (CR)	Estimated Revenues (DR)
Other Financing Sources (CR) (Operating Transfers In) (Bond Issue Proceeds)	Estimated Other Financing Sources (DR)
Expenditures (DR)	Appropriations (CR) Encumbrances (DR)
Other Financing Uses (DR) (Operating Transfers Out)	Estimated Other Financing Uses (CR)
Residual Equity Transfers (DR) (CR) (Sometimes a direct debit or credit to Fund Balance)	Estimated Residual Equity Transfers (CR) (DR) (Sometimes this is not budgeted)
	Budgetary Fund Balance

Assuming $50,000 of the transfer was for principal repayment, this entry would require an entry in the General Long-Term Debt Account Group as follows

<u>General Long-Term Account Group</u>

Amount Available for Retirement of Bonds	50,000	
Amount to be Provided for Retirement of Bonds		50,000
(see p. 1043 for sale of bonds)		

The "Operating Transfers" accounts are closed at the end of the year. It is important to note that the account "Operating Transfers Out" is not an expenditure account, and that the account "Operating Transfers In" is not a revenue account. Both are considered "Other Financing Sources (Uses)." (See the Combined Statement of Revenues, Expenditures, and Changes in Fund Balance shown previously.) There is a complete discussion of interfund transactions and transfers later in this module.

c. The property tax levy is recorded as revenues, under the modified accrual basis, when the tax levy is enacted by the governmental unit, if collections will be in time to finance expenditures of the current period. The tax bills amount to $250,000, and $20,000 is estimated to be uncollectible.

Property Taxes Receivable--Current	250,000	
Allowance for Uncollectible		
Taxes--Current		20,000
Revenues		230,000

Under the modified accrual basis, revenues should be recorded in the period in which they are both measurable and available. The GASB requires that property taxes be recognized as a revenue if the taxes are

1) Available--collected soon enough to pay liabilities of the current period (within 60 days of the end of the fiscal year)
2) To finance the budget of the current period

To the extent the modified accrual criteria for recognition are not met, the property tax levy would be recorded with a credit to Deferred Revenues instead of Revenues.

If cash is needed to pay for expenditures before the property tax receivables are collected, it is not uncommon for governmental units to borrow on tax anticipation warrants. The receivable serves as security for this loan and, as taxes are collected, the anticipation warrants are liquidated, i.e., "Tax Anticipation Warrants or Notes Payable" is debited.

Note, also, the treatment of the allowance for uncollectible accounts. Expendable funds account for resource inflows (revenues) and resource outflows (expenditures). Expenses are not recorded. The allowance for uncollectible accounts represents an estimated reduction in a resource inflow and, accordingly, revenues are recorded net of estimated uncollectible taxes.

d. Revenues from fines, licenses, and permits amount to $40,000.

Cash	40,000	
Revenues (detail posted)		40,000

Resource inflows from fines, licenses, permits, etc. are usually not measurable until the cash is collected. Sometimes, it is possible to measure the potential resource inflow; however, because the availability is questionable, revenues are recorded when cash is collected.

e. The state owes the city $25,000 for the city's share of the state sales tax. The amount has not been received at year end, but it is expected within the first few months of the next fiscal year.

State Sales Tax Receivable	25,000	
Revenues (detail posted)		25,000

Sales taxes, income taxes, etc. are <u>not</u> accrued before collected by a governmental unit. However, once collected, it is appropriate for recipient governmental units to record the receivable and revenue. The amount due from the state is measurable, and it will soon be available to finance year-end liabilities which resulted from expenditures. Other firm commitments from the state or other governmental units for grants, etc. are also recorded.

f. Incurred liabilities for salaries, repairs, utilities, rent, and other regularly occurring items for $200,000.

Expenditures (detail posted)	200,000	
Vouchers Payable		200,000

Note that all resource outflows authorized in the appropriations budget are debited to "Expenditures." It makes no difference whether the outflow is for a fire truck or for rent. Remember, expendable funds do not have a capital maintenance objective. Also, note that the encumbrance accounts were not used in this example. There is usually no need to encumber appropriations for items that occur regularly, and which possess a highly predictable amount--e.g., salaries, rent, etc. It should be pointed out, however, that there is no hard and fast rule for when to use encumbrances, and encumbrance policies do vary tremendously, i.e., from every expenditure being encumbered to virtually no expenditures being encumbered.

g. Ordered one police car; estimated cost is $17,000. One month later, ordered second police car; estimated cost is $16,500.

Encumbrances	17,000	
Fund Balance Reserved for Encumbrances		17,000
Encumbrances	16,500	
Fund Balance Reserved for Encumbrances		16,500

Recording encumbrances prevents overspending line-item appropriations. In the case of the police cars, assume the appropriations budget authorized $34,000 for police vehicles. After the first police car was ordered, the unencumbered appropriation for police vehicles was reduced to $17,000. This placed a dollar limit on what could be spent on the second car.

h. Police car ordered first was received; actual cost is $16,800.

Fund Balance Reserved for Encumbrances	17,000	
Encumbrances		17,000
Expenditures	16,800	
Vouchers Payable		16,800

In order to achieve accountability and control over fixed assets acquired by expendable funds, the following entry would be made in the General Fixed Assets (GFA) Account Group.

Vehicles--Police Cars	16,800	
Investment in Fixed Assets--General		
Fund Revenues		16,800

i. Property tax collections amounted to $233,000, payments to other funds amounted to $50,000 (see Item B), and payments of vouchers were $190,000.

Cash	233,000	
Property Taxes Receivable--Current		233,000
Due to Debt Service Fund	50,000	
Cash		50,000
Vouchers Payable	190,000	
Cash		190,000
Allowance for Uncollectible Taxes--Current	3,000	
Revenues		3,000

The last entry above is required because the "Allowance for Uncollectible Taxes--Current" was overstated. Note that the estimate was $20,000 in entry "c." above. Tax revenues were estimated to be $230,000. Since property tax collections exceeded $230,000 for the current year, an increase in revenues is required.

j. Recorded $5,000 inventory of materials and supplies, reduced the allowance for uncollectible property taxes to $10,000, and reclassified uncollected property taxes to delinquent accounts.

Materials and Supplies Inventory*	5,000	
Fund Balance Reserved for Inventory of Materials and Supplies		5,000
Allowance for Uncollectible Taxes--Current	7,000	
Revenues		7,000
Property Taxes Receivable--Delinquent	17,000	
Allowance for Uncollectible Taxes--Current	10,000	
Allowance for Uncollectible Taxes-- Delinquent		10,000
Property Taxes Receivable--Current		17,000

One of the reasons for recording the inventory of materials and supplies is to inform the preparers of the budget that items purchased during the year and charged to expenditures (Item "f.") are still unused. The account "Fund Balance Reserved for Inventory of Materials and Supplies" is a reservation of Fund Balance. In this respect, it is similar to "Fund Balance Reserved for Encumbrances."

The second entry adjusts the estimate of uncollectible property taxes to $10,000. This is the result of collecting more property taxes than anticipated (see entries made in "c." and "i." above) and of an estimate that $7,000 will now be collected.

The third entry reclassifies property taxes receivable from current to delinquent at the end of the year. Generally, interest and penalty charges accrue on the unpaid taxes from the date they become delinquent. If these items have accrued at the end of a fiscal period, they would be recorded in the following way.

*The illustration covers the "purchase method" for materials and supplies. The "consumption method" is not covered in this illustration. Consult an advanced or governmental text for coverage of the latter method.

Interest and Penalties Receivable on Delinquent Taxes	xx	
Allowance for Uncollectible Interest and Penalties		xx
Revenues		xx

k. Appropriate closing entries are made.

Budgetary Fund Balance	10,000	
Appropriations	240,000	
Estimated Other Financing Uses	50,000	
Estimated Revenues		300,000
Revenues	305,000	
Expenditures		216,800
Encumbrances		16,500
Operating Transfers Out		50,000
Fund Balance--Unreserved		21,700

<u>Financial Statements</u>. Under the GASB <u>Codification</u>, individual fund statements should not be prepared that simply repeat information found in the combined or combining statements but would be prepared to present individual fund budgetary comparisons (not needed for the General Fund), to present prior year comparative data, or to present more detailed information than is found in the combined or combining statements.

The following balance sheet would represent the General Fund portion of the Combined Balance Sheet.

City of X
General Fund
Balance Sheet
At June 30, 19XX

<u>Assets</u>			<u>Liabilities and fund equity</u>		
Cash		$33,000	Liabilities:		
Property Taxes Receivable-- Delinquent	$17,000		Vouchers Payable		$26,800
			Fund Balance:		
Less: Allowance for Un- collectible Taxes-- Delinquent	10,000	7,000	Reserved for Inven- tory of Materials and Supplies	$ 5,000	
State Sales Tax Receivable		25,000			
			Reserved for Encum- brances	16,500	
Inventory of Materials and Supplies		5,000	Unreserved	21,700	
			Total Fund Equity		$43,200
			Total Liabilities and Fund		
Total Assets		$70,000	Equity		$70,000

Note the following points from the balance sheet.

1) The total fund balance is $43,200, but only $21,700 is unreserved. This $21,700 represents the appropriable component of total fund balance, i.e., the amount that can be used next period to help finance a deficit budget. The $21,700 represents unreserved net liquid resources.

2) The reason for crediting "Fund Balance Reserved for Inventory of Materials and Supplies" in item "j." previously should now be more meaningful. The inventory of materials and supplies is not a liquid resource which can be used to finance future expenditures. Consequently, if this asset is disclosed, it must be disclosed via a fund restriction.

3) The "Fund Balance Reserved for Encumbrances" which is disclosed on the balance sheet relates to the second police car which was ordered but not delivered at year end. When the car is received in the next period, the following journal entries could be made, assuming the actual cost is $16,600.

Expenditure--Prior Year	16,500	
Expenditures	100	
Vouchers Payable		16,600
Fund Balance Reserved for Encumbrances	16,500	
Expenditures--Prior Year		16,500

In the General Fixed Assets Account Group

Vehicles--Police Cars	16,600	
Investment in Fixed Assets--General Fund Revenues	16,600	

The following would be the General Fund Portion of the "Budget/Actual Combined Statement."

City of X
General Fund
Statement of Revenues, Expenditures, and Changes in Fund Balance--Budget and Actual
For Year Ended June 30, 19XX

	Budget	Actual	Variance Favor. (Unfav.)
Revenues:			
• • •			
• • •	$300,000	$305,000	$ 5,000
• • •			
Expenditures (and encumbrances):			
• • •			
• • •	240,000	233,300	(6,700)
• • •			
Excess of Revenues over Expenditures and Encumbrances	$ 60,000	$ 71,700	$11,700
Other Financing Uses;			
Operating Transfers Out	(50,000)	(50,000)	-0-
Excess of Revenues over Expenditures and Other Financing Uses	$ 10,000	$ 21,700	$11,700
Fund Balance-Unreserved at Beginning of Year	-0-	-0-	-0-
Fund Balance-Unreserved at End of Year	$ 10,000	$ 21,700	$11,700

Note that the Statement ends with the Unreserved Fund Balance. An acceptable alternative for this Statement or for the Statement of Revenues, Expenditures, and Changes in Fund Balances would be to end with total Fund Balance. If this were done, additions would be necessary to add back the increases in the reserves for inventory and encumbrances in the amounts of $5,000 and $16,500, respectively.

Note also that the current year expenditures "actual" column includes the outstanding encumbrances of $16,500. Recent CPA exam multiple choice questions distinguish between the "expenditures" reported in the Statement of Revenues, Expenditures, and Change in Fund Balances (GAAP Statement) and the Statement of Revenues, Expenditures, and Changes in Fund Balances--Budget and Actual (Budgetary Basis Statement). The GAAP Statement includes only the expenditures (both current and prior years) whereas the Budgetary Basis Statement includes the current year expenditures and outstanding current year encumbrances.

One additional point needs to be covered before going to Special Revenue Funds, i.e., how to account for the inventory of materials and supplies in the second or any subsequent year. Accordingly, assume that at the end of the second year, $4,000 of materials and supplies were unused. The adjusting entry would appear as follows.

Fund Balance Reserved for Inventory of		
Materials and Supplies	1,000	
Materials and Supplies Inventory		1,000

This entry, when posted, will result in a balance of $4,000 in the inventory and reserve accounts. Note the entry at the end of the first year established a $5,000 balance in these accounts. Thereafter, the inventory and reserve accounts are adjusted upward or downward to whatever the balance is at the end of the year.

2. Special Revenue Funds

Special Revenue Funds account for earmarked revenue as opposed to the many revenue sources which are accounted for in the General Fund. The earmarked revenue is then used to finance various authorized expenditures. For example, the proceeds from on-street parking meters might be placed in a Parking Meter Fund. The resources of this fund could be used for traffic law enforcement--traffic courts and police. Similarly, a city might place its share of the state's gasoline tax revenues into a State Gasoline Tax Fund, which could then be used to maintain streets. Note that a governmental unit has some discretion in terms of how many Special Revenue Funds it creates. Sometimes separate funds are required by law or grant requirements. Many federal and state grants are reported in Special Revenue Funds.

The accounting for Special Revenue Funds parallels that of the General Fund. In terms of financial reporting, when a governmental unit has more than one Special Revenue Fund, the GASB mandates combining fund reports for the Comprehensive Annual Financial Report.

A special problem relates to the receipt of grant proceeds and the recognition of revenues. A restricted revenue is not considered earned until the expenditure has taken place. The reasoning is that if the expenditure does not take place in accordance with grant guidelines, it will be necessary to return the grant proceeds. For example, if the City of X receives $100,000 in grant proceeds in 19X7, but expends those proceeds in FY 19X8, the entries for both years would be as follows.

19X7

Cash	100,000	
Deferred Revenues		100,000

19X8

Expenditures	100,000	
Cash		100,000
Deferred Revenues	100,000	
Revenues		100,000

Of course, if the funds were expended in FY 19X7, the revenue would also be recognized in that year.

3. Capital Projects Funds

Capital Projects Funds account for the acquisition and use of resources for the construction or purchase of major, long-lived fixed assets, except for those which are financed by Internal Service, Enterprise, and Nonexpendable Trust Funds. Resources for construction or purchase normally come from the issuance of general long-term debt and from government grants (federal, state, and local).

Budgets (long-term capital budgets) for estimated resources and appropriations must be approved before the project can begin. However, unlike the operating budgets of General and Special Revenue Funds, the capital projects budget may not be recorded formally in the accounts. The budget is often not recorded because a Capital Projects Fund is usually established for each project, and the number of revenue and other financing sources and expenditure outlays is small. However, it is permissible to record the budget if so desired by the governmental unit.

The following transactions illustrate the entries encountered in the Capital Projects Fund.

a. City Council approved the construction of a new city hall at an esti-
    mated cost of $10,000,000. General obligation long-term serial debt was
    authorized for issuance in the face amount of $10,000,000.

    No formal entry need be recorded for the project authorization, although
    a budgetary entry is permissible. Assume a "memorandum only" recording.

b. $10,000,000 in 8% general obligation serial bonds were issued for
    $10,100,000. Assume that the premium is transferred to a debt service
    fund for the eventual payment of the debt.

Cash	10,100,000	
Proceeds of Bonds		10,100,000
Operating Transfers Out	100,000	
Cash		100,000

Note the credit to "Proceeds of Bonds." This is an "Other Financing
Source" on the operating statement, whereas the "Operating Transfers
Out" is an "Other Financing Use." Both accounts are temporary accounts
that are closed to Unreserved Fund Balance at year end.

The sale of bonds and the transfer require entries in the Debt Service
Fund and the General Long-Term Debt Account Group.

Debt Service Fund

Cash	100,000	
Operating Transfer In		100,000

General Long-Term Debt Group

Amount Available for Retirement of Bonds	100,000	
Amount to be Provided for Retirement of Bonds	9,900,000	
8% General Obligation Serial Bonds Payable		10,000,000

These entries will be explained in more detail later.

c. The bond issue proceeds are temporarily invested in a Certificate of
    Deposit (CD) and earn $50,000. The earnings are authorized to be sent
    to the Debt Service Fund for the payment of bonds.

Capital Projects Fund			Debt Service Fund		
Investment in CD	10,000,000				
Cash		10,000,000			
Cash	50,000				
Revenues--Interest		50,000			
Operating Transfers Out	50,000		Cash		50,000
Cash		50,000	Operating Transfers in		50,000

General Long-Term Debt Account Group

Amount Available for Retirement of Bonds	50,000	
Amount to be Provided for Retirement of Bonds		50,000

d. The lowest bid, $9,800,000, is accepted from a general contractor.

Encumbrances	9,800,000	
Fund Balance Reserved for Encumbrances		9,800,000

e. $2,000,000 of the temporary investments are liquidated.

Cash	2,000,000	
Investment in CD		2,000,000

f. Progress billings due to the general contractor for work performed amount to $2,000,000. The contract allows 10% of the billings to be retained until final inspection and approval of the building. The contractor was paid $1,800,000.

Fund Balance Reserved for Encumbrances	2,000,000	
Encumbrances		2,000,000
Expenditures--Construction	2,000,000	
Contracts Payable		2,000,000
Contracts Payable	2,000,000	
Cash		1,800,000
Contracts Payable--Retained Percentage		200,000

The account "Contracts Payable--Retained Percentage" is a liability account. Note, also, that the fixed asset is not recorded in the Capital Projects Fund because this fund is expendable and does not have a capital maintenance objective. The fixed asset is recorded in the General Fixed Asset Account Group.

At this point (year end), note that construction in progress would be recorded in the GFA Account Group, as follows.

Construction in Progress--Buildings	2,000,000	
Investment in General Fixed Assets-- Capital Projects Fund--G.O. Bonds		2,000,000

When the project is finished, "Construction in Progress" is credited and "Buildings" is debited.

g. Interest accrued on a CD at the end of the year amounted to $40,000. This was authorized to be sent to the Debt Service Fund for the payment of debt.

Capital Projects Fund

Interest Receivable	40,000	
Revenues--Interest		40,000
Operating Transfers Out	40,000	
Due to Other Funds		40,000

Debt Service Fund

Due from Other Funds	40,000	
Operating Transfers In		40,000

General Long-Term Debt Account Group

Amount Available for Retirement of Bonds	40,000	
Amount to be Provided for Retirement of Bonds		40,000

The interest is recognized because it is measurable and will soon be available to finance Debt Service Fund expenditures.

h. Closing entries for the Capital Projects Fund would appear as follows.

1)
Revenues--Interest	90,000	
Proceeds of Bonds	10,100,000	
Fund Balance--Unreserved		10,190,000

2)
Fund Balance--Unreserved	9,800,000	
Encumbrances		7,800,000
Expenditures--Construction		2,000,000

3)
Fund Balance--Unreserved	190,000	
Operating Transfers Out		190,000

The GASB requires that the totals for all Capital Projects Funds appear in the Combined Balance Sheet, the Combined Statement of Revenues, Expenditures, and Changes in Fund Balances, and the Combined Statement of Revenues, Expenditures, and Changes in Fund Balances--Budget and Actual (if an annual budget is adopted). Combining Statements are required if the governmental unit has more than one Capital Projects Fund.

A "stand-alone" Statement of Revenues, Expenditures, and Changes in Fund Balances appears for the Capital Projects Fund example.

City of X
Capital Projects Fund
Statement of Revenues, Expenditures, and Changes
in Fund Balances
Year Ended June 30, 19XX

Revenues and Other Financing Sources:	
Revenues:	
Interest on Temporary Investments	$ 90,000
Other Financing Sources:	
Proceeds of General Obligations Bonds	10,100,000
Total Revenues and Other Financing Sources	$10,190,000
Expenditures and Other Financing Uses:	
Expenditures:	
Construction of City Hall	2,000,000
Other Uses:	
Transfer to Debt Service Fund	190,000
Total Expenditures and Other Financing Uses	$ 2,190,000
Excess of Revenues and Other Financing Sources over Expenditures and Other Uses	$ 8,000,000
Fund Balance at Beginning of Year	-0-
Deduct Fund Balance Reserved for Encumbrances	7,800,000
Unreserved Fund Balance at End of Year	$ 200,000

Note that the above operating statement classified "Other Financing Sources" with "Revenues" and "Other Uses" with "Expenditures." This is an acceptable alternative to the format shown for the General Fund on page 1166.

At the beginning of the second year, the following entry would be made to reestablish the "Encumbrances" balance.

Encumbrances	7,800,000	
Unreserved Fund Balance		7,800,000

The purpose of this entry is to permit the recording of expenditures in the normal manner; i.e., reverse the encumbrances before recording the expenditures.

When the city hall project is finished, the Capital Projects Fund should be terminated. Assuming there are no cost overruns, the excess cash left in the fund upon project completion must be transferred to some other fund, normally a debt service fund. This is called a residual equity transfer and is described along with other interfund transactions and transfers on pages 1182-1185. Finally, upon project completion, the GFA will record the fixed asset as follows.

```
Buildings--City Hall                        9,800,000
    Construction in Progress--Buildings                2,000,000
    Investment in General Fixed Assets--
        Capital Projects Fund--G.O. Bonds              7,800,000
```

4. Debt Service Funds

Debt Service Funds usually handle the repayment of general obligation long-term debt. This type of debt is secured by the good faith and taxing power of the governmental unit. Repayment of internal service and enterprise long-term debt is accounted for in these individual funds. Consequently, the type of debt for which the Debt Service Fund is established usually is the result of issuing general obligation bonds for capital projects. The Debt Service Fund is used to account for repayment of bond principal and the payment of interest.

The bond liability to be extinguished is not recorded in the Debt Service Fund until it matures. The purpose of this fund is to accumulate resources to liquidate general long-term debt. When the debt matures, it is transferred from the General Long-Term Debt (GLTD) Account Group to the Debt Service Fund. Remember, when the bonds were sold to finance the city hall project, the liability was recorded in the GLTD Account Group.

A Debt Service Fund often requires an annual operating budget for its estimated revenues, other financing sources, and appropriations. The resources usually come from an allocated portion of property taxes and from interfund transfers. The expenditures are made for matured bonds payable and for interest. Remember that the GASB permits governmental units to either record or not record the budget in the accounts of debt service funds. However, in the example which follows, the budget is recorded because of the importance of ensuring that funds are available for debt service payments.

Assume the City of X authorizes a Debt Service Fund for the general obligation serial bonds issued to finance the city hall project. The Debt Service Fund is also authorized to pay the 8% interest on the $10,000,000 of debt on December 31 and June 30. The fiscal year end is June 30. Note that the Debt Service Fund has received resources from the General and Capital Projects Funds. Transactions showing recognition and receipt of these resources were illustrated in the discussions of the General and Capital Projects Funds. They are repeated below as follows.

1) Due From General Fund   50,000   (Transaction "b."
      Operating Transfers In   50,000   on page 1034)
2) Cash   50,000   (Transaction "i."
      Due from General Fund   50,000   on page 1038)
3) Cash   100,000   (Transaction "b."
      Operating Transfers In   100,000   on page 1043)
4) Cash   50,000   (Transaction "c."
      Operating Transfers In   50,000   on page 1043)
5) Due from Capital Projects Fund   40,000   (Transaction "g."
      Operating Transfers In   40,000   on page 1044)

Assume the bonds were issued on July 1. In addition, assume that $250,000 of the bonds mature each six months, starting June 30.

a. The following entry records the budget for the first year.

Estimated Other Financing Sources	200,000	
Estimated Revenues (portion of property taxes)	850,000	
Appropriations (for two interest and one principal payment)		1,050,000

b. The property tax levy contains $870,000 portion allocable to the Debt Service Fund. $20,000 of this amount is estimated to be uncollectible.

Property Taxes Receivable--Current	870,000	
Allowance for Uncollectible Taxes--Current		20,000
Revenues--Property Taxes		850,000

c. $840,000 of property taxes are collected during the year. The remainder of the property taxes are reclassified as delinquent.

Cash	840,000	
Property Taxes Receivable--Current		840,000
Property Taxes Receivable--Delinquent	30,000	
Allowance for Uncollectible Taxes--Current	20,000	
Property Taxes Receivable--Current		30,000
Allowance for Uncollectible Taxes--Delinquent		20,000

Assuming that $50,000 of the tax revenues are for the payment of principal and the remainder is for the payment of interest, the following entry is required in the General Long-Term Debt Account Group.

Amount Available for the Retirement of Bonds	50,000	
Amount to be Provided for the Retirement of Bonds		50,000

This makes a total of $290,000 "Available" in the General Long-Term Debt Account Group.

d. The semi-annual interest is paid on December 31 and June 30. The following entries are made on December 31.

Expenditures--Interest	400,000	
Matured Interest Payable		400,000
Matured Interest Payable	400,000	
Cash		400,000

The following entries are made on June 30.

Expenditures--Interest	400,000	
Matured Interest Payable		400,000
Matured Interest Payable	400,000	
Cash		400,000

Note that if interest were paid on dates other than December 31 and June 30, interest would not be accrued to the end of the fiscal year.

e. On June 30, the first $250,000 principal payment became due of which $200,000 was paid. The following entries would be made in the Debt Service Fund and General Long-Term Debt Account Group.

Debt Service Fund

Expenditures--Principal	250,000	
Matured Bonds Payable		250,000
Matured Bonds Payable	200,000	
Cash		200,000

General Long-Term Debt Account Group

8% General Obligation Serial Bonds Payable	250,000	
Amount Available for Retirement of Bonds		250,000

If a bank were used as the fiscal agent, cash would first be transferred to a "Cash with Fiscal Agent" account, and payment would then be made from that account.

f. Appropriate closing entries are made based upon all information presented.

Appropriations	1,050,000	
Estimated Revenues		850,000
Estimated Other Financing Sources		200,000
Revenues--Property Taxes	850,000	
Operating Transfers In	240,000	
Expenditures--Interest		800,000
Expenditures--Principal		250,000
Fund Balance Designated for Debt Service		40,000

The balance sheet for the Debt Service Fund would appear as follows.

City of X
Debt Service Fund
Balance Sheet
June 30, 19XX

Assets		Liabilities and Fund Equity	
Cash	$40,000	Liabilities:	
Due from Capital Projects Fund	40,000	Matured Bonds Payable	$50,000
Property taxes receivable--delinquent (net of $20,000 allowance for uncollectible taxes)	10,000	Fund Equity: Fund Balance--Designated for Debt Service	40,000
		Total Liabilities	
Total Assets	$90,000	and Fund Equity	$90,000

Note that the $40,000 Fund Balance equals the "Amount Available for Retirement of Debt" in the General Long-Term Debt Account Group.

5. Special Assessments

  GASB <u>Statement No. 6: Accounting and Reporting for Special Assessments</u>
eliminated the Special Assessment Fund type, for financial reporting periods
beginning after June 15, 1987. In the past, separate Special Assessment
Funds were created for projects to be paid primarily by the property owners
who benefited (for example, a street lighting on sidewalk project). Special
assessment construction projects were accounted for entirely within the fund
including the bond liability, the construction activities, the levying of
the assessments (essentially like a multi-year property tax), and the
collection of the assessments and payment of principal and interest on the
debt.

  Under GASB <u>Statement 6</u>, the accounting for special assessment capital
projects depends on the liability of the governmental unit for the special
assessment debt. If the governmental unit is not obligated in any way for
the debt, the special assessment activities will be accounted for in an
agency fund. However, if the governmental unit is either <u>primarily</u> or
<u>potentially liable</u> for the debt, the accounting will take place as if it
were any other capital improvement and financing transaction. Construction
activities will be recorded in a capital projects fund and debt principal
and interest activities would be recorded in a Debt Service Fund. The
completed project would be recorded in the General Fixed Asset Account Group
or Enterprise Fund, as appropriate. The debt would be recorded in the
General Long-Term Debt Account Group or Enterprise Fund.

F. **Proprietary Funds**

  <u>Internal Service Funds</u> are established to account for the provision of goods
and services by one department of the government to other departments within the
government on generally a cost-reimbursement basis. Internal Service Funds are
budgeted through the budgets of the user departments. Internal Service Funds
are normally established for the following types of activities: central
garages, motor pools, central printing and duplicating, stores departments,
etc. <u>Enterprise Funds</u>, on the other hand, account for activities by which the
government provides goods and services which are (1) rendered primarily to the
general public, (2) financed substantially or entirely through user charges, and
(3) intended to be self-supporting. Enterprise Funds are usually established
for public utilities, toll roads and bridges, transit systems, golf courses,
etc.

Proprietary Funds use the accrual basis of accounting and are nonexpendable; capital is to be maintained. Revenues and expenses are recorded just as they would be in commercial enterprises. Fixed assets are recorded in Proprietary Funds, and depreciation expense is deducted from revenues. The GFA Account Group does not account for fixed assets of Proprietary Funds. These funds also report their own long-term liabilities. The GLTD Account Group is not used to report Proprietary Fund long-term debt because the debt is secured by present and future Proprietary Fund resources. This is even true if the debt is general obligation debt, when the debt is intended to be paid from proprietary fund resources.

When Proprietary Funds are initially established, a contribution or advance is usually received from the General Fund. A contribution is a residual equity transfer and would be recorded by the Internal Service or Enterprise Fund as follows.

```
Cash                                    xx
     Contribution from Government            xx
```

The contribution account is a permanent equity account on the balance sheet of a Proprietary Fund. It is equivalent to paid-in capital in a corporation. On the other hand, an advance from the General Fund is a long-term loan and would be recorded by an Internal Service or Enterprise Fund as follows.

```
Cash                                    xx
     Advance from General Fund               xx
```

The advance is a long-term liability on the Proprietary Fund's balance sheet and a long-term asset on the General Fund's balance sheet which would cause a reservation of Fund Balance. According to the GASB "Grants, entitlements, or shared revenues received before the revenue recognition criteria have been met should be reported as Deferred Revenue, a liability account." When meeting revenue recognition criteria, a grant for a capital asset will be credited to "Contributed Capital," a subdivision of fund equity, as follows.

```
Equipment, etc.                    100,000
     Contributed Capital--Capital Grants    100,000
```

As the asset is depreciated, the following entry would normally be made.

```
Accumulated Amortization--Contributed
  Capital--Capital Grants          10,000
     Accumulated Depreciation--Equipment     10,000
```

In other words, the depreciation is charged directly to the capital account.

It is also important to note that Proprietary Funds do not normally record their operating budgets. Encumbrance accounting need not be used, and a retained earnings account, often with several reserves or appropriations, reflects the accumulated earnings to date. Other journal entries relating to Proprietary

Funds will not be shown because of their similarity to entries for commercial enterprises.

The financial statements of Proprietary Funds include the following.

1) Balance Sheet
2) Statement of Revenues, Expenses, and Changes in Retained Earnings
3) Statement of Changes in Financial Position*

Totals for Internal Service and Enterprise Funds would be presented in the combined statements. Where more than one Internal Service or Enterprise Fund exists, combining statements would be required.

G. Fiduciary Funds--Trust and Agency

Trust Funds are similar to Agency Funds in that each type of fund is used to account for monies held for others, trust funds generally being used when assets are held for substantial periods of time. Trust and Agency Funds do not generally record their budgets formally except for some expendable Trust Funds.

There are three types of Trust Funds: Expendable, Nonexpendable, and Pension. An Expendable Trust Fund is accounted for as a Governmental Fund--modified accrual basis. Nonexpendable and Pension Trust Funds are accounted for as Proprietary Funds--accrual basis. An example of an Expendable Trust Fund is a Bond Guarantee Fund wherein performance bonds are held. The bond is returned to the contractor upon satisfactory performance, or remitted to the appropriate fund if there is unsatisfactory performance. When the bond is received, Fund Balance is credited. Fund Balance is debited when the bond is returned. Interest earned would be closed to the Fund Balance account.

Nonexpendable Trust Funds either permit earnings to be expended, e.g., Endowment Funds, or do not permit earnings to be expended, e.g., Loan Funds. Example entries for a Nonexpendable Trust Fund (principal remains intact) whose earnings are transferred to an Expendable Trust Fund would appear as follows.

Cash	10,000		(to record receipt of resources from
Endowment Fund Balance		10,000	a donor)
Investments	10,000		
Cash		10,000	
Cash	1,000		(to record earnings from invest-
Investment Revenue		1,000	ments)
Operating Transfer to			
Expendable Trust Fund	1,000		(to record authorized transfer of
Due to Expendable			earnings to the Expendable Trust
Trust Fund/Cash		1,000	Fund)

As of this writing, GASB is considering a change to a Statement of Cash Flows.

```
Investment Revenue          1,000       (to record closing entry)
   Operating Transfer
     to Expendable
   Trust Fund                         1,000
```

An important point to remember is that capital gains and losses are part of the Endowment Fund principal, i.e., they are not part of the expendable income. Example entries for the Expendable Trust Fund referred to above would appear as follows.

```
Due from Endowment Fund/Cash   1,000    (to record interest transferred
   Operating Transfer                      from Endowment Fund above)
     from Endowment Fund                1,000

Expenditures                    900     (to record expenditures autho-
   Cash                                900   rized in the trust agreement)

Operating Transfer from
   Endowment Fund              1,000    (to record closing entry)
     Expenditures                       900
     Fund Balance                       100
```

Agency Funds hold temporary deposits, such as employee wage withholdings, for subsequent payment. For example, if union dues had been withheld from employees for subsequent payment to the union, the following entries would be made in an Agency Fund.

```
Cash                            xx
   Union Dues Payable                  xx
Union Dues Payable              xx
   Cash                                xx
```

In addition to the example above, another common use of Agency Funds is to account for property taxes. Property taxes are usually remitted to a county treasurer who places the monies in a county Tax Agency Fund. The taxes are held until such time they are remitted to each of the political subdivisions located within the county. Another use for Agency Funds is to account for special assessment activities when the governmental unit is not obligated in any way for special assessment debt. Agency Funds have only assets and liabilities as accounts and do not record revenues, expenditures, or transfers.

Financial statements required for Trust and Agency funds depend upon their measurement focus. Nonexpendable and Pension Trust Funds are combined with the proprietary funds in the combined statements. Combining and individual fund statements would require

1) Balance Sheet
2) Statements of Revenues, Expenses, and Changes in Fund Balances
3) Statement of Changes in Financial Position

Expendable Trust Funds are combined with the governmental funds in the combined statements. Combining and individual fund statements would include

1) Balance Sheet
2) Statement of Revenues, Expenditures, and Changes in Fund Balances
3) Statement of Revenues, Expenditures, and Changes in Fund Balances Budget and Actual (if an annual budget is adopted)

Agency Funds would appear in the Combined Balance Sheet and should have a Combining Statement of Assets and Liabilities.

H. **The GFA and GLTD Account Groups**

Throughout the discussion of Governmental Funds, entries in the General Fixed Asset and General Long-Term Debt Account Groups were made when necessary. It is now important to review these two account groups.

In the governmental funds, acquisition of a general fixed asset is a use of expendable fund resources because the fixed assets are not appropriable resources and belong to the organization as a whole, not to a specific governmental fund. The assets are considered general fixed assets to be recorded in the General Fixed Assets Account Group. These assets never cause depreciation to be recorded as a charge in the governmental funds. It is permissible to show accumulated depreciation in the GFA Group, but not required (and almost never done).

Investments in general fixed assets are not recorded in the Governmental Funds listed below, but rather in the General Fixed Asset Account Group.

General   Review Note: These are all expendable
Special Revenue   funds. Emphasis is on expendable re-
Capital Projects   sources to provide goods and services.
Expendable Trust   Each uses the modified accrual method.

Fixed assets are recorded in the funds shown below and not in the General Fixed Asset Account Group. Depreciation is recorded on fixed assets in these funds (except on nonrevenue-producing property in Trust Funds).

Internal Service
Enterprise
Nonexpendable Trust
Pension Trust

The entries in the General Fixed Asset Group are very simple. Fixed assets are recorded at cost or fair market value, if donated. Debit the Fixed Asset Account purchased or constructed, e.g., land, building, etc., and credit Investment in Fixed Assets--(blank) Fund--Source.

Land	xx	
Building	xx	
Investment in General Fixed Assets--		
General Fund Revenues		xx

Uncompleted assets are recorded as "Construction in Progress" at year end, and are subsequently recorded as fixed assets when completed. When fixed assets are retired, simply reverse the entry in the General Fixed Asset Account Group. Remember, normally depreciation is not recorded. Any cash received for the asset when sold is generally recorded in the General Fund with a credit to Proceeds from Sale of Fixed Assets (an Other Financing Source) for the proceeds and the entry in the GFA Group recording the asset is reversed. Note that general fixed assets which represent infrastructure (sidewalks, streets, curbing, bridges, etc.) may but do not have to be given recognition in GFA. This is due to the observation that these assets have value only to the governmental unit. These assets are usually called "Improvements other than Buildings" in the GFA.

The governmental unit should present a schedule of its general fixed assets according to sources, as follows.

City of X
Schedule of General Fixed Assets by Sources
June 30, 19XX

General Fixed Assets:		Investment in General Fixed Assets from:	
Land	$x	General Fund Revenues	$x
Building	x	Special Revenue Fund Revenues	x
Improvements Other than		Capital Projects Funds:	
Buildings	x	General Obligation Bonds	x
Equipment	x	County Grants	x
Construction-in-Progress	x	Total Investment in	
Total General		General Fixed Assets	$x
Fixed Assets	$x		

Other statements include

(1) Schedule of General Fixed Assets--By Function and Activity
(2) Schedule of Changes in General Fixed Assets--By Function and Activity

The GLTD Account Group records long-term debt from the following funds.

General
Special Revenue
Capital Projects

Long-term debt is carried directly in the following funds.

Enterprise
Internal Service
Nonexpendable Trust

If long-term debt in one of these funds is guaranteed by the General Fund, note disclosure should be made in the General Purpose Financial Statements. The entry to record long-term debt in the General Long-Term Debt Account Group is

Amount to be Provided for Retirement of Bonds   xx
    Bonds Payable   xx

As monies are set aside for bond repayment (in the Debt Service Fund), the following entry is made.

    Amount Available for Retirement of Bonds   xx
        Amount to be Provided for Retirement of Bonds   xx

The entry to record retirement in GLTDAG is

    Bonds Payable   xx   (See discussion of
        Amount Available for Retirement of Bonds   xx   Debt Service Fund
                                                                for entries made
                                                                in that fund)

Thus, entries are required in GLTD when

    (1) Debt is incurred
    (2) Monies are set aside for debt repayment
    (3) Debt is repaid

Remember that the GLTDAG group records transactions involving debt principal, not interest.

I. **Capital Lease Obligations**

    Governmental units use the same criteria to determine whether a lease is capital or operating. Capital leases for proprietary fund operations are handled in the same manner as in business accounting; the asset and liability are generally recorded at the present value of the minimum lease payments (the asset is recorded at its fair market value, if lower than the PV of minimum lease payments). Each lease payment is partially interest expense and partially a payment of the lease obligation. The fixed asset is depreciated.

    The accounting for capital lease obligations for general government operations is more complex. Assume on January 1, 19X8, the general fund of the City of X leased a computer system, for which the present value of the minimum lease payments (and fair market value) amounted to $45,000. The applicable interest rate is 10%, and the first payment of $5,000 is due on December 31, 19X8. The following entries would be required:

1/1/X8

General Fund

Expenditures--Capital Lease	45,000	
Other Financing Sources--		
Capital Leases		45,000

General Fixed Asset Account Group

Equipment	45,000	
Investment in General Fixed Assets--		
General Fund--Capital Lease Obligations		45,000

General Long-Term Debt Account Group

Amount to be Provided for Payment of		
Capital Lease Obligations	45,000	
Capital Lease Obligations Payable		45,000

12/31/X88

General Fund

Expenditures--Interest	4,500	
Expenditures--Principal	500	
Cash		5,000

General Long-Term Debt Account Group

Capital Lease Obligations Payable	500	
Amount to be Provided for Payment		
of Capital Lease Obligations		500

Of the total $5,000 payment, $4,500 (45,000 x 10%) is for interest and $500 is for principal. The 12/31/X8 entry in the GLTDG could be preceded by an entry indicating that the funds are available, if desired.

J. **Interfund Transfers and Other Interfund Transactions**

Assuming appropriate authorization, a governmental unit's resources can be shifted among the various funds of a governmental unit for a variety of reasons. In addition, certain transactions involve more than one fund. There are six types of interfund transactions.

    (1) Loans
    (2) Quasi-external transactions
    (3) Expenditure/expense reimbursement transactions
    (4) Residual equity transfers
    (5) All other transfers which are not of the residual equity type
           (operating transfers)
    (6) Transactions affecting more than one fund/group

The first type of resource movement described above, <u>loans</u>, results in a shift (temporary or long-term) of the resource cash from one fund to another fund. The creditor fund sets up a receivable while the debtor fund establishes a payable. The receivable/payable descriptions for a short-term loan are: Due from...Fund/Due to...Fund Accounts.* As an example, suppose the General Fund, in order to alleviate a temporary cash flow problem, borrows $100,000 from an Enterprise Fund. The loan is to be paid in six months. The entries which would be made are

General Fund		Enterprise Fund	
Cash	100,000	Due from General Fund	100,000
Due to Enterprise Fund	100,000	Cash	100,000

If interest is charged at 10% on this loan, the following entries would be made at the end of six months.

*If the loan is long-term, "Due form...Fund" is changed to "Advance to...Fund" and "Due to...Fund" is changed to "Advance from...Fund".

General Fund			Enterprise Fund		
Due to Enterprise Fund	100,000		Cash		105,000
Expenditures	5,000		Interest Revenues		5,000
Cash		105,000	Due from General Fund		100,000

Note the expenditure/revenue treatment of the interest above. This treatment leads directly to the next type of resource movement, i.e., from quasi-external transactions.

Quasi-external transactions are accounted for as if the transaction were between an individual fund and an entity external to the particular governmental unit, i.e., as revenues and expenditures/expenses in the affected funds. In the loan example, the interest paid is treated the same way it would have been had the General Fund borrowed the money from a bank, i.e., an expenditure. Similarly, the interest received is treated the same way it would have been had the Enterprise Fund lent the money to an entity outside of the particular governmental unit, i.e., a revenue. Other examples which illustrate quasi-external transactions include the following.

(1) The General or a Special Revenue Fund's use of the services provided by Internal Service Funds, e.g., printing, data processing, motor vehicle, etc. services
(2) The General or a Special Revenue Fund's use of the services provided by enterprise funds, e.g., water and sewer, electricity, etc. services

To illustrate one of these transactions, suppose that General Fund personnel use motor vehicles owned by an Internal Service Fund. The latter fund's bill for these services amounts to $1,500. The following entries would be made.

General Fund		Internal Service	
Expenditures	1,500	Due from General Fund/Cash	1,500
Due to Internal Service Fund/Cash	1,500	Billings to Departments (Revenues)	1,500

The third type of interfund resource movement involves reimbursement for expenditures/expenses which were initially paid by one fund on behalf of some other fund. To illustrate, suppose that General and Special Revenue Fund personnel attend a conference together, for which the total cost is $10,000. The entire bill is paid by the General Fund, which results in a charge to expenditures for $10,000. However, suppose that $3,000 of the $10,000 was for Special Revenue Fund personnel. The Special Revenue Fund should reimburse the General Fund for the latter's expenditure of funds which relate to the Special Revenue Fund. The following entries would be made.

General Fund		Special Revenue Fund	
Due from Special Revenue		Expenditures	3,000
Fund/Cash	3,000	Due to General Fund/Cash	3,000
Expenditures	3,000		

Note that expenses, rather than expenditures, would be involved if the reimbursement affects Proprietary Funds, i.e., Internal Service and Enterprise Funds.

The fourth type of resource movement involves <u>residual equity transfers</u> between funds. Equity accounts are debited and credited in the paying and receiving funds, respectively. Typical examples which illustrate this type of transaction include the transfer of excess cash from Capital Projects and Debt Service Funds to the General Fund. This transfer occurs at the conclusion of the capital project or when the general obligation debt has been fully paid and cash balances remain in these funds. The following journal entries would be made.

General Fund		Debt Service		Capital Projects Fund	
Due from--Fund/Cash	xx	Fund Balance		Unreserved Fund	
Unreserved Fund		(Residual Equity		Balance (Residual	
Balance (Residual		Transfer)	xx	Equity Transfer)	xx
Equity Transfer)	xx	Due to General		Due to General	
		Fund/Cash	xx	Fund/Cash	xx

Another example which illustrates a residual equity transfer is the contribution made by the General Fund to an Internal Service Fund or to an Enterprise Fund. These contributions, which help to establish operations, are equivalent to paid-in capital in the proprietary funds being established. The following journal entries show how these contributions would be recorded.

General Fund		Internal Service/Enterprise Funds	
Unreserved Fund Balance		Due from General Fund/Cash	xx
(Residual Equity Transfer)	xx	Contribution from Government*	xx
Due to--Fund/Cash	xx		

Residual Equity Transfers are reported as adjustments of the beginning Fund Balance of a governmental fund. For example, in the statement on page 1032, a Residual Equity Transfer in the General Fund would be reported after the January 1 Fund Balance of $202,500 and would adjust the December 31 Fund Balance.

<u>Operating transfers</u> include all interfund transfers which are not residual equity transfers. As stated in the GASB <u>Codification</u> "for example, legally authorized transfers from a fund receiving revenue to the fund through which the

---

*"Contribution from Government" is reported in the equity section of the balance sheet fof Proprietary Funds. An alternative procedure would be to first credit "Residual Equity Transfers" and then to close that account to "Contribution from Government."

resources are to be expended transfers of tax revenues from a Special Revenue Fund to a Debt Service Fund, transfers from the General Fund to a Special Revenue or Capital Projects Fund, operating subsidy transfers from the General or a Special Revenue Fund to an Enterprise Fund, and transfers from an Enterprise Fund other than payments in lieu of taxes to finance General Fund expenditures."

Generally, these resource transfers require payments from the General Fund to various other funds. It is essential to note that expenditure/expense and revenue accounts are not used to record or report these operating transfers. Instead, special "Operating Transfers Out" and "Operating Transfers In" accounts are used. These accounts are temporary accounts and are closed at the end of the fiscal year. Examples which illustrate this type of resource movement include the following

(1) The General Fund's transfer of resources to a Capital Projects Fund for the governmental unit's share of the project's cost
(2) A Capital Projects' Fund transfer of resources, representing investment income, to a Debt Service Fund for debt repayment
(3) The General Fund's transfer to a Debt Service Fund of resources for payment of debt principal and interest

Journal entries for the first example would appear as follows

General Fund		Capital Projects Fund	
Operating Transfers Out	xx	Due from General Fund/Cash	xx
Due to Capital Projects		Operating Transfers In	xx
Fund/Cash	xx		

Operating transfers are classified as "Other Financing Sources/Uses" in the operating statements of governmental funds.

An example of transactions affecting more than one fund or group of accounts would be the example in this review of the construction of a new city hall. Entries were required in the Capital Projects and Debt Service Funds and the General Fixed Assets and General Long-Term Debt Account Groups. Review of interfund problems is necessary, as this type of question is common on the CPA exam.

K. STATE AND LOCAL GOVERNMENT FUND REVIEW CHECKLIST

	Governmental Funds				Proprietary Funds		Fiduciary Funds
	General	Special Revenue	Capital Projects	Debt Service	Internal Service	Enterprise	Trust & Agency
Accounting basis	Modified Accrual	Modified Accrual	Modified Accrual	Modified Accrual	Accrual	Accrual	See p. 1159
Land, Buildings, Equipment, etc.	No	No	No	No	Yes depreciation also	Yes depreciation also	See p. 1179
Long-term debt	No	No	No	No	Possibly	Yes	Possibly, See p. 1180
Budgetary Accounts	Yes See p. 1161	Yes See p.1168	Perhaps*	Perhaps*	None	None	Perhaps**
Encumbrances	Yes	Yes	Yes	No	No	No	Expendable Trust Funds (Possibly)

Nonfund Account Groups

General Fixed Asset Group

Land
Buildings
Etc.
  Investments in general fixed assets--(blank)
  Fund--source

General Long-term Debt

Amount to be provided for retirement of bonds
Amount available for retirement of bonds
Bonds Payable

*Required when a legally adopted annual budget is passed.

**For expendable trust funds only, when a legally adopted annual budget is passed.

NONPROFIT ACCOUNTING

Nonprofit organizations provide socially desirable services without the intention of realizing a profit. Some nonprofit organizations are financed partially by taxes and/or contributions from constituents. The nature and extent of the support depends upon the type of nonprofit organization.

The Financial Accounting Standards Board has authority to establish accounting principles for nongovernmental nonprofit organizations. The GASB has the authority to establish accounting principles for similar organizations if they are governmental (colleges, etc.) but, if the GASB has not acted, FASB Standards apply. Currently, the FASB has, in effect, adopted prior pronouncements of the AICPA and certain practitioner organizations as constituting GAAP until further action is taken.

The four types of nonprofit organizations that have been tested and the applicable sources of GAAP are

(1) Colleges and Universities (AICPA Audits of Colleges and Universities, AICPA Statements of Position, National Association of College and University Business Officers, College and University Business Administration)
(2) Hospitals (AICPA Hospital Audit Guide, AICPA Statements of Position, American Hospital Association, Chart of Accounts for Hospitals)
(3) Voluntary Health and Welfare Organizations (AICPA Audits of Voluntary Health and Welfare Organizations)
(4) Other Nonprofit Organizations (AICPA Statement of Position 78-10, contained in AICPA Audits of Certain Nonprofit Organizations)

Most nonprofit CPA exam questions can be answered adequately based on (1) a knowledge of governmental fund accounting and (2) familiarity with certain aspects of the four types of nonprofit organizations. Also, when nonprofit organizations are tested with a problem, it is customary for the problem to show the nonprofit organization's financial statements (or trial balance). Thus, the accounts used for journal entries can usually be found very quickly upon examining this information.

In order to prepare for the possibility of nonprofit organizations on the CPA exam, candidates should become familiar with (1) the fund structure, (2) the statement formats, and (3) the major unique accounting features of each of the four types of nonprofit organizations. In addition, candidates can use general accounting knowledge to answer many parts, using account titles given in the problems. Before proceeding further, candidates should review the outline of SFAC 6 Elements of Financial Statements.

Note: In August 1987, the FASB issued SFAS 93, Recognition of Depreciation by Not-for-Profit Organizations. This statement requires all not-for-profit organizations, including colleges which do not now depreciate, to record depreciation. In January 1988, GASB issued Statement No. 8, Applicability of SFAS 93 Recognition of Depreciation by Not-for-Profit Organizations to Certain State and

Local Governmental Entities. GASB Statement No. 8 provides that not-for-profit organizations that are governmental entities need not charge depreciation as a result of SFAS 93. More recently, the FASB passed SFAS 99 which defers the effective date of SFAS 93 to fiscal years beginning on or after January 1, 1990. These statements apply primarily to colleges and universities, as other not-for-profit organizations have charged depreciation for some time. Illustrated entries for depreciation, when charged, are indicated in the discussion related to each type of not-for-profit organization.

A. **College and University Accounting**

The Committee on College and University Accounting and Auditing of the AICPA states that

> Service, rather than profits, is the objective of an educational institution; thus, the primary obligation of accounting and reporting is one of accounting for resources received and used rather than for the determination of net income. Frequently, there is no relationship between the fees charged and the actual expenditures for program services (Audits of Colleges and Universities, p. 5).

This statement reflects the similarity between college and university accounting and that for the expendable, governmental funds for state and local governmental units.

The accounting and reporting for colleges and universities is done through fund groups. The fund groups below are usually maintained.

    (1) Current Funds

        (a) Unrestricted
        (b) Restricted

    (2) Loan Funds
    (3) Endowment and similar funds
    (4) Annuity and Life Income Funds
    (5) Plant funds

        (a) Unexpended
        (b) Investment in Plant
        (c) Funds for Retirement of Indebtedness
        (d) Funds for Renewals and Replacements

    (6) Agency Funds

The accrual basis of accounting should be used for all fund groups. The financial statements for colleges and universities include the following.

    (1) Balance Sheet (see following pages for example)
    (2) Statement of Changes in Fund Balances (see following pages for example)
    (3) Statement of Current Funds Revenues, Expenditures, and Other Changes (see following pages for example)

A discussion of each of the fund groups is presented on the following pages.

Current Funds are those ". . . which are expendable for any purpose in performing the primary objectives of the institution, i.e., instruction, research, extension, and public service . . ." (Audits of Colleges and Universities, p. 13). Current Funds--Unrestricted are only subject to the usual budgetary limitations, while Current Funds--Restricted are subject to provisions limiting their use. Examples of restricted funds are special purpose federal grants and private donations for a specific purpose. Current Funds--Unrestricted are internally designated in that a governing board determines how the resources are to be used. Current Funds--Restricted are externally restricted because donors or other outside parties determine how the resources are to be used.

Current funds revenues include tuition and fees, governmental appropriations and grants, private gifts and grants, endowment income, sales and services of educational departments and auxiliary enterprises, and expired term endowments. Current funds revenues are reduced by refunds; however, scholarships and tuition remissions are included in revenues and offset by expenditures.

All revenues of Current Funds--Unrestricted are recognized when earned. Revenues of Current Funds--Restricted are recognized when the expenditure takes place.

In addition, auxiliary enterprise activities (dormitories, cafeterias, bookstores, etc.) are accounted for in the Current Funds category and follow the accounting rules applicable to Current Funds rather than those of Enterprise Funds of governmental units.

Current Funds follow accrual accounting, but do record budget entries and encumbrances. Until SFAS 93 becomes effective, depreciation is not normally recorded in the Current Funds, even for assets of auxiliary enterprises (see discussion in Plant Funds). Grants made to Restricted Funds are recognized as revenues only when earned, by incurring the expenditure, as was the case for local governmental units.

Loan Funds are those from which cash may be loaned to students, faculty, and staff. Interest revenues increase the fund balance and provide a larger asset base for subsequent loans. Assets consist of cash, temporary investments, and notes receivable (less a provision for uncollectibles).

Endowment Funds include endowment, term endowment, and quasi-endowment funds. Endowment funds are those in which the principal is required to be kept intact in perpetuity. The earnings from the investment of the principal will normally be expended for current restricted or unrestricted purposes, depending upon the wishes of the donor. If expended for current restricted purposes, these resources are transferred to the Current Funds--Restricted group and expenditures are made there according to the donor restrictions. All income earned for current unrestricted purposes is recognized as Endowment Income. Term Endowment Funds are treated as endowment until a certain event or condition has been met (e.g., time passage), and then all or part of the principal may be expended. Quasi-Endowment Funds are similar to Endowment and Term Endowment funds. The difference lies in the control aspects. Quasi-Endowment Funds are controlled by the governing board of the college or university, not some external donor, and are unrestricted. It should be noted that an endowment must be under the control of the university to be recorded; a recent CPA exam question involved a trust established at a bank with the university as beneficiary. Only a memo entry was required.

Annuity and Life Income Funds, if not significant, are reported along with the Endowment Funds; otherwise, if material, they are reported separately. This fund group receives gifts or amounts from donors which constitute principal. In the case of Life Income Funds, all earnings from the principal are usually paid annually to the donor while living. Upon the donor's death, the principal is transferred to some other fund group, e.g., Current Funds, Endowment Funds, etc., by the governing board. In the case of Annuity Funds, both the term and the amount or percentage of income to be transferred to the donor may be fixed. As a result, the accounting is more complex; an Annuities Payable liability account must be established equal to the present value of the future payments.

Plant Funds usually consist of four independent, balancing sections, each section consisting of a self-balancing set of accounts.

(1) Unexpended Plant Funds which comprise funds restricted for physical plant expenditures
(2) Investment in Plant which accounts for past expenditures in plant
(3) Funds for the Retirement of Indebtedness which are similar to Debt Service Funds
(4) Funds for Renewals and Replacements used often by private colleges to accumulate resources on a long-term basis

When monies are set aside for plant acquisition, rehabilitation, etc., by other funds (e.g., Current, Endowment, Annuity, etc.), the cash is accounted for in the Unexpended Plant Fund section. When monies are spent for plant acquisition, the investment is recorded in the Investment in Plant Fund section. Note that these sections of the Plant Fund are not directly parallel to any specific state and local government funds. Liabilities may be recorded temporarily in the Unexpended Plant Fund section from the time monies are raised (e.g., sale of bonds) until expenditures ar emade to acquire physical facilities.

As indicated earlier, private universities will be required to charge depreciation; public colleges may or may not.

SFAS 93 did not indicate where, or how, depreciation should be charged. Most private universities will record depreciation in the investment in Plant section of the Plant Funds group. The entry would be:

Plant Fund Group--Investment in Plant

Investment in Plant--Depreciation Charge	xx	
Accumulated Depreciation		xx

Note that the debit to Fund Balance will cause an entry in the "Expenditures and Other Deductions" section of the Statement of Changes in Fund Balances (in the following sample set of FSs).

Agency Funds are used to account for funds not owned or controlled by the college or university but in the custody of the school, e.g.,g deposits, etc. They are quite similar to municipal agency funds.

Illustrative Transactions. Many entries for colleges and universities are similar to entries for state and local government. For example, the Revenues, Expenditures, Encumbrances, and various reserve accounts are used in the Current Funds Group, although full accrual accounting is employed. Some entries that are different and relate to situations unique to colleges and universities are presented below.

1. Bad Debts. Unlike local government, where estimates of uncollectible receivables are considered to be deductions from revenues, colleges and universities normally debit Expenditures. Assume that a college recorded tuition revenues of $10,000,000, of which $9,000,000 is collected in cash, and a 3% bad debt rate is used.

   Current Funds--Unrestricted

Cash	9,000,000	
Accounts Receivable--Student Fees	1,000,000	
Expenditures--Bad Debts	30,000	
Revenues--Student Fees		10,000,000
Allowance for Uncollectible Accounts		30,000

2. Summer School. If a session is offered in a term that is held during more than one fiscal year, GAAP requires that both revenues and expenditures be reported in the fiscal year in which most of the instruction takes place. In practice, this often means that revenues are deferred. For example, when summer session fees are collected for an institution that has a June 30 fiscal year end, the entry would be

Current Funds--Unrestricted

Cash	500,000	
Deferred Revenues		500,000

In the new fiscal year, as the expenditures are recognized for faculty salaries and other purposes, the revenues would be recognized

Deferred Revenues	500,000	
Revenues		500,000

3. Transfers--Mandatory and Nonmandatory. Assume that transfers are made from the Current Funds--Unrestricted to the Plant Funds. $340,000 represents a Mandatory Transfer to the Funds for Retirement of Indebtedness for debt service repayment and $170,000 represents a Nonmandatory Transfer to the Funds for Renewals and Replacements for future renovations.

Current Funds--Unrestricted

Mandatory Transfer to Funds for Retirement of Indebtedness	340,000	
Nonmandatory Transfer to Funds for Renewals and Replacements	170,000	
Cash		510,000

Funds for Retirement of Indebtedness

Cash	340,000	
Fund Balance--Mandatory Transfers		340,000

Funds for Renewals and Replacements

Cash	170,000	
Fund Balance--Nonmandatory Transfers		170,000

Note how this transaction would be reported in the Statement of Changes in Fund Balances in the following sample set of FSs.

SAMPLE EDUCATIONAL INSTITUTION BALANCE SHEET
June 30, 19X2 and 19X1

Assets	19X2	19X1	Liabilities and Fund Balances	19X2	19X1
Current funds:			Current funds:		
Unrestricted:			Unrestricted:		
Cash	$ 210,000	$ 110,000	Accounts payable	$ 145,000	$ 115,000
Investments	450,000	360,000	Students' deposits	60,000	55,000
Accounts receivable	228,000	175,000	Due to other funds	158,000	120,000
Inventories, at LCM	118,000	100,000	Fund balance	643,000	455,000
Total unrestricted	1,006,000	745,000	Total unrestricted	1,006,000	745,000
Restricted:			Restricted:		
Cash	145,000	101,000	Accounts payable	14,000	5,000
Investments	315,000	325,000	Fund balances	446,000	421,000
Total restricted	460,000	426,000	Total restricted	460,000	426,000
Total current funds	$1,466,000	$1,171,000	Total current funds	$1,466,000	$1,171,000
Loan funds:			Loan funds:		
Cash	$ 30,000	$ 20,000	Fund balances:		
Investments	100,000	100,000	U.S. Govt. grants refundable	$ 50,000	$ 33,000
Loans to students, faculty and staff	553,000	382,000	University funds	633,000	469,000
Total loan funds	$ 683,000	$ 502,000	Total loan funds	$ 683,000	$ 502,000
Endowment and similar funds:			Endowment and similar funds:		
Cash	$ 100,000	$ 101,000	Endowment fund balance	$ 7,800,000	$ 6,740,000
Investments	13,900,000	11,800,000	Term endowment fund balance	6,200,000	5,161,000
Total endowment and similar funds	$14,000,000	$11,901,000	Total endowment and similar funds	$14,000,000	$11,901,000
Annuity funds:			Annuity funds:		
Cash	$ 55,000	$ 45,000	Annuities payable	$2,150,000	$2,300,000
Investments	3,260,000	3,010,000	Fund balances	1,165,000	755,000
Total annuity funds	$3,315,000	$3,055,000	Total annuity funds	$3,315,000	$3,055,000
Plant funds:			Plant funds:		
Unexpended:			Unexpended:		
Cash	$ 425,000	$ 530,000	Accounts payable	$ 200,000	$ 120,000
Investments	1,285,000	1,590,000	Fund balances	1,510,000	2,000,000
Total unexpended	1,710,000	2,120,000	Total unexpended	$1,710,000	$2,120,000
Renewal and replacement:			Renewal and replacement:		
Cash	110,000	94,000	Fund balances:		
Investments	150,000	286,000	Restricted	25,000	180,000
			Unrestricted	235,000	200,000
Total renewal & replacement	260,000	380,000	Total renewal & replacement	260,000	380,000
Retirement of indebtedness:			Retirement of indebtedness:		
Cash	50,000	40,000	Fund balances:		
Deposits with trustees	250,000	253,000	Restricted	185,000	125,000
			Unrestricted	115,000	168,000
Total retirement of indebtedness	300,000	293,000	Total retirement of indebtedness	300,000	293,000
Investment in plant:			Investment in plant:		
Land	1,600,000	1,690,000	Mortgages payable	3,390,000	3,410,000
Buildings and equipment	40,000,000	38,260,000	Net investment in plant	38,210,000	36,540,000
Total investment in plant	41,600,000	39,950,000	Total investment in plant	41,600,000	39,950,000
Total plant funds	$43,870,000	$42,743,000	Total plant funds	$43,870,000	$42,743,000
Agency funds:			Agency funds:		
Cash	$ 50,000	$ 70,000	Deposits held in custody for others	$ 110,000	$ 90,000
Investments	60,000	20,000			
Total agency funds	$ 110,000	$ 90,000	Total agency funds	$ 110,000	$ 90,000

Source: See following page

Sample Educational Institution
Statement of Changes in Fund Balances
Year Ended June 30, 19—

	Current funds		Loan funds	Endowment and similar funds	Annuity and life income funds	Plant funds			Investment in plant
	Unrestricted	Restricted				Unexpended	Renewals and replacements	Retirement of indebtedness	
Revenues and other additions									
Unrestricted current fund revenues	$7,540,000	$ —	$ —	$ —	$ —	$ —	$ —	$ —	$ —
Expired term endowment—restricted	—	—	—	—	—	50,000	—	—	—
State appropriations—restricted	—	—	—	—	—	50,000	—	—	—
Federal grants and contracts—restricted	—	500,000	—	—	—	—	—	—	—
Private gifts, grants and contracts—restricted	—	370,000	100,000	1,500,000	800,000	115,000	—	65,000	15,000
Investment income—restricted	—	224,000	12,000	10,000	—	5,000	5,000	5,000	—
Realized gains on investments—unrestricted	—	—	—	109,000	—	—	—	—	—
Realized gains on investments—restricted	—	—	4,000	50,000	—	10,000	5,000	5,000	—
Interest on loans receivable	—	—	7,000	—	—	—	—	—	—
U.S. government advances	—	—	18,000	—	—	—	—	—	—
Expended for plant facilities (including $100,000 charged to current funds expenditures)	—	—	—	—	—	—	—	—	1,550,000
Retirement of indebtedness	—	—	—	—	—	—	—	—	220,000
Accrued interest on sale of bonds	—	—	—	—	—	—	—	3,000	—
Matured annuity and life income restricted to endowment	—	—	—	10,000	—	—	—	—	—
Total revenues and other additions	$7,540,000	$1,094,000	$141,000	$ 1,679,000	$ 800,000	$ 230,000	$ 10,000	$ 78,000	$ 1,785,000
Expenditures and other deductions									
Educational and general expenditures	4,400,000	1,014,000	—	—	—	—	—	—	—
Auxiliary enterprises expenditures	1,830,000	—	—	—	—	—	—	—	—
Indirect costs recovered	—	35,000	—	—	—	—	—	—	—
Refunded to grantors	—	20,000	10,000	—	—	—	—	—	—
Loan cancellations and write-offs	—	—	1,000	—	—	—	—	—	—
Administrative and collection costs	—	—	1,000	—	—	—	—	1,000	—
Adjustment of actuarial liability for annuities payable	—	—	—	—	75,000	—	—	—	—
Expended for plant facilities (including noncapitalized expenditures of $50,000)	—	—	—	—	—	1,200,000	300,000	—	—
Retirement of indebtedness	—	—	—	—	—	—	—	220,000	—
Interest on indebtedness	—	—	—	—	—	—	—	190,000	—
Disposal of plant facilities	—	—	—	—	—	—	—	—	115,000
Expired term endowments ($40,000 unrestricted, $50,000 restricted to plant)	—	—	—	90,000	—	—	—	—	—
Matured annuity and life income funds restricted to endowment	—	—	—	—	10,000	—	—	—	—
Total expenditures and other deductions	$6,230,000	$1,069,000	$ 12,000	$ 90,000	$ 85,000	$1,200,000	$300,000	$411,000	$ 115,000
Transfers among funds—additions/ (deductions)									
Mandatory:									
Principal and interest	(340,000)	—	—	—	—	—	—	340,000	—
Renewals and replacements	(170,000)	—	—	—	—	—	170,000	—	—
Loan fund matching grant	(2,000)	—	2,000	—	—	—	—	—	—
Unrestricted gifts allocated	(650,000)	—	50,000	550,000	—	50,000	—	—	—
Portion of unrestricted quasi-endowment funds investment gains appropriated	40,000	—	—	(40,000)	—	—	—	—	—
Total transfers	($1,122,000)	$ —	$ 52,000	$ 510,000	$ —	$ 50,000	$170,000	$340,000	$ —
Net increase/(decrease) for the year	$ 188,000	$ 25,000	$181,000	$ 2,099,000	$ 715,000	($ 920,000)	($120,000)	$ 7,000	$ 1,670,000
Fund balance at beginning of year	455,000	421,000	502,000	11,901,000	2,505,000	2,120,000	380,000	293,000	36,540,000
Fund balance at end of year	$ 643,000	$ 446,000	$683,000	$14,000,000	$3,220,000	$1,200,000	$260,000	$300,000	$38,210,000

Source: AICPA, *Audits of Colleges and Universities*, pp. 60-67.

Sample Educational Institution
Statement of Current Funds Revenues, Expenditures, and Other Changes
Year Ended June 30, 19--

| | Current Year | | | Prior |
	Unrestricted	Restricted	Total	Year total
Revenues:				
Tuition and fees	$2,600,000		$2,600,000	$2,300,000
Federal appropriations	500,000		500,000	500,000
State appropriations	700,000		700,000	700,000
Local appropriations	100,000		100,000	100,000
Federal grants and contracts	20,000	$ 375,000	395,000	350,000
State grants and contracts	10,000	25,000	35,000	200,000
Local grants and contracts	5,000	25,000	30,000	45,000
Private gifts, grants, and contracts	850,000	380,000	1,230,000	1,190,000
Endowment income	325,000	209,000	534,000	500,000
Sales and services of educational departments	190,000		190,000	195,000
Sales and services of auxiliary enterprises	2,200,000		2,200,000	2,100,000
Expired term endowment	40,000		40,000	
Other sources (if any)				
Total current revenues	$7,540,000	$ 1,014,000	$8,554,400	$8,180,000
Expenditures and mandatory transfers:				
Educational and general:				
Instruction	2,960,000	489,000	3,449,000	3,300,000
Research	100,000	400,000	500,000	650,000
Public service	130,000	25,000	155,000	175,000
Academic support	250,000		250,000	225,000
Student services	200,000		200,000	195,000
Institutional support	450,000		450,000	445,000
Operation and maintenance of plant	220,000		220,000	200,000
Scholarships and fellowships	90,000	100,000	190,000	180,000
Educational and general expenditures	$4,400,000	$ 1,014,000	$5,414,000	$5,370,000
Mandatory transfers for:				
Principal and interest	90,000		90,000	50,000
Renewals and replacements	100,000		100,000	80,000
Loan fund matching grant	2,000		2,000	
Total education and general	$4,592,000	$ 1,014,000	$5,606,000	$5,500,000
Auxiliary enterprises:				
Expenditures	1,830,000		1,830,000	1,730,000
Mandatory transfers for:				
Principal and interest	250,000		250,000	250,000
Renewals and replacements	70,000		70,000	70,000
Total auxiliary enterprises	$2,150,000	$ -0-	$2,150,000	$2,050,000
Total expenditures and mandatory transfers	$6,742,000	$ 1,014,000	$7,756,000	$7,550,000
Other transfers and additions/(deductions):				
Excess of restricted receipts over transfers to revenues		45,000	45,000	40,000
Refunded to grantors		(20,000)	(20,000)	
Unrestricted gifts allocated to other funds	(650,000)		(650,000)	(510,000)
Portion of quasi-endowment gains appropriated	40,000		40,000	
Net increase in fund balances	$ 188,000	$ 25,000	$ 213,000	$ 160,000

Source: See previous page

4. Grants for Current Purposes. Assume that a federal grant was received in
    the amount of $100,000 for cancer research. Of that amount, one half was
    expended this fiscal year, and the remainder will be expended in future
    years. Of the $50,000 expended this year, $10,000 represented indirect cost
    recoveries to the institution, and $40,000 was expended directly on the
    grant.

    Current Funds--Restricted

Cash	90,000	
Fund Balance--Governmental		
Grants and Contracts		50,000
Revenues--Governmental Grants and		
Contracts		40,000
Expenditures--Governmental Grants and		
Contracts	40,000	
Cash		40,000

    Current--Funds Unrestricted

Cash	10,000	
Revenues--Governmental Grants and		
Contracts--Indirect Cost Recoveries		10,000

    It can be seen that Current Funds--Restricted Revenues will always equal
    Expenditures.

5. Endowment Transactions. Assume that a wealthy alumnus contributed
    $1,000,000 in corporate stock to the institution, asking that the $1,000,000
    be maintained, that half the proceeds be used for student scholarships, and
    the remaining proceeds be used at the discretion of the institution. During
    the first year, $50,000 was received in dividends, and $20,000 was expended
    for scholarships.

    Endowment Funds

Investment in A Corporation Stock	1,000,000	
Fund Balance--Income Restricted		500,000
Fund Balance--Income Unrestricted		500,000

    Current Funds--Restricted

Cash	25,000	
Revenues--Endowment Income		20,000
Fund Balance--Restricted		5,000
Expenditures--Student Aid	20,000	
Cash		20,000

    Current Funds--Unrestricted

Cash	25,000	
Revenues--Endowment Income		25,000

6. <u>Plant Fund Transactions</u>. Assume that a college borrows $2,000,000 to construct a small dormitory.

<u>Unexpended Plant Funds</u>

Cash	2,000,000	
Bonds Payable		2,000,000
Construction Work in Progress	2,000,000	
Cash		2,000,000
Bonds Payable	2,000,000	
Construction Work in Progress		2,000,000

<u>Investment in Plant Funds</u>

Buildings	2,000,000	
Bonds Payable		2,000,000

Further, assume that a total of $200,000 was paid for debt service for this project, including $100,000 for principal and $100,000 for interest.

<u>Funds for Retirement of Indebtedness</u>

Fund Balance--Retirement of Indebtedness	100,000	
Fund Balance--Interest on Indebtedness	100,000	
Cash		200,000

<u>Investment in Plant Funds</u>

Bonds Payable	100,000	
Net Investment in Plant		100,000

Note that in all of the above entries, Revenue and Expenditures have been recorded only in the Current Funds (Restricted and Unrestricted). Fund Balance is debited and credited for similar entries in the other funds, indicating that those transactions appear in the Statement of Changes in Fund Balances.

B. **Hospital Accounting**

Hospitals generally have fewer funds than governments and colleges and universities. Additionally, they use the accrual basis including depreciation (expenses are matched with revenues). To summarize, hospital accounting is more similar to profit-oriented financial accounting than to governmental or college and university accounting because hospitals are similar to a business (hospitals provide services based primarily on user fees as do business enterprises). The financial statements have separate sections for each type of fund. Hospital statements include

(1) Statement of Revenues and Expenses (see following pages for examples)
(2) Balance Sheet (see following pages for example)
(3) Statement of Changes in Fund Balance

(4) Statement of Changes in Financial Position*

Hospitals generally make a major distinction between general and restricted funds. The balance sheet on page 1200 illustrates three categories of restricted funds: Specific Purpose Funds, Plant Replacement and Expansion Funds, and Endowment Funds.

General Funds. It is important to note that Unrestricted Funds have been used historically to identify those funds that are not restricted by donors or grantors; however, per Statement of Position 85-1, Unrestricted Funds should now be referred to as General Funds. Throughout this module we will use the term "General Funds." The General Funds account for all of the funds not restricted for identified purposes by donors or grantors, including resources that the governing board may use for any designated purpose and resources whose use is limited by agreement between the health care entity and an outside party other than a donor or grantor. All revenues and expenses of a hospital are reported in the General Funds. Full accrual accounting is used, and fixed assets are depreciated.

An understanding of some of the unique features of hospital accounting can be gained by looking at the Statement of Revenues and Expenses in the following sample set of FSs. Patient Service Revenues include all charges to all patients at the full rate, regardless of the amount eventually paid. Allowances and Uncollectible Accounts represent revenue deductions for bad debts, contractual adjustments by Medicare, Medicaid, Blue Cross, etc., and employee discounts. Net Patient Service Revenues reflects the difference between the Patient Service Revenues and Allowances and Uncollectible Accounts. Other Operating Revenues include amounts transferred from restricted funds, purchase discounts, tuition from nursing students, cafeteria and parking lot revenues, and donated materials. Nonoperating Revenues include unrestricted gifts, bequests, investment income from board designated assets, and donated services.

Donated services are recorded at the fair market value of the services received, if an employer-employee relationship exists. Note the difference: donated materials are recorded as Other Operating Revenues; donated services are recorded as Nonoperating Revenues.

Restricted Funds. As can be seen from the Balance Sheet in the following sample set of FSs, hospitals report three types of restricted funds. Specific Purpose Funds contain assets that have been restricted by granting agencies and

*As of this writing, the AICPA is considering a change to a Statement of Cash Flows in a proposed revision to Audits of Health Care Entities.

other donors for current purposes.   When expenditures take place, the funds are transferred to the General Funds, where the amounts are recognized as Other Operating Revenues and (normally) Operating Expenses.   <u>Plant Replacement and Expansion Funds</u> hold assets set aside by donors for the future construction of a hospital plant.   When expended, the funds are transferred to the General Funds, where the assets are capitalized.   <u>Endowment Funds</u> hold assets that are invested, the proceeds of which are to be available for either restricted or unrestricted purposes.

SAMPLE HOSPITAL BALANCE SHEET
December 31, 19--
(with Comparative Figures for 19--)
[in thousands]

General Funds

Assets	Current Year	Prior Year
Current:		
Cash	$ 133	$ 33
Receivables	1,382	1,269
Less estimated uncollectibles	(160)	(105)
	$ 1,222	$ 1,164
Due from restricted funds	225	--
Inventories	176	183
Prepaid expenses	68	73
Total current assets	$ 1,824	$ 1,453
Assets whose use is limited:		
Cash	$ 143	$ 40
Investments	1,427	$ 1,740
Property, plant, and equipment	11,028	10,375
Accumulated depreciation	(3,885)	(3,600)
Net property, plant, and equipment	$ 7,143	$ 6,775
Total	$10,537	$10,008

Liabilities and Fund Balances	Current Year	Prior Year
Current:		
Notes payable to banks	$ 237	$ 300
Current long-term debt	90	90
Accounts payable	450	463
Accrued expenses	150	147
Advances from third parties	300	200
Deferred revenue	10	10
Total current liabilities	$ 1,237	$ 1,210
Deferred revenue-- third-party reimbursement	200	90
Long-term debt:		
Housing bonds	500	520
Mortgage note	1,200	1,270
Total long-term debt	$ 1,700	$ 1,790
Fund balance	$ 7,400	$ 6,918
Total	$10,537	$10,008

Restricted Funds

Assets	Current Year	Prior Year
Specific purpose funds:		
Cash	$ 2	$ 1
Investments	200	70
Grants receivable	90	--
Total	$ 292	$ 71
Plant replacement and expansion funds:		
Cash	$ 10	$ 450
Investments	800	290
Pledges receivable, net of estimated uncollectibles	20	360
Total	$ 830	$ 1,100
Endowment funds:		
Cash	$ 50	$ 33
Investments	6,100	3,942
Total	$ 6,150	$ 3,975

Liabilities and Fund Balances	Current Year	Prior Year
Specific purpose funds:		
Due to general funds	$ 215	$ --
Fund balances:		
Research grants	15	30
Other	62	41
	77	71
Total	$ 292	$ 71
Plant replacement and expansion funds:		
Fund balances:		
Restricted by third-parties	$ 380	$ 150
Other	450	950
Total	$ 830	$ 1,100
Endowment funds:		
Fund balances:		
Permanent endowment	$ 4,850	$ 2,675
Term endowment	1,300	1,300
Total	$ 6,150	$ 3,975

Source: AICPA *Hospital Audit Guide*, pp. 40-43, as amended by SOP 85-1.

Sample Hospital
Statement of Changes in Fund Balances
Year Ended December 31, 19--
(with comparative figures for 19--)

	Current Year	Prior Year
Unrestricted Funds		
Balance at beginning of year	$6,918,000	$6,242,000
Excess of revenues over expenses	84,000	114,000
Transferred from plant replacement and expansion funds to finance property, plant, and equipment expenditures	628,000	762,000
Transferred to plant replacement and expansion funds to reflect third-party payor revenue restricted to property, plant, and equipment replacement	(230,000)	(200,000)
Balance at end of year	$7,400,000*	$6,918,000
Restricted Funds		
Specific purpose funds:		
Balance at beginning of year	$ 71,000	$ 50,000
Restricted gifts and bequests	35,000	20,000
Research grants	35,000	45,000
Income from investments	35,260	39,000
Gain on sale of investments	8,000	–
Transferred to:		
Other operating revenue	(100,000)	(80,000)
Allowances and uncollectible accounts	(8,000)	(3,000)
Balance at end of year	$ 76,260	$ 71,000
Plant replacement and expansion funds:		
Balance at beginning of year	$1,100,000	$1,494,000
Restricted gifts and bequests	113,000	150,000
Income from investments	15,000	18,000
Transferred to unrestricted funds (described above)	(628,000)	(762,000)
Transferred from unrestricted funds (described above)	230,000	200,000
Balance at end of year	$ 830,000	$1,100,000
Endowment funds:		
Balance at beginning of year	$3,975,000	$2,875,000
Restricted gifts and bequests	2,000,000	1,000,000
Net gain on sale of investments	175,000	100,000
Balance at end of year	$6,150,000	$3,975,000

---

*Composition of the balance may be shown here, on the balance sheet, or in a footnote.

Source: See previous page.

Sample Hospital
Statement of Revenues and Expenses
Year Ended December 31, 19--
(with comparative figures for 19--)

	Current year	Prior year
Patient service revenue:	$8,500,000	$8,000,000
Allowances and uncollectible accounts (after deduction of related gifts, grants, subsidies, and other income--$55,000 and $40,000)	(1,777,000)	(1,700,000)
Net patient service revenue	$6,723,000	$6,300,000
Other operating revenue (including $100,000 and $80,000 from specific purpose funds)	184,000	173,000
Total operating revenue	$6,907,000	$6,473,000
Operating expenses:		
Nursing services	$2,200,000	$2,000,000
Other professional services	1,900,000	1,700,000
General services	2,100,000	2,000,000
Fiscal services	375,000	360,000
Administrative services (including interest expense of $50,000 and $40,000)	400,000	375,000
Provision for depreciation	300,000	250,000
Total operating expenses	$7,275,000	$6,685,000
Loss from operations	$ (368,000)	$ (212,000)
Nonoperating revenue:		
Unrestricted gifts and bequests	$ 228,000	$ 205,000
Unrestricted income from endowment funds	170,000	80,000
Income and gains from board-designated funds	54,000	41,000
Total nonoperating revenue	$ 452,000	$ 326,000
Excess of revenues over expenses	$ 84,000	$ 114,000

Source: See previous page.

Illustrative Transactions. Entries in the General Funds generally parallel entries for business enterprises. Revenues and expenses are recorded on the full accrual basis. Fixed assets and long-term debt are recorded directly in the General Funds, and depreciation is recorded. Entries in the Restricted Funds record additions to and deductions from Fund Balance. Some entries that illustrate accounting for hospitals are presented below.

1. Unrestricted Revenues. Assume that $1,000,000 is received in cash from patients, an additional $1,000,000 is due from patients and third party payors, $100,000 is received from cafeteria sales, and $50,000 is received as an unrestricted gift.

> General Funds
>
> | | | |
> |---|---|---|
> | Cash | 1,150,000 | |
> | Accounts and Notes Receivable | 1,000,000 | |
> | Patient Service Revenues | | 2,000,000 |
> | Other Operating Revenues | | 100,000 |
> | Nonoperating Revenues | | 50,000 |

2. Revenue Deductions. Assume that the estimated provision for bad debts is $70,000, contractual adjustments are $80,000, and charity services $40,000.

General Funds

Provision for Bad Debts	70,000	
Contractual Adjustments	80,000	
Charity Services	40,000	
Allowance for Uncollectible Receivables		70,000
Accounts and Notes Receivable		120,000

The three debit accounts are revenue deductions, as Patient Service Revenue is to be recorded at the total amount that would be charged to full paying patients.

3. <u>Restricted Gifts and Grants</u>. Assume that a hospital received $90,000 to conduct cancer research. When the funds are received, the following entry would be made.

<u>Specific Purpose Funds</u>

Cash	90,000	
Fund Balance--Restricted Gifts and Bequests		90,000

Assume further that the funds are later expended for cancer research.

<u>Specific Purpose Funds</u>

Fund Balance--Transfer to General Funds	90,000	
Cash		90,000

<u>General Funds</u>

Cash	90,000	
Other Operating Revenues		90,000
Other Professional Services (Research)	90,000	
Cash		90,000

4. <u>Fixed Asset Transactions</u>. Assume that contributors gave $1,000,000 for a fund drive for a building addition. The funds would qualify as restricted gifts due to the intentions of the donor. Later, that amount plus $2,000,000 raised from the sale of bonds was used for the construction (on a turn-key basis) of a building addition.

<u>Plant Replacement and Expansion Funds</u>

Cash	1,000,000	
Fund Balance--Restricted Gifts and Bequests		1,000,000
Fund Balance--Transferred to General Funds	1,000,000	
Cash		1,000,000

<u>General Funds</u>

Cash	3,000,000	
Transfers from Restricted Funds for Capital Outlays		1,000,000
Bonds Payable		2,000,000
Buildings	3,000,000	
Cash		3,000,000

5. Endowment Fund Transactions. Assume that on the first day of a fiscal year,
    a wealthy patron gave $1,000,000 in corporate stocks to the hospital with the
    stipulation that half the proceeds be used for cancer research (restricted)
    and half be used in accordance with the wishes of the Board of Trustees.
    During the first year, $80,000 in dividends was received.

    Endowment Fund

Investment in Corporate Stocks	1,000,000	
Fund Balance--Income Restricted		500,000
Fund Balance--Income Unrestricted		500,000
Cash	80,000	
Due to Specific Purpose Funds		40,000
Due to General Funds		40,000

Assume further that the $80,000 was transferred during the same fiscal year.

    Endowment Fund

Due to Specific Purpose Funds	40,000	
Due to General Funds	40,000	
Cash		80,000

    Specific Purpose Fund

Cash	40,000	
Fund Balance--Income from Investments		40,000

    General Funds

Cash	40,000	
Nonoperating Revenues		40,000

When the research expense takes place, the accounting would be identical to
the $90,000 shown above in subsection "3."

An examination of these entries should indicate that all revenues, expenses, and other transactions of substance take place in the General Funds.
The three restricted funds are "holding" funds for monies restricted by
donors and grantors. As soon as those funds are expended, the transactions
are recorded in the General Funds.

C. Voluntary Health and Welfare Organizations

Voluntary health and welfare organizations perform voluntary services, e.g.,
Red Cross, Salvation Army, American Cancer Society, and local level counter-
parts. Their revenues are derived primarily from voluntary contributions from
the general public. The following financial reports are required.

(1) Statement of Support, Revenues and Expenses, and Changes in Fund
     Balances (see following pages for example)
(2) Statement of Functional Expenses
(3) Balance Sheet (see following pages for example)

The following funds are recommended for voluntary health and welfare
organizations.

(1) Current Unrestricted Funds account for all resources used in the opera-
     tions of the organization that are not restricted for special purposes
     by donors. Contributions, special events (net of direct costs),
     legacies and bequests, and net receipts from United Way and other
     campaigns are classified as Public Support. Membership dues, investment
     income, gains on sales of investments, and charges for services are
     classified as Revenues. Expenses are classified as program services and
     supporting services of the organization. Supporting services expenses
     are broken down further between management and general and fund raising.
(2) Current Restricted Funds account for resources available for specific
     current operations per donor or grantor specifications or restric-
     tions. Restricted income may also come from grants, income from endow-
     ment funds, or other sources.
(3) Land, Building, and Equipment Funds account for investment in fixed
     assets including unexpended resources contributed specifically for use
     of replacing land, building, and equipment. Additionally, land,
     building, and equipment and the related obligations are included in the
     fund. Depreciation should be recorded on fixed assets, and gains or
     losses on sale of fixed assets should be included as income in the plant
     fund accounts.
(4) Endowment Funds are accounted for as other endowment funds. However,
     these Endowment Funds include only amounts, the principal of which has
     been restricted by donors. There are no quasi-endowments or legally
     unrestricted amounts included in voluntary health and welfare Endowment
     Funds. Restricted income from Endowment Funds should be transferred to
     the Current Restricted Funds; unrestricted income from Endowment Funds
     should be transferred to the Current Unrestricted fund. If restrictions
     on endowment fund principal lapse, the resources released should be
     transferred to Unrestricted Funds.
(5) Custodian Funds are in effect agency funds which account for assets
     owned by others, i.e., not the property of the voluntary health or wel-
     fare organization.
(6) Loan and Annuity Funds are usually not significant to voluntary health
     and welfare organizations. If they are, they should be shown sepa-
     rately.

Voluntary Health and Welfare Service
Statement of Support, Revenue, and Expenses and Changes in Fund Balances
Year Ended December 31, 19X2
(with comparative totals for 19X1)

| | 19X2 | | | | Total all funds | |
| | Current funds | | Land, building and equip-ment fund | Endowment fund | 19X2 | 19X1 |
	Unrestricted	Restricted				
Public support and revenue:						
Public support:						
Contributions (net of estimated uncollectible pledges of $195,000 in 19X2 and $150,000 in 19X1)	$3,764,000	$162,000	$ —	$ 2,000	$3,928,000	$3,976,000
Contributions to building fund			72,000		72,000	150,000
Special events (net of direct costs of $181,000 in 19X2 and $163,000 in 19X1)	104,000	—	—	—	104,000	92,000
Legacies and bequests	92,000	—	—	4,000	96,000	129,000
Received from federated and nonfederated campaigns (which incurred related fund-raising expenses of $38,000 in 19X2 and $29,000 in 19X1)	275,000	—	—	—	275,000	308,000
Total public support	$4,235,000	$162,000	$ 72,000	$ 6,000	$4,475,000	$4,655,000
Revenue:						
Membership dues	17,000		—	—	17,000	12,000
Investment income	98,000	10,000	—	—	108,000	94,000
Realized gain on investment transactions	200,000	—	—	25,000	225,000	275,000
Miscellaneous	42,000	—	—	—	42,000	47,000
Total revenue	$ 357,000	$ 10,000	$ —	$ 25,000	$ 392,000	$ 428,000
Total support and revenue	$4,592,000	$172,000	$ 72,000	$ 31,000	$4,867,000	$5,083,000
Expenses:						
Program services:						
Research	1,257,000	155,000	2,000	—	$1,414,000	$1,365,000
Public health education	539,000	—	5,000	—	544,000	485,000
Professional education and training	612,000	—	6,000	—	618,000	516,000
Community services	568,000	—	10,000	—	578,000	486,000
Total program services	$2,976,000	$155,000	$ 23,000	—	$3,154,000	$2,852,000
Supporting services:						
Management and general	567,000	—	7,000	—	574,000	638,000
Fund raising	642,000	—	12,000	—	654,000	546,000
Total supporting services	$1,209,000	—	$ 19,000	—	$1,228,000	$1,184,000
Total expenses	$4,185,000	$155,000	$ 42,000	—	$4,382,000	$4,036,000
Excess (deficiency) of public support and revenue over expenses	407,000	17,000	30,000	31,000		
Other changes in fund balances:						
Property and equipment acquisitions from unrestricted funds	(17,000)		17,000	—		
Transfer of realized endowment fund appreciation	100,000		—	(100,000)		
Returned to donor		(8,000)		—		
Fund balances, beginning of year	5,361,000	123,000	649,000	2,017,000		
Fund balances, end of year	$5,851,000	$132,000	$696,000	$1,948,000		

Source: AICPA, *Audits of Voluntary Health and Welfare Organizations*, pp. 42–43.

VOLUNTARY HEALTH AND WELFARE SERVICE
BALANCE SHEETS
December 31, 19X2 and 19X1

CURRENT FUNDS
Unrestricted

Assets	19X2	19X1	Liabilities and Fund Balances	19X2	19X1
Cash	$2,207,000	$2,530,000	Accounts payable	$ 148,000	$ 139,000
Investments:			Research grants payable	596,000	616,000
For long-term purposes	2,727,000	2,245,000	Contributions for future periods	245,000	219,000
Other	1,075,000	950,000	Total liabilities	989,000	974,000
Pledges receivable	475,000	363,000	Fund balances designated for:		
Inventories of ed. materials	70,000	61,000	Long-term investments	2,800,000	2,300,000
Accrued interest and receivables	286,000	186,000	Purchases of new equipment	100,000	–
			Research purposes	1,152,000	1,748,000
			Available for general activities	1,799,000	1,313,000
			Total fund balance	5,851,000	5,361,000
Total	$6,840,000	$6,335,000	Total	$6,840,000	$6,335,000

Restricted

Assets	19X2	19X1	Liabilities and Fund Balances	19X2	19X1
Cash	$ 3,000	$ 5,000	Fund balances:		
Investments	71,000	72,000	Professional education	$ 84,000	$ –
Grants receivable	58,000	46,000	Research grants	48,000	123,000
Total	$ 132,000	$ 123,000	Total	$ 132,000	$ 123,000

LAND, BUILDING AND EQUIPMENT FUND

Assets	19X2	19X1	Liabilities and Fund Balances	19X2	19X1
Cash	$ 3,000	$ 2,000	Mortgage pay., 8% due 19XX	$ 32,000	$ 36,000
Investments	177,000	145,000	Fund balances:		
Pledges receivable	32,000	25,000	Expended	484,000	477,000
Land, buildings and equipment			Unexpended—restricted	212,000	172,000
less accumulated depreciation	516,000	513,000	Total fund balance	696,000	649,000
Total	$ 728,000	$ 685,000	Total	$ 728,000	$ 685,000

ENDOWMENT FUNDS

Assets	19X2	19X1	Liabilities and Fund Balances	19X2	19X1
Cash	$ 4,000	$ 10,000	Fund balance	$1,948,000	$2,017,000
Investments	1,944,000	2,007,000			
Total	$1,948,000	$2,017,000	Total	$1,948,000	$2,017,000

Source: See previous page.

A look at the financial statements should help point out some unique features of voluntary health and welfare organization accounting. First, note that the operating statement includes a "total" column. This total is required and highlights the fact that, unlike hospitals, these organizations may report support, revenues and expenses in all funds, except agency. Depreciation expense is normally reported in the Land, Building, and Equipment fund. Full accrual accounting is required. Like all other nonprofit organizations, assets must be restricted by donors or others external to the organization before being classified as "Restricted" on the financial statements.

In the Statement of Support, Revenue, and Expenses and Changes in Fund Balances, note that "Public Support" and "Revenue" are reported separately. "Public Support" includes contributions, special events, legacies and bequests, and indirect support. Contributions include cash, investments, donated materials, or donated services. Revenues include internally generated resources including dues, investment income, and charges for services. Also, note that expenses are classified as between "program" and "supporting," giving the potential contributor an idea of where his/her money would be expended.

"Other Changes in Fund Balances" include transfers and any other transactions that are not classified as public support, operating revenues, or expenses.

Illustrative Transactions. Unlike colleges and hospitals, voluntary health and welfare organizations may report revenues and expenses in any of their funds. Some illustrative entries that point out some of the unique features of these organizations follow.

1. Public Support and Revenues. Assume that a voluntary health and welfare organization reported the following: unrestricted cash donations, $50,000; unrestricted pledges, $40,000; restricted pledges, $30,000, of which one half is designated by the donor for future periods; unrestricted special events, $40,000 (less $15,000 costs); unrestricted membership dues, $10,000; restricted investment income, $5,000; and a realized gain on endowment investments of $2,000. All pledges are subject to a 2% uncollectible rate.

Unrestricted Current Funds

Cash	100,000	
Pledges Receivable	40,000	
Estimated Uncollectible Pledges Receivable		800
Public Support--Contributions		89,200
Public Support--Special Events		40,000
Revenues--Membership Dues		10,000
Cost of Special Events	15,000	
Cash		15,000

Restricted Current Funds

Cash	5,000	
Pledges Receivable	30,000	
Estimated Uncollectible Pledges Receivable		600
Public Support--Contributions		14,700
Support and Revenue Designated for Future Periods		14,700
Revenues--Investment Income		5,000

Endowment Funds

Cash	20,000	
Investments		18,000
Revenues--Realized Gain on Investments		2,000

2. Expenses. Expenses for voluntary health and welfare organizations may be
    reported in any of the funds, although Endowment Funds normally report
    transfers to other funds. Expenses are recorded both by object and by
    function, so that the Statement of Functional Expenses may be prepared.
    Assuming that a voluntary health and welfare organization had three
    programs, the expenses for a given period might be reported (by function) as
    follows.

    Unrestricted Current Funds

Public Health Education Expense	100,000	
Public Health Research Expense	110,000	
Community Services Expense	50,000	
Management and General Expense	30,000	
Fund Raising Expense	15,000	
Cash		300,000
Accounts Payable		5,000

    Restricted Current Funds

Public Health Education Expense	15,000	
Public Health Research Expense	20,000	
Community Services Expense	25,000	
Cash		60,000

    Assuming that $10,000 of the restricted expenses is from funds contributed
    in prior periods, the following entry would be required.

    Restricted Current Funds

Support and Revenue Designated for		
Future Periods	10,000	
Public Support--Contributions		10,000

3. Fixed Assets and Depreciation. Fixed assets and depreciation transactions
    are recorded in the Land, Building, and Equipment fund. The Fund Balance
    account in this fund is separated into two categories. The Fund Balance--
    Expended represents the net book value of the fixed assets not represented
    by indebtedness. The Fund Balance--Unexpended represents the assets
    available for future expenditure for plant.

    Assume that equipment is purchased for $100,000, of which $50,000 is
    paid from funds on hand (which were "offset" by a $50,000 credit balance in
    Fund Balance--Unexpended), and $50,000 is borrowed.

    Land, Building, and Equipment Fund

Equipment	100,000	
Mortgage Notes Payable		50,000
Cash		50,000
Fund Balance--Unexpended	50,000	
Fund Balance--Expended		50,000

    Assume that $10,000 was later paid to retire part of the mortgage note.

Land, Building, and Equipment Fund

Mortgage Note Payable	10,000	
Cash		10,000
Fund Balance--Unexpended	10,000	
Fund Balance--Expended		10,000

Assume finally that depreciation expense for this equipment amounted to $5,000.

Land, Building, and Equipment Fund

Depreciation Expense--Equipment	5,000	
Accumulated Depreciation--Equipment		5,000
Public Health Education Expense	1,000	
Public Health Research Expense	1,000	
Community Services Expense	2,000	
Management and General Expense	500	
Fund Raising Expense	500	
Depreciation Expense--Equipment		5,000
Fund Balance--Expended	5,000	
Fund Balance--Unexpended		5,000

At year end, public support, revenues, and expenses of the land, building, and equipment fund are closed out to the Fund Balance--Unexpended account. The first and second entries above illustrate how expenses can be charged to both objects of expenditure and functions.

D. **SOP 78-10 "Accounting Principles and Reporting Practices for Certain Nonprofit Organizations"**

The purpose of SOP 78-10 is to provide general accounting and reporting guidelines for all nonprofit entities other than those on which audit guides had previously been issued. The intent of this SOP is to state general principles for all nonprofit organizations rather than develop specialized techniques for each different type of nonprofit organization. Some examples of such nonprofit organizations are

Cemetery organizations
Civic organizations
Foundations
Fraternal organizations
Labor unions
Libraries
Museums
Other cultural institutions
Performing arts organizations
Political parties

Private elementary and secondary schools
Private and community foundations
Professional associations
Public broadcasting stations
Religious organizations
Research and scientific organizations
Social and country clubs
Trade associations
Zoological and botanical societies

Other organizations operating for the direct economic benefit of their member stockholders, e.g., mutual insurance companies, trusts, etc., are not covered by this SOP.

Financial statements required for these nonprofit organizations include

(1)   Balance Sheet
(2)   Statement of Activity (see example on next page)
(3)   Statement of Changes in Financial Position (the Statement of Cash Flows is not yet required for nonprofit organizations)

A great deal of flexibility is permitted in the fund structure and in the reporting format for these nonprofit organizations. Fund accounting is permitted but not required. If fund accounting is used, the reporting format may show all accounts separately for each fund (as is done for colleges, hospitals, etc.), or the fund balance alone may have separate balances. Some additional features of accounting for other nonprofit organizations include

(1)   Fund accounting may be used. If material restrictions exist and reporting is not on a fund basis, the restrictions should be disclosed.
(2)   Only assets restricted by outside donors or grantors should be classified as "Restricted." Restricted assets are offset by a liability, "Deferred Revenues," until expended, so that the revenue and expense are recognized in the same accounting period.
(3)   Fixed assets should be capitalized and depreciated. Exceptions include art collections, rare books, cathedrals, and similar items.
(4)   Investments may be carried at market. Increases and decreases in market value of investments are recorded as revenues and expenses.
(5)   Capital grants are shown separately after an "Excess from Current Endeavors" line in the operating statement. See the Statement of Activity.
(6)   Restricted capital additions should be treated as deferred capital support until used
(7)   Enforceable pledges should be valued at their estimated realizable value and recorded as support revenue
(8)   Donated materials and investments normally are recorded at FMV when received, unless the intent is to quickly pass the item through to a grantee
(9)   Donated services are generally not recorded unless the service would normally be purchased by the reporting or a similar organization
(10) Membership dues should be recognized by the organization over the period to which the dues relate. Nonrefundable initiation and life income fees are recognized in the period the fees are receivable, if not needed to cover anticipated expenses.

Illustrative Transactions. As mentioned earlier, a great deal of flexibility is permitted in the recording and reporting of transactions for other nonprofit organizations. A few transactions are illustrated below for a nonprofit organization that is choosing to report for the entire organization rather than by fund.

1. Revenue, Support, and Capital Additions. Assume that a nonprofit organization reported the following: dues received in cash, $30,000; unrestricted contributions received in cash, $50,000; snack bar sales, $15,000; contributions received for current capital additions, $10,000; contributions received for capital additions in the future, $60,000.

Cash	165,000	
Revenues--Membership Dues		30,000
Public Support--Contributions		50,000
Revenues--Snack Bar Sales		15,000
Capital Additions		10,000
Deferred Capital Support		60,000

The "Capital Additions" must be shown as a separate item after "Excess from Current Endeavors" on the Activity Statement. The "Deferred Capital Support" account is a liability.

Sample Performing Arts Organization
Statement of Activity
Years Ended June 30, 19X7, and 19X6

	19X7	19X6
Revenue and support from operations		
Admissions	$1,557,567	$1,287,564
Dividends and interest	21,555	2,430
Net realized gains and losses	54,700	18,300
Tuition	242,926	130,723
Concessions and other support	103,582	68,754
	$1,980,330	$1,507,771
Production costs	476,982	427,754
Operating expense	797,044	685,522
Ballet school	473,658	301,722
Neighborhood Productions	378,454	81,326
General and administrative expense	390,487	469,891
	$2,516,625	$1,966,215
Deficiency from operations	$ (536,295)	$ (458,444)
Donated services, materials, and facilities	$ --	$ 8,000
Annual giving	150,379	78,469
Grants	702,368	678,322
Fund-raising costs	(35,743)	(50,454)
	$ 817,004	$ 714,337
Excess from current endeavors	280,709	255,893
Capital additions	11,221	18,250
Total increase in entity capital	$ 291,930	$ 274,143

Source: AICPA, Statement of Position 78-10, *Accounting Principles and Reporting Practices for Certain Nonprofit Organizations.*

2.   <u>Investment Transactions</u>. Assume that a nonprofit organization received $20,000 in dividends for a given year, that investments were sold at a $15,000 loss, and that the remaining investments increased in market value by $10,000.

Cash	20,000	
Revenues--Investment Income		20,000
Cash	70,000	
Loss from Sale of Investments	15,000	
Investments		85,000
Investments	10,000	
Revenues--Unrealized Gain on Investments		10,000

Investments may be carried at market. If this is done, the unrealized gains and losses are reported in the same manner as realized gains and losses. Note that while gains and losses from the sale of investments are reported in the activity statement, gains are not normally available for unrestricted use unless specified by the donor.

E. OTHER NOT-FOR-PROFIT ENTITIES REVIEW CHECKLIST

	Colleges and Universities	Hospitals	Voluntary Health and Welfare Organizations	Other Non-profit Entities
Full Accrual Basis	Yes	Yes	Yes	Yes
Depreciation	*	Yes	Yes	Yes
Required Financial Statements	Balance Sheet; Statement of Current Funds Revenues, Expenditures, and Other Changes; Statement of Changes in Fund Balances	Balance Sheet; Statement of Revenues and Expenses; Statement of Changes in Fund Balances; Statement of Changes in Financial Position	Balance Sheet; Statement of Functional Expenses; Statement of Support, Revenues and Expenses, and Changes in Fund Balances	Balance Sheet; Statement of Activity; Statement of Changes in Financial Position
Fund Accounting	Yes	Yes	Yes	Optional (See Page 1211)
Types of Funds	Current, Restricted, Unrestricted; Loan; Endowment; Annuity; Life Income; Plant; Agency	General Funds; Restricted: Specific Purpose, Endowment, Plant Replacement and Expansion	Current: Unrestricted, Restricted; Land, Building, and Equipment; Endowment; Custodian; Loan and Annuity	(See Page 1211)

*Depreciation will be required for private colleges and universities for financial statements issued for fiscal years beginning after January 1, 1990. The GASB does not require public colleges and universities to record depreciation.

CHAPTER ELEVEN
TAXES

Introduction

Module 40/Individual Taxation (ITAX)

TAXES ON THE ACCOUNTING PRACTICE EXAMINATION

A minimum of 20% of the practice section of the examination (two of ten practice problems) tests federal income taxation. One problem will test individual taxation, while the other problem will test corporate and/or partnership taxation. Prior to May 1980, this was accomplished by a problem containing a series of multiple choice questions in one practice section, and a long computational tax problem in the other practice section. From May 1980 through November 1985, both tax problems consisted solely of multiple choice questions. However, on the May 1986 examination, one problem consisted of 20 multiple choice questions testing individual taxation, while the other problem required the use of a worksheet to convert a corporation's book income to taxable income. On the November 1986 and May 1987 examinations, one problem consisted of 20 multiple choice questions testing corporations, partnerships, and exempt organizations, while the other problem required the preparation of a detailed schedule to compute taxable income for individual taxpayers. On the May 1989 examination, one problem consisted of 20 multiple choice questions testing individual and estate taxation while the other problem required the detailed computation of a corporation's taxable income.

The multiple choice questions test detailed application of the Internal Revenue Code and tax regulations. The problem instructions indicate that "answers should be based on the Internal Revenue Code and Tax Regulations in effect for the tax period specified in the item. If no tax period is specified, use the current Internal Revenue Code and Tax Regulations." On recent examinations, approximately 60% of the multiple choice questions have specified the preceding taxable year, while the remaining 40% have no year specified. Although candidates are responsible for current tax law, it is important to note that the examiners generally avoid testing on recent tax law changes.

The AICPA Content Specification Outline of the coverage of taxes, including the authors' frequency analysis thereof (last nine exams), appears on the following pages. The frequency analysis should be used as an indication of the topics' relative importance on past Accounting Practice exams.

Immediately following the frequency analysis is a summary of accounting practice problems referenced to our study modules. The following symbols are used:

Q = Practice II Exam Problem

The summary tax outlines presented in this chapter begin by emphasizing individual taxation. Because of numerous common concepts, partnership and corporate taxation are later presented in terms of their differences from individual taxation (i.e., learn individual taxes thoroughly and then learn the special rules of partnership and corporate taxation). Interperiod and intraperiod tax allocation questions are presented in Module 27: Deferred Taxes.

The property transactions outline has been inserted between individual taxation and the partnership and corporate tax outlines because property transactions are common to all types of taxpayers, and generally are tested within every tax problem, both PTAX and CTAX, as well as ITAX.

The next section presents a detailed outline of the individual tax formula, and outlines of two basic federal income tax returns: Form 1065-Partnership; and Form 1120-Corporation. These outlines are an intermediary step between the simple formula outline (below) and the outlines of the detailed rules.

Formula Outline for Individuals

Gross income
    less "above the line" deductions
Adjusted gross income
    less total itemized deductions (or standard deduction)
    less exemptions
Taxable income
    times tax rates
    less tax credits
Tax liability

AICPA CONTENT SPECIFICATION OUTLINE/FREQUENCY ANALYSIS*
TAXES

	May 1985	Nov. 1985	May 1986	Nov. 1986	May 1987	Nov. 1987	May 1988	Nov. 1988	May 1989
I. Federal Taxation--Individuals, Estates, and Trusts									
A. Inclusions for Gross Income and Adjusted Gross Income									
1. Reporting Basis of Taxpayer--Cash, Accrual, or Modified	-	-	1	-	-	2	-	-	-
2. Compensation for Services	-	-	-	-	-	-	-	1	-
3. Business Income	1	-	1	-	-	-	-	1	-
4. Interest	1	1	-	-	-	-	1	1	-
5. Rents and Royalties	-	1	-	-	-	1	-	-	-
6. Dividends	1	1	-	-	-	1	1	1	1
7. Alimony	1	1	-	-	-	1	-	1	-
8. Capital Gains and Losses	2	2	2	-	-	-	-	1	1
9. Miscellaneous Income	-	1	-	-	-	1	2	2	-
B. Exclusions and Adjustments to Arrive at Adjusted Gross Income	3	-	5	-	-	3	4	3	2
C. Gain or Loss on Property Transactions									
1. Character	-	-	-	-	-	2	-	1	1
2. Recognition	1	3	1	-	-	-	2	-	1
3. Basis and Holding Period	3	1	3	-	-	2	-	-	1
D. Deductions from Adjusted Gross Income									
1. Interest**	1	1	-	-	-	-	-	-	-
2. Taxes**	1	1	-	-	-	-	-	1	1
3. Contributions**	-	1	1	-	-	-	1	-	-
4. Medical Expenses**	-	1	2	-	-	-	-	-	-
5. Casualty Losses**	-	1	-	-	-	-	-	1	1
6. Miscellaneous Deductions**	1	1	-	-	-	-	1	1	2
7. Other**	1	-	1	-	-	-	1	-	-
E. Filing Status and Exemptions	3	1	2	-	-	1	1	1	1
F. Tax Computations and Credits									
1. Tax Computations**	-	1	-	-	-	-	-	-	-
2. Tax Credits and Other Allowances**	-	-	1	-	-	-	2	-	2

*Except where noted, the line items in the outline are the AICPA's; the frequencies, tabulations, and actual percentages are the authors'.

**These line items in the outline have been added by the authors.

AICPA CONTENT SPECIFICATION OUTLINE/FREQUENCY ANALYSIS (CONTINUED)
TAXES

	May 1985	Nov. 1985	May 1986	Nov. 1986	May 1987	Nov. 1987	May 1988	Nov. 1988	May 1989
G. Statute of Limitations									
1. Claims for Refund	-	1	-	-	-	1	-	-	1
2. Assessments	-	-	-	-	-	1	-	-	1
H. Estate and Gift Taxation and Income Taxation of Estates and Trusts	-	-	-	-	-	4	4	4	4
Total MC Questions	20	20	20	-	-	20	20	20	20
Total Problems	-	-	-	1	1	-	-	-	-
Actual Percentage*** (AICPA 10%)	10	10	10	10	10	10	10	10	10

II. Federal Taxation--Corporations, Partnerships, and Exempt Organizations

Corporations

	May 1985	Nov. 1985	May 1986	Nov. 1986	May 1987	Nov. 1987	May 1988	Nov. 1988	May 1989
A. Determination of Taxable Income or Loss									[1]
1. Determination of Gross Income Including Capital Gains and Losses									
a. Sec. 1231 and Capital Gains and Losses**	1	2	-	1	2	1	1	-	-
b. Issuance of Stock (including treasury stock)**	1	-	-	-	-	1	1	1	-
2. Deductions from Gross Income									
a. Charitable Contributions**	-	2	-	2	-	1	1	2	-
b. Dividends Received**	1	1	-	1	1	1	1	1	-
c. Organization Expenditures**	1	-	-	-	-	1	-	-	-
d. Net Operating Loss**	-	-	-	-	-	-	-	-	-
e. Depreciation and Other**	3	1	-	2	3	1	2	1	-
3. Reconciliation of Taxable Income and Book Income	-	-	-	1 [1]	-	1	1	-	-
4. Reconciliation of Opening and Closing Retained Earnings	-	-	-	-	-	-	-	-	-
5. Consolidations	1	1	-	1	-	1	1	1	-

***The "actual percentage" is a measure of the relative coverage of the specific areas (i.e., I, II, etc.) on each Accounting Practice exam. This percentage includes both multiple choice questions and problems based on the point allocation used by the AICPA (i.e., multiple choice are assigned ½ point each and problems are 10 points each; note that the number of problems for each topic is shown in brackets right below the multiple choice questions for that topic).

AICPA CONTENT SPECIFICATION OUTLINE/FREQUENCY ANALYSIS (CONTINUED)
TAXES

	May 1985	Nov. 1985	May 1986	Nov. 1986	May 1987	Nov. 1987	May 1988	Nov. 1988	May 1989
B. Tax Computations and Credits									
1. Computations**	-	1	-	-	-	1	-	1	-
2. Credits**	-	1	-	1	1	-	1	-	-
C. S Corporations	1	3	-	2	1	1	1	1	-
D. Collapsible Corporations**	-	-	-	-	-	-	-	1	-
E. Personal Holding Companies	1	1	-	1	1	1	1	1	-
F. Accumulated Earnings Tax	1	1	-	1	1	1	1	1	-
G. Distributions	1	-	-	-	1	-	-	1	-
H. Tax-Free Incorporation	1	-	-	-	1	-	1	-	-
I. Reorganizations	1	-	-	1	1	1	-	1	-
J. Liquidations and Dissolutions	1	1	-	-	1	-	-	-	-
Partnerships									
K. Formation of Partnership									
1. Contribution of Capital	-	-	-	1	-	-	-	1	-
2. Contribution of Services	1	-	-	-	1	-	1	1	-
L. Basis of Partner's Interest									
1. Acquired through Contribution	1	-	-	-	1	-	1	1	-
2. Interest Acquired from Another Partner	-	-	-	-	-	-	-	-	-
3. Holding Period of Partner's Interest	-	-	-	-	-	-	-	-	-
4. Adjustments to Basis of Partner's Interest	1	-	-	-	-	-	-	-	-
M. Determination of Partnership Ordinary Income**	-	1	-	-	-	-	1	1	-
N. Determination of Partner's Taxable Income and Partner's Elections									
1. Partner's Distributive Share of Income**	-	1	-	-	-	-	-	-	-
2. Deductibility of Losses from Partnership**	-	-	-	-	-	-	-	-	-

AICPA CONTENT SPECIFICATION OUTLINE/FREQUENCY ANALYSIS (CONTINUED)
TAXES

	May 1985	Nov. 1985	May 1986	Nov. 1986	May 1987	Nov. 1987	May 1988	Nov. 1988	May 1989
O. Accounting Periods of Partnership and Partners	-	-	-	1	-	-	-	-	-
P. Partner Dealing with Own Partnership									
1. Sales and Exchanges	1	-	-	-	1	1	-	-	-
2. Guaranteed Payments	-	-	-	-	-	-	-	-	-
Q. Treatment of Liabilities	-	-	-	-	-	-	-	-	-
R. Distribution of Partnership Assets									
1. Current Distributions	-	-	-	-	-	1	-	-	-
2. Distributions in Complete Liquidation	1	1	-	-	-	-	-	-	-
3. Basis of Distributed Property	-	-	-	1	-	1	-	-	-
S. Termination of Partnership									
1. Change of Membership	-	1	-	-	-	-	-	-	-
2. Merger or Split-Up of Partnership	-	-	-	-	-	-	-	-	-
3. Sale or Exchange of Partnership Interest	-	-	-	-	-	1	1	-	-
4. Payments to a Retiring Partner	-	1	-	-	-	-	-	-	-
5. Payments to a Deceased Partner's Successor	-	-	-	-	-	-	-	-	-
Exempt Organizations									
T. Types of Organizations	-	-	-	1	2	1	1	1	-
U. Requirements for Exemption	-	-	-	1	1	1	1	1	-
V. Unrelated Business Income	-	-	-	1	-	1	1	1	-
Total MC Questions	20	20	-	20	20	20	20	20	-
Total Problems	-	-	1	-	-	-	-	-	1
Actual Percentage (AICPA 10%)	10	10	10	10	10	10	10	10	10

(Q) - Practice II Exam

TAXES
Problem Summary

Date	Mod 40 Individual Taxation	Mod 43 Corporate Taxation
5/89		Schedule of taxable income (Q)
11/88		
5/88		
11/87		
5/87	Schedules for (1) nonincludable receipts and expenditures (2) taxable income, and (3) projected tax liability or refund (Q)	
11/86	Schedules to compute (1) taxable income, and (2) tax liability	
5/86		Worksheet for taxable income (Q)
11/85		
5/85		

OVERVIEW OF FEDERAL TAX RETURNS

Problems requiring computation of taxable income require that you be familiar with the outlines below. The tax return outlines help you "pull together" all of the detailed tax rules. The schedule and form identification numbers are provided for reference only; they are not tested on the examination.

Review the outlines presented below. The outlines will introduce you to the topics tested on the exam and their relationship to final "tax liability."

Form 1040 - Individuals

A. **Income**

   1. Wages, salaries, tips, etc.
   2. Interest (Sch. B)
   3. Dividend income (Sch. B)
   4. Income other than wages, dividends, and interest (The gross income reported on the schedules below is already reduced by corresponding deductible expenses. Only the net income (or loss) is reported on Form 1040)

      a. State and local income tax refunds
      b. Alimony received
      c. Business income or loss (Sch. C)
      d. Capital gain or loss (Form 4797)
      e. Supplemental gains or losses (Form 4797)
      f. Fully taxable pensions and annuities
      g. Other pensions, annuities, rents, royalties (Sch. E)
      h. Unemployment compensation, social security
      i. Other

B. **Less "Above the Line" deductions** (also known as "Deductions for AGI")

   1. Reimbursed employee business expenses (Form 2106)
   2. Payments to an individual retirement arrangement (IRA)
   3. Self-employed health insurance deduction
   4. Payments to a Keogh retirement plan
   5. Forfeited interest penalty for premature withdrawals
   6. Alimony paid

C. **Adjusted Gross Income**

D. **Less Itemized Deductions** (Sch. A), (or standard deduction), including

   1. Medical and dental expenses
   2. Taxes
   3. Interest expense
   4. Contributions
   5. Casualty and theft losses
   6. Moving expenses
   7. Miscellaneous

      a. Subject to 2% of AGI limitation
      b. Not subject to 2% of AGI limitation

E. **Less Exemptions**

F. **Taxable Income**

   1. Find your tax in the tables, or
   2. Use tax rate schedules

G. Additional Taxes

1. Tax on accumulation distributions of trusts (Form 4970)
2. Lump-sum retirement plan distribution 5-year averaging

H. Less Tax Credits

1. General business credit

    a. Investment credit (Form 3468)
    b. Targeted jobs credit (Form 5884)
    c. Alcohol fuels credit
    d. Research credit
    e. Low-income housing credit

2. Credit for the elderly and the permanently disabled (Sch. R)
3. Credit for child care expenses (Form 2441)
4. Foreign tax credit (Form 1116)

I. Tax Liability

J. Other Taxes

1. Self-employment tax (Sch. SE)
2. Alternative minimum tax (Form 6251)
3. Investment credit recapture (Form 4255)
4. Social security tax on tip income (Form 4137)
5. Tax on individual retirement arrangements (Form 5329)

K. Less Payments

1. Tax withheld on wages
2. Estimated tax payments
3. Earned income credit
4. Amount paid with an extension
5. Excess FICA paid
6. Credit for federal tax on special fuels (Form 4136)
7. Credit from a regulated investment company (Form 2439)

L. Amount Overpaid or Balance Due

Form 1065 - Partnerships

A. Income

1. Gross sales less returns and allowances
2. Less cost of goods sold
3. Gross profit
4. Ordinary income from other partnerships and fiduciaries
5. Net farm profit
6. Ordinary gain or loss (including depreciation recapture)
7. Other

B. Less Deductions

1. Salaries and wages
2. Guaranteed payments to partners
3. Rents
4. Interest expense
5. Taxes
6. Bad debts
7. Repairs
8. Depreciation

9. Depletion
10. Retirement plans
11. Employee benefit program contributions
12. Other

C. **Ordinary Income (loss)** from trade or business activity

D. **Schedule K** (on partnership return) and Schedule K-1 to be prepared for each

partner

1. Ordinary income (loss) from trade or business activity
2. Income (loss) from rental real estate activity
3. Income (loss) from other rental activity
4. Portfolio income (loss)
    a. Interest
    b. Dividends
    c. Royalties
    d. Net short-term capital gain (loss)
    e. Net long-term capital gain (loss)
    f. Other portfolio income (loss)

5. Guarantee payments
6. Net gain (loss) under Sec. 1231 (other than casualty or theft)
7. Other
8. Charitable contributions
9. Sec. 179 expense deduction
10. Deductions related to portfolio income
11. Other
12. Credits
    a. Credit for income tax withheld
    b. Low-income housing credit
    c. Qualified rehabilitation expenditures related to rental real estate
    d. Credits related to rental real estate activities

13. Other

14a. Net earnings (loss) from self-employment
   b. Gross farming or fishing income
   c. Gross nonfarm income

15. Tax preference items

    a. Accelerated depreciation on property placed in service before 1/1/87
    b. Accelerated depreciation on leased personal property placed in service
       before 1/1/87
    c. Depreciation adjusted on property placed in service after 12/31/86

16. Investment interest expense
17. Foreign income taxes

Form 1120 - Corporations

A. Gross Income

1. Gross sales less returns and allowances
2. Less cost of goods sold
3. GROSS PROFIT
4. Dividends
5. Interest
6. Gross rents
7. Gross royalties
8. Net capital gains
9. Ordinary gain or loss
10. Other income

B. Less Deductions

1. Compensation of officers
2. Salaries and wages (net of jobs credit)
3. Repairs
4. Bad debts
5. Rents
6. Taxes
7. Interest
8. Charitable contributions
9. Depreciation
10. Depletion
11. Advertising
12. Pension, profit-sharing plan contributions
13. Employee benefit programs
14. Other
15. Net operating loss deduction
16. Dividends received deduction

C. TAXABLE INCOME times tax rates

D. Less tax credits equals TAX LIABILITY

I. GROSS INCOME ON INDIVIDUAL RETURNS

This section outlines (1) gross income in general, (2) exclusions from gross income, (3) items to be included in gross income, (4) tax accounting methods, and (5) items to be included in gross income net of deductions (e.g., business income, sales and exchanges).

A. **In General**

1. <u>Gross income</u> includes all income from whatever source derived, unless specifically excluded

    a. Includes all flow of wealth to the taxpayer
    b. Does not include a return of capital (e.g., if a taxpayer loans $6,000 to another and is repaid $6,500 at a later date, only the $500 difference is included in gross income)
    c. The income must be <u>realized</u>, i.e., there must be a transaction which gives rise to the income

        (1) Mere accretions in value of property are not income (e.g., value of one's home increases $2,000 during year. Only if the house is sold will the increase in value be realized)
        (2) A transaction may be in the form of

            (a) Actual receipt of cash or property
            (b) Accrual of a receivable
            (c) Sale or exchange

    d. The income must also be <u>recognized</u> (i.e., the transaction must be a taxable event, and not a transaction for which nonrecognition is provided in the Internal Revenue Code)
    e. An <u>assignment of income</u> will not be recognized for tax purposes

        (1) If income from property is assigned, it is still taxable to the owner of the property

            EXAMPLE: X owns a building and assigns the rents to Y. X remains taxable on the rents, even though the rents are received by Y

        (2) If income from services is assigned, it is still taxable to the person who earns it

            EXAMPLE: X earns $200 per week. To pay off a debt owed to Y, he assigns half of it to Y. $200 per week remains taxable to X

2. Distinction between exclusions, deductions, and credits

    a. <u>Exclusions</u>--income items which are not included in gross income

        (1) Exclusions must be specified by law. Remember, gross income includes all income except that specifically excluded.
        (2) Although exclusions are exempt from income tax, they may still be taxed under other tax rules (e.g., gifts may be subject to the gift tax)

    b. <u>Deductions</u>--amounts that are subtracted from income to arrive at adjusted gross income or taxable income

        (1)   Deductions for adjusted gross income (above the line deductions)--amounts deducted from gross income to arrive at adjusted gross income

        (2)   Itemized deductions (below the line deductions)--amounts deducted from adjusted gross income to arrive at taxable income

   c. <u>Credits</u>--amounts subtracted from the computed tax to arrive at taxes payable

B. **Exclusions from Gross Income** (not reported)

   1. Payments received for <u>support</u> of minor children

      a. Must be children of the parent making the payments

      b. Decree of divorce or separate maintenance must specify the amount to be treated as child support, otherwise payments are generally treated as alimony

   2. <u>Property settlement</u> (division of capital) received in a divorce

   3. <u>Annuities</u> and pensions are excluded to the extent they are a return of capital

      a. Excluded portion of each payment is

$$\frac{\text{Net Cost of Annuity}}{\text{Expected Total Annuity Payments}} \quad x \quad \text{Payment Received}$$

      b. "Expected total annuity payments" is calculated by multiplying the annual return by

         (1)   The number of years receivable if an annuity for a definite period

         (2)   A life expectancy multiple (from IRS tables) if an annuity for life

      c. Once this exclusion ratio is determined, it remains constant until the cost of the annuity is completely recovered. Any additional payments will be fully taxable

        EXAMPLE: Mr. Jones purchased an annuity contract for $3,600 that will pay him $1,500 per year beginning in 1989. His expected return under the contract is $10,800. Mr. Jones' exclusion ratio is $3,600 ÷ $10,800 = 1/3. For 1989 Mr. Jones will exclude $1,500 x 1/3 = $500; and will include the remaining $1,000 in gross income.

      d. If taxpayer dies before total cost is recovered, unrecovered cost is allowed as a deduction on taxpayer's final tax return

      e. Dividends received before the annuity starting date are included in income to the extent of the increase in the cash value of the contract (for contracts issued after 8/13/82)

   4. <u>Life insurance proceeds</u> (face amount of policy) are generally excluded if paid by reason of death

      a. If beneficiary elects to receive the benefits in <u>installments</u>, use annuity exclusion ratio using the face amount of policy as cost (i.e., only the interest will be included in income)

      b. Life insurance dividends on unmatured policies are excluded as long as the dividends do not exceed the premiums paid

   5. Certain <u>employee benefits</u> are excluded

      a. Payment of <u>death benefits</u> by employer to employee's beneficiary

        (1)   Exclusion not applicable to amounts to which employee had a non-forfeitable right before death
        (2)   Limited to $5,000 per employee (not per beneficiary)
        (3)   If more than one employer, limit is $5,000 total and must be allocated pro rata to all beneficiaries

    b.   <u>Group-term life insurance</u> premiums paid by employer (up to $50,000 of insurance coverage). Exclusion not limited if beneficiary is the employer or a qualified charity
    c.   Premiums employer pays to fund an accident or health plan for employees are excluded
    d.   <u>Accident and health benefits</u> provided by employer are excluded if benefits are for

        (1)   Permanent injury or loss of bodily function
        (2)   Reimbursement for medical care of employee, his spouse, or dependents

            (a)   Employee cannot take itemized deduction for reimbursed medical expenses
            (b)   Exclusion may not apply to highly compensated individuals if reimbursed under a discriminatory self-insured medical plan

    e.   <u>Meals or lodging</u> furnished for the convenience of the employer on the employer's premises are excluded

        (1)   For the convenience of the employer means there must be a noncompensatory reason such as the employee is required to be on duty during this period
        (2)   In the case of lodging, it also must be a condition of employment

    f.   Employer contributions to, and benefits derived from a <u>group legal services plan</u> are excluded through 1988. However, the exclusion value of any insurance-type protection against legal expenses for any individual in a taxable year is limited to $70.
    g.   Benefits for payment of tuition, fees, etc., derived from an employer's qualified <u>educational assistance program</u>, are excluded through 1988; annual limit is $5,250 per person. The exclusion does not apply to any payment of benefits with respect to any graduate level courses of a kind normally taken by an individual pursuing an advanced academic or professional degree.
    h.   Employer payments to an employee for <u>dependent care assistance</u> are excluded from an employee's income if made under a written, nondiscriminatory plan. Maximum exclusion is $5,000 per year ($2,500 for a married person filing a separate return)
    i.   <u>Employee fringe benefits</u> are generally excluded if--

        (1)   <u>No additional-cost services</u>--e.g., airline pass
        (2)   <u>Employee discount</u> that is nondiscriminatory
        (3)   <u>Working condition fringes</u>--excluded to the extent that if the amount had been paid by the employee, the amount would be deductible as an employee business expense
        (4)   <u>De minimis fringes</u>--small value, impracticable to account for (e.g., coffee, personal use of copying machine)

    j.   Workers' compensation is excluded

6. Accident and health insurance benefits derived from policies <u>purchased by the taxpayer</u> are excluded; but not excluded if the medical expenses were deducted in a prior year and the tax benefit rule applies

7. Compensation for <u>damages</u> resulting from personal injury
   a. Damages for slander of personal or business reputation are generally excluded from income
   b. Damages for personal injury that compensate the taxpayer for lost earnings are generally excluded. If there was no personal injury, damages that compensate for lost earnings are generally included in income
   c. Damages for loss of property are excluded, except to the extent they exceed the basis of the property destroyed
   d. Punitive damages are not excluded (e.g., treble damages in antitrust recovery)

8. <u>Gifts, bequests, devises, or inheritances</u> are excluded
   a. Income from property so acquired is not excluded (e.g., interest or rent)
   b. "Gifts" from employer except for death benefits and holiday presents are generally not excluded

9. The receipt of <u>stock dividends</u> (or stock rights) is generally excluded from income (see page 1286 for basis and holding period); but, the FMV of the stock received will be included in income if the distribution
   a. Is on preferred stock
   b. Is payable, at the election of any shareholder, in stock or property
   c. Results in the receipt of preferred stock by some common shareholders, and the receipt of common stock by other common shareholders
   d. Results in the receipt of property by some shareholders, and an increase in the proportionate interests of other shareholders in earnings or assets of the corporation

10. Certain <u>interest income</u> is excluded
    a. Interest on obligations of a state or one of its political subdivisions (e.g., municipal bonds), the District of Columbia, and U.S. possessions is generally excluded from income if the bond proceeds are used to finance traditional governmental operations
    b. Other state and local government-issued obligations (private activity bonds) are generally fully taxable. An obligation is a private activity bond if (1) more than 10% of the bond proceeds are used (directly or indirectly) in a private trade or business and more than 10% of the principal or interest on the bonds is derived from, or secured by, money or property used in the trade or business, or (2) the lesser of 5% or $5 million of the bond proceeds is used (directly or indirectly) to make or finance loans to private persons or entities
    c. The following bonds are excluded from the private activity bond category even though their proceeds are not used in traditional government operations. The interest from these bonds is excluded from income:
       (1) Qualified bonds issued for the benefit of schools, hospitals, and other charitable organizations
       (2) Bonds used to finance certain exempt facilities, such as airports, docks, wharves, mass commuting facilities, etc.

    (3) Qualified redevelopment bonds, small-issue bonds (i.e., bonds not exceeding $1 million), and student loan bonds
    (4) Qualified mortgage and veterans' mortgage bonds

  d. Interest on U.S. obligations is included in income

11. Savings bonds for higher education

  a. After 1989, the accrued interest on Series EE U.S. savings bonds that are redeemed by the taxpayer is excluded from gross income to the extent that the aggregate redemption proceeds (principal plus interest) are used to finance the higher education of the taxpayer, taxpayer's spouse, or dependents.

    (1) The bonds must be issued after December 31, 1989 to an individual age 24 or older at date of issuance.
    (2) The exclusion is available only to the original purchaser of the bond or purchaser's spouse.
    (3) The redemption proceeds must be used to pay qualified higher education expenses (i.e., tuition and required fees less scholarships, fellowships, and employer-provided educational assistance) at an accredited university, college, junior college, or other institution providing post-secondary education, or at an are a vocational education school.
    (4) If the redemption proceeds exceed the qualified higher education expenses, only a pro rata amount of interest can be excluded.

    EXAMPLE: During the year, a married taxpayer redeems Series EE bonds receiving $6,000 of principal and $4,000 of accrued interest. Assuming qualified higher education expenses total $9,000, accrued interest of $3,600 ($9,000/$10,000 x $4,000) can be excluded from gross income.

  b. If the taxpayer's modified AGI exceeds a specified level, the exclusion is subject to phase-out as follows:

Filing Status	AGI Phase-out Range
Married filing jointly	$60,000 - $90,000
Single (including head of household)	$40,000 - $55,000

    (1) The reduction of the exclusion is computed as:

$$\left(\frac{\text{Excess AGI}}{\begin{array}{c}\$15,000\\(\$30,000 \text{ for joint returns})\end{array}}\right) \times \left(\begin{array}{c}\text{Otherwise}\\\text{excludable}\\\text{interest}\end{array}\right) = \text{Reduction}$$

    (2) Married taxpayers must file a joint return to qualify for the exclusion
    (3) If the taxpayer's modified AGI exceeds the applicable $90,000 or $55,000 level, no exclusion is available

    EXAMPLE: Assume the joint return of the married taxpayer in the above Example has modified AGI of $70,000. The reduction would be $1,200 ($10,000/$30,000 x $3,600). Thus, of the $4,000 of interest received, a total of $2,400 could be excluded from gross income

12. Scholarships and fellowships

    a. A degree candidate can exclude the amount of a scholarship or fellowship that is used for tuition and course-related fees, books, supplies and equipment. Amounts used for other purposes including room and board are included in income

    b. Amounts received as a grant or a tuition reduction that represent payment for teaching, research, or other services are not excludable

    c. Nondegree students may not exclude any part of a scholarship or fellowship grant

13. Political contributions received by candidates' campaign funds are excluded from income, but included if put to personal use

14. Rental value of parsonage or cash rental allowance for a parsonage is excluded by a minister

15. Discharge of indebtedness normally results in income to debtor, but may be excluded if

    a. A discharge of certain student loans pursuant to a loan provision providing for discharge if the individual works in a certain profession for a specified period of time

    b. A discharge of a corporation's debt by a shareholder (treated as a contribution to capital)

    c. The discharge is a gift

    d. The discharge is qualified indebtedness of a solvent farmer

    e. The discharge is a purchase money debt reduction (treat as a reduction of purchase price)

    f. Debt is discharged in bankruptcy proceeding, or debtor is insolvent both before and after discharge

        (1) If debtor is insolvent before but solvent after discharge of debt, income is recognized to the extent that the FMV of assets exceeds liabilities after discharge

        (2) The amount excluded from income in "d." above must be applied to reduce tax attributes in the following order

            (a) NOL for taxable year and loss carryovers to taxable year

            (b) General business credit

            (c) Capital loss of taxable year and carryovers to taxable year

            (d) Reduction of the basis of property

            (e) Foreign tax credit carryovers to or from taxable year

        (3) Instead of reducing tax attributes in the above order, taxpayer may elect to first reduce the basis of depreciable property

16. Lease Improvements. Increase in value of property due to improvements made by lessee are excluded from lessor's income unless improvements are made in lieu of rent

C. Items to be Included in Gross Income

    Gross income includes all income from any source except those specifically excluded. The more common items of gross income are listed below. Those items requiring a detailed explanation are discussed in the following pages.

1. Compensation for services, including wages, salaries, bonuses, commissions, fees and tips

    a. Property received as compensation is included in income at FMV
    b. Bargain purchases by an employee from an employer are included in income at FMV less price paid
    c. Life insurance premiums paid by employer must be included in an employee's gross income except for group-term life insurance coverage of $50,000 or less
    d. Employee expenses paid or reimbursed by the employer unless the employee has to account to the employer for these expenses and they would qualify as deductible business expenses for employee
    e. Tips must be included in gross income

        (1) If an individual receives less than $20 in tips while working for one employer during one month, the tips do not have to be reported to the employer and the tips must be included in the individual's gross income when received
        (2) If an individual receives $20 or more in tips while working for one employer during one month, the individual must report the total amount of tips to the employer by the 10th day of the following month for purposes of withholding of income tax and social security tax. Then the total amount of tips must be included in the individual's gross income for the month in which reported to the employer.

2. Gross income derived from business or profession

3. Distributive share of partnership or S corporation income

4. Gain from the sale or exchange of real estate, securities, or other property

5. Rents and royalties

6. Dividends

7. Interest including

    a. Earnings from savings and loan associations, mutual savings banks, credit unions, etc.
    b. Interest on bank deposits, corporate or U.S. government bonds and treasury bills (note that interest from U.S. obligations is included, while interest on state and local obligations is generally excluded)
    c. Interest on tax refunds
    d. Imputed interest from interest-free and low-interest loans

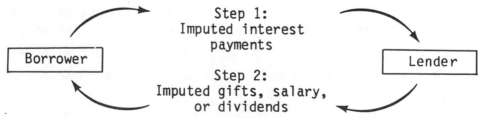

        (1) Borrower is treated as making imputed interest payments (subject to the same deduction restrictions as actual interest payments) which the lender reports as interest income
        (2) Lender is treated as making gifts (for personal loans) or paying salary or dividends (for business-related loans) to the borrower

(3) Rate used to impute interest is tied to average yield on certain federal securities; if federal rate greater than the interest rate charged on a loan (i.e., a low-interest loan) imputed interest only for the excess

(a) For demand loans, the deemed transfers are generally treated as occurring at the end of each year, and will fluctuate with interest rates

(b) For term loans, the interest payments are determined at the date of the loan and then allocated over the term of the loan; lender's payments are treated as made on date of loan

(4) No interest is imputed to either the borrower or the lender for any day on which the aggregate amount of loans between such individuals (and their spouses) does not exceed $10,000

(5) For any day that the aggregate amount of loans between borrower and lender (and their spouses) does not exceed $100,000, imputed interest is limited to borrower's "net investment income;" no imputed interest if borrower's net investment income does not exceed $1,000

EXAMPLE: Parents make a $200,000 interest-free demand loan to their unmarried daughter on January 1, 1989. Assume the average federal short-term rate is 7% for 1989. If the loan is outstanding for the entire year, under Step 1, the daughter is treated as making a $14,000 ($200,000 x 7%) interest payment on 12/31/89 which is included as interest income on the parents' 1989 tax return. Under Step 2, the parents are treated as making a $14,000 gift to their daughter on 12/31/89. (Note that the gift will be offset by annual exclusions totaling $20,000 for gift tax purposes as discussed on page 1350.)

8. Alimony and separate maintenance payments

a. Alimony is included in the recipient's gross income and is deductible toward AGI by the payor. In order for a payment to be considered as alimony, the payment must

(1) Be made in <u>cash</u> and received by or on behalf of the payee spouse
(2) Be made under a decree of divorce or written separation instrument
(3) Not be made to a member of the same household at the time the payments are made
(4) Not be characterized in the decree or written instrument as other than alimony
(5) Not be made to a person with whom the taxpayer is filing a joint return
(6) Terminate upon the death of the recipient

b. If the alimony payments in the first calendar year that payments are made exceed the average payments in the second and third years by more than $15,000, the excess amounts are recaptured in the third year by requiring the payor to include the excess in income and allowing the payee a deduction in computing AGI. A similar rule applies to the extent the payments in the second year exceed the payments in the third year by more than $15,000

(1) When computing the amount of recapture for the first year, any amount recaptured with respect to the second year is treated as a reduction in the alimony paid for the second year
(2) Recapture will not apply to any year in which payments terminate as a result of the death of either spouse or the remarriage of the payee

(3) Recapture does not apply to payments that may fluctuate over 3 years or more and are not within the control of the payor spouse (e.g., 20% of the net income from a business)

EXAMPLE: If a payor makes alimony payments of $50,000 in 1987 and no payments in 1988 or 1989, $50,000 - $15,000 = $35,000 will be recaptured in 1989 (assuming none of the exceptions apply).

EXAMPLE: If a payor makes alimony payments of $50,000 in 1987, $20,000 in 1988, and nothing in 1989, the recapture amount for 1988 is $20,000 - $15,000 = $5,000. The recapture amount for 1987 is $50,000 - ($15,000 + $7,500) = $27,500. The $7,500 is the average payments for 1988 and 1989 after reducing the $20,000 1988 payment by the $5,000 of recapture for 1988. The recapture amounts for 1987 and 1988 total $32,500 and are reported in 1989.

c. Any amounts specified as "child support" are not treated as alimony

(1) Child support is not gross income to the payee, and is not deductible by the payor
(2) If the decree or instrument specifies both alimony and child support, but less is paid than required, then amounts are first allocated to child support, with any remainder allocated to alimony
(3) If a specified amount of alimony is to be reduced upon the happening of some contingency relating to a child, then an amount equal to the specified reduction will be treated as child support rather than alimony

EXAMPLE: A divorce decree provides that payments of $1,000 per month will be reduced by $400 per month when a child reaches age 21. Here, $400 of each $1,000 monthly payment will be treated as child support.

9. Social security, pensions, annuities (other than excluded recovery of capital)

a. A portion of social security retirement benefits may be included in gross income if the recipient's AGI (plus tax-exempt interest) plus 50% of the benefits

(1) Exceeds a base amount of

(a) $32,000 for married individuals filing a joint return
(b) Zero for a married individual filing a separate return
(c) $25,000 for all other individuals

(2) Amount included in gross income is lesser of

(a) One-half of social security benefits, or
(b) One-half of the excess of the taxpayer's combined income (i.e., modified AGI plus 50% of benefits) over the base amount

b. An individual may make a one-time election to use 5-year forward averaging with respect to a single lump-sum distribution from an employer's qualified retirement plan received on or after age 59 1/2

10. Income in respect of a decedent and from an interest in an estate or trust. Income in respect of a decedent is income which would have been income of the decedent before death but was not includible in income under the decedent's method of accounting (e.g., installment payments that are paid to

estate after his death). Such income has the same character as it would have had if the decedent had lived and must be included in gross income by the person who receives it.

11. Employer supplemental unemployment benefits or strike benefits from union funds

12. Fees, including those received by an executor, administrator, director, or for jury duty or precinct election board duty

13. Income from discharge of indebtedness unless specifically excluded (see page 1233)

14. Stock Options

    a. An incentive stock option receives favorable tax treatment

        (1) The option must meet certain technical requirements to qualify

        (2) No income is recognized by employee when option is granted or exercised

        (3) If employee holds the stock acquired through exercise of the option at least 2 years from the date the option was granted, and holds the stock itself at least 1 year, the

            (a) Employee's realized gain will be long-term capital gain

            (b) Employer receives no deduction

        (4) If the holding period requirements above are not met, the employee has ordinary income to the extent that the FMV at date of exercise exceeds the option price

            (a) Remainder of gain is short-term or long-term capital gain

            (b) Employer receives a deduction equal to the amount employee reports as ordinary income

        (5) An incentive stock option may be treated as a nonqualified stock option if a corporation so elects at the time the option is issued

    b. A nonqualified stock option is included in income when received if option has a determinable FMV

        (1) If option has no ascertainable FMV when received, then income arises when option is exercised; to the extent of the difference between the FMV when exercised and the option price

        (2) Amount recognized (at receipt or when exercised) is treated as ordinary income to employee; employer is allowed a deduction equal to amount included in employee's income

    c. An employee stock purchase plan which does not discriminate against rank and file employees

        (1) No income when employee receives or exercises option

        (2) If the employee holds the stock at least 2 years after the option is granted and at least 1 year after exercise, then

            (a) Employee has ordinary income to the extent of the lesser of

                1] FMV at time option granted over option price, or

                2] FMV at disposition over option price

            (b) Capital gain to the extent realized gain exceeds ordinary income

        (3)   If the stock is not held for the required time, then

            (a)   Employee has ordinary income at the time of sale for the difference between FMV when exercised and the option price. This amount also increases basis

            (b)   Capital gain or loss for the difference between selling price and increased basis

15.   <u>Prizes and awards</u> are generally taxable

    a.   Prizes and awards received for religious, charitable, scientific, educational, artistic, literary, or civic achievement can be excluded only if the recipient

        (1)   Was selected without any action on his/her part
        (2)   Is not required to render substantial future services, and
        (3)   Designates that the prize or award is to be transferred by the payor to a governmental unit or a tax-exempt charitable, educational, or religious organization
        (4)   The prize or award is excluded from the recipient's income, but no charitable deduction is allowed for the transferred amount

    b.   Employee achievement awards are excluded from an employee's income if the cost to the employer of the award does not exceed the amount allowable as a deduction (generally from $400 to $1,600, see page 1245)

        (1)   The award must be for length of service or safety achievement, and must be in the form of tangible personal property (cash does not qualify)
        (2)   If the cost of the award exceeds the amount allowable as a deduction to the employer, the employee must include in gross income the greater of:

            (a)   The portion of cost not allowable as a deduction to the employer, or
            (b)   The excess of the award's FMV over the amount allowable as a deduction

16.   <u>Tax benefit rule</u>. A recovery of an item deducted in an earlier year must be included in gross income to the extent that a tax benefit was derived from the prior deduction of the recovered item

    a.   A tax benefit was derived if the previous deduction reduced the taxpayer's income tax
    b.   A recovery is excluded from gross income to the extent that the previous deduction did not reduce the taxpayer's income tax

        (1)   A deduction would not reduce a taxpayer's income tax if the taxpayer was subject to the alternative minimum tax and the deduction does not reduce AMT
        (2)   A recovery of state income taxes, medical expenses, or other items deductible on Schedule A (Form 1040) will be excluded from gross income if an individual did not itemize deductions for the year the item was paid

            EXAMPLE: Individual X, a single taxpayer, did not itemize deductions but instead used the standard deduction of $3,000 for 1988.   In 1989 a refund of $300 of 1988 state income taxes is received.   X would exclude the $300 refund from income in 1989.

> *EXAMPLE: Individual Y, a single taxpayer, had total itemized deductions of $3,200 for 1988, including $500 of state income taxes. In 1989 a refund of $300 of 1988 state income taxes is received. Y must include $200 ($3,200 - $3,000) of the refund in income for 1989.*

17. Embezzled or other illegal income

18. Gambling winnings

19. <u>Unemployment compensation</u> is fully included in gross income by the recipient

D. Tax Accounting Methods

Tax accounting methods often affect the period in which an item of income or deduction is recognized. Note that the classification of an item is not changed, only the time for its inclusion in the tax computation

1. Cash method or accrual method is commonly used

   a. <u>Cash method</u> recognizes income when first received or constructively received; expenses when paid out

      (1) Constructive receipt means that an item is unqualifiedly available without restriction (e.g., interest on bank deposit is income when credited to account)

      (2) Not all receipts are income

         (a) Loan proceeds
         (b) Recovery of capital

      (3) Not all payments are deductible

         (a) Loan repayment
         (b) Expenditures benefiting future years (fixed assets and prepaid expenses) must generally be capitalized and deducted over their useful lives as under accrual accounting

   b. The cash method of accounting cannot generally be used by C corporations, partnerships that have a C corporation as a partner, tax shelters, and certain tax-exempt trusts. However, the following may continue to use the cash method:

      (1) An individual (including a sole proprietorship business)
      (2) S corporations
      (3) A qualifying partnership (i.e., a partnership that does not have a C corporation as a partner)
      (4) A qualified personal service corporation if substantially all its activities consist of the performance of services in the field of health, law, engineering, architecture, accounting, actuarial science, performing arts or consulting, and at least 95% of the value of its stock is owned by specified shareholders including present or retired employees of the corporation or their estates
      (5) A small business if for every year after 1985 it does not have more than $5 million in average annual gross receipts for any prior three-year period, and provided it does not have inventories for sale to customers

   c. <u>Accrual method</u> recognizes income when the "right to receive payment" has occurred; expenses when the "obligation to pay" has occurred

        (1) Accrual method must be used for purchases and sales when inventories are required to clearly reflect income

        (2) Accrual method differs somewhat from that used in financial accounting

2. <u>Special rules</u> regarding methods of accounting

    a. Rents and royalties received in advance are included in gross income in the year received under both the cash and accrual methods

        (1) A security deposit is included in income when not returned to tenant

        (2) An amount called a "security deposit" that is to be used as final payment of rent is considered to be advance rent and included in income when received

    EXAMPLE: In 1989, a landlord signs a 5-year lease. During 1989, the landlord receives $5,000 for that year's rent, and $5,000 as advance rent for the last year (1993) of the lease. All $10,000 will be included in income for 1989.

    b. Dividends are included in gross income in the year received under both the cash and accrual methods

    c. No advance deduction is generally allowed accrual method taxpayers for estimated or contingent expenses; the obligation must be "fixed and determinable"

3. The <u>installment method</u> of reporting income applies to dispositions of property where at least one payment is to be received after the year in which the disposition occurs

    a. The installment method is required, unless taxpayer makes a negative election to report the full amount of gain in year of sale

    b. The amount to be reported in each year is determined by the formula

$$\frac{\text{Gross Profit of Entire Sale}}{\text{Total Contract Price}} \times \text{Amount Received in Year}$$

        (1) <u>Contract price</u> is the selling price reduced by the amount of any indebtedness which is assumed or taken subject to by the buyer, to the extent not in excess of the seller's basis in the property

    EXAMPLE: Taxpayer sells property with a basis of $80,000 to buyer for a selling price of $150,000. As part of the purchase price, buyer agrees to assume a $50,000 mortgage on the property and pay the remaining $100,000 in 10 equal annual installments together with adequate interest.

    The contract price is $100,000 ($150,000 - $50,000); the gross profit is $70,000 ($150,000 - $80,000); and the gross profit ratio is 70% ($70,000 ÷ $100,000). Thus, $7,000 of each $10,000 payment is reported as gain from the sale.

    EXAMPLE: Assume the same facts as above except that the seller's basis is $30,000.

    The contract price is $120,000 ($150,000 - mortgage assumed but only to extent of seller's basis of $30,000); the gross profit is $120,000 ($150,000 - $30,000); and the gross profit ratio is 100% ($120,000 ÷ $120,000). Thus, 100% of each $10,000 payment is reported as gain from the sale. In addition, the amount by which

*the assumed mortgage exceeds the seller's basis ($20,000) is deemed
to be a payment in year of sale.   Since the gross profit ratio is
100%, all $20,000 is reported as gain in the year the mortgage is
assumed.*

(2) Use of the installment method does not change the character of the
income to be reported (e.g., ordinary income, capital gain, etc.)

(3) Any depreciation recapture under Secs. 1245, 1250, and 291 must be
included in income in the year of sale

(a) Amount of recapture included in income is treated as an
increase in the basis of the property for purposes of
determining the gross profit ratio

(b) Remainder of gain, if any, is spread over installment payments

(4) If depreciable property is sold between a person and a more than
50% owned corporation or partnership, the purchaser may not
increase the property's basis for any amount until the seller has
included such amount in income

(5) If installment obligations are pledged as security for a loan, the
net proceeds of the loan are treated as payments received on the
installment obligations

(6) The installment method can not be used for revolving credit plan
sales (e.g., department store credit card sales) and for sales of
certain publicly traded property (e.g., stock or securities traded
on an established securities market)

(7) The installment method can not be used by _dealers_ in personal and
real property (other than farm property, timeshares, and
residential lots) for installment sales after 1987

(8) Installment obligations arising from nondealer sales of property
used in the taxpayer's trade or business or held for the production
of rental income (e.g., factory building, warehouse, office
building, apartment building) are subject to an interest charge on
the tax that is deferred on such sales to the extent that the
amount of deferred payments arising from all dispositions of such
property during a taxable year and outstanding as of the close of
the taxable year exceeds $5,000,000. This provision does not apply
to installment sales of property if the sales price does not exceed
$150,000, to sales of personal-use property, and to sales of farm
property

4. Special methods are allowable for contracts that are not completed within
the year they are started

a. Percentage-of-completion method recognizes income each year based on the
percentage of the contract completed that year

b. Completed-contract method recognizes income only when the contract is
completed and accepted. To qualify for this method, the contract must
be

(1) For the construction or improvement of real property expected to be
completed within two years and the contractor's average annual
gross receipts cannot exceed $10 million for the three taxable
years prior to the year the contract is entered into, or

(2) A home construction contract (i.e., 80% of the costs are for
buildings with four or fewer dwelling units)

c. Percentage-of-completion--capitalized-cost method is a hybrid method;
90% of the contract is reported under the percentage-of-completion
method and 10% under the completed-contract method

E. **Business Income and Deductions**

1. Gross income for a business includes sales less cost of goods sold plus
    other income. In computing cost of goods sold

    a. Inventory is generally valued at (1) cost, or (2) market, whichever is
        lower
    b. Specific identification, FIFO, and LIFO are allowed
    c. If LIFO is used for taxes, it must also be used on books
    d. Lower of cost or market cannot be used with LIFO

2. All ordinary (customary and not a capital expenditure) and necessary
    (appropriate and helpful) expenses incurred in a trade or business are de-
    ductible

    a. Business expenses that violate public policy (fines or illegal kick-
        backs) are not deductible
    b. Business expenses must be reasonable

        (1) If salaries are excessive (unreasonable compensation), they may be
            disallowed as a deduction to the extent unreasonable
        (2) Reasonableness of compensation issue generally arises only when the
            relationship between the employer and employee exceeds that of the
            normal employer-employee relationship (e.g., employee is also a
            shareholder)
        (3) Use test of what another enterprise would pay under similar cir-
            cumstances to an unrelated employee
    c. In the case of an individual, any charge (including taxes) for basic
        local telephone service with respect to the first telephone line
        provided to any residence of the taxpayer shall be treated as a
        nondeductible personal expense

        (1) Disallowance does not apply to charges for long-distance calls,
            charges for equipment, rental, and optional services provided by a
            telephone company, or charges attributable to additional telephone
            lines to a taxpayer's residence other than the first telephone line
        (2) The above provision is effective for taxable years beginning after
            1988
    d. The trade or business expenses of a self-employed individual include a
        deduction for AGI for up to 25% of the premiums paid for medical
        insurance for the individual, the individual's spouse, and dependents

        (1) The deduction cannot exceed the individual's net earnings from the
            trade or business with respect to which the plan providing for
            health insurance was established
        (2) The deduction does not reduce the income base for purposes of the
            self-employment tax
        (3) No deduction is allowed if the self-employed individual or spouse
            is eligible to participate in an employer's subsidized health plan
        (4) Any medical insurance premiums not deductible under the above rules
            are deductible as an itemized medical expense deduction from AGI
    e. Uniform capitalization rules generally require that all costs incurred
        (both direct and indirect) in manufacturing or constructing real or
        personal property, or in purchasing or holding property for sale, must
        be capitalized as part of the cost of the property

(1) These costs become part of the basis of the property and are recovered through depreciation or amortization, or are included in inventory and recovered through cost of goods sold as an offset to selling price

(2) The rules apply to inventory, noninventory property produced or held for sale to customers, and to assets or improvements to assets constructed by a taxpayer for the taxpayer's own use in a trade or business or in an activity engaged in for profit

(3) Taxpayers subject to the rules are required to capitalize not only direct costs, but also most indirect costs that benefit the assets produced or acquired for resale, including general, administrative, and overhead costs

(4) Retailers and wholesalers must include in inventory all costs incident to purchasing and storing inventory such as wages of employees responsible for purchasing inventory, handling, processing, repackaging and assembly of goods, and off-site storage costs. These rules do not apply to "small retailers and wholesalers" (i.e., a taxpayer who acquires personal property for resale if the taxpayer's average annual gross receipts for the three preceding taxable years do not exceed $10,000,000)

(5) Interest must be capitalized if the debt is incurred or continued to finance the construction or production of real property, property with a recovery period of 20 years, property that takes more than 2 years to produce, or property with a production period exceeding one year and a cost exceeding $1 million

(6) The capitalization rules do not apply to research and experimentation expenditures, property held for personal use, and to free-lance authors, photographers, and artists

f. Business meals, entertainment, and travel

(1) Receipts must be maintained for all lodging expenditures and for other expenditures of $25 or more except transportation expenditures where receipts are not readily available

(2) Adequate contemporaneous records must be maintained for business meals and entertainment to substantiate the amount of expense, i.e., who, when, where, why (the 4 Ws)

(3) Business meals and entertainment must be directly related or associated with the active conduct of a trade or business to be deductible. The taxpayer or a representative must be present to satisfy this requirement

(4) The amount of otherwise allowable deduction for business meals or entertainment must be reduced by 20%. This 20% reduction rule applies to all food, beverage, and entertainment costs (even though incurred in the course of travel away from home) after determining the amount otherwise deductible. The 20% reduction rule will not apply if:

   (a) The full value of the meal or entertainment is included in the recipient's income or excluded as a fringe benefit

   (b) An employee is reimbursed for the cost of a meal or entertainment (the 20% reduction rule applies to the party making the reimbursement)

   (c) A traditional employer paid employee recreation expense (e.g., a company Christmas party)

   (d) The cost is for samples and other promotional activities made available to the public

      (e)   The expense is for a sports event that qualifies as a charitable fund raising event

      (f)   The cost is for meals or entertainment sold for full consideration

      (g)   The cost is for a meal provided during 1987 or 1988 as an integral part of a qualified banquet meeting

(5)   The cost of a ticket to any entertainment activity is limited (prior to the 20% reduction rule) to its face value

(6)   No deduction is generally allowed for expenses with respect to an entertainment, recreational, or amusement facility

      (a)   Entertainment facilities include yachts, hunting lodges, fishing camps, swimming pools, etc.

      (b)   If the facility is used for a business purpose, the related out-of-pocket expenditures are deductible even though depreciation, etc. of the facility is not deductible

      (c)   Proportional part of membership fees paid to social, athletic, luncheon, sporting, or country clubs is deductible if club is used more than 50% for business, and then only the portion attributable to directly related use is deductible

> *EXAMPLE: A taxpayer paid dues of $500 to a country club. During the year, he used the club 30 days for personal use, 45 days for entertainment directly related to his business, and 25 days for entertainment associated with his business.   Since the club was used more than 50% for business purposes (70 of 100 days), he can deduct the part of his dues that is directly related to his business use of the club (subject to the 20% reduction rule).*

$$\$500 \left(\frac{45}{100} \right) = \begin{array}{r} \$225 \\ \times\ 80\% \\ \hline \underline{\$180} \end{array}$$

(7)   <u>Transportation and travel expenses</u> are deductible if incurred in the active conduct of a trade or business

      (a)   Deductible transportation expenses include local transportation between two job locations, but excludes commuting expenses between residence and job

      (b)   Deductible travel expenses are those incurred while temporarily "away from tax home" overnight including meals, lodging, transportation, and expenses incident to travel (clothes care, etc.)

          1]   Travel expenses to and from domestic destination are fully deductible if business is the primary purpose of trip

          2]   Actual automobile expenses can be deducted, or taxpayer can use standard mileage rate of 24¢/mile for first 15,000 business miles per year, and 11¢/mile in excess of 15,000 miles (plus parking and tolls)

          3]   No deduction is allowed for travel as a form of education. This rule applies when a travel expense would otherwise be deductible only on the ground that the travel itself serves educational purposes

          4]   No deduction is allowed for expenses incurred in attending a convention, seminar, or similar meeting for investment purposes

(8)   An employee's unreimbursed business meal, entertainment, transportation, and travel expenses are only deductible as miscellaneous itemized deductions (subject to a 2% of AGI floor; see page 1216)

g.   Deductions for <u>business gifts</u> are limited to $25 per recipient each year

(1)   Advertising and promotional gifts costing $4 or less are not limited

(2)   Gifts of tangible personal property costing $400 or less are deductible if awarded as an employee achievement award for length of service or safety achievement

(3)   Gifts of tangible personal property costing $1,600 or less are deductible if awarded as an employee achievement award under a qualified plan for length of service or safety achievement

(a)   Plan must be written and nondiscriminatory
(b)   Average cost of all items awarded under the plan during the tax year must not exceed $400

h.   <u>Bad debts</u> are generally deducted in the year they become worthless

(1)   There must have been a valid "debtor-creditor" relationship
(2)   A <u>business</u> bad debt is one that is incurred in the trade or business of the lender

(a)   Deductible against ordinary income (toward AGI)
(b)   Deduction allowed for partial worthlessness

(3)   Business bad debts must be deducted under the specific charge-off method

(a)   A deduction is allowed when a specific debt becomes partially or totally worthless
(b)   A bad debt deduction is available for accounts or notes receivable only if the amount owed has already been included in gross income for the current or a prior taxable year. Since receivables for services rendered of a <u>cash method</u> taxpayer have not yet been included in gross income, the receivables cannot be deducted when they become uncollectible

(4)   A <u>nonbusiness</u> bad debt (not incurred in trade or business) can only be deducted

(a)   If totally worthless
(b)   As a short-term capital loss

(5)   Guarantor of debt who has to pay, takes same deduction as if the loss were from a direct loan

(a)   Business bad debt if guarantee related to trade, business, or employment
(b)   Nonbusiness bad debt if guarantee entered into for profit but not related to trade or business

i.   Expenses may exceed income resulting in a deductible loss if the activity is engaged in for profit

(1)   Expenses of an activity not engaged in for profit (a <u>hobby</u>) are deductible if they are

(a)   Allowable anyway (e.g., interest, taxes, casualty losses)

(b) Other hobby operating expenses are deductible to the extent they do not exceed gross income from the hobby reduced by the interest, taxes, and casualty losses above. These hobby expenses are aggregated with other miscellaneous itemized deductions that are subject to a 2% of AGI floor

(2) An activity is presumed to be for profit if it produces profit in at least 3 out of 5 consecutive years (2 out of 7 years for horses)

3. Net operating loss (NOL)

a. A net operating loss may occur even if an individual is not engaged in a separate trade or business (e.g., a NOL created by a personal casualty loss)

b. NOLs may be carried back 3 years and carried forward 15 years to offset profits in other years

(1) Carryback is first made to the third preceding year
(2) May elect not to carryback and only carryforward 15 years

c. To compute the NOL, begin with the loss using all income items and deductions (including the standard deduction)

(1) Then reduce this loss by adding back

(a) Any NOL carryover or carryback from another year
(b) Excess of capital losses over capital gains. Excess of nonbusiness capital losses over nonbusiness capital gains even if overall gains exceed losses
(c) Personal exemptions
(d) Excess of nonbusiness deductions (usually itemized deductions) over nonbusiness income

1] The standard deduction is treated as a nonbusiness deduction
2] Contributions to a self-employed retirement plan are considered nonbusiness deductions
3] Casualty losses (even if personal) are considered business deductions
4] Dividends are nonbusiness income; salary and rent are business income

(2) Any remaining loss is a NOL and must be carried back first, unless election is made to carryforward only

4. Limitation on deductions for business use of home. To be deductible

a. A portion of the home must be used exclusively and regularly as the principal place of business or as a meeting place for patients, clients, or customers

(1) Exclusive use rule does not apply to a place of regular storage of business inventory or a day-care center
(2) If an employee, the exclusive use must be for the convenience of the employer

b. Deduction is limited to the excess of gross income derived from the business use of the home over deductions otherwise allowable for taxes, interest, and casualty losses

c. Any business expenses not allocable to the use of the home (e.g., wages, transportation, supplies) must be deducted before home use expenses

d. Any business use of home expenses that are disallowed due to the gross income limit can be carried forward and deducted in future years subject to the same restrictions

EXAMPLE: Taxpayer uses 10% of his home exclusively for business purposes. Gross income from his business totaled $750, and he incurred the following expenses

	Total	10% Business
Interest	$4,000	$400
Taxes	2,500	250
Utilities, insurance	1,500	150
Depreciation	2,000	200

Since total deductions for business use of the home are limited to business gross income, the taxpayer can deduct the following for business use of his home: $400 interest; $250 taxes; $100 utilities and insurance; and $-0- depreciation (operating expenses such as utilities and insurance must be deducted before depreciation). The remaining $50 of utilities and insurance, and $200 of depreciation can be carried forward and deducted in future years subject to the same restrictions.

5. Loss deductions incurred in a trade or business, or in the production of income are limited to the amount a taxpayer has "at risk"

   a. Applies to all activities except the leasing of personal property by a closely held corporation (5 or fewer individuals own more than 50% of stock)
   b. Applies to individuals and closely held regular corporations
   c. Amount "at risk" includes

      (1) The cash and adjusted basis of property contributed by the taxpayer, and
      (2) Liabilities for which the taxpayer is personally liable; excludes nonrecourse debt

   d. For real estate activities, a taxpayer's amount at risk includes "qualified" nonrecourse financing secured by the real property used in the activity

      (1) Nonrecourse financing is qualified if it is borrowed from a lender engaged in the business of making loans (e.g., bank, savings and loan) provided that the lender is not the promoter or seller of the property or a party related to either; or is borrowed from or guaranteed by any Federal, State, or local government or instrumentality thereof
      (2) Nonrecourse financing obtained from a qualified lender who has an equity interest in the venture is treated as an amount at risk, as long as the terms of the financing are commercially reasonable
      (3) The nonrecourse financing must not be convertible, and no person can be personally liable for repayment

   e. Excess losses can be carried over to subsequent years (no time limit) and deducted when the "at risk" amount has been increased
   f. Previously allowed losses will be recaptured as income if the amount at risk is reduced below zero

6. Losses and credits from passive activities may generally only be used to offset income from (or tax allocable to) passive activities. Except for a

phase-in rule, passive losses may not be used to offset active income (e.g., wages, salaries, professional fees, etc.) or portfolio income (e.g., interest, dividends, annuities, royalties, etc.)

EXAMPLE: Individual X has salary income, a loss from a partnership in whose business he does not actively participate, and income from a limited partnership. X may offset the partnership loss against the income from the limited partnership, but not against X's salary income.

EXAMPLE: Individual Y has dividend and interest income of $40,000 and a passive-activity loss of $30,000. The passive-activity loss cannot be offset against the dividend and interest income.

a. Applies to individuals, estates, trusts, closely held C corporations, and personal service corporations

   (1) A closely held C corporation is one with 5 or fewer shareholders owning more than 50% of stock
   (2) Personal service corporation is an incorporated service business with more than 10% of its stock owned by shareholder-employees

b. Passive activity is any activity that involves the conduct of a trade or business in which the taxpayer does "not materially participate," any rental activity, and any limited partnership interest

   (1) Material participation is the taxpayer's involvement in an activity on a regular, continuous, and substantial basis considering such factors as time devoted, physical duties performed, and knowledge of or experience in the business
   (2) Passive activity does not include (1) a working interest in any oil or gas property that a taxpayer owns directly or through an entity that does not limit the taxpayer's liability; (2) operating a hotel or transient lodging if significant services are provided; or (3) operating a short-term equipment rental business

c. Losses from passive activities may be deducted only against income from passive activities

   (1) If there is insufficient passive-activity income to absorb passive-activity losses, the excess losses are carried forward indefinitely to future years
   (2) If there is insufficient passive-activity income in subsequent years to fully absorb the loss carryforwards, the unused losses from a passive activity may be deducted when the taxpayer's entire interest in the activity that gave rise to the unused losses is finally disposed of in a fully taxable transaction
   (3) Other dispositions

       (a) A transfer of a taxpayer's interest in a passive activity by reason of the taxpayer's death results in suspended losses being allowed (to the decedent) to the extent they exceed the amount of the step-up in basis allowed
       (b) If the disposition is by gift, the suspended losses are added to the basis of the gift property. If less than 100% of an interest is transferred by gift, an allocable portion of the suspended losses is added to the basis of the gift
       (c) An installment sale of a passive interest triggers the recognition of suspended losses in the ratio that the gain recognized in each year bears to the total gain on sale

            (d)   If a formerly passive activity becomes an active one, suspended losses are allowed against income from the now active business (if the activity remains the same)

   d. <u>Credits</u> from passive activities can only be used to offset the tax liability attributable to passive activity income

      (1)   Excess credits are carried forward indefinitely (subject to limited carryback during the phase-in period)

      (2)   Excess credits (unlike losses) cannot be used in full in the year in which the taxpayer's entire passive activity interest is disposed of. Instead, excess credits continue to be carried forward

      (3)   Credits allowable under the passive activity limitation rules are also subject to the general business credit limitation

   e. Although <u>rental activity</u> is defined as a passive activity regardless of the property owner's participation in the operation of the rental property, a special rule permits an individual to offset up to $25,000 of income that is <u>not</u> from passive activities by losses or credits from rental real estate if the individual <u>actively participates</u> in the rental real estate activity

      (1)   "Active participation" is less stringent than "material participation" and is met if the taxpayer personally operates the rental property; or, if a rental agent operates the property, the taxpayer participates in management decisions or arranging for others to provide services

      (2)   The active participation requirement must be met in both the year that the loss arises and the year in which the loss is allowed

      (3)   For losses, the $25,000 amount is reduced by 50% of AGI in excess of $100,000, and fully phased out when AGI exceeds $150,000

      (4)   For low-income housing and rehabilitation credits, the $25,000 amount is reduced by 50% of AGI in excess of $200,000, and fully phased out when AGI exceeds $250,000

   f. For passive activity interests acquired before 10/23/86, the limitations are phased-in over a five-year period. The portion of a passive activity loss or credit that is disallowed is 65% for 1987; 40% in 1988; 20% in 1989, 10% in 1990; and 0% in 1991

      (1)   The deduction for passive activity interests acquired before 10/23/86 is the applicable percentage times the lesser of (a) the net loss from pre-10-23-86 activities (disregarding suspended losses from previous years, or (b) the net loss from all passive activities (disregarding suspended losses from previous years)

      (2)   In computing the $25,000 deduction under e. above, losses from pre-10-23-86 interests are applied first, with any remaining pre-10-23-86 losses then subject to the percentage phase-in as determined in (1)

   g. The passive activity limitation rules do not apply to losses disallowed under the at-risk rules

F. Depreciation, Depletion, and Amortization

Depreciation is an allowance for the exhaustion, wear and tear of property used in a trade or business, or of property held for the production of income. The Tax Reform Act of 1986 significantly lengthened the ACRS depreciation periods for real property and certain long-life equipment placed in service after 1986. The ACRS depreciation class of property is generally determined by reference to its Asset Depreciation Range (ADR) guideline class. Statutory tables listing depreciation percentages are no longer provided. Taxpayers must determine annual deductions based on the applicable property class, depreciation method, and averaging convention

1. For property placed in service <u>prior to 1981</u>, the basis of property reduced by salvage value would be recovered over its useful life using the straight-line, declining balance, or sum-of-the-years'-digits method. Whether an accelerated method of depreciation could be used depended on the classification and useful life of the property, and whether it was new or used when acquired

2. <u>Accelerated Cost Recovery System (ACRS)</u>

   a. ACRS is <u>mandatory</u> for most depreciable property placed in service <u>after 1980</u>. Taxpayers will continue to use facts and circumstances or Class Life Asset Depreciation Range (CLADR) for property placed in service prior to 1981

   b. Salvage value is completely ignored under ACRS; the method of cost recovery and the recovery period are the same for both new and used property

   c. <u>Recovery property</u> includes all property other than land, intangible assets, and property the taxpayer elects to depreciate under a method not expressed in terms of years (e.g., unit of production or income forecast methods). Recovery property placed in service after 1986 is divided into six classes of personal property based on ADR midpoint life, and into two classes of real property. This is referred to as Modified ACRS or MACRS. Each class is assigned a recovery period and a depreciation method. Recovery deductions for the first six classes are based on the declining balance method, switching to the straight-line method to maximize deductions

      (1) <u>3-year, 200% class</u>. Includes property with an ADR midpoint of 4 years or less (except for autos and light trucks) and certain horses

      (2) <u>5-year, 200% class</u>. Includes property with an ADR midpoint of more than 4 and less than 10 years. Also included are autos and light trucks, certain technological equipment, and research and experimentation property

      (3) <u>7-year, 200% class</u>. Includes property with an ADR midpoint of at least 10 and less than 16 years. Also included are property having no ADR midpoint and not classified elsewhere

      (4) <u>10-year, 200% class</u>. Includes property with an ADR midpoint of at least 16 and less than 20 years

      (5) <u>15-year, 150% class</u>. Includes property with an ADR midpoint of at least 20 years and less than 25 years

      (6) <u>20-year, 150% class</u>. Includes property with an ADR midpoint of 25 years or more, other than real property with an ADR midpoint of 27.5 years or more

      (7) <u>27 1/2-year, straight-line class</u>. Includes residential rental property (i.e., a building or structure with 80% or more of its rental income from dwelling units)

        (8) <u>31 1/2-year, straight-line class</u>. Includes nonresidential real property and real property having an ADR midpoint life of less than 27.5 years

d. Instead of using the declining balance method for 3-year through 20-year property, taxpayers can elect to use the straight-line method over the ACRS class life. This is an annual class-by-class election

e. Instead of using the 200% declining balance method for 3-year through 10-year property, taxpayers can elect to use the 150% declining balance method using ADS class lives. This is an annual class-by-class election

f. An <u>alternative depreciation system</u> (ADS) provides for straight-line depreciation over the property's ADS class life (12 years for personal property with no ADS class life, and 40 years for real property)

        (1) A taxpayer may elect to use the alternative system for any class of property placed in service during a taxable year. For real property, the election is made on a property-by-property basis

        (2) Once made, the election is irrevocable and continues to apply to that property for succeeding years, but does not apply to similar property placed in service in a subsequent year, unless a new election is made

        (3) The alternative system must be used for foreign-use property, property used 50% or more for personal use, and for purposes of computing earnings and profits

g. An <u>averaging convention</u> is used to compute depreciation for the taxable year in which property is placed in service or disposed of under both the regular ACRS and alternative depreciation system

        (1) Personal property is treated as placed in service or disposed of at the midpoint of the taxable year, resulting in a half-year of depreciation for the year in which the property is placed in service or disposed of. However, no depreciation is allowed for personal property disposed of in the same taxable year in which it was placed in service

           EXAMPLE: A calendar-year taxpayer purchases machinery (5-year, 200% class) for $10,000 in January, 1989. Because of the averaging convention, the depreciation for 1989 will be ($10,000 x 40% x 1/2) = $2,000.

        (2) Real property is treated as placed in service or disposed of in the middle of a month, resulting in a half-month of depreciation for the month disposed of or placed in service

        (3) A midquarter convention applies if more than 40% of all personal property is placed in service during the last quarter of the taxpayer's taxable year. Under this convention, property is treated as placed in service (or disposed of) in the middle of the quarter in which placed in service (or disposed of)

           EXAMPLE: In January 1988 a calendar-year taxpayer purchased machinery for $10,000. In December 1988 the taxpayer purchased additional machinery for $30,000. All machinery was assigned to the 5-year, 200% class. No other depreciable assets were purchased during the year.

           Since the machinery placed in service during the last three months of the year exceeded 40% of the depreciable basis of all personal property placed in service during the taxable year, all machinery is depreciated under the mid-quarter convention. The taxpayer may *claim 3 1/2 quarters depreciation on the machinery acquired in January ($10,000 x 40% x 3.5/4 = $3,500), and only 1/2 quarter of depreciation for the machinery acquired in December ($30,000 x 40% x 1/8 = $1,500).*

h. The cost of <u>leasehold improvements</u> made by a lessee must be recovered over the ACRS recovery period of the underlying property without regard to the lease term. Upon the expiration of the lease, any unrecovered adjusted basis in abandoned leasehold improvements will be treated as a loss

i. <u>Sec. 179 expense election.</u> A taxpayer (other than a trust or estate) may annually elect to treat the cost of qualifying depreciable property as an expense rather than a capital expenditure

  (1) Qualifying property is generally recovery property that is tangible personal property acquired by purchase from an unrelated party for use in the active conduct of a trade or business

  (2) The maximum cost that can be annually expensed is $10,000, but is reduced dollar-for-dollar by the cost of qualifying property that is placed in service during the taxable year that exceeds $200,000

  (3) The amount of expense deduction is further limited to the taxable income derived from the active conduct by the taxpayer of any trade or business. Any expense deduction disallowed by this limitation is carried forward to the succeeding taxable year

  (4) If property is converted to nonbusiness use at any time, the excess of the amount expensed over the ACRS deductions that would have been allowed must be recaptured as ordinary income in the year of conversion

j. For a passenger automobile acquired after 1986, the amount of ACRS (including expensing) deductions is limited to $2,560 in the year placed in service, $4,100 for the second year, $2,450 for the third year, and $1,475 for each year thereafter

  (1) These limits are reduced to reflect personal use [e.g., if auto used 30% for personal use and 70% for business use, limits are (70% x $2,560) = $1,792 for the year of acquisition, (70% x $4,100) = $2,870 for the second year, etc.]

  (2) If automobile not used more than 50% for business use, ACRS is limited to straight-line depreciation over 5 years

    (a) Use of the automobile for income-producing purposes is not counted in determining whether the more than 50% test is met, but is considered in determining the amount of allowable depreciation

      EXAMPLE: An automobile is used 40% in a business, 35% for production of income, and 25% for personal use. The 200% declining balance method cannot be used because business use is not more than 50%. However, depreciation limited to the straight-line method is allowed based on 75% of use.

    (b) If the more than 50% test is met in year of acquisition, but business use subsequently falls to 50% or less, ACRS deductions in excess of 5-year straight-line method are recaptured

k. Transportation property other than automobiles (e.g. airplanes, trucks, boats, etc.), entertainment property (including real property), and any computer or peripheral equipment not used exclusively at a regular business establishment are subject to the same more than 50% business use requirement and consequent restrictions on depreciation as are applicable to automobiles

   (1)   Failure to use these assets more than 50% for business purposes will limit the deductions to the straight-line method
   (2)   If the more than 50% test is met in year of acquisition, but business use subsequently falls to 50% or less, ACRS deductions in excess of the applicable straight-line method are recaptured

3.   Depletion

   a.   Depletion is allowed on timber, minerals, oil, and gas, and other exhaustible natural resources or wasting assets
   b.   There are 2 basic methods to compute

      (1)   Cost method divides the adjusted basis by the total number of recoverable units and multiplies by the number of units sold (or payment received for, if cash basis) during the year

         (a)   Adjusted basis is cost less accumulated depletion (not below zero)

            EXAMPLE: Land cost $10,050,000 of which $50,000 is the residual value of the land.   There are 1,000,000 barrels of oil recoverable.   If 10,000 barrels were sold, cost depletion would be ($10,000,000 ÷ 1,000,000 barrels) x 10,000 = $100,000.

      (2)   Percentage method uses a specified percentage of gross income from the property during the year

         (a)   Deduction may not exceed 50% of the taxable income (before depletion) from the property
         (b)   May be taken even after costs have been recovered and there is no basis
         (c)   May be used for domestic oil and gas wells by "independent producer" or royalty owner; cannot be used for timber
         (d)   The percentage is a statutory amount and generally ranges from 5% to 20% depending on the mineral

4.   Amortization is allowed for several special types of capital expenditures

   a.   A corporation's or partnership's organizational expenses can be amortized over 60 or more months.   Otherwise deductible only when corporation or partnership is dissolved
   b.   Business investigation and start-up costs are deductible in the year paid or incurred if the taxpayer is currently in a similar line of business as the start-up business.   If not in a similar line of business and the new business is --

      (1)   Acquired by the taxpayer, investigation and start-up costs are capitalized and may be amortized over not less than 60 months beginning with the month that business begins
      (2)   Not acquired by the taxpayer, investigation costs are not deductible

   c.   Pollution control facilities can be amortized over 60 months if installed on property that was placed in operation prior to 1976.   The pollution control investment must not increase output, capacity, or the useful life of the asset

    d. Patents and copyrights may be amortized over their useful life

      (1) 17 years for patents; life of author plus 50 years for copyrights
      (2) If become obsolete early, deduct in that year

    e. Research and experimental expenses may be amortized over 60 months or more. Alternatively, may be expensed at election of taxpayer if done so for year in which such expenses are first incurred or paid

    f. Intangible assets for which the Code does not specifically provide for amortization are amortizable over their useful lives. If an intangible asset does not have a determinable useful life and the Code does not specifically provide for amortization, no amortization is allowed (e.g., goodwill can not be amortized for tax purposes

II.   "ABOVE THE LINE" DEDUCTIONS

"Above the line" deductions are taken from gross income to determine adjusted gross income. Adjusted gross income is important, because it may affect the amount of allowable charitable contributions, medical expense, casualty loss, and miscellaneous itemized deductions. The deductions which reduce gross income to arrive at adjusted gross income are

    1) Business deductions of a self-employed person (see Business Income and Deductions, page 1242)
    2) Losses from sale or exchange of property (discussed in Sales and Exchanges and in Capital Gains and Losses, pages 1286 and 1295)
    3) Reimbursed employee business expenses
    4) Deductions attributable to rents and royalties
    5) Self-employed health insurance deduction
    6) Jury duty pay remitted to employer
    7) Contributions to self-employed retirement plans and IRAs
    8) Penalties for premature withdrawals from time deposits
    9) Alimony payments

A. **Reimbursed Employee Business Expenses**

    1. <u>Reimbursed expenses</u> are deductible "above the line" if the reimbursement is included in gross income

    2. If employee travel, transportation, entertainment, and other business expenses (including outside salesman expenses) exceed the reimbursement, the excess can only be deducted as a miscellaneous itemized deduction

    3. Reimbursements do not have to be included in income and the reimbursed expenses are not deducted if an employee adequately "accounts" to the employer

      a. Employee must submit a report describing each element of the expense

        (1) Remember the 4 Ws: who, when, where, and why; plus the amount
        (2) Receipts must be maintained for all lodging expenditures and for other travel and entertainment expenditures of $25 or more, except transportation expenditures whose receipts are not readily available

      b. Per diem and per mile arrangements satisfy this, e.g., reimbursement not in excess of $44 per day and 24¢ per mile

B. **Expenses attributable to property held for the production of rents or royalties are deductible "above the line"**

1. <u>Rental of vacation home</u>

   a. If there is any personal use, the <u>amount deductible</u> is

      (1) $\dfrac{\text{No. of days rented}}{\text{Total days used}}$ x Total expenses = Amount deductible

      (2) Personal use is by taxpayer, or any other person to whom a fair rent is not charged

   b. If used as a residence, amount deductible is further limited to rental income less deductions otherwise allowable for interest, taxes, and casualty losses

      (1) Used as a residence if personal use exceeds greater of 14 days or 10% of number of days rented
      (2) These limitations do not apply if rented or held for rental for a continuous 12 month period with no personal use

      EXAMPLE: Use house as a principal residence and then begin to rent in June. As long as rental continues for 12 consecutive months, limitations do not apply in year converted to rental.

   c. If used as a residence (above) and rented for less than 15 days per year, then income therefrom is not reported, and rental expense deductions are not allowed

      EXAMPLE: Taxpayer rents his condominium for 120 days for $2,000 and used it himself for 60 days. The rest of the year it is vacant. His expenses are

Mortgage interest	$1,800
Real estate taxes	600
Utilities	300
Maintenance	300
Depreciation	2,000
	$5,000

   Taxpayer may deduct the following expenses.

	Rental Expense	Itemized Deduction
Mortgage interest	$1,200	$ 600
Real estate taxes	400	200
Utilities	200	-0-
Maintenance	200	-0-
Depreciation	-0-	-0-
	$2,000	$ 800

   Taxpayer may not deduct any depreciation because his rental expense deductions are limited to rental income when he has made personal use of the condominium in excess of the 14-day or 10% rule.

C. **Jury Duty Pay Remitted to Employer**

1. An employee is allowed to deduct the amount of jury duty pay that was surrendered to an employer in return for the employer's payment of compensation during the employee's jury service period.

2. This above-the-line deduction applies to taxable years beginning after 1986.

D. **Contributions to Certain Retirement Plans**

   1. <u>Self-employed</u> individuals (sole proprietors and partners) may contribute to a qualified retirement plan (called H.R.-10 or Keogh Plan)

      a. The maximum contribution and deduction is the lesser of

         (1) $30,000, or 25% of earned income

         (2) The definition of "earned income" includes the retirement plan deduction (i.e., earnings from self-employment must be reduced by the retirement plan contribution for purposes of determining the maximum deduction). To simplify the computation, multiply earnings from self-employment by 20%

         EXAMPLE: A CPA has earnings from self-employment of $140,000 for 1989. The maximum that can be deducted for contributions to the CPA's self-employed retirement plan for 1989 would be $140,000 x 20% = $28,000 [i.e., ($140,000 - $28,000) x 25% = $28,000]

      b. A taxpayer may elect to treat contributions made up until the due date of the tax return (including extensions) as made for the taxable year for which the tax return is being filed, if the retirement plan was established by the end of that year

   2. Contributions to an <u>Individual Retirement Account</u> (IRA)

      a. If neither the taxpayer nor the taxpayer's spouse are active participants in an employer-sponsored retirement plan or a Keogh plan, there is no phase-out of IRA deductions

         (1) The maximum deduction for contributions is the lesser of

            (a) $2,000, or

            (b) 100% of compensation (including alimony)

         (2) For a taxpayer with a nonworking spouse (or a spouse who consents to be treated as having no compensation), a <u>spousal IRA</u> may be established in addition to the taxpayer's IRA. Then the maximum contribution allowed as a deduction on a joint return is the lesser of

            (a) $2,250, or

            (b) 100% of taxpayer's compensation (including alimony)

            (c) However, the deduction for either the taxpayer's IRA or the spouse's IRA cannot exceed $2,000

         (3) If both spouses are working and each have at least $2,000 of compensation, the maximum deduction on a joint return is $4,000

      b. If the taxpayer, or taxpayer's spouse, is an active participant in an employer-sponsored retirement plan or a Keogh plan, the IRA deduction is proportionately phased-out for

         (1) Married taxpayers with AGI between $40,000 and $50,000

         (2) Single taxpayers with AGI between $25,000 and $35,000

         (3) Married taxpayers filing separately with AGI between $-0- and $10,000

      c. Under the phase-out rule, the $2,000 maximum deduction is reduced by a percentage equal to adjusted gross income in excess of the lower AGI amount (above) divided by $10,000. The deduction limit is rounded to the next lowest multiple of $10

(1)   A taxpayer is not considered married for a year in which the
taxpayer and taxpayer's spouse (1) file separate returns and (2)
did not live together at any time during the year

(2)   A taxpayer whose AGI is not above the applicable phase-out range
can make a $200 deductible contribution regardless of the
proportional phase-out rule. This $200 minimum applies separately
to taxpayer and taxpayer's spouse

(3)   A taxpayer who is partially or totally prevented from making
deductible IRA contributions can make <u>nondeductible IRA
contributions</u>

(4)   <u>Total IRA contributions</u> (whether deductible or not) are subject to
the $2,000 ($2,250 spousal) or 100% of compensation limit

> *EXAMPLE: For 1989, a single individual who has compensation income
> (and AGI) of $32,000, and who is an active participant in an
> employer-sponsored retirement plan, would be subject to a limit
> reduction of $1,400 computed as follows: $2,000 x [($32,000 –
> $25,000) ÷ $10,000)] = $1,400. Thus, the individual's deductible
> IRA contribution would be limited to $2,000 – $1,400 = $600.
> However, the individual could make nondeductible IRA contributions
> of up to $1,400 more.*

> *EXAMPLE: For 1989, a single individual who has compensation income
> (and AGI) of $34,600, and who is an active participant in an em-
> ployer-sponsored retirement plan, would normally be limited to an
> IRA deduction of $2,000 – [($34,600 – $25,000) ÷ $10,000] x
> $2,000 = $80. However, because of the special rule in (1) above,
> a $200 IRA contribution deduction is allowable.*

3. An employer's contributions to an employee's <u>simplified employee pension
plan</u> are deductible by the employer up to the lesser of 15% of compensation,
or $30,000

   a.   SEP may contain a salary reduction provision allowing an employee to
take a reduced salary and to have the reduction (up to $7,000 indexed by
inflation) deposited in the plan as an employer contribution
   b.   The up to $30,000 of employer SEP contributions (including up to $7,000
of employee salary reduction contributions) are excluded from the
employee's gross income
   c.   In addition, the employee may make deductible IRA contributions subject
to the IRA phase-out rules

E. **Penalties for Premature Withdrawals from Time Deposits**

1.   Full amount of interest is included in gross income

2.   Forfeited interest is then subtracted "above the line"

F. **Alimony** or separate maintenance payments are deducted "above the line"

III.   ITEMIZED DEDUCTIONS FROM ADJUSTED GROSS INCOME

Itemized deductions reduce adjusted gross income, and are sometimes referred to
as   "below the line" deductions because they are deducted from adjusted gross income.
Itemized deductions (or a standard deduction) along with personal exemptions are
subtracted from adjusted gross income to arrive at taxable income.

A taxpayer will itemize deductions only if the taxpayer's total itemized deductions exceed the applicable standard deduction which is available to nonitemizers. The amount of standard deduction is based on the filing status of the taxpayer, and whether the taxpayer is a dependent, and for taxable years beginning after 1988 will be indexed for inflation. Additional standard deductions are allowed for age and blindness.

	Filing Status	Basic Standard Deduction	
		1988	1989
a)	Married, filing jointly; or surviving spouse	$5,000	$5,200
b)	Married, filing separately	$2,500	$2,600
c)	Head of household	$4,400	$4,550
d)	Single	$3,000	$3,100

The basic standard deduction of an individual who is eligible to be claimed as a dependency exemption on another taxpayer's return is limited to the greater of earned income (up to the basic standard deduction) or $500.

An unmarried individual who is either age 65 or older or blind, receives an additional standard deduction of $750. The standard deduction is increased by $1,500 if the individual is both elderly and blind. The increase is $600 for each married individual who is age 65 or older or blind ($1,200 if elderly and blind). An elderly or blind individual who may be claimed as a dependent on another taxpayer's return may claim the basic standard deduction plus the additional standard deduction(s) (e.g., an unmarried dependent aged 65 with only unearned income would have a standard deduction of $500 + $750 = $1,250).

The major itemized deductions are outlined below. It should be remembered that some may be deducted "above the line" if they are incurred by a self-employed taxpayer in a trade or business, or for the production of rents or royalties.

A. **Medical and Dental Expenses**

1. Medical and dental expenses paid by taxpayer for himself, spouse, or dependent (relationship, support, and citizenship tests are met) are deductible in year of payment, if not reimbursed by insurance, employer, etc. A child of divorced or separated parents is treated as a dependent of both parents for this purpose

2. Computation--unreimbursed medical expenses (including <u>prescribed</u> medicine and insulin, and medical insurance premiums) are deducted to the extent in excess of <u>7.5%</u> of adjusted gross income

    EXAMPLE: Ralph and Alice Jones, who have Adjusted Gross Income of $20,000, paid the following medical expenses: $900 for hospital and doctor bills (above reimbursement), $250 for prescription medicine, and $600 for medical insurance. The Joneses would compute their medical expense deduction as follows:

Prescribed medicine	$ 250
Hospital, doctors	900
Medical insurance	600
	$1,750
Less 7.5% of AGI	-1,500
Medical expense deduction	$ 250

3. Expenses incurred by physically handicapped individuals for removal of structural barriers in their residences to accommodate their handicapped condition are fully deductible as medical expenses. Qualifying expenses include constructing entrance or exit ramps, widening doorways and hallways, the installation of railings and support bars, and other modifications

4. Capital expenditures for special equipment (other than in 3 above) installed for medical reasons in a home or automobile are deductible as medical expenses to the extent the expenditures exceed the increase in value of the property

5. Deductible medical expenses include

   a. Fees for doctors, surgeons, dentists, osteopaths, ophthalmologists, optometrists, chiropractors, chiropodists, podiatrists, psychiatrists, psychologists, and Christian Science practitioners
   b. Fees for hospital services, therapy, nursing services (including nurses' meals you pay for), ambulance hire, and laboratory, surgical, obstetrical, diagnostic, dental, and X-ray services
   c. Meals and lodging provided by a hospital during medical treatment, and meals and lodging provided by a center during treatment for alcoholism or drug addiction
   d. Amounts paid for lodging (but not meals) while away from home primarily for medical care provided by a physician in a licensed hospital or equivalent medical care facility. Limit is $50 per night for each individual
   e. Medical and hospital insurance premiums
   f. Prescribed medicines and insulin
   g. Transportation for needed medical care (actual expenses or 9¢/mile if you use your car)
   h. Special items and equipment, including false teeth, artificial limbs, eyeglasses, hearing aids, crutches, guide dogs, motorized wheelchairs, hand controls on a car, and special telephones for deaf

6. Items not deductible as medical expenses include

   a. Bottled water, maternity clothes, and diaper service
   b. Household help, and care of a normal and healthy baby by a nurse (but a portion may qualify for child or dependent care tax credit)
   c. Toothpaste, toiletries, cosmetics, etc.
   d. Program to stop smoking or lose weight (unless prescribed to alleviate a specific illness)
   e. Trip, social activities, or health club dues for general improvement of health
   f. Nonprescribed medicines and drugs (e.g., over the counter medicines)
   g. Illegal operation or treatment
   h. Funeral and burial expenses

7. Reimbursement for expenses deducted in an earlier year may be gross income in the period received under the tax benefit rule

8. Reimbursement in excess of expenses is includible in income to the extent the excess reimbursement was paid by policies provided by employer

B. **Taxes**

1. The following taxes are deductible as a tax in year paid if they are imposed on the taxpayer:

   a. Income tax (state, local, or foreign)

      (1) The deduction for state and local taxes includes amounts withheld from salary, estimated payments made during the year, and payments made during the year on a tax for a prior year
      (2) A refund of a prior year's taxes is not offset against the current year's deduction, but is generally included in income under the tax benefit rule

   b. Real property tax (state, local, or foreign). When real property is sold, the deduction is apportioned between buyer and seller on a daily basis within the real property tax year, even if the parties do not apportion the taxes at the closing

   c. Personal property tax (state or local, not foreign)

2. The following taxes are deductible only as an expense incurred in a trade or business or in the production of income (above the line)

   a. Social security and other employment taxes paid by employer
   b. Federal excise taxes on automobiles, tires, telephone service, and air transportation
   c. Customs duties and gasoline taxes
   d. State and local taxes not deductible as such (stamp or cigarette taxes) or charges of a primarily regulatory nature (licenses, etc.)
   e. Sales taxes incurred on the acquisition or disposition of property are treated as part of the cost of the acquired property or as a reduction in the amount realized on the dispostion

3. The following taxes are not deductible

   a. Federal income taxes
   b. Federal, state, or local estate or gift taxes
   c. Social security and other Federal employment taxes paid by employee (including self-employment taxes)
   d. Social security and other employment taxes paid by an employer on the wages of an employee who only performed domestic services (maid, etc.)

C. **Interest Expense**

1. Personal interest. The deduction for personal interest is phased out over a five-year period beginning in 1987. The percentage of personal interest that is deductible is 65% for 1987, 40% for 1988, 20% for 1989, and 10% for 1990. After 1990, no deduction will be allowed for personal interest

   a. Personal interest includes interest paid or incurred to purchase an asset for personal use, credit card interest for personal purchases, interest incurred as an employee, and interest on income tax underpayments

b. Personal interest <u>excludes</u> qualified residence interest, investment interest, interest properly allocable to a trade or business (other than as an employee), interest incurred in a passive activity subject to the passive activity rules, and interest on deferred estate taxes

> *EXAMPLE: X, a self-employed consultant, finances a new automobile used 80% for business and 20% for personal use. X would treat 80% of the interest as deductible business interest expense (toward AGI), and 20% as personal interest subject to the above phase-out rules.*

> *EXAMPLE: Y, an employee, finances a new automobile used 80% for use in his employer's business and 20% for personal use. All of the interest expense on the auto loan would be considered personal interest subject to the above phase-out rules.*

2. <u>Qualified residence interest</u>. The disallowance of personal interest above does not apply to interest paid or accrued on acquisition indebtedness or home equity indebtedness secured by a security interest perfected under local law on the taxpayer's principal residence or a second residence owned by the taxpayer

a. <u>Acquisition indebtedness</u>. Interest is deductible on up to $1,000,000 ($500,000 if married filing separately) of loans secured by the residence if such loans were used to acquire, construct, or substantially improve the home

  (1) Acquisition indebtedness is reduced as principal payments are made and cannot be restored or increased by refinancing the home
  (2) If the home is refinanced, the amount qualifying as acquisition indebtedness is limited to the amount of acquisition debt existing at the time of refinancing plus any amount of the new loan which is used to substantially improve the home

b. <u>Home equity indebtedness</u>. Interest is deductible on up to $100,000 ($50,000 if married filing separately) of loans secured by the residence (other than acquisition indebtedness) regardless of how the loan proceeds are used (e.g., for a personal car, education expenses, medical expenses, etc.). The amount of home equity indebtedness cannot exceed the FMV of the home as reduced by any acquisition indebtedness

> *EXAMPLE: Allan purchased a home for $380,000, borrowing $250,000 of the purchase price which was secured by a 15 year mortgage. In 1989, when the home was worth $400,000 and the balance of the first mortgage was $230,000, Allan obtained a second mortgage on the home in the amount of $120,000, using the proceeds for a car and to pay off personal loans.*

> *Allan may deduct the interest on the balance of the first mortgage acquisition indebtedness of $230,000. However, Allan can deduct interest on only $100,000 of the second mortgage because it is considered home equity indebtedness since the loan proceeds were not used to acquire, construct, or substantially improve a home.*

c. <u>Transitional rules</u>. All debt incurred before October 13, 1987 which is secured by a first or second residence is considered acquisition indebtedness. For this purpose, the $1,000,000 (or $500,000) limitation on acquisition indebtedness does not apply. Additionally, any debt incurred to refinance pre-October 13, 1987 debt secured by a first or second residence is considered acquisition indebtedness to the extent of the principal refinanced

EXAMPLE: Beth used cash to purchase a residence in 1980. During 1986, she obtained a $150,000 loan secured by a mortgage on her home. She used the $150,000 of loan proceeds to pay off the loans on her car and airplane. In 1988, the interest on Beth's mortgage on her home is fully deductible since the entire $150,000 mortgage constitutes acquisition indebtedness under the transitional rules.

EXAMPLE: In 1989, when the balance of the mortgage was $130,000, Beth refinanced the debt by borrowing $160,000, using the additional $30,000 to buy a mink coat. Only interest on the $130,000 of mortgage principal refinanced is deductible as interest on acquisition indebtedness under the transitional rules. However, interest on the additional $30,000 of mortgage principal would also be deductible because it is considered home equity indebtedness.

    d. The term "residence" includes houses, condominiums, cooperative housing units, and any other property that the taxpayer uses as a dwelling unit (e.g., mobile home, motor home, boat, etc.)

    e. In the case of a residence used partly for rental purposes, the interest can only be qualified residence interest if the taxpayer's personal use during the year exceeds the greater of 14 days or 10% of the number of days of rental use (unless the residence was not rented at any time during the year)

    f. Qualified residence interest does not include interest on unsecured home improvement loans

3. <u>Investment interest</u>. The deduction for investment interest expense for noncorporate taxpayers is limited to the amount of net investment income. Interest disallowed is carried forward indefinitely and is allowed only to the extent of net investment income in a subsequent year

    a. Investment interest is interest paid or accrued on indebtedness properly allocable to property held for investment including

        (1) Interest expense allocable to portfolio income, and

        (2) Interest expense allocable to a trade or business in which the taxpayer does not materially participate, if that activity is not treated as a passive activity

    b. Investment interest excludes interest expense taken into account in determining income or loss from a passive activity, interest allocable to rental real estate in which the taxpayer actively participates, qualified residence interest, and personal interest

    c. Net investment income includes

        (1) Interest, dividends, rents, and royalties in excess of any related expenses (using the actual amount of depreciation or depletion allowable)

        (2) The amount of recaptured depreciation or amortization on the disposition of depreciable property, and

        (3) Short-term and long-term capital gain from the disposition of investment property

           (a) Income or expenses taken into account in computing income or loss from a passive activity is excluded from net investment income

(b) Net investment income is generally reduced by a percentage of the amount of loss from passive activities that is allowed as a deduction due to the phase-in of the passive loss rule, but is not reduced by losses attributable to rental real estate activity in which the taxpayer actively participates. Net investment income is reduced 35% of deductible passive losses in 1987, 60% in 1988, 80% in 1989, 90% in 1990, and 100% in 1991 and later years.

d. The disallowed investment interest caused solely by the repeal of the $10,000 allowance under prior law ($5,000 for a married individual filing separately) is phased in as follows: 35% disallowed in 1987, 60% in 1988, 80% in 1989, 90% in 1990, with a full disallowance after 1990

EXAMPLE: For 1988, a single taxpayer has investment interest expense of $40,000 and net investment income of $24,000, resulting in excess investment interest expense of $16,000. However, under the phase-in rule, only (60% x $10,000) = $6,000 of the first $10,000 of excess investment interest expense is disallowed. Thus, the deductible investment interest expense for 1988 is $24,000 + $4,000 = $28,000; the remaining $12,000 is disallowed.

D. Charitable Contributions

Contributions to qualified domestic charitable organizations are deductible in the year actually paid or donated (for both accrual and cash basis taxpayers) with some carryover allowed. A "pledge" is not a payment. Charging the contribution on your bank card does constitute payment

1. Qualified organizations include
    a. A state, a U.S. possession, or political subdivision, or the District of Columbia if made exclusively for public purposes
    b. A community chest, corporation, foundation, etc., operated exclusively for charitable, religious, educational, scientific, or literary purposes, or for the prevention of cruelty to children or animals, or for fostering national or international amateur sports competition (unless they provide facilities or equipment)

    (1) No part of the earnings may inure to any individual's benefit
    (2) May not attempt to influence legislation or intervene in any political campaign

    c. Church, synagogue, or other religious organizations
    d. War veterans' organizations
    e. Domestic fraternal societies operating under the lodge system (only if contribution used exclusively for the charitable purposes listed in "b." above)
    f. Nonprofit cemetery companies if the funds are irrevocably dedicated to the perpetual care of the cemetery as a whole, and not a particular lot or mausoleum crypt

2. Dues, fees, or assessments paid to qualified organizations are deductible to the extent that payments exceed benefits received. Not deductible to
    a. Veterans' organizations
    b. Lodges
    c. Fraternal organizations
    d. Country clubs

3. Out of pocket expenses to maintain a <u>student</u> (domestic or foreign) in a taxpayer's home are deductible (limited to $50/month for each month the individual is a full-time student) if

    a. Student is in 12th or lower grade, and not a dependent or relative
    b. Based on written agreement between taxpayer and qualified organization
    c. Taxpayer receives no reimbursement

4. Payments to qualified organizations for goods or services are deductible to the extent the amount paid exceeds the fair market value of benefits received

5. A taxpayer who makes a payment to or for the benefit of a college or university and is thereby entitled to purchase tickets to athletic events is allowed to deduct 80% of the payment as a charitable contribution. Any payment that is attributable to the actual cost of tickets is not deductible as a charitable contribution

6. Unreimbursed out of pocket expenses incurred while rendering services to a charitable organization without compensation are deductible, including actual auto expenses or a standard rate of 12¢ per mile may be used

7. <u>Nondeductible</u> contributions include contributions to/for/of

    a. Civic leagues, social clubs, and foreign organizations
    b. Communist organizations, chambers of commerce, labor unions
    c. The value of your time or services
    d. The use of property, or less than an entire interest in property
    e. Blood donated
    f. Tuition or amounts in place of tuition
    g. Payments to a hospital for care of particular patients
    h. "Sustainer's gift" to retirement home
    i. Raffles, bingo, etc. (but may qualify as gambling loss)
    j. Fraternal societies if the contributions are used to defray sickness or burial expenses of members
    k. Political organizations
    l. Travel, including meals and lodging (e.g., trip to serve at charity's national meeting), if there is any significant element of personal pleasure, recreation, or vacation involved

8. Gifts of property to qualified organizations are <u>deductible</u>

    a. At fair market value when FMV is below basis
    b. At basis when fair market value exceeds basis and if sold gain would be short-term capital gain or ordinary income (e.g., gain would be ordinary because of depreciation recapture or if property is inventory)
    c. At fair market value if long-term capital gain property, but

        (1) Contribution must be reduced by the entire amount of any long-term capital gain or Sec. 1231 gain that would have been realized if the property had been sold <u>if</u>

             (a) Contribution is tangible personal property and is unrelated to the purpose or the function of the charity, or

(b) Contributed to certain private nonoperating foundations (except qualified appreciated stock)

d. The contribution must be reduced by interest prepaid or interest liability on a loan assumed by the donee
e. Appraisal fees on donated property are a miscellaneous deduction

9. The overall limitation for contribution deductions is 50% of adjusted gross income (before any net operating loss carryback). A second limitation is that contributions of long-term capital gain property to "8.a." charities (where gain is not reduced) are limited to 30% of AGI. A third limitation is that some contributions to certain charities are limited to 20% of AGI or a lesser amount

a. Contributions to the following are taken first and may be taken up to 50% of AGI limitation

(1) Public charities

(a) Churches
(b) Educational organizations
(c) Tax exempt hospitals
(d) Medical research
(e) States or political subdivisions
(f) U.S. or District of Columbia

(2) All private operating foundations (i.e., foundations that spend their income directly for the active conduct of their exempt activities, e.g., public museums)
(3) Certain private nonoperating foundations that distribute proceeds to public and private operating charities

b. Deductions for contributions of long-term capital gain property (when the gain is not to be reduced) to organizations in "8.a." above are limited to 30% of adjusted gross income; but, taxpayer may elect to reduce all appreciated long-term capital gain property by the potential gain and not be subject to this 30% limitation
c. Deductions for contributions to charities that do not qualify in "8.a." above (generally private nonoperating foundations) are subject to special limitations

(1) The deduction limitation for gifts of

(a) Ordinary income property is the lesser of (1) 30% of AGI, or (2) (50% x AGI) - gifts to "8.a." charities
(b) Capital gain property is lesser of (1) 20% of AGI, or (2) (30% x AGI) - gifts of long-term capital gain property to "8.a." charities where no reduction is made for appreciation

(2) These deductions are taken after deductions to organizations in "8.a." above without the 30% limitation on capital gain property in "8.b." above

EXAMPLE: An individual with AGI of $9,000 made a contribution of capital gain appreciated property with a FMV of $5,000 to a church, and gave $2,000 cash to a private nonoperating foundation. Since the contribution to the church (before the 30% limit) exceeds 50% of AGI, no part of the contribution to the foundation is deductible this year.

Assuming no election is made to reduce the contribution of the capital gain property by the amount of its appreciation, the current deduction for the contribution to the church is limited to 30% x $9,000 = $2,700.

10. Contributions in excess of the 50%, 30%, or 20% limitation can be carried forward for <u>5 years</u> and remain subject to the 50%, 30%, or 20% limitation in the carryforward years

EXAMPLE: Your adjusted gross income is $50,000. During the year you gave your church $2,000 cash and land (held for investment more than one year) having a fair market value of $30,000 and a basis to you of $22,000. You also gave $5,000 cash to a private foundation to which a 30% limitation applies.

Since your contributions to an organization to which the 50% limitation applies (disregarding the 30% limitation for capital gain property) exceed $25,000 (50% of $50,000), your contribution to the private foundation is not deductible this year.

The $2,000 cash donated to the church is deducted first. The donation for the gift of land is not required to be reduced by the appreciation in value, but is limited to $15,000 (30% x $50,000). Thus, you may deduct only $17,000 ($2,000 + $15,000). The unused portion of the land contribution ($15,000) and the gift to the private foundation ($5,000) are carried over to the next year, still subject to their respective 30% limitations.

Alternatively, you may elect to reduce the land by its appreciation of $8,000 and not be subject to the 30% limitation for capital gain property. In such case your current deduction would be $25,000 ($2,000 cash + $22,000 land + $1,000 cash to private foundation), but only the remaining $4,000 cash to the private foundation would be carried over to the next year.

E. Personal Casualty and Theft Gains and Losses

Gains and losses from casualties and thefts of property held for personal use are no longer subject to the Sec. 1231 netting process. Instead, personal casualty and theft gains and losses are separately netted, without regard to the holding period of the converted property

1. A casualty loss must be identifiable, damaging to property, and sudden, unexpected, or unusual. Casualty losses include

    a. Damage from a fire, storm, accident, mine cave-in, sonic boom, or loss from vandalism
    b. Damage to trees and shrubs if there is a decrease in the total value of the real estate
    c. A loss on personal residence that has been rendered unsafe by reason of a disaster declared by President and has been ordered demolished or relocated by a state or local government

2. Losses not deductible as casualties include

    a. Losses from the breakage of china or glassware through handling or by a family pet
    b. Disease, termite, or moth damage
    c. Expenses incident to casualty (temporary quarters, etc.)
    d. Progressive deterioration through a steadily operating cause and damage from normal process. Thus, the steady weakening of a building caused by normal or usual wind and weather conditions is not a casualty loss

    e. Losses from nearby disaster (property value reduced due to location near a disaster area)

    f. Loss of future profits from, for example, ice storm damage to standing timber that reduces the rate of growth or the quality of future timber is not deductible. To qualify as a casualty, the damage must actually result in existing timber being rendered unfit for use

3. Casualty loss is deductible in the year the loss occurs

    a. Theft loss is deductible in the year the loss is discovered

    b. Loss in a declared disaster area is deductible either in the year loss occurs or the preceding year (by filing an amended return)

4. The amount of loss is the lesser of (1) the decrease in the FMV of the property resulting from the casualty, or (2) the adjusted basis of the property. The amount of loss must be reduced by

    a. Any insurance or reimbursement, and

    b. $100 floor for each separate nonbusiness casualty

5. An individual is not permitted to deduct a casualty loss for damage to insured property not used in a trade or business or in a transaction entered into for profit unless the individual files a timely insurance claim with respect to the loss

6. If personal casualty and theft gains exceed losses (after the $100 floor for each loss), then all gains and losses are treated as capital gains and losses

    EXAMPLE: An individual incurred a $5,000 personal casualty gain, and a $1,000 personal casualty loss during the current taxable year. Since there was a net gain, the individual will report the gain and loss as a $5,000 capital gain and a $1,000 capital loss.

7. If losses (after the $100 floor for each loss) exceed gains, the losses-- (1) offset gains, and (2) are an ordinary deduction from AGI to the extent in excess of 10% of AGI

    EXAMPLE: An individual had AGI of $40,000 (before casualty gains and losses), and also had a personal casualty loss of $12,000 (after the $100 floor) and a personal casualty gain of $3,000. Since there was a personal casualty net loss, the net loss will be deductible as an itemized deduction of [$12,000 − $3,000 − (10% x $40,000)] = $5,000.

    EXAMPLE: Frank Jones' lakeside cottage which cost him $13,600 (including $1,600 for the land) on April 30, 1975, was partially destroyed by fire on July 12, 1989. The value of the property immediately before the fire was $46,000 ($24,000 for the building and $22,000 for the land), and the value immediately after the fire was $36,000. He collected $7,000 from the insurance company. It was Jones' only casualty for 1989 and his AGI was $25,000. Jones' casualty loss deduction from the fire would be $400, computed as follows.

        1. Value of entire property before fire $46,000

        2. Value of entire property after fire   36,000

        3. Decrease in fair market value of entire property $10,000

A CHARITABLE CONTRIBUTION FLOWCHART FOR INDIVIDUALS

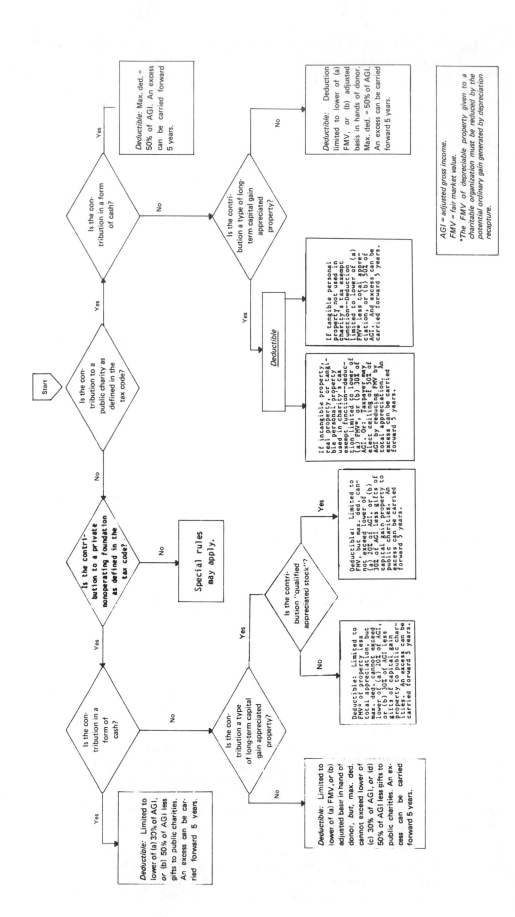

4. Adjusted basis (cost in this case)	$13,600
5. Loss sustained (lesser of 3 or 4)	$10,000
6. Less insurance recovery	- 7,000
7. Casualty loss	$ 3,000
8. Less $100 limitation	- 100
9. Loss after $100 limitation	$ 2,900
10. Less 10% of AGI	- 2,500
11. Casualty loss deduction	$ 400

F. Moving expenses

1. The distance between the former residence and new job (d_2) must be at least 35 miles farther than from the former residence to the former job (d_1) (i.e., $d_2 - d_1 \geq 35$ miles). If no former job, new job must be at least 35 miles from former residence

2. Employee must be employed at least 39 weeks out of the 12 months following the move. Self-employed individual must be employed 78 weeks out of the 24 months following the move (in addition to 39 weeks out of first 12 months). Time test does not have to be met in case of death, taxpayer's job at new location ends beacuse of disability, or taxpayer is laid off for other than willful misconduct

3. Deductible expenses are

   a. Travel expenses for family to move (including 80% of meal expenses)
   b. Costs of moving household goods and personal assets
   c. Costs of househunting including transportation, meals, and lodging
   d. Temporary living expenses during any 30-day period after obtaining employment
   e. Residence sale and purchase related expenses, e.g., real estate commissions

      (1) (c) and (d) are limited to $1,500
      (2) (c), (d), and (e) are limited to $3,000

G. Miscellaneous Deductions

1. The 1986 TRA substantially changed this category of itemized deductions by reclassifying unreimbursed employee travel and transportation expenses, and outside salesman expenses as miscellaneous itemized deductions. Thus, for taxable years beginning after 1986, taxpayers must itemize to deduct these expenses

2. The 1986 TRA additionally provided that miscellaneous itemized deductions are generally deductible only to the extent that (in the aggregate) they exceed 2% of AGI

3. The following miscellaneous expenses are not subject to the 2% floor, but instead are deductible in full

   a. Gambling losses to the extent of gambling winnings

    b. Impairment-related work expenses for handicapped employees
    c. Estate tax related to income in respect of a decedent
    d. Certain adjustments when a taxpayer restores amounts held under a claim of right
    e. Amortization of bond premium
    f. Certain costs of cooperative housing corporations
    g. Certain expenses of short sales
    h. The balance of an employee's investment in an annuity contract where the employee dies before recovering the entire investment

4. The following miscellaneous expenses are only deductible to the extent they (in the aggregate) exceed 2% of AGI

    a. Outside salesman expenses include all business expenses of an employee who principally solicits business for his/her employer while away from the employer's place of business
    b. All unreimbursed employee expenses including

        (1) Employee education expenses if

            (a) Incurred to maintain or improve skills required in employee's present job, or to meet requirements to keep job
            (b) Deductible expenses include unreimbursed transportation, travel, tuition, books, supplies, etc.
            (c) Education expenses are not deductible if required to meet minimum educational requirements in employee's job, or the education qualifies the employee for a new job (e.g., CPA Review Course) even if a new job is not sought
            (d) Travel as a form of education is not deductible

        (2) Other deductible unreimbursed employee expenses include

            (a) Transportation and travel (including 80% of meals and entertainment)
            (b) Uniforms not adaptable to general use
            (c) Employment agency fees to secure employment in same occupation
            (d) Subscription to professional journals
            (e) Dues to professional societies, union dues and initiation fees
            (f) Physical examinations required by employer
            (g) A college professor's research, lecturing, and writing expenses
            (h) Amounts teacher pays to a substitute
            (i) Surety bond premiums
            (j) Malpractice insurance premiums
            (k) A research chemist's laboratory breakage fees
            (l) Small tools and supplies

    c. Tax counsel, assistance, and tax return preparation fees
    d. Expenses for the production of income other than those incurred in a trade or business or for production of rents and royalties (e.g., investment counsel fees, clerical help, safe deposit box rent, etc.)

5. Examples of nondeductible expenses include

    a. Fees and licenses, such as auto licenses, marriage licenses, and dog tags
    b. Home repairs, insurance, rent
    c. Personal legal expenses
    d. Life insurance

    e. Burial expenses
    f. Capital expenditures
    g. Illegal bribes and kickbacks
    h. Fines and tax penalties
    i. Collateral
    j. Commuting to and from work
    k. Professional accreditation fees
    l. Bar examination fees and incidental expenses in securing admission to the bar
    m. Medical and dental license fees paid to obtain initial licensing
    n. Campaign expenses of a candidate for any office are not deductible, nor are registration fees for primary elections, even if taxpayer is the incumbent of the office to be contested
    o. Cost of midday meals while working late (except while traveling away from home)
    p. Political contributions

IV.   EXEMPTIONS

Personal exemptions are like itemized deductions in that they are deducted from adjusted gross income ("below the line" deductions). Personal exemptions are allowed for the taxpayer, spouse, and dependents if taxpayer is a U.S. citizen or resident.

1. The personal exemption amount is $1,950 for 1988, and $2,000 for 1989. Beginning in 1990, the amount will be indexed for inflation

2. Beginning in 1988, the personal exemption amounts claimed on a return are phased out if TI exceeds the amount where the 15% bracket is eliminated

Filing Status	Phase-out begins if TI exceeds	
	1988	1989
Single	$ 89,560	$ 93,130
Head of household	123,790	128,810
Married, filing jointly	149,250	155,320
Married, filing separately	113,300	117,895

    a. The phase-out is accomplished by a 5% additional tax on TI exceeding the threshold amount
    b. For 1988, the tax benefit of one personal exemption ($1,950 x 28% = $546) will be lost for each additional $10,920 of TI above the threshold amount ($11,200 for 1989)
    c. In the case of a married individual filing a separate return, the maximum amount of additional income tax liability resulting from the phaseout of the deduction for personal exemptions is determined as if the taxpayer was allowed a personal exemption for the taxpayer's spouse

3. Personal exemption for taxpayer

    a. Full exemption even if birth or death occurred during the year
    b. No personal exemption for taxpayer if eligible to be claimed as a dependent on another taxpayer's return

4. Exemption for spouse

    a. Exemption on joint return

b. Not allowed if divorced or legally separated at end of year
c. If a separate return is filed, taxpayer may claim spouse exemption only
    if the spouse had no gross income and was not the dependent of another
    taxpayer

5. Exemptions for dependents

a. Full exemption even if death or birth occurred during the year
b. Each dependent must meet 5 tests

    (1) Support. Taxpayer must furnish over one-half of support

         (a) Support includes lodging, meals, clothing, medical, etc.
         (b) Support excludes scholarships, life insurance, taxes, etc.

    (2) Gross income. Dependent had less than $1,950 gross income for 1988
         ($2,000 for 1989)

         (a) Does not apply to child of the taxpayer less than 19 at end of
              year
         (b) Does not apply to taxpayer's child if a full-time student (at
              least 5 months out of the year) whatever child's age. Begin-
              ning in 1989, this exception does not apply if the taxpayer's
              child has attained the age of 24 by the close of the calendar
              year
         (c) Gross income does not include tax-exempt income (e.g.,
              nontaxable social security)

    (3) Household or relationship. Dependent must either be of specified
         relationship (closer than cousin), or live with taxpayer the entire
         year

         (a) A person who is temporarily absent for vacation, school, or
              sickness, or is indefinitely confined in a nursing home meets
              the member of household test
         (b) A person who died during the year but was a member of
              household until death, and a child who is born during the year
              and was a member of household for the rest of year, meet the
              member of household test

    (4) Citizenship. Dependent must be a citizen, resident, or national of
         U.S., or a resident of Canada or Mexico
    (5) Joint return. Dependent cannot file a joint return, unless joint
         return is filed solely for refund of tax withheld

c. A multiple support agreement can be used if no single taxpayer furnishes
    more than 50% of the support of a dependent. Then any taxpayer (who
    meets the other requirements) contributing more than 10% can claim the
    dependent provided others furnishing more than 10% agree not to claim
    the dependent as an exemption
d. Child of divorced or separated parents

    (1) Treated as receiving over one-half of support from parent who has
         custody for the greater part of the year
    (2) Parent who does not have custody will be treated as providing over
         one-half of support if

(a) Pre-1985 divorce decree or written agreement entitles that parent to the exemptions and that parent provides $600 or more for the child's support, or

(b) Custodial parent signs a written declaration waiving the right to claim such child as a dependent, and the written declaration is attached to the noncustodial parent's return

V. TAX COMPUTATION

A. **Tax Tables**

1. Tax tables contain precomputed tax liability based on taxable income

    a. AGI less itemized deductions and exemptions
    b. Filing status

       (1) Single
       (2) Head of household
       (3) Married filing separately
       (4) Married filing joint return (even if only one had income)
       (5) Surviving spouse (qualifying widow(er) with dependent child)

2. Tax tables must be used by taxpayers unless taxable income is $50,000 or more

B. **Tax Rate Schedules**

1. Beginning in 1988, only two rates will apply

Tax Rates	Joint Returns	Married Separate	Head of Household	Single
		Taxable Income		
15%	Up to $29,750	Up to $14,875	Up to $23,900	Up to $17,850
28%	Over $29,750	Over $14,875	Over $23,900	Over $17,850

   a. Beginning in 1988, the 15% bracket is phased out for taxpayers with high taxable income. This is accomplished by an additional tax of 5% on taxable income within certain ranges. The additional 5% tax applies to TI levels between $71,900 and $149,250 for joint returns, $35,950 and $113,300 for married filing separately, $61,650 and $123,790 for heads of household, and between $43,150 and $89,560 for single taxpayers

   b. The dollar amounts for the tax rate brackets and the phase-out of the 15% bracket will be adjusted for inflation beginning in 1989

   EXAMPLE: A married couple filing a joint return have taxable income for 1988 of $149,250. Their tax would be computed as follows

Bracket	Rate	Tax
$0 to $29,750	15%	$ 4,463
$29,751 to $71,900	28%	11,802
$71,901 to $149,250	33%	25,525
Total tax		$41,790

   Note that the 5% additional tax effectively eliminated the 15% bracket and the taxpayers will pay an effective rate of 28% on their taxable income ($149,250 x 28%) = $41,790.

2. <u>Income of children under age 14</u>. The earned income of a child of any age and the unearned income of a child 14 years or older as of the end of the taxable year is taxed at the child's own marginal rate. However, the

unearned income in excess of $1,000 of a child under age 14 is generally taxed at the rates of the child's parents

a. The amount taxed at the parents' rates equals the child's unearned income less the sum of (1) any penalty for early withdrawal of savings, (2) $500, and (3) the greater of $500 or the child's itemized deductions directly connected with the production of unearned income

    (1) Directly connected itemized deductions are those expenses incurred to produce or collect income, or maintain property that produces unearned income, including custodian fees, service fees to collect interest and dividends, and investment advisory fees. These are deductible as miscellaneous itemized deductions subject to a 2% of AGI limitation

    (2) The amount taxed at the parents' rates cannot exceed the child's taxable income

EXAMPLE: Brian (age 12) is claimed as a dependent on his parents' return, has interest income of $15,000 and itemized deductions of $1,200 that are directly connected to the production of the interest income. The amount taxed at his parents' rates is $13,300 [$15,000 - ($500 + $1,200)]

EXAMPLE: Kerry (age 10) is claimed as a dependent on her parents' return, has interest income of $12,000, an early withdrawal penalty of $350, and itemized deduction of $400 that are directly connected to the production of the interest income. The amount taxed at her parents' rates is $10,650 [$12,000 - ($350 + $500 + $500)]

b. A child's tax liability on unearned income taxed at the parents' rates is the child's share of the increase in tax (including alternative minimum tax) that would result from adding to the parents' taxable income the unearned income of their children under age 14

c. If the child's parents are divorced, the custodial parent's taxable income will be used in determining the child's tax liability

d. If child's parents are divorced and both parents have custody, the taxable income of the parent having custody for the greater portion of the calendar year will be used in determining the child's tax liability

3. <u>Reporting unearned income of child on parent's return</u>. For taxable years beginning after 1988, parents may elect to include on their return the unearned income of their child under age 14 whose income consists solely of interest and dividends and is between $500 and $5,000

a. The child is treated as having no gross income and does not have to file a tax return for the year the election is made

b. The electing parents must include the child's gross income in excess of $1,000 on their return for the tax year, resulting in the taxation of that income at the parents' highest marginal rate. Also, the parents must report additional tax liability equal to the lesser of (1) $75, or (2) 15% of the child's income between $500 and $1,000

c. The election cannot be made if estimated tax payments were made for the tax year in the child's name and social security number, or if the child is subject to backup withholding

C. **Filing Status**

1. Married persons (married at year end or at death of spouse) can file joint return or separate returns

2. Surviving spouse (i.e., qualifying widow(er) with dependent child) can use joint return rates for two years after death of spouse if

   a. Dependent child lives with surviving spouse, and
   b. Surviving spouse was eligible to file joint return in year of spouse's death, and
   c. Surviving spouse pays over one-half of cost of maintaining household, and
   d. Surviving spouse does not remarry before year end

3. Head of household status applies to unmarried person not qualifying for surviving spouse status but who maintains a household for more than one-half of the taxable year for

   a. An unmarried child or other descendant (who need not be a dependent), or
   b. Relative (closer than cousin) who is a dependent; including a married child or married descendant
   c. Parents need not live with head of household, but parents' household must be maintained by taxpayer, e.g., nursing home
   d. Unmarried requirement is satisfied if spouses are living apart under a separate maintenance decree

D. **Alternative Minimum Tax (AMT)**

1. The alternative minimum tax is computed by applying a 21% tax rate to alternative minimum taxable income (AMTI) after exemption

   a. Applies only if it exceeds the amount of regular tax
   b. Is reduced by only foreign tax credits attributable to foreign-source income included in AMTI

2. Computation. The AMT is generally the amount by which 21% of alternative minimum taxable income (AMTI) as reduced by an exemption, exceeds the regular tax (i.e., regular tax liability reduced by the regular foreign tax credit). AMTI is equal to taxable income computed with specified adjustments and increased by tax preferences

3. Exemption. AMTI is offset by an exemption. However, the AMT exemption amount is phased out at the rate of 25% of AMTI between certain specified levels

Filing status	AMT exemption	Phase-out range
Married filing jointly; Surviving Spouse	$40,000	$150,000 – $310,000
Single; Head of Household	$30,000	$112,500 – $232,500
Married filing separately	$20,000	$ 75,000 – $155,000

4. Adjustments. In determining AMTI, taxable income must be computed with various adjustments. Example of adjustments include

a. For real property placed in service after 1986, the excess of accelerated depreciation over straight-line using a 40 year life
b. For personal property placed in service after 1986, the excess of accelerated depreciation over the amount determined using the 150% declining balance method (switching to straight-line when necessary to maximize the deduction)
c. Passive activity losses deductible for regular tax purposes are added back to TI
d. For long-term contracts, the excess of income under the percentage of completion method over the amount reported using the completed contract method
e. The installment method cannot be used for sales of dealer property
f. The medical expense deduction is computed using a 10% floor (instead of the 7.5% floor used for regular tax)
g. Personal interest is disallowed entirely, rather than being phased out over 4 years
h. No deduction is allowed for personal state and local taxes, and miscellaneous itemized deductions subject to the 2% floor for regular tax purposes
i. No deduction is allowed for personal exemptions and the standard deduction

5. Preference items. The following are examples of preference items added to taxable income (as adjusted above) in computing AMTI

a. Accelerated depreciation on real property and leased personal property placed in service before 1987--excess of accelerated depreciation over straight-line
b. The excess of percentage depletion over the property's adjusted basis
c. The excess of intangible drilling costs using a 10-year amortization over 65% of net oil and gas income
d. The untaxed appreciation on long-term capital gain property donated to charity if taxpayer did not elect to reduce FMV by appreciation
e. Tax-exempt interest on certain private activity bonds reduced by related interest expense that is disallowed for regular tax purposes

6. Minimum tax credit. The amount of AMT paid (net of exclusion preferences) is allowed as a credit against regular tax liability in future years

a. The amount of the AMT credit to be carried forward is the excess of the AMT paid over the AMT that would be paid if AMTI included only exclusion preferences (e.g., disallowed itemized deductions, and the preferences for excess percentage depletion, tax-exempt interest, and charitable contributions)
b. The credit can be carried forward indefinitely, but not carried back
c. The AMT credit can only be used to reduce regular tax liability, not future AMT liability

E. **Other Taxes**

1. Social security (FICA) tax is imposed on both employers and employees (withheld from wages) at a rate of 7.51% on first $48,000 of wages for 1989

2. Federal unemployment (FUTA) tax is imposed only on employers at a rate of 6.2% of the first $7,000 of wages paid each employee. A credit of up to 5.4% is available for unemployment taxes paid to a state, leaving a net federal tax of 0.8%

3. <u>Self-employment</u> tax is imposed on individuals who work for themselves (e.g., sole proprietor, independent contractor, partner) at a rate of 13.02% on first $48,000 of self-employment income for 1989

   a. Income from self-employment generally includes all items of business income less business deductions. Does not include personal interest, dividends, rents, capital gains and losses, gains and losses on the disposition of business property, and the self-employment tax
   b. Wages subject to FICA tax are deducted from $48,000 in determining the amount of income subject to self-employment tax
   c. No tax if net earnings from self-employment are less than $400

F. **Supplemental Medicare Premiums**

   1. After 1988, individuals eligible for Medicare Part A (hospital benefits) for more than six full months during a taxable year are subject to a surcharge on their federal income tax liability to help finance the benefits provided by the Medicare Catastrophic Coverage Act of 1988

      a. The surcharge (i.e., supplemental premium) is $22.50 ($27.14 for 1990) for each $150 of federal income tax liability
      b. The maximum supplemental premium is $800 for 1989 ($850 for 1990). In the case of a married couple where both spouses are Medicare-eligible, the maximum is $1,600 for 1989 ($1,700 for 1990)

   2. The supplemental premium is considered a tax for estimated tax purposes, but is not considered to be a tax for purposes of the alternative minimum tax on deducting tax credits

   3. The supplemental premium cannot be deducted as a medical expense, and applies regardless of whether an individual has ever received any Medicare benefits

   EXAMPLE: H and W are both Medicare-eligible and have an income tax liability of $12,000 for 1989. Their supplemental premium is the lesser of (1) $1,600, or (2) ($12,000/$150) x $22.50 = $1,800. Thus, their total tax liability is $13,600.

VI.   TAX CREDITS/ESTIMATED TAX PAYMENTS

Tax credits directly reduce tax liability. The tax liability less tax credits equals tax payable. Taxes which have already been withheld on wages, and estimated tax payments are credited against tax liability without limitation, even if the result is a refund due the taxpayer.

A. **General Business Credit**

   1. It is comprised of the (1) investment credit (regular, energy, and rehabilitation), (2) targeted jobs credit, (3) alcohol fuels credit, (4) research credit, and (5) low-income housing credit

   2. The general business credit is allowed to the extent of "net income tax" less the greater of (1) the tentative minimum tax, or (2) 25% of "net regular tax liability" above $25,000

      a. "Net income tax" means the amount of the regular income tax plus the alternative minimum tax, and minus nonrefundable tax credits (except the alternative minimum tax credit)

      b. "Net regular tax liability" is the taxpayer's regular tax liability reduced by nonrefundable tax credits (except the alternative minimum tax credit)

EXAMPLE: An individual (not subject to the alternative minimum tax) has a net income tax of $65,000. The individual's general business credit cannot exceed $65,000 - [25% x ($65,000 - $25,000)] = $55,000.

B. Regular Investment Tax Credit (ITC)

1. The 1986 TRA generally repealed (subject to numerous transition rules) the regular ITC for property placed in service after 1985, although it did not repeal the ITC for energy property and for qualified rehabilitation expenditures for real property

    a. For a taxpayer's first taxable year beginning after June 30, 1987, any regular ITC carryforwards are reduced by 35%. This 35% reduction permanently reduces the amount of regular ITC that can be utilized

2. The recoverable basis of ITC property must be reduced by 100% of the regular ITC taken after 1986

3. All or a part of the <u>ITC may be recaptured</u> if ACRS property is disposed of before the end of the recapture period, or other property is disposed of before the end of its estimated life

    a. Each full year that ACRS property is held before disposition earns 1/5 of the ITC for 5, 10, and 15-year property

    b. If 3-year ACRS property is held

Years	Recapture %
Less than 1 year	100%
1, but less than 2	66%
2, but less than 3	33%
3 or more	0%

    c. Recapture for other property is the excess of the credit allowed over the credit that would have been allowed based on the time the property was actually held

EXAMPLE: A taxpayer acquired 5-year property in 1985 and deducted an ITC of $2,000 on the property. If the property is disposed of after being held three full years, the ITC recapture would be ($2,000 x 2/5) = $ 800

C. Business Energy Credit

1. The business energy credit is <u>10%</u> or <u>15%</u> for qualified investment in energy property through December 31, 1989, depending on the type of property (e.g., 15% for ocean thermal property; 10% for solar energy property)

2. The recoverable basis of energy property must be reduced by 100% of the amount of business energy credit

D. **Credit for Rehabilitation Expenditures**

  1. Special investment credit (in lieu of regular ITC and energy credits) for qualified expenditures incurred to substantially rehabilitate old buildings. Credit percentages are (1) 10% for residential and nonresidential buildings placed in service before 1936 (other than certified historic structures), and (2) 20% for residential and nonresidential certified historic structures

  2. <u>To qualify</u> for credit on other than certified historic structures

     a. 75% of external walls must remain in place as external or internal walls
     b. 50% or more of existing external walls must be retained in place as external walls
     c. 75% or more of existing internal structural framework must be retained in place

  3. A building's recoverable basis must be reduced by 100% of the amount of rehabilitation credit

E. **Targeted Jobs Credit**

  1. The targeted jobs credit is generally 40% of the first $6,000 of qualified first-year wages paid or accrued to each qualified new employee who begins work for an employer before 1990

  2. For qualified summer youth employees, the credit is 85% (40% after 1988) of up to $3,000 of wages during any 90-day period between May 1 and September 15

     a. Qualified new employees include vocational rehabilitation referrals, economically disadvantaged youth, Vietnam-era veterans, ex-convicts, SSI recipients, general assistance recipients, youth in co-op education programs, eligible work incentive employees, involuntarily terminated CETA employees, and qualified summer youth employees
     b. The employee must either be (1) employed by the employer for at least 90 days (14 days for qualified summer youth employees), or (2) perform services for the employer for at least 120 hours (20 hours for qualified summer youth employees)
     c. Excess credit carried back 3 and forward 15 years
     d. For employees of a trade or business only; wage deduction reduced by amount of credit
     e. Taxpayer can elect not to take this credit

F. **Alcohol Fuels Credit**

  1. The amount of credit is generally 60¢ per gallon of alcohol used in a fuel mixture, or used as a fuel by the taxpayer in a trade or business or sold at retail for use as a vehicle's fuel

  2. The 60¢ per gallon rate is subject to reduction depending upon the proof of the alcohol

G. Research Credit

1. Credit consists of two parts

a. 20% of the excess of the qualified research expenses (in-house research expenses plus 65% of contract research expenses) for the taxable year over the average of research expenses for the previous three-year base period

(1) Expenses must be incurred to discover information which is technological and useful in developing new or improved business products, processes, software, techniques, or formulas. The costs of efficiency surveys, management studies, or market research, testing, or development do not qualify

(2) Base period research expenses are deemed to be not less than 50% of research expenses for current year

(3) Unused credits are carried back 3 years and forward 15 years

EXAMPLE: Taxpayer incurred qualified research expenses of $100,000 in 1988. He had never before incurred any research expenses. The research credit for 1988 would be [20% ($100,000 - $50,000 deemed average base period expenses)] = $10,000.

b. 20% of the excess of university basic research payments over the greater of two minimum amounts reflecting past research expenditures, plus an amount reflecting any decrease in nonresearch charitable donations made to universities as compared to such given during a fixed base period

2. Credit is available for expenditures incurred through December 31, 1989 regardless of whether taxpayer elected to expense or amortize the research expenditures

3. For taxable years beginning after 1988, the deduction for allowable research expenses is reduced by 50% of the research credit

a. This reduction also applies to taxpayers who capitalize research expenses

b. If 50% of the research credit exceeds the amount of qualified research expenses and basic research expenses allowable as a deduction, the excess reduces the amount of capitalized research costs

4. A taxpayer may elect not to claim the research credit in order to avoid the reduction in 3. above

H. **Low-Income Housing Credit**

1. The amount of credit for owners of low-income housing projects depends upon (1) whether the taxpayer acquires existing housing or whether the housing is newly constructed or rehabilitated, and (2) whether or not the housing project is financed by tax-exempt bonds or other federally-subsidized financing

Type of Project	Maximum Credit
New construction and rehabilitation of existing housing (Unsubsidized)	9% per year for 10 years
New construction and rehabilitation of existing housing (Subsidized)	4% per year for 10 years
Acquisition cost of existing housing	4% per year for 10 years

2.   The amount on which the credit is computed is the portion of the total
     depreciable basis of a qualified housing project that reflects the portion
     of the housing units within the project that are occupied by qualified low-
     income individuals

     *EXAMPLE: A taxpayer who is first eligible for the low-income housing credit
     on $100,000 of unsubsidized qualifying costs to rehabilitate low-income
     property on January 1, 1987 would generally be eligible for a 9% x $100,000
     = $9,000 credit for each year from 1987 through 1996.*

3.   The rate of credit will be redetermined for projects placed in service or
     acquired after 1987

I. **Credit for the Elderly and the Disabled**

1.   Eligible taxpayers are those who are either (1) 65 or older, or (2) per-
     manently and totally disabled

     a.   Permanent and total disability is the inability to engage in substantial
          gainful activity for a period that is expected to last for a continuous
          12-month period
     b.   Married individuals must file a joint return to claim the credit unless
          they have not lived together at all during the year
     c.   Credit cannot be claimed if Form 1040A or 1040EZ is filed

2.   Credit is <u>15%</u> of an initial amount reduced by certain amounts excluded from
     gross income and AGI in excess of certain levels

     a.   Initial amount varies with filing status

          (1) $5,000 for single or joint return where only one spouse is 65 or
               older
          (2) $7,500 for joint return where both spouses are 65 or older
          (3) $3,750 for married filing a separate return
          (4) Limited to disability income for taxpayers under age 65

     b.   Reduced by annuities, pensions, social security, or disability income
          that is excluded from gross income
     c.   Also reduced by 50% of the excess of AGI over

          (1) $7,500 if single
          (2) $10,000 if joint return
          (3) $5,000 for married individual filing separate return

     *EXAMPLE: H, age 67, and his wife, W, age 65, file a joint return and
     have adjusted gross income of $12,000. H received social security
     benefits of $2,000 during the year. The computation of their credit
     would be as follows.*

Initial amount		$7,500
Less: social security	$2,000	
50% of AGI over $10,000	1,000	3,000
Balance		4,500
		x 15%
Amount of credit		$ 675

J. **Child Care Credit**

1. The credit may vary from <u>20% to 30%</u> of the amount paid for qualifying household and dependent care expenses incurred to enable taxpayer to be gainfully employed. Credit is 30% if AGI is $10,000 or less, but is reduced by 1 percentage point for each $2,000 (or portion thereof) of AGI in excess of $10,000 (but not reduced below 20%)

    EXAMPLE: Able, Baker, and Charlie have AGIs of $10,000, $20,000, and $40,000 respectively, and each incurs child care expenses of $2,000. Able's child care credit is $600 (30% x $2,000); Baker's credit is $500 (25% x $2,000); and Charlie's credit is $400 (20% x $2,000).

2. <u>Eligibility</u> requirements include:

    a. Expenses must be incurred to enable taxpayer to be gainfully employed
    b. Married taxpayer must file joint return. If divorced or separated, credit available to parent having custody longer time during year
    c. Taxpayer must furnish more than half the cost of maintaining a household that is the principal residence of both taxpayer and <u>qualifying individual</u>, who is

        (1) Dependent under 13 years of age, or
        (2) Dependent or spouse who is physically or mentally incapable of self-care

    d. <u>Qualifying expenses</u> are those incurred for care of qualifying individual, and for household services that were partly for care of qualifying individual

        (1) Expenses incurred outside taxpayer's household qualify only if incurred for (1) a dependent under age 15, or (2) any other qualifying individual who regularly spends at least 8 hours each day in taxpayer's household
        (2) Payments to taxpayer's child under age 19 do not qualify
        (3) Payments to a relative do not qualify if taxpayer is entitled to a dependency exemption for that relative

3. <u>Maximum amount of expenses</u> that qualify for credit is lesser of

    a. Actual expenses incurred, or
    b. $2,400 for one, $4,800 for two or more qualifying individuals, or
    c. Taxpayer's earned income (or spouse's earned income if smaller)
    d. If spouse is a student or incapable of self-care and thus has little or no earned income, spouse is treated as being gainfully employed and having earnings of not less than $200 per month for one, $400 per month for two or more qualifying individuals

    EXAMPLE: Husband and wife have earned income of $10,000 each, resulting in AGI of $20,000. They have one child, age 3. They incurred qualifying household service expenses of $1,500 and child care expenses at a nursery school of $1,200.

Household expenses	$1,500
Add child care outside home	1,200
Total employment-related expenses	$2,700
Maximum allowable expenses	$2,400
Credit = 25% x $2,400	$ 600

K. **Foreign Tax Credit**

1. Foreign income taxes on U.S. taxpayers can either be deducted or used as a credit at the option of the taxpayer each year

2. The credit is limited to the overall limitation of

    $$\frac{\text{TI From All Foreign Countries}}{\text{Taxable Income + Exemptions}} \times \text{(U.S. tax - credit for elderly)}$$

3. The limitation must be computed separately for passive income

4. Foreign tax credit in excess of the overall limitation are subject to a 2-year carryback and a 5-year carryover

5. There is no limitation if foreign taxes are used as a deduction

L. **Earned Income Credit**

1. The credit is 14% of the first $6,500 of earned income reduced by (1) 10% of earned income (or adjusted gross income if larger) that exceeds $10,240, and (2) the amount of the taxpayer's alternative minimum tax liability

2. The $6,500 earned income amount and the $10,240 phase-out amount are subject to adjustment for inflation

3. To be eligible a taxpayer must

    a. Maintain a household for him/herself and child in the U.S., and be

        (1) A married person entitled to a dependency exemption for the child, or
        (2) A surviving spouse, or
        (3) A head of household and child is either unmarried, or a married child for whom the taxpayer may claim a dependency exemption

    b. File a joint return if married

4. Credit in excess of tax liability will be <u>refunded</u>

M. **Estimated Tax Payments**

1. An individual whose regular and alternative minimum tax liability is not sufficiently covered by withholding on wages must pay estimated tax in quarterly installments or be subject to penalty

2. Quarterly payments of estimated tax are due by the 15th day of the 4th, 6th, and 9th month of the taxable year, and by the 15th day of the 1st month of the following year

3. There will be no penalty if the amount of tax withheld plus estimated payments are at least equal to the lesser of

    a. 90% of the current year's tax (80% for 1987),
    b. 100% of the prior year's tax, or
    c. 90% of the tax determined by annualizing current-year taxable income through each quarter

4. The penalty is based on the difference between the required annual payment (i.e., lesser of a., b., or c. above) and the amount paid

5. IRS can waive penalty if failure to pay was the result of casualty, disaster, illness, or death of the taxpayer

VII. FILING REQUIREMENTS

A. Form 1040 must generally be filed if gross income at least equals the sum of the taxpayer's standard deduction plus personal exemptions allowable (e.g., generally $3,100 + $2,000 = $5,100 for single taxpayer for 1989)

1. The additional standard deduction for age ($750 or $600) is included in determining an individual's filing requirement; the additional standard deduction for blindness and dependency exemptions are not included

    EXAMPLE: A single individual age 65 and blind who can <u>not</u> be claimed as a dependency exemption by another taxpayer must file a return for 1989 if the individual's gross income is $3,100 + $2,000 + $750 = $5,850

2. An individual who can be claimed as a dependency exemption by another tax-payer must file a return if the individual has (1) unearned income in excess of the sum of $500 plus any additional standard deduction allowed for age or blindness, or (2) total gross income in excess of the individual's standard deduction (i.e, earned income up to the amount of the basic standard deduction plus additional standard deductions for age and blindness)

    EXAMPLE: A single individual age 65 who can be claimed as a dependency exemption by another taxpayer must file a return if the individual has unearned income (e.g., interest and dividends) in excess of $1,250 ($2,000 if 65 or over and blind)

    EXAMPLE: A single individual under age 65 who can be claimed as a dependency exemption by another taxpayer must file a return if the individual has unearned income of $1 or more and has total gross income in excess of $500

    EXAMPLE: A single individual age 65 with earned income of at least $3,000 who can be claimed as a dependency exemption by another taxpayer must file a return if the individual has total gross income in excess of $3,750 ($4,500 if 65 or over and blind)

3. Self-employed individual must file if net earnings from self-employment are $400 or more

B. Return must be filed by 15th day of 4th calendar month following close of taxable year

C. An automatic 4-month extension of time for filing the return can be obtained by filing Form 4868 by the due date of the return, and paying any estimated tax due

VIII. STATUTE OF LIMITATIONS

A. **Claims for Refund**

1. A taxpayer must file a claim for refund within 3 years from date return was filed, or 2 years from payment of tax, whichever is later

    a. A return filed before its due date is treated as filed on the due date
    b. The 3-year period is extended to 7 years for claims resulting from worthless securities or bad debts
    c. If the refund claim is the result of a carryback (e.g., NOL, ITC, corporate capital loss), the 3-year period begins with the return for the year in which the carryback arose

B. **Assessments**

1. The normal period for assessment of a tax deficiency is 3 years after the due date of the return, or 3 years after the return is filed, whichever is later

    a. The assessment period is extended to 6 years if gross income omissions exceed 25% of the gross income stated on the return
    b. There is no time limit for assessment if no return is filed, if the return is fraudulent, or if there is a willful attempt to evade tax

TRANSACTIONS IN PROPERTY

A. Sales and Other Dispositions

A sale or other disposition is a transaction which generally gives rise to the recognition of gain or loss. Gains or losses may be categorized as ordinary or capital. If an exchange is nontaxable, the recognition of gain or loss is generally deferred until a later sale of the newly acquired property. This is accomplished by giving the property received the basis of the old property exchanged.

1. The <u>basis of property</u> to determine gain or loss is generally its cost or purchase price

   a. The cost of property is the amount paid for it in cash or the FMV of other property, plus expenses connected with the purchase
   b. If property is acquired subject to a debt, or the purchaser assumes a debt, this debt is also included in cost
   c. If acquired by <u>gift</u>, the basis for gain is the basis of the donor (substituted basis) increased by any gift tax paid attributable to the net appreciation in the value of the gift

   (1) Basis for loss is lesser of gain basis (above), or FMV on date of gift
   (2) Because of this rule, no gain or loss is recognized when use of the basis for computing loss results in a gain, and use of the basis for computing gain results in a loss

   EXAMPLE: A taxpayer received a boat from his father as a gift. Father's adjusted basis was $10,000 and FMV was $8,000. If taxpayer sells the boat for $9,200, no gain or loss is recognized.

   d. If <u>acquired from decedent</u>, basis is property's FMV on date of decedent's death, or alternate valuation date (6 months after death)

   (1) Use FMV on date of disposition if alternate valuation date is elected and property is distributed, sold, or otherwise disposed of during 6-month period following death
   (2) FMV rule not applicable to appreciated property acquired by the decedent by gift within one year before death if such property then passes from the donee-decedent to the original donor or donor's spouse. The basis of such property to the original donor (or spouse) will be the adjusted basis of the property to the decedent immediately before death.

   e. The basis of <u>stock received as a dividend</u> depends upon whether it was included in income when received

   (1) If included in income, basis is its FMV at date of distribution
   (2) If nontaxable when received, the basis of shareholder's original stock is allocated between the dividend stock and the original stock in proportion to their relative FMVs. The holding period of the original stock "tacks on" to the holding period of the dividend stock.

   EXAMPLE: T owns 100 shares of X Corp. common stock that was acquired in 1988 for $12,000. In 1989, T receives a nontaxable distribution of 10 X Corp. preferred shares. At date of distribution the FMV of the 100 common shares was $15,000, and the FMV of *the 10 preferred shares was $5,000. The portion of the $12,000 basis allocated to the preferred and common shares would be*

$$Preferred = \frac{\$\ 5,000}{\$20,000}\ (\$12,000)\ =\ \$3,000$$

$$Common = \frac{\$15,000}{\$20,000}\ (\$12,000)\ =\ \$9,000$$

    f. The basis of <u>stock rights</u> depends upon whether they were included in income when received

       (1) If rights were nontaxable and allowed to expire, they are deemed to have no basis and no loss can be deducted

       (2) If rights were nontaxable and exercised or sold

          (a) Basis is zero if FMV of rights is less than 15% of FMV of stock, unless taxpayer elects to allocate basis

          (b) If FMV of rights at date of receipt is at least 15% of FMV of stock, or if taxpayer elects, basis is

$$\frac{FMV\ of\ rights}{FMV\ of\ rights\ +\ FMV\ stock}\quad \times\quad \begin{array}{c}basis\ in\\ stock\end{array}$$

       (3) If rights were taxable and included in income, basis is their FMV at date of distribution

    g. Detailed rules for basis are included in following discussions of exchanges and involuntary conversions

2. In a <u>sale</u>, the gain or loss is generally the difference between

    a. The cash or fair market value received, and the adjusted basis of the property sold

    b. If the property sold is mortgaged (or encumbered by any other debt) and the buyer assumes or takes the property subject to the debt

       (1) Include the amount of the debt in the amount realized because the seller is relieved of the obligation

       EXAMPLE: Property with a $10,000 mortgage, and a basis of $15,000, is sold for $10,000 cash and buyer assumes the mortgage. The amount realized is $20,000, and the gain is $5,000.

       (2) If the amount of the mortgage exceeds basis, use the same rules

       EXAMPLE: Property with a $15,000 mortgage, and a basis of $10,000, is given away subject to the mortgage. The amount realized is $15,000, and the gain is $5,000.

    c. Casual sellers of property (as opposed to dealers) reduce selling price by any selling expenses

3. In a <u>taxable exchange</u>, the gain or loss is the difference between the adjusted basis of the property exchanged and the FMV of the property acquired. The basis of property received in a taxable exchange is its FMV.

4. <u>Nontaxable exchanges</u> generally are not taxed in the current period. Questions concerning nontaxable exchanges usually require a determination of the basis of property received, and the effect of "boot" on the recognition of gain.

4
1

a. Like-kind exchange--an exchange of business or investment property for property of a like-kind

  (1) Does not apply to property held for personal use, inventory, stocks, bonds, notes, intangible evidences of ownership, and interests in a partnership

  (2) Property held for business use may be exchanged for investment property; or, vice versa

  (3) Like-kind means "same class of property"

   (a) Real estate must be exchanged for real estate; personal property exchanged for personal property, e.g.

    1] Land held for investment exchanged for apartment building
    2] Real estate exchanged for a lease on real estate to run 30 years or more
    3] Truck exchanged for a truck

   (b) Exchange of personal property for real property does not qualify

  (4) To qualify as a like-kind exchange (1) the property to be received must be identified within 45 days after the date on which the old property is relinquished, and (2) the exchange must be completed within 180 days after the date on which the old property is relinquished, but not later than the due date of the tax return (including extensions) for the year that the old property is relinquished

  (5) The basis of like-kind property received is the basis of like-kind property given

   (a) + Gain recognized
   (b) + Basis of boot given (money or property not of a like-kind)
   (c) - Loss recognized
   (d) - FMV of boot received

  (6) If un-like property (i.e., boot) is received, its basis will be its FMV on the date of the exchange

  (7) If property is exchanged solely for other like-kind property, no gain or loss is recognized. The basis of the property received is the same as the basis of the property transferred.

  (8) If "boot" (money or property not of a like-kind) is given, no gain or loss is generally recognized. However, gain or loss is recognized if the "boot" given consists of property with a FMV different from its basis.

   EXAMPLE: Land held for investment plus shares of stock are exchanged for investment real estate with a FMV of $13,000. The land transferred had an adjusted basis of $10,000 and FMV of $11,000; the stock had an adjusted basis of $5,000 and FMV of $2,000. A $3,000 loss is recognized on the transfer of stock. The basis of the acquired real estate is $12,000 ($10,000 + $5,000 - $3,000).

  (9) If "boot" is received

   (a) Any realized gain is recognized to the extent of the lesser of (1) the realized gain, or (2) the FMV of the "boot" received
   (b) No loss is recognized due to the receipt of boot

EXAMPLE: Land held for investment with a basis of $10,000 was exchanged for other investment real estate with a FMV of $9,000, an automobile with a FMV of $2,000, and $1,500 in cash.   The realized gain is $2,500.   Even though $3,500 of "boot" was received, the recognized gain is only $2,500 (limited to the realized gain).   The basis of the automobile (un-like property) is its FMV $2,000; while the basis of the real estate acquired is $9,000 ($10,000 + $2,500 gain recognized - $3,500 boot received).

(10) Liabilities assumed (or liabilities to which property exchanged is subject) on either or both sides of the exchange are treated as "boot"

(a) Boot received--if the liability was assumed by the other party
(b) Boot given--if the taxpayer assumed a liability on the property acquired
(c) If liabilities are assumed on both sides of the exchange, they are offset to determine the net amount of "boot" given or received

EXAMPLE: A owns investment land with an adjusted basis of $50,000, FMV of $70,000, but which is subject to a mortgage of $15,000.   B owns investment land with an adjusted basis of $60,000, FMV of $65,000, but which is subject to a mortgage of $10,000.   A and B exchange real estate investments with A assuming B's $10,000 mortgage, and B assuming A's $15,000 mortgage.   The computation of realized gain, recognized gain, and basis for the acquired real estate for both A and B is as follows.

	A		B
FMV of real estate received	$65,000		$70,000
+ Liability on old real estate assumed by other party (boot received)	15,000	(1)	10,000
Amount realized on the exchange	$80,000		$80,000
- Adjusted basis of old real estate transferred	-50,000		-60,000
- Liability assumed by taxpayer on new real estate (boot given)	-10,000	(2)	-15,000
Gain realized	$20,000		$ 5,000
Gain recognized (1) minus (2)	$ 5,000		$ -0-
Basis of old real estate transferred	$50,000		$60,000
+ Liability assumed by taxpayer on new real estate (boot given)	10,000		15,000
+ Gain recognized	5,000		-0-
- Liability on old real estate assumed by other party (boot received)	-15,000		-10,000
Basis of new real estate acquired	$50,000		$65,000

(d) Boot given in the form of an assumption of a liability does not offset boot received in the form of cash or un-like property; however, boot given in the form of cash or un-like property does offset boot received in the form of a liability assumed by the other party

EXAMPLE: Assume same facts as above except that the mortgage on B's old real estate was $6,000, and that A paid B cash of $4,000 to make up the difference. The tax effects to A remain unchanged. However, since the $4,000 cash cannot be offset by the liability assumed by B, B must recognize a gain of $4,000, and will have a basis of $69,000 for the new real estate.

b. Involuntary conversions

(1) Occur when money or other property is received for property that has been destroyed, damaged, stolen, or condemned (even if property is transferred only under threat or imminence of condemnation)

(2) If payment is received and gain is realized, taxpayer may <u>elect</u> not to recognize <u>gain</u> if converted property is replaced with property of similar or related use

(a) Gain is recognized only to the extent that the amount realized exceeds the cost of the replacement

(b) The replacement must be purchased within a period beginning with the earlier of the date of disposition or the date of threat of condemnation, and ending 2 years after the close of the taxable year in which gain is first <u>realized</u> (3 years for condemned business or investment real property, other than inventory or property held primarily for resale)

(c) Basis of replacement property is the cost of the replacement decreased by any gain not recognized

EXAMPLE: Taxpayer had unimproved real estate (with an adjusted basis of $20,000) which was condemned by the county. The county paid him $24,000 and he reinvested $21,000 in unimproved real estate. $1,000 of the $4,000 realized gain would not be recognized. His tax basis in the new real estate would be $20,000 ($21,000 - $1,000).

EXAMPLE: Assume the same facts as above except the taxpayer reinvested $25,000 in unimproved real estate. None of the $4,000 realized gain would be recognized. His basis in the new real estate would be $21,000 ($25,000 - $4,000).

(3) If property is converted directly into property similar or related in service or use, complete nonrecognition of gain is mandatory. The basis of replacement property is the same as the property converted.

(4) The meaning of <u>property similar or related in service or use</u> is more restrictive than "like-kind"

(a) For an owner-user--property must be functionally the same and have same end use (business vehicle must be replaced by business vehicle that performs same function)

(b) For a lessor--property must perform same services for <u>lessor</u> (lessor could replace a rental manufacturing plant with a rental-wholesale grocery warehouse even though tenant's functional use differs)

(c) A purchase of at least 80% of the stock of a corporation whose property is similar or related in service or use also qualifies

(d) More liberal "like-kind" test applies to real property held for business or investment (other than inventory or property held primarily for sale) that is converted by seizure, con-

demnation, or threat of condemnation (e.g., improved real
estate could be replaced with unimproved real estate)

(5) If property is not replaced within the time limit, an amended
return is filed to recognize gain in the year realized

(6) Losses on involuntary conversions are recognized whether the property is replaced or not. However, a loss on condemnation of
property held for personal use (e.g., personal residence) is not
deductible

c. Sale or exchange of residence

(1) Gain on the sale or exchange of a principal residence is not recognized to the extent an amount equal to the adjusted sales price is
reinvested in another principal residence 2 years before or after
date of sale

(2) If more than one residence is purchased within the time period,
generally only the last residence purchased will qualify as a
replacement unless the taxpayer has relocated for employment
purposes, in which case any sale incident to such a move will
qualify

(3) The adjusted sales price is the sales price less
 (a) Selling expenses (e.g., sales commissions, advertising)
 (b) Fixing-up expenses (i.e., the expenses for work performed on
     the old residence in order to assist its sale, made within 90
     days before contract to sell is entered into and paid no later
     than 30 days after sale)
 (c) Any gain excluded under "(5)" below

(4) Basis in the new house is its cost less gain not recognized

*EXAMPLE: Taxpayer's house cost $100,000 in 1980. In preparation
for sale, he had it painted for $5,000 in May 1989. He sold the
house on June 15, 1989, for $240,000 and paid a $10,000 sales
commission. He bought another house for $110,000 on July 14,
1989. The following computations would be made.*

Selling price	*$240,000*		
- Selling expenses	*-10,000*		
Amount realized	*$230,000*	*Adjusted sales price*	*$225,000*
- Basis of old house	*-100,000*	*- Cost of new house*	*-110,000*
Gain realized	*$130,000*	*Gain recognized*	*$115,000*
Amount realized	*$230,000*	*Cost of new house*	*$110,000*
- Fixing-up expenses	*- 5,000*	*- Gain not recognized*	*- 15,000*
Adjusted sales price	*$225,000*	*Basis of new house*	*$ 95,000*

(5) Taxpayer age 55 or older may elect to exclude up to $125,000 of the
gain realized on the sale or involuntary conversion of a principal
residence

 (a) Election may only be made once in lifetime
 (b) Taxpayer must have owned and occupied the residence for at
     least 3 of the 5 years ending on date of sale
 (c) Periods during which a physically or mentally incapacitated
     individual owns a residence but resides in a licensed care
     facility (e.g., nursing home) are counted toward meeting the 3
     of 5 years test, if the individual actually lives in the
     residence for periods aggregating at least 1 year during the
     5-year period.

(d)   Exclusion reduces the gain realized and adjusted sales price, but does not reduce the basis of replacement property

(e)   If taxpayer and spouse own residence in joint tenancy and file joint return for year of sale, exclusion may be elected even though only one of them satisfies the age, holding, and use tests

EXAMPLE: In the example above, if taxpayer had made the once-in-lifetime election to exclude $125,000 of gain, the realized gain would be $5,000, the adjusted sales price would be $100,000, the recognized gain would be zero, and the basis of the new house would be ($110,000 - $5,000 of gain not recognized) = $105,000.

(6)   Loss on sale of personal residence is not deductible; does not affect basis of new home

d.   Exchange of insurance policies.   No gain or loss is recognized on an exchange of certain life, endowment, and annuity contracts to allow taxpayers to obtain better insurance

5.   Sales and exchanges of securities

a.   Stocks and bonds are not included under like-kind exchanges
b.   Exchange of stock of same corporation

(1)   Common for common, or preferred for preferred is nontaxable
(2)   Common for preferred, or preferred for common is taxable, unless exchange qualifies as a recapitalization (see p. 1345)

c.   Exercise of conversion privilege in convertible stock or bond is generally nontaxable
d.   Wash sales

(1)   Wash sale occurs when stock or securities (or options to acquire stock or securities) are sold at a loss and within 30 days before or after the sale, substantially identical stock or securities or options to acquire them in the same corporation are purchased
(2)   Wash sale loss is not deductible, but is added to the basis of the new stock
(3)   Wash sale rules do not apply to gains

EXAMPLE: C purchased 100 shares of X Corporation stock for $1,000. C later sold the stock for $700, and within 30 days acquired 100 shares of X Corporation stock for $800. The loss of $300 on the sale of stock is not recognized. However, the unrecognized loss of $300 is added to the $800 cost of the new stock to arrive at the basis of the new stock of $1,100. The holding period of the new stock includes the time the old stock was held.

(4)   Does not apply to dealers in stock and securities where loss is sustained in ordinary course of business

e.   Worthless stock and securities

(1)   Treated as a capital loss as if sold on the last day of the taxable year they become worthless
(2)   Treated as an ordinary loss if stock and securities are those of an 80% or more owned corporate subsidiary that derived more than 90% of its gross receipts from active-type sources

    f.   The first-in, first-out (FIFO) method is used to determine the basis of securities sold unless the taxpayer can specifically identify the securities sold and uses specific identification

6. Losses on deposits in insolvent financial institutions

    a.   A loss resulting from a deposit in a nonbusiness account in an insolvent financial institution is generally treated as a nonbusiness bad debt deductible as a short-term capital loss in the year in which there is no prospect of recovery

    b.   However, a qualified individual can elect to treat losses on deposits in insolvent financial institutions as personal casualty losses for the year in which the amount of loss can be determined with reasonable accuracy

        (1)   A qualified individual is any individual other than a 1% or more owner of the institution in which the loss was sustained, an officer of such institution, and certain relatives and other related persons to such owner or officer

        (2)   The loss is subject to the $100 floor and 10% of AGI limitation that applies to personal casualty losses

        (3)   If the election is made, no bad debt deduction can be claimed for the loss

    c.   In lieu of the election in "b." above, a qualified individual can elect to treat up to $20,000 ($10,000 if married filing separately) of the loss as an ordinary loss arising out of a transaction entered into for profit

        (1)   This election is only available if the deposit was not federally insured

        (2)   The amount of loss in excess of $20,000 ($10,000 if married filing separately) is treated as a nonbusiness bad debt deductible as a short-term capital loss

7. Losses, expenses, and interest between related taxpayers

    a.   <u>Loss is disallowed</u> on the sale or exchange of property to a related taxpayer

        (1)   Transferee's basis is cost; holding period begins when transferee acquires property

        (2)   On a later resale, any gain recognized by the transferee is reduced by the disallowed loss (unless the transferor's loss was from a wash sale, in which case no reduction is allowed)

        (3)   <u>Related taxpayers</u> include

            (a)   Members of a family, including spouse, brothers, sisters, ancestors, and lineal descendents

            (b)   A corporation and a more than 50% shareholder

            (c)   Two corporations which are members of the same controlled group

            (d)   A person and an exempt organization controlled by that person

            (e)   Certain related individuals in a trust, including the grantor or beneficiary and the fiduciary

            (f)   A C corporation and a partnership if the same persons own more than 50% of the corporation, and more than 50% of the capital and profits interest in the partnership

            (g)   Two S corporations if the same persons own more than 50% of each

(h) An S corporation and a C corporation if the same persons own more than 50% of each

> *EXAMPLE: During August 1988, Bob sold stock with a basis of $4,000 to his brother Ray for $3,000, its FMV. During January 1989, Ray sold the stock to an unrelated taxpayer for $4,500. Bob's loss of $1,000 is disallowed; Ray recognizes a STCG of ($4,500 - $3,000) - $1,000 disallowed loss = $500.*

(4) <u>Constructive stock ownership rules</u> apply in determining if taxpayers are related. For purposes of determining stock ownership

(a) Stock owned, directly or indirectly, by a corporation, partnership, estate, or trust is considered as being owned proportionately by its shareholders, partners, or beneficiaries.

(b) An individual is considered as owning the stock owned, directly or indirectly, by his brothers and sisters (whole or half blood), spouse, ancestors, and lineal descendants.

(c) An individual owning stock in a corporation [other than by (b) above] is considered as owning the stock owned, directly or indirectly, by his partner.

b. The disallowed loss rule in "a." above does not apply to transfers between spouses, or former spouses incident to divorce, as discussed on the next page.

c. Any loss from the sale or exchange of property between corporations that are members of the same <u>controlled group</u> is deferred (instead of disallowed) until the property is sold outside the group. Use controlled group definition found at CTAX, "D.2.," but substitute "more than 50%" for "at least 80%."

> *EXAMPLE: Mr. Gudjob is the sole shareholder of X Corp. and Y Corp. During 1988, X Corp. sells nondepreciable property with a basis of $8,000 to Y Corp. for $6,000, its FMV. During 1989, Y Corp. sells the property to an unrelated taxpayer for $6,500. X Corp.'s loss in 1988 is deferred. In 1989, X Corp. recognizes the $2,000 of deferred loss, and Y Corp. recognizes a gain of $500.*

d. An accrual-basis payor is effectively placed on the cash method of accounting for purposes of deducting accrued interest and other expenses owed to a related cash-basis payee

(1) No deduction is allowable until the year the amount is actually paid

(2) This rule applies to pass-through entities (e.g., a partnership and <u>any</u> partner; two partnerships if the same persons own more than 50% of each; an S corporation and <u>any</u> shareholder) in addition to the related taxpayers described in "a.(3)" above, but does not apply to guaranteed payments to partners. This rule also applies to a personal service corporation and <u>any</u> employee-owner.

> *EXAMPLE: An S corporation accrues a $500 bonus owed to an employee-shareholder in 1988, but does not make payment until February 1989. The $500 bonus will be deductible by the S corporation in 1989, when the employee-shareholder reports the $500 as income.*

8. Transfer between spouses

   a. No gain or loss is generally recognized on the transfer of property from an individual to (or in trust for the benefit of)

      (1) A spouse (other than a nonresident alien spouse), or
      (2) A former spouse (other than a nonresident alien former spouse), if the transfer is related to the cessation of marriage, or occurs within one year after marriage ceases

   b. Transfer is treated as if it were a gift from one spouse to the other
   c. Transferee's basis in the property received will be the transferor's basis (even if FMV is less than the property's basis)

      EXAMPLE: H sells property with a basis of $6,000 to his spouse, W, for $8,000.   No gain is recognized to H, and W's basis for the property is $6,000.   W's holding period includes the period that H held the property.

   d. If property is transferred to a <u>trust</u> for the benefit of a spouse or former spouse (incident to divorce)

      (1) Gain is recognized to the extent that the amount of liabilities assumed, or to which the property is subject, exceeds the total adjusted basis of property transferred
      (2) Gain or loss is recognized on the transfer of installment obligations

9. Gain from the sale or exchange of property will be entirely ordinary gain (no capital gain) if the property is depreciable in hands of transferee and the sale or exchange is between

   a. A person and a more than 50% owned corporation or partnership
   b. A taxpayer and any trust in which such taxpayer or spouse is a beneficiary, unless such beneficiary's interest is a remote contingent interest
   c. Constructive ownership rules apply--use rules at "6.a.(4)(a) and (b)" above

10. Installment sales (see Tax Accounting Methods)

B. **Capital Gains and Losses**

   Although the preferential rate treatment for capital gains has been eliminated, the 1986 TRA did not eliminate the many Code provisions concerning the characterization of income or loss as ordinary or capital, or the provisions that require differentiating between long-term and short-term capital gains and losses.   The long-term vs. short-term capital gain structure has been retained in order to facilitate the reinstatement of a capital gains differential in the event of a future tax rate increase.

1. Capital gains and losses result from the "sale or exchange of capital assets."   The term <u>capital assets</u> includes investment property and property held for personal use.   The term specifically <u>excludes</u>

   a. Stock in trade, inventory, or goods held primarily for sale to customers in the normal course of business

b. Depreciable or real property used in a trade or business
c. Copyrights or artistic, literary, etc., compositions created by the taxpayer

   (1) They are capital assets only if purchased by the taxpayer
   (2) Patents are generally capital assets in the hands of the inventor

d. Accounts or notes receivable arising from normal business activities
e. An agreement (i.e., covenant) not to compete for a fixed number of years that is separable from goodwill

2. Whether short-term or long-term depends upon the <u>holding period</u>

a. Long-term if held more than 1 year
b. The day property was acquired is excluded and the day it is disposed of is included
c. Use calendar months (e.g., if held from January 4 to January 4 it is held exactly 1 year)
d. If stock or securities which are traded on an established securities market (or other property regularly traded on an established market) are sold, any resulting gain or loss is recognized on the date the trade is executed (transaction date) by both cash and accrual taxpayers.
e. The holding period of property received in a nontaxable exchange (e.g., like-kind exchange, involuntary conversion) includes the holding period of the property exchanged, if the property that was exchanged was a capital asset or Sec. 1231 asset
f. If the basis of property to a prior owner carries over to the present owner (e.g., gift), the holding period of the prior owner "tacks on" to the present owner's holding period
g. If using the lower FMV on date of gift to determine loss, then holding period begins on date of gift

   EXAMPLE: X purchased property on July 14, 1988, for $10,000.   X made a gift of the property to Z on January 10, 1989, when its FMV was $8,000. Since Z's basis for gain is $10,000, his holding period for a disposition at a gain extends back to July 14, 1988.   Since Z's $8,000 basis for loss is determined by reference to FMV at January 10, 1989, his holding period for a disposition at a loss begins on that date.

h. Property acquired from a decedent is always given long-term treatment, regardless of how long the property was held by the decedent or beneficiary

3. Computation of capital gains and losses for <u>all taxpayers</u>

a. First net STCG with STCL and net LTCG with LTCL to determine

   (1) Net short-term capital gain or loss (NSTCG or NSTCL)
   (2) Net long-term capital gain or loss (NLTCG or NLTCL)

b. Then net these two together to determine whether there is a NCG or NCL

4. The following rules apply to <u>individuals</u>

a. If there is a <u>net capital gain</u>, the net capital gain (including a NLTCG) is fully included in income.

   EXAMPLE: An individual has a NLTCG of $8,000, and a NSTCL of $1,000. The net capital gain is $7,000, and increases the individual's adjusted gross income by $7,000.

b. If there is a <u>net capital loss</u> the following rules apply

   (1) A net capital loss is an above the line deduction, but limited to the lesser of

      (a) $3,000 ($1,500 if married filing separately), or
      (b) The excess of capital losses over capital gains

   (2) The 1986 TRA repealed the two-for-one offset requirement for a NLTCL. Both a NSTCL and a NLTCL are used dollar-for-dollar in computing the capital loss deduction.

> *EXAMPLE: An individual had $2,000 of NLTCL and $500 of NSTCL for 1988. The capital losses are combined and the entire net capital loss of $2,500 is deductible in computing the individual's AGI.*

   (3) Short-term losses are used before long-term losses. The amount of net capital loss that exceeds the allowable deduction may be carried over for an unlimited period of time. The carryovers retain their identity as long-term or short-term in carryover years.

> *EXAMPLE: An individual has a $4,000 STCL and a $5,000 LTCL for 1988. The $9,000 net capital loss results in a capital loss deduction of $3,000 for 1988, while the remainder is a carryover to 1989. Since $3,000 of the STCL would be used to create the capital loss deduction, there is a $1,000 STCL carryover and a $5,000 LTCL carryover to 1989.*

   (4) For purposes of determining the amount of excess net capital loss that can be carried over to future years, the taxpayer's net capital loss for the year is reduced by the lesser of (1) $3,000 ($1,500 if married filing separately), or (2) adjusted taxable income.

      (a) Adjusted taxable income is taxable income increased by $3,000 ($1,500 if married filing separately) and the amount allowed for personal exemptions.
      (b) An excess of deductions allowed over gross income is taken into account as negative taxable income.

> *EXAMPLE: For 1988, a single individual with no dependents had a net capital loss of $8,000, and had allowable deductions that exceeded gross income by $4,000. For 1988, the individual is entitled to a net capital loss deduction of $3,000, and will carry over a net capital loss of $7,050 to 1989. This amount represents the 1988 net capital loss of $8,000 reduced by the lesser of (1) $3,000, or (2) $-4,000 + $3,000 + $1,950 = $950.*

5. <u>Corporations</u> have special capital gain and loss rules

  a. Capital losses are only allowed to offset capital gains, not ordinary income.
  b. A net capital loss is carried back 3 years, and forward 5 years to offset capital gains in those years. All capital loss carrybacks and carryovers are treated as short-term capital losses.

> *EXAMPLE: A corporation has a NLTCL of $8,000 and a NSTCG of $2,000, resulting in a net capital loss of $6,000 for 1988. The $6,000 NLTCL is not deductible for 1988, but is first carried back as a STCL to 1985 to offset capital gains. If not used up in 1985, the STCL is carried to*

1986 and 1987, and then forward to 1989, 1990, 1991, 1992, and 1993 to offset capital gains in those years.

    c. Although an alternative tax computation still exists for a corporation with a net capital gain, the alternative tax computation applies the highest corporate rate (34%) to a net capital gain and thus currently provides no benefit.

C. Personal Casualty and Theft Gains and Losses

Gains and losses from casualties and thefts of property held for personal use are separately netted, without regard to the holding period of the converted property.

1. If gains exceed losses (after the $100 floor for each loss), then all gains and losses are treated as capital gains and losses, short-term or long-term depending upon holding period

    EXAMPLE: An individual incurred a $25,000 personal casualty gain, and a $15,000 personal casualty loss during the current taxable year. Since there was a net gain, the individual will report the gain and loss as a $25,000 capital gain and a $15,000 capital loss.

2. If losses (after the $100 floor for each loss) exceed gains, the losses (1) offset gains, and (2) are an ordinary deduction from AGI to the extent in excess of 10% of AGI

    EXAMPLE: An individual had AGI of $40,000 (before casualty gains or losses), and also had a personal casualty loss of $25,000 (after the $100 floor) and a personal casualty gain of $15,000. Since there was a net personal casualty loss, the net loss will be deductible as an excess itemized deduction of [$25,000 - $15,000 - (10% x $40,000)] = $6,000.

D. Gains and Losses on Business Property

Although property used in a business is excluded from the definition of "capital assets," Sec. 1231 extends capital gain and loss treatment to business assets if the gains from these assets exceed losses. However, before Sec. 1231 becomes operative, Sections 1245, 1250, and 291 provide for recapture of depreciation (i.e., gain is taxed as ordinary income to the extent of certain depreciation previously deducted).

1. All gains and losses are <u>ordinary</u> on business property <u>held 1 year or less</u>

2. <u>Section 1231</u>

    a. All property included must have been held for <u>more than 1 year</u>

        (1) Section 1231 gains and losses include those from

            (a) Sale or exchange of property used in trade or business (or held for production of rents or royalties) and which is not

                1] Inventory
                2] A copyright or artistic composition

            (b) Casualty, theft, or condemnation of

             1] Property used in trade or business
             2] Capital assets held in connection with a trade or business, or a transaction entered into for profit

     (c) Infrequently encountered items such as cut timber, coal and domestic iron ore, livestock, and unharvested crop

b. The combining of Sec. 1231 gains and losses is accomplished in <u>two steps</u>. <u>First</u>, net all casualty and theft gains and losses on property held for more than 1 year

   (1) If the losses exceed gains, treat them all as ordinary losses and gains and do not net them with other Sec. 1231 gains and losses
   (2) If the gains exceed losses, the net gain is combined with other Sec. 1231 gains and losses

c. <u>Second</u>, net all Sec. 1231 gains and losses (except casualty and theft net loss per above)

   (1) Include casualty and theft net gain
   (2) Include gains and losses from condemnations (other than condemnations on nonbusiness, non-income-producing property)
   (3) Include gains and losses from the sale or exchange of property used in trade or business

d. If losses exceed gains, treat all gains and losses as ordinary
e. If gains exceed losses, treat the Sec. 1231 net gain as a long-term capital gain

EXAMPLE: Taxpayer has a gain of $10,000 from the sale of land used in his business, a loss of $4,000 on the sale of depreciable property used in his business, and a $2,000 (noninsured) loss when a car used in his business was involved in a collision.

The net gain or loss from casualty or theft is the $2,000 loss. The net casualty loss of $2,000 is treated as an ordinary loss and not netted with other Sec. 1231 gains and losses.

The $10,000 gain is netted with the $4,000 loss resulting in a net Sec. 1231 gain of $6,000, which is then treated as a long-term capital gain.

f. Net Sec. 1231 gain will be treated as ordinary income (instead of LTCG) to the extent of nonrecaptured net Sec. 1231 losses for the five most recent taxable years. Losses will be deemed to be recaptured in the chronological order in which they arose.

EXAMPLE: Corp. X, on a calendar year, has a net Sec. 1231 gain of $10,000 for 1988. For the years 1983 through 1987, Corp. X had net Sec. 1231 losses totaling $8,000. Of the $10,000 net Sec. 1231 gain for 1988, the first $8,000 will be treated as ordinary income, with only the remaining $2,000 treated as long-term capital gain.

3. <u>Section 1245 Recapture</u>

a. Requires the recapture as <u>ordinary income</u> of all gain attributable to

   (1) <u>Post-1961 depreciation</u> on the disposition of Sec. 1245 property
   (2) <u>Post-1980 recovery deductions</u> on the disposition of Sec. 1245 recovery property (including amount expensed under Sec. 179 expense election)

b. <u>Sec. 1245 property</u> generally includes depreciable tangible and intangible <u>personal property</u>, e.g.

    (1) Desks, machines, equipment, cars, and trucks
    (2) Special purpose structures, storage facilities, and other property (but not buildings and structural components) e.g., oil and gas storage tanks, grain storage bins and silos, and escalators and elevators

c. <u>Sec. 1245 recovery property</u> means <u>all</u> ACRS recovery property placed in service before 1987 other than

    (1) 19-year real residential rental property
    (2) 19-year real property used outside the U.S.
    (3) 19-year subsidized low-income housing
    (4) 19-year real property for which a straight-line election was made

    NOTE: If the cost of 19-year nonresidential real property was recovered using the prescribed percentages of ACRS, all gain on disposition is ordinary income to extent of all ACRS deductions. Such recapture is not limited to the excess of accelerated depreciation over straight-line. However, if the straight-line method was elected for 19-year real property, there is no recapture and all gain is Sec. 1231 gain if property held over 12 months. If property held 12 months or less, gain is recaptured as ordinary income to the extent of all depreciation (including straight-line) because of a special rule under Sec. 1250 that treats all depreciation as excess when the property is held 12 months or less.

d. Sec. 1245 does not apply to residential rental property and nonresidential real property placed in service after 1986 because only straight-line depreciation is allowed

e. Upon the disposition of property subject to Sec. 1245, any recognized gain will be ordinary income to the extent of post-1961 depreciation or post-1980 recovery deductions

    (1) Any remaining gain after recapture will be Sec. 1231 gain if property held more than 1 year
    (2) If the disposition is not by sale, use FMV of property (instead of selling price) to determine gain

        (a) When boot is received in a like-kind exchange, Sec. 1245 will apply to the recognized gain

            EXAMPLE: Taxpayer exchanged his old machine (adjusted basis of $2,500) for a smaller new machine worth $5,000 and received $1,000 cash. Depreciation of $7,500 had been taken on the old machine. The realized gain of $3,500 ($6,000 - $2,500) will be recognized to the extent of the $1,000 "boot," and will be treated as ordinary income as the result of Sec. 1245.

        (b) In the case of an involuntary conversion, the recognized gain under Sec. 1245 shall not exceed

            1] The gain recognized without regard to Sec. 1245, plus
            2] The FMV of property acquired which is not Sec. 1245 property, and which is not taken into account in "1]"

            EXAMPLE: Taxpayer received $117,000 of insurance proceeds as a result of a fire that destroyed his machinery. After deducting depreciation of $15,000, the machinery had an adjusted basis of $100,000 when destroyed. Taxpayer spent

> *$105,000 for replacement machinery and $9,000 for stock of a corporation that qualifies as replacement property. Ordinary income of $12,000 would be recognized (i.e., $3,000 without regard to Sec. 1245 + $9,000 FMV non-Sec. 1245 property acquired). If, instead of buying $9,000 in stock, taxpayer had bought $9,000 more of replacement machinery, only $3,000 of ordinary income would be recognized above.*

    (c) Sec. 1245 recapture does not apply to transfers by gift (including charitable contributions) or transfers at death

4. Section 1250 Recapture

    a. Applies to all real property (e.g., buildings and structural components) that is not Sec. 1245 recovery property

      (1) If Sec. 1250 property was held 12 months or less, gain on disposition is recaptured as ordinary income to extent of all depreciation (including straight-line)

      (2) If Sec. 1250 property was held more than 12 months, gain is recaptured as ordinary income to the extent of post-1969 <u>additional depreciation</u> (generally depreciation in excess of straight-line)

> *EXAMPLE: An office building with an adjusted basis of $200,000 was sold by <u>individual X</u> in 1989 for $350,000. The property had been purchased for $300,000 in 1980 and $100,000 of depreciation had been deducted. Straight-line depreciation would have totaled $70,000.*

Total gain ($350,000 - $200,000)	*$150,000*
Post-1969 additional depreciation	
recaptured as ordinary income	*(30,000)*
Remainder is Sec. 1231 gain	*$120,000*

5. Section 291 Recapture

    a. The ordinary income element on the disposition of Sec. 1250 property by <u>corporations</u> is increased by 20% of the additional amount which would have been ordinary income if the property had been Sec. 1245 property or Sec. 1245 recovery property. (Not applicable to the disposition of a pollution control facility for which a 5-year amortization election was made.)

> *EXAMPLE: Assuming the same facts as in the above example except that the building was sold by <u>Corporation X</u> in 1989, the computation of gain would be*

Total gain ($350,000 - $200,000)	*$150,000*
Post-1969 additional depreciation	
recaptured as ordinary income	*(30,000)**
Additional ordinary income--	
20% of $70,000 (the additional	
amount that would have been ordi-	
nary income if the property were	
Sec. 1245 property)	*(14,000)**
Remainder is Sec. 1231 gain	*$106,000*

> **All $44,000 ($30,000 + $14,000) of recapture is referred to as Sec. 1250 ordinary income.*

6. <u>Summary of Gains and Losses</u>. The treatment of gains and losses (other than personal casualty and theft) on property held for <u>more than 1 year</u> is summarized in the following <u>4 steps</u> (also enumerated on flowchart at end of this section).

a. Separate all recognized gains and losses into four categories

    (1) Ordinary gain and loss
    (2) Sec. 1231 casualty and theft gains and losses
    (3) Sec. 1231 gains and losses other than by casualty or theft
    (4) Gains and losses on capital assets (other than by casualty or theft)

    NOTE: "(2)" and "(3)" are only temporary classifications and all gains and losses will ultimately receive ordinary or capital treatment.

b. Any gain (casualty or other) on Sec. 1231 property is treated as ordinary income to extent of Sec. 1245, 1250, and 291 depreciation recapture

c. After depreciation recapture, any remaining Sec. 1231 casualty and theft gains and losses are netted

    (1) If losses exceed gains--the losses and gains receive ordinary treatment
    (2) If gains exceed losses--the net gain is combined with other Sec. 1231 gains and losses in "d." below

d. After recapture, any remaining Sec. 1231 gains and losses (other than by casualty or theft), are combined with any net casualty or theft gain from "c." above

    (1) If losses exceed gains--the losses and gains receive ordinary treatment
    (2) If gains exceed losses--the net gain receives LTCG treatment

    EXAMPLE: Taxpayer incurred the following transactions during the current taxable year.

Loss on condemnation of land used in business held 15 months	($ 500)
Loss on sale of machinery used in business held 2 months	($1,000)
Bad debt loss on loan made 3 years ago to friend	($2,000)
Gain from insurance reimbursement for tornado damage to business property held 10 years	$3,000
Loss on sale of business equipment held 3 years	($4,000)
Gain on sale of land held 4 years and used in business	$5,000

    The gains and losses would be treated as follows. Note that the loss on machinery is ordinary because it was not held more than 1 year.

Ordinary	Sec. 1231 casualty	Other Sec. 1231	Capital L-T	S-T
($1,000)	$3,000	($ 500)		($2,000)*
		(4,000)		
		5,000		
	⟶	3,000		
		⟶	$3,500	
($1,000)			$3,500	($2,000)

*Note: A nonbusiness bad debt is always treated as a STCL.

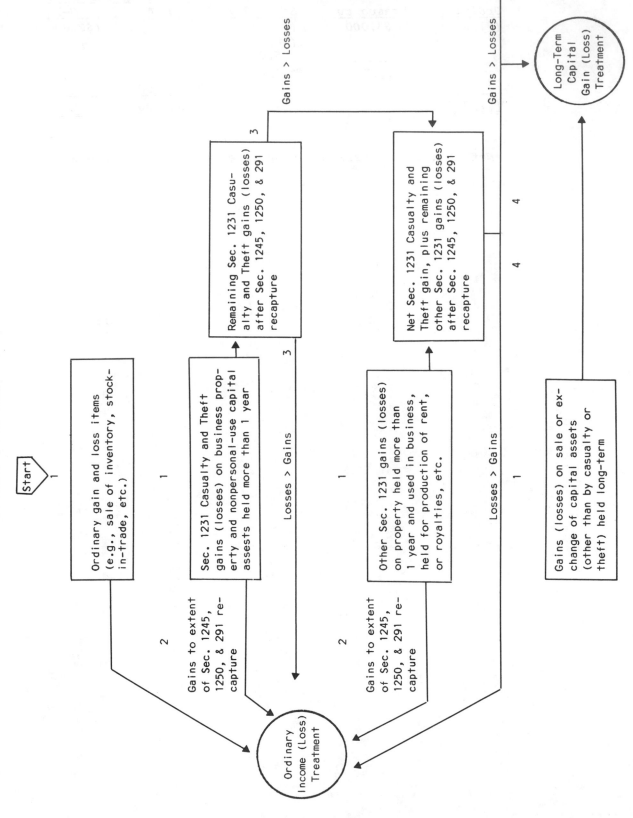

TAX TREATMENT OF GAINS AND LOSSES (OTHER THAN PERSONAL CASUALTY AND THEFT) ON PROPERTY HELD MORE THAN 1 YEAR

PARTNERSHIPS

Partnerships are organizations of two or more persons to carry on business activities. For tax purposes, partnerships also include a syndicate, joint venture, or other unincorporated business through which any business or financial operation is conducted. If a partnership is found to be an association for tax purposes, it will be taxed as a corporation. A partnership will be treated as an association if it has more than two of the following corporate characteristics: continuous life, centralized management, unrestricted transferability of interests, no personal liability of owners.

Partnerships do not pay any income tax; they are merely conduits to "flow-through" tax items to the partners. Partnerships file an informational return (Form 1065), and partners report their share of partnership taxable income or loss and other items on their individual returns. The nature or character (e.g., taxable, nontaxable) of income or deductions is not changed by the "flow-through" nature of the partnership.

A. **Partnership Formation**

    1. As a general rule, no gain or loss is recognized by a partner when there is a contribution of property to the partnership in exchange for an interest in the partnership. There are three situations where gain must be recognized

        a. A partner must recognize income when property is contributed which is subject to a liability, and the resulting decrease in his individual liability exceeds his basis [see p. 1311 "2.d.(1)"]

            (1) The excess of liability over adjusted basis is generally treated as a capital gain from the sale or exchange of a partnership interest

            (2) The gain will be treated as ordinary income to the extent the property transferred was subject to depreciation recapture under Sec. 1245 or 1250

EXAMPLE: A partner acquires a 20% interest in a partnership by contributing property worth $10,000 but with an adjusted basis of $4,000. There is a mortgage of $6,000 that is assumed by the partnership. The partner must recognize a gain of $800, and has a zero basis for his partnership interest, calculated as follows.

Adjusted basis of contributed property	$4,000
Less: portion of mortgage allocated to other partners (80% x $6,000)	(4,800)
	$ (800)
Plus recognized gain	800
Partner's basis	$ -0-

        b. Gain will be recognized on a contribution of property to a partnership in exchange for an interest therein if the partnership would be an investment company if incorporated

        c. Partner must recognize compensation income when an interest in partnership capital is received in exchange for services rendered

42

> *EXAMPLE: X received a 10% capital interest in the ABC Partnership in exchange for services rendered. On the date X was admitted to the partnership, ABC's net assets had a basis of $30,000 and a FMV of $50,000. X must recognize ordinary income of $5,000.*

2. Property contributed to the partnership has the same basis as it had in the contributing partner's hands (a carryover basis)

   a. The basis for the partner's partnership interest is increased by the adjusted basis of property contributed
   b. No gain or loss is generally recognized by the partnership upon the contribution

3. The partnership's holding period for contributed property includes the period of time the property was held by the partner

4. A partner's holding period for a partnership interest includes the holding period of property contributed, if the contributed property was a capital asset or Sec. 1231 asset in the contributing partner's hands

B. **Partnership Income and Loss**

1. Since a partnership is not a separate taxable entity, but instead acts as a conduit to "flow-through" items of income and deduction to individual partners, the partnership's reporting of income and deductions requires a two-step approach

   a. First, all items having special tax characteristics (i.e., subject to partial or full exclusion, % or dollar limitation, etc.) must be segregated and taken into account separately by each partner so that any special tax characteristics are preserved

      (1) These special items are listed separately on Schedule K of the partnership return and include

         (a) Capital gains and losses
         (b) Sec. 1231 gains and losses
         (c) Charitable contributions
         (d) Foreign income taxes
         (e) Sec. 179 expense deduction for recovery property (generally $10,000 per partnership)
         (f) Interest, dividend, and royalty income
         (g) Interest expense on investment indebtedness
         (h) Net income (loss) from rental real estate activity
         (i) Net income (loss) from other rental activity

   b. Second, all remaining items (since they have no special tax characteristics) are ordinary in nature and are netted in the computation of partnership taxable income (referred to as "ordinary income or loss" on Form 1065)

      (1) Frequently encountered ordinary income and deductions found in the computation of partnership taxable income include

         (a) Sales less cost of goods sold
         (b) Business expenses such as wages, rents, bad debts, and repairs
         (c) Guaranteed payments to partners
         (d) Depreciation

(e) Amortization (over 60 months or more) of partnership organization expenses. Note that syndication fees (expenses of selling partnership interests) are neither deductible nor amortizable

(f) Sec. 1245, 1250, etc., recapture

(g) See Form 1065 outline at beginning of chapter for more detail

2. The character of any gain or loss recognized on the disposition of property is generally determined by the nature of the property in the hands of the partnership. However, for contributed property, the character may be based on the nature of the property to the contributing partner before contribution

    a. If a partner contributes unrealized receivables, the partnership will recognize ordinary income or loss on the subsequent disposition of the unrealized receivables

    b. If the property contributed was inventory property to the contributing partner, any gain or loss recognized by the partnership on the disposition of the property within 5 years will be treated as ordinary income or loss

    c. If the contributed property was a capital asset, any loss later recognized by the partnership on the disposition of the property within 5 years will be treated as a capital loss to the extent of the contributing partner's unrecognized capital loss at the time of contribution. This rule applies to losses only, not to gains

3. A person sitting for the examination should be able to calculate book income of the partnership by adjusting partnership ordinary income (or partnership ordinary income by adjusting book income)

EXAMPLE: A partnership's accounting income statement discloses net income of $75,000 (i.e., book income). The three partners share profit and losses equally. Supplemental data indicate the following information has been included in net income.

	DR.	CR.
Net sales		$160,000
Cost of goods sold	$ 88,000	
Tax-exempt income		1,500
Sec. 1231 casualty gain		9,000
Section 1231 gain (other than casualty)		6,000
Section 1250 gain		20,000
Long-term capital gain		7,500
Short-term capital loss	6,000	
Guaranteed payments ($8,000 per partner)	24,000	
Charitable contributions	9,000	
Advertising expense	2,000	
	$129,000	$204,000

Partnership ordinary income is $66,000, computed as follows:

Book income		$ 75,000
Add		
Charitable contributions	$ 9,000	
Short-term capital loss	6,000	15,000
		$ 90,000
Deduct		
Tax-exempt income	$ 1,500	
Sec. 1231 casualty gain	9,000	
Section 1231 gain (other than casualty)	6,000	
Long-term capital gain	7,500	24,000
Partnership ordinary income		$ 66,000

Each partner's share of partnership ordinary income is $22,000.

4. Three sets of rules may limit the amount of partnership loss that a partner can deduct

   a. A partner's distributive share of partnership ordinary loss and special loss items is deductible by the partner only to the extent of the partner's basis in the partnership at the end of the taxable year [Sec. 704(d)]

      (1) Th flow through of loss is considered to be the last event during the partnership's taxable year; all positive basis adjustments are made prior to determining the amount of deductible loss
      (2) Unused losses are carried forward and can be deducted when the partner obtains additional basis for the partnership interest

      EXAMPLE: A partner who materially participates in the partnership's business has a distributive share of partnership capital gain of $200 and partnership ordinary loss of $3,000, but the partner's basis in the partnership is only $2,400 before consideration of these items. The partner can deduct $2,600 of the ordinary loss ($2,400 of beginning basis + $200 net capital gain). The remaining $400 of ordinary loss must be carried forward.

   b. The deductibility of partnership losses is also limited to the amount of the partner's at-risk basis [Sec. 465]

      (1) A partner's at-risk basis is generally the same as the partner's regular partnership basis with the exception that liabilities are inluded in at-risk basis only if the partner is personally liable for such amount
      (2) Nonrecourse liabilities are generally excluded from at-risk basis
      (3) Qualified nonrecourse real estate financing is included in at-risk basis

   c. The deductibility of partnership losses may also be subject to the passive activity loss limitations [Sec. 469]. Passive activity losses are deductible only to the extent of the partner's income from other passive activities [See ITAX page 1247]

      (1) Passive activities include (a) any partnership trade or business in which the partner does not materially participate, and (b) any rental activity
      (2) A limited partnership interest generally fails the material participation test

(3) To qualify for the $25,000 exception for active participation in a rental real estate activity, a partner (and spouse) must own at least 10% of the value of the partnership interests

C. **Partnership Agreements**

1. A partner's distributive share of income or loss is generally determined by the partnership agreement. Such agreement

   a. Can have different ratios for income or loss, and may agree to allocate other items (e.g., credits and deductions) in varying ratios
   b. Special allocations must have substantial economic effect

      (1) Economic effect is measured by an analysis of the allocation on the partners' capital accounts. The special allocation (a) must be reflected in the partners' capital accounts, (b) liquidation distributions must be based upon the positive capital account balances of partners, and (c) there must be a deficit payback agreement wherein partners agree to restore any deficit capital account balances
      (2) An allocation's economic effect will <u>not</u> be substantial if the net change recorded in the partners' capital accounts does not differ substantially from what would have been recorded without the special allocation, and the total tax liability of all partners is less

   c. If no allocation is provided, or if the allocation of an item does not have substantial economic effect, the partners' distributive shares of that item shall be determined by the ratio in which the partners generally divide the income or loss of the partnership
   d. If property is contributed by a partner to a partnership, related items of income, deduction, gain, or loss must be allocated among partners in a manner that reflects the difference between the property's tax basis and its fair market value at the time of contribution

   EXAMPLE: Partner X contributes property with a tax basis of $1,000 and a fair market value of $10,000 to the XYZ Partnership. If the partnership subsequently sells the property for $12,000, the first $9,000 of gain must be allocated to X, with the remaining $2,000 of gain allocated among partners according to their ratio for sharing gains.

   e. If there was any change in the ownership of partnership interests during the year, distributive shares of partnership interest, taxes, and payments for services or for the use of property must be allocated among partners by assigning an appropriate share of each item to each day of the partnership's taxable year

   EXAMPLE: Z becomes a 40% partner in calendar-year Partnership XY on December 1. Previously, X and Y each had a 50% interest. Partnership XY uses the cash method of accounting and on December 31 pays $10,000 of interest expense that relates to its entire calendar year. Z's distributive share of the interest expense will be ($10,000 ÷ 365 days) x 31 days x 40% = $340.

2. Distributable shares of income and guaranteed payments are reported by partners for their taxable year during which the end of the partnership fiscal
   year occurs

   a. Guaranteed payments are payments to a partner determined without regard
      to income of the partnership. Guaranteed payments are deductible by the
      partnership and reported as income by the partners

      *EXAMPLE: Z (on a calendar-year) has a 20% interest in a partnership
      that has a fiscal year ending May 31. Z received a guaranteed payment
      for services rendered of $1,000 a month from 6/1/88 to 12/31/88, and
      $1,500 a month from 1/1/89 to 5/31/89. After deducting the guaranteed
      payment, the partnership had ordinary income of $50,000 for its fiscal
      year ended 5/31/89. Z must include $24,500 in income on her calendar-
      year 1989 return ($50,000 x 20%) + ($1,000 x 7) + ($1,500 x 5).*

   b. Partners are generally not considered to be employees for purposes of
      employee fringe benefits (e.g., $5,000 employee death benefit exclusion,
      cost of $50,000 of group-term life insurance, etc.)

3. Family partnerships are subject to special rules because of their potential
   use for tax avoidance

   a. If the business is primarily service oriented (capital is not a material
      income-producing factor), a family member will be considered a partner
      only if the family member shares in the management or performs needed
      services, in addition to possibly contributing some capital
   b. A family member is generally considered a partner if he actually owns a
      capital interest in a business in which capital is a material income-
      producing factor
   c. Where a capital interest in a partnership in which capital is a material
      income-producing factor is treated as created by gift, the distributive
      shares of partnership income of the donor and donee are determined by
      first making a reasonable allowance for services rendered to the part-
      nership, and then allocating the remainder according to the relative
      capital interests of the donor and donee

D. **Partner's Basis in Partnership**

1. A partner's original basis is generally the amount of money plus adjusted
   basis of property contributed

   a. Plus gain recognized
   b. Adjusted for liabilities (see "2.d." below)

2. As the partnership operates, the partner's basis increases or decreases

   a. A partner's basis is increased by the adjusted basis of any subsequent
      capital contributions
   b. Also, a partner's basis is increased by any distributive share of

      (1) Partnership ordinary income
      (2) Capital gains and other special income items
      (3) Tax-exempt income of the partnership
      (4) The excess of the deduction for depletion over the partnership's
          basis of the property subject to depletion

   c. A partner's basis is decreased (but not below zero) by

(1) Distributions received from the partnership
(2) Any distributive share of any losses of the partnership
(3) Distributive share of special expense items
(4) Amount of partner's deduction for depletion on oil and gas wells

EXAMPLE: In the xxx example in "3." on page 1307, one partner's tax basis (who had a $15,000 tax basis at the beginning of the year) would be $40,000 at the end of the year, calculated as shown below.

Beginning partnership basis		$15,000
Add:		
Distributive share of partnership ordinary income	$22,000	
Tax-exempt income	500	
Sec. 1231 casualty gain	3,000	
Section 1231 gain (other than casualty)	2,000	
Long-term capital gain	2,500	30,000
		$45,000
Less:		
Short-term capital loss	$ 2,000	
Charitable contributions	3,000	5,000
Ending partnership basis		$40,000

d. **Changes in liabilities** affect a partner's basis

(1) Any decrease in a partner's <u>individual</u> liability by reason of the assumption by the partnership of such individual liabilities is considered to be a distribution of money to the partner by the partnership (i.e., partner's basis is reduced)
(2) Any increase in a partner's <u>individual</u> liability by reason of the assumption by the partner of partnership liabilities is considered to be a contribution of money to the partnership by the partner. Thus, the partner's basis is increased
(3) An increase in the <u>partnership's</u> liabilities, (e.g., loan from the bank, increase in accounts payable) increases each partner's basis in his partnership interest by his share of the increase
(4) Any decrease in the <u>partnership's</u> liabilities is considered to be a distribution of money to each partner and reduces his basis in the partnership by his share of the decrease

EXAMPLE: The XYZ partnership owns a warehouse with an adjusted basis of $120,000 subject to a mortgage of $90,000. Partner X (one of three equal partners) has a basis for his partnership interest of $75,000. If the partnership transfers the warehouse and mortgage to Partner X as a current distribution, X's basis for his partnership interest immediately following the distribution would be $15,000, calculated as follows.

Beginning basis	$ 75,000
Individual assumption of mortgage	+ 90,000
	$165,000
Distribution of warehouse	-120,000
Partner's share of decrease in partnership's liabilities	- 30,000
Basis after distribution	$ 15,000

> *EXAMPLE: Assume in the example above that one of the other one-third partners had a basis of $75,000 immediately before the distribution. What would the partner's basis be immediately after the distribution to Partner X? $45,000 (i.e., $75,000 less 1/3 of the $90,000 decrease in partnership liabilities).*

E. Transactions With Controlled Partnerships

1. If a person engages in a transaction with a partnership other than as a member of such partnership, any resulting gain or loss is generally recognized. However, if the transaction involves a <u>more than 50% owned partnership</u>, one of three special rules may apply. Constructive ownership rules [page 1294, a.(4)(a) and (4)(b)] apply in determining whether a transaction involves a more than 50% owned partnership

    a. No losses are deductible from sales or exchanges of property between a partnership and a person owning (directly or indirectly) more than 50% of the capital or profits interest in such partnership, or between two partnerships in which the same persons own (directly or indirectly) more than 50% of the capital or profits interest. A gain later realized on a subsequent sale by the transferee will not be recognized to the extent of the disallowed loss

    > *EXAMPLE: Partnership X is owned by three <u>equal</u> partners, A, B, and C, who are brothers. Partnership X sells property at a loss of $5,000 to C. Since C owns a more than 50% interest in the partnership (i.e., C constructively owns his brothers' partnership interests), the $5,000 loss is disallowed to Partnership X.*

    > *EXAMPLE: Assume the same facts as in the above example. C later resells the property to Z, an unrelated taxpayer, at a gain of $6,000. C's realized gain of $6,000 will not be recognized to the extent of the $5,000 disallowed loss to the Partnership X.*

    b. If a person related to a partner does not indirectly own a more than 50% partnership interest, a transaction between the related person and the partnership is treated as occurring between the related person and the partners individually

    > *EXAMPLE: X owns 100% of X Corp. and also owns a 25% interest in WXYZ Partnership. X Corp. sells property at a $1,200 loss to the WXYZ Partnership. Since X Corp. is related to partner X (i.e., X owns more than 50% of X Corp.), the transaction is treated as if it occurred between X Corp. and partners W, X, Y, and Z individually. Therefore, the loss disallowed to X Corp. is $1,200 x 25% = $300.*

    c. A gain recognized on a sale or exchange of property between a partnership and a person owning (directly or indirectly) more than 50% of the capital or profits interest in such partnership, or between two partnerships in which the same persons own (directly or indirectly) more than 50% of the capital or profits interests, will be treated as ordinary income if the property is not a <u>capital asset</u> in the hands of the transferee

    > *EXAMPLE: Assume the same facts as in the above example. Further assume that F is the father of W, Y, and Z. F sells investment property to Partnership WXYZ at a gain of $10,000. If the property will not be a*

capital asset to Partnership WXYZ, F must report the $10,000 gain as ordinary income because F constructively owns a more than 50% partnership interest (i.e., F constructively owns his children's partnership interests).

    d. A gain recognized on a sale or exchange of property between a partnership and a person owning (directly or indirectly) more than 50% of the capital or profits interest in such partnership, will be treated as ordinary income if the property is <u>depreciable property</u> in the hands of the transferee

F. Taxable Year of Partnership

1. A partnership must determine its taxable year in the following order:

    a. A partnership must adopt the taxable year used by one or more of its partners owning an aggregate interest of more than 50% in profits and capital (but only if the taxable year used by such partners has been the same for the lesser of 3 taxable years or the period the partnership has existed)

EXAMPLE: A partnership is formed by a corporation (which receives a 55% partnership interest) and five individuals (who each receive a 9% partnership interest). The corporation has a fiscal year ending June 30, while the individuals have a calendar year. The partnership must adopt a fiscal year ending June 30.

    b. If partners owning a more than 50% interest in partnership profits and capital do not have the same year end, the partnership must adopt the same taxable year as used by all of its principal partners (i.e., a partner with a 5% or more interest in capital or profits)

    c. If its principal partners have different taxable years, the partnership must adopt a calendar year

EXAMPLE: A partnership is owned by three equal partners--X, Y, and Z. X has a fiscal year ending January 31, Y has a fiscal year ending September 30, and Z has a calendar year. The partnership must adopt a calendar year.

2. A different taxable year than the year determined above can be used by a partnership if a valid business purpose can be established and IRS permission is received. The business purpose test will be met if a partnership receives at least 25% of its gross receipts in the last two months of a 12-month period, and this "25% test" has been satisfied for three consecutive years

EXAMPLE: Partnership X is owned by three equal partners--A, B, and C, who use a calendar year. Partnership X has received at least 25% of its gross receipts during the months of June and July for each of the last three years. Partnership X may change to a fiscal year ending July 31.

3. A partnership that otherwise would be required to adopt or change its tax year (normally to the calendar year) may elect to use a fiscal year if the election does not result in a deferral period longer than three months, or, if less, the deferral period of the year currently in use. However, a

partnership that had a taxable year beginning in 1986 could have elected to retain that same taxable year even though the deferral exceeds three months

a. The "deferral period" is the number of months between the close of the fiscal year elected and the close of the required year (e.g., if a partnership elects a tax year ending September 30 and a tax year ending December 31 is required, the deferral period of the year ending September 30 is three months)

b. A partnership that elects a tax year other than a required year must make a "required payment" which is in the nature of a refundable, non-interest bearing deposit that is intended to compensate the government for the revenue lost as a result of tax deferral

   (1) The required payment is due on May 15 each year and is recomputed for each subsequent year

   (2) If the amount of the required payment increases, the partnership must pay the amount of increase. Conversely, if the amount of deferred tax decreases relative to the previous year, the partnership is entitled to a refund

   (3) Thus, a partnership that elects this procedure maintains a deferred payment balance with the government and adjusts it annually. No interest accrues on the balance, and partners do not receive any type of credit for the tax deposit

c. The amount of <u>required payment</u> is computed as:

   Net base year income
    x Highest individual rate + 1% (e.g., 29% for 1988 and 1989)

   _____

   = Deferred tax and "toll charge" for current year
   <u>- Required payment of preceding year</u>
   Required payment (refund) for current year

d. A partnership's <u>net base income</u> is generally the amount of income in the prior taxable year that is deferred and is computed as follows:

   Net income of the partnership for prior taxable year
    <u>+ Certain payments</u> included in partners' income
   Balance
    x Deferral ratio (months of deferral/months in taxable year)

   _____

   <u>Net base year income</u>

e. No payment need be made if the required payment does not exceed $500. The required payment is generally phased in over four years--

Taxable year beginning in	Percentage to be paid
1987	25%
1988	50
1989	75
1990	100

EXAMPLE: A partnership that otherwise would be required to adopt a calendar year elects to retain its fiscal year ended August 31. Its net income for the year ended August 31, 1987 was $120,000. It made no payment to its partners during the year. The partnership's net base income is $120,000 x 4/12 = $40,000. Its required payment due April 15, 1988 is $40,000 x 36% x 25% (phase-in) = $3,600.

4. The taxable year of a partnership ordinarily will not close as a result of the death or entry of a partner, or the liquidation or sale of a partner's interest. But the partnership's taxable year closes as to the individual partner whose <u>entire</u> interest is sold or liquidated

EXAMPLE: A partner sells his entire interest in a calendar-year partnership on March 31. His pro rata share of partnership income up to March 31 is $15,000. Since the partnership year closes with respect to him at the time of sale, the $15,000 is includible in his income and increases the basis of his partnership interest for purposes of computing gain or loss on the sale. However the partnership's taxable year does not close as to its remaining partners.

EXAMPLE: X (on a calendar year) is a partner in the XYZ Partnership which uses a June 30 fiscal year. X dies on October 31, 1988. Since the partnership year does not close with respect to X at his death, X's final return for the period January 1 thru October 31 will only include his share of partnership income for the partnership year ended June 30, 1988. His share of partnership income after June 30 will be reported by his estate or other successor in interest.

G. Partnership's Use of Cash Method

1. The cash method of accounting can not generally be used by a partnership that has a C corporation (i.e., regular corporation) as a partner. It must use the accrual method of tax accounting

2. A partnership that has a C corporation as a partner can use the cash method if its average annual gross receipts for the 3-year period (or the period in existence if less) ending with the taxable year does not exceed $5,000,000.

H. Termination or Continuation of Partnership

1. A partnership will terminate when it no longer has at least two partners

2. A partnership and its taxable year will terminate for all partners if there is a sale of 50% or more of the total interest in partnership capital and profits within a 12-month period

3. In a merger of partnerships, the resulting partnership is a continuation of the merging partnership whose partners have a more than 50% interest in the resulting partnership

EXAMPLE: Partnerships AB and CD merge on April 1, forming the ABCD Partnership in which the partners' interests are as follows: Partner A, 30%; B, 30%; C, 20%; and D, 20%. Partnership ABCD is a continuation of the AB Partnership. The CD Partnership is considered terminated and its taxable year closed on April 1.

4. In a division of a partnership, a resulting partnership is a continuation of the prior partnership if the resulting partnership's partners had a more than 50% interest in the prior partnership

EXAMPLE: Partnership ABCD is owned as follows: A, 40%; and B, C, and D
each own a 20% interest. The partners agree to separate and form two
partnerships--AC and BD. Partnership AC is a continuation of ABCD. BD is
considered a new partnership and must adopt a taxable year, as well as make
any other necessary tax accounting elections.

I. Sale of a Partnership Interest

1. Since a partnership interest is usually a capital asset, sale of a partner-
    ship interest generally results in capital gain or loss

    a. Gain is excess of amount realized over the adjusted basis for the
        partnership interest
    b. Include the selling partner's share of partnership liabilities in the
        amount realized because the selling partner is relieved of them

2. Gain is ordinary (instead of capital) to extent attributable to substan-
    tially appreciated inventory or unrealized receivables (Sec. 751 items)

    a. "Unrealized receivables" generally refer to the accounts receivable of a
        cash method taxpayer, but for this purpose also include any potential
        recapture under Secs. 1245, 1250, 1251, and 1252
    b. "Inventory" includes all assets except capital assets and Section 1231
        assets. Thus unrealized receivables are included in this definition of
        "inventory"
    c. Inventory is substantially appreciated if its fair market value

        (1) Exceeds 120% of its adjusted basis, and
        (2) Exceeds 10% of the fair market value of all assets except money

EXAMPLE: X has a 40% interest in the XY Partnership. Partner X sells
his 40% interest to Z for $50,000. X's basis in his partnership is
$22,000 and the cash-method partnership had the following receivables
and inventory.

	Adjusted Basis	Fair Market Value
Accounts receivable	$ 0	$10,000
Inventory	4,000	10,000
Potential Sec. 1250 recapture	0	10,000
	$4,000	$30,000

X's total gain is $28,000 (i.e., $50,000 - $22,000). Since the Sec.
1250 recapture is treated as "unrealized receivables" and the inventory
is substantially appreciated, X will recognize ordinary income to the
extent that his selling price attributable to Sec. 751 items ($30,000 x
40% = $12,000) exceeds his basis in those items ($4,000 x 40% = $1,600),
i.e., $10,400. The remainder of X's gain ($28,000 - $10,400 = $17,600)
will be treated as capital gain.

J. Pro Rata Distributions from Partnership

1. Partnership recognizes no gain or loss on a distribution
2. Partner recognizes gain only to the extent money received exceeds the
    partner's partnership basis

    a. Relief from liabilities is deemed a distribution of money

      b. Gain is capital except for gain attributable to unrealized receivables and substantially appreciated inventory

      c. If property other than money is received, gain is not recognized until disposition of the property

  3. Partner recognizes loss only upon complete liquidation of a partnership interest through receipt of only money, unrealized receivables, or inventory

      a. The amount of loss is the basis for the partner's partnership interest less the money and the partnership's basis in the unrealized receivables and inventory received by the partner

      b. The loss is generally treated as a capital loss

  4. If property other than money, unrealized receivables, or inventory is distributed in complete liquidation of a partner's interest, no loss is recognized

      a. The partner's basis for any receivables or inventory received will generally be the same as the partnership's former basis for those items

      b. The basis for the partner's partnership interest is reduced by the amount of money and the partnership's former basis for any unrealized receivables and inventory received, with any remaining basis allocated to other property received in proportion to their adjusted bases (not FMV) to the partnership

  5. In nonliquidating (current) distributions, a partner's basis in distributed property is the same as the partnership's former basis in the property; but limited to the basis for the partner's partnership interest less any money received

     EXAMPLE: S receives a current distribution from her partnership at a time when the basis for her partnership interest is $10,000.   The distribution consists of $7,000 cash and Sec. 1231 property with an adjusted basis of $5,000 and a FMV of $9,000.   No gain is recognized by S since the cash received did not exceed her basis.   After being reduced by the cash, her partnership basis of $3,000 is reduced by the basis of the property (but not below zero).   Her basis for the property is limited to $3,000.

  6. Payments to a retiring partner are allocated between amounts paid for the partner's interest in partnership property (resulting in capital gain or loss), and other payments (resulting in ordinary income)

      a. Amounts received for a partner's share of unrealized receivables and substantially appreciated inventory are treated as ordinary income

      b. Amounts treated as ordinary income by retiring partner are either

         (1) Deductible by the partnership, or

         (2) Reduce the income allocated to remaining partners

K. **Non Pro Rata Distributions from Partnership**

  1. A non pro rata (disproportionate) distribution occurs when

      a. A distribution is disproportionate as to a partner's share of substantially appreciated inventory or unrealized receivables

         (1) Partner may receive more than the partner's share of these assets, or

    (2)   Partner may receive more than the partner's share of other assets, in effect giving up a share of unrealized receivables or substantially appreciated inventory

  b. The partner may recognize gain or loss

    (1)   The gain or loss is the difference between the FMV of what is received and the basis of what is given up

    (2)   The gain or loss is limited to the disproportionate amount of unrealized receivables or substantially appreciated inventory which is received or given up

    (3)   The character of the gain or loss depends upon the character of the property given up

  c. The partnership may similarly recognize gain or loss when there is a disproportionate distribution with respect to substantially appreciated inventory or unrealized receivables

EXAMPLE: A, B, and C each own a one-third interest in a partnership. The partnership has the following assets.

	Adjusted Basis	FMV
Cash	$ 6,000	$ 6,000
Inventory	6,000	12,000
Land	9,000	18,000
	$21,000	$36,000

Assume that A has a $7,000 basis for his partnership interest and that all inventory is distributed to A in liquidation of his partnership interest. He is treated as having exchanged his 1/3 interest in the cash and the land for a 2/3 increased interest in the substantially appreciated inventory. He has a gain of $3,000. He received $8,000 (2/3 x $12,000) of inventory for his basis of $2,000 (1/3 x $6,000) in cash and $3,000 (1/3 x $9,000) of land. The gain is capital if the land was a capital asset. The partnership is treated as having received $8,000 (FMV of A's 1/3 share of cash and land) in exchange for inventory with a basis of $4,000 (basis of inventory distributed in excess of A's 1/3 share). Thus, the partnership will recognize ordinary income of $4,000.

L. **Optional Adjustment to Basis of Partnership Property**

  1. On a distribution of property to a partner, or on a sale by a partner of a partnership interest, the partnership may elect to adjust the basis of its assets to prevent any inequities that otherwise might occur. Once election is made, it applies to all similar transactions unless IRS approves revocation of the election

  2. Upon the distribution of partnership property, the basis of remaining partnership property will be adjusted for <u>all</u> partners

    a. Increased by

      (1)   The amount of gain recognized to a distributee partner, and

      (2)   The excess of the partnership's basis in the property distributed over the basis of that property in the hands of distributee partner

EXAMPLE: If election were made under facts in the example on page 1317, $2,000 of basis that otherwise would be lost will be allocated to remaining partnership Sec. 1231 property.

b. Decreased by

(1) The amount of loss recognized to a distributee partner, and
(2) The excess of basis of property in hands of distributee over the prior basis of that property in the partnership

3. Upon the sale or exchange of a partnership interest, the basis of partnership property to the <u>transferee</u> (not other partners) will be

a. Increased by the excess of the basis of the transferee's partnership interest over the transferee's share of the adjusted basis of partnership property
b. Decreased by the excess of transferee's share of adjusted basis of partnership property over the basis for the transferee's partnership interest

EXAMPLE: Assume X sells his 40% interest to Z for $80,000 when the partnership balance sheet reflects the following.

XY Partnership

Assets	Basis	FMV
Accounts Receivable	$ -0-	$100,000
Real Property	30,000	100,000
Capital		
X (40%)		$ 80,000
Y (60%)		120,000

Z will have a basis for his partnership interest of $80,000, while his share of the adjusted basis of partnership property will only be $12,000. If the partnership elects to adjust the basis of partnership property, it will increase the basis of its assets by $68,000 ($80,000 – $12,000) solely for the benefit of Z. The basis of the receivables will increase from -0- to $40,000 with the full adjustment allocated to Z. When the receivables are collected, Y will have $60,000 of income and Z will have none. The basis of the real property will increase by $28,000 to $58,000, so that Z's share of the basis will be $40,000 (i.e., $12,000 + $28,000).

CORPORATIONS

Corporations are separate taxable entities, organized under state law. Although corporations may have many of the same income and deduction items as individuals, corporations are taxed at different rates and some tax rules are applied differently. There also are special provisions applicable to transfers of property to a corporation, and issuance of stock.

A. **Transfers to a Controlled Corporation (Sec. 351)**

1. No gain or loss is recognized if property is transferred to a corporation solely in exchange for stock or securities and immediately after the exchange those persons transferring property control the corporation

    a. "Property" includes everything but services
    b. "Securities" are corporate debt obligations with at least a 5-year maturity
    c. "Control" means ownership of at least 80% of the total combined voting power and 80% of each class of nonvoting stock
    d. Receipt of boot (e.g., cash, short-term notes, etc.) will cause recognition of gain (but no loss)

        (1) Corporation's assumption of liabilities treated as boot only if there is a tax avoidance purpose, or no business purpose
        (2) Shareholder recognizes gain if liabilities assumed by corporation exceed the total basis of property transferred by the shareholder

2. Shareholder's basis for stock and securities = adjusted basis of property transferred

    a. + gain recognized
    b. - boot received (assumption of liability always treated as boot for purposes of determining stock basis)

3. Corporation's basis in property = transferor's adjusted basis + gain recognized to transferor

    EXAMPLE: *Individuals A, B, & C form ABC Corp. and make the following transfer to their corporation.*

Item transferred	A	B	C
Property - FMV	$10,000	$ 8,000	$ -0-
- Adjusted basis	1,500	3,000	-0-
Liability assumed by ABC Corp.	2,000	-0-	-0-
Services	-0-	-0-	1,000
Consideration received			
Stock (FMV)	$ 8,000	$ 7,600	$ 1,000
2-year note (FMV)	-0-	400	-0-
Gain recognized to shareholder	$ 500[a]	$ 400	$ 1,000[b]
Basis of stock received	-0-	$ 3,000	$ 1,000
Basis of property to corp.	2,000	3,400	1,000[c]

    a. Liability in excess of basis: $2,000 - $1,500 = $500
    b. Ordinary compensation income
    c. Expense or asset depending on nature of services rendered

B. **Section 1244 - Small Business Corporation (SBC) Stock**

   1. Sec. 1244 stock permits shareholders to deduct an ordinary loss on sale or worthlessness of stock

      a. Shareholder must be the original holder of stock, and an individual or partnership
      b. Stock can be common or preferred
      c. Ordinary loss limited to $50,000 ($100,000 on joint return); any excess is capital loss
      d. The corporation during the 5-year period before the year of loss, received less than 50% of its total gross receipts from royalties, rents, dividends, interest, annuities, and gains from sales or exchanges of stock or securities

   2. SBC is any domestic corporation whose aggregate amount of money and adjusted basis of other property received for stock, as a contribution to capital, and as paid-in surplus, does not exceed $1,000,000. If more than $1 million of stock is issued, up to $1 million of qualifying stock can be designated as Sec. 1244 stock

C. **Variations from Individual Taxation**

   1. Filing and payment of tax

      a. A corporation must file a return (Form 1120) every year even though it has no taxable income
      b. The return must be filed by the 15th day of the third month following the close of its taxable year (e.g., March 15 for calendar-year corporation)

         (1) An automatic six-month extension may be obtained by filing Form 7004
         (2) Any balance due on the corporation's tax liability must be paid with the request for extension

      c. Estimated tax payments must be made by every corporation whose estimated tax is expected to be $40 or more

         (1) Quarterly payments are due on the 15th day of the fourth, sixth, ninth, and twelfth months of its taxable year (April 15, June 15, September 15, and December 15 for a calendar-year corporation). Any balance due must be paid by the due date of the return
         (2) A corporation with $1 million or more of taxable income in any of its three preceding tax years must pay at least 90% of its current year's tax liability as estimated tax

   2. Corporations are subject to

      a. <u>Regular tax rates</u>. For taxable years beginning on or after July 1, 1987, corporate tax rates are

	Taxable income	Rate
(1)	$0 - $50,000	15%
(2)	$50,001 - $75,000	25
(3)	$75,001 +	34

4
3

        (4)   The less-than-34% brackets are phased out by adding an additional tax of 5% of the excess of taxable income over $100,000, up to a maximum additional tax of $11,750

   b. Certain personal service corporations are not eligible to use the less-than-34% brackets and their taxable income is taxed at a flat 34% rate

   c. <u>Alternative minimum tax (AMT)</u>

      (1) <u>Computation</u>. The AMT is generally the amount by which 20% of alternative minimum taxable income (AMTI) as reduced by an exemption, exceeds the regular tax (i.e., regular tax liability reduced by the foreign tax credit). AMTI is equal to taxable income computed with specified adjustments and increased by tax preferences

      (2) <u>Exemption</u>. AMTI is offset by a $40,000 exemption. However, the exemption is reduced by 25% of AMTI over $150,000, and completely phased out once AMTI reaches $310,000

      (3) <u>Adjustments</u>. In determining AMTI, taxable income must be computed with various adjustments. Examples of adjustments include

          (a) For real property placed in service after 1986, the excess of depreciation over straight-line using a 40-year life

          (b) For personal property placed in service after 1986, the excess of accelerated depreciation over the amount determined using the 150% declining balance method (switching to straight-line when necessary to maximize the deduction)

          (c) One-half of the excess of a corporation's adjusted net book income over its pre-book AMTI

> EXAMPLE: Acme, Inc. has adjusted net book income of $100,000 and alternative minimum taxable income (without regard to the book income preference) of $60,000. Since adjusted net book income exceeds the AMTI by $40,000, one-half of this amount must be added to Acme's AMTI. Thus, Acme's AMTI for the year is $80,000 [$60,000 + ($40,000 x ½)].

      (4) <u>Preference items</u>. The following are examples of preference items added to taxable income (as adjusted above) in computing AMTI:

          (a) The excess of percentage depletion over the property's adjusted basis

          (b) The excess of intangible drilling costs using a 10-year amortization over 65% of net oil and gas income

          (c) The untaxed appreciation on capital gain property donated to charity

          (d) Tax-exempt interest income (net of related expenses) from private activity bonds

   d. See subsequent discussion for penalty taxes on

      (1) Accumulated earnings

      (2) Personal holding companies

3. <u>Gross income</u> for a corporation is quite similar to the rules for an individual taxpayer. However, there are a few differences

   a. A corporation does not recognize gain or loss on the issuance of its own stock (including treasury stock), or on the lapse or acquisition of an option to buy or sell its stock (including treasury stock)

(1) It generally recognizes gain (but not loss) if it distributes appreciated property to its shareholders

(2) Assessments against shareholders are not income (they are capital contributions)

(3) Capital contributions by other than a shareholder are excluded from income, and the basis of the contributed property is zero

  (a) If money is received, the basis of property purchased within 1 year afterwards is reduced by the money contributed

  (b) Any money not used reduces the basis of the corporation's other property beginning with depreciable property

b. No gain or loss is recognized on the issuance of <u>debt</u>

(1) Premium or discount on bonds payable is amortized as income or expense over the life of bonds

(2) Ordinary income/loss is recognized by a corporation on the repurchase of its bonds, determined by the relationship of the repurchase price to the net carrying value of the bonds (issue price plus or minus the discount or premium amortized)

(3) Interest earned and gains recognized in a bond sinking fund are income to the corporation

c. A property dividend received by a domestic corporation is included in income at its FMV on date of distribution

d. Gains are treated as ordinary income on sales to or from a more than 50% shareholder, or between corporations which are more than 50% owned by the same individual, if the property is subject to depreciation in the hands of the buyer

4. Deductions for a corporation are much the same as for individuals. However, there are some major differences

a. Adjusted gross income is not applicable to corporations

b. <u>Organizational expenditures</u> may be amortized over 60 months or longer if elected in the first tax return; otherwise deductible only in year of liquidation

(1) Election applies to expenditures incurred before the end of the corporation's first tax year (even if the amounts have not yet been paid by a cash-method corporation)

(2) Amortization period starts with the month that the corporation begins business

(3) Expenditures connected with issuing or selling shares of stock, or listing stock on an exchange are neither deductible nor amortizable

c. The deduction for <u>charitable contributions</u> is limited to 10% of taxable income before the contributions deduction, the dividends received deduction, a net operating loss carryback (but after carryover), and a capital loss carryback (but after carryover)

(1) Generally the same rules apply for valuation of contributed property as for individuals except

  (a) Deduction for donations of inventory and other appreciated ordinary income-producing property is the donor's basis plus one-half of the unrealized appreciation but limited to twice the basis, provided

                1]   Donor is a corporation (but not an S corporation)
                2]   Donee must use property for care of ill, needy, or infants
                3]   Donor must obtain a written statement from the donee that the use requirement has been met
                4]   No deduction allowed for unrealized appreciation that would be ordinary income under recapture rules

        (b) Deduction for donation of appreciated scientific personal property to a college or university is the donor's basis plus one-half the unrealized appreciation but limited to twice the basis, provided

                1]   Donor is a corporation (but not an S corporation, PHC, or service organization)
                2]   Property was constructed by donor and contributed within 2 years of substantial completion, and donee is original user of property
                3]   Donee must use property for research or experimentation
                4]   Donor must obtain a written statement from the donee that the use requirement has been met
                5]   No deduction allowed for unrealized appreciation that would be ordinary income under recapture rules

    (2) Contributions are deductible in period paid (subject to 10% limitation) unless corporation is an accrual method taxpayer and then deductible (subject to 10% limitation) when authorized by board of directors if payment is made within 2 1/2 months after tax year end, and corporation elects to deduct contributions when authorized

    (3) Excess contributions over the 10% limitation may be carried forward for up to five years

    EXAMPLE: The books of a calendar-year, accrual method corporation for 1988 disclose net income of $350,000 after deducting a charitable contribution of $50,000. The contribution was authorized by the Board of Directors on December 24, 1988, and was actually paid on January 31, 1989. The allowable charitable contribution deduction for 1988 (if the corporation elects to deduct it when accrued) is $40,000, calculated as follows: ($350,000 + $50,000) x .10 = $40,000. The remaining $10,000 is carried forward for up to 5 years.

 d. A 100% DRD is permitted for dividends received from affiliated corporations

    (1) There must be at least 80% ownership
    (2) See page 1330 for discussion of affiliated corporations

 e. An 80% dividends received deduction (DRD) is allowed for qualified dividends from taxable domestic unaffiliated corporations that are at least 20% owned

    (1) DRD may be limited to 80% of taxable income before the dividends received deduction, the net operating loss deduction, and a capital loss carryback
    (2) Exception: The 80% of taxable income limitation does not apply if the full 80% DRD creates or increases a net operating loss

    EXAMPLE: A corporation has income from sales of $20,000 and dividend income of $10,000, along with business expenses of

$22,000.   Since taxable income before the DRD would be $8,000 (less than the dividend income), the DRD is limited to $6,400 (80% x $8,000).   Thus, taxable income would be: $1,600 ($8,000 - $6,400).

EXAMPLE: In the example above, assume that all facts are the same except that business expenses are $22,001.   Since the full DRD ($8,000) would create a $1 net operating loss ($7,999 - $8,000), the exception would apply and the full DRD ($8,000) would be allowed.

f. Only a 70% dividends received deduction (instead of 80%) is allowed for qualified dividends from taxable domestic unaffiliated corporations that are less than 20% owned

   (1) A 70% of taxable income limitation (instead of 80%) and a limitation exception for a net operating loss apply as in e.(1) and (2) above

   (2) If dividends are received from both 20% owned corporations and corporations that are less than 20% owned, the 80% DRD and 80% DRD limitation for dividends received from 20% owned corporations is computed first. Then the 70% DRD and 70% DRD limitation is computed for dividends received from less than 20% owned corporations. For purposes of computing the 70% DRD limitation, taxable income is reduced by the total amount of dividends received from 20% owned corporations

EXAMPLE: A corporation has taxable income before the dividends received deduction of $100,000.   Included in taxable income are $65,000 of dividends from a 20% owned corporation and $40,000 of dividends from a less than 20% owned corporation.   First, the 80% DRD for dividends received from the 20% owned corporation is computed.   That deduction equals $52,000 [i.e., the lesser of 80% of the dividends received (80% x $65,000), or 80% of taxable income (80% x $100,000)].

Second, the 70% DRD for the dividends received from the less than 20% owned corporation is computed.   That deduction is $24,500 [i.e., the lesser of 70% of the dividends received (70% x $40,000), or 70% of taxable income after deducting the amount of dividends from the 20% owned corporation (70% x [$100,000 - $65,000])].

Thus, the total dividends received deduction is $52,000 + $24,500 = $76,500.

g. A portion of a corporation's 80% (or 70%) DRD will be disallowed if the dividends are directly attributable to debt-financed portfolio stock

   (1) "Portfolio stock" is any stock (except not stock of a corporation if the taxpayer owns at least 50% of the voting power and at least 50% of the total value of such corporation)

   (2) The DRD percentage for debt-financed portfolio stock = [80% (or 70%) x (100% - Average % of indebtedness on the stock)]

EXAMPLE: P Inc. purchased 25% of T Inc. for $100,000, paying with $50,000 of its own funds and $50,000 borrowed from its bank.

During the year P received $9,000 in dividends from T, and paid $5,000 in interest expense on the bank loan. No principal payments were made on the loan during the year. If the stock were not debt financed, P's DRD would be $9,000 x 80% = $7,200. However, because half of the stock investment was debt financed, P's DRD is $9,000 x [80% x (100% - 50%)] = $3,600.

(3) The reduction in the DRD can not exceed the interest deduction allocable to the portfolio stock indebtedness

EXAMPLE: Assume the same facts as above except that the interest expense on the bank loan was only $3,000. The reduction in the DRD would be limited to the $3,000 interest deduction on the loan. The DRD would be ($9,000 x 80%) - $3,000 = $4,200.

h. No DRD is allowed if the stock is held 45 days or less (90 days or less for preferred stock if the dividends received on it are for a period of more than one year)

i. The basis of stock held by a corporation must be reduced by the nontaxed portion of a non-liquidating extraordinary dividend received with respect to the stock, unless the corporation has held the stock for more than two years before the dividend is announced. To the extent the nontaxed portion of an extraordinary dividend exceeds the adjusted basis of the stock, the excess is recognized as gain when the stock is sold or otherwise disposed of

(1) The nontaxed portion of a dividend is generally the amount that is offset by the DRD

(2) A dividend is considered "extraordinary" when it equals or exceeds 10% (5% for preferred stock) of the stock's adjusted basis (or FMV on the day preceding the ex-dividend date if greater)

(3) Aggregation of dividends

(a) All dividends received that have ex-dividend dates that occur within a period of 85 consecutive days are treated as one dividend

(b) All dividends received within 365 consecutive days are treated as extraordinary dividends if they in total exceed 20% of the stock's adjusted basis

(4) This provision is not applicable to dividends received from an affiliated corporation, and does not apply if the stock was held during the entire period the paying corporation (and any predecessor, was in existence

EXAMPLE: Corporation X purchased 30% of the stock of Corporation Y for $10,000 during January 1988. During July 1988, X received a $20,000 dividend from Y. X sold its Y stock for $5,000 in March 1989.

Because the dividend from Y is an extraordinary dividend, the nontaxed portion (equal to the DRD allowed to X) $20,000 x 80% = $16,000 has the effect of reducing the Y stock basis from $10,000 to $0, with the remaining $6,000 to be recognized as gain when the Y stock is sold in 1989. At time of sale, the excess of sale proceeds over the reduced stock basis $5,000 - $0 = $5,000 is also recognized as gain, resulting in total gain of $11,000 in 1989.

j. <u>Losses</u> in the ordinary course of business are deductible

  (1) Loss is <u>disallowed</u> if the sale or exchange of property is between

    (a) A corporation and a more than 50% shareholder,

    (b) A C corporation and an S corporation if the same persons own more than 50% of each, or

    (c) A corporation and a partnership if the same persons own more than 50% of the corporation, and more than 50% of the capital and profits interest in the partnership

    (d) In the event of a disallowed loss, the transferee on subsequent disposition only recognizes gain to the extent it exceeds the disallowed loss

  (2) Any loss from the sale or exchange of property between corporations that are members of the same <u>controlled group</u> is <u>deferred</u> (instead of disallowed) until the property is sold outside the group. See controlled group definition in CTAX, "D.2.," except substitute "more than 50%" for "at least 80%"

  (3) An accrual method C corporation is effectively placed on the cash method of accounting for purposes of deducting accrued interest and other expenses owed to a related cash-method payee. No deduction is allowable until the year the amount is actually paid

    EXAMPLE: A calendar-year corporation accrues $10,000 of salary to an employee (a 60% shareholder) during 1988, but does not make payment until February 1989.   The $10,000 will be deductible by the corporation and reported as income by the employee-shareholder in 1989.

  (4) <u>Capital losses</u> are deductible only to the extent of capital gains (i.e., may not offset ordinary income)

    (a) Unused capital losses are carried back 3 years and then carried forward 5 years to offset capital gains

    (b) All corporate capital loss carrybacks and carryforwards are treated as <u>short-term</u>

  (5) Bad debt losses are treated as ordinary deductions

  (6) Casualty losses are treated the same as for an individual except

    (a) There is no $100 floor

    (b) If property is completely destroyed, the amount of loss is the property's adjusted basis

    (c) A partial loss is measured the same as for an individual (i.e., the lesser of the decrease in FMV, or the property's adjusted basis)

  (7) A corporation's <u>net operating loss</u> is computed the same way as its taxable income

    (a) The dividends received deduction is allowed without limitation

    (b) No deduction is allowed for a NOL carryback or carryover from other years

    (c) A NOL may be carried back 3 years and forward 15 years to offset taxable income in other years

    (d) Carryback is first made to third preceding year, but corporation may elect to forego carryback and only carryforward 15 years

k. Depreciation and depletion computations are same as for individuals

1. Research and development expenditures of a corporation (or individual) may be treated under one of three alternatives

    (1) Currently expensed in year paid or incurred
    (2) Amortized over a period of 60 months or more if life not determinable
    (3) Capitalized and depreciated over determinable life

m. Contributions to a pension or profit sharing plan

    (1) Defined benefit plans

        (a) Maximum deductible contribution is actuarially determined
        (b) There also are minimum funding standards

    (2) Defined contribution plans

        (a) <u>Maximum deduction</u> for contributions to qualified profit-sharing or stock bonus plans is generally limited to 15% of the compensation paid or accrued during the year to covered employees
        (b) If more than 15% is paid, the excess can be carried forward as part of the contributions of succeeding years to the extent needed to bring the deduction up to 15%

5. In working a corporate problem, certain calculations must be made in a specific order [e.g., charitable contributions (CC) must be computed before the dividends received deduction (DRD)]. The following memory device is quite helpful

Gross income
     <u>less deductions (except CC and DRD)</u>
     = Taxable income before CC and DRD
        less charitable contributions (CC): limited to 10% of TI before CC,
     <u>   DRD, capital loss carryback, and NOL carryback</u>
     = Taxable income before DRD
        less dividends received deduction (DRD): may be limited* to 80% (or 70%) of
     <u>   TI before DRD, capital loss carryback, and NOL carryover or carryback</u>
     = Taxable income
     <u>   times applicable rates</u>
     = Tax liability before tax credits
     <u>   less tax credits</u>
     <u>= Tax liability</u>

     *Limitation not applicable if full 80% (or 70%) of dividends received creates or increases a NOL

6. A person sitting for the CPA examination should be able to reconcile book and taxable income

    a. If you begin with book income to calculate taxable income, make the following adjustments

(1) Increase book income by

    (a) Federal income tax expense
    (b) Excess of capital losses over capital gains because a net capital loss is not deductible
    (c) Income items in the tax return not included in book income (e.g., prepaid rents, royalties, interest)
    (d) Charitable contributions in excess of the 10% limitation
    (e) Expenses deducted on the books but not on the tax return (e.g., amount of business gifts in excess of $25, nondeductible life insurance premiums paid, provision for cash discounts)

(2) Deduct from book income

    (a) Income reported on the books but not on the tax return (e.g., tax exempt interest, life insurance proceeds)
    (b) Expenses deducted on the tax return but not on the books (e.g., ACRS depreciation above straight-line, charitable contribution carryover)
    (c) The dividends received deduction

b. When going from taxable income to book income, the above adjustments would be reversed
c. Schedule M-1 of Form 1120 provides a reconciliation of income per books with taxable income before the NOL and DRD. There are two types of Schedule M-1 items

(1) Permanent differences (e.g., tax-exempt interest)
(2) Temporary differences--items are reflected in different periods (e.g., accelerated depreciation on tax return and straight-line on books)

> *EXAMPLE: A corporation discloses that it had net income after taxes of $36,000 per books. Included in the computation were deductions for charitable contributions of $10,000, a net capital loss of $5,000, and federal income taxes paid of $9,000. What is the corporation's TI?*

Net income per books after tax	$36,000
Nondeductible net capital loss	+ 5,000
Federal income tax expense	+ 9,000
Charitable contributions	+10,000
Taxable income before CC	$60,000
CC (limited to 10% X 60,000)	− 6,000
Taxable income	$54,000

d. Schedule M-2 of Form 1120 analyzes changes in a corporation's Unappropriated Retained Earnings per books between the beginning and end of the year

    Balance at beginning of year
    Add: Net income per books
          Other increases (e.g., refund of a prior year's federal income tax)
    Less: Dividends to shareholders
          Other decreases (e.g., addition to reserve for contingencies)
    Balance at end of year

D. Affiliated and Controlled Corporations

1. An <u>affiliated group</u> is a parent-subsidiary chain of corporations in which at least 80% of the combined voting power <u>and</u> total value of all stock (except nonvoting preferred) are owned by includible corporations

   a. They may elect to file a consolidated return. Election is binding on all future returns
   b. If affiliated corporations file a consolidated return, intercompany dividends are eliminated in the consolidation process. If separate tax returns are filed, dividends from affiliated corporations are eligible for a 100% dividends received deduction.
   c. Possible advantages of a consolidated return include the deferral of gain on intercompany transactions and offsetting operating/capital losses of one corporation against the profits/capital gains of another

   EXAMPLE: P Corp. owns 80% of the stock of A Corp., 40% of the stock of B Corp., and 45% of the stock of C Corp. A Corp. owns 40% of the stock of B Corp. A consolidated tax return could be filed by P, A, and B.

2. A <u>controlled group</u> of corporations is limited to an aggregate of $75,000 of taxable income taxed at less than 34%, one $250,000 accumulated earnings credit, one $10,000 Sec. 179 expense deduction, etc. There are three basic types of controlled groups

   a. Parent-subsidiary--basically same as P-S group eligible to file consolidated return, except ownership requirement is 80% of combined voting power <u>or</u> total value of stock. Affiliated corporations are subject to the controlled group limitations if the corporations file separate tax returns
   b. Brother-sister--two or more corporations at least 80% owned by 5 or fewer individuals, estates, or trusts, who also own more than 50% of each corporation when counting only identical ownership in each corporation. The 80% test is applied by including only the shares of those shareholders that hold stock in each corporation of the group being tested. The percentage tests are based on voting power <u>or</u> total value

   EXAMPLE:

Individual Shareholder	Corporations W	X	Stock Considered for 50% Test
A	30%	20%	20%
B	5%	40%	5%
C	30%	35%	30%
D	15%	5%	5%
E	20%	–	–
	100%	100%	60%

   Corporations W and X are a controlled group since five or fewer individuals own at least 80% of each, and also own more than 50% when counting only identical ownership.

   EXAMPLE:

Individual Shareholder	Corporations Y	Z	Stock Considered for 50% Test
F	79%	100%	79%
G	21%	--	--
	100%	100%	79%

Y and Z are not a controlled group because the 80% test is not met for Corporation Y. Since G owns no stock in Z, G's stock in Y cannot be added to F's Y stock for purposes of applying the 80% test.

    c. Combined--the parent in a P-S group is also a member of a brother-sister group of corporations

        EXAMPLE: Individual H owns 100% of the stock of Corporations P and Q. Corporation P owns 100% of the stock of Corporation S. P, S, and Q are members of one controlled group.

E. Dividends and Distributions

1. Corporate distributions to shareholders on their stock are taxed as dividends to the extent of the corporation's current and/or accumulated earnings and profits

2. Most distributions fall into the dividend category

    a. But if a distribution exceeds the corporation's earnings and profits, it is a nontaxable return of capital

        (1) If a return of capital, it reduces the shareholder's stock basis
        (2) If return of capital exceeds stock basis, the excess is treated as capital gain

        EXAMPLE: Corporation X has earnings and profits of $6,000 and makes a $10,000 distribution to its sole shareholder, A, who has a stock basis of $3,000. The $10,000 distribution to A will be treated as a dividend of $6,000, a nontaxable return of stock basis of $3,000, and a capital gain of $1,000.

    b. The distributing corporation recognizes gain on the distribution of appreciated property as if such property were sold at its FMV

    EXAMPLE: A corporation distributes property with a FMV of $10,000 and a basis of $3,000 to a shareholder. The corporation recognizes a gain of $10,000 - $3,000 = $7,000.

        (1) If the distributed property is subject to a liability (or if the distributee assumes a liability) and the FMV of the distributed property is less than the amount of liability, then the gain is the difference between the amount of liability and the property's basis

        EXAMPLE: A corporation distributes property with a FMV of $10,000 and a basis of $3,000 to a shareholder, who assumes a liability of $12,000 on the property. The corporation recognizes a gain of $12,000 - $3,000 = $9,000.

        (2) The type of gain recognized (e.g., ordinary, Sec. 1231, capital) depends on the nature of the property distributed (e.g., recapture rules may apply)

    c. Both noncorporate and corporate distributees include in income the amount of cash, plus the fair market value of other property received; reduced by any liabilities assumed, or liabilities to which property is subject
    d. The distributee's tax basis for the property received will be the property's FMV at date of distribution (not reduced by liabilities)

3. <u>Earnings and Profits</u>

   a. Current earnings and profits (CEP) are similar to book income, but are computed by making adjustments to taxable income

     (1) Add--tax-exempt income, dividends received deduction, excess of ACRS depreciation over straight-line, etc.

     (2) Deduct--federal income taxes, net capital loss, excess charitable contributions, expenses relating to tax-exempt income, penalties, etc.

   b. Accumulated earnings and profits (AEP) represent the sum of prior years' CEP, reduced by distributions and NOLs of prior years

   c. CEP are increased by the gain recognized on a distribution of appreciated property (excess of FMV over basis)

   d. Distributions reduce earnings and profits (but not below zero) by

     (1) The amount of money

     (2) The face amount (or issue price if less) of obligations of the distributing corporation, and

     (3) The adjusted basis (or FMV if greater) of other property distributed

     (4) Above reductions must be adjusted by any liability assumed by the shareholder, or the amount of liability to which the property distributed is subject

> EXAMPLE: Z Corp. has two 50% shareholders--B Corp. and Mr. C.   Z Corp. distributes a parcel of land (held for investment) to each shareholder.   Each parcel of land has a FMV of $12,000, basis of $8,000; and each shareholder assumes a liability of $3,000 on the property received.   Z Corp. will recognize a gain of $4,000 on the distribution of each property.

	B Corp.	Mr. C
Dividend	$ 9,000	$ 9,000
Tax basis for property received	12,000	12,000
Effect (before tax) on Z's earnings & profits:		
Increased by gain (FMV-basis)	4,000	4,000
Increased by liabilities distributed	3,000	3,000
Decreased by FMV of property		
distributed	(12,000)	(12,000)

4. <u>Stock Redemptions</u>

   a. A stock redemption is treated as an exchange, generally resulting in capital gain or loss treatment to the shareholder if at least one of the following five tests is met. Constructive stock ownership rules generally apply in determining whether the following tests are met

     (1) The redemption is not essentially equivalent to a dividend [this has been interpreted by Revenue Rulings to mean that a redemption must reduce a shareholder's right to vote, share in earnings, and share in assets upon liquidation; and after the redemption the shareholder's stock ownership (both direct and constructive) must not exceed 50%], or

     (2) The redemption is substantially disproportionate (i.e., after redemption, shareholder's percentage ownership is less than 80% of shareholder's percentage ownership prior to redemption, and less than 50% of shares outstanding), or

      (3)   All of the shareholder's stock is redeemed, or

      (4)   The redemption is from a noncorporate shareholder in a partial liquidation, or

      (5)   The distribution is a redemption of stock to pay death taxes under Sec. 303

    b. If none of the above tests are met, the redemption proceeds are treated as an ordinary Sec. 301 distribution, taxable as a dividend to the extent of the distributing corporation's earnings and profits

    c. A corporation cannot deduct amounts paid or incurred in connection with a redemption of its stock (except for interest expense on loans used to purchase stock)

5. Complete Liquidations

    a. Amounts received by <u>shareholders</u> in liquidation of a corporation are treated as received in exchange for stock, generally resulting in capital gain or loss. Property received will have a basis equal to FMV

    b. A <u>liquidating corporation</u> generally recognizes gain or loss on the sale or distribution of its assets in complete liquidation

      (1)   If a distribution, gain or loss is computed as if the distributed property were sold to the distributee for FMV

      (2)   If distributed property is subject to a liability (or a shareholder assumes a liability) in excess of the basis of the distributed property, FMV is deemed to be not less than the amount of liability

    c. Small closely-held corporations

      (1)   Generally no gain or loss will be recognized by a liquidating small closely-held corporation if completely liquidated before 1989. Even if this exception applies, nonrecognition does not apply to dispositions that result in ordinary gain or loss, short-term capital gain or loss, and gain from the distribution of installment obligations

      (2)   "Small closely-held" means (a) more than 50% in value of stock is held by 10 or fewer individuals, estates, or certain trusts on August 1, 1986 and at all times thereafter, and (b) the value of the corporation's stock does not exceed $10 million

      (3)   Nonrecognition [except as noted in (1) above] is fully available if the value of the corporation's stock does not exceed $5 million, but is proportionately phased out for a corporation with a stock FMV between $5 million and $10 million

    d. Distributions to related persons

      (1)   No loss is generally recognized to a liquidating corporation on the distribution of property to a related person if

          (a)   The distribution is not pro rata, or

          (b)   The property was acquired by the liquidating corporation during the 5-year period ending on the date of distribution in a Sec. 351 transaction or as a contribution to capital. This includes any property whose basis is determined by reference to the adjusted basis of property described in the preceding sentence

      (2)   Related person is a shareholder who owns (directly or constructively) more than 50% of the corporation's stock

e. Carryover basis property

    (1) If a corporation acquires property in a Sec. 351 transaction or as a contribution to capital after the date that is 2 years before the date of the adoption of the plan of liquidation, any loss resulting from the property's sale, exchange, or distribution can be recognized only to the extent of the decline in value that occurred subsequent to the date that the corporation acquired the property

    (2) The above rule applies only where the loss is not already completely disallowed by d.(1) above

    EXAMPLE: A shareholder makes a capital contribution of property with a basis of $15,000 and a FMV of $10,000 on the contribution date.   Within 2 years the corporation adopts a plan of liquidation and sells the property for $8,000.   The liquidating corporation will recognize a loss of $10,000 - $8,000 = $2,000.

f. Liquidation of subsidiary

    (1) No gain or loss is recognized to a parent corporation under Sec. 332 on the receipt of property in complete liquidation of an 80% or more owned subsidiary. The subsidiary's basis for its assets along with all tax accounting attributes will carry over to the parent corporation

    (2) No gain or loss is recognized to a subsidiary corporation on the distribution of property to its parent if Sec. 332 applies to the parent corporation

        (a) If the subsidiary has debt outstanding to the parent, nonrecognition also applies to property distributed in satisfaction of the debt

        (b) Gain (but not loss) is recognized on the distribution of property to minority (20% or less) shareholders

    (3) A parent corporation may elect to treat the sale, exchange, or distribution of all the stock of an 80% or more owned subsidiary as a disposition of all the subsidiary's assets

        (a) No gain or loss will be recognized on the disposition of the subsidiary's stock

        (b) Gain or loss will be recognized on the deemed disposition of the subsidiary's assets

6. Stock purchases treated as asset acquisitions

a. An acquiring corporation that has purchased at least 80% of a target corporation's stock within a 12-month period may elect under Sec. 338 to have the purchase of stock treated as an acquisition of assets

b. Old target corporation is deemed to have sold all its assets on the acquisition date, and is treated as a new corporation that has purchased those assets on the day after the acquisition date

    (1) Acquisition date is the date on which at least 80% of the target's stock has been acquired by purchase within a 12-month period

    (2) Gain or loss is generally recognized to old target corporation on deemed sale of assets

    (3) The deemed sales price for the target corporation's assets is generally the FMV of the target's assets as of the close of the acquisition date

F. **Collapsible Corporations**

    1. Rules to prevent taxpayers from using corporations to convert ordinary income into capital gain by

        a. Forming or using an existing corporation to construct or produce property

        b. Before corporation realizes <u>two-thirds</u> of the taxable income from the property, shareholders sell stock or liquidate corporation

        c. Thus, shareholders attempt to realize a capital gain on the sale or liquidation instead of recognizing ordinary income through continued operation of the corporation

    2. May result in what would otherwise be reported by shareholder as capital gain must instead be reported as ordinary income if corporation is collapsible

G. **Personal Holding Company and Accumulated Earnings Taxes**

    1. Personal holding companies (PHC) are subject to a penalty tax on undistributed PHC income to discourage taxpayers from accumulating their investment income in a corporation taxed at lower than individual rates

        a. A <u>personal holding company</u> is any corporation (except certain banks, financial institutions, and similar corporations)

            (1) During anytime in the last half of the tax year, 5 or fewer individuals own more than 50% of the value of the outstanding stock directly or indirectly, <u>and</u>

            (2) The corporation receives at least 60% of its adjusted ordinary gross income as "personal holding company income" (e.g., dividends, interest, rents, royalties, and other passive income)

        b. Taxed

            (1) At ordinary corporate rates on taxable income, plus

            (2) 28% of undistributed PHC income

        c. The PHC tax

            (1) Is self-assessing (i.e., computed on Sch. PH and attached to Form 1120); a 6-year statute of limitations applies if no Sch. PH is filed

            (2) May be avoided by dividend payments sufficient in amount to reduce undistributed PHC income to zero

    2. Corporations may be subject to an <u>accumulated earnings tax</u> (AET), in addition to regular income tax, if they accumulate earnings beyond reasonable business needs in order to avoid shareholder tax on dividend distributions

        a. The tax is not self-assessing, but is based on a determination of the existence of tax avoidance intent

        b. AET may be imposed without regard to the number of shareholders of the corporation, but is not applicable to PHCs

        c. Accumulated earnings credit allowed for greater of

            (1) $250,000 ($150,000 for personal service corporations) minus the accumulated earnings and profits at end of prior year, or

(2) Reasonable needs of the business (e.g., expansion, working capital, to retire debt, etc.)

d. Balance of accumulated taxable income is taxed at the rate of 28%
e. The AET may be avoided by dividend payments sufficient in amount to reduce accumulated taxable income to zero

H. S Corporations

The Subchapter S Revision Act of 1982 made fundamental changes in the tax treatment of Subchapter S corporations and their shareholders. The changes make their treatment similar to partnership taxation. Electing small business corporations are designated as S corporations; all other corporations are referred to as C corporations

1. Eligibility requirements for S corporation status

   a. Domestic corporation
   b. Not a member of an affiliated group (but inactive affiliated subsidiaries are allowed if they have not begun business and do not have any gross income)
   c. Only one class of stock issued and outstanding. A corporation will not be treated as having more than one class of stock solely because of differences in voting rights among the shares of common stock.
   d. Shareholders must be individuals, estates, or certain trusts including a

      (1) Voting trust
      (2) A trust created by will (i.e., testamentary trust) is allowed for a 60 day period
      (3) Subpart E trust (i.e., a trust all of which is treated as owned by one individual)

         (a) May continue to be a shareholder for 60 days beginning with date of death of deemed owner, or,
         (b) For 2 years if entire corpus of trust is includible in the deemed owner's estate

      (4) Qualified Subchapter S Trust (QSST)

   e. No nonresident alien shareholders
   f. Number of shareholders limited to 35

      (1) Husband and wife (and their estates) are counted as one shareholder
      (2) Each beneficiary of a voting trust is considered a shareholder
      (3) If a trust is treated as owned by an individual, that individual (not the trust) is treated as the shareholder

2. An election must be filed anytime in the preceding taxable year or on or before the 15th day of the third month of the year for which effective

   a. All shareholders on date of election, plus any shareholders who held stock during the taxable year but before the date of election, must consent to the election

      (1) If an election is made on or before the 15th day of the third month of taxable year, but either (1) a shareholder who held stock during the taxable year and before the date of election does not consent to the election or (2) the corporation did not meet the eligibility requirements during the part of the year before the date of

election, then the election is treated as made for the following taxable year

    (2) An election made after the 15th day of the third month of the taxable year is treated as made for the following year

b. If a corporation's taxable year is less than 2 1/2 months' duration, an election will be timely if made within 2 1/2 months after the first day of the taxable year

c. A valid election is effective for all succeeding years until terminated

3. <u>LIFO recapture</u>. A C corporation using LIFO that converts to S status must recapture the excess of the inventory's value using a FIFO cost flow assumption over its LIFO tax basis as of the close of its last tax year as a C corporation

    a. The LIFO recapture is included in the C corporation's gross income and the tax attributable to its inclusion is payable in four equal installments

    b. The first installment must be paid by the due date of the tax return for the last C corporation year, with the three remaining installments due by the due dates of the tax returns for the three succeeding taxable years

4. For tax year beginning after 1986, S corporation must generally adopt or change to a <u>calendar taxable year</u>. However, an S corporation can use a fiscal year if a valid business purpose can be established and IRS permission is received. The business purpose test will be met if an S corporation receives at least 25% of its gross receipts in the last two months of a 12-month period, and this "25% test" has been satisfied for three consecutive years

EXAMPLE: An S corporation, on a calendar-year, has received at least 25% of its gross receipts during the months of May and June for each of the last three years. The S corporation may change to a fiscal year ending June 30.

    a. An S corporation that otherwise would be required to adopt or change its tax year (normally to the calendar year) may elect to use a fiscal year if the election does not result in a deferral period longer than three months, or, if less, the deferral period of the year currently in use. However, an S corporation that had a taxable year beginning in 1986 could have elected to retain that same taxable year even though the deferral period exceeds three months

        (1) The "deferral period" is the number of months between the close of the fiscal year elected and the close of the required year (e.g., if an S corporation elects a tax year ending September 30 and a tax year ending December 31 is required, the deferral period of the year ending September 30 is three months)

        (2) An S corporation that elects a tax year other than a required year must make a "required payment" which is in the nature of a refundable, non-interest-bearing deposit that is intended to compensate the government for the revenue lost as a result of tax deferral

(a) The required payment is due on May 15 each year and is recomputed for each subsequent year

(b) If the amount of the required payment increases, the S corporation must pay the amount of increase. Conversely, if the amount of deferred tax decreases relative to the previous year, the S corporation is entitled to a refund

(c) Thus, an S corporation that elects this procedure maintains a deferred payment balance with the government and adjusts it annually. No interest accrues on the balance, and shareholders do not receive any type of credit for the tax deposit

b. The amount of <u>required payment</u> is computed as:

Net base year income
<u>x Highest individual rate + 1% (e.g., 29% for 1988 and 1989)</u>
= Deferred tax and "toll charge" for current year
<u> - Required payment of preceding year</u>
Required payment (refund) for current year

c. An S corporation's <u>net base income</u> is generally the amount of income in the prior taxable year that is deferred and is computed as follows:

Net income of the S corporation for prior taxable year
<u>+ Certain payments included in S shareholders' income</u>
= Balance
<u> x Deferral ratio (months of deferral/months in taxable year)</u>
Net base year income

d. No payment need be made if the required payment does not exceed $500. The required payment is generally phased in over four years--

Taxable year beginning in	Percentage to be paid
1987	25%
1988	50
1989	75
1990	100

EXAMPLE: An S corporation that otherwise would be required to adopt a calendar-year elected to retain its fiscal year ended September 30. Its net income for the year ended September 30, 1988 was $120,000. It made no payments to its shareholders during the year. The S corporation's net base income is $120,000 x 3/12 = $30,000. Its required payment due May 15, 1989 is $30,000 x 29% x 50% (phase-in) = $4,350.

5. <u>Termination</u> of S corporation status may be caused by

a. Shareholders holding more than 50% of the shares of stock of the corporation consent to revocation of the election

(1) A revocation made on or before the 15th day of the third month of the taxable year is generally effective on the first day of such taxable year

(2) A revocation made after the 15th day of the third month of the taxable year is generally effective as of the first day of the following taxable year

(3)   Instead of the dates mentioned above, a revocation may specify an effective date on or after the date on which the revocation is filed

> *EXAMPLE: For a calendar-year S corporation, a revocation not specifying a revocation date that is made on or before 3/15/89 is effective as of 1/1/89. A revocation not specifying a revocation date that is made after 3/15/89 is effective as of 1/1/90. If a revocation is filed 3/11/89 and specifies a revocation date of 7/1/89, the corporation ceases to be an S corporation on 7/1/89.*

b.   The corporation failing to satisfy any of the eligibility requirements listed in "1." Termination is effective on the date an eligibility requirement is failed

c.   Passive investment income exceeding 25% of gross receipts for 3 consecutive taxable years if the corporation has Subchapter C earnings and profits

(1)   Subchapter C earnings and profits are earnings and profits accumulated during a taxable year for which a Subchapter S election was not in effect

(2)   Termination is effective as of the first day of the taxable year beginning after the third consecutive year of passive investment income in excess of 25% of gross receipts

> *EXAMPLE: An S corporation with Subchapter C earnings and profits had passive investment income in excess of 25% of its gross receipts for its calendar-years 1987, 1988, and 1989. Its S corporation status would terminate 1/1/90.*

d.   Generally once terminated, an S corporation status can only be reelected after 5 non-S corporation years

(1)   The corporation can request IRS for an earlier reelection
(2)   IRS may treat an inadvertent termination as if it never occurred

6.   An <u>S corporation</u> generally pays no federal income taxes, but may have to pay a tax on its built-in gain, its capital gain, or on its excess passive investment income if certain conditions are met (see page 1351)

a.   The S corporation is treated as a <u>conduit</u>--the character of any item of income, expense, gain, loss, or credit is determined at the corporate level, and passes through to shareholders retaining its identity

b.   The taxable income of an S corporation is computed the same as for an individual except (1) certain items must be separately stated for each shareholder; (2) deductions are denied for personal exemptions, charitable contributions, net operating losses, itemized deductions, and deductions (or credits) for foreign taxes; and (3) a deduction is allowed for amortization of organizational expenses

c.   An S corporation must recognize gain on the distribution of appreciated property (other than its own obligations) to its shareholders. Gain is recognized in the same manner as if the property had been sold to the distributee at its FMV

> *EXAMPLE: An S corporation distributes property with a FMV of $900 and an adjusted basis of $100 to its sole shareholder. Gain of $800 will be recognized by the corporation. The character of the gain will be determined at the corporate level, and passed through and reported by its shareholder. The shareholder is treated as receiving a $900 distribution, subject to the distribution rules discussed on page 1342.*

d. Expenses and interest owed to any cash-basis shareholder are deductible by an accrual-basis S corporation only when paid

> *EXAMPLE: A calendar-year S corporation accrues $2,000 of salary to an employee (a 1% shareholder) during 1988, but does not make payment until February 1989. The $2,000 will be deductible by the corporation in 1989, and reported by the shareholder-employee as income in 1989.*

e. An S corporation will not generate any earnings and profits for taxable years after 1982. All items are reflected in adjustments to the basis of shareholders' stock and/or debt

7. A <u>shareholder</u> of an S corporation must separately take into account (for the shareholder's taxable year in which the taxable year of the S corporation ends) (1) the shareholder's pro rata share of the corporation's items of income (including tax-exempt income), loss, deduction, or credit the separate treatment of which could affect the tax liability of <u>any</u> shareholder, plus (2) the shareholder's pro rata share of all remaining items which are netted together into "nonseparately computed income or loss"

a. Some of the items which must be separately passed through to retain their identity include

(1) Net long-term capital gain (loss)
(2) Net short-term capital gain (loss)
(3) Net gain (loss) from Sec. 1231 casualty or theft
(4) Net gain (loss) from other Sec. 1231 transactions
(5) Tax-exempt interest
(6) Charitable contributions
(7) Foreign income taxes
(8) Depletion
(9) Investment interest expense
(10) Dividend, interest, and royalty income
(11) Net income (loss) from real estate activity
(12) Net income (loss) from other rental acivity

b. All separately stated items plus the nonseparately computed income or loss are allocated on a <u>daily per share basis</u> to anyone who was a shareholder during the year. Items are allocated to shareholders' stock (both voting and nonvoting); but not to debt

> *EXAMPLE: Alan owned 100% of a calendar-year S corporation's stock from January 1, 1988 until February 1, 1988 at which time Alan sold all his stock to Betty. Assuming the S corporation had $366,000 of nonseparately computed income for the entire 1988 calendar year, the amount allocated to Alan would be $31,000 (31 days x $1,000 per day), and the amount allocated to Betty would be $335,000 (335 days x $1,000 per day).*

(1) The daily per share rule will not apply if

(a) A shareholder's interest is completely terminated, and all persons who were shareholders during the year consent to allocate items as if the corporation's taxable year consisted of two years, the first of which ends on the date the shareholder's interest was terminated

EXAMPLE: Assume in the above example that the S Corporation had net income of $40,000 for the month of January. If both Alan and Betty consent, $40,000 would be allocated to Alan, and $326,000 would be allocated to Betty.

    (b) An S Corporation's election is terminated on other than the first day of the taxable year, and all shareholders during the S short year and all persons who were shareholders on the first day of the C short year consent to allocate items using the corporation's financial accounting records

(2) The daily per share rule can <u>not</u> be used if:

    (a) There is a sale or exchange of 50% or more of the stock of the corporation during an S termination year. Financial accounting records must be used to allocate items

    (b) If a Sec. 338 election is made, gains and losses resulting from the election must be reported on a C Corporation return

8. Three sets of rules may limit the amount of S Coporation loss that a shareholder can deduct

  a. A shareholder's allocation of the aggregate <u>losses and deductions</u> of an S corporation can be deducted by the shareholder to the extent of the shareholder's basis for stock plus basis of any debt owed the shareholder by the corporation [Sec. 1366 (d)]

    (1) An excess of loss over combined basis for stock and debt can be carried forward indefinitely and deducted when there is basis to absorb it

    (2) Once reduced, the basis of debt is later increased (but not above its original basis) by net income items before any increase is made to the stock basis

EXAMPLE: An S corporation incurred losses totaling $50,000. Its sole shareholder (who materially participates in the business and is at-risk) had a stock basis of $30,000 and debt with a basis of $15,000. The shareholder's loss deduction is limited to $45,000. The losses first reduce stock basis to zero, then debt basis is reduced to zero. The excess loss of $5,000 can be carried forward and deducted when there is basis to absorb it.

  b. The deductibility of S Corporation losses is also limited to the amount of the shareholder's at-risk investment at the end of the taxable year [Sec. 465]

    (1) A shareholder's amount at-risk includes amounts borrowed and reloaned to the S Corporation if the shareholder is personally liable for repayment of the borrowed amount, or has pledged property not used in the activity as security for the borrowed amount

    (2) A shareholder's amount at-risk does not include any debt of the corporation to any person other than the shareholder, even if the shareholder guarantees the debt

c. The deductibility of S Corporation losses may also be subject to the passive activity loss limitations [Sec 469]. Passive activity losses are deductible only to the extent of the shareholder's income from other passive activities [See ITAX page 1247]

    (1) Passive activities include (a) any S Corporation trade or business in which the shareholder does not materially participate, and (b) any rental activity

    (2) If a shareholder "actively participates" in a rental activity and owns at least 10% of the value of an S Corporation's stock, up to $25,000 of rental losses may be deductible

9. A shareholder's S corporation <u>stock basis</u> is

  a. Increased by all income items (including tax-exempt income), plus depletion in excess of the basis of the property subject to depletion

  b. Decreased by distributions which were not includible in income, all loss and deduction items, nondeductible expenses not charged to capital, and the shareholder's deduction for depletion on oil and gas wells

10. The treatment of <u>distributions</u> (cash + FMV of other property) to shareholders depends upon whether the corporation has accumulated earnings and profits

  a. S corporation <u>without</u> accumulated earnings and profits

    (1) Distributions are nontaxable and are applied to reduce the shareholder's stock basis

    (2) Distributions in excess of stock basis are treated as gain from the sale of stock

  b. S corporation <u>with</u> accumulated earnings and profits

    (1) Distributions are nontaxable to the extent of the Accumulated Adjustments Account (AAA) and are applied to reduce the AAA and the shareholder's stock basis

      (a) The AAA represents the cumulative total of undistributed net income items for S corporation taxable years beginning after 1982

      (b) If there is more than one distribution during the year, a pro rata portion of each distribution is treated as made from the AAA

      (c) The AAA can have a negative balance if expenses and losses exceed income. No adjustment is made to the AAA for tax-exempt income and related expenses, and Federal taxes attributable to a year in which the corporation was a C corporation

    (2) Distributions in excess of the AAA are treated as ordinary dividends to the extent of the corporation's accumulated earnings and profits (AEP). These amounts generally represent earnings and profits that were accumulated (and never taxed to shareholders) during C Corporation taxable years

    (3) Distributions are next nontaxable and are applied to reduce the basis of stock

    (4) Distributions in excess of stock basis are treated as gain from the sale of stock

c.   Before applying the above distribution rules, the basis of a shareholder's stock and the AAA are first adjusted for the corporate items
passed through from the taxable year of the corporation during which the
distribution is made

*EXAMPLE: A calendar-year S corporation had accumulated earnings and
profits of $10,000 at December 31, 1988.   During calendar year 1989, the
corporation had net income of $20,000, and distributed $38,000 to its
sole shareholder on June 20, 1989.   Its shareholder had a stock basis of
$15,000 at January 1, 1989.*

*The $20,000 of net income passes through and is includible in gross in-
come by the shareholder for 1989.   The shareholder's stock basis is
increased by the $20,000 of income (to $35,000), as is the AAA which is
increased to $20,000.   Of the $38,000 distribution, the first $20,000 is
nontaxable and (1) reduces stock basis to $15,000, and (2) the AAA to
zero; the next $10,000 of distribution is reported as dividend income
(no effect on stock basis); while the remaining $8,000 of distribution
is nontaxable and reduces stock basis to $7,000.*

*EXAMPLE: Assume the same facts as above except that the corporation had
no accumulated earnings and profits.   The $20,000 of income increases
stock basis to $35,000.   Of the distribution of $38,000 the first
$35,000 is nontaxable and reduces stock basis to zero; while the re-
maining $3,000 is treated as gain from the sale of stock.*

11. An employee-shareholder owning (directly or by attribution) more than 2% of
an S corporation's stock is treated the same as a partner in a partnership
for purposes of employee <u>fringe benefits</u> (i.e., an S corporation's fringe
benefit payments for a more than 2% employee-shareholder are
nondeductible).   Examples of these benefits include the cost of up to
$50,000 of group-term life insurance, the cost of meals and lodging
furnished for the convenience of the employer, amounts paid to or for
certain accident and health plans, and the $5,000 death benefit exclusion

12. An S corporation (that previously was a C corporation) is taxed on its <u>net</u>
<u>recognized built-in gain</u> if the gain is (1) attributable to an excess of the
FMV of its assets over their aggregate adjusted basis as of the beginning of
its first taxable year as an S corporation, and (2) is recognized within 10
years after the effective date of its S corporation election

a.   This provision generally applies to C corporations that make an S
corporation election after December 31, 1986

(1) Corporations that qualify as "small corporations" (i.e., more than
50% of the value of the corporation's stock is held by 10 or fewer
qualified persons, and the value of the corporation does not exceed
$10 million) and elect S corporation status prior to January 1,
1989 are only taxed on net recognized built-in gain resulting from
ordinary income assets, capital assets held short-term, and the
disposition of installment obligations.

(2) A corporation that is an S corporation for each of its taxable
years (i.e., has never been a C corporation) will not be subject to
this provision

b. Tax is computed by applying the highest corporate rate to the lesser of (1) the net recognized built-in gain for the taxable year, or (2) taxable income (including the business credit and NOL carryforwards)

c. Recognized built-in gain does not include gain from the disposition of an asset if

(1) The asset was not held by the corporation when its S election became effective (e.g., an asset was purchased after the first day of its S election), or

(2) The gain is attributable to appreciation that occurred after the S election became effective (e.g., an asset is sold for a gain of $1,000, but $600 of its appreciation occurred after the first day of its S election; the corporation would be taxed on only $400 of gain)

d. The total amount of net recognized built-in gain that will be taxed to an S corporation is limited to the aggregate net built-in gain when the S election became effective

e. The tax paid by the corporation reduces the gain passed through to shareholders

13. An S corporation not subject to the tax on built-in gain (see above), may have to pay a capital gains tax if

a. NLTCG exceeds NSTCL by more than $25,000; exceeds 50% of TI; and, TI exceeds $25,000

b. Tax is lesser of (1) [(NLTCG - NSTCL) - ($25,000)] x 34%; or, (2) TI x regular corporate rates

c. It is computed the same as for a C corporation except that the NOL and dividends received deductions are not allowed

d. Tax won't apply if corporation had a subchapter S election for 3 preceding years or has had a subchapter S election for entire period of existence

e. The tax paid reduces the amount of LTCG passed through to shareholders

EXAMPLE: James Corporation, organized in 1980, is in its second year of subchapter S election. It had TI of $40,000 for 1988, of which $30,000 was NLTCG. Its capital gain tax is $1,700 (i.e., $5,000 x 34%). The amount of NLTCG passed through to shareholders would be $30,000 - $1,700 = $28,300.

14. If an S corporation has Subchapter C accumulated earnings and profits, and its <u>passive investment income</u> exceeds 25% of gross receipts, a tax is imposed at the highest corporate rate on the lesser of (1) excess net passive income (ENPI), or (2) taxable income

a. $$\text{ENPI} = \left(\begin{matrix} \text{Net Passive} \\ \text{Income} \end{matrix} \right) \left[\frac{(\text{Passive Investment Income}) - (25\% \text{ of Gross Receipts})}{\text{Passive Investment Income}} \right]$$

b. The tax paid reduces the amount of passive investment income passed through to shareholders

EXAMPLE: An S corporation has gross receipts of $80,000, of which $50,000 is interest income. Expenses incurred in the production of this passive income total $10,000. The ENPI is $24,000.

$$\text{ENPI} = (\$50,000 - \$10,000) \left[\frac{(\$50,000) - (25\% \times \$80,000)}{\$50,000} \right]$$

I. Corporate Reorganizations

Certain exchanges, usually involving the exchange of one corporation's stock for the stock or property of another, result in deferral of gain or loss

1. There are seven types of reorganizations given nonrecognition treatment under the IRC

   a. Statutory mergers or consolidations (Type "A")

      (1) Merger is where one corporation absorbs another
      (2) Consolidation is where two corporations form a new corporation, the former ones dissolving

   b. The acquisition of at least 80% of the voting power and 80% of each non-voting class of stock of one corporation by another, in exchange solely for all or a part of its voting stock. No "boot" may be exchanged (Type "B")

   c. The acquisition of substantially all the properties of one corporation by another, in exchange solely for all or a part of its voting stock (Type "C")

      (1) In determining whether the acquisition is made solely for stock, the assumption by the acquiring corporation of a liability of the other, or the fact that the property acquired is subject to a liability is disregarded
      (2) "Substantially all" means at least 90% of the FMV of the net assets and at least 70% of the FMV of the gross assets
      (3) The acquired corporation must distribute the consideration it receives, as well as all of its other properties, in pursuance of the plan of reorganization

   d. A transfer by a corporation of all or a part of its assets to another if immediately after the transfer the transferor, or one or more of its shareholders, or both, own at least 80% of the voting power and 80% of each nonvoting class of stock (Type "D")

   e. A recapitalization (where the capital structure of one corporation is readjusted in amount, priority, etc.) (Type "E")

   f. A mere change in identity, form, or place of organization (Type "F")

   g. A bankruptcy reorganization (Type "G")

2. For the reorganization to be tax-free, it must meet one of the above definitions and the exchange must be made under a plan or reorganization involving the affected corporations as parties to the reorganization. It must satisfy the judicial doctrines of continuity of shareholder interest, business purpose, and continuity of business enterprise

3. No gain or loss is generally recognized to a transferor corporation on the transfer of its property pursuant to a plan of reorganization

   a. Gain is recognized to the extent that boot (i.e., consideration other than stock or securities in a party to the reorganization) is received, but not distributed to the corporation's shareholders or creditors pursuant to the plan of reorganization

   b. The transferee corporation's basis for property received equals the transferor's basis plus gain recognized to the transferor

4. No gain or loss is recognized by a corporation on the disposition of stock or securities in another corporation that is a party to the reorganization

    a. No gain or loss is recognized on the distribution of stock or securities of a controlled subsidiary in a qualifying spin-off, split-off, or split-up
    b. Gain is recognized on the distribution of appreciated boot property

5. If a shareholder receives boot in a reorganization, gain is recognized (but not loss)

    a. Boot includes the FMV of an excess of principal (i.e., face) amount of securities received over the principal amount of securities surrendered

        EXAMPLE: In a recapitalization, a bondholder exchanges a bond with a face amount and basis of $1,000, for a new bond with a face amount of $1,500 and a fair market value of $1,575. Since an excess face amount of security ($500) has been received, the bondholder's realized gain of $575 will be recognized to the extent of the fair market value of the excess [($500/$1,500) x $1,575] = $525.

    b. Recognized gain will generally be treated as a dividend to the extent of the shareholder's ratable share of earnings and profits of the acquired corporation

6. A shareholder's basis for stock and securities received equals the basis of stock and securities surrendered, plus gain recognized, and minus boot received

    EXAMPLE: Pursuant to a merger of Corporation T into Corporation P, Smith exchanged 100 shares of T that he had purchased for $1,000, for 80 shares of P having a FMV of $1,500 and also received $200 cash, which was not in excess of Smith's ratable share of T's earnings and profits. Smith's realized gain of $700 is recognized to the extent of the cash received of $200, and is treated as a dividend. Smith's basis for his P stock is $1,000 ($1,000 + $200 recognized gain - $200 cash received).

7. Carryover of tax attributes

    a. The tax attributes of the acquired corporation (e.g., NOL carryovers, earnings and profits, accounting methods, etc.) generally carry over to the acquiring corporation in an acquisitive reorganization
    b. The amount of an acquired corporation's NOL carryovers that can be utilized by the acquiring corporation for its first taxable year ending after the date of acquisition is limited by Sec. 381 to

$$\left[\begin{array}{c}\text{Acquiring}\\\text{corporation's}\\\text{TI before}\\\text{NOL deduction}\end{array}\right] \times \left(\frac{\text{Days after acquisition date}}{\text{Total days in taxable year}}\right)$$

    EXAMPLE: Corporation P (on a calendar year) acquired Corporation T in a statutory merger on October 19, 1988, with the former T shareholders receiving 60% of P's stock. If T had a NOL carryover of $70,000, and P has taxable income (before a NOL deduction) of $91,500, the amount of T's $70,000 NOL carryover that can be deducted by P for 1988 would be

$$(\$91,500) \quad \left(\frac{73}{366}\right) = \$18,250$$

c. If there is a more than 50% change in ownership of a loss corporation, the taxable income for any year of the new loss (or surviving) corporation may be reduced by a NOL carryover from the old loss corporation only to the extent of the value of the old loss corporation's stock on the date of the ownership change multiplied by the "long-term tax-exempt rate"(Sec. 382 limitation)

   (1) An ownership change has occurred when the percentage of stock owned by an entity's 5% or more shareholders has increased by more than 50 percentage points relative to the lowest percentage owned by such shareholders at any time during the preceding 3-year testing period

   (2) For the year of acquisition, the Sec. 382 limitation amount is available only to the extent allocable to days after the acquisition date

$$\begin{bmatrix} \text{Sec. 382} \\ \text{limitation} \end{bmatrix} \times \left(\frac{\text{Days after acquisition date}}{\text{Total days in taxable year}} \right)$$

EXAMPLE: If T's former shareholders received only 30% of P's stock in the preceding example, there would be a more than 50 pecentage point change of ownership in T Corporation, and T's NOL carryover would be subject to a Sec. 382 limitation. If the FMV of T's stock on October 19, 1988 were $500,000 and the long-term tax-exempt rate were 8%, the Sec. 382 limitation for 1988 would be ($500,000 x 8%) x (73/366 days) = $7,978.

Thus, only $7,978 of T's NOL carryover could be deducted by P for 1988. The remaining $70,000 - $7,978 = $62,022 of T's NOL would be carried forward by P and could be used to offset P's taxable income for 1989 to the extent of the Sec. 382 limitation (i.e., $500,000 x 8% = $40,000)

J. **Exempt Organizations**

1. Tax-exempt organizations are specifically identified in the Internal Revenue Code and include charities, labor organizations, social clubs, employees' pension and profit-sharing trusts, political organizations, private foundations, etc.

   a. An exempt organization may be in the form of a corporation or trust
   b. An organization is exempt only if it applies for and receives an exemption
   c. Exempt organizations (except churches) must generally file annual information returns specifically stating items of gross income, receipts, and disbursements if gross receipts exceed $25,000. If an exempt organization is required to file an information return, it must annually report the total amount of contributions received as well as the identity of all substantial contributors.
   d. An organization must operate exclusively for a tax-exempt purpose. Feeder organizations and organizations that primarily attempt to influence legislation generally do not qualify for exempt status
   e. Although generally tax-exempt, an exempt organization will be taxed on its unrelated business income (UBI) and debt-financed income
   f. A private foundation is a tax exempt organization other than a public charity. Generally, a private foundation is a tax exempt organization which receives less than 1/3 of its annual support from its members and the general public

2. To determine whether income is UBI, it is necessary to determine (1) whether it is income from a business regularly carried on, and (2) whether the business is unrelated

   a. A business is substantially related only if the activity (not its proceeds) contributes importantly to the accomplishment of the exempt purposes of the organization

   b. Activities specifically treated as resulting in related income include

      (1) An activity where substantially all work is performed without compensation (e.g., a church runs a second-hand clothing store with all the work performed by volunteers)

      (2) A trade or business carried on for the convenience of the students or members of a charitable, religious, or scientific organization

      (3) The sale of merchandise received as gifts or contributions

   c. Dividends, interest, annuities, and royalties are generally excluded from UBI; but will be included if they result from debt-financed investments

   d. Income from conducting games of chance in a locality where such games are legal is excluded from UBI if conducted in a state that confines such activity to nonprofit organizations

   e. Income from debt financed property unrelated to the exempt function of the organization is included in UBI. The amount of such income to be included in UBI is based on the proportion of average acquisition indebtedness to the property's average adjusted basis

3. UBI is taxed at regular corporate rates if the organization is a corporation; taxed at rates applicable to trusts if the organization is a trust. Unrelated business income is subject to tax to the extent in excess of $1,000

I. GIFT AND ESTATE TAXATION

The federal gift tax is an excise tax (imposed on donor) on the transfer of property by gift during a person's lifetime. The federal estate tax is an excise tax on the transfer of property upon death. The Tax Reform Act of 1976 combined these taxes into a unified transfer tax rate schedule that applies to both life and death transfers. To remove relatively small gifts and estates from the imposition of tax, a unified transfer tax credit of $192,800 is allowed against gift and estate taxes. This is equivalent to exempting the first $600,000 of taxable gifts or taxable estate from the unified transfer tax.

A. **The Gift Tax**

1. Gift Tax Formula

Gross gifts (cash plus FMV of property at date of gift)		$XXX
Less:		
One-half of gifts treated as given by spouse	$ X	
Annual exclusion (up to $10,000 per donee)	X	
Unlimited exclusion for educational or medical expenses paid on behalf of donee	X	
Charitable gifts (remainder of charitable gifts after annual exclusion)	X	
Marital deduction (remainder of gifts to spouse after annual exclusion)	X	XX
Taxable gifts for current year		$ XX
Add: Taxable gifts for prior years		X
Total taxable gifts		$ XX
Unified transfer tax on total taxable gifts		$ XX
Less: Unified transfer tax on taxable gifts made prior to current year		X
Unified transfer tax for current year		$ XX
Unified transfer tax credit	$XX	
Less: Unified transfer tax credit used in prior years	X	X
Net gift tax liability		$ XX

2. Gross gifts include any transfer for less than an adequate and full consideration

    a. The creation of joint ownership in property is treated as a gift to the extent the donor's contribution exceeds the donor's retained interest
    b. The creation of a joint bank account is not a gift; but a gift results when the noncontributing tenant withdraws funds

3. Gross gifts less the following deductions equal taxable gifts

   a. Gift-splitting--a gift by either spouse to a third party may be treated as made one-half by each, if both spouses consent to election. Gift-splitting has the advantage of using the other spouse's annual exclusion and unified transfer tax credit.

   b. Annual exclusion--of up to $10,000 per donee is allowed for gifts of present interests (not future interests)

      EXAMPLE: H is married and has three sons. H could give $20,000 per year to each of his sons without incurring any gift tax if H's spouse consents to gift-splitting.

	H	W
Gifts	$60,000	
Gift-splitting	(30,000)	$30,000
Annual exclusion (3 x $10,000)	(30,000)	(30,000)
Taxable gifts	$ -0-	$ -0-

   c. Educational and medical exclusion--an unlimited exclusion is available for amounts paid on behalf of a donee (1) as tuition to an educational organization, or (2) to a health care provider for medical care of donee

   d. Charitable gifts--(net of annual exclusion) are deductible without limitation

   e. Marital deduction--is allowed without limitation for gifts to a donor's spouse

      (1) The gift must not be a terminable interest (i.e., donee spouse's interest ends at death with no control over who receives remainder)

      (2) If donor elects, a gift of qualified terminable interest property (i.e., property placed in trust with income to donee spouse for life and remainder to someone else at donee spouse's death) will qualify for the marital deduction if the income is paid at least annually to spouse and the property is not subject to transfer during the donee spouse's lifetime

      (3) The marital deduction for gifts to an alien spouse is limited to $100,000 per year.

4. The tax computation reflects the cumulative nature of the gift tax. A tax is first computed on lifetime taxable gifts, then is reduced by the tax on taxable gifts made in prior years in order to tax the current year's gifts at applicable marginal rates. Any available transfer tax credit is then subtracted to arrive at the gift tax liability.

5. A gift tax return must be filed on a calendar-year basis, with the return due and tax paid on or before April 15th of the following year. If donor subsequently dies, the gift tax return is due not later than the date for filing the federal estate tax return (generally 9 months after date of death).

6. The basis of property acquired by gift

   a. Basis for gain (and depreciation)--basis of donor plus gift tax attributable to appreciation

   b. Basis for loss--lesser of gain basis or FMV at date of gift

B. The Estate Tax

1. Estate Tax Formula

Gross estate (cash plus FMV of property at date of death, or alternate valuation date)		$XXX
Less:		
Funeral expenses	$X	
Administrative expenses	X	
Debts and mortgages	X	
Casualty losses	X	
Charitable bequests (unlimited)	X	
Marital deduction (unlimited)	X	XX
Taxable estate		$XXX
Add: Post-76 adjusted taxable gifts		XX
Total taxable life and death transfers		$XXX
Unified transfer tax on total transfers		$ XX
Less:		
Unified transfer tax on post-76 taxable gifts	$X	
Unified transfer tax credit	X	
State death, foreign death, and prior transfer tax credits	X	X
Net estate tax liability		$ XX

2. Gross estate includes the FMV of all property in which the decedent had an interest at time of death

a. Jointly-held property

(1) If property was held by tenancy in common, only the FMV of the decedent's share is included

(2) Include one-half the FMV of community property, and one-half the FMV of property held by spouses in joint tenancy or tenancy by the entirety

(3) Include one-half of FMV if the property held by two persons in joint tenancy was acquired by gift, bequest, or inheritance (1/3 if held by three persons, etc.)

(4) If property held in joint tenancy was acquired by purchase by other than spouses, include the FMV of the property multiplied by the percentage of total cost furnished by the decedent

b. The FMV of transfers with retained life estates and revocable transfers are included in the gross estate

c. Include the FMV of transfers intended to take effect at death (i.e., the donee can obtain enjoyment only by surviving the decedent, and the decedent prior to death had a reversionary interest of more than 5% of the value of the property)

d. Include any property over which the decedent had a general power of appointment (i.e., decedent could appoint property in favor of decedent, decedent's estate, or creditors of decedent or decedent's estate)

e. Include the value of life insurance proceeds from policies payable to the estate, and policies over which the decedent possessed an "incident of ownership" (e.g., right to change beneficiary)

f. Income in respect of a decedent.

3. Property is included at FMV at date of decedent's death; or executor may elect to use FMV at alternate valuation date (a date six months subsequent

to death), if such election will reduce both the gross estate and the
federal estate tax liability

   a. If alternate valuation date is elected, but property is disposed of
      within six months of death, then use FMV on date of disposition
   b. Election is irrevocable and applies to all property in estate; cannot be
      made on an individual property basis

4. Estate tax <u>deductions</u> include funeral expenses, administrative expenses,
debts and mortgages, casualty losses during the estate administration,
charitable bequests (no limit), and an unlimited marital deduction for the
FMV of property passing to a surviving spouse

   a. A terminable interest granted to surviving spouse will not generally
      qualify for marital deduction
   b. If executor elects, the FMV of "qualified terminable interest property"
      is eligible for the marital deduction if the income from the property is
      paid at least annually to spouse and the property is not subject to
      transfer during the surviving spouse's lifetime
   c. Property passing to a surviving spouse who is not a U.S. citizen is not
      eligible for the estate tax marital deduction, except for property
      passing to an alien spouse through a qualified domestic trust (QDT).
   d. Property passing from a nonresident alien to a surviving spouse who is a
      U.S. citizen is eligible for the estate tax marital deduction.

5. Post-76 taxable gifts are added back to the taxable estate at date of gift
FMV. Any gift tax paid is <u>not</u> added back.

6. A unified transfer tax is computed on total life and death transfers, then
is reduced by the tax already paid on post-76 gifts, the unified transfer
tax credit, state death taxes (limited to table amount), foreign death
taxes, and prior transfer taxes (i.e., percentage of estate tax paid on the
transfer to the present decedent from a transferor who died within past 10
years)

7. An estate tax return must be filed if the decedent's gross estate exceeds
$600,000. The return must be filed within 9 months of decedent's death,
unless extension of time has been granted.

8. The <u>basis</u> of property received from a decedent is generally the FMV at date
of decedent's death, or the alternate valuation date if elected for estate
tax purposes

   a. The above rule does not apply to appreciated property acquired by the
      decedent by gift within one year before death if such property then
      passes from the donee-decedent to the original donor or donor's
      spouse. The basis of such property to the original donor (or spouse)
      will be the adjusted basis of the property to the decedent immediately
      before death.
   b. *EXAMPLE: Son gives property with FMV of $40,000 (basis of $5,000) to
      terminally ill father within one year before father's death. The
      property is included in father's estate at FMV of $40,000. If property
      passes to son or son's spouse, basis will remain at $5,000. If passed to
      someone else, the property's basis will be $40,000.*

II. INCOME TAXATION OF ESTATES AND TRUSTS

Although estates and trusts are separate taxable entities, they will not pay an income tax if they distribute all of their income to beneficiaries. In this respect they act as a conduit, since the income taxed to beneficiaries will have the same character as it had for the estate or trust.

A. **An estate or trust must file U.S. Fiduciary Income Tax Return Form 1041 if it has gross income of $600 or more**

1. Return is due by the 15th day of the fourth month following the close of the estate or trust's taxable year

2. A trust must adopt a calendar year as its taxable year. An estate may adopt a calendar year or any fiscal year.

3. Estates and trusts are taxed as follows:

    a. First $5,000 of taxable income is taxed at 15%
    b. Taxable income in excess of $5,000 is taxed at 28%
    c. The 15% bracket is phased out by adding an additional 5% tax on taxable income between $13,000 and $26,000

4. Estates and trusts are generally required to make estimated tax payments using the rules applicable to individuals. However, estates do not have to make estimated payments for taxable years ending within 2 years of the decedent's death.

B. **If estate or trust income is**

1. Not distributed to beneficiaries, the income is taxable to the estate or trust

2. Distributed to beneficiaries, the estate or trust receives a deduction for the distribution, and the income is taxable to beneficiaries for their taxable year in which the estate or trust taxable year ends. Income has the same character for beneficiaries as it had for the estate or trust.

C. **Computation of taxable income**

1. <u>Gross income</u> for an estate or trust is generally the same as for individual taxpayers

    a. No gain or loss is recognized on the transfer of property to beneficiaries to satisfy specific bequests
    b. Gain or loss is recognized on the transfer of property to beneficiaries in lieu of cash to satisfy specific cash bequests

2. <u>Allowable deductions</u> for an estate or trust are generally the same as for an individual taxpayer

    a. A personal exemption is allowed

        (1) $600 for estate

        (2) $300 for simple trust (i.e., a trust required to distribute all income currently)

        (3) $100 for a complex trust (i.e., a trust other than a simple trust)

  b. Charitable contributions can be deducted without limitation if paid out of income

      (1) Contributions are not deductible to the extent paid out of tax-exempt income

      (2) Only complex trusts can make charitable contributions

  c. Medical and funeral expenses of a decedent are not allowed as deductions on estate's Form 1041, but if medical expenses are paid within 12 months of decedent's death they are deductible on decedent's final Form 1040

  d. Any unused capital loss and NOL carryovers from the decedent's final Form 1040 are not allowed as deductions

3. An <u>income distribution deduction</u> is allowed for distributions of income to beneficiaries.

  a. Distributable net income (DNI) sets the limit on the amount of the deduction for distributions to beneficiaries in any taxable year, and also determines the amounts and character of the income reported by the beneficiaries

  b. Generally, <u>DNI is taxable income</u> before the income distribution deduction with the following modifications

      (1) Add back

          (a) Exemption

          (b) Any net capital loss deduction

          (c) Tax-exempt interest reduced by related nondeductible expenses

      (2) Subtract

          (a) Net capital gains allocable to corpus

          (b) Dividends allocated to corpus of simple trust

  c. Deduction will be the lesser of DNI or the taxable income distributed to beneficiaries (i.e., taxable income required to be distributed, plus other amount of taxable income distributed)

D. **Tax Treatment of Beneficiaries**

1. Beneficiaries are taxed on income distributions to the extent of DNI

2. A two-tier income distribution system is used

  a. First tier--all required income distributions

  b. Second tier--all other income distributions

3. DNI is first allocated to first tier distributions, then to second tier distributions. Distributions in excess of DNI are nontaxable.

E. **Termination of estate or trust**

1. An estate or trust is not entitled to a personal exemption on its final return

2. Any unused carryovers (e.g., NOL or capital loss) are passed through to beneficiaries for use on their individual tax returns

3. Any excess deductions for its final year are passed through to beneficiaries and can be deducted as miscellaneous itemized deductions

ABBREVIATIONS

AAA	Accumulated Adjustments Account	CPI	Consumer Price Index
AAA	American Accounting Association	CPU	Central Processing Unit
AC	Absorption Costing	CRE	Consolidated Retained Earnings
ACRS	Accelerated Cost Recovery System	CRT	Cathode Ray Tube
AcSEC	Accounting Standards Executive Committee (AICPA)	CSE	Common Stock Equivalent
		CSV	Cash Surrender Value
AEP	Accumulated Earnings & Profits	CVP	Cost-Volume-Profit
AET	Accumulated Earnings Tax	DB	Declining Balance
AGI	Adjusted Gross Income	DBA	Data-Base Administrator
AH	Actual Hours	DBMS	Data-Base Management System
AICPA	American Institute of CPAs	DC	Direct Costing
AJE	Adjusting Journal Entry	DDB	Double Declining Balance
AMTI	Alternative Minimum Taxable Income	DL	Direct Labor
A/P	Accounts Payable	DLH	Direct Labor Hours
AP	Actual Price	DM	Direct Materials
APB	Accounting Principles Board	DNI	Distributable Net Income
AQ	Actual Quantity	DRD	Dividends Received Deduction
A/R	Accounts Receivable	EAPV	Estimated Audited Populations Value
AR	Actual Rate, Analytical Review, Accounting and Review Services (Citation for AICPA Professional Standards Volume)	EDA	Excess Deductions Account
		EDP	Electronic Data Processing
		EI	Ending Inventory
ARB	Accounting Research Bulletin (AICPA)	ENPI	Excess Net Passive Income
ARR	Accounting Rate of Return	EOQ	Economic Order Quantity
ARS	Accounting Research Study (AICPA)	E&P	Earnings and Profits
ASOBAT	A Statement of Basic Accounting Theory	EPS	Earnings Per Share
ASR	Accounting Series Release (SEC)	ERISA	Employee Retirement Income Security Act
AT	Attestation (Citation for AICPA Professional Standards Volume)	ESIC	Enterprise Standard Industrial Classification
AU	Auditing (Citation for AICPA Professional Standards Volume)	ESOP	Employee Stock Option Plan
		EU	Equivalent Units
AudSEC	Auditing Standards Executive Committee (AICPA)	EUP	Equivalent Units of Production
		EWIP	Ending Work in Process
AVGP	Analysis of Variation in Gross Profit	F	Favorable
BFP	Bona Fide Purchaser	FA	Fixed Asset
BI	Beginning Inventory	FAS	Free Along Side
B of D	Board of Directors	FASB	Financial Accounting Standards Board
BV	Book Value	FC	Fixed Cost
BWIP	Beginning Work in Process	FCPA	Foreign Corrupt Practices Act
CA	Current Assets	FCU	Foreign Currency Unit
CAFR	Comprehensive Annual Financial Report	FDEPS	Fully Diluted Earnings Per Share
CAP	Committee on Accounting Procedures	FEI	Financial Executives Institute
CASB	Cost Accounting Standards Board	FG	Finished Goods
CC	Charitable Contributions	FICA	Federal Insurance Contribution Act
CD	Certificate of Deposit	FIFO	First-In, First-Out
CEP	Current Earnings and Profits	FMV	Fair Market Value
CETA	Comprehensive Employment and Training Act	FOB	Free on Board
CGM	Cost of Goods Manufactured	FPC	Finite Population Correction Factor
CGS	Cost of Goods Sold	FUTA	Federal Unemployment Tax Act
CIF	Cost, Insurance, and Freight	FV	Future Value
CIP	Construction in Progress	FY	Fiscal Year
CL	Current Liabilities	GAAFR	Governmental Accounting, Auditing, and Financial Reporting
CLADR	Class Life Asset Depreciation Range		
CM	Contribution Margin	GAAP	Generally Accepted Accounting Principles
CMA	Certified Management Accountant	GAAS	Generally Accepted Auditing Standards
CMA	Cumulative Monetary Amount	GAO	General Accounting Office
CNI	Consolidated Net Income	GASB	Governmental Accounting Standards Board
COD	Collect on Delivery	GCAP	Generalized Computer Audit Programs
COM	Computer Output to Microfilm	GFA	General Fixed Asset (Group of Accounts)
CPA	Certified Public Accountant	GI	Gross Income
CPFF	Cost Plus Fixed Fee (Contract)	G/L	General Ledger

GLTD	General Long-Term Debt (Group of Accounts)	R&D	Research and Development
GNP	Gross National Product	RE	Retained Earnings
GP	Gross Profit	REITs	Real Estate Investment Trusts
GW	Goodwill	REV	Revenue
HDC	Holder in Due Course	RM	Raw Materials
IC	Internal Control	ROI	Return on Investment
ICS	Internal Control Structure, Internal Control System	ROM	Read Only Memory
		S	Sales
IFCO	Income From Continuing Operations	SARs	Stock Appreciation Rights
INV	Inventory	SAS	Statement on Auditing Standards (AICPA)
IRA	Individual Retirement Account	SBC	Small Business Corporation
IRC	Internal Revenue Code	SCF	Statement of Cash Flows
IRR	Internal Rate of Return	SDLC	Systems Development Life Cycle
IRS	Internal Revenue Service	SE	Stockholders' Equity
ITC	Investment Tax Credit	SEC	Securities and Exchange Commission
ITF	Integrated Test Facility	SFAC	Statement of Financial Accounting Concepts (FASB)
LCM	Lower of Cost or Market		
LIFO	Last-In, First-Out	SFAS	Statement of Financial Accounting Standards (FASB)
LTCG	Long-Term Capital Gain		
LTCL	Long-Term Capital Loss	SFR	Standard Fixed Rate
MAS	Management Advisory Services	SH	Standard Hours
MAT	Material	SI	Sampling Interval
MC	Marginal Cost	SIC	Standard Industrial Classification
MFOA	Municipal Finance Officers Association	S&L	Savings and Loan
MI	Minority Interest	SL	Straight-Line
MOH	Manufacturing Overhead	SOP	Statements of Position
MS	Management Advisory Services (Citation for AICPA Professional Standards Volume)	SP	Standard Price
		SQ	Standard Quantity
		SQCS	Statements on Quality Control Standards (AICPA)
MU	Markup		
N/A	Not Applicable	SR	Standard Rate
NAA	National Association of Accountants	SS	Social Security
NBV	Net Book Value	SSARS	Statement on Standards for Accounting and Review Services (AICPA)
NCA	Noncurrent Asset		
NCG	Net Capital Gain	SSI	Supplemental Security Income
NCGA	National Council on Governmental Accounting	SSMAS	Standards for Management Advisory Services
NCL	Noncurrent Liability	SSN	Social Security Number
NCL	Net Capital Loss	ST	Short-Term
NI	Net Income	STCG	Short-Term Capital Gain
NLTCG	Net Long-Term Capital Gain	STCL	Short-Term Capital Loss
NLTCL	Net Long-Term Capital Loss	STR	Standard Total Rate
NOL	Net Operating Loss	SVR	Standard Variable Rate
NPV	Net Present Value	SYD	Sum-of-the-Years'-Digits
N/R	Note Receivable	TC	Total Cost
NRV	Net Realizable Value	TD	Test of Detail
NSF	Nonsufficient Funds	TE	Tolerable Error
NSTCG	Net Short-Term Capital Gain	TI	Taxable Income
NSTCL	Net Short-Term Capital Loss	TRA	Tax Reform Act
OCR	Optical Character Recognition	TS	Treasury Stock
O/H(OH)	Overhead	TVMF	Time Value of Money Factor
OLRT	Online Real-Time	TX	Tax Practice (Citation for AICPA Professional Standards Volume)
O/S	Outstanding		
PBGC	Pension Benefit Guarantee Corporation	U	Unfavorable
PC	Purchase Commitments	UBI	Unrelated Business Income
PEPS	Primary Earnings Per Share	UCC	Uniform Commercial Code
PHC	Personal Holding Company	ULPA	Uniform Limited Partnership Act
PIC	Paid-in Capital	UPA	Uniform Partnership Act
P&L	Profit and Loss	UR	Ultimate Risk
POC	Percentage-of-Completion	UTI	Undistributed Taxable Income
PP&E	Property, Plant, and Equipment	VAR	Variance
PPS	Probability Proportional to Size	VC	Variable Cost
PTI	Previously Taxed Income	WA	Weighted-Average
PV	Present Value	WC	Working Capital
RAM	Random Access Memory	WIP	Work in Process

FREE

 FREE

ADDITIONAL PUBLICATION
FOR CPA CANDIDATES

A Complimentary Service for Users of
Gleim/Delaney's CPA EXAMINATION REVIEW, Volumes I and II

CPA EXAMINATION REVIEW UPDATING SUPPLEMENT

This booklet will be published in February to update the Sixteenth Edition of *CPA Examination Review* for present owners of the text. Contents of this supplement include:

- Outlines of new FASB pronouncements.
- Outlines of new Auditing pronouncements.
- New developments in Business Law.
- New developments in Federal Taxation.

If you would like to receive, free of charge, the above booklet, complete this form and mail it to CPA EXAMINATION REVIEW, P.O. Box 886, DeKalb, Illinois 60115.

Date _____

Full Name _____

Address _____
(Street)

_____
(City)   (State)   (Zip)

0471-51380-6

Feedback to Authors

We invite your suggestions, corrections, typographical errors, etc. Please send these to Patrick R. Delaney, c/o CPA Examination Review, P.O. Box 886, DeKalb, Illinois 60115 before **April 1, 1990,** for inclusion in the *CPA Examination Review,* 17th Edition.

1.

2.

3.

4.

5.

6.

7.

8.

9.

10.

11.

12.

13.

14.

15.